Sunset

NORTHEASTERN

GARDEN

BOOK

Edited by Anne Halpin

SUNSET BOOKS • MENLO PARK, CALIFORNIA

Hardy geraniums and roses are focal points in this New York garden.

Sunset Books

VP, General Manager: Richard A. Smeby
VP, Editorial Director: Bob Doyle
Production Director: Lory Day
Art Director: Vasken Guiragossian

Sunset Northeast Garden Book

was produced by Roundtable Press, Inc., New York, New York

Directors: Marsha Melnick, Susan E. Meyer, Julie Merberg
Editor: Anne Halpin
Principal Horticultural Consultant: Robert S. Hebb
Horticultural Consultants: Thomas Burford, John Emmanuel, Gary Koller,
      Nan Sinton, Kathy Tracy
Managing Editor: Lori Stein
Art Director: Areta Buk
Encyclopedia Designer: Laura Smyth
Photography Editor: Jane A. Martin
Editorial Production: John Glenn
Editorial Assistants: Carrie Glidden, Sara Newberry, Erica Toth
Production: Bill Rose
Writers: Barbara Ellis, Leslie Garisto, Jane Mintzer Hoffman, Penny
      O'Sullivan, Roseanne Scott, Robert Speziale (A Garden for All Seasons)
Production Coordinator: Patricia S. Williams
Copy Editor: Patricia Woodruff
Indexer: Lina Burton
Illustrators: Mary Davey Burkhardt, Ireta Cooper, Edward Lam,
      Lois Lovejoy, Dennis Nolan, Bill Oetinger, Mimi Osborne
Maps: Reineck & Reineck

Special thanks to: Pam Cornelison, Suzanne Normand Eyre, Marianne
      Lipanovich, Alice Rogers, Janet Sanchez, Britta Swartz

Cover photograph: Syringa vulgaris *'Sensation' (lilac),*
Harry Haralambou
Title page photograph: Catmint, lilies, and other summer flowers
in a Cape Cod garden, Karen Bussolini

Box turtle in garden of wild geraniums.

Foreword

Welcome to a unique one-stop reference on gardening in the Northeast. Since 1954, gardeners in the West have relied on the climate-specific information available in the *Western Garden Book*. In 1997 Sunset extended its coverage with the *National Garden Book*. Now, a team of horticultural experts across the northeastern United States and southeastern Canada have developed the same highly detailed plant information for gardeners in this region.

What sets this book apart from others is its system of climate zones, developed with help from university climatologists, the National Weather Service, and agricultural extension agents. Most other zoning schemes are based on minimum winter temperatures, providing a useful—but limited—plant hardiness index. Another system relies on heat zones based on maximum summer temperatures, but its maps must be used along with a cold hardiness map. The *Sunset* system is both simpler to use and more detailed. It recognizes that other factors are just as important as temperature in determining how well a particular plant will grow in a given region. Humidity, rainfall patterns, elevation, land formations, length of growing seasons, and proximity to oceans or other large bodies of water all play their part. The *Sunset* system incorporates all these factors to produce a single zone rating for your particular area.

The *Sunset* climate maps organize the United States and the southern part of Canada into 53 climate zones, 14 of which are in the Northeast. To learn more about these zones and find your zone, see the chapter that begins on page 30.

For each entry in the A to Z Plant Encyclopedia, we note the zones where that plant grows best. So once you've found your zone on one of the regional maps, you can easily learn whether a particular plant is likely to perform well for you.

The encyclopedia includes detailed information about more than 5,000 plants—some widely available and commonly grown, others harder to find but worth seeking out. But this book also contains much more. A Garden for All Seasons takes you on an inspiring tour that captures the spirit of this region. The Plant Selection Guide will help you choose the right plants for special situations—such as damp soil or deep shade—and for special purposes, such as providing winter interest or attracting birds and butterflies. The Practical Gardening Dictionary offers the latest advice on everything from watering and fertilizing plants to managing garden pests in environmentally friendly ways. And the Resource Directory lists, among other things, outstanding botanic gardens and mail-order suppliers of seeds and plants.

We hope that you will find in the *Sunset Northeastern Garden Book* a complete, easy-to-use reference to guide you in all your gardening efforts.

Bob Doyle
Editorial Director,
Sunset Books

Anne Halpin
Editor

CONTENTS

Summer blooms of hydrangeas, hollyhocks, daisies, lilies, and a shrub rose among the boat sheds supply subtle spots of color to a tranquil view of Edgartown Harbor on Martha's Vineyard.

A Garden for ALL SEASONS

The Northeast encompasses a large region, from Canada in the north to Virginia in the south, the Ohio border in the west and eastward to the Atlantic Ocean. This vast terrain ranges from flat coastal plains and mountain valleys to rolling hillsides and brookside banks. Such gorgeous diversity is a boon to gardeners who benefit from a growing season that lasts roughly from April through September, winter cold that provides the necessary dormancy for many types of flowering plants, adequate moisture throughout the year with few periods of drought, and seasons of dramatically striking contrast.

The sheer variety of gardens in the Northeast defies simple characterization, but the best of them take their visual cues from the natural landscape surrounding them. A garden in rural New England may meander about a hilly landscape dotted with stands of old beech and oak. A Japanese-inspired oasis with rock gardens, a koi pond, and a simple waterspout may fit perfectly behind a contemporary house in suburban Maryland. Roses and daylilies straddling a roadside fence in southern Maine will tell you that someone's solitary labors have been well rewarded. A clearing at the edge of a woodland filled with native wildflowers, bulbs, mountain laurel, and tough, but exotic-looking foliage of all shapes and sizes can offer shady repose in the Berkshires or the foothills of the Blue Ridge. And if the heavens are smiling down on you, you just may find a lady's slipper or two rising from the woodland floor.

Good gardens serve their makers well. They satisfy the basic human need for serenity and refuge from the pressures and pace of modern life. In addition to being a place of privacy and repose, a garden can be an outlet for creative endeavor. Gardening, after all, is an expression of hope, a belief that no matter what delights the present holds, the future can and will be better, perhaps more perfect, and yield untold and unimagined pleasures. In every corridor and corner of the Northeast, you'll discover gardens as singular, charming, and surprising as the people who create them.

▼ A clay pot chock full of annuals including pink petunias, magenta nicotiana, and 'Victoria Blue' salvia and edged with violet-blue *Lobelia erinus* forms a miniature garden in a sunny spot.

▲ Deep yellow flowers of the self-sowing perennial celandine poppy emerge from a hollow tree stump surrounded by the parasol-like foliage of May apple in early spring.

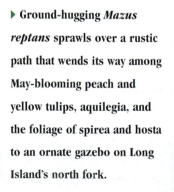

▶ Ground-hugging *Mazus reptans* sprawls over a rustic path that wends its way among May-blooming peach and yellow tulips, aquilegia, and the foliage of spirea and hosta to an ornate gazebo on Long Island's north fork.

The Garden Comes to Life

Spring arrives quickly in the Northeast. Before the leaf canopy emerges overhead, the angle and intensity of daylight changes, awakening a succession of blooms beginning with the earliest of spring bulbs such as snowdrop, crocus, hyacinth, and scilla, swiftly followed by the many members of the narcissus clan. In the more northerly latitudes, where winter ice and cold linger on through April, the joys of spring are fleeting indeed. But wherever you may find yourself in early spring, you can count for sure on one thing—rain, rain, and more rain.

Brilliant yellow and lime green seem to be the colors in abundance at this time of year. Lemony blooms of forsythia and the electric chartreuse of euphorbia finally yield to spots of pastels, in the pale blue blooms of a ground hugger like lungwort, the drooping, half-hidden flowers of epimedium, and the ever-so-pink sprays of little heart shapes on native bleeding heart *(Dicentra eximia)*.

In dry shade, a notoriously difficult location for plants, the Northeast can host gems like May apple and false Solomon's seal. In a moist area near a shaded brook, native trilliums make their appearance. Once the lilacs, dogwoods, and the sturdy star magnolia *(Magnolia stellata)* burst forth in bloom, along with flowering fruit trees like crabapple and cherry, spring has truly reached its height.

The clever gardener gets a head start on the growing season by using a cold frame. Whether it be a simple construction using a storm window over a few supports or a more elaborate, store-bought contraption, a cold frame allows a gardener to enjoy those plants that require a growing season longer than the local climate provides. It is a comforting sight, seeing the annuals, biennials, and edibles to be set out in summer snuggling contentedly under a few panes of glass despite the cold gusts swirling about them.

▲ The end of a border of parrot tulips in Charlottesville, Virginia *(above left)*, leads to a vista of blooming redbud and the rolling hills beyond. A weeping Higan cherry in full spring splendor *(above right)* takes center stage in a garden at the edge of a Connecticut woodland.

◄ Tidy clumps of pure white daffodils with egg-yolk yellow centers bloom before an unmortared granite wall in a New England valley.

9

▲ A swallow tail butterfly alights on the cushiony, heart-shaped leaves of purplish-blue flowering violets.

▼ The luminous pastel blooms of Japanese primroses and white woodland forget-me-nots brighten a small pond backed by shade-loving hosta and Japanese maple leaves.

The Bravura of Late Spring

Come May, the visual display accelerates despite the possibility of a late frost to daunt a gardener's best efforts. Virtually anywhere in the Northeast, it's a simple task to choreograph a succession of colorful blooms. Flowering shrubs such as weigela and mock orange and perennials like bleeding heart and poppies are rapidly followed by later-blooming ones, such as peonies and iris, leaving little or no gap in flower interest.

By June, many gardens in the Northeast reach a peak of color and form matched only by the intricate patterns of greenery against which they're seen. In the June border, successful gardeners start by grouping plants with similar cultural needs of soil, sunlight, and moisture. From then on, it's anyone's guess what will be planted.

Making a border an artful part of the landscape seems to be playful sport in the Northeast. Color combinations in peaceful pastels of pink, cool blue-greens, and violets that seem to recede from the eye compete with a neighbor's yen for startling contrasts of red, orange, and magenta that appear to lurch forward and confront you. The more circumspect border designer may limit the color palette to three colors plus, of course, green, and then use countless tints and shades of each for a harmonious whole. Adventurous gardeners may ignore conventional wisdom and plant a few tall plants at the front of the

◄ The showstopping pink-violet flowers of an Empress-tree *(Paulownia tomentosa)* in full spring regalia crown the end of a border blooming with pink, rose-pink, and white peonies, lavender, and a flowering weigela in late spring on Long Island.

border, maybe spires of foxglove, a clump of slender, elegant lilies, or a tall, commanding mullein, that don't fully obscure the back of the border.

It's hard to imagine wandering more than a mile or so in the residential townships of the Northeast without spotting the tried-and-true beauties of the June border. Starting a week or two before Memorial Day, you're sure to delight in the breathtakingly enormous blooms of lilacs and tree peonies. A fortnight or so later you're awash in the buxom blooms of their herbaceous cousins, foxgloves of all descriptions, mounds of phlox, and bearded iris buds unfurling on 2–3-foot stalks in hues from the deepest, darkest purple to the palest pink and purest white. Even florists will tell you that you'll rarely find these splendid specimens in their shops, because it is impossible to ship blossoms as beautiful, fragile, and ephemeral as these.

Well-designed paths assume paramount importance during this season. To view the blooms of late spring gardeners venture forth, enjoying the rewards of their efforts up close, no longer from the confines of their homes. More than one gardener has surely been tempted to step from a well-constructed path at some opportune point, to wonder at the forget-me-nots and lily-of-the-valley that have sprung from the soil, unaided by human hand, and naturalized with merry abandon.

Fences, too, whether they be long-standing structures of stacked fieldstone in rural Pennsylvania or white picket fences in suburban Massachusetts, serve aesthetic objectives as well as functional ones. They frame the visual space the garden occupies, suggesting that the gardener has succeeded in making her world distinguishable from the natural land-scape around it. More impenetrable barriers of netting and wire announce to marauding rodents and mammals that snapping off the tulip and fritillaria blooms, devouring the first, juicy shoots of hosta poking through the soil, or grazing on the tasty, early lettuces and beet greens will not be an indulgence easily gratified.

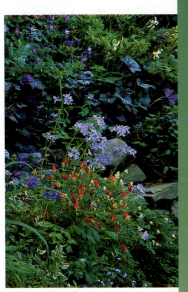

▲ Pale blue phlox and the glossy leaves of 'Pewter Moon' heuchera contrast with the nodding reddish orange and yellow flowers of native columbine.

Chartreuse foliage of dwarf variegated bamboo *(right foreground)* offers a stunning counterpoint to blooms of vibrant orange butterfly weed, bright yellow 'Zagreb' coreopsis, pink blooms of the rose 'Carefree Delight', and dusky purple spires of 'Provence' lavender flanking a grassy path on the eastern slope of the Blue Ridge Mountains in central Virginia.

Congenial Companions

Roses and herbs, two of the most fragrant kinds of plants, have been garden companions for thousands of years. In the Northeast, they make supremely suitable mates. Give these partners the bright, sunny location most roses and herbs prefer, and they will flourish, even in cool areas.

Species roses—the narcotically fragrant ancestors of today's modern hybrids—belong in every Northeast garden. Musk roses such as spring-blooming *Rosa gallica officinalis*, which is hardy to southern Canada (and probably the Arctic Circle), and later-blooming *Rosa moschata,* as well as the richly scented Bourbons, pair delightfully with herbs such as lovage, lavender, and calendula, whose scents attract beneficial insects that help protect roses from pests and diseases. Classic partners such as comfrey, hyssop, feverfew, and germander camouflage the unsightly bare legs of shrub roses.

Gardeners in northern latitudes should consider planting the hardier roses hybridized to withstand severe winter weather. The cold-hardy Explorer roses developed in Canada and the Dr. Buck roses hybridized at Iowa State by the botanist of the same name, as well as the wild rugosas and eglantines naturalized in North America, have proved their mettle in less than hospitable growing conditions.

▼ Aromatic 'Six Hills Giant' catmint edges a border contained by an open arbor of cedar poles, abloom with white, red, and deep pink roses and leading to a lattice-work pool house.

The uses of roses in the garden are as diverse as their growth habits and bloom colors, and gardeners take full advantage of their versatility. Pink 'Bonica' and cherry red 'John Cabot' can be planted as hedges; the whitest of white beauties such as 'Madame Alfred Carrière' and 'Frau Karl Druschki' make eye-popping specimen plants in a mixed border; and the ultrahardy, bright pink, creeping 'Max Graf' quickly forms a dense ground cover for sunny slopes and the rocky terrain so often found in the Northeast.

As landscape plants, roses with long canes and those known as climbers, such as the light pink 'Dr. W. van Fleet' and its ever-blooming relative 'New Dawn', blanket garden structures with ease, cloaking an arbor, a trellis, or a pergola. They can be coaxed to climb a *tuteur*, espaliered against a wall, or trained to be standards, in much the same way their prized garden colleagues rosemary and myrtle can be fashioned into topiary.

▲ **A brilliant red rambler scales an arbor and 'The Fairy', a light pink shrub rose, forms mounds of cool color on either side of a brick path leading to an enclosed vegetable garden in upstate New York.**

Summer Splendor

Heat-sensitive annuals such as pansies, lobelia, and sweet peas, which would wilt and perish in most other parts of the United States, persist in Northeast gardens when summer temperatures are moderate unless there are extended periods of drought. The summer garden is also ablaze with saturated hues of red, orange, and yellow, which plants like daylilies, crocosmia, and red-hot poker possess in abundance. The pale blue, lavender, silver, and white of perennials such as eryngium and echinops, and annuals such as nicotiana and tree mallow provide a calming counterpoint.

Many wildflowers of the Northeast come into full bloom during the summer months. Clusters of deep yellow flowers hovering atop the upright stems of goldenrod *(Solidago canadensis),* the purple flower heads of ironweed *(Vernonia noveboracensis),* the circular lavender, pink, or white flowers of wild bergamot *(Monarda* spp.), and the flattened, mauve blooms of Joe Pye weed *(Eupatorium purpureum)* look best planted in tall clusters. Seeing these hardy natives massed along a rough-hewn fence or by the roadside of a semirural property signals at once that you are in a very particular place in the world.

Equally at home are plants that arrived on these shores from distant lands. Bamboos and ornamental grasses imbue Northeast gardens with an exotic mood, and they are as hardy as any native. In full summer sun, there are few plants quite as showstopping as the red-stemmed annual castor bean *(Ricinus communis)* with its huge, bronze-streaked, palmate leaves, and the ghostly, spiny-leafed, silver gray biennial Scotch thistle *(Onopordum acanthium),* both of which may make you want to check your map to be sure you haven't taken a detour to the tropics.

▲ **Magenta clematis** *(top)* **and white sweet peas surround a lamp post. 'Golden Orange' zinnias and darker orange 'Queen Sophia' marigolds enliven a planting of violet-blue 'Victoria' salvia.**

▶ **A swath of showy yellow evening primrose competes for attention with orange and yellow 'Royal Standard' kniphofia, hot pink foxglove, lavender larkspur, and sheer white *Chrysanthemum leucanthemum* in a Chester County, Pennsylvania, border.**

Junipers in southern Canada play host to a colorful and dramatic assembly of annuals, including lemony mopheads of amaranthus, spikes of golden yellow celosia, and clusters of the vanilla-scented, deep purple flowers of heliotrope.

Peaceful Gardens

Flowers need not be the dominant feature of a garden. There are locations where a garden decorated with foliage bestows a visually welcome alternative to the riot of spring and summer blooms. In a region where all sorts of natural water features—rivers, brooks, lakes, ponds, and, of course, the Atlantic Ocean—influence the landscape, and stone outcroppings and woodland divides are the rule rather than the exception, you'll find many gardens relying on the ornamental value of foliage.

In an intimate, shaded setting, especially near a stream or running water, cream-tipped hosta leaves, silver-and-burgundy fronds of Japanese painted fern, the erect, vase-shaped American native ostrich fern, the broad-fronded sensitive fern, and the finely incised foliage of masterwort *(Astrantia major)* build on the sense of tranquility. In slightly more sunlight, Northeast gardeners rely on perennials with striking foliage such as the rodgersias, especially the aptly named giant, round-leafed species *tabularis*. Equally valuable are sea kale *(Crambe maritima)* with broad, wrinkled, glaucous blue leaves, and the easily grown ligularias with rounded or kidney-shaped foliage.

Some gardens in the Northeast offer only a slight hint of the larger landscape in which they exist. Taking advantage of the rocky soil that abounds throughout many areas, a city courtyard may reveal a garden for meditation, with a simple armless bench situated amid raked gravel or pebbles punctuated with smooth, shapely boulders that have been heaved to the surface during the freeze and thaw cycles common to the region. Accents of evergreen foliage, mosses, and perhaps a small, weeping shrub like stephanandra help evoke thoughtful repose.

▼ **A cherub pouring water into a small pool surrounded by variegated hosta, ferns, and white bleeding heart adds a note of whimsy to a partly shaded corner of a New Jersey garden.**

▲ A simple wooden bench before a border blooming with giant purple-lilac alliums, white Shasta daisies, and lemon yellow trollius overlooking a coastal inlet in Sprucehead, Maine, provides a spot for repose.

◀ An allée brimming with pink honeysuckle, sweet autumn clematis, and white hydrangeas leads to a secluded, rough-hewn sitting area.

Summer Bounty

Because the growing season for vegetables is not as long as it is in other parts of the country, Northeast gardeners know they must site their vegetable gardens with great care. Full sun, at the very least six hours a day, rewards the gardener with the widest choice of tasty vegetables to grow. An especially productive site is a south-facing slope, where sunlight strikes the ground at a more direct angle, warming the soil earlier in the spring and keeping it warm later into the fall.

For the sake of convenience, nothing beats growing vegetables near your kitchen door. You can easily check on the garden every day, watering as needed, pulling weeds, and harvesting the ripening bounty. For more than two centuries, savvy farmers in New England have placed their vegetable plots between the farmhouse and the barn, where a steady source of manure is available. You can build on their wisdom by having the compost pile close by the vegetable garden and the kitchen, since both generate organic waste for composting.

Opinions on what to plant and how to plant it elicit as much discussion as they do elsewhere in the United States. Traditionalists may swear that hardy, old-fashioned heirloom varieties of tomatoes, lettuces, and potatoes, whose seeds grow true and have been passed down for generations untampered with by human hand, taste better than newer hybrids.

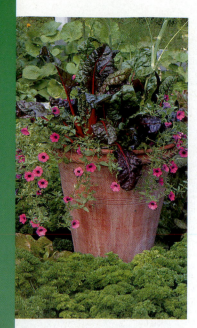

▲ **Ruby chard, bronze fennel, and magenta petunias fill a tall terra cotta planter ringed with a planting of curly leaf parsley.**

▶ **Vegetables, herbs, and ornamentals including corn, zucchini, scarlet runner beans, basil, thyme, nasturtiums, red coleus, Joe Pye weed, rudbeckia, castor bean, and sunflowers disport harmoniously in a Hudson Valley kitchen garden.**

These same gardeners wouldn't let a growing season pass without tending to the highbush blueberries, black raspberries, and alpine strawberries that have been grown in the Northeast for ages.

More contemporary souls may look instead for the most dramatic-looking produce—Chioggia beets, Malabar spinach, white eggplants, bronze fennel, and purple kohlrabi, for example—and mix these plants with herbs and flowering ornamentals in a handsome raised bed. Gardeners with limited space may choose to go vertical, draping an arch with pole beans, training summer squash up a trellis, and planting potatoes at several levels in a whiskey barrel.

Perhaps the only aspect of vegetable gardening that is agreed upon is the face of the enemy—voracious nuisance mammals and rodents, including deer, woodchucks, raccoons, rabbits, and squirrels, to name only a few. It takes only one growing season to realize that there is no such thing as deer-proof or rodent-proof fencing. Gardeners who seek revenge sometimes plant chili peppers throughout the other edibles, to give these pests the shock they so richly deserve.

▲ A formal potager combines symmetrical blocks of yellow and orange marigolds, red and pink zinnias, and rows of leeks, chard, onions, and salad greens. Wire mesh on the white board fence keeps unwanted critters out.

21

Cherry tomatoes trained on a twig trellis, a tripod with pole beans, and pots of rosemary, coreopsis, and 'Vera Jameson' sedum mingle with tall bronze fennel, magenta petunias, 'Silver Mound' artemisia, and 'Blue Mist' caryopteris in a casual, sunny garden in Warren, Connecticut.

City Gardens

In the cities of the Northeast, where space is at a premium, devoted gardeners find ways to make the most of their property. Whether planting in containers or wherever there's a patch of earth, no matter how impoverished the soil may be, there are surprises to be seen behind streetside gates or high on a rooftop.

Dust and air pollution, poor air circulation, and—on rooftops and elevated terraces—wind and dessication add to the challenges city gardeners face. Small details assume more importance. Choosing plants with one spectacular trait such as a weeping habit, waxy fruit, or flamboyant color makes a planting memorable. A fruit tree espaliered against the side of a house or a wall can add unique interest. Natural elements such as driftwood, mulches of wood chips or pine needles, and weathered rock suggest the rural in the city, linking the garden with the natural world.

For nighttime enjoyment, white flowers, those with dramatic shapes like lilies, or a potted tropical like angel's trumpet (*Brugmansia* spp.) will stand out. For even more drama, the specimens you wish to showcase can be illuminated with strategically placed lights. Fragrant plants such as heliotrope, four o'clock, and mignonette add another dimension to the city garden, especially when the night scents are held captive in a confined space.

In addition to townhouse and roof gardens, decks, terraces, and porches are common architectural features of the urban landscape. Container plants alone may make a deck or terraced garden a cherished spot, but a trellis, so often partly shaded in the city, hosting Dutchman's pipe and akebia, or the side of a screened-in porch covered by a climbing hydrangea will make your outdoor living space even more distinctive. A pergola attached to the sunny rear of a residence and covered with grapes, passion flower, honeysuckle, or clematis can lift the spirit of a city garden in countless ways.

▶ **White-flowering mandevilla and roses cascade from the walls and latticework surrounding a penthouse garden in New York City. Pots of geraniums, chrysanthemums, petunias, and dainty hydrangeas add to the intimacy of this rooftop dining terrace.**

A colorful assortment of plants including honeysuckle, weigela, ferns, roses, and honey locust make a slate-paved townhouse garden in the Vinegar Hill neighborhood of Brooklyn a verdant oasis.

Autumn Glory

In autumn, when summer heat is gone, lawns become lush and strikingly green once again. Expanses of cold-season turf grass are an indisputable feature of the urban, suburban, and rural landscape of the Northeast. With the exception of the coastal Northwest, there is no other region of the country in which such lovely lawn areas can be created.

Many roses bloom until the first frost, and shrubs native to the Northeast such as chokeberry *(Aronia arbutifolia)* and highbush cranberry *(Viburnum trilobum)* bear tantalizing fruit that attracts scores of hungry birds and other wildlife. Fall beds and borders are abloom with the flowers of cosmos, gaillardia, zinnias, dahlias, asters, monkshood, toad lily, anemones, alliums, and chrysanthemums, and bulbs such as autumn crocus, nerine, and colchicum come into full flower. The stunning blooms of peegee hydrangea and its slightly less regal garden brethren dry in the sunlight, adding beauty to the northeastern

▲ The gold-mottled, ruby red foliage of a Japanese maple such as *Acer palmatum* 'Ichigyoji' makes fall in the Northeast an unparalleled delight.

▶ Fountain grass with bristly, copper fruitheads begins its display in fall and lasts through the winter in a sylvan Maryland meadow anchored with majestic river birch.

▶ An unruly but graceful bundle of striped, variegated miscanthus shares a sunny spot with the early fall blooms of deep yellow rudbeckia and rosy purple Joe Pye weed.

▲ Sugar maples alongside a stately white picket fence in Bennington, Vermont, begin their autumn display.

◄ The vivid autumn scarlet of 'Compacta' burning bush outshines the crimson foliage of barberry and the rusty red of a Japanese maple.

landscape. In a sunny location, the seed heads of annual grasses such as foxtail millet, Job's tears, quaking grass, and variegated corn stand ready for harvesting for winter bouquets.

In the vegetable patch, pumpkins, winter squash, onions, and gourds of every imaginable shape and size grow fat and handsome. Apple and pear trees bear ripened fruit. And after the first hint of winter wind and freezing temperatures, the foliage of deciduous trees shows a new color scheme.

Nowhere else in the United States is the display of autumn foliage as extravagant as it is in the Northeast. Sugar maples, hickory, beech, chestnut, and hornbeam, to name only a few magnificent specimens, glow in the crisp, clear light with the reds, oranges, russets, and yellows that signal the end of another growing season.

The Garden in Winter

The garden may look more austere in winter, but it need not look barren. Color is first muted by frost; later, the snow provides a backdrop against which the bare bones of deciduous trees and shrubs are seen. Stately conifers including spruces and false cypress come in greens, blue-greens, and yellow-greens to enliven and structure the scene, and the bark of trees such as shellbark hickory and mountain ash supply textural contrast. The upright stems of yellowtwig and redtwig dogwood glow luminously against the snow, and the heavy seed heads of ornamental grasses rustle in the wind, contributing movement to the winter display.

▶ **The northeastern natives red osier dogwood** *(Cornus sericea)* **with richly hued twigs and winterberry** *(Ilex verticillata)* **with bright red fruits carry the show of a barnside garden into December.**

▶ **A dusting of snow on two** *Syringa meyeri* **trained into standards and spheres of boxwood wrapped in burlap for winter protection highlights the elegant structure of a formal parterre.**

◀ Ice frosts the two *Kerria japonica* flanking the birdhouse, the limbs of a dogwood, and the sedges in the foreground of an Annapolis, Maryland, garden after a December storm.

▲ Blue-violet flowers of *Iris reticulata* hover above the crusty snowcover of March in a Connecticut garden.

With the growing season's raiment stripped away, winter reveals the garden's formal design or lack of it. Walls and fences no longer adorned with summer's opulent foliage suddenly appear more prominent, indicating whether the garden's focus and sightlines are balanced or out of kilter. Hedges of boxwood, yew, and privet and the carpet of ivy stand out, allowing a no-nonsense assessment of what has become unruly and needs to be trimmed back. The sudden sight of your neighbor's garage or toolshed may spur plans for next year's planting schemes.

Finally in late winter, when the bleakness of the season begins to seem interminable, nature comes to the rescue with those cold-blooming plants that offer gentle reassurance. One of the showiest is the hellebore, whose nodding, cup-shaped flowers, in pale pink, greenish white, lime green, and green-speckled purple, bloom as early as January. A month later, the red-and-yellow flowers of witch hazel bloom on its bare branches. Gardeners in the more southerly reaches of the Northeast can count on shrubby camellias and their large, waxy red, pink, and white blooms to remind them that the garden will once again awaken to the splendor of spring.

THE CLIMATE ZONES
of the Northeast

When an unfamiliar plant strikes your fancy, your first question is likely to be, "Can I grow it?" You may have no trouble learning its soil preference, its water needs, and whether it thrives in full sun or does better in a shadier spot—but this information accounts for only part of the answer. Influencing the entire can-I-grow-it issue is the matter of climate. Are your summers hot or mild, dry or humid? Is winter a time of snow and ice cover, or drying, frigid winds? You can modify soil, apply or withhold water, or create shade in an attempt to satisfy the needs of certain plants, but the weather—the year-round climate—is in true control of your garden. And if the climate isn't right, some plants may fail to prosper despite your best efforts.

With the 1954 publication of Sunset's first *Western Garden Book,* gardeners west of the Continental Divide had the chance to read plant descriptions keyed to a map that organized the West into a set of actual climate zones. Until that time, gardening references addressed the issue of plant adaptability exclusively in terms of cold tolerance, following hardiness-zone maps created by the United States Department of Agriculture and the Arnold Arboretum based on winter low temperatures and annual first-frost dates. The statement

"hardy through Zone 8," for instance, identified a plant that could withstand lows to 10°F/−12°C, but revealed nothing about its preference, if any, for the climate of central California over that of the southeastern states. The system treated these regions alike, presenting gardeners in both areas with the same list of "hardy in Zone 8" plants. The *Western Garden Book* system, however, assigned these two regions to different zones, giving gardeners in each a far more accurate idea of which plants would and would not flourish for them.

Based on the success of the climate zones in the West, Sunset extended its climate research to the parts of the United States and Canada east of the Continental Divide and now, in the *Northeastern Garden Book,* presents the 14 climate zones in the northeastern U.S. and southeastern Canada. The region covered in this book is bounded by Virginia in the south, Ohio in the west, runs through the mid-Atlantic and New England states, and includes parts of southeastern Canada. All the climate zones are described and shown on the following pages.

Overlooking the Susquehannah River in Lancaster County, Pennsylvania.

Early morning in the Adirondack Mountains near Lake Placid, in upstate New York.

WHAT MAKES CLIMATE?

Weather and climate are two different, although obviously related, occurrences. Weather is a day-to-day happening, the conditions described in the daily reports we read in the newspaper or hear on the radio or TV. Climate refers to the prevailing weather conditions of a particular place, determined by averaging weather data over a period of years.

To grasp the complexities (and, therefore, the importance) of climate, you need to know some weather basics and understand how weather patterns are influenced by topography.

Three factors have a general influence on climate:

Latitude. The farther north of the equator a place is, the colder its winters are likely to be, and the longer the wintry weather is likely to last.

Elevation. Temperatures in both summer and winter tend to decrease with elevation. Mountain locations are cooler in summer, colder in winter than adjacent lowlands.

Wind patterns. In the middle latitudes of the Northern Hemisphere, winds move in a general west-to-east direction. Various high-altitude air currents known as jet streams are important in weather creation; their speed and strength make them express conduits for air of all qualities— moist, dry, warm, cold. In their predictable latitudinal migration, they tend to dip farther south in winter and move more to the north in summer, following the movement of the sun. The so-called storm track follows the jet streams' path, accounting for rainy and dry seasons.

Several other, more localized factors modify the basic patterns: influence of the Gulf of Mexico (in the eastern half of the U.S.), ocean currents, proximity to one or more of the Great Lakes, and location of mountain ranges.

THE TOPOGRAPHY OF THE NORTHEAST

From Nova Scotia to West Virginia and farther south, the Appalachian mountain system rises up and forms a natural barrier between the eastern seaboard and the expansive lowlands of the continental interior. The Appalachians don't reach soaring heights—Mt. Washington in New Hampshire, the highest mountain in the northern division of the Appalachians, is a relatively modest 6,288 feet. But these mountains

The Appalachian Mountains in the Northeast are older, more rounded, and not as high as the Rockies in the West.

Along Lake Erie in Ohio, the Allegheny Plateau flattens out; farther west is prairie land.

pervade the northeastern sensibility, giving it a flinty endurance. Rivers and deep, glacier-carved lakes, including the Great Lakes, dot the North and serve as conduits and reservoirs for rain and melted snow. On either side of the mountain range are plains. The coastal plain stretches to the east from New Jersey to the Chesapeake Bay and south, and has sandy, sometimes boggy soil. To the west, from western New York, Pennsylvania, and West Virginia and through Ohio, runs the hilly Allegheny Plateau, which descends into prairie in western Ohio and the fertile Ohio River Valley in southern Ohio. Long barrier islands, such as Long Island in New York and Assateague Island in Virginia, stretch along the Atlantic Coast.

CLIMATE IN THE NORTHEAST

Northeastern gardeners can expect cold winters, hot, muggy summers, and drier autumns. Rainfall is plentiful, from 30 to 50 inches per year, with much precipitation taking the form of snow in the Great Lakes, Hudson Bay, and St. Lawrence River areas. Drought, therefore, is generally less of a problem than winter cold. The air in the Northeast is more humid than the air in many parts of the West, and humid air is generally best for plants. Humidity moderates temperature—humid air cools more slowly at night than dry air, and heats up more slowly in the morning. High humidity can be harmful, however, when the air is very still, as it can be in summer. Fungi and other disease pathogens can develop into rusts, mildew, and other diseases when they sit on leaves undisturbed by wind or rain.

In much of the Northeast—northern Maine, New Hampshire, Vermont, New York, and southern Canada—winter temperatures range from 0° to −20°F/−18° to −29°C. In the warmer Chesapeake Bay area of Maryland and Virginia the coldest winter temperatures hover between 0° and 10°F/−18° to −12°C. The greatest risk to plants in the Northeast comes not from cold temperatures in winter, but from a combination of cold and drying winds when no snow cover is present. Dry cold is very damaging to plants. Dry winter winds draw moisture out of plant leaves, and when the soil is frozen, roots cannot draw up more moisture from the soil to replace what's been lost. Broadleaf evergreens are especially at risk of winter damage. Anti-desiccant sprays and in extreme cases, burlap windbreaks, can help. Roses can be protected with a mound of soil over their roots and a thick blanket of loose mulch held in place by a wire mesh cylinder surrounding the plant. To avoid winter damage, grow plants known to be hardy in your area. If you experiment with plants of borderline hardiness, give them winter protection (see Frost Protection, on page 464).

In late summer and fall, a coastal storm season begins as tropical storms from the Gulf of Mexico track up the Atlantic coast; "nor'easters" from the North Atlantic batter the coast in winter.

THE INFLUENCE OF MICROCLIMATES

"Microclimate" refers to local conditions resulting in a different climate within a single garden or slightly larger area in a neighborhood—all within one climate zone. For instance, south-facing portions of a garden are typically warmer than those facing north, and areas near walls and fences tend to be drier than those in the middle of a garden bed. Look for the following microclimates:

Unusually warm sections. A courtyard that receives full afternoon sun and is surrounded by high walls on all four sides will be a garden hot spot. Even a single cement or brick wall may warm part of a garden if it receives several hours of afternoon sun each day—the wall absorbs heat during the day, then gradually releases it during the cooler nighttime hours. A hot spot is not a good location for some early bloomers, such as peach trees, that might be prodded into bloom during an early spring mild spell, only to have the flowers damaged by a late frost.

Cool pockets. Because cool air travels downward, the bottom of a slope is colder than the top—so the base of a hill isn't the place for heat-loving summer vegetables. A cold air pocket may also develop halfway down a slope if a hedge or wall impedes air flow. If you garden in an area with many frosty days and nights each year, be particularly careful not to plant tender plants or vegetables in such cool pockets.

Windy areas. The placement of buildings on your property can generate a local wind tunnel. Wind is especially problematic in cities, where plants growing in rooftop or courtyard gardens are often buffeted by the strong winds that whip around tall buildings. Even if the enhanced wind isn't especially severe, it can still damage the leaves of sensitive plants and dry out the soil, resulting in a need for extra water. To neutralize a wind tunnel, you can plant fast-growing trees or shrubs facing into the wind. Don't construct a solid wall; it will simply deflect the wind briefly, then drop it back into the garden a few feet away.

Large bodies of water such as Lake Champlain (shown here) moderate the climate in surrounding areas.

The 14 Northeast
CLIMATE ZONES

Map labels:
Quebec Page 46
Ontario Page 43
Maine Page 46
Vermont Page 46
New Hampshire Page 46
New York Page 43
Massachusetts Page 46
Rhode Island Page 46
Connecticut Page 46
Pennsylvania Page 42, 43
New Jersey Page 43
New York City Page 44–45
Ohio Page 42
Maryland Page 42, 43
Delaware Page 41
West Virginia Page 42
Virginia Page 41, 42

In the following pages, the variety of northeastern gardening in the United States and Canada is presented in 14 distinct climate zones, numbered 32, 34–45. Zone 33 falls outside the boundaries of the Northeast region and is not included in this book. One small corner of southeastern Virginia falls into very mild Zone 31, and gardeners there can grow many plants more commonly associated with the Deep South, including camellias and the showy trademark tree of the South, *Magnolia grandiflora.* The 14 zones of the Northeast organize the land mass into cohesive climatic regions as they relate to gardening.

Each description in the A to Z Plant Encyclopedia (beginning on page 113) states the zones in which that plant can be expected to thrive, given the garden culture it needs. Remember, too, that each garden has its own microclimates, areas in which exposure to sun, wind, and frost vary according to the terrain and the orientation of the house. Such microclimates may be critical to the survival of plants.

In the climate zone descriptions that follow, each zone's growing season—the average number of days between the last frost in spring and the first frost in fall—

is shown as a light green band on a bar at the end of the zone description. The yellow parts of the bands indicate shoulder seasons, when light frosts would not be likely to bother cool-season crops, though more tender plants would be damaged.

Although growing season data offer a guide to the timing of some planting and choice of plants, it is just one piece of the climate puzzle. The expected growing season weather—hot, cool, wet, dry, windy—will affect plant success and your gardening practices.

Locator Map

To find your garden's climate zone, start with this locator map and then turn to the page listed for your area. If you garden in a microclimate, adjust your zone accordingly.

At Home in the Northeast

Cold winters and humid, moist summers are fine for, left to right, *Clematis jackmanii,* tomatoes, and coneflowers (*Rudbeckia hirta* and *Echinacea purpurea*).

ZONE 32 — Mid-Atlantic States; Chesapeake Bay, Southeastern Pennsylvania, Southern New Jersey

For the most part, this region is a gardener's delight. It gets some snow, but usually not much; winter lows are typically in the 20s north of Virginia. Thanks to the barrier of the Appalachians, Arctic freezes rarely move through—but when they do, temperatures typically drop to 0° to 10°F/−18° to −12°C (record lows range from −9° to −17°F/−23° to −27°C). The growing season is usually long enough (180 to 240 days) and warm enough to offer grand gardening and a choice of plants to satisfy the most demanding of gardeners.

The northern cut-off line for Bermuda grass and traditional camellias runs through Zone 32. Both plants are popular in the zone's southern reaches, rare or entirely absent in Baltimore, Philadelphia, and Atlantic City. This is also the northernmost climate in which a wide variety of vegetables, flowers, and ornamental trees and shrubs can be planted in fall as well as in spring.

Precipitation comes fairly evenly year-round in Zone 32. Throughout the zone, the annual average rainfall is a consistent 40 to 50 inches.

Gentle Climate

Zone 32 is blessed with a mild climate and a long growing season. There's usually plenty of moisture, with rainfall distributed evenly through the year. Blasts of Arctic air are rare in winter, but summers are humid and often muggy.

ZONE 34 — Lowlands and Coast from Gettysburg to North of Boston

Winters in Zone 34 are so mild that some of the hardier camellias survive, along with many evergreen hollies, common boxwood, *Clerodendrum trichotomum,* and the hardier selections of *Magnolia grandiflora.*

This happy clime has predictable and temperate seasons, with generous precipitation year-round (30 to 50 inches annually). The weather here results from three major sources: first, cold air moving down from Canada in winter; second, warm and moist air coming all the way up from the Gulf of Mexico; and third, some damp ocean air that occasionally moves inland from the North Atlantic.

In those winters when Zone 34 gets no freezing arctic air, winter minimums are in the low 20s; when Arctic air moves in, lows range from −3° to −22°F/−19° to −30°C. North of Philadelphia and Atlantic City, 12 National Oceanic and Atmospheric Administration stations typically record 100 or fewer days with freezing temperatures each year, and those 12 stations are all in Zone 34.

La Guardia Airport records just 65 annual days of freezing temperatures; Central Park, 80; JFK Airport, 81; Mineola, NY, 85; Newark, NJ, 86; New Bedford, MA, 87; Jersey City, NJ, 89; Long Branch, NJ, 98; Boston, 98; Islip, NY, 98; Dobbs Ferry, NY, 99; and Bridgeport, CT, 100.

In elevation, most towns in this zone range from sea level to 600 feet—another factor resulting in milder winters here than in climates farther inland. New York, Newark, Boston, and Bridgeport lie essentially at sea level and get more marine air (bringing fog, mist, and moderate temperatures) than the zone's other cities do.

Coastal Lowlands

Coastal areas in the Northeast enjoy milder conditions than locations farther inland. Long Island Sound moderates the climate in southern Connecticut *(seen here)* and northern Long Island. Though mild, coastal gardens are also often windy.

ZONE **35** Southern Ohio

Most of Zone 35 runs through the Oua-chita Mountains, northern Okla-homa, and southern Kansas to north central Kentucky. But it also includes southern Ohio, which is part of the Northeast region covered in this book. Throughout the central region of the United States and Canada, the climate in each area is determined by its latitude; by how much air from the Gulf of Mexico it gets midyear; and by how much Arctic air it gets in winter. In Zone 35, these factors combine to produce a climate with hot, humid summers (with highs from 103° to 114°F/39° to 46°C) and winters with typical lows of 19° to 24°F/−7° to −4°C. When Arctic air masses come through every few years, however, temperatures may drop as low as −20°F/−29°C.

Gardeners here enjoy success with a huge number of perennials; top-notch dependables include columbine, coreopsis, sunflower, hellebore, daylily, hosta, bee

balm, peony, phlox, and Stokes' aster. Many rhododendrons and azaleas do well in shady gardens, except in very windy areas and in those with alkaline soil. Roses do nicely, too; if adequately fertilized, they'll produce four or five flushes of bloom per year, though the fifth one is likely to be a bit weak.

Zone 35's normal annual rainfall is 36 to 42 inches. The growing season ranges from 150 to 240 days.

Farm Country

The hilly Allegheny Plateau in south-eastern Ohio is dotted with farms. Many perennials grow well in gardens here.

ZONE **36** Appalachian Mountains

In the eastern half of the United States, the Appalachian chain plays a part in determining the weather. When cold air masses move down through central North America, they don't always make it over or through the mountains—thus sparing the land on the lee (southeastern) side of the range some of the deep cold that settles to the west. When Arctic air does make it up and over the Appalachians, it tends to warm up as it moves, so that winters on the mountains' southeast side are still milder than those to the west. Minimum temperatures range from 0° to −20°F/−18° to −29°C.

Within the Appalachians themselves, the higher elevation produces cooler summers and colder winters than in the surrounding regions. The area's biggest gardening challenge, though, lies in accommodating a weather pattern that crops up throughout winter and on into April: a few warm days will be followed by a freeze. Appalachian native plants can take this sort of inconsistency, and scores of handsome and enjoyable choices are sold by the region's native plant nurseries.

Many of the hardier azaleas and rhododendrons also do well. The deciduous forests here are rich in species and luxuriant in growth, and an equally rich variety of shrubs and perennials flourishes beneath the trees.

The zone's second notable gardening problem, especially in the slightly lower elevations, is its sporadic rainfall, particularly between the end of the normally rainy spring and the beginning of winter. Again, native plants can help gardeners cope with this problem. Other solutions include double digging, incorporating ample organic matter in garden beds, mulching, and using drip and/or seepage irrigation.

The growing season varies from 120 to 160 days in Zone 36.

The Blue Ridge

Catawba and rosebay rhododendron (*R. catawbiense* and *R. maximum*) grace summer woodlands along the Blue Ridge Parkway. This area is subject to late frosts in spring.

ZONE 37   Hudson Valley and Appalachian Plateau

Covering parts of Pennsylvania, New York, and Connecticut, Zone 37 is too far inland to get much of the Atlantic's mild influence, but its elevation is low enough to let it largely escape the harshness of the neighboring mountains. Valleys in this zone are fine for gardening. In the valleys, the last frosts of spring typically come in early or mid-May, while the first frosts of autumn arrive in early to mid-October. Over the region as a whole, the growing season varies from about 120 to 180 days. Winters here are cold; low temperatures average in the high teens, though they may dip as low as −5° to −15°F/−20° to −26°C with the arrival of the occasional Arctic air mass.

Autumn Color

Northeastern hardwood forests are colorful in fall, as shown in this woodland view in Ulster County, New York. The valleys here boast many lush and varied gardens.

The Magnificent Hudson

The Hudson Valley is known for fine apples and is home to an increasing number of small farms raising gourmet produce for sophisticated markets.

A wide range of trees, shrubs, vines, and perennials perform beautifully in Zone 37. Examples of sure-thing choices include this gardener's dozen: azalea, coreopsis, delphinium, flowering quince, hydrangea, lilac, mountain laurel, rhododendron, rudbeckia, Shasta daisy, spiraea, viburnum, and weigela. Thanks to its location near a major metropolitan area, the Hudson Valley is increasingly popular among growers of

quality produce for on-site sale to city buyers. Tomatoes can be planted in late April or early May and harvested from mid-July through August. Some discerning tomato fans claim that, variety for variety, tomatoes raised in the Hudson Valley clay-soil areas taste better than those grown anywhere else. Apples, the big commercial crop here, grow successfully in home gardens across the region as well.

ZONE **38** New England Interior and Lowland Maine

Gardeners here have only 4 or 5 months to work with: summers start quickly and end just as rapidly. Short though it is, the season offers some substantial horticultural pleasures. For one thing, growing cool-season lawn grass is supremely easy. When the locals say "just throw the seed on the ground and walk away," they're exaggerating only slightly. There is another plus: regular rainfall often eliminates the need for irrigation, keeping moisture in the root zone throughout the growing season. (When rainfall is irregular, watering will be necessary in July and August.)

Zone 38 offers another advantage, too. Some of the native soils are just about perfect: slightly acidic and rich in organic matter. On the down side, the soil is incredibly rocky—and indeed, rock removal has always been part of New England gardening.

This area is world-famous for the autumn color of its deciduous trees, among them sugar maple, red maple, beeches, and oaks.

Normal lows in Zone 38 range from −2°F/−19°C to perhaps 16° to 18°F/−9° to −8°C. Record lows (always due to Arctic air) range from −19° to −30°F/−28° to −34°C. The cold means that most fruit trees become chancier as you move north within the zone. Apples make it all the way, but peaches and other stone fruits perform well only in the southern parts: either the trees themselves are not sufficiently cold-hardy, or the blossoms are killed by spring frosts in most years. Hardier rhododendrons thrive here if carefully sited; exposure to the north keeps plants shaded in winter, avoiding freeze-and-thaw damage from southern sun. Provide protection from north winds.

Rocky Coast of Maine

In this part of New England, rocky soil is the norm. Many plants bloom together during the short growing season.

ZONE **39** Shoreline Regions of the Great Lakes

Lake Effects

The areas east and south of the Great Lakes enjoy milder conditions than other locations at similar latitudes. Lake-effect snows blanket the region in winter.

From late spring through late fall and into the start of winter, the Great Lakes moderate the climate of some of the regions surrounding them—an effect felt more to the east and south of the lakes than to their north and west, since weather generally moves from west to east. Where this influence is strongest, a definably different garden climate exists, designated in this book as Zone 39.

Compared to the adjoining areas, Zone 39 has milder, later springs, and it is less likely to experience the late spring freezes that kill flower buds. It also has cooler summers and milder, longer autumns. The growing season varies from 180 to 210 days.

Year-round, gardens here—in Cleveland and Buffalo, for example—experience an average of 21 fewer freezing days than do those located at the same latitude (41° to 42° north) but beyond the lakes' influence—such as in Albany and Worcester. Winter lows range from 0° to 10°F/−18° to −12°C.

ZONE 40 Inland Plains of Lake Erie and Lake Ontario

The second-mildest of the Great Lakes climates, Zone 40 covers parts of Ohio, Pennsylvania, New York, and Ontario. Typical winters see temperatures dropping to −10° to −20°F/−23° to −29°C; when Arctic air moves in, lows may fall to −30°F/−34°C. The growing season begins in mid- to late May and generally ends in mid-September or soon thereafter.

Gardeners in Zone 40 can grow some fruits and berries: apples, pears, plums, blueberries, grapes. Nurseries sell about 60 kinds of ornamentals; those available in greatest variety are flowering crabapple, lilac, juniper, spiraea, maple, and viburnum.

Fertile Fields

The soil in this Ohio wheat field is rich and fertile, in part the result of glacial deposits.

ZONE 41 Northern Ohio

Here the climate results from two primary forces: warm, moist air moving north from the Gulf of Mexico during spring, summer, and fall; and frigid Arctic air descending from Canada in winter. A lesser (but still noteworthy) influence is the dry, usually warm air that sometimes moves in from the West or Southwest. Average annual minimum temperatures range from 11° to 20°F/−12° to −7°C, with record lows from −26° to −37°F/−32° to −38°C. The growing season averages 120 to 180 days.

In this part of Ohio, Lake Erie does influence the weather (though its effect is not as strong here as it is in Zone 39). Areas of Zone 41 closer to the lake have summers that are cooler, wetter, and later to arrive, while winters are somewhat milder and likewise later in arriving.

Zone 41 marks the northern boundary for many deciduous fruit trees (though not for apples and sour cherries), either because the trees are not hardy there or because springtime frosts kill the blossoms.

Zone 41's temperature extremes vary from extremely cold to very hot (as high as 112°F/44°C)—conditions that rule out a number of popular permanent landscaping plants. Regional native plants, however, have the stamina and disposition to survive through every season. Handsome, durable natives of this area include, among many others, various kinds of columbine, gayfeather, and rudbeckia.

Northwestern Ohio at one time contained a huge swamp, full of marsh vegetation. Draining the swamp allowed the land to be farmed. Soils, though fertile, often have a high lime content ideal for lilacs and delphiniums, but difficult for rhododendrons and other acid-soil lovers. Grow the latter in raised beds heavily amended with peat moss or other organic matter. Protect these and other evergreens from freeze-and-thaw winters and harsh winds by mulching and using wind screens.

Spring Beauty

Trilliums carpet the floor of a woodland in Zone 41, in northern Ohio. Soil here tends to be alkaline.

ZONE 42 Mountains of Interior Pennsylvania and New York, St. Lawrence Valley

The United States part of Zone 42 is mountainous country, a continuation of the Appalachian range (Zone 36). Though lower in elevation than Zone 36, it is farther from the equator, so its minimum temperatures are lower. Winters are harsher and summers more humid than those in the surrounding areas. Still, numerous flowering native plants thrive to delight gardeners in this zone. You can grow excellent tomatoes here, too; plant them in late May for harvest in August and September. The growing season ranges from 90 to 120 days.

In Canada, much of the St. Lawrence Valley (as far north as 48° north latitude) experiences the general conditions just described, although the Canadian region of Zone 42 typically records lower temperatures than does the U.S. part. Over the zone as a whole, minimums range from −20° to −40°F/−29° to −40°C.

Roses for the North

Hardy and disease free, fragrant rugosa roses are good choices for Zone 42 gardens.

Serene Mountain Lakes

Yellow flag iris *(I. pseudacorus)* blooms beside a tranquil lake in upstate New York *(left)*.

ZONE 43 Southern Ontario and Quebec

Here, as in Zone 41 to the south, gardening is influenced by frigid Arctic air coming south in winter. Expected winter lows range from −20° to −30°F/−29° to −34°C, but in unusually cold years, temperatures may drop to −40°F/−40°C or lower. Given temperatures like these, the best shade trees for the region are its native maples, oaks, birches, and conifers, as well as some species from northern Europe and Asia. This far north, the one really dependable fruit tree is the apple. Those that do best are early-ripening varieties on semidwarf rootstocks.

Tomatoes grown in this region are sweet and tasty. With the last frosts expected in late May, set out started plants in early June for harvest in late August and early September. The first frosts usually arrive in mid- to late September.

Roses bloom quite nicely during the summer. For many gardeners, the reward of warm-season blossoms is well worth the trouble of protecting the plants each autumn against winter's freezes. Or seek out extra-hardy varieties.

Depending on the weather, lawns may well get through the summer without watering. An inch or more of rain each week will sustain the grass; less than that, and you'll need to water your lawn to keep it green.

Autumn Begins

The Niagara River gorge, not far from the Falls, begins to show its autumn colors in September. Garden plants must be hardy to survive winters here. Provide winter protection for roses (see Frost Protection on page 464) and they will reward you with summer blossoms. Other plants for Zone 43 include achillea, monkshood, coreopsis, hostas, lilies, lamb's ears, and veronica.

ZONE 44 Mountains of New England and Southeastern Quebec

"Ski country" is what many people would call the southern half of Zone 44. Winters are very cold (with lows from −20° to −40°F/−29° to −40°C) and summers comparatively cool (highs from 60°F/16°C to 70°F/21°C or higher), thanks both to the region's northerly latitude and to its frequently high elevations. Mt. Washington (elevation 6,288 ft.), in the White Mountains, has been known to get freezing weather and snow during every month of the year.

But the region has its gardening life as well. If you want to grow a summer garden, wait until June 1 or the apparent last frost—and then plant immediately, since the year's first frost looms only about 3 months away (or even sooner, in the occasional extra-cold year). Get tomatoes and peppers into the ground as soon as possible, along with the hardier potatoes, broccoli, cauliflower, and cabbage. Lawn grass grows well in May and June, then often slows a little in July. In August, cool, wet weather promotes fresh growth again.

Among roses, most popular hybrid teas, grandifloras, and floribundas are too tender to survive winters unless they are heavily protected. The most satisfactory roses for this climate are the hardiest species (such as *Rosa rugosa*) and cold-tolerant shrub roses developed in the Midwest and Canada.

Northern Meadow

A field of lupines with New Hampshire's White Mountains in the background demonstrates the beauty of the mountains-and-lakes country of New England.

ZONE 45 Northern and Central Ontario and Quebec

No other garden climate in eastern North America matches Zone 45 for winter cold or briefness of the frost-free season. Temperatures often fall to −30° to −40°F/−34° to −40°C. The soil freezes in early December—often to a depth of 5 to 6 feet—and thaws in mid-April. The last spring frosts come in early or even mid-June, with the first frosts of fall arriving in early September. If you want to grow frost-delicate crops such as tomatoes, peppers, and corn, you will need to choose short-season varieties. Among fruits and berries, some good choices for Zone 45 are blueberries and native raspberries, cherries, and plums.

Gardeners in this region enjoy a number of dependable and beautiful flowering shrubs, including lilac, viburnum, and redtwig dogwood. Flowering trees are few, but two hawthorns, *Crataegus ambigua* and *C.* 'Toba', reliably show off their white flowers and red fruit. Spring-blooming bulbs perform beautifully; native wildflowers and rock garden plants are popular, too. The consistently low winter temperatures and a good snow cover aid in the survival of many perennials and low shrubs.

Broadleaf evergreens are the major garden element lacking in this zone, but many conifers and berry-producing shrubs provide winter color. Recent work at the University of Minnesota has extended the cold tolerance of deciduous azaleas to −40°F/−40°C in the Northern Lights Hybrids (such as 'Golden Lights,' 'Orchard Lights,' 'White Lights').

Winter Dreams

The quiet beauty of snow-covered conifers reflects a landscape asleep for the winter in this part of Canada.

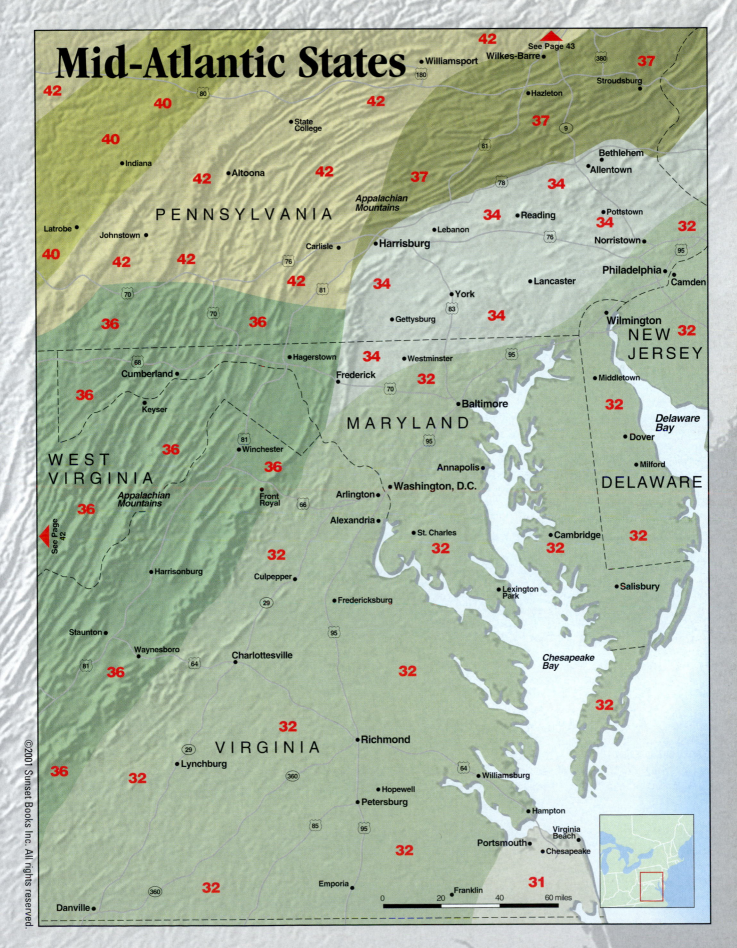

Mid-Atlantic States

PENNSYLVANIA

Williamsport
Wilkes-Barre
See Page 43
Stroudsburg
Hazleton
State College
Indiana
Bethlehem
Allentown
Altoona
Appalachian Mountains
Reading
Pottstown
Norristown
Philadelphia
Latrobe
Johnstown
Lebanon
Harrisburg
Lancaster
Camden
Carlisle
York
Wilmington
NEW JERSEY
Gettysburg
Hagerstown
Westminster
Cumberland
Frederick
Middletown
Keyser
MARYLAND
Baltimore
DELAWARE
Dover
Winchester
Delaware Bay
WEST VIRGINIA
Annapolis
Milford
Appalachian Mountains
Front Royal
Arlington
Washington, D.C.
Alexandria
See Page 42
St. Charles
Cambridge
Harrisonburg
Culpepper
Lexington Park
Salisbury
Fredericksburg
Chesapeake Bay
Staunton
Waynesboro
Charlottesville
Richmond
VIRGINIA
Lynchburg
Williamsburg
Hopewell
Petersburg
Hampton
Virginia Beach
Portsmouth
Chesapeake
Emporia
Franklin
Danville

0   20   40   60 miles

42 40 42 37 42 37 40 40 42 42 37 34 34 34 34 32 40 42 42 42 36 36 34 32 36 34 32 32 32 36 36 36 36 36 32 32 32 32 32 36 32 32 32 31

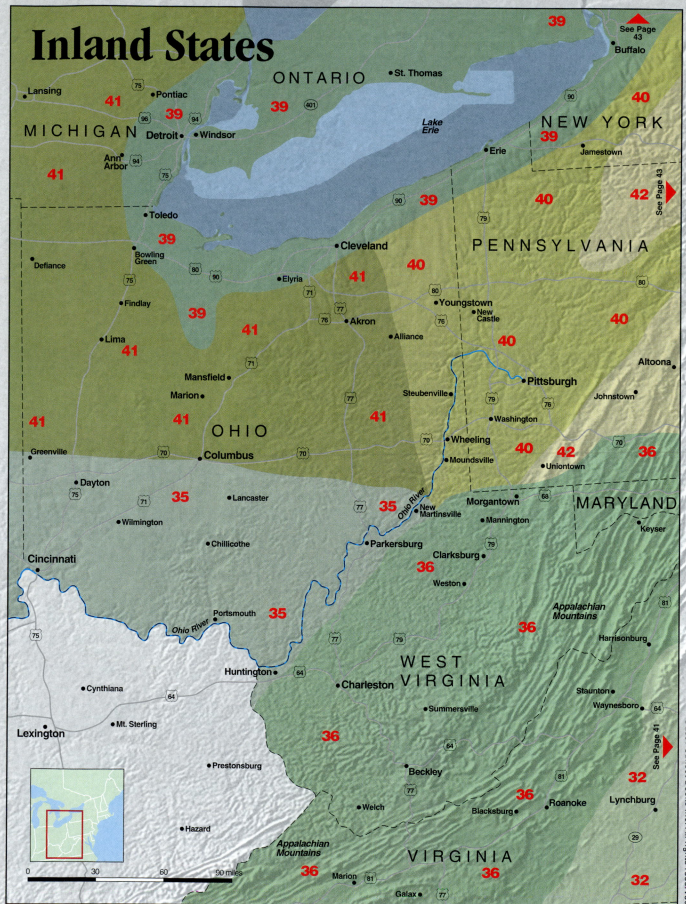

Inland States

ONTARIO

39

See Page 43
Buffalo

St. Thomas

Lansing

41

Pontiac
39

39

40

NEW YORK

MICHIGAN
Detroit • Windsor

39

Jamestown

Ann Arbor

Lake Erie

Erie

41

39

40

PENNSYLVANIA

Toledo

39

Cleveland

42

See Page 43

Defiance

Bowling Green

Elyria

40

41

Findlay

Youngstown
New Castle

40

39

Akron

Lima

41

41

Alliance

40

Altoona

Mansfield

41

Steubenville

Pittsburgh

Marion

41

Johnstown

Greenville

41

41

OHIO

41

Washington

40

42

36

Dayton

Columbus

Wheeling

MARYLAND

Lancaster

35

Moundsville

40

Uniontown

Keyser

Wilmington

35

Morgantown

Chillicothe

Martinsville
New

Mannington

Cincinnati

Parkersburg

36

Clarksburg

Appalachian Mountains

Portsmouth

35

Weston

36

Ohio River

Harrisonburg

Huntington

WEST VIRGINIA

Cynthiana

Charleston

Staunton

Lexington

Mt. Sterling

Summersville

Waynesboro

Prestonsburg

36

Beckley

36

Roanoke

Lynchburg

32

Welch

Blacksburg

Hazard

Appalachian Mountains

36

VIRGINIA

36

32

Marion

Galax

0   30   60   90 miles

New York, Pennsylvania, New Jersey

45

QUEBEC

Ste.-Agathe-des-Monts **43**

45

Joliette **42**

Hull
Ottawa

Laval • Montreal **44**

Salaberry-de-Valleyfield
St.-Jean-sur-Richelieu

43

Cornwall

43 **43**

Massena

ONTARIO

Lake Champlain

42

Burlington

44

40

Peterborough

Kingston

Adirondack Mountains

39

Belleville

Watertown

39

40

44

Scarborough
York • Toronto
Mississauga

Lake Ontario

38

Glens Falls

Kitchener

Hamilton
St. Catharines

40

Brantford

Rochester

Oneida Lake

Syracuse

Utica

Saratoga Springs

42

Schenectady
Troy
Albany

39

Niagara Falls **39**

Buffalo

39

Lake Erie

40

Geneseo

Finger Lakes

NEW YORK

Ithaca

42

Oneonta

37

Catskill Mountains

Kingston

Erie **39**

Jamestown

Corning • Elmira

Binghamton

37

Poughkeepsie

40

42

Newburgh

34

Scranton

Pocono Mountains

37

42

42

Wilkes-Barre

Williamsport

Hazleton

Stroudsburg

37

Long Island

Paterson
Newark

New York

40

42

State College

PENNSYLVANIA

37

Bethlehem
Allentown

34

See Pages 44 & 45

Youngstown
New Castle

Pittsburgh

Altoona

Appalachian Mountains

Reading

Princeton
Trenton

Steubenville
Washington

42

Johnstown

42

Lebanon

Pottstown

Harrisburg

Norristown

NEW JERSEY

Wheeling

42

Philadelphia
Camden

Atlantic Ocean

Moundsville **40**

Uniontown

36

York
Lancaster

34

Wilmington

32

Vineland

36

Morgantown

Cumberland

Gettysburg

36

Hagerstown

Westminster

Middletown

Atlantic City

WEST VIRGINIA

Keyser

MARYLAND

Baltimore

See Page 42

DELAWARE

32

Winchester

32

New York City and Long Island

37

See Page 43

84

37

• Danbury

84

37

37

87

684

N E W   Y O R K

34

Hudson River

87

34

Norwalk •

95

Bridgep•

684

37

Stamford •

See Page 43

Greenwich •

287

• White
Plains

95

• Paterson

• Yonkers

80

87

95

37

Fort
Lee •

34
Bronx

• New
Rochelle

Oyster
Bay •

95

95

• Huntington
Station

34

495

678

495

34

495

• Plainview

N E W   J E R S E Y

34
Manhattan

278

495

Deer
Park •

• Newark

34
Queens

678

Long
Island

27

Bay
Shore

Jersey
City •

• Hempstead

• West
Babylon

78

34

Massapequa
Park •

Elizabeth •

Valley
Stream

27

• Freeport

Brooklyn

95

34

278

34

Long
Beach

Staten
Island

95

34

See Page 42

32

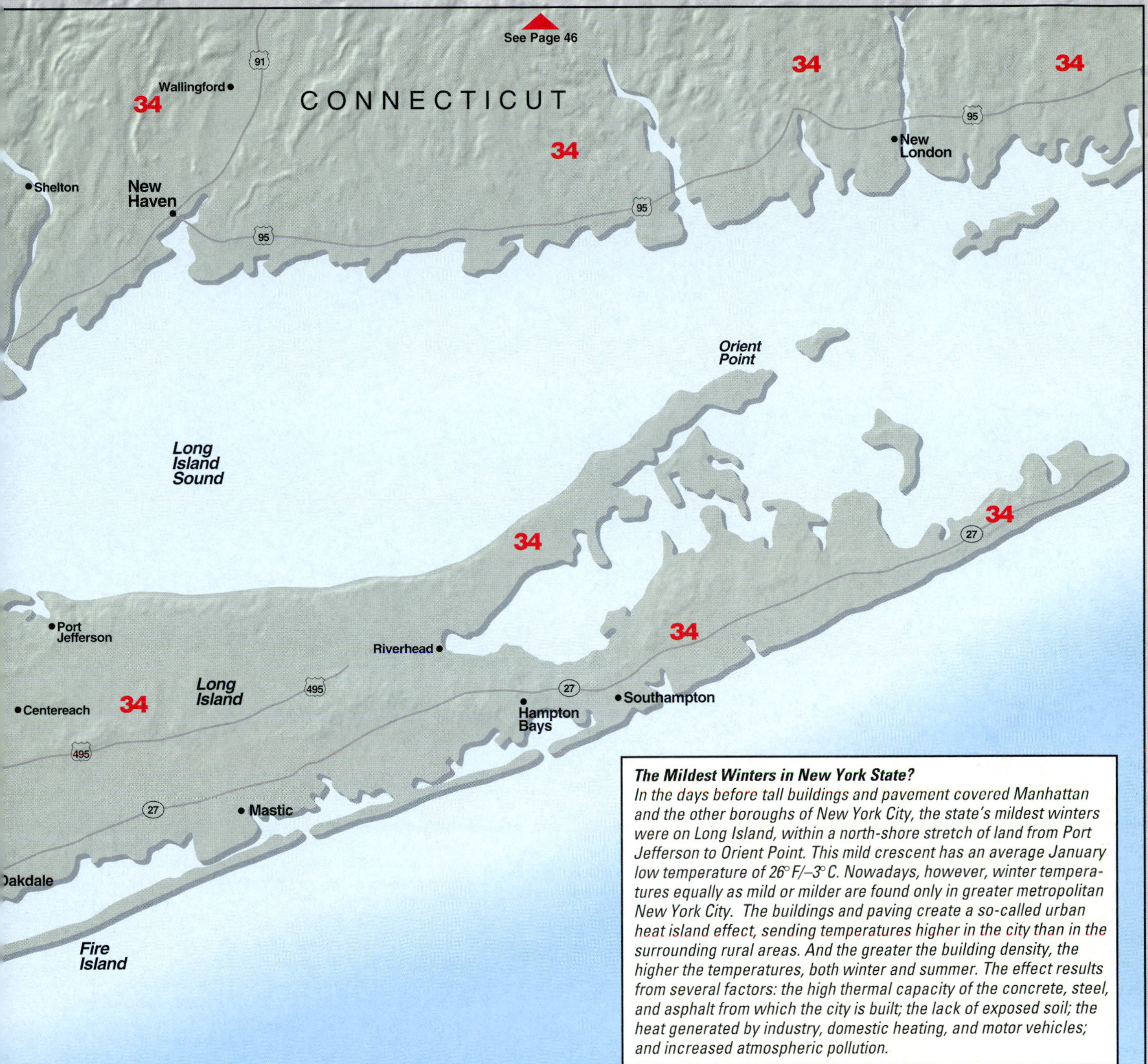

See Page 46

34

34

34

34

CONNECTICUT

91

Wallingford

34

Shelton

New
Haven

95

95

New
London

95

Orient
Point

Long
Island
Sound

34

34

27

34

Port
Jefferson

Riverhead

Long
Island

495

27

Southampton

Hampton
Bays

34

Centereach

495

27

Mastic

Oakdale

Fire
Island

Atlantic
Ocean

The Mildest Winters in New York State?
In the days before tall buildings and pavement covered Manhattan
and the other boroughs of New York City, the state's mildest winters
were on Long Island, within a north-shore stretch of land from Port
Jefferson to Orient Point. This mild crescent has an average January
low temperature of 26° F/–3° C. Nowadays, however, winter temperatures equally as mild or milder are found only in greater metropolitan
New York City. The buildings and paving create a so-called urban
heat island effect, sending temperatures higher in the city than in the
surrounding rural areas. And the greater the building density, the
higher the temperatures, both winter and summer. The effect results
from several factors: the high thermal capacity of the concrete, steel,
and asphalt from which the city is built; the lack of exposed soil; the
heat generated by industry, domestic heating, and motor vehicles;
and increased atmospheric pollution.

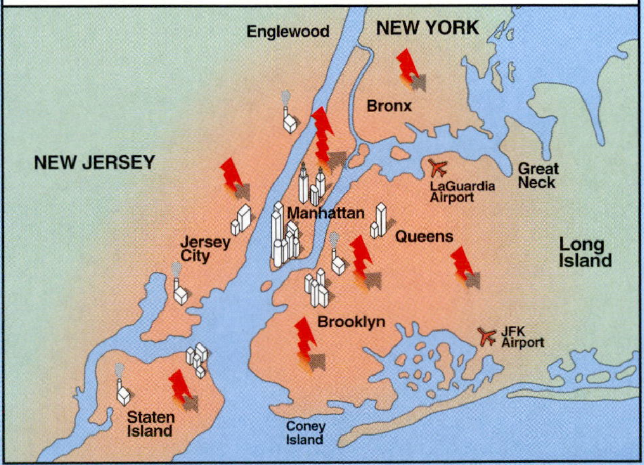

Englewood NEW YORK

NEW JERSEY

Bronx

Jersey
City

Manhattan

LaGuardia
Airport

Great
Neck

Queens

Long
Island

Brooklyn

JFK
Airport

Staten
Island

Coney
Island

0   5   10   15 miles

New England

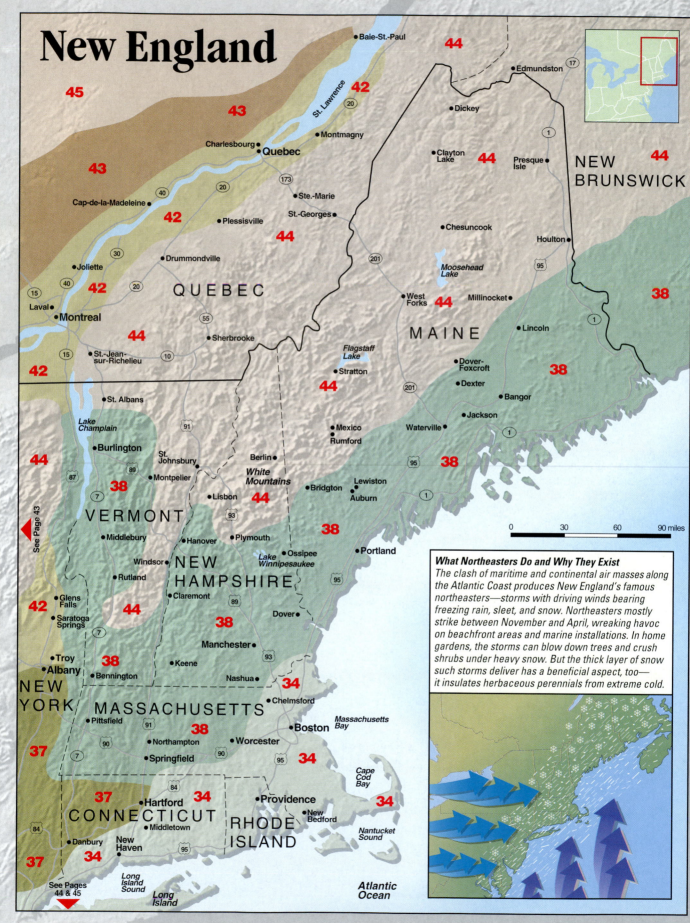

45

Baie-St.-Paul

44

Edmundston ·

43

42

St. Lawrence

Dickey ·

44

Presque Isle ·

NEW BRUNSWICK

44

Charlesbourg ·
Quebec
Montmagny ·

43

Clayton Lake ·

44

Cap-de-la-Madeleine ·

42

Plessisville ·
Ste.-Marie ·
St.-Georges ·

Chesuncook ·

Houlton ·

38

Joliette ·
Drummondville ·

44

Moosehead Lake

42

QUEBEC

West Forks ·

Millinocket ·

44

MAINE

Laval ·
Montreal ·

44

Sherbrooke ·

Lincoln ·

38

42

St.-Jean-sur-Richelieu ·

Flagstaff Lake

Dover-Foxcroft ·

Dexter ·

38

St. Albans ·

Stratton ·

44

Bangor ·

Jackson ·

Lake Champlain

Waterville ·

Mexico ·
Rumford ·

Burlington ·

St. Johnsbury ·

Berlin ·

White Mountains

Bridgton ·

Lewiston ·
Auburn ·

38

44

Montpelier ·

38

44

Lisbon ·

VERMONT

Middlebury ·
Hanover ·
Plymouth ·

Ossipee ·

38

Portland ·

Windsor ·

NEW HAMPSHIRE

Lake Winnipesaukee

Rutland ·

42

Glens Falls ·

Claremont ·

Saratoga Springs

44

Dover ·

38

Troy ·
Albany ·

38

Bennington ·

Manchester ·

Keene ·

Nashua ·

34

NEW YORK

MASSACHUSETTS

Chelmsford ·

Massachusetts Bay

Pittsfield ·

38

Boston ·

37

Northampton ·
Worcester ·

Springfield ·

34

Cape Cod Bay

37

Hartford ·

34

Providence ·

34

CONNECTICUT

Danbury ·

Middletown ·

New Bedford ·

RHODE ISLAND

Nantucket Sound

37

34

New Haven ·

Long Island Sound

Long Island

Atlantic Ocean

See Page 43

See Pages 44 & 45

0   30   60   90 miles

What Northeasters Do and Why They Exist

The clash of maritime and continental air masses along the Atlantic Coast produces New England's famous northeasters—storms with driving winds bearing freezing rain, sleet, and snow. Northeasters mostly strike between November and April, wreaking havoc on beachfront areas and marine installations. In home gardens, the storms can blow down trees and crush shrubs under heavy snow. But the thick layer of snow such storms deliver has a beneficial aspect, too— it insulates herbaceous perennials from extreme cold.

A GUIDE TO
PLANT SELECTION

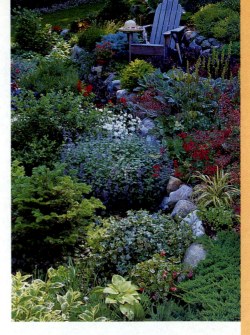

The thousands of plants described in the A to Z Plant Encyclopedia (beginning on page 113) include an infinitely varied assortment of sizes, shapes, textures, and colors. The pleasure of choosing from this rich assortment is available to anyone with a sense of adventure and a bit of earth. But such abundance can sometimes lead to bewilderment. The lists of plants that follow, used with the plant encyclopedia, will help you to select the right plants, whether you are looking to achieve a special effect with flowers or foliage, tackling a difficult landscape situation, or starting out with the basics.

The symbols in the lists will help you choose plants most suitable for your garden. How much sun a plant needs for best performance is shown by one or more of three symbols:

☼ Grows best with unobstructed sunlight all day long or almost all day— you can overlook an hour or so of shade at the beginning or end of a summer day

◑ Needs partial shade—that is, shade for half the day or for at least 3 hours during the hottest part of the day

● Prefers little or no direct sunlight— for example, it does best on the north side of a house or beneath a broad, dense tree

A plant's approximate moisture needs are indicated by one or more of three symbols:

◌ Thrives with less than regular moisture—moderate amounts for some plants, little for those with greater drought tolerance

◍ Performs well with regular moisture—the soil doesn't become too wet or too dry

◍◍ Takes more than regular moisture—includes plants needing constantly moist soil, bog plants, and aquatic plants.

A plant's climate adaptability is shown after the ⚡. The numbers refer to the climate zones (see pages 30–46) where the plant will grow best. Other information, such as flower or leaf color, is explained in legends on the individual lists.

Aesculus pavia

Abeliophyllum distichum

LANDSCAPE PLANTS
with Showy Flowers

Trees, shrubs, ground covers, and vines are the backbones of the garden, but that doesn't mean they serve only as a neutral backdrop to showy annuals and perennials. Many permanent landscape plants put on a striking show of blooms, which provide changing interest throughout the year. In this list, plants are arranged by the time of year in which they flower. Use it to plan your garden's permanent floral display according to season and flower color.

Chionanthus retusus

Spring
TREES

Aesculus
HORSECHESTNUT
NEEDS, ZONES VARY — p. 121

Amelanchier arborea
SERVICEBERRY
☼ ◐ ● ● ⚡ 31, 32, 34–45 — p. 128

Cercis canadensis
REDBUD
☼ ◐ ● ⚡ 32, 34–41 — p. 178

Chionanthus retusus
CHINESE FRINGE TREE
☼ ● ● ⚡ 31, 32, 34, 39 — p. 182

Cladrastis lutea
YELLOW WOOD
☼ ● ⚡ 31, 32, 34–45 — p. 186

Cornus
DOGWOOD
☼ ◐ ● ⚡ ZONES VARY — p. 194

Crataegus
HAWTHORN
☼ ● ⚡ MANY ZONES — p. 198

Davidia involucrata
DOVE TREE
☼ ● ⚡ 31, 32, 34 — p. 207

Halesia
SILVERBELL
☼ ◐ ● ⚡ 31, 32, 34–41 — p. 249

Laburnum
GOLDENCHAIN TREE
☼ ◐ ● ⚡ ZONES VARY — p. 282

Magnolia (most deciduous)
☼ ◐ ● ⚡ ZONES VARY — p. 302

Malus
CRABAPPLE
☼ ● ⚡ 31, 32, 34–43 — p. 308

Prunus (flowering)
☼ ● ⚡ ZONES VARY — p. 368

Pyrus calleryana
ORNAMENTAL PEAR
☼ ● ⚡ 31, 32, 34–41 — p. 375

Robinia pseudoacacia
BLACK LOCUST
☼ ● ● ⚡ 31, 32, 34–43 — p. 385

Styrax
SNOWBELL
☼ ◐ ● ⚡ ZONES VARY — p. 418

Spring
SHRUBS

Abeliophyllum distichum
WHITE FORSYTHIA
☼ ● ⚡ 31, 32, 34–41 — p. 114

Berberis
BARBERRY
☼ ◐ ● ● ⚡ ZONES VARY — p. 154

Calycanthus floridus
SPICE BUSH
☼ ◐ ● ⚡ 31, 32, 34–41 — p. 166

Camellia (many)
☼ ◐ ● ⚡ ZONES VARY — p. 166

Caragana
PEA SHRUB
☼ ● ● ⚡ 31, 32, 34–45 — p. 169

Chaenomeles
FLOWERING QUINCE
☼ ● ● ⚡ 31, 32, 34–43 — p. 179

Chionanthus virginicus
FRINGE TREE
☼ ● ● ● ⚡ 31, 32, 34–41 — p. 182

Cornus mas
CORNELIAN CHERRY
☼ ● ⚡ 32, 34–41 — p. 194

Corylopsis
WINTER HAZEL
☼ ◐ ● ● ⚡ ZONES VARY — p. 195

Cytisus
BROOM
☼ ● ● ⚡ ZONES VARY — p. 204

Malus purpurea

Camellia japonica 'Kumasaka'

Corylopsis spicata

Laburnum anagyroides

Magnolia soulangiana

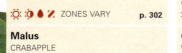
For growing symbol explanations, please see page 47.

Enkianthus campanulatus

Kerria japonica 'Pleniflora'

Ledum groenlandicum 'Compactum'

Neillia sinensis

Daphne
NEEDS, ZONES VARY   p. 206

Enkianthus
☀ ◐ ● ⚡ ZONES VARY   p. 219

Erica carnea
HEATH
☀ ◐ ● ⚡ 31, 32, 34, 36, 39   p. 221

Exochorda
PEARL BUSH
☀ ◐ ● ⚡ 31, 32, 34–41   p. 228

Forsythia
☀ ◐ ● ⚡ ZONES VARY   p. 232

Fothergilla
☀ ◐ ● ⚡ 31, 32, 34–39   p. 233

Hamamelis
WITCH HAZEL
☀ ◐ ● ⚡ ZONES VARY   p. 249

Jasminum nudiflorum
WINTER JASMINE
☀ ◐ ● ⚡ 31, 32, 34, 39   p. 274

Kalmia latifolia
MOUNTAIN LAUREL
☀ ◐ ● ⚡ 31, 32, 34–41   p. 280

Kerria japonica
☀ ◐ ● ⚡ 31, 32, 34–41   p. 281

Kolkwitzia amabilis
BEAUTY BUSH
☀ ◐ ● ⚡ 31, 32, 34–41   p. 282

Ledum
☀ ◐ ● ● ⚡ 34–45   p. 287

Leucothoe
☀ ◐ ● ⚡ ZONES VARY   p. 289

Lindera benzoin
SPICEBUSH
☀ ◐ ● ● ⚡ 31, 32, 34–43   p. 293

Lonicera
HONEYSUCKLE
☀ ◐ ● ⚡ ZONES VARY   p. 297

Lonicera fragrantissima
WINTER HONEYSUCKLE
☀ ◐ ● ⚡ 31, 32, 34–41   p. 297

Mahonia
NEEDS, ZONES VARY   p. 307

Neillia
☀ ◐ ● ⚡ 31, 32, 34, 39   p. 324

Paeonia suffruticosa
TREE PEONY
☀ ◐ ● ⚡ 31, 32, 34–43   p. 332

Philadelphus (some)
MOCK ORANGE
☀ ◐ ● ● ⚡ ZONES VARY   p. 347

Photinia
☀ ◐ ● ⚡ ZONES VARY   p. 349

Pieris
☀ ◐ ● ⚡ ZONES VARY   p. 351

Poncirus trifoliata
HARDY ORANGE
☀ ◐ ● ⚡ 31, 32, 34–41   p. 362

Prinsepia
☀ ◐ ● ⚡ ZONES VARY   p. 365

Prunus
☀ ◐ ⚡ ZONES VARY   p. 368

Rhododendron
AZALEA, RHODODENDRON
☀ ◐ ● ● ⚡ ZONES VARY   p. 380

Rosa
ROSE
NEEDS, ZONES VARY   p. 386

Spiraea (some)
☀ ◐ ● ⚡ ZONES VARY   p. 412

Syringa
LILAC
☀ ◐ ● ⚡ ZONES VARY   p. 420

Viburnum (some)
NEEDS, ZONES VARY   p. 439

Weigela
☀ ◐ ● ⚡ 32, 34–41   p. 443

Spiraea

Aubrietia deltoidea

Brunnera macrophylla

Spring
GROUND COVERS, VINES

Ajuga
CARPET BUGLE
☀ ◐ ● ⚡ 31, 32, 34–45   p. 123

Akebia
☀ ◐ ● ● ⚡ 31, 32, 34–43   p. 124

Arabis
ROCKCRESS
☀ ◐ ● ⚡ ZONES VARY   p. 139

Armeria maritima
THRIFT, SEA PINK
☀ ◐ ● ⚡ 34–43   p. 141

Aubrieta deltoidea
COMMON AUBRIETA
☀ ◐ ● ⚡ 36–43   p. 148

Bergenia
☀ ◐ ● ⚡ 31, 32, 34–45   p. 154

Brunnera macrophylla
BRUNNERA
☀ ◐ ● ⚡ 31, 32, 34–45   p. 160

Campanula portenschlagiana
DALMATIAN BELLFLOWER
☀ ◐ ● ● ⚡ 31, 32, 34–41   p. 168

Campanula portenschlagiana

Plant listings continue ▶

Cornus kousa

Caryopteris clandonensis

Hydrangea macrophylla

Franklinia alatamaha

Cerastium tomentosum
SNOW-IN-SUMMER
32, 34–45   p. 178

Clematis (some)
ZONES VARY   p. 187

Convallaria majalis
LILY-OF-THE-VALLEY
31, 32, 34–45   p. 191

Deutzia gracilis 'Nikko'
31, 32, 34–41   p. 209

Epigaea repens
TRAILING ARBUTUS
31, 32, 34–45   p. 220

Epimedium
31, 32, 34–43   p. 220

Erica carnea
HEATH
31, 32, 34, 36–39   p. 221

Forsythia viridissima 'Bronxensis'
31, 32, 34–41   p. 232

Gelsemium sempervirens
CAROLINA JESSAMINE
31, 32   p. 237

Hydrangea anomala petiolaris
CLIMBING HYDRANGEA
31, 32, 34–41   p. 262

Iberis sempervirens
CANDYTUFT
31, 32, 34–45   p. 264

Iris cristata
CRESTED IRIS
32, 34, 39   p. 269

Lamium galeobdolon
YELLOW ARCHANGEL
32, 34–43   p. 284

Lonicera (some)
HONEYSUCKLE
ZONES VARY   p. 297

Omphalodes verna
BLUE-EYED MARY
31, 32, 34–41   p. 328

Phlox
(CREEPING AND MAT-FORMING TYPES)
ZONES VARY   p. 348

Pulmonaria
LUNGWORT
32, 34–43   p. 373

Rosa
ROSE
NEEDS, ZONES VARY   p. 386

Schisandra chinensis
CHINESE MAGNOLIA VINE
31, 32, 34–43   p. 403

Sedum acre
GOLDEN CARPET
31, 32, 34–43   p. 404

Vinca
PERIWINKLE
ZONES VARY   p. 441

Wisteria
ZONES VARY   p. 444

Summer TREES

Albizia julibrissin 'Ernest Wilson'
SILK TREE
31, 32, 34–41   p. 124

Catalpa
31, 32, 34–41   p. 174

Cornus kousa
KOUSA DOGWOOD
31, 32, 34   p. 194

Cornus rutgersensis
STELLAR DOGWOOD
31, 32, 34–41   p. 194

Franklinia alatamaha
31, 32, 34–41   p. 233

Kalopanax septemlobus
CASTOR ARALIA
32, 34–41   p. 280

Koelreuteria paniculata
GOLDENRAIN TREE
31, 32, 34–41   p. 282

Lagerstroemia indica
CRAPE MYRTLE
31, 32   p. 283

Maackia
ZONES VARY   p. 301

Magnolia grandiflora
SOUTHERN MAGNOLIA
31, 32   p. 302

Oxydendrum arboreum
SORREL TREE
31, 32, 34, 35, 37, 39   p. 332

Sophora japonica
JAPANESE PAGODA TREE
31, 32, 34–41   p. 410

Stewartia
ZONES VARY   p. 415

Vitex agnus-castus
CHASTE TREE
31, 32, 34, 39   p. 442

Summer SHRUBS

Abelia
ZONES VARY   p. 114

Aesculus parviflora
BOTTLEBRUSH BUCKEYE
31, 32, 34–41   p. 121

Amorpha
31, 32, 34–45   p. 129

Amorpha fruticosa
INDIGO BUSH
31, 32, 34–45   p.129

Aralia spinosa
HERCULES' CLUB
31, 32, 34–41   p. 139

Buddleia davidii
BUTTERFLY BUSH
32, 34, 35, 37, 39   p. 161

Caryopteris clandonensis
BLUEBEARD
31, 32, 34, 39   p. 173

Ceanothus americanus
NEW JERSEY TEA
31, 32, 34–43   p. 175

Chionanthus virginicus
31, 32, 34–41   p. 182

Clerodendrum trichotomum
GLORYBOWER
31, 32, 34–41   p. 189

Clethra
ZONES VARY   p. 189

Cotinus coggygria
SMOKE BUSH
31, 32, 34–41   p. 196

Deutzia (some)
31, 32, 34–41   p. 209

Diervilla sessilifolia
BUSH HONEYSUCKLE
31, 32, 34–43   p. 212

Elliottia racemosa
GEORGIA PLUME
31, 32, 34, 39   p. 218

Genista
BROOM
ZONES VARY   p. 237

Hedysarum coronarium
FRENCH HONEYSUCKLE
31, 32, 34–43   p. 250

Helianthemum nummularium
SUNROSE
32, 34   p. 251

Hibiscus (hardy)
ZONES VARY   p. 257

Holodiscus discolor
OCEAN SPRAY
31, 32, 34, 39   p. 258

Hydrangea
ZONES VARY   p. 262

Hypericum
ST. JOHNSWORT
ZONES VARY   p. 263

For growing symbol explanations, please see page 47.

Indigofera
INDIGO BUSH
☼ ◑ ◐ ⚡ ZONES VARY   p. 268

Itea virginica
VIRGINIA SWEETSPIRE
☼ ◑ ◐ ⚡ 31, 32, 34, 39   p. 273

Lavandula
LAVENDER
☼ ◐ ⚡ ZONES VARY   p. 286

Lavatera
TREE MALLOW
☼ ◐ ◐ ⚡ ZONES VARY   p. 287

Lespedeza

☼ ◐ ⚡ ZONES VARY   p. 288

Lonicera bella
BELLE HONEYSUCKLE
☼ ◑ ◐ ◐ ⚡ 32, 34–43   p. 297

Lonicera brownii

☼ ◐ ◐ ⚡ 31, 32, 34–45   p. 297

Lonicera maackii
AMUR HONEYSUCKLE
☼ ◑ ◐ ◐ ⚡ 31, 32, 34–41   p. 297

Lyonia mariana
STAGGERBUSH
☼ ◑ ◐ ◐ ⚡ 31, 32, 34–41   p. 300

Neviusia alabamensis
SNOW WREATH
☼ ◑ ◐ ◐ ⚡ 31, 32, 34–41   p. 325

Philadelphus (some)
MOCK ORANGE
☼ ◑ ◐ ◐ ◐ ⚡ ZONES VARY   p. 347

Potentilla fruticosa
CINQUEFOIL
☼ ◐ ⚡ 32, 34–45   p. 364

Punica granatum 'Nana'
POMEGRANATE
☼ ◐ ◐ ⚡ 31, 32   p. 373

Rhododendron maximum
ROSEBAY RHODODENDRON
☼ ◑ ◐ ◐ ⚡ 31, 32, 34–43   p. 380

Rhus typhina 'Laciniata'
STAGHORN SUMAC
☼ ◐ ⚡ 31, 32, 34–45   p. 384

Rosa (some)
ROSE
NEEDS, ZONES VARY   p. 386

Sambucus
ELDERBERRY
☼ ◑ ◐ ⚡ ZONES VARY   p. 399

Sinocalycanthus chinensis

☼ ◑ ◐ ◐ ⚡ 31, 32, 34, 39   p. 408

Sorbaria
FALSE SPIRAEA
☼ ◑ ◐ ◐ ⚡ ZONES VARY   p. 410

Spiraea (some)

☼ ◑ ◐ ◐ ◐ ⚡ ZONES VARY   p. 412

Styrax americanum
AMERICAN SNOWBELL
☼ ◑ ◐ ◐ ⚡ 31, 32, 34, 39   p. 418

Styrax obassia
FRAGRANT SNOWBELL
☼ ◑ ◐ ◐ ⚡ 32, 34, 35, 37, 39   p. 418

Yucca

☼ ◐ ◐ ⚡ ZONES VARY   p. 446

Summer
GROUND COVERS, VINES

Adlumia fungosa
ALLEGHENY VINE, MOUNTAIN FRINGE
☼ ◐ ◐ ⚡ 32, 34–43   p. 121

Calluna vulgaris
HEATHER
☼ ◐ ⚡ 34–43   p. 165

Campsis
TRUMPET VINE
☼ ◑ ◐ ◐ ◐ ⚡ ZONES VARY   p. 168

Ceratostigma plumbaginoides
DWARF PLUMBAGO
☼ ◑ ◐ ◐ ◐ ⚡ 32, 34–41   p. 178

Chamaemelum nobile
ROMAN CHAMOMILE
☼ ◑ ◐ ◐ ⚡ 31, 32, 34–43   p. 179

Clematis (some)

☼ ◑ ◐ ⚡ ZONES VARY   p. 187

Delosperma cooperi
ICE PLANT
☼ ◐ ◐ ⚡ 31, 32   p. 208

Lamium maculatum
DEAD NETTLE, SPOTTED NETTLE
☼ ◑ ◐ ◐ ◐ ⚡ 32, 34–43   p. 284

Lantana montevidensis

☼ ◐ ◐ ⚡ ALL ZONES   p. 284

Liriope spp.
LILY TURF
☼ ◐ ◐ ◐ ◐ ⚡ ZONES VARY   p. 295

Lonicera
HONEYSUCKLE
☼ ◑ ◐ ◐ ⚡ ZONES VARY   p. 297

Ophiopogon spp.
LILY TURF
☼ ◐ ◐ ◐ ◐ ⚡ ZONES VARY   p. 295

Passiflora incarnata
PASSION VINE
☼ ◐ ◐ ⚡ ALL ZONES   p. 336

Polygonum aubertii
SILVER LACE VINE
☼ ◐ ◐ ◐ ⚡ 31, 32, 34–41   p. 361

Rosa spp. (some)
CLIMBING ROSES
☼ ◑ ◐ ◐ ⚡ ALL ZONES   p. 386

Schizophragma hydrangeoides
JAPANESE HYDRANGEA VINE
☼ ◐ ⚡ 31, 32, 34, 39   p. 403

Fall
TREES

Franklinia alatamaha
☼ ◑ ◐ ◐ ⚡ 31, 32, 34–41   p. 233

Koelreuteria paniculata 'September'
☼ ◐ ◐ ◐ ⚡ 31, 32, 34–41   p. 282

Prunus subhirtella 'Autumnalis'
☼ ◐ ⚡ 31, 32, 34–41   p. 368

Fall
SHRUBS

Abelia
☼ ◑ ◐ ◐ ⚡ ZONES VARY   p. 114

Buddleia davidii
BUTTERFLY BUSH
☼ ◑ ◐ ◐ ◐ ⚡ 32, 34, 35, 37, 39   p. 161

Camellia sasanqua
☼ ◐ ⚡ 31, 32   p. 166

Erica (some)
☼ ◑ ◐ ◐ ⚡ ZONES VARY   p. 221

Hibiscus (hardy)
☼ ◐ ◐ ◐ ⚡ ZONES VARY   p. 257

Potentilla atrosanguinea
CINQUEFOIL
☼ ◐ ◐ ⚡ 31, 32, 34–43   p. 364

Rosa (some)
ROSE
NEEDS, ZONES VARY   p. 386

Salvia (some)
SAGE
NEEDS, ZONES VARY   p. 396

Fall
GROUND COVERS, VINES

Ceratostigma plumbaginoides
DWARF PLUMBAGO
☼ ◑ ◐ ◐ ⚡ 31, 32, 34–41   p. 178

Clematis (some)
☼ ◑ ◐ ⚡ ZONES VARY   p. 187

Lonicera (some)
HONEYSUCKLE
☼ ◑ ◐ ◐ ⚡ ZONES VARY   p. 297

Mandevilla (some)
☼ ◑ ◐ ⚡ ALL ZONES   p. 312

Polygonum aubertii
SILVER LACE VINE
☼ ◐ ◐ ◐ ⚡ 31, 32, 34–41   p. 361

Rosa spp. (some)
CLIMBING ROSES
☼ ◑ ◐ ◐ ⚡ ALL ZONES   p. 386

Sorbaria

Buddleia 'Nanho Purple'

Hibiscus syriacus 'Aphrodite'

Ceratostigma plumbaginoides

AUTUMN
Foliage Color

Plants that change leaf color in fall do so in varying degrees, depending on the nature of the plant, the climate it grows in, and the exact weather each fall. Generally, the change is less pronounced in mild-winter areas than in cold-winter regions. The plants listed below display a notable autumn foliage change; many are worth planting for that reason alone. Leaf color can vary within a species, so it's best to shop for plants when they are changing color.

Acer circanatum

Cladrastis lutea

Fagus sylvatica 'Asplenifolia'

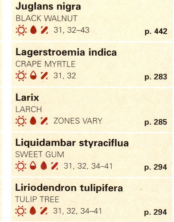

Fraxinus americana 'Autumn Purple'

Ginkgo biloba

Juglans nigra

Lagerstroemia indica

Liquidambar styraciflua

TREES

Acer (many)
MAPLE
ZONES VARY — p. 116

Amelanchier
JUNEBERRY
31, 32, 34–45 — p. 128

Asimina triloba
PAWPAW
31, 32, 34–41 — p. 144

Betula
BIRCH
ZONES VARY — p. 155

Carpinus
HORNBEAM
ZONES VARY — p. 172

Carya ovata
SHAGBARK HICKORY
31, 32, 34–44 — p. 173

Catalpa
31, 32, 34–41 — p. 174

Celtis
HACKBERRY
ZONES VARY — p. 176

Cercidiphyllum japonicum
KATSURA TREE
31, 32, 34–41 — p. 178

Cercis canadensis
REDBUD
31, 32, 34–41 — p. 178

Chionanthus
FRINGE TREE
ZONES VARY — p. 182

Cladrastis lutea
YELLOW WOOD
31, 32, 34–43 — p. 186

Cornus (many)
DOGWOOD
ZONES VARY — p. 194

Cotinus obovatus
AMERICAN SMOKE TREE
31, 32, 34–43 — p. 196

Crataegus (many)
HAWTHORN
ZONES VARY — p. 198

Fagus
BEECH
ZONES VARY — p. 229

Franklinia alatamaha
31, 32, 34, 39 — p. 233

Fraxinus
ASH
ZONES VARY — p. 234

Ginkgo biloba
MAIDENHAIR TREE
31, 32, 34–43 — p. 240

Gleditsia triacanthos
HONEY LOCUST
32, 34–43 — p. 242

Gymnocladus dioica
KENTUCKY COFFEE TREE
32, 34–43 — p. 248

Juglans nigra
BLACK WALNUT
31, 32–43 — p. 442

Lagerstroemia indica
CRAPE MYRTLE
31, 32 — p. 283

Larix
LARCH
ZONES VARY — p. 285

Liquidambar styraciflua
SWEET GUM
31, 32, 34–41 — p. 294

Liriodendron tulipifera
TULIP TREE
31, 32, 34–41 — p. 294

Magnolia denudata
YULAN MAGNOLIA
31, 32, 34, 35, 37, 39 — p. 302

For growing symbol explanations, please see page 47.

Metasequoia glyptostroboides
DAWN REDWOOD
31, 32, 34–41   p. 316

Morus
MULBERRY
ZONES VARY   p. 319

Nyssa sylvatica
SOUR GUM
31, 32, 34–41   p. 327

Oxydendrum arboreum
SOURWOOD
31, 34, 35, 37, 39   p. 332

Parrotia persica
PERSIAN PARROTIA
31, 32, 34–41   p. 335

Persimmon
ZONES VARY   p. 345

Phellodendron amurense
AMUR CORK TREE
31, 32, 34–45   p. 347

Pistacia chinensis
CHINESE PISTACHE
31, 32   p. 352

Populus (some)
POPLAR
ZONES VARY   p. 363

Prunus sargentii
31, 32, 34–41   p. 368

Pseudolarix kaempferi
GOLDEN LARCH
31, 32, 34–41   p. 371

Ptelea trifoliata
WAFER ASH
31, 32, 34–43   p. 372

Pyrus
ORNAMENTAL PEAR
31, 32, 34–41   p. 375

Quercus
OAK
ZONES VARY   p. 375

Robinia
LOCUST
31, 32, 34–45   p. 385

Salix
WILLOW
ZONES VARY   p. 395

Sassafras albidum
SASSAFRAS
31, 32, 34–41   p. 401

Sorbus
MOUNTAIN ASH
ZONES VARY   p. 410

Stewartia
ZONES VARY   p. 415

Styrax japonicus
JAPANESE SNOWBELL
31, 32, 34, 39   p. 418

Taxodium distichum
BALD CYPRESS
31, 32, 34–41   p. 422

Tilia
LINDEN
ZONES VARY   p. 427

Ulmus (most)
ELM
ZONES VARY   p. 435

Walnut
ZONES VARY   p. 442

Zelkova serrata
SAWLEAF ZELKOVA
31, 32, 34–41   p. 447

SHRUBS

Acer palmatum
JAPANESE MAPLE
31, 32, 34–41   p. 116

Amelanchier
JUNEBERRY
31, 32, 34–45   p. 128

Aronia
CHOKEBERRY
ZONES VARY   p. 142

Berberis thunbergii
JAPANESE BARBERRY
31, 32, 34–43   p. 154

Blueberry
ZONES VARY   p. 157

Callicarpa
BEAUTYBERRY
ZONES VARY   p. 164

Calycanthus floridus
31, 32, 34–41   p. 166

Chaenomeles
FLOWERING QUINCE
31, 32, 34–41   p. 179

Chimonanthus praecox
WINTERSWEET
31, 32   p. 182

Clethra alnifolia
SUMMERSWEET
31, 32, 34–43   p. 189

Cornus alba 'Sibirica'
SIBERIAN DOGWOOD
31, 32, 34–45   p. 194

Cotinus coggygria
SMOKE TREE
31, 32, 34–41   p. 196

Cotoneaster (most deciduous)
ZONES VARY   p. 196

Cyrilla racemiflora
LEATHERWOOD
31, 32, 34–41   p. 204

Nyssa sylvatica

Oxydendrum arboreum

Parrotia persica

Sassafras albidum

Stewartia monadelpha

Acer palmatum

Berberis thunbergii

Cornus alba 'Sibirica'

Plant listings continue ▶

Euonymus alatus 'Compactus'

Fothergilla major

Gaultheria procumbens

Hydrangea quercifolia

Disanthus cercidifolius
31, 32, 34, 39   p. 213

Enkianthus campanulatus
31, 32, 34–41   p. 219

Euonymus (several)
ZONES VARY   p. 226

Fothergilla
31, 32, 34–41   p. 233

Hamamelis
WITCH HAZEL
ZONES VARY   p. 249

Hydrangea quercifolia
OAKLEAF HYDRANGEA
31, 32, 34–41   p. 262

Ilex verticillata
WINTERBERRY
31, 32, 34–43   p. 265

Itea virginica
VIRGINIA SWEETSPIRE
31, 32, 34, 39   p. 273

Kerria japonica
31, 32, 34–41   p. 281

Lagerstroemia indica
CRAPE MYRTLE
31, 32   p. 283

Leucothoe racemosa
SWEETBELLS
31, 32, 34–41   p. 289

Lindera
SPICEBUSH
ZONES VARY   p. 293

Lonicera
HONEYSUCKLE
ZONES VARY   p. 297

Magnolia stellata
STAR MAGNOLIA
31, 32, 34–41   p. 302

Mahonia aquifolium
OREGON GRAPE
31, 32, 34–41   p. 307

Nandina domestica
HEAVENLY BAMBOO
31, 32, 34, 39   p. 322

Paxistima canbyi
32, 34–41   p. 337

Philadelphus
MOCK ORANGE
ZONES VARY   p. 347

Photinia villosa
31, 32, 34–41   p. 349

Prunus
ZONES VARY   p. 368

Pseudocydonia sinensis
CHINESE QUINCE
31, 32, 34, 39   p. 371

Punica granatum 'Nana'
POMEGRANATE
31, 32   p. 373

Rhododendron
AZALEA, DECIDUOUS
ZONES VARY   p. 380

Rhus
SUMAC
ZONES VARY   p. 384

Rosa (some)
ROSE
NEEDS, ZONES VARY   p. 386

Spiraea (many)
ZONES VARY   p. 412

Stephanandra incisa 'Crispa'
31, 32, 34–43   p. 414

Syringa oblata dilatata
KOREAN EARLY LILAC
31, 32, 34–45   p. 420

Vaccinium
NEEDS, ZONES VARY   p. 436

Viburnum (many)
NEEDS, ZONES VARY   p. 439

Zenobia pulverulenta (Andromeda speciosa)
31, 32, 34–41   p. 447

Ziziphus jujuba
CHINESE JUJUBE
31, 32   p. 448

VINES

Actinidia arguta
HARDY KIWI
31, 32, 34–41   p. 120

Celastrus
BITTERSWEET
ZONES VARY   p. 176

Gaultheria procumbens
WINTERGREEN, CHECKERBERRY
31, 32, 34–45   p. 236

Parthenocissus quinquefolia
VIRGINIA CREEPER
31, 32, 34–43   p. 336

Parthenocissus tricuspidata
BOSTON IVY
31, 32, 34–41   p. 336

Vitis coignetiae (Grape)
CRIMSON GLORY VINE
31, 32, 34–41   p. 244

Wisteria
ZONES VARY   p. 444

Itea virginica 'Henry's Garnet'

Rhus typhina

Celastrus orbiculatus

Parthenocissus tricuspidata

For growing symbol explanations, please see page 47.

Anemone tomentosa 'Robustissima'

Achillea millefolium 'Paprika'

SHOWY PERENNIALS
for Beds and Borders

Year after year, these perennial garden mainstays provide spectacular flowers that inspire artists and photographers to attempt to capture their fleeting beauty. Perennials are distinguished from annuals and biennials by their longevity—they live for more than two years and usually bloom every year. Depending on the plant and the climate, they may be evergreen, or they may die to the ground every winter and regrow from the roots the next spring.

Adenophora liliifolia

Acanthus 'Summer Beauty'
BEAR'S BREECH
☼ ◐ ◖ ◖ ⬤ ⚡ 31, 32, 34, 39   **p. 115**

Achillea
YARROW
☼ ◖ ⚡ 31, 32, 34–45   **p. 118**

Aconitum
MONKSHOOD
☼ ◐ ◖ ⚡ ZONES VARY   **p. 119**

Adenophora
LADY BELLS
☼ ◐ ◖ ◖ ⚡ ZONES VARY   **p. 120**

Adonis
PHEASANT'S EYE
☼ ◖ ⚡ ZONES VARY   **p. 121**

Agapanthus 'Headbourne Hybrids'   LILY-OF-THE-NILE
☼ ◐ ◖ ◖ ⚡ 31, 32   **p. 122**

Agastache
GIANT HYSSOP
☼ ◐ ◖ ◖ ⚡ ZONES VARY   **p. 122**

Alchemilla
LADY'S-MANTLE
☼ ◐ ◖ ⚡ ZONES VARY   **p. 124**

Alstroemeria
☼ ◖ ⚡ ZONES VARY   **p. 127**

Alyssum
☼ ◐ ◖ ⚡ 31, 32, 34–43   **p. 127**

Amsonia
BLUE STAR FLOWER
☼ ◐ ◖ ⚡ ZONES VARY   **p. 129**

Anaphalis
PEARLY EVERLASTING
◐ ◖ ◖ ◖ ⚡ ZONES VARY   **p. 130**

Anemone hybrida
JAPANESE ANEMONE
◐ ◖ ⚡ 31, 32, 34–41   **p. 131**

Anthemis
☼ ◖ ⚡ ZONES VARY   **p. 133**

Aquilegia
COLUMBINE
☼ ◐ ◖ ⚡ ZONES VARY   **p. 138**

Arenaria montana
SANDWORT
☼ ◐ ◖ ⚡ 31, 32, 34–45   **p. 140**

Armeria
THRIFT
☼ ◖ ◖ ⚡ ZONES VARY   **p. 141**

Aruncus
GOAT'S BEARD
☼ ◐ ⬤ ⚡ 31, 32, 34–43   **p. 143**

Asclepias tuberosa
BUTTERFLY WEED
☼ ◖ ◖ ⚡ ALL ZONES   **p. 144**

Aster
☼ ◖ ⚡ ZONES VARY   **p. 146**

Astilbe
FALSE SPIRAEA
☼ ◐ ◖ ⚡ ZONES VARY   **p. 147**

Aubrieta deltoidea
COMMON AUBRIETA
☼ ◐ ◖ ⚡ 31, 32, 34–43   **p. 148**

Aurinia saxatilis
BASKET-OF-GOLD
☼ ◐ ◖ ⚡ 32, 34–43   **p. 148**

Baptisia
FALSE INDIGO, WILD INDIGO
☼ ◖ ⚡ 31, 32, 34–43   **p. 151**

Begonia grandis
HARDY BEGONIA
☼ ◐ ◖ ⚡ 31, 32, 34, 39   **p. 153**

Bergenia
☼ ◐ ◖ ⚡ 31, 32, 34–45   **p. 154**

Bidens ferulifolia
☼ ◖ ◖ ⚡ 31, 32, 34–45   **p. 155**

Bletilla striata
CHINESE GROUND ORCHID
☼ ◐ ◖ ⚡ 31, 32, 34, 39   **p. 157**

Aquilegia 'Music Box'

Aster novae-angliae 'Alma Potschke'

Agastache foeniculum

Bidens ferulifolia 'Compact'

Amsonia tabernaemontana

Plant listings continue ▶

Chrysanthemum x *superbum*

Echinacea purpurea

Euphorbia griffithii 'Fireglow'

Hemerocallis 'Silent Entry'

Knautia

Brunnera macrophylla
☼ ◑ ● ⚡ 32, 34–45   **p.160**

Campanula (some)
BELLFLOWER
☼ ◑ ● ◐ ⚡ ZONES VARY   **p. 168**

Catananche caerulea
CUPID'S DART
☼ ● ⚡ 31, 32, 34–45   **p. 174**

Centaurea macrocephala
☼ ● ⚡ 31, 32, 34–45   **p. 177**

Centranthus ruber
RED VALERIAN
☼ ◑ ● ⚡ 32, 34–43   **p. 177**

Cephalaria gigantea
GIANT SCABIOUS, YELLOW SCABIOUS
☼ ● ⚡ 31, 32, 34–45   **p. 177**

Cerastium tomentosum
SNOW-IN-SUMMER
☼ ◑ ● ⚡ 31, 32, 34–45   **p. 178**

Ceratostigma plumbaginoides
DWARF PLUMBAGO
☼ ◑ ● ● ⚡ 31, 32, 34–41   **p. 178**

Chelone glabra
TURTLEHEAD
☼ ● ● ⚡ 31, 32, 34–43   **p. 180**

Chrysanthemum
NEEDS, ZONES VARY   **p. 183**

Chrysanthemum serotinum
☼ ● ⚡ 31, 32, 34–43   **p. 183**

Chrysopsis
☼ ● ● ⚡ 31, 32, 34–43   **p. 185**

Claytonia
SPRING BEAUTY
● ● ⚡ 31, 32, 34–41   **p. 187**

Clematis recta
☼ ● ⚡ 31, 32, 34–45   **p. 187**

Convallaria majalis
LILY-OF-THE-VALLEY
◑ ● ● ⚡ 31, 32, 34–45   **p. 191**

Coreopsis
☼ ● ⚡ ZONES VARY   **p. 192**

Corydalis
◑ ● ● ⚡ ZONES VARY   **p. 195**

Crambe cordifolia
☼ ● ⚡ 31, 32, 34–41   **p. 197**

Crinum
☼ ● ● ⚡ ZONES VARY   **p. 198**

Crocosmia
☼ ● ● ⚡ 31, 32, 34, 39   **p. 199**

Cynara cardunculus
CARDOON
☼ ● ⚡ 31, 32   **p. 202**

Delphinium
☼ ● ⚡ ZONES VARY   **p. 208**

Dianthus
PINK
☼ ◑ ● ● ⚡ 31, 32, 34–45   **p. 209**

Dicentra
BLEEDING HEART
☼ ● ● ● ⚡ 31, 32, 34–45   **p. 211**

Dictamnus albus
GAS PLANT
☼ ◑ ● ⚡ 31, 32, 34–45   **p. 211**

Dierama
FAIRY WAND
☼ ● ⚡ 31, 32   **p. 211**

Digitalis
FOXGLOVE
◑ ● ⚡ ZONES VARY   **p. 212**

Doronicum
LEOPARD'S BANE
◑ ● ⚡ 31, 32, 34–43   **p. 213**

Echinacea purpurea
PURPLE CONEFLOWER
☼ ● ⚡ 31, 32, 34–45   **p. 216**

Echinops
GLOBE THISTLE
☼ ● ● ⚡ 32, 34–45   **p. 217**

Eremurus
FOXTAIL LILY, DESERT CANDLE
☼ ● ⚡ 31, 32, 34–43   **p. 221**

Erinus alpinus
☼ ◑ ● ⚡ 31, 32, 34–43   **p. 224**

Erodium
CRANESBILL
☼ ◑ ● ⚡ ZONES VARY   **p. 224**

Eryngium amethystinum
SEA HOLLY
☼ ● ⚡ 31, 32, 34–45   **p. 224**

Eupatorium
☼ ◑ ● ● ⚡ ZONES VARY   **p. 226**

Euphorbia
NEEDS, ZONES VARY   **p. 227**

Filipendula
☼ ◑ ● ● ⚡ ZONES VARY   **p. 231**

Gaillardia grandiflora
BLANKET FLOWER
☼ ● ⚡ 31, 32, 34–45   **p. 235**

Gaura lindheimeri
GAURA
☼ ● ● ⚡ 31, 32, 34, 39   **p. 237**

Gentiania
GENTIAN
☼ ◑ ● ⚡ 34, 36–43   **p. 238**

Geranium
CRANESBILL
☼ ◑ ● ⚡ ZONES VARY   **p. 238**

Geum
☼ ◑ ● ⚡ 32, 34–43   **p. 240**

Glaucidium palmatum
◑ ● ● ⚡ 32, 34–41   **p. 241**

Glaucium flavum
YELLOW HORNED POPPY
☼ ● ⚡ 31, 32, 34, 39   **p. 241**

Gypsophila
☼ ● ● ⚡ ZONES VARY   **p. 248**

Helenium autumnale
COMMON SNEEZEWEED
☼ ● ⚡ 31, 32, 34–45   **p. 251**

Helianthemum nummularium
SUNROSE
☼ ● ⚡ 32, 34, 39   **p. 251**

Helianthus
SUNFLOWER
☼ ● ⚡ ZONES VARY   **p. 251**

Heliopsis helianthoides
OX-EYE
☼ ◑ ● ⚡ 33, 34–45   **p. 252**

Helleborus
HELLEBORE
☼ ● ● ● ⚡ ZONES VARY   **p. 253**

Hemerocallis
DAYLILY
☼ ◑ ● ⚡ 31, 32, 34–45   **p. 253**

Heuchera
CORAL BELLS
☼ ◑ ● ⚡ ZONES VARY   **p. 256**

Hibiscus moscheutos
ROSE-MALLOW
☼ ● ⚡ 31, 32, 34–41   **p. 257**

Iberis sempervirens
EVERGREEN CANDYTUFT
☼ ● ⚡ 31, 32, 34–45   **p. 264**

Inula
ELECAMPANE
☼ ◑ ● ● ● ⚡ 31, 32, 34–45   **p. 268**

Iris
NEEDS, ZONES VARY   **p. 269**

Kalimeris pinnatifida
JAPANESE ASTER
☼ ◑ ● ⚡ 31, 32, 34, 39   **p. 280**

Kirengeshoma palmata
YELLOW WAX BELLS
◑ ● ⚡ 31, 32, 34, 37, 39   **p. 281**

Knautia macedonica
☼ ◑ ● ⚡ 31, 32, 34–41   **p. 281**

Kniphofia uvaria
RED-HOT POKER
☼ ◑ ● ● ⚡ 31, 32, 34–41   **p. 281**

For growing symbol explanations, please see page 47.

Lavandula
LAVENDER
☼ ◗ ◖ ╱ ZONES VARY   p. 286

Liatris
GAYFEATHER
☼ ◗ ◖ ╱ 31, 32, 34–45   p. 290

Ligularia
☼ ◗ ◖ ╱ ZONES VARY   p. 290

Limonium
SEA LAVENDER
☼ ◗ ◖ ╱ ZONES VARY   p. 293

Linaria purpurea
TOADFLAX
☼ ◗ ◖ ╱ 31, 32, 34–41   p. 293

Linum perenne
PERENNIAL BLUE FLAX
☼ ◗ ◖ ╱ 31, 32, 34–41   p. 294

Lobelia cardinalis
CARDINAL FLOWER
☼ ◗ ◖ ◖ ╱ 31, 32, 34–45   p. 295

Lupinus
LUPINE
☼ ◗ ◖ ╱ ZONES VARY   p. 298

Lychnis chalcedonica
MALTESE CROSS
☼ ◗ ◖ ◖ ╱ 31, 32, 34–43   p. 299

Lysimachia clethroides
GOOSENECK LOOSESTRIFE
☼ ◗ ◖ ╱ 31, 32, 34–45   p. 300

Macleaya cordata
PLUME POPPY
☼ ◗ ◖ ╱ 31, 32, 34–43   p. 301

Malva (most)
MALLOW
☼ ◗ ◖ ╱ 31, 32, 34–45   p. 312

Monarda
BEE BALM
☼ ◗ ◖ ◖ ╱ ZONES VARY   p. 319

Nepeta
☼ ◗ ◖ ╱ 32, 34–43   p. 325

Oenothera
EVENING PRIMROSE
NEEDS, ZONES VARY   p. 327

Origanum
NEEDS, ZONES VARY   p. 329

Paeonia (herbaceous)
PEONY
☼ ◗ ◖ ╱ 31, 32, 34–45   p. 332

Papaver orientale
ORIENTAL POPPY
☼ ◖ ╱ 31, 32, 34–45   p. 335

Penstemon (many)
BEARD TONGUE
☼ ◗ ◖ ◖ ╱ ZONES VARY   p. 344

Perovskia
RUSSIAN SAGE
☼ ◖ ╱ 31, 32, 34, 37, 39   p. 345

Phlomis
JERUSALEM SAGE
NEEDS, ZONES VARY   p. 347

Phlox
☼ ◗ ◖ ╱ ZONES VARY   p. 348

Phygelius
CAPE FUCHSIA
☼ ◗ ◖ ╱ 31, 32   p. 349

Physostegia virginiana
FALSE DRAGONHEAD
☼ ◗ ◖ ╱ 31, 32, 34–45   p. 350

Platycodon grandiflorus
BALLOON FLOWER
☼ ◗ ◖ ╱ 31, 32, 34–45   p. 357

Polemonium
◗ ◖ ◖ ╱ 31, 32, 34–43   p. 361

Polygonum
KNOTWEED
☼ ◗ ◖ ╱ ZONES VARY   p. 361

Potentilla
CINQUEFOIL
☼ ◗ ◖ ╱ ZONES VARY   p. 364

Primula (many)
PRIMROSE
NEEDS, ZONES VARY   p. 365

Prunella
SELF-HEAL
☼ ◗ ◖ ╱ 31, 32, 34–43   p. 367

Pulmonaria
LUNGWORT
◗ ◖ ◖ ╱ 31, 32, 34–43   p. 373

Pulsatilla
PASQUE FLOWER
☼ ◗ ◖ ╱ 31, 32, 34–45   p. 373

Ranunculus
NEEDS, ZONES VARY   p. 377

Ratibida columnifera
MEXICAN HAT
☼ ◖ ╱ 31, 32, 34–43   p. 378

Rhexia virginica
MEADOW BEAUTY
☼ ◖ ╱ 31, 32, 34–41   p. 379

Rudbeckia
☼ ◗ ◖ ◖ ╱ ZONES VARY   p. 393

Salvia
SAGE
NEEDS, ZONES VARY   p. 396

Scabiosa
PINCUSHION FLOWER
☼ ◗ ◖ ╱ ZONES VARY   p. 402

Schizostylis coccinea
☼ ◗ ◖ ◖ ╱ 31, 32   p. 403

Sedum spectabile (varieties)
☼ ◗ ◖ ╱ 31, 32, 34–43   p. 404

Sedum telephium (varieties)
☼ ◗ ◖ ╱ 31, 32, 34–43   p. 404

Sidalcea
CHECKERBLOOM
☼ ◗ ◖ ╱ 31, 32, 34–41   p. 407

Silene
NEEDS, ZONES VARY   p. 408

Sisyrinchium
☼ ◗ ◖ ◖ ╱ ZONES VARY   p. 408

Solidago
GOLDENROD
☼ ◗ ◖ ╱ ZONES VARY   p. 409

Solidaster luteus
☼ ◗ ◖ ╱ 31, 32, 34–45   p. 409

Stachys officinalis
BETONY
☼ ◗ ◖ ╱ 31, 32, 34–45   p. 414

Stokesia laevis
STOKES' ASTER
☼ ◖ ╱ 31, 32, 34–43   p. 415

Symphytum officinale
COMFREY
☼ ◗ ◖ ╱ 31, 32, 34–43   p. 420

Teucrium chamaedrys
GERMANDER
☼ ◗ ◖ ╱ 31, 32, 34–41   p. 423

Thalictrum
MEADOW RUE
☼ ◗ ◖ ╱ ZONES VARY   p. 424

Thymus
THYME
☼ ◗ ◖ ╱ ZONES VARY   p. 426

Tradescantia virginiana
SPIDERWORT
☼ ◗ ◖ ◖ ◖ ╱ 31, 32, 34–43   p. 430

Trollius
GLOBEFLOWER
☼ ◗ ◖ ◖ ╱ 31, 32, 34–43   p. 431

Tulbaghia
☼ ◖ ╱ 31, 32   p. 432

Verbascum
MULLEIN
☼ ◗ ◖ ╱ ZONES VARY   p. 437

Verbena
☼ ◗ ◖ ╱ ZONES VARY   p. 437

Veronica
SPEEDWELL
☼ ◗ ◖ ╱ ZONES VARY   p. 438

Veronicastrum virginicum
CULVER'S ROOT
☼ ◗ ◖ ╱ 31, 32, 34–43   p. 439

Viola odorata
SWEET VIOLET
☼ ◖ ╱ 31, 32, 34–43   p. 441

Oenethera speciosa

Papaver orientale

Rudbeckia fulgida

Scabiosa columbaria 'Butterfly Blue'

Thalictrum aquilegiifolium

SHOWY PERENNIALS FOR BEDS AND BORDERS

57

Centaurea cyanus

ANNUALS
for Seasonal Color

Flowering annuals provide the quick, showy color that can bring almost instant drama to an otherwise quiet part of the garden. Available in every size and color imaginable, annuals make delightful fillers between shrubs, colorful companions to perennials, or stunning plantings just by themselves. Some plants on this list are biennials or perennials commonly grown as annuals. Cool-season annuals grow best in cool soils and mild temperatures—fall through spring in mild-winter climates. Warm-season annuals are planted after the last frost and generally grow best between late spring and fall.

Matthiola incana

Dimorphotheca

Nemesia strumosa

Eschscholzia californica

Iberis umbellata

Nigella damascena

Viola wittrockiana

COLD-SEASON ANNUALS

Adonis aestivalis
SUMMER ADONIS
☼ ☼ ◑ ✂ ALL ZONES   p. 121

Ammi majus
BISHOP'S FLOWER
☼ ☼ ◑ ◑ ◑ ✂ ALL ZONES   p. 128

Antirrhinum majus
SNAPDRAGON
☼ ◑ ✂ ALL ZONES   p. 134

Bellis perennis
☼ ☼ ◑ ✂ ALL ZONES   p. 153

Cabbage, flowering
☼ ☼ ◑ ✂ ALL ZONES   p. 162

Calendula officinalis
POT MARIGOLD
☼ ◑ ✂ ALL ZONES   p. 163

Campanula medium
CANTERBURY BELL
☼ ☼ ◑ ✂ ZONES 32, 34–41   p. 168

Centaurea cyanus
CORNFLOWER
☼ ◑ ✂ ALL ZONES   p. 177

Consolida ambigua
LARKSPUR
☼ ◑ ✂ ALL ZONES   p. 191

Cynoglossum amabile
CHINESE FORGET-ME-NOT
☼ ◑ ✂ ALL ZONES   p. 203

Dianthus (some)
☼ ☼ ◑ ✂ ALL ZONES   p. 209

Dimorphotheca
AFRICAN DAISY
☼ ◑ ✂ ALL ZONES   p. 212

Eschscholzia californica
CALIFORNIA POPPY
☼ ◑ ◑ ✂ ALL ZONES   p. 225

Iberis umbellata
GLOBE CANDYTUFT
☼ ◑ ◑ ✂ ALL ZONES   p. 264

Lathyrus odoratus
SWEET PEA
☼ ◑ ✂ ALL ZONES   p. 285

Lavatera trimestris
ANNUAL MALLOW
☼ ◑ ◑ ✂ ALL ZONES   p. 287

Linaria maroccana
TOADFLAX
☼ ◑ ◑ ✂ ALL ZONES   p. 293

Matthiola incana
STOCK
☼ ☼ ◑ ✂ ALL ZONES   p. 313

Myosotis sylvatica
FORGET-ME-NOT
☼ ☼ ◑ ✂ ALL ZONES   p. 321

Nemesia strumosa
☼ ◑ ✂ ALL ZONES   p. 324

Nigella damascena
☼ ◑ ◑ ✂ ALL ZONES   p. 326

Papaver (some)
POPPY
☼ ◑ ◑ ✂ ALL ZONES   p. 335

Primula (many)
PRIMROSE
☼ ☼ ◑ ◑ ◑ ✂ ZONES VARY   p. 365

Schizanthus pinnatus
POOR MAN'S ORCHID
◑ ◑ ✂ ALL ZONES   p. 403

Viola
PANSY, VIOLA
NEEDS, ZONES VARY   p. 441

Catharanthus roseus

Celosia argentea var. *cristata*

Lobelia erinus 'Crystal Palace'

Petunia hybrida 'Sugar Daddy'

WARM-SEASON ANNUALS

Ageratum houstonianum
FLOSS FLOWER
ALL ZONES — p. 123

Brachycome iberidifolia
SWAN RIVER DAISY
ALL ZONES — p. 158

Browallia speciosa
AMETHYST FLOWER
ALL ZONES — p. 160

Callistephus chinensis
CHINA ASTER
ALL ZONES — p. 164

Catharanthus roseus
MADAGASCAR PERIWINKLE
ALL ZONES — p. 174

Celosia
COCKSCOMB
ALL ZONES — p. 176

Cleome hasslerana
SPIDER FLOWER
ALL ZONES — p. 188

Coreopsis tinctoria
CALLIOPSIS
ALL ZONES — p. 192

Cosmos
ALL ZONES — p. 196

Datura
THORN APPLE
32, 34–43 — p. 207

Dolichos lablab
HYACINTH BEAN
ALL ZONES — p. 213

Eustoma grandiflorum
LISIANTHUS
ALL ZONES — p. 228

Gaillardia pulchella
BLANKET FLOWER
ALL ZONES — p. 235

Gazania
ALL ZONES — p. 237

Gomphrena
GLOBE AMARANTH
ALL ZONES — p. 243

Gypsophila elegans
ALL ZONES — p. 248

Helianthus annuus
COMMON SUNFLOWER
ALL ZONES — p. 251

Helichrysum bracteatum
STRAWFLOWER
ALL ZONES — p. 252

Heliotropium arborescens
COMMON HELIOTROPE
ALL ZONES — p. 252

Impatiens
BALSAM
NEEDS VARY, ALL ZONES — p. 267

Ipomoea
MORNING GLORY
ALL ZONES — p. 269

Limonium (some)
STATICE
ALL ZONES — p. 293

Lobelia erinus
ALL ZONES — p. 295

Lobularia maritima
SWEET ALYSSUM
ALL ZONES — p. 295

Luffa cylindrica
32, 34, 39 — p. 298

Nicotiana
ALL ZONES — p. 326

Petunia hybrida
PETUNIA
ALL ZONES — p. 346

Phlox drummondii
ANNUAL PHLOX
ALL ZONES — p. 348

Portulaca grandiflora
ROSE MOSS
ALL ZONES — p. 363

Salpiglossis sinuata
PAINTED TONGUE
ALL ZONES — p. 396

Salvia splendens
SCARLET SAGE
ALL ZONES — p. 396

Sanvitalia procumbens
CREEPING ZINNIA
ALL ZONES — p. 400

Scabiosa atropurpurea
PINCUSHION FLOWER
ALL ZONES — p. 402

Tagetes
MARIGOLD
ALL ZONES — p. 421

Thunbergia alata
BLACK-EYED SUSAN VINE
ALL ZONES — p. 426

Tithonia rotundifolia
MEXICAN SUNFLOWER
ALL ZONES — p. 427

Tropaeolum majus
GARDEN NASTURTIUM
ALL ZONES — p. 432

Verbena
ALL ZONES — p. 437

Zinnia
ALL ZONES — p. 448

Phlox drummondii 'Palona Rose'

Salvia splendens 'Flare'

Verbena canadensis 'Roseum'

Zinnia elegans

BULBS
and Bulblike Plants

Allium aflatunense

Arisaema sikokianum

Camassia

Hyacinthoides hispanicus

S ome of a garden's showiest flowers appear from bulbs, corms, tubers, rhizomes, and tuberous roots (often lumped together as bulbs). These humble-looking structures store food, allowing the plants to survive underground until it's time to send out shoots and flowers. Bulbs thrive in many different environments. Daffodils and iris, for example, thrive equally well in both desert and mountain regions. Other bulbs have more specific growing needs. You can successfully grow many bulbs out of their range by planting them in containers and growing them indoors (amaryllis is a common example) or by providing a period of chilling in the refrigerator to simulate winter (in mild-winter climates crocus, hyacinths, and tulips should be chilled for 6 weeks).

Fritillaria meleagris

Iris

Leucojum vernum

Lilium 'Cinnabar'

FALL-PLANTED BULBS	
Allium ORNAMENTAL ALLIUM ☼ ◑ ● ∕ ZONES VARY **p. 125**	**Fritillaria** FRITILLARY ☼ ◑ ● ∕ ZONES VARY **p. 234**
Anemone WINDFLOWER NEEDS, ZONES VARY **p. 131**	**Galanthus** SNOWDROP ☼ ◑ ● ∕ ZONES VARY **p. 235**
Anemone coronaria POPPY-FLOWERED ANEMONE ☼ ◑ ● ∕ 31, 32, 34–41 **p. 131**	**Hyacinthoides** ☼ ◑ ● ∕ ZONES VARY **p. 261**
Arisaema ◑ ● ● ● ∕ ZONES VARY **p. 140**	**Hyacinthus orientalis** COMMON HYACINTH ☼ ◑ ● ∕ ALL ZONES **p. 262**
Arisarum MOUSE PLANT ◑ ● ∕ 31, 32 **p. 141**	**Ipheion uniflorum** SPRING STAR FLOWER ☼ ◑ ● ∕ 32, 34, 39 **p. 268**
Camassia CAMASS ☼ ● ●● ∕ 31, 32, 34, 39 **p. 166**	**Iris** NEEDS, ZONES VARY **p. 269**
Chionodoxa GLORY-OF-THE-SNOW ◑ ● ∕ 31, 32, 34–43 **p. 182**	**Iris danfordiae** ☼ ● ● ∕ 31, 32, 34–41 **p. 269**
Corydalis solida ☼ ◑ ● ∕ 32, 34–43 **p. 195**	**Iris histrioides** ☼ ◑ ● ∕ 31, 32, 34–41 **p. 269**
Crocus ☼ ◑ ● ∕ 31, 32, 34–45 **p. 199**	**Iris, English Irises** I. LATIFOLIA ☼ ◑ ● ● ∕ 31, 32 **p. 269**
Dracunculus vulgaris DRAGON ARUM ☼ ● ●● ∕ 31, 32 **p. 215**	**Iris reticulata** ☼ ● ● ∕ 31, 32, 34–41 **p. 269**
Erythronium DOG-TOOTH VIOLET ☼ ◑ ● ● ●● ∕ ZONES VARY **p. 225**	**Leucojum** SNOWFLAKE ☼ ◑ ● ∕ ZONES VARY **p. 289**
	Lilium LILY ◑ ● ∕ 31, 32, 34–45 **p. 291**

For growing symbol explanations, please see page 47.

Narcissus 'Jack Snipes'

Tulipa 'Apricot Beauty'

Dahlia pinnata

Canna 'Delaware'

Gladiolus communis ssp. *byzantinus*

Crocosmia 'Citronella'

Zantedeschia aethiopica

Colchicum autumnale 'Waterfall'

Muscari
GRAPE HYACINTH
ZONES VARY — p. 320

Narcissus
DAFFODIL
ZONES VARY — p. 322

Ornithogalum umbellatum
STAR OF BETHLEHEM
31, 32 — p. 330

Oxalis (some)
NEEDS, ZONES VARY — p. 331

Paeonia (herbaceous)
PEONY
31, 32, 34–45 — p. 332

Puschkinia scilloides
31, 32, 34–43 — p. 374

Rhodohypoxis baurii
31, 32 — p. 383

Scilla
SQUILL
ZONES VARY — p. 404

Tulipa
TULIP
31, 32, 34–45 — p. 433

SPRING–PLANTED BULBS

Alocasia
ELEPHANT'S EAR
ALL ZONES — p. 126

Amorphophallus konjac
DEVIL'S TONGUE, SNAKE PALM,
ALL ZONES — p. 129

Begonia, tuberous
ALL ZONES — p. 153

Caladium bicolor
FANCY-LEAFED CALADIUM
ALL ZONES — p. 162

Canna
ALL ZONES — p. 168

Cardiocrinum giganteum
HEART LILY
ALL ZONES — p. 169

Colocasia esculenta
TARO, ELEPHANT'S EAR
ALL ZONES — p. 191

Crocosmia
31, 32, 34, 39 — p. 199

Dahlia
ALL ZONES — p. 205

Eucomis
PINEAPPLE FLOWER
ALL ZONES — p. 225

Gladiolus
ALL ZONES — p. 241

Hymenocallis
ALL ZONES — p. 263

Ixia
CORN LILY
ALL ZONES — p. 273

Liatris
GAYFEATHER
ALL ZONES — p. 290

Lilium, Oriental hybrids
ALL ZONES — p. 291

Pinellia
31, 32, 34, 39 — p. 352

Polianthes tuberosa
TUBEROSE
ALL ZONES — p. 361

Ranunculus asiaticus
TURBAN RANUNCULUS
ALL ZONES — p. 377

Sauromatum venosum
VOODOO LILY
ALL ZONES — p. 401

Sparaxis tricolor
HARLEQUIN FLOWER
ALL ZONES — p. 411

Tigridia pavonia
MEXICAN SHELL FLOWER
ALL ZONES — p. 427

Watsonia
ALL ZONES — p. 443

Zantedeschia
CALLA
NEEDS VARY, ALL ZONES — p. 446

Zephyranthes
ZEPHYR FLOWER
ALL ZONES — p. 447

SUMMER-PLANTED BULBS

Colchicum
MEADOW SAFFRON
31, 32, 34–43 — p. 190

Crocus (fall-flowering)
31, 32, 34–45 — p. 199

Cyclamen
ZONES VARY — p. 201

Lycoris
SPIDER LILY
ZONES VARY — p. 300

Sternbergia lutea
32, 34, 39 — p. 415

Arachniodes simplicior

Athyrium nipponicum 'Pictum'

Cyrtomium falcatum

FERNS
for Foliage Interest

Think of ferns, and you probably think of a lush and shady forest nook. What you may not imagine, though, is the stunning diversity that these typically shade-loving plants have to offer. In size, they range from forest-floor creepers to the majestic tree ferns that seem to belong to the age of dinosaurs. Their leaves (fronds) may look like a hand with outstretched fingers (palmate) or like feathers of a bird (pinnate); texture varies from silky-soft to thick and leathery. Most ferns have a filigreed look, but some kinds have undivided fronds resembling green spearpoints.

Adiantum
MAIDENHAIR FERN
ZONES VARY   p. 120

Arachniodes simplicior
'Variegata' VARIEGATED HOLLY FERN
32, 34, 39   p. 139

Asplenium
SPLEENWORT
ZONES VARY   p. 146

Asplenium rhizophyllum
WALKING FERN
32, 34–43   p. 146

Asplenium scolopendrium
HART'S-TONGUE FERN
32, 34–41   p. 146

Athyrium
LADY FERN, GLADE FERN
32, 34–43   p. 148

Athyrium nipponicum 'Pictum'
JAPANESE PAINTED FERN
32, 34–43   p. 148

Blechnum
HARD FERN
32, 34–41   p. 156

Cheilanthes
ZONES VARY   p. 180

Cyrtomium falcatum
HOLLY FERN
32, 34, 39   p. 204

Dennstaedtia punctilobula
HAY-SCENTED FERN
32, 34–45   p. 209

Dryopteris
WOOD FERN
ZONES VARY   p. 215

Lygodium
CLIMBING FERN
ZONES VARY   p. 300

Matteuccia struthiopteris
OSTRICH FERN
32, 34–45   p. 313

Onoclea sensibilis
SENSITIVE FERN
32, 34–43   p. 328

Osmunda cinnamomea
CINNAMON FERN
32, 34–45   p. 330

Osmunda claytoniana
INTERRUPTED FERN
32, 34–45   p. 330

Osmunda regalis
ROYAL FERN, FLOWERING FERN
31, 32, 34–45   p. 330

Polypodium
POLYPODY
ZONES VARY   p. 362

Polystichum
ZONES VARY   p. 362

Polystichum acrostichoides
CHRISTMAS FERN
31, 32, 34–45   p. 362

Pteridium aquilinum
BRACKEN
32, 34–43   p. 372

Selaginella
SPIKE MOSS
ZONES VARY   p. 405

Thelypteris
ZONES VARY   p. 424

Woodsia obtusa
32, 34–43   p. 445

Woodwardia
CHAIN FERN
32, 34–41   p. 445

For growing symbol explanations, please see page 47.

Osmunda cinnamomea

Polystichum

Pteridium aquilinum

Woodwardia areolata

Artemisia absinthium

Caryopteris clandonensis 'Blue Mist'

Santolina

Vitex agnus-castus

Plants with
COLORED FOLIAGE

Not all color comes from flowers or fruit. The plants listed below offer long-term garden accents in the form of colored leaves: gray or silver; bronze, red, or purple; yellow or gold; blue; and variegated. They can be used to enliven the basic green of other garden foliage, to form contrasting combinations with one another (such as gray and red), to complement flower colors in season, and to provide eye-catching focal points throughout the growing season.

Gray, silver TREES, SHRUBS

Andromeda polifolia
BOG ROSEMARY
36–45 — p. 130

Artemisia
ZONES VARY — p. 142

Caryopteris clandonensis
BLUE MIST
31, 32, 34–41 — p. 173

Elaeagnus angustifolia
RUSSIAN OLIVE
31, 32, 34–45 — p. 218

Elaeagnus 'Coral Silver'
31, 32, 34–41 — p. 218

Elaeagnus pungens
SILVERBERRY
31, 32 — p. 218

Hippophae rhamnoides
SEA BUCKTHORN
31, 32, 34–45 — p. 257

Holodiscus discolor
ROCK SPIREA, OCEAN SPRAY
31, 32, 34, 39 — p. 258

Juniperus (many)
JUNIPER
ZONES VARY — p. 275

Populus alba
WHITE POPLAR
31, 32, 34–45 — p. 363

Salix elaeagnos
ROSEMARY WILLOW
31, 32, 34–43 — p. 395

Santolina chamaecyparissus
LAVENDER COTTON
32, 34, 39 — p. 399

Vitex agnus-castus
CHASTE TREE
31, 32, 34, 39 — p. 442

Gray, silver PERENNIALS, ANNUALS

Achillea (many)
YARROW
31, 32, 34–45 — p. 118

Anaphalis
PEARLY EVERLASTING
34–45 — p. 130

Antennaria
PUSSYTOES
36–45 — p. 133

Centaurea
NEEDS, ZONES VARY — p. 177

Cerastium tomentosum
SNOW-IN-SUMMER
31, 32, 34–45 — p. 178

Crambe maritima
SEA KALE
31, 32, 34–41 — p. 197

Cynara cardunculus
CARDOON
31, 32 — p. 202

Dianthus (many)
ZONES VARY — p. 209

Helichrysum petiolare
LICORICE PLANT
ALL ZONES — p. 252

Holcus mollis 'Albovariegatus'
VARIEGATED CREEPING SOFT GRASS
31, 32, 34, 39 — p. 258

Lamium (some)
DEAD NETTLE
32, 34–43 — p. 284

Lavandula (most)
LAVENDER
ZONES VARY — p. 286

Lychnis coronaria
CROWN-PINK
31, 32, 34–43 — p. 299

Plant listings continue ▶

Centaurea cineraria

Helichrysum petiolare

Holcus mollis

Lamium maculatum 'White Nancy'

Fagus sylvatica 'Atropurpurea'

Ajuga reptans 'Burgundy Glow'

Setcreasea pallida 'Purple Heart'

Acer shirasawanum 'Aureum'

Chamaecyparis lawsoniana

Panicum virgatum 'Heavy Metal'
SWITCH GRASS
31, 32, 34–43   p. 334

Perovskia
RUSSIAN SAGE
31, 32, 34, 39   p. 345

Rudbeckia maxima
31, 32, 34–43   p. 393

Salvia argentea
SILVER SAGE
31, 32, 34–45   p. 396

Sempervivum
HOUSELEEK
31, 32, 34–41   p. 405

Senecio cineraria
DUSTY MILLER
31, 32 OR ANNUAL   p. 406

Stachys byzantina
LAMB'S EARS
31, 32, 34–43   p. 414

Thymus (several)
THYME
ZONES VARY   p. 426

Verbascum (some)
31, 32, 34–41   p. 437

Yucca glauca
SOAPWEED
31, 32, 34–43   p. 446

Bronze, Red, Purple
TREES, SHRUBS

Acer palmatum (some)
JAPANESE MAPLE
31, 32, 34–41   p. 116

Acer platanoides (some)
NORWAY MAPLE
31, 32, 34–43   p. 116

Berberis thunbergii (several)
JAPANESE BARBERRY
31, 32, 34–43   p. 154

Cercis canadensis 'Forest Pansy'
EASTERN REDBUD
31, 32, 34–41   p. 178

Corylus avellana 'Fusco-rubra'
31, 32, 34–45   p. 196

Corylus maxima 'Purpurea'
31, 32, 34–45   p. 196

Cotinus coggygria (some)
SMOKE TREE
31, 32, 34–41   p. 196

Euonymus fortunei 'Colorata'
31, 32, 34–41   p. 226

Fagus sylvatica (some)
EUROPEAN BEECH
31, 32, 34–41   p. 229

Malus purpurea 'Lemoinei'
31, 32, 34–43   p. 308

Nandina domestica 'Firepower'
31, 32   p. 322

Prunus blireiana
31, 32, 34–41   p. 368

Prunus cerasifera (some)
CHERRY PLUM
31, 32, 34–43   p. 368

Sambucus nigra 'Purpurea'
BLACK ELDER
32, 34, 39   p. 399

Spiraea bumalda (several)
31, 32, 34–43   p. 412

Weigela florida 'Purpurea'
31, 32, 34–41   p. 443

Bronze, Red, Purple
PERENNIALS, ANNUALS

Acalypha wilkesiana
COPPER LEAF
ALL ZONES   p. 115

Ajuga reptans (several)
CARPET BUGLE
31, 32, 34–45   p. 123

Astilbe 'Fanal'
32, 34–45   p. 147

Caladium bicolor
FANCY-LEAFED CALADIUM
DIG/STORE   p. 162

Canna (some)
31, 32 OR DIG/STORE   p. 168

Carex (several)
SEDGE
31, 32, 34–45   p. 169

Cimicifuga ramosa 'Atropurpurea'
BUGBANE
31, 32, 34–45   p. 185

Euphorbia amygdaloides 'Purpurea'
31, 32, 34, 39   p. 227

Foeniculum vulgare 'Purpurascens'   BRONZE FENNEL
31, 32, 34–41   p. 232

Heuchera micrantha 'Palace Purple'
31, 32, 34–43   p. 256

Imperata 'Red Baron'
31, 32, 34, 39   p. 267

Ipomoea batatas 'Blackie'
SWEET POTATO VINE
ALL ZONES   p. 269

Ocimum basilicum (some)
SWEET BASIL
ALL ZONES   p. 327

Pennisetum setaceum 'Rubrum'
ALL ZONES   p. 343

Perilla frutescens
SHISO
ALL ZONES   p. 345

Phormium tenax (several)
NEW ZEALAND FLAX
DIG/STORE   p. 349

Ricinus communis 'Carmencita'
CASTOR BEAN
ALL ZONES   p. 385

Sedum spathulifolium 'Purpureum'
31, 32, 34, 39   p. 404

Sedum spurium (some)
31, 32, 34–43   p. 404

Sedum 'Vera Jameson'
31, 32, 34–43   p. 404

Setcreasea pallida 'Purple Heart'
PURPLE HEART, PURPLE QUEEN
ALL ZONES   p. 406

Strobilanthes dyerianus
ALL ZONES   p. 416

Yellow, gold
TREES, SHRUBS

Acer shirasawanum 'Aureum'
GOLDEN FULLMOON MAPLE
31, 32, 34, 37, 39   p. 116

Aucuba japonica (some)
31, 32   p. 148

Berberis thunbergii 'Aurea'
31, 32, 34–43   p. 154

Chamaecyparis (some)
ZONES VARY   p. 179

Chamaecyparis lawsoniana (some)
PORT ORFORD CEDAR
31, 32, 34, 39   p. 179

Gleditsia triacanthos 'Sunburst'
SUNBURST HONEY LOCUST
31, 32, 34–43   p. 242

Juniperus (several)
JUNIPER
ZONES VARY   p. 275

Ligustrum vicaryi
VICARY GOLDEN PRIVET
32, 34–41   p. 290

Lonicera nitida 'Baggesen's Gold'   BOXLEAF HONEYSUCKLE
31, 32, 34, 39   p. 297

For growing symbol explanations, please see page 47.

Philadelphus coronarius 'Aureus'
☼ ◑ ● ● ✔ 31, 32, 34–43   p. 347

Platycladus orientalis (several)
ORIENTAL ARBORVITAE
☼ ◑ ● ✔ 31, 32, 34–41   p. 356

Robinia pseudoacacia 'Frisia'
BLACK LOCUST
☼ ● ✔ 31, 32, 34–43   p. 385

Salix alba tristis
GOLDEN WEEPING WILLOW
☼ ◑ ● ✔ 31, 32, 34–45   p. 395

Sambucus canadensis 'Aurea'
☼ ◑ ● ✔ 31, 32, 34–45   p. 399

Spiraea bumalda (several)
☼ ◑ ● ● ✔ 31, 32, 34–43   p. 412

Spiraea japonica 'Goldflame'
☼ ◑ ● ● ✔ 31, 32, 34–43   p. 412

Taxus baccata (several)
ENGLISH YEW
☼ ◑ ● ● ✔ 31, 32, 34, 39   p. 422

Thuja occidentalis 'Rheingold'
AMERICAN ARBORVITAE
☼ ◑ ● ● ✔ 31, 32, 34–45   p. 425

Thuja plicata 'Aurea'
WESTERN RED CEDAR
☼ ◑ ● ● ✔ 31, 32, 34–41   p. 425

Thymus vulgaris 'Aureus'
☼ ● ● ✔ 31, 32, 34–43   p. 426

Viburnum opulus 'Aureum'
EUROPEAN CRANBERRY BUSH
☼ ◑ ● ✔ 31, 32, 34–43   p. 439

Blue TREES

Cedrus atlantica 'Glauca'
☼ ◑ ● ✔ 31, 32, 34, 39   p. 175

Chamaecyparis lawsoniana
PORT ORFORD CEDAR
☼ ◑ ● ✔ 32, 34, 39   p. 179

Cunninghamia lanceolata 'Glauca'
☼ ◑ ✔ 31, 32   p. 200

Juniperus (some)
JUNIPER
☼ ● ✔ ZONES VARY   p. 275

Picea pungens (some)
COLORADO SPRUCE
☼ ● ● ✔ 31, 32, 34–45   p. 350

Blue PERENNIALS

Elymus magellanicus
☼ ● ✔ 31, 32, 34, 39   p. 219

Festuca glauca
BLUE FESCUE
☼ ◑ ● ✔ 31, 32, 34–45   p. 230

Hosta (several)
PLANTAIN LILY
◑ ● ● ✔ ZONES VARY   p. 259

Ilex meserveae
HOLLY
☼ ◑ ● ● ✔ 31, 32, 34, 35, 37–39 p. 265

Ruta graveolens 'Jackman's Blue' RUE
☼ ● ● ✔ 31, 32, 34–41   p. 394

Schizachyrium scoparium 'The Blues'
☼ ● ● ✔ 31, 32, 34–45   p. 403

Sorghastrum nutans
'SIOUX BLUE'
☼ ● ● ✔ 31, 32, 34–43   p. 411

Variegated TREES, SHRUBS

Abelia 'Confetti'
☼ ◑ ● ✔ 31, 32, 34, 39   p. 114

Acanthopanax sieboldianus 'Variegatus'
☼ ◑ ● ● ● ✔ 31, 32, 34–41   p. 115

Acer negundo 'Variegatum'
VARIEGATED BOX ELDER
☼ ◑ ● ● ✔ 31, 32, 34–45   p. 116

Acer palmatum 'Butterfly'
JAPANESE MAPLE
☼ ◑ ● ● ✔ 31, 32, 34–41   p. 116

Aralia elata 'Aureovariegata'
☼ ◑ ● ● ✔ 31, 32, 34–41   p. 139

Aralia elata 'Variegata'
☼ ◑ ● ✔ 31, 32, 34–41   p. 139

Aucuba japonica (several)
JAPANESE AUCUBA
◑ ● ● ● ✔ 31, 32   p. 148

Cornus alba 'Argenteomarginata'
☼ ◑ ● ✔ 31, 32, 34–45   p. 194

Cornus alba 'Spaethii'
☼ ◑ ● ✔ 31, 32, 34–45   p. 194

Cornus alternifolia 'Argentea'
VARIEGATED PAGODA DOGWOOD
☼ ◑ ● ✔ 31, 32, 34–43   p. 194

Cornus controversa 'Variegata'
VARIEGATED GIANT DOGWOOD
☼ ◑ ● ✔ 31, 32, 34–41   p. 194

Cornus florida (several)
FLOWERING DOGWOOD
☼ ◑ ● ✔ 31, 32, 34–41   p. 194

Cotoneaster horizontalis 'Variegatus'
☼ ◑ ● ✔ 31, 32, 34–41   p. 196

Daphne burkwoodii 'Carol Mackie'
☼ ◑ ● ● ✔ 31, 32, 34–41   p. 206

Daphne odora 'Marginata'
WINTER DAPHNE
◑ ● ✔ 31, 32   p. 206

Elaeagnus pungens (some)
SILVERBERRY
☼ ◑ ● ● ✔ 31, 32   p. 218

Euonymus (some)
NEEDS, ZONES VARY   p. 226

Fagus sylvatica 'Tricolor'
TRICOLOR BEECH
☼ ◑ ● ● ✔ 31, 32, 34–41   p. 229

Hydrangea macrophylla 'Tricolor'
GARDEN HYDRANGEA
☼ ◑ ● ✔ 31, 32, 34, 39   p. 262

Ilex (several)
HOLLY
☼ ◑ ● ✔ ZONES VARY   p. 265

Leucothoe fontanesiana 'Rainbow' DROOPING LEUCOTHOE
◑ ● ● ✔ 31, 32, 34–41   p. 289

Pieris japonica 'Variegata'
LILY-OF-THE-VALLEY SHRUB
◑ ● ✔ 31, 32, 34–41   p. 351

Pinus densiflora 'Oculus-draconis'
DRAGON EYE PINE
☼ ● ● ✔ 31, 32, 34–41   p. 352

Pinus wallichiana 'Zebrina'
VARIEGATED HIMALAYAN WHITE PINE
☼ ● ✔ 31, 32, 34, 37, 39   p. 352

Weigela florida (some)
☼ ◑ ● ✔ 31, 32, 34–41   p. 443

Plant listings continue ▶

Juniperus squamatus 'Blue Star'

Picea pungens

Festuca ovina 'Elijah Blue'

Acanthopanax sieboldianus 'Variegatus'

Acer negundo 'Flamingo'

PLANTS WITH COLORED FOLIAGE

Asarum shuttleworthii

Euonymus fortunei

Arrhenatherum elatius

Coleus hybridus

Variegated GROUND COVERS, VINES

Actinidia kolomikta
☼ ◐ ◑ ● ⚡ 31, 32, 34–41 **p. 120**

Ampelopsis brevipedunculata 'Elegans'
☼ ◐ ● ◑ ● ⚡ 31, 32, 34–41 **p. 129**

Asarum shuttleworthii
WILD GINGER
◑ ● ● ● ⚡ 31, 32, 34–37, 39 **p. 144**

Epimedium (some)
◑ ● ⚡ 31, 32, 34–43 **p. 220**

Euonymus fortunei (some)
☼ ◐ ● ● ◑ ● ⚡ 31, 32, 34–41 **p. 226**

Hedera (some)
IVY
◑ ● ● ◑ ● ⚡ ZONES VARY **p. 250**

Lonicera japonica 'Aureo-reticulata' GOLDNET HONEYSUCKLE
☼ ◑ ● ⚡ 31, 32, 34–41 **p. 297**

Pachysandra terminalis 'Silver Edge'
◑ ● ● ⚡ 31, 32, 34–43 **p. 332**

Vinca (some)
PERIWINKLE
◑ ● ● ⚡ ZONES VARY **p. 441**

Variegated PERENNIALS, ANNUALS

Ajuga (several)
CARPET BUGLE
☼ ◑ ● ⚡ 31, 32, 34–45 **p. 123**

Amoracia rusticana 'Variegata'
HORSERADISH
☼ ● ⚡ 31, 32, 34–41 **p. 258**

Arrhenatherum elatius ssp. bulbosum 'Variegatum'
☼ ◑ ● ⚡ 31, 32, 34–41 **p. 142**

Arum italicum 'Pictum'
◑ ● ⚡ 31, 32, 34, 39 **p. 143**

Arundo donax 'Variegata'
☼ ●● ⚡ 31, 32, 34, 39 **p. 143**

Astrantia major 'Sunningdale Variegated'
☼ ◑ ● ⚡ 31, 32, 34–41 **p. 147**

Brunnera macrophylla 'Variegata'
☼ ◑ ● ⚡ 31, 32, 34–45 **p. 160**

Cabbage, flowering
☼ ◑ ● ⚡ ALL ZONES **p. 162**

Caladium bicolor
FANCY-LEAFED CALADIUM
◑ ● ● ⚡ ALL ZONES **p. 162**

Canna
☼ ● ◑ ⚡ 31, 32, DIG/STORE **p. 168**

Carex (many)
SEDGE
NEEDS, ZONES VARY **p. 169**

Coleus hybridus
COLEUS
☼ ◑ ● ⚡ ALL ZONES **p. 190**

Holcus mollis 'Albovariegatus'
☼ ◑ ● ⚡ 31, 32, 34, 39 **p. 258**

Hosta (many)
PLANTAIN LILY
◑ ● ◑ ⚡ ZONES VARY **p. 259**

Houttuynia cordata 'Variegata'
☼ ◑ ● ● ◑ ⚡ 31, 32, 34–41 **p. 260**

Humulus japonicus 'Variegatus'
☼ ◑ ● ⚡ 31, 32, 34–43 **p. 261**

Hypoestes
FRECKLE FACE, PINK POLKA-DOT PLANT
☼ ◑ ● ⚡ ALL ZONES **p. 264**

Impatiens (some)
☼ ◑ ● ⚡ ALL ZONES **p. 267**

Iris 'Pallida Variegata'
☼ ◑ ● ⚡ 31, 32, 34–41 **p. 269**

Lamium (several)
DEAD NETTLE
◑ ● ● ⚡ 31, 32, 34–43 **p. 284**

Liriope muscari (some)
LILY TURF
◑ ● ● ◑ ● ⚡ 31, 32, 34, 39 **p. 295**

Miscanthus sinensis (several)
EULALIA GRASS
☼ ● ⚡ 31, 32, 34–41 **p. 317**

Pelargonium (some)
☼ ● ⚡ ALL ZONES **p. 341**

Physostegia virginiana 'Variegata'
☼ ◑ ● ⚡ 31, 32, 34–45 **p. 350**

Polygonum virginianum (some)
◑ ● ⚡ 31, 32, 34–41 **p. 361**

Pulmonaria (several)
LUNGWORT
◑ ● ● ⚡ 31, 32, 34–43 **p. 373**

Sedum (several)
☼ ◑ ● ● ⚡ ZONES VARY **p. 404**

Symphytum (some)
☼ ◑ ● ⚡ 31, 32, 34–43 **p. 420**

Yucca (several)
☼ ◑ ● ⚡ ZONES VARY **p. 446**

Hosta 'June'

Hypoestes phyllostachya 'White Splash'

Liriope muscari 'Variegata'

Miscanthus sinensis 'Zebrinus'

For growing symbol explanations, please see page 47.

Calamagrostis acutifolia 'Karl Foerster'

ORNAMENTAL GRASSES

Denizens of prairie, marsh, seashore, and forest, the ornamental grasses are enormously varied. In contrast to the familiar lawn grasses, these decorative cousins are not for mowing. Their beauty lies in their fountains and shaving brushes of foliage, in their range of texture, color, and character. Many mount a significant floral display, producing reedlike stems with plumes or pendants of tiny floral structures. And some even offer colorful fall foliage.

Molinia caerulea 'Variegatus'

Carex elata 'Bowles Golden'

Arrhenatherum elatius bulbosum
BULBOUS OAT GRASS
☼ ◑ ● ⚡ 36–41   **p. 142**

Arundo donax
GIANT REED
☼ ● ⚡ 31, 32, 34, 39   **p. 143**

Bamboo

☼ ◑ ● ● ⚡ ZONES VARY   **p. 149**

Bouteloua gracilis
BLUE GRAMA GRASS
☼ ● ⚡ 35, 41, 43, 45   **p. 158**

Briza maxima
RATTLESNAKE GRASS
☼ ● ● ⚡ 31, 32, 34–45   **p. 159**

Calamagrostis acutifolia
FEATHER REED GRASS
☼ ● ⚡ 31, 32, 34–41   **p. 163**

Carex
SEDGE
☼ ◑ ● ● ⚡ ZONES VARY   **p. 169**

Chasmanthium latifolium
SEA OATS
☼ ◑ ● ⚡ 31, 32, 34–43   **p. 180**

Coix lacryma-jobi
JOB'S TEARS
☼ ◑ ● ⚡ ALL ZONES   **p. 190**

Cortaderia selloana
PAMPAS GRASS
☼ ● ● ● ⚡ 31, 32   **p. 195**

Deschampsia
HAIR GRASS
☼ ◑ ● ● ⚡ 31, 32, 34–41   **p. 209**

Elymus magellanicus
BLUE WHEATGRASS
☼ ● ● ⚡ 31, 32, 34, 39   **p. 219**

Festuca
FESCUE
☼ ● ⚡ 31, 32, 34–45   **p. 230**

Hakonechloa macra 'Aureola'
JAPANESE FOREST GRASS
◑ ● ● ⚡ 31, 32, 34–41   **p. 248**

Helictotrichon sempervirens
BLUE OAT GRASS
☼ ● ⚡ 31, 32, 34–41   **p. 252**

Imperata cylindrica 'Rubra'
JAPANESE BLOOD GRASS
☼ ◑ ● ⚡ 31, 32, 34, 39   **p. 267**

Juncus effusus
SOFT RUSH
☼ ◑ ● ● ⚡ 31, 32, 34–43   **p. 275**

Lagurus ovatus
HARE'S TAIL GRASS
☼ ● ⚡ ALL ZONES   **p. 284**

Milium effusum 'Aureum'
BOWLES' GOLDEN GRASS
◑ ● ● ⚡ 31, 32, 34, 39   **p. 317**

Miscanthus
EULALIA GRASS
☼ ◑ ● ● ● ⚡ 31, 32, 34–41 **p. 317**

Molinia caerulea
PURPLE MOOR GRASS
☼ ◑ ● ● ● ⚡ 31, 32, 34, 39   **p. 318**

Muhlenbergia
☼ ◑ ● ⚡ ZONES VARY   **p. 320**

Panicum virgatum
SWITCH GRASS
☼ ● ● ● ⚡ 31, 32, 34–43   **p. 334**

Pennisetum
FOUNTAIN GRASS
NEEDS, ZONES VARY   **p. 343**

Phalaris arundinacea
RIBBON GRASS
☼ ◑ ● ● ● ⚡ 31, 32, 34–43 **p. 347**

Saccharum ravennae
RAVENNA GRASS
☼ ● ⚡ 31, 32, 34, 39   **p. 394**

Sporobolus
DROPSEED
☼ ● ● ⚡ 31, 32, 34–45   **p. 413**

Stipa
FEATHER GRASS
☼ ● ● ⚡ 31; 32   **p. 415**

Muhlenbergia lindheimeri

Pennisetum alopecuroides 'Hameln'

Miscanthus sinensis 'Silberfeder'

Elymus magellanicus

Pennisetum orientale

67

Magnolia soulangiana

Malus 'Jewelberry'

Poncirus trifoliata

Prunus persica

FRAGRANT PLANTS

A garden's fragrance can be as memorable as its appearance; even years later, the scent of a particular blossom can evoke the memory of a past experience. Flower fragrance is usually most pronounced on warm and humid days and least noticeable when weather is dry and hot. Use fragrant plants where they're most likely to be noticed: in containers on a patio, or beneath a window so the pleasant aroma can drift into the house.

Calycanthus floridus 'Athens'

TREES

Albizia julibrissin 'Rosea'
SILK TREE
31, 32, 34, 39   p. 124

Chionanthus virginicus
FRINGE TREE
31, 32, 34–41   p. 182

Cladrastis lutea
YELLOW WOOD
31, 32, 34–43   p. 186

Crataegus laevigata
ENGLISH HAWTHORN
31, 32, 34–41   p. 198

Elaeagnus angustifolia
RUSSIAN OLIVE
31, 32, 34–45   p. 218

Franklinia alatamaha
31, 32, 34, 39   p. 233

Gleditsia triacanthos
31, 32, 34–43   p. 242

Laburnum watereri
GOLDENCHAIN TREE
31, 32, 34–39   p. 282

Magnolia (many)
ZONES VARY   p. 302

Malus (some)
CRABAPPLE
31, 32, 34–43   p. 308

Poncirus trifoliata
TRIFOLIATE ORANGE
31, 32, 34, 39   p. 362

Prunus (many)
ZONES VARY   p. 368

Robinia pseudoacacia
BLACK LOCUST
31, 32, 34–45   p. 385

Styrax japonicus
JAPANESE SNOWBELL
31, 32, 34, 39   p. 418

Styrax obassia
FRAGRANT SNOWBELL
31, 32, 34, 39   p. 418

Tilia
LINDEN
ZONES VARY   p. 427

SHRUBS

Buddleia
ZONES VARY   p. 161

Calycanthus floridus
CAROLINA ALLSPICE
31, 32, 34–41   p. 166

Cephalanthus occidentalis
BUTTONBUSH
31, 32, 34–41   p. 177

Chimonanthus praecox
WINTERSWEET
31, 32   p. 182

Clethra alnifolia
SUMMERSWEET
31, 32, 34–43   p. 189

Corylopsis
WINTER HAZEL
ZONES VARY   p. 195

Cytisus
BROOM
ZONES VARY   p. 204

Daphne (many)
NEEDS, ZONES VARY   p. 206

Elaeagnus
ZONES VARY   p. 218

Epigaea repens
TRAILING ARBUTUS
31, 32, 34–45   p. 220

Clethra barbinervis

Corylopsis pauciflora

Daphne odora

For growing symbol explanations, please see page 47.

Fothergilla major

Lavandula

Philadelphus virginalis 'Natchez'

Ribes odoratum

Fothergilla

☼ ◐ ● ⚡ 31, 32, 34–41   **p. 233**

Hamamelis
WITCH HAZEL

☼ ◐ ● ⚡ ZONES VARY   **p. 249**

Illicium
ANISE TREE

● ● ● ⚡ 31, 32   **p. 266**

Itea virginica
VIRGINIA SWEETSPIRE

☼ ◐ ● ⚡ 31, 32, 34, 39   **p. 273**

Lavandula (most)
LAVENDER

☼ ● ⚡ ZONES VARY   **p. 286**

Lindera
SPICEBUSH

☼ ◐ ● ⚡ ZONES VARY   **p. 293**

Lonicera
HONEYSUCKLE

☼ ◐ ● ⚡ ZONES VARY   **p. 297**

Magnolia stellata
STAR MAGNOLIA

☼ ◐ ● ⚡ 31, 32, 34–41   **p. 302**

Osmanthus heterophyllus
HOLLY-LEAF OSMANTHUS

☼ ◐ ● ● ⚡ 31, 32   **p. 330**

Philadelphus (most)
MOCK ORANGE

☼ ◐ ● ● ⚡ ZONES VARY   **p. 347**

Rhododendron alabamense
ALABAMA AZALEA

● ● ●● ⚡ 31, 32   **p. 380**

Rhododendron arborescens
SWEET AZALEA

◐ ● ●● ⚡ 31, 32, 34–41   **p. 380**

Rhododendron Dexter Hybrids (some)

◐ ● ⚡ 31, 32, 34, 39   **p. 380**

Rhododendron, Viscosum Hybrids   DECIDUOUS AZALEAS

● ●● ● ⚡ 31, 32, 34–41   **p. 380**

Ribes odoratum

☼ ● ● ⚡ 31, 32, 34–45   **p. 384**

Rosa (many)
ROSE
NEEDS, ZONES VARY   **p. 386**

Sarcococca
SWEET BOX

◐ ● ● ● ⚡ 31, 32   **p. 400**

Skimmia japonica (esp. males)

◐ ● ● ⚡ 31, 32   **p. 409**

Syringa (many)
LILAC

☼ ◐ ● ⚡ ZONES VARY   **p. 420**

Viburnum carlcephalum
FRAGRANT SNOWBALL

☼ ● ● ⚡ 31, 32, 34, 39   **p. 439**

Viburnum carlesii
KOREAN SPICE VIBURNUM

☼ ◐ ● ⚡ 31, 32, 34–41   **p. 439**

Viburnum farreri (V. fragrans)

☼ ◐ ● ⚡ 31, 32, 34, 37, 39   **p. 439**

Vitex agnus-castus
CHASTE TREE

☼ ● ⚡ 31, 32, 34, 39   **p. 442**

VINES

Akebia

☼ ◐ ● ● ⚡ 31, 32, 34–41   **p. 124**

Clematis armandii
EVERGREEN CLEMATIS

☼ ● ⚡ 31, 32   **p. 187**

Clematis terniflora
SWEET AUTUMN CLEMATIS

☼ ● ⚡ 31, 32, 34–41   **p. 187**

Gelsemium sempervirens
CAROLINA JESSAMINE

☼ ◐ ● ● ⚡ 31, 32   **p. 237**

Ipomoea alba
MOONFLOWER

☼ ◐ ● ⚡ ALL ZONES   **p. 269**

Jasminum spp.
JASMINE

☼ ◐   ● ⚡ ZONES VARY   **p. 274**

Lonicera (some)
HONEYSUCKLE

☼ ◐ ● ⚡ ZONES VARY   **p. 297**

Mandevilla laxa
CHILEAN JASMINE

☼ ◐ ● ⚡ BRING INDOORS   **p. 312**

Passiflora alatocaerulea
PASSION VINE

☼ ● ● ⚡ BRING INDOORS   **p. 336**

Rosa (climbing, some)

☼ ● ⚡ ZONES VARY   **p. 386**

Wisteria

NEEDS, ZONES VARY   **p. 444**

PERENNIALS, ANNUALS, BULBS

Allium neapolitanum
ORNAMENTAL ALLIUM

☼ ◐ ● ⚡ 31, 31, 32, 34, 39   **p. 125**

Allium tuberosum
CHINESE CHIVES

☼ ● ⚡ 31, 32, 34–41   **p. 125**

Centaurea moschata
SWEET SULTAN

☼ ● ⚡ ALL ZONES   **p. 177**

Centranthus ruber
RED VALERIAN, JUPITER'S BEARD

☼ ● ● ⚡ 31, 32, 34–43   **p. 177**

Skimmia japonica

Viburnum carlesii 'Cayuga'

Clematis dioscoreifolia

Lonicera heckrottii

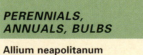
Plant listings continue ▶

FRAGRANT PLANTS

Dianthus caryophyllus 'Daydream'

Hedychium

Heliotropum arborescens

Hesperis matronalis

Convallaria majalis
LILY-OF-THE-VALLEY
☼ ◑ ● ⚡ 31, 32, 34–45   p. 191

Crinum
☼ ◑ ● ● ⚡ ZONES VARY   p. 198

Crocus chrysanthus
☼ ◑ ● ⚡ 31, 32, 34–45   p. 199

Dianthus (some)
PINK
☼ ◑ ● ⚡ 31, 32, 34–45   p. 209

Dictamnus albus
GAS PLANT
☼ ◑ ● ⚡ 31, 32, 34–45   p. 211

Erysimum cheiri
ENGLISH WALLFLOWER
☼ ◑ ● ● ⚡ 32, 34–45   p. 224

Filipendula (some)
☼ ◑ ● ● ⚡ ZONES VARY   p. 231

Hedychium
GINGER LILY
☼ ◑ ● ● ⚡ 31, 32   p. 250

Heliotropium arborescens
COMMON HELIOTROPE
☼ ◑ ● ⚡ ALL ZONES   p. 252

Hemerocallis lilio-asphodelus
LEMON DAYLILY
☼ ◑ ● ⚡ 31, 32, 34–43   p. 253

Hesperis matronalis
DAME'S ROCKET
☼ ◑ ● ⚡ ALL ZONES   p. 256

Hosta plantaginea
FRAGRANT PLANTAIN LILY
◑ ● ● ⚡ 31, 32, 34–45   p. 259

Hyacinthus
HYACINTH
☼ ◑ ● ⚡ ALL ZONES   p. 262

Hymenocallis
☼ ◑ ● ⚡ DIG AND STORE   p. 263

Iberis amara
HYACINTH-FLOWERED CANDYTUFT
☼ ◑ ● ⚡ 31, 32, 34–45   p. 264

Ipomoea alba
MOONFLOWER
☼ ◑ ● ● ⚡ ALL ZONES   p. 269

Iris, bearded (many)
☼ ◑ ● ⚡ 31, 32, 34–45   p. 269

Lathyrus odoratus
SWEET PEA
☼ ◑ ● ⚡ ALL ZONES   p. 285

Lilium (many)
LILY
☼ ● ⚡ 31, 32, 34–45   p. 291

Lobularia maritima
SWEET ALYSSUM
☼ ● ⚡ ALL ZONES   p. 295

Lycoris
SPIDER LILY, NAKED LADY
☼ ◑ ● ⚡ ZONES VARY   p. 300

Matthiola
STOCK
☼ ◑ ● ⚡ ALL ZONES   p. 313

Mentha
MINT
☼ ◑ ● ⚡ ZONES VARY   p. 315

Mirabilis jalapa
FOUR O'CLOCK
☼ ◑ ● ⚡ ALL ZONES   p. 317

Monarda didyma
BEE BALM, OSWEGO TEA, HORSEMINT
☼ ◑ ● ● ⚡ 31, 32, 34–43   p. 319

Narcissus (many)
DAFFODIL
☼ ◑ ● ⚡ ZONES VARY   p. 322

Nelumbo
LOTUS
☼ ◑ ● ● ⚡ 31, 32, 34–45   p. 324

Nepeta spp.
☼ ◑ ● ⚡ ZONES VARY   p. 325

Nicotiana
☼ ◑ ● ⚡ ALL ZONES   p. 326

Ocimum
BASIL
☼ ● ⚡ ALL ZONES   p. 327

Origanum
OREGANO
☼ ◑ ● ⚡ ALL ZONES   p. 329

Paeonia (many)
PEONY
☼ ◑ ● ⚡ ZONES VARY   p. 332

Phlox paniculata (esp. light colors)   SUMMER PHLOX
☼ ◑ ● ⚡ 31, 32, 34–45   p. 348

Polianthes tuberosa
TUBEROSE
☼ ● ⚡ ALL ZONES   p. 361

Primula vulgaris
ENGLISH PRIMROSE
☼ ◑ ● ● ⚡ 31, 32, 34–41   p. 365

Reseda odorata
MIGNONETTE
☼ ◑ ● ⚡ ALL ZONES   p. 379

Scabiosa
PINCUSHION FLOWER
☼ ◑ ● ● ⚡ ZONES VARY   p. 402

Thymus
THYME
☼ ◑ ● ⚡ ZONES VARY   p. 426

Tropaeolum majus
GARDEN NASTURTIUM
☼ ◑ ● ⚡ ALL ZONES   p. 432

Viola odorata
SWEET VIOLET
☼ ● ⚡ 31, 32, 34–43   p. 441

Hyacinthus orientalis 'Amethyst'

Origanum vulgare 'Aureum'

Paeonia 'Largo'

Thymus x *citriodorus*

For growing symbol explanations, please see page 47.

COLORFUL FRUITS AND BERRIES

Crataegeus laevigata

Aronia melanocarpa

The plants listed below offer a showy display of color in the form of fruit or berries that, depending on the plant, may be red, orange, yellow, purple, pink, blue, black, or white. Many produce this fruit in addition to striking flowers; in others, it comes as a surprise following an inconspicuous blossoming. Mountain ash, pyracantha, holly, and certain other plants produce fruits that especially appeal to birds. Trees like persimmon yield familiar edible crops.

Ilex opaca 'Canary'

Callicarpa dichotoma

TREES		
Amelanchier JUNEBERRY	31, 32, 34–45	p. 128
Cornus DOGWOOD	ZONES VARY	p. 194
Crataegus HAWTHORN	31, 32, 34–41	p. 198
Evodia daniellii	31, 32, 34–41	p. 228
Ilex (many) HOLLY	ZONES VARY	p. 265
Kalopanax septemlobus CASTOR ARALIA	31, 32, 34–41	p. 280
Koelreuteria	31, 32, 34–41	p. 282
Magnolia	ZONES VARY	p. 302
Malus CRABAPPLE	31, 32, 34–43	p. 308
Oxydendrum arboreum SORREL TREE	31, 32, 34–41	p. 332
Persimmon	ZONES VARY	p. 345
Phellodendron CORK TREE	ZONES VARY	p. 347
Sorbus MOUNTAIN ASH	ZONES VARY	p. 410

SHRUBS		
Arctostaphylos uva-ursi BEARBERRY, KINNIKINNICK	31, 32, 36–45	p. 140
Aronia CHOKEBERRY	ZONES VARY	p. 142
Berberis thunbergii JAPANESE BARBERRY	31, 32, 34–41	p. 154
Callicarpa BEAUTYBERRY	ZONES VARY	p. 164
Chionanthus virginicus VIRGINIA FRINGE TREE	31, 32, 34–41	p. 182
Clerodendrum trichotomum fargesii HARLEQUIN GLORYBOWER	31, 32, 34, 39	p. 189
Cornus kousa KOUSA DOGWOOD	31, 32, 34–41	p. 194
Cornus mas CORNELIAN CHERRY	31, 32, 34–41	p. 194
Corylus FILBERT, HAZELNUT	ZONES VARY	p. 196
Cotoneaster	ZONES VARY	p. 196
Decaisnea fargesii	31, 32	p. 208
Elaeagnus	ZONES VARY	p. 218
Euonymus (many) EUONYMUS	NEEDS, ZONES VARY	p. 226

Malus

Cornus mas

Sorbus aria

Cotoneaster divaricatus

Plant listings continue ▶

COLORFUL FRUITS AND BERRIES

Ilex cornuta

Mahonia bealei

Pyracantha 'Mohave'

Sambucus

Euscaphis japonica
SWEETHEART TREE
☼ ● ◓ ✂ 31, 32, 34, 39   **p. 228**

Gaultheria procumbens
WINTERGREEN, CHECKERBERRY
◐ ◓ ✂ 31, 32, 34–45   **p. 236**

Heptacodium miconioides
SEVEN SONS FLOWER
☼ ● ✂ 31, 32, 34–41   **p. 254**

Hippophae rhamnoides
SEA BUCKTHORN
☼ ● ◓ ✂ 31, 32, 34–45   **p. 257**

Ilex (many)
HOLLY
☼ ● ◓ ✂ ZONES VARY   **p. 265**

Kolkwitzia amabilis
BEAUTY BUSH
☼ ● ✂ 31, 32, 34–41   **p. 282**

Lindera
SPICEBUSH
☼ ◐ ● ✂ ZONES VARY   **p. 293**

Lonicera (most shrubby types)
HONEYSUCKLE
☼ ◐ ● ✂ ZONES VARY   **p. 297**

Lycium chinense
MATRIMONY VINE
☼ ◐ ● ✂ 31, 32, 34–41   **p. 299**

Mahonia
NEEDS, ZONES VARY   **p. 307**

Mitchella repens
PARTRIDGEBERRY
◐ ● ◓ ◔ ✂ 31, 32, 34–45   **p. 318**

Myrica
BAYBERRY
☼ ◐ ● ◓ ✂ ZONES VARY   **p. 321**

Nandina domestica
HEAVENLY BAMBOO
☼ ● ◐ ◓ ✂ 31, 32   **p. 322**

Pernettya mucronata
☼ ● ◓ ✂ 31, 32, 34   **p. 345**

Photinia villosa
☼ ● ◓ ✂ 31, 32, 34–41   **p. 349**

Poncirus trifoliata
HARDY ORANGE
☼ ● ✂ 31, 32, 34, 39   **p. 362**

Prinsepia sp.
☼ ● ✂ ZONES VARY   **p. 365**

Prunus maritima
BEACH PLUM
☼ ● ✂ 31, 32, 34–45   **p. 368**

Punica granatum 'Nana'
POMEGRANATE
☼ ● ◓ ✂ 31, 32   **p. 373**

Pyracantha
FIRETHORN
☼ ● ◓ ✂ ZONES VARY   **p. 374**

Rosa (many, especially rugosas)
ROSE
NEEDS, ZONES VARY   **p. 386**

Sambucus
ELDERBERRY
☼ ◐ ● ◓ ✂ ZONES VARY   **p. 399**

Sarcococca hookeriana humilis
SWEET BOX
◐ ● ◔ ◓ ✂ 31, 32   **p. 400**

Skimmia japonica
◐ ● ◓ ✂ 31, 32   **p. 409**

Symphoricarpos
SNOWBERRY
NEEDS, ZONES VARY   **p. 419**

Symplocos paniculata
SAPPHIREBERRY
☼ ● ✂ 31, 32, 34–41   **p. 420**

Taxus
YEW
☼ ◐ ● ◓ ✂ ZONES VARY   **p. 422**

Vaccinium
NEEDS, ZONES VARY   **p. 436**

Viburnum (many)
NEEDS, ZONES VARY   **p. 439**

PERENNIALS, VINES

Actaea
BANEBERRY
◐ ● ◔ ◓ ✂ 32, 34–45   **p. 119**

Ampelopsis brevipedunculata
PORCELAIN BERRY
☼ ◐ ● ◓ ✂ 32, 34–41   **p. 129**

Arisaema
JACK-IN-THE-PULPIT
◐ ● ✂ ZONES VARY   **p. 140**

Arum italicum
ITALIAN ARUM
◐ ● ◓ ✂ 31, 32, 34, 39   **p. 143**

Belamcanda chinensis
BLACKBERRY LILY
☼ ● ◓ ✂ 31, 32, 34–43   **p. 153**

Celastrus
BITTERSWEET
☼ ● ✂ ZONES VARY   **p. 176**

Dolichos lablab
HYACINTH BEAN
☼ ● ✂ ALL ZONES   **p. 213**

Iris foetidissima
GLADWIN IRIS
☼ ◐ ● ◓ ✂ 31, 32, 34, 39   **p. 269**

Lonicera (some)
HONEYSUCKLE
☼ ◐ ● ✂ ZONES VARY   **p. 297**

Schisandra chinensis
CHINESE MAGNOLIA VINE
☼ ◐ ● ✂ 31, 32, 34–43   **p. 403**

Taxus media

Viburnum dilatatum

Actaea alba

Schisandra chinensis

For growing symbol explanations, please see page 47.

Salix alba 'Vitellina'

TREES AND SHRUBS
for Winter Interest

Acer griseum

Even in the dead of winter, even in the coldest zones, you can have a lively landscape. With no flowers and foliage to steal the show, the beauties of stem, bark, and branch structure come to the fore. Locate these trees and shrubs strategically in your garden, and you'll create a landscape that transforms itself each winter into a striking display of color and sculptural beauty. In addition to these plants, needled and broadleaf evergreens and ornamental grasses can provide winter color and texture.

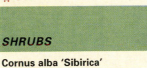
Betula nigra

Lagerstroemia indica 'Natchez'

Pinus bungeana

TREES

Acer davidii
DAVID'S MAPLE
☼ ◐ ◊ ⁄ 31, 32, 34–41   p. 116

Acer griseum
PAPERBARK MAPLE
☼ ◐ ◊ ⁄ 31, 32, 34–41   p. 116

Acer palmatum 'Sango Kaku'
CORAL BARK MAPLE
☼ ◐ ◊ ⁄ 31, 32, 34–41   p. 116

Betula (most)
BIRCH
☼ ◊ ◊◊ ⁄ ZONES VARY   p. 155

Carya ovata
SHAGBARK HICKORY
☼ ◊ ◊ ⁄ 31, 32, 34–44   p. 173

Crataegus viridis 'Winter King'
WINTER KING HAWTHORN
☼ ◊ ⁄ 31, 32, 34–41   p. 198

Lagerstroemia
CRAPE MYRTLE
☼ ◊ ⁄ 31, 32   p. 283

Malus 'Donald Wyman'
DONALD WYMAN CRABAPPLE
☼ ◊ ⁄ 31, 32, 34–43   p. 308

Parrotia
☼ ◊ ◊ ⁄ 31, 32, 34–41   p. 335

Pinus bungeana
LACEBARK PINE
☼ ◊ ◊ ⁄ 31, 32, 34–44   p. 352

Platanus acerifolia
PLANE TREE, SYCAMORE
☼ ◐ ◊ ⁄ 31, 32, 34–41   p. 356

Prunus sargentii
SARGENT CHERRY
☼ ◊ ⁄ 31, 32, 34–41   p. 368

Prunus serrulata
JAPANESE FLOWERING CHERRY
☼ ◊ ⁄ 31, 32, 34, 39   p. 368

Salix (some)
WILLOW
☼ ◊◊ ⁄ ZONES VARY   p. 395

Stewartia
☼ ◐ ◊ ⁄ ZONES VARY   p. 415

Ulmus parvifolia
CHINESE ELM
☼ ◊ ⁄ 31, 32, 34–41   p. 435

SHRUBS

Cornus alba 'Sibirica'
TATARIAN DOGWOOD
☼ ◐ ◊ ⁄ 31, 32, 34–45   p. 194

Cornus sericea 'Flaviramea'
YELLOWTWIG DOGWOOD
☼ ◐ ◊ ⁄ 31, 32, 34–45   p. 194

Corylus avellana 'Contorta'
HARRY LAUDER'S WALKING STICK
☼ ◐ ◊ ⁄ 31, 32, 34–41   p. 196

Cytisus
BROOM
☼ ◊ ⁄ ZONES VARY   p. 204

Euonymus alata
WINGED EUONYMUS
☼ ◐ ◊ ◊ ◊ ⁄ 31, 32, 34–45   p. 226

Ilex verticillata
WINTERBERRY
☼ ◊ ⁄ 31, 32, 34–43   p. 265

Jasminum nudiflorum
WINTER JASMINE
☼ ◐ ◊ ⁄ 31, 32, 34, 39   p. 274

Kerria japonica
☼ ◐ ◊ ⁄ 31, 32, 34–41   p. 281

Pyracantha
FIRETHORN
☼ ◊ ◊ ⁄ ZONES VARY   p. 374

Syringa reticulata
JAPANESE TREE LILAC
☼ ◐ ◊ ⁄ 31, 32, 34–43   p. 420

Stewartia monadelpha

Cornus alba 'Sibirica'

Cornus sericea 'Flaviramea'

Daphne

Plants that
TOLERATE SHADE

S hady spots, whether created by leafy trees, sun-blocking walls, or an overhead structure, are darker and cooler than sunny locations. Many plants that thrive in sunlight and warmth fail to prosper in the different environment that shade provides—either dwindling away or becoming leggy and sparse. In the lists below are trees, shrubs, ground covers, vines, perennials, bulbs, and annuals that prefer or accept some degree of shade. No matter what degree of shade is present in your garden there is a plant that will flourish there.

Acer palmatum

Cercis

TREES

Acer palmatum
JAPANESE MAPLE
31, 32, 34–41   p. 116

Acer pensylvanicum
MOOSEWOOD
31, 32, 34–45   p. 116

Cercis canadensis
EASTERN REDBUD
31, 32, 34–41   p. 178

Franklinia alatamaha
31, 32, 34, 39   p. 233

Halesia
31, 32, 34–41   p. 249

Stewartia
ZONES VARY   p. 415

Tsuga
HEMLOCK
ZONES VARY   p. 432

Tsuga diversifolia

SHRUBS

Abelia grandiflora
31, 32, 34, 39   p. 114

Acanthopanax sieboldianus 'Variegatus'
32, 34–41   p. 115

Aucuba japonica
JAPANESE AUCUBA
31, 32   p. 148

Buxus
BOXWOOD
ZONES VARY   p. 162

Camellia
ZONES VARY   p. 166

Clethra alnifolia
SUMMERSWEET
31, 32, 34–43   p. 189

Corylopsis
WINTER HAZEL
ZONES VARY   p. 195

Daphne
ZONES VARY   p. 206

Enkianthus campanulatus
31, 32, 34–41   p. 219

Euonymus fortunei
31, 32, 34–41   p. 226

Fothergilla
31, 32, 34–41   p. 233

Gaultheria procumbens
31, 32, 34–45   p. 236

Hamamelis
WITCH HAZEL
ZONES VARY   p. 249

Hydrangea
ZONES VARY   p. 262

Ilex
HOLLY
ZONES VARY   p. 265

Kalmia latifolia
MOUNTAIN LAUREL
31, 32, 34–41   p. 280

Leucothoe
NEEDS, ZONES VARY   p. 289

Hydrangea arborescens 'Annabelle'

Ilex meserveae 'Blue Girl'

Kalmia latifolia 'Pink Charm'

For growing symbol explanations, please see page 47.

Rhododendron 'Dexter's Victoria'

Stachyurus praecox

Chrysogonum virginianum

Epimedium

Lindera
SPICEBUSH
☼ ◐ ♦ ⚡ ZONES VARY   p. 293

Mahonia
NEEDS, ZONES VARY   p. 307

Nandina domestica
HEAVENLY BAMBOO
☼ ◐ ● ♦ ♦ ⚡ 31, 32   p. 322

Osmanthus
☼ ◐ ♦ ♦ ⚡ 31, 32   p. 330

Pieris
◐ ♦ ⚡ ZONES VARY   p. 351

Rhododendron
AZALEA, RHODODENDRON
◐ ♦ ♦ ⚡ ZONES VARY   p. 380

Ribes
CURRANT, GOOSEBERRY
☼ ◐ ♦ ⚡ ZONES VARY   p. 384

Skimmia japonica
◐ ● ♦ ⚡ 31, 32   p. 409

Stachyurus praecox
☼ ◐ ♦ ⚡ 31, 32   p. 414

Symphoricarpos (some)
SNOWBERRY
NEEDS, ZONES VARY   p. 419

Taxus
YEW
☼ ◐ ♦ ● ⚡ ZONES VARY   p. 422

Vaccinium
NEEDS, ZONES VARY   p. 436

Viburnum
NEEDS, ZONES VARY   p. 439

GROUND COVERS, VINES

Actinidia kolomikta
☼ ◐ ♦ ♦ ⚡ 31, 32, 34–41   p. 120

Aegopodium podagraria
BISHOP'S WEED
☼ ◐ ♦ ♦ ⚡ 31, 32, 34–45   p. 121

Ajuga
CARPET BUGLE
☼ ◐ ♦ ⚡ 31, 32, 34–45   p. 123

Akebia quinata
☼ ◐ ♦ ♦ ⚡ 31, 32, 34–41   p. 124

Ampelopsis brevipedunculata
PORCELAIN BERRY
☼ ◐ ♦ ♦ ⚡ 31, 32, 34–41   p. 129

Asarum
WILD GINGER
☼ ◐ ● ♦ ⚡ ZONES VARY   p. 144

Athyrium nipponicum 'Pictum'
JAPANESE PAINTED FERN
◐ ● ♦ ⚡ 31, 32, 34–43   p. 148

Chrysogonum virginianum
GREEN AND GOLD
☼ ◐ ♦ ⚡ 31, 32, 34–39   p. 185

Clematis (some)
☼ ♦ ⚡ ZONES VARY   p. 187

Cornus canadensis
BUNCHBERRY
◐ ● ♦ ⚡ 31, 32, 34–45   p. 194

Cymbalaria muralis
KENILWORTH IVY
◐ ● ♦ ⚡ 31, 32, 34, 36–39   p. 202

Epimedium
◐ ● ♦ ⚡ ZONES VARY   p. 220

Euonymus fortunei
☼ ◐ ♦ ♦ ⚡ 31, 32, 34–41   p. 226

Hedera
IVY
☼ ◐ ● ♦ ♦ ⚡ ZONES VARY   p. 250

Hosta (some)
PLANTAIN LILY
☼ ◐ ● ♦ ⚡ ZONES VARY   p. 259

Liriope
LILY TURF
◐ ● ♦ ♦ ⚡ ZONES VARY   p. 295

Mitchella repens
PARTRIDGEBERRY
◐ ● ♦ ♦ ⚡ 31, 32, 34–45   p. 318

Pachysandra terminalis
JAPANESE SPURGE
◐ ● ♦ ⚡ 31, 32, 34–41   p. 332

Parthenocissus
☼ ◐ ● ♦ ⚡ ZONES VARY   p. 336

Sarcococca
SWEET BOX
◐ ● ♦ ♦ ⚡ 31, 32   p. 400

Vinca
PERIWINKLE
◐ ● ♦ ⚡ ZONES VARY   p. 441

PERENNIALS, BULBS, ANNUALS

Aconitum
MONKSHOOD
☼ ◐ ● ⚡ 31, 32, 34–45   p. 119

Ajuga
CARPET BUGLE
☼ ◐ ♦ ⚡ 31, 32, 34–45   p. 123

Alchemilla
LADY'S-MANTLE
☼ ◐ ♦ ⚡ ZONES VARY   p. 124

Anemone
WINDFLOWER
NEEDS, ZONES VARY   p. 131

Hedera helix 'Fan'

Pachysandra terminalis

Sarcococca hookeriana var. *humilis*

Vinca major

Plant listings continue ▶

75

PLANTS THAT TOLERATE SHADE

Campanula lactiflora

Coleus hybridus

Corydalis lutea

Gillenia trifoliata

Aquilegia
COLUMBINE
☼ ◐ ● ▲ ✂ ZONES VARY — p. 138

Arisaema
◐ ● ▲ ▲ ✂ ZONES VARY — p. 140

Arum
◐ ● ▲ ✂ ZONES VARY — p. 143

Aruncus
GOAT'S BEARD
☼ ◐ ● ▲ ✂ 31, 32, 34–45 — p. 143

Asarum
WILD GINGER
◐ ● ● ▲ ✂ ZONES VARY — p. 144

Aspidistra elatior
CAST-IRON PLANT
◐ ● ▲ ✂ 31, 32 — p. 145

Astilbe
FALSE SPIRAEA
☼ ◐ ● ▲ ✂ 31, 32, 34–45 — p. 147

Astrantia
MASTERWORT
☼ ◐ ● ▲ ✂ 31, 32, 34–41 — p. 147

Begonia grandis
◐ ● ▲ ✂ 31, 32, 34, 39 — p. 153

Bergenia
☼ ◐ ● ▲ ✂ 31, 32, 34–45 — p. 154

Bletilla striata
CHINESE GROUND ORCHID
◐ ● ▲ ✂ 31, 32, 34, 39 — p. 157

Browallia
AMETHYST FLOWER
◐ ● ▲ ✂ ALL ZONES — p. 160

Brunnera macrophylla
BRUNNERA
☼ ◐ ● ▲ ✂ 31, 32, 34–45 — p. 160

Caladium bicolor
FANCY-LEAFED CALADIUM
☼ ◐ ● ▲ ▲ ✂ ALL ZONES — p. 162

Campanula (some)
BELLFLOWER
☼ ◐ ● ▲ ✂ 31, 32, 34–45 — p. 168

Carex
SEDGE
☼ ◐ ● ▲ ✂ 31, 32, 34–45 — p. 169

Cimicifuga
☼ ◐ ● ▲ ✂ 31, 32, 34–45 — p. 185

Coleus hybridus
COLEUS
☼ ◐ ● ▲ ✂ ALL ZONES — p. 190

Colocasia esculenta
ELEPHANT'S EAR
● ▲ ▲ ✂ ALL ZONES — p. 191

Convallaria majalis
LILY-OF-THE-VALLEY
◐ ● ▲ ✂ 31, 32, 34–45 — p. 191

Corydalis
◐ ● ▲ ✂ ZONES VARY — p. 195

Cyclamen
☼ ◐ ● ▲ ✂ 31, 32, 34, 39 — p. 201

Dicentra (most)
BLEEDING HEART
◐ ● ▲ ✂ 31, 32, 34–45 — p. 211

Digitalis
FOXGLOVE
☼ ◐ ● ▲ ✂ ZONES VARY — p. 212

Doronicum
LEOPARD'S BANE
☼ ◐ ● ▲ ✂ 31, 32, 34–43 — p. 213

Epimedium
◐ ● ▲ ✂ ZONES VARY — p. 220

Erythronium
☼ ◐ ● ▲ ▲ ✂ ZONES VARY — p. 225

Ferns
NEEDS, ZONES VARY — p. 230

Filipendula
☼ ◐ ● ▲ ▲ ✂ 31, 32, 34–45 — p. 231

Galax urceolata
☼ ◐ ● ▲ ✂ 31, 32, 34–43 — p. 236

Galium odoratum
SWEET WOODRUFF
☼ ◐ ● ▲ ✂ 31, 32, 34–43 — p. 236

Gillenia trifoliata
BOWMAN'S ROOT
☼ ◐ ● ▲ ✂ 31, 32, 34–43 — p. 240

Geranium (some)
CRANESBILL
☼ ◐ ● ▲ ✂ ZONES VARY — p. 238

Hakonechloa macra 'Aureola'
JAPANESE FOREST GRASS
☼ ◐ ● ▲ ✂ 31, 32, 34–41 — p. 248

Helleborus
HELLEBORE
☼ ◐ ● ● ▲ ✂ ZONES VARY — p. 253

Hepatica
LIVERLEAF
☼ ◐ ● ▲ ✂ ALL ZONES — p. 254

Heuchera
CORAL BELLS
☼ ◐ ● ● ▲ ✂ ZONES VARY — p. 256

Hosta
PLANTAIN LILY
◐ ● ▲ ✂ 31, 32, 34–45 — p. 259

Impatiens (most)
NEEDS VARY, ALL ZONES — p. 267

Inula helenium
ELECAMPANE
☼ ◐ ● ▲ ✂ 31, 32, 34–45 — p. 268

Heuchera villosa

Hosta 'Platinum Tiara'

Impatiens 'New Guinea'

Inula helenium

For growing symbol explanations, please see page 47.

Podophyllum peltatum

Primula vulgaris

Rhexia virginica

Smilacina racemosa

Iris foetidissima
GLADWIN IRIS
☼ ◐ ● ◌ ✂ 31, 32   **p. 269**

Iris, crested species
☼ ◐ ● ◌ ✂ 31, 32, 34–41   **p. 269**

Kirengeshoma palmata
◐ ● ✂ ZONES 31, 32, 34–41   **p. 281**

Lamium maculatum
DEAD NETTLE
◐ ● ● ✂ 32, 34–43   **p. 284**

Ligularia
◐ ● ◐ ✂ ZONES VARY   **p. 290**

Lilium
LILY
◐ ● ✂ 31, 32, 34–45   **p. 291**

Lobelia (most)
☼ ◐ ● ◐ ◐ ✂ ZONES VARY   **p. 295**

Lysimachia
☼ ◐ ● ◌ ✂ ZONES VARY   **p. 300**

Mertensia virginica
VIRGINIA BLUEBELLS
◐ ● ● ✂ 31, 32, 34–45   **p. 316**

Milium effusum 'Aureum'
BOWLES' GOLDEN GRASS
◐ ● ◐ ◐ ✂ 31, 32, 34, 39   **p. 317**

Muscari
GRAPE HYACINTH
☼ ◐ ● ◌ ✂ ZONES VARY   **p. 320**

Myosotis
FORGET-ME-NOT
◐ ● ◌ ✂ 32, 34–45   **p. 31, 321**

Nicotiana alata
☼ ◐ ● ◌ ✂ ALL ZONES   **p. 31, 326**

Ophiopogon
◐ ● ● ◌ ✂ ZONES VARY   **p. 295**

Ophiopogon jaburan
◐ ● ● ◌ ✂ 31, 32   **p. 295**

Ophiopogon japonicus
◐ ● ● ◌ ✂ 31, 32   **p. 295**

Ophiopogon planiscapus 'Nigrescens'
◐ ● ● ◌ ✂ 31, 32, 34, 39   **p. 295**

Oxalis
NEEDS, ZONES VARY   **p. 331**

Phormium
NEW ZEALAND FLAX
☼ ◐ ● ◐ ● ✂ ZONES VARY   **p. 349**

Podophyllum
◐ ● ● ◌ ✂ ZONES VARY   **p. 360**

Polemonium
◐ ● ◌ ✂ 31, 32, 34–43   **p. 361**

Polygonatum
SOLOMON'S SEAL
◐ ● ● ◌ ✂ 31, 32, 34–43   **p. 361**

Primula
PRIMROSE
☼ ◐ ● ● ◐ ◐ ✂ ZONES VARY   **p. 365**

Prunella
SELF-HEAL
☼ ◐ ● ✂ 31, 32, 34–43   **p. 367**

Pulmonaria
LUNGWORT
◐ ● ◌ ✂ 32, 34–43   **p. 373**

Rhexia virginica
MEADOW BEAUTY
☼ ◐ ● ● ✂ 31, 32, 34–41   **p. 379**

Rodgersia
◐ ● ◌ ✂ 32, 34–41   **p. 385**

Saxifraga
SAXIFRAGE
NEEDS, ZONES VARY   **p. 402**

Scilla
SQUILL, BLUEBELL
☼ ◐ ● ◌ ✂ ZONES VARY   **p. 404**

Smilacina racemosa
FALSE SOLOMON'S SEAL
◐ ● ● ◌ ✂ 31, 32, 34–43   **p. 409**

Spigelia marilandica
PINKROOT, INDIAN PINK
◐ ● ◌ ✂ 31, 32, 34, 39   **p. 411**

Thalictrum
MEADOW RUE
☼ ◐ ● ◌ ✂ ZONES VARY   **p. 424**

Tiarella
FOAMFLOWER
◐ ● ✂ ZONES VARY   **p. 426**

Tolmiea menziesii
PIGGY-BACK PLANT
◐ ● ● ● ◌ ✂ 31, 32, 34, 39   **p. 427**

Torenia fournieri
WISHBONE FLOWER
◐ ● ◌ ✂ ALL ZONES   **p. 429**

Tradescantia
NEEDS, ZONES VARY   **p. 430**

Tricyrtis
TOAD LILY
◐ ● ◌ ✂ ZONES VARY   **p. 430**

Trillium
WAKE ROBIN
◐ ● ● ◌ ✂ 31, 32, 34–43   **p. 430**

Trollius
GLOBEFLOWER
☼ ◐ ● ● ◐ ✂ 32, 34–43   **p. 431**

Viola
VIOLA, PANSY
NEEDS, ZONES VARY   **p. 441**

Spigelia marilandica

Tradescantia

Trillium grandiflorum

Viola tricolor

Plants for DAMP SOIL

Taxodium distichum

Swamps, bogs, and marshes may be standard settings in gothic novels—but in your own backyard, they're distinctly lacking in romantic appeal. More often, they present problems that must be solved before you can plant or plan a garden. Fortunately, there are many attractive plants that will thrive in the oxygen-poor soils characteristic of these watery environs—as well as in damp ground alongside ponds and streams. Any of these "swamp creatures" may adapt to poorly drained soils, too.

TREES		SHRUBS	
Acer rubrum SCARLET MAPLE 32, 34–44	p. 116	**Amelanchier** JUNEBERRY 32, 34–45	p. 128
Alnus ALDER ZONES VARY	p. 126	**Andromeda polifolia** BOG ROSEMARY 36–45	p. 130
Betula nigra RIVER BIRCH 32, 34–43	p. 155	**Aronia arbutifolia** RED CHOKEBERRY 32, 34–45	p. 142
Liquidambar styraciflua AMERICAN SWEET GUM 32, 34–41	p. 294	**Cephalanthus occidentalis** BUTTONBUSH 32, 34–41	p. 177
Magnolia virginiana SWEET BAY 32, 34–41	p. 302	**Clethra alnifolia** SUMMERSWEET 32, 34–43	p. 189
Metasequoia glyptostroboides DAWN REDWOOD 31, 32, 34–45	p. 316	**Cornus sericea** REDTWIG DOGWOOD 32, 34–45	p. 194
Nyssa sylvatica SOUR GUM 32, 34–41	p. 327	**Ilex glabra** INKBERRY 32, 34–43	p. 265
Quercus bicolor SWAMP WHITE OAK 32, 34–43	p. 374	**Ilex verticillata** WINTERBERRY 32, 34–43	p. 265
Quercus nigra WATER OAK 32, 34, 39	p. 374	**Itea virginica** VIRGINIA SWEETSPIRE 32, 34, 39	p. 273
Salix WILLOW ZONES VARY	p. 395	**Lindera** SPICEBUSH ZONES VARY	p. 293
Taxodium ZONES VARY	p. 422	**Rhododendron vaseyi** PINKSHELL AZALEA 32, 34–41	p. 379
Thuja occidentalis AMERICAN ARBORVITAE 32, 34–45	p. 426	**Rhododendron viscosum** SWAMP AZALEA 32, 34–41	p. 379

Acer rubrum 'October Sunset'

Metasequoia glyptostroboides

Nyssa sylvatica

Salix

Amelanchier

Cephalanthus occidentalis

Cornus sericea 'Isanti'

For growing symbol explanations, please see page 47.

Caltha palustris

Carex siderosticha 'Variegata'

Cimicifuga racemosa

Dodecatheon meadia 'Album'

Salix
WILLOW
☼ ◐ ♦ ⚡ ZONES VARY   p. 395

Sambucus canadensis
AMERICAN ELDERBERRY
☼ ◐ ♦ ⚡ 32, 34–45   p. 399

Thuja occidentalis
AMERICAN ARBORVITAE
☼ ◐ ♦ ♦ ⚡ 32, 34–45   p. 426

Vaccinium

NEEDS, ZONES VARY   p. 436

Zenobia pulverulenta

◐ ♦ ♦♦ ⚡ 32, 34–41   p. 447

PERENNIALS, BULBS

Acorus calamus 'Variegatus'
VARIEGATED SWEET FLAG
☼ ♦ ♦♦ ⚡ 32, 34–43   p. 119

Arisaema

◐ ● ♦ ♦♦ ⚡ ZONES VARY   p. 140

Aruncus dioicus
GOAT'S BEARD
☼ ◐ ● ♦ ⚡ 32, 34–43   p. 143

Asclepias incarnata
SWAMP MILKWEED
☼ ♦♦ ⚡ 32, 34–45   p. 144

Aster novae-angliae
NEW ENGLAND ASTER
☼ ♦ ⚡ 32, 34–43   p. 146

Astilbe
FALSE SPIRAEA
☼ ◐ ♦ ⚡ 32, 34–45   p. 147

Caltha palustris
MARSH MARIGOLD
☼ ◐ ● ♦♦ ⚡ 32, 34–45   p. 165

Carex
SEDGE
☼ ◐ ● ♦♦ ⚡ 32, 34–45   p. 169

Chelone glabra

☼ ◐ ♦ ♦♦ ⚡ 32, 34–43   p. 180

Cimicifuga racemosa
BLACK SNAKEROOT
☼ ◐ ● ♦ ⚡ 32, 34–45   p. 185

Darmera peltata
UMBRELLA PLANT
◐ ● ♦♦ ⚡ 32, 34–41   p. 207

Dodecatheon meadia
SHOOTING STAR
☼ ◐ ● ♦♦ ⚡ 32, 34–45   p. 213

Equisetum hyemale
HORSETAIL
☼ ◐ ● ♦ ⚡ 32, 34–45   p. 221

Eupatorium

☼ ◐ ● ♦♦ ⚡ ZONES VARY   p. 226

Filipendula
☼ ◐ ● ♦ ♦♦ ⚡ 32, 34–45   p. 231

Geum rivale 'Lionel Cox'
WATER AVENS
☼ ◐ ● ♦ ⚡ 32, 34–43   p. 240

Helianthus angustifolius
SWAMP SUNFLOWER
☼ ● ♦ ⚡ 32, 34, 39   p. 251

Hibiscus moscheutos
ROSE-MALLOW
☼ ● ♦ ⚡ 32, 34–41   p. 257

Iris (several)
☼ ◐ ● ♦ ⚡ ZONES VARY   p. 269

Juncus effusus
SOFT RUSH
☼ ◐ ● ♦ ⚡ 32, 34–43   p. 275

Ligularia

◐ ● ♦♦ ⚡ ZONES VARY   p. 290

Lobelia cardinalis
CARDINAL FLOWER
☼ ◐ ● ♦ ⚡ 32, 34–45   p. 295

Lobelia siphilitica

☼ ◐ ● ♦ ⚡ 32, 34–43   p. 295

Lysimachia

☼ ◐ ● ♦ ⚡ ZONES VARY   p. 300

Matteuccia struthiopteris
OSTRICH FERN
☼ ◐ ● ♦ ♦♦ ⚡ 32, 34–45   p. 313

Mimulus hybridus
MONKEY FLOWER
☼ ◐ ● ♦ ♦ ⚡ ALL ZONES   p. 317

Monarda didyma
BEE BALM
☼ ◐ ● ♦ ⚡ 32, 34–45   p. 319

Myosotis scorpioides
FORGET-ME-NOT
☼ ● ♦ ⚡ 32, 34–45   p. 321

Petasites japonicus
JAPANESE COLTSFOOT
☼ ◐ ● ♦ ♦♦ ⚡ 32, 34–41   p. 346

Primula japonicus

☼ ◐ ● ♦♦ ⚡ 32, 34–43   p. 365

Rodgersia

☼ ◐ ● ⚡ 32, 34–41   p. 385

Sarracenia
PITCHER PLANT
☼ ◐ ♦♦ ⚡ ZONES VARY   p. 400

Tradescantia virginiana
SPIDERWORT
☼ ◐ ● ♦ ♦♦ ⚡ 32, 34–43   p. 430

Vernonia noveboracensis
IRONWEED
☼ ◐ ● ♦ ♦♦ ⚡ 32, 34–41   p. 438

Iris pseudocorus

Lobelia cardinalis

Rodgersia aesculifolia

Sarracenia leucophylla

Cedrus atlantica 'Glauca'

Fraxinus

Gymnocladus dioica

Koelreutia paniculata

Plants for
DRY GARDENS

Not all of the country receives rainfall that amounts to "regular watering." Scant rainfall, long dry seasons, or periodic drought years may leave gardeners slaves to watering or scrambling for supplies for garden use, even in the Northeast where rainfall is usually abundant. Fortunately, many fine plants, once they are established in the garden, are naturally equipped to grow well with far less than regular water during the growing season. Here are some proven performers in all plant categories.

Robinia pseudoacacia 'Frisia'

Artemisia 'Powis Castle'

Berberis 'Wildfire'

Chaenomeles

TREES

Albizia julibrissin 'Rosea'
SILK TREE
☼ ◐ ● ◢   31, 32, 34, 39   p. 124

Betula populifolia
GRAY BIRCH
☼ ◐ ● ◢   31, 32, 34–45   p. 155

Cedrus
CEDAR
☼ ● ◢   ZONES VARY   p. 175

Celtis
HACKBERRY
☼ ◐ ● ◢   ZONES VARY   p. 176

Elaeagnus angustifolia
RUSSIAN OLIVE
☼ ◐ ● ● ◢   31, 32, 34–45   p. 218

Fraxinus (most)
ASH
☼ ● ● ◢   ZONES VARY   p. 234

Ginkgo biloba
MAIDENHAIR TREE
☼ ● ◢   31, 32, 34–44   p. 240

Gymnocladus dioica
KENTUCKY COFFEE TREE
☼ ● ● ◢   32, 34–43   p. 248

Juniperus rigida 'Pendula'
NEEDLE JUNIPER
☼ ● ● ◢   31, 32, 34–41   p. 275

Koelreuteria paniculata
GOLDENRAIN TREE
☼ ● ● ◢   31, 32, 34–41   p. 282

Lagerstroemia indica
CRAPE MYRTLE
☼ ● ◢   31, 32   p. 283

Maclura pomifera
OSAGE ORANGE
☼ ● ● ◢   31, 32, 34–41   p. 301

Pinus (many)
PINE
☼ ● ● ◢   ZONES VARY   p. 352

Pistacia chinensis
CHINESE PISTACHE
☼ ● ◢   31, 32   p. 352

Quercus marilandica
BLACKJACK OAK
☼ ● ● ◢   31, 32, 34, 39   p. 375

Robinia
LOCUST
☼ ● ◢   31, 32, 34–45   p. 385

Sophora japonica
JAPANESE PAGODA TREE
☼ ◐ ● ◢   31, 32, 34–41   p. 410

Tilia tomentosa
SILVER LINDEN
☼ ● ◢   31, 32, 34–41   p. 427

SHRUBS

Amorpha
☼ ● ● ◢   31, 32, 34–45   p. 129

Artemisia
☼ ● ◢   31, 32, 34–45   p. 142

Berberis
BARBERRY
☼ ◐ ● ● ◢   ZONES VARY   p. 154

Buddleia alternifolia
FOUNTAIN BUTTERFLY BUSH
☼ ◐ ● ● ◢   31, 32, 34–41   p. 161

Caragana arborescens
SIBERIAN PEASHRUB
☼ ● ◢   31, 32, 34–45   p. 169

Caryopteris clandonensis
BLUE MIST
☼ ● ◢   31, 32, 34–41   p. 173

For growing symbol explanations, please see page 47.

Nandina domestica

Phlomis russeliana

Tamarix

Teucrium

Chaenomeles
FLOWERING QUINCE
☼ ◗ ◗ ◪ 31, 32, 34–41   p. 179

Chimonanthus praecox
WINTERSWEET
☼ ◑ ◗ ◪ 31, 32, 34   p. 182

Cotinus coggygria
SMOKE TREE
☼ ◗ ◪ 31, 32, 34–41   p. 196

Cotoneaster
☼ ◗ ◪ ZONES VARY   p. 196

Cytisus
BROOM
☼ ◗ ◪ ZONES VARY   p. 204

Elaeagnus (some)
☼ ◑ ◗ ◗ ◪ ZONES VARY   p. 218

Genista
☼ ◗ ◪ ZONES VARY   p. 237

Jasminum nudiflorum
WINTER JASMINE
☼ ◑ ◗ ◗ ◪ 31, 32, 34, 39   p. 274

Juniperus (some)
JUNIPER
☼ ◗ ◗ ◪ ZONES VARY   p. 275

Lavandula
LAVENDER
☼ ◗ ◪ ZONES VARY   p. 286

Mahonia (most)
NEEDS, ZONES VARY   p. 307

Nandina domestica
HEAVENLY BAMBOO
☼ ◑ ◗ ◗ ◗ ◪ 31, 32   p. 322

Phlomis
JERUSALEM SAGE
☼ ◗ ◪ ZONES VARY   p. 347

Pyracantha
FIRETHORN
☼ ◗ ◪ ZONES VARY   p. 374

Rhamnus
☼ ◑ ◗ ◪ 31, 32, 34–45   p. 379

Rhus
SUMAC
☼ ◗ ◪ ZONES VARY   p. 384

Rosa rugosa
RAMANAS ROSE
☼ ◑ ◗ ◪ 31, 32, 34–45   p. 386

Rosmarinus officinalis
ROSEMARY
☼ ◗ ◪ 31, 32   p. 393

Rubus
BRAMBLE
☼ ◑ ◗ ◗ ◪ ZONES VARY   p. 393

Salvia (some)
SAGE
NEEDS, ZONES VARY   p. 396

Santolina chamaecyparissus
LAVENDER COTTON
☼ ◗ ◗ ◪ 32, 34, 39   p. 399

Tamarix
TAMARISK
☼ ◗ ◪ ZONES VARY   p. 421

Teucrium
GERMANDER
☼ ◗ ◪ ZONES VARY   p. 423

Vitex agnus-castus
CHASTE TREE
☼ ◗ ◪ 31, 32   p. 442

GROUND COVERS, VINES

Arctostaphylos uva-ursi
BEARBERRY
☼ ◑ ◗ ◪ 31, 32, 34–45   p. 140

Cerastium tomentosum
SNOW-IN-SUMMER
☼ ◑ ◗ ◪ 31, 32, 34–45   p. 178

Ceratostigma plumbaginoides
DWARF PLUMBAGO
☼ ◑ ◗ ◪ 31, 32, 34–41   p. 178

Delosperma
ICE PLANT
☼ ◗ ◪ ZONES VARY   p. 208

Deutzia gracilis 'Nikko'
☼ ◑ ◗ ◗ ◪ 31, 32, 34–41   p. 209

Euonymus fortunei
☼ ◑ ◗ ◗ ◪ 31, 32, 34–41   p. 226

Gelsemium sempervirens
CAROLINA JESSAMINE
☼ ◑ ◗ ◗ ◪ 31, 32   p. 237

Helianthemum nummularium
SUNROSE
☼ ◗ ◪ 31, 32, 34, 39   p. 251

Phlox subulata
MOSS PINK
☼ ◗ ◗ ◪ 31, 32, 34–45   p. 348

Polygonum aubertii
SILVER LACE VINE
☼ ◗ ◪ 31, 32, 34–41   p. 361

Robinia hispida
BRISTLY LOCUST
☼ ◗ ◗ ◪ 31, 32, 34–41   p. 385

Rosmarinus officinalis (dwarf)
ROSEMARY
☼ ◗ ◪ 31, 32   p. 393

Stephanandra incisa 'Crispa'
☼ ◑ ◗ ◗ ◪ 31, 32, 34–43   p. 414

Verbena canadensis
☼ ◗ ◪ 31, 32, 34–41   p. 437

Wisteria
☼ ◗ ◗ ◪ ZONES VARY   p. 444

Arctostaphylos uva-ursi 'Vancouver Gold'

Delosperma cooperi

Phlox subulata

Verbena canadensis

Plant listings continue ▶

PLANTS FOR DRY GARDENS

Achillea 'Moonshine'

Euphorbia cyparissias

Gaillardia grandiflora

Hesperaloe parviflora

PERENNIALS, BULBS, ANNUALS

Achillea
YARROW
☼ ♦ ✂ 31, 32, 34–45 p. 118

Agapanthus 'Headbourne Hybrids' LILY-OF-THE-NILE
☼ ◑ ♦ ♦ ✂ 31, 32 p. 122

Agave parryi huachucensis
☼ ♦ ♦ ✂ 31, 32 p. 122

Antennaria dioica
PUSSY TOES
☼ ♦ ♦ ✂ 36–45 p. 133

Artemisia
☼ ♦ ✂ 31, 32, 34–45 p. 142

Baptisia
FALSE INDIGO
☼ ♦ ✂ 31, 32, 34–43 p. 151

Callirhoe involucrata
WINE CUPS
☼ ♦ ♦ ✂ 32, 34–43 p. 164

Centranthus ruber
RED VALERIAN
☼ ◑ ♦ ✂ 32, 34–43 p. 177

Coreopsis
☼ ♦ ✂ ZONES VARY p. 192

Echinacea
PURPLE CONEFLOWER
☼ ♦ ✂ ZONES VARY p. 216

Euphorbia (most)
NEEDS, ZONES VARY p. 227

Festuca glauca
BLUE FESCUE
☼ ◑ ♦ ✂ 31, 32, 34–45 p. 230

Gaillardia
☼ ♦ ✂ ALL ZONES p. 235

Gaura lindheimeri
GAURA
☼ ♦ ♦ ✂ 31, 32, 34, 37–39 p. 237

Geranium sanguineum
☼ ◑ ♦ ✂ ALL ZONES p. 238

Gomphrena globosa
GLOBE AMARANTH
☼ ◑ ♦ ✂ ALL ZONES p. 243

Hemerocallis
DAYLILY
☼ ◑ ♦ ♦ ✂ 31, 32, 34–45 p. 253

Hesperaloe parviflora
☼ ♦ ✂ 31, 32 p. 256

Iris, bearded
☼ ◑ ♦ ♦ ✂ 31, 32, 34–45 p. 269

Kniphofia uvaria
RED-HOT POKER
☼ ◑ ♦ ♦ ✂ 31, 32, 34–41 p. 281

Liatris
GAYFEATHER
☼ ♦ ✂ 31, 32, 34–45 p. 290

Linum
FLAX
☼ ♦ ✂ 31, 32, 34–41 p. 294

Melampodium paludosum
☼ ♦ ✂ ALL ZONES p. 315

Oenothera
EVENING PRIMROSE
☼ ♦ ✂ ZONES VARY p. 327

Pennisetum
FOUNTAIN GRASS
☼ ♦ ♦ ✂ 31, 32, 34, 37, 39 p. 343

Pennisetum setaceum
FOUNTAIN GRASS
☼ ♦ ✂ 31, 32, 34–45 p. 343

Penstemon
BEARD TONGUE
☼ ◑ ♦ ♦ ✂ ZONES VARY p. 344

Perovskia
RUSSIAN SAGE
☼ ♦ ✂ 31, 32, 34, 37, 39 p. 345

Portulaca
PORTULACA, ROSE MOSS
☼ ◑ ♦ ♦ ✂ ALL ZONES p. 363

Salvia (most)
SAGE
NEEDS, ZONES VARY p. 396

Santolina
☼ ♦ ♦ ✂ ZONES VARY p. 399

Sedum (many)
STONECROP
NEEDS, ZONES VARY p. 404

Stachys byzantina
LAMB'S EARS
☼ ◑ ♦ ✂ 31, 32, 34–43 p. 414

Stipa (some)
☼ ♦ ✂ ZONES VARY p. 415

Tithonia rotundifolia
MEXICAN SUNFLOWER
☼ ♦ ✂ ALL ZONES p. 427

Verbascum
MULLEIN
☼ ◑ ♦ ✂ ZONES VARY p. 437

Verbena
☼ ♦ ✂ ZONES VARY p. 437

Yucca (most)
☼ ♦ ♦ ✂ ZONES VARY p. 446

Zinnia grandiflora
☼ ♦ ✂ ALL ZONES p. 448

Melampodium paludosum 'Showstar'

Oenethera fruticosa

Sedum spurium

Yucca filamentosa

For growing symbol explanations, please see page 47.

Carpinus betulus

Picea abies

Plants for WINDY AREAS

Strong winds can wreak havoc on plants. Wind causes water stress in plants by increasing transpiration and evaporation from leaves. A gale-force wind can defoliate or uproot plants, or snap off branches with such force that stems or trunks can split. Whether you live on the coast or inland, if wind is common in your area you'll want to choose plants that can take it. Listed below are plants tough enough to withstand strong winds, while still providing plenty of ornamental value in the garden. Some trees and large shrubs are tough enough to serve as windbreaks, allowing more delicate plants to thrive in their shelter.

Tilia cordata

Aralia

TREES

Acer (some)
MAPLE
31, 32, 34–41   p. 116

Calocedrus decurrens
INCENSE CEDAR
31, 32, 34, 37, 39   p. 165

Caragana arborescens
SIBERIAN PEASHRUB
31, 32, 34–45   p. 169

Carpinus betulus
HORNBEAM
31, 32, 34–41   p. 172

Chamaecyparis lawsoniana
PORT ORFORD CEDAR
31, 32, 34, 39   p. 179

Cupressocyparis leylandii
31, 32, 34, 39   p. 201

Elaeagnus angustifolia
RUSSIAN OLIVE
31, 32, 34–45   p. 218

Juniperus
JUNIPER
ZONES VARY   p. 275

Maclura pomifera
OSAGE ORANGE
31, 32, 34–41   p. 301

Picea abies
NORWAY SPRUCE
32, 34–45   p. 350

Picea omorika
SERBIAN SPRUCE
32, 34–41   p. 350

Pinus (many)
PINE
ZONES VARY   p. 352

Populus nigra 'Italica'
LOMBARDY POPLAR
31, 32, 34–45   p. 363

Pseudotsuga menziesii glauca
DOUGLAS FIR
31, 32, 34–43   p. 371

Quercus phellos
WILLOW OAK
31, 32, 34–41   p. 375

Thuja (many)
ARBORVITAE
ZONES VARY   p. 425

Tilia cordata
LINDEN
ZONES VARY   p. 427

Ulmus pumila
SIBERIAN ELM
31, 32, 34–45   p. 435

SHRUBS

Aralia elata
JAPANESE ANGELICA TREE
31, 32, 34–41   p. 139

Artemisia
31, 32, 34–45   p. 142

Berberis
BARBERRY
ZONES VARY   p. 154

Buxus
BOXWOOD
ZONES VARY   p. 162

Pinus wallichiana

Populus nigra 'Italica'

Buxus 'Elegantissima'

Cotoneaster horizontalis

Plant listings continue ▶

PLANTS FOR WINDY AREAS

Lavandula

Pyracantha 'Mohave'

Carex morowii 'Goldband'

Cortaderia selloana 'Pumila'

Chamaecyparis
FALSE CYPRESS
☼ ◐ ◖ ⚡ ZONES VARY   **p. 179**

Cotoneaster
☼ ◐ ◖ ⚡ ZONES VARY   **p. 196**

Elaeagnus
☼ ◐ ◖ ◖ ⚡ ZONES VARY   **p. 218**

Euonymus (several)
EUONYMUS
☼ ◐ ◖ ⚡ ZONES VARY   **p. 226**

Hippophae rhamnoides
SEA BUCKTHORN
☼ ◐ ◖ 31, 32, 34–45   **p. 257**

Juniperus
JUNIPER
☼ ◐ ◖ ⚡ ZONES VARY   **p. 275**

Lavandula
LAVENDER
☼ ◖ ⚡ ZONES VARY   **p. 286**

Ligustrum
PRIVET
☼ ◖ ⚡ ZONES VARY   **p. 290**

Lonicera tatarica
HONEYSUCKLE
☼ ◐ ◖ ⚡ 31, 32, 34–43   **p. 297**

Myrica pensylvanica
BAYBERRY
☼ ◐ ◖ ⚡ 31, 32, 34–44   **p. 321**

Nandina domestica
HEAVENLY BAMBOO
☼ ◐ ◖ ◖ ⚡ 31, 32   **p. 322**

Pyracantha
FIRETHORN
☼ ◖ ⚡ ZONES VARY   **p. 374**

Rhamnus
☼ ◐ ◖ ⚡ 31, 32, 34–45   **p. 379**

Rhus (some)
SUMAC
☼ ◐ ◖ ⚡ ZONES VARY   **p. 384**

Rosmarinus officinalis
ROSEMARY
☼ ◖ ⚡ 31, 32   **p. 393**

Syringa vulgaris
COMMON LILAC
☼ ◖ ◖ ⚡ 31, 32, 34–45   **p. 420**

Viburnum cassinoides
WITHE-ROD
☼ ◐ ◖ ◖ 31, 32, 34–43   **p. 439**

Viburnum dentatum
ARROWWOOD VIBURNUM
☼ ◐ ◖ ⚡ 31, 32, 34–45   **p. 439**

GROUNDCOVERS, VINES

Arctostaphylos uva-ursi
BEARBERRY
☼ ◐ ◖ ◖ 31, 32, 34–45   **p. 140**

Clematis terniflora
SWEET AUTUMN CLEMATIS
☼ ◖ ⚡ 31, 32, 34–41   **p. 187**

Delosperma
ICE PLANT
☼ ◖ ⚡ ZONES VARY   **p. 208**

Juniperus (many)
☼ ◖ ◖ ⚡ ZONES VARY   **p. 275**

PERENNIALS, ACCENT PLANTS

Baptisia
FALSE INDIGO
☼ ◖ ⚡ 31, 32, 34–43   **p. 151**

Carex
SEDGE
☼ ◐ ◖ ◖ ⚡ 31, 32, 34–45   **p. 169**

Cerastium tomentosum
SNOW-IN-SUMMER
☼ ◖ ⚡ 31, 32, 34–45   **p. 178**

Cortaderia selloana 'Pumila'
PAMPAS GRASS
☼ ◐ ◖ ◖ 31, 32   **p. 195**

Eryngium
SEA HOLLY
☼ ◖ ⚡ 31, 32, 34–43   **p. 224**

Euphorbia
NEEDS, ZONES VARY   **p. 227**

Hemerocallis
DAYLILY
☼ ◖ ⚡ 31, 32, 34–45   **p. 253**

Iris sibirica
SIBERIAN IRIS
☼ ◖ ◖ ⚡ ALL ZONES   **p. 269**

Kniphofia uvaria
RED-HOT POKER
☼ ◐ ◖ ◖ ⚡ 31, 32, 34–41   **p. 281**

Phlomis
JERUSALEM SAGE
☼ ◐ ◖ ⚡ ZONES VARY   **p. 347**

Salvia
SAGE
NEEDS, ZONES VARY   **p. 396**

Santolina
☼ ◖ ◖ ⚡ ZONES VARY   **p. 399**

Sedum (most)
STONECROP
☼ ◐ ◖ ◖ ⚡ ZONES VARY   **p. 404**

Sempervivum (most)
HENS AND CHICKS
☼ ◐ ◖ ◖ ⚡ ZONES VARY   **p. 405**

Thymus
☼ ◖ ⚡ 31, 32, 34–43   **p. 426**

Yucca
NEEDS, ZONES VARY   **p. 446**

Eryngium giganteum

Santolina chamaecyparissus

Sedum kamtschaticum

Sempervivum tectorum

For growing symbol explanations, please see page 47.

Chamaecyparis pisifera 'Gold Spangle'

Plants for
COASTAL GARDENS

A walk on the beach is a pleasure in fine weather, but on less pleasant days, blustery, salt-laden winds can send you scurrying for shelter. Plants, unfortunately, have no escape: they have to tough it out. Even on the breeziest coastlines, though, some plants look fresh and healthy whatever the weather. A number of these sturdy choices are listed below.

Thuja occidentalis

Pinus cembra

Pinus nigra

Platycladus orientalis

TREES

Aesculus hippocastanum
COMMON HORSECHESTNUT
☼ ◑ ✹   32, 34–43   p. 121

Amelanchier canadensis
SHADBLOW
☼ ◑ ◐ ◐ ✹   32, 34–45   p. 128

Chamaecyparis pisifera
SAWARA FALSE CYPRESS
☼ ◑ ◐ ✹   32, 34–43   p. 179

Crataegus crus-galli
COCKSPUR THORN
☼ ◐ ✹   32, 34–41   p. 198

Cryptomeria japonica
☼ ◐ ✹   32, 34, 39   p. 200

Ilex opaca
AMERICAN HOLLY
☼ ◑ ◐ ✹   32, 34–41   p. 265

Nyssa sylvatica
TUPELO
☼ ◑ ◐ ◐ ✹   32, 34–41   p. 327

Pinus (many)
PINE
☼ ◐ ◐ ✹   ZONES VARY   p. 352

Platycladus orientalis
ORIENTAL ARBORVITAE
☼ ◑ ◐ ✹   32, 34–41   p. 356

Robinia pseudoacacia
BLACK LOCUST
☼ ◐ ✹   32, 34–45   p. 385

Thuja occidentalis
AMERICAN ARBORVITAE
☼ ◑ ◐ ◐ ✹   32, 34–45   p. 426

Tilia cordata
LITTLE-LEAF LINDEN
☼ ◐ ✹   32, 34–43   p. 427

Ulmus parvifolia
CHINESE ELM
☼ ◐ ✹   32, 34–41   p. 435

Ulmus pumila
SIBERIAN ELM
☼ ◐ ✹   32, 34–45   p. 435

SHRUBS

Arctostaphylos uva-ursi
BEARBERRY
☼ ◑ ◐ ✹   32, 34–45   p. 140

Aronia arbutifolia
RED CHOKEBERRY
☼ ◑ ◐ ◐ ✹   32, 34–41   p. 142

Baccharis halimifolia
SALT BUSH
☼ ◐ ◐ ✹   32, 34–41   p. 149

Berberis thunbergii
JAPANESE BARBERRY
☼ ◑ ◐ ◐ ✹   32, 34–41   p. 154

Buddleia
BUTTERFLY BUSH
☼ ◐ ◐ ✹   ZONES VARY   p. 161

Chaenomeles
FLOWERING QUINCE
☼ ◐ ◐ ✹   32, 34–41   p. 179

Clethra alnifolia
SUMMERSWEET
☼ ◑ ◐ ◐ ✹   32, 34–43   p. 189

Cornus stolonifera
REDTWIG DOGWOOD
☼ ◐ ◐ ✹   32, 34–45   p. 194

Cotoneaster
☼ ◐ ✹   ZONES VARY   p. 196

Cytisus
BROOM
☼ ◐ ✹   ZONES VARY   p. 204

Elaeagnus
☼ ◑ ◐ ◐ ✹   ZONES VARY   p. 218

Hibiscus syriacus
ROSE OF SHARON
☼ ◐ ✹   32, 34–45   p. 257

Cotoneaster adpressus

Elaeagnus pungens 'Maculata'

Genista

Plant listings continue ▶

Juniperus davurica 'Expansa'

Lonicera nitida 'Baggesens' Gold'

Wisteria sinensis

Armeria maritima 'Laucheana'

Hippophae rhamnoides
SEA BUCKTHORN
☼ ◑ ♦ ◊ 32, 34–45   p. 257

Hydrangea (several)
☼ ◑ ♦ ◊ ZONES VARY   p. 262

Ilex glabra
INKBERRY
☼ ◑ ♦ ◊ 32, 34–43   p. 265

Juniperus
JUNIPER
☼ ◑ ♦ ◊ ZONES VARY   p. 275

Lavandula angustifolia
ENGLISH LAVENDER
☼ ♦ ◊ 32, 34, 39   p. 286

Ligustrum (some)
PRIVET
☼ ◑ ♦ ◊ ZONES VARY   p. 290

Myrica pensylvanica
BAYBERRY
☼ ◑ ♦ ◊ 32, 34–44   p. 321

Pinus mugo
SWISS MOUNTAIN PINE
☼ ♦ ◊ 32, 34–45   p. 352

Prunus maritima
BEACH PLUM
☼ ♦ ◊ 32, 34–45   p. 368

Rhamnus
☼ ◑ ♦ ◊ ZONES VARY   p. 379

Rhus
☼ ♦ ◊ ZONES VARY   p. 384

Rosa rugosa
SALTSPRAY ROSE
☼ ◑ ♦ ◊ 32, 34–45   p. 386

Tamarix
TAMARISK
☼ ♦ ◊ ZONES VARY   p. 421

Taxus cuspidata
JAPANESE YEW
☼ ◑ ♦ ◊ 32, 34–41   p. 422

VINES

Clematis terniflora
SWEET AUTUMN CLEMATIS
☼ ♦ ◊ 32, 34–41   p. 187

Lonicera (several)
☼ ◑ ♦ ◊ ZONES VARY   p. 297

Parthenocissus quinquefolia
VIRGINIA CREEPER
☼ ◑ ♦ ◊ 32, 34–43   p. 336

Polygonum aubertii
SILVER LACE VINE
☼ ♦ ◊ 32, 34–41   p. 361

Wisteria sinensis
CHINESE WISTERIA
☼ ◑ ♦ ◊ 32, 34–41   p. 444

PERENNIALS

Armeria maritima
COMMON THRIFT
☼ ♦ ◊ 32, 34–43   p. 141

Artemisia (most)
☼ ♦ ◊ 32, 34–45   p. 142

Baptisia australis
BLUE FALSE INDIGO
☼ ♦ ◊ 32, 34–43   p. 151

Chrysanthemum (most)
☼ ♦ ◊ ZONES VARY   p. 183

Dianthus
PINK
☼ ♦ ◊ 32, 34–45   p. 209

Dictamnus albus
GAS PLANT
☼ ◑ ♦ ◊ 32, 34–45   p. 211

Eryngium
SEA HOLLY
☼ ♦ ◊ 32, 34–45   p. 224

Festuca glauca
BLUE FESCUE
☼ ◑ ♦ ◊ 32, 34–45   p. 230

Gypsophila
☼ ♦ ◊ ZONES VARY   p. 248

Helianthemum nummularium
SUNROSE
☼ ♦ ◊ 32, 34, 39   p. 251

Hibiscus moscheutos
ROSE-MALLOW
☼ ♦ ◊ 32, 34–41   p. 257

Hosta
PLANTAIN LILY
◑ ♦ ◊ 32, 34–45   p. 259

Kniphofia uvaria
RED-HOT POKER
☼ ◑ ♦ ◊ ZONES VARY   p. 281

Limonium
SEA LAVENDER
☼ ♦ ◊ ZONES VARY   p. 293

Liriope and Ophiopogon
LILY TURF
◑ ♦ ◊ ZONES VARY   p. 295

Santolina
☼ ♦ ◊ ZONES VARY   p. 399

Sedum
STONECROP
NEEDS, ZONES VARY   p. 404

Stachys byzantina
LAMB'S EARS
☼ ◑ ♦ ◊ 32, 34–43   p. 414

Yucca
☼ ♦ ◊ ZONES VARY   p. 446

Chrysanthemum pacificum

Eryngium

Helianthemum 'Henfield Brilliant'

Liriope muscari

For growing symbol explanations, please see page 47.

Good Choices for
ROCK GARDENS

Small or tiny shrubs, miniature bulbous plants, annuals and perennials that form low tufts or creeping mats of foliage—these are the choices listed here. Classic European rock and alpine garden plants can be easily grown in some parts of the Northeast; but climates made less favorable by heat, dryness, humidity, or cold call for a different assortment of plants. Read the climate zone adaptations carefully.

Pinus albicaulis

Pinus strobus 'Nana'

Juniperus sabina var. tamariscifolia

Daphne caucasica

Helianthemum nummularium

Alchemilla alpina

Aster alpinus

TREES

Abies balsamea 'Nana'
DWARF BALSAM FIR
☼ ◐ ◯ ◐ ⁄ 34–44   p. 114

Acer palmatum (dwarf)
JAPANESE MAPLE
☼ ◐ ◯ ◐ ⁄ 32, 34–41   p. 116

Betula pendula 'Trost's Dwarf'
☼ ◐ ◐ ⁄ 32, 34–45   p. 155

Chamaecyparis obtusa (dwarf)
HINOKI FALSE CYPRESS
☼ ◐ ◯ ⁄ 32, 34–41   p. 179

Picea (many dwarf types)
SPRUCE
☼ ◐ ◯ ◐ ⁄ ZONES VARY   p. 350

Pinus (many dwarf types)
PINE
☼ ◐ ◯ ⁄ ZONES VARY   p. 352

Tsuga canadensis (dwarf)
CANADA HEMLOCK
☼ ◐ ◯ ⁄ 32, 34–43   p. 432

SHRUBS, SHRUBLETS

Berberis thunbergii (some)
JAPANESE BARBERRY
☼ ◐ ◯ ◐ ⁄ 32, 34–41   p. 154

Calluna vulgaris (dwarf)
SCOTCH HEATHER
☼ ◐ ⁄ 32, 34–41   p. 165

Daphne (some)
HEATH
☼ ◐ ◯ ⁄ ZONES VARY   p. 206

Erica (dwarf)
HEATH
☼ ◐ ◯ ⁄ ZONES VARY   p. 221

Helianthemum nummularium
SUNROSE
☼ ◐ ⁄ 32, 34, 39   p. 251

Ilex crenata (several dwarf types)
DWARF JAPANESE HOLLY
☼ ◐ ◯ ⁄ 32, 34, 39   p. 265

Juniperus (many dwarf types)
JUNIPER
☼ ◐ ◯ ⁄ ZONES VARY   p. 275

Pieris japonica (dwarf)
LILY-OF-THE-VALLEY SHRUB
◐ ◯ ◐ ⁄ 32, 34–41   p. 351

Teucrium (low-growing)
GERMANDER
☼ ◐ ⁄ ZONES VARY   p. 423

PERENNIALS

Aethionema
STONECRESS
☼ ◐ ⁄ 32, 34–45   p. 122

Ajuga genevensis
CARPET BUGLE
☼ ◐ ◯ ⁄ 32, 34–45   p. 123

Alchemilla alpina
LADY'S-MANTLE
☼ ◐ ◯ ⁄ 36–43   p. 124

Androsace
ROCK JASMINE
☼ ◐ ⁄ 36–45   p. 131

Arabis procurrens
☼ ◐ ⁄ 32, 34–45   p. 139

Arenaria
SANDWORT
☼ ◐ ◯ ⁄ 32, 34–45   p. 140

Armeria
THRIFT
☼ ◐ ◯ ⁄ ZONES VARY   p. 141

Aster alpinus
☼ ◐ ⁄ 36–45   p. 146

Aubrieta deltoidea
COMMON AUBRIETA
☼ ◐ ◯ ⁄ 36–43   p.148

Plant listings continue ▶

GOOD CHOICES FOR ROCK GARDENS

Lewisia cotyledon

Lithodora diffusa

Mazus reptans

Saponaria ocymoides

Aurinia saxatilis
BASKET-OF-GOLD
☼ ◐ ♦ 32, 34–43   **p. 148**

Campanula (smallest)
BELLFLOWER
☼ ◐ ♦ ♦ 32, 34–45   **p. 168**

Cerastium tomentosum
SNOW-IN-SUMMER
☼ ◐ ♦ 32, 34–45   **p. 178**

Dianthus (smallest)
PINK
☼ ◐ ♦ 32, 34–45   **p. 209**

Dodecatheon meadia
SHOOTING STAR
☼ ◐ ♦ ♦ 32, 34–45   **p. 213**

Draba
☼ ♦ 34, 36–43   **p. 214**

Dryas
☼ ♦ 36–45   **p. 215**

Erinus alpinus
☼ ◐ ♦ 32, 34–43   **p. 224**

Euphorbia myrsinites
☼ ♦ 32, 34–43   **p. 227**

Gentiana
GENTIAN
☼ ◐ ♦ ZONES VARY   **p. 238**

Geranium (smallest)
CRANESBILL
☼ ◐ ♦ ZONES VARY   **p. 238**

Herniaria glabra
GREEN CARPET
☼ ◐ ♦ ♦ 32, 34–45   **p. 255**

Iberis sempervirens
EVERGREEN CANDYTUFT
☼ ♦ 32, 34–45   **p. 264**

Lewisia
☼ ◐ ♦ ZONES VARY   **p. 289**

Lithodora diffusa
☼ ♦ 32, 34, 39   **p. 295**

Mazus reptans
☼ ◐ ♦ 31, 32, 34, 39   **p. 314**

Papaver alpinum
ALPINE POPPY
☼ ♦ 32, 34–41   **p. 335**

Phlox (trailing or creeping)
☼ ◐ ♦ ZONES VARY   **p. 348**

Polemonium reptans
◐ ♦ ZONES VARY   **p. 361**

Potentilla (some)
CINQUEFOIL
☼ ◐ ♦ ZONES VARY   **p. 364**

Primula (most)
PRIMROSE
☼ ◐ ♦ ♦ ♦ ZONES VARY   **p. 365**

Pulsatilla vulgaris
PASQUE FLOWER
☼ ◐ ♦ 32, 34–45   **p. 373**

Saponaria ocymoides
☼ ♦ 32, 34–45   **p. 400**

Saxifraga
SAXIFRAGE
NEEDS, ZONES VARY   **p. 402**

Sedum (many)
STONECROP
NEEDS, ZONES VARY   **p. 404**

Sempervivum
HOUSELEEK
☼ ♦ ♦ 32, 34–41   **p. 405**

Silene acaulis
CUSHION PINK
☼ ◐ ♦ 32, 34–45   **p. 408**

Thalictrum alpinum
MEADOW RUE
◐ ♦ 32, 34–41   **p. 424**

Thymus
THYME
☼ ◐ ♦ ZONES VARY   **p. 426**

Veronica (mat-forming)
SPEEDWELL
NEEDS, ZONES VARY   **p. 438**

BULBS, BULBLIKE PLANTS

Allium (smallest)
ORNAMENTAL ALLIUM
☼ ◐ ♦ ZONES VARY   **p. 125**

Chionodoxa
GLORY-OF-THE-SNOW
◐ ♦ 32, 34–43   **p. 182**

Crocus
☼ ◐ ♦ 32, 34–45   **p. 199**

Galanthus
SNOWDROP
☼ ◐ ♦ 32, 34–45   **p. 235**

Iris (smallest)
NEEDS, ZONES VARY   **p. 269**

Muscari
GRAPE HYACINTH
☼ ◐ ♦ ZONES VARY   **p. 320**

Narcissus (small)
DAFFODIL
☼ ◐ ♦ ZONES VARY   **p. 322**

Tulipa (species only)
TULIP
☼ ♦ 32, 34–45   **p. 433**

Zephyranthes
ZEPHYR FLOWER
☼ ♦ 32   **p. 447**

Sedum 'Vera Jameson'

Thymus pseudolanuginosus

Galanthus nivalis

Tulipa turkestanica

For growing symbol explanations, please see page 47.

Arctostaphylos uva-ursi

Plants that Attract

BIRDS

Watching birds enjoy your garden increases your enjoyment as well. Give feathered visitors a warm welcome by choosing plantings that provide favorite natural bird foods—seeds, berries, nectar. To keep the guests dropping in year-round, select your plants carefully, making sure the garden offers flowers, fruit, or seeds in every season.

Cotoneaster salicifolius

Lonicera tatarica

Acer cappadocicum 'Aureum'

Cornus canadensis

Fruit/seed-eating birds
GROUND COVERS/VINES

Ampelopsis brevipedunculata
PORCELAIN BERRY
☼ ☼ ● ◗ ● ◗ ✎ 31, 32, 34–41   p. 129

Arctostaphylos uva-ursi
BEARBERRY
☼ ☼ ◗ ✎ 31, 32, 34–45   p. 140

Celastrus scandens
AMERICAN BITTERSWEET
☼ ◗ ✎ 31, 32, 34–44   p. 176

Euonymus fortunei
☼ ☼ ● ◗ ● ◗ ✎ 31, 32, 34–41   p. 226

Grape
☼ ◗ ✎ ZONES VARY   p. 244

Lonicera
HONEYSUCKLE
☼ ☼ ◗ ✎ ZONES VARY   p. 297

Parthenocissus
☼ ☼ ◗ ● ◗ ✎ ZONES VARY   p. 336

Fruit/seed-eating birds
SHRUBS, TREES

Acer
MAPLE
☼ ☼ ◗ ● ◗ ✎ ZONES VARY   p. 116

Alnus
ALDER
☼ ☼ ◗ ● ● ◗ ✎ ZONES VARY   p. 126

Amelanchier
JUNEBERRY
☼ ☼ ◗ ● ◗ ✎ 31, 32, 34–45   p. 128

Aronia
CHOKEBERRY
☼ ☼ ◗ ● ◗ ✎ ZONES VARY   p. 142

Berberis
BARBERRY
☼ ☼ ◗ ● ◗ ✎ ZONES VARY   p. 154

Betula
BIRCH
☼ ☼ ◗ ● ◗ ✎ ZONES VARY   p. 155

Callicarpa
BEAUTYBERRY
☼ ☼ ◗ ● ◗ ✎ ZONES VARY   p. 164

Carpinus
HORNBEAM
NEEDS, ZONES VARY   p. 172

Celtis
HACKBERRY
☼ ☼ ◗ ● ✎ ZONES VARY   p. 176

Cornus
DOGWOOD
☼ ☼ ◗ ● ✎ ZONES VARY   p. 194

Cotoneaster
☼ ☼ ◗ ✎ ZONES VARY   p. 196

Crataegus
HAWTHORN
☼ ◗ ● ✎ ZONES VARY   p. 198

Elaeagnus
☼ ☼ ◗ ● ◗ ✎ ZONES VARY   p. 218

Euonymus
NEEDS, ZONES VARY   p. 226

Euscaphis japonica
SWEETHEART TREE
☼ ☼ ◗ ● ✎ 31, 32, 34, 39   p. 228

Ilex
HOLLY
☼ ☼ ◗ ● ✎ ZONES VARY   p. 265

Juniperus
JUNIPER
☼ ☼ ◗ ● ✎ ZONES VARY   p. 275

Ligustrum
PRIVET
☼ ☼ ◗ ● ✎ ZONES VARY   p. 290

Lindera
SPICEBUSH
☼ ☼ ◗ ● ✎ 31, 32, 34–41   p. 293

Crataegus phaenopyrum

Ilex altaclarensis 'Balearica'

Lindera obtusiloba

Plant listings continue ▶

PLANTS THAT ATTRACT BIRDS

Malus zumi

Ribes sanguineum

Rubus

Vaccinium corymbosum

Liquidambar styraciflua
AMERICAN SWEET GUM
☼ ● ● ✂ 31, 32, 34–41   **p. 294**

Lonicera
HONEYSUCKLE
☼ ◐ ● ✂ ZONES VARY   **p. 297**

Magnolia
☼ ● ✂ ZONES VARY   **p. 302**

Mahonia
NEEDS, ZONES VARY   **p. 307**

Malus
CRABAPPLE
☼ ● ● ✂ 31, 32, 34–43   **p. 308**

Morus
MULBERRY
☼ ● ● ✂ ZONES VARY   **p. 319**

Myrica
WAX MYRTLE
☼ ◐ ● ● ● ✂ ZONES VARY   **p. 321**

Myrica pensylvanica
BAYBERRY
☼ ◐ ● ✂ 31, 32, 34–44   **p. 321**

Photinia
☼ ● ● ✂ ZONES VARY   **p. 349**

Prunus
☼ ● ● ✂ ZONES VARY   **p. 368**

Pyracantha
FIRETHORN
☼ ● ✂ ZONES VARY   **p. 374**

Quercus
OAK
☼ ● ● ✂ ZONES VARY   **p. 375**

Ribes
☼ ● ● ✂ ZONES VARY   **p. 384**

Rosa (some)
NEEDS, ZONES VARY   **p. 386**

Rubus
BRAMBLE
☼ ● ● ● ✂ ZONES VARY   **p. 393**

Sambucus
ELDERBERRY
☼ ● ● ✂ ZONES VARY   **p. 399**

Sorbus
MOUNTAIN ASH
☼ ● ● ● ✂ ZONES VARY   **p. 410**

Symphoricarpos
SNOWBERRY
NEEDS, ZONES VARY   **p. 419**

Vaccinium
NEEDS, ZONES VARY   **p. 436**

Viburnum
NEEDS, ZONES VARY   **p. 439**

For growing symbol explanations, please see page 47.

Hummingbirds
ANNUALS, PERENNIALS, BULBS

Abutilon
FLOWERING MAPLE
☼ ◐ ● ✂ ALL ZONES   **p. 115**

Alcea rosea
HOLLYHOCK
☼ ● ✂ 31, 32, 34–45   **p. 124**

Alstroemeria
☼ ◐ ● ✂ ZONES VARY   **p. 127**

Antirrhinum majus
SNAPDRAGON
☼ ● ✂ ALL ZONES   **p. 134**

Aquilegia
COLUMBINE
☼ ◐ ● ✂ ZONES VARY   **p. 138**

Asclepias tuberosa
BUTTERFLY WEED
☼ ● ✂ 31, 32, 34–45   **p. 144**

Cleome hasslerana
SPIDER FLOWER
☼ ● ✂ ALL ZONES   **p. 188**

Crocosmia crocosmiiflora
MONTBRETIA
☼ ◐ ● ✂ 31, 32, 34, 39   **p. 199**

Delphinium
☼ ● ✂ ZONES VARY   **p. 208**

Digitalis
FOXGLOVE
◐ ● ✂ ZONES VARY   **p. 212**

Fuchsia
☼ ● ✂ ALL ZONES   **p. 235**

Gladiolus
☼ ● ✂ DIG AND STORE   **p. 241**

Heuchera
CORAL BELLS
☼ ◐ ● ✂ ZONES VARY   **p. 256**

Hibiscus (perennial and annual)
HARDY AND TROPICAL HIBISCUS
☼ ● ✂ ZONES VARY   **p. 257**

Impatiens
BALSAM
NEEDS, ZONES VARY   **p. 267**

Ipomopsis aggregata
☼ ● ● ✂ ALL ZONES   **p. 269**

Iris
NEEDS, ZONES VARY   **p. 269**

Kniphofia uvaria
RED-HOT POKER
☼ ◐ ● ● ✂ 31, 32, 34–41   **p. 281**

Lantana montevidensis
☼ ● ● ✂ ALL ZONES   **p. 284**

Abutilon pictum 'Thompsonii'

Aquilegia canadensis

Fuschia hybrida 'Lord Beacon'

Lantana montevidensis

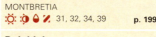
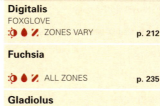

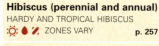

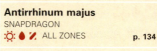

Lobelia cardinalis

Lobelia cardinalis
CARDINAL FLOWER
☼ ● ● ● ✂ 31, 32, 34, 35 p. 295

Lupinus
LUPINE
☼ ● ● ✂ ZONES VARY p. 298

Lychnis
☼ ◑ ● ● ✂ ZONES VARY p. 299

Mertensia virginica
VIRGINIA BLUEBELLS
◑ ● ● ✂ 31, 32, 34–45 p. 316

Mirabilis jalapa
FOUR O'CLOCK
☼ ● ✂ ALL ZONES p. 317

Monarda
BEE BALM
☼ ◑ ● ● ✂ ZONES VARY p. 319

Nicotiana
☼ ◑ ● ✂ ALL ZONES p. 326

Pelargonium
GERANIUM
☼ ◑ ● ● ✂ ALL ZONES p. 341

Penstemon (many)
BEARD TONGUE
☼ ● ● ● ✂ ZONES VARY p. 344

Phlox
☼ ◑ ● ✂ ZONES VARY p. 348

Salvia coccinea
☼ ● ✂ ALL ZONES p. 396

Salvia splendens
SCARLET SAGE
☼ ● ✂ ALL ZONES p. 396

Silene virginica
FIRE PINK
☼ ◑ ● ● ✂ ZONES VARY p. 408

Tropaeolum majus
GARDEN NASTURTIUM
☼ ● ● ✂ ALL ZONES p. 432

Veronica
SPEEDWELL
NEEDS, ZONES VARY p. 438

Zinnia
☼ ● ✂ ALL ZONES p. 448

Lupinus 'Russell Hybrids'

Pelargonium 'Clorinda'

Salvia

Hummingbirds
GROUND COVERS, VINES

Bean, scarlet runner
☼ ● ✂ ALL ZONES p. 152

Campsis
TRUMPET VINE
☼ ◑ ● ● ✂ ZONES VARY p. 168

Ipomoea
MORNING GLORY
☼ ● ● ✂ ALL ZONES p. 269

Ipomoea quamoclit
CYPRESS VINE
☼ ● ● ✂ ALL ZONES p. 269

Lonicera
HONEYSUCKLE
☼ ◑ ● ✂ ZONES VARY p. 297

Hummingbirds
SHRUBS

Abelia
☼ ◑ ● ✂ ZONES VARY p. 114

Buddleia
☼ ◑ ● ● ✂ ZONES VARY p. 161

Cephalanthus occidentalis
BUTTONBUSH
☼ ● ● ● ✂ 32, 34–41 p. 177

Chaenomeles
FLOWERING QUINCE
☼ ● ● ✂ 31, 32, 34–41 p. 179

Cotoneaster
☼ ● ✂ ZONES VARY p. 196

Kolkwitzia amabilis
BEAUTY BUSH
☼ ● ✂ 31, 32, 34–41 p. 282

Lavandula (many)
LAVENDER
☼ ● ✂ ZONES VARY p. 286

Lonicera
HONEYSUCKLE
☼ ◑ ● ✂ ZONES VARY p. 297

Ribes sanguineum
RED FLOWERING CURRANT
☼ ◑ ● ✂ 31, 32, 34–41 p. 384

Rosmarinus officinalis
ROSEMARY
☼ ● ✂ 31, 32 p. 393

Sambucus
ELDERBERRY
☼ ◑ ● ● ✂ ZONES VARY p. 399

Syringa
LILAC
☼ ● ✂ ZONES VARY p. 420

Weigela
☼ ◑ ● ✂ 31, 32, 34–41 p. 443

Hummingbirds
TREES

Aesculus
HORSECHESTNUT
NEEDS, ZONES VARY p. 121

Albizia julibrissin 'Rosea'
SILK TREE
☼ ● ● ✂ 31, 32, 34, 39 p. 124

Liriodendron tulipifera
TULIP TREE
☼ ● ✂ 31, 32, 34–41 p. 294

Tropaeolum majus

Veronica 'Waterperry Blue'

Campsis radicans

Weigela florida 'Eve Supreme'

Alcea rosea

Asclepias syriaca

Foeniculum vulgare

Lavatera thuringiaca 'Barnsley'

Plants that Attract
BUTTERFLIES

Butterflies are always welcome garden visitors. Choose the right plants and you can encourage them to stay a while and return each year. Butterfly larvae (caterpillars) need food plants; adult butterflies need plants that offer nectar-bearing flowers. Sunny areas such as meadows that are sheltered from the wind and contain such amenities as leaf litter, rock crevices, brush piles, damp places, and even weeds are the most welcoming of gardens for butterflies. When you choose plants, keep in mind that not every plant will attract butterflies in every region. And never use pesticides, unless you can target the specific pest without harming the butterflies or their larvae.

Butterfly larvae
ANNUALS, BIENNIALS, PERENNIALS

Alcea rosea
HOLLYHOCK
☼ ◐ ⚡ 31, 32, 34–45   p. 124

Antirrhinum majus
SNAPDRAGON
☼ ◐ ⚡ ALL ZONES   p. 134

Asclepias (esp. natives)
NEEDS, ZONES VARY   p. 144

Aster
☼ ◐ ⚡ 31, 32, 34–43   p. 146

Cleome hasslerana
SPIDER FLOWER
☼ ◐ ⚡ ALL ZONES   p. 188

Dicentra
BLEEDING HEART
◑ ● ◐ ⚡ 31, 32, 34–45   p. 211

Digitalis purpurea
COMMON FOXGLOVE
◑ ◐ ⚡ 31, 32, 34–41   p. 212

Foeniculum vulgare
COMMON FENNEL
☼ ◐ ⚡ 31, 32, 34–41   p. 232

Geum
☼ ◑ ◐ ⚡ 31, 32, 34–43   p. 240

Helianthus
SUNFLOWER
☼ ◐ ⚡ ZONES VARY   p. 251

Heliotropium arborescens
COMMON HELIOTROPE
☼ ◑ ● ⚡ ALL ZONES   p. 252

Lavatera
ANNUAL MALLOW
☼ ◐ ⚡ ALL ZONES   p. 287

Lupinus
LUPINE
☼ ◐ ● ⚡ ZONES VARY   p. 298

Malva
☼ ◑ ◐ ⚡ ZONES VARY   p. 312

Sidalcea
CHECKERBLOOM
☼ ◐ ⚡ 31, 32, 34–41   p. 407

Tropaeolum majus
GARDEN NASTURTIUM
☼ ◑ ◐ ⚡ ALL ZONES   p. 432

Veronica
SPEEDWELL
NEEDS, ZONES VARY   p. 438

Butterfly larvae
GROUND COVERS, VINES

Fragaria
STRAWBERRY
☼ ◐ ● ⚡ ALL ZONES   p. 233

Passiflora
PASSION VINE
☼ ◐ ◐ ⚡ 31, 32   p. 336

Wisteria
☼ ◐ ◐ ⚡ ZONES VARY   p. 444

Butterfly larvae
SHRUBS

Hibiscus syriacus
ROSE OF SHARON
☼ ◐ ⚡ 31, 32, 34–41   p. 257

Lupinus polyphyllus

Malva alcea 'Fastigiata'

Veronica austriaca 'Crater Lake Blue'

Fragaria 'Pink Panda'

For growing symbol explanations, please see page 47.

Spiraea nipponica 'Snowmound'

Viburnum carlcephalum

Pinus thunbergiana

Quercus palustris

Ribes
CURRANT, GOOSEBERRY
ZONES VARY · p. 384

Rosa
ROSE
NEEDS, ZONES VARY · p. 386

Spiraea
ZONES VARY · p. 412

Viburnum
NEEDS, ZONES VARY · p. 439

Butterfly larvae TREES

Aesculus
HORSECHESTNUT
NEEDS, ZONES VARY · p. 121

Betula
BIRCH
ZONES VARY · p. 155

Celtis
HACKBERRY
ZONES VARY · p. 176

Cornus
DOGWOOD
NEEDS, ZONES VARY · p. 194

Crataegus
HAWTHORN
31, 32, 34–41 · p. 198

Malus
CRABAPPLE
31, 32, 34–43 · p. 308

Pinus
PINE
ZONES VARY · p. 352

Platanus
PLANE TREE, SYCAMORE
ZONES VARY · p. 356

Prunus
ZONES VARY · p. 368

Pseudotsuga menziesii glauca
DOUGLAS FIR
34–41 · p. 371

Quercus
OAK
ZONES VARY · p. 375

Salix
WILLOW
ZONES VARY · p. 395

Adult Butterflies ANNUALS, PERENNIALS, GRASSES

Achillea
YARROW
31, 32, 34–45 · p. 118

Agastache foeniculum
ANISE HYSSOP
31, 32, 34–41 · p. 122

Antirrhinum majus
SNAPDRAGON
ALL ZONES · p. 134

Aquilegia
COLUMBINE
ZONES VARY · p. 138

Asclepias tuberosa
BUTTERFLY WEED
31, 32, 34–45 · p. 144

Aster
31, 32, 34–43 · p. 146

Astilbe
FALSE SPIRAEA
32, 34–45 · p. 147

Borago officinalis
BORAGE
ALL ZONES · p. 158

Centranthus ruber
RED VALERIAN
32, 34–43 · p. 177

Ceratostigma plumbaginoides
DWARF PLUMBAGO
32, 34–41 · p. 178

Chelone
TURTLEHEAD
31, 32, 34–43 · p. 180

Chrysanthemum maximum
SHASTA DAISY
31, 32, 34–43 · p. 183

Coreopsis
ZONES VARY · p. 192

Cosmos
ALL ZONES · p. 196

Delphinium
ZONES VARY · p. 208

Dianthus
PINK
31, 32, 34–45 · p. 209

Echinacea purpurea
PURPLE CONEFLOWER
31, 32, 34–45 · p. 216

Echinops
GLOBE THISTLE
31, 32, 34–45 · p. 217

Eryngium amethystinum
SEA HOLLY
31, 32, 34–45 · p. 224

Eupatorium
ZONES VARY · p. 226

Gaillardia grandiflora
BLANKET FLOWER
31, 32, 34–45 · p. 235

Heliotropium arborescens
COMMON HELIOTROPE
ALL ZONES · p. 251

Achillea millefolium 'Apple Blossom'

Agastache foeniculum

Aster novi-belgii

Borago officinalis

Plant listings continue ▶

PLANTS THAT ATTRACT BUTTERFLIES

Monarda didyma 'Croftway Pink'

Rudbeckia fulgida 'Goldsturm'

Salvia nemorosa

Solidago 'Golden Fleece'

Hesperis matronalis
DAME'S ROCKET
☼ ◑ ◔ ✄ ALL ZONES   p. 256

Lathyrus odoratus
SWEET PEA
☼ ◔ ✄ ALL ZONES   p. 285

Lobelia
☼ ◑ ◔ ◔◔ ✄ ZONES VARY   p. 295

Lobularia maritima
SWEET ALYSSUM
☼ ◑ ◔ ✄ ALL ZONES   p. 295

Monarda
BEE BALM
☼ ◑ ◔ ◔◔ ✄ ZONES VARY   p. 319

Nepeta
☼ ◑ ◔ ✄ 32, 34–43   p. 325

Origanum vulgare
OREGANO
☼ ◔ ✄ 31, 32, 34–45   p. 329

Phlox
☼ ◑ ◔ ✄ ZONES VARY   p. 348

Rudbeckia hirta
GLORIOSA DAISY
☼ ◑ ◔ ◔ ✄ 31, 32, 34–45   p. 393

Salvia
SAGE
NEEDS, ZONES VARY   p. 396

Scabiosa
PINCUSHION FLOWER
☼ ◔ ◔ ✄ ZONES VARY   p. 402

Sedum (tall)
STONECROP
NEEDS, ZONES VARY   p. 404

Solidago
GOLDENROD
☼ ◔ ✄ ZONES VARY   p. 409

Tagetes
MARIGOLD
☼ ◔ ✄ ALL ZONES   p. 421

Tithonia rotundifolia
MEXICAN SUNFLOWER
☼ ◔ ✄ ALL ZONES   p. 427

Verbena bonariensis
☼ ◔ ✄ 31, 32   p. 437

Adult Butterflies
SHRUBS

Abelia
☼ ◑ ◔ ✄ ZONES VARY   p. 114

Buddleia
☼ ◑ ◔ ◔ ✄ ZONES VARY   p. 161

Caryopteris
BLUEBEARD
☼ ◔ ✄ ZONES VARY   p. 173

Clethra alnifolia
SUMMERSWEET
☼ ◑ ◔ ◔ ✄ 31, 32, 34–43   p. 189

Hibiscus rosa-sinensis
CHINESE HIBISCUS
☼ ◔ ✄ ALL ZONES   p. 257

Kolkwitzia amabilis
BEAUTY BUSH
☼ ◑ ◔ ✄ 31, 32, 34–41   p. 282

Lantana
☼ ◔ ✄ ALL ZONES   p. 284

Lavandula
LAVENDER
☼ ◔ ✄ ZONES VARY   p. 286

Lonicera
HONEYSUCKLE
☼ ◑ ◔ ✄ ZONES VARY   p. 297

Philadelphus (single-flowered)
MOCK ORANGE
☼ ◑ ◔ ◔ ✄ ZONES VARY   p. 347

Potentilla
CINQUEFOIL
☼ ◑ ◔ ✄ ZONES VARY   p. 364

Rhododendron
◑ ◔ ✄ ZONES VARY   p. 379

Sambucus
ELDERBERRY
☼ ◑ ◔ ✄ ZONES VARY   p. 399

Spiraea
☼ ◑ ◔ ✄ ZONES VARY   p. 412

Syringa
LILAC
☼ ◔ ✄ ZONES VARY   p. 420

Vitex agnus-castus
CHASTE TREE
☼ ◔ ✄ 31, 32, 34, 39   p. 442

Adult Butterflies
TREES

Acer
MAPLE
☼ ◑ ◔ ◔ ✄ ZONES VARY   p. 116

Aesculus
HORSECHESTNUT
NEEDS, ZONES VARY   p. 121

Albizia julibrissin 'Rosea'
SILK TREE
☼ ◑ ◔ ✄ 31, 32, 34, 39   p. 124

Apple
☼ ◔ ✄ ZONES VARY   p. 134

Salix
WILLOW
☼ ◔◔ ✄ ZONES VARY   p. 395

Vitex
CHASTE TREE
☼ ◔ ✄ 31, 32, 34, 39   p. 442

Verbena bonariensis

Kolkwitzia amabilis

Rhododendron maximum

Acer

For growing symbol explanations, please see page 47.

Plants that Resist
DEER

Browsing deer are charming to watch, but they can do considerable damage to gardens. There are various ways you can attempt to discourage or repel deer, but the best tactic may be to grow plants that deer will find unpalatable. However, deer in different areas seem to have somewhat different tastes. To complicate the picture further, young plants may be eaten but older ones left alone; plants untouched in spring may be eaten in fall. As a final frustration, tastes change: what deer pass by one year they may find irresistible the next. Despite these variables, a number of plants can be considered "best bets" in deer country. These are listed below.

Betula papyrifera

Gleditsia triacanthos

Leucothoe fontanesiana 'Rollissonii'

Convallaria majalis

Galium odoratum

Pachysandra procumbens

Tiarella cordifolia

TREES, SHRUBS

Amelanchier
SHADBLOW
31, 32, 34–35 — p. 128

Asimina triloba
PAWPAW
31, 32, 34–41 — p. 144

Betula albo-sinensis
31, 32, 34–41 — p. 155

Betula nigra 'Heritage'
HERITAGE RIVER BIRCH
31, 32, 34–43 — p. 155

Betula papyrifera
CANOE BIRCH
31, 32, 34–45 — p. 155

Chamaecyparis pisifera
SAWARA FALSE CYPRESS
31, 32, 34–43 — p. 179

Cryptomeria japonica
JAPANESE CRYPTOMERIA
31, 32, 34, 39 — p. 200

Gleditsia triacanthos
HONEY LOCUST
32, 34–43 — p. 242

Leucothoe
ZONES VARY — p. 289

Picea abies
NORWAY SPRUCE
32, 34–45 — p. 350

Picea pungens
COLORADO SPRUCE
32, 34–45 — p. 350

Pinus mugo
SWISS MOUNTAIN PINE
32, 34–45 — p. 352

Pinus nigra
AUSTRIAN BLACK PINE
31, 32, 34–41 — p. 352

Pinus sylvestris
SCOTCH PINE
31, 32, 34–45 — p. 352

Pseudotsuga menziesii glauca
DOUGLAS FIR
34–41 — p. 371

GROUND COVERS

Convallaria majalis
LILY-OF-THE-VALLEY
31, 32, 34–45 — p. 191

Epimedium
ZONES VARY — p. 220

Galium odoratum
SWEET WOODRUFF
31, 32, 34–43 — p. 236

Pachysandra
31, 32, 34–43 — p. 332

Phlox subulata
MOSS PINK
31, 32, 34–45 — p. 348

Thymus
THYME
31, 32, 34–43 — p. 426

Tiarella cordifolia
FOAMFLOWER
31, 32, 34–43 — p. 426

Plant listings continue ▶

PLANTS THAT RESIST DEER

Buxus sempervirens

Cephalotaxus harringtonia

Forsythia

Pieris

SHRUBS, VINES

Aesculus parviflora
BOTTLEBRUSH BUCKEYE
☼ ◐ ◔ ✂ 31, 32, 34–41   p. 121

Berberis
BARBERRY
☼ ◐ ◔ ◔ ✂ ZONES VARY   p. 154

Buxus
BOXWOOD
☼ ◐ ◔ ◔ ✂ ZONES VARY   p. 162

Caryopteris clandonensis
BLUE MIST
☼ ◔ ◔ ✂ 31, 32, 34, 39   p. 173

Celastrus
BITTERSWEET
☼ ◔ ✂ ZONES VARY   p. 176

Cephalotaxus harringtonia
PLUM YEW
☼ ◐ ◔ ◔ ✂ 31, 32, 34, 39   p. 178

Cornus sericea (stolonifera)
REDTWIG DOGWOOD
☼ ◔ ✂ 31, 32, 34–45   p. 194

Daphne
☼ ◐ ◔ ◔ ✂ ZONES VARY   p. 206

Elaeagnus angustifolia
RUSSIAN OLIVE
☼ ◔ ◔ ✂ 31, 32, 34–45   p. 218

Forsythia
☼ ◔ ◔ ✂ ZONES VARY   p. 232

Gaultheria procumbens
WINTERGREEN
◐ ◔ ✂ 31, 32, 34–45   p. 236

Hibiscus syriacus
ROSE OF SHARON
☼ ◔ ✂ 31, 32, 34–41   p. 257

Kolkwitzia amabilis
BEAUTY BUSH
☼ ◔ ◔ ✂ 31, 32, 34–41   p. 282

Ligustrum vulgare
COMMON PRIVET
☼ ◔ ✂ 31, 32, 34–41   p. 290

Myrica
WAX MYRTLE, BAYBERRY
☼ ◐ ◔ ◔ ◔ ✂ ZONES VARY   p. 321

Pieris japonica
LILY-OF-THE-VALLEY SHRUB
◐ ◔ ✂ 31, 32, 34–41   p. 351

Rhamnus cathartica
COMMON BUCKTHORN
☼ ◔ ◔ ✂ 31, 32, 34–45   p. 379

Sambucus canadensis
AMERICAN ELDERBERRY
☼ ◔ ◔ ✂ 31, 32, 34–45   p. 399

Syringa vulgaris
COMMON LILAC
☼ ◔ ✂ 31, 32, 34–45   p. 420

ANNUALS, PERENNIALS, BULBS

Achillea
YARROW
☼ ◔ ✂ 31, 32, 34–45   p. 118

Aconitum
MONKSHOOD
☼ ◐ ◔ ◔ ✂ 31, 32, 34–45   p. 119

Agastache foeniculum
ANISE HYSSOP
☼ ◐ ◔ ◔ ✂ 31, 32, 34–41   p. 122

Ageratum houstonianum
FLOSS FLOWER
☼ ◐ ◔ ✂ ALL ZONES   p. 123

Allium (several)
ORNAMENTAL ALLIUM
☼ ◔ ◔ ✂ ZONES VARY   p. 125

Anemone hybrida
JAPANESE ANEMONE
☼ ◐ ◔ ◔ ✂ 31, 32, 34–41   p. 131

Anethum graveolens
DILL
✂ ALL ZONES   p. 132

Antirrhinum majus
SNAPDRAGON
☼ ◔ ◔ ✂ ALL ZONES   p. 134

Arabis
ROCKCRESS
☼ ◔ ◔ ✂ 31, 32, 34–45   p. 139

Arisaema
◐ ◔ ◔ ◔ ✂ ZONES VARY   p. 140

Asclepias tuberosa
BUTTERFLY WEED
☼ ◔ ✂ 31, 32, 34–45   p. 144

Aubrieta deltoidea
COMMON AUBRIETA
☼ ◐ ◔ ◔ ✂ 36–43   p. 148

Aurinia saxatilis
BASKET-OF-GOLD
☼ ◐ ◔ ◔ ✂ 32, 34–43   p. 148

Bergenia
☼ ◐ ◔ ◔ ✂ 31, 32, 34–45   p. 154

Ceratostigma plumbaginoides
DWARF PLUMBAGO
☼ ◐ ◔ ◔ ◔ ✂ 31, 32, 34–41   p. 178

Cimicifuga racemosa
BLACK SNAKEROOT
☼ ◐ ◔ ◔ ✂ 31, 32, 34–45   p. 185

Colchicum
AUTUMN CROCUS
☼ ◐ ◔ ◔ ✂ 31, 32, 34–43   p. 190

Consolida ambigua
LARKSPUR
☼ ◐ ◔ ✂ 31, 32, 34–45   p. 191

Coreopsis 'Moonbeam'
☼ ◔ ◔ ✂ 31, 32, 34–45   p. 192

Allium tuberosum

Anemone tomentosa 'Robustissima'

Bergenia cordifolia 'Purpurea'

Coreopsis verticillata 'Moonbeam'

For growing symbol explanations, please see page 47.

Echinacea purpurea 'Bravo'

Euphorbia polychroma

Hyacinthus 'Delft Blue'

Narcissus 'Dutch Master'

Cyclamen hederifolium
31, 32, 34, 39   p. 201

Datura
THORN APPLE
ALL ZONES   p. 207

Dicentra spectabilis
COMMON BLEEDING HEART
31, 32, 34–45   p. 211

Digitalis
FOXGLOVE
ZONES VARY   p. 212

Dryopteris marginalis
MARGINAL SHIELD FERN
31, 32, 34–41   p. 215

Echinacea purpurea
PURPLE CONEFLOWER
31, 32, 34–45   p. 216

Euphorbia
ZONES VARY   p. 227

Fritillaria
FRITILLARY
ZONES VARY   p. 234

Galium odoratum
SWEET WOODRUFF
31, 32, 34–43   p. 236

Helleborus
HELLEBORE
ZONES VARY   p. 253

Hesperis matronalis
DAME'S ROCKET
ALL ZONES   p. 256

Hyacinthus orientalis
HYACINTH
31, 32, 34–45   p. 262

Lamium maculatum
DEAD NETTLE
31, 32, 34–43   p. 284

Lantana
ALL ZONES   p. 284

Lavandula
LAVENDER
ZONES VARY   p. 286

Lobularia maritima
SWEET ALYSSUM
ALL ZONES   p. 295

Lychnis coronaria
ROSE CAMPION
31, 32, 34–43   p. 299

Matteuccia struthiopteris
OSTRICH FERN
31, 32, 34–45   p. 313

Narcissus
DAFFODIL
ZONES VARY   p. 322

Nicotiania
ALL ZONES   p. 326

Opuntia compressa
PRICKLY PEAR
31, 32, 34–41   p. 329

Osmunda regalis
REGAL FERN
31, 32, 34–45   p. 330

Papaver
POPPY
ZONES VARY   p. 335

Pelargonium
GERANIUM
ALL ZONES   p. 341

Perovskia
RUSSIAN SAGE
31, 32, 35, 37, 39   p. 345

Ranunculus
ZONES VARY   p. 377

Rheum palmatum
ORNAMENTAL RHUBARB
31, 32, 34–41   p. 379

Ricinus communis
CASTOR BEAN
ALL ZONES   p. 385

Rudbeckia
ZONES VARY   p. 393

Salvia
SAGE
ZONES VARY   p. 396

Santolina
ZONES VARY   p. 399

Scilla
SQUILL, BLUEBELL
ZONES VARY   p. 404

Sempervivum
HOUSELEEK
31, 32, 34–41   p. 405

Stachys
LAMB'S EARS, BETONY
ZONES VARY   p. 414

Tagetes
MARIGOLD
ALL ZONES   p. 421

Tanacetum vulgare
TANSY
31, 32, 34–43   p. 422

Thymus
THYME
ZONES VARY   p. 426

Tropaeolum majus
NASTURTIUM
ALL ZONES   p. 432

Yucca
ZONES VARY   p. 446

Zinnia elegans
ALL ZONES   p. 448

Papaver somniferum

Perovskia atriplicifolia

Santolina rosmarinifolia

Tagetes tenuifolia

FLOWERS
for Cutting

Arctotis hybrida 'Flame'

Cleome hasslerana

Cosmos sulphureus 'Sunny Orange'

Gerbera jamesonii 'Advantage Mix'

A large bouquet of fresh flowers is a satisfying reward for your gardening efforts. Many kinds of flowers are good for cutting. The ones listed here will generally last a week in water. Annuals and biennials must be planted every year, although a few, such as larkspur and cosmos, may reseed themselves. Perennials and most bulbs provide flowers for cutting year after year. Peak flower season can come earlier or later than indicated, depending on climate and care. Stand flower stems in a bucket of water as soon as you cut them.

ANNUALS, BIENNIALS

Ageratum houstonianum
FLOSS FLOWER
ALL ZONES — p. 123

Arctotis
AFRICAN DAISY
ALL ZONES — p. 140

Calendula officinalis
POT MARIGOLD
ALL ZONES — p. 163

Callistephus chinensis
CHINA ASTER
ALL ZONES — p. 164

Centaurea cyanus
CORNFLOWER
ALL ZONES — p. 177

Cleome hasslerana
SPIDER FLOWER
ALL ZONES — p. 188

Consolida ambigua
LARKSPUR
ALL ZONES — p. 191

Cosmos bipinnatus
ALL ZONES — p. 196

Dianthus (some)
ALL ZONES — p. 209

Eustoma grandiflorum
LISIANTHUS
ALL ZONES — p. 228

Gerbera jamesonii
TRANSVAAL DAISY
ALL ZONES — p. 239

Gomphrena globosa
GLOBE AMARANTH
ALL ZONES — p. 243

Helianthus annuus
COMMON SUNFLOWER
ALL ZONES — p. 251

Helichrysum bracteatum
STRAWFLOWER
ALL ZONES — p. 252

Lathyrus odoratus
SWEET PEA
ALL ZONES — p. 285

Lavatera trimestris
ANNUAL MALLOW
ALL ZONES — p. 287

Limonium sinuatum
ALL ZONES — p. 293

Matthiola
STOCK
ALL ZONES — p. 313

Moluccella laevis
BELLS-OF-IRELAND
ALL ZONES — p. 318

Nigella damascena
LOVE-IN-A-MIST
ALL ZONES — p. 326

Osteospermum
AFRICAN DAISY
ALL ZONES — p. 331

Phlox drummondii
ANNUAL PHLOX
ALL ZONES — p. 348

Tagetes (most)
MARIGOLD
ALL ZONES — p. 421

Tithonia rotundifolia
MEXICAN SUNFLOWER
ALL ZONES — p. 427

Zinnia
ALL ZONES — p. 448

Osteospermum fruticosum

Phlox drummondii

Tithonia rotundifolia

Zinnia haageana 'Chippendale'

For growing symbol explanations, please see page 47.

Astilbe chinensis 'Pumila'

Campanula perscifolia

Delphinium 'Pacific Giants'

Kniphofia uvaria

PERENNIALS, BULBS

Achillea filipendulina
FERNLEAF YARROW
:☼: ◐ ✎   32, 34–45   p. 118

Alstroemeria
:☼: :◐: ◐ ✎   ZONES VARY   p. 127

Anemone coronaria
POPPY-FLOWERED ANEMONE
:☼: :◐: ◐ ✎   31, 32, 34–41   p. 131

Aquilegia
COLUMBINE
:☼: :◐: ◐ ✎   ZONES VARY   p. 138

Aster
:☼: ◐ ✎   31, 32, 34–43   p. 146

Astilbe
FALSE SPIRAEA
:☼: :◐: ◐ ✎   ZONES VARY   p. 147

Campanula (some)
BELLFLOWER
:☼: :◐: ◐ ◐ ✎   ZONES VARY   p. 168

Chrysanthemum (some)
NEEDS, ZONES VARY   p. 183

Coreopsis (most)
:☼: ◐ ✎   ZONES VARY   p. 192

Dahlia
:☼: :◐: ◐ ✎   DIG AND STORE   p. 205

Delphinium
:☼: ◐ ✎   ZONES VARY   p. 208

Dianthus (many)
:☼: :◐: ◐ ✎   31, 32, 34–45   p. 209

Dicentra
BLEEDING HEART
◐ ◐ ◐ ✎   31, 32, 34–45   p. 211

Digitalis
FOXGLOVE
◐ ◐ ✎   ZONES VARY   p. 212

Echinacea purpurea
PURPLE CONEFLOWER
:☼: ◐ ✎   31, 32, 34–45   p. 216

Echinops
GLOBE THISTLE
:☼: ◐ ◐ ✎   31, 32, 34–45   p. 217

Gaillardia grandiflora
BLANKET FLOWER
:☼: ◐ ✎   31, 32, 34–45   p. 235

Gladiolus
:☼: ◐ ✎   DIG AND STORE   p. 241

Gypsophila paniculata
BABY'S BREATH
:☼: ◐ ✎   31, 32, 34–45   p. 248

Heliopsis helianthoides
OX-EYE
:☼: ◐ ◐ ✎   31, 32, 34–45   p. 252

Iris
NEEDS, ZONES VARY   p. 269

Kniphofia uvaria
RED-HOT POKER
:☼: ◐ ◐ ✎   31, 32, 34–41   p. 281

Lavandula
LAVENDER
:☼: ◐ ✎   ZONES VARY   p. 286

Liatris
GAYFEATHER
:☼: ◐ ◐ ✎   31, 32, 34–45   p. 290

Lilium
LILY
:☼: ◐ ✎   31, 32, 34–45   p. 291

Limonium
SEA LAVENDER
:☼: ◐ ✎   ZONES VARY   p. 293

Narcissus
DAFFODIL
NEEDS, ZONES VARY   p. 322

Paeonia
PEONY
:☼: ◐ ✎   ZONES VARY   p. 332

Papaver orientale
ORIENTAL POPPY
:☼: ◐ ◐ ✎   31, 32, 34–45   p. 335

Phlox paniculata
SUMMER PHLOX
:☼: ◐ ✎   31, 32, 34–43   p. 348

Platycodon grandiflorus
BALLOON FLOWER
:☼: :◐: ◐ ◐ ✎   31, 32, 34–45 p. 357

Ranunculus asiaticus
PERSIAN RANUNCULUS
:☼: ◐ ✎   ALL ZONES   p. 377

Rudbeckia hirta
GLORIOSA DAISY
:☼: :◐: ◐ ◐ ✎   31, 32, 34–43 p. 393

Scabiosa (some)
PINCUSHION FLOWER
:☼: ◐ ◐ ✎   ZONES VARY   p. 402

Stokesia laevis
STOKES' ASTER
:☼: ◐ ✎   31, 32, 34–43   p. 415

Thalictrum aquilegiifolium
MEADOW RUE
:☼: :◐: ◐ ✎   31, 32, 34–41   p. 424

Tulipa
TULIP
:☼: ◐ ✎   ALL ZONES   p. 433

Veronica spicata
SPEEDWELL
:☼: ◐ ✎   31, 32, 34–43   p. 438

Zantedeschia aethiopica
CALLA
:☼: ◐ ◐ ✎   31, 32   p. 446

Lilium 'Connecticut King'

Paeonia 'Bev'

Ranunculus asiaticus

Veronica 'Sunny Border Blue'

Abutilon hybridum

Bacopa

Brachycome iberidifolia

Convolvulus tricolor 'Ensign'

Plants for HANGING BASKETS AND WINDOW BOXES

Lantana camara

T he charm of a garden in the air—whether it perches at the edge of a window or hangs suspended from an arbor—derives from the choice of plants. You want a full (and probably colorful) display, with foliage that is lax enough to soften the edges of the container or even spill over it. Here's a selection of proven aerial artists, drawn from a variety of annuals, perennials, and woody plants.

ANNUALS

Abutilon hybridum
FLOWERING MAPLE
☼ ☼ ● ● ✂ ALL ZONES   p. 115

Bacopa (Sutera)
☼ ☼ ● ● ✂ ALL ZONES   p. 149

Bidens ferulifolia
☼ ● ● ✂ ALL ZONES   p. 155

Begonia, tuberous
☼ ● ● ✂ ALL ZONES   p. 153

Brachycome iberidifolia
SWAN RIVER DAISY
☼ ● ✂ ALL ZONES   p. 158

Browallia
AMETHYST FLOWER
☼ ● ✂ ALL ZONES   p. 160

Calibrachoa
MILLION BELLS
☼ ● ● ✂ ALL ZONES   p. 164

Coleus hybridus
☼ ☼ ● ● ✂ ALL ZONES   p. 190

Convolvulus tricolor
DWARF MORNING GLORY
☼ ● ✂ ALL ZONES   p. 192

Evolvulus glomeratus
BLUE DAZE
☼ ☼ ● ● ✂ ALL ZONES   p. 228

Fuchsia hybrida
HYBRID FUCHSIA
☼ ● ● ✂ ALL ZONES   p. 235

Helichrysum petiolare
LICORICE PLANT
☼ ● ● ✂ ALL ZONES   p. 252

Hypoestes phyllostachya
FRECKLE FACE
☼ ● ● ✂ ALL ZONES   p. 264

Impatiens walleriana
BUSY LIZZIE
☼ ● ● ✂ ALL ZONES   p. 267

Lantana
☼ ● ✂ ALL ZONES   p. 284

Linaria maroccana
☼ ☼ ● ✂ ALL ZONES   p. 293

Lobelia erinus
☼ ☼ ● ● ● ✂ ALL ZONES   p. 295

Lobularia maritima
SWEET ALYSSUM
☼ ☼ ● ✂ ALL ZONES   p. 295

Mimulus hybridus
MONKEY FLOWER
☼ ● ● ● ✂ ALL ZONES   p. 317

Nemophila
☼ ☼ ● ✂ ALL ZONES   p. 324

Nicotiana alata
☼ ☼ ● ✂ ALL ZONES   p. 326

Linaria maroccana

Nemophila maculata

Nicotiana alata 'Domino Crimson'

For growing symbol explanations, please see page 47.

Nierembergia
CUP FLOWER
☼ ◐ ● ⚡ ALL ZONES   p. 326

Pelargonium peltatum
IVY GERANIUM
☼ ◐ ● ● ⚡ ALL ZONES   p. 341

Petunia
☼ ● ⚡ ALL ZONES   p. 346

Sanvitalia procumbens
CREEPING ZINNIA
☼ ● ● ⚡ ALL ZONES   p. 400

Senecio cineraria
☼ ◐ ● ⚡ ALL ZONES   p. 406

Strobilanthes dyerianus
☼ ◐ ● ⚡ ALL ZONES   p. 416

Torenia fournieri
WISHBONE FLOWER
◐ ● ● ⚡ ALL ZONES   p. 429

Tropaeolum majus
GARDEN NASTURTIUM
☼ ◐ ● ⚡ ALL ZONES   p. 432

Verbena hybrida
GARDEN VERBENA
☼ ● ⚡ ALL ZONES   p. 437

Viola wittrockiana
PANSY
☼ ◐ ● ⚡ ALL ZONES   p. 441

Zinnia angustifolia
☼ ● ⚡ ALL ZONES   p. 448

PERENNIALS, BULBS

Alchemilla mollis
LADY'S-MANTLE
☼ ◐ ● ⚡ 31, 32, 34–43   p. 124

Asparagus (some)
☼ ◐ ● ● ⚡ ZONES VARY   p. 145

Aurinia saxatilis
BASKET-OF-GOLD
☼ ● ● ⚡ 32, 34–43   p. 148

Begonia, semperflorens
◐ ● ● ⚡ ALL ZONES   p. 153

Begonia, tuberous
◐ ● ● ⚡ ALL ZONES   p. 153

Campanula (many)
BELLFLOWER
☼ ◐ ● ● ⚡ ZONES VARY   p. 168

Campanula portenschlagiana
DALMATIAN BELLFLOWER
◐ ● ● ⚡ 32, 34–41   p. 168

Campanula poscharskyana
SERBIAN BELLFLOWER
◐ ● ⚡ 32, 34–45   p. 168

Cymbalaria muralis
KENILWORTH IVY
☼ ● ● ⚡ ZONES VARY   p. 202

Gazania
☼ ● ⚡ ZONES VARY   p. 237

Glechoma hederacea
GROUND IVY
☼ ◐ ● ● ⚡ ALL ZONES   p. 242

Helichrysum petiolare
LICORICE PLANT
☼ ● ⚡ ALL ZONES   p. 252

Iberis sempervirens
EVERGREEN CANDYTUFT
☼ ● ⚡ 31, 32, 34–45   p. 264

Lamium maculatum
DEAD NETTLE
◐ ● ● ⚡ 32, 34–43   p. 284

Lotus berthelotii
PARROT'S BEAK
☼ ◐ ● ⚡ ALL ZONES   p. 298

Lysimachia nummularia
MONEYWORT
☼ ◐ ● ⚡ 31, 32, 34–43   p. 300

Primula (some)
PRIMROSE
☼ ◐ ● ● ● ⚡ ZONES VARY   p. 365

Saxifraga stolonifera
STRAWBERRY GERANIUM
◐ ● ⚡ 31, 32   p. 402

Scaevola
☼ ◐ ● ⚡ ZONES VARY   p. 402

Sedum (some)
☼ ◐ ● ⚡ ZONES VARY   p. 404

Senecio mikanioides
GERMAN IVY
☼ ◐ ● ⚡ ALL ZONES   p. 406

Tradescantia
WANDERING JEW
◐ ● ● ⚡ ZONES VARY   p. 430

Vinca minor
DWARF PERIWINKLE
◐ ● ● ⚡ 31, 32, 34–43   p. 441

SHRUBS, VINES

Hedera helix
ENGLISH IVY
☼ ◐ ● ● ● ⚡ ZONES VARY   p. 250

Mandevilla
☼ ◐ ● ⚡ ALL ZONES   p. 312

Passiflora
☼ ◐ ● ⚡ ALL ZONES   p. 336

Thunbergia alata
BLACK-EYED SUSAN VINE
☼ ◐ ● ⚡ ALL ZONES   p. 426

Petunia 'Purple Wave'

Sanvitalia

Senecio

Strobilanthes dyerianus

Alchemilla mollis

Sedum telephium

Mandevilla 'Alice du Pont'

Passiflora

Centranthus ruber

Cosmos

Dicentra eximia

Heliotropum

Plants for COTTAGE GARDENS

More and more gardeners are discovering the delights of cottage gardens full of old-fashioned flowers. These cheerful, exuberant gardens are the perfect place for favorite flowers and heirloom varieties. The only "design" needed is to enclose the garden with a fence and make a path through it. Then fill it with a mix of perennials, annuals (self-sowers are especially welcome), bulbs, roses, and vines. Add some herbs and vegetables, too, if you like.

Alcea rosea
HOLLYHOCK
☀ ◐ ▮ ALL ZONES   p. 124

Alchemilla mollis
LADY'S-MANTLE
☀ ◐ ◓ ▮ 31, 32, 34–43   p. 124

Antirrhinum majus
SNAPDRAGON
☀ ◐ ▮ ALL ZONES   p. 134

Aquilegia hybrids
COLUMBINE
☀ ◐ ◓ ▮ 32, 34–45   p. 138

Calendula officinalis
POT MARIGOLD
☀ ◐ ▮ 32, 34–44   p. 163

Centaurea cyanus
BACHELOR'S BUTTON
☀ ◐ ▮ ALL ZONES   p. 177

Centranthus ruber
RED VALERIAN, JUPITER'S BEARD
☀ ◐ ◓ ▮ ALL ZONES   p. 177

Consolida ambigua
LARKSPUR
☀ ◐ ▮ ALL ZONES   p. 191

Cosmos
☀ ◐ ▮ ALL ZONES   p. 196

Dianthus barbatus
SWEET WILLIAM
☀ ◐ ◓ ▮ 31, 32, 34–43   p. 209

Dicentra spectabilis
BLEEDING HEART
☀ ◐ ◓ ▮ 31, 32, 34–45   p. 211

Digitalis purpurea
FOXGLOVE
◐ ◓ ▮ 31, 32, 34–41   p. 212

Heliotropium arborescens
COMMON HELIOTROPE
☀ ◐ ◓ ▮ ALL ZONES   p. 252

Hemerocallis
DAYLILY
☀ ◐ ◓ ▮ 31, 32, 34–45   p. 253

Lobularia maritima
SWEET ALYSSUM
☀ ◐ ◓ ▮ ALL ZONES   p. 295

Lychnis coronaria
ROSE CAMPION
☀ ◐ ◓ ◓ ▮ ALL ZONES   p. 299

Mirabilis jalapa
FOUR O'CLOCK
☀ ◐ ▮ ALL ZONES   p. 317

Nigella damascena
LOVE-IN-A-MIST
☀ ◐ ◓ ◓ ▮ ALL ZONES   p. 326

Paeonia lactiflora
PEONY
☀ ◐ ◓ ▮ 32, 34–45   p. 332

Papaver
POPPY
☀ ◐ ◓ ▮ 32, 34–45   p. 335

Platycodon grandiflorus
BALLOON FLOWER
☀ ◐ ◓ ▮ 32, 34–45   p. 357

Rosa spp.
ROSE
☀ ◐ ◓ ▮ ALL ZONES   p. 386

Stokesia
STOKES' ASTER
☀ ◐ ◓ ▮ ZONES VARY   p. 415

Viola tricolor
JOHNNY JUMP-UP
☀ ◐ ◓ ◓ ▮ ALL ZONES   p. 441

For growing symbol explanations, please see page 47.

Hemerocallis

Platycodon grandiflorum

Rosa 'Harrison's Yellow'

Stokesia

TREES

Acer circinatum

Betula pendula

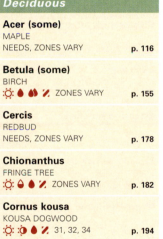
Cercis chinensis

Euonymus europaeus

The best trees are well suited to their sites. Patio trees are generally small, as trees go, and look good at close range. Many have showy flowers, fruit, or both; some have striking fall foliage or decorative bark. All are well-mannered: root systems are not likely to crack pavement; branches do not shed lots of leaves or drop messy fruit. All patio trees are fine candidates for garden planting, but the list of garden trees includes others of moderate size that fail to meet all the patio criteria. Some may shed leaves or fruit that would require frequent cleanup on a patio but pose no problem in a garden. Others may have roots that interfere with paving or other plantings.

Large landscape trees are generally too massive for small gardens but are worth planting on larger properties where their majesty can be appreciated.

Malus 'Snowdrift'

Morus alba 'Pendula'

Salix 'Hatsu Nigiri'

Styrax

SMALL TREES FOR PATIOS AND GARDENS *Deciduous*	
Acer (some) MAPLE NEEDS, ZONES VARY p. 116	**Hovenia dulcis** JAPANESE RAISIN TREE ☼ ◐ ∕ 31, 32, 34–41 p. 260
Betula (some) BIRCH ☼ ◐ ◐ ∕ ZONES VARY p. 155	**Koelreuteria** ☼ ◐ ◐ ∕ ZONES VARY p. 282
Cercis REDBUD NEEDS, ZONES VARY p. 178	**Lagerstroemia indica hybrids** CRAPE MYRTLE ☼ ◐ ∕ 31. 32 p. 283
Chionanthus FRINGE TREE ☼ ◐ ◐ ∕ ZONES VARY p. 182	**Maackia amurensis** AMUR MAACKIA ☼ ◐ ∕ 32, 34–43 p. 301
Cornus kousa KOUSA DOGWOOD ☼ ◑ ◐ ∕ 31, 32, 34 p. 194	**Magnolia (some)** ☼ ◑ ◐ ∕ ZONES VARY p. 302
Corylus (some) FILBERT, HAZELNUT ☼ ◑ ◐ ∕ ZONES VARY p. 196	**Malus** CRABAPPLE ☼ ◐ ◐ ∕ 31, 32, 34–43 p. 308
Cotinus coggygria SMOKE TREE ☼ ◐ ∕ 31, 32, 34–41 p. 196	**Morus alba** WHITE MULBERRY ☼ ◐ ◐ ∕ 31, 32, 34–43 p. 319
Crataegus HAWTHORN ☼ ◐ ∕ 31, 32, 34–41 p. 198	**Oxydendrum arboreum** SOURWOOD ☼ ◐ ∕ 31, 32, 34, 35. 37. 39 p. 332
Davidia involucrata DOVE TREE ☼ ◑ ◐ ∕ 31, 32, 34 p. 207	**Parrotia persica** PERSIAN PARROTIA ☼ ◐ ◐ ∕ 31, 32, 34–41 p. 335
Euonymus europaeus SPINDLE TREE ☼ ◑ ◐ ◐ ∕ 31, 32, 34–45 p. 226	**Prunus (some)** ☼ ◐ ◐ ∕ ZONES VARY p. 368
Halesia carolina SILVER BELL ◑ ◐ ∕ 31, 32, 34–41 p. 249	**Salix (many)** WILLOW ☼ ◐ ◐ ∕ ZONES VARY p. 395
	Styrax SNOWBELL ☼ ◑ ◐ ∕ ZONES VARY p. 418

Plant listings continue ▶

TREES

Thuja 'Techny'

Magnolia stellata

Prunus

Tilia

Picea omorika

Syringa reticulata
JAPANESE TREE LILAC
☼ ◑ ● ⚡ 32, 34–43   p. 420

Viburnum lentago
NANNYBERRY
☼ ◑ ● ⚡ 32, 34–45   p. 439

Xanthoceras sorbifolium
YELLOWHORN
☼ ● ⚡ 31, 32, 34–41   p. 445

SMALL TREES FOR PATIOS AND GARDENS
Evergreen

Chamaecyparis obtusa
HINOKI FALSE CYPRESS
☼ ◑ ● ⚡ 31, 32, 34–45   p. 179

Juniperus (several)
JUNIPER
☼ ◑ ● ● ⚡ ZONES VARY   p. 275

Ligustrum lucidum
GLOSSY PRIVET
☼ ◑ ● ⚡ 31, 32   p. 290

Photinia fraseri
REDTIP
☼ ● ● ⚡ 31, 32   p. 349

Pinus densiflora 'Umbraculifera'
TANYOSHO PINE
☼ ● ● ⚡ 32, 34–41   p. 352

Pinus mugo mugo
MUGHO PINE
☼ ● ● ⚡ 32, 34–45   p. 352

Thuja occidentalis
AMERICAN ARBORVITAE
☼ ◑ ● ● ⚡ 32, 34–45   p. 425

Trochodendron aralioides
WHEEL TREE
☼ ◑ ● ⚡ 32, 34, 39   p. 431

MEDIUM SIZE TREES
Deciduous

Acer davidii
DAVID'S MAPLE
☼ ◑ ● ⚡ 32, 34, 39   p. 116

Aesculus carnea
RED HORSECHESTNUT
☼ ● ⚡ 32, 34–45   p. 121

Albizia julibrissin
SILK TREE
☼ ◑ ● ⚡ 31, 32   p. 124

Amelanchier arborea
DOWNY SERVICEBERRY
☼ ◑ ● ● ⚡ 31, 32, 34–45   p. 128

Asimina triloba
PAWPAW
☼ ● ⚡ 31, 32, 34–41   p. 144

Broussonetia papyrifera
PAPER MULBERRY
☼ ● ● ⚡ 31, 32, 34, 39   p. 159

Carpinus
HORNBEAM
NEEDS, ZONES VARY   p. 172

Catalpa

NEEDS, ZONES VARY   p. 174

Celtis
HACKBERRY
☼ ◑ ● ⚡ ZONES VARY   p. 176

Cercidiphyllum japonicum
KATSURA TREE
☼ ◑ ● ⚡ 32, 34–41   p. 178

Cladrastis lutea
YELLOW WOOD
☼ ● ⚡ 31, 32, 34–45   p. 186

Cornus controversa
GIANT DOGWOOD
☼ ◑ ● ⚡ 31, 32, 34   p. 194

Diospyros kaki
PERSIMMON
☼ ● ● ⚡ 31, 32   p. 345

Eucommia ulmoides
HARDY RUBBER TREE
☼ ● ⚡ 31, 32, 34–41   p. 226

Firmiana simplex
CHINESE PARASOL TREE
☼ ◑ ● ⚡ 31, 32   p. 232

Fraxinus holotricha
ASH
☼ ● ● ⚡ 31, 32, 34–41   p. 234

Gleditisia triacanthos inermis
HONEY LOCUST
☼ ● ● ⚡ 32, 34–43   p. 242

Laburnum
GOLDENCHAIN TREE
☼ ◑ ● ⚡ ZONES VARY   p. 282

Maackia amurensis

☼ ● ⚡ 32, 34–43   p. 301

Maclura pomifera
OSAGE ORANGE
☼ ● ● ⚡ 31, 32, 34–41   p. 301

Magnolia (many)

☼ ◑ ● ⚡ ZONES VARY   p. 302

Nyssa sylvatica
SOUR GUM
☼ ● ● ● ⚡ 31, 32, 34–43   p. 327

Ostrya
HOP HORNBEAM
☼ ◑ ● ● ⚡ ZONES VARY   p. 331

Oxydendrum arboreum
SOURWOOD, SORREL TREE
☼ ● ⚡ 31, 32, 34, 37, 39   p. 332

Phellodendron
CORK TREE
☼ ● ⚡ ZONES VARY   p. 347

Populus tremula
EUROPEAN ASPEN
☼ ● ⚡ 35–45   p. 363

Prunus
FLOWERING CHERRY
☼ ● ● ⚡ ZONES VARY   p. 368

Pseudolarix
GOLDEN LARCH
☼ ● ⚡ 32, 34–41   p. 371

Pyrus calleryana
ORNAMENTAL PEAR
☼ ◑ ● ⚡ 31, 32, 34–41   p. 375

Sassafras albidum

☼ ◑ ● ⚡ 31, 32, 34–41   p. 401

Sophora japonica
JAPANESE PAGODA TREE
☼ ◑ ● ⚡ 31, 32. 34–41   p. 410

Sorbus alnifolia
KOREAN MOUNTAIN ASH
☼ ◑ ● ● ⚡ ZONES 32, 34–43 p. 410

Sorbus aucuparia
EUROPEAN MOUNTAIN ASH, ROWAN
☼ ◑ ● ● ⚡ 34–43   p. 410

Stewartia pseudocamellia

☼ ◑ ● ⚡ 32, 34, 39   p. 415

Styrax

☼ ◑ ● ⚡ ZONES VARY   p. 418

Tilia (several)
LINDEN
☼ ● ⚡ ZONES VARY   p. 427

MEDIUM SIZE TREES
Evergreen

Abies (some)

☼ ◑ ● ● ⚡ ZONES VARY   p. 114

Cryptomeria japonica

☼ ● ⚡ 32, 34–41   p. 200

Ilex (many)
HOLLY
☼ ◑ ● ⚡ ZONES VARY   p. 265

Juniperus virginiana
JUNIPER
☼ ● ● ● ⚡ ZONES VARY   p. 275

Picea (several)
SPRUCE
☼ ◑ ● ● ● ⚡ ZONES VARY   p. 350

Pinus (several)
PINE
☼ ● ● ⚡ ZONES VARY   p. 352

Platycladus orientalis
ORIENTAL ARBORVITAE
☼ ● ● ⚡ 31, 32, 34–41   p. 356

Thuja occidentalis
AMERICAN ARBORVITAE
☼ ◑ ● ⚡ 32, 34–45   p. 425

Torreya
KAYA
☼ ◑ ● ⚡ 31, 32, 34–41   p. 429

Tsuga
HEMLOCK
☼ ◑ ● ● ⚡ ZONES VARY   p. 432

For growing symbol explanations, please see page 47.

LARGE LANDSCAPE TREES
Deciduous

Acer negundo
BOX ELDER
☼ ◐ ● ● ✎ 31, 32, 34–45   **p. 116**

Acer nigrum
BLACK MAPLE
☼ ◐ ● ● ✎ 35-45   **p. 116**

Acer platanoides
NORWAY MAPLE
☼ ◐ ● ● ✎ 31, 32, 34–45   **p. 116**

Acer saccharum
SUGAR MAPLE
☼ ◐ ● ● ✎ 32, 34–45   **p. 116**

Betula
BIRCH
☼ ● ● ● ✎ ZONES VARY   **p. 155**

Carya ovata
SHAGBARK HICKORY
☼ ● ● ✎ 31, 32, 34–44   **p. 173**

Castanea mollissima
CHINESE CHESTNUT
☼ ● ● ✎ 31, 32 34–43   **p. 173**

Fagus sylvatica
EUROPEAN BEECH
☼ ◐ ● ● ● ✎ 32, 34–43   **p. 229**

Fraxinus americana
WHITE ASH
☼ ● ● ✎ 31, 32, 34–43   **p. 234**

Fraxinus excelsior
EUROPEAN ASH
☼ ● ● ✎ 31, 32, 34–43   **p. 234**

Gymnocladus dioica
KENTUCKY COFFEE TREE
☼ ● ● ✎ 32, 34–43   **p. 248**

Kalopanax septemlobus
CASTOR ARALIA
☼ ● ✎ 32, 34–41   **p. 280**

Larix laricina
AMERICAN LARCH
☼ ✎ 37–45   **p. 285**

Liquidambar
SWEET GUM
☼ ● ✎ ZONES VARY   **p. 294**

Liriodendron tulipifera
TULIP TREE
☼ ● ● ✎ 31, 32, 34–41   **p. 294**

Magnolia acuminata
CUCUMBER TREE
☼ ● ● ✎ 31, 32, 34–43   **p. 302**

Metasequoia glyptostroboides
DAWN REDWOOD
☼ ● ✎ 31, 32, 34–41   **p. 316**

Paulownia tomentosa
EMPRESS TREE
☼ ◐ ● ● ✎ 31, 32, 34, 35, 37, 39 **p. 337**

Pistacia chinensis
CHINESE PISTACHE
☼ ● ✎ 31, 32   **p. 352**

Platanus acerifolia
LONDON PLANE TREE
☼ ◐ ● ✎ 31, 32, 34–41   **p. 356**

Platanus occidentalis
SYCAMORE
☼ ◐ ● ✎ 31, 32, 34–43   **p. 356**

Populus alba
WHITE POPLAR
☼ ● ✎ 31, 32, 34–45   **p. 363**

Populus tremula
EUROPEAN ASPEN
☼ ✎ 35–45   **p. 363**

Pterocarya fraxinifolia
CAUCASIAN WINGNUT
☼ ● ✎ 31, 32, 34–41   **p. 372**

Quercus acutissima
SAWTOOTH OAK
☼ ● ✎ 31, 32, 34–41   **p. 375**

Quercus alba
WHITE OAK
☼ ● ✎ 31, 32, 34–43   **p. 375**

Quercus coccinea
SCARLET OAK
☼ ● ✎ 31, 32, 34–41   **p. 375**

Quercus palustris
PIN OAK
☼ ● ✎ 31, 32, 34–43   **p. 375**

Quercus velutina
BLACK OAK
☼ ● ✎ 31, 32, 34–43   **p. 375**

Robinia pseudoacacia
BLACK LOCUST
☼ ● ✎ 31, 32, 34–43   **p. 385**

Salix alba
WHITE WILLOW
☼ ● ● ✎ 31, 32, 34–45   **p. 395**

Taxodium distichum
BALD CYPRESS
☼ ● ● ● ✎ 31, 32, 34–45   **p. 422**

Tilia tomentosa
SILVER LINDEN
☼ ● ✎ 32, 34–43   **p. 427**

Ulmus (several)
ELM
☼ ● ✎ ZONES VARY   **p. 435**

Walnut
☼ ● ✎ ZONES VARY   **p. 442**

Zelkova serrata
SAWLEAF ZELKOVA
☼ ● ● ✎ 31, 32, 34–41   **p. 447**

LARGE LANDSCAPE TREES
Evergreen

Abies concolor
WHITE FIR
☼ ◐ ● ● ✎ 32, 34–43   **p. 114**

Abies homolepis
NIKKO FIR
☼ ◐ ● ● ✎ 32, 34, 36–38   **p. 114**

Abies veitchii
VEITCH FIR
☼ ◐ ● ● ✎ 32, 34–41   **p. 114**

Cedrus atlantica
ATLAS CEDAR
☼ ● ✎ 31, 32, 34   **p. 175**

Cedrus deodara
DEODOR CEDAR
☼ ✎ 31, 32   **p. 175**

Chamaecyparis lawsoniana
PORT ORFORD CEDAR
☼ ◐ ● ✎ 31, 32, 34–41   **p. 179**

Chamaecyparis nootkatensis
NOOTKA CYPRESS
☼ ◐ ● ✎ 31, 32, 34–43   **p. 179**

Chamaecyparis thyoides
WHITE CEDAR
☼ ● ✎ 31, 32, 34, 36–42   **p. 179**

Cunninghamia
CHINA FIR
☼ ● ✎ 31, 32   **p. 200**

Cupressocyparis leylandii
LEYLAND CYPRESS
☼ ● ✎ 31, 32, 34, 39   **p. 201**

Picea abies
NORWAY SPRUCE
☼ ● ✎ 32, 34–45   **p. 350**

Picea glauce
WHITE PRUCE
☼ ● ● ✎ 35–45   **p. 350**

Pinus densiflora
JAPANESE RED PINE
☼ ● ● ✎ 32, 34–41   **p. 352**

Pinus strobus
WHITE PINE
☼ ● ● ✎ 32, 34–41   **p. 352**

Pinus sylvestris
SCOTCH PINE
☼ ● ● ✎ 32, 34–45   **p. 352**

Pinus thunbergiana
JAPANESE BLACK PINE
☼ ● ● ✎ 32, 34–37, 39   **p. 352**

Pinus wallichiana
HIMALAYAN WHITE PINE
☼ ● ● ✎ 32, 34, 37, 39   **p. 352**

Pseudotsuga menziesii glauca
DOUGLAS FIR
☼ ◐ ● ● ✎ 34–43   **p. 371**

Sciadopitys verticillata
UMBRELLA PINE
☼ ◐ ● ● ✎ 32, 34–37, 39   **p. 403**

Thuja plicata
WESTERN RED CEDAR
☼ ● ✎ 32, 34–37, 39   **p. 425**

Tsuga canadensis
CANADA HEMLOCK
☼ ◐ ● ✎ 32, 34–43   **p. 432**

Tsuga caroliniana
CAROLINA HEMLOCK
☼ ● ✎ 32, 34–41   **p. 432**

Fagus

Liriodendron tulipifera

Platanus

Sciadopitys

Tsuga canadensis

VINES AND
Vinelike Plants

Vines are some of the most tractable of plants. Unlike shrubs and trees, which have fairly rigid stems, the flexible stems of most vines can be guided to grow where you want them. You can train a vine to grow upward or outward (or both) on a flat, vertical surface; up and around a post or tree trunk; or up and over a pergola. Many will perform alternative duty as a ground cover.

Though vines are all tractable and long-limbed, they climb in different manners: some with tendrils, some by twining, some by clinging. Some have no means of attachment at all; they will climb only if you tie them to a support.

Clematis jackmanii

Grape

Hydrangea anomala

Lonicera

Euonymus fortunei

Hedera helix

Ampelopsis brevipedunculata

Campsis radicans

EVERGREEN

Anisostichus capreolata
CROSSVINE
☼ ◑ ♦ ✂ 31, 32, 34, 39 — p. 133

Clematis armandii
EVERGREEN CLEMATIS
☼ ♦ ✂ 31, 32 — p. 187

Euonymus fortunei
☼ ◑ ● ♦ ♦ ✂ 31, 32, 34–41 — p. 226

Hedera (many)
IVY
☼ ◑ ● ♦ ♦ ✂ ZONES VARY — p. 250

Jasminum officinale
JASMINE
☼ ◑ ♦ ✂ ALL ZONES — p. 274

Lonicera henryi
HENRY HONEYSUCKLE
☼ ◑ ♦ ✂ 31, 32, 34–43 — p. 297

DECIDUOUS

Actinidia arguta
KIWI
☼ ◑ ♦ ● ✂ 31, 32, 34–41 — p. 120

Actinidia kolomikta
KIWI
☼ ◑ ♦ ● ✂ 31, 32, 34–43 — p. 120

Actinidia polygama
SILVER VINE
☼ ◑ ♦ ● ✂ 31, 32, 34–43 — p. 120

Akebia quinata
FIVELEAF AKEBIA
☼ ◑ ● ♦ ✂ 31, 32, 34–43 — p. 124

Ampelopsis brevipedunculata
PORCELAIN BERRY
☼ ◑ ♦ ● ♦ ✂ 31, 32, 34–43 — p. 129

Aristolochia macrophylla
DUTCHMAN'S PIPE
☼ ● ♦ ● ✂ 31, 32, 34–43 — p. 141

Campsis
TRUMPET VINE
☼ ◑ ♦ ● ✂ ZONES VARY — p. 168

Celastrus
BITTERSWEET
☼ ♦ ✂ ZONES VARY — p. 176

Clematis (most)
☼ ♦ ✂ ZONES VARY — p. 187

Clerodendrum thomsoniae
GLORYBOWER
● ♦ ✂ ALL ZONES — p. 189

Clerodendrum trichotomum
HARLEQUIN GLORYBOWER
◑ ♦ ✂ 31, 32, 34–43 — p. 189

Decumaria barbara
CLIMBING HYDRANGEA
◑ ● ♦ ✂ 31, 32, 34, 39 — p. 208

Grape
☼ ♦ ✂ ZONES VARY — p. 244

Hydrangea anomala
CLIMBING HYDRANGEA
☼ ◑ ♦ ✂ 31, 32, 34–41 — p. 262

Lathyrus latifolius
PERENNIAL SWEET PEA
☼ ◑ ♦ ✂ 31, 32, 34–45 — p. 285

Lonicera (many)
HONEYSUCKLE
☼ ◑ ♦ ● ✂ ZONES VARY — p. 297

For growing symbol explanations, please see page 47.

Parthenocissus quinquefolia

Rosa

Wisteria frutescens

Dolichos lablab

Lonicera heckrotti
GOLDFLAME HONEYSUCKLE
☼ ◑ ◌ ⚡ 31, 32, 34–41   p. 297

Lonicera pericylnenum
WOODBINE HONEYSUCKLE
☼ ◑ ◌ ⚡ 31, 32, 34–41   p. 297

Lonicera sempervirens
TRUMPET HONEYSUCKLE
☼ ◑ ◌ ⚡ 31, 32, 34–43   p. 297

Lonicera tellmanniana
TELLMAN HONEYSUCKLE
☼ ◑ ◌ ⚡ 31, 32, 34   p. 297

Lycium chinense
MATRIMONY VINE
☼ ◌ ◐ ⚡ 31, 32, 34   p. 299

Menispermum canadense
CANADA MOONSEED
☼ ◑ ◌ ⚡ ZONES 32, 34–41   p. 315

Parthenocissus henryana
SILVERVEIN CREEPER
☼ ◑ ● ◌ ⚡ 31, 32   p. 336

Parthenocissus quinquefolia
VIRGINIA CREEPER
☼ ◑ ● ◌ ⚡ 31, 32, 34–43   p. 336

Passiflora incarnata
WILD PASSION VINE, MAYPOP
☼ ◌ ● ⚡ 31, 32, 34, 39   p. 336

Polygonum aubertii
SILVER LACE VINE
☼ ● ⚡ 31, 32, 34–41   p. 361

Rosa (climbers)
ROSE
NEEDS, ZONES VARY   p. 386

Schisandra chinensis
CHINESE MAGNOLIA VINE
☼ ◑ ● ⚡ ZONES 32, 34–43   p. 403

Schizophragma hydrangeoides
JAPANESE HYDRANGEA VINE
◑ ● ⚡ 31, 32, 34, 39   p. 403

Vitis (several)
ORNAMENTAL GRAPE
☼ ◑ ● ⚡ ZONES VARY   p. 244

Wisteria
☼ ◌ ● ⚡ ZONES VARY   p. 444

ANNUALS

Allamanda
☼ ● ⚡ ALL ZONES   p. 125

Asarina
CLIMBING SNAPDRAGON
☼ ◑ ● ⚡ ALL ZONES   p. 144

Bean, scarlet runner
☼ ● ⚡ ALL ZONES   p. 152

Cardiospermum halicacabum
LOVE IN A PUFF
☼ ● ⚡ ALL ZONES   p. 169

Cobaea scandens
CUP-AND-SAUCER VINE
☼ ● ⚡ ALL ZONES   p. 189

Dolichos lablab
HYACINTH BEAN
☼ ● ⚡ ALL ZONES   p. 213

Humulus lupulus
COMMON HOP
☼ ● ⚡ ALL ZONES   p. 261

Ipomoea alba
MOONFLOWER
☼ ● ● ⚡ ALL ZONES   p. 269

Ipomoea batatas
SWEET POTATO VINE
☼ ● ● ⚡ ALL ZONES   p. 269

Ipomoea lobata (Mina lobata)
SPANISH FLAG, EXOTIC LOVE
☼ ● ● ⚡ ALL ZONES   p. 269

Ipomoea multifida
CARDINAL CLIMBER
☼ ● ● ⚡ ALL ZONES   p. 269

Ipomoea nil
MORNING GLORY
☼ ● ● ⚡ ALL ZONES   p. 269

Ipomoea quamoclit
CYPRESS VINE
☼ ● ● ⚡ ALL ZONES   p. 269

Ipomoea tricolor
MORNING GLORY
☼ ● ● ⚡ ALL ZONES   p. 269

Lagenaria siceraria
GOURDS
☼ ● ⚡ ALL ZONES   p. 283

Lathyrus odoratus
SWEET PEA
☼ ● ● ⚡ ALL ZONES   p. 285

Mandevilla
☼ ◑ ● ◌ ⚡ ALL ZONES   p. 312

Momordica charantia
BITTER MELON
☼ ● ⚡ ALL ZONES   p. 318

Passiflora (several)
PASSION VINE
☼ ● ● ⚡ ALL ZONES   p. 336

Rhodochiton atrosanguineum
PURPLE BELLS, PURPLE BELL VINE
☼ ● ⚡ ALL ZONES   p. 380

Thunbergia alata
BLACK-EYED SUSAN VINE
☼ ◑ ● ⚡ ALL ZONES   p. 426

Tropaeolum majus
NASTURTIUM
NEEDS VARY, ALL ZONES   p. 432

Tropaeolum peregrinum
CANARY CREEPER
☼ ◑ ● ⚡ ALL ZONES   p. 432

Vinca major
◑ ● ● ⚡ ALL ZONES   p. 441

Ipomoea lobata

Passiflora

Thunbergia alata

Tropaeolum majus

GROUND COVERS AND LAWN SUBSTITUTES

Ajuga pyramidalis 'Metallica Crispa'

Arabis

Arenaria verna

Bamboo

GROUND COVERS AND *Lawn Substitutes*

Lawn is unsurpassed as a surface to walk and play on. But where foot traffic is infrequent or undesirable, many other plants can offer much of a lawn's neatness and uniformity with considerably less maintenance. Some ground covers spread by underground runners or roots as they grow. Others grow from clumps and must be planted close together to achieve the effect of a ground cover. Not all of them are low mats; the taller ones function as barriers rather than carpets.

GROUND COVERS

Abelia grandiflora 'Prostrata'
☼ ◐ ⬤ ╱ 32, 34, 35   p. 114

Aegopodium podagraria
BISHOP'S WEED
☼ ◐ ⬤ ⬤ ╱ 31, 32, 34–45   p. 121

Ajuga reptans
CARPET BUGLE
☼ ◐ ⬤ ╱ 31, 32, 34–45   p. 123

Anemone nemorosa
WOOD ANEMONE
☼ ◐ ⬤ ⬤ ╱ 31, 32, 34–43   p. 131

Antennaria
PUSSYTOES
☼ ⬤ ⬤ ╱ 36–45   p. 133

Arabis
ROCKCRESS
☼ ⬤ ╱ ZONES VARY   p. 139

Arctostaphylos uva-ursi
BEARBERRY
☼ ◐ ⬤ ╱ 34, 36–45   p. 140

Arenaria montana
SANDWORT
☼ ◐ ⬤ ╱ 32, 34–45   p. 140

Armeria maritima
COMMON THRIFT
☼ ⬤ ╱ 34–43   p. 141

Aronia melanocarpa
BLACK CHOKEBERRY
☼ ◐ ⬤ ⬤ ╱ 31, 32, 34–43   p. 142

Artemisia (several)
☼ ⬤ ╱ ZONES VARY   p. 142

Asarum
WILD GINGER
◐ ⬤ ⬤ ⬤ ╱ ZONES VARY   p. 144

Aurinia saxatilis
BASKET-OF-GOLD
☼ ⬤ ╱ 32, 34–43   p. 148

Bamboo (some)
☼ ◐ ⬤ ⬤ ╱ ZONES VARY   p. 149

Begonia grandis
HARDY BEGONIA
◐ ⬤ ⬤ ╱ 31, 32, 34, 39   p. 153

Bergenia
☼ ◐ ⬤ ╱ 31, 32, 34–45   p. 154

Brunnera macrophylla
☼ ◐ ⬤ ╱ 31, 32, 34–45   p. 160

Calluna vulgaris (some)
SCOTCH HEATHER
☼ ⬤ ╱ 34–43   p. 165

Carex (several)
SEDGE
☼ ◐ ⬤ ⬤ ╱ 31, 32, 34–45   p. 169

Cerastium tomentosum
SNOW-IN-SUMMER
☼ ◐ ⬤ ╱ 32, 34–45   p. 178

Ceratostigma plumbaginoides
DWARF PLUMBAGO
☼ ◐ ⬤ ╱ 32, 34–41   p. 178

Chelone lyonii
☼ ◐ ⬤ ⬤ ╱ 31, 32, 34–43   p. 180

Chrysanthemum pacificum
GOLD AND SILVER CHRYSANTHEMUM
☼ ◐ ⬤ ╱ 31, 32, 34–41   p. 183

Begonia grandis

Calluna vulgaris 'Corbett's Red'

Carex flacca

Chelone lyonii

For growing symbol explanations, please see page 47.

Epimedium alpinum

Geranium cinereum var. incana

Hedera colchica

Helleborus argutifolius

Chrysogonum virginianum
GOLDEN STAR
☼ ☼ ● ✿ 31, 32, 34–39   p. 185

Conradina verticillata
CUMBERLAND ROSEMARY
☼ ● ✿ 31, 32   p. 191

Convallaria majalis
LILY-OF-THE-VALLEY
☼ ☼ ● ✿ 31, 32, 34–45   p. 191

Cornus canadensis
BUNCHBERRY
☼ ☼ ● ● ✿ 32, 34–45   p. 194

Coronilla varia
CROWN VETCH
☼ ● ✿ 31, 32, 34–45   p. 195

Cotoneaster (some)
☼ ● ✿ ZONES VARY   p. 196

Cymbalaria muralis
KENILWORTH IVY
☼ ● ● ✿ 31, 32, 34, 39   p. 202

Delosperma
ICE PLANT
☼ ● ✿ ZONES VARY   p. 208

Dryas
☼ ● ✿ 36–45   p. 215

Dryopteris erythrosora
AUTUMN FERN
☼ ● ● ✿ 31, 32, 34–41   p. 215

Duchesnea indica
INDIAN MOCK STRAWBERRY
☼ ☼ ● ● ✿ 31, 32, 34–43   p. 216

Epimedium
☼ ● ✿ 31, 32, 34–43   p. 220

Erica (some)
HEATH
☼ ☼ ● ✿ ZONES VARY   p. 221

Euonymus fortunei (some)
☼ ☼ ● ● ● ✿ 31, 32, 34–41   p. 226

Euphorbia cyparissias
☼ ☼ ● ✿ 31, 32, 34–43   p. 227

Festuca
FESCUE
☼ ● ✿ 31, 32, 34–45   p. 230

Forsythia 'Arnold Dwarf'
F. INTERMEDIA 'GOLDTIDE'
☼ ● ● ✿ 31, 32, 34–41   p. 232

Galax urceolata
● ● ● ✿ 31, 32, 34–43   p. 236

Galium odoratum
SWEET WOODRUFF
● ● ● ✿ 31, 32, 34–43   p. 236

Gaultheria procumbens
● ● ✿ 32, 34–45   p. 236

Genista (some)
BROOM
☼ ● ✿ ZONES VARY   p. 237

Geranium (some)
CRANESBILL
☼ ● ● ✿ ZONES VARY   p. 238

Glechoma hederacea
GROUND IVY
☼ ☼ ● ● ✿ 31, 32, 34–45   p. 242

Gypsophila repens
☼ ● ✿ 31, 32, 34–43   p. 248

Hedera
IVY
☼ ☼ ● ● ● ✿ ZONES VARY   p. 250

Helleborus orientalis
LENTEN ROSE
● ● ● ● ✿ 31, 32, 34–41   p. 253

Heuchera americana cultivars
☼ ☼ ● ✿ 32, 34–43   p. 256

Hosta
PLANTAIN LILY
● ● ● ✿ 31, 32, 34–45   p. 259

Houttuynia cordata 'Variegata'
☼ ☼ ● ● ● ● ✿ 31, 32, 34–41   p. 260

Iberis sempervirens
EVERGREEN CANDYTUFT
☼ ● ✿ 31, 32, 34–45   p. 264

Juniperus (low-growing)
JUNIPER
☼ ☼ ● ● ✿ ZONES VARY   p. 275

Lamium maculatum (several)
DEAD NETTLE
☼ ● ● ✿ 32, 34–43   p. 284

Liriope spicata
CREEPING LILY TURF
☼ ● ● ● ✿ 32, 34, 39   p. 295

Lysimachia
☼ ☼ ● ✿ ZONES VARY   p. 300

Mazus reptans
☼ ☼ ● ✿ 31, 32, 34, 39   p. 314

Microbiota decussata
SIBERIAN CARPET CYPRESS
☼ ☼ ● ✿ 32, 34–45   p. 317

Nierembergia
CUP FLOWER
☼ ● ✿ ALL ZONES   p. 326

Oenothera (many)
EVENING PRIMROSE
NEEDS, ZONES VARY   p. 327

Omphalodes verna
BLUE-EYED MARY
☼ ● ✿ 31, 32, 34–41   p. 328

Ophiopogon japonicus
MONDO GRASS
☼ ● ✿ 32   p. 295

Microbiota decussata

Nierembergia hippomanica 'Mont Blanc'

Oenothera macrocarpa

Omphalodes cappadocica

Plant listings continue ▶

GROUND COVERS AND LAWN SUBSTITUTES

Paxystima canbyi

Phlox pilosa

Polygonatum biflorum

Pulmonaria angustifolia

Origanum (some)
ZONES VARY — p. 329

Pachysandra terminalis
JAPANESE SPURGE
31, 32, 34–43 — p. 332

Parthenocissus quinquefolia
VIRGINIA CREEPER
31, 32, 34–43 — p. 336

Paxistima canbyi
32, 34–43 — p. 337

Phlox (mat-forming)
ZONES VARY — p. 348

Polygonatum biflorum
SOLOMON'S SEAL
31, 32, 34–43 — p. 361

Polygonum (several)
KNOTWEED
NEEDS, ZONES VARY — p. 361

Potentilla (several)
CINQUEFOIL
ZONES VARY — p. 364

Prunella
SELF-HEAL
31, 32, 34–43 — p. 367

Pulmonaria (several)
LUNGWORT
32, 34–43 — p. 373

Pyracantha (low-growing)
FIRETHORN
ZONES VARY — p. 374

Ranunculus repens 'Pleniflorus'
CREEPING BUTTERCUP
31, 32, 34–43 — p. 377

Rhus aromatica 'Gro-low'
31, 32, 34–43 — p. 384

Rosa (some)
NEEDS, ZONES VARY — p. 386

Rubus calycinoides
'EMERALD CARPET'
32 — p. 393

Saponaria ocymoides
34–45 — p. 400

Sarcococca hookeriana humilis
SWEET BOX
31, 32 — p. 400

Saxifraga
SAXIFRAGE
NEEDS, ZONES VARY — p. 402

Sedum (many)
STONECROP
NEEDS, ZONES VARY — p. 404

Smilacina racemosa
FALSE SOLOMON'S SEAL
31, 32, 34–43 — p. 409

Spiraea japonica 'Alpina'
DAPHNE SPIRAEA
32, 34–41 — p. 412

Stephanandra incisa 'Crispa'
32, 34–43 — p. 414

Taxus baccata 'Repandens'
SPREADING ENGLISH YEW
32, 34 — p. 422

Teucrium chamaedrys
GERMANDER
31, 32, 34, 39 — p. 423

Thymus
THYME
31, 32, 34–43 — p. 426

Tiarella cordifolia
FOAMFLOWER
32, 34–43 — p. 426

Tolmiea menziesii
PIGGY-BACK PLANT
31, 32, 34, 39 — p. 427

Vaccinium vitis-idaea
COWBERRY
32, 34–41 — p. 436

Verbena
ZONES VARY — p. 437

Veronica (several)
SPEEDWELL
NEEDS, ZONES VARY — p. 438

Vinca
PERIWINKLE
ZONES VARY — p. 441

Viola (several)
VIOLET
NEEDS, ZONES VARY — p. 441

Viola labradorica
31, 32, 34–45 — p. 441

Waldsteinia fragarioides
BARREN STRAWBERRY
32, 34–41 — p. 442

Xanthorhiza simplicissima
YELLOWROOT
32, 34–43 — p. 445

WALK-ON LAWN SUBSTITUTES

Carex flacca
BLUE SEDGE
31, 32, 34–45 — p. 169

Chamaemelum nobile
CHAMOMILE
31, 32, 34–43 — p. 179

Sagina subulata
IRISH MOSS, SCOTCH MOSS
32, 34–43 — p. 395

Zoysia tenuifolia
KOREAN GRASS
31, 32, 34, 39 — p. 448

Rubus calycinoides

Smilacina

Tolmiea menziesii 'Taff's Gold'

Chamaemelum nobile

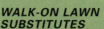

For growing symbol explanations, please see page 47.

Plants for HEDGES AND SCREENS

Berberis thunbergii 'Kobold'

Caragana arborescens

Chaenomeles

Cotinus coggygria 'Purple Cloak'

Plants that maintain dense foliage from top to bottom are good candidates for providing a screen in your landscape. Some are knee-high shrublets, mainly useful for edging a walk or path; others are large shrubby trees that, grouped closely, can block an objectionable view or direct your attention to a focal point in the garden. Shearing can transform some of these plants into formal hedges; or, leave them in their natural habit for an informal look.

Ilex verticillata

Larix laricina

Lespedeza

Rosa 'Bonica'

DECIDUOUS

Acanthopanax sieboldianus 'Variegatus'
☼ ◐ ● ● ● ● 🌡 32, 34–41   **p. 115**

Acer campestre
HEDGE MAPLE
☼ ◐ ● ● 🌡 34–41   **p. 116**

Berberis thunbergii
JAPANESE BARBERRY
☼ ◐ ● ● 🌡 31, 32, 34–41   **p. 154**

Caragana arborescens
SIBERIAN PEASHRUB
☼ ● 🌡 31, 32, 34–45   **p. 169**

Carpinus betulus
EUROPEAN HORNBEAM
☼ ◐ ● 🌡 31, 32, 34–41   **p. 172**

Chaenomeles
FLOWERING QUINCE
☼ ● ● 🌡 31, 32, 34–43   **p. 179**

Cotinus (some)
☼ ● 🌡 ZONES VARY   **p. 196**

Cotoneaster (some)
☼ ● 🌡 ZONES VARY   **p. 196**

Crataegus monogyna
HAWTHORN
☼ ● 🌡 31, 32, 34–41   **p. 198**

Euonymus (some)
NEEDS, ZONES VARY   **p. 226**

Fagus sylvatica
EUROPEAN BEECH
☼ ◐ ● ● 🌡 32, 34–43   **p. 229**

Hibiscus syriacus
ROSE OF SHARON
☼ ● 🌡 31, 32, 34–41   **p. 257**

Hippophae rhamnoides
SEA BUCKTHORN
☼ ● 🌡 34, 37–45   **p. 257**

Ilex verticillata
WINTERBERRY
☼ ◐ ● 🌡 31, 32, 34–43   **p. 265**

Laburnum
LARCH
☼ ◐ ● 🌡 ZONES VARY   **p. 282**

Larix laricina
AMERICAN LARCH
☼ ● 🌡 37–45   **p. 285**

Lespedeza
BUSH CLOVER
☼ ● 🌡 ZONES VARY   **p. 288**

Ligustrum (some)
PRIVET
☼ ◐ ● 🌡 ZONES VARY   **p. 290**

Lonicera (shrubs)
HONEYSUCKLE
☼ ◐ ● 🌡 ZONES VARY   **p. 297**

Prinsepia uniflora
HEDGE PRINSEPIA
☼ ● 🌡 35–38, 40, 41   **p. 365**

Prunus laurocerasus
ENGLISH LAUREL
☼ ● ◐ 🌡 ZONES VARY   **p. 368**

Rhamnus frangula 'Columnaris'
TALLHEDGE BUCKTHORN
☼ ◐ ● 🌡 32, 34–45   **p. 379**

Rosa (shrub)
ROSE
NEEDS, ZONES VARY   **p. 386**

Plant listings continue ▶

Stephanandra incisa 'Crispa'

Cryptomeria japonica 'Globus'

Euonymus fortunei

Juniperus conferta

Salix purpurea 'Gracilis'
DWARF PURPLE OSIER
☼ ◑ ✿ 34–43   p. 395

Spiraea (some)
☼ ◑ ● ◑ ✿ ZONES VARY   p. 412

Stephanandra incisa 'Crispa'
CUT-LEAVED STEPHANANDRA
☼ ◑ ● ◑ ✿ 32, 34–43   p. 414

Syringa (most)
LILAC
☼ ● ✿ ZONES VARY   p. 420

Weigela
☼ ◑ ● ✿ 32, 34–41   p. 443

EVERGREEN

Abelia grandiflora
GLOSSY ABELIA
☼ ◑ ● ✿ 32, 34, 39   p. 114

Abies (some)
FIR
☼ ◑ ● ◑ ✿ ZONES VARY   p. 114

Bamboo (many)
☼ ◑ ● ◑ ✿ ZONES VARY   p. 149

Berberis julianae
WINTERGREEN BARBERRY
☼ ◑ ● ◑ ✿ 31, 32, 34, 39   p. 154

Buxus
BOXWOOD
☼ ◑ ● ◑ ✿ ZONES VARY   p. 162

Calocedrus decurrens
INCENSE CEDAR
☼ ◑ ● ✿ 32, 34, 36, 37   p. 165

Camellia
◑ ● ✿ 31, 32, 34   p. 166

Chamaecyparis (many)
FALSE CYPRESS
☼ ◑ ● ✿ ZONES VARY   p. 179

Cryptomeria japonica
☼ ◑ ● ✿ 32, 34–41   p. 200

Cupressocyparis leylandii
☼ ◑ ● ◑ ✿ 31, 32, 34, 39   p. 201

Elaeagnus (some)
☼ ◑ ● ◑ ✿ ZONES VARY   p. 218

Euonymus (some)
NEEDS, ZONES VARY   p. 226

Ilex
HOLLY
☼ ◑ ● ✿ ZONES VARY   p. 265

Juniperus (shrub, columnar)
JUNIPER
☼ ◑ ● ◑ ✿ ZONES VARY   p. 275

Kalmia latifolia
MOUNTAIN LAUREL
☼ ◑ ● ✿ 31, 32, 34–41   p. 280

Leucothoe
◑ ● ● ◑ ◑ ✿ ZONES VARY   p. 289

Ligustrum (some)
PRIVET
☼ ◑ ● ✿ ZONES VARY   p. 290

Mahonia (tall)
NEEDS, ZONES VARY   p. 307

Myrica cerifera
WAX MYRTLE
☼ ◑ ● ◑ ✿ 31, 32, 34, 39   p. 321

Myrica pensylvanica
BAYBERRY
☼ ◑ ● ◑ ✿ 32, 34–44   p. 321

Nandina domestica
HEAVENLY BAMBOO
☼ ◑ ● ● ◑ ✿ 31, 32   p. 322

Osmanthus heterophylls
☼ ◑ ● ◑ ✿ ZONES 31, 32   p. 330

Photinia fraseri
REDTIP
☼ ◑ ● ✿ 31, 32   p. 349

Pieris
◑ ● ✿ ZONES VARY   p. 351

Pinus (many)
PINE
☼ ◑ ● ✿ ZONES VARY   p. 352

Platycladus orientalis
ORIENTAL ARBORVITAE
☼ ◑ ● ✿ 31, 32, 34–41   p. 356

Prunus (some)
☼ ◑ ● ✿ ZONES VARY   p. 368

Pyracantha
FIRETHORN
☼ ◑ ● ✿ ZONES VARY   p. 374

Rhamnus alaternus
ITALIAN BUCKTHORN
☼ ◑ ● ✿ 31, 32   p. 379

Rhododendron (many)
◑ ● ● ✿ ZONES VARY   p. 379

Taxus
YEW
☼ ◑ ● ● ✿ ZONES VARY   p. 422

Thuja
ARBORVITAE
☼ ◑ ● ● ✿ ZONES VARY   p. 425

Tsuga canadensis
CANADA HEMLOCK
☼ ◑ ● ◑ ✿ 32, 34–43   p. 432

Viburnum (several)
NEEDS, ZONES VARY   p. 439

Ligustrum vicaryi

Pinus banksiana 'Uncle Foggy'

Taxus media 'Hatfieldii'

Thuja occidentalis 'George Peabody'

For growing symbol explanations, please see page 47.

A TO Z PLANT ENCYCLOPEDIA

Paeonia
Double Type

This encyclopedia describes a wide spectrum of plants—
from majestic trees to small, gemlike perennials for rock
gardens, from familiar summer annuals to such oddities as the devil's tongue
(*Amorphophallus*). There are also tropical plants to grow outdoors in summer
and move indoors in fall to use as winter houseplants. Many of the more than
5,000 plants included here are widely available; others are sold by specialty
nurseries or are obtainable through seed exchanges run by horticultural societies.

Plants are listed alphabetically by scientific name (genus and
species). Common fruits, vegetables, and berries are an exception;
these are listed by common name (apple or pumpkin, for example). If you know only a common name, look that up—either in
the A to Z Plant Encyclopedia or in the Index of Scientific and
Common Names—to find a reference to the plant entry.

The scientific names we use are based on the *New Royal
Horticultural Society Dictionary of Gardening* (London:
Macmillan; Portland, OR: Timber Press, Inc., 1994). We also have
consulted local plant indexes. Although some scientific names may
not be familiar to every reader, their use makes it easier for gardeners to speak a common language. (For help in understanding
scientific names, see pages 540–541).

The sample entry below illustrates the format used throughout
the encyclopedia. For the convenience of plant shoppers, former (and
perhaps better-known) scientific names are shown in parentheses
after the scientific name and are also cross-referenced. Next comes
the plant's common name or names, followed by the family name in
italics. The type of plant is described on the next line.

Climate adaptability is shown in the line that begins with ✓. The
zone numbers refer to the climate zones (explained and mapped on
pages 30–47) where the plant will grow. "Zones 32, 34–43," for
example, gives the inclusive zones for which the plant is recommended. "All zones" means the plant is an annual (or treated as
one in the Northeast) and will grow everywhere.

Recommended exposure is shown by one or more of the three
symbols indicating how much sun a plant needs for best performance. ☼ means the plant grows best with unobstructed sunlight all
day long or almost all day; you can overlook an hour or so of shade
at the beginning or end of a summer day. ◐ means that the plant
needs partial shade—shade for half the day or for at least 3 hours
during the hottest part of the day. ● indicates that a plant prefers little or no direct sunlight—for example, it does best on the north
side of a house or beneath a broad, dense-foliaged tree.

Approximate moisture needs, which can be supplied by irrigation or rainfall, are symbolized as follows. ◖ indicates the plant
thrives with less than regular moisture—moderate amounts for
some plants, little for those with greater drought tolerance. ● means
the plant performs well with regular moisture: the soil shouldn't
become too dry or too wet. ●● means the plant takes more than regular moisture; this category includes plants requiring constantly
moist soil (such as many ferns), bog plants (such as cardinal
flower), and aquatic plants (such as pickerel weed). Many plants
show a range; for example, ● ●● means the plant can take regular
moisture or wetter conditions.

If a plant or any of its parts is known to be poisonous, the toxicity is noted in the last line, next to the symbol ◊. Plants not marked
with this symbol may have poisonous parts, but their toxicity is not
well known.

The drawings that accompany the entries give a general idea of
the appearance of one or more members of a genus. Not all members will necessarily look alike, so be sure to read the individual
species descriptions.

Plant families are also included in the alphabetical listings. A
family name may be omitted if only one member of the family is
given in the plant encyclopedia; in these instances, the listed plant
adequately illustrates family characteristics. When authorities differ
on the correct names for certain plant families, we list both.

There are boxes throughout the encyclopedia offering advice on
matters such as plant selection, garden usage, planting and culture,
and harvesting.

CONSOLIDA ambigua
(Delphinium ajacis)

LARKSPUR, ANNUAL DELPHINIUM

Ranunculaceae

ANNUAL

✓ ALL ZONES

☼ FULL SUN

● REGULAR WATER

◊ ALL PARTS, ESPECIALLY SEEDS, ARE POISONOUS IF
INGESTED

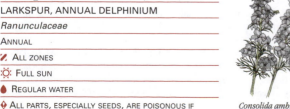

Consolida ambigua

A

ABELIA

Caprifoliaceae

EVERGREEN OR DECIDUOUS SHRUBS

ZONES VARY BY SPECIES

BEST IN SUN, TOLERATE SOME SHADE

REGULAR WATER

Abelia grandiflora

Graceful, arching branches densely clothed with oval, usually glossy leaves ½–1½ in. long; bronzy new growth. Tubular or bell-shaped flowers in clusters at ends of branches or among leaves. Though small, blossoms are plentiful enough to be showy, mostly during summer and early fall. When blooms drop, they usually leave purplish or copper-colored sepals that provide color into the fall months. Leaves also may take on bronzy tints in fall.

To keep the shrub's graceful form, prune selectively; don't shear. The more stems you cut to the ground in winter or early spring, the more open and arching next year's growth will be.

Abelias are adaptable plants, useful in shrub borders, as space dividers and visual barriers, and near house walls; lower kinds are good bank or ground covers.

A. chinensis. Deciduous. Zones 32, 34. Grows to 4–5 ft. tall with fragrant, pink-tinted white flowers in summer and fall. Exceptionally attractive to butterflies.

A. grandiflora. GLOSSY ABELIA. Evergreen to semievergreen. Zones 32, 34, 35. Hybrid of two species from China. Best known and most popular of the abelias. Grows to 8 ft. or taller; spreads to 5 ft. or wider. Flowers white or faintly tinged pink. Stems freeze at about 0°F/−18°C, but plant will usually recover to bloom the same year, making a graceful border plant 10–15 in. tall.

'Francis Mason' is a compact (3–4 ft. high and wide), densely branched variety, with pink flowers and yellow-variegated leaves. 'Golden Glow' is similar, but with entirely yellow foliage. 'John Creech' forms a dwarf mound to about 30 in. high and wide, covered from midsummer to after first frosts with white flowers that open from pink buds; makes a good ground cover. 'Prostrata' is a low-growing (1½–2-ft.), smaller-leafed variety useful as ground cover, bank planting, low foreground shrub. 'Sherwoodii' grows 3–4 ft. tall, 5 ft. wide. Hybrid 'Edward Goucher' is less hardy (Zone 32 only), lower growing (to 3–5 ft.), and lacier than its *A. grandiflora* parents, with glossy, 2-in. leaves and small trumpet-shaped flowers, lilac pink with orange throats.

ABELIOPHYLLUM distichum

WHITE FORSYTHIA

Oleaceae

DECIDUOUS SHRUB

ZONES 31, 32, 34–41

FULL SUN

REGULAR WATER

Abeliophyllum distichum

Resembles forsythia in miniature and blooms in early spring but its flowers are white, not yellow. Native to Korea and now well established in southern New England, this shrub grows to 3 ft. and features fragrant four-petaled flowers, each about ½ in. across, which cluster on thin, twiggy branches. Leaves are opposite, glossy, and look similar to those of abelia. Shows best against an evergreen background. Thrives in ordinary well-drained garden soil and requires little, if any, pruning, which can be done after the flowers fade. 'Roseum' has pale pink flowers.

ABELMOSCHUS

SILK FLOWER

Malvaceae

ANNUAL

ALL ZONES

FULL SUN

REGULAR WATER

Abelmoschus moschatus

Bushy plants resemble small tropical hibiscus. Like good garden soil, heat, and a sunny location; bloom most profusely in hot summer weather. Sow seed indoors 6 to 8 weeks before transplanting outdoors after frost danger is past (or grow from seed sown outdoors as soon as ground is warm). Flowering begins 100 days after sowing and continues to frost or cold weather.

A. manihot. SUNSET HIBISCUS. Tropical native grown as annual; grows to 7 ft.; disklike flowers of white to light yellow, to 5 in. across; palmately lobed leaves to 1½ ft. long. Self-sows in Zones 31, 32.

A. moschatus. About 1½ ft. tall and wide, with deep green, deeply cut leaves. Five-petaled, 3–4½-in. flowers, cherry red or pink, with white centers. Can be grown as houseplant in a 6-in. pot; set on a windowsill in bright light. 'Oriental Red' has red flowers; 'Oriental Pink' is pink.

ABIES

FIR

Pinaceae

EVERGREEN TREES

ZONES VARY BY SPECIES

FULL SUN OR LIGHT SHADE

REGULAR TO MODERATE WATER

Abies concolor

In nature, firs are tall, erect, symmetrical trees with uniformly spaced branch whorls. Though sometimes confused with spruces *(Picea)*, they have softer needles that fall directly from the stems (spruces leave short pegs behind), and their large cones grow up rather than down. The cones shatter after ripening, leaving a spiky stalk. Most (but not all) native firs are high-mountain plants that grow best in or near their natural environments. Some species adapt well to warmer, drier conditions.

Christmas tree farms grow native firs for cutting, and nurseries in "fir country" grow a few species for the living Christmas tree trade. Licensed collectors in the Northwest dig picturesque, contorted firs at high elevations near the timberline and market them through nurseries as "alpine conifers." Use these in rock gardens; small specimens are good container or bonsai subjects. Birds are attracted by fir seeds.

A. alba. SILVER FIR. Zones 32, 34–43. Native to central and southeastern Europe. Columnar tree to 150 ft.; dark green needles with silver underside.

A. balsamea. BALSAM FIR. Zones 36–38, 42–44. Native to northeastern U.S. Pyramidal tree to 50 ft.; dark green needles. Does not thrive in hot-summer climates, but where it is adapted, its legendary fragrance makes it a favorite for Christmas trees and wreaths. Dwarf variety 'Nana' is used as a rock garden or container plant.

A. concolor. WHITE FIR. Zones 32, 34–43. Native to mountain regions of West and Southwest, but succeeds in the humid-summer Northeast. Grows 50–70 ft. tall in gardens. Bluish green, 1–2-in.-long needles; 'Argentea' (syn. 'Candicans') is bluish white. 'Violacea' foliage is bluish white when young.

A. firma. JAPANESE FIR, MOMI FIR. Zones 32, 34. Native to Japan. Broadly pyramidal to 40–50 ft., with branches slightly above horizontal. Needles dark green above, lighter beneath. Can tolerate hot, moist climates.

A. fraseri. SOUTHERN BALSAM FIR, FRASER FIR, SOUTHERN FIR. Zones 36, 37. Native to higher, cooler elevations of the Appalachian Mountains.

Attractive pyramidal tree resembling *A. balsamea* in both looks and fragrance. Widely grown as a Christmas tree where summers are not too hot.

A. homolepis. NIKKO FIR. Zones 32, 34, 36–38. Native to Japan. Broad, dense, rather formal fir to 80 ft. Needles are densely arranged, forward pointing. Adapted to warm, moist regions.

A. koreana. KOREAN FIR. Zones 32, 34–41. Native to Korea. Slow-growing, compact, pyramidal tree seldom over 30 ft. Shiny, short green needles. Sets cones on young, small trees. 'Aurea', with gold-green foliage, is even smaller, slower growing.

A. nordmanniana. NORDMANN FIR. Zones 32, 34, 39. Native to the Caucasus, Asia Minor, Greece. Vigorous, densely foliaged fir, 30–50 ft. tall and 20 ft. wide in cultivation. Dark green, shiny, ¾–1½-in.-long needles, with whitish bands beneath, densely cover branches. Adapts well to humid mid-Atlantic states, but does best with regular water. Will submit to long-term container growing.

A. pinsapo. SPANISH FIR. Zones 32, 34, 39. Native to Spain. Thrives in warm, dry regions as well as cool, moist "fir country." Slow grower, reaching 50 ft. after many years. Thanks to its dense, symmetrical form, it's sometimes mistaken for a spruce. Stiff, deep green, ½–¾-in.-long needles are set uniformly around branches. 'Glauca' is blue gray.

A. procera (A. nobilis). NOBLE FIR. Zones 34–41. This fir will grow satisfactorily—if slowly—in the Northeast, though it performs best in its native Northwest range, where it is a narrow, graceful tree reaching well over 100 ft. in gardens. Blue-green, 1-in.-long needles; short, stiff branches. Cones 6–10 in. long, 3 in. wide, with extended bracts.

A. veitchii. VEITCH FIR. Zones 34–41. Native to Japan. Conical, fast-growing, to 70 ft., with dense, soft, glossy green needles upturned at the tips and silver on the underside. Cones 2–3 in. long, bluish gray.

ABUTILON

FLOWERING MAPLE, CHINESE BELLFLOWER, CHINESE LANTERN

Malvaceae

EVERGREEN VINE-SHRUBS

ALL ZONES

PART SHADE IN HOT-SUMMER AREAS

REGULAR TO MODERATE WATER

Abutilon hybridum

Mostly native to South America. Planted primarily for their flowers. Need good drainage. Growth rapid, coarse, and rangy; control by pinching out branch tips.

Can be used as container plants indoors in winter, out on terrace in summer. Control whitefly and scale insects with light oil spray.

A. hybridum. The best-known species. Upright, arching growth to 8–10 ft., with equal spread. Broad maplelike leaves. Drooping bell-like flowers in white, yellow, pink, and red. Main blooming season is spring, but white and yellow forms seem to bloom almost continuously.

A. megapotamicum. Leaves are arrowlike, 1½–3 in. long. Flowers resembling red-and-yellow lanterns gaily decorate the long, rangy branches in spring and summer. This vine-shrub is more graceful in detail than in entirety but can be trained to an interesting pattern. Good hanging-basket plant. 'Marianne' has superior form; 'Variegata' has leaves mottled with yellow; 'Victory' is compact and floriferous with small, deep yellow flowers.

A. pictum 'Thompsonii'. Similar to *A. hybridum* but foliage strikingly variegated with creamy yellow. Blooms almost continuously, bearing pale orange bells veined with red.

ABYSSINIAN BANANA. See ENSETE ventricosum

ABYSSINIAN SWORD LILY. See GLADIOLUS callianthus

PRACTICAL GARDENING DICTIONARY

PLEASE SEE PAGES 449–523

ACALYPHA wilkesiana (A. tricolor)

COPPER LEAF

Euphorbiaceae

TROPICAL SHRUB GROWN AS ANNUAL

ALL ZONES

FULL SUN OR PARTIAL SHADE

REGULAR TO MODERATE WATER

Acalypha hispida

Native to South Pacific Islands. Foliage more colorful than many flowers. Tropical and quite tender, it is used as an annual, substituting for flowers from late spring to frost. Or grow it in pots moved outdoors in summer, indoors in winter. Leaves to 8 in.; may be bronzy green mottled with shades of red and purple, red with crimson and bronze, or green edged with crimson and stippled with orange and red. In a warm, sheltered spot, can grow to 3 ft. or more. Container plants need fast-draining potting mix, kept slightly dry through winter.

'Marginata' has leaves edged in red, pink, or white; 'Mooreana' has broad, wavy, reddish black leaves, with copper highlights and scalloped edges; 'Obovata' has pink-edged bronzy green leaves.

Acanthaceae. The acanthus family consists of herbs and shrubs, generally from warm or tropical areas. Many have showy flowers or foliage. Examples are bear's breech *(Acanthus), Hypoestes,* and *Thunbergia.*

ACANTHOPANAX sieboldianus (Eleutherococcus sieboldianus)

Araliaceae

DECIDUOUS SHRUB

ZONES 31, 32, 34–41

SUN OR SHADE

MUCH OR LITTLE WATER

Acanthopanax sieboldianus

Grows 8–10 ft. tall and wide; erect, eventually arching stems have short thorns below each leaf. Leaves bright green, with five to seven leaflets 1–2½ in. long arranged like fingers on a hand. Clustered white flowers are small and inconspicuous, only rarely followed by clusters of small black berries. This plant's great virtues are its somewhat tropical appearance and high tolerance for difficult conditions. It can thrive in bright sun or dense shade, with much or little water, in rich or poor soil. It is remarkably tolerant of urban air pollution. 'Variegatus', a showy 6–8-ft. plant with white-bordered leaflets, is grown more often than the species.

ACANTHUS

BEAR'S BREECH

Acanthaceae

PERENNIALS

ZONES VARY BY SPECIES

FULL SUN OR PARTIAL SHADE

REGULAR TO MODERATE WATER

Acanthus mollis

Spreading, clump-forming perennials with basal clusters of deeply lobed and cut leaves, and rigid spikes of tubular flowers. Cut them back after flowering. To keep foliage through summer, cut off flower stalks and soak roots occasionally. Plantings are very vigorous on the West Coast, but better behaved in the Northeast. If necessary, divide crowded clumps in spring, handling with great care. Acanthus is effective with bamboo, large-leafed ferns.

A. mollis. Zone 32. Native to southern Europe. Fast-growing to 5 ft. high. Leaves are lobed and deeply cut, shining dark green, to 2 ft. long. In late spring or early summer, 1½-ft. spikes of whitish, lilac, or rose flowers with spiny green or purplish bracts top 2–3-ft. stems. Variety 'Oak Leaf' is very similar to species; 'Latifolius' has larger leaves, is hardier.

A. spinosus. Zones 31, 32, 34, 39. Native from Italy to western Turkey and hardier than *A. mollis*. Grows to 5 ft. high, with leaves cut almost to the midrib and spiny-edged. Tall spikes of tubular white flowers with purple bracts bloom in late spring to midsummer.

A. 'Summer Beauty'. Zones 31, 32, 34, 39. Recent introduction of hybrid origin (probably *A. mollis × A. spinosus*). Very vigorous in hot-summer areas, producing 6-ft.-wide clumps of shiny dark green leaves. White flowers with purple calyces on 6-ft.-tall stems.

ACER

MAPLE

Aceraceae

DECIDUOUS OR EVERGREEN TREES OR SHRUBS

ZONES VARY BY SPECIES

FULL SUN OR PARTIAL SHADE

REGULAR TO MODERATE WATER

Acer palmatum

When you talk about maples, you're talking about many trees—large and midsize deciduous shade trees; smaller evergreen and deciduous trees; and dainty, picturesque shrub-trees. Maples of one type or another will grow over much of the country, the limiting factors being heat, dryness, and lack of winter cold. For a good fall leaf display, look for a maple that colors well in your area; visit local nurseries while the foliage is changing hue.

All maples prefer well-drained soil but must have moisture available in the root zone throughout their leafy period. Most have shallow, competitive roots, and the sizable ones cast dense shade; it's not easy to maintain a garden beneath them. They are subject to various problems, including anthracnose and verticillium wilt.

A. buergeranum. TRIDENT MAPLE. Deciduous tree. Zones 32, 34, 39. Native to China, Japan. Grows 20–25 ft. high. Roundish crown of 3-in.-wide, glossy, three-lobed leaves that are pale beneath. Fall color usually red, sometimes orange or yellow. Attractive flaking bark on older wood. Low, spreading growth; stake and prune to make it branch high. A decorative, useful patio tree and favorite bonsai subject.

A. campestre. HEDGE MAPLE. Deciduous tree. Zones 32, 34–41. Native to Europe, western Asia. Slow growing to 70 ft., seldom over 30 ft. in cultivation. Usually rounded, dense habit. Leaves 2–4 in. wide, with three to five lobes, dull green above; turn yellow in fall. 'Queen Elizabeth' has glossier foliage, more erect habit. 'Compactum', Zones 32, 34, is a densely branched, dwarf form, slightly broader than tall, ranging from 2–4 ft. high at maturity amd spreading 3–5 ft. Less hardy than the species.

A. capillipes. Deciduous tree. Zones 32, 34–41. Native to Japan. Moderate growth rate to 30 ft. Young branches red, turning brown with white stripes with age. Young leaves red; leafstalks and midribs red. Shallowly three-lobed leaves, 3–5 in. long; turn scarlet in fall. In warmer climates, does best in part shade.

A. cappadocicum. COLISEUM MAPLE. Deciduous tree. Zones 31, 32, 34, 39. Native to western Asia. Known here in its variety 'Rubrum', red coliseum maple. Grows to 35 ft.; forms compact, rounded crown. Leaves with five to seven lobes, 5½ in. wide. Bright red spring foliage turns rich dark green.

A. carpinifolium. HORNBEAM MAPLE. Deciduous tree. Zones 32, 34–41. Native to Japan. Grows from 20 to 30 ft. in height with a rounded or vase-shaped crown spreading as far. Bears dark green, oval leaves with toothed margins unlike those typical of maples. Good golden brown fall color. Attractive, smooth gray bark. Tiny, greenish flowers in spring. Best in

moist, well-drained soil with some shade. A good understory tree for the shade garden.

A. circinatum. VINE MAPLE. Deciduous shrub or small tree to about 25 ft. Zones 31, 32, 34, 39. Spreading, with one or several trunks. Leaves nearly circular, to 6 in. across, with 5–11 lobes; red tinted when new, light green as they mature, then orange, scarlet, or yellow in fall. Tiny reddish purple spring flowers are followed by red winged seeds. 'Monroe' has deeply cut foliage.

A. crataegifolium. HAWTHORN MAPLE. Deciduous tree. Zones 32, 34, 39. Native to Japan. Small, 25- to 30-ft. tall tree with a rounded, spreading crown. Bears rounded, dark green leaves to 3 in. long with three shallow lobes and toothed margins. Orange fall color. Handsome green-and-white-striped bark. Tiny, pale yellow flowers in spring.

A. davidii. DAVID'S MAPLE. Deciduous tree. Zones 32, 34, 39. Native to central China. This 20–35-ft.-high maple is distinctive on several counts. Bark is shiny green striped with silvery white, particularly striking in winter. Leaves are glossy green, oval or lobed, 2–7 in. long, 1½–4 in. wide, deeply veined. New foliage bronze tinted; fall color of bright yellow, red-orange, and purple. Clustered greenish yellow flowers showy in spring. Part shade in warmer areas. 'Ernest Wilson' is compact, to 25 ft., with roughly triangular, unlobed light green leaves that turn orange in fall.

A. ginnala. AMUR MAPLE. Deciduous shrub or small tree. Zones 35–45. Native to Manchuria, north China, Japan. To 20 ft. high. Three-lobed, toothed leaves to 3 in. long, 2 in. wide. Striking red fall color. Clusters of small, fragrant yellowish flowers in early spring are followed by handsome bright red, winged seeds. Grown as staked, trained single-trunked tree or multiple-trunked tall shrub. 'Flame', 15–20 ft. tall, shows fiery red fall color. Tough trees, tolerating heat and cold.

A. griseum. PAPERBARK MAPLE. Deciduous tree. Zones 32, 34–41. Native to China. Grows to 25 ft. or higher with narrow to rounded crown. In winter it makes a striking silhouette with bare branches angling out and up from main trunk, and cinnamon-colored bark peeling away in paper-thin sheets. Late to leaf out in spring; leaves are divided into three coarsely toothed leaflets 1½–2½ in. long, dark green above, silvery below. Inconspicuous red flowers in spring develop into showy winged seeds. Foliage turns brilliant red in fall unless caught by early frosts. Not drought-tolerant.

A. japonicum. FULLMOON MAPLE. Deciduous shrub or small tree. Zones 31, 32, 34–41. Native to Japan. To 20–30 ft. Nearly round, 2–5-in.-long leaves cut into 7–11 lobes. Give regular moisture, part shade in warm regions. The following varieties are small, slow growing, and best placed as shrubs.

'Aconitifolium'. FERNLEAF FULLMOON MAPLE. Leaves are deeply cut, almost to leafstalk; each lobe is also cut and toothed. Fine fall color where adapted.

'Aureum'. GOLDEN FULLMOON MAPLE. See *A. shirasawanum* 'Aureum'.

'Vitifolium' bears large, grapelike leaves, 6–10 in. wide, that are not as deeply cut as 'Aconitifolium'. Features outstanding fall color in shades of purple, orange, red, and yellow.

A. mandschuricum. MANCHURIAN MAPLE. Deciduous tree. Zones 32, 34–43. Native to Manchuria and Korea. A 30–40-ft. tree with an upright to spreading crown. Three-leaflet leaves, to 5 in. long, with oval leaflets that have saw-toothed edges. Excellent pinkish red foliage color in early fall. Tiny yellowish spring flowers. Smooth, gray bark. Good small specimen tree.

A. maximowiczianum (A. nikoense). NIKKO MAPLE. Deciduous tree. Zones 32, 34, 39. Native to Japan and China. Slow-growing 20- to 30-ft. tree with a vase-shaped to round-headed crown. Bears three-leaflet leaves with oval leaflets. Foliage is bronze-green in spring and turns red, yellow, and purple in fall. Tiny yellow spring flowers. Attractive smooth gray bark. Interesting small specimen tree.

A. mono. PAINTED MAPLE. Deciduous tree. Zones 32, 34–41. Native to Japan, Korea, and China. A small, rounded to vase-shaped tree that ranges from 30 to 40 ft. and spreads as far. Bears leaves with heart-shaped bases and five to seven pointed lobes. Good yellow-orange fall color in some years. Tiny greenish yellow flowers in spring. Handsome silvery gray bark with darker fissures.

A. negundo. BOX ELDER. Deciduous tree. Zones 32–45. Native to most of U.S. Where you can grow other maples of your choice, do so. This is a weed tree of many faults—it seeds readily, hosts box elder bugs, suckers badly, and is subject to breakage. Fast growing to 60 ft., usually less. Leaves divided into three to five (or seven to nine) oval, 2–5-in.-long leaflets with toothed margins; yellow in fall.

'Flamingo'. Has white and pink leaf markings. Some shade in warm areas.

'Variegatum'. VARIEGATED BOX ELDER. Not as large or weedy as the species. Combination of green and creamy white leaves stands out in any situation. Large, pendent clusters of white fruit are spectacular.

A. nigrum. BLACK MAPLE. Zones 35–45. Similar to sugar maple (*A. saccharum*), but more resistant to heat and drought. Light green leaves turn yellow in fall. 'Greencolumn' can reach 65 ft. tall, 25 ft. wide.

A. palmatum. JAPANESE MAPLE. Deciduous shrub or tree. Zones 31, 32, 34–41. Native to Japan and Korea. Slow growing to 20 ft.; normally many stemmed. Most airy and delicate of all maples. Leaves 2–4 in. long, deeply cut into five to nine toothed lobes. All-year interest: young spring growth is glowing red; summer's leaves are soft green; fall foliage is scarlet, orange, or yellow. Slender leafless branches in greens and reds provide winter interest. Japanese maples are inclined to grow in flat, horizontal planes, so pruning to accentuate this growth habit is easy. Plants fare best in filtered shade, though full sun can be satisfactory.

Grafted garden varieties are popular, but common seedlings have uncommon grace and usefulness: they are more rugged, faster growing, and more drought tolerant than named forms, and they stand more sun and wind. Grafted forms are usually smaller, more weeping and spreading in form, brighter in foliage color, and more finely cut in leaf. The following list includes the best known of the numerous varieties available.

'Atropurpureum'. RED JAPANESE MAPLE. Purplish or bronze to bronzy green leaves, brighter in sun. Color tends to fade in summer heat.

'Bloodgood'. Vigorous, upright growth to 15 ft. Deep red spring and summer foliage, scarlet in fall. Bark blackish red.

'Bonfire'. Orange-pink spring and fall foliage; twisted trunk, short branches, drooping branchlets.

'Burgundy Lace'. Leaves purplish, more deeply cut than those of 'Atropurpureum'; branchlets bright green.

'Butterfly'. Small (to 7 ft.) shrub with small bluish green leaves edged in white. Cut out growth that reverts to plain green. Needs some shade.

'Crimson Queen'. Small, shrubby, with finely cut reddish leaves that hold color all summer, turn scarlet before dropping off in fall.

'Dissectum' ('Dissectum Viridis'). LACELEAF JAPANESE MAPLE. Small shrub with drooping branches, green bark; pale green, finely divided leaves turn gold in autumn.

'Ever Red' ('Dissectum Atropurpureum'). Small mounding shrub with weeping branches. Finely divided, purple-tinged, lacy foliage turns crimson in fall.

'Filiferum Purpureum'. Mounding shrub to 10 ft. with threadlike leaf segments opening dark red and aging bronzy green.

'Garnet'. Similar to 'Crimson Queen' and 'Ever Red'; somewhat more vigorous grower.

'Ornatum' ('Dissectum Atropurpureum'). RED LACELEAF JAPANESE MAPLE. Like 'Dissectum' but with red leaves turning brighter red in autumn.

'Oshio Beni'. Like 'Atropurpureum' but more vigorous; has long, arching branches.

'Sango Kaku' ('Senkaki'). CORAL BARK MAPLE. Vigorous, upright, treelike. Fall foliage yellow. Twigs, branches striking coral red in winter.

A. pensylvanicum. STRIPED MAPLE, MOOSEWOOD. Deciduous tree or large shrub. Zones 34–45. Native to eastern North America. In cultivation, a 15- to 20-ft. tree with a rounded crown, although plants reach 30 to 40 ft. or more in the wild. Rounded leaves with heart-shaped bases and three shallow lobes. Outstanding yellow fall foliage color. Bears tiny yellow-green spring flowers. Handsome, green-and-white-striped bark. Best in partial shade with moist, cool, slightly acid, well-drained soil. Does not tolerate heat and humidity. Can be difficult to transplant successfully. Suitable for use as an understory tree in the shade garden or wild areas.

A. pentaphyllum. Deciduous tree. Zone 32. Rare plant to 20–30 ft., with leaves divided into five narrow, 3-in. leaflets spread like fingers on a hand. Medium green leaves turn pale orange to red in fall.

A. platanoides. NORWAY MAPLE. Deciduous tree. Zones 31, 32, 34–43. Native to Europe, western Asia. Broad-crowned, densely foliaged tree to 50–60 ft. Leaves five-lobed, 3–5 in. wide, deep green above, paler beneath; turn yellow in fall. Showy clusters of small, greenish yellow flowers in early spring. Very adaptable, tolerating many soil and environmental conditions. Once widely recommended, especially as street tree, but now strongly objected to because of voracious roots, self-sown seedlings, and aphid-caused honeydew drip and sooty mold. Here are some of the best horticultural varieties:

'Cavalier'. Compact, round headed, to 30 ft.

'Cleveland' and 'Cleveland II'. Shapely, compact, well-formed trees about 50 ft. tall.

'Columnare'. Slower growing and narrower in form than the species.

'Crimson King'. Holds purple foliage color until leaves drop. Slower growing, more compact than the species.

'Deborah'. Like 'Schwedler' but faster growing, straighter.

'Drummondii'. Leaves are edged with silvery white; unusual and striking. Some shade in warm areas.

'Faassen's Black'. Pyramidal in shape, with dark purple leaves.

'Globe'. Slow growing with dense, round crown; eventual height 20–25 ft.

'Green Lace'. Finely cut, dark green leaves; moderate growth rate to about 40 ft.

'Jade Glen'. Vigorous, straight-growing form with bright yellow fall color.

'Parkway'. A broader tree than 'Columnare', with a dense canopy.

'Royal Red Leaf'. Another good red- or purple-leafed form.

'Schwedler' ('Schwedleri'). Purplish red leaves in spring turn to dark bronzy green, gold in autumn.

'Summershade'. Fast-growing, upright, heat-resistant selection.

A. pseudoplatanus. SYCAMORE MAPLE. Deciduous tree. Zones 31, 32, 34–41. Native to Europe, western Asia. Moderate growth to 40 ft. or more. Leaves 3–5 in. wide, five-lobed, thick, prominently veined, dark green above, pale below. No particular fall color. The variety 'Atropurpureum' ('Spaethii') has leaves that are rich purple underneath.

A. pseudosieboldianum. PURPLEBLOOM MAPLE. Deciduous tree. Zones 32, 34–41. Native to Manchuria and Korea. A small, 15- to 20-ft. tree resembling *A. japonicum*. Bears lobed, maplelike leaves that turn attractive shades of red and orange in fall. Tiny, reddish spring flowers. A good substitute for *A. japonicum* in northern zones.

A. rubrum. RED MAPLE, SCARLET MAPLE, SWAMP MAPLE. Deciduous tree. Zones 31, 32, 34–44. Native to low, wet areas of eastern North America. Fairly fast growth to 60 ft. or more, 40 ft. or wider. Faster growing than Norway or sycamore maples. Red twigs, branchlets, and buds; quite showy flowers. Fruit dull red. Leaves 2–4 in. long, with three to five lobes, shiny green above, pale beneath; brilliant scarlet fall color in frosty areas. Often among the first trees to color up in fall. Very soil tolerant. Not at its best in urban pollution. Selected forms include the following:

'Armstrong' and 'Armstrong II'. Hybrids between red and silver maple. Tall, very narrow trees with often poor, orange to red fall color.

'Autumn Radiance'. Broad oval form, orange-red fall color.

'Bowhall'. Tall, narrow, cone shaped, with orange-red foliage color in fall.

'Columnare'. Tall, broadly columnar.

'Gerling'. Broadly pyramidal, to 35 ft. with 20-ft. spread.

'Karpick'. Narrow grower with red twigs, yellow to red fall color.

'Northwood'. Rounded form. Extremely cold hardy.

'October Glory'. Tall, round-headed tree; last to turn color in fall.

'Red Sunset'. Upright, vigorous branching pattern.

'Scarlet Sentinel'. Hybrid between red and silver maple. Columnar, fast-growing form.

'Schlesingeri'. Tall, broad, fast growing, with regular form; orange-red fall color.

'Shade King'. Very fast grower to 50 ft. Pale green foliage turns bright red in fall.

'Tilford'. Nearly globe-shaped crown if grown in the open; pyramidal when crowded.

A

'V. J. Drake'. Unusual fall color: leaf borders turn red and violet while center is still green. Leaves eventually turn completely red.

A. rufinerve. REDVEIN MAPLE. Deciduous tree. Zones 32, 34, 39. Native to Japan. A 25- to 30-ft. tree with arching, green-and-white-striped branches and a rounded crown. Rounded leaves with three shallow lobes. Good yellow-orange fall color some years. Tiny, greenish yellow spring flowers followed by red-winged fruit in fall. Best in partial shade.

A. saccharinum. SILVER MAPLE. Deciduous tree. Zones 31, 32, 34–44. Native to eastern North America. Grows fast to 40–100 ft. with equal spread. Open form, with semipendulous branches; casts fairly open shade. Silvery gray bark peels in long strips on old trees. Leaves 3–6 in. wide, five lobed, light green above, silvery beneath. Autumn color is usually poor, pale yellow. Aggressive roots hard on sidewalks, sewers.

You pay a penalty for the advantage of fast growth: weak wood and narrow crotch angles make this tree break easily. Unusually susceptible to aphids and cottony scale. Many rate it among the least desirable of maples. Nevertheless, it is often planted for fast growth and graceful habit.

'Silver Queen'. More upright than the species, seedless. Bright gold fall color.

'Wieri' ('Laciniatum'). WIER MAPLE, CUTLEAF SILVER MAPLE. Same as species but leaves are much more finely cut; provides open shade.

A. saccharum. SUGAR MAPLE. Deciduous tree. Zones 32, 34–45. Native to eastern North America. The source of maple sugar in the Northeast, this tree is renowned for spectacular fall color in cold-winter climates. Moderate growth to 60 ft. and more, with stout branches and upright-oval to rounded canopy. Leaves 3–6 in. wide, with three to five lobes, green above, pale below. Brilliant autumn foliage ranges from yellow and orange to deep red and scarlet. Intolerant of road salt. These are some of the most commonly available varieties.

'Arrowhead'. Erect pyramid with yellow to orange leaves in fall.

'Bonfire'. Tall, spreading tree with bright red fall foliage.

'Commemoration'. Heavy leaf texture; orange, yellow, and red fall color.

'Green Mountain'. Tolerant of heat and drought; autumn leaves are yellow to orange to reddish orange.

'Legacy'. Fast growing, drought resistant, and multihued in fall; the best variety for the South.

'Monumentale' ('Temple's Upright'). Narrow, erect form with yellow-orange fall leaves.

'Seneca Chief'. Narrow form, orange to yellow fall color.

A. shirasawanum 'Aureum'. GOLDEN FULLMOON MAPLE. Deciduous shrub or small tree. Zones 32, 34–41. Leaves open pale gold in spring and remain a pale chartreuse yellow all summer. Some shade in warm areas.

A. spicatum. MOUNTAIN MAPLE. Deciduous shrub or small tree. Native to eastern North America. Zones 32, 34–45. A bushy, 15- to 25-ft.-tall shrub or short-trunked tree with lobed, maplelike leaves. Bears tiny, creamy white flowers in spring. Good red, purple, and orange fall color. Best in cool, shady spots with moist, acid soil.

A. tataricum. TATARIAN MAPLE. Deciduous shrub or small tree. Zones 34–43. Resembles *A. ginnala* in size and habit. Leaves toothed, lobed only on young plants, 2–3½ in. long. Winged seeds red in summer, showy; fall color yellow to reddish brown.

A. tegmentosum. MANCHU STRIPED MAPLE. Deciduous tree. Native to northeast Asia. Zones 32, 34–43. A small, 20- to 30-ft. tree with a spreading, rounded to oval crown. Bears rounded leaves with three to five lobes. Golden yellow fall color some years. Tiny, yellow-green spring flowers. Green-and-white-striped bark on branches.

A. triflorum. THREE-FLOWER MAPLE. Deciduous tree. Native to northeast Asia. Zones 32, 34–41. An upright to spreading, 20- to 30-ft. tree. Bears three-leaflet leaves that turn rich red, orange, and yellow in fall. Clusters of tiny, yellow-green flowers in spring. Handsome, peeling bark in shades of brown to golden brown with vertical fissures. Good small specimen tree or effective addition to a shrub border.

A. truncatum. Deciduous tree. Zones 32, 34–43. Native to China. Grows fairly rapidly to 25 ft. Like a small Norway maple with more deeply lobed leaves to 4 in. wide. Expanding leaves are purplish red, summer leaves green, autumn leaves dark purplish red. A good lawn or patio tree.

Aceraceae. The maple family consists of deciduous, rarely evergreen, trees and shrubs with paired opposite leaves and paired, winged seeds.

ACHILLEA

YARROW

Asteraceae (Compositae)

PERENNIALS

🌱 ZONES 31, 32, 34–45

☀️ FULL SUN

💧 MODERATE WATER

Achillea tomentosa

Yarrows are among the most carefree and generously blooming perennials for summer and early fall, several being equally valuable in the garden and as cut flowers (taller kinds may be cut and dried for winter bouquets). Leaves are gray or green, bitter-aromatic, usually finely divided (some with toothed edges). Flower heads usually in flattish clusters. Drought tolerant once established. Cut back after bloom, dividing when clumps get crowded.

A. ageratifolia. GREEK YARROW. Native to Balkan region. Low mats of silvery leaves, toothed or nearly smooth edged. White flower clusters ½–1 in. across on stems 4–10 in. tall.

A. clavennae. SILVERY YARROW. Mats of silvery gray, silky leaves, lobed somewhat like chrysanthemum leaves. Loose, flat-topped clusters of ½–¾-in.-wide ivory white flower heads on 5–10-in.-high stems. Often sold as *A. argentea*.

A. filipendulina. FERNLEAF YARROW. Tall, erect plants 4–5 ft. high, with deep green, fernlike leaves. Bright yellow flower heads in large, flat-topped clusters. Dried or fresh, they are good for flower arrangements. Several horticultural varieties are available. 'Gold Plate', a tall plant, has flower clusters up to 6 in. wide; 'Coronation Gold', to about 3 ft., also has large flower clusters.

A. kellereri. Gray-green ferny leaves on a low (6-in.) plant. Clusters of flower heads look like tiny white daisies with yellow centers.

A. millefolium. COMMON YARROW, MILFOIL. This species may spread a bit or grow erect to 3 ft. Narrow, fernlike, green or gray-green leaves on 3-ft. stems. White flower clusters grow on long stems. 'Rosea' has rosy flower heads. One of the more successful garden varieties is 'Fire King', about 3 ft. tall with gray foliage and dark reddish flowers. 'Cerise Queen' has brighter red flowers. 'Paprika' is red-orange. 'Salmon Beauty' is salmon pink. Hybrids, many of them named, have extended the color range. Summer Pastels and Debutante strains show white and cream to lighter shades of yellow and red; they can grow from seed. Galaxy hybrids exhibit deeper colors; 'Appleblossom' is lilac pink.

A LAWN-MEADOW DOTTED WITH WILDFLOWERS

That's the effect you get with common yarrow (*Achillea millefolium*) treated as a sometimes-mowed ground cover. Install in spring, like this: Prepare soil as for a new lawn. Use ½ lb. of seed per 1,000 sq. ft. Mix it with an equal amount of sand and broadcast the mix with a handheld spreader. Press seeds in with a lawn roller. Mow two to eight times a year (the less often you mow, the more flowers can form). Use a rotary mower at a 3–4-in. setting.

A. 'Moonshine'. Upright growth to 2 ft. Gray-green foliage and light yellow flowers. Like *A. 'Taygetea'* but flowers are deeper yellow.

A. ptarmica. Erect plant up to 2 ft. high. Narrow leaves with finely toothed edges. White flower heads in rather open, flattish clusters. 'The Pearl' has double flowers.

A. 'Taygetea'. Native to the eastern Mediterranean. Grows to 1½ ft. Gray-green, divided leaves 3–4 in. long. Dense clusters of bright yellow flower heads fade to primrose yellow—excellent contrast in color shades until it's time to shear off old stalks. Good cut flowers.

A. tomentosa. WOOLLY YARROW. Makes a flat, spreading mat of fernlike, deep green, hairy leaves. Golden flower heads in flat clusters top 6–10-in. stems in summer. 'Primrose Beauty' has pale yellow flowers; 'King George' has cream flowers. A good edging and a neat ground cover for small areas; used in rock gardens. Shear off dead flowers to leave attractive green mat.

ACHNATHERUM
calamagrostis

SILVER SPIKE GRASS, SILVER SPEAR GRASS

Poaceae (Gramineae)

PERENNIAL

▨ ZONES 32, 34–41

☼ FULL SUN

🌢 REGULAR WATER

Acnatherum calamagrostis

Ahandsome ornamental grass native to southern and central Europe. Forms fountainlike, 2- to 2½-ft.-tall clumps of fine-textured, gray-green leaves. Arching, silvery green flowerheads appear above the leaves in early to midsummer and turn tan in fall. Plants reach 3 ft. in bloom. Tolerates very light shade, but plants become floppy if they do not receive enough sun. Requires well-drained, average soil. Best in areas with cool nights and low humidity. Use in drifts, on slopes, and in semiwild areas. Flowerheads are attractive for cutting. Cut foliage to the ground in late winter.

ACIDANTHERA bicolor. See GLADIOLUS callianthus

ACONITUM

ACONITE, MONKSHOOD

Ranunculaceae

PERENNIALS

▨ ZONES 34–45

☼ ◐ FULL SUN OR PARTIAL SHADE

🌢 REGULAR WATER

⬧ ALL PARTS ARE POISONOUS IF INGESTED

Aconitum napellus

Leaves, usually lobed, in basal clusters. Flowers shaped like hoods or helmets, along tall, leafy spikes. Monkshood has a definite place in rich soil under trees, at the back of flower beds, or even at the edge of a bog garden. Substitute for delphinium in shade. Combines effectively with ferns, meadow rue, astilbe, and hosta.

Needs some winter chill. Hard to establish in warm, dry climates. Sow seeds in spring; or sow in late summer or early fall for bloom the next year. Moist, fertile soil for best growth and bloom. Divide in early spring or late fall, or leave undivided for years. Completely dormant in winter; mark site.

A. 'Bressingham Spire'. Hybrid, to 3 ft. high. Deep green, lobed leaves; upright clusters of deep blue-violet flowers in midsummer to early fall.

A. cammarum 'Bicolor'. Grows to 3 ft., with broad, branching spires of blue-and-white flowers in summer.

A. carmichaelii (A. fischeri). Native to central China. Densely leafy stems 2–4 ft. high. Leaves leathery, dark green, lobed and coarsely toothed. Blooms late summer into fall; deep purple-blue flowers form dense, branching clusters 4–8 in. long. 'Wilsonii' grows 6–8 ft. high, has more open flower clusters 10–18 in. long.

A. 'Carneum' has pink flowers.

A. hemsleyonum. Native to central and western China. Climbing, twining, to 10 ft. Lobed leaves. Clusters of deep violet flowers in midsummer to early autumn.

A. henryi (A. bicolor) 'Sparks'. Grows 4–5 ft. tall, with purple-blue flowers on a widely branching plant. Summer bloom.

A. napellus. GARDEN MONKSHOOD. Native to Europe. Upright leafy plants 2–5 ft. high. Leaves 2–5 in. wide, divided into narrow lobes. Flowers usually blue or violet, in spikelike clusters in late summer.

A. 'Newry Blue' has deep blue flowers.

ACORUS

Araceae

PERENNIAL

▨ ZONES VARY BY SPECIES

☼ FULL SUN

🌢 MUCH WATER

Acorus gramineus

Native to Japan, northern Asia. Related to callas, but fans of sword-shaped leaves more nearly resemble tufts of iris. Flowers are inconspicuous. Aquatic plants for bog gardens or pool edges.

A. calamus. SWEET FLAG. Zones 31, 32, 34–43. Native to southeast Asia. Sword-shaped leaves to 5 ft. high. 'Variegatus' has leaves striped with creamy white and pale yellow, and resembles a large, variegated iris. Plant in shallow water at the edge of a pond.

A. gramineus. GRASSY-LEAVED SWEET FLAG. Zones 31, 32, 34–41. Native to Japan, northern Asia. Narrower, grassy leaves to 14 in. high. 'Ogon' has rich golden yellow leaves. 'Pusillus' is tiny, its green leaves seldom more than 1 in. long. It is used in planting miniature landscapes and dish gardens. 'Albovariegatus' is dwarf, with white-striped leaves. 'Variegatus', with cream-striped, ¼-in.-wide leaves to 1½ ft. long, is also useful with collections of grasses, bamboos, or sword-leafed plants among gravel and boulders.

ACTAEA

BANEBERRY

Ranunculaceae

PERENNIALS

▨ ZONES 32, 34–45

◐ ⬤ PARTIAL OR FULL SHADE

🌢 REGULAR WATER

⬧ ALL PARTS ARE POISONOUS IF INGESTED

Actaea rubra

Woodland plants native to the U.S. and useful primarily for the wild or native plant garden, baneberries grow to 2½ ft. tall, with gracefully divided leaves, somewhat like those of astilbe, and clusters of small white blossoms in spring. Principal feature is the attractive (but poisonous) fruit that follows the flowers. Use as a background for smaller native plants. Give soil rich in humus.

A. alba (A. pachypoda). WHITE BANEBERRY, DOLL'S EYES. Showy ¼-in. berry is white with a dark spot at the end; berry stalks are swollen and red.

A. rubra. RED BANEBERRY. Similar to *A. alba,* but berries are somewhat larger, scarlet in color, and borne on slender stems.

FOR INFORMATION ON SELECTING PLANTS

PLEASE SEE PAGES 47–112

A

ACTINIDIA

Actinidiaceae

DECIDUOUS VINES

ZONES VARY BY SPECIES

FULL SUN OR PARTIAL SHADE

REGULAR TO MODERATE WATER

Actinidia

Native to eastern Asia. Handsome foliage. Plant in rich soil. Supply sturdy supports for vines to twine upon, such as a trellis, an arbor, or a patio overhead. You can also train them to cover walls and fences; guide and tie vines to the support as necessary. Thin occasionally to shape or to control pattern.

In winter, prune and shape plant for form and fruit production. Shape to one or two main trunks; cut out closely parallel or crossing branches. Fruit is borne on shoots from year-old or older wood; cut out shoots that have fruited for 3 years and shorten younger shoots, leaving from three to seven buds beyond previous summer's fruit. In summer, shorten overlong shoots and unwind shoots that twine around main branches.

A. arguta. HARDY KIWI. Zones 31, 32, 34–41. Native to eastern Asia. Twining, climbing to 20 ft. Dark green, oval leaves to 5 in. long. Clusters of fragrant white flowers in early summer. Fruit 1–1½ in. long, fuzzless (eat skin and all). Female varieties 'Ananasnaja' and 'Hood River' need male varieties, such as 'Meader Male', for pollen. The rare variety 'Issai' is self-fertile. Fruiting is satisfactory even in mild winters.

A. kolomikta. Zones 31, 32, 34–43. Rapid growth to 15 ft. or more to produce a wondrous foliage mass made up of heart-shaped, 3–5-in.-long, variegated leaves. Male varieties are generally sold, since they are said to have better color than females. Some leaves are all white, some are green splashed with white, and others have rose, pink, or even red variegation. Color is best in cool spring weather. In warm regions, color is apparent only in light shade. Clusters of fragrant, small white flowers in early summer.

A. polygama. SILVER VINE. Zones 31, 32, 34–43. Native to Japan. Climbing, to 15 ft. Oval leaves to 6 in. long, deep green with silvery white tips; most colorful on male plants. Clusters of fragrant white flowers in early summer. Egg-shaped yellow-green fruit produced on female plants.

HOW VINES TWINE

Many of the vines we grow in gardens climb by twining-wrapping their stems around a nearby support. Actinidias, honeysuckle, pole beans, morning glories, and wisteria are all twiners. Charles Darwin noted that the tip of the twining stem actually moves around in all directions until reaching a support—a movement known as circumnutation.

Most twiners, including actinidias, twine in a clockwise direction. A vine species will always twine in the same direction. If you twist the stems the wrong way around a support, they will unwrap themselves and turn in the right direction.

ADENOPHORA

LADY BELLS

Campanulaceae (Lobeliaceae)

PERENNIALS

ZONES 31, 32, 34–43

FULL SUN OR LIGHT SHADE

REGULAR TO MODERATE WATER

Adenophora liliifolia

Campanula relatives, mostly from the Far East; erect plants with narrow, leafy stems bearing fragrant blue bells along their upper portions. Useful in the shade garden

but tolerate sun as well. Long lived, they resent moving once well established. Provide well-drained soil.

A. confusa. To 2½ ft., with deep blue flowers in mid- to late summer.
A. liliifolia. To 1½ ft., with pale blue (rarely white) flowers.
A. tashiroi. To 1 ft., with violet flowers.

ADIANTUM

MAIDENHAIR FERN

Polypodiaceae

FERNS

ZONES VARY BY SPECIES

PARTIAL OR FULL SHADE

AMPLE WATER

Adiantum aleuticum

Most are native to tropics; some originate in North America. Stems thin, wiry, and dark; fronds finely cut; leaflets mostly fan shaped, bright green, thin textured. Plants need shade, steady moisture, and soil rich in organic matter. Leaves of even hardy varieties die back in hard frosts. Kinds listed as tender or indoor plants sometimes succeed in sheltered places in mild-winter areas.

A. aleuticum (A. pedatum aleuticum). FIVE-FINGER FERN, WESTERN MAIDENHAIR. Zones 36–40. Native to North America. Fronds fork to make a fingerlike pattern atop slender 1–2½-ft. stems. General effect airy and fresh; excellent in containers or shaded beds.

A. capillus-veneris. SOUTHERN MAIDENHAIR. Zones 31, 32, 34, 36, 37. Native to North America. To 1½ ft. tall, fronds twice divided but not forked.

A. mairisii. Zones 31, 32, 34, 39. Hybrid, to 1½ ft. high, with broadly triangular fronds divided into triangular segments.

A. pedatum. AMERICAN MAIDENHAIR. Zones 31, 32, 34–45. Native to eastern North America. To 1½ ft. high; lance-shaped to broadly oval, medium green fronds divided into narrow triangular segments, on dark stems. Wonderful in masses as a textural contrast to hostas in a shade garden.

A. venustum. HIMALAYAN MAIDENHAIR. Zones 31, 32, 34, 39. Native to the Himalayas. Grows to 2½ ft. high, with triangular, medium green fronds divided into triangular segments. This species is evergreen in mild climates, semievergreen throughout the Northeast. Young fronds are pinkish.

ADINA rubella

GLOSSY ADINA, CHINESE BUTTONBUSH

Rubiaceae

DECIDUOUS SHRUBS

ZONES 31, 32, 34–41

FULL SUN TO PARTIAL SHADE

REGULAR TO MODERATE WATER

Adina rubella

Native to China, this underused shrub is most often planted for its attractive, glossy green foliage. Clusters of small, white, buttonlike flowers are lightly fragrant and borne throughout much of the summer. In more northerly gardens, it overwinters best in a protected location. Little pruning is necessary; if desired, prune to shape in early spring before evidence of new growth. Growing more wide than tall, it reaches a mature height of 4 to 5 feet in about 10 years.

FOR INFORMATION ON YOUR CLIMATE ZONE

PLEASE SEE PAGES 30–46

ADLUMIA fungosa

ALLEGHENY VINE, MOUNTAIN FRINGE

Fumariaceae (Papaveraceae)

BIENNIAL

ZONES 32, 34–43

PARTIAL SHADE

REGULAR WATER

Adlumia fungosa

Twining vine grown for blue-green ferny foliage and hanging clusters of long, pale pink, heart-shaped flowers, similar to fringed bleeding heart (a close relative). Used as a screen, on fences and arches, or scrambling through shrubs at the woodland's edge. Forms a 12-in. mound of leaves the first year and blooms the second. Grows 10–15 ft. with lacy leaves made up of many leaflets grouped near 4–6-in. flower clusters that bloom from June to September. Thrives in sheltered woodland sites where soil is cool, moist, well-drained, and rich in humus or decaying leaves. Sow seed outdoors in spring, covering thinly with soil. Thin seedlings to 18 in. Self-sows in ideal conditions. Aphids may be a problem. Native to eastern North America but endangered in some areas. Do not collect in the wild.

WHERE ADONIS GOT ITS NAME

Adonis is named for a mythological character, a handsome young man of whom Venus became enamored. When Adonis was fatally gored by a wild boar while hunting, Venus was unable to save his life. But to keep his memory alive, she decreed that his blood would be transformed into flowers that would bloom each year. Red blossoms grew at once in the bloody ground—and today are known as *Adonis aestivalis,* or the annual *Adonis annuua.*

ADONIS

ADONIS, PHEASANT'S EYE

Ranunculaceae

PERENNIALS AND ANNUALS

ZONES VARY BY SPECIES

FULL SUN OR LIGHT SHADE

REGULAR WATER

Adonis

Native to Europe and Asia, adonises are upright plants with very finely cut, fernlike leaves and solitary, cup-shaped, red or yellow flowers. The foliage of some species, including the perennials listed here, dies back by midsummer. Plant the perennials in drifts in beds and borders, rock gardens, or wild gardens; annuals are best used in flower gardens and are suitable for cutting. Once planted, perennials are best left undisturbed, but they can be divided carefully immediately after flowering. Perennials form 1-ft.-wide clumps with time.

A. aestivalis. SUMMER ADONIS. Annual. All Zones. Erect, 1- to 1½-ft.-tall species. Bears 1- to 1½-in.-wide, deep red flowers with dark centers in midsummer. Sow seeds outdoors in early spring where the plants are to grow. Best in full sun with neutral to slightly alkaline soil.

A. amurensis. AMUR ADONIS. Perennial. Zones 31, 32, 34–43. Clump-forming, ½- to 1½-ft.-tall plant producing bright yellow, cup- to bowl-shaped, 1- to 2-in.-wide blooms in very early spring. Plants can even bloom before snows have melted. 'Fukajukai' bears semidouble to double flowers that are sterile, meaning they produce no seeds. 'Pleniflora', also sold as 'Plena', bears double flowers with green eyes.

A. vernalis. SPRING ADONIS, PHEASANT'S EYE. Perennial. Zones 31–32. Clump-forming, 6- to 15-in.-tall species bearing golden yellow, 2- to 3-in.-wide flowers from mid to late spring. Best in full sun.

AEGOPODIUM podagraria

BISHOP'S WEED, GOUT WEED

Apiaceae (Umbelliferae)

DECIDUOUS PERENNIAL

ZONES 31, 32, 34–45

SUN OR SHADE

MODERATE WATER

Aegopodium podagraria 'Variegatum'

Very vigorous ground cover, especially in rich soil. Spreads by creeping underground rootstocks and very invasive. Not recommended. If planted, contain behind underground barrier of wood, concrete, or heavy tar paper. Many light green, divided leaves make a low (to 6-in.), dense mass; leaflets are ½–3 in. long. To keep it low and even, mow it two or three times a year.

'Variegatum' is the most widely planted form. Leaflets are edged white, giving a luminous effect in shade. Pull plants that revert to solid green leaves. Can become invasive, but takes longer to do so than the species. Lovely in a hanging basket.

AESCULUS

HORSECHESTNUT, BUCKEYE

Hippocastanaceae

DECIDUOUS TREES OR LARGE SHRUBS

ZONES VARY BY SPECIES

FULL SUN

REGULAR WATER

SEEDS OF ALL ARE SLIGHTLY TOXIC IF INGESTED

Aesculus carnea

Leaves are divided fanwise into large, toothed leaflets. Springtime flowers, in long, dense, showy clusters at the ends of branches, attract hummingbirds. Leathery fruit capsules enclose glossy seeds.

A. carnea. RED HORSECHESTNUT. Zones 32, 34–45. Hybrid between *A. hippocastanum* and *A. pavia.* To 40 ft. high and 30 ft. wide—smaller than *A. hippocastanum* and a better fit for small gardens. Round headed with large, dark green leaves, each divided into five leaflets; casts dense shade. Gets leaf scorch, defoliates in warm, humid regions. Bears hundreds of 8-in.-long plumes of soft pink to red flowers. 'Briotii' has rosy crimson flowers; 'O'Neill Red' has bright red blooms.

A. glabra. OHIO BUCKEYE. Zones 32, 34–43. To 40 ft., possibly taller, with dense, rounded form. Low branching, casts dense shade. Early to leaf out. Bright green expanding leaves mature to dark green, then turn yellow to orange in autumn. Flowers greenish yellow in 4–7-in. clusters. Prickly seed capsules enclose shiny brown buckeyes.

A. hippocastanum. COMMON HORSECHESTNUT. Native to Europe. Zones 32, 34–43. To 60 ft. high with a 40-ft. spread, this bulky, densely foliaged tree gives heavy shade. Leaves divided into five to seven toothed, 4–10-in.-long leaflets. Gets leaf scorch, defoliates in warm, humid regions. Spectacular flower show: ivory blooms with pink markings in 1-ft.-long plumes. Invasive roots can break up walks. 'Baumannii' has double flowers, sets no seeds.

A. parviflora. BOTTLEBRUSH BUCKEYE. Zones 31, 32, 34–41. Native to southeastern U.S. Shrub to 12–15 ft. tall, spreading by suckers, with dark green leaves divided into five to seven 3–8-in.-long leaflets. Very showy white flower clusters (8–12 in. tall, 2–4 in. wide). Bright yellow fall foliage. Good choice for massing, shrub borders, or specimen planting.

Var. *serotina* blooms a few weeks later; 'Rogers' also blooms later, with flower clusters to 2½ ft. long.

A. pavia. RED BUCKEYE. Zones 31, 32, 34–45. Native to eastern U.S. Bulky shrub or tree to 12–20 ft., with irregular rounded crown. Narrow, erect 10-in. clusters of bright red or orange-red (rarely yellow) flowers. Best foliage for warm, humid climates.

AETHIONEMA

STONECRESS	
Brassicaceae (Cruciferae)	
PERENNIALS	
⚘ ZONES 32, 34–45, EXCEPT AS NOTED	
☼ FULL SUN	
⬤ MODERATE TO LITTLE WATER	

Aethionema

Native to Mediterranean region and Asia Minor. Choice shrublets, attractive in or out of bloom, best adapted to colder climates; a favorite among rock gardeners. Grow best in a light, porous soil with considerable lime. Bloom late spring to summer. Deadhead flowers.

A. cordifolium. Similar to *A. grandiflorum,* but a bit smaller, to just 8 in. high.

A. grandiflorum (A. pulchellum). PERSIAN STONECRESS. Zones 31, 32, 34, 39. Evergreen or semievergreen, to 10 in. high, upright or spreading. Narrow blue-green leaves to 1½ in. long, clusters of very light pink to deep rose pink flowers.

A. saxatile. Zones 31, 32. Annual or perennial to 1 ft. high, with light purplish white flowers.

A. schistosum. Erect, unbranched stems 5–10 in. high, densely clothed with narrow, slate blue, ½-in.-long leaves. Fragrant, rose-colored flowers; petals about ¼ in. long.

A. warleyense (A. 'Warley Rose'). Hybrid form; neat, compact plant to 8 in. high. Pink flowers in dense clusters. Widely used.

AFRICAN CORN LILY. See IXIA

AFRICAN DAISY. See ARCTOTIS, DIMORPHOTHECA, OSTEOSPERMUM

AGAPANTHUS

LILY-OF-THE-NILE	
Amaryllidaceae	
TENDER BULBS	
⚘ ALL ZONES	
☼ ◑ FULL SUN OR LIGHT SHADE	
⬤ REGULAR TO MODERATE WATER	

Agapanthus

All form fountainlike clumps of strap-shaped leaves, from which rise bare stems ending in spherical clusters of funnel-shaped flowers in summer. Each bloom cluster resembles a burst of blue (sometimes white) fireworks.

Adaptable. Will bloom in full sun or light shade. Best in loamy soil but will grow in heavy soils. Thrive with regular water. Divide infrequently; every 5 or 6 years is usually sufficient. Lift and store over winter and replant in spring. Some may be perennial in warmest areas. Superb container plants. Good near pools.

A. africanus. Leaves shorter, narrower than those of *A. orientalis;* flower stalks shorter (to 1½ ft. tall) with blue flowers in fewer numbers (20–50 to a cluster). Often sold as *A. umbellatus.* 'Albus' is white.

A. Headbourne Hybrids. Deciduous. Zones 31, 32. Flowers come in a range of blues and in white on 2–2½-ft.-tall stems above fairly narrow, rather upright foliage.

A. inapertus. Deep blue blossoms in drooping clusters atop 4–5-ft. stems.

A. orientalis. Most commonly planted. Broad, arching leaves in big clumps. Stems to 4–5 ft. tall bear up to 100 blue flowers. There are white ('Albus'), double ('Flore Pleno'), and giant blue varieties. Often sold as *A. africanus, A. umbellatus.*

A. 'Peter Pan'. Outstanding dwarf. Foliage clumps 8–12 in. tall; profuse blue flowers top 1–1½-ft. stems.

AGASTACHE

GIANT HYSSOP	
Lamiaceae (Labiatae)	
PERENNIALS	
⚘ ZONES VARY BY SPECIES	
☼ ◑ FULL SUN OR PARTIAL SHADE	
⬤ ◖ REGULAR TO MODERATE WATER	

Agastache foeniculum

Aromatic summer-blooming tender perennials somewhat resembling salvias, with whorls of purple, blue, or yellow flowers forming spikelike clusters. Provide well-drained soil. Grow as annuals where plants are not hardy.

A. barberi. Zones 31, 32, 34, 39. Woody-based perennial to 2 ft., with 2-in. leaves and reddish purple flowers on 6–12-in. spikes. 'Firebird' has coppery orange-red flowers. Purple-flowered 'Tutti-Frutti' is a good substitute for purple loosestrife (*Lythrum*).

A. cana. HUMMINGBIRD'S MINT. Zones 31, 32, 34–41. Branched perennial to 3 ft., with 1-in. leaves and deep pink to rosy purple flowers.

A. foeniculum. ANISE HYSSOP. Zones 31, 32, 34, 39–41. Erect, narrow clumping perennial to 5 ft., with anise- or licorice-scented foliage and dense clusters of lilac blue flowers on 4-in. spikes. Decorative and useful in perennial borders or herb gardens.

A. mexicana. Zones 31, 32. Grows to 2 ft., with 2½-in. toothed leaves and rose pink inch-long flowers on spikes to 1 ft. long. 'Champagne' has apricot flowers.

A. nepetoides. YELLOW GIANT HYSSOP. Native to eastern North America. Zones 31, 32, 34–41. To 5½ ft. high, sturdy stems, with leaves to 6 in. long, and greenish yellow flowers.

AGATHAEA coelestis. See FELICIA amelloides

Agavaceae. The agave family contains rosette-forming, sometimes treelike plants generally from dry regions. Flower clusters are spikes or spikelike; leaves often contain tough fibers.

AGAVE parryi huachucensis

MESCAL	
Agavaceae	
SUCCULENT PERENNIAL	
⚘ ZONES 31, 32	
☼ FULL SUN; PROTECT FROM WIND	
⬤ MODERATE WATER	

Agave

A century plant relative from the mountains of southern Arizona, has proven to be hardy as far north as Washington, D.C. Forms beautiful, large rosettes of blue-gray, 1-ft.-long leaves tipped with sharp, dark spines. The flower stems may reach 10 ft. or more in height and bear numerous funnel-shaped, creamy colored blossoms. The rosette dies after flowering, but produces offsets.

Plant in full sun in moderately fertile, well-drained soil. Sites protected from winter wind help ensure minimum winter burn to the leaves. An excellent plant for gardeners who like to experiment with the unusual and push the limits of hardiness beyond normal expectations.

AGERATUM, HARDY. See EUPATORIUM coelestinum

AGERATUM houstonianum

FLOSS FLOWER	
Asteraceae (Compositae)	
ANNUAL	
✂ ALL ZONES	
☼ ◑ FULL SUN OR PARTIAL SHADE	
● REGULAR WATER	

Ageratum houstonianum

Reliable favorite for summer and fall in borders and containers. Leaves roundish, often heart shaped at the base, soft green, hairy. Tiny blue, white, or pink tassel-like flowers in dense clusters. A few tall types, such as 2½-ft. 'Blue Horizon', are sold but most varieties offered are low growers. Dwarf kinds (4–6 in. high) with blue flowers include 'Blue Blazer', 'Blue Danube' ('Blue Puffs'), 'Blue Surf', and 'Royal Delft'. Somewhat taller (9–12-in.) blues include 'Blue Mink' and 'North Sea'. Good varieties in other colors are 'Pink Powder-puffs' and white-blooming 'Summer Snow', both 9 in. high.

Best in rich, moist soil. Easy to transplant even when in bloom. Low growers make excellent edgings or pattern plantings with other similar-size annuals. Tall types provide good cut flowers.

AGROSTEMMA githago

CORN COCKLE	
Caryophyllaceae	
ANNUAL	
✂ ALL ZONES	
☼ FULL SUN	
● ● REGULAR TO MODERATE WATER	
☙ ALL PARTS ARE POISONOUS IF INGESTED	

Agrostemma githago

The species is an attractive weed of roadside and grain field. Variety 'Milas' is a superior plant with 3-in. flowers of deep purplish pink, lined and spotted with deep purple and centered with a white eye. Stems 6–12 in. long make it a good cut flower. Plants wispy but sturdy, 2–3 ft. tall. Sow seed in spring or early summer for summer and fall bloom in most climates; sow in fall for winter–spring bloom in warmest climates. Mass at rear of border, among shrubs, or in front of fence or hedge.

AGROSTIS

BENT, BENT GRASS	
Poaceae (Gramineae)	
LAWN GRASSES	
✂ ZONES 34–45	
☼ FULL SUN	
● ● AMPLE WATER	

Agrostis stolonifera

All except redtop make beautiful velvety lawns under proper conditions and with constant care. They need frequent close mowing, frequent feeding, occasional top-dressing, and much water. In hot weather they succumb to fungal diseases. Best putting greens are of bent grass.

A. gigantea. REDTOP. Coarser than other bents, not generally used in lawns. Has been used as quick-sprouting nurse grass in mixtures or for winter overseeding of Bermuda and other winter-dormant grasses.

A. stolonifera. CREEPING BENT. Premium lawn but requires the most care, including frequent mowing to ½ in. tall with special mower. Seed-grown strains include Emerald, Penncross, and Seaside. In some areas you can buy sod of choice strains, Congressional, Old Orchard.

A. tenuis. COLONIAL BENT. More erect than *A. stolonifera;* somewhat easier to care for but still fussy. Astoria and Highland are best-known strains; latter is tougher, hardier, more disease resistant. Mow to ¾ in.

AILANTHUS altissima

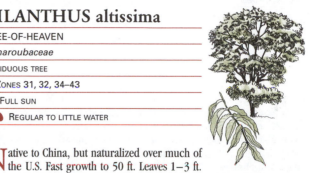

TREE-OF-HEAVEN	
Simaroubaceae	
DECIDUOUS TREE	
✂ ZONES 31, 32, 34–43	
☼ FULL SUN	
● ● REGULAR TO LITTLE WATER	

Ailanthus altissima

Native to China, but naturalized over much of the U.S. Fast growth to 50 ft. Leaves 1–3 ft. long are divided into 13–25 leaflets 3–5 in. long. Flowers on male trees are smelly. On female trees, the inconspicuous greenish flowers are usually followed by handsome clusters of red-brown, winged seedpods in late summer and fall; great for dried arrangements. Though often condemned as a weed tree because it suckers profusely and self-seeds, it must be praised for its ability to create beauty and shade under adverse conditions, including extreme air pollution and every type of difficult soil. It is the tree that survived against all odds in *A Tree Grows in Brooklyn.*

AJUGA

CARPET BUGLE	
Lamiaceae (Labiatae)	
PERENNIALS	
✂ ZONES 31, 32, 34–45	
☼ ◑ FULL SUN OR PARTIAL SHADE	
● REGULAR WATER	

Ajuga reptans

One species is a rock garden plant; the others are ground covers. Of the latter, the highly variable *A. reptans* is better known and more useful, though it will escape into lawns unless contained. All bloom spring to early summer.

A. genevensis. Rock garden plant 5–14 in. high, does not spread by runners. Grayish, hairy stems and coarse-toothed leaves to 3 in. long. Flowers in blue spikes; rose and white forms are also sold.

A. pyramidalis. Erect plant 2–10 in. high; does not spread by runners. Stems, with long grayish hairs, have many roundish, 1½–4-in.-long leaves. Violet blue flowers are not obvious among the large leaves. 'Metallica Crispa' has reddish brown leaves with a metallic glint.

A. reptans. The popular ground cover ajuga. Spreads quickly by runners, making a mat of dark green leaves that grow 2–3 in. wide in full sun, 3–4 in. wide in part shade. Varieties with bronze- or metallic-tinted leaves keep color best in full sun. Flowers, usually blue, borne in 4–5-in.-high spikes. Plant in spring or early fall 6–12 in. apart. Mow or trim off old flower spikes. Subject to root-knot nematodes; also subject to rot and fungal diseases where drainage or air circulation is poor. Many varieties of this species are available, some sold under several names. The following are among the best choices: 'Alba', flowers are white. 'Burgundy Glow', leaves flushed with burgundy. 'Caitlin's Giant', large leaves to 6 in. long of deep purple-bronze, 8-in.-long flower spikes. 'Jungle Beauty', purple-tinged leaves and 15-in. spikes of blue flowers. 'Multicolor' has dark bronze leaves with cream-and-pink mottling. 'Purpurea', usually has somewhat larger leaves tinted bronze or purple; often sold as 'Atropurpurea'. 'Rosea', pink flowers. 'Silver Beauty', silver green and white leaves, light blue flower spikes; grows 6 in. high. 'Variegata', leaves edged and splotched with creamy yellow.

AKEBIA quinata

FIVELEAF AKEBIA

Lardizabalaceae

DECIDUOUS VINE

ZONES 31, 32, 34–43

SUN OR SHADE

REGULAR WATER

Akebia quinata

Native to Japan, China, and Korea. Twines to 15–20 ft. Grows fast in mild regions, slower where winters are cold. Dainty leaves on 3–5-in. stalks, each divided into five deep green leaflets 2–3 in. long, notched at tips. Clusters of quaint dull purple flowers in spring are more a surprise than a show. The edible fruit, if produced, looks like a thick, 2½–4-in.-long, purplish sausage.

Give support for climbing; keep plant under control to prevent it from becoming rampant. Benefits from annual pruning. Recovers quickly when cut to the ground. For a tracery effect on post or column, prune out all but two or three basal stems.

A. trifoliata. THREELEAF AKEBIA. Like the above but with three instead of five leaflets per leaf.

ALASKA CEDAR. See CHAMAECYPARIS nootkatensis

ALBIZIA (Albizzia)

Fabaceae (Leguminosae)

DECIDUOUS TREE

ZONES VARY BY SPECIES; CULTIVARS, ZONES 31, 32, 34–41

FULL SUN OR PARTIAL SHADE

WATER NEEDS VARY BY SPECIES

Albizia julibrissin

Twice-divided, finely textured foliage and powder-puff flowers that are attractive to birds. Weak-wooded. Main branches may break with heavy snow. Cut back broken branches almost to ground level and new growth will quickly replace them.

A. julibrissin. SILK TREE. Deciduous. Zones 31, 32. Native to Asia from Iran to Japan. This is the "mimosa" of eastern U.S., though it's also grown in the West. Rapid growth to 40 ft. with wider spread. Can be headed back to make a 10–20-ft. umbrella. Fluffy pink flowers like pincushions on ferny-leafed branches in summer. Light-sensitive leaves fold at night. The species is disease prone and not very hardy; plant cultivars instead. 'Rosea' has richer pink flowers and is considered hardier. 'E. H. Wilson' is also hardier, with dense clusters of bright pink flowers. Silk tree does best with high summer heat. With regular water, it grows fast; on skimpy moisture, it usually survives but grows slowly, and eventually starts to look yellowish.

Unique flat-topped, spreading canopy makes it a good patio tree, despite fallen leaves, flowers, and pods. Tree can be short lived because of a wilt disease; check with a local nursery.

MAKE HOLLYHOCKS BLOOM TWICE

In July, after blooms fade, cut off flower stems just above the ground. Continue to feed and water the plants. Roots will push out another flush of growth, which will rebloom in September. This technique demands a lot from the plants, so feed two or three times during the regular growing season, and water as needed all along.

ALCEA (Althaea rosea)

HOLLYHOCK

Malvaceae

BIENNIAL OR SHORT-LIVED PERENNIAL

ALL ZONES

FULL SUN

REGULAR WATER

Alcea rosea

These old-fashioned favorites have their place against a fence or wall or at the back of a border or cottage garden. Old single varieties can reach 9 ft.; newer strains and selections are shorter.

A. ficifolia grows to 8 ft. high. Its lobed leaves have prominent veins. Spikes of single or double yellow flowers to 3 in. across bloom in early summer.

A. rosea, the best-known species, has big, rough, roundish heart-shaped leaves more or less lobed; single, semidouble, or double flowers 3–6 in. wide in white, pink, rose, red, purple, creamy yellow, apricot. Summer bloom. Destroy rust-infected leaves as soon as disease appears.

A. rugosa is similar to A. rosea, but has hairier stems and deeply lobed leaves. Flowers are yellow to yellow-orange.

Chater's Double is a fine perennial strain; 6-ft. spires have 5–6-in. flowers. So-called annual strains (biennials treated as annuals) bloom first year from seed sown in early spring: Summer Carnival strain is 5–6 ft. tall with double 4-in. flowers; Majorette strain is 2½ ft. tall with 3–4-in. flowers; Pinafore strain (mixed colors) branches freely from base, has five to eight bloom stalks per plant. Sow seeds in ground in August or September for next season's bloom. Other good varieties include 'Appleblossom', with double, soft pink flowers; 'Nigra', with single flowers of deep maroon-black; and 'Peaches 'n' Dreams', with double peach flowers flushed with raspberry pink.

ALCHEMILLA

LADY'S-MANTLE

Rosaceae

PERENNIALS

ZONES VARY BY SPECIES

TOLERATE SUN IN COOL-SUMMER CLIMATES

REGULAR WATER

Alchemilla mollis

Rounded pale green lobed leaves have a silvery look; after rain or overhead watering they hold beads of water on their surfaces. Summer flowers are yellowish green, in large branched clusters, individually inconspicuous but attractive as a mass. Useful for edgings in shady places, as ground cover, and as soothing contrast to brightly colored flowers.

A. alpina. Zones 36–43. Mat-forming plant creeping by runners, with flowering stems 6–8 in. tall. Leaves 2 in. wide, divided into five or seven leaflets.

A. erythropoda. Zones 36–40. Resembles *A. glaucescens* but has more deeply lobed leaves and red-tinted flowering stems.

A. glaucescens (A. pubescens). Zones 36–40. Dense grower. Flowering stems to 8 in. tall. Leaves nearly round; seven to nine lobes.

A. mollis. Zones 31, 32, 34–43. To 2 ft. or more, with equal spread and nearly circular, scallop-edged leaves to 6 in. across.

ALDER. See ALNUS

ALDER BUCKTHORN. See RHAMNUS frangula

ALEXANDRIAN LAUREL. See DANAE

ALLAMANDA

Apocynaceae

EVERGREEN VINES OR SHRUBS

⚡ ALL ZONES

☼ FULL SUN

💧 REGULAR WATER

💧 ALL PARTS ARE POISONOUS IF INGESTED

Allamanda cathartica

These handsome tropical plants tolerate very little frost and require considerable heat for proper growth; warm nights as well as warm days seem necessary. Both foliage and flowers are imposing. Purchase plants to grow as summer annuals, or move them indoors for winter.

A. blanchetii. Shrubby, with climbing stems to 10 ft. Leaves grow to 5 in. long, and the trumpet-shaped flowers are purple-pink.

A. cathartica. ALLAMANDA, GOLDEN TRUMPET. Can grow to great heights as a vine, but often pinched back as a large free-standing shrub. Leaves are glossy, leathery, 4–6 in. long. Trumpet-shaped yellow flowers are 5 in. wide, 3 in. long. 'Hendersonii' has exceptionally attractive orange-yellow flowers.

A. schottii (A. neriifolia). BUSH ALLAMANDA. Shrubby, to 5 ft., with occasional climbing stems. Flowers 3 in. wide, tinted orange or reddish.

ALLIUM

ORNAMENTAL ALLIUM

Liliaceae

BULBS

⚡ ZONES VARY BY SPECIES; OR DIG AND STORE; OR GROW IN POTS

☼ ◖ FULL SUN OR PARTIAL SHADE

💧 REGULAR WATER DURING GROWTH AND BLOOM

Allium giganteum

About 500 species, all from the Northern Hemisphere. Relatives of the edible onion, peerless as cut flowers (fresh or dried) and useful in borders; smaller kinds are effective in rock gardens. Most ornamental alliums are hardy, sun loving, easy to grow; they thrive in deep, rich, sandy loam. Plant bulbs in fall. Lift and divide only after they become crowded. Alliums bear small flowers in compact or loose roundish clusters at ends of leafless stems 6 in.–5 ft. tall or more. Many are delightfully fragrant; those with onion odor must be bruised or cut to give it off. Various species provide flowers from late spring through summer, in white and shades of pink, rose, violet, red, blue, yellow. All alliums die to the ground after bloom, even in mild climates. In areas colder than stated hardiness, dig and store; or grow in pots and protect during winter.

A. aflatunense. Zones 31, 32, 34–43. Round clusters of lilac flowers on stems 2½–5 ft. tall. Resembles *A. giganteum* but with smaller (2–3-in.) flower clusters; blooms in late spring.

A. atropurpureum. Zones 31, 32, 34, 39. Stems to 2½ ft. tall carry 2-in. clusters of dark purple to nearly black flowers in late spring.

A. caeruleum (A. azureum). BLUE ALLIUM. Zones 31, 32, 34–45. Cornflower blue flowers in dense, round clusters 2 in. across on 1-ft. stems. Late spring bloom.

A. carinatum pulchellum (A. pulchellum). Zones 31, 32, 34–41. Tight clusters of reddish purple flowers on 2-ft. stems, late spring.

A. cepa. See Onion

A. cernuum. NODDING ONION. Zones 31, 32, 34–43. Loose clusters of nodding pink flowers in summer on stems to 2 ft. high. Good for naturalizing.

A. christophii (A. albopilosum). STAR OF PERSIA. Zones 31, 32, 34–41. Distinctive. Very large clusters (6–12 in. across) of lavender to deep lilac, starlike flowers with metallic sheen. Late spring bloom. Stems 12–15 in. tall. Leaves to 1½ ft. long, white and hairy beneath. Dried flower cluster looks like an elegant ornament.

A. cyaneum. Zones 31, 32, 34–41. To 10 in. high. Small clusters of blue flowers in summer. Narrow, threadlike, deep green leaves.

A. flavum. Zones 31, 32, 34–43. To 14 in. high. Loose clusters of bright yellow flowers in summer. Narrow, gray-green leaves.

A. giganteum. GIANT ALLIUM. Zones 31, 32, 34. Spectacular ball-like clusters of bright lilac flowers on stems 5 ft. tall or more. Summer bloom. Leaves 1½ ft. long, 2 in. wide.

'Globemaster'. Zones 31, 32, 34, 39. Produces large (to 8 in. across) clusters of star-shaped deep purple flowers in summer, on 2½-ft. stems.

A. karataviense. TURKESTAN ALLIUM. Zones 31, 32, 34–41. Large, dense, round flower clusters in midspring, varying in color from pinkish to beige to reddish lilac. Broad, flat, recurved leaves, 2–5 in. across.

A. moly. GOLDEN GARLIC. Zones 31, 32, 34–45. Bright, shining, yellow flowers in open clusters on 9–18-in.-tall stems. Late spring bloom. Flat leaves 2 in. wide, almost as long as flower stems.

A. narcissiflorum. Zones 31, 32, 34–43. Foot-tall stems with loose clusters of ½-in. bell-shaped, bright rose flowers, summer.

A. neapolitanum. Zones 31, 32, 34, 39. Spreading clusters of large white flowers on 1-ft. stems bloom in midspring. Leaves 1 in. wide. Variety 'Grandiflorum' is larger, blooms earlier. A form of 'Grandiflorum' listed as 'Cowanii' is considered superior. Grown commercially as cut flowers.

A. nutans. Zones 31, 32, 34–41. Bears round clusters of lilac to rose pink flowers, to 2 ft. high.

A. oreophilum (A. ostrowskianum). Zones 31, 32, 34–43. Large, loose clusters of rose-colored flowers on 8–12-in. stems in late spring; two or three narrow, gray-green leaves. 'Zwanenburg' has deep carmine red flowers, 6-in. stems. Good for rock gardens, cutting.

A. porrum. See Leek

A. rosenbachianum. Zones 31, 32, 34–43. Similar to *A. giganteum* but slightly smaller; blooms in late spring.

A. sativum. See Garlic

A. schoenoprasum. See Chives

A. schubertii. Zones 31, 32, 34–43. Large clusters (to 1 ft. across) of soft rose purple flowers with long stamens in early summer. Stems vary in height from 1–2 ft.

A. scorodoprasum. See Garlic

A. sphaerocephalum. DRUMSTICKS, ROUND-HEADED GARLIC. Zones 31, 32, 34–43. Tight, dense, spherical red-purple flower clusters on 2-ft. stems, early summer. Spreads freely.

A. tuberosum. CHINESE CHIVES, GARLIC CHIVES, ORIENTAL GARLIC. Zones 31, 32, 34–43. Spreads by tuberous rootstocks and by seeds. Clumps of gray-green, flat leaves ¼ in. wide, 1 ft. long or less. Abundance of 1–1½-ft.-tall stalks bear clusters of white flowers in summer. Flowers have scent of violets, are excellent for fresh or dry arrangements. Leaves have mild garlic flavor, are useful in salads and cooked dishes. Grow like chives.

ALLSPICE, CAROLINA. See CALYCANTHUS floridus

ALMOND, FLOWERING. See PRUNUS triloba

A

ALNUS

ALDER

Betulaceae

DECIDUOUS TREES

ZONES VARY BY SPECIES

SUN OR SHADE

AMPLE WATER

Alnus cordata

Moisture loving, thriving in moist or wet soils, even tolerating periodic flooding. Very fast growing. In all species, clusters of tassel-like, greenish yellow male flower catkins give interesting display before leaf-out. Female flowers develop into small woody cones that decorate bare branches in winter; these delight flower arrangers. Seeds attract birds.

A. cordata. ITALIAN ALDER. Zones 31, 32, 34–41. Native to Italy, Corsica. Young growth vertical; older trees to 40 ft., spreading to 25 ft. Heart-shaped, 4-in. leaves, glossy rich green above, paler beneath. Short deciduous period.

A. glutinosa. BLACK ALDER. Zones 34–45. Native to Europe, North Africa, Asia. Probably best as multistemmed tree. Grows to 70 ft. Roundish, 2–4-in., coarsely toothed leaves, dark lustrous green. Makes dense mass from ground up. Good for screen. 'Laciniata' has lobed leaves. 'Pyramidalis' is very erect, with upright branches, and grows to 50 ft. high.

A. incana. WHITE ALDER, GRAY ALDER. Zones 34–45. Native to Europe and the Caucasus. Good tree for cold, wet sites. Forms a pyramid to 40–60 ft. high. Dull green leaves 2–4 in. long. Varieties are more often planted than the species; these include one with yellow leaves, one with a weeping habit ('Pendula'), and many cut-leaf forms, including 'Laciniata'.

ALOCASIA

ELEPHANT'S EAR

Araceae

PERENNIALS

ALL ZONES

FILTERED SUNLIGHT

AMPLE WATER

PLANT JUICES ARE POISONOUS IF INGESTED

Alocasia macrorrhiza

Native to tropical Asia. Handsome, lush plants for tropical effects. Flowers like those of calla (*Zantedeschia*). Grow them outdoors in summer and as houseplants in winter. Provide ample organic matter in soil and light, frequent feedings. Tropical plant specialists sell many kinds with leaves in coppery and purplish tones, often with striking white veins.

A. amazonica. AFRICAN MASK. Leathery, deep bronzy green leaves to 16 in. long have wavy edges, heavy white main veins. This species is the one most commonly available as a house plant.

A. cuprea. GIANT CALADIUM. Large, arrow-shaped leaves to 1½ ft. long on 2-ft. stalks have deep green veins and zones, copper shading, and reddish purple undersides.

A. macrorrhiza. Large, arrow-shaped leaves to 2 ft. or longer, on stalks to 5 ft. tall, form a dome-shaped plant 4 ft. across. Tiny flowers on spike surrounded by greenish white bract. Flowers followed by reddish fruit, giving spike the look of corn on the cob.

A. odora. Similar to *A. macrorrhiza* but not quite as hardy. Flowers fragrant.

A. sanderiana. KRIS PLANT. Large, arrow-shaped leaves to 16 in. long on 2-ft. stems are deep green with wavy or lobed edges, silver veins and margins, and an overall silvery sheen.

A. watsoniana. Large, oblong, blue-green leaves and blue-green stems, to 3 ft. long. The leaves are puckered, veined and edged in silver, and reddish purple on the underside.

ALOE

Liliaceae

SUCCULENTS

ALL ZONES

FULL SUN OR PARTIAL SHADE

REGULAR TO LITTLE WATER

LATEX BENEATH THE SKIN IS AN IRRITANT

Aloe arborescens

Aloes range from 6-in. miniatures to trees; all form clumps of fleshy, pointed leaves and bear branched or unbranched clusters of orange, yellow, cream, or red flowers. Most are South African. Showy, easy to grow in well-drained soil in reasonably frost-free areas. Need little water but can take more. Most kinds make outstanding container plants. Some species in bloom every month; biggest show midwinter through summer. Leaves may be green or gray green, often strikingly banded or streaked with contrasting colors. Where winters are too cool, grow in pots and shelter from frosts. Aloes listed here are only a few of the many kinds.

A. arborescens. TREE ALOE. Branching stems with rosettes of gray-green, spiny-edged leaves. Flowers (late spring to early summer) in long, spiky clusters, bright vermilion to clear yellow. Withstands salt spray. Tolerates shade.

A. barbadensis. See *A. vera*

A. saponaria. Short-stemmed, clumps of broad, thick, 8-in.-long leaves with white spots. Branched flower stalk 1½–2½ ft. tall. Orange-red to shrimp pink flowers over long period.

A. variegata. PARTRIDGE-BREAST ALOE, TIGER ALOE. Foot-high, triangular rosette of fleshy, triangular, dark green, 5-in.-long leaves strikingly banded and edged with white. Loose clusters of pink to dull red flowers in summer.

A. vera (A. barbadensis). MEDICINAL ALOE, BARBADOS ALOE. Clustering rosettes of narrow, fleshy, stiffly upright leaves 1–2 ft. long. Yellow flowers in dense spike atop 3-ft. stalk in summer. Favorite folk medicine plant used to treat burns, bites, inflammation, and a host of other ills.

ALONSOA

MASK FLOWER

Scrophulariaceae

PERENNIALS USUALLY GROWN AS ANNUALS

ALL ZONES

FULL SUN OR PARTIAL SHADE

REGULAR WATER

Alonsoa warscewiczii

Mask flowers are usually grown as summer bedding plants, as fillers in the perennial border, or as indoor or outdoor container plants. Sprawling or erect to 3 ft., freely branching, with wispy foliage and open clusters of oddly shaped, roundish flowers. All are fairly easy to grow from seed, blooming the first year if started early and continuing to frost or cold weather.

A. linearis. Flowers brick red.

A. meridionalis. Flowers are orange to dark red, somewhat less than 1 in. wide. Seed-grown Firestone Jewels strain has flowers ranging from white through yellow to salmon, pink, and red. 'Shell Pink' and 'Salmon' are offered as nursery plants.

A. warscewiczii (A. grandiflora). Flowers scarlet to peach or sometimes white, with dark eye, to ½ in. across.

'Compacta' has scarlet flowers.

PRACTICAL GARDENING DICTIONARY

PLEASE SEE PAGES 449–523

ALOYSIA triphylla (Lippia citriodora)

LEMON VERBENA

Verbenaceae

DECIDUOUS OR PARTIALLY EVERGREEN HERB-SHRUB

⚡ ALL ZONES

☼ FULL SUN

💧 REGULAR WATER

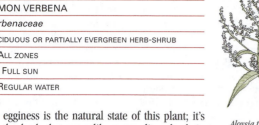

Aloysia triphylla

Legginess is the natural state of this plant; it's the herb that grew like a gangling shrub in grandmother's garden. Prized for its lemon-scented leaves. When you read of the scent of verbena in literature about the antebellum South, lemon verbena is the plant being described. Grows to 6 ft. or taller; narrow leaves to 3 in. long are arranged in whorls of three or four along branches. Bears open clusters of very small lilac or whitish flowers in summer. Needs well-drained soil.

Grow it as a houseplant (pinch frequently) and let it spend warm months outdoors.

LEMON VERBENA LEAVES FOR FRAGRANCE AND FLAVOR

This plant is prized for its lemon-scented leaves, which scent the area around them in the garden. The long, shiny leaves add lemony flavor to teas and iced drinks. Dry the leaves for potpourri. When making apple jelly, try placing a big fresh leaf in the bottom of each glass or jar. For all these purposes, pick the fresh-looking leaves from near top of stem.

ALSTROEMERIA

Liliaceae

PERENNIALS

⚡ WARMER PARTS OF ZONES 32, 34

☼ ◑ FULL SUN OR PARTIAL SHADE

💧 REGULAR WATER

⚠ CAUSES DERMATITIS IN ALLERGIC PEOPLE

Alstroemeria aurantiaca

Ligtu hybrids bloom on leafy stems 2–5 ft. tall, topped with broad, loose clusters of azalealike flowers in beautiful colors—orange, yellow, and shades of pink, rose, red, lilac, and creamy white to white; many are streaked and speckled with darker colors. Masses of color in borders from midspring to midsummer. Long-lasting cut flowers. Tops wither after bloom; flowerless shoots dry up even sooner.

Evergreen hybrids (Cordu, Meyer) have a long bloom season if spent flowering stems are pulled, not cut. Colors include white to pink, red, lilac, and purple, usually bicolored and spotted.

A Connecticut-bred group of hybrids called the Constitution Series has proved fairly hardy (with heavy mulching) along the Atlantic seaboard. Flowers are in the white to pink and purple color range, heavily marked with darker streaks.

A few nurseries offer 3–4-ft.-tall Peruvian lily (*A. aurea, A. aurantiaca*). 'Orange King' has orange-yellow, brown-spotted flowers; 'Lutea' has yellow flowers, 'Splendens' red. *A. psittacina (A. pulchella)* is 1–1½ ft. tall, more or less evergreen, with dark red flowers tipped green and spotted deep purple. It can be invasive. *A. p.* 'Variegata' has green leaves beautifully edged in white, and spreads much less rapidly than the species. The tubular flowers are speckled maroon and green, and appear on 3-ft. spikes in June. Where hardy, it is one of the most beautiful of all variegated plants.

All types grow best in cool, moist, deep, sandy to medium loam. Plant roots in fall; if you buy alstroemeria in a pot, you can plant outdoors any time in mild-winter climates. Set roots 6–8 in. deep, 1 ft. apart; handle brittle roots gently. Leave clumps undisturbed for many years because they reestablish slowly after transplanting. You can easily start alstroemerias by sowing seed where the plants are to grow or in individual pots for later transplanting. Sow in fall, winter, or earliest spring. All are hardy in cold-winter climates indicated if planted at proper depth and kept mulched in winter. Ligtu hybrids can be allowed to dry off after bloom. Evergreen kinds need moisture for continued bloom; cool summers also prolong bloom.

PICK ALSTROEMERIA FLOWERS IN A SPECIAL WAY

When you pick flowers of the evergreen kinds of alstroemeria, don't cut them. Instead, grasp each flower stem several inches above the soil and gently twist and pull upward to break the stem's base cleanly away from the rhizome. Cutting slows growth, but this technique encourages new bud growth and flower production.

ALTERNANTHERA ficoidea

Amaranthaceae

TROPICAL PERENNIAL TREATED AS ANNUAL

⚡ ALL ZONES

☼ FULL SUN

💧 REGULAR WATER

Alternanthera ficoidea 'Bettzickiana'

Colorful foliage somewhat resembles that of coleus but leaves of most cultivars are smaller. Plants grow 6–12 in. tall and should be planted 4–10 in. apart for colorful effect. Where winters are cold, plant only after soil warms up. Tolerates heat well. Keep low and compact by shearing. Grow from cuttings. Often sold as *A. bettzickiana*. 'Aurea Nana' is low grower with yellow-splotched foliage. 'Rosea Nana' has rose coloring. 'Bettzickiana' has spoon-shaped leaves with red and yellow markings. 'Magnifica' is a red-bronze dwarf. 'Parrot Feather' and 'Versicolor' have broad green leaves with yellow markings and pink veins.

ALTHAEA rosea. See **ALCEA rosea**

ALUM ROOT. See **HEUCHERA**

ALYSSUM

Brassicaceae (Cruciferae)

PERENNIALS

⚡ ZONES 31, 32, 34–43

☼ ◑ FULL SUN OR JUST A LITTLE SHADE

💧 MODERATE WATER

Alyssum montanum

Mostly native to Mediterranean region. Mounding plants or shrublets that brighten spring borders and rock gardens with their cheerful bloom. They thrive in poor, rocky, well-drained soil.

A. montanum. Stems to 8 in. high; leaves gray, hairy (denser on underside); flowers yellow, fragrant, in dense short clusters.

A. saxatile. See *Aurinia saxatilis*

A. wulfenianum. Prostrate and trailing, with fleshy, silvery leaves and sheets of pale yellow flowers.

A

ALYSSUM, SWEET. See LOBULARIA maritima

AMARACUS dictamnus. See ORIGANUM dictamnus

Amaranthaceae. The amaranth family largely consists of herbaceous plants, many of them weedy. Flowers are small and chaffy, often effective when massed.

AMARANTHUS

AMARANTH

Amaranthaceae

ANNUALS

⚡ ALL ZONES

☼ ◑ FULL SUN OR PARTIAL SHADE

🔴 REGULAR WATER

Amaranthus caudatus

Coarse, sometimes weedy plants; a few ornamental kinds are grown for their brightly colored foliage or flowers. Sow seed in early summer—soil temperature must be above 70°F/21°C for germination.

Picked when young and tender, leaves and stems of many species (even some of the weedy ones) can be cooked like spinach, taking its place in hot weather. Some species have seeds that look like sesame seeds, have a high protein content, and can be used as grain.

A. caudatus. LOVE-LIES-BLEEDING, TASSEL FLOWER. Sturdy, branching plant 3–8 ft. high; leaves 2–10 in. long, ½–4 in. wide. Red flowers in drooping, tassel-like clusters. 'Viridis' has green tassels. A curiosity rather than a pretty plant. One of the amaranths that produce grain.

A. hypochondriacus. PRINCE'S FEATHER. To 5 ft. high with leaves 1–6 in. long, ½–3 in. wide, usually reddish. Flowers red or brownish red in many-branched clusters. Some strains grown as spinach substitute or for grain. 'Erythrostachys' has deep red flowers and purple coloration on the leaves. 'Pygmy Torch' has upright flower spikes of deep maroon on dwarf plants.

A. tricolor. JOSEPH'S COAT. Branching plant 1–4 ft. high. Leaves 2½–6 in. long, 2–4 in. wide, blotched in shades of red and green. Selections such as 'Early Splendor', 'Flaming Fountain', and 'Molten Fire' bear masses of yellow to scarlet foliage at tops of main stems and principal branches. 'Aurora' is green, with the top leaves turning creamy yellow. 'Illumination' has upper leaves of brilliant rose red topped with yellow and bronzy brown lower leaves. Green-leafed strains used as spinach substitute under the name "tampala."

AMELANCHIER

JUNEBERRY, SHADBLOW, SERVICEBERRY

Rosaceae

DECIDUOUS SHRUBS OR SMALL TREES

⚡ ZONES 31, 32, 34–45

☼ ◑ FULL SUN OR PARTIAL SHADE

🔴 🔴 REGULAR TO MODERATE WATER

Amelanchier laevis

Graceful, airy trees provide year-round interest. Drooping clusters of white or pinkish flowers in early spring, just before or during leaf-out, are showy, though short lived. These are followed in early summer by edible blueberry-flavored fruits excellent in pies—if you can get to them before the birds do. Purplish new spring foliage turns deep green in summer, then fiery in fall; drops to reveal attractive silhouette in winter. Silvery gray bark with darker striations adds to the all-season beauty of these plants.

Plant against dark background to show off form, flowers, fall color. Noninvasive roots and light shade make these good trees to garden under.

Especially lovely in woodland gardens. Those with upright habit make excellent patio trees. All need a definite period of winter chill. Serviceberry is often pronounced "sarvisberry."

A. alnifolia. SASKATOON. Native to western Canada and mountainous parts of the western U.S. To 20 ft., spreading by rhizomes. 'Regent', 4–6 ft. tall, bears heavy crop of fruit in early summer. Red-and-yellow fall foliage.

A. arborea. DOWNY SERVICEBERRY. Native to eastern North America. Rounded tree to 25 ft. high. Oval leaves are hairy and gray when young, turning medium green, then yellow to red in fall. Drooping clusters of fragrant white flowers in spring. Reddish purple fruit.

A. canadensis. Narrowish, to 25 ft. tall, with short, erect flower clusters. Plants offered under this name may actually belong to other species.

A. grandiflora. APPLE SERVICEBERRY. Hybrid between *A. arborea* and *A. laevis*. Named selections—more than a dozen are available—may be sold under any of these species names. Most grow to 25 ft., with drooping clusters of white flowers opening from pinkish buds. 'Autumn Brilliance' has blue-green foliage that turns orange red in fall. 'Cole's Selection' and 'Princess Diana' are similar.

A. laevis. ALLEGHENY SERVICEBERRY. Native to eastern North America. Narrow shrub or small tree to 40 ft. with nodding or drooping, 4-in. white flower clusters. Leaves are bronzy purple when new, dark green in summer, yellow to red in autumn. Small black-purple fruit is very sweet.

AMERICAN SWEET GUM. See LIQUIDAMBAR styraciflua

AMETHYST FLOWER. See BROWALLIA

AMMI majus

BISHOP'S FLOWER

Apiaceae (Umbelliferae)

ANNUAL

⚡ ALL ZONES

☼ ◑ FULL SUN OR PARTIAL SHADE

🔴 🔴 REGULAR TO AMPLE WATER

Ammi majus

This native of the Mediterranean is a good garden substitute for Queen Anne's Lace. Rounded, 5–6-in. umbels of tiny, pure white flowers sit atop strong 1–3-ft. stems with ferny foliage. Prefers cool to moderate climates and grows best in moist, fertile soil. Sow seeds outdoors where plants will grow, just before last frost date, or start indoors in March or April; thin to 6–9 in. apart. Useful in informal and naturalistic plantings and cottage or cutting gardens.

AMMOBIUM alatum

WINGED EVERLASTING

Asteraceae (Compositae)

TENDER PERENNIAL GROWN AS ANNUAL OR BIENNIAL

⚡ ALL ZONES

☼ FULL SUN

🔴 REGULAR WATER

Ammobium alatum

A plant covered in tiny white hairs with daisy-like, papery flower heads and winged or angled stalks, grown for cutting and drying or occasionally massed in beds and borders. Blooms have yellow centers surrounded by silvery bracts. Plants grow 2–3 ft. tall and flower heads are about 1 in. across. Var. *grandiflorum*, a better garden plant than the species, has 2-in.-wide flowers. Stems emerge from a 12-in.-high basal rosette of narrow, tapered leaves 6–8 in. long. Stem leaves are short, sparse, and lancelike. Main and side stems start producing terminal blooms in early summer, with new branches appearing as old ones are cut. Flowers are long-lasting but eventually centers fade from golden yellow to reddish brown. Stems may bend under the weight of mature flowers, so cultivate with more *Ammobium* for support or let stems weave through stronger plants. This Australian native prefers a dry, sandy site but will grow in ordinary well-drained soil.

Start plants indoors from seed 6–8 weeks before the last frost and transplant into the garden 12 in. apart when soil is warm. In warm climates, sow outdoors in September where you want them to grow. In cold-winter areas, sow outdoors in early spring. Thin seedlings to 1 ft. apart. To use in dried arrangements, cut long stems or entire branches before flowers fully open. Bind the stems with string or a rubber band and hang upside down in a warm, dry, preferably darkened room until brittle.

AMORACIA RUSTICANA 'VARIEGATA'. See HORSERADISH

AMORPHA

Fabaceae (Leguminosae)

DECIDUOUS SHRUBS

🌡 ZONES 31, 32, 34–45

☼ FULL SUN

💧💧 REGULAR TO MODERATE WATER

Amorpha fruticosa

Shrubs with leaves divided featherwise into many leaflets; 3–6-in.-long spikelike clusters of single-petaled flowers in early summer are blue or purple. In cold weather, plants may die back nearly to the ground; in warmer regions, they should be cut back severely to prevent lankiness. Tough and undemanding, withstanding heat and wind.

A. canescens. LEAD PLANT. Native to the high plains from Canada to Texas. About 3 ft. tall and wide, with silvery, downy foliage.

A. fruticosa. INDIGO BUSH, FALSE INDIGO. Native to eastern U.S. Lanky growth to 10–15 ft. tall, with light green foliage. Needs hard pruning in winter or early spring to maintain some degree of compactness.

A. nana. Native from Minnesota to the Rocky Mountains. To 2 ft. high, with oblong leaves. Young shoots are reddish brown.

AMORPHOPHALLUS konjac

DEVIL'S TONGUE, SNAKE PALM, UMBRELLA ARUM

Araceae

PERENNIAL

🌡 ZONES 31, 32, OR HOUSEPLANT

☼ PARTIAL SHADE

💧 MORE THAN REGULAR WATER

Amorphophallus konjac

In cold zones, grow this native of southern China as a pot plant in a greenhouse, or transplant outdoors when all threat of frost has passed. Formerly known as *A. rivieri konjac*, it is grown mostly as a curiosity for its striking, though fetid, single bloom, appearing on a 2-ft. mottled stalk of brownish green. The inflorescence, which can reach 3 ft. in height, consists of a purple spadix (or central spike) nestled in a brown-and-white-spotted green spathe (modified leaf) with a purplish outer edge. On older, well-grown specimens, it is followed by a single dramatic leaf that rises to about 6 ft. in height. Indoors, plants need ample room for the large tubers and a combination of rich potting soil and compost; repot at the beginning of each growing season or transplant outdoors into moist, humusy soil, keeping

well watered until growth tapers off. Over the winter, when the plant is fully dormant, soil should be kept nearly dry but not arid. Outdoors, the plant requires ample moisture while growing, and benefits from a winter mulch where it can be safely left in the ground.

AMPELOPSIS
brevipedunculata

PORCELAIN BERRY

Vitaceae

DECIDUOUS VINE

🌡 ZONES 31, 32, 34–43

☼ ◐ ● SUN OR SHADE

💧 💧 REGULAR TO MODERATE WATER

Ampelopsis brevipedunculata

Rampant climber with twining tendrils. To 20 ft. Large, handsome, three-lobed, 2½–5-in.-wide leaves are dark green. In warm climates, leaves turn red and partially drop in fall; more leaves come out, redden, and drop all winter. Many clusters of small grapelike berries turn from greenish ivory to brilliant metallic blue in late summer and fall. Needs strong support. Highly invasive and not recommended, especially near woods, natural areas. Attracts birds. Japanese beetles can be a problem. 'Elegans' has leaves variegated with white and pink. Smaller, less vigorous, and less hardy than the species, it is a splendid hanging-basket plant.

Boston ivy and Virginia creeper, formerly included in genus *Ampelopsis,* are now placed under genus *Parthenocissus* because, unlike *Ampelopsis,* both have disks at ends of their tendrils.

AMSONIA

BLUE STAR FLOWER

Apocynaceae

PERENNIALS

🌡 ZONES VARY BY SPECIES

☼ ◐ FULL SUN OR LIGHT SHADE

💧 REGULAR TO MODERATE WATER

Amsonia tabernaemontana

Elegant milkweed relatives with narrow leaves and erect stems topped by clusters of small, star-shaped, pale blue flowers. Most bloom in late spring. All are tough plants that tolerate ordinary soil and occasional lapses in watering. Bright yellow fall foliage color is a bonus.

A. ciliata (A. hubrectii). Zones 31, 32, 34–41. To 2½–3 ft. tall, with crowded, needlelike (but soft), 2-in. leaves; has exceptional fall color.

A. illustris. Zones 31, 32, 34–41. Like *A. tabernaemontana* but has shiny, leathery leaves.

A. tabernaemontana. Zones 31, 32, 34–45. To 2–2½ ft. tall, with narrow, willowlike foliage. 'Montana' is more compact and blooms earlier.

AMUR CHOKECHERRY. See PRUNUS maackii

Anacardiaceae. The cashew family includes evergreen or deciduous trees, shrubs, and vines with small, unshowy, but often profuse flowers. Foliage is attractive; fruits are sometimes showy or edible. Many have poisonous or irritating sap. Mango (*Mangifera*) and poison ivy (*Toxicodendron*) indicate the diversity of the family.

FOR INFORMATION ON SELECTING PLANTS

PLEASE SEE PAGES 47–112

A

ANACYCLUS depressus
(A. pyrethrum depressus)

MOUNT ATLAS DAISY

Asteraceae (Compositae)

PERENNIAL

ZONES 31, 32, 34, 39

FULL SUN

MODERATE TO LITTLE WATER

Anacyclus depressus

Slowly forms dense, spreading mat somewhat like *Chamaemelum*. Grayish leaves finely divided. Single daisylike flowers to 2 in. across, with yellow center disks and white ray-type petals (red on reverse side). Blooms in summer. Good in sunny, dry, hot rock gardens. May freeze in extremely severe winters or rot in cold, wet, heavy soil. Dislikes humidity.

ANAGALLIS

PIMPERNEL

Primulaceae

ANNUALS OR PERENNIALS

ALL ZONES

FULL SUN

REGULAR TO MODERATE WATER

Anagallis monelli linifolia

Two species sometimes seen, one a weed. Less aggressive type attractive in rock gardens.

A. arvensis. SCARLET PIMPERNEL. Annual. Low-growing weed with ¼-in. flowers of brick red. *A. a. caerulea* has deep blue, larger flowers.

A. monelli. Perennial or biennial to 1½ ft., with ¾-in. flowers of bright blue. 'Pacific Blue' is a superior selection; 'Phillipsii' is compact, 1 ft. tall; *A. m. linifolia* has narrower leaves than the species.

ANAPHALIS

PEARLY EVERLASTING

Asteraceae (Compositae)

PERENNIALS

ZONES VARY BY SPECIES

PARTIAL OR FULL SHADE

REGULAR TO MODERATE WATER

Anaphalis triplinervis

Furry gray foliage is the outstanding characteristic of the pearly everlastings. Most are mounding, heat-tolerant plants with erect, branching stems carrying attractively displayed (though not showy) clusters of papery daisies. These may be cut in summer for use in dried arrangements. Plants spread to form broad mats and are useful as foreground plants or in the rock garden. Since they withstand lower light than is typical for gray-leafed plants, they are ideal for semishady borders where other gray plants will fail. They are not fussy about soil, needing only reasonably good drainage.

A. margaritacea. Zones 31, 32, 34–45. To 3 ft. high. Leaves, to 6 in. long, are green above, white and woolly beneath. Pearly white flowers with yellow centers. *A. m. yedoensis (A. yedoensis, A. cinnamomea)* has smaller leaves than the species and brown-tinted flowers; it is less cold hardy (Zones 32, 34, 39).

A. triplinervis. Zones 31, 32, 34–43. Slightly shorter than *A. margaritacea*, with similar flowers and somewhat smaller, silvery leaves. 'Sulphur Light' has pale yellow blooms centered with deeper yellow. 'Summer Snow' bears bright white flowers.

FOR INFORMATION ON YOUR CLIMATE ZONE

PLEASE SEE PAGES 30–46

ANCHUSA

Boraginaceae

ANNUALS, BIENNIALS, OR PERENNIALS

ZONES VARY BY SPECIES

FULL SUN

REGULAR TO MODERATE WATER

Anchusa capensis

Related to forget-me-not *(Myosotis)* but larger and showier. Worth growing for vibrant blue color; rate high for purest blue among easier plants. Grow in well-drained soil. High humidity inhibits performance.

A. azurea (A. italica). Perennial. Zones 31, 32, 34–45. Coarse, open, spreading, 3–5 ft. tall. Leaves 6 in. or longer, covered with bristly hairs. Clusters of bright blue blossoms, ½–¾ in. across, bloom in summer and fall. Horticultural forms include 'Dropmore', gentian blue; 'Opal', sky blue; and 'Loddon Royalist' (a newer variety), rich blue. Not for small areas: once established, it is difficult to eradicate.

A. capensis. CAPE FORGET-ME-NOT, SUMMER FORGET-ME-NOT. Biennial in warm climates; annual throughout the Northeast. Native to South Africa. To 1½ ft. high. Leaves narrow, to 5 in. long, ½ in. wide. Flowers bright blue, white throated, ¼ in. across, in clusters 2 in. long. Use for vivid clean blue in summer borders with marigolds, petunias.

ANDROMEDA polifolia

BOG ROSEMARY

Ericaceae

EVERGREEN SHRUB

ZONES 36–45

FULL SUN OR LIGHT SHADE

AMPLE WATER

Andromeda polifolia

Erect or spreading shrub, usually 4–6 in. tall, rarely to 1 ft. Narrow, leathery leaves are ½–2 in. long, dark green above, blue gray beneath. Flowers flask shaped, nodding, white to pink, up to eight in a cluster at top of stems. Plant requires strongly acid soil with ample moisture, sun (but with protection from hottest sun) or light shade. Connoisseur's plant for rock garden, pot culture, or streamside or bog garden. Varieties usually offered are 'Grandiflora', a dwarf form with blue-green leaves and large, creamy, pink-shaded flowers; and 'Nana', very compact and vigorous, with nearly round pink flowers.

ANDROPOGON glomeratus
(A. virginicus)

BUSHY BEARD GRASS, BUSHY BLUESTEM

Poaceae (Gramineae)

PERENNIAL

ZONES 32, 34–41

FULL SUN OR PARTIAL SHADE

MORE THAN REGULAR WATER

Andropogon glomeratus

Handsome grass native to streamsides and bogs in the eastern and southern U.S. Produces attractive clumps with narrow, grassy leaves that range from 1 to 2 ft. in height. Clumps spread to 2 ft. Foliage is topped by fluffy, densely branched, cottonlike plumes of white flowers in early fall. Foliage turns attractive shades of orange-brown in fall. Grows best in rich, moist soil and full sun, although plants will also tolerate some shade. Can become invasive and is best in wild areas, where it will naturalize. Cut foliage back to the ground in late winter or very early spring.

ANDROSACE

ROCK JASMINE

Primulaceae

PERENNIALS

⬥ ZONES 36–45

☼ FULL SUN

⬥ MODERATE WATER

Androsace lanuginosa

Choice rock garden miniatures grown mostly by alpine plant specialists. Summer bloomers. All types require perfect drainage and are best adapted to gravelly banks in rock gardens. Protect from more aggressive rockery plants such as alyssum, rockcress, aubrieta.

A. carnea. Tufted plant just 2 in. high, to 6 in. wide. Leaves are evergreen, to ¾ in. wide, hairy along the edges. Clusters of pink flowers with yellow eye in late spring.

A. lanuginosa. Trailing plant forms mats 3 ft. across. Silvery leaves to ¾ in. long, covered with silky white hairs. Pink flowers in dense clusters on 2-in. stems. *A. l. leichtlinii* has white flowers with crimson eye.

A. primuloides. Trailing; forms 4-in.-long runners. Leaves ½–2 in. long in rosettes covered with silvery hairs. Flowers pink, to ½ in. across, in clusters on 5-in. stems.

A. sarmentosa. Spreads by runners. Leaves to 1½ in. long, in rosettes, covered with silvery hairs when young. Flowers rose colored, ¼ in. across, in clusters on stems 5 in. tall. *A. s. chumbyi* forms dense clump, has woolly leaves.

A. sempervirens. Spreads by stolons and forms mats to 8 in. across. Evergreen leaves are leathery and spoon-shaped. Clusters of fragrant, pink to mauve flowers bloom in spring.

A. villosa. Forms mats or cushions to 8 in. across. Evergreen leaves are oblong and hairy on the underside. In spring bears clusters of white flowers with yellow eye that may turn pink or red as flowers age.

ANEMONE

WINDFLOWER, ANEMONE

Ranunculaceae

PERENNIALS WITH TUBEROUS OR FIBROUS ROOTS

⬥ ZONES VARY BY SPECIES

☼ ◑ ● EXPOSURE NEEDS VARY BY SPECIES

⬥ REGULAR WATER

⬥ ALL PARTS ARE POISONOUS IF INGESTED

Anemone blanda

A rich and varied group of plants ranging in size from alpine rock garden miniatures to tall Japanese anemones grown in borders; bloom extends from very early spring to fall, depending on species.

Of the species listed here, *A. blanda, A. coronaria,* and *A. fulgens* are grown from tubers; in general, tuberous types are short lived in warm regions, where they may best be treated as annuals. Plant them in a spot that gets some shade every day. Set out tubers October or November; wait until spring to set out *A. coronaria* and *A. fulgens.* (Or, if planting in November, mulch with 6–8 in. of leaf mold or peat moss after first hard frost.)

Plant tubers 1–2 in. deep, 8–12 in. apart, in rich, light, well-drained garden loam. Or start in flats of damp sand; set out in garden when leaves are a few inches tall. Keep soil moist. Protect from birds until leaves toughen. In high-rainfall areas, excess moisture induces rot.

A. altaica. Zones 32, 34–45. Creeping, to 8 in. high and 1 ft. across. Lobed and toothed leaves to 1½ in. long. In spring, white flowers veined with purple inside.

A. blanda. GRECIAN WINDFLOWER. Zones 31, 32, 34–43. Stems rise 2–8 in. from tuberous roots. Finely divided leaves covered with soft hairs. In spring, one sky blue flower, 1–1½ in. across, on each stem. Sometimes

confused with *A. apennina,* which has more pointed leaf segments. Grow with and among Japanese maples, azaleas, and other light shrubbery in partial shade. Associate with miniature daffodils, tulips, and scillas; or grow in pots. Selections with 2-in. flowers (in blue and other colors) on 10–12-in. plants include 'Blue Star', 'Pink Star', 'White Splendor', and purplish red 'Radar'.

A. canadensis. Zones 31, 32, 34–45. Grows 1–2 ft. tall, with divided leaves and inch-wide white flowers springing in twos and threes from the upper leaf joints; summer bloom. Partial shade.

A. coronaria. POPPY-FLOWERED ANEMONE. Zones 31, 32, 34, 39. Tuberous rooted. Common large-flowered, showy anemone valued for cutting and for spectacular color in spring borders. Finely divided green leaves. Flowers red, blue, tones and mixtures of these colors, and white, 1½–2½ in. across, borne singly on 6–18-in. stems. Most popular strains are De Caen (with single flowers) and St. Brigid (with semidouble to double flowers). Full sun or partial shade.

A. fulgens. SCARLET WINDFLOWER. Zones 31, 32, 34, 39. To 1 ft. high from tuberous roots. Leaves entirely or slightly divided. Flowers 2½ in. across, brilliant scarlet with black stamens, late spring or early summer. St. Bavo strain comes in unusual color range including pink and rusty coral. Partial shade.

A. hybrida (A. japonica, A. hupehensis japonica). JAPANESE ANEMONE. Zones 31, 32, 34–43. A long-lived, fibrous-rooted perennial indispensable for fall color in partial shade. Graceful, branching stems 2–4 ft. high rise from clump of dark green, three- to five-lobed leaves covered with soft hairs. Flowers semidouble, in white, silvery pink, or rose. Many named varieties. Slow to establish but once started spreads readily if roots not disturbed. Mulch in fall where winters are extremely severe. Increase by divisions in fall or early spring or by root cuttings in spring. May need staking. Effective in clumps in front of tall shrubbery or under high-branching trees. Good cultivars include 'Alice' (white, double), 'Honorine Jobert' (white), 'Konigin Charlotte' (pink, semidouble), 'Kriemhilde' (light purplish pink, semidouble), 'Margarette' (pink, nearly double), 'Max Vogel' (light pink), 'Prinz Heinrich' (medium pink), 'September Charm' (pale pink), and 'Whirlwind' (white, semidouble).

A. nemorosa. WOOD ANEMONE. Zones 31, 32, 34–43. To 1 ft., with creeping rhizomes, deeply cut leaves, and inch-wide white (rarely pinkish or blue) spring flowers held above the foliage. Spreads slowly to make an attractive woodland ground cover. Many named varieties exist; 'Allenii' has large blue flowers, and there are double forms. Partial to full shade.

WHICH SIDE OF AN ANEMONE TUBER IS UP?

Locating the top side of an anemone tuber can be difficult because of its irregular shape. The important sign to look for is the depressed scar left by the base of last year's stem (sometimes you really have to search for it); plant the tuber with the scarred side up.

A. pulsatilla. See *Pulsatilla vulgaris.*

A. quinquefolia. Zones 31, 32, 34–45. American native. Attractive woodland ground cover resembling *A. nemorosa,* with inch-wide white flowers in spring. *A. q. oregana* is similar, but blooms are sometimes blue or pink.

A. ranunculoides. Zones 32, 34–43. Spreading, to 4 in. high and 1½ ft. across. Deeply lobed leaves, rich yellow flowers in spring. Nice for naturalizing in a woodland garden.

A. sylvestris. SNOWDROP ANEMONE. Zones 31, 32, 34–45. European native growing to 1½ ft. tall. White, fragrant, 1½–3-in. flowers appear in spring; attractive cottony seed heads follow. Partial to full shade.

A. tomentosa (A. vitifolia 'Robustissima'). Zones 32, 34–43. Native to China. To 5 ft. high. Lobed and toothed leaves are hairy on the underside. Clusters of pale pink flowers bloom in late summer to early fall.

A. virginica. Zones 32, 34–43. American native to 2 ft. high, with segmented leaves and, in summer, white flowers.

A. vitifolia. GRAPE-LEAVED ANEMONE. Zones 32, 34–41. To 3 ft. high. Deep green, lobed leaves resemble grape leaves. White flowers bloom in late summer to early fall.

ANEMONELLA thalictroides

RUE ANEMONE
Ranunculaceae
PERENNIAL
⚘ ZONES 32, 34–43
◑ ● PARTIAL OR FULL SHADE
💧 REGULAR WATER

Anemonella thalictroides

Delicate woodland plant native to eastern North America. Grows to 9 in. high, with finely divided leaves resembling those of meadow rue (*Thalictrum*). Loose clusters of inch-wide white (usually) or pink flowers appear in early spring. Attractive for close-up viewing. The selection known as either 'Rosea Plena' or 'Schoaff's Double Pink' has long-lasting, fully double pink flowers like tiny roses.

ANEMONOPSIS macrophylla

FALSE ANEMONE
Ranunculaceae
PERENNIAL
⚘ ZONES 32, 34–43
◑ ● PARTIAL TO FULL SHADE
💧 REGULAR WATER

Anemonopsis macrophylla

Airy summer-blooming perennial resembling a small Japanese anemone and grown for its nodding, lavender flowers rising on long dark stems from a clump of large, shiny, dark green leaves. Long-stalked waxy flowers on thin stems appear like delicate wands, while the feathery, deep-cut leaves have a bolder look. This rare Japanese native grows up to 3 ft. tall.

Plant at the bog's edge, in small gardens and shady woodland borders, or near the front of raised beds to view the underside of the flowers. Use with plants of contrasting foliage such as hosta, pulmonaria, and other shade lovers. Prefers protected woodsy setting with moist loose loam, rich in humus or decaying leaves. Wind and dry spells can kill it. Propagate in spring by division or by fresh seed in late summer.

ANETHUM graveolens

DILL
Apiaceae (Umbelliferae)
ANNUAL HERB
⚘ ALL ZONES
☀ FULL SUN
💧 REGULAR WATER

Anethum graveolens

To 3–4 ft. Soft, feathery leaves; umbrellalike, 6-in.-wide clusters of small yellow flowers. Seeds and leaves have pungent fragrance. Sow seed where plants are to be grown; for constant supply, sow several times during spring and summer. Thin seedlings to 1½ ft. apart. Sprouts and grows better in spring than summer. An easy way to grow it in a casual garden is to

let a few plants go to seed. Seedlings appear here and there at odd times and can be pulled and chopped as "dill weed." Use seeds in pickling and vinegar; use fresh or dried leaves with fish or lamb, in salads, stews, sauces.

ANGELICA'S CULINARY USES

Angelica leaves (*A. archangelica*) are good in salads; leafstalks can be cooked and eaten like celery. Both leafstalks and hollow flower stems can be candied and used to decorate pastries. The seeds are used commercially to flavor wines, vermouth, and liqueurs (Benedictine and Chartreuse).

ANGELICA

ANGELICA
Apiaceae (Umbelliferae)
BIENNIAL
⚘ ZONES 31, 32, 34–43
◑ PARTIAL SHADE
💧 REGULAR WATER

Angelica archangelica

Angelicas are big, architectural plants that like a moist location. Grow them in a large border or alongside a pond. Give them moist, rich soil in partial shade.

A. archangelica. A perennial often treated as a biennial. Its candied stems are used in confectionery. It grows to 6 ft. high with divided and toothed, yellow-green leaves 2–3 ft. long. Greenish white flowers in large umbrellalike clusters. Cut flowers before buds open to prolong plant's life. Propagate from seed sown as soon as ripe in autumn.

A. atropurpurea. An American native, this perennial grows to 6 ft. or more, with purple stems and white flowers. The green leaves are toothed and divided.

A. gigas. Native to Korea, a biennial or short-lived perennial to 6 ft. Plants have toothed and divided green leaves, and in late summer to early fall bear deep purple flower clusters on dark reddish purple stems. Flowers highly attractive to bees, wasps, hornets, and other stinging insects.

ANGEL'S HAIR. See ARTEMISIA schmidtiana

ANGEL'S TEARS. See NARCISSUS triandrus

ANISE. See PIMPINELLA anisum

ANISE TREE. See ILLICIUM

ANISODONTEA

CAPE MALLOW
Malvaceae
EVERGREEN SHRUBS
⚘ ALL ZONES
☀ FULL SUN
💧 REGULAR TO LITTLE WATER

Anisodontea hypomandarum

These quick-growing South Africans, grown as annuals in the Northeast, are notable for producing vast quantities of flowers over a long period. Growth is rounded, rather open but freely branching, with small lobed leaves. Flowers are shaped like miniature individual hollyhock flowers and are borne throughout the summer. Use in shrub perennial borders or in large containers. Dig and overwinter in a cool greenhouse, or purchase new plants in early spring.

A. capensis. Grows to 3 or more ft., with 1-in. lobed leaves and 1-in. flowers of purplish pink, with deeper veining and a dark basal spot. Blooms from summer to autumn.

A. hypomandarum. To 5 ft., with 1½-in. leaves and inch-wide pink flowers with dark veins and eyes. Flowering is continuous and profuse. Sometimes trained as single-trunk standards. 'Tara's Pink' has larger leaves and larger, lighter flowers.

ANISOSTICHUS capreolata (Bignonia capreolata)

CROSSVINE

Bignoniaceae

EVERGREEN OR SEMIEVERGREEN VINE

ZONES 31, 32, 34, 39

FULL SUN OR LIGHT SHADE

REGULAR WATER

Anisostichus capreolata

Often still sold as *Bignonia capreolata*. Native to the South and lower Midwest. Climbs rapidly to 30 ft. or more by tendrils and holdfast disks. Useful for covering fences, poles, masonry walls, and outbuildings; can also grow up the trunk of an established tree. Shiny dark green leaves consist of two 6-in.-long, lance-shaped leaflets and a tendril; leaf cover is not dense. In winter, leaves turn purplish; they will fall off in severe weather. Clustered, 2-in., trumpet-shaped flowers, typically brownish red or brownish orange, appear in spring. 'Tangerine Beauty', with bright apricot orange flowers, is exceptionally bright colored and free blooming. 'Atropurpurea' has long, narrow leaves and deep brownish purple flowers.

ANNUAL MALLOW. See LAVATERA trimestris

ANTENNARIA

PUSSY TOES

Asteraceae (Compositae)

PERENNIALS

ZONES 36–45

FULL SUN

REGULAR TO LITTLE WATER

Antennaria dioica

Mat-forming plants with rosettes of woolly foliage and small furry puffs of flower heads. Tough and tolerant of heat, cold, and poor soil, they spread slowly but surely among rocks or along crevices in paving. Useful small-scale bulb cover or ground cover. Flowerheads can be dried and used in dried-flower arrangements. Accept regular water if soil is well drained.

A. dioica. COMMON PUSSYTOES. The most commonly grown species. Native to Europe, Asia, and the Aleutian Islands. Inch-high gray mats produce pinkish white flower puffs. 'Rosea' bears rose pink flowers. 'Rubra' has deep pink flowers.

A. neglecta. SMALLER PUSSYTOES. Native to the northern U.S. White flower puffs atop 3-in. stems in mid- to late spring.

FOR GROWING SYMBOL EXPLANATIONS

PLEASE SEE PAGE 113

ANTHEMIS

Asteraceae (Compositae)

PERENNIALS

ZONES VARY BY SPECIES

FULL SUN

REGULAR TO MODERATE WATER

Anthemis tinctoria

Aromatic foliage, especially when bruised. Leaves divided into many segments. Flowers daisylike or buttonlike. Some are weedy, but the following species are choice garden plants. All need good drainage.

A. carpatica (A. cretica carpatica). Zones 31, 32, 34, 39. Green to gray-green mounds with 1½-in. white, yellow-centered daisies on 6-in. stems in spring and summer.

A. marschalliana (A. biebersteiniana). Zones 31, 32. Rounded plant 1 ft. tall and as wide, with finely cut, fernlike, silvery leaves and 1-in. brilliant yellow, daisylike blooms in summer.

A. nobilis. See *Chamaemelum nobile*

A. punctata cupaniana. Zones 31, 32, 34, 39. Foot-tall, spreading mounds of silvery foliage topped by a long show of white daisies.

A. sancti-johannis. Zones 31, 32, 34–43. Clump-forming plant to 3 ft. high. Leaves are white-tipped and covered with gray hairs; bright orangey yellow flowers all summer.

A. tinctoria. GOLDEN MARGUERITE. Zones 32, 34–45. Erect, shrubby. Grows to 2–3 ft. Angular stems. Light green, much-divided leaves. Golden yellow, daisylike flowers, to 2 in. across, bloom in summer and fall. Short lived; divide and replant frequently. Grow from seed, stem cuttings, or divisions in fall or spring. Varieties include 'Beauty of Grallagh', golden orange flowers; 'E. C. Buxton', white with yellow centers; 'Kelwayi', golden yellow; 'Moonlight', soft, pale yellow.

ANTHERICUM liliago

ST. BERNARD'S LILY

Liliaceae

PERENNIAL

ZONES 31, 32, 34, 39

FULL SUN

REGULAR WATER

Anthericum liliago

Comprised of more than 50 species, anthericums are native to America, Europe, and Africa. They do not have bulbs like other members of the lily family but tuberous roots instead. Small, white, lilylike flowers bloom in late spring and early summer and stand out against long, narrow, grasslike leaves. *A. liliago* is the most frequently cultivated species and grows to 3 ft., with clustered flowers to 1¼ in. across. Easy to cultivate, it thrives in rich loam with minimal attention and will not spread appreciably. Excellent for borders, container gardens, and informal landscape settings.

A NATURAL DYE FROM ANTHEMIS

Golden marguerite (*Anthemis tinctoria*) is also known as yellow chamomile. Like its relative, true chamomile (*Chamaemelum nobile,* formerly *Anthemis nobilis*), the flowers of golden marguerite can be used to produce a yellow dye. To dye 1 pound of yarn, boil 8 quarts of fresh flowers in 4–4½ gallons of soft water. Simmer ½–1 hour, then strain. Before dyeing, mordant the yarn by simmering in 4 gallons of soft water with ½ ounce of potassium dichromate and ½ ounce cream of tartar. Or, for a brighter yellow, substitute 4 ounces potassium aluminum sulfate and 1 ounce cream of tartar.

A

ANTHRISCUS cerefolium

CHERVIL
Apiaceae (Umbelliferae)
ANNUAL HERB
⧄ ALL ZONES
◑ PARTIAL SHADE
● REGULAR WATER

Anthriscus cerefolium

Grows 1–2 ft. high. Finely cut, fernlike leaves resembling parsley; white flowers. Use like parsley, fresh or dried; flavor milder than parsley. Grow from seed in raised bed near kitchen door, in box near barbecue, or in vegetable garden. Quickly goes to seed in hot weather. Keep flower clusters cut to encourage vegetative growth.

ANTIRRHINUM majus

SNAPDRAGON
Scrophulariaceae
PERENNIAL USUALLY TREATED AS ANNUAL
⧄ ALL ZONES
☼ FULL SUN
● REGULAR WATER

Antirrhinum majus

Among best flowers for sunny borders and cutting, reaching greatest perfection in spring and early summer. Individual flower of basic snapdragon has five lobes, which are divided into unequal upper and lower "jaws"; slight pinch at sides of flower will make dragon open its jaws. Later developments include double flowers; the bell-shaped kind, with round, open flowers; and the azalea-shaped bloom, which is a double bellflower.

Snapping snapdragons in tall (2½–3-ft.) range include Pocket and Topper strains (single flowers) and Double Supreme strain. Intermediate (12–20 in.) are Cinderella, Coronette, Minaret, 'Princess White with Purple Eye', Sprite, and Tahiti. Dwarfs (6–8 in.) include Dwarf Bedding Floral Carpet, Kim, Kolibri, and Royal Carpet.

Bell-flowered strains include Bright Butterflies and Wedding Bells (both 2½ ft.); Little Darling and Liberty Bell (both 15 in.); and Pixie (6–8 in.). Azalea-flowered strains include Madame Butterfly (2½ ft.) and Sweetheart (1 ft.).

> ### FIVE WAYS TO AVOID SNAPDRAGON RUST
> Snapdragons, like lawns, roses, and hollyhocks, can fall victim to rust (orange pustules on undersides of leaves). Here are five ways to avoid or minimize it: Start with rust-resistant varieties (even that's not foolproof). Keep plants well watered. Avoid overhead watering (or do it only in the morning or on sunny days). Feed regularly. If necessary, change planting locations from one year to the next.

Sow seed in flats indoors, in very early spring for later transplanting or buy started plants at nursery. Set out plants midspring.

Valuable cut flowers. Tall and intermediate forms are splendid vertical accents in borders with delphinium, iris, daylily, peach-leafed bluebell (*Campanula persicifolia*), Oriental poppy. Dwarf kinds are effective as edgings and in rock gardens and raised beds, or pots.

Apiaceae. This family, formerly known as Umbelliferae, comprises nearly 3,000 plants, most of them annuals and perennials. All have flowers in umbels—flat- or round-topped clusters whose individual flower stems all originate at a single point. Many are vegetables (carrot, parsnip, celery, fennel) or aromatic herbs (parsley, coriander, dill). Others are grown for ornament, such as wild buckwheat (*Eryngium*) and blue lace flower (*Trachymene*).

Apocynaceae. The dogbane family contains shrubs, trees, and vines with milky, often poisonous sap. Flowers are often showy and fragrant, as in *Allamanda* and *Mandevilla*.

Aponogetonaceae. Only the following genus is of importance in this small family of aquatic plants.

APONOGETON distachyus

CAPE PONDWEED, WATER HAWTHORN
Aponogetonaceae
AQUATIC PLANT
⧄ ALL ZONES
☼ ◑ FULL SUN OR PARTIAL SHADE
● LIVES IN WATER

Aponogeton distachyus

Native to South Africa. Suitable for small water gardens. Like miniature water lily, it produces floating leaves from submerged tuber. Leaves are long and narrow; ⅓-in.-long white, fragrant flowers stand above water in double-branched clusters. In hot-summer climates, blooms in cool weather and is dormant in hottest weather; where winters are cold, blooms in summer and is dormant in winter. Same culture as water lily (*Nymphaea*); will bloom in part shade.

APPLE

Rosaceae
DECIDUOUS FRUIT TREES
⧄ ZONES BY VARIETY
☼ FULL SUN
● REGULAR WATER
▸ SEE CHART NEXT PAGE

Apple

When the colonists arrived on the east coast of the New World, the apple as we know it today was not found. Only a few native crabapples existed. Apple seeds, saplings, and cuttings were brought from the Old World and became the orchards of young America.

In the history of the apple in America it is significant that apple trees were planted not to produce fruit to eat, but fruit to drink. Cider production was the purpose of orchards. It was not until known dessert varieties were brought from the British Isles and Europe and the classic America dessert apples appeared in the cider orchards as chance seedlings, that the colonists began to use this king of fruits for eating.

Every apple seed is a new apple variety and to duplicate any variety it must be grafted from a tree of the variety wanted. From the millions and millions of apple seeds planted in the cider orchards of America came thousands of meritorious trees given telling names: Black Gilliflower, Blue Pearmain, Cathead, Crow's Egg, Graniwinkle, Hightop Sweet, Horse, Hubbardston Nonesuch, Limbertwig, Magnum Bonum, Maiden Blush,

Mother, Pumpkin Sweet, Smokehouse, Westfield Seek-No-Further. An accounting made about 1900 listed 17,000 varieties.

When planting apple varieties in the home orchard, consider location, soil, season of ripening, taste preferences and use, pollination, and rootstocks.

Location. The ideal site is frost-free, sheltered from strong winds, well drained and, above all, located in full sun to develop flavor and color. Cooking apples can be allocated to the less sunny planting site because color and flavor is not as vital. If necessary, plant windbreaks to provide shelter for the insects that will pollinate the fruit. Bees cannot work the blossoms on windswept slopes. The slope will allow cold air to drain downward and not pocket around the budding or blooming trees. Avoid planting in frost zones at the bottom of slopes.

Soil. Apple trees are tolerant of many soil types, whether sand or clay, but the ideal is a well-drained loam that has been worked about 2 ft. deep with a pH factor from 6 to 7. Soil amendments should be made at planting time and will make a remarkable growth difference. Also, preparation of the planting site in the fall for spring planting is good planning.

Season of ripening. Select varieties that will provide a supply of fresh apples throughout the growing season. If apples for use during the winter and early spring are wanted, plant varieties that have long keeping quality like 'Baldwin', 'McIntosh', 'Northern Spy', 'Roxbury Russet', 'Spartan', 'Stayman', and 'Winesap'. Tree selection should be made to reflect taste preferences and use.

Pollination. Many apple varieties are self-fruitful, but planting a pollinator variety in the orchard enhances fruit production. Some good pollinators are 'Golden Delicious', 'Grimes Golden', 'McIntosh', 'Melrose', 'Newtown Pippin', 'Winter Banana', and many of the crabapples. 'Crispin', 'Gravenstein', 'Jonagold', 'Stayman', and 'Winesap' have specific pollinator requirements.

For these, pollen from two compatible varieties named above is needed for fruit set. In existing plantings that are not fruiting because of the absence of viable pollen, grafts of a pollinator can be placed throughout the tree or bouquets of flowers from a blooming variety can be placed beneath the pollen-sterile tree.

Tree size and rootstocks. Generally, apple trees are available in standard (seedling), semidwarf, and dwarf sizes that range in height from 30 to 40 ft. 'East Malling' and 'Merton Malling' rootstocks were developed in England and some, like 'Mark' and 'Geneva', are U.S. developments. Rootstocks not only reflect the size control but have other characteristics like early bearing, cold hardiness, and drought and pest resistance. Dwarf rootstocks or those of about 50 percent tree size require not only anchoring, but a permanent irrigation system. Also, the life span of the dwarf tree is much shorter than those larger than 50 percent size. The chart below describes a few of the more popular rootstocks.

Planting. Apple trees should be planted in the spring in all regions of the Northeast except the warmer southern area, where late fall and early winter planting can be done. The planting hole should be large enough to accommodate the root system and planted at the same level as it grew in the nursery. The soil line should be obvious. Under no circumstances plant the tree above the graft union because the rooting above it will override the rootstock characteristics and a standard tree will be the result. Use the topsoil and any compost around the root system and place the subsoil on top. Do not use any fertilizer at the time of planting, but water well to settle the soil.

A 4–6-in. mulch of organic material at least 3 ft. out from the trunk of the tree will not only conserve moisture, but create a positive growing environment for the young plant. Keep the mulch a few inches away from the trunk to prevent mice from damaging the stem. A hardware cloth screen will also stop nibbling by mice and other varmints. A fertilization and spray program is available from the bulletin of the state agricultural extension service or from many of the agricultural websites on fruits.

The first few years of an apple tree must be devoted to the production of wood, not fruit. Early fruiting will stymie development of the framework that will support the later crops. Generally, prune to a central leader or modified leader design or to develop the espalier form. Pruning demonstrations are available at horticultural workshops, from agricultural bulletins and in textbooks. The objective of pruning is to stimulate the tree and to open it for the circulation of air to reduce fungal and bacteria growth and to permit sunshine to enter. One indication that a mature apple tree has been successfully pruned is that a robin can fly through without its wingtips touching a branch. Three salient points in successful fruit tree growing are variety selection, proper pruning and thinning, and orchard sanitation.

Taste preferences and use. Tart, sweet, subacid, vinous, sprightly, complex, crisp, juicy, mild, tender, spicy, and sugary are some of the descriptive words that emerge in biting into an apple. In planning a home orchard select varieties that reflect personal preference and family diversity. Taste is subjective and each person has a taste spectrum. Apple tastings at historic sites and orchards are growing in popularity and afford an opportunity to find one's taste spectrum before planting the apple trees. The use of the apples will often dictate variety selection. Plant varieties that are appropriate for one's purpose in planting: fresh eating, sauce, butter, drying, baking, pie making, or cider. Blemished fruit should be used for processing, and unblemished apples picked just before fully ripe can be stored for later use. One way to determine the time of ripening is to examine the seed. If it is still white or greenish, the fruit is immature. When the seed begins to color, the apple is ready for harvest. The color of the skin of the fruit is not an indicator of ripeness.

MAKE YOUR OWN APPLESAUCE

Once you taste homemade applesauce you'll never want to go back to the supermarket kind. Less-than-perfect apples are fine for applesauce; just cut out any bad spots before using them. An assortment of different varieties makes the best sauce: Try to include some tart apples along with some sweeter varieties.

Wash the apples, remove the stems and the bottom, and cut each apple into quarters. There's no need to peel or core the fruit. Place the apples in a large pot with just enough water to cover the bottom of the pot and prevent the apples from sticking. Bring to a boil and simmer until the apples are soft (cooking time depends on ripeness; the riper the apples, the faster they'll soften). Drain the cooked apples. Place several pieces at a time into a coarse sieve and press the pulp through. The seeds and skins will stay behind.

Sweeten to taste and add a small amount of butter. The applesauce freezes well for long-term storage.

APPLE ROOTSTOCKS

TREE SIZE	SPACING	ANCHORAGE	BEARING TIME	TREE SIZE	SPACING	ANCHORAGE	BEARING TIME
Seedling 100%	20–30 ft.	Excellent	6–10 years	EMLA or M7 60–70%	0–14 ft.	Fair	3–4 years
EMLA or MM 111 75%	14–18 ft.	Excellent	4–6 years	EMLA or M26 50%	8–12 ft.	Staking Required	2–4 years
EMLA or MM 106 75%	14–18 ft.	Excellent	3–5 years	EMLA or M9 35%	4–8 ft.	Staking Required	2–3 years

Some other apple rootstocks are designated: Mark, Bud 9, Geneva 16, Geneva 30, M27.

APPLE

VARIETY	ZONES	RIPENING DATE	FRUIT	COMMENTS
'Ashmead's Kernel'	All zones	Midseason to late	Medium size, golden brown russet with orange-red cheek. Yellowish flesh, crisp and juicy with sweet-tart flavor	Originated in England about 1700. Growing in popularity among russet apple varieties; stores well
'Baldwin'	All zones	Late	Large and round; skin yellow-and-red striped, nearly covered with crimson. Flesh crisp, tender and subacid	Originated near Boston, late 18th century. A major commercial variety before 'McIntosh' was introduced. Usually a biennial cropper. Stores well
'Braeburn'	All zones	Late	Red striped with red blush on yellow background; pale cream-colored flesh, crisp and juicy, breaks off cleanly when bitten	From New Zealand;, there are a number of cultivars. Makes a good low or no sugar applesauce. Stores well
'Crispin' ('Mutsu')	All zones	Midseason to late	Large to very large; greening yellow skin, waxy and clear, sometimes with a reddish blush. Dense, crisp, juicy flesh; coarse-grained; sprightly flavor	From Japan, a triploid that needs a pollinator to fruit. Good common storage
'Empire'	All zones	Midseason to late	Medium size; most cultivars dark red skinned. White flesh crisp and juicy with a light tartness	From Geneva Fruit Test Station in New York, Empire is a cross of 'McIntosh' and 'Red Delicious'; introduced in 1966
'Esopus Spitzenburg'	All zones	Midseason	Medium size, oblong shape. Smooth skin is lively brilliant red, covered with small yellow specks. Yellow flesh is rich, juicy, and sprightly.	Originated in Esopus, New York, early 18th century. Reputed favorite of Thomas Jefferson, planted it at Monticello in 1790. Ranks high in apple tastings; likely a parent of the 'Jonathan'. Fair keeper
'Gala'	All zones	Early to midseason	Small to medium with long stem; coloration varies among cultivars; reddish orange background with red striping or reddish blush. Creamy yellow flesh, crisp, dense, aromatic. Subacid flavor	Raised in New Zealand in 1934, named in 1965. With 'Fuji' and 'Braeburn' it has become a major commercial variety worldwide. Good storage
'Ginger Gold'	All zones	Early	Medium to large size, clear yellow skin, crisp, firm flesh with mild flavor	Originated in Nelson County, Virginia. Ripens over 2-3 weeks. Unlike many yellow apples, has some resistance to sunburn. Good storage
'Golden Delicious' ('Yellow Delicious')	All zones	Midseason	Usually large and conic in shape; golden yellow skin. Flesh firm, crisp, juicy with mild, sweet flavor. Skin dry, bruises easily; natural tendency to russet	Many strains, sports, and cultivars. Second most popular apple in U.S. Appeared in 1912 as a chance seedling, likely of 'Grimes Golden', on a farm in West Virginia. Somewhat self-fertile, an excellent pollinator. Shrivels in storage
'Granny Smith'	31, 32, 34, 35	Late. Not suitable for the Upper Northeast	Large bright green apple with peened surface, sometimes flushed purplish brown with conspicuous large white dots. White flesh is very crisp and juicy.	Noted cooking and sauce apple, came from Australia in 1860s. Harvest time 190 days after full bloom. Resistant to bruising and cedar apple rust. Long keeper
'Gravenstein'	All zones	Early	The slightly lopsided fruit has yellow skin marked with bright red and copper or orange and the yellowish white flesh is tender, fine-grained, and crisp. The acid-sugar content is well balanced. The skin becomes greasy in storage.	A 17th century variety from Italy it migrated to Denmark via Germany and was introduced into the United States in 1790. From the northeast it was taken to Sonoma County, California, in 1820. It is a triploid that must have pollinators. Storage is short-term.

APPLE

VARIETY	ZONES	RIPENING DATE	FRUIT	COMMENTS
'Grimes Golden'	All zones	Midseason	Roundish fruit, medium size; skin greenish yellow ripening to clear yellow with yellow or russet dots Yellowish flesh, crisp, spicy, sweet flavor	Found in West Virginia in 1804. All-purpose fruit, exceptional cider maker. Excellent pollinator, resists fireblight and cedar-apple rust. Fair keeper
'Jonagold'	All zones	Midseason to late	Large fruit, orange-red blush, with hint of stripes on a yellow background. Juicy and crisp, creamy yellow flesh, sweet-tart balance of flavor	Developed at New York State Fruit Station in 1943, introduced in 1968. Tetraploid. Stores for about 3 months
'Jonathan'	All zones	Midseason to late	Medium size; yellow skin nearly covered with bright red stripes, red blush. Some nearly all red strains. White flesh, firm, tender, and juicy with sprightly subacid flavor	Originated about 1820, Ulster County, New York. Bears early, annually, and heavily. Subject to fireblight, some resistance to scab
'Liberty'	All zones	Midseason to late	Large to medium size, 90% red blush on yellow background. Creamy white flesh, crisp, juicy, sweet	From New York Experiment Station in 1978; cross of Macoun and Purdue 54-12. Considered scab immune; resists mildew, fireblight, cedar-apple rust. Good keeper, storage enhances flavor
'Macoun'	39–45	Late. Suitable for the cooler regions of Northeast	Medium size. Waxy, smooth, tough skin, blushed and striped red over green; bluish bloom. Greenish white flesh, crisp, juicy, and easily bruised	Originated in Geneva, New York, introduced in 1923. Some resistance to fireblight and mildew. Has a tendency for biennial bearing. High-quality dessert apple, stores well
'McIntosh'	All zones	Midseason	Medium to large size; pale yellow skin, flushed and striped deep bright red. Many strains. White flesh, sometimes tinged red, fine, crisp and tender with tartness and spiciness that has become the 'McIntosh' flavor	John McIntosh discovered the variety in 1796 in Ontario. Introduced and named in 1870. Good pollinator, blooms early and bears heavy crop
'Newtown Pippin'	All zones	Late	Classic American variety with yellow and green strains. Generally, round with short stem. Solid green, becomes yellow or greenish yellow with a reddish blush on ripening. Yellowish flesh, very firm, crisp, and juicy	Also known as 'Albemarle Pippin' and 'Yellow Newtown Pippin'. Noted in 1759; originated on Long Island, New York. George Washington and Thomas Jefferson planted pippins. All-purpose fruit, flavor improved by long storage
'Northern Spy'	All zones	Late	Large size, variable fruit color, generally clear yellow with bright red tints, streaked with yellow. White flesh very juicy, crisp, and sweet with rich subacid flavor	Found in an orchard in East Bloomfield, New York, about 1800. Blooms late, escapes frost, but is slow to bear on standard rootstocks. Several strains. Stores exceptionally well
'Red Delicious'	All zones	Midseason	Enormous variation in shape and color. Early strains striped and less pointed, modern ones nearly or all red, elongated, with five prominent points on blossom end. White flesh tender, crisp and juicy with distinctive mild flavor and aroma	Most popular and widely grown apple in the world, more than 300 strains. From a chance seedling found in 1872 near Peru, Iowa, originally named Hawkeye. Renamed 'Red Delicious' in 1894. Some resistance to fireblight and cedar-apple rust. Not a long keeper
'Rome Beauty'	All zones	Late	Medium to large in size and uniformly round in shape, the greenish yellow skin is mottled and flushed with bright red which deepens to a solid red where sun exposed. It is conspicuously striped bright carmine. The creamy yellow flesh is coarse-textured and juicy and the skin is tough	'Rome' was recorded in 1848 and originated near Proctorville, Ohio. It is somewhat self-fruitful and blooms late, escaping late frosts. An all-purpose apple noted for its baking qualities, it stores well

A

APPLE

VARIETY	ZONES	RIPENING DATE	FRUIT	COMMENTS
'Roxbury Russet'	All zones	Late	Medium size, elliptical shape. Green skin, tinged bronze, overspread with brownish yellow russet. Sometimes has reddish blush on sun side. Greenish yellow flesh, coarse, sugary, high flavored	May be the oldest named American apple variety, probably from Roxbury, Massachusetts; noted in 1649. Ranks high in apple tastings. Nearly 13% sugar, one of few varieties that singly make a high quality cider. Long keeper
'Spartan'	All zones	Midseason to late	Large size; yellow skin almost entirely flushed purplish red with indistinct striping. Surface covered with heavy bloom; aromatic skin. Very white flesh, crisp and fine-textured with subacid flavor	Raised in 1926 in British Columbia, a cross of 'McIntosh' and 'Newtown Pippin'. Some resistance to apple diseases; pollination with 'Lodi' will increase yields. Good pollinator for 'Jonagold'. Stores well
'Winesap'	All zones	Late	Small to medium size; deep red or maroon skin with yellow background showing on shaded side. Indistinct flushes and stripes of darker red, sometimes netting of russet. Yellow flesh is sweet, crisp, and aromatic with a vinous flavor	Described as a cider fruit in 1804; likely originated in Virginia. Several strains. A dependable bearer, produces heavy crops annually, suitable for cooking, dessert and cidermaking. Stores well throughout winter

APPLE-OF-PERU. See NICANDRA

Aquifoliaceae. The holly family contains evergreen trees or shrubs with berrylike fruit. *Ilex* (holly) is the only important genus.

AQUILEGIA

COLUMBINE

Ranunculaceae

PERENNIALS

◪ ZONES VARY BY SPECIES

☼ ◑ FULL SUN OR FILTERED SHADE

🔴 REGULAR WATER

Aquilegia McKana Giant

Columbines have a fairylike, woodland quality with their lacy foliage and beautifully posed flowers in exquisite pastels, deeper shades, and white. Erect, 2 in.–4 ft. high, depending on species or hybrid. Fresh green, blue-green, or gray-green divided leaves reminiscent of maidenhair fern. Slender, branching stems carry flowers to 3 in. across, erect or nodding, often with sepals and petals in contrasting colors; they usually have backward-projecting, nectar-bearing spurs. Some columbines have large flowers and very long spurs; these have an airier look than short-spurred and spurless kinds. Double-flowered types lack the delicacy of those with single blossoms, but they make a bolder color mass. Bloom season for most columbines is late spring to early summer, but some bloom in mid- to late spring.

Plants are not fussy about soil as long as it is well drained. On all columbines, cut back old stems for second crop of flowers. All kinds attract hummingbirds. Most columbines are not long-lived perennials; replace plants every 3 or 4 years. If you allow spent flowers to form seed capsules, you'll ensure a crop of volunteer seedlings. If you're growing hybrids, the seedlings won't necessarily duplicate the parent plants; seedlings from species (if grown isolated from other columbines) should closely resemble the originals. Leaf miners are a potential pest, especially on hybrids.

A. alpina. ALPINE COLUMBINE. Zones 32, 34–45. Native to the Alps. Grows 1–2 ft. tall. Nodding, bright blue flowers to 2 in. across, with curved spurs to 1 in. long. Good rock garden plant. 'Hensol Harebell' is a cross between this species and *A. vulgaris;* flowers are deep blue on stems that may reach 3 ft. tall.

A. bertolonii. Zones 32, 34–41. Native to Italy and southern France. Grows to 1 ft. high and bears deep violet flowers with incurved spurs.

A. caerulea. ROCKY MOUNTAIN COLUMBINE. Zones 32, 34–45. State flower of Colorado. Grows 1½–3 ft. high. Flowers upright, 2 in. or more across, blue and white. Spurs straight or spreading, to 2 in. long. This species is an important parent of many long-spurred hybrids.

A. canadensis. Zones 32, 34–45. Native to much of eastern and central North America. Grows 1–2 ft. tall, occasionally taller. Red-and-yellow, 1½-in., nodding flowers have slightly curved, 1-in. spurs. Red color may wash out to pink in areas with warm nighttime temperatures. Less susceptible to leaf miners than most columbines. 'Corbett' (*A. c. flavescens*) has creamy yellow flowers.

A. chrysantha. GOLDEN COLUMBINE, GOLDEN-SPURRED COLUMBINE. Zones 31, 32, 34–45. Native to Arizona, New Mexico, and adjacent Mexico. One of showiest species. Large, many-branched plant to 3–4 ft. tall. Leaflets densely covered with soft hairs beneath. Upright, clear yellow, 1½–3 in. flowers, with slender, hooked spurs 2–2½ in. long. 'Silver Queen' has white flowers; double-flowered forms are white (sometimes pink-tinged) 'Alba Plena' and yellow 'Flore Pleno'.

A. flabellata. Zones 31, 32, 34–43. Native to Japan. Stocky, 9-in. plant with nodding lilac blue and creamy white flowers and hooked spurs to 1 in. long. Differs from most other columbines in having thicker, darker leaves with often overlapping segments. *A. f. pumila* is a very dwarf (4-in.) form. Good rock garden plants.

A. hinckleyana. HINCKLEY'S COLUMBINE. Zones 31, 32, 34–41. Native to Big Bend country of Texas. To 1½–2 ft. high, with blue-gray foliage and long-spurred, chartreuse yellow flowers.

A. hybrids. Zones 32, 34–45. Derived from several species. Preferred tall hybrid strains are graceful, long-spurred McKana Giants and double-flowering Spring Song (both to 3 ft.). Lower-growing strains include Biedermeier and Dragonfly (1 ft.); long-spurred Music (1½ ft.); and single to double, upward-facing Fairyland (15 in.). One of the most unusual hybrids is 2–2½-ft.-tall 'Nora Barlow', which has spurless, double, dahlialike flowers of reddish pink with a white margin.

A. longissima. Zones 31, 32, 34–45. Native to southwest Texas and northern Mexico. Grows to 2½–3 ft. tall. Similar to *A. chrysantha*. Flowers numerous, erect, pale yellow, spurs very narrow, drooping, 4–6 in. long. 'Maxistar', the variety mostly commonly offered, has clear yellow flowers and is strong growing.

A. saximontana. Zones 32, 34–45. In effect, a miniature *A. caerulea*, 4–8 in. high.

A. sibirica. Zones 32, 34–45. Native to Siberia and very hardy. Grows 9 in. to over 2 ft. high. Blue or white flowers with curved blue spurs.

A. vulgaris. EUROPEAN COLUMBINE. Zones 32, 34–45. Naturalized in eastern U.S. Grows to 1–2½ ft. tall. Nodding, blue or violet flowers to 2 in. across; short, knobby spurs are about ¾ in. long. Many selections and hybrids, from single to fully double and either short spurred or spurless. Some nurseries offer a mix of flower forms in white and shades of pink, red, and violet.

ARABIS

ROCKCRESS

Brassicaceae (Cruciferae)

PERENNIALS

☀ ZONES VARY BY SPECIES

☀ FULL SUN

🌢 MODERATE WATER

Arabis caucasica

Low-growing, spreading plants for edgings, rock gardens, ground covers, and pattern plantings. All kinds have attractive foliage and clusters of white, pink, or rose purple flowers that bloom in spring. Provide good drainage.

A. alpina. MOUNTAIN ROCKCRESS. Zones 36–45. Low, tufted plant, rough-hairy, with leafy stems 4–10 in. high and basal leaves in clusters. White flowers in dense, short clusters. 'Rosea', 6 in. high, has pink flowers; 'Variegata' has variegated leaves. Plants sold as *A. alpina* are often really *A. caucasica*.

A. arendsii. Zones 31, 32, 34–41. This hybrid is similar to *A. caucasica*, but with pink flowers. It grows 6–9 in. high.

A. blepharophylla. CALIFORNIA ROCKCRESS, ROSE CRESS. Zones 32, 34. Native to rocky hillsides and ridges along Northern California coast. Tufted plant 4–8 in. high. Basal leaves 1–2¾ in. long. Rose purple flowers, fragrant, ½–¾ in. wide, in short, dense clusters. Good in rock garden, containers.

A. caucasica (A. albida). WALL ROCKCRESS. Zones 31, 32, 34–35. Native Mediterranean region to Iran. Dependable old favorite. Forms mat of gray leaves to 6 in. high. White, ½-in. flowers almost cover plants in early spring. Excellent ground cover and base planting for spring-flowering bulbs such as daffodils and paper white narcissus. Start plants from cuttings or sow seeds in spring or fall. Provide some shade in hot climates. Short lived where winters are warm and summers humid.

'Variegata' has gray leaves with creamy white margins. 'Flore Plena' has double flowers; 'Rosabella' and 'Pink Charm' have pink blooms. Latter two are popular rock garden plants in cold climates.

A. ferdinandi-coburgii. Zones 31, 32, 34–43. Tight clumps to 4 in. Commonest form is 'Variegata', with leaves heavily edged and splashed with white.

A. procurrens. Zones 31, 32, 34–35. Creeping plant with 1–1¼-in. leaves and white flowers clustered on stems 4–12 in. tall.

Araceae. The arum family contains plants ranging from tuberous or rhizomatous perennials to shrubby or climbing tropical foliage plants. Leaves are often highly ornamental; while variable in shape, they tend to be arrow-like. Inconspicuous flowers cluster tightly on a club-shaped spadix within an often showy leaflike bract (spathe). Examples are *Alocasia*, calla (*Zantedeschia*), and *Arisaema*. Sap of many is highly irritating to mouth and throat.

ARACHIS HYPOGAEA. See PEANUT

ARACHNIODES

Dryopteridaceae

FERN

☀ ZONES VARY BY SPECIES

☀ ● PARTIAL OR FULL SHADE

🌢 🌢 AMPLE WATER

Arachniodes simplicior
'Variegata'

A genus of Asian ferns with creeping rhizomes, sometimes called holly ferns. Grow them in pots where they are not hardy, moving them indoors for winter.

A. aristata. EAST INDIAN HOLLY FERN. Zones 31, 32, 34, 39. Broadly oval fronds to 1½ ft. long and 10 in. wide, divided into two or three segments.

A. simplicior. 'Variegata' is the variety usually grown. Zones 31, 32, 34, 39. Grows 10–16 in. tall, with broadly triangular, once-divided fronds, deeply divided subdivisions. Base of each subdivision is yellow green, creating a strong two-tone effect. Goes dormant in winter.

A. standishii. UPSIDE-DOWN FERN. Zones 31, 32, 34–43. Bright green, oblong to triangular fronds to 2 ft. long and 1 ft. wide, leathery and divided into three segments.

ARALIA

Araliaceae

DECIDUOUS SHRUBS OR PERENNIALS

☀ ZONES 31, 32, 34–41

☀ ☀ FULL SUN OR PARTIAL SHADE

🌢 🌢 REGULAR TO MODERATE WATER

Aralia chinensis

Three of the species described below are striking, bold-leafed, shrubby plants that may eventually grow to 25 ft. under ideal conditions (15 ft. is more common in the Northeast). *A. racemosa* and *A. nudicaulis* are smaller and perennial. Branches are nearly vertical or slightly spreading, usually very spiny. Huge leaves, clustered at ends of branches and divided into many leaflets, have effective pattern value. White flowers, small but in such large, branched clusters that they are showy in midsummer, are followed by purplish berrylike fruit.

Grow in well-drained soil. Not good near swimming pools because of spines; even leafstalks are sometimes prickly. Protect plants from wind to avoid burning foliage.

A. chinensis. CHINESE ANGELICA. Only moderately spiny. Leaves 2–3 ft. long, divided into 2–6-in.-long toothed leaflets without stalks. Flower clusters grow 1–2 ft. wide.

A. elata. JAPANESE ANGELICA TREE. Native to northeast Asia. Similar to *A. chinensis* but leaflets are narrower, have fewer teeth. 'Variegata' has leaflets strikingly bordered with creamy white; 'Aureovariegata' has yellow-edged leaves.

A. elegantissima. See *Schefflera elegantissima*

A. nudicaulis. WILD SARSAPARILLA. North American native growing to 1 ft. high. Woody perennial with compound leaves containing three to five oblong, toothed leaflets. Clusters of flowers at tips of stems.

A. racemosa. SPIKENARD. Native to eastern U.S. Unlike the other species, a rhizomatous perennial to 6 ft., with long (2½-ft.) leaves divided into many coarse leaflets. Tiny white flowers are clustered into balls on branching stems. Tiny fruits are black or brown.

A. spinosa. HERCULES' CLUB, DEVIL'S WALKING STICK. Native to eastern U.S. Has a few usually unbranched spiny stems, each crowned by 2–6-ft. leaves. Tiny flowers form huge, branched clusters. Spreads by suckers. One of the most tropical-looking, genuinely hardy trees.

Araliaceae. The aralia family of herbaceous and woody plants is marked by leaves that are divided fanwise into leaflets or veined in pattern like the fingers of a hand. Individually tiny flowers are in round clusters or in large compound clusters. Examples are English ivy *(Hedera helix)*, *Fatshedera*, and *Schefflera*.

ARBORVITAE. See PLATYCLADUS orientalis, THUJA

ARCTANTHEMUM. See CHRYSANTHEMUM arcticum

ARCTOSTAPHYLOS uva-ursi

BEARBERRY, KINNIKINNICK

Ericaceae

EVERGREEN SHRUB

✂ ZONES 34, 36–45

☼ ◐ FULL SUN OR LIGHT SHADE

💧 MODERATE WATER

Arctostaphylos uva-ursi

Native to the northern regions of the world, extending south to the northern U.S. and down into California. Small white or pink urn-shaped flowers in late winter to early spring, followed by berrylike red or brown fruits. Requires excellent drainage but can tolerate poor soil, preferring rocky, or sandy, acid soils to heavy, rich ones.

Good ground or bank cover at seashore, in mountains. Prostrate, spreading and rooting as it grows, eventually making broad mats a few inches deep. Small, glossy, leathery leaves are bright green, turning red or purplish in winter. White or pinkish flowers are followed by red or pink fruits. Slow to become established; mulch heavily between plants to keep down weeds until branches provide cover. Named, cutting-grown varieties provide uniform appearance in large plantings. These include:

'Alaska'. Flat grower with small, round dark green leaves.

'Massachusetts'. Small leafed, flat growing. Abundant pinkish white flowers, red fruit.

'Wood's Red'. Reliable producer of large bright red berries. Small dark green leaves turn reddish in cold weather.

ARCTOTIS

AFRICAN DAISY

Asteraceae (Compositae)

ANNUALS

✂ ALL ZONES

☼ FULL SUN

💧 MODERATE WATER

Arctotis hybrid

The term "African daisy" can refer to any of several plants; names and identities of the plants are often confused, even by seed companies and nurseries. *Arctotis* species have lobed leaves that are rough, hairy, or woolly; their flower heads usually have a contrasting ring of color around central eye. *Dimorphotheca* species have smooth green foliage; their flowers are in the yellow-orange-salmon range or are white. Trailing ground cover African daisies and woody, shrubby white-and-blue African daisies are *Osteospermum*.

In cold-winter areas, the following annuals are planted in spring for summer bloom. They do not withstand extreme heat and humidity.

A. hybrids (Harlequin hybrids). Most garden plants are hybrids 1–1½ ft. tall. Their 3-in. flowers come in white, pink, red, purplish, cream, yellow, and orange, usually with a dark ring around the nearly black eyespot. Will self-sow but tend to revert to orange. You can perpetuate colors you like by taking cuttings. Plants survive as perennials in mildest climates but bloom best in their first year.

Named hybrid cultivars include 'Bacchus', with red-purple flowers; 'China Rose', dusty rose, and 'Flame', bright red-orange.

A. stoechadifolia grandis. Bushy growth to 2 ft., with gray-green, slightly hairy leaves and 3-in. white daisies in which yellow ring surrounds deep blue central eye.

ARENARIA

SANDWORT

Caryophyllaceae

PERENNIAL GROUND COVERS

✂ ZONES 32, 34–45

☼ ◐ PARTIAL SHADE IN HOT CLIMATES

💧 REGULAR WATER

Arenaria montana

Low evergreen plants carpet ground with dense mats of mosslike foliage, have small white flowers in late spring and summer. They are often used as lawn substitutes, between stepping-stones, or for velvety green patches in rock gardens. Provide well-drained soil.

A. montana. Grows 2–4 in. high; weak stems up to 1 ft. long, usually covered with soft hairs. Leaves grayish, ½–¾ in. long. White flowers, 1 in. across, profuse in late spring or early summer. Good plant to let trail over sunny rock or tumble over low wall.

A. purpurascens. PINK SANDWORT. Grows to 2 in. high, 8 in. across. Covered with clusters of star-shaped pink flowers ½ in. wide in midsummer.

A. verna (A. v. caespitosa). See under *Sagina subulata*

ARGEMONE

PRICKLY POPPY

Papaveraceae

ANNUALS OR BIENNIALS

✂ ALL ZONES

☼ FULL SUN

💧 MODERATE TO LITTLE WATER

Argemone mexicana

Prickly leafed and prickly stemmed plants with large, showy poppy flowers. Native to desert or dry areas, Wyoming to Mexico and west to California. Grow easily from seed sown in spring where plants are to bloom or from seed sown in pots; transplant gently. Need sun and good drainage. Bloom mostly in summer. To 3 ft.

A. intermedia. See *A. polyanthemos*

A. mexicana. Annual. Yellow to orange flowers.

A. platyceras. Annual. White flowers. Most common kind.

A. polyanthemos (A. intermedia). Annual or biennial. White flowers.

ARGYRANTHEMUM. See CHRYSANTHEMUM frutescens

ARISAEMA

Araceae

TUBEROUS-ROOTED PERENNIALS

✂ ZONES VARY BY SPECIES

◐ ● PARTIAL OR FULL SHADE

💧 AMPLE WATER DURING ACTIVE GROWTH

Eerie-looking woodland plants from the eastern U.S. and the Far East. All have leaves divided into segments and summer flowers somewhat resembling otherworldly callas, with a much-modified leaflike bract (spathe) surrounding a spike of minute flowers on

Arisaema triphyllum

a fleshy stalk (spadix). The native Jack-in-the-pulpit is a familiar example, but species from Asia attract connoisseurs of the odd. Fruits that follow the blossoms resemble small, bright red ears of corn. All die down in winter and tend to reappear late in spring. Use in the woodland garden or grow in pots for close-up viewing. All like rich soil, with abundant organic matter and plenty of water.

A. candidissimum. Zones 32, 34–41. China native growing to 16 in. high. Spathe is fragrant, white striped with purple-pink, and appears in early summer. Followed by three-part leaves of oval leaflets to 8 in. long.

A. consanguineum. Zones 32, 34–41. Native to Himalayas to central China. Grows to 3 ft. high. Hooded, white-striped green spathe tinged with brown, purple inside, appears in summer, followed by red berries. Leaves are composed of up to 20 oval leaflets to 8 in. long.

A. dracontium. DRAGON ROOT. Zones 32, 34–43. Native to eastern North America. Grows 2½ ft. high, with a hooded, slender green spathe in spring. Lobed leaf divided into as many as 15 lance-shaped segments.

A. ringens. Zones 32, 34–41. Native to China, Japan, and Korea. Grows to 1 ft. high, with a large, hooded spathe striped in green and purple in early summer. Leaves are glossy and made up of three oblong leaflets.

A. sikokianum. Zones 31, 32, 34–41. Native to Japan. Grows to 20 in. Plant has two leaves, one with three leaflets, the other with five; leaflets grow 6 in. long, 4 in. wide. Flower stem, as tall (or nearly) as leafstalks, bears a 6-in. spathe—deep purple outside, yellowish within. Tip of spathe curves over a white spadix with a rounded, club-shaped tip.

A. speciosum. SHOWY COBRA LILY. Zones 31, 32. Native to Himalayas, western China. Grows 2–3 ft., with a single 1½-ft. leaf bearing three leaflets with reddish edges. Leafstalk marbled dark purple. Spathe to 8 in., dark purple striped white. Whitish spadix terminates in a slender 2-ft. tail.

A. thunbergii. Zones 31, 32. Native to Japan. Grows to 2 ft. high, with reddish purple to deep purple spathe in spring. Leaves are composed of up to 15 oblong leaflets.

A. tortuosum. Zones 31, 32. Native to Himalayas, western China. Grows 3–4 ft. tall. Each leaf has 5–15 narrow leaflets. Green or purplish, 6-in. spathe is strongly curved downward at tip; green or purplish spadix thrusts out and upward in a strong curve.

A. triphyllum. JACK-IN-THE-PULPIT, INDIAN TURNIP. Zones 31, 32, 34–43. Native to eastern North America. Each of the two 2-ft. leafstalks bears three 6-in. leaflets. Flowering stems, usually taller than leaves, carry a hooded spathe to 6 in., green or purple with white stripes (the pulpit), and a green or purple spadix (Jack). A common woodland plant. The name "Indian turnip" refers to the plant's root. It contains calcium oxalate crystals that sting the tongue and throat, but is edible if thoroughly boiled.

ARISARUM

Araceae

PERENNIALS

⚡ ZONES 31, 32, 34, 39

☼ PARTIAL SHADE TO SHADE

🔴 AVERAGE MOISTURE

Used mostly in rock or woodland gardens, these European natives grow from rhizomes *Arisarum* or tubers and form dense, low carpets of foliage that disappears in summer. The small, hooded flowers resemble those of Jack-in-the-pulpit *(Arisaema)*. Where soil temperatures fall below freezing, apply protective winter mulch.

A. proboscideum. MOUSE PLANT. Arrow-shaped, lustrous, dark green leaves. Appearing in spring, hooded, brownish purple spathes with slender gray tips resemble the hindquarters of mice. Plant in moist, humus-rich soil in partial shade

A. vulgare. FRIAR'S COWL. To 6 in. tall. Arrow- to heart-shaped leaves are yellow-green and sometimes mottled with purple. Produces green or dull purple, hooded spathes in late winter or very early spring. Plant in full sun and well-drained to dry soil.

ARISTOLOCHIA

Aristolochiaceae

DECIDUOUS OR EVERGREEN VINES

⚡ ZONES VARY BY SPECIES

☼ ◐ ● EXPOSURE NEEDS VARY BY SPECIES

🔴 🔴 AMPLE WATER

Aristolochia elegans

Curiously shaped flowers in rather sober colors resemble curved pipes with flared bowls or birds with bent necks.

A. macrophylla (A. durior). DUTCHMAN'S PIPE. Deciduous. Zones 31, 32, 34–43. Native to eastern U.S. Will cover 15 by 20 ft. in one season. Easily grown from seed. Kidney-shaped, 6–14-in.-long, deep green, glossy leaves are carried in shinglelike pattern to form dense cover on trellis. Blooms late spring to early summer. Flower is yellowish green, 3-in. curved tube that flares into three brownish purple lobes about 1 in. wide; flowers almost hidden by leaves. Thrives in full sun to heavy shade. Generous feeding and watering will speed growth. Cut back in winter if too heavy. Short lived in warm-winter areas. Will not stand strong winds.

A. elegans (A. littoralis). CALICO FLOWER. Evergreen house or greenhouse plant; move outdoors in summer. Twines to 6 ft. or more. Wiry, slender stems; heart-shaped leaves 3 in. long. Whitish buds shaped like little pelicans open to 3-in.-wide, heart-shaped flowers of deep purple veined creamy white; summer bloom. Needs rich soil, partial shade.

A. grandiflora. PELICAN FLOWER. Evergreen house or greenhouse plant; move outdoors in summer. Twines to 6 ft. or more. Heart-shaped deep green leaves to 10 in. long. Flowers are white with long tails, purple brown veins and deep purple eye, to 7 in. across; summer bloom.

Aristolochiaceae. This family includes *Aristolochia* and wild ginger *(Asarum)*. All display odd-shaped flowers in low-key colors.

ARMERIA

THRIFT, SEA PINK

Plumbaginaceae

PERENNIALS

⚡ ZONES VARY BY SPECIES

☼ FULL SUN

🔴 REGULAR TO LITTLE WATER

Armeria maritima

Narrow, stiff, evergreen leaves grow in compact tufts or basal rosettes; small white, pink, rose, or red flowers in dense globular heads. Main bloom period is spring to early summer, but removing faded flowers may prolong blooming into fall. Sturdy, dependable plants for edging walks or borders and for tidy mounds in rock gardens or raised beds. Attractive in containers. Need excellent drainage. Propagate by divisions or from seeds in spring or fall.

A. alliacea. Zones 32, 34–37. Leaf clumps 2–6 in. tall produce 8–16-in. flowering stalks with deep pink flowers. 'Leucantha' has white flowers.

A. arenaria (A. plantaginea). Zones 34–43. Leaves narrow, 2–6 in. long. Flowering stems 8–24 in. tall, with purplish pink or white blossoms. 'Bee's Ruby' has bright, darker pink flowers on 1-ft. stems.

A. girardii (A. juncea, A. setacea). Zone 32. Low, dense mounds of narrow, needlelike foliage produce lavender pink flowers.

A. juniperifolia (A. caespitosa). Zones 32, 34, 36–39. Stiff, needle-shaped leaves ½ in. long in low, extremely compact rosettes. Flowers rose pink or white on 2-in. stems. This little mountain native is very touchy about drainage; apply mulch of fine gravel around plants to prevent basal stem rot, especially in summer. Selections include 'Alba', with white flowers; 'Bevan's Variety', deep rose pink flowers on 2-in. stems, on compact plants; and 'Rubra', very dark pink flowers.

A. maritima (Statice armeria, Armeria vulgaris). COMMON THRIFT. Zones 34–43. Tufted mounds spreading to 1 ft. with 6-in.-long, stiff, grasslike leaves. Small white to rose pink flowers in tight clusters at top of 6–10-in. stalks. 'Alba' (with white flowers), 'Bloodstone' (rose red), 'Cotton Tail' (white), and 'Dusseldorf Pride' (rose pink flowers) are selections.

A. pseudarmeria. Zones 31, 32, 34, 39. Clump-forming, to 20 in. high. Basal rosette of lance-shaped green leaves, white to light pink flowers in dome-shaped clusters in summer.

ARONIA

CHOKEBERRY

Rosaceae

DECIDUOUS SHRUBS

ZONES VARY BY SPECIES

FULL SUN OR LIGHT SHADE

MUCH OR LITTLE WATER

Aronia melanocarpa

Chokeberries, native to southern Canada and the eastern U.S., are tough, undemanding shrubs useful as fillers or background plantings. They tolerate a wide variety of soils and can thrive on much or little water. All tend to spread by suckering, but are somewhat leggy (good for planting beneath). Small white or pinkish flowers are followed by showy fruits that last well into winter. Fall foliage is brightly colored.

A. arbutifolia. RED CHOKEBERRY. Zones 31, 32, 34–41. Clumping shrub to 6–8 ft., with many erect stems bearing shiny foliage that is rich green above, paler beneath. Fruits are clustered, ¼ in. wide, brilliant red, long lasting. Fall foliage is also bright red; plants tend to color early. 'Brilliantissima' ('Brilliant') is a selected form with exceptionally fine fall color.

A. melanocarpa. BLACK CHOKEBERRY. Zones 31, 32, 34–43. Lower growing than *A. arbutifolia*, to just 3–5 ft. tall, rarely taller. Purple-red fall color; shiny black ½-in. fruits.

A. prunifolia. PURPLE CHOKEBERRY. Zones 31, 32, 34–41. Hybrid growing to 10 ft. high, with deep green leaves that turn dark purple red in fall. Fruits are ⅜ in. across, dark purple black, and carried in clusters.

ARRHENATHERUM elatius bulbosum 'Variegatum'

BULBOUS OAT GRASS

Poaceae (Gramineae)

PERENNIAL

ZONES 32, 34–41

FULL SUN OR PARTIAL SHADE

REGULAR WATER

Arrhenatherum elatius bulbosum 'Variegatum'

With its narrow leaves boldly edged and striped in white, it is attractive in the perennial border or large rock garden and can brighten a dark place under trees or big shrubs. Makes a graceful foliage clump about 1 ft. high. Flowering stems in summer double the plant's height. Performs best in cool seasons and cool climates. If it flops over in heat, shear for fresh growth in fall. Clumps spread by rhizomes, which may periodically need curtailing. Divide and replant as needed.

ARROWHEAD. See SAGITTARIA

FOR INFORMATION ON SELECTING PLANTS

PLEASE SEE PAGES 47–112

ARTEMISIA

Asteraceae (Compositae)

PERENNIALS

ZONES VARY BY SPECIES

FULL SUN

MODERATE WATER

Artemisia abrotanum

Several species are valuable for interesting leaf patterns and silvery gray or white aromatic foliage. Most of those described here have woody stems; *A. dracunculus, A. frigida, A. lactiflora, A. ludoviciana albula,* and *A. stellerana* are herbaceous. Most kinds excellent for use in mixed border where white or silvery leaves soften harsh reds or oranges and blend beautifully with blues, lavenders, and pinks. Divide in spring and fall.

A. abrotanum. SOUTHERNWOOD, OLD MAN. Zones 31, 32, 34–41. To 3–5 ft. Beautiful lemon-scented, green, feathery foliage; yellowish white flower heads. Use for pleasantly scented foliage in shrub border. Hang sprigs in closet to discourage moths. Burn a few leaves on stove to kill cooking odors.

A. absinthium. COMMON WORMWOOD. Zones 31, 32, 34–41. To 2–4 ft. Silvery gray, finely divided leaves with bitter taste, pungent odor. Tiny yellow flowers. Prune to get better-shaped plant. Divide every 3 years. Background shrub; good gray feature in flower border, particularly fine with delphiniums. 'Lambrook Silver' is a 1½-ft. form with especially finely cut, silver white leaves.

A. arborescens. Zones 31, 32. To 3 ft. or a little more in height, 2 ft. wide, with silvery white, very finely cut foliage. Most attractive but more tender than other artemisias.

A. caucasica. SILVER SPREADER. Zones 31, 32, 34–41. To 3–6 in. tall, spreading to 2 ft. in width. Silky, silvery green foliage; small yellow flowers. Bank or ground cover; plant 1–2 ft. apart. Needs good drainage. Takes extremes of heat and cold.

A. dracunculus. FRENCH TARRAGON, TRUE TARRAGON. Zones 31, 32, 34–41. To 1–2 ft.; spreads slowly by creeping rhizomes. Shiny dark green, narrow leaves are very aromatic. Flowers greenish white in branched clusters. Attractive container plant. Cut sprigs in June for seasoning vinegar. Use fresh or dried leaves to season salads, egg and cheese dishes, fish. Divide plant every 3 or 4 years to keep it vigorous. Propagate by divisions or by cuttings. Plants grown from seed are not true culinary tarragon.

A. frigida. FRINGED WORMWOOD. Zones 31, 32, 34–43. To 1–1½ ft. with white, finely cut leaves. Small yellow flowers. Young plants are compact; cut back when they become rangy.

A. lactiflora. WHITE MUGWORT. Zones 31, 32, 34–41. Tall, straight column to 4–5 ft. One of few artemisias with attractive flowers: creamy white in large, branched, 1½-ft. sprays in late summer. Leaves dark green with broad, tooth-edged lobes.

A. ludoviciana albula (A. albula). SILVER KING ARTEMISIA. Zones 31, 32, 34–41. Bushy growth to 2–3½ ft., with slender, spreading branches and silvery white, 2-in. leaves. The lower leaves have three to five lobes; the upper ones are narrow and unlobed. Cut foliage useful in arrangements. 'Valerie Finnis' is a compact grower (to 2 ft. tall), with broader silvery leaves slightly lobed toward the tips.

A. pontica. ROMAN WORMWOOD. Zones 31, 32, 34–41. To 4 ft. Feathery, silver gray leaves. Heads of nodding, whitish yellow flowers in long, open, branched clusters. Leaves used in sachets.

A. 'Powis Castle'. Zones 31, 32, 34. A hybrid, with *A. absinthium* as a probable parent. Silvery, lacy mound to 3 ft. tall, 6 ft. wide. Splendid background plant for bright flowers and tough enough to use as a bank or berm cover.

A. schmidtiana. ANGEL'S HAIR. Zones 31, 32, 34–41. Forms dome, 2 ft. high and 1 ft. wide, of woolly, silvery white, finely cut leaves. Flowers insignificant. 'Silver Mound' is 1 ft. high.

A. stellerana. BEACH WORMWOOD, OLD WOMAN, DUSTY MILLER. Zones 31, 32, 34–45. Dense, silvery gray plant to 2½ ft. with 1–4-in. lobed leaves. Hardier than *Senecio cineraria* (another dusty miller), this artemisia is often used in its place in colder climates. Yellow flowers in spikelike clusters. 'Silver Brocade' is a superior, densely growing selection.

ARTICHOKE

Asteraceae (Compositae)

PERENNIAL VEGETABLE WITH LANDSCAPE VALUE

ALL ZONES

FULL SUN

REGULAR WATER TO PRODUCE CROP

Artichoke

Big ferny-looking plant with irregular, somewhat fountainlike form to 4 ft. high, 6–8 ft. wide. Leaves are silvery green. In warm climates, big flower buds form at tops of stalks; they are the artichokes you cook and eat. Except in some locations along the Atlantic Coast, gardeners in the Northeast can grow artichoke as an annual foliage plant, for its architectural value.

Crops have been raised from seed with some success in cool-summer, mild-winter areas of the Eastern Seaboard (Zones 34, 38). Start seed indoors 8 to 12 weeks before last frost; set outdoors when soil has warmed and frost danger is past. Choose a variety that yields a crop in its first season, such as 'Imperial Star', which takes 90 to 100 days from transplanting. Before first frost, cut stalks close to ground; protect with several inches of compost, manure, or straw. Replace plants every few years.

A close relative of artichoke, also grown for its dramatic foliage, is cardoon (*Cynara cardunculus*).

ARUGULA

ROCKET, ROQUETTE, RUGOLA

Brassicaceae (Cruciferae)

ANNUAL

ALL ZONES

FULL SUN

REGULAR WATER

Arugula

Leaves of this weedy plant supply 1–4-in.-long leaves, like small mustard leaves, that give a nutty zing to green salads. Pick small leaves; the bigger ones have sharp taste. Grows to 3 ft. high. Start from seed in winter or spring. Grows best in cool weather. Reseeds.

ARUM

Araceae

PERENNIALS WITH TUBEROUS ROOTS

ZONES VARY BY SPECIES

PARTIAL OR FULL SHADE

REGULAR WATER DURING ACTIVE GROWTH

SAP IS AN IRRITANT IF INGESTED

Arum italicum

Arrow-shaped or heart-shaped leaves. Curious callalike blossoms on short stalks. Flower bract (spathe) half encloses thick, fleshy spike (spadix), which bears tiny flowers. Use in shady flower borders or woodland gardens where hardy.

A. creticum. Zones 31, 32. Grows to 1½ ft. high. Deep green, arrow-shaped leaves. Deep yellow or ivory spathes to 10 in. long in spring. The yellow spadix inside is fragrant.

A. italicum. ITALIAN ARUM. Zones 31–34, 39. Arrow-shaped leaves, 8 in. long and wide, emerge in fall or early winter. Very short stem; white or greenish white (sometimes purple-spotted) flowers in spring and early summer. Spathe first stands erect, then folds over and conceals short yellow spadix. Dense clusters of bright red fruit follow. Lasting long after leaves have faded, these are the most conspicuous feature of the plant. They resemble small, bright red ears of shucked corn. In variety 'Marmoratum' ('Pictum'), leaves are veined with white.

A. maculatum. Zones 31, 32, 34, 39. Glossy green, arrow-shaped leaves to 8 in. long and often with dark spots. Green spathes to 10 in. long, with purple-black spots and purple edges in spring.

A. pictum. BLACK CALLA. Zones 31, 32. Tuberous-rooted plant to 10 in. high. Arrow- to heart-shaped leaves are glossy dark green, with creamy veins, to 1 ft. long. Dark purple-black spathes to 10 in. long in fall.

ARUNCUS

GOAT'S BEARD

Rosaceae

PERENNIALS

ZONES 31, 32, 34–43

CAN TAKE SUN IN COOL-SUMMER AREAS

REGULAR WATER

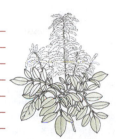

Aruncus dioicus

Resemble *Astilbe,* with slowly spreading clumps of finely divided leaves topped in summer by plumy branched clusters of tiny white or creamy flowers. Good in perennial borders or at edge of woodland; especially handsome against a dark background. Require moist but not boggy soil.

A. aethusifolius. Deep green, finely divided leaves make foot-tall mounds. White flower plumes reach 16 in. Useful in rock garden, as edging or small-scale ground cover.

A. dioicus (A. sylvester). Grows to 6 ft., with a foam of white flowers in 20-in., much-branched clusters. 'Kneiffii' is half as tall, with more finely divided, almost ferny, leaves. 'Child of Two Worlds' ('Zweiweltenkind'), often sold as *A. chinensis,* grows to 5 ft.; branched flower clusters droop gracefully.

ARUNDO donax

GIANT REED

Poaceae (Gramineae)

PERENNIAL

ZONES 31, 32, 35–39

FULL SUN

AMPLE WATER

Arundo donax

One of largest grasses, planted for bold effects in garden fringe areas or by watersides. Often called a bamboo. Strong, somewhat woody stems, 6–20 ft. high. Leaves to 2 ft. long, flat, 3 in. wide. Flowers in rather narrow, erect clusters to 2 ft. high. 'Variegata', less hardy than species (Zones 31, 32, 34), has leaves with white or yellowish stripes. Plants need rich soil. Protect roots with mulch in cold-winter areas. Cut out dead stems and thin occasionally to get look-through quality. Extremely invasive in warm climates, less problematic in the Northeast. Still, plant only where you can control it. Stems have some utility as plant stakes or, if woven together with wire, as fencing or shade canopy.

FOR GROWING SYMBOL EXPLANATIONS

PLEASE SEE PAGE 113

ASARINA

CLIMBING SNAPDRAGON, CHICKABIDDY

Scrophulariaceae

PERENNIALS

⚡ ALL ZONES, EXCEPT AS NOTED

☼ ◐ CAN TAKE FULL SUN IN COOL-SUMMER AREAS

💧 REGULAR WATER

Asarina antirrhinifolia

Climbing, sprawling, or trailing tender plants with tubular flowers that flare at the mouth like snapdragons (a close relative). *A. procumbens* is hardy, but the other three species are not; grow them as annuals. Plants from early sowings will bloom in late spring and through the summer. Grow them on a trellis or brushy twigs or in window boxes or hanging pots. They can also trail over a wall or serve as a small-scale ground cover.

A. antirrhinifolia. Flowers are lavender to purple, 1 in. long, with white throats marked yellow. A mixed-color seed strain offers red-and-yellow or blue-and-white flowers.

A. barclaiana. Vigorous grower to 8–10 ft., with white to pink or purple flowers. 'Angel's Trumpet' has 2-in. pink flowers.

A. procumbens. Zones 31, 32, 35, 39. Trailing stems to 2 ft. long. Pairs of heart- to kidney-shaped leaves, softly hairy and grayish green, with toothed edges. In summer, pale yellow flowers veined in purple.

A. scandens. Resembles *A. barclaiana*, with flowers that range from white to pink and dark blue.

ASARUM

WILD GINGER

Aristolochiaceae

PERENNIALS

⚡ ZONES VARY BY SPECIES

◐ ● PARTIAL OR FULL SHADE

💧 💧💧 AMPLE WATER

Asarum

Roots and leaves of the wild gingers have a scent somewhat like that of ginger, but are not used as seasoning. Low, creeping plants with roundish or heart-shaped leaves, they make attractive woodland ground covers. Flowers are oddly shaped, with three spreading, leathery lobes that may be brownish, purplish, or greenish; hidden among the leaves, blossoms are curious rather than showy. Of the many species, only a few are available to gardeners. Asiatic species with beautifully variegated leaves, now grown as connoisseur's plants in Japan, may eventually make their way here.

A. arifolium. Zones 32, 34–41. Native to the southeastern U.S. Evergreen leaves to 5 in. long are mottled with light green to silver between the veins. Flowers in spring.

A. asaroides. Zones 32, 34, 39. Native to Japan. Evergreen leaves are attractively variegated silver and white in various patterns, to 5 in. long. Flowers are purple green and bloom in spring.

A. canadense. Zones 31, 32, 34–45. Native to eastern North America. Deciduous, kidney-shaped, dark green leaves to 6 in. wide. Flowers are purplish brown. The hardiest species.

A. europaeum. Zones 31, 32, 34–45. Native to Europe. Evergreen, shiny, kidney-shaped, dark green leaves 2–3 in. wide. Small brown flowers. Slow spreader.

A. maximum. Zones 31, warmer parts of 32. Heart-shaped, deep green leaves mottled with gray, to 8 in. across. Maroon flowers in spring.

A. shuttleworthii. Zones 31, 32, 34–37, 39. Native to the Appalachians. Evergreen, 4-in. heart-shaped or roundish leaves usually variegated with silvery markings. Brown flowers with red spots. Slow growing. 'Callaway' spreads more quickly.

A. splendens. Zones 31, 32, 35, 39. Dark green leaves heavily mottled with silver. Vigorous grower; makes a good ground cover.

A. virginicum. Zones 31, 32, 34–41. Small dark green leaves to 3 in. across, usually mottled with purple and silver. Purple flowers to 1 in. long in spring.

Asclepiadaceae. Best-known family members are the milkweeds (*Asclepias*), but other garden plants also belong to this group, among them many succulents and some perennials and vines, including *Stephanotis*.

ASCLEPIAS

Asclepiadaceae

PERENNIALS

⚡ ZONES VARY BY SPECIES

☼ FULL SUN

💧 💧 💧💧 WATER NEEDS VARY BY SPECIES

💧 ALL PARTS OF MANY SPECIES ARE POISONOUS IF INGESTED

Asclepias tuberosa

Milkweeds are the best-known representatives of this group of plants. Just a few are cultivated in gardens, some as annuals.

A. curassavica. BLOOD FLOWER. All zones. Subshrub to 3 ft. high, often grown as an annual. Oblong leaves and clusters of red to red-orange (sometimes yellow or white) flowers, summer into fall.

A. incarnata. SWAMP MILKWEED. Zones 31, 32, 34–45. Native to the eastern U.S. Grows 3–5 ft. tall, with narrow, long-pointed leaves and clustered pink flowers in joints of upper leaves. Needs plenty of moisture, even withstands wet soil. 'Ice Ballet', with white flowers, is a more compact 3½-ft. plant.

A. syriaca. COMMON MILKWEED. Zones 31, 32, 34–43. Weedy perennial found in meadows and grown in butterfly gardens. To 6 ft. high, with oblong leaves and clusters of fragrant, greenish purple and pinkish flowers. The bumpy green pods that follow open to release seeds on silky "parachute" hairs.

A. tuberosa. BUTTERFLY WEED. Zones 31, 32, 34–43. Many stems to 3 ft. rise every year from perennial root. Broad clusters of bright orange flowers appear in midsummer, attracting swarms of butterflies. Prefers good drainage and moderate water. Flowers of Gay Butterflies strain are yellow to red. 'Hello Yellow' is a selected form with bright yellow flowers.

ASH. See FRAXINUS

ASH, MOUNTAIN. See SORBUS

ASIMINA triloba

PAWPAW

Annonaceae

DECIDUOUS TREE

⚡ ZONES 31, 32, 34–41

☼ FULL SUN, EXCEPT AS NOTED

💧 REGULAR WATER

Asimina triloba

The pawpaw (sometimes known as Michigan banana) is the only hardy representative of a tropical family that has given us the cherimoya. It grows to 30 ft., generally broad and spreading when grown alone, but often narrow and erect in thickets that arise from suckering. Leaves are oval, somewhat drooping, 4–10 in. long, medium green, turning bright yellow in fall. Foliage has an unpleasant odor when crushed. Flowers are large but not showy, purplish or brownish (sometimes green), with three prominent petals. Fruits are roughly oval, yellowish green turning brown,

3–5 in. long. The soft, custardlike flesh has a flavor somewhat like that of banana and a number of large brown seeds.

If possible, get grafted plants of named varieties such as 'Prolific' and 'Taylor'. Seedlings are highly variable.

ASPARAGUS

Liliaceae

PERENNIAL VEGETABLE

⚡ ALL ZONES

☼ FULL SUN

💧 💧 AMPLE WATER

Asparagus

One of most permanent and dependable of home garden vegetables. Plants take 2 to 3 years to come into full production but then furnish delicious spears every spring for 10 to 15 years. They take up considerable space but do so in the grand manner: plants are tall, feathery, graceful, highly ornamental. Use asparagus along sunny fence or as background for flowers or vegetables.

Seeds grow into strong young plants in one season (sow in spring), but roots are far more widely used. Set out seedlings or roots (not wilted, no smaller than an adult's hand) in fall (mild climates), or in early spring (cold winters). Make trenches 1 ft. wide and 8–10 in. deep. Space trenches 4–6 ft. apart. Heap loose, manure-enriched soil at bottoms of trenches and soak. Space plants 1 ft. apart, setting them so that tops are 6–8 in. below top of trench. Spread roots out evenly. Cover with 2 in. of soil and water again.

As young plants grow, gradually fill in trench, taking care not to cover growing tips. Soak deeply whenever soil begins to dry out at root depth. Don't harvest any spears the first year; object at this time is to build big root mass. When plants turn brown in late fall or early winter, cut stems to ground. In cold-winter areas, permit dead stalks to stand until spring; they will help trap and hold snow, which will furnish protection to root crowns.

The following spring you can cut your first spears; cut only for 4 to 6 weeks or until appearance of thin spears indicates that roots are nearing exhaustion. Then permit plants to grow. Cultivate, feed, and irrigate heavily. The third year you should be able to cut spears for 8 to 10 weeks. Spears are ready to cut when they are 5–8 in. long. Thrust knife down at 45° angle to soil; flat cutting may injure adjacent developing spears. If asparagus beetles appear during cutting season, handpick them, knock them off the plant with water jets, or spray with rotenone or (carefully noting label precautions) malathion.

Asparagus seed and roots are sold as "traditional" ('Martha Washington' and others) and "all-male" ('Jersey Giant' and others). The latter kinds are bred to produce more and larger spears because they don't have to put energy into seed production. Such varieties still produce an occasional female plant.

HOW TO BLANCH ASPARAGUS

Fresh white asparagus is a delicacy. It's not a special variety; blanching makes it white. In early spring before spears emerge, mound soil 8 in. high over a row of asparagus. When tips emerge from the top of the mounded soil, push a long-handled knife into the base of the mound to cut each spear well below the surface. Pull cut shoots out by the tips. Level mounds after the harvest season.

ASPEN. See POPULUS

ASPERULA odorata. See GALIUM odoratum

ASPHODELINE lutea

YELLOW ASPHODEL, KING'S SPEAR

Liliaceae

PERENNIAL

⚡ ZONES 31, 32, 34, 39

☼ ◐ FULL SUN OR PARTIAL SHADE

💧 REGULAR WATER

Asphodeline lutea

This rhizomatous rootstock forms a clump of dark green, grassy, 1-ft. leaves. The 3-ft. flower stalk is topped in spring by an 8-in. narrow cluster of yellow, fragrant flowers a little more than 1 in. across. These peer from a shag of buff or reddish brown bracts. Use it in perennial borders.

ASPHODELUS

ASPHODEL

Liliaceae

PERENNIAL

⚡ ZONES 31, 32, 34, 39

☼ FULL SUN

💧 LESS THAN REGULAR WATER

Asphodelus

The perennial species of asphodels covered here are tall, stately plants grown for their erect clusters of small flowers. The individual blooms range from ¾ to 1½ in. wide and are densely packed along leafless stalks. Leaves are grassy and borne at the base of the plant. Perennial asphodels grow from fleshy, congested rhizomes and require soil that is deeply prepared and well drained, but not too rich in organic matter. Grow them in perennial beds and borders or naturalize them in sunny wildflower meadows or grassy areas.

A. aestivus (A. microcarpus). Native to the Mediterranean and western Turkey. Forms clumps of flat, leathery, foot-long green leaves. The white to pink-tinted, star-shaped flowers appear in late spring or early summer on branched stems about 3 ft. high.

A. albus. A clump-forming perennial native to central and southern Europe as well as northern Africa. Produces 2–3-ft. stalks of starry, white, ¾-in. flowers in early summer.

ASPIDISTRA elatior (A. lurida)

CAST-IRON PLANT

Liliaceae

PERENNIAL

⚡ ZONES 31, 32, OR INDOORS

◐ ● TOLERATES VERY LOW LIGHT

💧 MODERATE WATER

Aspidistra elatior

Sturdy, long-lived evergreen foliage plant remarkable for its ability to thrive under conditions unacceptable to most kinds of plants. It can be grown outdoors as far north as Washington, D.C., in a sheltered location. Elsewhere, use it outdoors in summer and as a house plant in winter. Leaf blades 1–2½ ft. long, 3–4 in. wide, tough, glossy dark green and arching, with distinct parallel veins; each blade is supported by a 6–8-in.-long grooved leafstalk. Inconspicuous brownish flowers bloom in spring close to ground. Although extremely tolerant, requiring minimal care, cast-iron plant grows best in porous soil enriched with organic matter and responds to feeding in spring and summer. Will grow in dark, shaded areas (under decks or stairs) anywhere, as well as in filtered sun. A good porch plant.

A

Keep leaves dust free and glossy by hosing them off, or clean with a soft brush or cloth. Variegated form ('Variegata'), with leaves striped with white, loses its variegation if it is planted in soil that's too rich.

ASPLENIUM

Polypodiaceae

FERNS

🌿 ZONES VARY BY SPECIES

◐ ● PARTIAL OR FULL SHADE

💧 💧 AMPLE WATER

Asplenium bulbiferum

Widespread and variable group. These resemble each other only in botanical details and need for shade and liberal watering. Common name "spleenwort" refers to alleged medicinal value.

A. bulbiferum. MOTHER FERN. Houseplant. From New Zealand. Graceful, very finely cut light green fronds produce plantlets that can be removed and planted. Grow potted plant indoors in winter, move to shady patio in summer.

A. ebenoides (Asplenosorus ebenoides). SCOTT'S SPLEENWORT. Zones 31, 32, 34–43. Hybrid between *A. platyneuron* and *A. rhizophyllum.* Small evergreen fern of variable appearance, with unevenly divided leaves.

A. platyneuron. EBONY SPLEENWORT. Zones 31, 32, 34–43. Native to eastern U.S. Evergreen, to 1½ ft. tall. Erect, once-divided dark green fronds have blackish brown midribs.

A. rhizophyllum (Camptosorus rhizophyllus). WALKING FERN. Zones 31, 32, 34–43. Native to North America. An oddity with long, slender undivided fronds that taper to the tips; where they touch soil, tips take root and produce new plantlets. Needs some lime in the soil. Best results often obtained when grown among moist limestone rocks.

A. scolopendrium (Phyllitis scolopendrium). HART'S TONGUE FERN. Zones 31, 32, 34–41. Native to Europe (rare native in eastern U.S.). Strap-shaped leaves 9–18 in. long. Dwarf, crested, puckered, and forked varieties are collector's items. Needs humus; add limestone chips to acid soil. Good woodland plant, likes to grow among moist rocks. Often establishes new plants from spores in such conditions. Also fine pot plant.

A. trichomanes. MAIDENHAIR SPLEENWORT. Zones 34–43. Native to much of the Northern Hemisphere. Delicate evergreen fern with narrow, bright green fronds 8–12 in. long. Leaflets are round or nearly so, only ½ in. long. Likes lime. Attractive in shady rock garden or on a wall where it can be seen close up.

ASTER

Asteraceae (Compositae)

PERENNIALS

🌿 ZONES 31, 32, 34–43, EXCEPT AS NOTED

☀ FULL SUN, EXCEPT AS NOTED

💧 REGULAR WATER

Aster frikartii

There are more than 600 species of true asters, ranging from alpine kinds forming compact mounds 6 in. high, to open-branching plants 6 ft. tall, to the odd tall climber. Flowers come in white or shades of blue, red, pink, lavender, or purple, mostly with yellow centers. Bloom is late summer to early fall, except as noted. Taller asters are invaluable for abundant color in large borders or among shrubs. Large sprays are effective in arrangements. Compact dwarf or cushion types make tidy edgings, mounds of color in rock gardens, good container plants.

Adapted to most soils. Most luxuriant in fertile soil. Few problems except for mildew on leaves in late fall. Strong-growing asters have invasive roots, need control. Divide clumps yearly in late fall or early spring. Replant vigorous young divisions from outside of clump; discard old center. Divide smaller, tufted, less vigorously growing kinds every 2 years.

A. alpinus. Zones 36–45. Mounding plant 6–12 in. tall. Leaves ½–5 in. long, mostly in basal tuft. Several stems grow from basal clump, each carrying one violet blue flower 1½–2 in. across. Late spring to early summer bloom. Best in cold-winter areas. White and pink forms are uncommon.

A. amellus. ITALIAN ASTER. Sturdy, hairy plant to 2 ft. Branching stems with violet, yellow-centered flowers 2 in. across.

A. carolinianus. CLIMBING ASTER. Zones 31, 32. Unusual climber to 10–20 ft., with grayish green leaves and pink flowers aging to purplish blue. Fall bloom.

A. cordifolius. BLUE WOOD ASTER. Grows to 6 ft., with loose, branching clusters of inch-wide flower heads. 'Little Carlow' is lower growing (to 3½ ft). Sun or light shade.

A. divaricatus. WHITE WOOD ASTER. Broadly spreading plant with dark stems and a generous show of small flowers in pure white aging to pink. Thrives in shade.

A. ericoides. HEATH ASTER. To 3 ft., with narrow leaves and strong horizontal branching. Flower heads are small and profusely borne, in white, pink, or blue.

A. frikartii. One of the finest, most useful and widely adapted perennials. Hybrid between *A. amellus* and *A. thomsonii,* a hairy-leafed, lilac-flowered, 3-ft. species native to the Himalayas. Abundant clear lavender to violet blue single flowers are 2½ in. across. Open, spreading growth to 2 ft. high. Blooms early summer to fall—almost all year in mild-winter areas if dead flowers are removed regularly. May be short lived. 'Wonder of Stafa' and 'Mönch' are lavender blue favorites.

A. laevis. Zones 31, 32, 34–45. To 3½ ft., with smooth, mildew-free foliage and clustered, 1-in. flower heads of deep purple blue.

A. lateriflorus. Zones 31, 32, 34–45. Species grows to 4 ft.; garden selections are smaller, to 2½ ft. 'Horizontalis' is a twiggy, mounding plant with spreading branches bearing small pale blue flowers. Foliage turns purplish in fall, at height of flowering. 'Prince' is similar in form, with dark purple foliage and white flower heads centered in dark red.

A. novae-angliae. NEW ENGLAND ASTER. Stout-stemmed plant to 3–5 ft. with hairy leaves to 5 in. long. Flowers variable in color, pink to deep purple, 2 in. across. Good in wet areas. Reseeds. 'Alma Potschke', bright, warm pink flowers; 'Harrington's Pink', light pink; 'Treasure', light purple.

A. novi-belgii. NEW YORK ASTER. To 3 ft., similar to New England aster but with smooth leaves. Full clusters of bright blue violet flowers. 'Audrey' has lavender blue flowers; 'Climax', lavender blue; 'Ernest Ballard', carmine red; 'Jenny', double, red violet.

Michaelmas daisy is the name applied to hybrids of *A. novae-angliae* and *A. novi-belgii.* They are tall (3–4-ft.), graceful, branching plants. Many horticultural varieties with flowers in white, pale to deep pink, rose, red, and many shades of blue, violet, and purple.

A. dumosus hybrids, sometimes known as Oregon-Pacific hybrids, are splendid garden plants developed by crossing some well-known Michaelmas daisies with a dwarf aster species native to the West. Dwarf, intermediate, and taller forms range in height from under 1 ft. to 2½ ft. Compact, floriferous, blooming late spring to fall. Many named varieties are available in white, blue, lavender, purple, rose, pink, cream.

A. oblongifolius. Native to the midwestern and western U.S., and as far east as Pennsylvania. To 16 in. high. Oblong, hairy leaves; violet, blue, or rose pink flowers in late summer to fall.

A. pringlei. Eastern U.S. native known in cultivation through the variety 'Monte Cassino', a familiar florist's cut flower. Stems are long (sometimes to 5 ft.) and narrowish, freely set with very short branches bearing starry white, ¾-in. flower heads. Usually sold as *A. ericoides* 'Monte Cassino'.

A. sericeus. Native to mountainous areas in the midwestern and southeastern U.S. To 2 ft. high. Narrow, oblong leaves; rosy purple to deep violet flowers.

A. tataricus. A giant (to 5–7 ft.) with 2-ft. leaves and sheaves of inch-wide blue flower heads in flat clusters in fall. Sun or shade.

A. tongolensis. EAST INDIES ASTER. Zones 31, 32, 34–41. Native to China and the Himalayas. To 1½ ft. high, spreads by rhizomes to form clumps. Dark green, hairy leaves, mostly in basal clumps. Blue violet flowers.

A. yunnanensis 'Napsbury'. An improved garden variety of this Chinese species. Leaves dark green in basal tufts. Stems to 1½ ft., each bearing a single lavender blue, orange-centered flower. Blooms in late spring to early summer.

For the common annual or China aster, sold in six-packs at nurseries, see *Callistephus*.

Asteraceae. The sunflower or daisy family, one of the largest plant families, is characterized by flowers borne in tight clusters (heads). In the most familiar form, these heads contain two types of flowers—small, tightly clustered disk flowers in the center of the head, and larger, strap-shaped ray flowers around the edge. The sunflower *(Helianthus)* is a familiar example. The family was formerly called Compositae.

ASTILBE

FALSE SPIRAEA, MEADOWSWEET

Saxifragaceae

PERENNIALS

ZONES 32, 34–43 (SEE BELOW)

FULL SUN OR PARTIAL SHADE

MOIST BUT NOT BOGGY SOIL

Astilbe arendsii

Valued for light, airy quality of plumelike flower clusters and attractive foliage, ability to provide color from late spring through summer. Leaves divided, with toothed or cut leaflets; leaves in some species simply lobed with cut margins. Small white, pink, or red flowers are carried in graceful, branching, feathery plumes held on slender, wiry stems ranging from 6 in. to 3 ft. or taller.

Astilbes are the mainstay of the shady perennial border, although in cool-summer climates they can withstand full sun if given plenty of moisture. Combine them with columbine, meadow rue, hosta, and bergenia in shady borders; with peonies, delphinium, and iris in sunnier situations. Effective at the edge of pools, along shady paths, and in containers. They require rich soil with ample humus. Cut off faded flowering stems and divide clumps every 4 to 5 years. Survival in zone 43 depends on good snow cover.

A. arendsii. Most astilbes sold belong to this hybrid group or are sold as such. Most of the earliest blooming varieties belong to *A. japonica* and some of the later bloomers to *A. chinensis* or *A. thunbergii*. The plants differ chiefly in technical details. Here are some of the many varieties in use:

'Amethyst'. Late. Lavender, 3–4 ft.

'Bonn'. Early. Medium pink, 1½–2 ft.

'Bremen'. Midseason. Dark rose, 1½–2 ft.

'Bressingham Beauty'. Late midseason. Drooping pink clusters, 3 ft.

'Bridal Veil'. Midseason to late. Full white plumes, 3 ft.

'Deutschland'. Early. White, 1½ ft.

'Erica'. Midseason. Slender pink plumes, 2½–3 ft.

'Fanal'. Early. Blood red flowers, bronzy foliage, 1½–2½ ft.

'Hyacinth'. Midseason. Purplish pink, 2–3 ft.

'Koblenz'. Early to midseason. Bright red, 1½–2½ ft.

'Ostrich Plume' ('Straussenfeder'). Midseason to late. Drooping pink clusters, 3–3½ ft.

'Peach Blossom'. Midseason. Light salmon pink, 2 ft.

'Rheinland'. Early. Deep pink, 2–2½ ft.

'White Gloria'. Early to midseason. Creamy white, 2 ft.

A. biternata. FALSE GOATSBEARD. Native to North America. Grows to 6 ft. high, with long, drooping clusters of white to ivory flowers in summer.

A. chinensis. Resembles the *A. arendsii* hybrids, but generally blooms in late summer, grows taller, and tolerates dryness a little better. Varieties include:

A. c. davidii. Late, with dense, narrow pink plumes 3 ft. tall. Finale, pink-flowered, blooms latest, grows 18–20 in. tall.

A. c. pumila is a dwarf, to 10 in. high, with reddish pink flowers.

A. c. taquetii 'Superba'. Bright pinkish purple flowers in spikelike clusters 4–5 ft. tall. 'Purple Candles' is deeper purple, slightly shorter.

A. simplicifolia. Grows to 16 in., with leaves merely cut or lobed instead of divided into leaflets. Known for its garden varieties. 'Bronze Elegance', to 1½ ft. high; bronze-tinted leaves, deep reddish pink flowers on reddish stems in late summer. 'Dunkellachs', to 14 in. high; dark pink flowers, deeply cut maroon leaves, blooms in midsummer. 'Sprite', the best known, is a low, compact plant with abundant pink, drooping, 1-ft. spires above bronze-tinted foliage; summer bloomer. 'Hennie Graefland' is similar, but grows a few inches taller and blooms somewhat earlier.

A. taquetii 'Superba'. See *A. chinensis taquetii* 'Superba'

ASTILBOIDES tabularis
(Rodgersia tabularis)

Saxifragaceae

PERENNIAL

ZONES 32, 34–41

PARTIAL SHADE TO FULL SUN

AMPLE WATER

Astilboides tabularis

Formerly classified as *Rodgersia*, this imposing plant is now in a genus by itself. Grow it for the sculptural leaves, which are shield-shaped and round, up to 2 ft. or more wide, and sit like broad umbrellas on top of their 3–4-ft.-high stems. In early to midsummer it bears 3–4-ft. plumes of white flowers similar to those of astilbe. Give the plant moist, rich soil and a good winter mulch. In colder climates it can tolerate full sun; elsewhere, partial shade is best. Striking alongside a pond or stream.

ASTRANTIA

MASTERWORT

Apiaceae (Umbelliferae)

PERENNIALS

ZONES 32, 34–41

FULL SUN OR PARTIAL SHADE

REGULAR WATER

Astrantia major

Flowers in dense, tight clusters surrounded by papery bracts resemble pincushions or, superficially, daisies. Flowers are attractive in arrangements and can be dried for winter use. Plants are useful in woodland gardens. Winter dormant.

A. carniolica. To 15–18 in. tall, with finely divided leaves. Bracts around flower heads shorter than in other species. 'Rubra' has dark red flowers with silvery accents.

A. major. Grows to 2–3 ft. tall, with inch-wide clusters of white and green or white and pink flowers. 'Primadonna' has flowers in shades of purple; 'Rosensinfonie', rose pink; 'Sunningdale Variegated', pale pink bracts, leaves edged in creamy yellow.

A. maxima. Slightly larger than *A. major*, with pink flowers.

ASTRANTIA FOR CUTTING AND DRYING

Astrantia makes a charming filler in fresh bouquets and arrangements, and dries well, too. Cut flowers before they open fully. Condition fresh flowers before arranging by standing stems in cool water nearly to the lowest flower stem. Remove lower leaves. Or air-dry by hanging stems upside down in bunches in a dry, airy place.

A

ATHYRIUM

Polypodiaceae

FERNS

ZONES 31, 32, 34–43, EXCEPT AS NOTED

PARTIAL OR FULL SHADE, EXCEPT AS NOTED

AMPLE WATER

Evergreen in mildest areas, these ferns turn brown after repeated frosts. Leave dead fronds on plant to provide mulch and to shelter emerging fronds in early spring, then cut back. Prefer rich, damp soil and shade. Propagate by dividing old clumps in early spring.

Athyrium filix-femina

A. filix-femina. LADY FERN. Grows to 4 ft. or more. Rootstock rises up on older plants to make short trunk. Vertical effect; narrow at bottom, spreading at top. Thin fronds, finely divided. Vigorous; can be invasive. Tolerates full sun in constantly moist soil. Specialists stock many varieties with oddly cut and feathered fronds. 'Cristata' has crests at the ends of the pinnae (segments). In 'Frizelliae', divisions of fronds are reduced to balls; fronds look like strings of beads. 'Vernoniae Cristatum' has crested and feathered fronds. In 'Victoriae' the divided leaf segments branch at the base to form crosses.

A. nipponicum 'Pictum' (A. goeringianum 'Pictum'). JAPANESE PAINTED FERN. Fronds grow to 1½ ft. long, making a tight, slowly spreading clump. Leaflets are purplish at base, then lavender, then silvery greenish gray toward ends.

A. otophorum. EARED LADY FERN. Zones 31, 32, 34–41. Actually a native of the Orient. To 2 ft. tall. It resembles Japanese painted fern, but its triangular bluish green fronds have a reddish or purple midrib. Fronds are chartreuse when they emerge and darken as they mature. Needs moist soil, neutral pH.

A. pycnocarpon. GLADE FERN, SILVERY SPLEENWORT. Zones 31, 32, 34–45. Attractive rosette-forming deciduous fern with once-divided fronds to 4 ft. long. New spring fronds are silvery light green; they turn darker in summer, then russet before dying back. Tolerates full sun in constantly moist soil.

A. spinulosum. Fronds to 1 ft. long are divided into narrow leaflets with toothed edges. Stems are pale yellowish.

AUBRIETA deltoidea

COMMON AUBRIETA

Brassicaceae (Cruciferae)

PERENNIAL

ZONES 36–43

FULL SUN OR LIGHT SHADE

REGULAR WATER

Aubrieta deltoidea

Native from eastern Mediterranean region to Iran. Low, spreading, mat-forming perennial; charming with other spring bloomers such as basket-of-gold, rockcress, perennial candytuft, and moss pink. Ideal for chinks in dry stone walls or between patio flagstones. Grows 2–6 in. high, 1–1½ ft. across. Small gray-green leaves with a few teeth at top. Tiny rose to deep red, pale to deep lilac, or purple flowers. 'Argenteovariegata' has purple flowers and silver-edged leaves. 'Aureomarginata' has mauve pink flowers and gold-edged leaves. 'Novalis Blue' is a fine seed-grown variety.

Provide good drainage. Needs regular moisture before and during bloom; takes some drought later on. After bloom, shear off flowers before they set seed. Don't cut back more than half—always keep some foliage. After trimming, top-dress with mixture of gritty soil and bone meal. Sow seeds in late spring for blooms the following spring. Difficult to divide clumps; make cuttings in late summer. Short lived, especially in warm, humid regions.

AUCUBA japonica

JAPANESE AUCUBA

Cornaceae

EVERGREEN SHRUB

ZONES 31, 32

PERFORMS WELL IN DEEP SHADE

MODERATE WATER

Aucuba japonica

Native from Himalayas to Japan. Good foliage plant. In most of the Northeast region, grow it in a container moved outdoors in summer and indoors in fall. Seedlings vary in leaf form and variegations; many varieties offered. Standard green-leafed aucuba grows at moderate rate to 6 ft. tall in a container and almost as wide. Buxom shrub, densely clothed with polished, dark green, toothed leaves 3–8 in. long, 1½–3 in. wide.

Minute, dark maroon flowers in spring are followed by clusters of bright red, ¾-in. berries hidden in leaves in fall and winter. Both sexes must be planted to ensure fruit crop. Green-leafed 'Rozannie' is reportedly self-fertile.

Other green-leafed varieties include 'Longifolia' ('Salicifolia'), narrow willowlike leaves (female); 'Nana', dwarf to about 3 ft. (female); 'Serratifolia', long leaves, coarsely toothed edges (female).

Variegated varieties (usually slower growing) include 'Crotonifolia', leaves heavily splashed with white and gold (male); 'Fructu Albo', leaves variegated with white, berries pale pinkish buff (female); 'Picturata' ('Aureo-maculata'), leaves centered with golden yellow, edged with dark green dotted yellow (female); 'Sulphur', green leaves with broad yellow edge (female); 'Variegata', gold dust plant, best-known aucuba, dark green leaves spotted with yellow (male or female). 'Mr. Goldstrike' has heavier gold splashings.

Tolerant of wide range of soils. Requires shade from hot sun, accepts deep shade. Tolerates low light level under trees, competes successfully with tree roots. Gets mealybug and mites. Prune to control height or form by cutting back to a leaf joint (node).

All aucubas make choice tub plants for shady patio or in the house. Use variegated forms to light up dark corners. Associate with ferns, hydrangeas.

AURICULA. See PRIMULA auricula

AURINIA saxatilis (Alyssum saxatile)

BASKET-OF-GOLD

Brassicaceae (Cruciferae)

PERENNIAL

ZONES 32, 34–43

FULL SUN OR LIGHT SHADE

MODERATE WATER

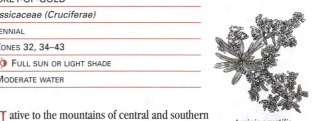

Native to the mountains of central and southern Europe, Russia, and Turkey. Stems 8–12 in. high. Gray, hairy leaves, 2–5 in. long, appear in rosettes. Dense clusters of tiny golden yellow flowers in spring and early summer. Use as foreground plant in borders, in rock gardens, atop walls. Shear lightly (not more than half) right after bloom to avoid legginess. Generally hardy but may be killed in extremely cold winters. Self-sows readily. Short lived in hot, humid areas.

Aurinia saxatilis

Varieties include 'Citrina' ('Lutea'), with pale yellow flowers; 'Compacta', dwarf, tight growing; 'Plena' ('Flore Pleno'), double flowered; 'Silver Queen', compact, with pale yellow flowers; 'Sunnyborder Apricot', with apricot-shaded flowers; 'Dudley Neville Variegated', with flower color similar to that of 'Sunnyborder Apricot' but leaves with whitish or creamy edges.

AUSTRIAN BRIER. See ROSA foetida

AZALEA. See RHODODENDRON

AZTEC LILY. See SPREKELIA formosissima

BABY BLUE EYES. See NEMOPHILA menziesii

BABY'S BREATH. See GYPSOPHILA paniculata

BABY SNAPDRAGON. See LINARIA maroccana

BACCHARIS halimifolia

GROUNDSEL, SALT BUSH

Asteraceae (Compositae)

DECIDUOUS SHRUB

⚡ ZONES 31, 32, 34–41

☼ FULL SUN

💧💧 WATER NEEDS VARY BY SPECIES

Baccharis halimifolia

Main value of this plant is its toughness and ability to grow in difficult conditions. Withstands heat, wind, poor soil. Native from Massachusetts south to Florida and Texas. Grows 5–12 ft. tall and wide, with gray-green, coarsely toothed, 1–3-in. leaves. Tolerates saline soil in dunes, tidal flats, and ditches. Valuable in windy coastal gardens. Regular to moderate water. Male and female flowers, borne on separate plants, are inconspicuous. Beautiful silvery seedheads from midautumn to early winter.

BACHELOR'S BUTTON. See CENTAUREA cyanus

BACOPA

Scrophulariaceae

ANNUAL

⚡ ALL ZONES

☼ ◐ FULL SUN TO PARTIAL SHADE

💧💧 REGULAR TO AMPLE WATER

Bacopa

The species is a bog plant, native from New Jersey to Florida, with small blue flowers blooming from late spring through early fall; of greater interest to the gardener are the Sutera hybrids, dependable, highly vigorous plants with compact, olive green foliage and abundant flowers, each with five rounded petals and a bright yellow center. Especially useful in hanging baskets and window boxes and at the front of the border. Plant in well-drained, slightly acidic soil; in containers use a peat/perlite mix. Apply a balanced fertilizer monthly (biweekly in containers). In areas with moderate summer temperatures they bloom heavily throughout the growing season, but in high-heat regions, results may not be favorable.

'Giant Snowflake', large white flowers. 'Lavender Storm', low-spreading with large lavender flowers, slightly raised above the foliage. 'Snowstorm', prolific bloomer with large white flowers.

BALD CYPRESS. See TAXODIUM distichum

BALLOON FLOWER. See PLATYCODON grandiflorus

BALLOTA nigra

Lamiaceae (Labiatae)

SHRUBBY PERENNIAL

⚡ ZONES 31, 32

☼ FULL SUN

💧💧 MODERATE TO LITTLE WATER

Ballota

Tough, shrubby 4-ft. perennial with rounded, hairy leaves that exude an unpleasant smell when rubbed. Bears white, ½-in.-long flowers from early summer to fall. 'Variegata', also sold as 'Archer's Variety', has leaves with white streaks and spots and purple flowers. Suitable for warm, sunny spots with poor, dry soil. Plants can be grown outdoors year round where hardy; elsewhere, treat them as annuals or as tender perennials overwintered indoors. To overwinter, take cuttings in summer or dig plants in early fall and grow them indoors until the following spring. Cut back plants hard in spring. Use in sunny beds and borders and with herbs such as lavender or other Mediterranean plants.

BALSAM. See IMPATIENS balsamina

Balsaminaceae. The touch-me-not family embraces herbaceous or shrubby plants with juicy stems, irregular flowers with spurs, and explosive seed capsules. *Impatiens* is the only important member.

BALSAM PEAR. See MOMORDICA charantia

BAMBOO

Poaceae (Gramineae)

GIANT GRASSES

⚡ ZONES VARY

☼ ◐ FULL SUN OR LIGHT SHADE

💧💧 REGULAR TO LITTLE WATER

Phyllostachys aurea

Large, woody stems (culms) divided into sections (internodes) by obvious joints (nodes). Upper nodes produce buds that develop into branches; these, in larger bamboos, divide into secondary branches that bear leaves. Bamboos spread by underground stems (rhizomes) that, like the aboveground culms, are jointed and carry buds. Manner in which rhizomes grow explains difference between running and clump bamboos.

In running bamboos (*Phyllostachys, Pleioblastus,* and *Sasa)*, underground stems grow rapidly to varying distances from parent plant before sending up new vertical shoots. These bamboos eventually form large patches or groves unless spread is curbed. They are generally fairly hardy plants from temperate regions in China and Japan, and they are tolerant of a wide variety of soils.

In clump bamboos, such as *Fargesia,* underground stems grow only a short distance before sending up new stems. These form clumps that slowly expand around the edges. Most are tropical or subtropical.

See plant descriptions for hardiness. Figures indicate temperatures at which leaf damage occurs. Stems and rhizomes may be considerably hardier.

Plant container-grown bamboos at any time of year. Best time to propagate from existing clumps is just before growth begins in spring; divide hardy kinds in March or early April. (Transplanting at other times is possible, but risk of losing divisions is high in summer heat.) Cut or saw out divisions with roots and at least three connected culms. If divisions are large, cut back tops to balance loss of roots and rhizomes. Foliage may wilt or wither, but culms will send out new leaves.

Rhizome cutting is another means of propagation. In clump bamboos, this cutting consists of the rooted base of a culm; in running bamboos, it

149

B

is a foot-long length of rhizome with roots and buds. Plant in rich mix with ample organic material added.

Culms of all bamboos have already attained their maximum diameter when they poke through ground; in mature plants, they usually reach their maximum height within a month. Many do become increasingly leafy in subsequent years, but not taller. Plants are evergreen, but there is considerable dropping of older leaves; old plantings develop nearly weedproof mulch of dead leaves. Individual culms live for several years but eventually die and should be cut out.

Mature bamboos grow phenomenally fast during their brief growth period—culms of giant types may increase in length by several feet a day. Don't expect such quick growth the first year after transplanting, though. To get fast growth and great size, water frequently and feed once a month with high-nitrogen or lawn fertilizer; to restrict size and spread, water and feed less. Once established, plants tolerate considerable drought, but rhizomes will not spread into dry soil (or into water). The plant descriptions list two heights for each bamboo. Controlled height, listed first, means average height under dry conditions with little feeding, or with rhizome spread controlled by barriers. Uncontrolled height, given in parentheses, refers to plants growing under best conditions without confinement.

Difficult to mass-produce and little known, most bamboos are hard to find in nurseries. Inquire about specialists in your area. The American Bamboo Society has chapters in various regions. Society members often propagate rare varieties for sales in connection with their meetings. Arboretum and botanical garden sales are another source. Plants may be offered under the principal name listed or under one of the synonyms. Plant names change so frequently that vendors cannot always keep up.

In the case of bamboo, disregard the rule of never buying root-bound plants: the more crowded the plant in the container, the faster its growth when planted. Both running and clump types grow well when roots are confined.

Scale, mealybugs, and aphids are occasionally found on bamboo but seldom do any harm; if they excrete honeydew in bothersome amounts, spray with insecticidal soap or summer oil. To control mites, release predatory mites.

The plant descriptions classify each bamboo by habit of growth, which, of course, determines its use in the garden. In Group I are the dwarf or low-growing ground cover types. These can be used for erosion control or, in small clumps (carefully confined in a long section of flue tile), in border or rock garden. Group II includes clump bamboos with fountainlike habit of growth. These have widest use in landscaping. They require no more space than the average strong-growing shrub. Clipped, they make hedges or screens that won't spread much into surrounding soil. When unclipped, they line up as informal screens or grow singly to show off their graceful form.

Bamboos in Group III are running bamboos of moderate size and more or less vertical growth. Use them as screens, hedges, or (if curbed) alone. The giant bamboos are not covered in plant descriptions but are best used for Oriental effects on a grand scale, or for tropical looks.

Some of the smaller bamboos bloom on some of their stalks every year and continue to grow. Some bloom partially and at erratic intervals. Some have never been known to bloom. Others bloom heavily, set seed, and die. Species of *Phyllostachys* bloom at rare intervals of 30 to 60 years, produce flowers for a long period, and become enfeebled. They may recover very slowly or die. There is evidence that very heavy feeding and watering may speed their recovery.

Bamboos are not recommended for year-round indoor culture, but container-grown plants can spend extended periods indoors in cool, bright rooms. You can revive plants by taking them outdoors, but it is important to avoid sudden changes in temperature and light.

There are several ways to eliminate unwanted bamboo. Digging it out with mattock and spade is the surest method, though sometimes difficult. Rhizomes are generally not deep, but they may be widespread. Remove them all or regrowth will occur. Starve out roots by cutting off all shoots before they exceed 2 ft. in height; repeat as needed—probably many times over the course of a year. Contact herbicide sprays that kill leaves have the same effect as removing culms. Full-strength glyphosate weed killer poured into freshly cut stumps is another good control.

Fargesia murielae *(Sinarundinaria murielae)*. UMBRELLA BAMBOO. Clumping, 6–8 ft. (15 ft.), ½-in.-diameter stems; −20°F/−29°C. Group III. Handsome, gracefully arching, green culms with evergreen foliage, but some leaves turn yellow and drop each fall. Forms dense, shrublike clumps that increase in diameter by only 2–3 in. per year. *F. nitida* (fountain bamboo) is another hardy slow spreader.

Phyllostachys aurea. GOLDEN BAMBOO. Running, 6–10 ft. (10–20 ft.), 2-in. stems; 0°F/−18°C. Group III. Erect, stiff culms, usually with crowded joints at base. Dense foliage makes it good screen or hedge. Can take drought but looks better with regular water. Grows well in tubs.

RUNNING BAMBOO CAN BE CONTAINED

Make 2–3-ft.-deep barriers with strips of galvanized sheet metal, 30-mil plastic, or poured concrete; or plant in long flue tiles or bottomless oil drums. You can limit spread by periodically inserting a spade down to its full depth around the clump. New shoots break off easily; they do not resprout. Another way to limit spread of large running bamboos: Dig a foot-deep trench around plant and sever any rhizomes that grow into it; the trench will fill with a loose mulch of leaves. Sift through leaves with gloved hands to find roving rhizomes.

P. dulcis. SWEET SHOOT BAMBOO. Running, 25–35 ft. (35–40 ft.), 3-in. stems; −10°F/−23°C. Group III. Vigorous and fast spreading, with upright, edible culms. Does not tolerate dry conditions.

P. flexuosa. ZIGZAG BAMBOO. Running, 6–25 ft. (25–35 ft.), 2½-in. stems; −20°F/−29°C. Group III. Produces spreading clumps of arching culms that often form a zig-zag pattern between joints. Culms emerge green, turn yellow-brown, are nearly black at maturity. Good for hedges.

P. rubromarginata. Running, 45–50 ft. (50–55 ft.), 3½-in. stems; −20°F/−29°C. Group III. Shoots are red-margined when young. Culms are edible when young. They are strong and have long, straight internodes, making them ideal for use as garden stakes.

P. viridiglaucescens. Running, 12–30 ft. (30–40 ft.), 1–2-in. stems; 0°F/−18°C. Group III. Produces clumps of upright green culms covered with waxy white powder below the leaf nodes.

Pleioblastus auricomus *(Arundinaria viridistriata, Pleioblastus viridistriatus)*. KAMURO-ZASA BAMBOO. Running, 3–4 ft. (4–5 ft.), ½-in. stems; 0°F/−18°C. Group I. Fast-spreading species with purple-green culms and green leaves striped bright yellow. Use as a ground cover in controlled situations or in containers.

P. pygmaeus *(Sasa pygmaea)*. Running, ½–1 ft. (1–1½ ft.), ⅛-in. stems; 0°F/−18°C. Group I. Aggressive spreader; good bank holder and erosion control. Can be mowed every few years to keep it from growing stemmy and unattractive.

P. simonii *(Arundinaria simonii)*. SIMON BAMBOO, MEDAKE. Running, to 10 ft. (20 ft.), 1½-in. stems; 0°F/−18°C. Group III. Vertical growth pattern, moderate spreader. Screens, hedges; garden stakes.

Sasa palmata *(S. senanensis)*. PALMATE BAMBOO. Running, 4–5 ft. (8–12 ft.), ⅜-in. stems; 0°F/−18°C. In class by itself. Grows bigger in moist or cool-summer areas than in very hot or dry areas. Broad, handsome leaves (to 15 in. long by 4 in. wide) spread fingerlike from stem and branch tips. Rampant spreader; curb it.

S. veitchii. Running, 2–3 ft. (2–3 ft.), ½-in. stems; 0°F/−18°C. Group I. Rampant spreader with large (7-in.-by-1-in.) dark green leaves that turn whitish.

BAMBUSA. See BAMBOO

BANANA. See ENSETE, MUSA

BANEBERRY. See ACTAEA

BAPTISIA

FALSE INDIGO, WILD INDIGO

Fabaceae (Leguminosae)

PERENNIALS

🌿 ZONES 31, 32, 34–43

☼ FULL SUN

💧 MODERATE WATER

Baptisia australis

Native to eastern and midwestern U.S. The false indigos somewhat resemble lupines, but have deep taproots that enable them to survive difficult conditions. Long lived, they eventually become large clumps with many stems and bloom spikes. They resent transplanting once established. Bluish green leaves are divided into three leaflets. Flower spikes to 1 ft. long top the plants in late spring or early summer. Flowers resemble small sweet peas and are followed by inflated seedpods; both flowers and pods are interesting in arrangements. Remove spent flowers to encourage repeat bloom.

B. alba. WHITE FALSE INDIGO. 3 ft. tall, with clusters of white flowers.

B. australis (B. minor). BLUE FALSE INDIGO. Grows 3–6 ft. tall; flowers are indigo blue. 'Purple Smoke', a hybrid between this species and *B. alba*, grows 4½ ft. tall and has violet flowers with dark purple centers.

B. bracteata (B. leucophaea). To 2½ ft. tall. Leaves divided into spoon-shaped leaflets to 4 in. long. White or cream-colored flowers in spring.

B. lactea (B. leucantha). WHITE FALSE INDIGO. To 6 ft. tall. Leaves covered with waxy bloom and divided into wavy oblong leaflets to 2½ in. long. White flowers 1 in. long, sometimes tinged purple, in early summer.

B. minor. Very similar to *B. australis,* but with smaller leaves.

BARBERRY. See BERBERIS

BARREN STRAWBERRY. See WALDSTEINIA

BASEBALL PLANT. See EUPHORBIA obesa

BASELLA alba

MALABAR SPINACH

Basellaceae

PERENNIAL VINE GROWN AS ANNUAL

🌿 ALL ZONES

☼ FULL SUN

💧 REGULAR WATER

Basella alba

Heat- and humidity-loving malabar spinach is native to tropical Africa and Southeast Asia, where it can climb to as much as 30 ft. in height. When grown in the Northeast as an annual, it reaches 4–6 ft. in a single season. Plants bear fleshy, rounded, dark green, edible leaves and small, white, insignificant flowers. Young leaves have an appealing, mild flavor even when temperatures exceed 90°F/32°C (when spinach and lettuce fail) provided they receive adequate water. Plants require a trellis and climb by twining stems.

Sow seeds indoors six weeks before the last frost date and transplant after all danger of frost is past. Use as a screen plant or train over a fence. Plants engulf nearby neighbors that are less vigorous.

'Rubra' bears dark green leaves with purple stems.

BASIL. See OCIMUM

BASKET FLOWER. See CENTAUREA americana, HYMENOCALLIS narcissiflora

---

BASKET-OF-GOLD. See AURINIA saxatilis

BASSWOOD. See TILIA americana

BAY. See LAURUS

BAYBERRY. See MYRICA pensylvanica

BEACH WORMWOOD. See ARTEMISIA stellerana

BEAN, BROAD

FAVA BEAN, HORSE BEAN

Fabaceae (Leguminosae)

ANNUAL

🌿 ALL ZONES

☼ FULL SUN

💧 MODERATE WATER

🔥 SOME PEOPLE HAVE SEVERE REACTIONS

Fava Bean

This bean (actually a giant vetch) was known in ancient and medieval times; it is a Mediterranean plant, while all other familiar beans are New World plants. Bushy growth to 2–4 ft. You can cook and eat immature pods like edible-pod peas; prepare immature and mature seeds in same way as green or dry limas.

Unlike true beans, this is a cool-season plant. In cold-winter areas, plant as early in spring as soil can be worked. In Zones 31 and 32 seeds may be planted as early as the middle of February. Matures in 120 to 150 days, depending on temperature. Space rows 1½–2½ ft. apart. Plant seeds 1 in. deep, 4–5 in. apart; thin to 8–10 in. apart. Watch for and control aphids.

Most people can safely eat fava beans, though a very few (principally of Mediterranean ancestry) have an enzyme deficiency that can cause severe reactions to the beans and even the pollen.

BEAN, DRY

Fabaceae (Leguminosae)

ANNUAL

🌿 ALL ZONES

☼ FULL SUN

💧 REGULAR WATER AFTER SEEDLINGS EMERGE

Dry Bean

Same culture as bush form of snap bean. Let pods remain on bush until they turn dry or begin to shatter; thresh beans from pods, dry, store to soak and cook later. 'Pinto', 'Red Kidney', and 'White Marrowfat' belong to this group.

GROW A BEAN TEPEE

From July to September, children can play in the cool, shady confines of a bean tepee (it will be especially colorful if scarlet runner beans are used). Place a vertical 10-ft. center pole 1½ ft. deep in the soil. Pack it in well. Place bases of at least four 10-ft.-long bamboo poles (or other skinny wooden sticks) 4½ ft. out from base of center pole and tie their tops together 6–12 in. below top of center pole. In a circle just outside pole bases, plant the beans 1 in. deep and 1–3 in. apart. Train the vines up the outside of the tepee, keeping main stems out of its interior.

B

BEAN, GREEN. See BEAN, SNAP

BEAN, LIMA

Fabaceae (Leguminosae)

ANNUAL

ALL ZONES

FULL SUN

REGULAR WATER AFTER SEEDLINGS EMERGE

Lima Bean

L ike snap beans (which they resemble), limas come in either bush or vine (pole) form. They develop more slowly than string beans—bush types require 65 to 75 days from planting to harvest, pole kinds 78 to 95 days—and do not produce as reliably in extremely dry, hot weather. They must be shelled before cooking—a tedious chore but worth it if you like fresh limas.

Among bush types, 'Burpee's Improved Bush', 'Henderson Bush', and 'Fordhook 242' are outstanding; the last two are especially useful in hot-summer areas. 'Prizetaker' and 'King of the Garden' are fine, large-seeded climbing forms; 'Small White Lima', ('Sieva'), usually grown for drying, gives heavy yields of shelled beans. Grow like snap beans.

BEAN, SCARLET RUNNER

Fabaceae (Leguminosae)

PERENNIAL TWINING VINE GROWN AS ANNUAL

ALL ZONES

FULL SUN

REGULAR WATER AFTER SEEDLINGS EMERGE

Scarlet Runner Bean

S howy and ornamental with bright scarlet flowers in slender clusters and with bright green leaves divided into three roundish, 3–5-in.-long leaflets. Use to cover fences, arbors, outbuildings; provides quick shade on porches. Pink- and white-flowered varieties exist.

Flowering may be sporadic during muggy weather in Zones 31 and 32, but improves dramatically when summer nights become cooler. Flowers are followed by flattened, very dark green pods that are edible and tasty when young but toughen as they reach full size. Beans from older pods can be shelled for cooking like green limas. Culture is same as for snap beans.

BEAN, SNAP

STRING BEAN, GREEN BEAN

Fabaceae (Leguminosae)

ANNUAL

ALL ZONES

FULL SUN

REGULAR WATER AFTER SEEDLINGS EMERGE

Snap Bean

S nap bean are among the most widely planted and most useful for home gardens. Snap beans have tender, fleshy pods with little fiber; they may be green, yellow (wax beans), or purple. Purple kinds turn green in cooking. Plants grow as self-supporting bushes (bush beans) or as climbing vines (pole beans). Bush types bear earlier, but vines are more productive. Plants resemble scarlet runner bean, but white or purple flowers are not showy.

Pole bean varieties include the following. Green: 'Fortex', 'Garden of Eden','Kentucky Wonder', 'Kentucky Blue'. Yellow: 'Goldmarie', 'Kentucky Wonder Wax'. Purple: 'Purple Peacock', 'Trionfo Violetto'.

Bush bean varieties include the following. Green: 'Bountiful', 'Bush Blue Lake', 'Bush Romano', 'Jade', 'Provider', 'Roma II', 'Tendergreen'. Yellow: 'Dragon Tongue', 'Goldkist', 'Gold Rush', 'Pencil Pod'. Purple: 'Purple Queen', 'Royal Burgundy'.

Plant seeds as soon as soil is warm, in full sun and good soil. The seeds must push heavy seed leaves through soil, so see that soil is reasonably loose and open. Plant seeds of bush types an inch deep and 1–3 in. apart in rows, with 2–3 ft. between rows. Pole beans can be managed in a number of ways: set three or four 8-ft. poles in the ground and tie together at top in wigwam fashion; or set single poles 3 or 4 ft. apart and sow six or eight beans around each, thinning to three or four strongest seedlings; or insert poles 1 or 2 ft. apart in rows and sow seeds as you would bush beans; or sow along sunny wall, fence, or trellis and train vines on web of light string supported by wire or heavy twine. Moisten ground thoroughly before planting; do not water again until seedlings have emerged.

Once growth starts, keep soil moist. In absence of rainfall, occasional deep soaking is preferable to frequent light sprinklings, which may encourage mildew. Feed after plants are in active growth and again when pods start to form. Pods are ready in 50 to 70 days, depending on variety. Pick every 5 to 7 days; if pods mature, plants will stop bearing. Mexican bean beetles are often a problem in the eastern U.S. A trap crop is an effective control: set out a few bean plants earlier than the bean crop you intend to harvest, wait until the trap beans are infested, and then dispose of them, pests and all. If the small, copper-colored beetles with 16 spots appear on your good crop, shake them loose onto a cloth, then discard it. Control aphids, cucumber beetles, and whiteflies as needed.

BEARBERRY. See ARCTOSTAPHYLOS uva-ursi

BEARD TONGUE. See PENSTEMON

BEAR'S BREECH. See ACANTHUS mollis

BEAUTYBERRY. See CALLICARPA

BEAUTY BUSH. See KOLKWITZIA amabilis

BEE BALM. See MONARDA

BEECH. See FAGUS

BEET

Chenopodiaceae

BIENNIAL GROWN AS ANNUAL

ALL ZONES

FULL SUN

REGULAR WATER

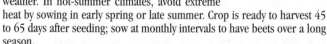

Beet

R aised for edible root and tender young leaves, beet grows best in relatively cool weather. In hot-summer climates, avoid extreme heat by sowing in early spring or late summer. Crop is ready to harvest 45 to 65 days after seeding; sow at monthly intervals to have beets over a long season.

Grow in fertile, well-drained soil without lumps or rocks. Sow seed 1 in. apart and cover with ¼ in. of compost, sand, or vermiculite. Thin to 2 in. apart while plants are small—the thinnings (tops as well as roots) are edible. To keep roots tender, keep soil evenly moist. Begin harvesting when roots are 1 in. wide; complete harvesting before they exceed 3 in. (they will be woody if allowed to grow bigger). In cold climates, harvest all beets before hard frosts in fall.

Types with round, red roots include 'Detroit Dark Red' and 'Crosby's Egyptian' (both old favorites) as well as 'Red Ace' and many newer varieties. Novelties include 'Cylindra' and 'Forma Nova' (with long, cylindrical roots) and 'Chioggia' (striped with pink-and-white rings inside). There are also varieties with golden yellow or white roots, such as 'Burpee's Golden'.

B

BEGONIA

Begoniaceae

PERENNIALS

🌿 TREAT AS ANNUALS, EXCEPT AS NOTED

◐ ● BEST IN FILTERED SHADE

💧 MOIST SOIL AND HUMID AIR

Begonia

This huge genus includes many tender plants that are popular houseplants in all but the warmest U.S. climates. There is also one species that is hardy in the warmer parts of the Northeast region. Wax or Semperflorens begonias and tuberous begonias are widely grown as annuals or houseplants in the Northeast. They thrive in filtered shade, with rich, porous, fast-draining soil, consistent but light feeding, and enough water to keep the soil moist but not soggy.

Hardy begonia. Unique among begonias is *B. grandis* (*B. evansiana*, *B. grandis evansiana*). Suitable for Zones 31, 32, 34, 39, it is the only begonia that is hardy outside the mildest parts of the U.S. Grows from a tuber; reaches 2–3 ft. tall, with branching red stems carrying large, smooth coppery green leaves with red undersides. Summer flowers are pink or white, borne in drooping clusters. Tops die down after frost; mulch to protect roots. Grow with ferns, hosta, bergenia, and similar shade plants.

Semperflorens begonias. Fibrous or bedding begonias, often called wax begonias. Dwarf (6–8-in.) and taller (10–12-in.) strains grown in garden beds or containers as annuals, producing lots of small flowers spring through fall in a white-through-red range. Foliage can be green, red, bronze, or variegated. Thrives in full sun in coolest summer areas. Prefers broken shade elsewhere, but dark-foliaged kinds will take sun if well watered. Take cuttings in fall to pot up for winter houseplants.

Wax begonia varieties include the Cocktail hybrids, with bronze leaves and scarlet, pink, or white flowers; Lotto hybrids, green leaves, large red or pink flowers; Senator series, bronze leaves, rose, pink, white, or scarlet flowers, early blooming; Super Olympia series (replaces Olympia hybrids), early blooming, green leaves, red, pink, coral, white; and Varsity series, green leaves, rose, pink, scarlet, white, and rose-and-white bicolor.

Tuberous begonias. These magnificent large-flowered hybrids grow from tubers. Types range from plants with saucer-size blooms and a few upright stems to multistemmed hanging-basket types covered with flowers. Except for some rare kinds, they are summer- and fall-blooming in almost any flower color except blue.

Grow tuberous begonias in filtered shade, such as under lath or in the open with eastern exposure. Not suited to areas of extreme heat and humidity. For best bloom in dry regions, mist with water several times a day. Watch for fuzzy white spots on leaves, which signal powdery mildew. In fall, when leaves begin to yellow and wilt, reduce watering. When stems have fallen off the plant on their own, lift tuber; shake off dirt; dry tuber in the sun for 3 days; and store in cool, dry place, such as a garden shed or garage, with its label until spring, when little pink buds will become visible. In April and May you can buy small seedling plants and plant them directly in pots.

HOW AND WHEN TO START BEGONIA TUBERS

In early February, place dormant tubers in shallow flats and cover ½–1 in. deep with coarse organic matter such as leaf mold. Water the flats regularly and keep them in broken shade (in mild climates) or under lights indoors (in cold-winter climates). As each plant reaches 3 in. high, repot into 8–10-in. pot with rich, humusy, fast-draining potting mix. Stake upright types. Water to keep potting mix moist but not soggy. Fertilize weekly with quarter-strength high-nitrogen fertilizer until mid-May; then switch to a bloom-producing fertilizer.

Strains are sold as hanging or upright. The former bloom more profusely; the latter have larger flowers. Colors are white, red, pink, yellow, and peach; shapes are frilly (carnation), formal double (camellia), and tight-centered (rose). Some have petal edges in contrasting colors (picotee). Popular strains are Double Trumpet (improved rose form), Prima Donna (improved camellia), and Hanging Sensation.

Another tender tuberous begonia is the species *B. sutherlandii*. This large plant grows to 4 ft. high, with long stems and bright green, lance-shaped, toothed leaves. Sprays of small orange flowers appear all summer.

BELAMCANDA chinensis

BLACKBERRY LILY

Iridaceae

PERENNIAL WITH RHIZOME

🌿 ZONES 31, 32, 34–43

☼ ◐ FULL SUN OR PARTIAL SHADE

💧 REGULAR WATER

Belamcanda

Like its iris relatives, forms clumps of sword-shaped leaves in fanlike sheaves from slowly creeping rhizomes. In summer, zigzagging, 3–4-ft. stems carry sprays of 1½-in. yellowish orange flowers dotted with red. Each flower lasts only a day, but new blossoms keep opening for weeks. As blooms fade, rounded seed capsules develop; they split open to expose shiny black seeds resembling blackberries (hence the plant's common name). Cut seed-bearing stems for unique dried arrangements. Plant is effective in clumps in border. Plant rhizomes 1 in. deep in porous soil.

Blackberry lily was crossed with vesper iris (*Pardanthopsis dichotoma,* formerly *Iris dichotoma*) to create a group of hybrids, *Pardancanda norrisii,* sometimes called candy lily. This plant produces the same general effect as blackberry lily, but bears flowers in an expanded color range, including white, yellow, red, pink, and purple.

BELLFLOWER. See CAMPANULA

BELLIS perennis

ENGLISH DAISY

Asteraceae (Compositae)

PERENNIAL OFTEN TREATED AS ANNUAL

🌿 ZONES 34–43

☼ ◐ LIGHT SHADE IN WARM AREAS

💧 💧 MODERATE TO LOTS OF WATER

Bellis perennis

Native to Europe and Mediterranean region. The original English daisies have small, single white flowers. Plump, fully double ones sold in nurseries are horticultural varieties. Rosettes of dark green leaves 1–2 in. long. Pink, rose, red, or white double flowers on 3–6-in. stems, in spring and early summer. Edging or bedding plant; effective with bulbs.

BELLS-OF-IRELAND. See MOLUCCELLA laevis

BELLWORT. See UVULARIA

BENT, BENT GRASS. See AGROSTIS

Berberidaceae. The barberry family contains both shrubs and herbaceous perennials. Barberry (*Berberis*) and heavenly bamboo (*Nandina*) are typical of the former; *Epimedium* of the latter.

B

BERBERIS

BARBERRY

Berberidaceae

EVERGREEN, SEMIEVERGREEN, DECIDUOUS SHRUBS

ZONES VARY BY SPECIES

FULL SUN OR LIGHT SHADE

REGULAR TO MODERATE WATER

Berberis

Ability of barberries, especially the deciduous species, to take punishment from climate and soil extremes makes them worth attention in all "hard" climates. They require no more than ordinary garden care. Vigorous growers can take a lot of cutting back for growth renewal; if plants are left to their own devices, some inner branches die and plants become ratty. The following species all bear yellow spring flowers and spiny branches typical of the genus. (Barberries with much-divided leaves are classified under *Mahonia* in this book.)

B. candidula. Evergreen. Zones 31, 32, 34–41. Forms a dense mound to 2 ft. high and 4 ft. wide. Glossy, dark green leaves, yellow flowers, and purple fruit. Excellent for rock gardens or the front of a shrub border.

B. chenaultii. Evergreen. Zones 31, 32, 34–41. To 5 ft. high and wide. Dense shrub, with glossy, dark green leaves that may turn reddish bronze in winter. Flowers are yellow and fruits are deep blue black. One of the most reliable evergreens for the Northeast.

B. darwinii. DARWIN BARBERRY. Evergreen. Zones 31, 32. Hardy to 10°F/−12°C. Showiest barberry, handsome in flower. Fountainlike growth to 5–10 ft. high and 4–7 ft. wide. Leaves small (1 in.), crisp, dark green, hollylike. Orange-yellow flowers are so thick along branches that it's difficult to see foliage. Berries dark blue and numerous—popular with birds. Wonderful as background for Oregon grape (*Mahonia aquifolium*). Spreads by underground runners.

B. gagnepainii. Evergreen. Zones 31, 32, 34–41. Upright shrub to 5 ft. high. Lance-shaped leaves to 4 in. long, grayish green on top with yellow-green underside. Flowers are abundant and yellow, and fruits are deep purple black. Thrives in a variety of climates, but needs good soil.

B. gladwynensis 'William Penn'. Evergreen; loses some of its leaves at 0° to 10°F/−18° to −12°C. Zones 31, 32, 34, 35, 39. Hardy to about −10°F/−23°C. Resembles *B. julianae* in general effect, but is faster growing, with denser growth to 4 ft. high and broader, glossier leaves. Good show of bright yellow flowers.

B. julianae. WINTERGREEN BARBERRY. Evergreen or semievergreen. Zones 31, 32, 34, 39. Hardy to 0°F/−18°C, but foliage damaged by winter cold. Dense, upright, to 6 ft., with slightly angled branches. Very leathery, spine-toothed, 3-in.-long, dark green leaves. Fruit bluish black. Reddish fall color. One of the thorniest—formidable as barrier hedge.

B. koreana. KOREAN BARBERRY. Deciduous. Zones 31, 32, 34–45. Dense shrub to 6 ft. high, spreads by suckers to form clumps. Deep green leaves to 3 in. long turn reddish purple in fall. Flowers are yellow and fruits are bright red.

B. mentorensis. Evergreen; loses some or all leaves below about −5°F/−21°C. Zones 31, 32, 34–41. Hardy to −20°F/−29°C. Hybrid with rather compact growth to 7 ft. and as wide. Leaves dark green, 1 in. long; beautiful red fall color in cold climates. Berries dull dark red. Easy to maintain as hedge at any height. Tolerates hot, dry weather.

B. thunbergii. JAPANESE BARBERRY. Deciduous. Zones 31, 32, 34–41. Hardy to −20°F/−29°C. Graceful growth habit with slender, arching, spiny branches; if not sheared, usually reaches 4–6 ft. tall with equal spread. Dense foliage with roundish, ½–1½-in.-long leaves, deep green above, paler beneath, turning to yellow, orange, and red. Beadlike, bright red berries stud branches in fall and through winter. Hedge, barrier planting, or single shrub. Many attractive varieties include the following:

'Atropurpurea'. RED-LEAF JAPANESE BARBERRY. Plants sold as such vary in size and leaf color, from bronzy red to purplish red. Hold color all summer. Must have sun to develop color.

'Aurea'. Bright golden yellow foliage, best in full sun. Will tolerate light shade. Slow growing to 2½–3 ft.

'Cherry Bomb'. Resembles 'Crimson Pygmy', but taller (to 4 ft.), with large leaves and more open growth.

'Crimson Pygmy' ('Atropurpurea Nana'). Selected miniature form, generally less than 1½ ft. high and 2½ ft. wide as 10-year-old. Mature leaves bronzy blood red; new leaves bright red. Must have sun to develop color.

'Helmond Pillar'. Resembles 'Atropurpurea' but columnar in form; grows to 6 ft. tall, less than 1 ft. wide.

'Kobold'. Extra-dwarf bright green variety. Like 'Crimson Pygmy' in habit but fuller and rounder.

'Rose Glow'. New foliage marbled bronzy red and pinkish white, deepening to rose and bronze. Colors best in full sun or lightest shade.

'Sparkle'. To 5 ft. tall and 4–6 ft. wide, with rich green foliage that turns vivid yellow, orange, and red in fall.

B. wisleyensis (B. triacanthophora). THREESPINE BARBERRY. Evergreen. Zones 31, 32, 34–41. To 5 ft. high and wide. Narrow, bright green leaves, often turning purple in winter. Light yellow flowers and blue-black fruits.

BERCKMAN DWARF ARBORVITAE. See PLATYCLADUS orientalis

BERGENIA

Saxifragaceae

PERENNIALS

ZONES 31, 32, 34–45, EXCEPT AS NOTED

TOLERATE FULL SUN IN COOL-SUMMER AREAS

REGULAR WATER FOR BEST APPEARANCE

Bergenia

Native to Himalayas and mountains of China. Thick rootstocks; large, ornamental, glossy green leaves, evergreen except in coldest areas. Thick leafless stalks, 1–1½ ft. high, bear graceful nodding clusters of small white, pink, or rose flowers. Strong, substantial textural quality in borders, under trees, as bold-patterned ground cover. Effective with ferns, hellebores, hostas, and as foreground planting for aucubas, rhododendrons, Japanese aralia.

Prefers partial shade but will take full sun in cool-summer climates. *B. cordifolia* and *B. crassifolia* endure neglect, poor soil, cold, but respond to good soil, regular watering, feeding, grooming. Cut back yearly to prevent legginess. Divide crowded clumps and replant vigorous divisions.

B. ciliata (B. ligulata). Zones 31, 32, 34, 39. Choicest, most elegant. To 1 ft. Lustrous, light green leaves to 1 ft. across, smooth on edges but fringed with soft hairs; young leaves bronzy. White, rose, or purplish flowers bloom late spring, summer. Slightly tender; leaves burn in severe frost. Plants sold under this name may be garden hybrids.

B. cordifolia. HEARTLEAF BERGENIA. Leaves, to 1 ft. across, are glossy, roundish, heart shaped at base, with wavy, toothed edges. In spring, rose or lilac flowers in pendulous clusters partially hidden by leaves. Plant grows to 20 in. 'Morning Red' ('Morgenrote') has leaves with bronzy tones, dark red flowers.

B. crassifolia. WINTER-BLOOMING BERGENIA. Leaves dark green, 8 in. or more across, with wavy, sparsely toothed edges. Flowers rose, lilac, or purple in dense clusters on erect stems standing well above leaves. Plants 20 in. high. Blooms any time from midwinter to early spring, depending on climate.

B. hybrids. Many hybrids of English or German origin are available. Choices include 'Abendglut' ('Evening Glow'), with dark reddish leaves with crimped edges, dark red flowers; 'Ballawley', with green leaves turning bronze-purple in winter, bright dark red flowers on red stems; 'Bressingham White', with deep green leaves and white flowers; and 'Silberlicht' ('Silver Light'), with large, slightly toothed leaves and white flowers with pink tints. 'Sunningdale' has green leaves with red undersides, turning reddish bronze in winter, and bright lilac pink flowers.

BERMUDA, BERMUDA GRASS. See CYNODON dactylon

BETHLEHEM SAGE. See PULMONARIA saccharata

BETULA

BIRCH

Betulaceae

DECIDUOUS TREES

🌡 ZONES VARY BY SPECIES

☀ FULL SUN

💧 💧 AMPLE WATER

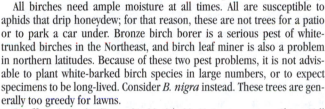

Betula

The white-barked European white birch—the tree that comes to mind when most people think of birches—has relatives that resemble it in graceful habit, thin bark that peels in layers, and small-scale, finely toothed leaves that turn from green to glowing yellow in fall. After leaf drop, the delicate limb structure, handsome bark, and small conelike fruit of birches provide a winter display.

All birches need ample moisture at all times. All are susceptible to aphids that drip honeydew; for that reason, these are not trees for a patio or to park a car under. Bronze birch borer is a serious pest of white-trunked birches in the Northeast, and birch leaf miner is also a problem in northern latitudes. Because of these two pest problems, it is not advisable to plant white-barked birch species in large numbers, or to expect specimens to be long-lived. Consider *B. nigra* instead. These trees are generally too greedy for lawns.

B. albo-sinensis. Zones 31, 32, 34, 39. Native to western China. Tall tree (to 100 ft.) grown chiefly for beautiful pinkish brown to coppery bark covered with powdery gray bloom. Leaves 3 in. long. *B. a. septentrionalis* has flaking bark that is orange to orange brown.

B. ermanii. ERMAN'S BIRCH. Zones 31, 32, 34–41. Native to Russia, Korea, and Japan. Conical tree to 70 ft., with attractive, peeling, pinkish to white bark. Dark green leaves to 4 in. long turn yellow in fall.

B. jacquemontii (B. utilis jacquemontii). Zones 31, 32, 34, 39. Native to northern India. Tall, narrow tree with brilliant white bark. Grows about 2 ft. a year to 40 ft., then more slowly to an eventual 60 ft. Seedlings vary in bark color; buy grafted trees. Not thoroughly tested in the East, but promising.

B. lenta. SWEET BIRCH, BLACK BIRCH, CHERRY BIRCH. Zones 32, 34–45. Native to eastern U.S. Seldom sold. An attractive tree with shiny reddish to blackish brown bark; grows 40–50 ft. tall. Rich yellow fall foliage color. Most country children in the eastern states have tasted the bark, which has a sweet wintergreen flavor and was once used to make a soft drink known as birch beer.

B. maximowicziana. MONARCH BIRCH. Zones 31, 32, 34, 39. Native to Japan. Fast growing; open growth when young. Can reach 80–100 ft. Bark flaking, orange brown, eventually gray or white. Leaves up to 6 in. long. Plants sold under this name are not always the true species.

B. nana. DWARF BIRCH. Zones 35–45. Native to northern North America and Eurasia. Shrub growing 2 ft. high and 4 ft. wide. Rounded, glossy, green leaves with toothed edges turn yellow or red in fall. Very hardy.

B. nigra. RIVER BIRCH, RED BIRCH. Zones 31, 32, 34–43. Native to eastern U.S. Very fast growth in first years; eventually reaches 50–90 ft. Trunk often forks near ground, but tree can be trained to single stem. Young bark is apricot to pinkish, very smooth, and shiny. On older trees bark flakes and curls in cinnamon brown to blackish sheets. Diamond-shaped leaves, 1–3 in. long, are bright glossy green above, silvery below. 'Heritage' has darker leaves and tan-and-apricot bark; keeps apricot color longer than the species. These are the best birches for hot, humid climates. Both *B. nigra* and 'Heritage' are also resistant to bronze birch borer and birch leaf miner and are excellent substitutes for white-barked species, although their bark is not pure white. Tolerate poor or slow drainage.

B. papyrifera. CANOE BIRCH, PAPER BIRCH. Zones 37–45. Native to northern part of North America. Somewhat similar to *B. pendula* but taller (to 100 ft.), more open, less weeping, with a stouter trunk that is creamy white. Bark peels off in papery layers. Leaves are larger (to 4 in. long), more sparse. Excellent fall color. More resistant to bronze birch borer than *B. pendula*.

B. pendula. EUROPEAN WHITE BIRCH. Zones 31, 32, 34–45. Native from Europe to Asia Minor. Delicate and lacy. Upright branching with weeping side branches. Average mature tree 30–40 ft. high, spreading to half its height. Bark on twigs and young branches is golden brown. Bark on trunk and main limbs becomes white, marked with black clefts; oldest bark at base is blackish gray. Rich green, glossy leaves to 2½ in. long, diamond shaped, with slender tapered point. Often sold as weeping birch, although trees vary somewhat in habit and young trees show little inclination to weep. Very susceptible to bronze birch borer. The following are some of the varieties offered.

'Dalecarlica' ('Laciniata'). CUTLEAF WEEPING BIRCH. Leaves deeply cut. Branches strongly weeping; graceful open tree. Weeping forms are more affected by dry, hot weather than is the species. Foliage shows stress by late summer.

'Fastigiata' (*B. alba* 'Fastigiata'). PYRAMIDAL WHITE BIRCH. Branches upright; habit somewhat like Lombardy poplar. Excellent screening tree.

'Purpurea' (*B. alba* 'Purpurea'). PURPLE BIRCH. Twigs purple black. New foliage rich purple maroon, fading to purplish green in summer; striking effect against white bark. Best in cool to cold climates.

'Trost's Dwarf'. True dwarf (3 ft. tall and wide) for bonsai, container, rock garden. Needs excellent drainage.

'Youngii'. YOUNG'S WEEPING BIRCH. Slender branches hang straight down. Form like weeping mulberry's, but tree is more graceful. Decorative display tree. Trunk must be staked to desired height. Same climate limitations as that of 'Dalecarlica'.

B. platyphylla japonica. JAPANESE WHITE BIRCH. Zones 31, 32, 34–41. Native to Japan. Fast growth to 40–50 ft.; narrow, open habit. Leaves to 3 in. long, glossy green. Bark white. 'Whitespire' is a narrowly pyramidal, heat-tolerant selection resistant to bronze birch borer.

B. populifolia. GRAY BIRCH. Zones 34–45. Native to eastern North America. Narrow, pyramidal tree to 30 ft. high. Grayish white bark and drooping branches. Triangular, glossy green leaves turn yellow in fall. Tolerates poor soils.

Betulaceae. The birch family includes deciduous trees and shrubs with inconspicuous flowers in tight clusters (catkins). Representatives are alder (*Alnus*), birch (*Betula*), filbert (*Corylus*), and hornbeam (*Carpinus*).

BIDENS ferulifolia

Compositae

ANNUALS

🌡 ALL ZONES

☀ FULL SUN

💧 💧 REGULAR TO AMPLE WATER

Bidens ferulifolia

Unlike the species, which is an unshowy plant native to pond margins and river edges, the *Ferulifolia* hybrids are attractive annual or biennial plants bearing colorful clusters of bright yellow flowers. Easily propagated from seed and tolerant of high temperatures, they have an erect but compact habit, growing to 6 in. high and 12 to 14 in. wide. Keep moist in especially hot weather, and check for whiteflies, which can sometimes be a problem. Plant in beds, borders, and hanging baskets in neutral to slightly acid soil. 'Peter's Gold Carpet' has a compact habit and brilliant yellow-gold flowers.

B

BIGNONIA capreolata. See ANISOSTICHUS capreolata

Bignoniaceae. The bignonia family includes vines (mostly), trees, shrubs, and (rarely) perennials or annuals—all with trumpet-shaped, often two-lipped flowers. The family gets its name from the genus *Bignonia,* which once included most of the trumpet vines; though most of these have been reclassified, they are often still sold as *Bignonia.* For *B. chinensis,* see *Campsis grandiflora,* and for *B. radicans,* see *Campsis radicans.*

BIG TREE. See SEQUOIADENDRON giganteum

BIRCH. See BETULA

BIRCH BARK CHERRY. See PRUNUS serrula

BIRD'S FOOT TREFOIL. See LOTUS corniculatus

BIRD'S NEST FERN. See ASPLENIUM nidus

BISHOP'S HAT. See EPIMEDIUM grandiflorum

BISHOP'S WEED. See AEGOPODIUM podagraria

BITTER MELON. See MOMORDICA charantia

BITTERROOT. See LEWISIA rediviva

BITTERSWEET. See CELASTRUS

BLACK ALDER. See ILEX verticillata

BLACKBERRY

Rosaceae

DECIDUOUS SHRUBS OR VINES

🔆 ZONES 31, 32, 34–41, EXCEPT AS NOTED

☀️ FULL SUN

💧 REGULAR WATER

Blackberry

Blackberries grow in areas of North America where summers are not too hot and dry, and winters not too harsh. They thrive in cool, humid regions along the eastern coast, as well as in cool-night areas of moderate-elevation mountains.

Varieties from the eastern states tend to be hardy, upright, and stiff caned; they usually grow 4–6 ft. tall. Some semierect varieties are also suitable.

Blackberries bear fruit in summer. For good crops, blackberries need full sun; deep, well-drained soil; and regular water throughout the growing season. The fruit makes excellent pies, fine jams and jellies, tangy syrups, and even good wines.

Blackberries are subject to many pests and diseases, so start with healthy plants from a reputable supplier. Also look for resistant varieties. Because of their susceptibility to verticillium wilt, blackberries should not be planted where potatoes, tomatoes, eggplants, or peppers have grown in the last two years.

Blackberries are usually planted in spring. Set new bare-root plants an inch deeper than they grew at the nursery, their crowns covered with an inch of soil.

When growing beyond certain hardiness, bury the first-year canes under a heavy mulch. In hard-winter areas, blackberries are best located on slight slopes with good air drainage. Northern exposures help keep plants dormant until spring freezes are past. Don't put plants where they will get standing water during the dormant season.

Though blackberry roots are perennial, the canes are biennial; they develop and grow one year, flower and fruit the second. Erect types can be tied to wire, though they don't need support. First-year canes can be headed back a little in midsummer to encourage side branches; the lateral branches can then be cut to 1 ft. long in early spring.

Trailing and semierect types are best grown on some kind of trellis. Train 1-year-old canes on the structure; after harvest, cut to the ground all canes that have fruited. The canes of the current season, those growing beneath the trellis, should now be trained onto it; thin to desired number of canes and prune to 6–8 ft., spreading them fanwise on trellis. Canes of semierect types often become more upright as plant matures.

The following includes some of the best blackberry varieties. (For ornamental relatives, see *Rubus.*)

'Arapaho'. Erect, thornless. Large, firm berries. Disease resistant.

'Black Satin'. Semierect, thornless, vigorous. Shiny black, very tart fruit.

'Cherokee'. Erect, thorny. Firm berries with excellent flavor. Resists anthracnose.

'Chester'. Semierect, thornless, heavy bearing, and resistant to cane blight. Very cold tolerant.

'Cheyenne'. Erect, thorny. Sweet, medium to large berries. Reliable to southern New England. Bears early.

'Choctaw'. Reliable to Zones 34, 39. Erect, thorny. Large, flavorful berries. Bears early. Resists root rot, orange rust, anthracnose.

'Darrow'. Erect. A heavy bearer, with large fruit ripening over a long season.

'Illini Hardy'. Erect, very thorny. Cold-hardy variety introduced by University of Illinois.

'Shawnee'. Reliable to Zones 34, 39. Erect, thorny. Produces exceptionally heavy crops of large, flavorful, soft fruits. Bears late.

'Smoothstem'. Semierect, thornless. Tart, large-seeded berries.

'Thornfree'. Semierect, thornless canes bearing large crop of tart berries.

BLACKBERRY LILY. See BELAMCANDA chinensis

BLACK-EYED SUSAN. See RUDBECKIA hirta

BLACK-EYED SUSAN VINE. See THUNBERGIA alata

BLACK LILY. See FRITILLARIA camschatcensis

BLACK SNAKEROOT. See CIMICIFUGA racemosa

BLADDERNUT. See STAPHYLEA

BLANKET FLOWER. See GAILLARDIA grandiflora

BLAZING STAR. See MENTZELIA

BLECHNUM

HARD FERN

Blechnaceae

FERN

🔆 ZONES 32, 34–41

◐ 💧 PARTIAL TO FULL SHADE

💧 MORE THAN REGULAR WATER

Blechnum

Evergreen ferns from both tropical and temperate regions with rosettes of erect fronds. The two species described here are both hardy. Ideal for a shade garden with rich, moist soil with an acidic pH. Water regularly during dry weather. Mulch to help retain soil moisture.

B. penna-marina. LITTLE HARD FERN. Native to South America and Australasia and hardy through much of the Northeast. Low-growing species with erect, arching, 4–8-in.-long fronds. Spreads by rhizomes to form drifts.

B. spicant. DEER FERN, HARD FERN. Native to North America, Europe, and Asia. Produces clumps of leathery, stiff, dark green fronds.

BLEEDING HEART. See DICENTRA

BLESSED THISTLE. See SILYBUM

BLETILLA striata
(B. hyacinthina)

CHINESE GROUND ORCHID

Orchidaceae

TERRESTRIAL ORCHID

✎ ZONES 31, WARMER PARTS OF 32

☼ UNDER HIGH-BRANCHING TREES OR LATH

💧 FREQUENT WATER DURING GROWTH

Bletilla striata

A terrestrial orchid native to China and Japan. Lavender, cattleyalike, 1–2-in. flowers, up to a dozen on 1½–2-ft. stem, produced for about 6 weeks beginning in May or June. Pale green leaves, three to six to a plant. 'Alba' is a white-flowered form. 'Variegata' has white-striped leaves.

Plant the tuberlike roots outdoors in early spring for spring and early summer bloom. Grow in pot or in ground under high-branching trees or under lath. Hardy to about 20°F/−7°C (to 0°F/−18°C if soil is well drained and plant is mulched). Dies back to ground each winter. In time will develop large clumps if grown in light shade and in a moist soil rich in humus. Can be divided in early spring before growth starts, but don't do it too often; blooms best when crowded.

BLOODLEAF. See IRESINE

BLOODROOT. See SANGUINARIA canadensis

BLUEBEARD. See CARYOPTERIS

BLUEBELL. See ENDYMION, SCILLA

BLUEBERRY

Ericaceae

DECIDUOUS SHRUBS

✎ ZONES VARY BY TYPE

☼ FULL SUN

💧 DON'T LET SOIL SURFACE DRY OUT

Blueberry

Native to eastern North America, blueberries thrive under conditions that suit rhododendrons and azaleas, to which they are related. Require sun and cool, moist, well-drained acid soil (pH 4.5–5.5). Outside their favored regions, either create proper soil conditions or grow plants in containers.

Most blueberries grown for fruit are also handsome plants suitable for hedges or shrub borders. Dark green or blue-green leaves change to red, orange, or yellow combinations in autumn. Spring flowers are tiny, white or pinkish, urn shaped. Summer fruit is very decorative.

Blueberries are available bare-root or in containers. Plant in early spring in cold regions, autumn in mild climates. Position crown so that it is no deeper than ½ in. below the ground. Grow at least two varieties for better pollination, resulting in larger berries and bigger yields per plant. Choose varieties that ripen at different times, for a long harvest season. Blueberries have fine roots near the soil surface; keep them moist but don't subject them to standing water. A 4–6-in.-thick mulch of sawdust, ground bark, or the like will protect roots and help conserve soil moisture. Don't cultivate around the plants.

Prune to prevent overbearing. Plants shape themselves but often produce so many fruit buds that berries are undersized and growth of plants slows down. Keep first-year plants from bearing by stripping off flowers. On older plants, cut back ends of twigs to point where fruit buds are widely spaced. Or simply remove some of oldest branches each year. Also get rid of all weak shoots. Plants don't usually have serious problems requir-

ing regular controls in home gardens. Netting will keep birds from getting the berries before you do.

The following are the major types of blueberries grown in the Northeast. (For ornamental relatives, see *Vaccinium.*)

Lowbush blueberries. Zones 34, 37–45. Varieties of this ground cover species *(Vaccinium angustifolium)* exist, but seedlings or wild plants are most commonly cultivated. In Maine and Canada's Maritime Provinces, fruit from wild plants is harvested in commercial quantities. Very sweet bluish black berries in summer. Plants grow from a few inches to 2 ft. tall; they spread by underground roots to cover large areas. They can thrive in poor, rocky, thin soil as long as it is acid and drains well. Rejuvenate plants by cutting all growth back to 1–2 in. every few years.

Lowbush has been hybridized with highbush varieties to produce very hardy types called half-high blueberries, growing to 2–4 ft. tall. The hybrids include 'North Country', 'Northblue', 'Northland', 'Northsky', and 'St. Cloud'.

Highbush blueberries. Selections of *V. corymbosum*, these are the blueberries found in grocery stores. Most varieties grow upright to 6 ft. or more; a few are rather sprawling and under 5 ft. The majority are northern varieties (Zones 32, 34–43), requiring definite winter cold and ripening their berries between June and late August.

'Berkeley'. Midseason. Open, spreading, tall. Large light berries.

'Bluecrop'. Midseason. Erect, tall growth. Large berries. Excellent flavor. Attractive shrub.

'Blueray'. Midseason. Vigorous, tall. Large, highly flavored, crisp berries. Attractive shrub.

'Bluetta'. Early. More cold hardy than 'Earliblue', but fruit not as tasty.

'Collins'. Midseason. Erect, attractive bush. Small clusters of large, very tasty fruit.

'Concord'. Midseason. Upright to spreading growth. Attractive. Large berry, tart flavored until fully ripe.

'Coville'. Late. Tall, open, spreading. Unusually large leaves. Very attractive. Long clusters of very large, light blue berries.

'Dixi'. Late. Not attractive plant—tall and open. Needs heavy pruning. Berries, among largest and tastiest, are medium blue, firm and sweet.

'Earliblue'. Early. Tall, erect. Large, heavy leaves. Large berries of excellent flavor.

'Elliott'. Late. Tall, upright. Medium to large berries of excellent flavor.

'Herbert'. Late. Vigorous, open, spreading. Among the biggest, best-flavored berries.

'Ivanhoe'. Early. Large, sweet-flavored, light blue berries. Erect, vigorous bush.

'Jersey'. Late. Tall, erect growing. Large, light blue berries. Very bland.

'Northland'. Early. Small, delicious fruit on a spreading bush to 5 ft. high.

'Patriot'. Midseason. Large, firm, tasty berries. Consistently high yields.

'Rancocas'. Midseason. Tall, erect, open, arching habit. Excellent shrub. Leaves smaller than most. Needs heavy pruning. Berries mild and sweet. Dependable old-timer.

'Weymouth'. Early. Ripens all berries quickly. Erect, medium height. Large, dark blue berries of fair quality; lack aroma.

BLOODY DOCK, BLOODY SORREL. See RUMEX

BLUE BUTTONS. See KNAUTIA arvensis

BLUE DAZE. See EVOLVULUS glomeratus

BLUE-EYED GRASS. See SISYRINCHIUM

BLUE-EYED MARY. See OMPHALODES verna

BLUE FESCUE. See FESTUCA glauca

BLUE GRAMA GRASS. See BOUTELOUA gracilis

BLUEGRASS. See POA

BLUE INDIAN GRASS. See SORGHASTRUM

BLUE LACE FLOWER. See TRACHYMENE coerulea

B

BLUE MARGUERITE. See FELICIA amelloides

BLUE MIST. See CARYOPTERIS clandonensis

BLUE PALMETTO. See RHAPIDOPHYLLUM

BLUE SPIRAEA. See CARYOPTERIS incana

BLUE STAR FLOWER. See AMSONIA

BLUETS. See HOUSTONIA caerulea

BLUEWEED. See ECHIUM vulgare

BOCCONIA cordata. See MACLEAYA cordata

BOG ROSEMARY. See ANDROMEDA polifolia

BOLTONIA asteroides

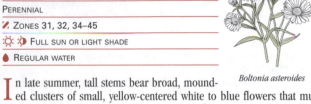

Asteraceae (Compositae)

PERENNIAL

ZONES 31, 32, 34–45

FULL SUN OR LIGHT SHADE

REGULAR WATER

Boltonia asteroides

In late summer, tall stems bear broad, mounded clusters of small, yellow-centered white to blue flowers that much resemble Michaelmas daisies. Plants grow to 6 ft. or more; may be floppy with overhead watering. 'Snowbank' is more compact (to 5 ft. tall) and upright, with larger flowers of a clearer white. 'Pink Beauty' has lilac pink flowers. Var. *latisquoma* has mauve to lilac purple or white flowers 1 in. across; 'Pink Beauty' has pink flowers. Plants survive in poor soil and with reduced water, but may bloom feebly on 2-ft. stems.

BONESET. See EUPATORIUM perfoliatum

BONNET BELLFLOWER. See CODONOPSIS clematidea

Boraginaceae. The borage family consists of annuals and perennials (rarely shrubs or trees), most of which have small flowers in coiled clusters that straighten as bloom progresses. Forget-me-not *(Myosotis)* is a familiar example.

BORAGO officinalis

BORAGE

Boraginaceae

ANNUAL HERB

ALL ZONES

SUN OR SHADE

REGULAR TO MODERATE WATER

Borago officinalis

Grows 1–3 ft. high. Bristly, gray-green leaves up to 4–6 in. long are edible, with a cucumberlike flavor. Blue, saucer-shaped, nodding flowers in leafy clusters on branched stems are also edible.

Usually sown in spring after frost danger; best as a fall–spring crop in climates with mild winters and hot, humid summers. Tolerates poor soil. Seeds itself but doesn't transplant easily. Use small tender leaves in salads; you can also pickle them or cook them as greens. Cut flowers for arrangements or use as an attractive garnish. In dry climates, makes a good drought-tolerant ground cover and soil binder.

BOSTON IVY. See PARTHENOCISSUS tricuspidata

BOULDER RASPBERRY. See RUBUS deliciosus

BOUNCING BET. See SAPONARIA officinalis

BOUTELOUA gracilis

BLUE GRAMA GRASS, MOSQUITO GRASS

Poaceae (Gramineae)

BUNCHING GRASS

ZONES 35, 41, 43, 45

FULL SUN

MODERATE TO LITTLE WATER

Bouteloua gracilis

Ornamental perennial grass native to the prairies of the Americas. Attractive additions to beds and borders or meadow gardens. Drought tolerant; need good drainage, especially in winter.

B. curtipendula. To 2½ ft. tall, forms clumps to 2 ft. wide. Narrow, grayish green leaves. In midsummer to early autumn, bears clusters of flat, reddish green flower spikes.

B. gracilis. To 20 in. high, with very narrow, semievergreen leaves and 1½-in.-long, dark red to purple flower spikes. Spikes are held at right angle to slender stems and have the look of hovering mosquitoes. Also used as pasture grass. If mowed at 1½ in., makes a fair lawn requiring little maintenance or water; most useful in sunny, arid, alkaline-soil regions. Sow seed at 1 lb. per 1,000 sq. ft.

BOWLES' GOLDEN GRASS. See MILIUM effusum 'Aureum'

BOWMAN'S ROOT. See GILLENIA trifoliata

BOX, BOXWOOD. See BUXUS

BOX ELDER. See ACER negundo

BOX HUCKLEBERRY. See GAYLUSSACIA brachycera

BOXTHORN. See LYCIUM chinense

BRACHYCOME

SWAN RIVER DAISY

Asteraceae (Compositae)

ANNUALS AND PERENNIALS

ZONES VARY BY SPECIES

FULL SUN

REGULAR WATER

Brachycome

Neat, charming Australian daisies make mounds 1 ft. tall, 1½ ft. across, with finely divided leaves and a profusion of inch-wide flowers in spring and summer. Use in rock garden, at front of border, in containers or raised beds. Often spelled *Brachyscome*.

B. iberidifolia. Annual. All zones. Flowers are blue, white, or pink. Sow seed where plants are to grow. For best results in regions with mild winters and steamy summers, grow between fall and spring.

Cultivars include 'Blue Star', which has blue flowers with quilled petals; and 'White Splendor', white flowers. Other Splendor series cultivars have lavender pink, purple, or black-centered flowers.

B. multifida. Perennial. Zones 14–24, 28. Very similar to *B. iberidifolia*. Blue flowers most common. Propagate by cuttings.

Cultivars include 'Break O' Day', with purple-pink flowers; and 'Lemon Mist', bearing flowers of soft yellow.

BRACKEN. See PTERIDIUM aquilinum

BRAMBLE. See RUBUS

BRASSAIA actinophylla. See SCHEFFLERA actinophylla

Brassicaceae. The mustard, or cress, family contains many food plants and ornamentals as well as a number of weeds. The notable characteristic is a four-petaled flower resembling a cross. Familiar members include all the cabbage group, radishes, turnips, stock *(Matthiola)*, and sweet alyssum *(Lobularia)*. This family was formerly called Cruciferae.

BREYNIA disticha (B. nervosa)

SNOW BUSH

Euphorbiaceae

EVERGREEN SHRUB

✓ ALL ZONES; OR INDOORS

☼ PARTIAL SHADE

◆ ◑ REGULAR TO MODERATE WATER

Breynia disticha

Usually seen as a houseplant or indoor/outdoor plant, except in the mildest frost-free climates. Open grower 3–4 ft. tall, with zigzag red branches set with ½–2-in. roundish leaves neatly arranged in two ranks. Leaves are liberally splashed with white; 'Roseo-Picta' has leaves splashed with white and pink. Likes humidity in the air and usually does poorly in hot, dry rooms.

BRIMEURA amethystina (Hyacinthus amethystinus)

Liliaceae

BULB

✓ ZONES 31, 32, 34–43

☼ FULL SUN

◆ REGULAR WATER DURING GROWTH AND BLOOM

Brimeura amethystina

Bulbs, leaf rosettes exactly resemble small hyacinths. For rock gardens or naturalizing. Plants bloom in spring or early summer, bearing loose spikes of clear blue bells with paler blue streaks on 6–8-in.-tall stems. Plant in mid- to late autumn, 2 in. deep, 3 in. apart. Mulch in areas where winters are very cold.

BRIZA maxima

RATTLESNAKE GRASS, QUAKING GRASS

Poaceae (Gramineae)

ANNUAL

✓ ALL ZONES

☼ FULL SUN

◆ ◑ MUCH TO LITTLE WATER

Briza maxima

Native to Mediterranean region. Ornamental grass of delicate, graceful form; used effectively in dry arrangements and bouquets. Grows 1–2 ft. high. Leaves are ¼ in. wide, to 6 in. long. Clusters of nodding, seed-bearing spikelets, ½ in. long (or longer), papery and straw colored when dry, dangle on threadlike stems. Spikelets resemble rattlesnake rattles. Scatter seed where plants are to grow; thin seedlings to 1 ft. apart. Often grows wild along roadsides, in fields. *B. media* is similar but perennial.

BROCCOLI

Brassicaceae (Cruciferae)

BIENNIAL GROWN AS ANNUAL

✓ ALL ZONES

☼ FULL SUN

◆ REGULAR WATER

Broccoli

Among cole crops (cabbage and its close relatives), broccoli is the best all-round choice for the home gardener; bears over long season, is not difficult to grow. Grows to 4 ft. and has branching habit. Central stalk bears cluster of green flower buds that may reach 6 in. in diameter. When central cluster is removed, side branches will lengthen and produce smaller clusters. Good varieties are 'Calabrese', 'Cleopatra', 'De Cicco', 'Green Goliath', 'Italian Green Sprouting', 'Premium Crop', and 'Waltham 29'. 'Packman' is a widely grown commercial variety that is also suited to home gardens.

Broccoli is a cool-season plant that tends to bolt into flower when temperatures are high, so plant it to mature during cool weather. In mild climates plant in late summer, fall, or winter for winter or early spring crops. In cold-winter areas set out young plants about 2 weeks before last frost.

Young plants resist frost but not hard freezes. Good guide to planting time is appearance of young plants in nurseries. Young plants ready to be planted take 4 to 6 weeks to develop from seed. One pack of seed will produce far more plants than even the largest home garden can handle, so save surplus seed for later plantings. A dozen plants will supply a family of four.

Choose a sunny location; space plants 1½–2 ft. apart in rows and leave 3 ft. between rows. Keeps plants growing vigorously with regular deep irrigation during dry periods and one or two fertilizer applications before heads start to form. Harvest 50 to 100 days after setting out plants. Cut heads before clustered buds begin to open, including 5–6 in. of edible stalk and leaves. Subject to same pests as cabbage.

BRONZE DRACAENA. See CORDYLINE australis 'Atropurpurea'

BROOM. See CYTISUS, GENISTA

BROUSSONETIA papyrifera

PAPER MULBERRY

Moraceae

DECIDUOUS TREE

✓ ZONES 31, 32, 34, 39

☼ FULL SUN

◆ ◑ MUCH TO LITTLE WATER

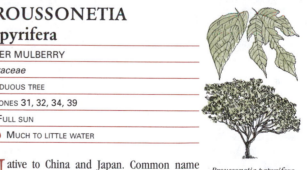
Broussonetia papyrifera

Native to China and Japan. Common name comes from inner bark, used for making paper and Polynesian tapa cloth. Has been sold as *Morus papyrifera*. Valuable as shade tree where soil and climate limit choices. Tolerates heat, drought, strong winds, city pollution, and stony, sterile, or alkaline soils.

Moderate to fast growth to 50 ft., with dense, broad crown to 40 ft. across. Often considerably smaller and more shrublike in gardens. Suckering habit can be problem in rainy climates and highly cultivated gardens. Good in rough bank plantings. Smooth gray bark can become ridged and furrowed with age, as seen in handsome old specimens in Colonial Williamsburg. Heart-shaped, 4–8-in., rough leaves, gray and velvety beneath; edges toothed, often lobed when young. Flowers on male trees are catkins; on female trees, rounded flower heads are followed by red fruits if a male tree is growing nearby.

B

BROWALLIA

AMETHYST FLOWER

Solanaceae

ANNUALS

🗡 ALL ZONES

◑ WARM SHADE OR FILTERED SUNLIGHT

💧 REGULAR WATER

Browallia

Choice plant for connoisseur of blue flowers. Bears one-sided clusters of lobelialike blooms in brilliant blue, violet, or white; blue flowers are more striking because of contrasting white eye or throat. Blooms profusely in warm shade or filtered sunlight. Graceful in hanging basket or pots.

Sow seeds in early spring for summer bloom, in fall for winter color indoors or in greenhouses. Plants need warmth, regular moisture. You can lift vigorous plants in fall, cut back, and pot; new growth will produce flowers through winter in warm spot. Rarely sold as plants in nurseries; get seeds from specialists.

B. americana. Branching, 1–2 ft. high; roundish leaves. Violet or blue flowers ½ in. long, ½ in. across, borne among leaves. 'Sapphire', dwarf compact variety, dark blue with white eye, is very free blooming. This species and its variety are often listed in catalogs as *B. elata* or *B. e.* 'Sapphire'.

B. speciosa. Sprawling, to 1–2 ft. high. Flowers dark purple above, pale lilac beneath, 1½–2 in. across. 'Blue Bells Improved', lavender blue, grows 10 in. tall, needs no pinching to make it branch. 'Marine Bells' has deep indigo flowers, 'Silver Bells' white flowers.

B. viscosa. Grows to 2 ft. high; oval leaves. Violet blue flowers to 1 in. long, with white eye. 'Alba' has white flowers. 'Sapphire' has sapphire blue flowers.

BROWN-EYED SUSAN. See RUDBECKIA triloba

BRUGMANSIA (Datura)

ANGEL'S TRUMPET

Solanaceae

EVERGREEN TO SEMIEVERGREEN SHRUBS

🗡 ALL ZONES

☼ ◑ ● SUN OR SHADE

💧 REGULAR WATER

☣ ALL PARTS ARE POISONOUS IF INGESTED

Brugmansia (Datura)

Related to the annual or perennial jimsonweeds. All are large, tender shrubs that can be trained as small trees. With their outsize leaves and big tubular flowers, they are dominating plants that will astonish your visitors. Main bloom period is summer and fall.

Grows in tubs. Provide sheltered position outdoors in summer; wind tatters foliage. Move indoors or to a frost-free site in cold weather. Tubbed plants can be wintered indoors with a little light and very little water. Prune in early spring; cut back branchlets to one or two buds.

B. arborea. Plants usually offered under this name are either *B. candida* or *B. suaveolens*. The true *B. arborea* has smaller flowers.

B. candida. Native to Peru. Fast and rank growing with soft, pulpy growth to 6 ft. in a container. Dull green, large leaves in the 8–12-in. range. Heavy, single or double white trumpets, to 8 in. long or more, are fragrant, especially at night. Shrub is showy in moonlight.

B. sanguinea. Native to Peru. Fast growing to 6 ft. in a container. Leaves bright green to 8 in. long. Trumpets, orange red with yellow veinings, about 10 in. long, hang straight down like bells from new growth. Rare.

B. suaveolens. Native to Brazil. Similar to *B. candida*, but leaves and flowers are somewhat larger and flowers less fragrant.

B. versicolor. To 6 ft. tall in a container. Flowers white or peach colored. Named versions of uncertain origin include 'Charles Grimaldi' (pale orange yellow) and 'Frosty Pink' (cream deepening to pink).

BRUNNERA macrophylla

BRUNNERA

Boraginaceae

PERENNIAL

🗡 ZONES 31, 32, 34–45

☼ ◑ WILL TAKE FULL SUN IN COOL-SUMMER AREAS

💧 REGULAR WATER

Brunnera macrophylla

Reaches 1½ ft. tall; leaves heart shaped, dark green, 3–4 in. wide. Variegated forms also available. In spring, plants produce airy clusters of tiny clear blue forget-me-not flowers with yellow centers.

'Dawson's White' ('Variegata') has leaves edged in creamy white. 'Hadspen's Cream' has narrower leaves, also white-edged. 'Langtrees', the easiest to grow of the variegated cultivars, has white spots on the leaves. All variegated cultivars need consistent shade and evenly moist soil.

Uses: informal ground cover under high-branching deciduous trees; among spring-flowering shrubs such as forsythia, deciduous magnolias; filler between newly planted evergreen shrubs. Freely self-sows once established. Planted seeds often difficult to germinate (try freezing them before sowing). Needs well-drained, moisture-retentive soil. Increase by dividing clumps in fall.

BRUSSELS SPROUTS

Brassicaceae (Cruciferae)

BIENNIAL GROWN AS ANNUAL

🗡 ALL ZONES

☼ FULL SUN

💧 REGULAR WATER

Brussels Sprouts

A cabbage relative of unusual appearance. Mature plant has crown of fairly large leaves, and its tall stem is completely covered with tiny sprouts. Fairly easy to grow where summers are not too hot, long, or dry. 'Jade Cross Hybrid' is easiest to grow and most heat tolerant; 'Long Island Improved' ('Catskill') is standard market variety. 'Rubine' bears reddish purple sprouts. You may have to grow your own from seed. Sow outdoors or in flats in April; transplant young plants in June or early July to sunny place. Sprouts are ready in fall.

Treat the same as broccoli. When big leaves start to turn yellow, begin picking. Snap off little sprouts from bottom first—best when slightly smaller than golf ball. Leave little sprouts on upper stem to mature. After picking, remove only leaves below harvested sprouts. A single plant will yield from 50 to 100 sprouts. Subject to same pests as cabbage.

BUCHLOE dactyloides

BUFFALO GRASS

Poaceae (Gramineae)

PERENNIAL GRASS

🗡 DRIER PARTS OF ZONES 35, 41, 43

☼ FULL SUN

💧 MODERATE TO LITTLE WATER

Buchloe dactyloides

Makes a low-maintenance, low-water-need lawn. Slow to sprout and fill in, it spreads rapidly by surface runners once established and makes matted, reasonably dense turf that takes hard wear and looks fairly good with very little irrigation during dry periods. Gray-green from late spring to hard frost, straw colored through late fall and winter. Runners can invade surrounding garden beds. Given minimum water, it grows to 4 in. tall and requires little or no mowing. More water means higher growth, some mowing. Sow 2 lb. per 1,000 sq. ft. In absence of rain, soak occasionally to 1 ft. while grass is getting started. To start from sod, plant 4-in.-wide plugs 3–4 ft. apart in prepared soil in spring; cover should be complete in two seasons.

BUCKEYE. See AESCULUS

BUCKTHORN. See RHAMNUS

BUDDLEIA

Loganiaceae

EVERGREEN, SEMIEVERGREEN, OR DECIDUOUS SHRUBS

🌿 ZONES VARY BY SPECIES

☼ ◐ FULL SUN OR LIGHT SHADE

💧 💧 REGULAR TO MODERATE WATER

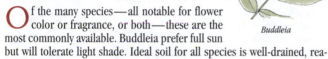
Buddleia

Of the many species—all notable for flower color or fragrance, or both—these are the most commonly available. Buddleia prefer full sun but will tolerate light shade. Ideal soil for all species is well-drained, reasonably fertile, and contains some organic matter.

B. alternifolia. FOUNTAIN BUTTERFLY BUSH. Deciduous. Zones 31, 32, 34–41. It can reach 12 ft. or more, with arching, willowlike branches rather thinly clothed with 1–4-in.-long leaves, dark dull green above, gray and hairy beneath. Blooms in spring from previous year's growth; profuse small clusters of mildly fragrant, lilac purple flowers make sweeping wands of color. Tolerates many soils; does very well in poor, dry gravels. Prune after bloom: remove some of oldest wood down to within few inches of ground. Or train up into small single- or multiple-trunked tree. So trained, it somewhat resembles a small weeping willow. 'Argentea' has silvery leaves and is exceptionally beautiful, even when not in flower.

B. davidii. BUTTERFLY BUSH, SUMMER LILAC. Deciduous or semievergreen. Zones 31, 32, 34–41. Fast, rank growth each spring and summer to 3, 4, or even 10 ft. Leaves tapering, 4–12 in. long, dark green above, white and felted beneath. In midsummer, branch ends adorned with small, fragrant flowers (lilac with orange eye) in dense, arching, spikelike, slender clusters 6–12 in. long or more. Needs good drainage and enough water to maintain growth but little else. Cut back plants heavily in late winter to early spring to promote strong new growth for good flowering. In cold climates, plants may freeze to the ground but will regrow each year from the roots. Butterflies often visit flowers. Many varieties are available with pink, lilac, blue, purple, or white flowers.

'African Queen' has deep violet flowers; 'Black Knight' is deep violet-purple; 'Bonnie', lavender; 'Border Beauty', low growing, lilac purple flowers; 'Charming', lavender blue; 'Darkness', deep blue to violet; 'Dartmoor' has narrow, deeply cut leaves and reddish purple flowers; 'Dubonnet', deep purple with orange eye; 'Empire Blue', violet-blue with orange eye; 'Fascinating', lavender pink; 'Fortune', light lavender blue; 'Harlequin', young leaves edged yellow fading to cream, deep reddish purple flowers; 'Nanho Blue', pale lilac blue; 'Nanho Purple', compact plant with bright purple flowers; 'Nanho White', compact plant, white flowers; 'Petite Plum', red-purple with orange eye; 'Pink Delight', bright pink with orange eye; 'Pink Pearl', lilac pink with orange eye; 'Potter's Purple', long panicles of clear violet flowers; 'Royal Red', long clusters of red-violet flowers; 'Snowbank', bright white; 'Summer Beauty', silvery leaves, dark rose pink flowers; 'White Bouquet', white with yellow eye.

B. globosa. ORANGE BUTTERFLY BUSH. Evergreen or semievergreen. Zones 4–24, 28–31. Grows 10–15 ft. tall. Fragrant orange-yellow flowers are tightly clustered in ¾-in. balls, which in turn are carried in narrow, spikelike 6–8-in. clusters. Blooms late spring or early summer. Flowers produced on previous year's wood, so prune as for *B. alternifolia*.

B. 'Lochinch'. Deciduous. Zones 3–24, 28–33. Hybrid between *B. davidii* and an Asian species. To 10–15 ft. tall. Displays woolly white new growth and branching foot-long clusters of intensely fragrant lilac blossoms with orange eyes. Produces summer flowers on current year's growth, so prune as for *B. davidii*.

B. pikei 'Hever' ('Hever Castle'). Deciduous. Zones 4–24, 28–31. Hybrid between *B. alternifolia* and a Himalayan species. Resembles a smaller *B. alternifolia*, with a profusion of fragrant, orange-centered lilac flowers in mid- to late spring. Leaves gray green. Prune as for *B. alternifolia*.

B. weyeriana 'Sungold'. Zones 3–24, 28–32. Hybrid between *B. davidii* and *B. globosa*. Resembles latter parent but deciduous and probably hardier, with somewhat less globular orange-yellow flower clusters. Blooms on old wood, so cut back after flowering as for *B. alternifolia*. (In coldest part of range, however, it freezes to the ground and so blooms on new wood.)

BUFFALOBERRY. See SHEPHERDIA

BUFFALO GRASS. See BUCHLOE dactyloides

BUGBANE. See CIMICIFUGA

BULL BAY. See MAGNOLIA grandiflora

BUNCHBERRY. See CORNUS canadensis

BUNNY EARS. See OPUNTIA microdasys

BUNYA-BUNYA. See ARAUCARIA bidwillii

BUPLEURUM angulosum

THOROUGHWAX

Apiaceae (Umbelliferae)

PERENNIAL

🌿 ZONES 31, 32, 34–43

☼ FULL SUN

💧 REGULAR TO MODERATE WATER

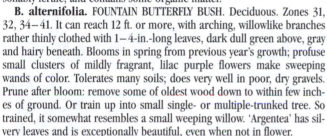
Burpleurum angulosum

This semievergreen perennial forms clumps to 1 ft. high and equally wide. The erect, branched stems rise from a clump of elongated, bluish green basal leaves, and are lined with heart-shaped blue-green leaves to 2 in. long. Branched clusters of tiny yellow or greenish flowers surrounded by green bracts form at tips of stems in mid- to late summer.

Bupleurum is valued by flower arrangers as a neutral-colored filler in bouquets and arrangements. Grow it in a sunny bed or border in well-drained soil. Plants may self-sow if not deadheaded.

BURRO TAIL. See SEDUM morganianum

BUTCHER'S BROOM. See RUSCUS aculeatus

BUTTERCUP TREE. See COCHLOSPERMUM vitifolium

BUTTERFLY BUSH. See BUDDLEIA

BUTTERFLY FLOWER. See SCHIZANTHUS pinnatus

BUTTERFLY WEED. See ASCLEPIAS tuberosa

BUTTERNUT. See WALNUT

BUTTONBUSH, BUTTON WILLOW. See CEPHALANTHUS occidentalis

BUTTONWOOD. See PLATANUS occidentalis

Buxaceae. The boxwood family comprises principally evergreen shrubs with inconspicuous flowers (fragrant in *Sarcococca*). Other members include boxwood (*Buxus*) and *Pachysandra*.

C

BUXUS

BOXWOOD, BOX

Buxaceae

EVERGREEN SHRUBS

ZONES VARY BY SPECIES

SUN OR SHADE

REGULAR WATER

Buxus

Widely used for edging and hedging. When not clipped, most grow soft and billowing. All are easy to grow where adapted and therefore are often neglected. Foliage is pleasantly aromatic, especially in warm weather.

B. microphylla. This species is rarely planted. Its widely planted varieties include the following:

B. m. japonica. JAPANESE BOXWOOD. Zone 3. Hardy to −10°F/−23°C but poor winter appearance in cold areas. It takes dry heat and alkaline soil. Compact foliage (small, ⅓–1-in., round-tipped leaves) is lively bright green in summer, brown or bronze in winter in many areas. Grows slowly to 4–6 ft. if not pruned, making a pleasing informal green shrub. Most often clipped as low or medium hedge or shaped into globes, tiers, pyramids in containers. Can be held to 6-in. height as a hedge or border edging.

'Compacta'. Extra-dwarf plant with tiny leaves. Slow growing; good rock garden plant.

'Green Beauty'. Holds its deep green color in coldest weather and is considerably greener than *B. m. japonica* in summer heat.

'Kingsville Dwarf'. Exceptionally compact and low growing.

'Winter Gem'. Hardiest of Japanese boxwoods.

B. m. koreana. KOREAN BOXWOOD. Hardy to −20°F/−29°C. Slower and lower growing than Japanese boxwood. Leaves smaller (¼–½ in.). This species is noted for its hardiness and will live where others freeze.

'Tide Hill'. Hardy and maintains good green color—even in New England if sheltered from harsh winter wind. Slow grower to 3 ft. tall and twice as wide.

'Wintergreen' is very hardy and maintains good deep green color in winter.

B. sempervirens. COMMON BOXWOOD. Zones 31, 32, 34, 39. Dies out in alkaline soils, arid hot-summer areas. Will grow to height of 15–20 ft. with equal spread. Dense foliage of medium-size, lustrous, dark green, oval leaves. Can be trained as a small tree. Plants labeled "American boxwood" will grow as described here.

'Graham Blandy', narrow upright form, good for topiary.

'Suffruticosa'. This is the plant often referred to as "English boxwood." Slower growing than the species; to 4–5 ft. but generally clipped lower. Small leaves, dense form and texture. A variegated form with silver-edged foliage is available.

'Newport Blue'. Dense low grower with bluish green foliage.

'Pendula' is small and treelike with weeping branches.

'Vardar Valley'. Zones 3–6, 15–17, 31–35, 37, 39. Dark green foliage. Grows 2–3 ft. tall, nearly twice as wide. Considered hardiest common boxwood. Native to the Vardar Valley in Macedonia.

CABBAGE

Brassicaceae (Cruciferae)

BIENNIAL GROWN AS ANNUAL

ALL ZONES

TOLERATE LIGHT SHADE IN HOT CLIMATES

NEVER LET PLANTS WILT

Cabbage

Early varieties mature in 7 to 8 weeks from transplanting into garden; late varieties require 3 to 4 months. In addition to green cabbage you can get red and curly-leafed (Savoy) varieties. To avoid overproduction,

set out a few plants every week or two or plant both early and late kinds. Time plantings so heads will form either before or after hot summer months. Sow seeds ½ in. deep about 6 weeks before planting-out time. Transplant to rich, moist soil, spacing plants 2–2½ ft. apart. Give frequent light applications of nitrogen fertilizer. Mulch helps keep soil moist and cool. Light frost doesn't hurt cabbage, but harvest and store before heavy freezes occur.

To avoid pest buildup, plant in different site each year. Row covers will protect plants from some pests such as cabbage loopers, imported cabbageworms, root maggots. Another way to prevent root maggots (a pest mainly in northern climates) is by ringing the base of the plant with a tar paper collar; the adult flies don't like to lay eggs on it. Collars also deter cutworms, which chew seedlings off at the base. *Bt* will control young larvae of loopers and cabbageworms if they get on the plants.

Good varieties include the following (days to maturity are from transplanting seedlings):

'Dynamo', early, uniform small, round heads stand well without splitting; 65–70 days to maturity.

'Primax', early, improved strain of 'Golden Acre', small to medium heads stand without splitting for about two weeks; 60 days to maturity.

'Savoy Ace', lightly savoyed leaves of medium blue-green, good flavor; 74 days to maturity.

'Storage No. 4', late, medium bluish green heads store well; 95 days to maturity.

For ornamental relatives, see Cabbage, Flowering.

CABBAGE, FLOWERING

Brassicaceae (Cruciferae)

BIENNIAL GROWN AS ANNUAL

ALL ZONES

BEST IN FULL SUN, TOLERATE SOME SHADE

REGULAR WATER

Flowering Cabbage

Flowering cabbage and flowering kale are grown for their highly ornamental, highly colored leaf rosettes, which look like giant peonies in deep blue green, marbled and edged with white, cream, rose, or purple. Kale differs from cabbage in that its head is slightly looser and its leaf edges are more heavily fringed. Both are spectacular in the autumn garden. They appreciate same soil, care, and timing as conventional cabbage. Plant 15–18 in. apart in open-ground beds, singly in 8-in. pots, or several in a large container. Colors are strongest after first frosts touch plants. Single rosette cut and placed on spike holder in bowl makes striking harvest arrangement. Foliage is edible raw or cooked and is highly decorative as a salad garnish.

CALADIUM bicolor

FANCY-LEAFED CALADIUM

Araceae

TENDER BULB

ALL ZONES

SOME VARIETIES ARE BRED FOR SUN

CAREFUL, FREQUENT WATERING

JUICES CAN CAUSE SWELLING IN MOUTH, THROAT

Caladium bicolor

Native to tropical America. Not grown for flowers. Entire show comes from large (to 1½-ft.-long), arrow-shaped, long-stalked, almost translucent leaves colored in bands and blotches of red, rose, pink, white, silver, bronze, and green. Most varieties sold in nurseries are derived from *C. bicolor (C. hortulanum)*—usually 2 ft. tall, occasionally 4 ft. Most require shade. New sun-tolerant varieties include 'Red Flash', 'Fire Chief',

C

'Rose Bud', and 'White Queen'. Other varieties include 'Candidum', which has white leaves with dark green veins; 'Freida Hemple', leaves have red centers and green edges; 'Pink Beauty', leaves have bright green edges splashed with pink, pink centers, and red veins. Combine all types with ferns, coleus, alocasias, colocasias, and tuberous begonias for a tropical look.

Caladiums need rich soil, high humidity, heat (above 70°F/21°C during days and rarely below 60°F/16°C at night), and ample water. Dig and store tubers after leaf dieback, or grow in pots and bring indoors during cold weather.

To grow in ground, plant tubers when days lengthen in spring; place tubers with knobby side up so tops are even with soil surface. Keep well watered and feed lightly throughout growing season. Foliage may be cut back in autumn. Where freezes are likely, dig tubers, remove most of soil, dry in semishade for 10 days, and store in dry peat moss or vermiculite at 50° to 60°F/10° to 16°C.

To grow in pots, start tubers indoors in March, outdoors in May. Pot in mix of equal parts coarse sand, leaf mold, and ground bark or peat moss. Use 5-in. pot for 2½-in. tuber, 7-in. pot for one or two large tubers. Fill pot halfway with mix; stir in heaping teaspoon of fish meal. Add 1 in. of mix, place tuber on top, cover with 2 in. of mix. Water thoroughly. Pots can go outdoors when nighttime temperatures no longer drop below 60°F.

C. esculentum. See *Colocasia esculenta*

CALAMAGROSTIS
acutifolia 'Stricta'

FEATHER REED GRASS
Poaceae (Gramineae)
PERENNIAL
☀ ZONES 31, 32, 34–41
☼ FULL SUN
● REGULAR WATER

Calamagrostic acutifolia 'Stricta'

One of the most effective and handsome ornamental grasses. Erect, somewhat arching clumps of narrow, bright green leaves grow 1½–4 ft. in height. Evergreen in mild climates, partly so in colder areas. Upright flowering stems rise 3–4 ft. above foliage in late spring or early summer, remain upright until first snow. Green with purplish tones, they age to golden yellow, turn buff by winter.

'Karl Foerster' grows to 6 ft. high and has pinkish bronze flower panicles. 'Overdam' grows to 4 ft., with leaves edged and striped with pale yellow fading gradually to pinkish white; flowers are purplish brown.

CALAMINTHA

CALAMINT
Lamiaceae (Labiatae)
PERENNIALS
☀ ZONES 31, 32, 34–41
☼ ☼ FULL SUN OR LIGHT SHADE
● MODERATE WATER

Calamintha grandiflora

Perennials in the mint family with pleasant-scented foliage and pretty, tubular, two-lipped flowers borne in clusters. Herb fanciers brew tea from the leaves. Plants need well-drained soil.

C. grandiflora. Creeping rhizomes give rise to slender stems to 2 ft. tall. Summer flowers are pink, 1½ in. long. Better in partial shade than full sun. Forms with variegated leaves exist.

C. nepetoides. Bushy plant with many tough, slender, 1½-ft. stems that grow outward, then erect. The upper portion of the plant carries a profusion of ½-in. pale lilac to white flowers in late summer and fall.

CALANDRINIA

Portulaceae
PERENNIALS USUALLY GROWN AS ANNUALS
☀ ALL ZONES
☼ FULL SUN
●● REGULAR TO LITTLE WATER

Calandrina umbellata

Portulaca relatives with fleshy leaves and a profusion of brilliant, short-lived flowers that appear over a long period. Most are native to desert or semidesert areas of Chile and Peru, but one is native to southwestern U.S. Tolerate poor soils. Can take regular garden watering or extended periods of drought once established. Use as temporary fillers in rock gardens or flower borders, or as edgings in hot, dry areas. Easy from seed.

C. grandiflora. To 1–3 ft. tall, with leaves to 8 in. long. Stems tinged red. Bright magenta flowers, 1½ in. wide, in summer.

C. umbellata. To 6 in. high, with very narrow leaves less than ½ in. long. Bright magenta flowers, ¾ in. wide, in summer.

CALENDULAS IN COOKING

In times past, calendula leaves and flowers went into vegetable stews, and the vivid petals are still popular today for the tangy flavor they bring to salads, fish, and egg dishes. If cooked with rice, they give the grain a saffron color.

CALENDULA officinalis

CALENDULA, POT MARIGOLD
Asteraceae (Compositae)
ANNUAL
☀ ALL ZONES
☼ FULL SUN
● MODERATE WATER

Calendula officinalis

Sure, easy color from spring to midsummer. Besides familiar daisylike, orange and bright yellow double blooms 2½–4½ in. across, calendulas come in more subtle shades of apricot, cream, and soft yellow. Plants somewhat branching, 1–2 ft. high. Leaves are long, narrow, round on ends, slightly sticky, and aromatic. Plants effective in masses of single colors in borders and parking strips, along drives, in containers. Long-lasting cut flowers.

Sow seed in place or in flats in spring, or buy seedlings at nurseries. Adapts to most soils if drainage is fast. Remove spent flowers to prolong bloom. Although it is an excellent pot plant, the common name is actually derived from the plant's earlier use as a "pot herb"—a vegetable to be used in the cooking pot.

Dwarf strains (12–15 in.) include Bon Bon (earliest), Dwarf Gem, and Fiesta (Fiesta Gitana). Taller (1½–2 ft.) are Kablouna (pompom centers with looser edges), Pacific Beauty, and Radio (quilled, "cactus" blooms).

CALIFORNIA POPPY. See **ESCHSCHOLZIA** *californica*

CALLA. See **ZANTEDESCHIA**

PRACTICAL GARDENING DICTIONARY

PLEASE SEE PAGES 449–523

C

CALIBRACHOA 'Million Bells'

Solanaceae	
ANNUAL	
⚡ ALL ZONES	
☀ FULL SUN	
💧💧 REGULAR TO AMPLE WATER	

Calibrachoa 'Million Bells'

Vigorous, self-cleaning, and heavy-blooming, these low-growing or trailing plants can be used in beds and at the front of borders, as well as in hanging baskets and window boxes. Leaves are small and bright green; trumpet-shaped flowers with yellow centers resemble petunias but are more abundant. Plant in well-drained, slightly acid soil (or in a peat/perlite mix in containers); apply a balanced fertilizer monthly (biweekly in containers).

'Million Bells Cherry Pink', cerise pink flowers. 'Million Bells Trailing Blue', royal purple flowers; excellent in hanging baskets or as an annual ground cover. 'Million Bells Trailing Pink', like 'Trailing Blue' but with soft lavender pink flowers. 'Million Bells Trailing White', like 'Trailing Blue' but with pure white flowers. Cultivars offered may change from year to year.

CALLA pallustris

WATER ARUM	
Araceae	
PERENNIAL	
⚡ ZONES 31, 32, 34–43	
☀ FULL SUN	
💧 MORE THAN REGULAR MOISTURE	

Calla pallustris

Wetland plant, native to the Northeast, grown to soften edges of bog gardens and ornamental ponds. Also suited to swamps, moors, marshes, lakesides, and muddy places in rock gardens. Distant relative of calla lily, with a stubby flower cluster clasped below the base by a large, white, pointed spathe flaring out to one side. Blooms in late spring to early summer and bears dull-red berry cluster in fall. Foliage is glossy, heart shaped, dark green on thin stems, arising from roots scrambling through mud or water up to 10 in. deep. Flower stalk grows up to 12 in. high.

Grow in muddy or wet areas free of lime and preferably with plenty of peat and organic matter. Cultivate in containers in shallow, still, or slowly moving water. Easily increased by division of clumps in spring, stem cuttings stuck in mud in summer, or by sowing seed in submerged pots in late summer.

CALLICARPA

BEAUTYBERRY	
Verbenaceae	
DECIDUOUS SHRUBS	
⚡ ZONES 31, 32, 34–41, EXCEPT AS NOTED	
☀ ◑ FULL SUN OR LIGHT SHADE	
💧 💧 REGULAR TO MODERATE WATER	

Callicarpa bodinieri

These graceful shrubs with arching branches are cultivated for their pleasing fruit display. Small, lilac flowers in summer are followed by tight clusters of small, round, lavender to violet purple fruits persisting into winter. Plants bloom and fruit on new wood, so prune in spring. In cold-winter areas, plants may freeze to the ground, but they come back from roots; in these regions, treat as herbaceous perennials and cut to the ground yearly. Beautyberry is effective in woodland gardens or massed in shrub borders.

C. americana. AMERICAN BEAUTYBERRY. Zones 31, 32. To 6 ft. tall, with leaves to 6 in. long that turn purplish in fall. Fruits are purple. Biggest, coarsest foliage of the species listed here.

C. bodinieri. BODINIER BEAUTYBERRY. Zones 31, 32, 34, 39. Grows to 6 ft. or more, with willowlike leaves to 5 in. long that turn pink or orange to purple in fall. Berries are violet. 'Profusion' is a heavy-fruiting variety.

C. dichotoma. PURPLE BEAUTYBERRY. To 3–4 ft. tall and slightly wider in sun (as tall as 8 ft. in shade), with slender branches sweeping the ground. Resembles a finer-textured *C. bodinieri*. Leaves to 3 in. long. 'Issai' is a select variety. *C. d. albifructus* is a white-fruited form.

C. japonica. JAPANESE BEAUTYBERRY. Upright, to 3–5 ft., with pink flowers, purple fruits. Leaves to 5 in. long; fall color varies from yellowish to deep reddish purple. 'Leucocarpa' has white fruits.

CALLIOPSIS. See COREOPSIS tinctoria

CALLIRHOE involucrata

POPPY MALLOW, WINE CUPS	
Malvaceae	
PERENNIAL	
⚡ ZONES 32, 34, 35, 41, 43	
☀ FULL SUN	
💧 💧 REGULAR TO LITTLE WATER	

Callirhoe involucrata

Thick, fleshy root produces a spreading plant 6 in. tall by 2–3 ft. wide, with roundish, deeply cut leaves and quantities of 2-in. purplish red mallow flowers during hot weather. Needs superb drainage but survives in infertile soil and intense heat. Useful on hot slopes or areas that get little attention.

C. papaver. Grows to 3 ft. high and has violet-red flowers.

CALLISTEPHUS chinensis

CHINA ASTER	
Asteraceae (Compositae)	
ANNUAL	
⚡ ALL ZONES	
☀ FULL SUN	
💧 REGULAR WATER; AVOID OVERWATERING	

Callistephus chinensis

Splendid cut flower and effective bedding plant when well grown and free of disease. Plants 1–3 ft. high. Some kinds are branching; others (developed mainly for florists) have strong stems and no side shoots. Leaves deeply toothed or lobed. Summer is bloom season. Many different flower forms: quilled, curled, incurved, ribbonlike, or interlaced rays; some have crested centers. Varieties classified as peony flowered, pompom, anemone flowered, ostrich feather. Colors range from white to pastel pink, rose pink, lavender, lavender blue, violet, purple, crimson, wine, and scarlet.

Cultivars include Asteroid Series, large, 4-in. flowers in scarlet, carmine, rose pink, dark blue, light blue, silver, or white, on 10-in.-high plants; 'Dwarf Queen', double flowers of deep red, rose pink, scarlet, deep blue, light blue, or white, on 10-in. plants; Love-Me Series, large flowers with thin, spidery rays of red, rose, pink, white, or deep blue on 10-in. plants; Pot N' Patio Series, double blue, white, pink, or scarlet flowers on 6-in. plants; Seastar Mix, large flowers with curled petals creating a swirled effect, in dark rose, light pink, salmon, blue, and white on 2-ft. plants.

Plant in rich, loamy, or sandy soil. After frosts, sow seed in place or set out plants started in flats. Keep growth steady; sudden checks in growth are harmful. Subject to aster yellows, a viral disease carried by leafhoppers. Discard infected plants. Spray or dust to control leafhoppers. All but wilt-resistant types are subject to aster wilt or stem rot, caused by parasitic fungus that lives in soil and is transmitted through roots into plants. Overwatering produces ideal condition for diseases, especially in heavy soil. Never plant in same location in successive years.

CALLUNA vulgaris

SCOTCH HEATHER

Ericaceae

EVERGREEN SHRUB

Ⓩ ZONES 34–43

☼ FULL SUN

🌢 REGULAR WATER

Calluna vulgaris

This, the true and only Scotch heather, has crowded, tiny, scalelike, dark green leaves and one-sided spikes of bell-shaped, rosy pink flowers. Garden varieties (far more common than wild kind) include dwarf ground cover and rock garden plants ranging from 2 in. to 3 ft. tall. Taller varieties make good backgrounds for lower kinds and are attractive cut flowers. Flower colors include white, pale to deep pink, lavender, and purple. Foliage—paler and deeper greens, yellow, chartreuse, gray, or russet—often changes color in winter. Most bloom in mid- to late summer; a few bloom into late fall. To prune, shear off faded flowers and branch tips immediately after bloom (with latest-flowering varieties, delay pruning until spring).

HEATHER FOR THE HOLIDAYS

Spikes of rosy heather make a lovely addition to garlands and wreaths. Or try a topiary tree: fill a cone of chicken wire with floral foam cut to fit. Then poke in small bunches of heather (strip off bottom 1 in. of foliage to make a stem), starting at top and working your way down in a spiral.

Heathers thrive in the cool, moist climates found in parts of New England and also succeed in other areas that aren't too hot. They languish in heat, whether dry or extremely humid. Plants do best in sandy, peaty, fast-draining soil. Light feeding with acid plant food—once in late winter or early spring, a second time in late spring or early summer—will encourage good growth and bloom.

Here are a few of the scores of varieties obtainable from specialists. All begin blooming in summer, except as noted.

'Alba Jae'. Sprawler to 1½ ft., with bright green leaves, white flowers.

'Alba Plena'. Loose, medium green mound to 1 ft. Double white flowers. Fast growing.

'Alison Yates'. Compact, vigorous to 1½ ft. Silver foliage. White flowers.

'Aurea'. Spreading, twiggy, 8–12-in. plant with gold foliage turning russet in winter. Sparse purple bloom.

'Aureafolia'. Upright, to 1½–2 ft. Chartreuse foliage, tinged gold in summer. White flowers.

'Blazeaway'. Compact, 12–15 in., with pale foliage with apricot tints, emerging bronzy. Lavender flowers.

'Corbett Red'. Compact growth to 10 in. with dark green foliage. Violet-red flowers.

'County Wicklow'. Mounding, 9–18 in., medium green. Pink double flowers from white buds.

'Dainty Bess'. Tiny gray leaves form mat 2–4 in. tall; shapes itself to rocks, crevices. Lavender flowers.

'Darkness'. Compact; to 1½ ft. Dark green foliage; dark purple flowers.

'David Eason'. Spreading mound, 1–1½ ft. Light green foliage; reddish purple flowers, October–November.

'Else Frye'. Erect plant to 2 ft. Medium green foliage; double white flowers.

'Foxii Nana'. Small mound to 6 in. Dark green foliage; purple flowers. A dwarf pincushion.

'Goldsworth Crimson'. Mounding, 1½–2 ft. Dark or smoky green foliage; crimson flowers, October–November.

'H. E. Beale'. Loose mound to 2 ft. Dark green foliage; soft pink double flowers. Long spikes are good for cutting.

'J. H. Hamilton'. Prostrate, bushy, to 9 in. Deep green foliage; profuse double pink bloom.

'Mair's Variety'. Erect, 2–3 ft. Medium green foliage; white flowers. Easy to grow, good background.

'Martha Herman'. Compact, to 4–9 in., with lime green leaves. White flowers.

'Minima Prostrata'. Nearly flat habit. Foliage dark green in summer, bronze in winter. Light rose purple flowers.

'Mrs. Pat'. Bushy, to 8 in. Light green foliage; pink new growth. Light purple flowers.

'Mrs. Ronald Gray'. Creeping mound, to 3 in. Dark green foliage; reddish purple flowers. Excellent ground cover.

'Mullion'. Tight mound to 9 in. Dark green foliage, rosy purple flowers. Fine ground cover.

'Nana'. Low, spreading, to 4 in. Dark green foliage; purple flowers. Often called carpet heather.

'Nana Compacta'. Tight mound to 4 in. Medium green. Purple flowers. Pincushion heather for rockery.

'Roma'. Compact, to 9 in. Dark green foliage; deep pink flowers.

'Searlei'. Bushy, 1–1½ ft. Yellow-green feathery foliage. White flowers.

'Silver King', 'Silver Knight', 'Silver Queen'. All grow 1–1½ ft. high, with light gray-green foliage and pink flowers.

'Tib'. Rounded, bushy, to 1–1½ ft. Medium green foliage; deepest rosy purple double flowers.

CALOCEDRUS decurrens (Libocedrus decurrens)

INCENSE CEDAR

Cupressaceae

EVERGREEN TREE

Ⓩ ZONES 32, 34, 36, 37

☼ ◐ FULL SUN OR LIGHT SHADE

🌢 REGULAR WATER

Calocedrus decurrens

Unlike most of its native associates—white fir, Douglas fir, sugar pine—this Far West native adapts to many climates. Takes blazing summer heat, drought. Tolerates a variety of soils, but does best in deep, well-drained soil, especially if climate is humid. Symmetrical tree to 75–90 ft. with dense, narrow, pyramidal crown. Rich green foliage in flat sprays, reddish brown bark. Tree gives pungent fragrance to garden in warm weather. When open, the small, yellowish brown to reddish brown cones resemble ducks' bills. Good tree to make green wall, high screen, windbreak. May get a heart rot in some regions.

CALONYCTION aculeatum. See IPOMOEA alba

CALTHA palustris

MARSH MARIGOLD

Ranunculaceae

PERENNIAL

Ⓩ ZONES 31, 32, 34–45

☼ ◐ 🌢 SUN OR SHADE

🌢 BOG OR MARSH PLANT IN NATURE

🌢 SAP IS AN IRRITANT

Caltha palustris

Native to eastern U.S., Europe, Asia. To 2 ft. tall, well adapted to edges of pools, ponds, streams, other moist situations. With sufficient water it can be grown in borders; good with bog irises, moisture-loving ferns. Green leaves 2–7 in. across, rounded with a heart-shaped base. Vivid yellow flowers are 2 in. across, in clusters. Lush, glossy foliage gives an almost tropical effect. Plant is vigorous; increase by divisions or sow seed in boggy soil. The variety *alba* has white flowers. 'Flore Pleno' has double yellow flowers.

Calycanthaceae. The calycanthus family contains shrubs with paired opposite leaves and flowers that somewhat resemble small water lilies—each bloom has an indefinite number of segments which are not easily defined as petals or sepals. *Calycanthus* and wintersweet (*Chimonanthus*) are typical.

CALYCANTHUS floridus

CAROLINA ALLSPICE, STRAWBERRY SHRUB, SWEETSHRUB

Calycanthaceae

DECIDUOUS SHRUBS

Calycanthus

☀️ ◐ ● SUN OR SHADE

🔴 REGULAR WATER

◆ SEEDS CAN PRODUCE CONVULSIONS

Native Virginia to Florida. This deciduous shrub is a bulky plant with lush foliage and flowers worthwhile for their fragrance and form. Stiffly branched to 6–10 ft. tall and as wide or wider. Suckering, fast spreading. Leaves oval to 5 in., glossy dark green above, grayish green beneath. Blooms at some time May–July, depending on climate and exposure. Flowers reddish brown, 2 in. wide, often with heady strawberry fragrance; carried at ends of leafy branchlets. Blooms followed by brownish, pear-shaped capsules, fragrant when crushed. Plant in shrub border or around outdoor living space where flower scent can be appreciated. Aroma varies, so buy when plants are in bloom. 'Michael Lindsay' is reliably fragrant. 'Athens' has yellow flowers.

CAMASSIA

CAMASS

Liliaceae

BULBS

Camassia quamash

🔷 ZONES 31, 32, 34, 39, EXCEPT AS NOTED

☀️ FULL SUN

🔴🔴 AMPLE WATER DURING GROWTH AND BLOOM

Most species native to moist meadows, marshes, fields in Northern California and Northwest. Starlike, slender-petaled blossoms are carried on spikes in late spring, early summer; grasslike basal leaves dry quickly after bloom. Plant in moist situation, fairly heavy soil, where bulbs can remain undisturbed for many years. Set bulbs 4 in. deep, 6 in. apart. To avoid premature sprouting, plant after weather cools in fall.

C. cusickii. Dense clusters of pale blue flowers on stems 2–3 ft. tall. 'Zwanenburg' has deep blue flowers.

C. leichtlinii. Large, handsome clusters of creamy white flowers on stems 2–4 ft. tall. 'Alba' has whiter flowers than species, and 'Plena' has double greenish yellow blooms. *C. l. suksdorfii* is attractive blue form.

C. quamash (C. esculenta). Loose clusters of deep blue flowers on 1–2-ft. stems; flowers of 'Orion' are deeper blue, those of 'San Juan Form' deeper still.

C. scilloides (C. fraseri). WILD HYACINTH. Zones 31, 32, 34–43. Native to the eastern and central U.S. Upright clusters of violet or white flowers in late summer; plants variable in height, from 8–32 in.

CAMELLIA

Theaceae

EVERGREEN SHRUBS

Camellia japonica

🔷 ZONES 31 AND WARMER PARTS OF 32; NEW HARDY TYPES THROUGHOUT 32 AND WARMER PARTS OF 34 (AND POSSIBLY A BIT COLDER)

◐ PART SUN

🔴 REGULAR WATER

Native to eastern and southern Asia. There are over 3,000 named kinds; range in color, size, and form is remarkable. Most of the Northeast is outside generally recognized camellia territory. However, bold gardeners are succeeding with certain of these exotic shrubs in such areas as the Delmarva Peninsula, the New Jersey shore, Long Island, coastal Connecticut, and Cape Cod. The few hardiest *C. japonica* cultivars noted here are grown in these colder regions with careful attention to proper siting and winter protection, but the newer hardy hybrids derived from *C. oleifera* represent a safer choice.

Camellias need well-drained soil rich in organic material. Never plant camellias so the trunk base is below the soil line, and never permit soil to wash over and cover this base. Keep roots cool with a 2-in.-thick mulch.

Camellias thrive and bloom best when sheltered from strong, hot sun and drying winds, especially in winter. The best sites include the partial shade of tall pine or oak trees, under lath cover, or on the north side of a building. Regular watering is necessary for the first few years, but established plants survive on natural rainfall. Fertilize with a commercial acid plant food. Read the fertilizer label for complete instructions. Don't use more than called for and run the risk of tender growth at the end of the growing season when plants should be hardening off. Young camellias are more easily damaged by cold than older, established plants. Unusually cold winters occasionally may kill thriving old specimens to the ground, but they often sprout back and grow vigorously from the roots.

A carefully chosen hardy variety that is well nourished, well watered, and properly sited can offer the best chance for beautiful camellia blossoms in many a northern garden.

C. japonica. This is the plant most gardeners have in mind when they mention camellias. Naturally a large shrub or small tree, but variable in size, growth rate, and habit; they bear single, semidouble to double blossoms (as illustrated on the following page). Flowers vary in size from over 5 in. across to 2½ in. or less, according to variety, and may appear from midwinter through spring. Only the hardiest varieties are listed here, but remember that these elegant, spring-blooming plants should be considered "experimental" beyond Zone 32.

'April Blush'. Early to midseason. Semidouble, shell pink blossoms. Slow to medium grower.

'April Dawn'. Formal double, variegated flowers with pink, stripelike markings in a random pattern on a white to pale pink background. Flowers open over a long period in spring. Upright growth habit.

'April Kiss'. Early. Small, formal double, red flowers. Compact habit and medium growth rate.

'April Remembered'. Early to midseason. Semidouble to rose-form blossoms are shades of cream pink. Bushy, vigorous growth and upright habit.

'April Rose'. Midseason. Beautiful, formal double flowers of rich rose red.

'Bette Sette'. Midseason. Formal double. Pink flowers about 3½-in. diameter on a medium-size shrub with an upright, dense growth habit.

'Glen 40'. Midseason to late. Profuse, large, formal double, deep red flowers. One of the best reds for corsages. Slow, compact, upright growth. Handsome even out of flower. Very good in containers.

'Kumasaka'. Midseason to late. Fairly large, rose form to peony form, rosy pink flowers. Vigorous, compact, upright growth and remarkably heavy blossom production make it a choice landscape plant. One of the hardiest japonicas of all and perhaps the first one for the novice to try.

'Lady Claire' ('Akashigata'). Early midseason. Large, semidouble, carmine rose blossoms with a crepelike texture. Striking in bloom. Rapid growth and imposing, upright habit. A particularly "good doer" in Zone 32.

'Lady Van Stittart'. Midseason to late. Semidouble, medium-size, white to blush pink flowers with dark pink stripes and broad, wavy petals. Rather coarse, hollylike foliage.

'Professor Charles Sargent'. Midseason. Full, rounded, peony shape, deep red flowers. Vigorous growth, upright habit; quite an eye-catcher in bloom.

C. oleifera. A large shrub or small tree to 20 ft. tall, with glossy, dark green leaves and fragrant, 2-inch white flowers in the autumn. The name means "oil bearing"; oil extracted from the large seeds has been used in China for cooking or as a hair conditioner. Probably the hardiest of all camellias. A parent of the hardy hybrids. 'Lushan Snow' is the plant at the National Arboretum from which the hardy hybrids were bred. It has become a handsome small tree with slightly pendulous branches, and is a virtual snowstorm of small, white flowers in the autumn.

C. sasanqua. Densely bushy, spreading to upright shrubs 8–12 ft. tall, and with dark green, shiny leaves. The flowers are produced from autumn to early winter, according to variety. Most sasanquas tolerate much sun if watering is adequate. May be slightly less cold hardy than *C. japonica*, but garden conditions will determine survival.

'Apple Blossom'. Single, white flowers blushed with pink, from pink buds. Spreading growth habit.

'Kanjiro'. Large, semidouble flowers of rose pink, shading to rose red at petal edges. Erect growth habit.

'Setsuga'. Large, white, semidouble flowers with fluted petals. Considerable substance to flowers; cut sprays hold well in water. Shrub's growth habit is upright and rather bushy.

'Yuletide'. A profusion of small, single, bright red flowers are borne on a dense, compact, upright plant.

Hardy hybrids. Dr. William Ackerman, National Arboretum, Washington, D.C., and Dr. Clifford Parks, University of North Carolina, Chapel Hill, bred a number of species, especially the hardy *C. oleifera*, to produce a race of very hardy camellias. The hybrids withstand temperatures as low as -15°F/ -26°C with little or no damage, provided they are given some shelter from winter sun and wind. Shelter from winter sun is especially important and may be the key to success in many locations. All these plants bloom at the end of the growing season, from early autumn to early winter, according to variety.

'Ashton's Pride'. Midseason. Flowers lavender pink, single. Extremely hardy. Reported to have survived 16°F without much damage. Upright, spreading growth habit.

'Carolina Moonmist'. Midseason to late. Flowers salmon pink, single. Dense, upright growth habit.

'Frost Prince'. Midseason. Flowers pink, semidouble. Upright, spreading growth habit.

'Polar Ice'. Midseason. Flowers white, anemone form. Spreading growth habit.

'Snow Flurry'. Very early. Flowers white, anemone to peony form, with blooms smaller than 'Polar Ice'. Heavy bloomer. Spreading growth habit.

'Twilight Glow'. Midseason. Sizeable, frilly, rose pink blossoms. Very shiny foliage on a plant of spreading, but compact, growth habit.

'Winter's Beauty'. Midseason. Flowers pink, frilly, peony to anemone form. Upright growth habit.

'Winter's Charm'. Early. Flowers pink, peony form. Upright growth habit.

'Winter's Cupid'. Midseason. The small, semidouble flowers are white, flushed pink near the tips. Tidy, upright growth habit.

'Winter's Dream'. Midseason. Flowers pink, semidouble, of medium size. Growth habit is upright and compact.

'Winter's Fancy'. Early. Semidouble, pink flowers of medium size. Growth habit is spreading but upright.

'Winter's Fire'. Midseason. Single to semidouble, deep pink flowers in abundance. Moderate growth rate and bushy, upright habit.

'Winter's Hope'. Late. The blossoms are white, semidouble, and of medium size. Spreading growth habit.

'Winter's Interlude'. Midseason. Flowers pink, anemone form, medium size. Spreading, upright growth habit.

'Winter's Joy'. Midseason. Semidouble, bright pink flowers. Vigorous growth, upright habit.

'Winter's Snowman'. Midseason. White, anemone-form flowers of medium size. Upright growth habit.

'Winter's Star'. Midseason. The medium-size flowers are reddish pink, single, and some have white centers. Tidy, upright growth habit.

'Winter's Starlight'. Midseason. The abundant, single flowers are white to pale pink and may be flecked with deeper pink. A vigorous grower with an upright growth habit. A sport of 'Winter's Star'.

'Winter's Sunset'. Midseason. The flowers are large, single, lavender pink, and relatively abundant. Vigorous upright growth. Very hardy, and proving to be one of the best.

'Winter's Waterlily'. Late. White, formal double flowers with somewhat incurving petals. Upright growth habit, but slow growing.

CHOCOLATE CAMELLIA LEAVES

Camellia leaves make perfect "molds" for a pretty dessert garnish. Spread melted semisweet chocolate over undersides of washed, dried leaves; refrigerate or freeze until chocolate is hard, then carefully peel off leaves. Keep chocolate leaves chilled or frozen until you're ready to use them.

Flower Forms of *Camellia japonica* *Single* flowers have a single row of petals and prominent stamens. *Semidouble* flowers have at least two rows of large petals and a center made up of stamens and loose petals. *Formal double* flowers have rows of overlapping petals and no visible stamens. *Peony* flowers are domed and consist of petals, petaloids, and stamens. *Anemone* form flowers have at least one row of petals and a center composed of stamens and petaloids. *Rose* form flowers have rows of overlapping petals, with stamens visible in fully open flowers.

Single   Semidouble   Formal Double   Peony Form   Anemone Form   Rose Form

C

CAMPANULA

BELLFLOWER

Campanulaceae (Lobeliaceae)

MOSTLY PERENNIALS; SOME BIENNIALS OR ANNUALS

ZONES 31, 32, 34–45, EXCEPT AS NOTED

TOLERATE FULL SUN IN COOLEST AREAS

REGULAR TO MODERATE WATER

SEE CHART ON FOLLOWING PAGES

Campanula isophylla

Vast and varied group (nearly 300 species) encompassing trailers, creeping or tufted miniatures, and erect kinds 1–6 ft. tall. Flowers generally bell shaped, but some star shaped, cup shaped, or round and flat. Usually blue, lavender, violet, purple, or white; some pink. Bloom period from spring to fall.

Uses are as varied as the plants. Gemlike miniatures deserve special settings—close-up situations in rock gardens, niches in dry walls, raised beds, containers. Trailing kinds are ideal for hanging pots or baskets, wall crevices; vigorous spreading growers serve well as ground covers. Upright growers are valuable in borders, for cutting, occasionally in containers.

In general, campanulas grow best in good, well-drained soil and cooler climates. Most species are fairly easy to grow from seed sown in flats in spring or early summer, transplanted to garden in fall for bloom the following year; also may be increased by cuttings or divisions. Divide clumps in fall every 3 to 4 years; some may need yearly division.

Campanulaceae. The campanula, or bellflower, family contains perennials or biennials, typically with bell-shaped or saucer-shaped flowers in shades of blue to purple, lilac, and white. This family includes plants formerly grouped under Lobeliaceae.

CAMPSIS

TRUMPET CREEPER, TRUMPET VINE

Bignoniaceae

DECIDUOUS VINES

ZONES VARY BY SPECIES

FULL SUN OR PARTIAL SHADE

REGULAR TO MODERATE WATER

Campsis

Vigorous climbers that cling to wood, brick, and stucco surfaces with aerial rootlets. Unless thinned, old plants sometimes become top heavy and pull away from supporting surface. Will spread through garden and into neighbor's by suckering roots. If you try to dig up suckers, any remaining piece of root will grow another plant. Can be trained as big shrub or flowering hedge if branches are shortened after first year's growth. Use for large-scale effects, quick summer screen. All produce open, arching sprays of trumpet-shaped flowers in summer.

C. grandiflora (Bignonia chinensis). CHINESE TRUMPET CREEPER. Zones 31, 32. Not as vigorous, large, or hardy as the American native *C. radicans,* but with slightly larger, more open scarlet flowers. Leaves divided into seven to nine leaflets, each 2½ in. long. 'Morning Calm' has peach-colored flowers.

C. radicans (Bignonia radicans). COMMON TRUMPET CREEPER. Zones 31, 32, 34–41. Native to southeastern U.S. Most widely used in cold-winter areas. Hard freeze will kill to ground but new stems grow quickly. Leaves divided into 9–11 toothed leaflets, each 2½ in. long. Flowers, growing in clusters of 6–12, are 3-in.-long orange tubes with scarlet lobes that flare to 2 in. wide. Grows fast to 40 ft. or more, bursting with health and vigor. Blossoms of 'Flava' are yellow to pale orange.

C. tagliabuana. Zones 31, 32, 34. Hybrid between the two above species. 'Mme Galen', best-known variety, has attractive salmon red flowers. 'Crimson Trumpet' bears pure red blooms.

CAMPTOSORUS rhizophyllus. See ASPLENIUM rhizophyllus

CANARY BIRD FLOWER. See TROPAEOLUM peregrinum

CANDYTUFT. See IBERIS

CANNA

Cannaceae

TUBEROUS-ROOTED PERENNIALS

ZONES 31, WARMER PARTS OF 32; OR DIG AND STORE

FULL SUN

AMPLE WATER DURING GROWTH AND BLOOM

Canna

Native to tropics and subtropics. Best adapted to warm- to hot-summer climates; in areas where soil freezes deeply, lift and store roots over winter. An old favorite that can add a tropical touch in the right place. Large, rich green to bronzy red leaves resemble those of banana *(Musa)* or ti plant *(Cordyline terminalis)*. Spikes of large, showy, irregularly shaped flowers bloom on 3–6-ft. stalks in summer, fall. Many varieties in a wide range of sizes and shapes, in near-white, ivory, yellow, orange, pink, apricot, coral, salmon, and red. Bicolors include 'Cleopatra', with flowers strikingly streaked and spotted red on yellow. Low-growing strains are Grand Opera (26 in.), Pfitzer's Dwarf (2½–3 ft.), and Seven Dwarfs (1½ ft.); grow Seven Dwarfs strain from seed. 'Bengal Tiger' ('Praetoria'), green leaves striped with yellow; yellow-orange flowers. 'Durban', bronze leaves striped with yellow, orange, and red; red flowers. 'Phaison', purple leaves striped with yellow and red; bright orange flowers. 'Pink Sunburst', green leaves striped with yellow and having a reddish cast; salmon pink flowers. 'Stuttgart', green leaves variegated with deep green, ivory, and white; flowers combine green-striped pink sepals and yellow-orange petals flushed with red. 'Tropical Rose', rosy pink flowers. 'Red King Humbert' ('Roi Humbert'), purple-bronze leaves; red flowers.

C. glauca. Less well-known and less flashy, grows to 6 ft., with gray-green leaves edged in white, with light yellow flowers that are narrower than those of hybrids. 'Panache' has salmon pink flowers and grows with an open, airy appearance for those who dislike the coarseness of other cannas.

Most effective in groups of single colors against plain background. Grow in borders, near poolside, in large pots or tubs on terrace or patio. Leaves useful in arrangements; cut flowers do not keep well. Plant rootstocks in spring after frost danger is past, in rich, loose soil. Set 5 in. deep, 10 in. apart. Remove faded flowers after bloom. After all flower clusters have bloomed, cut stalk to ground.

CANTALOUPE. See MELON, MUSKMELON, CANTALOUPE

CANTERBURY BELL. See CAMPANULA medium

CAPE FORGET-ME-NOT. See ANCHUSA capensis

CAPE FUCHSIA. See PHYGELIUS

CAPE MALLOW. See ANISODONTEA

CAPE MARIGOLD. See DIMORPHOTHECA, OSTEOSPERMUM

CAPE PONDWEED. See APONOGETON distachyus

Capparaceae. The caper family includes the caper plant *(Capparis spinosa)* as well as *Cleome hasslerana,* commonly known as spider flower.

Caprifoliaceae. The honeysuckle family of shrubs and vines contains many ornamentals in addition to honeysuckle *(Lonicera);* among them are *Abelia, Viburnum,* and *Weigela.*

C

CAPSICUM annuum

ORNAMENTAL PEPPER

Solanaceae

ANNUAL

ALL ZONES

FULL SUN

REGULAR WATER

Capsicum annuum

Handsome foliage and eye-catching fruit make peppers ideal plants for adding season-long color to plantings of annuals or mixed beds of perennials and annuals. All peppers are native to tropical regions in North and South America. Even common vegetable-garden-type peppers are attractive and can be used in edible landscaping schemes. Shrubby plants range from 1 to 4 ft. tall and bear rounded leaves. Flowers are small, white or yellow, and star or bell shaped. Peppers developed for ornamental use have especially showy fruit that often is extremely hot and not meant to be eaten. Fruit range from marble-size to 6 in. or more long. Although many peppers bear pendant fruits, ornamental types generally have erect fruit that covers the tops of the plants. Some feature variegated foliage.

'Sweet Pickle' bears sweet red, yellow, orange, and purple 2-in. fruits on 1–1½-ft. plants. 'Pretty Purple' bears red-and-purple fruits the size and shape of marbles on 2½-ft. plants. 'Tri-Fetti' (sometimes sold as 'Variegata') bears variegated green, white, and purple leaves on mounding 1½- ft. plants with small purple and red fruits. 'Prairie Fire' has upright, cone-shaped fruits in abundance that ripen from yellow to orange to red; plants are 6 in. high and 14 in. wide. 'Treasures Red' grows 8 in. high and 10 in. wide; the upright fruits mature from white to brilliant red.

Start seeds indoors 8 weeks before the last spring frost date and transplant after all danger of frost has passed. Use in mixed plantings, as edgings, or as fillers in perennial beds and borders.

CARAGANA

PEASHRUB

Fabaceae (Leguminosae)

DECIDUOUS SHRUBS OR SMALL TREES

ZONES 31, 32, 34–45

FULL SUN

MODERATE TO LITTLE WATER

Caragana arborescens

Native to Russia, Manchuria, Siberia. Leaves divided into small leaflets. Spring flowers shaped like bright yellow sweet peas. Useful where choice is limited by cold, heat, wind, bright sun; nearly indestructible in desert, mountain, and prairie climates. Use as windbreak, clipped hedge, cover for wildlife.

C. arborescens. SIBERIAN PEASHRUB. Fast growing to 20 ft., with 15-ft. spread. Leaves to 3 in. long, each with four to six pairs of leaflets. 'Lorbergii' has long leaves with narrow leaflets to 14 in. long. 'Nana' is dwarf, to 5 ft. high, with twisted stems. 'Pendula' grows to 5 ft., with weeping stems.

C. frutex. RUSSIAN PEASHRUB. To 10 ft.; leaves have one or two pairs of 1-in. leaflets.

CARAWAY. See CARUM carvi

CARDINAL CLIMBER. See IPOMOEA quamoclit

CARDINAL FLOWER. See LOBELIA cardinalis

FOR GROWING SYMBOL EXPLANATIONS

PLEASE SEE PAGE 113

CARDIOCRINUM giganteum

HEART LILY

Liliaceae

BULB

ZONES 34–41

FILTERED SUNLIGHT, PARTIAL SHADE

MORE THAN REGULAR WATER

Cardiocrinum giganteum

This genus includes two other species of the bulbous perennials, all native to the cooler woodlands of Asia. Spectacular clusters of fragrant, white, trumpet-shaped flowers, as many as 20 per plant and each as long as 6 in., bloom in summer on stems that can grow to 12 ft. and feature glossy, heart-shaped, veined leaves. Brown seed capsules, oblong and up to 2½ in. long, follow flowers. Bulbs take 3–4 years before blossoming, then die leaving several offsets. To ensure blooms each year, plant bulbs of different sizes in a cool and sheltered site, and in soil rich with humus that is moist, but well-drained. Intolerant to heat and drought.

CARDIOSPERMUM halicacabum

BALLOON VINE, HEART SEED, LOVE-IN-A-PUFF

Sapindaceae

ANNUAL OR BIENNIAL

ALL ZONES

FULL SUN

REGULAR

Cardiospermum halicacabum

This woody tendril climber, the most commonly cultivated among the 14 species, grows to 12 ft. and has bright green leaves, 6–8 in. long, each divided into seven to nine oblong and deeply toothed leaflets. Bears small, greenish white flowers from summer to autumn. They are followed by three-angled balloonlike capsules up to 1¼ in. long that change from light green to brown. Naturalized in the southern U.S. and often found growing wild near streams and riverbanks, vines can be started from seed indoors in northern climates 2 months before planting out. Requires fertile, well-drained soil. Vines are ideal over trellises and fences.

CAREX

SEDGE

Cyperaceae

PERENNIALS

ZONES 31, 32, 34–45

MIDDAY SHADE IN HOT CLIMATES

CONSTANTLY MOIST SOIL

Carex

Grasslike, clumping plants grown for foliage effect in borders, rock gardens, containers, water gardens. Long, narrow evergreen leaves are often striped or oddly colored. Specialists offer many varieties.

C. buchananii. LEATHER LEAF SEDGE. Curly tipped, arching blades 2–3 ft. tall make clumps of striking reddish bronze. Use with gray foliage or with deep greens.

C. comans (C. albula). NEW ZEALAND HAIR SEDGE. Dense, finely textured clumps of narrow leaves are silvery green. Leaves, usually 1 ft. long, may reach 6 ft.; on slopes, they look like flowing water. Also sold as 'Frosty Curls'. 'Bronze' is similar but has coppery brown leaves.

CAMPANULA

NAME, TYPE	GROWTH HABIT, SIZE	FOLIAGE	FLOWERS	USES, COMMENTS
Campanula alliariifolia Perennial	Forms clumps 1–2 ft. high	Oval to kidney-shaped, toothed leaves, 3 in. long	¾ in. long, tubular, bell-shaped, drooping, white. Summer.	A vigorous grower. Use in naturalistic and informal gardens
C. alpestris (C. allionii) Perennial	Rosettes spring from creeping rhizomes. Stems 2–5 in. long	Leaves 2 in. long in rosettes	1¾ in. long, erect or horizontal, blue or white. Summer	Rock gardens, borders, edging
C. barbata Short-lived perennial or biennial	Clumps of erect stems, 4–18 in. high	Leaves mostly at base of stem, 2–5 in. long, narrow, hairy	Bell-shaped, lilac blue, bearded inside, 1 in. long, nodding. Few near top of each stem. Summer	Foreground in borders, rock gardens. Taprooted; needs good drainage. White forms may appear from seed.
C. carpatica (C. turbinata) TUSSOCK BELLFLOWER Perennial	Compact leafy tufts, stems branching and spreading. Usually about 8 in. tall, may reach 1–1½ ft.	Leaves smooth, bright, green, wavy, toothed, 1–1½ in. long	Open bell- or cup-shaped, blue or white, 1–2 in. across, single and erect on stems above foliage. Late spring	Rock gardens, foreground in borders, edging. Variable in flower size and color. 'Blue Clips' and 'White Clips' good dwarf varieties. Easily grown from seed; sometimes sold as 'Blue Clips', 'White Clips'
C. cochleariifolia Perennial	Creeping and mat-forming, tufted, low growing, to 3 in. high	Oval to rounded or heart-shaped, bright green, to 3 in. long in rosettes	¾-in.-long, drooping, bell-shaped, purplish blue to light lavender blue. Summer	Use in rock gardens or dry stone walls.
C. elatines garganica (C. garganica) Perennial Zones 31, 32, 34, 39	Low (3–6 in. high), with outward spreading stems	Small, gray or green, sharply toothed, heart-shaped leaves	Flat, star-shaped, violet blue. One or a few at top of stem. Late spring to fall	Rock gardens. Usually sold as *C. garganica*. Somewhat like a miniature, prostrate *C. poscharskyana*
C. glomerata Perennial	Upright, with erect side branches to 1–2 ft.	Basal leaves broad, wavy-edged. Stem leaves broad, toothed. Both somewhat hairy	Narrow, bell-shaped, flaring at the mouth, 1 in. long, blue violet, tightly clustered at tops of stems. Summer	Shaded borders or large rock gardens. Plants have proportionately more foliage than flowers. Seed-grown strains. Superba and Alba are deepest purple and white, respectively.
C. lactiflora Perennial Zones 31, 32, 34, 39	Erect, branching, leafy, 3½–5 ft. tall	Oblong, pointed, toothed leaves 2–3 in. long	Broadly bell-shaped to star-shaped, 1 in. long, white to pale blue in drooping clusters at ends of branches. Summer	Rear of borders in sun or partial shade. Endures even dry shade and is long lived. 'Loddon-Anna' has pale pink flowers.
C. latifolia Perennial	Upright, sturdy stems to 4 ft. high	Oval to oblong, toothed, medium green, to 6 in. long in basal clumps	Tubular to bell-shaped, to 2 in. long, purple blue or white. Summer	Big, bold, and vigorous
C. medium CANTERBURY BELL, CUP-AND-SAUCER Biennial or annual	Sturdy, hairy, leafy, with erect stems 2½–4 ft. tall	Lance-shaped basal leaves 6–10 in.; stem leaves 3–5 in.; wavy-margined, lance-shaped	Bell-shaped or urn-shaped, 1–2 in. across, single or double, held upright in long, loose open clusters. Purple, violet, blue, lavender, pink, white. Late spring or early summer	Sow seed in May or June for bloom next year, or set out plants from nursery 15–18 in. apart. Good for cutting. 'Calycanthema', commonly called cup-and-saucer, is very popular. Annual variety with bell-shaped flowers (not cup-and-saucer) blooms in 6 months from seed.
C. persicifolia PEACH-LEAVED BLUEBELL Perennial	Strong-growing, slender, erect stems 2–3 ft. tall. Plants leafy at base	Basal leaves smooth-edged, green, 4–8 in. long. Stem leaves 2–4 in. long, shaped like leaves of peach tree	Open, cup-shaped, about 1 in. across, held erect on short side shoots on sturdy stems. Blue, pink, or white. Summer	Choice plant for borders. Easy to grow from seed sown in late spring. 'Telham Beauty', old but still popular, has 3-in. blue flowers. 'Blue Gardenia' and 'White Pearl' have double flowers.

C

CAMPANULA

NAME, TYPE	GROWTH HABIT, SIZE	FOLIAGE	FLOWERS	USES, COMMENTS
C. portenschlagiana (C. muralis) DALMATIAN BELLFLOWER Perennial Zones 31, 32, 34–41	Low, leafy, mounding mats 4–7 in. high	Roundish, heart-shaped, deep green leaves with deeply toothed, slightly wavy edges	Flaring bell-shaped, violet blue flowers to 1 in. long; 2 or 3 on each semierect stem. Late spring into summer, sometimes blooming again in fall	Fine plant for edging or as small-scale ground cover. In warm regions best in partial shade. Spreads moderately fast; is sturdy, permanent, and not invasive. Easily increased by dividing. 'Resholt' has larger, darker flowers
C. poscharskyana SERBIAN BELLFLOWER Perennial	Spreading, many branched, leafy, with semiupright flowering stems 1 ft. tall or taller	Long heart-shaped, irregularly toothed, slightly hairy leaves 1–3½ in. long, ¾–1 in. wide	Star-shaped, ½–1 in. across blue-lilac or lavender. Spring to early summer. There also is a white-flowered form	Very vigorous. Shaded border near pools, shaded rock gardens, with fuchsias and begonias. Needs little water. Small area ground cover.
C. punctata Perennial	Forms clumps of erect stems to 2 ft. high, with creeping rhizomes	Oval to heart-shaped, toothed, dark green, to 5 in. long in rosettes	Bell-shaped, drooping, white to lilac or pink, dark red spots inside. Summer	Can become invasive
C. raddeana Perennial Zones 31, 32, 34–41	Low growing, mat forming	Small, shiny, sharp-toothed, long-stemmed, dark green leaves	Bell-shaped, drooping, profuse on foot-tall stems; deep violet blue. Summer	Good in rock garden or foreground. Needs good drainage, some lime in acid soil
C. rapunculoides ROVER BELLFLOWER Perennial	Clumps of long-stemmed leaves send up 3-ft. spires of blue-purple bells	Leaves medium green, large, heart-shaped at base	Funnel-shaped flowers, 1 in. long. Sometimes pale blue or white. Summer	Tough, invasive plant, useful in difficult soils, climates. Don't locate near delicate plants
C. rotundifolia BLUEBELL OF SCOTLAND, HAREBELL Perennial	Upright or spreading, simple or with many branches, 6–20 in. tall	Leaves green or sometimes slightly grayish. Basal leaves roundish, long-stalked, 1 in. across. Stem leaves grasslike, 2–3 in. long. May dry up before blooming time	Broad, bell-shaped, bright blue, 1 in. across, one or a few nodding in open clusters. Summer	Flower color variable, sometimes in lavender, purple, or white shades. Rock gardens, borders, naturalized under deciduous trees. Self-sows in favorable situations
C. sarmatica Perennial	Clumps of upright, unbranched stems to 1½ ft. high	Elongated, heart-shaped, toothed, to 3 in. long	Bell-shaped, to 2 in. long, pale grayish blue. Late spring to midsummer	Similar to *C. alliariifolia* but not as vigorous
C. takesimana Perennial	Clumping, to 2 ft. high, spreading freely by underground runners	Large, roundish, toothed leaves	Large, drooping, bell-shaped, pale lilac with dark red spots inside. Early summer	Vigorous spreader. Useful in borders, but don't place near delicate plants
C. trachelium Perennial	Upright, to 3 ft. high	Oval, toothed, bristly, similar to nettles, to 5 in. long	Tubular, to 1¼ in. long, blue to lilac purple or white. Late summer	Best in informal planting

C

C. conica 'Snowline' ('Marginata'). A 6-in. dwarf sedge with white-margined leaves.

C. elata 'Aurea' ('Bowles Golden'). Clumps up to 2 ft. have narrow leaves that emerge bright yellow in spring and hold some color until late summer. Needs much moisture; will grow in water.

C. flacca (C. glauca). BLUE SEDGE. Creeping perennial with blue-gray grasslike foliage 6–12 in. tall; evergreen only in mildest climates. Tolerant of many soils and irrigation schemes; best in moist soil. Not invasive but spreads slowly and can be clipped like a lawn. Endures light foot traffic, moderate shade, competition with tree roots.

C. morrowii expallida (C. m. 'Variegata'). VARIEGATED JAPANESE SEDGE. Drooping leaves striped with green and white make 1-ft. mound. Edging plant; single clumps attractive among rocks. 'Ice Dance' looks just like 'Variegata', but is spreading instead of clump-forming. 'Aurea-variegata' ('Goldband') has gold-striped leaves. *C. m. temnolepis* 'Silk Tassel' grows to 2 ft.; thin, threadlike leaves striped green and white.

C. muskingumensis. PALM BRANCH SEDGE. Zones 31, 32, 34–43. Deciduous, tufted, slightly spreading, with horizontal, bright green leaves to 2½ ft. long on upright stems. Golden brown flower spikes to 1 in. long in summer.

C. oshimensis 'Evergold' (C. hachijoensis 'Evergold'). Zones 31, 32, 34, 39. Forms a low mound of narrow, evergreen, deep green leaves to 1 ft. or more long, each having a light yellow stripe down the middle. The leaves are weeping and graceful. Brown flower spikes to 1 in. long in spring.

C. siderosticha 'Variegata'. Zones 31, 32, 34, 39. Spreads slowly by rhizomes to form clumps of deciduous, broadly lance-shaped, light green leaves to 10 in. long. Leaves are edged and striped in white, with a pink flush at the base of the leaf. New shoots are red tinged. Light brown flower spikes in late spring.

CARNATION. See DIANTHUS caryophyllus

CAROLINA ALLSPICE. See CALYCANTHUS floridus

CAROLINA JESSAMINE. See GELSEMIUM sempervirens

CARPET BUGLE. See AJUGA

CARPINUS

HORNBEAM

Betulaceae

DECIDUOUS TREES

ZONES VARY BY SPECIES

EXPOSURE NEEDS VARY BY SPECIES

REGULAR WATER

Carpinus betulus

Well-behaved, relatively small shade trees. Long life and good habits as street trees. Slow to moderate growth rate. Very hard, tough wood. Dark green, sawtooth-edged leaves color up agreeably in cold-winter climates, hang on late in season. Fruits (small, hard nutlets in leaflike bracts) are carried in attractive drooping clusters to 5 in. long.

C. betulus. EUROPEAN HORNBEAM. Zones 31, 32, 34–41. Excellent landscape tree to 40 ft. tall. Dense pyramidal form, eventually becoming broad with drooping outer branches. Handsome, furrowed gray bark somewhat similar to that of *C. caroliniana.* Very clean leaves, 2–5 in. long, turn yellow or dark red in autumn. Best in full sun, but tolerates light shade. 'Fastigiata' is the variety commonly sold; though name implies very upright growth, tree develops an oval-vase shape with age.

C. caroliniana. AMERICAN HORNBEAM. Zones 31, 32, 34–43. Native from Nova Scotia to Minnesota, southward to Texas and Florida. Also known as blue beech and ironwood in its native range, where it is often found at forest edges or as understory plant along rivers and streams (in this location, it withstands periodic flooding). Those common names refer to the tree trunk, which is blue gray and smooth, with undulations that look like muscles flexing beneath the surface. To 25–30 ft. tall with round head; can be grown as single or multitrunked tree. Leaves, 1–3 in. long, turn mottled yellow and red in fall. Drops leaves before *C. betulus.* Does well in exposures from full sun to heavy shade. Best in natural gardens.

CARROT

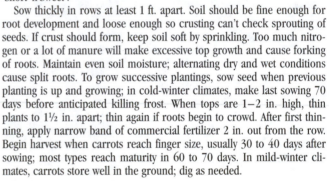

Apiaceae (Umbelliferae)

BIENNIAL GROWN AS ANNUAL

ALL ZONES

FULL SUN

MAINTAIN EVEN SOIL MOISTURE

Carrot

The variety to plant depends on the soil's condition: carrots reach smooth perfection only in good-textured soil free of stones and clods. Plant long market kinds only if you can give them a foot of this ideal, light soil. If you can provide only a few inches, plant half-long varieties such as 'Nantes' and 'Chantenay' or miniatures 'Amstel', 'Lady Finger', or 'Short 'n Sweet'.

Sow thickly in rows at least 1 ft. apart. Soil should be fine enough for root development and loose enough so crusting can't check sprouting of seeds. If crust should form, keep soil soft by sprinkling. Too much nitrogen or a lot of manure will make excessive top growth and cause forking of roots. Maintain even soil moisture; alternating dry and wet conditions cause split roots. To grow successive plantings, sow seed when previous planting is up and growing; in cold-winter climates, make last sowing 70 days before anticipated killing frost. When tops are 1–2 in. high, thin plants to 1½ in. apart; thin again if roots begin to crowd. After first thinning, apply narrow band of commercial fertilizer 2 in. out from the row. Begin harvest when carrots reach finger size, usually 30 to 40 days after sowing; most types reach maturity in 60 to 70 days. In mild-winter climates, carrots store well in the ground; dig as needed.

CARROT THINNINGS TO EAT

Carrot harvesting actually starts with thinning—the removal of excess seedlings when the tops are about 1–2 in. tall to make space for others to grow. Steam the tiny carrots in butter. Or chop the entire miniature plants, tops and all; add to tossed salads for a fresh surprise.

CARTHAMUS tinctorius

SAFFLOWER, FALSE SAFFRON

Asteraceae (Compositae)

ANNUAL

ALL ZONES

FULL SUN

MODERATE WATER

Carthamus tinctorius

This relative of the thistles is ornamental as well as useful. Erect, spiny-leafed stems, 1–3 ft. tall, bear orange-yellow flower heads above leafy bracts; inner bracts are spiny. Durable cut flower, fresh or dried. Grown commercially for oil extracted from the seeds. The dried flowers have been used for seasoning in place of true saffron, which they somewhat resemble in color and flavor. Sow seeds in place in spring after frosts. An ornamental spineless safflower is also available.

CARUM carvi

CARAWAY

Apiaceae (Umbelliferae)

BIENNIAL HERB

☘ ALL ZONES

☼ FULL SUN

💧 REGULAR WATER

Carum carvi

Mound of carrotlike leaves, 1–2 ft. high, in first year. Umbrellalike clusters of white flowers rise above foliage in second year. Plant dies after seeds ripen in midsummer. Start from seed sown in place in fall or spring. Thrives in well-drained soil. Thin seedlings to 1½ ft. To harvest seed, pick dry heads and rub off seeds. Sift to remove chaff, dry thoroughly, and store in jars. Use dried seeds for flavoring pickles, vegetables, cookies, rye bread.

CARYA

PECAN, HICKORY

Juglandaceae

DECIDUOUS TREES

☘ ZONES VARY BY SPECIES

☼ FULL SUN

💧💧 REGULAR TO MODERATE WATER

Carya

Large trees with leaves divided featherwise into many leaflets, inconspicuous flowers, and nuts enclosed in husks that usually break away at maturity. Nuts of pecan and hickory are delicious, and the former is an important commercial crop. Trees are too large for smaller home plots, but are attractive where space is available. All develop deep taproots and should be planted while young and not moved later.

C. glabra. PIGNUT HICKORY. Zones 32, 34–41. Native to the eastern U.S. Spreading tree to 80 ft. tall and 70 ft. wide. Furrowed gray bark is shaggy but not ornamental. Compound leaves to 1 ft. long, with oblong leaflets, turn yellow in autumn. Nuts are thin shelled and bitter.

C. illinoensis. PECAN. Native to southern and central U.S. Grow for nut crop in Zones 31, 32, hardiest varieties in 35; may also be grown as an ornamental in Zones 34, 36, 37, 39, 41. Graceful, shapely tree to 70 ft. tall and equally wide. Foliage like that of English walnut but prettier, with more (11–17) leaflets that are narrower and longer (4–7 in.); foliage pattern is finer textured, casts less shade. Trees need well-drained, deep soils (6–10 ft. deep); won't stand salinity. Prune to shape or remove dead wood.

C. ovata. SHAGBARK HICKORY. Zones 31, 32, 34–44. Grows to 60–100 ft. Most conspicuous feature is bark, which is gray and shaggy, with large plates curving out and away from the trunk. The hard-shelled nuts are sweet. Autumn foliage is an attractive yellow and brown. Wood is proverbially tough and hard. *C. laciniosa*, shellbark hickory, is a similar but smaller tree.

Caryophyllaceae. The pink family includes many garden annuals and perennials as well as a few weeds. Leaves are borne in opposite pairs at joints that are often swollen; leaves are often joined together at their bases. Pinks and carnations are typical representatives, along with snow-in-summer (*Cerastium*) and *Lychnis*.

CARYOPTERIS

BLUEBEARD

Verbenaceae

DECIDUOUS SHRUBS

☘ ZONES VARY BY SPECIES

☼ FULL SUN

💧 MODERATE WATER

Caryopteris

Valued for contribution of cool blue to flower borders from August to frost. Generally grown as shrubby perennials. If plant is not frozen back in winter, cut nearly to ground in spring. Cut back growth after each wave of bloom to encourage more flowers. Provide good drainage; can rot in wet soils.

C. clandonensis. BLUE MIST. Zones 31, 32, 34, 39. Low-growing mound (to 2 ft. tall and wide) of narrow, 3-in.-long leaves. Clusters of small blue flowers top upper parts of stems. Selected forms 'Azure' and 'Heavenly Blue' have deep blue flowers. 'Dark Knight' and 'Longwood Blue' have deep blue flowers and silvery foliage. 'Worcester Gold' has yellow leaves, blue flowers.

C. incana (C. mastacanthus). COMMON BLUEBEARD, BLUE SPIRAEA. Zones 31, 32, 34. Taller than *C. clandonensis*, with looser, more open growth to 3–4 ft. Lavender blue flowers.

CASTANEA

CHESTNUT

Fagaceae

DECIDUOUS TREES OR SHRUBS

☘ ZONES VARY BY SPECIES

☼ FULL SUN, EXCEPT AS NOTED

💧 REGULAR TO MODERATE WATER

Castanea

The American chestnut (*C. dentata*) has become nearly extinct as a result of chestnut blight, but other members of the genus also supply edible nuts (they are actually fruits), and are less susceptible to blight. They make wonderful, dense shade trees where there is space to accommodate them and where their litter and rank-smelling pollen won't be as noticeable—at large country places, for example. All have handsome dark to bright green foliage. Small, creamy white flowers in long (8–10-in.), slim catkins make quite a display in early summer. The large edible nuts are enclosed in prickly burrs. Plant two or more trees to ensure pollination and a substantial crop. Single trees bear lightly or not at all. Somewhat drought tolerant.

C. mollissima. CHINESE CHESTNUT. Zones 31, 32, 34–43. Native to northern China and Korea. Grows to 40–60 ft. high and 40 ft. wide, with a spreading, rounded form. Oblong, toothed leaves to 6 in. long and 3 in. wide, rich deep green and turning yellow to bronze in autumn. The grayish brown bark is deeply furrowed. Sweet-flavored nuts mature in fall— the prickly burrs split open when nuts are ripe. Trees begin bearing in 3 to 5 years. Prefers well-drained, loamy, acidic soil, but tolerates a range of conditions except for alkaline soil, including hot, dry sites.

Hybrid chestnuts. Zones 31, 32, 34–41. Dunstan hybrids, developed in the South during the 1950s, are hybrids between American and Chinese and Japanese chestnuts that are resistant to blight. Other resistant American-Oriental hybrids are also offered in nursery catalogs. Hybrids have the same oblong, toothed leaves and round nuts as American and Chinese chestnuts.

C. pumila. ALLEGHENY CHINAPIN, CHINQUAPIN. Deciduous shrub or small tree. Zones 31, 32, 34–41. Native to the eastern U.S., from Pennsylvania to Florida. Usually grows as a shrub to 10 ft. high, but may be a 20–25-ft. tree. Dark green leaves are oval and toothed, to 5 in. long. Bears small brown nuts that are edible and attractive to wildlife. Grow in a

C

woodland garden or a naturalistic mixed border. Needs well-drained soil, tolerates partial to light shade.

CAST-IRON PLANT. See ASPIDISTRA elatior

CASTOR ARALIA. See KALOPANAX septemlobus

CASTOR BEAN. See RICINUS communis

CATALPA

Bignoniaceae

DECIDUOUS TREES

ZONES 31, 32, 34–41

FULL SUN OR LIGHT SHADE

REGULAR TO MODERATE WATER

Catalpa

Catalpas are among the few truly deciduous trees that can compete in flower and leaf with subtropical species. Bloom in late spring and summer, bearing large, upright clusters of trumpet-shaped, 2-in.-wide flowers in pure white striped and marked with yellow and soft brown; flowers held above large, bold, heart-shaped leaves. Long, bean-shaped seed capsules, sometimes called Indian beans or Indian stogies, follow the blossoms.

Unusually well adapted to extremes of heat and cold, and to all soils. Where winds are strong, plant in lee of taller trees or buildings to protect leaves from damage. Some gardeners object to litter of fallen flowers in summer and seed capsules in autumn. Plants need shaping while young, seldom develop a well-established dominant shoot. Shorten side branches as tree grows. When branching begins at desired height, remove lower branches.

For the tree sometimes called desert catalpa, see *Chilopsis linearis*. Another tree sometimes mistakenly called catalpa is the very similar *Paulownia tomentosa*, or empress tree, with lavender flowers. *Paulownia* shows flower buds in winter; catalpa does not.

C. bignonioides. COMMON CATALPA, INDIAN BEAN. Native to southeastern U.S. Generally smaller than *C. speciosa,* 20–50 ft. according to climate or soil, with somewhat smaller spread. Leaves 5–8 in. long, often in whorls, give off odd odor when crushed. Chlorotic in alkaline soil. Yellow leaves of 'Aurea' are showier where summers are cool.

'Nana'. UMBRELLA CATALPA. A dense globe form usually grafted high on *C. bignonioides.* Almost always sold as *C. bungei.* It never blooms. Cut it back to keep it in scale.

C. erubescens 'Purpurea'. Selection of hybrid between *C. bignonioides* and a Chinese species. Tree resembles *C. bignonioides* parent. Young leaves and branchlets are deep blackish purple, turning purple-toned green in summer.

C. speciosa. WESTERN CATALPA. Native to central and southern Midwest. Round headed; 40–70 ft. tall. Leaves 6–12 in. long; no odor when crushed. Fewer flowers per cluster than for *C. bignonioides.* Early training and pruning will give tall trunk and umbrella-shaped crown.

CATANANCHE caerulea

CUPID'S DART

Asteraceae (Compositae)

PERENNIAL

ALL ZONES

FULL SUN

MODERATE WATER

Catananche caerulea

Sturdy, free-flowering plant for summer borders and arrangements. Needs well-drained soil, not too much moisture; self-sows freely. Narrow gray-green leaves, 8–12 in. long, mostly at base of stem. Leafless,

---

2-ft. stems carry lavender blue, 2-in. flower heads reminiscent of cornflowers and surrounded by strawlike, shining bracts. Flowers dry well for everlasting bouquets. Remove faded flowers to prolong bloom. 'Alba' is white flowered. 'Major' has purple-blue flowers with dark purple centers.

CATHARANTHUS roseus (Vinca rosea)

MADAGASCAR PERIWINKLE

Apocynaceae

PERENNIAL OFTEN GROWN AS ANNUAL

ALL ZONES

FULL SUN OR PARTIAL SHADE

MODERATE WATER

Catharanthus roseus

Good for summer–fall color in hot climates. Thrives in dry or humid heat. Glossy leaves 1–3 in. long cover bushy plant 1–2 ft. high. Phloxlike flowers 1½ in. wide in pure white, white with rose or red eye, blush pink, clear cotton-candy pink, or bright rose. The Little series grows 8–10 in. high. Pacific and Cooler series are compact, 15-in. plants with large (2-in. or wider) flowers. The Tropicana series is early blooming (60 days from seed). Creeping strains, including the Carpet series, grow 4–8 in. tall, 1½ ft. wide. All types will bloom first season from seed sown early indoors, in greenhouse or cold frame. Nurseries sell plants in late spring.

Blooms all summer and keeps flowering after zinnias and marigolds have gone, until Thanksgiving if weather stays mild. Lives over in frost-free areas but may look ragged in winter. Self-sows readily. Provide good drainage and avoid overwatering.

USEFUL IN MORE WAYS THAN ONE

Madagascar periwinkle is a workhorse in the garden, bearing its colorful blooms over a long season and outlasting other summer annuals. It doesn't even need deadheading to keep the show going; the blossoms drop cleanly on their own. The plant's usefulness goes beyond the garden: in the 1950s, its alkaloids were discovered to be valuable in treating leukemia.

CATMINT. See NEPETA faassenii

CATNIP. See NEPETA cataria

CAT'S CLAW. See MACFADYENA unguis-cati

CATTAIL. See TYPHA

CAULIFLOWER

Brassicaceae (Cruciferae)

ANNUAL OR BIENNIAL GROWN AS ANNUAL

ALL ZONES

FULL SUN

REGULAR WATER

Cauliflower

Related to broccoli and cabbage; has similar cultural requirements but is more difficult to grow. Easiest in cool, humid regions. Where summers are hot, grow it to harvest well before or well after midsummer; also look for heat-tolerant varieties. Home gardeners usually plant one of the several 'Snowball' varieties or hybrids such as 'Early White Hybrid' and 'Snow Crown Hybrid'. An unusual variety is

'Purple Head', a large plant with a deep purple head that turns green in cooking. 'Romanesco' makes cone-shaped heads of light green flowerets that are less tightly packed than those of other cauliflowers. Considered to have a fine flavor.

Grow cauliflower like broccoli. Start with small plants; space them 1½–2 ft. apart in rows and leave 3 ft. between rows. Be sure to keep plants actively growing; any check during transplanting or later growth is likely to cause premature setting of undersized heads. When heads first appear, tie up the large leaves around them to keep them white. On self-blanching varieties, leaves are supposed to curl over developing heads without assistance, but you may have to help them. Harvest heads as soon as they reach full size. Most varieties are ready in 50 to 100 days after transplanting; overwintering types may take 6 months. Cauliflower is subject to same pests as cabbage.

CAULOPHYLLUM thalictroides

BLUE COHOSH

Berberidaceae

PERENNIAL

ZONES 32, 34–45

PARTIAL SHADE, FULL SHADE

REGULAR WATER

Caulophyllum thalictroides

Native of mountain woodlands in the Northeast, grown for decorative deep blue berries and handsome leaves in wild gardens and shady borders. Massed plantings look best. Grows up to 2 ft. high. Foliage unfurls dark purple, changing to green. Drab clusters of tiny yellow-green flowers at the stem tips in spring. Long-lasting berries appear in fall.

Grows best in deep shade in moist, acidic, well-drained soil rich in organic matter. Propagate by dividing in spring before growth begins, after blooming, or in early fall. Or sow seed in a cold frame as soon as it is ripe, although this method is less reliable. Plants multiply slowly.

CEANOTHUS americanus

NEW JERSEY TEA

Rhamnaceae

DECIDUOUS SHRUB

ZONES 31–32, 34–43

FULL SUN OR LIGHT SHADE

REGULAR TO MODERATE WATER

Ceanothus americanus

Probably the hardiest species in a genus of 60 species and many hybrids grown along the West Coast. Dense, compact, rounded plant to 3 ft. tall, 5 ft. wide. Leaves are dark green, prominently veined. Tiny white flowers in 2-in. clusters at branch tips in summer. Attractive but not showy. Tough, tolerant plant for banks or wild areas. Regular to moderate water. Hybrids between this and tender blue *C. caeruleus* are occasionally tried. One, 'Gloire de Versailles', a tall deciduous shrub with light blue flowers, might survive in the zones noted above with special care.

CEDAR. See CEDRUS

CEDAR, EASTERN RED. See JUNIPERUS virginiana

CEDAR, INCENSE. See CALOCEDRUS decurrens

CEDAR, WESTERN RED. See THUJA plicata

CEDAR OF LEBANON. See CEDRUS libani

CEDRUS

CEDAR

Pinaceae

EVERGREEN TREES

ZONES VARY BY SPECIES

FULL SUN

MODERATE WATER

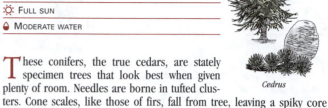

Cedrus

These conifers, the true cedars, are stately specimen trees that look best when given plenty of room. Needles are borne in tufted clusters. Cone scales, like those of firs, fall from tree, leaving a spiky core behind. Male catkins produce prodigious amounts of pollen that may cover you with yellow dust on a windy day. Plant in deep, well-drained soil. All species are deep rooted and drought tolerant once established.

C. atlantica (C. libani atlantica). ATLAS CEDAR. Zones 31, 32, 34. Native to North Africa. Slow to moderate growth to 60 ft. or more. Open, angular in youth. Branches usually get too long and heavy on young trees unless tips are pinched or cut back. Growth naturally less open with age. Less spreading than other true cedars, but still needs 30-ft. circle.

Needles, less than 1 in. long, are bluish green. Varieties: 'Aurea', needles with yellowish tint; 'Glauca', silvery blue; 'Glauca Pendula', weeping form with blue needles; 'Pendula', vertically drooping branches. Untrained, spreading, informally branching plants are sold as "rustics." All types stand up well to hot, humid weather.

C. deodara. DEODAR CEDAR. Zones 31, 32. (Best bet is an extrahardy variety such as 'Shalimar'.) Native to the Himalayas. Fast growing to 80 ft., with 40-ft. spread at ground level. Lower branches sweep down to ground, then upward. Upper branches openly spaced, graceful. Nodding tip identifies it in skyline. Softer, lighter texture than other cedars. Planted in small lawn, it soon overpowers area. You can control spread of tree by cutting new growth of side branches halfway back in late spring. This pruning also makes tree more dense.

Although deodars sold by nurseries are very similar in form, many variations occur in a group of seedlings—from scarecrowlike forms to compact low shrubs. Needles, to 2 in. long, may be green or have blue, gray, or yellow cast. Following three variations are propagated by cuttings or grafting: 'Aurea', with yellow new foliage turning golden green in summer; 'Descanso Dwarf' ('Compacta'), a slow-growing form reaching 15 ft. in 20 years; and 'Pendula' ('Prostrata'), which grows flat on ground or will drape over rock or wall. Deodar cedar can be pruned to grow as spreading low or high shrub. Annual late-spring pruning will keep it in the shape you want. This is the best species for hot, humid climates.

C. libani. CEDAR OF LEBANON. Zones 32, 34. Native to Asia Minor. To 80 ft., but slow—to 15 ft. in 15 years. Variable in habit. Usually a dense, narrow pyramid in youth. Spreads picturesquely as it matures to become majestic skyline tree with long horizontal arms and irregular crown. In young trees, needles, less than 1 in. long, are brightest green of the cedars; in old trees, they are dark gray green. Rather scarce and expensive because of time it requires to reach salable size. Routine garden care. No pruning needed. 'Sargentii' ('Pendula Sargentii') grows even more slowly, has a short trunk and crowded, pendulous branches; choice container or rock garden plant. 'Pendula' is a weeping form.

C. l. stenocoma. Zones 31, 32, 34–41. Hardiest of the cedars. More stiffly branched than species, with good green color.

CELANDINE POPPY. See STYLOPHORUM diphyllum

Celastraceae. This family of evergreen or deciduous woody plants has undistinguished flowers, but fruit is often brightly colored. Bittersweet (*Celastrus*) and *Euonymus* are examples.

C

CELASTRUS

BITTERSWEET

Celastraceae

DECIDUOUS VINES

✂ ZONES VARY BY SPECIES

☼ FULL SUN

💧 REGULAR WATER

Celastrus

Grown principally for clusters of handsome summer fruit—yellow to orange capsules that split open to display brilliant red-coated seeds inside. Branches bearing fruit are much prized for indoor arrangements. Since birds seem uninterested in fruit, display extends into winter. To get fruit, you need a male plant near the female; self-fertile forms of *C. orbiculatus* are available, but this species is so invasive it is no longer recommended for planting.

Vigorous and twining with ropelike branches; need support. Will become tangled mass of intertwining branches unless pruned constantly. Cut out fruiting branches in winter; pinch out tips of vigorous branches in summer.

C. orbiculatus. ORIENTAL BITTERSWEET. Zones 31, 32, 34−43. To 30−40 ft. Leaves roundish, toothed, to 4 in. Fruit on short side shoots is partially obscured until leaves drop. Foliage may turn an attractive yellow in fall. A very aggressive grower that has escaped gardens and become a weed in the northeastern U.S.

C. rosthornianus (C. loeseneri). CHINESE BITTERSWEET. Zones 31, 32, 34. To 20 ft. Dark green, oval leaves to 5 in. long. Fruit heavily borne. Similar to *C. orbiculatus* but not as rampant.

C. scandens. AMERICAN BITTERSWEET. Zones 31, 32, 34−44. Native to eastern U.S. To 20 ft.; even higher if plant has something to grow on. If allowed to climb shrubs or small trees, it can kill them by girdling the stems. Leaves very light green, oval, toothed, to 4 in. Fruit in scattered dense clusters is held above leaves, looks showy before foliage falls.

CELERIAC

Apiaceae (Umbelliferae)

BIENNIAL GROWN AS ANNUAL

✂ ALL ZONES

☼ FULL SUN

💧 KEEP SOIL EVENLY MOIST

Celeriac

A form of celery grown for its large, rounded, edible roots rather than for leafstalks; is usually displayed in markets as "celery root." Roots are peeled, then cooked or used raw in salads.

Growth requirements are same as for celery. Grow plants 6−8 in. apart in rows spaced 1½−2 ft. apart. Harvest when roots are 3 in. across or larger—in about 120 days. 'Giant Prague' and 'Alabaster' are recommended varieties.

CELERY

Apiaceae (Umbelliferae)

BIENNIAL GROWN AS ANNUAL

✂ ALL ZONES

☼ FULL SUN

💧 KEEP SOIL EVENLY MOIST

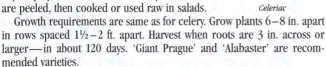

Celery

Needs long period of warm but not high heat; not suited to hot, humid climates. Plant seeds in flats in early spring; where winters are mild, start in summer for winter crop. Seedlings are slow to reach planting size; to save time, purchase seedlings. Plant seedlings 6 in. apart in rows 2 ft. apart. Enrich planting soil with fertilizer. Every 2 to 3 weeks apply liquid fertilizer with irrigation water. Work some soil up around plants as they grow

to keep them upright. For whitened stalks, set bottomless milk carton, tar paper cylinder, or similar device over plants to exclude light from stalks (leaves must have sunlight). Or look for self-blanching varieties. Harvest 105 to 130 days after transplanting. Row covers will exclude many pests.

CELERY ROOT. See CELERIAC

CELOSIA

COCKSCOMB, CHINESE WOOLFLOWER

Amaranthaceae

ANNUAL

✂ ALL ZONES

☼ FULL SUN

💧 MODERATE WATER

Celosia

Richly colored tropical plants, some with flower clusters in bizarre shapes. Although attractive in cut arrangements with other flowers, in gardens the traditional bright-colored cultivars of celosia are most effective by themselves. Newer cultivars in softer colors are better choices to grow with other flowers. Cut blooms can be dried for winter bouquets. Sow seed in place in late spring or early summer, or set out started plants.

There are three kinds of cockscombs, all derived from *C. argentea,* a species with silvery white flowers and narrow leaves to 2 in. or longer. One group, the plume cockscombs (often sold as *C.* 'Plumosa'), has plumy flower clusters. Some of these, like Chinese woolflower (sometimes sold as *C.* 'Childsii'), have flower clusters that look like tangled masses of yarn. Flowers come in brilliant shades of pink, orange red, gold, crimson. Cultivars in gentler colors include apricot orange 'Apricot Brandy' and pastel pink 'Pink Castle'. You can get 2½−3-ft.-high forms or dwarf, more compact varieties. The latter grow about 1 ft. high and bear heavily branched plumes.

Spicata cultivars bear cylindrical flower spikes on 3−3½-ft. stems. Called wheat or foxtail celosias, they include 'Flamingo Purple', deep pink-purple; and 'Pink Tassels', light silvery pink.

The other group is the crested cockscombs (often sold as *C.* 'Cristata'). These have velvety, fan-shaped flower clusters, often much contorted and fluted. Flowers are yellow, orange, crimson, purple, and red. Tall kinds grow to 3 ft., dwarf varieties to 10 in. high.

CELTIS

HACKBERRY

Ulmaceae

DECIDUOUS TREES

✂ ZONES VARY BY SPECIES

☼ ◐ FULL SUN OR PARTIAL SHADE

💧 MODERATE WATER

Celtis

Related to elms and similar to them in most details, but smaller. All have virtue of deep rooting; old trees in narrow planting strips expand in trunk diameter and nearly fill strips without surface roots or any sign of heaving the sidewalk or curb. Good choice for street or lawn tree, even near buildings or paving. Canopy casts moderate shade in spring and summer; leaves turn yellow in fall. Mature trees have picturesque bark with corky warts and ridges. Small berrylike fruit attracts birds.

Hackberry is exceptionally tough, taking strong winds (stake young trees until well established), heat, and dry, alkaline soils. Bare-root plants, especially in larger sizes, sometimes fail to leaf out. Buy in containers or try for small bare-root trees with big root systems.

C. laevigata. SUGARBERRY, SUGAR HACKBERRY. Zones 31, 32, 34–41. Native to southern Midwest and South. Grows to 60 ft. or more with rounded crown. Similar to *C. occidentalis,* but resistant to witches'-broom (ugly clusters of dwarfed twigs). A desirable street or park tree.

C. occidentalis. COMMON HACKBERRY. Zones 32, 34–45. Native from Rocky Mountains to the Atlantic, north to Quebec and south to Alabama. Grows to form rounded crown 50 ft. high or more and nearly as wide. Branches are spreading and sometimes pendulous. Leaves oval, light green, 2–5 in. long, finely toothed on edges. Tree leafs out fairly late. Withstands urban pollution. Endures adverse conditions, including extreme cold, winds, soggy soil. Often disfigured by witches'-broom in the East.

C. sinensis. CHINESE HACKBERRY, YUNNAN HACKBERRY. Zones 31, 32. Similar in growth habit to *C. occidentalis,* but smaller. Leaves to 4 in. long, smoother and glossier than those of other hackberries, with scallop-toothed edges.

CENTAUREA

Asteraceae (Compositae)

PERENNIALS AND ANNUALS

ZONES VARY BY SPECIES

FULL SUN

MODERATE WATER, EXCEPT AS NOTED

Centaurea

Out of some 500 species, only dozen or so are widely cultivated. Of these, annuals are grown mainly for cut flowers; perennial kinds are used principally for soft, silvery foliage. All are relatively easy to grow. For best performance, add lime to acid soils. Sow seeds of annuals or set out plants of perennial kinds in spring (or in fall, in mild-winter climates).

C. americana. BASKET FLOWER. Annual. All zones. Native to central and southwestern U.S. To 5–6 ft. high, with rather rough, oval leaves to 4 in. long. Flower heads to 4 in. wide are rose pink, paler toward center. Good in arrangements, fresh or dried.

C. cineraria (C. candidissima). DUSTY MILLER. Perennial grown as annual in the Northeast. (This common name applies to many plants with whitish foliage; see Dusty Miller, page 216.) Compact plant to 1 ft. or more. Velvety white leaves, mostly in basal clump, are strap shaped, with broad, roundish lobes. Solitary 1-in. flower heads (purple, occasionally yellow) in summer. Trim back after flowering. Attracts bees.

C. cyanus. CORNFLOWER, BACHELOR'S BUTTON. Annual. All zones. To 1–2½ ft., branching if given sufficient space. Narrow gray-green leaves, 2–3 in. long. Flower heads 1–1½ in. across, blue, pink, rose, wine red, and white. Blue varieties are traditional favorites for boutonnieres. 'Jubilee Gem' is bushy, compact, 1 ft. tall, with deep blue flowers; Polka Dot strain has all cornflower colors on 16-in. plants. Sow seed in early spring in cold-winter areas, late summer or fall where winters are mild.

C. dealbata. Perennial. Zones 32, 34–43. To 3 ft.; light green leaves are divided, with oblong segments, to 8 in. long. Flower heads to 1¼ in. across, pink with white center, in midsummer. Tall stems need staking. Good cut flower.

C. hypoleuca 'John Coutts'. Zones 32, 34–43. Resembles *C. montana* but has deeply lobed leaves and deep rose flower heads. Sometimes offered as a variety of *C. dealbata.*

C. macrocephala. Perennial. Zones 32, 34–43. Coarse-foliaged, leafy plant 3–4 ft. tall, with 2-in. clusters of yellow flowers tightly enclosed at the base by papery, overlapping, shiny brown bracts. Flower heads resemble thistles. Use in fresh or dried arrangements.

C. montana. Perennial. Zones 32, 34–43. Clumps 1½–2 ft. tall and as wide, with grayish green leaves to 7 in. long. Flowers resembling ragged 3-in. blue cornflowers top the stems. Divide every other year. Cool-season plant that is very weedy in North, less vigorous in warmer climates. Regular water.

C. moschata (Amberboa moschata). SWEET SULTAN. Annual. All zones. Erect, branching at base, to 2 ft.; Imperialis strain to 3 ft. Green, deeply toothed leaves; thistlelike, 2-in. flower heads mostly in shades of lilac through rose, sometimes white or yellow. Musklike fragrance. Splendid cut flower. Sow seed directly on soil in spring or set out as transplants. Needs lots of heat.

CENTRANTHUS ruber (Valeriana rubra)

RED VALERIAN, JUPITER'S BEARD

Valerianaceae

PERENNIAL

ZONES 32, 34–43

FULL SUN OR PARTIAL SHADE

MODERATE TO LITTLE WATER

Centranthus ruber

Trouble-free plant. Self-sows prolifically because of small dandelion-like parachutes on seeds. Forms a bushy clump with upright stems to 3 ft. high bearing 4-in.-long bluish green leaves. Small, dusty crimson or rose pink flowers about ½ in. long in dense terminal clusters in late spring, early summer. 'Albus' is white; 'Atrococcineus' is deep red. Plants give long, showy bloom in difficult situations. Will grow in poor, dry soils; accept almost any condition except damp shade. Cut off old flowering stems to shape plants, prolong bloom, and prevent seeding.

CEPHALANTHUS occidentalis

BUTTONBUSH

Rubiaceae

DECIDUOUS SHRUB

ZONES 32, 34–41

FULL SUN OR LIGHT SHADE

MOIST TO WET SOIL

Cephalanthus occidentalis

Remarkable for wide distribution—eastern Canada to Florida, Minnesota south through Oklahoma and west to California, with outposts in Cuba, Mexico, and Asia. Grows 3–15 ft. or taller, with rounded, rather open habit and bright green paired or whorled leaves 2–6 in. long. Leafs out late in spring. Creamy white, slender-tubed flowers crowded in rounded, 1–1½-in.-wide heads in late summer. Projecting stigmas produce a pincushion effect. Attracts butterflies. Useful for naturalizing in wet areas.

CEPHALARIA gigantea

GIANT SCABIOUS, YELLOW SCABIOUS

Dipsacaceae

PERENNIAL

ZONES 32, 34–45

FULL SUN

REGULAR WATER

Cephalaria gigantea

Native to the Caucasus and northern Turkey. Clumps of sturdy stems can exceed 6 ft. in height, but stand erect and require no staking. Coarse featherlike leaves grow up to 16 in. long. Round pale yellow flowers open to 2 in. across in summer with larger, radiating outer florets. Requiring only moderately moist and fertile soil, cephalaria is best suited, because of its striking size, to larger herbaceous borders, informal gardens, and parks.

FOR INFORMATION ON SELECTING PLANTS

PLEASE SEE PAGES 47–112

C

CEPHALOTAXUS

PLUM YEW

Cephalotaxaceae

EVERGREEN SHRUBS OR TREES

🌡 ZONES VARY BY SPECIES

☀️ ◐ PARTIAL SHADE IN HOT-SUMMER AREAS

💧 MODERATE WATER

Cephalotaxus

S low-growing plants related to yews *(Taxus);* differ from yews in larger, brighter green needles and (on female plants only) larger fruit that resembles small green or brown plums. May not bear fruit in all areas. Very heat tolerant.

C. fortunei. CHINESE PLUM YEW. Zones 31, 32, 34, 39. Big shrub or small tree to 10 ft. tall (rarely more), with soft, needlelike leaves up to 3½ in. long.

C. harringtonia. Zones 31, 32, 34–41. Spreading shrub or small tree to 10 ft. (possibly 20 ft.) tall, with needles 1–2½ in. long. Spreading ('Prostrata') and columnar ('Fastigiata') forms are sometimes seen. When young, the latter resembles Irish yew (*Taxus baccata* 'Fastigiata'). 'Korean Gold' has golden new foliage, columnar habit. 'Duke Gardens' is low and wide spreading, to 3 ft. high and 4 ft. across.

CERASTIUM tomentosum

SNOW-IN-SUMMER

Caryophyllaceae

PERENNIAL

🌡 ZONES 32, 34–45

☀️ ◐ PARTIAL SHADE IN HOT CLIMATES

💧 REGULAR MOISTURE FOR FAST GROWTH

Cerastium tomentosum

L ow-growing plant that performs reliably everywhere except in hot, humid South. Spreading, dense, tufty mats of silvery gray, ¾-in.-long leaves. Masses of snow-white flowers, ½–¾ in. across, in early summer. Plant grows 6–8 in. high, spreads 2–3 ft. in a year. Use as ground cover on slopes or level ground, as bulb cover, in rock gardens, as edging for paths, between stepping-stones. Avoid extensive planting in prominent situations, since plant is not long lived.

In warmest areas, provide some shade. Takes any soil as long as drainage is good: standing water causes root rot. Set divisions or plants 1–1½ ft. apart, or sow seed. Feed two or three times a year to speed growth. Shear off faded flower clusters. May look a bit shabby in winter but revives rapidly in spring. Divide in fall or early spring.

CERATOSTIGMA plumbaginoides

DWARF PLUMBAGO

Plumbaginaceae

PERENNIAL GROUND COVER

🌡 ZONES 32, 34–41

☀️ ◐ FULL SUN OR PARTIAL SHADE

💧 MODERATE WATER

Ceratostigma plumbaginoides

W iry-stemmed ground cover 6–12 in. high. In loose soil and where growing season is long, spreads rapidly by underground stems, eventually covering large areas. Bronzy green to dark green, 3-in.-long leaves turn reddish brown with frosts. Intense blue, ½-in. phloxlike flowers from July until first frosts. Most effective in early or midautumn, when blue flowers contrast with red autumn foliage. Blooms well only in areas

with a long growing season. Semievergreen only in the mildest-winter areas; best to cut back after bloom. Dies back elsewhere; leafs out late in spring. In coldest climates, apply a winter mulch. When plants show signs of aging, remove old crowns and replace with rooted stems. Often sold as *Plumbago larpentae*.

For Cape plumbago, see *Plumbago auriculata*.

CERCIDIPHYLLUM japonicum

KATSURA TREE

Cercidiphyllaceae

DECIDUOUS TREE

🌡 ZONES 32, 34–41

☀️ ◐ FULL SUN OR LIGHT SHADE

💧 REGULAR WATER

Cercidiphyllum japonicum

N ative to Japan. A specimen tree of many virtues if given regular moisture, especially during youth, and sheltered from intense sun and wind. Light, dainty branch and leaf pattern. Foliage, always fresh looking, changes color during the growing season: new growth emerges reddish purple, becomes bluish green in summer, then turns yellow to apricot in autumn. To enhance fall color, water less frequently in late summer. Trees grown in acid soil will have the best color. Foliage of some katsura trees smells like burnt sugar on warm autumn days during leaf fall.

Rather slow growing, eventually to 40 ft. or more. Pyramidal form when young; growth may remain upright or become more spreading with maturity. Some specimens have single trunk, but multiple trunks are more usual. Nearly round, 2–4-in. leaves neatly spaced in pairs along arching branches. Flowers inconspicuous. Brown bark somewhat shaggy on old trees. No serious pest or disease problems. There is a weeping form known as forma *pendulum*. Var. *magnificum* is smaller, to 30 ft., with larger leaves to 5 in. long.

CERCIS

REDBUD

Fabaceae (Leguminosae)

DECIDUOUS SHRUBS OR TREES

🌡 ZONES VARY BY SPECIES

☀️ ◐ FULL SUN OR LIGHT SHADE

💧 REGULAR WATER, EXCEPT AS NOTED

Cercis

V alued for flowers, fruit, foliage. Clusters of small, sweet pea–shaped, rosy to purplish pink blossoms in early spring. Where plant is adapted, blooms are borne in great profusion on bare twigs, branches, sometimes even on main trunk. Flowers are followed by clusters of flat, beanlike pods that persist into winter. Attractive broad, rounded leaves are heart shaped at base. All provide fall color with first frosts. All are attractive in naturalized settings.

C. canadensis. EASTERN REDBUD. Zones 31, 32, 34–41. Native to eastern U.S. Largest (to 25–35 ft. tall) and fastest growing of the redbuds, and the most apt to take tree form. Round headed but with horizontally tiered branches in age. Rich green, 3–6-in.-long leaves have pointed tips. Small (½-in.-long), rosy pink flowers. Needs some winter chill to flower profusely. Valuable for filling the gap between the early-flowering fruit trees (flowering peach, flowering plum) and the crabapples and late-flowering cherries. Effective as specimen or understory tree. Varieties include 'Alba' (white flowers); 'Flame' (double pink flowers); 'Forest Pansy' (purple foliage, needs some shade in Zone 31 and warmer parts of

Zone 32); 'Rubye Atkinson' (pure pink flowers); 'Silver Cloud' (leaves marbled with white); and 'Wither's Pink Charm' (bright pink flowers).

C. chinensis. CHINESE REDBUD. Zones 32, 34. Native to China, Japan. Seen mostly as light, open shrub to 10–12 ft. Flower clusters (3–5 in. long) are deep rose, almost rosy purple. Leaves are sometimes glossier and brighter green than those of *C. canadensis,* with transparent line around the edge. 'Avondale' is a superior form with deep purple flowers. 'Alba' has white flowers. Full sun.

C. siliquastrum. JUDAS TREE. Zone 32. Native to Europe and western Asia. Performs best with some winter chill. Generally of shrubby habit to 25 ft., occasionally a taller, slender tree with single trunk. Purplish rose, ½-in.-long flowers; 3–5-in. leaves, deeply heart shaped at base, rounded or notched at tip. Fairly drought tolerant.

CHAENOMELES

FLOWERING QUINCE

Rosaceae

DECIDUOUS SHRUBS

🌡 ZONES 31, 32, 34–43

☀ FULL SUN

💧 REGULAR TO MODERATE WATER

Chaenomeles

Bloom time—as early as March in the warmest parts of the region—is the only time flowering quince calls attention to itself. The plant is bland-looking the rest of the year, though judicious pruning improves its looks. Blossoms are 1½–2½ in. across, single to semidouble or double, in colors ranging from soft to vibrant.

Practically indestructible shrubs with shiny green leaves (red tinged when young) and varying growth habit. Some grow to 10 ft. and spread wider; others are compact and low growing. Most are thorny, a few thornless. Some bear small quincelike fruit. All are useful as hedges and barriers. Easy to grow; tolerant of extremes in cold and heat, light to heavy soil. In humid regions, lower leaves may drop in summer. Prune any time to shape, limit growth, or gain special effects. Good time to prune is in bud and bloom season—use cut branches for indoor arrangements. New growth that follows will bear next year's flowers. Blossoms attract birds.

The following list of choice varieties notes both height and flower color. Tall types are 6 ft. and over; low are 2–3 ft. All are garden hybrids (some formerly called *Cydonia*); specialists can furnish even more varieties.

'Apple Blossom'. Tall. White and pink.

'Cameo'. Low, compact. Double, soft apricot pink.

'Contorta'. Low. White to pink; twisted branches. Good as bonsai.

'Corallina' ('Coral Glow'). Tall. Reddish orange.

'Coral Sea'. Tall. Large, coral pink.

'Enchantress'. Tall. Large, shell pink.

'Falconet Charlot'. Tall, thornless. Double, salmon pink.

'Hollandia'. Tall. Large red flowers; reblooms in fall.

'Jet Trail'. Low. Pure white.

'Low-n-White'. Low, spreading. White.

'Minerva'. Low, spreading. Cherry red.

'Nivalis'. Tall. Large, pure white.

'Orange Delight' ('Maulei'). Low, spreading. Orange to orange red.

'Pink Beauty'. Tall. Purplish pink.

'Pink Lady'. Low. Rose pink blooms from deeper-colored buds.

'Red Ruffles'. Tall, almost thornless. Large, ruffled, red.

'Rowallane'. Low. Darkest red.

'Snow'. Tall. Large, pure white.

'Stanford Red'. Low, almost thornless. Tomato red.

'Super Red'. Tall, upright. Large, bright red.

'Texas Scarlet'. Low. Tomato red.

'Toyo Nishiki'. Tall. Pink, white, pink and white, red all on same branch.

CHAMAECYPARIS

FALSE CYPRESS

Cupressaceae

EVERGREEN SHRUBS OR TREES

🌡 ZONES VARY BY SPECIES

☀ ◐ FULL SUN OR PARTIAL SHADE

💧 REGULAR WATER

Chamaecyparis

False cypress is sometimes mistaken for arborvitae *(Thuja),* but leaf undersides of false cypress have white lines, while those of arborvitae are entirely green. Most false cypresses have two distinct types of leaves: juvenile and mature. Juvenile leaves (short, needlelike, soft but often prickly) appear on young plants and some new growth of larger trees. Mature foliage consists of tiny, scalelike, overlapping leaves. Cones are small and round.

All of the many varieties sold are forms of five species—one from the eastern U.S., two from the western U.S., and two from Japan. New varieties appear each year, while older ones lose market share. Many closely resemble each other and are often mislabeled. Many dwarf and variegated kinds are available, providing rich source of bonsai and rock garden material. All need good drainage and protection from wind.

C. lawsoniana. PORT ORFORD CEDAR, LAWSON CEDAR. Zones 31, 32, 34–41. The 60-ft. pyramidal western timber tree with lacy, drooping foliage is seldom seen in gardens. Blue-green forms include 'Allumii', slow growing to 30 ft.; 'Ellwoodii', dense, compact growth to 6–8 ft.; and 'Wisselii', to 15–18 ft., with twisted, irregular growth. Golden-leafed forms are 'Golden King', 'Lutea', and 'Stewartii', all conical to 30 ft. or more.

C. nootkatensis. NOOTKA CYPRESS, ALASKA CEDAR. Zones 32, 34–43. Pyramidal tree to 80 ft., coarser than *C. lawsoniana;* stands poorer soil. 'Pendula', a weeping form, slowly grows to 10 ft., possibly to 30 ft.; it is the form most commonly sold in the eastern U.S.

C. obtusa. HINOKI FALSE CYPRESS. Zones 31, 32, 34–45. There are dozens of golden, dwarf, and fern-leafed forms, but two varieties are the most important in landscaping. 'Gracilis', slender hinoki cypress, has slender, upright growth to 20 ft. with nodding branch tips; 'Nana Gracilis' is a miniature of the former to 4 ft. in height.

C. pisifera. SAWARA FALSE CYPRESS. Zones 31, 32, 34–45. Japanese tree to 20–30 ft., rarely seen except in its garden varieties. 'Cyano-Viridis' ('Boulevard') is a slow, dense bush to 6–8 ft., with silvery blue-green foliage; 'Filifera', to 8 ft., has drooping, threadlike branchlets; 'Filifera Aurea' has similar branchlets in yellow.

C. thyoides. WHITE CEDAR. Zones 31, 32, 34, 36–42. Eastern U.S. timber tree, columnar to 75 ft. tall, found in wet sites in the wild. Garden forms include 'Andelyensis', dense, columnar, gray-green shrub to 10 ft., turning bronze in cold weather; and 'Heather Bun', broader than 'Andelyensis', turning intense plum purple in winter.

CHAMAEMELUM nobile (Anthemis nobilis)

ROMAN CHAMOMILE

Asteraceae (Compositae)

EVERGREEN PERENNIAL

🌡 ZONES 31, 32, 34–43

☀ ◐ FULL SUN OR PARTIAL SHADE

💧 MODERATE WATER

Chamaemelum nobile

Forms soft-textured, spreading, 3–12-in. mat of bright light green, finely cut, aromatic leaves. Most commonly grown form has small yellow buttons of summer-blooming flower heads; some forms have little daisylike flower heads. Makes lawn substitute for nontraffic areas if mowed or sheared occasionally. 'Treneague' is a nonflowering variety that needs no mowing. Also used between stepping-stones. Plant divisions 1 ft. apart.

C

Chamomile tea is made from dried flower heads, but sweeter, more flavorful tea comes from flowers of German chamomile, *Matricaria recutita* (*M. chamomilla*).

CHAMOMILE. See CHAMAEMELUM nobile; MATRICARIA recutita

CHARD. See SWISS CHARD

CHASMANTHIUM
latifolium (Uniola latifolia)

SEA OATS, BAMBOO GRASS

Poaceae (Gramineae)

PERENNIAL GRASS

🌡 ZONES 31, 33. 34–43

☼ ◑ PARTIAL SHADE IN HOT-SUMMER AREAS

💧 REGULAR WATER

Chasmanthium latifolium

Ornamental clump-forming grass. Broad, bamboolike leaves are topped by arching flowering stems, 2–5 ft. tall, carrying showers of silvery green flower spikelets that resemble flattened clusters of oats (or flattened armadillos). Flowering stems dry to an attractive greenish straw color and look good in dried arrangements. Clumps broaden slowly and are not aggressive like bamboo. Leaves turn brown in winter, when plants should be cut back almost to ground. Divide clumps when they become overgrown and flowering diminishes. Stake if flowering stems sprawl too far. Self-sows extensively and can become invasive.

CHASTE TREE. See VITEX

CHECKERBERRY. See GAULTHERIA procumbens

CHECKERED LILY. See FRITILLARIA meleagris

CHEILANTHES

LIP FERN, RESURRECTION FERN

Pteridaceae (Adiantiaceae)

PERENNIALS

🌡 ZONES VARY BY SPECIES

◑ ☼ PARTIAL SHADE TO FULL SUN

💧 LESS THAN REGULAR WATER

Cheilanthes

More than 150 species of ferns native throughout the world. Ground dwellers, often growing between rocks in dry places. Rolled down leaf edges or lips protect reproductive units, located at edges of the fronds. A collector's plant, occasionally grown in dry spots in stone walls or rock gardens where a species is native. Easy to grow in the right conditions. Cultivate in full sun in very well drained, sandy or gravelly soil rich in humus. Avoid overwatering, especially in winter, and shelter from snow and rain. Increase the number of plants by sowing spores as soon as they are ripe, or carefully dividing the thick roots, which resent disturbance, in spring.

C. lanosa. HAIRY LIP FERN. Zones 31, 32, 34, 39. Grows to 12 in. tall and 16 in. wide. Deciduous leaves like deep gray-green lances, 6–12 in. long and about 2 in. wide. Leaf tops have few hairs, undersides woolly with glossy white hairs. Purple-tinged black stems. Often confused with the next species in nurseries.

C. tomentosa. WOOLLY LIP FERN. Zones 31, 32, 34, 39. Forms a beautiful clump of erect, deciduous leaves 12–14 in. high, and with dense mats of white to gray hairs and scales below. Easy to grow.

CHEIRANTHUS. See ERYSIMUM

CHELIDONIUM majus

GREATER CELANDINE

Papaveraceae

PERENNIAL OR BIENNIAL

🌡 ZONES 31, 32, 34–41

☼ ◑ TOLERATES SUN IN COOL CLIMATES

💧 REGULAR WATER

🜄 SAP CAUSES SKIN IRRITATION

Chelidonium majus

Grows 2–3 ft. tall, with several erect stems rising from the rootstock. Leaves are attractively cut and lobed, smooth bright green. Profuse yellow to orange-yellow flowers to 1 in. wide; summer bloom. Orange sap is irritating to the skin. Self-sows freely and naturalizes (sometimes too well). Double-flowered 'Flore Pleno' also seeds itself freely; var. *laciniatum* has deeply cut leaves. All forms are best in wild gardens.

CHELONE

TURTLEHEAD

Scrophulariaceae

PERENNIALS

🌡 ZONES 31, 32, 34–43

☼ ◑ FULL SUN OR LIGHT SHADE

💧 AMPLE WATER

Chelone

Leafy, clump-forming perennials related to penstemon. All are native to the eastern U.S. and grow in damp places in sun or light shade. Frequently used in bog gardens. All bloom in late summer and autumn. Common name comes from the oddly formed flowers—inch-long, puffy, and two lipped, with a fancied resemblance to a turtle's or snake's head. Useful for cut flowers, shade gardens, wild gardens.

C. glabra. Grows 2–3 ft. tall, occasionally much taller. Flowers are white or palest pink.

C. lyonii. Reaches 3 ft. tall. Rose pink flowers. 'Hot Lips' is lipstick pink.

C. obliqua. To 2–2½ ft. tall, with deep pink flowers. The latest bloomer among these three species. 'Alba' is a compact, white-flowered variety.

Chenopodiaceae. The goosefoot family contains many annuals and perennials (some of them weeds) and a few shrubs. Flowers are inconspicuous. Many will tolerate salty or alkaline soil, and some are useful food plants, notably beet and spinach.

CHENOPODIUM
bonus-henricus

GOOD KING HENRY, WILD SPINACH

Chenopodiaceae

PERENNIAL

🌡 ZONES 31, 32, 34–41

☼ ◑ FULL SUN TO PARTIAL SHADE

💧 REGULAR WATER

Chenopodium bonus-henricus

Grown for its dark green, edible leaves, Good King Henry is native to Europe but naturalized in eastern North America. Plants form low clumps of arrow-shaped leaves that reach 1 ft. across. Clumps topped by 2–2½-ft. spikes of tiny, insignificant flowers in spring, which can be harvested and prepared like asparagus. Young leaves are best: Harvest them in spring. Best in rich, evenly moist soil and full sun, but tolerates poor soil and partial shade. Grow in edible landscaping plantings or at one end of the vegetable garden, to avoid disturbing plants in spring when the rest of the garden is being prepared.

CHERRY

Rosaceae

DECIDUOUS FRUIT TREES

ZONES VARY BY TYPE

FULL SUN

REGULAR, DEEP WATERING

Cherry

Cherries belong to the genus Prunus of the rose family *Rosaceae*. Fruits are small, round to heart shaped and vary in color from red to yellow to black. They are botanically designated drupes (stone fruits), as are the closely related peach, apricot, and plum.

There are hundreds of cherry varieties, mostly derived from two species, the *P. avium* (sweet cherry) and the *P. cerasus* (sour cherries).

Sweet cherries are classified as Hearts or Genas with soft flesh and a heart shape and Biggerreaus with crisp, sweet flesh. Sour cherries are divided into the Amarelles with red skin and yellow flesh, like the variety 'Montmorency' and Morellos with dark skin and acid flesh, like the cherry 'English Morello'.

Both of these species are thought to have originated in western Asia and eastern Europe, but there are a number of species of American cherries that include the chokecherries, pin cherry, and wild black cherries. The varieties called dukes are considered crosses of the sweet and sour cherries.

Rootstocks. There are two major rootstocks, the 'Mazzard' and the 'Mahaleb'. Both sweets and sours are budded to the 'Mazzard', which is suitable for heavier soils with some nematode and oak root fungus resistance. Most sour cherries are budded to the Mahaleb and result in a larger tree more tolerant of wet ground. It will also bear earlier than the Mazzard. If there are light and dry soils, the Mahaleb is preferred. There are also other cherry rootstocks that produce more dwarf size plants.

Site & Location. Select a well-drained deep clay to loam soil with a pH of 6 to 8. Poor soil should be amended with organic matter. Sweet cherries particularly must have good soil to produce good fruit. If the site is sloping, plant the tree near the top of the slope for good air drainage. Frost pockets will develop at the bottom.

Tree Development and Cropping. From a 1- or 2-year-old tree, a sweet cherry will begin to crop 3 to 4 years after planting with an increase for the next 10 to 12 years and, when mature, will produce 3 to 4 bushels. The sour cherry tree will begin to crop in 2 to 3 years and will ultimately produce a bushel or more. With proper nutrition, sweets should grow 2 to 3 ft. for the first few years and sours should produce 1 to 2 ft. of new shoots. When fruiting begins, production of shoot growth will slow down.

Pollination. Sour cherries, like 'Montmorency', 'Early Richmond', and 'North Star', are considered self-pollinating and do not need a pollinator. However, sweet cherries will not set fruit unless they receive pollen from a specific variety. One variety, 'Stella', is somewhat self-pollinating but will produce more with a pollinator. These varieties will not pollinate each other: 'Bing', 'Lambert', 'Royal Ann', and 'Emperor Francis'. Varieties that can pollinate each other are 'Windsor', 'Schmidt', and 'Hedelfingen'. It also must be considered that when two compatible varieties are selected, the bloom period must overlap. Consult nursery catalogs or a local extension agent for suitable varieties.

Pests and diseases. Birds can quickly destroy a crop of cherries, and netting may become necessary. Some success has been reported by planting mulberries that ripen about the same time at a distance as a decoy. Some insects to be concerned about are the black cherry aphid found in curled leaves, tent caterpillars that will strip a limb in a day, cherry maggots, borers, and scale. Diseases like the fungus cherry leaf spot, also called shot hole, can defoliate a young tree and make it more susceptible to winter injury. Repeated defoliation will kill the tree. Brown rot fungus, the plague of stone fruits, must be fought. The spray schedule of the local extension service publications can be consulted.

SOUR CHERRY VARIETIES

'Montmorency' is bright red with yellow flesh. A premier pie-making cherry it has some resistance to cracking. Late ripening.

'Early Richmond' is an old variety with bright red fruit that ripens usually a week before Montmorency. The tree often sets a crop the second year after planting. Late ripening.

'North Star', a natural dwarf that matures at 10 ft., is a deep crimson color and it has some resistance to cherry leaf spot. Late ripening.

'English Morello' also remains small in size and the fruit is nearly black with dark flesh and juice. It freezes well. Late ripening.

SWEET CHERRY VARIETIES

'Bing' is large, nearly black in color with dark flesh, and is considered the premier dessert cherry. Heart-shaped, it needs a pollinator like 'Black Tartarian'. Midseason ripening.

'Black Tartarian' is smaller than the 'Bing' and is purplish black. Like the 'Bing', it may crack in wet weather. It is a good pollinator. Early ripening.

'Emperor Francis' is large and yellow with a pink blush. The flesh is very sweet and there is some resistance to cracking. Midseason ripening.

'Hedelfingen' is a large nearly black cherry with sweet, dark flesh. It resists cracking and bacterial canker. A good pollinator, it may be biennial bearing. Late ripening.

'Lambert' bears heavy crops annually and is large, purple-red in color and has pale flesh. Very sweet and juicy, it is a rival for the 'Bing'. Late ripening

'Royal Ann' ('Napoleon') is yellow skinned with bright red cheeks. Birds are not as attracted to the fruit—perhaps because of the yellow color. It is bud tender and may crack. Midseason ripening.

'Rainier' is yellow with a pink blush and resists cracking. 'Royal Ann' is a good pollinator for this variety. The flower buds are more frost hardy than other varieties. Early ripening.

'Schmidt' is a large cherry with black skin and reddish flesh. It is susceptible to brown rot and can be a shy bearer. Excellent fresh and frozen. Midseason ripening.

'Stella', like 'Lambert', is large with black skin and a heart shape. It is a good pollinator for other varieties. Midseason ripening.

CHERRY, FLOWERING. See PRUNUS

CHERRY PLUM. See PLUM and PRUNE; PRUNUS cerasifera

CHERVIL. See ANTHRISCUS cerefolium

CHESTNUT. See CASTANEA

CHICKABIDDY. See ASARINA

CHICORY

Asteraceae (Compositae)

PERENNIAL HERB

ZONES 31, 32, 34–45

FULL SUN

REGULAR TO MODERATE WATER

Chicory

Botanically known as *Cichorium intybus*. Dried ground roots can be roasted and used as substitute for coffee. Wild form grows as 3–6-ft. perennial roadside weed and is recognized by its pretty sky blue flowers that close by midday. Grown for its leaves, it is known as chicory, endive, or curly endive; grown for its blanched sprouts, it's known as Belgian or French endive, endive hearts, or witloof ("white leaf"). For culture, see Endive.

Radicchio is the name given to a number of red-leafed chicories grown for salads. 'Rossa de Verona', or 'Rouge de Verone', is the best known. It forms lettucelike heads that color to a deep rosy red as weather grows cold in autumn or winter. Slight bitterness lessens as color deepens. Sow in early summer to mature in cold weather. Sow seeds of the similar 'Giulio' in spring to harvest in summer, 'Cesare' in midsummer for fall, winter harvest.

CHILEAN JASMINE. See MANDEVILLA laxa

C

CHIMONANTHUS praecox
(C. fragrans, Meratia praecox)

WINTERSWEET

Calycanthaceae

DECIDUOUS SHRUB

ZONES 31, 32, 34

FULL SUN OR PARTIAL SHADE

MODERATE WATER

Chimonanthus praecox

Native to China and Japan. Winter-blooming shrub with wonderfully spicy-scented blossoms. Needs some winter cold. Tall, open, slow growing to 10–15 ft. high and 6–8 ft. wide, with many basal stems. Flowers appear on leafless branches late winter to early spring, depending on climate; bloom lasts for many months if not frosted. Blossoms are 1 in. wide, with pale yellow outer sepals and smaller, chocolate-colored inner sepals. Tapered leaves are rough to the touch, medium green, 3–6 in. long and half that wide; turn yellow green in fall. 'Luteus' has conspicuous bright yellow flowers.

Plant in sheltered site to prevent frost damage, and locate plant where its winter fragrance can be enjoyed. Some possible locations: near a much-used entrance or path, under a bedroom window. Keep plant lower by cutting back during bloom; shape as a small tree by removing excess basal stems; rejuvenate leggy plant by trimming to within a foot of the ground in late winter. Needs good drainage.

CHINA ASTER. See CALLISTEPHUS chinensis

CHINA FIR. See CUNNINGHAMIA lanceolata

CHINA LILY. See RHODEA japonica

CHINESE BELLFLOWER. See ABUTILON

CHINESE CABBAGE

Brassicaceae (Cruciferae)

BIENNIAL GROWN AS ANNUAL

ALL ZONES

TOLERATES LIGHT SHADE IN HOT CLIMATES

REGULAR WATER

Chinese cabbage

Makes head somewhat looser than usual cabbage; sometimes called celery cabbage. Raw or cooked, it has more delicate flavor than cabbage. There are two kinds: pe-tsai, with tall, narrow heads; and wong bok, with short, broad heads. Favored pe-tsai variety is 'Michihli'; wong bok varieties include 'Springtime', 'Summertime', and 'Wintertime' (early to late maturing). Definitely cool-season crop; very prone to bolt to seed in hot weather or in long days of spring and early summer. In cold-winter regions, plant seeds directly in open ground in July; in August or September in milder climates. Sow seeds thinly in rows 2–2½ ft. apart and thin plants to 1½–2 ft. apart. Heads should be ready in 70 to 80 days. Subject to same pests as cabbage.

CHINESE CHIVES. See ALLIUM tuberosum

CHINESE ELM. See ULMUS parvifolia

CHINESE FLAME TREE. See KOELREUTERIA bipinnata

CHINESE FORGET-ME-NOT. See CYNOGLOSSUM amabile

CHINESE GROUND ORCHID. See BLETILLA striata

CHINESE LANTERN. See ABUTILON

CHINESE LANTERN PLANT. See PHYSALIS alkekengi

CHINESE MAGNOLIA VINE. See SCHISANDRA chinensis

CHINESE PARASOL TREE. See FIRMIANA simplex

CHINESE PARSLEY. See CORIANDRUM sativum

CHINESE REDBUD. See CERCIS chinensis

CHINESE RHUBARB. See RHEUM palmatum

CHINESE SCHOLAR TREE. See SOPHORA japonica

CHINESE SWEET GUM. See LIQUIDAMBAR formosana

CHINESE WOOLFLOWER. See CELOSIA

CHIONANTHUS

FRINGE TREE

Oleaceae

DECIDUOUS SHRUBS OR SMALL TREES

ZONES VARY BY SPECIES

FULL SUN

REGULAR TO MODERATE WATER

Chionanthus retusus

Spectacular flowering plants requiring some winter chill. Earn common name from narrow, fringelike white petals on flowers that are borne in impressive, ample, lacy clusters. There are male and female plants. Males have larger flowers. If both are present, female plants produce fruit like clusters of small dark olives, favored by birds. Broad leaves turn bright to deep yellow in fall. Both species tolerate city pollution.

C. pygmaeus. DWARF FRINGE TREE. Zones 31, 32. Similar to *C. virginicus* but smaller and less hardy. To about 4 ft. high, covered with clusters of white flowers in spring.

C. retusus. CHINESE FRINGE TREE. Zones 31, 32, 34, 39. Grows to about 20 ft. tall; not quite as wide spreading as *C. virginicus.* Usually seen as a big multistemmed shrub, but can be grown as small tree. Produces pure white flower clusters to 4 in. long in late spring or early summer, 2 to 3 weeks before *C. virginicus.* Magnificent in bloom, something like a tremendous white lilac. Handsome gray-brown bark (sometimes golden on young stems) provides winter interest.

C. virginicus. FRINGE TREE. Zones 31, 32, 34–41. Native Pennsylvania to Florida and Texas. Leaves and flower clusters often twice as big as those of *C. retusus,* and the blooms appear a little later. Slightly fragrant flowers are more greenish than white. Can reach 30 ft., but in cultivation usually 12–20 ft. high with equal spread. Variation in habit, from very shrubby and open to more treelike. In Zones 38–41, where it grows very slowly (the most you can hope for is 12 ft. in 10 years), it is best used as an airy shrub; blooms profusely when just 2–3 ft. tall. One of the last deciduous plants to leaf out in spring. Susceptible to borers when growing in dry sites.

CHIONODOXA

GLORY-OF-THE-SNOW

Liliaceae

BULBS

ZONES 31, 32, 34–43

PARTIAL SHADE

REGULAR WATER DURING GROWTH AND BLOOM

Chionodoxa luciliae

Native to alpine meadows in Asia Minor. Charming small bulbous plants 4–6 in. high; among first to bloom in spring. Narrow basal leaves, two or three to each flower stalk. Blue or white, short, tubular,

open flowers in loose spikes. Plant bulbs 3 in. deep in September or October in half shade; keep moist. Under favorable conditions, plants self-sow freely.

C. forbesii. (**C. luciliae** of gardens). Most generally available. Brilliant blue, white-centered, starlike flowers. 'Alba' offers larger white flowers; 'Gigantea' has larger leaves, larger flowers of violet blue with white throat. 'Rosea' has pink flowers.

C. sardensis. Deep, true gentian blue flowers with very small white eye.

CHIVES

Liliaceae

PERENNIAL HERB

ZONES 31, 32, 34–45

FULL SUN OR LIGHT SHADE

REGULAR WATER

Chives

Leaves are grasslike in general appearance but round and hollow in cross section. Clumps may reach 2 ft. in height but are usually shorter. Cloverlike, rose purple spring flowers are carried in clusters atop thin stems. Plant is pretty enough to use as edging in sunny or lightly shaded flower border or herb garden. Does best in moist, fairly rich soil. May be increased by divisions or grown from seed. Evergreen (or nearly so) in mild regions; goes dormant where winters are severe, but small divisions may be potted in rich soil and grown on kitchen windowsill. Chop or snip leaves; use as garnish or add to salads, cream cheese, cottage cheese, egg dishes, gravies, and soups for delicate onion-like flavor. For garlic chives (Chinese chives), see *Allium tuberosum*.

CHOCOLATE LILY. See FRITILLARIA camschatcensis

CHOKEBERRY. See ARONIA

CHOKECHERRY. See PRUNUS virginiana

CHRISTMAS FERN. See POLYSTICHUM acrostichoides

CHRISTMAS ROSE. See HELLEBORUS niger

CHRYSANTHEMUM

Asteraceae (Compositae)

PERENNIALS AND ANNUALS

ZONES VARY BY SPECIES

BEST IN FULL SUN, EXCEPT AS NOTED

REGULAR WATER, EXCEPT AS NOTED

There are about 160 species of chrysanthemum, mostly native to China, Japan, and Europe. Included are some of most popular and useful of garden plants—top favorite being *C. grandiflorum*, whose modern descendants are known as florists' chrysanthemums. Botanists have split *Chrysanthemum* into many new genera. More and more growers are using the new names but because many gardeners still use the old names we have included all the species here. The new names are listed immediately after the old.

Chrysanthemum

C. arcticum (Arctanthemum arcticum). Perennial. Zones 32, 34–45. Very hardy autumn bloomer; forms clump with stems 6–12 in. high. Spoon-shaped leaves, usually three-lobed, 1–3 in. long, leathery in texture. White or pinkish flower heads 1–2 in. across. Developed from this species is a group of hybrids known as Northland daisies, with single flowers 3 in. across or more, in shades of pink, rose, rosy purple, and yellow. *C. arcticum* itself is primarily rock garden plant. Taller-growing varieties serve best in borders.

C. balsamita (Tanacetum balsamita). COSTMARY. Perennial. Zones 31, 32, 34–41. Weedy plant with sweet-scented foliage that justifies its presence in herb garden (use leaves in salads and sachets). If leggy stems are cut back, gray-green basal leaves with tiny scalloped margins can make herb garden edging. Divide clumps and reset divisions in late summer or fall.

C. carinatum. SUMMER CHRYSANTHEMUM, TRICOLOR CHRYSANTHEMUM. Annual. All zones. Grows 1–3 ft. high, about 3 ft. wide. Summer and fall bloom; in mild-winter areas, can be planted for winter and spring bloom. Deeply cut foliage; showy, single, daisylike, 2-in.-wide flower heads in purple, orange, scarlet, salmon, rose, yellow, and white, with contrasting bands around dark center. Satisfactory, long-lasting cut flowers. Sow seeds in spring either in pots or in open ground. Where winters are mild, do sowing in fall. Court Jesters is an excellent strain.

C. coccineum (Tanacetum coccineum, Pyrethrum roseum). PYRETHRUM, PAINTED DAISY. Perennial. Zones 32, 34–41. Bushy plant to 2–3 ft., with very finely divided, bright green leaves and single, daisylike, long-stemmed flowers in pink, red, and white. Also available in double and anemone-flowered forms. Starts blooming in late April in Zone 32, in May or June in colder areas; if cut back, blooms again in late summer. Excellent for cutting, borders. Needs summer heat to perform well (but does not take high humidity). Divide clumps or sow seeds in spring. Double forms may not come true from seed; they may revert to single flowers.

C. coronarium. CROWN DAISY. Annual. All zones. To 2½ ft., with light green, coarsely cut leaves and yellow daisies. A variety is the vegetable known as shungiku, chop-suey greens, or edible chrysanthemum; it can be cooked like spinach.

C. frutescens (Argyranthemum frutescens). MARGUERITE, PARIS DAISY. Short-lived shrubby perennial grown as summer annual in the Northeast. Bright green, coarsely divided leaves; abundant daisies 1½–2½ in. across in white, yellow, or pink. 'Snow White', double anemone type, has pure white flowers, more restrained growth habit; 'White Lady' and 'Pink Lady' produce buttonlike flower heads; 'Silver Leaf' has gray-green leaves and masses of very small white flowers. Also dwarf varieties. All types are splendid in containers and for quick effects in borders, mass displays in new gardens. For continued bloom, prune lightly at frequent intervals.

C. grandiflorum (C. morifolium, Dendranthema grandiflorum). FLORISTS' CHRYSANTHEMUM. Perennial. Zones 31, 32, 34–41. This species was briefly reclassified as *Dendranthema*, but it is officially *Chrysanthemum* again. The most useful of all autumn-blooming perennials for borders, containers, and cutting, and the most versatile and varied of all chrysanthemum species, available in many flower forms, colors, plant and flower sizes, and growth habits. Colors include white, yellow, red, pink, orange, bronze, purple, and lavender, as well as multicolors. Following are flower forms as designated by chrysanthemum hobbyists:

Chrysanthemum morifolium

Anemone. One or more rows of rays with large raised center disk or cushion. Center disk may be same color as rays or different. (Disbud to encourage very large flowers.)

Brush. Narrow, rolled rays give brush or soft cactus dahlia effect.

Decorative. Long, broad rays overlap in shingle effect to form broad, full flower.

Incurve. Big double flowers with broad rays curving upward and inward.

Irregular curve. Like above, but with looser, more softly curving rays.

Laciniated. Fully double, with rays fringed and cut at tips in carnation effect.

Pompom. Globular, neat, compact flowers with flat, fluted, or quilled rays. Usually small, they can reach 5 in. with disbudding.

Quill. Long, narrow rolled rays; like spider but less droopy.

Reflex. Big double flowers with rays that curl in, out, and sideways, creating shaggy effect.

C

Semidouble. Somewhat like single or daisy, but with two, three, or four rows of rays around a yellow center.

Single or daisy. Single row of rays around a yellow center. May be large or small, with broad or narrow rays.

Spider. Long, curling, tubular rays ending in fish-hook curved tips.

Spoon. Tubular rays flatten at tip to make little disks, sometimes in colors that contrast with body of flower.

GARDEN CULTURE

It's easy to grow chrysanthemums, not so easy to grow prize-winning chrysanthemums. The latter need more water, feeding, pinching, pruning, grooming, and pest control than most perennials. Many gardeners prefer to treat mums as annuals, buying new plants each year for fall color.

Plant in good, well-drained garden soil improved by organic matter and a complete fertilizer dug in 2 or 3 weeks before planting. Don't plant near large trees or hedges with invasive roots.

Set out young plants (rooted cuttings or vigorous, single-stem divisions) in early spring. When dividing clumps, take divisions from outside; discard woody centers. Water deeply at intervals determined by your soil structure—frequently in porous soils, less often in heavy soils. Too little water causes woody stems and loss of lower leaves; overwatering causes leaves to yellow, then blacken and drop. Aphids are the only notable pest in all areas. Feed plants in ground two or three times during the growing season; make last application with low-nitrogen fertilizer not less than 2 weeks before bloom.

Sturdy plants and big flowers are result of frequent pinching, which should begin at planting time with removal of new plant's tip. Lateral shoots will form; select one to four of these for continued growth. Continue pinching all summer, nipping top pair of leaves on every shoot that reaches 5 in. in length. On some early-blooming cushion varieties, or in coldest regions, pinching should be stopped earlier. Stake plants to keep them upright. To produce huge blooms, remove all flower buds except for one or two in each cluster—this is called disbudding.

POT CULTURE

Pot rooted cuttings February–April, using porous, fibrous, moisture-holding planting mix. Move plants to larger pots as growth requires—don't let them become root-bound. Pinch as directed above; stake as required. Plants need water daily in warm weather, every other day in cool conditions. Feed with liquid fertilizer every 7 to 10 days until buds show color.

CARE AFTER BLOOM

Cut back plants to within 8 in. of ground. Where soils are heavy and likely to remain wet in winter, dig clumps with soil intact and set on top of ground in inconspicuous place. Cover with sand or sawdust if you wish. Take cuttings from early to late spring (up until May for some varieties), or when shoots are 3–4 in. long. As new shoots develop, you can make additional cuttings of them. In cold-winter areas, store plants in cold frame or mulch them with a light, noncompacting material such as excelsior.

Off-season, potted chrysanthemums. Florists and stores sell potted chrysanthemums in bloom every day of the year, even though by nature a chrysanthemum blooms in late summer or fall. Growers force these plants to bloom out of season by subjecting them to artificial day lengths, using lights and dark cloths. You can plunge the potted flowering plants right into a garden bed or border for an immediate (but expensive) display, or you can enjoy them in the house while the flowers remain fresh and then plant them out. Either way, they will not bloom again at the same off-season time the next year. Instead, they will revert to their natural inclination and commence fall bloom once again.

Cut off flowers when they fade, leaving stems about 6–8 in. long. Remove soil clump from pot and break apart the several individual plants that were grown in the pot. Plant these individual plants. When new growth shows from the roots, cut off remainder of old flower stems.

C. leucanthemum (Leucanthemum vulgare). OX-EYE DAISY, COMMON DAISY. Perennial. Zones 31, 32, 34–43. European native naturalized in many places. To 2 ft., with bright green foliage, yellow-centered daisies from late spring through fall. 'May Queen' begins blooming in early spring.

C. maximum (Leucanthemum superbum). SHASTA DAISY. Perennial. Zones 31, 32, 34–43. Summer and fall bloomer. Original 2–4-ft.-tall Shasta daisy, with coarse, leathery leaves and gold-centered, white flower heads 2–4 in. across, has been largely superseded by varieties with larger, better-formed, longer-blooming flowers. They are available in single, double, quilled, and shaggy-flowered forms. All are white, but two show a touch of yellow. Some bloom May–October. Shasta daisies are splendid in borders and cut arrangements.

Following are some of the varieties available in nurseries:

'Esther Read', most popular double white, long bloom; 'Marconi', large frilly double; 'Aglaya', similar to 'Marconi', long blooming season; 'Alaska', big, old-fashioned single; 'Horace Read', 4-in.-wide, dahlialike flower; 'Majestic', large yellow-centered flower; 'Thomas Killin', 6-in.-wide (largest) yellow-centered flower.

'Cobham's Gold' has distinctive flowers in yellow-tinted, off-white shade. 'Canarybird', another yellow, is dwarf, with attractive dark green foliage.

Most popular varieties for cut flowers are 'Esther Read', 'Majestic', 'Aglaya', and 'Thomas Killin'.

Shasta daisies are easy to grow from seed. Catalogs offer many strains, including Roggli Super Giant (single) and Diener's Strain (double). 'Marconi' (double), also available in seed, nearly always blooms double. 'Silver Princess' (also called 'Little Princess' and 'Little Miss Muffet') is 12–15-in. dwarf single. 'Snow Lady' (single), an All-America winner, 10–12 in. tall, begins to bloom in 5 months from seed, then blooms nearly continuously.

Set out divisions of Shasta daisies in fall or early spring, container-grown plants any time. Thrive in fairly rich, moist, well-drained soil. Prefer sun, but do well in partial shade in hot-summer climates; double-flowered kinds hold up better in very light shade. In coldest regions, mulch around plants but do not smother foliage. Divide clumps every 2 to 3 years in early spring

Flower Forms of *Chrysanthemum*

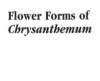

 Anemone *Brush* *Decorative* *Incurve* *Laciniated*

Pompom *Reflex* *Semidouble* *Single* *Spider* *Spoon*

(or in fall in mild-winter areas). Shasta daisies are generally easy to grow but have a few problems. Disease called "gall" causes root crown to split into many weak, poorly rooted growing points that soon die. Dig out and dispose of affected plants; don't replant Shasta daisies in the same spot.

C. nipponicum (Nipponanthemum nipponicum). NIPPON CHRYSANTHEMUM, MONTAUK DAISY. Perennial. Zones 31, 32, 34–41. Resembles a large (up to 3-ft.), rounded, shrubby Shasta daisy with a dense mass of nearly succulent bright green leaves. White daisy flowers on long stems form in fall. In Zones 31, 32, 34, and 39, you may cut back after bloom. Where winters are colder, do not disturb plants until they put on strong new growth in spring; at that time, you may cut back partway to maintain compactness.

C. pacificum (Ajania pacificum, Dendranthema pacificum). GOLD AND SILVER CHRYSANTHEMUM. Perennial. Zones 31, 32, 34–41. Semitrailing and semishrubby, with stems to 2–3 ft. densely clad in lobed, dark green leaves apparently edged white (woolly white undersides show at edges). Broad clusters of yellow flowers appear in fall; lacking rays, they resemble clustered brass buttons. 'Pink Ice' is a pale pink–flowered variety with short petals. Use as bank or ground cover or at front of perennial border. In mild-winter regions, you may cut back after bloom. Where winters are cold, do not disturb plants until they put on strong new growth in spring; at that time, you may cut back partway to maintain compactness.

C. paludosum (Leucanthemum paludosum). Annual, sometimes living over for a second bloom season. All zones. In summer, bears white daisies 1–1½ in. wide on 8–10-in. stems above dark green, deeply toothed leaves. Look like miniature Shasta daisies.

C. parthenium (Tanacetum parthenium). FEVERFEW. Perennial. Zones 31, 32, 34–45. Compact, leafy, aggressive; once favored in Victorian gardens. Leaves have strong odor, offensive to some. Named varieties range from 1 to 3 ft. tall. 'Golden Ball' has bright yellow flower heads and no rays; 'Silver Ball' is completely double with only the white rays showing. In 'Aureum', commonly sold in flats as 'Golden Feather', chartreuse-colored foliage is principal attraction. Sow seeds in spring for bloom by midsummer, or plant from divisions in fall or spring. Can also grow from cuttings. Full sun or light shade.

C. ptarmiciflorum (Tanacetum ptarmiciflorum). DUSTY MILLER, SILVER LACE. Perennial grown as annual. To 6–10 in. tall, 8–10 in. wide. Very finely cut, silvery white leaves. Where hardy, produces white daisy flowers on 1½-ft. stems in summer. Somewhat drought tolerant.

C. rubellum (Dendranthema zawadskii). Perennial. Zones 31, 32, 34–43. To 2 ft. tall, with finely cut leaves and pink flowers over a long blooming season beginning in late summer. 'Clara Curtis' is the best-known variety.

C. serotinum (C. uliginosum). Perennial. Zones 31, 32, 34–43. Grows 5–6 ft. tall, producing sheaves of 3-in., yellow-eyed white daisies in late summer. Useful for late flowers in back of perennial border. Can tolerate damp soil better than most daisies.

C. weyrichii (Dendranthema weyrichii). Perennial. Zones 32, 34–41. Mat-forming; for rock garden. Leaves finely cut. Single daisies about 2 in. wide, with white to pink rays and yellow centers, appear just above foliage in autumn. 'Pink Bomb' has rosy pink rays, 'White Bomb' creamy white ones.

CHRYSANTHEMUMS AS HOUSEPLANTS

Commercial growers are so skilled at forcing mums into bloom in greenhouses that blooming plants are available practically any time of year. If you buy a chrysanthemum plant from a florist, here's how to get the longest life from it: choose a plant that has many buds but few open flowers—it will bloom for up to a month. Look for a compact, bushy, well-shaped plant with good green foliage. Inspect carefully for signs of aphids, whiteflies, or other pests. Examine shoot tips, leaf axils, and undersides of leaves. At home, keep the plant on a sunny but cool windowsill. Keep soil evenly moist but not soggy.

CHRYSOGONUM virginianum

GOLDEN STAR, GREEN AND GOLD

Asteraceae (Compositae)

PERENNIAL

ZONES 31, 32, 34–39

PARTIAL SHADE IN WARMER AREAS

REGULAR WATER

Chrysogonum virginianum

Native to eastern U.S. Useful and attractive native plant for ground cover or foreground planting. Grows 8 in. tall and spreads freely. Bright green, toothed leaves, 1–3 in. long, make a good background for bright yellow flower heads. Blossoms have five rays, resemble stars more than daisies. Bloom is heavy in spring and fall, sporadic through summer months. Plant 1 ft. apart in rich soil high in organic matter for quick ground cover.

'Allen Bush' is a dwarf, carpeting form just 3–4 in. tall; makes a nice, low ground cover.

CHRYSOLARIX. See PSEUDOLARIX kaempferi

CHRYSOPSIS

GOLDEN ASTER

Asteraceae (Compositae)

PERENNIALS

ZONES 31, 32, 34–43

FULL SUN

REGULAR TO MODERATE WATER

Chrysopsis

Perennials native to eastern and central U.S. Tough, somewhat coarse plants. Drought and heat tolerance makes them useful for poor, dry soils and hot situations, yet bright yellow daisylike flowers are showy enough for garden use. Late summer and fall bloom.

C. mariana. Grows to 2 ft. or possibly 3 ft. high, with large (9-in.) basal leaves, smaller stem leaves, tight clusters of 1½-in. flowers.

C. villosa. Taller than *C. mariana* (to 3–4 ft.), with smaller, somewhat more scattered flowers.

CICHORIUM intybus. See CHICORY

CIGAR PLANT. See CUPHEA ignea

CILANTRO. See CORIANDRUM sativum

CIMICIFUGA

BUGBANE

Ranunculaceae

PERENNIALS

ZONES 32, 34–45

PARTIAL SHADE IN WARMER AREAS

REGULAR WATER

Cimicifuga

Stately, upright, slim spikes of small white flowers rise from clumps of shiny, dark green leaves divided into many 1½–3-in.-long, deeply toothed leaflets. The blossom spikes resemble elongated bottlebrushes. The various bugbane species bloom midsummer into fall. All are handsome planted among large ferns in woodland gardens; use the tallest types at the back of borders. Delicate, airy effect.

C

Best in rich, well-drained, moist soil. Will take considerable sun with plentiful water. Need some winter chill for best blooming. Clumps can remain undisturbed for many years. Divide in early spring before growth starts in cold-winter areas, in fall in milder climates. Dried seed clusters useful in flower arrangements.

C. americana. AMERICAN BUGBANE. Native to the eastern U.S. Height varies from 2 to 6½ ft. Loose wands of red-tinged white flowers, to 20 in. long, from late summer well into autumn.

C. japonica. Native to Japan. White flowers on purplish black, leafless stalks in autumn. About 3–4 ft. tall in bloom. 'Acerina' has white flowers opening from pink buds.

C. racemosa. BLACK SNAKEROOT. Native from Massachusetts south to Georgia and west to Missouri. Plant was once used medicinally by Native Americans. Flowering stems to 7 ft. tall. Starts blooming in midsummer in southern part of range, in late summer or early fall farther north.

C. ramosa. Fall bloomer with flowers on branched stems to 7 ft. tall. Narrow 1-ft. spires on each branch provide a long floral display. 'Atropurpurea' is lower growing (to 5 ft.), with dark reddish purple foliage.

C. simplex. KAMCHATKA BUGBANE. Native to Siberia and Japan. Fall bloomer, with plumes reaching 3–5 ft. high. 'White Pearl' has especially large flower spikes.

CINERARIA. See SENECIO cineraria

CINNAMON FERN. See OSMUNDA cinnamomea

CINQUEFOIL. See POTENTILLA

CITROFORTUNELLA microcarpa (Citrofortunella mitis)

CALAMONDIN
Rutaceae
EVERGREEN SHRUB
✕ ALL ZONES
☼ FULL SUN
⬤ DO NOT LET ROOT ZONE BECOME DRY OR SOGGY

A mandarin orange/kumquat hybrid with fruit like a very small orange but a sweet, edible rind. Juicy, tart flesh has some seeds. Grow in a large container moved outdoors in summer, overwinter indoors as house plant in a sunny window, sunporch, or greenhouse. The plant thrives, blossoms, and fruits indoors where night temperatures can be maintained around 50°F/10°C. Fertilize monthly with a dilute liquid all-purpose fertilizer. 'Variegata' is especially ornamental, with leaves mottled with white, and fruits mottled with green.

Citrofortunella microcarpa

CLADRASTIS

YELLOW WOOD
Fabaceae (Leguminosae)
DECIDUOUS TREE
✕ ZONES VARY BY SPECIES
☼ FULL SUN
⬤ REGULAR WATER

Deciduous trees of moderate size, grown for their summer flowers and colorful autumn foliage. Even if it never blooms, yellow wood is useful and attractive as a lawn tree. It's deep rooted, so you can grow other plants beneath it. Tolerates alkaline soils. Established trees withstand some drought.

Cladrastis

Prune when young to shorten side branches or to correct narrow, weak branch crotches, which are susceptible to breakage in ice storms. Usually low branching; you can remove lower branches entirely when tree reaches the height you want. Confine any pruning to summer, since cuts made in winter or spring bleed profusely.

C. lutea (C. kentukea) YELLOW WOOD. Zones 31, 32, 34–45. Native to Kentucky, Tennessee, and North Carolina. Slow growing to 30–50 ft. with broad, rounded head. Big leaves, 8–12 in. long, divided into many (usually 7–11) oval leaflets. Yellowish green new foliage turns to beautiful bright green in summer, then brilliant yellow in fall. Mature trees have handsome smooth gray bark; common name refers to color of freshly cut heartwood.

Tree may not flower until 10 years old and may skip bloom some years, but when floral display does come (possibly every 2 to 3 years), it's spectacular. In late spring to early summer, the tree produces big clusters (to 14 in. long) of fragrant white flowers that look like wisteria blossoms. ('Rosea' is pink flowered.) Blooms are followed by flat, 3–4-in.-long seedpods.

C. platycarpa. JAPANESE YELLOW WOOD. Zones 31, 32, 34–43. Native to Japan and China. Rounded, to 40 ft. tall. Light green leaves to 1 ft. long, composed of numerous oblong leaflets, turn yellow or orange in fall. Upright clusters to 10 in. long of white, pealike flowers in summer.

C. sinensis. CHINESE YELLOW WOOD. Zones 31, 32, 34–41. Native to China. Taller and narrower than the two other species described here, to 70 ft. high and 20 ft. wide, but still rounded in form. Medium green leaves to 1 ft. long, divided into many oblong leaflets and covered with soft hairs, turn bright yellow in autumn. In summer bears upright pyramidal clusters of white flowers flushed with pink.

CLARKIA (includes Godetia)

Onagraceae
ANNUALS
✕ ALL ZONES
☼ ◐ LIGHT SHADE IN HOTTEST CLIMATES
⬤ KEEP SOIL MOIST FROM SEEDING TO FLOWERING

Native to western South and North America. They grow in the cool season, bloom in spring and early summer. Attractive in mixed borders or in mass displays, alone or with love-in-a-mist, cornflower, violas, sweet alyssum. Cut branches keep for several days; cut when top bud opens (others open successively).

Clarkia

Sow seed in place in fall (mild-winter areas) or spring. Seedlings are difficult to transplant, but volunteer seedlings grow very well. Best in well-drained soil without added fertilizer.

C. amoena (Godetia amoena, G. grandiflora). FAREWELL-TO-SPRING, GODETIA. Two wild forms: one coarse stemmed and sprawling, 4–5 in. high; the other slender stemmed, 1½–2½ ft. high. Tapered leaves are ½–2 in. long. On both forms, upright buds open into cup-shaped, slightly flaring, white, red, pink, or lavender flowers, 2 in. across, usually blotched or penciled in crimson. Although seeds of named varieties are rarely sold in the U.S. (more available in England), strains of mixed colors are easy to find. Dwarf Gem grows 10 in. tall; Tall Upright reaches 2–3 ft.

C. unguiculata (C. elegans). CLARKIA, MOUNTAIN GARLAND. Erect, to 1–4 ft. Reddish stems, 1–1¾-in.-long leaves, 1-in.-wide flowers in rose, purple, white. Some varieties have double white, orange, salmon, crimson, purple, rose, pink, or creamy yellow flowers. Double-flowered kinds are ones usually sold in seed packets.

PRACTICAL GARDENING DICTIONARY

PLEASE SEE PAGES 449–523

C

CLAYTONIA

SPRING BEAUTY

Portulacaceae

PERENNIALS

⚡ ZONES 31, 32, 34–41

● SHADE

💧 MORE THAN REGULAR WATER

Claytonia

A genus of about 20 diminutive, spring-flowering, rather succulent plants; they grow from thick taproots, corms, tubers, or stolons. There are anywhere from one to several basal leaves and usually an opposite pair of leaves on the stem. Small, starlike, pink or white flowers bloom in summer on terminal racemes. Best suited to shady woodlands and rock gardens with moist, humusy soil.

C. caroliniana. Native to eastern North America, grows to 12 in. with stalked leaves 1–2 in. wide and pink flowers.

C. virginica. Native to eastern North America, does not exceed 8 in. high, with long, narrow leaves and white flowers tinged with pink.

CLEMATIS

Ranunculaceae

DECIDUOUS OR EVERGREEN VINES AND PERENNIALS

⚡ ZONES VARY BY SPECIES

☼ ROOTS NEED TO BE COOL; TOPS IN SUN

● REGULAR WATER

Clematis

Most of the 200-odd species are deciduous vines; the evergreen *C. armandii* and a few interesting freestanding or sprawling perennials and small shrubs are exceptions. All have attractive flowers, and most are spectacular. The flowers are followed by fluffy clusters of seeds with tails, often quite effective in flower arrangements. Leaves of vining kinds are dark green, usually divided into leaflets; leafstalks twist and curl to hold plant to its support.

Clematis are not demanding, but their few specific requirements should be met. Plant vining types next to a trellis, tree trunk, or open framework to give stems support for twining. Provide rich, loose, fast-draining soil; add generous quantities of organic matter such as decomposed ground bark. Add lime only where soil tests indicate calcium deficiency.

To provide cool area for roots, add mulch, place large flat rock over soil, or plant shallow-rooted ground cover over the root area. Put in support when planting and tie up stems at once. Stems are easily broken, so protect them with wire netting if child or dog traffic is heavy. Clematis need constant moisture and nutrients to make their great rush of growth; apply a complete liquid fertilizer monthly during the growing season.

Pruning clematis sounds complicated, but it need not be; plants are forgiving and will quickly repair mistakes. Do remember that dormant wood can look dead, and take care not to make accidental cuts. Watch for healthy buds at leaf bases and preserve them. The basic objective is to get the greatest number of flowers on the shapeliest plant.

The type of pruning you do depends on when your plants flower. If you don't know what kind you have, watch them for a year to see when they bloom; then prune accordingly.

Spring-blooming clematis bloom only on the previous year's wood. Cut back a month after flowering to restrict sprawl, preserving main branches.

Summer- and fall-blooming clematis bloom on wood produced in the spring. In mild-winter climates, cut back in late fall after flowering or in early spring as buds swell; wait until spring in cold climates. For the first 2 to 3 years, cut to within 6–12 in. of the ground, or to two or three buds; cut to 2 ft. or less on older plants.

Clematis that bloom in spring and again in summer or fall bloom on old wood in spring, new wood later. Do only light, corrective pruning in fall or

early spring; pinch or lightly shape portions that have bloomed to stimulate low branching and avoid a bare base.

Cut flowers are choice for indoors (float in bowl). Burn cut stems with match to make flowers last longer. Unless otherwise specified, flowers are 4–6 in. across.

C. alpina. Zones 31, 32, 34–43. To 8–12 ft., with dangling flowers borne singly on long stalks in spring. Flowers have four spreading, pointed, petal-like sepals and an inner cup of smaller modified stamens. Flowers may be blue, white, purple, pink, or red, depending on variety. 'Willy', pale pink, is best known. 'Helsingborg' is dark blue, 'Pamela Jackman' lavender blue.

C. armandii. EVERGREEN CLEMATIS. Zones 31, warmer part of 32. Native to China. Fast growing to 20 ft. Leaves divided into three glossy dark green leaflets, 3–5 in. long; they droop downward to create strongly textured pattern. Glistening white, 2½-in.-wide, fragrant flowers in large, branched clusters in spring. 'Hendersoni Rubra' has light pink flowers.

Slow to start; races when established. Needs constant pruning after flowering to prevent tangling and buildup of dead thatch on inner parts of vine. Keep and tie up stems you want, and cut out all others. Frequent pinching will hold foliage to eye level. Train along fence tops or rails, roof gables. Allow to climb tall trees. Trained on substantial frame, makes privacy screen if not allowed to become bare at base.

C. chrysocoma. Zones 31, 32. Native to western China. To 6–8 ft. or more in height; fairly open. Young branches, leaves, and flower stalks covered with yellow down. Flowers long stalked, white, shaded pink, 2 in. wide, in clusters from old wood in spring, with later flowers following from new wood. Will take considerable shade.

C. davidiana. See *C. heracleifolia davidiana*

C. dioscoreifolia See *C. terniflora*

C. durandii. Zones 31, 32, 34–41. Hybrid between *C. jackmanii* and *C. integrifolia;* a nonclimbing perennial. Scrambling rather than ascending, it should be tied to a support or permitted to ramble through a large shrub or sprawl in a large perennial border. Grows to 6 ft., with 4½–5-in. flowers in rich violet blue. Blooms over a long period in summer.

C. florida 'Sieboldii' (C. f. 'Bicolor'). Zones 31, 32, 34–39. Flowers 3–4 in. across, with a central puff of purple petal-like stamens, in summer. Vine is a somewhat delicate 8–12 ft. Not as rugged as other clematis, but bears striking flowers. 'Alba Plena' has double greenish white blooms.

C. heracleifolia davidiana (C. davidiana). Zones 31, 32, 34–43. Native to China. Woody-based perennial to 4 ft. high. Deep green leaves divided into three broad, oval, 3–6-in.-long leaflets. Dense clusters of 1-in.-long, tubular, medium to deep blue, fragrant flowers in summer. Use in perennial or shrub border.

C. integrifolia. Zones 31, 32, 34–43. Native to Europe and Asia. Woody-based perennial to 3 ft. with dark green, undivided, 2–4-in.-long leaves and nodding, urn-shaped, 1½-in.-long blue flowers in summer. 'Hendersonii' has larger flowers.

C. jackmanii. Zones 31, 32, 34–43. Series of hybrids between forms of *C. lanuginosa* and *C. viticella*. All are vigorous plants of rapid growth to 10 ft. or more in one season. The best known of the older large-flowered hybrids is known simply as *C. jackmanii*. It has a profusion of 4–5-in. rich purple flowers with four sepals. Blooms from early summer through fall, with heaviest bloom early in the season. Newer hybrids have larger flowers with more sepals, but none blooms as profusely. 'Comtesse de Bouchard' has silvery rose pink flowers; 'Mme. Edouard André' has purplish red blossoms. All flower on new wood; do best with severe pruning in early spring as buds begin to swell. Freeze to ground in cold-winter areas. (For more on large-flowered hybrid clematis, see discussion on next page.)

C. lanuginosa. Zones 31, 32, 34–39. Native to China. A parent of many of the finest large-flowered hybrids. Grows only to about 6–9 ft. but produces magnificent display of large (6-in.) lilac to white flowers, May–July. Best known for its variety 'Candida', with 8-in. white flowers and light yellow stamens. Blooms on new and old wood. Prune only to remove dead or weak growth in early spring. Then, after first flush of flowers (March–April in favorable climates), cut back flowered portions promptly for another crop later in the summer.

C. macropetala. DOWNY CLEMATIS. Zones 31, 32, 34–43. Native to China, Siberia. Variable in size; may reach 6–10 ft. high. In early spring, produces 4-in. lavender to powder blue flowers that look double, resembling a dancer's tutu. Blooms are followed by showy bronzy pink, silvery-tailed seed clusters. 'Markham Pink' has lavender pink flowers. Prune lightly in late winter to remove weak shoots and limit vigorous growth to sound wood.

C. maximowicziana. See *C. terniflora*

C. montana. ANEMONE CLEMATIS. Zones 31, 32, 34–39. Native to Himalayas, China. Vigorous to 20 ft. or more. Easy to grow. Massive early spring display of 2–2½-in. anemonelike flowers, opening white, turning pink. Flowers on old wood, so can be heavily thinned or pruned immediately after flowering to rejuvenate or reduce size.

Clematis montana

'Tetrarose' has large rich mauve flowers. 'Elizabeth' has pale pink blooms with the fragrance of vanilla. 'Grandiflora', vigorous growth to 40 ft., bears abundant pure white blooms. *C. m. rubens,* to 15–25 ft., has crimson new leaves maturing to bronzy green; fragrant rose red to pink flowers are carried throughout vine. In *C. m. rubens* 'Odorata', the blossoms are vanilla scented.

C. orientalis. Zones 31, 32, 34–41. Native to Russia, the Himalayas, China, Korea. Climbs or rambles, to 25 ft. Leaves to 8 in. long, divided into five or more oblong leaflets. Yellow flowers in summer to fall.

C. paniculata. See *C. terniflora*

C. recta. Zones 31, 32, 34–45. Not a climber but a perennial to 4–5 ft., with a profusion of small (¾-in.), fragrant white flowers in summer. It resembles a mounding, sprawling version of *C. terniflora*. Profuse, attractive, plumed seed heads follow the blossoms. 'Purpurea' has purple-tinted foliage.

C. tangutica. GOLDEN CLEMATIS. Zones 31, 32, 34–41. Native to Mongolia, northern China. To 10–15 ft., with gray-green, finely divided leaves. Bright yellow, 2–4-in., nodding, lantern-shaped flowers in great profusion from July to fall. They are followed by handsome, silvery-tailed seed clusters. Prune as for *C. terniflora*.

C. terniflora (C. dioscoreifolia, C. paniculata, C. maximowicziana). SWEET AUTUMN CLEMATIS. Zones 31, 32, 34–41. Native to Japan. Tall and vigorous (some would say rampant), forming billowy masses of 1-in.-wide, creamy white, fragrant flowers in late summer, fall. Attractive plumed seeds; self-sows freely. Dark green, glossy leaves divided into three to five oval leaflets, 1–2½ in. long. After bloom or in early spring, prune growth that has bloomed most recently to one or two buds. Good privacy screen, arbor cover.

C. texensis. SCARLET CLEMATIS. Zones 31, 32, 34–41. Native to Texas. Fast growing to 6–10 ft. Dense bluish green foliage. Bright scarlet, urn-shaped flowers to 1 in. long, early summer until frost. More tolerant of dry soils than most clematis. Hybrid 'Duchess of Albany' has flowers of bright pink shading to lilac at the edges.

C. viticella. Zones 31, 32, 34–41. Native to southern Europe, western Asia. To 12–15 ft. Purple or rose purple, 2-in. flowers in summer. Named varieties include 'Mme. Julia Correvon', rosy red, and 'Polish Spirit', deep purple blue with red center.

LARGE-FLOWERED HYBRID CLEMATIS

Best in Zones 31, 32, 34–41. Although well over a hundred varieties of large-flowered hybrid clematis are being grown today, your local nursery is not likely to offer more than a dozen of the old favorites. Mail-order catalogs remain the best source for collectors seeking the newest. Flowers on some of these may reach 10 in. wide. Most are summer bloomers.

Here are varieties to choose from—old favorites first, then newer offerings:

White. 'Henryi' and 'Candida' are standard. 'Marie Boisselot' or 'Mme. Le Coultre' (large, flat, round flowers) and 'Gillian Blades' (huge, star-shaped flowers) are newer.

Pink. 'Comtesse de Bouchard', the standard pink, has these rivals: 'Charissima' (veined pink with deeper bars); 'Hagley Hybrid' ('Pink Chiffon'), shell pink with pointed sepals; and 'Lincoln Star' (pink with paler edges).

Red. Red clematis have deep purplish red flowers that are best displayed where the sun can shine through them, as on the top of a fence. 'Mme. Edouard André', 'Ernest Markham', and 'Red Cardinal' are standards. 'Ville de Lyon' has full, rounded, velvety flowers; 'Niobe' is the darkest red of all.

Blue violet. Mid-blue 'Ramona' is always popular. Other varieties are 'Edo Murasaki' (deep blue); 'General Sikorski' (huge, with faint red bar); 'Lady Betty Balfour' (dark blue); 'Mrs. Cholmondeley' (big, veined sky blue); 'Piccadilly' (purplish blue); 'Prince Philip' (huge purplish blue with ruffled edges); and 'Will Goodwin' (lavender to sky blue).

Purple. Classic *C. jackmanii* is the most popular. 'Purpureus Superba' ('Jackmanii Superba') is larger, somewhat redder. Others include 'Gypsy Queen' (deepest purple); 'Mrs. M. Thompson' (deep bluish purple with red bar); and 'Richard Pennell' (rosy purple).

Bicolor. 'Nelly Moser' (purplish pink with reddish center bar) is deservedly one of the most popular clematis. 'Carnaby' (white with red bar) and 'Dr. Ruppel' (pink with red bar) are newer and splashier.

Double. Fully double, roselike blooms in early summer on old wood are usually followed later by single or semidouble flowers on new wood. 'Belle of Woking' is silvery blue; 'Duchess of Edinburgh', white; 'Mrs. P. T. James', deep blue; 'Teshio', lavender; and 'Vyvyan Pennell', deep blue with lavender blue center.

CLEMATIS ON SHRUBS

For a lovely effect, consider using clematis to dress up an uninteresting green hedge or shrub. Plant clematis at the base of the shrub or hedge and allow it to grow up and over the other plants, weaving its stems through their branches. Large-flowered clematis will perch its flowers among the branches like colorful birds. Small-flowered types like sweet autumn clematis will blanket the supporting plant with a froth of little flowers without harming the host.

CLEOME hasslerana (C. spinosa)

SPIDER FLOWER

Capparaceae

ANNUAL

◪ ALL ZONES

☼ FULL SUN

● REGULAR WATER

Cleome hasslerana

Shrubby, branching plant topped in summer and fall with many open, fluffy clusters of pink or white flowers with extremely long, protruding stamens. Slender seed capsules follow blossoms. Short, strong spines on stems; lower leaves divided, upper ones undivided. Leaves and stems feel clammy to the touch, have a strong but not unpleasant smell. Reaches 4–6 ft. tall, 4–5 ft. wide. Thrives in heat, tolerates some drought. Grow in background, as summer hedge, against walls or fences, in large containers. Flowers and dry seed capsules are useful in arrangements.

Sow seeds in place in spring; they sprout rapidly in warm soil. A number of varieties can be grown from seed. In most cases color is indicated

C

by variety name: 'Cherry Queen', 'Mauve Queen', 'Pink Queen', 'Purple Queen', 'Rose Queen', and 'Ruby Queen'. 'Helen Campbell' is snow-white. Plants self-sow to a fault.

CLERODENDRUM

GLORYBOWER

Verbenaceae

EVERGREEN OR DECIDUOUS SHRUBS OR TREES

ZONES VARY BY SPECIES

PARTIAL SHADE

REGULAR WATER

Clerodendrum

This relatively little known group of small trees, shrubs, and shrubby vines is cultivated for big clusters of showy, brightly colored flowers. They are grown in warm climates, but the two described here grow well in pots moved outdoors in summer and indoors in winter.

C. thomsoniae (C. balfouri). BLEEDING HEART GLORYBOWER. Evergreen vining shrub. All zones. Native to West Africa. Leaves oval, 4–7 in. long, dark green, shiny, distinctly ribbed. Flowers are a study in color contrast—scarlet, 1-in. tubes surrounded by large (¾-in.-long) white calyxes, carried in flattish, 5-in.-wide clusters, late summer to fall. Will flower in 6-in. pot. Can grow to 6 ft. or more if left untrimmed. Give support for twining. Needs rich, loose soil mix, plenty of water with good drainage. Prune after flowering.

C. trichotomum. HARLEQUIN GLORYBOWER. Deciduous shrub-tree hardy in Zones 31, 32, 34–41. (In the cooler parts of its range, it dies back to the ground each winter, but grows to 5–6 ft. during the growing season and produces flowers and fruit.) Native to Japan. Grows with many stems from base to 10–15 ft. or more; suckers freely. Leaves oval, to 5 in. long, dark green, soft, hairy. Fragrant clusters of white, tubular flowers almost twice as long as prominent, fleshy, ½-in.-long scarlet calyxes. Late-summer bloom. Calyxes hang on and contrast pleasingly with turquoise or blue-green, metallic-looking fruit. Give room to spread at top; plant under it to hide its legginess. *C. t. fargesii,* from China, is somewhat hardier and smaller; it has smooth leaves and green calyxes that later turn pink.

CLETHRA

Clethraceae

DECIDUOUS SHRUBS

ZONES VARY BY SPECIES

PREFERS PARTIAL SHADE BUT ADAPTABLE

AMPLE WATER

Clethra

These attractive shrubs are grown for the small, five-lobed, sweetly fragrant, white or pink flowers clustered at their branch ends in mid- to late summer. Fairly soil tolerant, but do best in moist, organic, slightly acid soil. Prefer partial shade but adapt well to less light as well as to full sun; need some shade where summers are very hot. No serious pest or disease problems. Routine pruning not required.

C. acuminata. CINNAMON CLETHRA. Zones 31, 32, 34–41. Native to southeastern U.S. Clump-forming shrub to 12 ft. high and wide, spreads by suckers. Attractive, cinnamon-colored bark and glossy, deep green, oval leaves to 6 in. long. Clusters of fragrant, white flowers, to 8 in. long, in mid-summer.

C. alnifolia. SUMMERSWEET, SWEET PEPPERBUSH. Zones 31, 32, 34–43. Native to eastern U.S. As the common names imply, this shrub's outstanding feature is its display of flowers with a sweet, spicy scent. Summersweet grows 4–10 ft. tall (it's more apt to reach the upper end of the range in moist soil and in shade), with thin, strong branches forming

a vertical pattern. The toothed, dark green, 2–4-in.-long leaves appear late in spring. In summer, each branch tip carries several 4–6-in.-long spires of tiny, gleaming white, perfumed blossoms. Fall foliage color ranges from golden yellow to brownish and can last for several weeks; old flower spikes hang on while the leaves are changing. Several varieties are commonly grown. 'Hummingbird' is a dense, compact plant; 'Paniculata' has clustered flower spires; 'Pink Spires' produces pale pink flowers from rose pink buds; 'Rosea' has pink buds opening pinkish white.

'Ruby Spice' has dark pink blooms. Tolerates seacoast conditions. Wonderful for borders, shade plantings. Prune in early spring, since flowers are produced on new growth. Spreads by suckers into a broad clump.

C. barbinervis. JAPANESE SWEET SHRUB. Zones 31, 32, 34, 39. Slow grower to 15–18 ft., with sharply toothed leaves that turn bright yellow in fall. Drooping, 4–6-in. clusters of fragrant, white flowers. Attractive glossy gray to brown bark. Beautiful plant, but rarely grown in U.S.

CLINTONIA

Liliaceae

PERENNIALS

ZONES VARY BY SPECIES

PARTIAL TO FULL SHADE

AMPLE WATER

Clintonia

Spreading by underground rhizomes, these woodland perennials produce basal clumps of glossy leaves and delicate bell- or star-shaped flowers followed by showy berries. Grow in rich, moist, neutral to acidic soil, and mulch in spring with compost or leaf mold. Best in naturalistic or woodland gardens.

C. borealis. CORN LILY, BLUEBEARD, YELLOW BEAD LILY. Zones 31, 32, 34–43. Native to Canada, New Jersey, Indiana, and the mountains of North Carolina. Long, glossy, dark green leaves, with nodding umbels of greenish yellow, star-shaped flowers that bloom in late spring and early summer and are followed by attractive, shiny blue berries.

C. umbellulata. SPECKLED WOOD LILY. Zones 32, 34–43. Similar to *C. borealis,* but with green- and purple-spotted flowers.

CLOVE PINK. See DIANTHUS caryophyllus

CLOVER. See TRIFOLIUM

COBAEA scandens

CUP-AND-SAUCER VINE

Polemoniaceae

TENDER PERENNIAL USUALLY GROWN AS ANNUAL

ALL ZONES

FULL SUN

REGULAR WATER

Cobaea scandens

Native to Mexico. Extremely vigorous growth to 25 ft. Bell-shaped flowers are first greenish, then violet or rose purple; there is also a white-flowered form. Called cup-and-saucer vine because 2-in.-long cup of petals sits in large, green, saucerlike calyx. Leaves divided into two or three pairs of oval, 4-in. leaflets. At ends of leaves are curling tendrils that enable vine to climb rough surfaces without support.

The hard-coated seeds may rot if sown outdoors in cool weather. Start indoors in 4-in. pots; notch seeds with a knife and press edgewise into moistened potting mix, barely covering seeds. Keep moist but not wet; transplant to warm, sunny location when weather warms up. Protect from wind. Blooms first year from seed. May not bloom until very late summer in coolest climates.

COCKSCOMB. See CELOSIA

COCKSPUR THORN. See CRATAEGUS crus-galli

CODIAEUM variegatum

CROTON

Euphorbiaceae

EVERGREEN SHRUB USUALLY GROWN AS
HOUSE PLANT

☘ ALL ZONES

☼ ◐ ● SOME FORMS TAKE SUN, OTHERS SHADE

● ●● AMPLE WATER

Codiaeum variegatum

Native to tropics. Can reach 6 ft. or more out-
doors in frost-free climates; elsewhere, usually seen as single-
stemmed house plant, 6–24 in. tall. Grown principally for coloring of
large, leathery, glossy leaves, which may be green, yellow, red, purple,
bronze, pink, or almost any combination of these colors. Leaves may be
oval, lance shaped, or very narrow; straight edged or lobed. Dozens of
named forms combine these differing features.

Outdoor exposure depends on the variety. Needs bright light, regular
misting indoors; does well in a warm, humid greenhouse. Can be brought
outdoors in warm season. Some people are sensitive to croton leaves.

CODONOPSIS clematidea

BONNET BELLFLOWER

Campanulaceae (Lobeliaceae)

PERENNIAL

☘ ZONES 34–41

☼ ◐ TOLERATES SUN IN COOL-SUMMER CLIMATES

● MODERATE WATER

Codonopsis clematidea

Of the many attractive members of this group, *C. clematidea* is the
only one generally grown in the U.S. It is a trailing or scrambling
plant that will drape over a wall or, if supported by a shrub, twine to
2–2½-ft. Stems appear in spring from a tuberous root; they bear inch-
long leaves and, at their tips, drooping, bell-shaped, inch-long light blue
flowers with striking interior markings of orange and maroon. The plant
has a slightly skunky odor when bruised. It prefers partial shade (though
can take sun in cool climates) and soil with ample organic material. Don't
neglect watering during protracted dry spells. Use in woodland garden or
rock garden.

COIX lacryma-jobi

JOB'S TEARS

Poaceae (Gramineae)

PERENNIAL GRASS

☘ ALL ZONES

☼ ◐ FULL SUN OR PARTIAL SHADE

● REGULAR WATER

Coix lacryma-jobi

A curiosity grown for its ornamental "beads,"
Job's tears is perennial in warm climates but
grown as an annual in the Northeast. Loose growing with smooth, prominently jointed stems to 6 ft. Sword-shaped leaves to 2 ft. long, 1½ in. wide.
Outside covering of female flower hardens as seed ripens; becomes shiny,
¼–1½-in. bead in pearly white, gray, or violet. Beads can be strung into
bracelets. Cut stems for winter arrangements before seeds dry and shatter.

COLCHICUM

MEADOW SAFFRON, AUTUMN CROCUS

Liliaceae

CORMS

☘ ZONES 34–43; OR INDOORS

☼ FULL SUN

● REGULAR WATER DURING GROWTH AND BLOOM

◆ ALL PARTS ARE HIGHLY POISONOUS IF INGESTED

Colchicum

Native to Mediterranean regions. Many species; sometimes called
autumn crocus, but not true crocuses. Shining, brown-skinned,
thick-scaled corms send up clusters of long-tubed, flaring, lavender pink,
rose purple, or white flowers to 4 in. across in late summer, whether corms
are sitting in dish on windowsill or planted in soil. When planted out,
broad, 6–12-in.-long leaves show in spring, last for a few months, and then
die long before flower cluster rises from ground. Best planted where they
need not be disturbed more often than every 3 years or so. Corms available
during brief dormant period in July and August. The two best varieties are
'The Giant', single lavender, and 'Waterlily', double violet. Plant 3–4 in.
deep. To plant in bowls, set upright on 1–2 in. of pebbles, or in special
fiber sold for this purpose, and fill bowl with water to base of corms.

COLEUS hybridus

COLEUS

Lamiaceae (Labiatae)

PERENNIAL TREATED AS ANNUAL OR INDOOR PLANT

☘ ALL ZONES

☼ ◐ MOST TAKE SHADE, SOME FULL SUN

● AMPLE WATER

Coleus hybridus

Native to tropics. Often sold as *C. blumei*. Grown for brilliantly colored leaves; blue flower spikes are attractive but spoil shape of plant
and are best pinched out in bud. Leaves may be 3–6 in. long in large-
leafed strains (1½–2 ft. tall), 1–1½ in. long in dwarf (1-ft.) strains.
Colors include green, chartreuse, yellow, buff, salmon, orange, red, purple, brown, often with many colors on one leaf. The more red pigment in
the leaves, the more sun tolerant the plant tends to be. 'Plum Parfait' and
'Burgundy Sun' are examples of varieties bred for full sun. Most coleus
perform best in strong, indirect light or filtered shade.

'Giant Exhibition' and 'Oriental Splendor' are large-leafed strains.
'Carefree' is dwarf, self-branching, with deeply lobed and ruffled, 1–1½-
in. leaves. Fairway series is also dwarf; 'Fairway Mosaic' has light green
leaves splashed with maroon. 'Salicifolius' has crowded, long, narrow
leaves; plant resembles foot-high feather duster. 'Golden Bedder' is greenish gold, easy to mix with other plants. 'Dark Star' has deep purple-black
leaves. 'Garnet Robe' is dark maroon with a narrow yellow-green edge and
cascading habit. Many other seed- and cutting-grown varieties also exist.

Useful for summer borders and as indoor/outdoor container and
hanging-basket plants. Plant in spring. Easy from seed sown indoors or,
with protection, outdoors in warm weather. Easy from cuttings, which root
in water as well as other media. Needs rich, loose, well-drained soil,
warmth. Feed regularly with high-nitrogen fertilizer. Pinch stems often to
encourage branching and compact habit; remove flower buds to ensure
vigorous growth. To keep plants in sunny sites compact, shear by a third
in midsummer. Recently renamed *Solenostemon scutellarioides*.

COLLARDS. See KALE

PRACTICAL GARDENING DICTIONARY

PLEASE SEE PAGES 449–523

C

COLLINSIA heterophylla
(Collinsia bicolor)

CHINESE HOUSES, INNOCENCE

Scrophulariaceae

ANNUALS

⚟ ALL ZONES

☼ ◑ FULL SUN, PARTIAL SHADE

🔴 REGULAR WATER

Collinsia heterophylla

A California wildflower in the snapdragon family, planted for its pretty, two-lipped bicolored flowers in informal beds, borders, wild gardens, and cutting gardens. Stems hairy and sticky, leaves lance-shaped, green to purple-green, up to 2 in. long. In summer, clustered blooms with white upper lip, violet or rosy purple lower lip, appear on weak stems up to 2 ft. tall.

'Alba' has white blooms with greenish white lower lip; 'Candidissima', all-white flowers; 'Marmorata' blossoms have vivid red spots and stripes; 'Multicolor', variegated white, pink, and lilac flowers.

Grow in a protected location in fertile, moist, well-drained soil. Water during drought to extend blooming. Stake with twigs for natural-looking support. Sow seed in place in fall or early spring for summer flowering. Plants grow about 12 in. wide. Thin seedlings in spring to give plants space to grow. Adequate air circulation helps prevent mildews and other fungal diseases.

COLOCASIA esculenta
(Caladium esculentum)

TARO, ELEPHANT'S EAR

Araceae

TUBEROUS-ROOTED PERENNIAL

⚟ ZONES 31, 32 (WARMER PARTS); OR DIG AND STORE, OR GROW IN POTS

◑ BEST IN WARM, FILTERED SHADE

🔴🔴 AMPLE WATERING

◈ JUICES CAN CAUSE SWELLING IN MOUTH, THROAT

Colocasia esulenta

Native to tropical Asia and Polynesia. Fast growing to 6 ft. tall. Mammoth (to 2-ft.-long), heart-shaped, gray-green leaves add lush effect to any tropical planting within a single season. Flowers resemble giant callas but are seldom seen as perennials, except in southern Florida. The starchy roots are a staple food in Hawaii and the Pacific area in general; taro is occasionally grown for food production by Hawaiians and other Americans of Pacific Island descent.

In most of the Northeast, colocasia is treated as a tender bulb or annual. Lift and store tubers in fall or grow in containers; shelter over winter. Effective with cannas and other large-leafed tropical plants. Handsome in large tubs, raised beds, near swimming pools. Protect from wind, which tears leaves. Feed lightly once a month during growing season. Needs constant, abundant moisture for most impressive growth.

COLONIAL BENT. See AGROSTIS tenuis

COLUMBINE. See AQUILEGIA

COMFREY. See SYMPHYTUM officinale

Commelinaceae. The spiderwort family is composed of herbaceous perennials, often fleshy, mostly tropical or subtropical. Wandering Jew (*Tradescantia albiflora* and *Zebrina*) and spiderwort (*Tradescantia virginiana*) are familiar examples. Flowers generally have three rounded petals.

COMPASS PLANT. See SILPHIUM laciniatum

Compositae. See Asteraceae

CONRADINA verticillata

CUMBERLAND ROSEMARY

Lamiaceae (Labiatae)

SHRUBBY PERENNIAL

⚟ ZONES 31–32

☼ FULL SUN

🔴 REGULAR WATER

Conradina verticillata

Native to sandy riverbanks of eastern Tennessee and Kentucky. Aromatic, freely branching plant that roots from trailing branches to make a small-scale ground cover. Dark green, narrow, needlelike leaves resemble those of rosemary *(Rosmarinus)* and have a minty scent. Lavender pink flowers top the 12–15-in. plant in spring or early summer.

CONSOLIDA ambigua
(Delphinium ajacis)

LARKSPUR, ANNUAL DELPHINIUM

Ranunculaceae

ANNUAL

⚟ ALL ZONES

☼ FULL SUN

🔴 REGULAR WATER

◈ ALL PARTS, ESPECIALLY SEEDS, ARE POISONOUS IF INGESTED

Consolida ambigua

Native to southern Europe. Upright, 1–5 ft. tall, with deeply cut leaves; blossom spikes densely set with 1–1½-in.-wide flowers (most are double) in white, blue-and-white, or shades of blue, lilac, pink, rose, salmon, carmine. Best bloom in cooler spring and early summer months. Giant Imperial strain has many 4–5-ft. vertical stalks compactly placed. Regal strain has 4–5-ft. base-branching stems, thick spikes of large flowers similar to perennial delphiniums. Super Imperial strain is base branching, has large flowers in 1½-ft. cone-shaped spikes. Steeplechase is base branching, has biggest double flowers on 4–5-ft. spikes, and is heat resistant. Sow seed where plants are to grow; fall planting is best except in heavy, slow-draining soils. Thin plants to avoid crowding, get biggest flowers.

CONVALLARIA majalis

LILY-OF-THE-VALLEY

Liliaceae

PERENNIAL GROWN FROM RHIZOME

⚟ ZONES 31, 32, 34–45; OR INDOORS

◑ PARTIAL SHADE

🔴 REGULAR WATER

◈ ALL PARTS ARE POISONOUS IF INGESTED

Convallaria majalis

Graceful, creeping, 6–8-in.-high ground cover puts up one-sided, arching stems of small, nodding, delightfully sweet-scented, waxy, white bells in spring. Pendent bells last only 2 to 3 weeks, but broad, bold, glossy green, deciduous leaves are attractive throughout growing season. Bright red berries may appear in autumn; they, like the rest of the plant, are poisonous. Double- and pink-flowered forms are available, as is a variegated type with cream-striped foliage. All are charming in woodland gardens; use as carpet

C

between camellias, rhododendrons, pieris, under deciduous trees or high-branching, not-too-dense evergreen trees. Where well adapted, lily-of-the-valley can become invasive—in fact, it has naturalized in many parts of the Northeast.

Plant clumps or single rhizomes (commonly called pips) in fall before the soil freezes. Give rich soil with ample humus. Set clumps 1–2 ft. apart, single pips 4–5 in. apart, 1½ in. deep. Cover yearly with leaf mold, peat moss, or ground bark. Large, prechilled pips for forcing, available in December and January, can be potted for bloom indoors. After bloom, plunge pots in ground in cool, shaded area. When dormant, either remove plants from pots and plant in garden, or wash soil off pips and store in plastic bags in vegetable compartment of refrigerator until time to repot in December or January.

Convolvulaceae. The morning glory family contains climbing or trailing plants, usually with funnel-shaped flowers. Morning glories (*Convolvulus* and *Ipomoea*) are typical examples.

CONVOLVULUS tricolor

DWARF MORNING GLORY
Convolvulaceae
ANNUAL
✿ ALL ZONES
☼ FULL SUN
⬤ REGULAR WATER

Convolvulus tricolor

Native to southern Europe. Bushy, branching, and somewhat trailing, to 1 ft. high and 2 ft. wide. Leaves are small and narrow. In summer, plant is covered with 1½-in. funnel-shaped morning glory blossoms; usually blue with white-centered yellow throat, though color does vary. 'Blue Flash' and Rainbow Flash strain (mixed colors) are lower growing, reaching just 6 in. tall. All types are good as edging, against low trellis, or at top of wall. Nick tough seed coats with a knife and plant in place when soil has warmed up.

COPPER LEAF. See ACALYPHA wilkesiana

CORAL BELLS. See HEUCHERA

CORALBERRY. See SYMPHORICARPOS orbiculatus

CORDYLINE

Agavaceae
EVERGREEN PALMLIKE SHRUBS OR TREES
✿ ALL ZONES
☼ ◐ ⬤ EXPOSURE NEEDS VARY BY SPECIES
◐ ⬤ ⬤ WATER NEEDS VARY BY SPECIES

Cordyline

Woody plants with swordlike leaves, related to yuccas and agaves. Grown outdoors in the warmest climates, but in the Northeast, grow in pots moved outdoors in summer and indoors in winter. Good next to swimming pools. Often sold as *Dracaena;* for true *Dracaena,* see that entry.

C. australis (Dracaena australis). Fountain of 3-ft.-long, narrow, swordlike leaves. Upper leaves are erect; lower leaves arch and droop. For more graceful plant, cut back when young to force multiple trunks. Grows fastest in soil deep enough for big, carrotlike root. Full sun. Tolerates some drought. Used for tropical effects, with boulders and gravel for desert look, near seashore.

'Atropurpurea'. BRONZE DRACAENA. Like the above, but with bronzy red foliage. Slower growth. Combine with gray or warm yellowish green to bring out color.

C. stricta. Slender, erect stems clustered at base or branching low. Swordlike, 2-ft.-long leaves are dark green with hint of purple. Long cuttings stuck in ground or pots of soil root quickly. Needs some shade except in coolest-summer areas. Regular water. Fine container plant indoors or out; good for tropical-looking background in narrow areas, side gardens.

C. terminalis. TI PLANT. Many named forms with red, yellow, or variegated leaves. Plants are usually started from "logs"—sections of stem imported from Hawaii. Lay short lengths in mixture of peat moss and sand, covering about one-half their diameter. Keep moist. When shoots grow out and root, cut them off and plant them. Ti plant takes ordinary house plant care; tolerates low light intensity.

GROOMING COREOPSIS

Early in the flowering season you can easily groom coreopsis by cutting off spent flowers with a pair of one-hand pruning shears. But by summer the dead flowers can outnumber the new until they're too much for one-hand shears. Cut back the waves of dead flowers with hedge shears. Such wholesale removals can bring on successive bloom.

COREOPSIS

Asteraceae (Compositae)
PERENNIALS AND ANNUALS
✿ ZONES VARY BY SPECIES
☼ FULL SUN
⬤ MODERATE WATER, EXCEPT AS NOTED

Coreopsis

Easily grown members of sunflower family yielding profusion of yellow, orange, maroon, or reddish flowers over long bloom season. Both annual and perennial kinds are easy to propagate—annuals from seed sown in place or in pots, perennials from seed or division of root crown. Tend to self-sow; seeds attract birds.

C. auriculata 'Nana'. Perennial. Zones 31, 32, 34–45. Makes 5–6-in.-high mat of leaves 2–5 in. long. Under ideal conditions, it will spread by stolons to form a 2-ft.-wide clump in a year. Bright orange-yellow flower heads, 1–2½ in. wide, rise well above foliage. Long and profuse blooming season from spring to fall if you remove faded flowers. Best used in foreground of taller plants, in border, or as edging.

C. grandiflora. COREOPSIS. Perennial. Zones 31, 32, 34–43. Grows 1–2 ft. high, spreading to 3 ft.; leaves narrow, dark green, with three to five lobes. Bright yellow, 2½–3-in.-wide flowers bloom all summer, carried on long slender stems high above foliage. 'Sunburst' has large, semidouble flowers; it will bloom the first year from seed sown early in spring, then spread by self-sowing. 'Early Sunrise' is similar and even earlier to bloom. Both are tough enough for use in roadside beautification.

C. lanceolata. COREOPSIS. Perennial. Zones 31, 32, 34–45. Grows 1–2 ft. high. Leaves somewhat hairy, narrow, mostly in tuft near base. Flower heads 1½–2 in. across, yellow, on pale green stems, spring–summer. Some leaves on lower stem have a few lobes. When well established, will persist year after year. Excellent cut flower.

C. rosea. Perennial. Zones 31, 32, 34–41. Finely textured plant 1½–2 ft. tall with pink, yellow-centered daisylike flowers from summer to fall. Unlike other species, prefers moist soil. Growth can be rampant in light soil.

C. tinctoria. ANNUAL COREOPSIS, CALLIOPSIS. Annual. All zones. Slender, upright, 1½–3 ft. tall with wiry stems; much like cosmos in growth habit. Leaves and stems smooth. Flowers similar to perennial coreopsis, in yellow, orange, maroon, bronze, and reddish, banded with

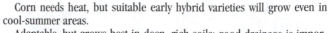

contrasting colors; purple-brown centers. Dwarf and double varieties. Flowers summer–fall, except where hot, humid weather shortens the show. Sow seed in place in full sun and dryish soil.

C. tripteris. ATLANTIC COREOPSIS. Perennial. Zones 31, 32, 34–43. Native to eastern and midwestern U.S. Sturdy, branching, to 8 ft. high and 2 ft. across. Medium green, three-part palmate leaves to 8 in. long. Light yellow flowers with yellow centers that darken to purple brown, from summer into fall.

C. verticillata. Perennial. Zones 31, 32, 34–45. Plant is 2½–3 ft. tall, half as broad. Many erect or slightly leaning stems carry many whorls of finely divided, very narrow leaves. At top are 2-in. bright yellow daisies, freely borne over long summer and autumn season. One of the most tolerant of drought, neglect. 'Moonbeam', 1½–2 ft. tall, has pale yellow flowers; 'Zagreb', 1 ft. tall, has golden yellow flowers.

CORIANDRUM sativum

CORIANDER, CHINESE PARSLEY, CILANTRO

Apiaceae (Umbelliferae)

ANNUAL HERB

🌱 ALL ZONES

☀️ FULL SUN

💧 REGULAR WATER

Coriandrum sativum

Grows 12–15 in. high. Delicate fernlike foliage; flat clusters of pinkish white flowers. Aromatic seeds crushed before use as seasoning for sausage, beans, stews, cookies, wines. Young leaves used in salads, soups, poultry recipes, and variety of Mexican and Chinese dishes. Grow in good, well-drained soil. Start from seed (including coriander seed sold in grocery stores); grows quickly, self-sows.

CORN

Poaceae (Gramineae)

ANNUAL

🌱 ALL ZONES

☀️ FULL SUN—ALWAYS

💧 SPECIAL WATERING TIMES; SEE BELOW

Corn

Sweet corn is the one cereal crop that home gardeners are likely to grow; it requires considerable space but is still well worth growing. Once most sweet corn is picked, its sugar changes to starch very quickly; only by rushing ears from garden directly to boiling water can you capture full sweetness. Examples are 'Merit' (yellow, midseason), 'Seneca Chief' (yellow, midseason), and the classic 'Silver Queen' (white, late).

Sugary enhanced (Se and Se+) varieties are sweeter and are slower to convert their sugar to starch after picking. Examples include 'Ambrosia' (bicolor, early), 'Argent' (white, late), 'Delectable' (bicolor, midseason), 'Precocious' (yellow, early), 'Silver King' (white, late), and 'Tuxedo' (yellow, midseason). Supersweet varieties of corn are actually sweeter than standard kinds and maintain their sweetness longer after harvest because of a gene that increases the quantity of sugar and slows its conversion to starch. A very few people find these varieties too sweet. Examples include 'Fantasy' (bicolor, early-midseason), 'First Snow' (white, early), 'Honey 'N Pearl' (bicolor, midseason), and 'Northern Xtra-Sweet' (yellow, early).

Where the growing season is brief, plant early varieties such as 'Aladdin' (bicolor), 'Earlivee' (yellow), 'Early Sunglow' (yellow), and 'Quickie' (bicolor).

Corn needs heat, but suitable early hybrid varieties will grow even in cool-summer areas.

Adaptable, but grows best in deep, rich soils; good drainage is important. Give full sun. Sow seed 2 weeks after average date of last frost, and make three or four more plantings at 2-week intervals; or plant early, midseason, and late varieties. Plant corn in blocks of short rows rather than single long rows; pollination is by wind, and unless good supply of pollen falls on silks, ears will be poorly filled. Don't plant popcorn near sweet corn; pollen of one kind can affect characteristics of other. For the same reason, some supersweet varieties have to be grown at a distance from other varieties. Either plant in rows 3 ft. apart and thin seedlings to stand 1 ft. apart, or plant in "hills" (actually clumps) 3 ft. apart each way. Place six or seven seeds in each hill and thin to three strongest plants. Give plants plenty of water and one high-nitrogen feeding when stalks are 7–8 in. tall. Make certain that you apply good deep watering that thoroughly wets entire root zone just as tassel emerges from stalk; repeat again when silk forms. Don't remove suckers that appear.

> ## FOR THE TASTIEST EAR OF CORN
> Check your crop when ears are plump and silks have withered; pull back husks and try popping a kernel with your thumb. Generally, corn is ready to eat 3 weeks after silks first appear. Kernels should squirt milky juice; watery juice means that corn is immature. Doughy consistency indicates overmaturity.

Corn earworm is a pest in all regions. Prevent by placing dropperful of mineral oil in tip of ear when silks have withered but before they turn brown. Or deter entry of worm by planting tight-husked varieties, or putting a clothes pin or rubber band on tip of husk. If damage occurs, just cut off damaged tips. European corn borer is a pest in most regions, including the Northeast. Caterpillars tunnel into plant stalks and sometimes into ears. Place *Bt* (or *Btk*) or diazinon granules in leaf whorls on stalks.

ORNAMENTAL CORN

Some kinds of corn are grown for the beauty of their shelled ears rather than for their eating qualities. Calico, Indian, Squaw, and rainbow corn are some names given to strains that have brightly colored kernels—red, brown, blue, gray, black, yellow, and many mixtures of these colors. Grow like sweet corn, but let ears ripen fully; silks will be withered, husks will turn straw color, and kernels will be firm. Cut ear from plant, including 1½ in. of stalk below ear; pull back husks (leave attached to ears) and dry thoroughly. Grow well away from late sweet corn; mix of pollen can affect its flavor.

Zea mays japonica includes several kinds of corn grown for ornamental foliage; one occasionally sold is 'Gracilis', a dwarf corn with bright green leaves striped white.

POPCORN

Grow and harvest popcorn just like ornamental corn described above. When ears are thoroughly dry, rub kernels off cobs and store in dry place. White and yellow popcorn resemble other corn in appearance. Strawberry popcorn, grown either for popping or for its ornamental value, has stubby, fat, strawberrylike ears packed with red kernels.

Cornaceae. The dogwood family consists of trees and shrubs with clustered inconspicuous flowers (sometimes surrounded by showy bracts) and berrylike fruit. *Aucuba* and dogwood *(Cornus)* are examples.

CORNELIAN CHERRY. See CORNUS mas

CORNFLOWER. See CENTAUREA cyanus

CORN PLANT. See DRACAENA fragrans

CORNUS

DOGWOOD

Cornaceae

DECIDUOUS OR EVERGREEN SHRUBS OR TREES AND A
GROUND COVER

ZONES VARY BY SPECIES

FULL SUN OR LIGHT SHADE, EXCEPT AS NOTED

REGULAR WATER, EXCEPT AS NOTED

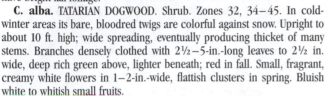

Cornus

All offer attractive foliage and flowers; some have spectacular fruit and winter bark. Many have bright fall foliage.

C. alba. TATARIAN DOGWOOD. Shrub. Zones 32, 34–45. In cold-winter areas its bare, bloodred twigs are colorful against snow. Upright to about 10 ft. high; wide spreading, eventually producing thicket of many stems. Branches densely clothed with 2½–5-in.-long leaves to 2½ in. wide, deep rich green above, lighter beneath; red in fall. Small, fragrant, creamy white flowers in 1–2-in.-wide, flattish clusters in spring. Bluish white to whitish small fruits.

Leaves of 'Gouchaultii' have yellow borders suffused with pink. 'Argenteomarginata' (*C.* 'Elegantissima') has showy green-and-white leaves on red stems. 'Sibirica', Siberian dogwood, less rampant than species, grows to about 7 ft. high with 5-ft. spread; has gleaming coral red branches in winter. In all types, new wood is brightest; cut back in spring to force new growth.

C. alternifolia. PAGODA DOGWOOD. Shrub or small tree. Zones 32, 34–43. Multitrunked, to 20 ft. high. Strong horizontal branching pattern makes attractive winter silhouette. Light green leaves turn red in fall. Small clusters of creamy spring flowers are not showy. Blue-black fruit. 'Argentea' has white-variegated leaves.

C. canadensis. BUNCHBERRY. Deciduous carpet plant. Zones 32, 34–45. Native to northern climates. It's difficult to believe this 6–9-in.-high perennial is related to dogwoods when you see it under trees by lakes and streams. Creeping rootstocks send up stems topped by whorls of oval or roundish, 1–2-in.-long, deep green leaves that turn yellow in fall, die down in winter. In late spring or early summer, plants bear small, compact clusters of tiny flowers surrounded by (usually) four oval, ½–¾-in. pure white bracts. Clusters of small, shiny red fruit appear in late summer.

For part or full shade in cool, moist climates, in acid soil with generous amounts of humus or rotten wood. Considered hard to establish, but when transplanted with piece of rotten log with bark attached, it establishes readily. Excellent with rhododendrons, ferns, trilliums, lilies.

C. controversa. GIANT DOGWOOD. Tree. Zones 31, 32, 34. From the Orient. Resembles big shrubby dogwoods in leaves, flowers, and fruit but grows rapidly into magnificent 40–60-ft. tree with picturesque horizontal branches. Luxuriant 3–6-in.-long oval leaves, 2–3 in. wide, are dark green above, silvery green beneath, glowing red in fall. Creamy white spring flowers are not spectacular but so abundant they give good show. They form in fluffy, flattish clusters 3–7 in. wide. Shiny, bluish black, ½-in.-wide fruit, enjoyed by birds, ripens in late summer. Plant in full sun for most flowers and best fall color.

'Variegata', WEDDING CAKE TREE, is a rare but highly desirable form; leaves have an irregular white-and-yellow margin.

C. florida. FLOWERING DOGWOOD, EASTERN DOGWOOD. Tree. Zones 31, 32, 34–41. Native to eastern U.S., from New England to central Florida. Has been called the most beautiful native tree of North America. May reach 40 ft. high and wide, but 20–30 ft. more common. Low-branching tree has fairly horizontal branch pattern and upturned branch tips; makes beautiful winter silhouette. Old trees broadly pyramidal but rather flat topped. Small springtime flower clusters are surrounded by four roundish, 2–4-in.-wide bracts with notched tips. White is the usual color in the wild, but named selections (see below) come in pink shades to nearly red, in addition to white. Flowers almost cover trees in midspring before leaves expand. Oval leaves, 2–6 in. long and 2½ in. wide, are bright green above, lighter beneath; they turn glowing red before they drop. Clusters of small, oval, scarlet fruit last into winter or until birds eat them.

Unfortunately, an anthracnose fungus has been infecting and destroying these trees throughout their range. Dieback symptoms show up first in lower branches and can spread to whole tree. Borers often attack trunks and limbs of stressed trees. *C. florida* has been bred with *C. kousa* to produce more disease-resistant hybrids; see *C. rutgersensis*.

'Cherokee Chief'. Deep rosy red bracts, paler at base.

'Cherokee Princess'. Gives unusually heavy display of white blooms.

'Cloud Nine'. Blooms young and heavily. Produces better in cold climates than other varieties of *C. florida;* also tolerates heat and lack of winter chill better than other varieties.

'Hohman's Gold'. Leaves edged yellow, turning reddish purple with scarlet edge in autumn. Bracts white.

'Pendula'. Drooping branches give it weeping look. White bracts.

'Pink Flame'. Leaves green and cream, deepening to dark green and red. Bracts pink.

'Purple Glory'. Leaves purple, turning deep purple-black in autumn. Bracts dark red.

'Rainbow'. Leaves strongly marked bright yellow on green. Heavy bloomer with large white bracts.

'Rubra'. Longtime favorite for its pink or rose bracts.

'Welchii'. TRICOLOR DOGWOOD. Best known for its variegated, 4-in.-long leaves of creamy white, pink, deep rose, and green throughout spring and summer; leaves turn deep rose to almost red in fall. Rather inconspicuous pinkish to white bracts are not profuse. Does best with some shade.

C. kousa. KOUSA DOGWOOD. Large shrub or small tree. Zones 31, 32, 34. Native to Japan and Korea. Later blooming (late spring or early summer) than other flowering dogwoods. Can be big multistemmed shrub or (with training) small tree to 20 ft. or higher. Delicate limb structure and spreading, dense horizontal growth habit. Lustrous, medium green leaves, 4 in. long, have rusty brown hairs at base of veins on undersurface. Yellow or scarlet fall color.

Flowers along tops of branches show above leaves. Creamy white, slender-pointed, 2–3-in.-long, rather narrow bracts surround flower cluster, turn pink along edges. In late summer–fall, red fruit hangs below branches like big strawberries. 'Milky Way' is more floriferous and has pure white bracts. 'Summer Stars' blooms later and is lavish in bloom. 'Satomi' ('Rosabella') has pink bracts. *C. k. chinensis,* native to China, has larger leaves and larger bracts. This species is less susceptible to diseases than *C. florida* and has been bred with the latter to produce resistant hybrids; see *C. rutgersensis.*

C. mas. CORNELIAN CHERRY. Zones 32, 34–41. Pest-free dogwood native to southern Europe and Asia. Usually an airy, twiggy shrub but can be trained as a small tree, 15–20 ft. high. Provides a progression of color throughout the year. One of earliest dogwoods to bloom, bearing clustered masses of small, soft yellow blossoms on bare twigs in late winter or early spring. Shiny green, 2–4-in.-long, oval leaves turn yellow in fall; some forms turn red. Autumn color is enhanced by clusters of bright scarlet, cherry-size fruits that hang on until birds get them. Fruits are edible and are frequently used in making preserves. In winter, flaking bark mottled gray and tan provides interest. 'Variegata' features leaves marbled creamy white.

C. rutgersensis. STELLAR DOGWOOD. Tree. Zones 31, 32, 34–41. This hybrid between *C. florida* and *C. kousa* has greater disease resistance than *C. florida*. Single-stemmed tree to about 20 ft. Bloom time falls between the midspring bloom of *C. florida* and the late-spring or early-summer bloom of *C. kousa;* flower bracts are produced with the leaves. 'Stellar Pink' has pink bracts; 'Aurora', 'Galaxy', and 'Ruth Ellen' bear broad-bracted white flowers; 'Constellation' and 'Stardust' have narrower white bracts. 'Constellation' has the most upright growth habit; other varieties are more rounded. All have brilliant red fall leaves.

C. sanguinea. BLOODTWIG DOGWOOD. Shrub. Zones 31, 32, 34–45. Big show comes in fall with dark bloodred foliage and in winter with bare, purplish to dark red twigs and branches. Prune severely in spring to produce new branches and twigs for winter color. Grows as big multistemmed shrub to 12 ft. high, about 8 ft. wide. Dark green leaves 1½–3 in. long. Late-spring flowers are greenish white in 2-in.-wide clusters. Black fruit.

'Viridissima'. Green winter shoots.

'Winter Beauty' ('Winter Flame'). Red and orange-yellow winter shoots.

C. sericea. (**C. stolonifera**). REDTWIG DOGWOOD, RED-OSIER DOGWOOD. Shrub. Zones 31, 32, 34–45. Native to moist places, eastern North America and Northern California to Alaska. Another dogwood with brilliant show of red fall foliage and bright red winter twigs striking against a snowy backdrop. Grows rapidly as a big multistemmed shrub, 7–9 ft. high and wide spreading. Leaves oval, 1½–2½ in. long, fresh deep green. The plant blossoms throughout the summer months, bearing small, creamy white flowers in 2-in.-wide clusters among the leaves; blooms are followed by white or bluish fruits.

Use this adaptable native as a space filler on moist ground (good for holding banks) or plant it along property line as a screen. Spreads widely by creeping underground stems and rooting branches. To control spread, use a spade to cut off roots; also trim branches that touch ground. Shade tolerant.

C. s. baileya. 6–8 ft. tall; exceptionally bright red twigs in winter.

'Cardinal'. Cherry red stems; originated in Minnesota.

C. s. coloradensis. COLORADO REDTWIG. Native from Yukon to New Mexico and California; 5–6 ft. high. Brownish red stems. Its variety 'Cheyenne' is redder.

'Flaviramea'. YELLOWTWIG DOGWOOD. Yellow twigs and branches.

'Isanti'. A compact 5 ft. tall, with bright red stems.

'Kelseyi' ('Nana'). Seldom over 1½ ft. tall; not as red as the species.

'Silver and Gold'. Yellow stems; green leaves with creamy border.

CORONILLA varia

CROWN VETCH	
Fabaceae (Leguminosae)	
DECIDUOUS PERENNIAL GROUND COVER	
🌿 ZONES 31, 32, 34–45	
☀️ FULL SUN	
💧 MODERATE WATER	

Coronilla varia

Related to peas, beans, and clovers. Creeping roots and rhizomes make it a tenacious ground cover. Straggling stems to 2 ft. high; leaves made up of 11–25 oval leaflets, ½–¾ in. long. Lavender pink flowers in 1-in. clusters soon become bundles of brown, slender, fingerlike seedpods. Dies back in winter, even in mild climates. For most attractive growth, mow early in spring. Too invasive and rank for flower beds. Use for covering erosion-prone banks and in fringes of garden. Once established, difficult to eliminate. 'Penngift' takes sun or shade.

CORTADERIA selloana

PAMPAS GRASS	
Poaceae (Gramineae)	
EVERGREEN GIANT ORNAMENTAL GRASS	
🌿 ZONES 31, WARMER PARTS OF 32, EXCEPT AS NOTED	
☀️ FULL SUN	
💧💧💧 ANY AMOUNT OF MOISTURE	

Cortaderia

Native to Argentina. Very fast growing in rich soil in mild climates; from gallon-can size to 8 ft. in one season. Established, may reach 20 ft. in height. Each plant is a fountain of saw-toothed, grassy leaves above which, in late summer, rise long stalks bearing 1–3-ft. white to chamois or pink flower plumes.

'Pumila' is dwarf and hardy throughout Zone 32 and often in Zone 34 with winter protection. 'Andes Silver' (silvery plumes) and 'Patagonia' (bluish gray-green leaves) are hardy in Zones 31, 32, 34, and 39.

There is a chance that, under certain circumstances, this plant—like its truly worthless cousin *C. jubata*—may seed itself freely, releasing its seeds into the wind to germinate and grow wherever they land. The result is a multitude of unwanted seedlings that can crowd out more desirable

plants. For this reason, nurseries in some areas no longer sell *Cortaderia* at all. Many horticulturists recommend against further landscaping with *C. selloana* and suggest removing it from gardens bordering wild lands, where it might threaten native plants. Grub out volunteer seedlings wherever they appear.

CORYDALIS

Fumariaceae	
PERENNIALS	
🌿 ZONES 32, 34, 35, 37, 39–43	
☀️ PARTIAL SHADE	
💧 MOIST, NOT SOGGY, SOIL	

Corydalis

Handsome clumps of dainty, divided leaves much like those of bleeding heart (to which it is closely related) or maidenhair fern. Clusters of small, spurred flowers. Plant in rich, moist soil. Effective in rock crevices, in open woodland, near pool or streamside. Combine with ferns, columbine, bleeding heart, primrose. Divide clumps or sow seed in spring or fall. Plants self-sow in garden.

C. cheilanthifolia. Hardy Chinese native, 8–10 in. high, with fernlike green foliage. Clusters of yellow, ½-in.-long flowers in spring.

C. flexuosa. Recently introduced from western China. Forms 1-ft. mound of blue-green, fernlike foliage. Narrow, erect clusters of sky blue flowers borne in early spring and sporadically during the growing season. Selections include 'Blue Panda' and 'Pere David'.

C. lutea. Native to southern Europe. To 15 in. tall. Many-stemmed plant with masses of gray-green foliage. Golden yellow, ¾-in.-long, short-spurred flowers throughout summer.

C. solida. To 10 in. high, with erect clusters of up to 20 purplish red, 1-in.-long flowers in spring. Grows from tubers that are sometimes available from bulb catalogs.

CORYLOPSIS

WINTER HAZEL	
Hamamelidaceae	
DECIDUOUS SHRUBS	
🌿 ZONES 31, 32, 34, EXCEPT AS NOTED	
☀️ FULL SUN OR PARTIAL SHADE	
💧 REGULAR WATER	

Corylopsis

Valued for sweet-scented, bell-shaped, soft yellow flowers hanging in short, chainlike clusters on bare branches in spring. New foliage that follows is often tinged pink before turning bright green. Toothed, nearly round leaves somewhat resemble those of filbert *(Corylus)*; fall color varies from none to poor to a good clear yellow. Rather open structure with attractive, delicate branching pattern. Give same soil conditions as for rhododendrons. Grow in wind-sheltered location in shrub border, at edge of woodland.

C. glabrescens. FRAGRANT WINTER HAZEL. Zones 31, 32, 34–41. Hardiest species. Grows 8–15 ft. high and wide. Can be trained as small tree. Flower clusters 1–1½ in. long.

C. pauciflora. BUTTERCUP WINTER HAZEL. Dainty plant to 4–6 ft. high, with spreading habit. Blossoms ¾ in. long, in clusters of two or three.

C. sinensis. To 15 ft. tall, with 3-in. flower clusters. 'Spring Purple' has purplish new growth that matures to green.

C. spicata. SPIKE WINTER HAZEL. New growth purple, turning bluish green. To 8 ft. high, spreading wider; 1–2-in.-long flower clusters, 6–12 blossoms per cluster.

FOR INFORMATION ON SELECTING PLANTS

PLEASE SEE PAGES 47–112

CORYLUS

FILBERT, HAZELNUT

Betulaceae

DECIDUOUS SHRUBS OR TREES

ZONES VARY BY SPECIES

FULL SUN OR PARTIAL SHADE

REGULAR WATER, EXCEPT AS NOTED

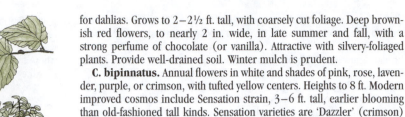

Corylus

Although filberts and hazelnuts are usually thought of as trees grown for their edible nuts (see Filbert, Hazelnut), the following types make pleasing ornamentals. The plants have separate female and male flowers: the female blossoms are inconspicuous, while the male ones, appearing in pendent catkins on bare branches in winter or early spring, are showy. Leaves are roundish to oval, with toothed margins.

C. americana. AMERICAN FILBERT. Shrub. Zones 31, 32, 34–43. Native to the eastern U.S. Multistemmed shrub to 15 ft. high. Heart-shaped to oval, pointed leaves with toothed edges. The autumn nuts are edible.

C. avellana. EUROPEAN FILBERT. Shrub. Zones 32, 34–41. To 10–15 ft. high and wide. One of the species grown for nuts. Its ornamental varieties, including the following two, are more widely grown than the species.

'Contorta'. HARRY LAUDER'S WALKING STICK. Rounded to 8–10 ft. tall. Grown for fantastically gnarled and twisted branches and twigs, revealed after its 2–2½-in. leaves turn yellow and drop in autumn. Branches are used in flower arrangements. Plants are almost always grafted, so suckers arising from the base below the graft should be removed; they won't have contorted form.

'Fusco-rubra' ('Atropurpurea'). To 10–15 ft. high and wide, with 3–4-in. leaves in reddish purple.

C. colurna. TURKISH HAZEL. Tree. Zones 32, 34, 37, 39. Pyramidal in form; usually 40–50 ft. (possibly 75 ft.) tall and about half as wide, with leaves to 6 in. long. Can be grown as a single- or multitrunked tree. Flaking, mottled bark provides winter interest. Produces small, clustered nuts. Flourishes in areas with hot summers and cold winters. Attractive tree in its own right, and a parent (with *C. avellana*) of hybrids called trazels. Quite drought tolerant once established.

C. maxima. Shrub or tree. Zones 31, 32, 34, 36–41; also eastern parts of 35. Native to southeastern Europe. One of the species grown for nuts. Suckering shrub to 12–15 ft. high; can be trained as small tree. Most widely grown ornamental form is 'Purpurea', which has leaves to 6 in. long in rich dark purple and heavily purple-tinted male catkins. Leaf color fades to green in hot climates.

COSMOS

Asteraceae (Compositae)

PERENNIALS AND ANNUALS

ALL ZONES, EXCEPT AS NOTED

FULL SUN

MODERATE WATER

Cosmos

Native to tropical America, mostly Mexico. Showy summer- and fall-blooming plants, open and branching in habit, with bright green divided leaves and daisylike flowers in many colors and forms (single, double, crested, and frilled). Heights vary from 2½ to 8 ft. Use for mass color in borders or background, or as filler among shrubs. Useful in arrangements if flowers are cut when freshly opened and placed immediately in deep cool water. Sow seed in open ground from spring to summer, or set out transplants from flats. Plant in not-too-rich soil. Plants self-sow freely, attract birds.

C. atrosanguineus. CHOCOLATE COSMOS. Tuberous-rooted perennial. Zones 31, 32 (warmer parts). Where winters are colder, dig and store as for dahlias. Grows to 2–2½ ft. tall, with coarsely cut foliage. Deep brownish red flowers, to nearly 2 in. wide, in late summer and fall, with a strong perfume of chocolate (or vanilla). Attractive with silvery-foliaged plants. Provide well-drained soil. Winter mulch is prudent.

C. bipinnatus. Annual flowers in white and shades of pink, rose, lavender, purple, or crimson, with tufted yellow centers. Heights to 8 ft. Modern improved cosmos include Sensation strain, 3–6 ft. tall, earlier blooming than old-fashioned tall kinds. Sensation varieties are 'Dazzler' (crimson) and 'Radiance' (rose with red center); white and pink are also available. 'Candystripe' has smaller (3-in.) white-and-rose flowers, blooms even earlier on smaller plants. Seashell strain has rolled, quilled ray florets like long, narrow cones.

C. sulphureus. YELLOW COSMOS. Annual. Grows to 7 ft., with yellow or golden yellow flowers with yellow centers. Tends to become weedy-looking at end of season. Klondike strain grows 3–4 ft. tall, with 2-in. semidouble flowers ranging from scarlet orange to yellow. Dwarf Klondike (Sunny) strain is 1½ ft. tall, with 1½-in. flowers.

COSTMARY. See CHRYSANTHEMUM balsamita

COTINUS coggygria (Rhus cotinus)

SMOKE TREE

Anacardiaceae

DECIDUOUS SHRUB OR SMALL TREE

ZONES 31, 32, 34–41

FULL SUN

MODERATE WATER

Cotinus coggygria

Unusual shrub-tree creating broad, urn-shaped mass usually as wide as high—typically 15 ft. tall, though it may eventually grow to 25 ft. Naturally multistemmed but can be trained to a single trunk. Common name derived from dramatic puffs of "smoke" from fading flowers: as the tiny, greenish blooms wither, they send out elongated stalks clothed in fuzzy lavender pink hairs. In the species, the roundish, 1½–3-in. leaves are bluish green in summer. Purple-leafed types are more commonly grown. Foliage of 'Purpureus' fades to green by midsummer; 'Royal Purple' (the variety with the deepest purple coloration) and 'Velvet Cloak' retain their purple leaves through summer. All types turn yellow or orange red in fall.

Plants are at their best under stress in poor or rocky soil. In cultivated gardens, provide fast drainage and avoid overly wet conditions.

A less widely grown American species is *C. obovatus*, American smoke tree. It is somewhat larger than C. *coggygria*, like a small tree with bigger leaves; fall color is equally striking.

COTONEASTER

Rosaceae

EVERGREEN, SEMIEVERGREEN, DECIDUOUS SHRUBS

ZONES VARY BY SPECIES

FULL SUN, EXCEPT AS NOTED

MODERATE WATER

Cotoneaster

Members of this genus range from low types used as ground covers to small, stiffly upright shrubs to tall-growing (18-ft.) shrubs of fountainlike form with graceful, arching branches. All grow vigorously and thrive with little or no maintenance, can tolerate poor soil and drought. White or pinkish springtime flowers resemble tiny single roses; though not showy, they are pretty because of their abundance. Usual color of fall and winter berries is red or orange red.

While some medium and tall growers can be sheared, they look best when allowed to maintain natural fountain shapes. Prune only to enhance graceful arch of branches. Keep medium growers looking young by pruning out portion of oldest wood each year. Prune ground covers to remove dead or awkward branches. Give flat growers room to spread. Don't plant near walk or drive where branch ends will need frequent cutting back.

Cotoneasters are useful if not striking shrubs, and can be attractive in the proper setting. Some are especially attractive in form and branching pattern (*C. congestus, C. horizontalis*), while others are notable for colorful, long-lasting fruit (*C. franchetii, C. microphyllus*). Trailing varieties make excellent ground cover plants.

C. acutifolius. PEKING COTONEASTER. Deciduous. Zones 32, 34–43. To 10 ft. tall and as wide, with glossy green foliage turning red in fall. Fruit is black. Useful as hedge or screen.

C. adpressus praecox. Deciduous. Zones 31, 32, 34–43. To 1½ ft. tall, 6 ft. wide, with shiny leaves turning maroon red in fall. Profuse, bright red, ½-in. fruit. Bank or ground cover. Tolerates some shade. *C. adpressus* is similar, somewhat smaller. 'Little Gem' forms a low cushion.

C. apiculatus. CRANBERRY COTONEASTER. Deciduous. Zones 31, 32, 34–43. Best in cold-winter climates. Dense grower to 3 ft. tall, 6 ft. wide, with small, round leaves turning deep red in autumn. Fruit is large, conspicuous, and abundant. Can take some shade. Use as bank cover, hedge, background planting.

C. congestus (C. microphyllus glacialis). PYRENEES COTONEASTER. Evergreen. Zones 31, 32, 34–39. Slow grower to 3 ft., with dense, downward-curving branches, tiny, dark green leaves, small, bright red fruit. Use in containers, rock gardens, above walls.

C. dammeri (C. humifusus). BEARBERRY COTONEASTER. Evergreen. Zones 31, 32, 34–41. Fast, prostrate growth to 3–6 in. tall, 10 ft. wide. Branches root along ground. Leaves are bright, glossy green; fruit bright red. Many varieties differ somewhat in height, rate of growth. 'Coral Beauty' is 6 in. tall; 'Eichholz', 10–12 in. tall with a scattering of red-orange leaves in fall; 'Lowfast', 1 ft. tall; 'Skogsholmen', 1½ ft. tall. All are good ground covers in sun or partial shade and can drape over walls, cascade down slopes.

C. divaricatus. SPREADING COTONEASTER. Deciduous. Zones 31, 32, 34–41. Stiff growth to 6 ft. tall and wide. Dark green leaves closely set on branches turn orange red in fall. Egg-shaped, bright red fruits are ½ in. long. Informal hedge, screen, bank planting.

C. franchetii. Evergreen. Zones 31, 32, 34, 39. Narrow habit to 10 ft. high with slender, erect stems arching outward toward the top. Foliage is gray green. Spring flowers are pinkish; orange-red fall fruits are long lasting.

C. horizontalis. ROCK COTONEASTER. Deciduous. Zones 31, 32, 34–43. Can be 2–3 ft. tall, 15 ft. wide, with stiff horizontal branches and many branchlets set in herringbone pattern. Leaves are small, round, bright green; turn orange and red before falling. Out of leaf very briefly. Showy red fruit. Effective when given enough room to spread; ugly when branches must be cut short to accommodate traffic. Fine bank cover or low traffic barrier. 'Variegatus' has leaves edged in white. *C. h. perpusillus* is smaller, more compact than species.

C. lucidus. HEDGE COTONEASTER. Deciduous. Zones 31, 32, 34–43. Erect shrub to 10 ft. high and as wide. Glossy, deep green, oval leaves to 2 in. long, turn yellow to red in fall. Black fruits in fall. Often planted as a hedge.

C. microphyllus. ROCKSPRAY COTONEASTER. Evergreen. Zones 31, 32, 34–41. Its horizontal branches trail and root to 6 ft.; secondary branches grow erect to 2–3 ft. Leaves are very small (⅓ in.), dark green, gray beneath. Fruit is rosy red. *C. m. thymifolius,* a smaller plant, has even tinier leaves, with edges rolled under. Both are effective in rock gardens, on banks.

C. multiflorus. Deciduous. Zones 31, 32, 34–43. Grows 6–10 ft. tall as spreading shrub with graceful arching and trailing branches. Dark green leaves are 2½ in. long. Clustered white flowers are showier than those of other cotoneasters. Pinkish red fruits follow. Var. *calocarpus* has larger leaves and a profusion of fruits.

C. salicifolius. WILLOWLEAF COTONEASTER. Evergreen or semievergreen. Zones 31, 32, 34, 39. An erect, spreading shrub to 15–18 ft., with narrow, dark green, 1–3½-in.-long leaves and bright red fruits. Graceful screening or background plant but can self-sow and become invasive.

Better known are the trailing forms used as ground cover. 'Emerald Carpet' is 12–15 in. tall, to 8 ft. wide, with compact habit and small leaves. 'Autumn Fire' ('Herbstfeuer') grows to 2–3 ft. 'Repens' is similar in appearance; it is sometimes grafted to a tall stem of some other cotoneaster species and used as a weeping tree.

COWBERRY. See VACCINIUM vitis-idaea

CRABAPPLE

Rosaceae

DECIDUOUS FRUIT TREES

☉ ZONES 32, 34–43

☉ FULL SUN

⬥ REGULAR WATER DURING FRUIT DEVELOPMENT

Crabapple

Crabapple is a small, usually tart apple. Many kinds are valued more for their abundant springtime flowers than for their fruit; these are flowering crabapples, described under *Malus*. One of the most popular crabapple varieties grown for fruit (used for jelly making and pickling) is 'Transcendent', with 2-in. red-cheeked yellow apples that ripen in summer. Red-fruited 'Maypole' is a newer colonnade apple variety. For information about colonnade types and general care, see Apple.

CRAMBE

Brassicaceae (Cruciferae)

PERENNIALS

☉ ZONES 31, 32, 34, 35, 37, 39–41

☉ FULL SUN

⬥ REGULAR WATER

Crambe

Two species of these big cabbagelike perennials are occasionally seen. Both have large, smooth leaves and much-branched clusters of small, honey-scented white flowers. They appreciate rich, well-drained garden soil and require considerable space.

C. cordifolia. Branching stems bearing dark green, 1-ft.-wide leaves on long stalks make 3-ft.-wide mounds. Flowering stem set with smaller leaves can reach 8 ft. tall. Broad, branching flower cluster, up to 5 ft. wide, somewhat resembles a gargantuan baby's breath. Requires a big garden and leaves a big vacancy when summer flowering is finished; plug in annuals to fill the space. Use in big borders to astonish your friends.

C. maritima. SEA KALE. Branched, purplish stems carry blue-gray leaves up to 1 ft. wide. In early summer, sends up 1–2½-ft.-tall stem with flower clusters to 1½ ft. wide. Once widely used as a vegetable; blanch the leafstalks by placing large pots or boxes over the emerging plants.

CRANBERRY BUSH. See VIBURNUM trilobum

CRANESBILL. See GERANIUM

CRAPE MYRTLE. See LAGERSTROEMIA

C

CRATAEGUS

HAWTHORN

Rosaceae

DECIDUOUS TREES

✔ ZONES 31, 32, 34–41, EXCEPT AS NOTED

☀ FULL SUN

🌢 MODERATE WATER

Crataegus

These small trees, members of the rose family, are known for pretty flower clusters after leaf-out in spring and for showy fruit resembling tiny apples in summer and fall, often into winter. Typically multitrunked, the trees have thorny branches that need some pruning to thin out excess twiggy growth. Hawthorns attract bees and birds.

Will grow in any soil as long as it is well drained. Better grown under somewhat austere conditions, since good soil, regular water, and fertilizer all promote succulent new growth that is most susceptible to fireblight. The disease makes entire branches die back quickly; cut out blighted branches well below dead part. The rust stage of cedar-apple rust can be a problem wherever eastern red cedar (*Juniperus virginiana*) grows nearby. Aphids and scale are widespread potential pests.

C. ambigua. RUSSIAN HAWTHORN. Zones 32, 34–45. Extremely cold hardy. Moderate growth to 15–25 ft. Vase form and twisting branches give attractive silhouette. Leaves to 2½ in. long, deeply cut. White flowers; profuse small red fruit.

C. 'Autumn Glory'. Hybrid origin. Vigorous growth to 25 ft. with 15-ft. spread. Twiggy, dense. Dark green leaves are similar to those of *C. laevigata* but more leathery. Clusters of single white flowers. Very large, glossy, bright red fruit, autumn into winter. Very susceptible to fireblight.

C. crus-galli. COCKSPUR THORN. Wide-spreading tree to 30 ft. Stiff thorns to 3 in. long. Smooth, glossy, toothed leaves are dark green, turning orange to red in fall. White flowers. Dull orange-red fruit. *C. c. inermis* is a thornless variety.

C. laevigata (C. oxyacantha). ENGLISH HAWTHORN. Native to Europe and North Africa. Moderate growth to 18–25 ft. high, 15–20 ft. wide. Best known through its varieties: 'Paul's Scarlet', clusters of double rose to red flowers; 'Double White'; 'Double Pink'. Double-flowered forms set little fruit. 'Crimson Cloud' ('Superba') has bright red single flowers with white centers, vivid red fruit. All have 2-in. toothed, lobed leaves lacking good fall color.

C. lavallei (C. carrierei). CARRIERE HAWTHORN. Zones 31, 32, 34, 35, 37, 39. Hybrid origin. To 25 ft., with 15–20-ft. spread. Very handsome. More erect and open branching than other hawthorns, with less twiggy growth. Leaves dark green, leathery, 2–4 in. long, toothed; turn bronze red after first sharp frost and hang on well into winter. White flowers are followed by loose clusters of large orange to red fruit that lasts all winter. Fruit is messy on walks.

C. mollis. DOWNY HAWTHORN. Big, broad tree to 30 ft.; looks like mature apple tree. Leaves to 4 in. long, lobed, toothed, covered with down. Flowers white, 1 in. wide. Red fruit 1 in. across, also downy; fruit doesn't last on tree as long as that of other species, but has value in jelly making.

C. monogyna. Native to Europe, North Africa, and western Asia. Classic hawthorn of English countryside for hedges and boundary plantings. Little known in the U.S., except for upright variety 'Stricta', 30 ft. tall and 8 ft. wide. White flowers. Small red fruit in clusters, rather difficult to see. Very prone to fireblight, mites, and leaf diseases.

C. nitida. GLOSSY HAWTHORN. Zones 34–39. Hybrid origin. Dense, rounded, thornless tree to 30 ft. Dark green, oval leaves with toothed edges turn orange or red in fall. Clusters of small white flowers in spring, followed by red fruit.

C. oxyacantha. See *C. laevigata*.

C. phaenopyrum (C. cordata). WASHINGTON THORN. Native to southeastern U.S. Moderate growth to 25 ft. with 20-ft. spread. Graceful, open limb structure. Glossy leaves 2–3 in. long with three to five sharp-pointed lobes (like some maples); foliage turns beautiful orange, scarlet,

or purplish in fall. Small white flowers in broad clusters. Shiny red fruit hangs on well into winter. One of the least prone to fireblight.

C. pinnatifida. Native to northeastern Asia. To 20 ft. high, 10–12 ft. wide. Leaves lobed like those of *C. laevigata* but bigger and thicker; they turn red in fall. Tree has more open, upright habit than *C. laevigata*. Flowers white, ¾ in. wide, in 3-in. clusters. Fruit slightly smaller than that of *C. lavallei*.

C. punctata inermis. THORNLESS DOTTED HAWTHORN. Native to eastern and midwestern U.S. Essentially thornless, to 30 ft. high. Plentiful white flowers followed by large (¾-in.), long-lasting dark red fruits.

C. 'Toba'. Zones 31, 34–45. Canadian hybrid of great cold tolerance. To 20 ft. Leaves similar to those of *C. lavallei*. White flowers age to pink. Sets sparse large fruit.

C. viridis 'Winter King'. GREEN HAWTHORN. Moderate growth to 25–30 ft., with rounded to vase-shaped form. Gray-green stems. Clustered white flowers followed by red fruit that lasts all winter. Among the most attractive and trouble-free hawthorns.

CREEPING BENT. See AGROSTIS stolonifera

CREEPING BUTTERCUP. See RANUNCULUS repens 'Pleniflorus'

CREEPING MINT. See MEEHANIA cordata

CREEPING JENNY. See LYSIMACHIA nummularia

CREEPING ZINNIA. See SANVITALIA procumbens

CRESS, GARDEN

Brassicaceae (Cruciferae)

ANNUAL

✔ ALL ZONES

☀ ◐ FULL SUN OR PARTIAL SHADE

🌢 🌢🌢 AMPLE WATER

Garden Cress

It is sometimes called pepper grass and tastes like watercress. Easy to grow as long as weather is cool. Sow seed as early in spring as possible. Plant in rich, moist soil. Make rows 1 ft. apart; thin plants to 3 in. apart (eat thinnings). Cress matures fast; make successive sowings every 2 weeks up to middle of May. Where frosts are mild, sow through fall.

Indoors, try growing garden cress in shallow pots of soil or planting mix in sunny kitchen window. It sprouts in a few days, can be harvested (with scissors) in 2 to 3 weeks. Or grow it by sprinkling seeds on pads of wet cheesecloth; keep damp until harvest in 2 weeks.

CRETE DITTANY. See ORIGANUM dictamnus

CRIMSON GLORY VINE. See VITIS coignetiae

CRINUM

Liliaceae

BULBS

✔ ZONES VARY BY SPECIES OR GROW IN POTS

☀ ◐ FULL SUN OR PARTIAL SHADE

🌢 🌢🌢 AMPLE WATER DURING GROWTH AND BLOOM

🌢 ALL PARTS ARE POISONOUS IF INGESTED

Crinum

Distinguished from their near relative amaryllis by long, slender flower tube that is longer than flower segments. Long-stalked cluster of lily-shaped, 4–6-in.-long, fragrant flowers rises in spring or summer from persistent clump of long, strap-shaped or sword-shaped leaves. Bulbs large, rather slender, tapering to stemlike neck; thick, fleshy roots. Bulbs generally available (from specialists) all year, but spring or fall planting is preferred.

Grow these tender plants in containers moved outdoors in summer, indoors or to a frost-proof location when weather turns cold in autumn. Provide soil with plenty of humus. Set bulbs 6 in. under surface; give ample space to develop. Divide infrequently.

Excellent for tropical effect. Mail-order nurseries offer a wide selection.

C. bulbispermum (C. longifolium). Zones 31, 32, 34. Long, narrow, twisting gray-green leaves tend to lie on the ground. Flowers are deep pink or white.

C. 'Ellen Bosanquet'. Zones 31, 32. Leaves are broad, bright green. Flowers are deep rose, nearly red.

C. powellii. Zones 31, 32, 34–41. Long, thin, wavy-edged bright green leaves. Bell-shaped, dark rose-colored flowers. 'Album' is a good pure white form, vigorous enough to serve as a tall ground cover in shade.

CROCOSMIA

Iridaceae

CORMS

ZONES 31, 32, 34–39; OR DIG AND STORE

PART SHADE IN HOTTEST CLIMATES

MODERATE TO LITTLE WATER

Crocosmia

Native to tropical and southern Africa. Formerly called tritonia and related to freesia, ixia, sparaxis. Sword-shaped leaves in basal clumps. Small orange, red, yellow flowers bloom in summer on branched stems. Useful for splashes of garden color and for cutting. Where winter temperatures remain above 10°F/−12°C, needs no winter protection. Grow in sheltered location and provide winter mulch where temperatures dip to 0°F/−18°C. In colder areas, dig and store over winter.

C. crocosmiiflora (Tritonia crocosmiiflora). MONTBRETIA. A favorite for generations, montbretias can still be seen in older gardens where they have spread freely, as though native, producing orange-crimson flowers 1½–2 in. across on 3–4-ft. stems. Sword-shaped leaves to 3 ft., ½–1 in. wide. Many once-common named forms in yellow, orange, cream, and near scarlet are making a comeback. Good for naturalizing on slopes or in fringe areas.

C. hybrids. Sturdy plants with branching spikes of large flowers. Often called Masoniorum Hybrids. 'Lucifer' is 4 ft. tall, with bright red flowers. 'Solfatare', to 2 ft., has bronze-tinted foliage and pale orange-yellow flowers.

C. masoniorum. Leaves 2½ ft. long, 2 in. wide. Flowers flaming orange to scarlet, 1½ in. across, borne in dense, one-sided clusters on 2½–3-ft. stems that arch over at the top. Buds open slowly from base to tip of clusters, and old flowers drop cleanly from stems. Flowers last about 2 weeks when cut.

Crocosmia masoniorum

CROCUS

Iridaceae

CORMS

ZONES 31, 32, 34–45; BEST IN COLD CLIMATES

FULL SUN OR PARTIAL SHADE

REGULAR WATER DURING GROWTH AND BLOOM

Crocus

Leaves are basal and grasslike—often with silvery midrib—and appear before, with, or after flowers, depending on species. Flowers with long stemlike tubes and flaring or cup-shaped petals are 1½–3 in. long; the short (true) stems are hidden underground.

Most crocus bloom in late winter or earliest spring, but some species bloom in fall, the flowers rising from bare earth weeks or days after planting. Mass them for best effect. Attractive in rock gardens, between stepping-stones, in containers. Set corms 2–3 in. deep in light, porous soil. Divide every 3 to 4 years. Won't naturalize where winters are warm.

C. ancyrensis. Flowers golden yellow, small, very early.

C. angustifolius. CLOTH OF GOLD CROCUS. Formerly *C. susianus*. Orange-gold, starlike flowers with dark brown center stripe. Starts blooming in January in warmest areas, in March in coldest climates.

C. chrysanthus. Orange yellow, sweet scented. Hybrids and selections of this plant range from white and cream through yellow and blue shades, often marked with deeper color. Usually even more freely flowering than *C. vernus*, but with smaller flowers. Spring bloom. Popular varieties are 'Blue Pearl', palest blue; 'Cream Beauty', pale yellow; 'E. P. Bowles', yellow with purple featherings; 'Ladykiller', outside purple edged white, inside white feathered purple; 'Princess Beatrix', blue with yellow center; and 'Snow Bunting', pure white.

C. imperati. Bright lilac inside, buff veined purple outside, saucer shaped. Early spring.

C. kotschyanus. Formerly *C. zonatus*. Pinkish lavender or lilac flowers in early fall.

C. sativus. SAFFRON CROCUS. Lilac. Orange-red stigma is true saffron of commerce. Interesting rather than showy. Autumn bloom. To harvest saffron, pluck the stigmas as soon as flowers open, dry them, and store them in glass or plastic vials. Stigmas from a dozen flowers will season a good-size paella or similar dish. To get continued good yield of saffron, divide corms as soon as leaves turn brown; replant in fresh or improved soil. Mark planting site with low-growing ground cover so you won't dig up dormant corms.

C. sieberi. Delicate lavender blue with golden throat. One of earliest.

C. speciosus. Showy blue-violet flowers in early fall. Lavender and mauve varieties available. Fast increase by seed and division. Showiest autumn-flowering crocus.

C. tomasinianus. Slender buds; star-shaped, silvery lavender-blue flowers, sometimes with dark blotch at tips of segments. Very early—January or February in milder climates.

C. vernus. DUTCH CROCUS. Familiar crocus in shades of white, yellow, lavender, and purple, often penciled and streaked. February–April (depending on climate). Most vigorous crocus, and only one widely sold in all areas.

AUTUMN CROCUS IN A LAWN

Autumn crocus can add little clusters of lavender pink to a lawn in September. How to create such a picture: in midsummer, peel back small pieces of sod, plant corms in well-amended soil beneath, then lay sod back down and water well. For a more permanent splash of color every spring, plant purple Dutch crocus in fall.

CROSSVINE. See ANISOSTICHUS capreolata

CROTON. See CODIAEUM variegatum

CROWN IMPERIAL. See FRITILLARIA imperialis

CROWN VETCH. See CORONILLA varia

Cruciferae. See Brassicaceae

GROWING SYMBOL EXPLANATIONS

PLEASE SEE PAGE 113

C

CRYPTOMERIA japonica

JAPANESE CRYPTOMERIA

Taxodiaceae

EVERGREEN TREE

ZONES 32, 34–41

FULL SUN

REGULAR WATER

Cryptomeria japonica

Graceful conifer, fast growing (3–4 ft. a year) in youth. Eventually skyline tree with straight columnar trunk, thin red-brown bark peeling in strips. Foliage soft bright green to bluish green in growing season, brownish purple in cold weather. Branches, slightly pendulous, are clothed with ½–1-in.-long needlelike leaves. Roundish, red-brown cones ¾–1 in. wide. These trees are sometimes used in closely planted groves for a Japanese garden effect.

'Elegans'. PLUME CEDAR, PLUME CRYPTOMERIA. Quite unlike species. Feathery, grayish green, soft-textured foliage. Turns rich coppery red or purplish in winter. Grows slowly into broad-based, dense pyramid, 20–60 ft. high. Trunks on old trees may lean or curve. For Oriental effect, prune out some branches to give tiered look. For most effective display, give it space.

'Lobbii Nana' ('Lobbii'). Upright, dwarf, very slow to 4 ft. Foliage dark green.

'Pygmaea' ('Nana'). DWARF CRYPTOMERIA. Bushy dwarf 1½–2 ft. high, 2½ ft. wide. Dark green, needlelike leaves, twisted branches.

'Vilmoriniana'. Slow-growing dwarf to 1–2 ft. Fluffy gray-green foliage turns bronze in late fall and winter. Rock garden or container plant.

CUCUMBER

Cucurbitaceae

ANNUAL VINE

ALL ZONES

FULL SUN

MAINTAIN EVEN SOIL MOISTURE

Cucumber

Each vine needs at least 25 sq. ft., but you can use a fence or trellis to conserve space. Both warm soil to sprout seeds and warmth for pollination are required.

There are long, smooth, green, slicing cucumbers; numerous small pickling cucumbers; and roundish, yellow, mild-flavored lemon cucumbers. Novelties include Oriental varieties (long, slim, very mild), Armenian cucumber (actually a long, curving, pale green, ribbed melon with cucumber look and mild cucumber flavor), and English greenhouse cucumber. This last type must be grown in greenhouse to avoid pollination by bees, with subsequent loss of form and flavor; when well grown it's the mildest of all cucumbers.

Bush cucumbers—varieties with compact vines—take up little garden space. Burpless varieties resemble hothouse cucumbers in shape and mild flavor but can be grown outdoors. Pickling cucumbers should be picked as soon as they have reached the proper size—tiny for sweet pickles (gherkins), larger for dills or pickle slices. They grow too large very quickly.

'Sweet Success' has quality of greenhouse cucumber but can be grown outdoors. Flowers are all female, but plants need no pollinator. Grow on trellis for long, straight cucumbers.

Plant seeds in sunny spot 1 or 2 weeks after average date of last frost. To grow cucumbers on trellis, plant seeds 1 in. deep and 1–3 ft. apart and permit main stem to reach top of support. Pick while young to ensure continued production.

Row covers will protect seedlings from various insect pests, including cucumber beetles and flea beetles; remove when flowering begins so that pollination can occur. Whiteflies are potential pest late in season; hose off plants regularly or hang yellow sticky traps. Misshapen fruit is usually due to uneven watering or poor pollination.

FRENCH CORNICHON PICKLES

For a gourmet pickle, buy seed of French cornichons from a specialty seed dealer. Plant when soil warms and all danger of frost is past; give full sun, fertile soil, consistent moisture. It's best to grow these little cucumbers on a trellis or in a 3-ft.-tall cage (two seedlings to a 14-in.-diameter cage). As plants mature, check daily for fruit. For pickling, take fruits at 1–2 in. long. Larger fruits, 2–2½ in., are best for eating fresh.

CUCUMBER TREE. See MAGNOLIA acuminata

CUCUMIS DIPSACEUS FLEXUOSUS. See GOURD

CUCURBITA FOETIDISSIMUS. See GOURD

Cucurbitaceae. The gourd family consists of vines with yellow or white flowers and large, fleshy, typically seedy fruits—chayote, cucumbers, gourds, melons, pumpkins, and squash.

CULVER'S ROOT. See VERONICASTRUM virginicum

CUDRANIA tricuspidata

CHE TREE

Moraceae

DECIDUOUS TREE

ZONES 31, 32, 34, 39

FULL SUN

REGULAR WATER

Cudrania tricuspidata

A small, spiny, rounded tree to 20 ft., native to China, Korea, and Japan. Little known to American gardeners and usually available only from specialist edible plant nurseries, che is an excellent small fruit tree with few insect or disease problems, and well suited for low-maintenance gardens. The tiny greenish to yellow flowers are crowded together in ball-like clusters in the axils of the leaves. In the grafted seedless form usually available, the blossoms give rise to rounded, bright red, rind-covered fleshy fruits that are sweet, juicy, and rather figlike in flavor. These shiny fruits are not attractive to birds and are produced in such quantity as to give the tree a decidedly ornamental appearance.

Adaptable and easy to grow, che tree requires only ordinary, well-drained soil and full sun in order to thrive.

CUNNINGHAMIA lanceolata

CHINA FIR

Taxodiaceae

EVERGREEN TREE

ZONES 31, 32

FULL SUN

REGULAR WATER

Cunninghamia lanceolata

Native to China. Picturesque conifer with heavy trunk, stout, whorled branches, and drooping branchlets. Stiff, needlelike, sharp-pointed leaves are 1½–2½ in. long, green above, whitish beneath. Brown, 1–2-in. cones are interesting but not profuse. Grows at moderate rate to 30 ft. with 20-ft. spread. Becomes less attractive as it ages. Prune out dead branchlets. Among palest of needled evergreens in spring and summer; turns red bronze in cold winters. Protect from wind. 'Glauca', which has striking blue-gray foliage, is more widely grown and hardier than the species.

CUP-AND-SAUCER. See CAMPANULA medium

CUP-AND-SAUCER VINE. See COBAEA scandens

CUP FLOWER. See NIEREMBERGIA

CUPHEA ignea

CIGAR PLANT

Lythraceae

PERENNIAL GROWN AS AN ANNUAL

ALL ZONES

POTTED PLANTS BEST IN LIGHT SHADE

REGULAR WATER

Cuphea ignea

Native to Mexico, Guatemala. Leafy, compact, 1 ft. high and wide. Leaves narrow, dark green, 1–1½ in. long. Flowers tubular, ¾ in. long, bright red with white tip and dark ring at end (hence name "cigar plant"). Blooms summer and fall. Interesting for summer color in small beds, as formal edging for border, along paths, in containers. Pinch tips for compact growth. Grow as an annual. Take cuttings late in the season to start house plants.

CUPID'S DART. See CATANANCHE caerulea

CUP PLANT. See SILPHIUM perfoliatum

Cupressaceae. The cypress family differs from the pine and yew families in having leaves that are usually reduced to scales and cones with few scales. Cones may even be berrylike, as in junipers (*Juniperus*).

CUPRESSOCYPARIS leylandii

LEYLAND CYPRESS

Cupressaceae

EVERGREEN TREE

ZONES 31, 32, 34, 39

FULL SUN

REGULAR TO MODERATE WATER

Cupressocyparis leylandii

Hybrid between *Chamaecyparis nootkatensis* and *Cupressus macrocarpa*. Grows very fast (from cuttings to 15–20 ft. in 5 years). Usually reaches 60–70 ft. in gardens. Most often planted as a quick screen. Long, slender, upright branches of flattened, gray-green foliage sprays give youthful tree narrow pyramidal form, though it can become open and floppy. Can be pruned into tall hedge, 10–15 ft. high, but will quickly get away from you without regular maintenance. Produces small cones composed of scales. Accepts wide variety of soil and climate conditions, strong wind. In warm-summer regions, loses stiff, upright habit and is subject to coryneum canker fungus. Bagworms are a potential problem. 'Naylor's Blue' has grayish blue foliage; 'Castlewellan' has golden new growth and narrow, erect habit; 'Emerald Isle' has bright green foliage on plant 20–25 ft. tall, 6–8 ft. wide.

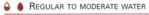

FOR INFORMATION ON YOUR CLIMATE ZONE

PLEASE SEE PAGES 30–46

CURRANT

Grossulariaceae (Saxifragaceae)

DECIDUOUS SHRUBS

ZONES 34–43 FOR BEST FRUIT PRODUCTION

FULL SUN TO PARTIAL SHADE

REGULAR WATER

Currant

Many-stemmed, thornless shrubs to 3–5 ft. high and equally wide, depending on vigor and variety. Attractive lobed, toothed leaves to 3 in. wide drop early in fall. Drooping clusters of yellowish flowers bloom in early spring, followed in summer by fruit used in jellies, jams, preserves.

Like other members of the *Ribes* tribe, currants may be hosts to white pine blister rust and are still banned in some areas where white pines grow; check with Cooperative Extension Office or a nursery for rules in your area. Black currants, derived from *R. nigrum* or *R. odoratum* (see descriptions under *Ribes*), are favored hosts. Rust-immune black currant hybrids are 'Consort', 'Coronet', and 'Crusader'; all have rich blackberry-like flavor and are good in jams and preserves. Red and white currants, derived from *R. sativum,* are less likely to be hosts; they are tart flavored and used mainly in jellies. Varieties include red-fruited 'Red Lake', 'Perfection', and 'Cherry' as well as 'White Imperial'.

Generally self-fertile. Do not grow where water or soil is high in sodium. Mulch well. Prune during dormant season. On red and white currants, cut to the ground stems older than 3 years; on black currants, remove stems older than 2 years. Older canes are often darker and peeling.

For ornamental relatives, see *Ribes*.

CUSHION PINK. See SILENE acaulis

CYCAS revoluta

SAGO PALM

Cycadaceae

CYCADS

ALL ZONES

PARTIAL SHADE

REGULAR WATER

Cycas revoluta

This evergreen plant is neither a fern nor a palm, but rather a primitive, cone-bearing relative of conifers. A rosette of dark green, featherlike leaves grows from a central point at the top of a single trunk (sometimes several trunks).

Native to Japan. In youth (2–3 ft. tall), has airy, lacy appearance of a fern; with age (grows very slowly to as high as 10 ft.), looks more like palm. Leaves are 2–3 ft. long (larger on very old plants), divided into many narrow, leathery segments.

Tough, tolerant house or patio plant; use it for tropical effect. Also good subject for bonsai. Leaf spot disease is a problem in rainy climates.

CYCLAMEN

Primulaceae

TUBEROUS-ROOTED PERENNIALS

ZONES VARY BY SPECIES

FULL SUN OR PARTIAL SHADE

KEEP SOIL MOIST DURING GROWTH

Cyclamen

Grown for pretty white, pink, rose, or red flowers carried atop attractive clump of basal leaves. Tender florists' cyclamen is best known, but species described here are smaller flowered, hardier. They bloom as described in listings that follow; all lose their leaves during part of year. Leaves may appear before or with flowers. Use cyclamen in rock gardens, in naturalized clumps under trees, or as carpets under rhododendrons and large noninvasive ferns. Or grow them in pots out of direct sun.

All kinds of cyclamen grow best in fairly rich, porous soil with lots of humus. Plant tubers 6–10 in. apart; cover with ½ in. soil. Best planting time is dormant period, June–August. Top-dress annually with light application of potting soil with complete fertilizer added. Do not cultivate around roots.

Cyclamen grow readily from seed; small-flowered hardy species take several years to bloom. Older strains of florists' cyclamen needed 15 to 18 months from seed to bloom; newer strains can bloom in as little as 7 months. Grown out-of-doors in open ground, cyclamen often self-sows.

C. cilicium. Zones 32, 34. Pale pink, purple-blotched, fragrant flowers on 2–6-in. stems, fall–winter. Leaves are mottled. There is a white-flowered variety, 'Album'.

C. coum. Zones 32, 34–41. Deep crimson rose flowers on 4–6-in. stems in winter and early spring; round, deep green leaves. White, pink varieties.

C. europaeum. See *C. purpurascens*

C. hederifolium (C. neapolitanum). 32, 34–41. Large light green leaves marbled silver and white. Rose pink flowers bloom on 3–4-in. stems, late summer–fall. There is a white variety. One of most vigorous and easiest to grow; very reliable in cold-winter climates. Set tubers a foot apart.

C. purpurascens (C. europaeum). Zones 32, 34, 39. Distinctly fragrant crimson flowers on 5–6-in. stems, late summer–fall. Bright green leaves mottled silvery white; almost evergreen.

C. repandum. Zone 32. Bright crimson flowers with long, narrow petals on 5–6-in. stems in spring. Rich green, ivy-shaped leaves, marbled silver, toothed on edges.

CYDONIA. See CHAENOMELES

CYDONIA oblonga. See QUINCE, FRUITING

CYMBALARIA muralis (Linaria cymbalaria)

Cymbalaria

KENILWORTH IVY

Scrophulariaceae

PERENNIAL USUALLY GROWN AS ANNUAL

✹ ZONES 31, 32, 34, 39

☼ ● PARTIAL OR FULL SHADE

💧 REGULAR WATER

Dainty creeper related to snapdragon. Leaves 1 in. wide or less, smooth, with three to seven toothlike lobes. Small lilac blue flowers carried singly on stalks a little longer than leaves. Trailing stems root at joints. Unshowy, but valuable as small-scale ground cover in cool, shady places or as decoration for terrarium or hanging basket. In ground, can be invasive, sometimes even sprouting in chinks of stone or brick wall.

CYMBOPOGON citratus

Cymbopogon citratus

LEMON GRASS

Poaceae (Gramineae)

TENDER PERENNIAL

✹ ALL ZONES

☼ FULL SUN

💧 REGULAR WATER

All plant parts are strongly lemon scented; widely used as an ingredient in Southeast Asian cooking. Very frost sensitive. Pot up a division and keep it indoors or in a greenhouse over winter. Or grow in pots year-round; repot each spring and move outdoors for summer when all danger of frost is past.

Clumps of inch-wide light bluish green leaves grow 2–3 ft. tall. Sheathed leaf bases are nearly bulbous in appearance.

CYMOPHYLLUS fraseri

Cymophyllus fraseri

FRASER'S SEDGE

Cyperaceae

PERENNIAL

✹ ZONES 31, 32

☼ ● PARTIAL TO FULL SHADE

💧 MORE THAN REGULAR WATER

Closely related to sedges (*Carex* spp.), Fraser's sedge is native to moist woodlands and streambanks in the southeastern U.S. Produces clumps of glossy, strap-shaped, 18–20-in.-long leaves that form a low, evergreen clump. Fluffy, white, 1-in.-long flower clusters are held on 15-in. stalks above the leaves in early summer. Requires evenly moist but well-drained soil very rich in organic matter. Mulch plants with evergreen boughs in early winter where they are marginally hardy or where winter sun will scorch the leaves. Use in woodland gardens, natural areas, or shaded rock gardens.

CYNARA cardunculus

Cynara cardunculus

CARDOON

Compositae

PERENNIAL VEGETABLE

✹ ZONES 31, 32, WARMER PARTS OF 34, OR AS ANNUAL

☼ FULL SUN

💧 MORE THAN REGULAR WATER

Related to the globe artichoke, the cardoon is hardy in the warmest parts of the Northeast, and cultivated throughout the rest of the region as a bold annual foliage plant. Leaves are silvery gray, spiny, shallowly lobed, and up to 20 in. long. Purple thistlelike flowerheads up to 3 in. across bloom on woolly gray stems and are suitable for dried flower arrangements. Blanched leaf stalks and midribs are edible. To blanch, secure leaf tops in a celerylike bunch, then shield the rest of the plant from sunlight with, for example, black plastic or a cardboard cylinder for 6–8 weeks beginning in fall. In cooler climates, dig up with a considerable rootball and replant safe from frost to complete blanching. Start plants indoors from seeds before planting out. Soil must be deep, fertile, and well drained.

PRACTICAL GARDENING DICTIONARY

PLEASE SEE PAGES 449–523

CYNODON dactylon

BERMUDA GRASS, BERMUDA

Poaceae (Gramineae)

LAWN GRASS

☀ ZONES 31, 32, 35

☼ FULL SUN

◐ WATER LESS THAN MOST LAWN GRASSES

Cynodon dactylon

Subtropical fine-textured grass that spreads rapidly by surface and underground runners. Tolerates heat; looks good if well maintained. It turns brown in winter; some varieties stay green longer than others, and most stay green longer if well fed. Bermuda grass can be overseeded with cool-season grasses or dyed green for winter color. Needs sun and should be cut low; ½ to 1 in. is desirable. Needs thatching—removal of matted layer of old stems and stolons beneath the leaves—to look its best.

Common Bermuda is good minimum-maintenance lawn for large area. Needs feeding, careful and frequent mowing to remove seed spikes. Roots invade shrubbery and flower beds if not carefully confined. Can become extremely difficult to eradicate. Plant from hulled seed or sprigs.

Hybrid Bermudas are finer in texture and better in color than common kind. They crowd out common Bermuda in time but are harder to overseed with rye, bluegrass, or red fescue. Help them stay green in winter by feeding in September and October and by removing thatch. Useful in areas with short dormant season. Grow from sprigs (stolons), plugs, or sod.

'Tifdwarf'. Extremely low and dense; takes very close mowing. Slower to establish than others, but slower to spread where it's not wanted. Useful as small-scale ground cover on banks, among rocks.

'Tifgreen'. Fine textured, deep blue green, dense. Few seed spikes; sterile seeds. Takes close mowing; preferred for putting greens.

'Tifway'. Low growth, fine texture, stiff blades, dark green, dense, wear resistant. Slow to start. Sterile (no seeds).

'U-3'. More finely textured than common Bermuda but with obvious and unattractive seed spikes. Very tough. Grow from sprigs; not dependable from seed, tending to revert to mixture of many types. Not up to other hybrids in quality.

CYNOGLOSSUM amabile

CHINESE FORGET-ME-NOT

Boraginaceae

BIENNIAL GROWN AS ANNUAL

☀ ALL ZONES; BEST IN COLDER CLIMATES

☼ FULL SUN

◐ REGULAR WATER

Cynoglossum amabile

Bedding, border, or wild garden plant, 1½–2 ft. high, with grayish green, soft, hairy, lance-shaped leaves. Loose sprays of blue, pink, or white flowers in spring, into summer where weather is cool. Not for hot, humid climates. Blossoms larger than those of forget-me-not *(Myosotis)*, a relative. 'Firmament', most widely available, has rich blue flowers on compact, 1½-ft.-tall plant. Blooms first year from seed sown (preferably where plants are to grow) in spring. Hardy in mild-winter climates, where seeds can be sown in autumn. Plants may self-sow and spread themselves, but unwanted seedlings are easily removed.

Cyperaceae. Members of the sedge family superficially resemble grasses, but their stems are usually three-sided and their leaves are arranged in three ranks. They generally grow in wet places; *Carex* and *Cyperus* are examples.

CYPERUS

Cyperaceae

TENDER PERENNIALS

☀ ALL ZONES

☀ ◐ ● SUN OR SHADE

◐ BOG PLANTS IN NATURE

Cyperus

These are sedges—grasslike plants distinguished from true grasses by three-angled, solid stems and very different flowering parts. Valued for striking form, silhouette, shadow pattern.

Most kinds grow in rich, moist soil or with roots submerged in water, in sun or shade. Groom plants by removing dead or broken stems. Divide plants at end of season; pot up divisions and keep them over the winter as house plants. Hardy outdoors in Zone 31.

C. alternifolius. UMBRELLA PLANT. Narrow, firm, spreading leaves arranged like ribs of umbrella at tops of 2–4-ft. stems. Flowers in dry, greenish brown clusters. Grows in or out of water. Effective near pools, in pots or planters, or in dry stream beds or small rock gardens. Self-sows. Can become weedy, take over a small pool. Dwarf form is 'Gracilis' ('Nanus'). 'Variegatus' has leaves striped or blotched with white.

C. papyrus. PAPYRUS. Tall, graceful, dark green stems 6–10 ft. high, topped with clusters of green threadlike parts to 1½ ft. long (longer than small leaves at base of cluster). Will grow quickly in 2 in. of water in shallow pool, or can be potted and placed on bricks or inverted pot in deeper water. Protect from strong wind. Also grows well in rich, moist soil out of water. Used by flower arrangers.

CYPRESS, FALSE. See CHAMAECYPARIS

CYPRESS, SUMMER. See KOCHIA scoparia

CYPRESS VINE. See IPOMOEA quamoclit

CYPRIPEDIUM

LADY'S SLIPPER, MOCCASIN FLOWER, RAM'S HEAD ORCHID

Orchidaceae

PERENNIALS

☀ ZONES VARY BY SPECIES

☼ PARTIAL SHADE

◐ REGULAR WATER

Cypripedium

Deciduous hardy orchids that grow, according to species, on shady ground in marshes or dry woodlands. Leaves are soft, often hairy, and pleated from top to bottom. Flowers distinguished by swollen, slipperlike sac in white, yellow, pink, or dark purple topped by three spreading red, pink, white, brownish or purple petal-like segments. Planted for their exotic-looking flowers and attractive leaves in informal shady borders, woodland gardens, and shaded parts of rock gardens. Apply thick leaf mold or shredded leaves in fall for winter mulch. Prefers to be left undisturbed but can be increased by division in spring if necessary. Replant divisions at once, keeping some soil from the original root mass with each transplant because it contains helpful fungal elements.

C. acaule. PINK LADY'S SLIPPER, NERVE ROOT. Zones 32, 34–35. Native to dry, acid woodlands in eastern North America. Short-lived and fragile, with single, nodding, 2-in. flowers. Blooms have greenish brown petals above a rosy pink pouch with dark red veins, produced in summer on erect 9-in. stems. Thrives in moist, leafy, neutral to acidic soil, rich with humus and in a sheltered location. Leave undisturbed in the wild. Difficult to propagate and cultivate, almost impossible to transplant from the wild.

C. calceolus var. parviflorum. SMALL YELLOW LADY'S SLIPPER, WHIPPOORWILL SHOE. Zones 32, 34–45. Native to eastern North America. Bears fragrant flowers with golden sacs topped with brownish

D

purple twisted petals in summer. Grows in clumps in the pebbly acidic soil of oak woods, often on north-facing hillsides. Relatively easy to grow in gardens. Purchase plants guaranteed to be propagated in nurseries, not dug from the wild.

C. kentuckiense. Zones 32, 34, 39. Native to the United States. Similar to yellow lady's slipper but bigger. In spring, white to pale cream blooms appear singly at ends of flower stems. Purchase plants guaranteed to be propagated in nurseries, not dug from the wild.

C. reginae. SHOWY LADY'S SLIPPER. Zones 32, 34–35. Native to eastern North America. White petals above a rosy pink pouch produced in early summer, singly or in pairs on erect 30-in. stems. Excellent for bog gardens. Relatively easy to grow in gardens in cool areas. Does not thrive in warm regions. Purchase plants guaranteed to be propagated in nurseries, not dug from the wild.

CYRILLA racemiflora

LEATHERWOOD

Cyrillaceae

DECIDUOUS SHRUB OR SMALL TREE

⚡ ZONES 31, 32, 34–41

☼ ◑ FULL SUN, PARTIAL SHADE

💧 REGULAR WATER

Cyrilla racemiflora

Native to swamps from Virginia to eastern South America but also thrives in moist, well-drained acid soil high in organic matter. A rounded, spreading shrub, usually 10–15 ft. high, for mixed or shrub borders. Leathery, glossy, dark green leaves are 4 in. long and lighter green underneath, turn red and orange in fall. From late summer to fall, 6-in. cylindrical clusters of small, white, scented flowers, followed by little round yellow fruit.

Make sure plants are hardy by choosing plants from northern stock. Protect plants from cold, drying winds. Sow seed directly in the ground or in containers set in a cold frame. Easy to grow from stem cuttings and root cuttings.

CYRTOMIUM

HOLLY FERN

Polypodiaceae

FERN

⚡ ZONES VARY BY SPECIES

◑ ● PARTIAL OR FULL SHADE

💧 REGULAR WATER

Cyrtomium

The ferns in this genus have fronds made up of pointed leaflets with toothed or notched edges. They somewhat resemble holly leaves and inspired the nickname, holly fern. The species described here are native to East Asia. Hardy in mild climates, in colder parts of the Northeast holly ferns are grown as house plants and moved outdoors to a shady deck or patio in summer.

C. caryotideum. Not hardy; grow as house plant, move outdoors in summer. Fronds to 1½ ft. long and 8 in. wide, divided into finely toothed leaflets.

C. falcatum. JAPANESE HOLLY FERN. Zones 31, 32. Coarse-textured but handsome fern, 2–3 ft. tall, sometimes taller. Fronds large, dark green, glossy, leathery. Takes indoor conditions well and thrives outside in milder areas; hardy to 14°F/–10°C. Provide good soil; take care not to plant too deeply. Protect from wind. 'Rochfordianum' has fringed leaflets.

C. fortunei. Hardy outdoors in Zones 31, 32, 34, 39. To 2 ft. high. Evergreen, light green fronds to 2 ft. long, divided into broad lance-shaped or sickle-shaped leaflets.

C. macrophyllum. LARGE-LEAFED HOLLY FERN. Zone 31. To 1½ ft. high. Wide, evergreen, medium green fronds grow to 20 in. long, with oblong leaflets to 8 in. long.

CYTISUS

BROOM

Fabaceae (Leguminosae)

EVERGREEN, SEMIEVERGREEN, DECIDUOUS SHRUBS

⚡ ZONES VARY BY SPECIES

☼ FULL SUN

💧 MODERATE WATER

Cytisus

Most widely planted brooms belong here, but look for other choice shrubs under *Genista*. Deciduous, semievergreen, or evergreen shrubs (many nearly leafless, but with green or gray-green stems). Sweet pea–shaped flowers, often fragrant. Plants tolerate wind, seashore conditions, and rocky, infertile soil. Prune after bloom to keep to reasonable size and form, lessen production of unsightly seedpods.

C. decumbens. Deciduous. Zones 31, 32, 34, 39. Spreading and low, to 1 ft. high and 3 ft. wide. Oblong leaves to ¾ in. long, on branched stems. In late spring to early summer, bears clusters of bright yellow flowers to ¾ in. long in leaf axils.

C. lydia. See *Genista lydia*

C. praecox. WARMINSTER BROOM. Zones 31, 32, 34–41. Deciduous. Compact growth to 3–5 ft. high and 4–6 ft. wide, with many slender stems. Plant resembles a mounding mass of pale yellow to creamy white flowers in spring. Small leaves drop early. Effective as informal screen or hedge, along drives, paths, garden steps. 'Allgold', slightly taller, has bright yellow flowers; 'Hollandia' has pink ones. 'Moonlight', formerly considered *C. praecox* variety, is now thought to be form of *C. scoparius*.

C. scoparius. SCOTCH BROOM. Evergreen. Zones 31, 32, 34. This species has given brooms a bad name in the West, where it escaped landscapes beginning in the early 20th century and spread into open land. It is less problematic in the Northeast, although still somewhat invasive. Upright-growing mass of wandlike green stems (often leafless or nearly so) may reach 10 ft. Golden yellow, ¾-in. flowers bloom in spring and early summer.

Much less aggressive than the species are lower-growing, more colorful forms. Most of these grow 5–8 ft. tall: 'Burkwoodii', red blossoms touched with yellow; 'Carla', pink and crimson lined white; 'Dorothy Walpole', rose pink and crimson; 'Lena', lemon yellow and red; 'Lilac Time', lilac pink, compact plant; 'Lord Lambourne', scarlet and cream; 'Minstead', white flushed lilac and deep purple; 'Moonlight', pale yellow, compact plant; 'Pomona', orange and apricot; 'St. Mary's', white; 'San Francisco' and 'Stanford', red.

DABOECIA cantabrica

IRISH HEATH

Ericaceae

EVERGREEN SHRUBS

⚡ ZONES 32, 34, 39

☼ ◑ TOLERATE FULL SUN IN COOL-SUMMER AREAS

💧 REGULAR WATER

Daboecia cantabrica

This member of the heath family is an erect-stemmed, slightly spreading plant 1½–2 ft. tall, with large, glossy, dark green leaves to ½ in. long. Pinkish purple egg-shaped flowers in narrow, 3–5-in. spikelike clusters, late spring to early autumn. Cut back in fall to keep compact. Varieties include 'Alba', white; 'Praegerae', pure pink; 'Rosea', deep pink. 'William Buchanan' is a prostrate grower with reddish purple flowers; 'William Buchanan Gold' is similar but with some yellow variegation in the foliage.

Irish heath require fast-draining, acid soil and is most useful on hillsides and in rock gardens or natural landscapes.

DAFFODIL. See NARCISSUS

DAHLBERG DAISY. See DYSSODIA tenuiloba

DAHLIA

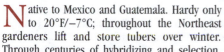

Asteraceae (Compositae)

TUBEROUS-ROOTED PERENNIALS

✿ ALL ZONES; SEE BELOW

☀ ◑ LIGHT AFTERNOON SHADE IN HOTTEST AREAS

🔴 REGULAR WATER

Dahlia

Native to Mexico and Guatemala. Hardy only to 20°F/−7°C; throughout the Northeast gardeners lift and store tubers over winter. Through centuries of hybridizing and selection, dahlias have become tremendously diversified, available in numerous flower types and in all colors but true blue. Sketches illustrate types based on flower form as classified by American Dahlia Society.

Informal decorative dahlias have twisted, curling, or wavy petal-like ray florets. Formal decoratives have regularly arranged ray florets that are flat and tend to curve back toward the stem. Cactus dahlias have pointed rays with downcurved edges for more than half their length, radiating out in all directions from the center. Semicactus dahlias have pointed rays with downcurved edges for up to half their length. Collarette dahlias have a single row of ray florets surrounding an inner ring of shorter rays that form a collar around the central disk. Single flowers have one row of rays around a central disk. Ball dahlias are round and full, with the edges of the rays curved inward for half their length. Anemone flowers have rays surrounding a central pincushionlike disk of tubular florets. Pompons are similar to balls but smaller, with ray edges more curled in.

Bush and bedding dahlias grow from 15 in. to over 6 ft. high. The tall bush forms are useful as summer hedges, screens, and fillers among shrubs; lower kinds give mass color in borders and containers. Modern dahlias, with their strong stems, long-lasting blooms that face outward or upward, and substantial, attractive foliage, are striking cut flowers. Leaves are generally divided into many large, deep green leaflets.

PLANTING

Most dahlias are started from tubers. Plant them after frost is past and soil is warm. Several weeks before planting, dig soil 1 ft. deep and work in organic matter such as ground bark or compost.

Dig holes 1 ft. deep and 3 ft. apart for most varieties; space largest kinds 4−5 ft. apart, smaller ones 1−2 ft. If you use fertilizer at planting time,

thoroughly mix ¼ cup of complete fertilizer in bottom of hole, then add 4 in. of plain soil. For tall types, drive a 5-ft. stake into hole; place tuber horizontally, 2 in. from stake, with eye (growth bud) pointing toward it. Cover tuber with 3 in. of soil. Water thoroughly. As shoots grow, gradually fill hole with soil.

Dahlias also can be started from seed. For tall types, plant seeds early indoors; transplant seedlings into garden beds after frosts are over. For dwarf dahlias, sow seed in place after soil is warm, or buy and plant started seedlings from the nursery. Dwarf dahlias are best replaced each year, though they can be lifted and stored.

THINNING, PINCHING

On tall-growing types, thin to strongest shoot or two shoots (you can make cuttings of removed shoots). When remaining shoots have three sets of leaves, pinch off tips just above top set; two side shoots develop from each pair of leaves. For large flowers, remove all but terminal flower buds on side shoots. Smaller-flowered dahlias, such as pompons, singles, and dwarfs, need only first pinching.

PLANT CARE

Start watering regularly after shoots are above ground, and continue throughout active growth. Dahlias planted in enriched soil don't need additional food. If soil lacks nutrients, side-dress plants with fertilizer high in phosphates and potash when first flower buds appear. Avoid high-nitrogen fertilizers: they result in soft growth, weak stems, tubers liable to rot in storage. Mulch to keep down weeds and to eliminate cultivating, which may injure feeder roots.

CUT FLOWERS

Pick nearly mature flowers in early morning or evening. Immediately place cut stems in 2−3 in. of hot water; let stand in gradually cooling water for several hours or overnight.

LIFTING, STORING

After tops turn yellow or are frosted, cut stalks to 4 in. above ground. Dig around plant 1 ft. from center, carefully pry up clump with spading fork, shake off loose soil, and let clump dry in sun for several hours. From that point, follow either of two methods:

Method 1: divide clumps immediately. This saves storage space; freshly dug tubers are easy to cut, and eyes (growth buds) are easy to recognize at this time. To divide, cut the stalks with a sharp knife, leaving 1 in. of stalk attached to each tuber. Each tuber must have an eye in order to produce a new plant. Dust cut surfaces with sulfur to prevent rot; bury tubers in sand, sawdust, or vermiculite; and store through winter in cool (40° to 45°F/ 4° to 7°C), dry place.

Method 2: leave clumps intact; cover them with dry sand, sawdust, peat moss, perlite, or vermiculite; store in cool, dry place. There is less danger of shrinkage with this storage method. About 2 to 4 weeks before planting in spring, separate tubers as described under method 1. Place tubers in moist sand to encourage development of sprouts.

Dahlia Flower Forms

Informal Decorative

Formal Decorative

Cactus

Semicactus

Collarette

Single

Ball

Anemone

Pompon

D

DANAE racemosa

ALEXANDRIAN LAUREL, POET'S LAUREL

Liliaceae

EVERGREEN PERENNIAL

🌡 ZONES 31, 32

◐ PARTIAL SHADE

💧💧 REGULAR TO AMPLE WATER

Danae racemosa

Growing 2–4 ft. tall, this dense, shrublike plant has graceful, arching stems supporting bright green foliage. In early summer, small creamy white flowers appear, giving way to orange-red berries, highly atttractive to birds, in the fall. Does best in moisture-retentive soil in a partially shaded location but tolerates sun and regular soil that isn't overly dry; if possible, mulch with compost or other organic material. A fine plant for winter interest in the shaded woodland garden.

DANDELION
(Taraxacum officinale)

Asteraceae (Compositae)

PERENNIAL

🌡 ZONES 31, 32, 34–45

☀ FULL SUN

💧 REGULAR WATER

Dandelion

A weed in lawns and flower beds, it can also be a cultivated edible-leaf crop. Seeds sold in packets. Cultivated forms have been selected for larger, thicker leaves than those of common weed form. Tie leaves together to blanch interiors; eat like endive. Add tender leaves to green salads; boil thick leaves like collards or other greens.

DAPHNE

Thymelaeaceae

EVERGREEN, SEMIEVERGREEN, DECIDUOUS SHRUBS

🌡 ZONES VARY BY SPECIES

☀◐ EXPOSURE NEEDS VARY BY SPECIES

💧💧 REGULAR TO MODERATE WATER, EXCEPT AS NOTED

💧 ALL PARTS, ESPECIALLY FRUITS, ARE POISONOUS IF INGESTED

Daphne

Of the many kinds, three (*D. burkwoodii, D. cneorum, D. odora*) are the most widely grown; the others tend to be choice rock garden subjects with more limited distribution in the nursery trade. Although some daphnes are easier to grow than others, all require excellent drainage, cool soil (use a mulch or noncompetitive ground cover), careful watering during dry spells, and shelter from wind and extreme sun.

D. burkwoodii. Evergreen or semievergreen to deciduous. Zones 31, 32, 34–41. Hybrid with erect, compact growth to 3–4 ft. Densely set, narrow leaves; numerous small clusters of fragrant flowers (white aging to pink) around branch ends in late spring and again in late summer. 'Somerset' is 4–5 ft. tall, with pink flowers. 'Briggs Moonlight' has leaves of pale yellow with a narrow border of green. 'Carol Mackie' has gold-edged green leaves. Use in shrub borders, at woodland edge, as foundation planting. Full sun or light shade.

D. caucasica. Deciduous. Zones 31, 32, 34, 39. Upright shrub to 4 ft. high and as wide. Light green, lance-shaped leaves to 3 in. long. Clusters of small, fragrant white flowers in spring and sporadically through summer. Use in a mixed border, in sun or shade.

D. cneorum. GARLAND DAPHNE. Evergreen. Zones 31, 32, 34–41. Matting and spreading; less than 1 ft. high and 3 ft. wide. Good container plant. Trailing branches covered with narrow, 1-in.-long, dark green leaves. Clusters of fragrant rosy light pink flowers appear in spring. Choice rock garden plant; give it light shade in warm areas, full sun in cool-summer areas. After bloom is through, top-dress with mix of peat moss and sand to keep roots cool and induce additional rooting of trailing stems.

Varieties include 'Eximia', lower growing than the species and with larger flowers; 'Pygmaea Alba', 3 in. tall, 1 ft. wide, with white flowers; 'Ruby Glow', with larger, more deeply colored flowers and with late-summer rebloom; and 'Variegata', with gold-edged leaves.

D. genkwa. LILAC DAPHNE. Deciduous. Zones 31, 32, 34, 39. Erect, open growth to 3–4 ft. high and as wide. Before leaves expand, clusters of lilac blue, scentless flowers wreathe branches, making foot-long wands of blossoms. White fruit follows flowers. Leaves are oval, 2 in. long. Use in rock garden, shrub border. Full sun or light shade.

D. mantensiana. Evergreen. Zones 31, 32, 34, 39. Hybrid growing slowly to 1½ ft., spreading to 3 ft. Clusters of perfumed purple flowers at branch tips, late spring (and often through summer). Densely branched and well foliaged, it can be used in same way as low-growing azaleas. Leaves narrow, to 1¼ in. long. Full sun or light shade.

D. mezereum. FEBRUARY DAPHNE. Deciduous. Zones 31, 32, 34–41. Rather gawky, stiffly twigged, erect growth to 4 ft., with roundish, 2–3-in.-long, thin leaves. Plant in groups. Full sun or light shade. Fragrant reddish purple flowers in short stalkless clusters are carried along branches in late winter to early spring before leaf-out. 'Alba' is the same but is less rangy and has white flowers, yellow fruit.

D. odora. WINTER DAPHNE. Evergreen. Zones 31, warmer parts of 32. Prized for the pervasive fragrance of its flowers. Very neat, handsome plant usually to about 4 ft. high and spreading wider; has reached 8–10 ft. under ideal conditions. Rather narrow, 3-in.-long leaves are thick and glossy. Nosegay clusters of charming flowers—pink to deep red on outside, with creamy pink throats—appear at branch ends in winter.

Give this species good growing conditions, since it's the fussiest of the lot. Locate the plant where it will get midday shade. To avoid water mold root rot (the chief cause of failure), roots need well-aerated, neutral-pH soil. Dig planting hole twice as wide as root ball and one and a half times as deep; refill with mixture of 1 part soil, 1 part sand, and 2 parts ground bark. Top of root ball should remain higher than soil level. Feed right after bloom with complete fertilizer but not acid plant food. During dry periods, water just enough to keep plant from wilting.

'Alba'. Plain green leaves, white flowers. Terminal growth sometimes distorted by fasciation (cockscomb-like growths).

'Leucanthe'. Vigorous and relatively disease resistant, with dark green leaves and a profusion of pale pink flowers with white interiors.

'Marginata' ('Aureo-Marginata'). More widely grown than species. Leaves are edged with band of yellow.

D. tangutica. Evergreen. Zones 31, 32. Upright to 3 ft. high and wide, form may be open or dense. Leathery, deep green, oblong leaves to 3 in. long. Clusters of fragrant white flowers flushed with pink or purple late spring to early summer, followed by round red fruits.

DAPHNE PRUNING? IT'S SPECIAL

Correct the shape of a *D. odora* by cutting late-winter flower clusters to wear as corsages or for indoor display. Make cuts to outward-facing buds to promote spreading, to inward-facing ones to promote upward growth. Cut stems of deciduous kinds for bouquets while they are in bud: put them in water indoors and buds will open.

PRACTICAL GARDENING DICTIONARY

PLEASE SEE PAGES 449–523

DAPHNIPHYLLUM

Daphniphyllaceae

EVERGREEN TREES AND SHRUBS

ZONES VARY BY SPECIES

PARTIAL SHADE

AMPLE TO REGULAR WATER

Daphniphyllum

With leathery, rhododendronlike leaves, often in whorls at the end of the branches, these natives of Asia are grown for their impressive foliage. Flowers, the male and female growing on different plants, are generally inconspicuous and are followed by equally unshowy blue-black fruits. Plant in moist but well-drained, slightly alkaline soil in a woodland or partially shaded location. Prune in spring, if necessary, to shape and to remove dead wood from the plant's center.

D. humile. Zones 31, 32. Can be grown as a ground cover in dense shade; in filtered light grows 2–3 ft. tall, occasionally to 5 ft. Glossy dark green leaves with whitish undersides; green flowers.

D. macropodum. Zones 31, 32, 34, 39. Depending on pruning and cultural conditions, either a tree growing up to 30 ft. tall or a broad, densely branched, rounded shrub. Oblong leaves, on reddish stalks, are dark green above with a whitish bloom below. Male plants bear purple-pink flowers, female green, both in late spring or early summer.

DARMERA peltata
(Peltiphyllum peltatum)

UMBRELLA PLANT, INDIAN RHUBARB

Saxifragaceae

PERENNIAL

ZONES 32, 34–41

PARTIAL SHADE

AMPLE WATER

ALL PARTS, ESPECIALLY FRUITS, ARE POISONOUS IF INGESTED

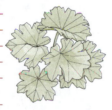

Darmera peltata

Native to mountains of Northern California and southern Oregon. Large, round clusters of pink flowers on bare stalks to 6 ft. tall in spring. Shield-shaped leaves 1–2 ft. wide appear later on 2–6-ft. stalks. Stout rhizomes to 2 in. thick grow in damp ground or even into streams. A spectacular plant for pond, stream, or damp, cool woodland site.

DATURA

THORN APPLE

Solanaceae

ANNUALS AND TENDER PERENNIALS

ALL ZONES

FULL SUN

REGULAR WATER

ALL PARTS ARE POISONOUS IF INGESTED; CAN BE FATAL

Datura

Also known as angel's trumpets, *Datura* species bear upward-facing, trumpet-shaped blooms that often are fragrant. (Closely related *Brugmansia* species, also called angel's trumpets, bear blooms that hang down.) While individual flowers are short-lived, plants bloom from midsummer to frost. Flowers often open in the evening and are pollinated by night-flying moths. Prickly or spiny seedpods follow the flowers, which come in white, purple-and-white, purple, violet, yellow, or red. The leaves are wavy, toothed, and ill-smelling when bruised. All parts of the plants, but especially the seeds, contain alkaloids and other compounds that have intoxicating and narcotic effects; ingestion can be fatal, so these plants are not suitable for gardens frequented by young children.

Use these shrub-size plants as unusual and attractive additions to beds and borders with annuals or perennials. They are grown as annuals: Sow seeds indoors in individual pots 8 to 10 weeks before the last spring frost date and transplant after all danger of frost is past. Or sow seeds outdoors where the plants will grow on the last frost date. To prolong bloom, remove the flowers as they fade to prevent seeds from forming.

D. innoxia. DOWNY THORN APPLE, INDIAN APPLE, ANGEL'S TRUMPET. A 3-ft.-tall species native to the southwestern U.S. and Central America with fragrant, 6–8-in.-long, white flowers tinged pink or lavender. Leaves and stems are grayish because of a covering of short, soft hairs.

D. metel. HORN OF PLENTY, DOWNY THORN APPLE. A 3–5-ft.-tall species native to Asia with white or sometimes yellow or lavender, 5–6-in.-long trumpets. Double-flowered forms have two or three additional trumpet-shaped corollas inserted inside the main one. 'Alba' bears white flowers; 'Aurea', yellow ones. 'Cornucopia' has purple-blushed leaves and stems and double purple flowers.

D. stramonium. JIMSON WEED, JAMESTOWN WEED, COMMON THORN APPLE. A weedy, musky-smelling species native to North America reaching 4–5 ft., with 2–5-in.-long white, or sometimes purple, flowers. One of the most poisonous species. 'Horn of Plenty' bears single lavender blooms.

See also *Brugmansia*.

> **DATURA IN AN EVENING GARDEN**
> Gardeners who like to be outdoors on warm summer evenings should consider planting a garden of night-blooming flowers to enjoy after dark. Many daturas bloom during the night and make lovely, exotic additions to a garden viewed under the moonlight. Plant datura with other fragrant night bloomers such as moonflower (*Ipomoea alba*), four o'clock (*Mirabilis jalapa*), evening stock (*Matthiola longipetala bicornis*), Nicotiana sylvestris, and night-blooming citron daylily (*Hemerocallis citrina*).

DAVIDIA involucrata

DOVE TREE

Nyssaceae

DECIDUOUS TREE

ZONES 31, 32, 34

PARTIAL SHADE IN HOT-SUMMER AREAS

REGULAR WATER

Davidia involucrata

Native to China. In gardens, grows 20–40 ft. tall, with pyramidal to rounded crown and strong branching pattern. Has clean look in and out of leaf. Roundish to heart-shaped, 3–6-in.-long leaves are vivid green. Comes into bloom in spring; general effect is that of white doves resting among green leaves—or, as some say, like handkerchiefs drying on branches. Small, clustered, red-anthered flowers are carried between two large, unequal, white or creamy white bracts; one 6 in. long, other about 4 in. long. Because leaves are already present at bloom time, the large blossoms aren't as showy as smaller flowers of deciduous fruit trees. Trees often take 10 years to come into flower, and then may bloom more heavily in alternate years. Brown fruits about the size of golf balls hang on tree well into winter. Unlike the species, *D. i. vilmoriniana*, which is more commonly grown, has leaves that are greenish yellow on the underside. It is hardier than the species, for Zones 31, 32, 34–41.

Plant this tree by itself; it should not compete with other flowering trees. Pleasing in front of dark conifers, where vivid green and white stand out.

DAWN REDWOOD. See **METASEQUOIA** glyptostroboides

DAYLILY. See **HEMEROCALLIS**

D

DEAD NETTLE. See LAMIUM maculatum

DECAISNEA fargesii

BLUE SAUSAGE FRUIT

Lardizabalaceae

DECIDUOUS SHRUB

✿ ZONES 31, 32, 34–41

☼ ◑ FULL SUN TO PARTIAL SHADE

💧 REGULAR WATER

Decaisnea fargesii

Erect stalks, often compared to walking sticks, long leaves (up to 2 ft.), and 3–4-in. cylindrical blue fruits are the hallmarks of this unusual shrub. Rapidly growing to 10 ft. or more in height and width, it bears panicles of small greenish flowers in spring. Of special interest are the blue cucumberlike fruits, whose yellow flesh is edible, though bland. Prefers rich, loamy soil; in full sun plants will require extra moisture.

DECUMARIA barbara

CLIMBING HYDRANGEA, WOOD-VAMP

Hydrangeaceae

DECIDUOUS SHRUB

✿ ZONES 31, 32, 34, 39

◑ ● PARTIAL SHADE TO SHADE

💧 REGULAR WATER

Decumaria barbara

A woody vine native to the southeastern U.S. that climbs to 30 ft. by attaching itself to walls, trees, or other supports with aerial rootlets. Bears handsome, glossy, rounded leaves and 2–4-in.-wide clusters of fragrant white flowers in late spring or early summer. Unlike most hydrangeas and Japanese hydrangea vine *(Schizophragma hydrangeoides),* both close relatives, it does not have a ring of large-petaled flowers around the outside of the cluster. Grows in well-drained soil rich in organic matter; evenly moist soil is best. Plants tolerate full sun with a constant, ready supply of moisture. They need little pruning other than to keep them in bounds. Plants are effective climbing trees, covering walls, or growing on sturdy trellises. They also make excellent ground covers.

DEERHORN CEDAR. See THUJOPSIS dolabrata

DELOSPERMA

ICE PLANT

Aizoaceae

SUCCULENT PERENNIALS

✿ ZONES VARY BY SPECIES

☼ FULL SUN

💧 TAKE CONSIDERABLE DROUGHT

Delosperma

This huge group of succulents includes two of the hardiest ice plants, described below. These and other types thrive in full sun with good drainage and just enough water to keep them looking bright and fresh.

D. cooperi. Zones 31, warmer parts of 32. Grows 5 in. tall, 2 ft. wide. Brilliant, shining purple flowers all summer long. Tolerates 0°F/−18°C if protected by snow or mulch.

D. nubigenum. Zones 31, 32, 34–41. Hardiest of all ice plants, it has withstood −25°F/−32°C. Barely 1 in. high, spreading to 3 ft. Fleshy, cylindrical, bright green leaves turn red in fall, then green up again in spring.

Bright golden yellow flowers, 1–1½ in. wide, blanket plants in spring. Effective in rock gardens.

DELPHINIUM

Ranunculaceae

PERENNIALS, SOME TREATED AS ANNUALS

✿ ZONES VARY BY SPECIES

☼ FULL SUN

💧 REGULAR WATER

Delphinium

Most people associate delphiniums with blue flowers, but color range also includes white and shades of red, pink, lavender, purple, and yellow. Leaves are lobed or fanlike, variously cut and divided. Taller hybrids offer rich colors in elegant spirelike form. Blossoms of all types attract birds. All kinds are effective in borders and make good cut flowers; lower-growing kinds serve well as container plants. For annual delphiniums (larkspurs), see *Consolida ambigua.*

All kinds are easy to grow from seed. In mild-winter areas, sow fresh seed in flats or pots of light soil mix in July or August; set out transplants in October for bloom in late spring and early summer. (Treat as fall-planted annuals in Zones 31–32.) In cold climates, refrigerate summer-harvested seed in airtight containers until time to sow. Sow seed in March or April, set out transplants in June or July for potential first bloom in September (and more bloom the following summer).

Delphiniums need rich, porous soil and regular fertilizing. Improve poor or heavy soils by blending in soil conditioners. Add lime to strongly acid soils. Work small handful of superphosphate into bottom of hole before setting out plant. Be careful not to cover root crown.

D. ajacis. See *Consolida ambigua*

HOW TO GROW CLOSE-TO-PERFECT DELPHINIUMS

When new shoots develop in spring, remove all but the two or three strongest and apply complete fertilizer alongside plants. Bait for slugs and snails. Stake flower stalks early. After bloom, cut back flower spikes, leaving foliage at the bottom; after new shoots are several inches high, cut old stalks to ground. Fertilize to encourage a possible good, but reduced, second bloom by the end of the growing season.

D. belladonna. Sturdy, bushy perennial. Zones 32, 34, 36–43. To 3–4 ft. Deeply cut leaves; short-stemmed, airy flower clusters. Varieties: 'Belladonna', light blue; 'Bellamosum', dark blue; 'Casa Blanca', white; 'Cliveden Beauty', deep turquoise blue. All have flowers 1½–2 in. across, are longer lived than tall hybrids listed under *D. elatum.*

D. elatum. CANDLE DELPHINIUM, CANDLE LARKSPUR. Perennial. Zones 32, 34, 36–41. Along with *D. cheilanthum* and others, this 3–6-ft. Siberian species, with small dark or dull purple flowers, is parent of modern tall-growing delphinium strains such as the spectacular Pacific strain.

Pacific strain delphinium hybrids (also called Giant Pacific, Pacific Hybrids, and Pacific Coast Hybrids) grow up to 8 ft. tall. They come in selected color series; members of these include 'Summer Skies', light blue; 'Blue Bird', medium blue; 'Blue Jay', medium to dark blue; 'Galahad', white with white center; 'Percival', white with black center. Other purple, lavender, pink named varieties also sold.

Like Pacific strain but shorter (2–2½ ft. tall) are the Blue Fountains, Blue Springs, and Magic Fountains strains. Even shorter is the Stand Up strain (15–20 in.). These shorter strains seldom require staking.

Other strains have flowers in shades of lilac pink to deep raspberry rose, clear lilac, lavender, royal purple, and darkest violet. Wrexham strain, tall growing with large spikes, was developed in England.

D. exaltatum. Perennial. Zones 31, 32, 34–41. Native to the eastern U.S. To 6½ ft. high. Lobed and divided leaves, in summer bears branched spikes of blue or purple flowers.

D. grandiflorum (D. chinense). CHINESE or BOUQUET DELPHINI-UM. Short-lived perennial treated as biennial or annual. All zones. Bushy, branching, 1 ft. tall or less. Varieties include 'Dwarf Blue Mirror', 1 ft., upward-facing flowers of deep blue; and 'Tom Thumb', 8 in. tall, pure gentian blue flowers.

DENDRANTHEMA. See CHRYSANTHEMUM grandiflorum, C. pacificum, C. rubellum, C. weyrichii

---

DENNSTAEDTIA
punctilobula

HAY-SCENTED FERN

Dennstaedtiaceae

FERN

📏 ZONES 31, 32, 34–45

🔆 LIGHT SHADE

💧 REGULAR TO MODERATE WATER

Dennstaedtia punctilobula

Native from eastern Canada to the Gulf states. Deciduous fern with finely divided fronds to 2 ft. tall arising from creeping rhizomes. Spreads quickly to make an attractive ground cover. Crushed fronds smell like freshly cut hay. Tolerates full sun in cool-summer regions. If given adequate water, thrives even in poor, rocky soil. Can form mats that cover rocks. You may see it growing along the roadside or under rail fences in partly shaded areas.

DEODAR CEDAR. See CEDRUS deodara

DESCHAMPSIA

HAIR GRASS

Poaceae (Graminae)

PERENNIAL GRASSES

📏 ZONES 31, 32, 34–41

🔆 FULL SUN OR PARTIAL SHADE

💧 REGULAR TO MODERATE WATER

Abelmoschus moschatus

Ornamental clumping grasses with narrow, rough leaves obscured by clouds of yellowish flower panicles in late spring or early summer. Use in mass plantings. Hair grass is best suited to cool-summer regions. Plants are evergreen in Zones 31, 32, 34, 35–39, semievergreen in Zone 41.

D. caespitosa. TUFTED HAIR GRASS. Native to much of North America, but most garden varieties are imports from European nurseries. Dark green foliage. Purple-tinged greenish yellow panicles persist into winter. Fountainlike clumps typically 2–3 ft. high in bloom. Varieties with golden yellow flowers include 'Goldgehaenge', 'Goldschleier', 'Goldstaub'. 'Bronzeschleier' ('Bronzy Veil') has bronzy yellow blooms. *D. c. vivipara* has the darkest green foliage; instead of flowers, it produces plantlets that droop to the ground.

D. flexuosa. CRINKLED HAIR GRASS. Wiry, glossy green leaves in tight clumps 1–2 ft. high. Nodding, purple-tinged flowers mature to yellowish brown.

FOR INFORMATION ON SELECTING PLANTS

PLEASE SEE PAGES 47–112

DEUTZIA

Saxifragaceae

DECIDUOUS SHRUBS

📏 ZONES 31, 32, 34–41

🔆 FULL SUN OR LIGHT SHADE

💧 REGULAR WATER

Deutzia

They are best used among evergreens, where they can make a show when in bloom, then blend back in with other greenery during the rest of the year. Their mid- to late spring flowering coincides with that of tulips and Dutch iris.

Prune after flowering. With low- or medium-growing kinds, cut some of oldest stems to ground every other year. Prune tall-growing kinds severely by cutting back wood that has flowered. Cut to outward-facing side branches.

D. crenata. Native to Japan. Similar to *D. scabra*, but with white flowers.

D. elegantissima. Bears pink flowers on a 6-ft. shrub. 'Rosealind', 4–5 ft. tall and spreading, has deep rose flowers.

D. gracilis. SLENDER DEUTZIA. Native to Japan. To 6 ft. or less. Many slender stems arch gracefully, carry bright green, 2½-in., sharply toothed leaves and clusters of snowy white flowers. 'Nikko' (*D. g. nakaiana*) grows only 1–2 ft. tall by 5 ft. wide and has deep burgundy fall color; effective as ground cover, over walls, in rock gardens.

D. 'Mont Rose'. Bushy and upright, to 4 ft. high. Narrow, oval, deep green leaves. Slender clusters of small rose purple flowers.

D. 'Pink-a-Boo'. Erect shrub to 6–8 ft. tall, 6 ft. wide, with large clusters of pink flowers.

D. rosea. Hybrid. Low growing (to 3–4 ft.), with finely toothed, 1–3-in. leaves. Flowers pinkish outside, white inside, in short clusters.

D. scabra. Native to Japan, China. This plant and its varieties are robust shrubs 7–10 ft. tall. Leaves oval, 3 in. long, dull green, roughish to touch, with scallop-toothed edges. Flowers are white or pinkish, in narrow, upright clusters. 'Pride of Rochester' has large clusters of small, frilled double flowers, rosy purple outside. 'Godsall' ('Godsall Pink') grows 4–6 ft. tall, bears pure pink double flowers.

DEVIL'S CLAW. See PROBOSCIDEA

DEVIL'S TONGUE. See AMORPHOPHALLUS

DIANTHUS

PINK

Caryophyllaceae

PERENNIALS, BIENNIALS, AND ANNUALS

📏 ZONES 31, 32, 34–45, EXCEPT AS NOTED

🔆 LIGHT AFTERNOON SHADE IN HOT AREAS

💧 REGULAR WATER

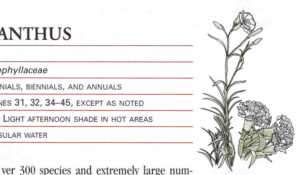
Dianthus

Over 300 species and extremely large number of hybrids, many with high garden value. Most kinds form attractive evergreen mats or tufts of grasslike green, gray-green, blue-green, or blue-gray leaves. Single, semidouble, or double flowers in white and shades of pink, rose, red, yellow, and orange; many have rich, spicy fragrance. Main bloom period for most is spring into early summer; some rebloom later in season or keep going into fall if faded flowers are removed.

Among dianthus are appealing border favorites such as cottage pink and sweet William, highly prized cut flowers such as carnation (clove pink), and rock garden miniatures. Many excellent named varieties not mentioned here are available locally.

D

All kinds of dianthus thrive in light, fast-draining soil. Carnations, sweet William, and cottage pinks need fairly rich soil; rock garden or alpine types require gritty growing medium, with added lime if soil is acid. Avoid overwatering. Sow seed of annual or biennial dianthus in flats or directly in garden. Propagate perennial types by cuttings made from tips of growing shoots, by division or layering, or from seed. Perennials are often short lived. Carnations and sweet William are subject to rust and fusarium wilt.

D. allwoodii. Group of modern pinks derived from *D. plumarius* and *D. caryophyllus*. Plants vary, but most have gray-green foliage and two blossoms on each stem; bloom over long period if deadheaded. Tend to be more compact and more vigorous than their *D. plumarius* parent. The many varieties include 'Aqua', which bears very fragrant, pure white double flowers on 10–12-in. stems. Plants sold as 'Allwoodii Alpinus' are the result of crossing *D. allwoodii* with dwarf species.

'Essex Witch'. Semidouble rose pink flowers on 5-in. stems.

D. alpinus. ALPINE PINK. Best suited to rock gardens. Low and cushiony, 3 in. high and 4 in. across. Deep green leaves to 1 in. long. In summer, bears dark pink to rosy red flowers with notched petals, to 1½ in. across. Short-lived and may need to be replaced every few years.

D. arenarius. Perennial. Tufted plant to 1½ ft. with narrow, grass green leaves and inch-wide fringed white flowers sometimes marked with green or purple. Highly fragrant; can tolerate some shade. 'Snow Flurries' has pure white flowers.

D. barbatus. SWEET WILLIAM. Vigorous biennial often grown as annual. Sturdy stems 10–20 in. high; leaves are flat, light to dark green, 1½–3 in. long. Dense clusters of white, pink, rose, red, purplish, or bicolored flowers, about ½ in. across, set among leafy bracts; not very fragrant. Sow seed in late spring for bloom following year. Double-flowered and dwarf strains are obtainable from seed. Indian Carpet strain is only 6 in. tall. Roundabout and Summer Beauty strains (1 ft.) bloom the first year from seed.

D. caryophyllus. CARNATION, CLOVE PINK. Perennial. There are two distinct categories of carnations: florists' and border types. Both have double flowers, bluish green leaves, and branching, leafy stems that often become woody at base.

Border carnations (Zones 32, 34–41, some to 39) are bushier and more compact than florists' type, 12–14 in. high. Flowers 2–2½ in. wide, fragrant, borne in profusion. Effective as shrub border edgings, in mixed flower border, and in containers. Hybrid carnations grown from seed are usually treated as annuals, but often live over. 'Juliet' makes compact, foot-tall clumps with long production of 2½-in. scarlet flowers; 'Luminette', 2 ft. tall, is similar. Pixie Delight strain also is similar but includes full range of carnation colors. Knight series has strong stems, blooms in 5 months from seed; Bambino strain is a little slower to bloom. There is also a strain called simply Hanging Mixed, with pink- or red-flowered plants that sprawl or hang from pot or window box.

Florists' carnations are grown commercially in greenhouses, outdoors in gardens in mild-winter areas. Greenhouse-grown plants reach 4 ft., have fragrant, 3-in.-wide flowers in many colors—white, shades of pink and red, orange, purple, yellow; some are variegated. For large flowers, leave only terminal bloom on each stem, pinching out all other buds down to fifth joint, below which new flowering stems will develop. Stake to prevent sprawling. Start with strong cuttings taken from the most vigorous plants of selected named varieties. Sturdy plants conceal supports, look quite tidy.

D. chinensis. CHINA PINK, RAINBOW PINK. Biennial or short-lived perennial; most varieties grown as annuals. Erect, 6–30 in. high; stems branch only at top. Stem leaves narrow, 1–3 in. long, ½ in. wide, hairy on margins. Basal leaves usually gone by flowering time. Flowers about 1 in. across, rose lilac with deeper colored eye; lack fragrance. Modern strains are compact (to 1 ft. tall or less) domes covered with bright flowers in white, pink, red, and all variations and combinations of those colors. 'Fire Carpet' is a brilliant solid red; 'Snowfire', white with a red eye. Telstar is an extra dwarf (6–8-in.) strain. Petals are deeply fringed on some, smooth edged on others. Some flowers have intricately marked eyes. Sow directly in ground in spring, in full sun, for summer bloom. Pick off faded flowers with their bases to prolong bloom.

D. deltoides. MAIDEN PINK. Hardy perennial (even though it blooms in just a few weeks from seed) forming loose mats. Flowering stems 8–12 in. high, with short leaves. Flowers, about ¾ in. across, with sharp-toothed petals, are borne at end of forked stems. Colors include light or dark rose to purple, spotted with lighter colors; and white. Can tolerate a half day of shade. Blooms in summer, sometimes again in fall. Useful, showy ground or bank cover.

THE STRONGLY FRAGRANT KINDS OF DIANTHUS

In addition to cheerful colors and striking patterns, most dianthus offer a strong, spicy, clovelike scent. Among those especially known for fragrance are *D. arenarius*, border carnations, *D. gratianopolitanus*, and *D. plumarius*.

Varieties include 'Albus', pure white; 'Vampire', deep red; 'Zing', bright scarlet; 'Zing Rose', rose red. Microchip is a mixture including pinks, reds, and white, often with contrasting eyes.

D. gratianopolitanus (D. caesius). CHEDDAR PINK. Zones 32, 34–43. Perennial. Neat, compact mound of blue-gray to green-gray foliage on weak, branching stems to 1 ft. long. Flowering stems erect, 9–12 in. high, bearing very fragrant, typically pink to rose single blooms with toothed petals. Bloom season lasts from spring to fall if flowers are deadheaded. Effective for ground cover, edging, rock gardens. Perform well in hot, humid weather.

'Bath's Pink'. An old variety rediscovered and renamed. Blue-green mat about 4 in. high topped by 12–15-in. stems bearing fringed single blossoms of soft pink with a red eye. Blooms profusely in spring, sporadically through summer.

'Fire Witch', bright pink flowers on 2-ft. stems above a 4-in. mound of foliage.

'Little Boy Blue'. To 1 ft. high, 2½ ft. wide, with intensely blue-gray leaves and single white flowers dotted pink.

'Little Joe'. Forms a clump of deep blue-gray foliage 4–6 in. high and about 6 in. across. Crimson single flowers. Especially effective with rock garden campanulas.

'Rose Bowl'. Very narrow leaves form a tight mat 2–3 in. high. Cerise rose flowers 1 in. across, carried on 6-in. stems.

'Spotty'. Resembles 'Rose Bowl', but the pink flowers are heavily spotted with white.

'Tiny Rubies'. Makes a low mat of gray-green foliage to 3 in. high, spreading to 4 in. Small, double, ruby red flowers on 4-in. stems.

D. knappii. Noteworthy for its surprising yellow flowers. Plants grow to 16 in. tall and as wide, with medium green leaves. Flowers bloom in summer and have toothed petals.

D. plumarius. COTTAGE PINK. Perennial. Charming, almost legendary plant, cultivated for hundreds of years, used in developing many hybrids. Typically has loosely matted gray-green foliage. Flowering stems 10–18 in. tall; flowers spicily fragrant, single or double, with petals more or less fringed, in rose, pink, or white with dark centers. Highly prized are old laced pinks, with spicy-scented white flowers in which each petal is outlined in red or pink. Blooms summer–fall if deadheaded. Indispensable edging for borders or for peony or rose beds. Perfect in small arrangements and old-fashioned bouquets.

'Dad's Favorite'. Centuries-old variety with double flowers on 10-in. stems. Blooms are white with ruby red edge and maroon center.

'Musgrave's White'. Classic variety two centuries old. Intensely fragrant single flowers, white with a pale green eye, on 1-ft. stems.

Three double-flowered cultivars are 'Pleno Alba', white flowers; 'Pleno Roseus', rose pink, and 'Pleno Ballade', mixed colors.

Diapensiaceae. The diapensia family contains a few perennials and tiny shrubs native to northern parts of the globe. Some, such as *Galax urceolata* and *Shortia*, are useful in shady gardens or rock gardens.

DIASCIA barberae

TWINSPUR

Scrophulariaceae

ANNUAL

✿ ALL ZONES

☼ ◑ PARTIAL SHADE IN HOT-SUMMER AREAS

◍ ◍ REGULAR TO MODERATE WATER

Diascia barberae

Summer-blooming South African native related to snapdragon and foxglove. Rich salmon to coral pink flowers, ¾ in. across, each with two curving, hornlike spurs on back of lower petals. Blossoms borne in spikelike clusters at ends of slender, 6–12-in.-tall stems. Toothed leaves are small, shiny, dark green.

Sow seed directly in ground after last frost. Also easy to grow from cuttings. After first flush of flowers, cut stems back to foliage mound to encourage more blossoms. Good plant for rock gardens, borders, pots.

DICENTRA

BLEEDING HEART

Fumariaceae

PERENNIALS

✿ ZONES 31, 32, 34–45

☼ ● PARTIAL OR FULL SHADE, EXCEPT AS NOTED

◍ REGULAR WATER

Dicentra

Graceful, divided, fernlike foliage. Dainty flowers, usually heart shaped, in pink, rose, or white on leafless stems. Combine handsomely with ferns, begonias, primroses, fuchsias, bergenias, hellebores. In general, bleeding heart needs rich, light, moist, porous soil. Never let water stand around roots. Foliage dies down in summer; mark clumps to avoid digging into roots in dormant season.

D. canadensis. SQUIRREL CORN. Native from Minnesota to Quebec and south to Missouri and North Carolina. To 1 ft. high and as wide. Heart-shaped white flowers tinged with mauve.

D. cucullaria. DUTCHMAN'S BREECHES. Native from Nova Scotia south to North Carolina and west to Kansas. Forms neat clumps to 8 in. high and 10 in. wide. Blue-green leaves. Flowers are white tipped with yellow, with two pointed lobes instead of heart shape; they resemble tiny pairs of pants hung upside down.

D. eximia. FRINGED BLEEDING HEART. Native to northeastern U.S. Forms tidy, nonspreading clumps 1–1½ ft. high. Blue-gray, finely divided leaves at base of plant. Deep rose pink flowers with short, rounded spurs bloom midspring into summer. Cut back for second growth and occasional repeat bloom. 'Alba' has white flowers. 'Bacchanal' is nearly everblooming during the growing season, with deep red blossoms. Pink-flowered 'Bountiful' ('Zestful') is an everbloomer tolerating considerable sun. White-blossomed 'Langtrees' and deep pink 'Luxuriant' are long blooming; the latter can endure drier soil and stronger light than most. 'Snowdrift' is a long-blooming white.

D. formosa. WESTERN BLEEDING HEART. Native to moist woods along Pacific coast. Blue-green foliage. Leafless flower stalks 8–18 in. high, with clusters of pendulous pale or deep rose flowers on reddish stems, spring. 'Sweetheart' has light green leaves and beautiful white flowers spring–fall. 'Tuolumne Rose' has large blue-green leaves and tall clusters of large rose pink blooms. *D. f. oregana,* about 8 in. high, has translucent blue-green leaves, cream-colored flowers with rosy-tipped petals.

D. spectabilis. COMMON BLEEDING HEART. Native to Japan. Old garden favorite; showiest and largest-leafed of all bleeding hearts. Plants grow 2–3 ft. high; stems are set with soft green leaves. In late spring, rose pink, pendulous, heart-shaped flowers, 1 in. long or longer, with protruding white petals, are borne on one side of arching stems. 'Alba' ('Pantaloons')

is a lovely pure white form. Both are beautiful with maidenhair ferns and in arrangements with tulips and lilacs. Plants generally die down and become dormant by midsummer; keep going longer in cool-summer climates if given adequate moisture. Plant summer-maturing perennials nearby to fill the gap. Best in partial shade.

DICTAMNUS albus

GAS PLANT, FRAXINELLA

Rutaceae

PERENNIAL

✿ ZONES 31, 32, 34–45

☼ ◑ FULL SUN OR PARTIAL SHADE

◍ REGULAR WATER

Dictamnus albus

Sturdy, long lived, extremely permanent in colder climates, needing little care once established. Forms clumps 2½–4 ft. high. In early summer, produces loose spires of blossoms at branch tips, each flower resembling a wild azalea with narrow petals and prominent, greenish stamens. Pink is the basic color, but nurseries offer lilac purple 'Purpureus' and white 'Albiflorus'. Seedpods that follow the blossoms can be left in place for fall interest. Attractive, glossy, olive green leaves with 9–11 leaflets, each 1–3 in. long, remain handsome throughout growing season. Plant emits strong lemony odor when rubbed or brushed against; however, the oils can cause allergic skin reactions in some people.

Effective in borders; combine with daylilies, Siberian iris, taller campanulas. Good cut flower. Divide infrequently; divisions are difficult to establish and often take 2 to 3 years before making a show. Propagate from seed (a slow process) sown in fall or spring, or from root cuttings in spring. Common name "gas plant" derives from this phenomenon: if a lighted match is held near flowers on warm, still evenings, volatile oil exuded from glands on that part of the plant will ignite and burn briefly.

DIDISCUS coeruleus. See TRACHYMENE coerulea

DIERAMA

FAIRY WAND

Iridaceae

CORMS

✿ ZONES 31, 32; ELSEWHERE, DIG AND STORE

☼ FULL SUN

◍ REGULAR WATER

Dierama

Native to South Africa. Evergreen; will die to the ground in extreme cold. Lift and store the bulbs as for dahlias. Swordlike, 2-ft.-long leaves; slender, tough, arching stems 4–7 ft. tall, topped with pendulous flowers in purplish pink to pink and white. Blooms in spring in mildest climates, in summer in areas with colder winters. Effective against background of dark green shrubs or at end of pool where graceful form can be displayed. Divide only when necessary and include several corms in each division.

D. pendulum. Fits the general description above; has bell-shaped flowers.

D. pulcherrimum. As for *D. pendulum,* but flowers are more funnel shaped. 'Album' has white flowers.

DIERVILLA sessilifolia

SOUTHERN BUSH HONEYSUCKLE

Caprifoliaceae

DECIDUOUS SHRUBS

ZONES 31, 32, 34–43

FULL SUN OR PARTIAL SHADE

REGULAR MOISTURE

Diervilla sessilifolia

A shrub native to eastern North America that spreads by suckers to form dense thickets. Plants range from 3 to 5 ft. tall and spread to 5 ft. or more. Bears dark green, opposite leaves that rarely exhibit fall color. Small, ½-in.-long flowers are produced in 2–3-in.-wide clusters from mid- to late summer. Tough and adaptable plant for shrub borders and wild areas as well as for holding soil on sloping sites. Prune in spring, immediately after flowering.

DIGITALIS

FOXGLOVE

Scrophulariaceae

PERENNIALS OR BIENNIALS

ZONES VARY BY SPECIES

LIGHT SHADE

REGULAR WATER

ALL PARTS ARE POISONOUS IF INGESTED

Digitalis

E rect plants 2–8 ft. high, with basal rosette of hairy, gray-green leaves. Spires of tubular flowers shaped like fingers of glove in purple, yellow, white, pastels; bloom comes in spring and summer. After first flowering, cut main spike; side shoots will develop and bloom late in the season.

Provide rich soil. Sow seed in spring for bloom the following year. Set out plants in early spring in cold-winter areas, in fall in mild climates. Plants self-sow freely. Use for vertical display among shrubs or with ferns, taller campanulas, meadow rue. Hummingbirds like the flowers.

D. ferruginea. RUSTY FOXGLOVE. Biennial or perennial. Zones 31, 32, 34–43. Very leafy stems to 6 ft. Leaves deeply veined. Flowers ¾–1¼ in. long, yellowish, netted with rusty red, in long, dense spikes.

D. grandiflora (D. ambigua). YELLOW FOXGLOVE. Biennial or perennial. Zones 31, 32, 34–43. To 2–3 ft. high. Toothed leaves wrap around stem. Flowers are 2–3 in. long, yellowish marked with brown.

D. laevigata. Perennial. Zones 31, 32, 34, 39. To 3 ft., with smooth, narrow dark green leaves and inch-long, creamy yellow flowers marked brownish purple.

D. lanata. GRECIAN FOXGLOVE. Perennial. Zones 31, 32, 34–41. To 3 ft., with dark green leaves and narrow spikelike clusters of small flowers. Blossoms are cream colored, with purplish or brownish veining and a small near-white lip.

D. lutea. Perennial. Zones 31, 32, 34–45. Native to Europe and northwestern Africa. To 2 ft. high. Toothed, oblong, deep green leaves to 8 in. long. In summer, slender spikes of light yellow flowers. Grows best in alkaline soil.

D. mertonensis. Perennial. Zones 31, 32, 34–43. Spikes to 2–3 ft. high, bearing odd yet attractive coppery rose blooms. Though a hybrid between two species, it comes true from seed.

D. purpurea. COMMON FOXGLOVE. Biennial, sometimes perennial. Zones 31, 32, 34–41. Naturalizes in shaded places. Variable, appears in many garden forms. Bold, erect, to 4 ft. high or more. Clumps of large, rough, woolly, light green leaves. Stem leaves have short stalks and become smaller toward top of plant; these leaves are source of digitalis, a valued but highly poisonous medicinal drug. Flowers 2–3 in. long, pendulous, purple, spotted on lower, paler side; borne in one-sided, 1–2-ft.-long spikes.

There are several garden strains. Excelsior, 5 ft., has fuller spikes than species, with flowers more horizontally held to show off interior spotting.

Foxy, 3 ft., performs as an annual, blooming in 5 months from seed; Gloxiniiflora, 4 ft., has flowers that are individually larger and open wider than the species. Monstrosa, 3 ft., has an unusual trait: the topmost flower of each spike is open or bowl shaped and 3 in. wide. Shirley is a tall (6-ft.), robust strain in full range of colors. Volunteer foxglove seedlings are frequently white or light colors.

D. thapsi. Perennial. Zones 31, 32, 34–41. To 2 ft. high. Oblong to lance-shaped leaves with scalloped edges. Spikes of purple flowers with red spots.

FOXGLOVES—SHOWY TOWERS

Flowers on spikes 3 ft. tall or more add charm and dimension to a garden. And foxgloves are perhaps the easiest of the towering flowering plants. An especially showy use for these plants is to fill a boxwood-edged flower bed with just one kind. Set the plants 1 ft. apart. Or mass them at the back of perennial borders.

DILL. See ANETHUM graveolens

DILL-LEAF URSINIA. See URSINIA anthemoides

DIMORPHOTHECA

AFRICAN DAISY, CAPE MARIGOLD

Asteraceae (Compositae)

ANNUALS

ALL ZONES

FULL SUN

MODERATE WATER

Dimorphotheca

G ay, free-blooming plants with daisy flowers that close when shaded, during heavy overcast, and at night. Use in broad masses as ground cover, in borders and parking strips, along rural roadsides, as filler among low shrubs. Broadcast seed in early spring (late fall or early winter in mildest climates) where plants are to grow. Does best in light soil. For other plants known as African daisy, see *Arctotis* and *Osteospermum*.

D. aurantiaca. See *D. sinuata*

D. fruticosa. See *Osteospermum fruticosum*

D. pluvialis (D. annua). Branched stems to 16 in. high. Leaves to 3½ in. long, 1 in. wide, coarsely toothed. Flower heads 1–2 in. across; rays white above, violet or purple beneath; yellow center. 'Glistening White', dwarf form with flower heads 4 in. across, is especially desirable.

D. sinuata. Best known of annual African daisies; usually sold as *D. aurantiaca*. Plants 4–12 in. high. Leaves narrow, 2–3 in. long, with a few teeth or shallow indentations. Flower heads 1½ in. across, with orange-yellow rays, sometimes deep violet at base, and yellow center. Hybrids between this species and *D. pluvialis* come in white and shades of yellow, apricot, and salmon, often with contrasting dark centers.

DIOSPYROS. See PERSIMMON

DIPLADENIA amoena, D. splendens. See MANDEVILLA 'Alice du Pont'

FOR INFORMATION ON YOUR CLIMATE ZONE

PLEASE SEE PAGES 30-46

DIPTERONIA sinensis

Aceraceae

DECIDUOUS SHRUB OR TREE

⚡ ZONES 31, 32, 34

☀ PREFERS AFTERNOON SHADE

💧 REGULAR WATER

Dipteronia sinensis

Unusual maple relative from central and western China; large shrub or tree to 30 ft. tall, 20 ft. wide. Leaves are in opposite pairs, as in maples, but are divided featherwise into 7–11 (rarely more) toothed, 3-in. leaflets. Leaves are coppery when they expand, maturing to bright green. Clusters of small greenish or whitish flowers are followed in autumn by large clusters of roundish winged fruits that turn from green to red.

DISANTHUS cercidifolius

Hamamelidaceae

DECIDUOUS SHRUB

⚡ ZONES 31, 32, 34–41

☀ FULL SUN OR LIGHT SHADE

💧 REGULAR WATER

Disanthus cercidifolius

Native to Japan. This slender-branched shrub, to 10–12 ft. tall and broad spreading with age, is grown for its magnificent fall color. The nearly round, smooth, 2–4-in.-wide bluish green leaves turn shades of deep red and purple, often suffused with orange. Tiny, purplish fall flowers are mildly scented. Provide rich soil—acid soil is best—light shade in hottest climates, and wind protection.

DISHCLOTH GOURD. See LUFFA

DISPORUM

FAIRY BELLS

Liliaceae

PERENNIALS

⚡ ZONES 31, 32, 34–43

💧 FILTERED SUNLIGHT

💧 MORE THAN REGULAR WATER

Disporum

Perfect for woodland settings, rock gardens, or other shady spots, these colonizing perennials feature slender ovate to lance-shaped leaves. Bell-shaped flowers are ½–1¼ in. long in white, greenish yellow, or purple red in late spring. Orange, red, or black berries follow. Humus-rich, acid soil is best.

D. lanuginosum. Native to eastern U.S. Narrow leaves to 5 in. long with pointed tips. Flowers are pale yellow to pale green. Black or red berries follow in autumn. Grows 1–3 ft. high.

D. maculatum. NODDING MANDARIN. Native to eastern and central U.S. Oblong to oval leaves to 4 in. long. Flowers are white with purple spots. Berries are yellow and hairy.

D. sessile. Oblong leaves grow to 6 in. long. Flowers are white or pale cream followed by black berries in autumn. 'Variegatum' features white-striped leaves and grows to 1½ ft.

S. smilacinum. Native to Korea and Japan. Oblong, elliptical leaves to 3 in. long. Flowers are white. Grows to 1½ ft. high.

DIZYGOTHECA elegantissima. See SCHEFFLERA elegantissima

DODECATHEON meadia

SHOOTING STAR

Primulaceae

PERENNIALS

⚡ ZONES 32, 34–45

☀ ☀ EXPOSURE NEEDS VARY BY SPECIES

💧 💧 AMPLE WATER DURING GROWTH AND BLOOM

Dodecatheon meadia

Most of the shooting stars are native to the western U.S., but this one grows successfully in the East. Leaves form a basal rosette and flowers are carried in clusters on leafless stalks to 1½ ft. high. Blossoms resemble small cyclamens, with swept-back petals and downward-thrusting stamens; color varies from white to pink, lavender, and magenta. Dies back completely at the onset of hot weather. Prefers rich, porous, well-drained alkaline soil and part shade.

DOG-TOOTH VIOLET. See ERYTHRONIUM dens-canis

DOGWOOD. See CORNUS

DOLICHOS lablab
(Lablab purpureus)

HYACINTH BEAN

Fabaceae (Leguminosae)

PERENNIAL VINE USUALLY GROWN AS ANNUAL

⚡ ALL ZONES

☀ FULL SUN

💧 REGULAR WATER

Dolichos lablab

Twining vine, with fast growth to 10 ft. Produces dense cover of purplish green leaves; each leaf divided fanwise into three broad, oval, 3–6-in.-long leaflets. Sweet pea–shaped purple or white flowers in loose, long-stemmed clusters stand out from foliage. Blossoms followed by showy edible pods in bright magenta purple; pods are velvety, beanlike, to 2½ in. long. Grow plants like string beans for quick screening. Needs good drainage. 'Darkness' has deep purple flowers; 'Daylight', white flowers.

DORONICUM

LEOPARD'S BANE

Asteraceae (Compositae)

PERENNIALS

⚡ ZONES 31, 32, 34–43

☀ PARTIAL SHADE

💧 REGULAR WATER

Doronicum

Summer is the season for most yellow daisies, but this one bears its profusion of showy flowers in early to midspring. The 2–3-in. blooms on long, slender, branching stems rise from low, dense clumps of toothed, rounded to heart-shaped dark green leaves. Good cut flowers.

Most types die back by midsummer, so best used in a strictly spring-flowering scheme or where summer annuals can fill the gap. Combine with white, purple, or lavender tulips, blue violas, or forget-me-nots; use in front of purple lilacs or with hellebores at edge of woodland or shade border. Mark location before plants die back; provide some moisture during dormancy. Divide clumps every 2 to 3 years; young plants bloom best. Tolerate full sun in cool-summer climates.

D

D

D. 'Mme Mason' ('Miss Mason'). Choice hybrid between *D. orientale* and another species. Large, bright yellow daisies on 2½-ft. plant. Leaves are a little less toothed, flowers a little bigger than those of *D. orientale;* plants also are less likely to die back in summer.

D. orientale (D. caucasium). Flower heads borne singly on 1–1½-ft. stems. 'Magnificum' and 'Finesse' a little taller, with bigger blossoms. Usually dies back in summer.

D. plantagineum. PLANTAIN LEOPARD'S BANE. Larger, coarser-leafed plant than the others, suitable for a wild garden. Each stout, 2½–3-ft.-tall stem bears a few 2–4-in.-wide flowers. 'Excelsum' ('Harpur Crewe') is taller than the species. Plants are dormant in summer.

DOROTHEANTHUS
bellidiformis

LIVINGSTONE DAISY

Aizoaceae

SUCCULENT ANNUAL

ALL ZONES

FULL SUN

TAKES CONSIDERABLE DROUGHT

Dorotheanthus bellidiformis

Ice plant, but unlike most others, an annual forming a pretty and useful temporary carpet. Trailing, a few inches high, with fleshy bright green leaves and daisylike, 2-in. flowers in white, pink, orange, red. Attracts bees. Sow seed in warm weather. Comes into bloom quickly. Tolerates poor, dry soil.

DOUGLAS FIR. See PSEUDOTSUGA menziesii

DOVE TREE. See DAVIDIA involucrata

DRABA

Brassicaceae (Cruciferae)

PERENNIALS

ZONES 32, 34, 36–43, EXCEPT AS NOTED

FULL SUN

REGULAR WATER

Draba

Some 300 species native to mountainous or subarctic regions of the world. All are low, mat- or cushion-forming plants with tightly clustered, tiny leaves in rosettes and four-petaled yellow (rarely white) flowers in short, spikelike clusters. All require perfect drainage, dislike soggy soil. Can endure great cold. Use in rock gardens. These are just a few of the most commonly planted species:

D. aizoides. Native to mountains of southern Europe. Tufts of tiny rosettes make clumps 2–4 in. across. Flowering stems to 4 in. hold four to ten or more bright yellow flowers.

D. oligosperma. One of more than a dozen species native to the Rocky Mountain area. Makes silvery mats up to 1 ft. wide topped with yellow flowers.

D. sibirica (D. repens). Zones 32, 34, 36–45. Native to Siberia, Greenland. Carpet-forming plant with trailing stems and a profusion of small yellow flowers in spring. Use in rock garden or between stepping-stones.

FOR GROWING SYMBOL EXPLANATIONS

PLEASE SEE PAGE 113

DRACAENA

Agavaceae

EVERGREEN, SMALL PALMLIKE TREES

INDOORS

FULL SUN OR PARTIAL SHADE

MODERATE WATER

Dracaena

Foliage plants that can go outdoors in summer and serve as house plants in winter. Some show graceful fountain forms with broad, curved, ribbonlike leaves, occasionally striped with chartreuse or white. Some have very stiff, swordlike leaves. Outdoors, plant all but *D. draco* in a wind-protected site. Seldom flower as house plants. In containers, water only when top ½–1 in. of soil is dry.

D. australis. See *Cordyline australis*

D. deremensis. Native to tropical Africa. Most commonly sold variety is 'Warneckii': erect, slow growing to an eventual 15 ft., with 2-ft.-long, 2-in.-wide leaves in rich green striped white and gray. 'Bausei' is green with white center stripe; 'Longii' has broader white center stripe; 'Janet Craig' has broad, dark green leaves. Compact versions of 'Janet Craig' and 'Warneckii' exist.

D. draco. DRAGON TREE. Native to Canary Islands. Stout trunk with upward-reaching or spreading branches topped by clusters of heavy, 2-ft.-long, sword-shaped leaves. Grows slowly to 20 ft. high and as wide. Makes odd but interesting silhouette. Clusters of greenish white flowers form at branch ends. After blossoms drop, stemmy clusters remain. Trim them off to keep plants neat.

D. fragrans. CORN PLANT. Native to West Africa. Upright, eventually to 20 ft. high, but slow growing. Heavy, ribbonlike, blue-green leaves to 3 ft. long, 4 in. wide. (Typical plant in 8-in. pot will bear leaves about 1½ ft. long.) 'Massangeana' has broad yellow stripe in center of each leaf. Other varieties with striped foliage are 'Lindenii' and 'Victoriae'.

D. marginata. Very easy to grow, very popular. Slender, erect, smooth gray stems to an eventual 12 ft. carry chevron markings where old leaves have fallen. Stems topped by crowns of narrow, leathery leaves to 2 ft. long, ½ in. wide. Leaves are deep glossy green with narrow margin of purplish red. If plant grows too tall, cut off crown and reroot it. New crowns will appear on old stem. 'Tricolor' ('Candy Cane') adds a narrow gold stripe to the green and red of the species.

D. sanderana. Native to West Africa. Neat and upright, to a possible 6–10 ft., somewhat resembling young corn plant. Strap-shaped, 9-in.-long leaves striped with white.

DRACOCEPHALUM

DRAGON'S HEAD

Lamiaceae (Labiatae)

ANNUALS, PERENNIALS, DWARF SHRUBS

ZONES VARY BY SPECIES

FILTERED SUN, PARTIAL SHADE

REGULAR WATER

Dracocephalum

Some 50 species of annuals, perennials, and small evergreen shrubs comprise this genus grown for their showy, densely packed, two-lipped blue or violet flowers. Blooms appear in summer on upright, terminal or axillary racemes that grow 1 ft. or more in length. Squarish stems feature green leaves that often are aromatic, to 3 in. long. While these plants are generally hardy, most prefer some shelter and well-drained loamy soil. Suitable for borders and rock gardens.

D. grandiflorum. Zones 31, 32, 34–45. Perennial with oblong radical leaves to 2 in. and smaller stem leaves. Spikes of deep blue flowers to 1½ in. long. Grows to 1 ft. high.

D. ruyschianum. Zones 31, 32, 34–43. Bushy perennial with leaves up to 2½ in. long and spikes of 1-in. purple flowers that bloom in early autumn. Tolerates dry soils. Grows to 2 ft. high.

D. tanguticum. Zones 31, 32, 34–43. Perennial with aromatic leaves that grow to 3 in., with spikes of violet flowers to 1¼ in. long. Blooms in early autumn. Grows to 16 in. high.

DRACUNCULUS vulgaris

SNAKE PLANT, DRAGON ARUM

Araceae

TUBEROUS PERENNIAL

ZONES 31, 32, 34–41

FULL SUN

REGULAR WATER

Dracunculus vulgaris

Known for its spectacular but foul-smelling flowers, or spathes, which can grow to 3 ft., this plant takes its name from the Latin for dragon. Dark green leaves deeply divide, are sometimes mottled with white, and grow 1 ft. or more long. Can reach an overall height of 5 ft. Grows best in full sun, but also in the open areas of sheltered woodlands in humus-rich, well-drained soil.

THE ALLURE OF AROIDS

Gardeners with a taste for adventure are planting *Dracunculus* and other members of the Arum family *(Araceae)* — known as aroids — in woodland gardens and other shady places. Aroids have long been familiar house plants — philodendron, Chinese evergreen *(Aglaonema)*, anthurium, and dieffenbachia are just a few of them. But hardier family members such as jack-in-the-pulpit or cobra lily *(Arisaema)*, arrow arum *(Peltandra)*, voodoo lily *(Sauromatum)*, and calla lily *(Zantedeschia)*, with their novel spathe-and-spadix flowers and in many cases, beautifully patterned foliage strike a note of mystery and exoticism in outdoor gardens.

DRAGON ARUM. See DRACUNCULUS

DRAGON'S HEAD. See DRACOCEPHALUM

DRAGON TREE. See DRACAENA draco

DROPSEED. See SPOROBOLUS

DROPWORT. See FILIPENDULA vulgaris

DRUMSTICKS. See ALLIUM sphaerocephalum

DRYAS

Rosaceae

PERENNIALS

ZONES 36–45

FULL SUN

MODERATE WATER

Dryas

Choice plants for rock gardens. Evergreen or partially so; somewhat shrubby at base, forming carpet of leafy creeping stems. Shiny white or yellow strawberrylike flowers, late spring–summer. Ornamental seed capsules with silvery white tails.

D. drummondii. To 4 in. high. Leaves oblong, 1½ in. long, white and woolly beneath. Flowers nodding, bright yellow, ¾ in. across.

D. octopetala. Mats to 2–3 ft. high. Leaves 1 in. long. Flowers white, 1½ in. across, erect.

D. suendermannii. Hybrid between the two species above. Leaves oblong, 1–1½ in. long, thick textured. Flowers yellowish in bud, white in full bloom, nodding.

DRYOPTERIS

WOOD FERN, SHIELD FERN, MALE FERN

Polypodiaceae

FERNS

ZONES VARY BY SPECIES

PARTIAL OR FULL SHADE

REGULAR WATER

Dryopteris

The wood or shield ferns number over 100 species and are found over most of the world, but only a few are generally offered by nurseries. Use them in shade or woodland gardens, where their fronds contrast with the coarser foliage of other perennials, especially such large-leafed plants as hosta and rodgersia. They prefer rich soil with adequate organic material and moisture.

D. affinis. SCALY MALE FERN. Semievergreen. Zones 31, 32, 34–43. Native to Europe and southwestern Asia. Grows to 5 ft. high. Finely cut fronds are chartreuse green with light brown scales when they unfold, dark green later. 'Cristata' ('Cristata The King'), arching, crested fronds to 6 in. wide. 'Crispa Gracilis', dwarf evergreen with twisted fronds and leaflets.

D. carthusiana. (D. spinulosa). SPINULOSE WOOD FERN, TOOTHED WOOD FERN, SHIELD FERN. Evergreen, except in harsh winters. Zones 34–43. Native to Europe, Asia, and North America. Coarsely cut yellowish green fronds grow 6–18 in. tall and have shaggy black scales on frond stem and lower part of midrib.

D. dilatata. BROAD BUCKLER FERN. Evergreen. Zones 32, 34, 36–43. Native to many areas in Northern and Southern Hemispheres. Grows 1–2 ft. tall, possibly much more, with finely cut, widely spreading fronds. 'Crispa Whiteside' has fronds with ruffled edges.

D. erythrosora. AUTUMN FERN. Evergreen. Zones 31, 32, 34–41. Native to China and Japan. Erect growth to 2 ft. One of the few ferns with seasonal color variation. Expanding fronds in spring are a blend of copper, pink, and yellow; they turn green in summer, then rusty brown in fall. Bright red spore cases, produced on leaf undersides in fall, are an attractive winter feature.

D. filix-mas. MALE FERN. Evergreen, sometimes becoming deciduous. Zones 31, 32, 34–45. Native to much of the Northern Hemisphere. Grows 2–5 ft. tall, with finely cut fronds to 1 ft. wide. 'Barnesii' to 4 ft. tall, has long, slender fronds. 'Crispa Cristata' has crested fronds, and the pinnae (segments) are both crested and ruffled. 'Grandiceps Wills' grows to 3 ft. tall; tips of fronds and pinnae are crested. 'Linearis Polydactyla' has narrow leaf divisions with spreading, fingerlike tips.

D. goldiana. GOLDIE'S WOOD FERN, GIANT WOOD FERN. Evergreen in milder climates, deciduous where winters are cold. Zones 32, 34–41. Robust grower to 4 ft., with arching fronds to 1½ ft. wide.

D. intermedia. Zones 31, 32, 34–45. Native to North America. Erect, arching, bright green fronds to 3 ft. long and 1 ft. wide, divided into many leaflets.

D. marginalis. MARGINAL SHIELD FERN, LEATHER WOOD FERN. Evergreen. Zones 32, 34–41. Grows 2–4 ft. tall. Finely cut, dark blue-green fronds.

D. sieboldii. Zone 31, 32, 34–39. Native to Japan and Taiwan. Grows to 1½ ft. high. Arching, semievergreen fronds to 20 in. long and 13 in. wide, divided into pairs of oval leaflets.

D. wallichiana. WALLICH'S WOOD FERN. Evergreen. Zones 31, 32, 34–41. Native to India, China. Stately fern to 3 ft. (possibly 5 ft.) high. Finely cut fronds emerge bright golden green on scaly brown stems, later turn dark green.

E

DUCHESNEA indica

INDIAN MOCK STRAWBERRY

Rosaceae

PERENNIAL GROUND COVER

⚡ ZONES 31, 32, 34–43

☼ ◐ ● SUN OR SHADE

💧 MODERATE WATER

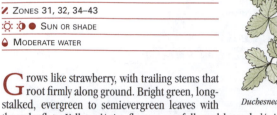

Duchesnea indica

Grows like strawberry, with trailing stems that root firmly along ground. Bright green, long-stalked, evergreen to semievergreen leaves with three leaflets. Yellow, ½-in. flowers are followed by red, ½-in., insipid-tasting fruit that stands above foliage rather than under leaves as in true strawberry. Grows readily without much care. Best used as ground cover among open shrubs or small trees. Plant 1–1½ ft. apart. In well-watered garden, can become rampant invader. Attracts birds.

DUCK-RATTEN. See VERATRUM

DUSTY MILLER. This name is given to a number of plants with gray foliage. The dusty miller of one region may be unknown in another. Among the many dusty millers are *Artemisia stellerana, Centaurea cineraria, Chrysanthemum ptarmiciflorum, Lychnis coronaria, Senecio cineraria*, and *S. vira-vira*.

DUTCHMAN'S PIPE. See ARISTOLOCHIA durior

DYSSODIA tenuiloba (Thymophylla tenuiloba)

DAHLBERG DAISY, GOLDEN FLEECE

Asteraceae (Compositae)

ANNUAL

⚡ ALL ZONES

☼ FULL SUN

💧 MODERATE WATER

Dyssodia tenuiloba

Southwest native. To 1 ft. high. Divided, threadlike leaves make dark green background for yellow flower heads, which look much like miniature golden marguerites. Use for massed display or pockets of color. Start in flats or plant in place, preferably in sandy soil. Blooms early summer to fall. Plants self-sow in warmest zones.

EARTHGALL. See VERATRUM

ECHEVERIA

Crassulaceae

SUCCULENTS

⚡ ALL ZONES

☼ ◐ FULL SUN OR PARTIAL SHADE

💧 MODERATE WATER, EXCEPT AS NOTED

Echeveria

All form rosettes of fleshy green or gray-green leaves, often marked or overlaid with deeper colors. Bell-shaped, nodding flowers, usually pink, red, or yellow, on long, slender, sometimes branched clusters. Good as accents in containers for deck or patio. Some make good house plants.

E. crenulata. Loose rosettes on short, thick stems. Pale green or white-powdered leaves to 1 ft. long and 6 in. wide, with wavy, crimped, purplish red edges. Flower clusters to 3 ft. high, with a few yellow-and-red flowers. Striking plant. Shelter from hottest sun; water frequently during warm weather.

E. elegans. MEXICAN GEM. Tight, grayish white rosettes to 4 in. across, spreading freely by offsets. Flowers pink, lined yellow, in clusters to 8 in. long. Common, useful for pattern planting, edging, containers. Or grow indoors. Can burn in hot sun.

E. hybrids. Generally have large, loose rosettes of big leaves on single or branched stems. Leaves are crimped, waved, wattled, or heavily shaded with red, bronze, or purple. All are splendid pot plants, indoors or out. Among them are 'Arlie Wright', with large, open rosettes of wavy-edged, pinkish leaves; 'Cameo', with large blue-gray leaves, each centered with a large raised lump of the same color; and 'Perle von Nürnberg', with pearly lavender blue foliage. Smaller, with short, close-set leaves, is 'Doris Taylor'; its leaves are densely covered with short hairs. Showy, nodding flowers are red and yellow.

ECHINACEA

PURPLE CONEFLOWER

Asteraceae (Compositae)

PERENNIALS

⚡ ZONES VARY BY SPECIES

☼ FULL SUN

💧 MODERATE WATER

Echinacea

Echinaceas are long-blooming and vigorous American natives. Use them on outskirts of garden or in wide borders with other robust perennials such as Shasta daisies, sunflowers, and Michaelmas daisies. Purple coneflower generally does not need staking. Performs well in summer heat. Good cut flower. Deadheading prolongs bloom. Can self-sow. Divide crowded clumps (usually after about 4 years) in spring or fall.

E. angustifolia. NARROW-LEAVED CONEFLOWER. Native to eastern North America. Zones 31, 32, 34–43. To 4½ ft. high. Lance-shaped leaves. Summer flowers are light purple to rose pink, the reflexed petal-like rays curving downward from the purple-brown center.

E. pallida. TALL CONEFLOWER. Native to eastern North America. Zones 31, 32, 34–43. To 5 ft. high. Narrow, lance-shaped leaves. Mauve pink flowers in late summer to fall, slender drooping rays.

E. purpurea. PURPLE CONEFLOWER. Zones 31, 32, 34–45. Native to east-central U.S. Coarse, stiff plant, forming large clumps of erect stems 4–5 ft. tall. Bristly, oblong leaves are 3–8 in. long. Blooms over long period in mid- to late summer, bearing very showy flower heads with drooping, rosy purple rays and a beehivelike, orange-brown central cone. Flowering may continue sporadically until frost. If left in place, bristly seed heads hang on into winter; seeds are favored by finches.

'Bravado' is rosy red; its rays are flat instead of curved. 'Bright Star' has 3–4-in. rosy pink rays. 'Finale White' has creamy white petals and a greenish central disc. 'Magnus', 3 ft. tall, has horizontally spreading rays and a low, dark center cone; 'WFF Strain' is similar in appearance. 'Robert Bloom' has horizontal, deep mauve pink rays surrounding a central disk of brownish orange. 'White Swan' and 'White Lustre' have white rays around an orange-yellow cone.

E. tennessiensis. TENNESSEE CONEFLOWER. Native to the southeastern U.S. Zones 31, 32, 34–45. Grows to about 1 ft. high, glowing deep rose flowers with broad, flat petals. Although endangered in the wild, it is a worthy addition to gardens on account of its low structure and vividly colored blossoms.

FOR INFORMATION ON YOUR CLIMATE ZONE

PLEASE SEE PAGES 30–46

ECHINOPS

GLOBE THISTLE

Asteraceae (Compositae)

PERENNIAL

❋ ZONES 31, 32, 34–45

☼ FULL SUN

💧 REGULAR TO MODERATE WATER

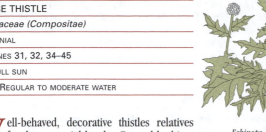

Echinops

Well-behaved, decorative thistles relatives for the perennial border. Rugged-looking, erect, rigidly branched plants 2–4 ft. tall with coarse, prickly, deeply cut gray-green leaves to 1 ft. long. Distinctive flower heads are spherical, like golf ball–size pincushions stuck full of tubular metallic blue pins. Bloom midsummer to late fall.

Plants may be offered as *E. exaltatus, E. humilis, E. ritro,* or possibly *E. sphaerocephalus.* Whatever name you encounter, you're likely to get a plant closely resembling the general description above. 'Taplow Blue' is a select form 4 ft. tall. 'Veitch's Blue' has smaller, more numerous flower clusters on a somewhat shorter plant.

Grow from divisions in spring or fall, or sow seed in flats or open ground in spring. Combine with Michaelmas daisies, phlox, yellow and orange rudbeckias, sneezeweed. Given good, well-drained soil and plenty of moisture, plants may grow so vigorously that they need staking. Established plants tolerate dry periods. Flowers are excellent for dried arrangements, but they must be cut before they open, then dried upside down. Many types will rebloom if cut to the ground immediately after the flowers fade. Clumps can be left in place, undivided, for many years.

ECHIUM vulgare

BLUEWEED, VIPER'S BUGLOSS

Boraginaceae

BIENNIAL GROWN AS ANNUAL

❋ ALL ZONES

☼ FULL SUN

💧 MODERATE TO LITTLE WATER

⚠ POISONOUS IF INGESTED

Echium vulgare

Bushy plant to 1–3 ft. high. Lance-shaped dark green leaves are covered with stiff white bristles. Clusters of blue, white, or pink flowers in summer. Blooms first year from seed; sow in place in late winter or earliest spring (fall in mild climates). Can become a pest if seedlings are not removed; has naturalized in eastern North America.

EDELWEISS. See LEONTOPODIUM alpinum

EGGPLANT

Solanaceae

ANNUAL

❋ ALL ZONES

☼ FULL SUN

💧 KEEP SOIL EVENLY MOIST

Eggplant

Few vegetable plants are handsomer than eggplant. Bushes resemble little trees, 2–3 ft. high and equally wide. Big leaves (usually lobed) are purple tinged; drooping violet flowers are 1½ in. across. And, of course, big purple fruit is spectacular. Plants are effective in large containers or raised beds; a well-spaced row of them makes distinguished border between vegetable and flower garden. Most people plant large roundish or oval varieties such as 'Black Beauty', 'Black Bell', 'Burpee Hybrid', 'Dusky', or 'Early Beauty'; Japanese and Italian eggplants are long and slender; cultivars include 'Ichiban', 'Orient Express', 'Pingtung Long' (lavender purple in color), and 'Violetta Lunga'.

Small-fruited "baby" cultivars that are excellent for container growing and whose fruits are ideal for grilling include 'Bambino' and 'Slim Jim'. Both are reliable, productive, and non-bitter.

Unusually colored varieties available from specialists in imported vegetable seeds and numerous regional seed companies include 'White Beauty' (full size white fruits), 'Osterei' (small, oval white fruits), and 'Snowy' (long, slender white fruits). 'Neon' bears medium-size fruits of arresting purple-pink; 'Machiaw' is similarly colored but long and thin. 'Violetta di Firenze' is lavender, sometimes with white stripes. 'Green Goddess' has slender green fruit. 'Green Tiger' and 'Kermit' bear small, round, light green fruits striped with darker green.

Can be grown from seed (sow indoors 8 to 10 weeks before date of last expected frost), but starting from nursery-grown plants is much easier. Eggplant needs 2 to 3 months of warm days and nights (minimum night temperatures of 65°F/18°C) to produce a crop. Set plants out in sun in spring when frosts are over and soil is warm. Space 3 ft. apart in loose, fertile soil. Feed once every 6 weeks with commercial fertilizer. Keep weeds out. Prevent too much fruit setting by pinching out some terminal growth and some blossoms; three to six large fruits per plant will result. A second crop for late summer–fall harvest can be grown in southernmost climates.

If you enjoy tiny whole eggplants, allow plants to produce freely. Harvest fruits after they develop some color but never wait until they lose their glossy shine. Flea beetles are often a problem on young plants; grow under row covers until plants are big enough to tolerate leaf damage. Control aphids and whiteflies.

EGLANTINE. See ROSA eglanteria

EICHHORNIA crassipes

WATER HYACINTH

Pontederiaceae

AQUATIC PLANT

❋ ALL ZONES AS ANNUAL

☼ FULL SUN

💧 LOCATE IN PONDS OR POOLS

Eichhornia crassipes

Native to tropical America. Floating leaves and feathery roots. Leaves ½–5 in. wide, nearly circular in shape; leaf stems inflated. Showy flowers, carried many to a spike, are lilac blue, about 2 in. long; upper petals have a yellow spot in center. Needs warmth to flower profusely. Can become a pest where it is perennial; in the Northeast it can be grown without problems as an annual.

Elaeagnaceae. This family contains trees and shrubs with a coating of tiny silvery or brown scales on leaves (and sometimes on flowers) and with small, tart-tasting, single-seeded fruits. Flowers are not showy but can be fragrant. Most are tough plants from arid or semiarid climates.

E

FOR GROWING SYMBOL EXPLANATIONS

PLEASE SEE PAGE 113

E

ELAEAGNUS

Elaeagnaceae

DECIDUOUS, EVERGREEN SHRUBS OR SMALL TREES

ZONES VARY BY SPECIES

FULL SUN OR PARTIAL SHADE

REGULAR TO LITTLE WATER

Elaeagnus

All are splendid screen plants. All grow fast when young, becoming dense, full, firm, and tough—and they do it with little upkeep. All tolerate seashore conditions, heat, and wind. Established plants will take considerable drought.

Foliage is distinguished in evergreen forms by silvery (sometimes brown) dots that cover leaves, reflecting sunlight to give plants a special sparkle. Deciduous kinds have silvery gray leaves. Small, insignificant, but usually fragrant flowers are followed by decorative fruit, typically red with silvery flecks. Evergreen kinds bloom in fall; in addition to their prime role as screen plants, they are useful as natural espaliers, clipped hedges, or high bank covers.

E. angustifolia. RUSSIAN OLIVE. Small deciduous tree. Zones 35, 41, 43, 45. To 20 ft. high, but can be clipped as medium-height hedge. Angular trunk and branches (sometimes thorny) are covered by shredding dark brown bark that is picturesque in winter. Bark contrasts with narrow, willowlike, 2-in.-long silvery gray leaves. Very fragrant, small greenish yellow flowers in early summer are followed by berrylike fruit resembling miniature olives. Can take almost any kind of punishment, including hot summers, bitterly cold winters, drought, poor soil. Doesn't do as well in mild winters or either cool or very humid summers. Good background plant, barrier.

E. commutata. SILVERBERRY. Deciduous shrub. Zones 35, 41, 43, 45. Native to Canada, northern plains, and Rocky Mountains. Upright to 12 ft., with open form and slender, spineless, red-brown branches that become coated with silvery scales. Oval leaves silvery gray on both surfaces. Tiny fragrant flowers in spring followed in early fall by dry, mealy, ⅓-in.-long oval fruits, also silver coated and a favorite of birds. Plant spreads by suckers to form colonies.

E. 'Coral Silver'. Zones 31, 32, 34–41. Large shrub, deciduous or partially deciduous. Has unusually bright gray foliage, coral red berries in fall.

E. ebbingei (E. macrophylla 'Ebbingei'). Evergreen shrub. Zones 31, 32. Hybrid derived from *E. pungens.* More upright (to 10–12 ft.) than its parent, with thornless branches. Leaves 2–4 in. long, silvery on both sides when young, are later dark green above and silvery beneath. Tiny, fragrant, silvery flowers. Red fruit makes good jelly. 'Gilt Edge' has striking yellow margins on its leaves.

E. multiflora. Deciduous shrub. Zones 31, 32, 34–41. To 6 ft.; leaves silvery green above, silvery and brown below. Small, fragrant spring flowers followed by attractive, ½-in.-long, bright orange-red berries on 1-in. stalks. Fruit is edible but tart, much loved by birds.

E. pungens. SILVERBERRY. Large evergreen shrub. Zones 31, 32. Has rather rigid, sprawling, angular habit of growth to height of 6–15 ft.; can be kept lower and denser by pruning. Even tolerates shearing into hedge. Grayish green, 1–3-in.-long leaves have wavy edges and brown tinting from rusty dots. Branches are spiny, also covered with rusty dots. Overall color of shrub is olive drab. Oval fruit, ½ in. long, red with silver dust. Tough container plant in reflected heat, wind. Variegated forms listed below are more widespread than the species and have a brighter, lighter look in the landscape; they are less hardy than the species, however, and may suffer cold damage in Zone 32. However, plants damaged in a cold winter recover quickly if pruned back hard. Be sure to cut out growth that reverts to green. Effective barrier plantings: growth is dense and twiggy, and spininess is a help, yet plants are not aggressively spiny.

'Fruitlandii'. Leaves large, silvery.

'Maculata'. GOLDEN ELAEAGNUS. Leaves have gold blotch in center.

'Marginata'. SILVER-EDGE ELAEAGNUS. Silvery white leaf margins.

'Variegata'. YELLOW-EDGE ELAEAGNUS. Yellowish white leaf margins.

E. umbellata. AUTUMN OLIVE. Zones 31, 32, 34–41. Deciduous shrub. To 12 or more ft. high, often thorny with gray-green leaves and fragrant yellow flowers followed by red fruits. This species, introduced from Asia, has escaped from cultivation and become an invasive pest in the Northeast. It is not recommended for planting.

ELDERBERRY. See SAMBUCUS

ELECAMPANE. See INULA

ELEPHANT'S EAR. See ALOCASIA, COLOCASIA esculenta

ELLIOTTIA racemosa

GEORGIA PLUME

Ericaceae

DECIDUOUS SHRUB OR SMALL TREE

ZONES 31, 32, 34, 39

FULL SUN TO PARTIAL SHADE

MORE THAN REGULAR WATER

Elliottia raemosa

Native to the Southeast and quite rare in cultivation, Georgia plume usually ranges from 4 to 12 ft. high, but in ideal conditions can reach 30 ft. Plants have elliptical leaves that turn scarlet to bronzy red in the fall, and produce showy, 6–10-in.-long panicles of slightly fragrant, white, four-petaled flowers in midsummer. Grow Georgia plume in moist, acid, sandy to peaty soil that is evenly moist but does not remain wet.

ELM. See ULMUS

ELSHOLTZIA stauntonii

MINT BUSH

Lamiaceae (Labiatae)

PERENNIAL

ZONES 31, 32, 34–41

FULL SUN

REGULAR WATER

Elsholtzia stauntonii

Not to be confused with the similar sounding *Eschscholzia* (California poppy), *Elsholtzia* is a discreet, semiwoody shrub that bears lavender pink flower spikes at the branch tips. The narrow, pointed blossom clusters, measuring 4–8 in. long and just 1 in. wide, occur from late summer into October. Standing 3–5 ft. high and wide, this deciduous shrub has an open, rounded habit. It blooms on new wood and grows best in well-drained, somewhat fertile soil in full sun. In most of the Northeast where the top dies back in winter, prune it like buddleia by cutting back almost to the ground in early spring. When crushed, the leaves and stems of elsholtzia, which is in the mint family, smell minty. Unlike most mints, however, this plant has round stems, not square ones.

Plant mint shrub in shrub borders and mixed borders of perennials, annuals, and shrubs. The cultivar 'Alba' has white blooms.

PRACTICAL GARDENING DICTIONARY

PLEASE SEE PAGES 449–523

ELYMUS magellanicus

MAGELLAN WHEATGRASS, BLUE WHEATGRASS

Poaceae (Gramineae)

Perennial grass

Zones 31, 32, 34, 39

Full sun, partial shade in hot climates

Regular water

Elymus magellanicus

Among several species of wheatgrass, only blue wheatgrass has major decorative value. This ice blue South American native makes a stunning accent in borders, rock gardens, coastal gardens, and containers, harmonizing beautifully with flowers of pink, white, blue, and pale lemon yellow. Effective massed on slopes or in beds underplanting taller grasses or flowers. Grows 6 in. high, 1½ ft. wide. Has wide leaves, loose mounded habit, and mature wheat-colored flower spikes. Tolerates moist to somewhat dry soil, but excellent drainage always a must. Declines in hot humid climates. To maintain, cut off dead leaves in spring and fertilize for strong growth. Divide for increase in spring or early fall. *Elymus arenarius,* blue wild rye, a handsome 2–3-ft. grassy ground cover native to eastern North America, is sometimes mistakenly called *E. glaucus*.

EMILIA coccinea (E. javanica)

TASSEL FLOWER, FLORA'S PAINTBRUSH

Asteraceae (Compositae)

Annual

All zones

Full sun

Regular water

Emilia coccinea

Grown for its ½-in. scarlet or orange-scarlet flower heads, tassel flower is a low-key, attractive plant suited to borders, flower beds, and rock gardens. Stands 2 ft. high and 1 ft. wide with flower stems emerging from a mound of foliage at the base. Lower leaves measure up to 5 in. long. Leaves higher on the stem are shorter and farther apart. The flowers are fluffy, without rays, and occur either singly or in loose groups all summer. Plants need no staking. Long-lasting cut flower; good in fresh and dried arrangements. Grow in ordinary, well-drained garden soil. Start seeds indoors 8 weeks before the last frost or sow seed outdoors in mid-spring after the danger of frost has passed. Thin seedlings to 6 in. apart. After the first year, plants may self-sow around the mother plant. A related species, *E. sonchifolia,* has a yellow cultivar, 'Lutea'.

EMPETRUM nigrum

BLACK CROWBERRY

Empetraceae

Evergreen shrub

Zones 34–45

Full sun

Regular water

Empetrum nigrum

Native to arctic regions in North America and Eurasia, black crowberry is a low, spreading, 10–12-in.-tall evergreen that resembles heaths or heathers. Plants bear narrow, ¼-in.-long dark green leaves and small, petalless flowers. Blooms are followed by ornamental displays of edible, black or dark purple, ¼-in. berries. Use black crowberry with heaths and heathers, in wild gardens, or as a ground cover in rock gardens. Plants require fairly moist, acid, somewhat sandy soil.

ENDIVE

Asteraceae (Compositae)

Biennial or annual

All zones

Full sun

Regular water

Endive

Botanically known as *Cichorium endivia.* This species includes curly endive and broad-leaf endive (escarole). Forms rosette of leaves. Tolerates more heat than lettuce, grows faster in cold weather. Matures in 90 to 95 days. In cold-winter areas, sow seed June–August; in Zones 31–32, sow in midsummer to mature in autumn, well after the hottest weather has passed. Space plants 10–12 in. apart in rows 15–18 in. apart. When plants have reached full size, pull outer leaves over center and tie them up; center leaves will blanch to yellow or white. 'Green Curled' is standard curly endive; 'Broad-leaved Batavian' is a good broad-leafed kind. Belgian or French endives are the blanched sprouts from roots of a kind of chicory. Roots are dug after a summer's growth, then stored in the dark to sprout. This forcing process produces the tight uniform heads known as Belgian endive. See Chicory.

ENDYMION. See HYACINTHOIDES

ENGLISH DAISY. See BELLIS perennis

ENKIANTHUS

REDVEIN ENKIANTHUS

Ericaceae

Deciduous shrubs

Zones vary by species

Full sun or partial shade

Ample water

Enkianthus

Genus of oriental woodland shrubs handsome in mixed borders or bright woodland gardens. Like rhododendrons, requires moist, well-drained, acid soil to which plenty of organic matter such as peat moss or ground bark has been added. Produces flowers on previous year's growth, so prune only to remove dead or broken branches. Plant in a location where silhouette and fall color can be enjoyed close-up.

E. campanulatus. Zones 31, 32, 34–41. Native to Japan. Slow-growing, handsome shrub typically grows 6–8 ft. tall in cold-winter regions, but in milder climates, it may reach 20 ft. in 20 years. Stems are upright, with tiers of nearly horizontal branches; habit is narrow in youth, broad in age, but always attractive. Bluish green leaves, 1½–3 in. long and whorled or crowded at branch ends, turn brilliant yellow to orange and red in autumn. Since color varies, choose plants in fall during color change. Blooms in spring (at approximately the time leaves are developing), producing pendulous clusters of yellow-green, red-veined, ½-in.-long bell-shaped blossoms. *E. c. palibinii* has deep red blooms, 'Albiflorus' creamy white ones. Flowers of 'Red Bells' are rosier at the tips than those of the species.

E. cernuus rubens. Zones 31, 32, 34, 39. Native to Japan. To 8 ft. high and as wide. Clusters of bright green, oval leaves to 2 in. long, with toothed edges, turn deep purple red in autumn. In late spring to early summer, bears drooping clusters of small, red, bell-shaped flowers.

E. perulatus. Zones 31, 32, 34, 39. Native to Japan. To 6 ft. high and as wide. Young stems are reddish. Clusters of oblong, medium green leaves turn bright red in autumn. Drooping clusters of small, bell-shaped white flowers in spring.

For information on selecting plants

please see pages 47–112

E

E

ENSETE ventricosum (Musa ensete)

ABYSSINIAN BANANA

Musaceae

LARGE, PALMLIKE PERENNIAL

✿ ALL ZONES

☼ ◖ FULL SUN OR PARTIAL SHADE

◉ WATER FREQUENTLY TO SPEED GROWTH

Ensete ventricosum

Lush, tropical-looking, dark green leaves 10–20 ft. long, 2–4 ft. wide, with stout midribs, grow out in arching form from single vertical stem, 6–20 ft. high. Fast growing. Leaves easily shredded by winds, so plant in wind-sheltered place. Typically blooms 2 to 5 years after planting; inconspicuous flowers form within cylinder of bronze red bracts at end of stem. Plant dies to roots after flowering. Possible then to grow new plants from shoots at crown, but easier to discard, replace with new nursery plants. 'Maurelii' has dark red leafstalks and leaves tinged with red on upper surface, especially along edges.

For a tropical effect in summer, grow in tub moved outdoors after frost danger is past and weather is warm, back indoors in fall. Attractive near swimming pools.

EPAULETTE TREE. See PTEROSTYRAX hispidus

EPHEDRA distachya

JOINT FIR

Ephedraceae

EVERGREEN SHRUB

✿ ZONES 31, 32, 34–45

☼ FULL SUN

◉ ◉ REGULAR TO MODERATE WATER

Ephedra distachya

Native to the Mediterranean, this low-growing shrub (1–2 ft. tall) is sometimes planted as a ground cover, especially in sandy soil. Spreading by underground rhizomes, it has leafless green stems and bears tiny yellow-green flowers in summer; the bright red, ¼-in. fruits are showier than the blooms. Does best in well-drained soil of low to normal fertility, in warm, dry climates.

EPIGAEA repens

TRAILING ARBUTUS, MAYFLOWER

Ericaceae

CREEPING, EVERGREEN SHRUB

✿ ZONES 31, 32, 34–45

☼ ◉ PARTIAL TO FULL SHADE

◉ REGULAR WATER

Epigaea repens

A treasured spring-blooming wildflower native to areas with poor, acid soil in the eastern U.S. The plants, which range from 2 to 3 in. tall, bear leathery, glossy green, rounded oblong leaves; both stems and leaves have bristly hairs. In spring they produce clusters of lightly fragrant, urn-shaped, white flowers that often are flushed with pink. Grow in a wild-flower or woodland garden. Plants demand acid soil that is poor and sandy, but will also tolerate evenly moist soil. Nursery-grown plants, started from seeds or cuttings, are fairly easy to establish in a site that provides the conditions these plants require.

EPIMEDIUM

Berberidaceae

PERENNIALS

✿ ZONES 31, 32, 34–43

◖ PARTIAL SHADE

◉ MODERATE WATER

Epimedium

Low-growing plants with creeping underground stems and thin, wiry stems holding leathery leaves divided into heart-shaped leaflets to 3 in. long. Foliage is bronzy pink in spring, green in summer, bronzy in fall; whether it is evergreen, semievergreen, or deciduous depends on the species. Even in deciduous types, leaves last late into the year. In spring, plants produce loose spikes of small, waxy flowers like tiny columbines in pink, red, red orange, creamy yellow, or white. The flowers have four petals, which may be spurred or hooded, and eight sepals—four inner ones resembling petals and four usually small, outer ones.

Use as ground cover under trees or among rhododendrons, azaleas, camellias; good in large rock gardens. Competes well with surface-rooted trees. Prefers partial shade, but tolerates heavy shade. Foliage, flowers long lasting in arrangements. Cut back foliage of semievergreen and deciduous types in late winter before bloom. Divide large clumps in spring or fall by severing tough roots with a sharp spade. Adaptable to containers.

E. acuminatum. To 1 ft. high and 1½ ft. across. Evergreen leaves to 7 in. long, light green mottled with brownish red. In spring and early summer, spurred lavender to purple-pink flowers.

E. alpinum. Evergreen. Rapidly spreading, 6–9 in. high, with small flowers. Like those of *E. rubrum*, the blossoms have red inner sepals and yellow petals.

E. cantabrigiense. Semievergreen hybrid. To 8–12 in. high, with olive-tinted foliage and small yellow-and-red flowers.

E. davidii. To 2 ft. high and as wide. Evergreen leaves to 3 in. long, coppery at first, then turning light green. Spurred yellow flowers in spring to early summer.

E. grandiflorum. BISHOP'S HAT, LONGSPUR EPIMEDIUM. Deciduous. About 1 ft. high. Flowers 1–2 in. across, shaped like bishop's hat; outer sepals red, inner sepals pale violet, petals white with long spurs. Varieties have white, pinkish, or violet flowers. 'Rose Queen', bearing crimson flowers with white-tipped spurs, is outstanding. 'White Queen', with silvery white blooms, is another good variety.

E. perralderianum. Evergreen. To 1 ft. tall and about 6 in. wide, with shiny leaves and bright yellow flowers. A hybrid of this species and *E. pinnatum colchicum* is *E. perralchicum* 'Frohnleiten', a 1½-ft. plant with large yellow flowers and leaves marked with brown in frosty weather.

E. pinnatum. Nearly evergreen. To 12–15 in. high. Flowers are ⅔ in. across, with bright yellow inner sepals and short red spurs. *E. p. colchicum* (often sold as *E. p. elegans*) is larger, with showier flowers.

E. rubrum. Semievergreen hybrid between *E. alpinum* and *E. grandiflorum*. To 1 ft. high. Flowers, borne in showy clusters, have bright crimson inner sepals, pale yellow or white slipperlike petals, upward-curving spurs. Rosy 'Pink Queen' and white 'Snow Queen' are desirable varieties offered by specialty nurseries.

E. sempervirens. Like *E. grandiflorum*, but evergreen. White flowers may be tinged with purple.

E. versicolor. Semievergreen. Several hybrids of *E. grandiflorum* and *E. pinnatum* bear this name. Best-known selection is the vigorous 'Sulphureum', 12–20 in. high with clusters of light yellow flowers and leaves marked with brownish red.

E. warleyense. Evergreen hybrid. To 1 ft. high. Light green foliage; clusters of coppery orange-red flowers. Also known as 'Ellen Wilmott'.

E. youngianum 'Niveum'. Deciduous. Low-growing (6–12-in.) plant with pure white blossoms.

PRACTICAL GARDENING DICTIONARY

PLEASE SEE PAGES 449–523

EQUISETUM hyemale

HORSETAIL

Equisetaceae

PERENNIAL

✎ ZONES 31, 32, 34–43

☼ ◐ FULL SUN OR PARTIAL SHADE

💧 LOCATE IN MARSHY AREAS OR POOLS

Equisetum hyemale

Rushlike survivor of Carboniferous Age. Slender, hollow, 4-ft. stems are bright green with black-and-ash-colored ring at each joint. Spores borne in conelike spikes at end of stem. Several species, but *E. hyemale* most common. Called horsetail because many of the species have bushy look from many whorls of slender, jointed green stems that radiate out from joints of main stem.

Although horsetail is effective in some garden situations, especially near water, use it with caution: it is extremely invasive and difficult to get rid of. Best confined to containers. In open ground, root-prune unwanted shoots rigorously and constantly.

Miniature *E. scirpoides* is similar, but only 6–8 in. tall.

ERANTHIS hyemalis

WINTER ACONITE

Ranunculaceae

TUBER

✎ ZONES 32, 34–43

◐ PARTIAL SHADE

💧 REGULAR WATER DURING GROWTH AND BLOOM

Eranthis hyemalis

Charming buttercuplike plant 2–8 in. high, blooming in early spring, even before crocuses. Single yellow flowers to 1½ in. wide, with five to nine petal-like sepals; each bloom sits on a single, deeply lobed bright green leaf that looks like a ruff. Round basal leaves divided into narrow lobes appear immediately after flowers. All traces of the plant disappear by the time summer arrives. Ideal companion for other small bulbs or bulblike plants that bloom at the same time, such as snowdrop and Siberian squill.

Plant tubers in August or early September before they shrivel. If tubers are dry, plump them up in wet sand before planting. When dividing, separate into small clumps rather than single tubers. Plant tubers 3 in. deep, 4 in. apart, in moist, porous soil. Can reseed in shady, damp conditions.

EREMURUS

FOXTAIL LILY, DESERT CANDLE

Liliaceae

PERENNIALS

✎ ZONES 32, 34–43

☼ FULL SUN

💧 MODERATE TO LITTLE WATER

Eremurus

Imposing lily relatives with spirelike flowering stems 3–9 ft. tall. Bell-shaped white, pink, or yellow flowers, ½–1 in. wide, massed closely in graceful, pointed spikes on upper third to half of stem. Plants bloom in late spring, early summer. Need winter cold to bloom well. Strap-shaped basal leaves in rosettes appear in early spring, fade away after bloom in summer. Magnificent in large borders against background of dark green foliage, wall, or solid fence. Dramatic in arrangements; cut when lowest flowers on spike open. Plant in rich, fast-draining soil; set crown just below surface in milder climates, 4–6 in.

deep in colder ones. Handle thick, brittle roots carefully; they tend to rot when bruised or broken. When leaves die down, mark spot; don't disturb roots. Provide winter mulch in coldest areas.

E. himalaicus. To 3–8 ft. tall, with white flowers. Bright green leaves to 1½ ft. long.

E. robustus. To 6–9 ft. tall, with clear pink flowers lightly veined with brown. Dense basal rosettes of leaves to 2 ft. long.

E. Shelford hybrids. To 4–5 ft. tall; flowers in white and shades of buff, pink, yellow, and orange.

E. stenophyllus (E. bungei). To 3–5 ft. tall, with flowers in bright yellow aging to orange brown. Leaves to 1 ft. long.

DRAMATIC ACCENTS

Thanks to their impressive height, spikes of eremurus add a dramatic accent to sizable floral arrangements. Cut spikes when about a quarter of lower flowers are open; recut stems regularly to encourage upper buds to bloom. Spikes should last up to 10 days; remove wilted blossoms as new ones open.

Ericaceae. The heath family contains shrubs and trees with rounded, bell-shaped, tubular, or irregular flowers, often showy, and fruits that are either capsules or berries. All share a preference, if not always a need, for acid soil with ample water and excellent aeration (a few plants from dry-summer climates are exceptions). Many are fine garden plants; azalea and rhododendron *(Rhododendron),* blueberry, heath *(Erica),* and heather *(Calluna)* are examples.

ERICA

HEATH

Ericaceae

EVERGREEN SHRUBS

✎ ZONES VARY BY SPECIES

☼ ◐ FULL SUN, PARTIAL SHADE IN WARMEST CLIMATES

💧 CONSISTENT, CAREFUL WATERING

▶ SEE CHART NEXT PAGE

Erica

Evergreen shrubs with small, needlelike leaves and abundant, usually small flowers that may be bell shaped, urn shaped, or tubular. Native to many regions of the world; those from northern and western Europe are most widely used in American gardens.

The most common heaths—the hardy European species—tend to be fairly low growing. In suitable climates, fanciers sometimes plant the shortest types in masses for a Persian-carpet effect. If you select your heath and heather *(Calluna)* varieties carefully, you can have color all year.

All heaths need excellent drainage; most require acid soil (exceptions noted in chart). Sandy soil with organic matter such as peat moss and compost added is ideal; heavy clay is usually fatal. They are not heavy feeders; an annual sifting of compost may be enough. If plants lose color, give a light feeding of acid plant food in early spring. They will not tolerate standing water on roots or absolute dryness. Give light shade or afternoon shade in hot-summer climates. After flowers fade, shear or cut off spent flower spikes. Don't cut back into leafless wood, since new growth may not sprout. Heaths attract bees.

FOR INFORMATION ON YOUR CLIMATE ZONE

PLEASE SEE PAGES 30–46

ERICA

NAME, ZONES	GROWTH HABIT, SIZE	LEAVES	FLOWER COLOR, SEASON	COMMENTS
E. carnea **(E. herbacea)** Zones 31, 32, 34, 36-39	Dwarf, 6–16 in. Upright branchlets rise from prostrate main branches	Medium green	Rosy red. Winter, spring	Unsightly unless pruned every year. This and its varieties tolerate neutral or slightly alkaline soil
E. c. 'Ruby Glow'	To 8 in.	Dark green	Deep ruby red. Winter, spring	One of richest in color
E. c. 'Springwood' **('Springwood White')**	Spreading, to 8 in. One of neatest heaths	Light green	White; creamy buds. Winter, early spring	Toughest, fastest-growing heath. More tolerant than others of hot, humid conditions
E. c. 'Springwood Pink'	Spreading mound, to 10 in.	Bright green	Pure pink. Winter, early spring	New growth pinkish rust. More tolerant than others of hot, humid conditions
E. c. 'Vivellii'	Spreading mound, to 1 ft.	Dark green; bronzy red in winter	Carmine red. Winter	Relatively tidy. Interesting for seasonal change in foliage color as well as for bloom
E. c. 'Winter Beauty' **('King George')**	Bushy, spreading, compact, to 15 in.	Dark green	Deep, rich pink. Winter, early spring	Often in bloom at Christmas
E. ciliaris DORSET HEATH Zones 31, 32, 34, 39	Trailing, 6–12 in.	Pale green	Rosy red. Summer	Good for massing
E. c. 'Mrs. C. H. Gill'	Spreading, to 1 ft.	Dark green	Deep red. Summer, early fall	Showy, bell-like flowers
E. c. 'Stoborough'	As above, but taller, to 1½ ft.	Medium green	White. Summer, early fall	Free blooming, showy
E. cinerea TWISTED HEATH Zones 31, 32, 34, 39	Spreading mound, to 1 ft.	Dark green, dainty	Purple. Summer	Forms low mat; good ground cover
E. c. 'Atrosanguinea'	Low, spreading, bushy, to 9 in.	Dark green, dainty	Scarlet. Summer, early fall	Dwarf, slow growing
E. c. 'C. D. Eason'	Compact, to 10 in.	Dark green	Red. Late spring, summer	Outstanding; good summer flower display

E

ERICA

NAME, ZONES	GROWTH HABIT, SIZE	LEAVES	FLOWER COLOR, SEASON	COMMENTS
E. c. 'P. S. Patrick'	Bushy, to 15 in.	Dark green	Purple. Summer	Long, sturdy spikes of large flowers
E. darleyenis 'Darley Dale' (E. mediterranea hybrida, E. purpurascens 'Darleyensis') Zones 31, 32, 34, 36-39	Bushy, to 1 ft.	Medium green	Light rosy purple. Fall to midspring	Tough, hardy plant that takes both heat and cold surprisingly well. Tolerates neutral soils. Hybrid between *E. carnea* and *E. mediterranea*
E. d. 'Furzey'	Bushy, 14–18 in.	Dark green	Deep rose pink. Winter, early spring	Spreading, vigorous plant
E. d. 'George Rendall'	Bushy, 1 ft.	Medium bluish green	Deeper purple than 'Darley Dale'. Fall to early spring	New growth gold tinted
E. d. 'Silberschmelze' ('Molten Silver', 'Alba', 'Mediterranea Hybrid White')	Vigorous, 1½–2 ft.	Medium green	White, fragrant. Winter, spring	Easy to maintain
E. 'Dawn' Zones 31, 32, 34, 39	Spreading mound, 1 ft.	Green; new growth golden	Deep pink. Summer, early fall	Excellent ground cover. Easy to grow. Hybrid between *E. ciliaris* and *E. tetralix*
E. tetralix CROSS-LEAFED HEATH Zones 32, 34, 39	Upright, to 1 ft.	Dark green, silvery beneath	Rosy pink. Summer, early fall	Other heaths are more cold-tolerant. New growth yellow, orange, or red. Needs moister conditions than other heaths
E. t. 'Alba Mollis'	Upright, slightly spreading, to 1 ft.	Silvery gray	Clear white. Summer, early fall	Foliage sheen pronounced in spring, summer
E. t. 'Darleyensis'	Spreading, open growth, to 8 in.	Gray green	Salmon pink. Summer	Good color. Do not confuse with *E. darleyensis,* which blooms fall–midspring
E. vagans CORNISH HEATH Zones 31, 32, 34, 39	Bushy, open, to 2–3 ft.	Bright green	Purplish pink. Summer	Robust and hardy
E. v. 'Lyonesse'	Bushy, rounded, to 1½ ft.	Bright, glossy green	White. Summer, early fall	Best white Cornish heath
E. v. 'Mrs. D. F. Maxwell'	Bushy, rounded, to 1½ ft.	Dark green	Cherry pink or red. Summer, early fall	Outstanding for color and heavy bloom; widely grown
E. v. 'St. Keverne'	Bushy, rounded, to 1½ ft.	Light green	Rose pink. Summer, early fall	Heavy bloom. Compact if pruned annually

E

E

ERINUS alpinus

Scrophulariaceae	
PERENNIAL	
◪ ZONES 32, 34–43	
☼ ◑ FULL SUN OR PARTIAL SHADE	
● REGULAR WATER	

Erinus alpinus

A short-lived perennial that reseeds itself freely, it can reach 1 ft. high, but usually grows in situations that restrict it to just 2–6 in. tall: in crevices in rock walls, in rock gardens, or between stepping-stones. Light green leaves are less than an inch long; narrow clusters of pink, purplish, or white flowers bloom in summer. Given the right conditions—cool, moist, not too sunny—it will reseed and form patches. It does not, however, become a pest. Especially attractive where flowers are at eye level, as on top of a wall or growing in chinks in the wall.

ERODIUM

CRANESBILL	
Geraniaceae	
PERENNIALS	
◪ ZONES VARY BY SPECIES	
☼ ◑ FULL SUN OR PARTIAL SHADE	
● REGULAR WATER	

Erodium

Plants in this genus are native to rocky or mountainous areas, and are usually grown in rock gardens. The five-petaled flowers resemble those of hardy geraniums, which are also called cranesbills.

E. manescaui (E. manescavii). Zones 31, 32, 34, 39. Native to the Pyrenees. To 1½ ft. tall. Medium green leaves to 12 in. long, divided into oval leaflets. Clusters of magenta flowers all summer into fall. Self-sows.

E. reichardii (E. chamaedryoides). Zones 31, 32. Native to Balearic Islands and Corsica. Dainty-looking but tough plant, forming dense foliage tuft 3–6 in. high, 1 ft. across. Long-stalked, roundish, dark green leaves ⅓ in. long with scalloped edges. Profuse, cup-shaped, ½-in.-wide flowers with white or rose pink, rosy-veined petals notched at tips, spring–fall. Good small-scale ground cover, rock garden plant. A double-flowered pink and a single white form exist. Plant in porous soil.

E. rupestre. Zones 31, 32, 34, 39. Native to the Pyrenees. To 4 in. high. Small, divided leaves with silver hairs in the upper surface, white flowers in summer.

ERYNGIUM

SEA HOLLY	
Apiaceae (Umbelliferae)	
PERENNIALS	
◪ ZONES 31, 32, 34–43, EXCEPT AS NOTED	
☼ FULL SUN	
● MODERATE WATER	

Eryngium

Most are erect, stiff-branched, thistlelike plants with summer show of striking oval, steel blue or amethyst flower heads surrounded by spiny blue bracts. Upper leaves and stems are also sometimes blue. Make long-lasting cut flowers and dry well for winter arrangements. Leaves are sparse, dark green, deeply cut, spiny toothed. Plant in borders or in fringe areas in deep, well-drained soil. Taprooted plants are difficult to divide; propagate by root cuttings or sow seed in place, thinning seedlings to 1 ft. apart. Plants often self-sow.

Another group of sea hollies has long, narrow, spine-edged leaves that resemble those of yucca. One of these is native to the U.S.

E. agavifolium. Zones 31, 32, 34, 39. To 5 ft. tall. Sword-shaped, toothed, dark green evergreen leaves from a rosette. Clusters of greenish white flowers surrounded by spiny bracts appear in late summer.

E. alpinum. To 2 ft., with 2-in. flower heads and large, deeply cut blue bracts. 'Blue Star' is a choice variety.

E. amethystinum. Zones 31, 32, 34–45. To 2½ ft. tall, with 1-in. flower heads in rich blue above finely cut leaves.

E. bromeliifolium. Zones 31, 32. To 3 ft. high. Narrow, spiny-toothed, sword-shaped leaves and in summer, blue-white flowers surrounded by stiff, sharp bracts.

E. bourgatii. Zones 31, 32, 34–41. To 1½ ft. high. Spiny, dark green leaves are veined in silver. Blue to silvery green flowers surrounded by narrow silver blue bracts on branched blue stems in mid- to late summer.

E. giganteum. MISS WILLMOTT'S GHOST. Zones 31, 32, 34–41. This species is a biennial or short-lived perennial. Grows to 3 ft. high. Basal leaves are heart shaped and medium green, with scalloped or toothed edges; spiny leaves grow farther up along the stems. In summer, bears branched clusters of flowers that start out light green and mature to steely blue, surrounded by prickly, toothed, silver bracts.

E. planum. To 3 ft. high. Flowers heads small, freely borne, dark blue, with dark blue bracts.

E. variifolium. To 16 in., with small, rounded blue-gray flower heads and bluish white bracts. Thistlelike leaves are evergreen and heavily veined with white.

E. yuccifolium. RATTLESNAKE MASTER. Native to eastern and central U.S. Long (to 3-ft.), narrow, spiny-edged leaves in a basal rosette. Erect stems to 3–4 ft. branch toward top and carry small balls of white flowers without significant bracts.

ERYNGIUM FLOWERS NEED LONGER STEMS

Eryngium flowers have such dramatic form and unusual color, they call out to be used in arrangements. But their individual flower stems are too short (3–6 in.) to be seen in long-stemmed company. Cut florists' wire as needed, and fasten pieces to the stems with florists' tape. Eryngiums are everlastings; their stems don't need to be in water.

ERYSIMUM

WALLFLOWER	
Brassicaceae (Cruciferae)	
PERENNIALS AND BIENNIALS, SOME GROWN AS ANNUALS	
◪ ZONES VARY BY SPECIES	
☼ ◑ FULL SUN OR LIGHT SHADE	
● ● WATER NEEDS VARY BY SPECIES	

Erysimum

This genus swallowed up *Cheiranthus*, which included the old-fashioned, sweetly fragrant bedding wallflowers. All species have the typical clustered, four-petaled flowers that give the crucifers their name.

E. allionii. SIBERIAN WALLFLOWER. Perennial grown as biennial. Zones 32, 34–45. To 2 ft. high and 1 ft. wide. Lance-shaped, toothed leaves. In spring, clusters of bright orange, spicy-scented flowers. Moderate to regular water.

E. 'Bowles Mauve'. Perennial. Zones 31, 32. Massed erect stems with narrow gray-green leaves form a plant to 3 ft. tall, 6 ft. wide; each stem is topped by 1½-ft.-long, narrow, spikelike clusters of mauve flowers. Best in areas with cool summers and mild winters, where bloom is practically continuous. Spring, summer bloom elsewhere. May be short lived. Moderate to little water. 'Wenlock Beauty' is smaller, with flowers varying from buff to purple in a single spike.

E. cheiri (Cheiranthus cheiri). ENGLISH WALLFLOWER. Perennial in Zones 32 and 34, but usually grown as a biennial or an annual. Best suited to cool, moist regions, such as the coastal Northeast. Branching, woody-based plants 1–2½ ft. tall, with narrow bright green leaves and broad clusters of showy, delightfully sweet-scented flowers in spring. Blossoms are yellow, cream, orange, red, brown, or burgundy, sometimes shaded or veined with contrasting color. Sow seeds in spring for bloom the following year (some strains flower the first year if seeded early); or set out plants in fall or earliest spring. May self-sow. Regular water. Cultivars include Bedder series, to 1 ft. high, flowers in shades of yellow, orange, and scarlet; Fair Lady series, flowers in yellow, pink, white, and red; Harlequin, to 10 in. high, flowers in various shades of yellow, orange, red, and creamy white, also some bicolors.

E. hieraciifolium (E. alpinum). SIBERIAN WALLFLOWER. Biennial or perennial (Zones 32, 34–43), frequently treated as an annual. This species (sometimes sold as *Cheiranthus allionii* or *E. asperum)* is more widely grown in the eastern U.S. than is *E. cheiri.* Narrow-leafed, branching plants 1–1½ ft. tall, covered with fragrant, rich orange flowers in spring. Sow seeds or set out plants as for *E. cheiri.* Often self-sows. Regular water. 'Moonlight' has bright yellow flowers that open from red buds.

E. kotschyanum. Perennial (Zones 31, 32, 34), often treated as an annual in warm climates. Light green leaves form 6-in. mats from which rise scented, deep yellow flowers on 2-in. stems in spring. Moderate water. Use in rock garden or with other small perennials between paving stones. If plants hump up, cut out central portions, transplant them, and press original plants flat again. Divide clumps in fall.

ERYTHRONIUM

| *Liliaceae* |
| CORMS |
| ◪ ZONES VARY BY SPECIES |
| ☼ ● PARTIAL OR FULL SHADE |
| ● ◖ AMPLE WATER |

Erythronium

Spring-blooming, dainty, nodding, lily-shaped flowers 1–1½ in. across, on stems usually 1 ft. high or less. All have two (rarely three) broad, tongue-shaped, basal leaves, mottled in many species. All need some subfreezing temperatures. Plant in groups under trees, in rock gardens, beside pools or streams. Set out corms in fall, 2–3 in. deep, 4–5 in. apart, in rich, porous soil; plant corms as soon as you receive them, and don't let them dry out.

E. albidum. Zones 32, 34–43. Native from Minnesota to Ontario south to Texas. White flowers, flushed yellow at the base. Blooms later in spring than most of the other species. Leaves infrequently mottled silver green. Spreads slowly to form colonies.

E. americanum. Zones 31, 32, 34–43. Native from Minnesota to Nova Scotia south to Florida. Shiny green leaves mottled brown and purple. Blooms in late spring at about the same time as *E. albidum,* bearing pale yellow blossoms sometimes flushed with purple.

E. dens-canis. DOG-TOOTH VIOLET. Zones 31, 32, 34–43. European species. Leaves mottled with reddish brown; purple or rose flowers on 6-in. stems. Specialists can supply named varieties with white, pink, rose, and violet blossoms. Needs more sun than others.

E. revolutum. Zones 32, 34–41. Western native. Leaves mottled with brown and white; large rose, pink, or lavender flowers are banded yellow at base. 'Rose Beauty' and 'White Beauty' are choice varieties.

E. tuolumnense. Zones 32 (colder parts), 34–41. Native to California. Solid green leaves. Flowers golden yellow, greenish yellow at base. Robust, with stems 12–15 in. tall. 'Kondo' and 'Pagoda' are extra-vigorous selections.

FOR INFORMATION ON SELECTING PLANTS

PLEASE SEE PAGES 47–112

ESCHSCHOLZIA
californica

| CALIFORNIA POPPY |
| *Papaveraceae* |
| PERENNIAL OFTEN GROWN AS ANNUAL |
| ◪ ALL ZONES |
| ☼ FULL SUN |
| ● ◗ REGULAR TO LITTLE WATER |

*Eschscholzia
californica*

State flower of California, where it grows wild on hillsides and along roads. Free branching from base; stems 8–24 in. long. Finely divided, lacy blue-green leaves. In the wild, plants produce satiny-petaled, 2-in.-wide single flowers in colors ranging from pale yellow to deep orange.

Garden forms available in yellow, pink, rose, flame orange, red, cream, and white. Sunset strain has single blooms, Mission Bells semidouble flowers, and Ballerina semidouble blooms with frilled and fluted petals. The Silk strain has bronze-tinted foliage and semidouble flowers in the full color range. Single-color varieties include 'Cherry Ripe', 'Milky White', and 'Purple-Violet'. Garden forms usually revert to the orange or yellow of wild plants when they reseed. Flowers of all types close at night and on overcast days.

In cold-winter areas, generally used as summer annual; pretty in cottage gardens, rock gardens. In mild climates, plants bloom from spring to summer and reseed freely; best suited for informal plantings and for naturalizing on hillsides, since foliage turns straw colored after bloom.

Does best in well-drained soil; in hot, humid regions, excellent drainage is essential. Sow seed where plants are to grow; brittle taproot makes it difficult to transplant successfully. Sow in early spring in cold-winter regions, in fall in milder climates. Plants often self-sow. Birds are attracted to the seeds.

EUCOMIS

| PINEAPPLE FLOWER |
| *Liliaceae* |
| BULBS |
| ◪ DIG AND STORE; OR GROW IN POTS, EXCEPT AS NOTED |
| ☼ ☼ FULL SUN OR LIGHT SHADE |
| ● REGULAR WATER DURING GROWTH AND BLOOM |

Eucomis

Unusual-looking plant: thick, 2–3-ft. spikes are closely set with ½-in.-long flowers and topped with clusters of leaflike bracts like a pineapple top. Bloom in summer, but persistent purplish seed capsules continue the show longer. Need rich soil with plenty of humus. Dormant in winter. Plant bulbs 5 in. deep; also fairly easy to grow from spring-sown seeds. Dig and store bulbs or grow in pots and protect during cold weather. Divide clumps when they become crowded. Interesting potted plants for outdoor or indoor use. Good cut flower.

E. autumnalis. To 1 ft. tall; flowers light greenish white maturing to green, in late summer and early fall. Light green leaves, 1½ ft. long with wavy edges.

E. bicolor. To 2 ft.; flowers green, each petal edged with purple. Attractive leaves 1 ft. long, 3–4 in. wide, with wavy edges.

E. comosa (E. punctata). Thick spikes 2–3 ft. tall are set with greenish white flowers tinged pink or purple. Stems are spotted purple at the base. Leaves grow to 2 ft. long and are less wavy than those of *E. bicolor.*

E. pallidiflora. GIANT PINEAPPLE FLOWER. Produces 2½-ft.-long straplike leaves and racemes of greenish white flowers.

E. 'Sparkling Burgundy'. PURPLE PINEAPPLE LILY. Zones 31, 32; 34, 39 with good winter protection from cold and wet. Grows to 20 in. tall, with a rosette of deep burgundy leaves and pale burgundy flowers in mid- to late summer.

E

EUCOMMIA ulmoides

HARDY RUBBER TREE

Eucommiaceae

DECIDUOUS TREE

⚡ ZONES 31, 32, 34–41

☀ FULL SUN

💧💧 REGULAR TO MODERATE WATER

Eucommia ulmoides

Though rubber can be made from the hardy rubber tree's sap, the process is not economically feasible. Instead, this tree is grown for its ornamental qualities. Attractive rounded habit; can reach 40–60 ft. in height, with nearly equal spread. Leaves resemble those of elm, but are glossier and more leathery. When a leaf is slowly torn in two, the sap from the veins congeals into threads of rubber, holding the two parts together. Summer foliage is attractive, fall color negligible. Flowers and fruit are not conspicuous. Requires good drainage but tolerates a wide variety of soils. Not troubled by pests.

EULALIA GRASS. See MISCANTHUS sinensis

EUONYMUS

Celastraceae

EVERGREEN, DECIDUOUS SHRUBS; EVERGREEN VINES

⚡ ZONES VARY BY SPECIES

☀◑● EXPOSURE NEEDS VARY BY SPECIES

💧💧 REGULAR TO MODERATE WATER

Euonymus

Deciduous and evergreen species are distinct; the characteristic squarish "hatbox" fruit provides the only hint that they're related. Deciduous types are valued for brilliant fall leaf color or prominent fruit; evergreen types, used mainly for landscape structure, include some of the most cold-tolerant broad-leafed evergreens. Most species tolerate a range of light conditions, from full sun to fairly deep shade; deciduous kinds with fall color give best display in sun. Scale can be a problem on any euonymus.

E. alatus. WINGED EUONYMUS. Deciduous shrub. Zones 31, 32, 34–45. Though nursery tags may indicate a much smaller plant, the species can reach 15–20 ft. high and wide. Dense, twiggy, flat topped, with horizontal branching. Twigs have flat, corky wings that disappear on older growth. Though fruit is smaller and less profuse than that of *E. europaeus*, fall color is impressive: the dark green leaves turn flaming red in autumn. (In shade, fall color is pink.) 'Compacta', a smaller plant (to 6–10 ft. high and a little narrower) with smaller corky wings, isn't quite as hardy. Use both species and variety as screen or alone, against dark evergreens for greatest color impact. 'Compacta' also makes a good unclipped hedge or foundation plant.

E. americana. STRAWBERRY BUSH. Deciduous shrub. Zones 31, 32, 34, 39. Native to eastern and southern U.S. Many-stemmed, suckering shrub with green stems. To 6 ft. high. Leaves medium green, to 3 in. long, lacking the fall color of *E. alatus*. Fruits are warty, bright red, up to ¾ in. in diameter. Tolerates much shade; use in native woodland plantings. Well-behaved plant.

E. bungeanus semipersistens. WINTERBERRY EUONYMUS. Semievergreen shrub. Zones 31, 32, 34–41. To 13 ft. high, with slender branches. Oval leaves to 4 in. long, lobed pinkish white fruits. Holds its leaves and fruits long in fall, but is susceptible to scale.

E. europaeus. SPINDLE TREE. Deciduous large shrub or small tree. Zones 31, 32, 34–45. Eventually reaches a possible 30 ft. tall; narrow when young, becoming rounded with age. Leaves are dark green; fall color varies from yellowish green to yellow to red. Fruits are the ornamental fea-ture: a profusion of four-chambered, pink to red capsules open to reveal bright orange seeds. 'Aldenham' ('Aldenhamensis') produces profuse large pink capsules on long stems; 'Red Cascade' bears rosy red capsules. Full sun or partial shade. Scale is often a serious problem.

E. fortunei. WINTER CREEPER EUONYMUS. Evergreen vine or shrub. Zones 31, 32, 34–41. One of the best broad-leafed evergreens where temperatures drop below 0°F/−18°C. Trails or climbs by rootlets. If this plant is used as shrub, its branches will trail and sometimes root; if allowed to climb, it will be a spreading mass to 20 ft. or more. Prostrate forms can be used to control erosion. Leaves dark rich green, 1–2½ in. long, with scallop-toothed edges; flowers inconspicuous. Mature growth, like that of ivy, is shrubby and bears fruit; cuttings taken from this shrubby wood produce upright plants.

The varieties of *E. fortunei*, several of which are listed here, are better known than the species itself. Many nurseries still sell them as forms of *E. radicans*, which was once thought to be the species but is now considered to be another variety (see *E. f. radicans* below).

'Canadale Gold'. Compact shrub with light green, yellow-edged leaves.

'Colorata'. PURPLE-LEAF WINTER CREEPER. Same sprawling growth habit as *E. f. radicans*, though makes a more even ground cover. Leaves turn dark purple in fall and winter.

'Emerald Gaiety'. Small, dense-growing, erect shrub with deep green leaves edged with white.

'Emerald 'n Gold'. Similar to above, but with gold-edged leaves.

'Golden Prince'. New growth tipped gold. Older leaves turn green. Extremely hardy; good hedge plant.

'Greenlane'. Low, spreading shrub with erect branches, deep green foliage, orange fruit in fall.

'Ivory Jade'. Resembles 'Greenlane' but has creamy white leaf margins that show pink tints in cold weather.

E. f. radicans. COMMON WINTER CREEPER. Zones 31, 32, 34, 39. Tough, hardy, trailing or vining shrub with dark green, thick-textured, 1-in.-long leaves. Given no support, it sprawls; given masonry wall to cover, it does the job completely.

E. kiautschovica (E. patens). SPREADING EUONYMUS. Semi-evergreen shrub. Zones 31, 32, 34, 35, 39. May retain leaves in warmest areas, drop them in coldest. About 8 ft. high and as wide or wider, with some low branches trailing on the ground and rooting. Relatively thin-textured, light green leaves and profusion of tiny, greenish cream flowers in late summer. Bloom followed by conspicuous pink to reddish fruits with red seeds. Two hybrids make good hedges: 'DuPont', a 4–6-ft.-high plant with large, dark green leaves; and 'Manhattan', an upright grower 6–8 ft. high with dark, glossy leaves.

E. nanus 'Turkestanicus'. DWARF EUONYMUS. Evergreen, semievergreen, or deciduous shrub. Zones 34–45. Small shrub to 3 ft. high. Blue-green leaves turn bright red in autumn. Lobed pink fruits.

EUPATORIUM

Asteraceae (Compositae)

PERENNIALS

⚡ ZONES 31, 32, 34–43. EXCEPT AS NOTED

☀◑ LIGHT SHADE IN HOT-SUMMER AREAS

💧 AMPLE MOISTURE, EXCEPT AS NOTED

Eupatorium

Medium-size to towering perennials with large clusters of small flower heads at the tops of leafy stems. Except as noted, these species are native to the eastern and central U.S. and have become popular not only in wild gardens and restored meadows, but also in more ordered perennial borders. All are easy to grow. Remove faded flower heads to avoid seedlings. Divide clumps in spring or fall.

E. cannabinum. HEMP AGRIMONY. Native to Europe. Grows 5–6 ft. tall, with opposite pairs of deeply cut leaves and broad clusters of fluffy white, pink, or purple flower heads in summer. 'Album' bears white flowers, 'Plenum' pinkish purple blooms.

E. coelestinum. HARDY AGERATUM. Grows to 3 ft. tall, with freely branching stems set with pairs of 4-in. dark green, toothed leaves. Broad clusters of fluffy blue flowers exactly resemble those of the annual ageratum. Vigorous, freely spreading plant needs division every 3 years or so. Prefers ample moisture, but will not thrive in soggy soil in winter. Late to appear in spring; blooms from late summer until frost. The 1½ – 2-ft.-high 'Album' bears pure white flowers; 2-ft.-high 'Cori' has exceptionally clear blue blossoms and comes into bloom later than the species; 'Wayside Form' is more compact, growing to 15 in. high.

E. maculatum. JOE PYE WEED. Similar to *E. purpureum,* but smaller (to 6 ft.), with green stems blotched with purple. Flat-topped clusters of pink, purple, or white flowers bloom from midsummer to early fall.

E. perfoliatum. BONESET. Zones 31, 32, 34–45. Grows 3–5 ft. tall. The long (8-in.), narrow leaves are joined at their bases, so that the stem appears to grow through the leaves. Fluffy white flowers borne in flat-topped clusters. This plant is attractive in meadow restoration, but poisonous to cattle and thus considered a nuisance by ranchers. Likes moisture but tolerates considerable drought. In the past, this plant was thought to have medicinal value for people, helping to knit broken bones—hence the common name.

E. purpureum. JOE PYE WEED. Zones 31, 32, 34–45. Often sold as *E. fistulosum.* An imposing plant of damp meadows in the eastern U.S. Grows 3–9 ft. tall, with clumps of hollow stems and whorls of strongly toothed leaves to 1 ft. long. Leaves have a vanilla scent when bruised. Pale purple flowers, attractive to butterflies, appear in large, dome-shaped clusters in late summer or early fall. Variety commonly sold is 'Gateway', a sensible 5 ft. in height, with dusky purplish rose flowers at the top of purple stems.

EUPHORBIA

Euphorbiaceae

SHRUBS, PERENNIALS, ANNUALS, AND SUCCULENTS

ZONES VARY BY SPECIES

EXPOSURE NEEDS VARY BY SPECIES

REGULAR TO MODERATE WATER, EXCEPT AS NOTED

SAP IS POISONOUS IN SOME SPECIES

Euphorbia

On euphorbia, what are called "flowers" are really groups of colored bracts. True flowers, centered in the bracts, are inconspicuous. Many euphorbias are succulents; these often mimic cacti in appearance and are as diverse as cacti in form and size. Only a couple of these are listed below, but specialists in cacti and succulents can supply scores of species and varieties. Plant euphorbias in well-drained soil. Give winter protection in cold climates.

E. amygdaloides. Perennial. Zones 31, 32, 34. To nearly 3 ft., resembling a smaller *E. characias* and also blooming late winter, early spring. 'Purpurea' has foliage heavily tinted purple, with bright green inflorescence. Best in sun, tolerates some shade. Dies back in winter.

E. characias. Evergreen perennial. Zones 31, warmer parts of 32. Upright stems make dome-shaped bush 4 ft. tall. Narrow blue-green leaves crowded along stems. Clustered flowers make dense, round to cylindrical masses of chartreuse or lime green in late winter, early spring. Color holds with only slight fading until seeds ripen; then stalks yellow and should be cut out at base, since new shoots have already made growth for next year's flowers. *E. c. wulfenii (E. veneta),* the most common form, has broader clusters of yellower flowers. Both species and variety are fairly drought resistant and perform best in full sun.

E. corollata. WILD SPURGE. Perennial. Zones 32, 34–43. To 3 ft. high. Medium green, oval leaves to 2½ in. long. Clusters of chartreuse flowers with white bracts below them, in summer. Sun to light shade.

E. cyparissias. Perennial. Zones 31, 32, 34–43. Produces clumps of erect stems to 16 in. high (often considerably less) from wide-roaming underground rhizomes. Narrow leaves to 1½ in. long are crowded on the stem to produce a feathery effect; stems somewhat resemble small pine trees. Clusters contain up to 18 greenish yellow or chartreuse yellow flowers, attractive over a long season in spring and summer. Covers ground rapidly and can become a pest among choice plants (so site carefully), but attractive along a road or at the edge of cultivated area. Can stand some shade but prefers sun. Needs little water once established. May become dormant in winter.

E. dulcis 'Chameleon'. PURPLE SPURGE. Perennial. Zones 31, 32, 34–43. To 1 ft. high, with oblong purple leaves whorled around the stems. Clusters of green bell-shaped flowers top the stems in early summer. Spreads to form clumps but is not invasive like the species. Provide light shade.

E. griffithii. Perennial. Zones 31, 32, 34–43. Erect stems to 3 ft., clad in narrow, medium green leaves and topped by clusters of brick red or orange bracts. Spreads by creeping roots but is not aggressive. Sun or light shade. Dies back in winter. 'Fireglow' is the variety commonly sold.

E. heterophylla. MEXICAN FIRE PLANT. Annual. All zones. To 3 ft. tall. Bright green leaves of varying shapes, larger ones resembling those of poinsettia; flowers unimportant. In summer, upper leaves are blotched bright red and white, giving appearance of second-rate poinsettia. Regular to little water. Useful in hot, dry, sunny borders in poor soil. Sow seed in place after frost danger is over.

E. 'Jade Dragon'. Perennial. Zones 31, 32, 34, 39. To 1½ ft. high with compact, chubby growth habit. New growth tinted purple. Large greenish flower heads to 11 in. wide. Sun to light shade.

E. lathyris. GOPHER PLANT, MOLE PLANT. Biennial. Zones 31, 32, 34–41. Legend claims that it repels gophers and moles. Stems have poisonous, caustic milky juice; keep away from skin and especially eyes, since painful burns can result. Juice could conceivably bother a gopher or mole enough to make it beat a hasty retreat. Grows as tall single stem—to 5 ft. high by second summer, when it sets a cluster of unspectacular yellow flowers at the top. Flowers soon turn to seed, after which the plant dies. Long, narrow-pointed leaves grow at right angles to stem and to each other. Grow from seed. Give sun or shade, regular to little water.

E. marginata. SNOW-ON-THE-MOUNTAIN. Annual. All zones. To 2 ft. Leaves light green, oval; upper ones striped and margined white, uppermost sometimes all white. Flowers unimportant. Used for contrast with bright-colored bedding dahlias, scarlet sage, or zinnias, or with dark cultivars of plume celosia. Before using in cut arrangements, dip stems in boiling water or hold in flame for a few seconds. Sow seed in place in spring, in sun or partial shade. Thin to only a few inches apart, as plants are somewhat rangy.

E. martinii. Evergreen perennial. Zones 31, 32. Hybrid between *E. amygdaloides* and *E. characias.* Resembles a compact *E. characias,* with dense clusters of chartreuse, brown-centered flowers in late winter, early spring. Has red stems in winter. Fairly drought resistant; takes full sun.

E. myrsinites. Evergreen perennial. Zones 31, 32, 34–43. Stems flop outward from central crown, then rise toward tip to 8–12 in. Leaves stiff, roundish, blue gray, closely set around stems. Flattish clusters of chartreuse to yellow flowers top stem ends in late winter, early spring. Cut out old stems as they turn yellow. Withstands cold and heat, but is short lived in warm-winter areas. Use in sunny rock gardens with succulents and gray-foliaged plants.

E. nicaeensis. Perennial. Zones 31, 32, 34–41. Evergreen or semievergreen, to 2½ ft. high, oblong to lance-shaped grayish green leaves, to 3 in. long, on reddish green stems. In late spring to midsummer, clusters of yellow-green flowers top the stems. Full sun.

E. palustris. Perennial. Zones 31, 32, 34. To 3 ft. (possibly 5 ft.) high, with many medium green, 2–3-in. leaves. Widely branching clusters of yellow flowers appear in spring, early summer. Will grow in sun or some shade, with regular to little water. Dies back in winter. Self-sows.

E. polychroma (E. epithymoides). CUSHION SPURGE. Perennial. Zones 31, 32, 34–43. To 16 in. high. Oblong, deep green leaves to 2 in. long, often turn purple, red, or orange in autumn. In midspring to midsummer, stems are tipped with clusters of bright yellow flowers backed by greenish yellow bracts. Full sun to light shade.

E

E. robbiae (E. amygdaloides robbiae). MRS. ROBB'S BONNET. Evergreen perennial. Zones 31, 32. Usually under 1 ft. high. The stems are closely set with leathery dark green leaves 1½−4 in. long, over 1 in. wide. Pale lime green flower clusters in late winter, early spring. Spreads slowly but surely from underground rhizomes. It can thrive in sun (but not the hottest sun) and in deep shade. Regular to little water.

E. seguieriana niciciana. Evergreen perennial. Zones 31, 32, 34. Resembles a delicate *E. characias*. To 1½ ft., with blue-gray, narrow, 1-in. leaves; chartreuse inflorescence in very early spring. Full sun.

E. veneta, E. characias wulfenii. See *E. characias*

Euphorbiaceae. The euphorbia family contains annuals, perennials, shrubs, and an enormous number of succulents. Most have milky sap, and many have unshowy flowers made decorative by bracts or bractlike glands. Poinsettia *(Euphorbia pulcherrima)* is the best-known example.

EUSCAPHIS japonica

SWEETHEART TREE

Staphyleaceae

DECIDUOUS SHRUB OR SMALL TREE

🗡 ZONES 31, 32, 34, 39

☼ ◑ FULL SUN OR PARTIAL SHADE

🔴 AVERAGE WATER

Euscaphis japonica

A 15−25-ft. shrub or small tree with reddish purple bark and pinnate, or featherlike, leaves that turn brown purple in fall. Bears 2−4½-in.-wide panicles of yellow-green or whitish flowers in late spring or early summer. Flowers are followed by large crops of decorative fruits in fall with reddish to red-purple pods that split to reveal handsome dark blue seeds. Use sweetheart tree in a shrub border or as a specimen. Plant in average, well-drained soil and prune, as necessary, in late winter.

EUSTOMA grandiflorum
(Lisianthus russellianus)

LISIANTHUS, TULIP GENTIAN,
TEXAS BLUEBELL

Gentianaceae

BIENNIAL OR SHORT-LIVED PERENNIAL OFTEN GROWN AS ANNUAL

🗡 ALL ZONES

☼ ◑ FULL SUN OR FILTERED LIGHT

🔴 REGULAR WATER

Eustoma grandiflorum

N ative to U.S. High Plains, but garden forms introduced from Japan. Plants grow better and have longer stems where nights are warm. Best cut flowers are produced in greenhouses.

In summer, clumps of gray-green foliage send up 1½-ft. stems topped by tulip-shaped, 2−3-in. flowers in purplish blue, pink, or white; plants bloom all summer if old blooms are cut off. Lion and Double Eagle strains have double flowers that look somewhat like roses. Heidi strain of F₁ hybrids are vigorous and long stemmed, and include yellow in addition to other flower colors. 'Red Glass' has rose red flowers. Picotee types are also available.

Buying started plants is easier, but lisianthus can be grown with much care from its dustlike seeds. Sprinkle seed on surface of potting soil; don't cover with soil. Soak well, then cover pot with glass or plastic until seeds germinate. At four-leaf stage (about 2 months), transplant three or four plants into each 6-in. pot. Needs good garden soil, good drainage, average fertilizer. Often grown as annual. Use in pots, border, cutting garden.

EVENING PRIMROSE. See OENOTHERA

EVERGREEN CANDYTUFT. See IBERIS sempervirens

EVERLASTING. See HELIPTERUM

EVODIA daniellii
(Tetradium daniellii)

Rutaceae

DECIDUOUS TREE

🗡 ZONES 31, 32, 34–41

☼ FULL SUN

🔴 REGULAR WATER

Evodia daniellii

N ative to northern China and Korea. Evodia is distantly related to citrus, but the leaves are more reminiscent of walnut. Grows to 30 ft. or taller and somewhat wider. The shiny dark green leaves are 1 ft. long or a little more, with five pairs of 2−5-in. leaflets plus a single leaflet at the end. Foliage is handsome throughout summer and early fall. No fall color; leaves drop while green. Blooms in early summer, bearing small white flowers in showy, 4−6-in., rather flat clusters; they are popular with bees. Fruits are small but attractive, aging from red to black. Although introduced nearly a century ago, the plant remains little known, despite its attractiveness, soil tolerance, and freedom from pests. *E. hupehensis* is a somewhat less hardy form from southern China.

EVOLVULUS glomeratus

BLUE DAZE

Convolvulaceae

TENDER PERENNIAL OFTEN GROWN AS ANNUAL

🗡 ALL ZONES

☼ ◑ FULL SUN OR LIGHT SHADE

🔴 REGULAR WATER

Evolvulus glomeratus

N ative to Brazil. Trailing stems to 20 in. are closely set with small gray-green leaves and spangled with blue morning glory flowers less than 1 in. wide. Flowers close in the evening and on darkly overcast days. Stems root where they touch the ground; cuttings root very easily in water or moist soil. Useful as an annual bedding plant, in summer borders, in hanging baskets. Often sold as *E. nuttallianus*.

EXOCHORDA

PEARL BUSH

Rosaceae

DECIDUOUS SHRUBS

🗡 ZONES 31, 32, 34–41

☼ FULL SUN

🔴 REGULAR WATER

Exochorda

L oose, spikelike clusters of 1½−2-in.-wide white flowers open from profusion of buds resembling pearls. Flowers bloom for a short time in spring, at about the same time the roundish, 1½−2-in.-long leaves expand. Foliage and arching growth suggest the related spiraea, but pearl bush's individual blossoms are considerably larger.

Showy during spring but undistinguished at other times of year, so choose your site accordingly. Prefers well-drained, acid soil; will take considerable neglect. Flowers are formed on previous year's growth, so prune after bloom to control size and form.

E. giraldii. Resembles the more widely grown *E. racemosa,* but with slightly smaller flowers, white, borne in upright clusters in spring. Red tints in leaf veins and flower stalks. *E. g. wilsonii* is more erect in habit and has green, not red stems.

E. macrantha. Hybrid between *E. racemosa* and another species. The only variety available, 'The Bride', is a compact shrub to about 4 ft. tall and as wide.

E. racemosa (E. grandiflora). COMMON PEARL BUSH. Native to China. Loose, open, slender; to 10–15 ft. tall and wide. In small gardens, remove lower branches to make upright, airy, multistemmed small tree.

Fabaceae. Previously called Leguminosae, the pea family is an enormous group containing annuals, perennials, shrubs, trees, and vines. Many are useful as food (beans, peas), while others furnish timber, medicines, pesticides, and a host of other products. Many are ornamental.

The best known kinds—sweet peas (Lathyrus), for example—have flowers shaped like butterflies, with two winglike side petals, two partially united lower petals (called the keel), and one erect upper petal (the banner or standard). Others have a more regular flower shape (Senna); still others have tightly clustered flowers that appear to be puffs of stamens, as in acacia and silk tree (Albizia). All bear seeds in pods (legumes). Many have on their roots colonies of bacteria that can extract nitrogen from the air and convert it into compounds useful as plant food; clovers (Trifolium) are a familiar example.

Fagaceae. The beech family contains evergreen or deciduous trees characterized by fruit that is either a nut enclosed in a cup, as in oak *(Quercus),* or a burr, as in beech *(Fagus)* and chestnut *(Castanea).*

FAGUS

BEECH	
Fagaceae	
DECIDUOUS TREES	
⚡ ZONES VARY BY SPECIES	
☼ ◑ FULL SUN OR LIGHT SHADE	
⬤ ⬤ REGULAR TO MODERATE WATER	

Fagus

Of the various beech types, those described here include a rarely seen Japanese species; a species native to the eastern U.S. that is widespread in nature but seldom planted in gardens; and the commonly planted European beech. Though all beeches are capable of growing to 90 ft. or more, they are usually considerably smaller. With the exception of selected horticultural varieties, they have a broad cone shape, with wide, sweeping lower branches that can reach the ground unless pruned off. Smooth gray bark contrasts well with glossy dark green foliage. Leaves color yellow to red brown in fall, then turn brown; many hang on the tree well into winter. Lacy branching pattern and pointed leaf buds provide an attractive winter silhouette. New foliage has a silky sheen. The nuts, enclosed in spiny husks, are edible but small; they will often fail to fill, especially on solitary trees.

All beeches cast heavy shade and have a dense network of fibrous roots near soil surface, inhibiting growth of lawn or other plants under the trees. Transplant from containers or, if moving an in-ground tree, dig with a substantial ball of earth. Give any good garden soil. Despite their size as trees, beeches can be closely planted and trimmed as dense, impassible hedges as low as 4 ft.

F. crenata. JAPANESE BEECH. Zones 32, 34–41. Leaves scallop edged, somewhat smaller than those of other beeches. Reddish brown fall color. Likes some shade in hot-summer areas, especially when young.

F. grandifolia. AMERICAN BEECH. Zones 31, 32, 34–45. A stately tree and a principal component of the vast hardwood forests that once covered much of the eastern U.S. More tolerant of summer heat than the other two species described here and can be grown farther south. Leaves are toothed, 3–6 in. long; golden bronze fall color. Allow plenty of room for this tree.

F. sylvatica. EUROPEAN BEECH. Zones 32, 34–43. Lustrous green leaves to 4 in. long, turning russet and bronzy in autumn. Many varieties, including the following:

'Asplenifolia'. FERNLEAF BEECH. Leaves narrow, deeply lobed or cut nearly to midrib. Delicate foliage on large, robust, spreading tree.

'Atropunicea'. COPPER BEECH, PURPLE BEECH. Leaves deep reddish or purple. Good in containers. Often sold as 'Riversii' or 'Purpurea'. Seedlings of copper beech are usually bronzy purple, turning bronzy green in summer.

'Dawck Gold'. Columnar, to 60 ft. hight and 20 ft. wide; young leaves are bright yellow, later turning green.

'Dawck Purple'. Columnar, to 70 ft. high and 15 ft. wide, with dark purple leaves.

'Fastigiata'. DAWYCK BEECH. Narrow, upright tree, like Lombardy poplar in form; 8 ft. wide when 35 ft. tall. Broader in great age, but still narrower than species.

'Laciniata'. CUTLEAF BEECH. Narrow green leaves, deeply cut.

'Pendula'. WEEPING BEECH. Irregular, spreading form. Long, weeping branches reach to ground, can root where they touch. Green leaves. Without staking to establish vertical trunk, it will grow wide rather than high.

'Purpurea Pendula'. WEEPING COPPER BEECH. Purple-leafed weeping form to 10 ft. tall. Splendid container plant.

'Tricolor'. TRICOLOR BEECH. Green leaves marked white and edged pink. Slow to 24–40 ft., usually much less. Foliage burns in hot sun or dry winds. Choice container plant.

'Zlatia'. GOLDEN BEECH. Young leaves yellow, aging to yellow green. Subject to sunburn. Good container plant.

FAIRY BELLS. See DISPORUM

FAIRY LILY. See ZEPHYRANTHES

FAIRY WAND. See DIERAMA

FALSE ANEMONE. See ANEMONOPSIS

FALSE CYPRESS. See CHAMAECYPARIS

FALSE DRAGONHEAD. See PHYSOSTEGIA virginiana

FALSE INDIGO. See AMORPHA fruticosa, BAPTISIA

FALSE LUPINE. See THERMOPSIS

FALSE SOLOMON'S SEAL. See SMILACINA racemosa

FALSE SPIRAEA. See ASTILBE, SORBARIA

FAREWELL-TO-SPRING. See CLARKIA amoena

FARFUGIUM. See LIGULARIA tussilaginea

BEECHES IN THE LANDSCAPE

Beeches are magnificent landscape trees in the right setting. Allow them plenty of space to show them off to best effect. A beech standing in a large, open expanse can be appreciated for its beautiful outline and sweeping branches. Try to avoid pruning the lower branches, especially of weeping cultivars. Use beeches as specimen trees on a large property. Do not plant them near the street or close to the house, where they would be cramped.

FATSHEDERA lizei

Araliaceae

EVERGREEN VINE, SHRUB, OR GROUND COVER

☒ ZONES 31, WARM PARTS OF 32

◐ ● PARTIAL OR FULL SHADE

● REGULAR WATER

Fatshedera lizei

Hybrid between Japanese aralia *(Fatsia japonica)* and English ivy *(Hedera helix)*, with characteristics of both parents. Highly polished, 4–10-in.-wide leaves with three to five pointed lobes look like giant ivy leaves; plant also sends out long, trailing or climbing stems like ivy, though without aerial holdfasts. Fatshedera inherited shrubbiness from Japanese aralia, though its habit is more irregular and sprawling than that of its parent. Several variegated forms exist.

Leaves are injured at 15°F/−9°C, tender new growth at 20 to 25°F/−7 to −4°C; seems to suffer more from late frosts than from winter cold. Give it protection from hot, drying winds. Good near swimming pools.

Fatshedera tends to grow in a straight line, but it can be shaped if you work at it. Pinch tip growth to force branching. About two or three times a year, guide and tie stems before they become brittle. If plant gets away from you, cut it back to ground; it will regrow quickly. If you use it as ground cover, cut back vertical growth every 2 to 3 weeks during growing season. Grown as vine or espalier, plants are heavy, so give them strong supports. Even a well-grown vine is leafless at base.

FAVA BEAN. See BEAN, BROAD

FEATHERED HYACINTH. See MUSCARI comosum 'Monstrosum'

FEATHER GRASS. See STIPA

FEATHER REED GRASS. See CALAMAGROSTIS acutifolia 'Stricta'

FELICIA

Asteraceae (Compositae)

SHRUBBY PERENNIALS AND ANNUALS

☒ ZONES VARY BY SPECIES

☼ FULL SUN

● ● REGULAR TO MODERATE WATER

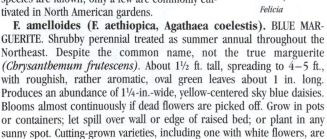

Felicia

Daisy relatives, typically with blue flowers; native to South Africa. Though more than 80 species are known, only a few are commonly cultivated in North American gardens.

F. amelloides (F. aethiopica, Agathaea coelestis). BLUE MARGUERITE. Shrubby perennial treated as summer annual throughout the Northeast. Despite the common name, not the true marguerite *(Chrysanthemum frutescens)*. About 1½ ft. tall, spreading to 4–5 ft., with roughish, rather aromatic, oval green leaves about 1 in. long. Produces an abundance of 1¼-in.-wide, yellow-centered sky blue daisies. Blooms almost continuously if dead flowers are picked off. Grow in pots or containers; let spill over wall or edge of raised bed; or plant in any sunny spot. Cutting-grown varieties, including one with white flowers, are sold in some areas.

F. bergeriana. KINGFISHER DAISY. Annual. All zones. Forms a mat of somewhat hairy foliage to 6–10 in. high and about as wide. Blue daisies about 1 in. across bloom over a long period in summer and fall. Tolerates wind but not extreme heat. Sow seed in early spring (fall in warm-winter climates). Use in pots, window boxes, borders, as edging.

FENNEL. See FOENICULUM vulgare

FERNLEAF YARROW. See ACHILLEA filipendulina

FERNS. Large group of perennial plants grown for their lovely and interesting foliage. They vary in height from a few inches to 50 ft. or more, and are found in all parts of the world; most are forest plants, but some grow in deserts, in open fields, or near the timberline in high mountains. Most have finely cut leaves (fronds). They do not flower but reproduce by spores that form directly on the fronds.

Ferns are divided into several families, according to botanical differences. Such technical differences aside, these plants fall into several groups based on general appearance.

Most spectacular are tree ferns, which display their finely cut fronds atop a treelike stem. These need rich, well-drained soil, moisture, and shade (except in cool-summer regions, where they can take sun). Most tree ferns are rather tender to frost, and all suffer in hot, drying winds and in extremely low humidity. Frequent watering of tops, trunks, and root area will help pull them through unusually hot or windy weather. They are not hardy outdoors in the Northeast.

Native ferns do not grow as tall as tree ferns, but their fronds are handsome and they can perform a number of landscape jobs. Naturalize them in woodland or wild gardens; or use them to fill shady beds, as ground cover, as interplantings between shrubs, or along a shady house wall. Many of those native to eastern North America take extreme cold and are usually deciduous. For native ferns, see *Adiantum, Asplenium, Athyrium, Dennstaedtia punctilobula, Dryopteris, Onoclea sensibilis, Osmunda, Polystichum, Pteridium, Thelypteris, Woodsia, Woodwardia.*

Many ferns from other parts of the world grow well in the U.S.; although some are house, greenhouse, or (in mildest climates) lathhouse subjects, many are fairly hardy. Use them as you would native ferns, unless some peculiarity of habit makes it necessary to grow them in baskets or on slabs. Some exotic ferns will be found under *Adiantum, Arachniodes, Asplenium, Cyrtomium, Polypodium, Polystichum.*

All ferns look best if groomed. Cut off dead or injured fronds near ground or trunk—but don't cut back hardy outdoor ferns until new growth begins, since old fronds protect growing tips. Natives growing outdoors don't need it, but feed others frequently during growing season, preferably with light applications of organic-base fertilizer such as blood meal or fish emulsion. Mulch with peat moss occasionally, especially if shallow fibrous roots are exposed by rain or irrigation.

FESTUCA

FESCUE

Poaceae (Gramineae)

GRASSES

☒ ZONES 31, 32, 34–45, EXCEPT AS NOTED

☼ FULL SUN, EXCEPT AS NOTED

● REGULAR WATER; TOLERATE SOME ARIDITY

Festuca

Several of these clumping grasses are used for cool-season lawns, erosion control, or pasture; others have use as ornamental plants. Lawn fescues are classified as fine or coarse. All fescues need good drainage.

F. amethystina, F. cinerea. These grasses form tight clumps of narrow bluish or grayish leaves. All are similar to *F. glauca* in appearance, culture, and uses; indeed, *F. glauca* may be the same plant as *F. amethystina* or *F. cinerea.* Named varieties abound; they vary in intensity of blue color and in height, ranging from 6 to 18 in. tall. 'Elijah Blue' is a popular powder blue variety.

F. elatior. TALL FESCUE. Coarse. Tall-growing (to 2½ ft.) pasture grass also used for erosion control when unmowed; or for moderately low-water-use lawns if planted close together and mowed to 2–3 in. high. Tough blades, tolerance of compacted soils make it good play or sports turf. Finer-textured strains are used as lawn grasses, either alone or mixed with bluegrass.

F. glauca (F. ovina glauca). BLUE FESCUE. Much like *F. ovina*, forms blue-gray tufts 4–10 in. tall. Use like *F. ovina*.

F. mairei. ATLAS FESCUE. Zones 31, 32. Forms clumps to 3 ft. tall of narrow, flat, gray-green leaves.

F. ovina. SHEEP FESCUE. Fine. Low-growing grass (to 1 ft.) with narrow, needle-fine, soft but tough leaves. *F. o. duriuscula,* hard fescue, is sometimes used as lawn grass. Useful ground cover for sunny or partially shaded areas, on slopes or level ground. Cannot tolerate foot traffic. Clip back near to the ground after flowering or any time plants look shabby. Does not make solid cover and needs frequent weeding. Dig overgrown clumps, pull apart, and replant as small divisions. Set 6–15 in. apart, depending on desired effect.

F. rubra. RED FESCUE. Fine. Principal use is in blends with bluegrass or other lawn grasses. Blades narrow, dark green. Not fussy about soil; takes some shade. Used alone, tends to grow clumpy; mow to 1½–2½ in. high. The type most commonly sold is sometimes called creeping red fescue; it is one of most shade tolerant of good lawn grasses. Unmowed, all types of red fescue make attractive meadow on slopes too steep to mow.

FEVERFEW. See CHRYSANTHEMUM parthenium

FIG, EDIBLE

Moraceae

DECIDUOUS TREES

🌡 ZONE 31, WARMER PARTS OF 32; OR IN POTS

☀ FULL SUN

🔴 REGULAR WATER

Fig, edible

Figs are not a common sight in the Northeast, but in favorable places such as the walled gardens at Colonial Williamsburg, picturesque old specimens with gnarled gray bark are a delightful surprise. Elsewhere in the warmer parts of the region, expect to see sizable shrubby plants up to 10 ft. high that have been killed to the ground in severe winters.

The large, rough, three- to five-lobed leaves give these plants a decidedly tropical look, and containerized specimens lend an exotic touch to decks, patios, or terraces. Fig trees can survive outdoors as far north as southern New England if a particularly cold-hardy variety is chosen, a sheltered site selected, and the stems are wrapped in burlap over the winter. The roots are hardy to about 0°F; where winter temperatures may dip below zero, mulch well or mound soil around the base of the plant for added protection.

Varieties differ in climate adaptability; most need prolonged high temperatures to bear good fruit, while some thrive in cooler conditions. The familiar dried 'Calimyrna' or imported Smyrna figs sold in markets require special pollinators (caprifigs) and special pollinating insects; not recommended for home gardens. Varieties with most tightly closed "eyes"—opening opposite stem end—resist invasion by dried fruit beetle, a pest in some areas. Such varieties are noted below.

'Blanche'. Developed for regions with cool, short growing seasons. The large, tasty, sweet fruits have a lemony flavor.

'Brown Turkey' ('San Pedro', 'Black Spanish'). Adaptable to most fig climates. Good garden tree; small, cold hardy. Fruit has purplish brown skin, pinkish amber flesh; good for fresh eating. Closed eye.

'Celeste' ('Blue Celeste', 'Celestial'). Cold-hardy plant. Bronzy, violet-tinged skin, rosy amber flesh; good for fresh eating. Closed eye.

'Hardy Chicago'. Succulent, sweet fruits ripen especially early, making it an excellent choice for container culture in northern gardens.

'Kadota' ('White Kadota'). Tough-skinned fruit has lemon yellow skin, light amber to yellow flesh. Commercial canning variety. Strong grower; needs little pruning. If pruned severely, will bear later, with fewer, larger fruits. Needs lots of heat.

'Long Island'. Discovered undamaged on Long Island after the winter of 1994 played havoc with most figs on the East Coast. Bears an excellent crop

of sweet green fruit. Good choice for gardeners along the coast to southern New England.

'LSU Purple'. The purple fruits of this very prolific variety are borne from very early to late in the season. Good hardiness and excellent in containers.

FILBERT, HAZELNUT

Betulaceae

DECIDUOUS NUT TREES

🌡 ZONES 32, 34–43

☀ FULL SUN

🔴 REGULAR WATER

Filbert, Hazelnut

For ornamental types, see *Corylus*. Those raised for nuts need winter chill for a good crop.

Gardeners in the eastern U.S. can grow either the blight-resistant, hardy native hazelnuts (*C. americana* or *C. cornuta*) or European-American hybrids. The principal hybrids are 'Bixby', 'Buchanan', 'Potomac', and 'Reed'; these have inherited some of the blight resistance and cold hardiness of their American parents, but they bear typically smaller, somewhat less flavorful nuts than the European type grown commercially in the Northwest. The nuts of American species are smaller and less flavorful still. *C. maxima* 'Purpurea' has purple leaves and bears nuts with purplish husks.

Most types grown for nuts are shrubby (10–18 ft. high) and will grow into thickets unless suckers are cleared out three or four times a year. For a boundary hedgerow, plant mixed varieties 4 ft. apart and permit suckers to grow. For best nut production, plant in deep, well-drained, fertile, slightly acid soil in a sunny spot (some afternoon shade is best in hottest climates). Since cross-pollination is necessary, plant at least two varieties (or two plants if growing a native). Don't plant a European variety if wild hazels are nearby; they carry eastern filbert blight even though they themselves are unaffected. The blight is evident as rows of black dots on the trunk. As protection, spray copper and dormant oil together at bud break, usually late March, and again in mid-April and early May.

Nuts ripen by the end of August and drop in early fall. Harvest by picking them from the ground, then dry them in the sun for a few days. Squirrels are a nuisance, often picking the nuts before they ripen.

FILIPENDULA

Rosaceae

PERENNIALS

🌡 ZONES 31, 32, 34–45, EXCEPT AS NOTED

☀◐ PARTIAL SHADE IN WARMER AREAS

🔴🔴 AMPLE WATER

Filipendula

Like related *Astilbe*, have plumes of tiny flowers above coarsely divided leaves that look like fern fronds. Dormant in winter, even in mild-winter areas. Most species prefer moist to constantly damp soil. Use in borders, naturalistic landscapes, beside ponds. Plant in full sun in northern latitudes and where summers are cool; give partial shade where summers are warm to hot.

F. hexapetala. See *F. vulgaris*

F. palmata. SIBERIAN MEADOWSWEET. Grows to 4 ft. high and 2 ft. wide, forming clumps of stems lined with toothed leaves divided into oblong leaflets. Plumes of fragrant, white to pale pink flowers on 6–10-ft. stems appear in midsummer to early fall. 'Nana' ('Digitata') has rose pink flowers and ferny leaves; 'Elegantissima' ('Elegans') has dark rose pink flowers followed by ornamental reddish bronze seed heads.

F. purpurea. Zones 31, 32, 34–43. Pink, 3–4-ft.-tall plumes rise above maplelike, 5–7-in. leaves. Varieties include 'Alba', with white plumes 2 ft. tall; 'Elegans', bearing 2-ft.-tall white flowers with red stamens; and 'Nana', with salmon pink plumes 12–15 in. tall.

F. rubra. QUEEN OF THE PRAIRIE. Given plenty of moisture and rich soil, can reach 8 ft. high in bloom; bears pink plumes. 'Venusta' has purplish pink flowers and is a little shorter, to 4–6 ft. high.

F. ulmaria. MEADOWSWEET, QUEEN OF THE MEADOW. To 6 ft. high, with 10-in. creamy white plumes. 'Flore Pleno', just 3 ft. tall, has dense plumes of double white flowers; 'Variegata' is similar, but with gold-speckled leaves. 'Aurea' is grown not for flowers but for bright golden leaves; protect from sun.

F. vulgaris (F. hexapetala). DROPWORT. White plumes on 3-ft. stems rise above 10-in., fernlike leaves with 1-in. leaflets. Double-flowered 'Flore Pleno' has heavier-looking plumes. Needs less water than the other species; also prefers full sun in all but the warmest regions.

FINOCCHIO. See FOENICULUM vulgare azoricum

FIR. See ABIES

FIRETAIL. See ACALYPHA pendula

FIRETHORN. See PYRACANTHA

FIRMIANA simplex
(F. platanifolia)

CHINESE PARASOL TREE

Sterculiaceae

DECIDUOUS TREE

☀ ZONES 31, WARMER PARTS OF 32

☼ ◑ FULL SUN OR MORNING SUN

💧 REGULAR WATER

Firmiana simplex

Native to China, Japan. Typically 30–45 ft. in gardens, usually slow growing, with unique light gray-green bark. Trunk often is unbranched for 4–5 ft. before dividing into three or more slender, upright, slightly spreading stems that carry lobed, tropical-looking, 1-ft. leaves. Each stem looks as if it could be cut off and carried away as a parasol. Large, loose, upright clusters of greenish white flowers appear at branch ends in early summer. Interesting fruit resembles two opened green pea pods with seeds on margins. Goes leafless for long period in winter—an unusual trait for a tropical-looking tree.

Tolerates all soil types. Does well in patios and courtyards protected from wind. Useful near swimming pools.

FIVE-FINGER FERN. See ADIANTUM aleuticum

FLAG. See IRIS

FLAX. See LINUM

FLAX, NEW ZEALAND. See PHORMIUM

FLOSS FLOWER. See AGERATUM houstonianum

FLOWERING ALMOND, CHERRY. See PRUNUS

FLOWERING CRABAPPLE. See MALUS

FLOWERING MAPLE. See ABUTILON

FLOWERING NECTARINE, PEACH, PLUM. See PRUNUS

FLOWERING QUINCE. See CHAENOMELES

FOAM FLOWER. See TIARELLA

IT FEEDS BENEFICIAL INSECTS

Common fennel is one of those prolific but valuable plants that provide pollen and nectar to beneficial insects when those insects aren't feeding on plant-damaging insects and mites. The good guys this plant sustains include hover flies, lacewings, ladybird beetles, paper wasps, and soldier bugs. It's also an important source of food for butterfly larvae.

FOENICULUM vulgare

COMMON FENNEL

Apiaceae (Umbelliferae)

PERENNIAL OR ANNUAL HERB

☀ ZONES VARY BY TYPE

☼ FULL SUN

💧 MODERATE WATER

Foeniculum vulgare

Two forms of fennel are commonly grown. One is a perennial, used for seasoning; the other is grown as an annual for its edible leaf bases.

The plain species is a perennial (Zones 31, 32, 34–41), cultivated for licorice-flavored seeds and young leaves. Grows to 3–5 ft. tall. Similar to dill, but coarser. Yellow-green, finely cut leaves; flat clusters of yellow flowers. Bronze fennel ('Purpurascens', 'Smokey'), to 6 ft. tall, has bronzy purple foliage. Start from seed where plants are to be grown. Sow in light, well-drained soil; thin seedlings to 1 ft. apart. Use seeds to season breads; use leaves as garnish for salads, fish. Fennel often grows as a roadside or garden weed; it's attractive until tops turn brown, and even then birds like the seeds. New stems grow in spring from perennial root.

F. v. azoricum, called Florence fennel or finocchio, is grown as a summer annual in all zones. It is lower growing (to 2 ft. high) than the species, with larger, thicker leafstalk bases that are used as a cooked or raw vegetable.

FORGET-ME-NOT. See MYOSOTIS

FORSYTHIA

Oleaceae

DECIDUOUS SHRUBS

☀ ZONES 31, 32, 34–41; HARDIEST TYPES IN 42, 43

☼ FULL SUN

💧 💧 REGULAR TO MODERATE WATER

Forsythia

From late winter to early spring, these fountain-shaped shrubs' bare branches are covered with yellow flowers. During rest of growing season, medium green foliage blends well with other shrubs in background of border plantings. Leaves rounded, with pointed tips. Use as screen, espalier, or bank cover; or plant in shrub border. Branches can be forced for indoor bloom in winter.

Tolerate most soils; respond to fertilizer. Prune established plants after bloom: cut a third of branches that have bloomed down to ground; remove oldest branches, weak or dead wood. In coldest winter climates, the flower buds may be destroyed by temperatures of −15 to −20°F/−26 to −29°C. The most bud-hardy varieties are noted below.

F. 'Arnold Dwarf'. Grows 1½–3 ft. high, to 6 ft. wide. Flowers are sparse and not especially attractive, but plant is a useful, fast-growing ground cover in cold climates.

Hardy hybrids. The spate of cold-hardy introductions in recent years includes the following:

'Meadowlark'. Semiarching, to 6–9 ft. tall. Flower buds hardy to −35°F/−37°C. Bright yellow blooms. Grown commercially in the upper Midwest.

'New Hampshire Gold'. Mounding habit to 5 ft. high, with drooping golden yellow blossoms.

'Northern Sun'. Upright, to 8–10 ft. tall. Reliable bloomer in areas where winter temperatures often drop to −30°F/−34°C.

F. intermedia. The most widely grown forsythias belong to this hybrid group. Most grow 7–10 ft. tall and have arching branches; smaller selections are also included in the following list.

'Beatrix Farrand'. Upright to 10 ft. tall, 7 ft. wide. Branches thickly set with 2–2½-in.-wide flowers in deep yellow marked with orange.

'Fiesta'. Grows 3–4 ft. high. Deep yellow flowers followed by green-and-yellow variegated leaves that hold their color all summer long.

'Goldtide'. Compact growth to 20 in. tall by 4 ft. wide; profuse bright yellow flowers.

'Goldzauber' ('Gold Charm'). Erect to 6–8 ft. high, with large, deep yellow flowers.

'Karl Sax'. Resembles 'Beatrix Farrand' but is lower growing, neater, more graceful.

'Lynwood' ('Lynwood Gold'). Stiffly upright to 7 ft., with 4–6-ft. spread. Profuse tawny yellow blooms survive spring storms.

'Spectabilis'. Dense, upright, vigorous to 9 ft. Deep yellow flowers; buds are cold hardy.

'Spring Glory'. To about 6 ft. tall, with heavy crop of pale yellow flowers.

'Tetragold'. Grows 3–5 ft. high. Deep yellow blossoms.

F. mandschurica 'Vermont Sun'. Exceptionally bud hardy. Erect growing to 6–8 ft.; blooms earlier than other forsythias, bearing lemon yellow flowers. Not as showy as the forsythia hybrids.

F. ovata. KOREAN FORSYTHIA. Shrub to 4–6 ft., spreading wider. Early bloomer, with a profusion of bright yellow flowers about a week after *F. mandschurica* 'Vermont Sun'.

F. suspensa. WEEPING FORSYTHIA. Dense, upright growth habit to 8–10 ft., with 6–8-ft. spread. Drooping, vinelike branches root where they touch damp soil. Golden yellow flowers. Useful large-scale bank cover. Can be trained as vine; if you support main branches, branchlets will cascade. 'Fortunei' is somewhat more upright, more available in nurseries.

F. viridissima. GREENSTEM FORSYTHIA. Stiff-looking shrub to 10 ft. with deep green foliage, olive green stems, greenish yellow flowers. 'Bronxensis' is slow-growing dwarf form to 16 in. tall, for smaller shrub borders or ground cover. *F. v. koreana (F. koreana),* to 8 ft., has larger, brighter yellow flowers and attractive purplish autumn foliage.

FOTHERGILLA

Hamamelidaceae

DECIDUOUS SHRUBS

ZONES 31, 32, 34–39

PARTIAL SHADE IN HOT-SUMMER AREAS

REGULAR WATER

Fothergilla

Native to southeastern U.S. Grown principally for fall foliage color, but small, honey-scented white flowers in brushlike, 1–2-in. clusters on zigzagging stems are pretty in spring. Performs best in moist, well-drained, acid soil.

F. gardenii. DWARF FOTHERGILLA. Typically 2–3 ft. high (though it can grow considerably taller) and as wide or wider. Inch-long flower clusters appear before the 1–2½-in.-long leaves. Fall foliage intense yellow and orange red. 'Mt. Airy' is taller than the species, with larger flower clusters, deeper blue-green leaves, and better fall color. 'Blue Mist' also has bluish summer foliage. 'Jane Platt' does not exceed 3 ft. high, with white flowers in spring and red to yellow fall color.

F. major. Erect shrub to 9 ft. with roundish, 2–4-in.-long leaves turning yellow to orange to purplish red in fall. Flowers appear with foliage. Plant formerly known as *F. monticola* is now treated as this species.

FOUNTAIN GRASS. See PENNISETUM setaceum

FOUR O'CLOCK. See MIRABILIS jalapa

FOXGLOVE. See DIGITALIS

FRAGARIA

ORNAMENTAL STRAWBERRIES

Rosaceae

PERENNIALS

ZONES 31, 32, 34–41

PARTIAL SHADE OR FULL SUN

REGULAR WATER

Fragaria

For strawberries to grow for their luscious fruit, see Strawberry. The varieties discussed here are grown primarily as ornamentals, although the alpine strawberry also produces delicious fruit. The other varieties also produce edible fruit, but it is not as tasty.

The plants form compact mats of dark green, toothed leaves with three toothed leaflets. White or pink flowers with yellow centers bloom in spring and in some cases are followed by small red fruits. Grow them in strawberry jars or other containers, or in the front of a shady garden.

Purchase plants locally or by mail, and plant them in moist but well-drained soil in spring or later during the growing season. Alpine strawberries can be started from seed sown indoors, then transplanted out when frost danger is past. Space plants 1–1 ½ ft. apart in the garden.

'Lipstick' grows to 8 in. tall and 1½–2 ft. across. From midspring into fall it bears rose red flowers, but seldom produces fruit.

'Pink Panda' grows to 6 in. tall and spreads, sometimes becoming invasive. Bears pink flowers from midspring into fall; seldom produces fruit.

F. vesca. ALPINE STRAWBERRY. The small red fruits have an intense flavor. Pick every few days all summer and sprinkle the succulent little fruits on cereal or eat them out of hand. Remove the oldest plants at the end of each growing season to prevent overcrowding and keep the planting vigorous and productive. Plants often self-sow. 'Variegata' has leaves variegated creamy white. 'Semperflorens' blooms in spring and again in fall.

F. virginiana. SCARLET STRAWBERRY. Unlike the other strawberries described here, this species has many stolons and spreads more. The small fruits are light pink or whitish.

FRANKLINIA alatamaha (Gordonia alatamaha)

Theaceae

DECIDUOUS TREE

ZONES 31, 32, 34–41

FULL SUN OR LIGHT SHADE

REGULAR WATER

Franklinia alatamaha

Unusual, very handsome tree once native to Georgia, but apparently extinct in the wilds before 1800. Open, airy form; may reach 30 ft., but more typically grows 10–20 ft. high. Tends to be fairly slender when grown with a single trunk, broad spreading with multiple trunks. Attractive dark gray bark has faint white vertical striping. Shiny dark green, spoon-shaped leaves, 4–6 in. long, turn orange and red in fall; they hang on for a long time before dropping. Fragrant, 3-in.-wide, five-petaled white flowers centered with clusters of yellow stamens open from round white buds in August–September, sometimes coinciding with fall foliage color.

F

Blossoms resemble single camellias—not surprising, since franklinia and camellia belong to the same family. Flowers are followed by small, woody capsules split into ten segments, each containing five seeds.

Provide moist, rich, light, acid soil. Good drainage is critical. Grows well in light shade, but has best bloom and fall color in full sun. Easy to grow from seed, blooming in 6 to 7 years. Highly decorative lawn or patio tree. Use for contrast in azalea or rhododendron plantings. In the northernmost part of its range, franklinia may be killed to the ground in severe winters. New growth from the roots will produce multistemmed, rounded specimens that can be quite picturesque, but more bushy than treelike.

FRASER'S SEDGE. See CYMOPHYLLUS

FRAXINELLA. See DICTAMNUS albus

FRAXINUS

ASH

Oleaceae

DECIDUOUS TREES

⚡ ZONES VARY BY SPECIES

☼ FULL SUN

💧 💧 REGULAR TO MODERATE WATER

Fraxinus

Trees grow fairly fast, and most tolerate hot summers, cold winters, and various soils. In many areas, ashes are susceptible to a number of serious problems, including anthracnose and borers, so check before planting. They are chiefly used as street trees, shade trees, lawn trees, patio shelter trees.

In most cases, leaves are divided into leaflets. Male and female flowers (generally inconspicuous, in clusters) grow on separate trees in some species, on same tree in others. In latter case, flowers are often followed by clusters of single-seeded, winged fruit, often in such abundance that they can be a litter problem. When flowers are on separate trees, you'll get fruit on female tree only if it grows near male tree.

F. americana. WHITE ASH. Zones 31, 32, 34–43. Native to eastern U.S. Grows to 80 ft. or more, with straight trunk and oval-shaped crown. Leaves 8–15 in. long, with five to nine oval leaflets; dark green above, paler beneath. Foliage turns purplish in fall. Male and female flowers on separate trees, but plants sold are generally seedlings, so you don't know what you're getting. If you end up with both male and female trees, you will get a heavy crop of seed; both litter and seedlings can be problem.

Seedless selections include 'Autumn Applause' and 'Autumn Purple', both with exceptionally good, long-lasting purple fall color; 'Champaign County', a dense grower with no appreciable fall color; 'Greenspire', narrow upright habit, deep orange fall color; 'Rosehill', with bronzy red fall color; 'Royal Purple', upright, with purple autumn leaves; and 'Skyline', an upright oval with brown and purple fall color. *F. texensis,* a drought-tolerant and fairly pest-resistant tree growing 30–45 ft. high, is considered a variety of *F. americana.*

F. angustifolia. NARROW-LEAVED ASH. Zones 31, 32, 34–39. To 80 ft. high. Glossy green leaves turn rich yellow in autumn.

F. excelsior. EUROPEAN ASH. Zones 31, 32, 34–43; best in colder part of range. Native to Europe, Asia Minor. Round-headed tree 60–80 ft. (possibly 140 ft.) tall. Black dormant buds. Leaves 10–12 in. long, divided into 7–11 oval, toothed leaflets, dark green above, paler beneath; do not change color but drop while green. 'Kimberley' is a seedless selection used as a shade tree. 'Pendula', weeping European ash, is a spreading, rather asymmetrical, umbrella-shaped tree with weeping branches that reach the ground.

F. holotricha. Zones 31, 32, 34–41. Native to eastern Balkan Peninsula. Upright, rather narrow tree to 40 ft. Leaves have 9–13 dull green, 2–3-in.-long leaflets with toothed edges. Casts light filtered shade.

Leaves turn yellow in fall, dry up, and sift down into lawn or ground cover, thus lessening litter. 'Moraine' is a neat, symmetrical tree with a rounded head and uniform bright yellow fall foliage; produces few seeds.

F. ornus. FLOWERING ASH. Zones 31, 32, 34–41. Native to southern Europe and Asia Minor. Grows rapidly to 40–50 ft. with broad, rounded crown 20–30 ft. wide. Supplies luxuriant mass of foliage. Leaves 8–10 in. long, divided into 7–11 oval, medium green, 2-in.-long leaflets with toothed edges. Foliage turns to soft shades of lavender and yellow in fall. In spring, displays quantities of fluffy, branched, 3–5-in.-long clusters of fragrant white to greenish white blossoms followed by unsightly seed clusters that hang on until late winter unless removed.

F. pennsylvanica (F. lanceolata). GREEN ASH, RED ASH. Zones 31, 32, 34–45. Native to eastern U.S. Typically 50–60 ft. tall, forming irregular oval crown. Gray-brown bark; dense, twiggy structure. Bright green leaves 10–12 in. long, divided into five to nine rather narrow, 4–6-in.-long leaflets. Inconsistent yellow fall color. Takes wet soil and severe cold, but foliage burns in hot, dry winds. Male and female flowers on separate trees.

Seedless varieties include 'Bergeson', fast growing, cold tolerant; 'Emerald', round headed, not as cold hardy as other selections; 'Marshall', fast growing, tapered crown, fewer insect problems than species; 'Patmore', tolerant of extreme cold; 'Summit', upright habit, good golden yellow fall color; and 'Urbanite', pyramidal shape and bronze fall color.

F. quadrangulata. BLUE ASH. Zones 35–41. Native to central U.S. Grows rapidly to 60–80 ft. or more. Branches distinctly square, usually with flanges along edges. Oval, dark green leaflets (7–11 per leaf), 2–5 in. long, with toothed edges. Foliage turns purplish in fall. Fruit may become litter problem if you have both female and male trees.

FRECKLE FACE. See HYPOESTES phyllostachya

FRENCH HONEYSUCKLE. See HEDYSARUM

FRINGE BELLS. See SHORTIA soldanelloides

FRINGED WORMWOOD. See ARTEMISIA frigida

FRINGE HYACINTH. See MUSCARI comosum

FRINGE TREE. See CHIONANTHUS

FRITILLARIA

FRITILLARY

Liliaceae

BULBS

⚡ ZONES VARY BY SPECIES

☼ ◐ FULL SUN OR LIGHT SHADE, EXCEPT AS NOTED

💧 REGULAR WATER DURING GROWTH AND BLOOM

Fritillaria

In spring, unbranched stems, 6 in.–4 ft. high, are topped by bell-like, nodding flowers, often unusually colored and mottled. Use in woodland gardens, rock gardens, or borders. In fall, plant bulbs in porous soil with ample humus. Set smaller bulbs 3–4 in. deep; set largest (*F. imperialis*) 4–5 in. deep. Bulbs sometimes rest a year after planting or after blooming, so put in enough for a yearly display.

F. camschatcensis. BLACK LILY, CHOCOLATE LILY. Zones 31, 32, 34–43. Native to areas around northern Pacific Ocean, Japan to northwestern U.S. Grows 9–18 in. tall, with whorls of leaves around the stem; one to six dark purple to black bells per stem. Prefers part shade.

F. imperialis. CROWN IMPERIAL. Zones 32, 34–43. Native to Europe. Stout stalk 3½–4 ft. tall, clothed with broad, glossy leaves and topped by circle of 2–3-in.-long bells in red, orange, or yellow; tuft of leaves above flowers. Bulb and plant have somewhat unpleasant odor. 'Argenteovariegata' has white-variegated leaves; 'Lutea', bright yellow flowers; 'Rubra Maxima', deep, glowing burnt orange blossoms.

F. meleagris. CHECKERED LILY, SNAKESHEAD. Zones 32, 34–43. Native to damp meadows in Europe, Asia; tolerates occasional flooding. Showy 2-in. bells, checkered and veined with reddish brown and purple, atop 1–1½-ft. stems. Lance-shaped leaves are 3–6 in. long. There is a white-blossomed form.

F. michailovskyi. Zones 32 (colder parts), 34–41. Native to northeastern Turkey. Grows 6 in. tall; each stem bears one to five 1–1¼-in. bells that are purplish brown on the lower portion, bright yellow on the top half.

F. pallidiflora. Zones 34–43. Native to Siberia, northern China. Slender stems 4–16 in. tall carry one to six (or more) pale yellow, green-tinted bells 1¼ in. long.

F. persica 'Adiyaman'. Zones 32 (colder parts), 34–41. Stems 2–3 ft. tall carry up to 30 deep plum purple, 1-in. flowers on upper half. Foliage is grayish. Plant is hardy and easy to grow—but in colder regions, emerging stems need protection from late frosts.

FUCHSIA

Onagraceae

SHRUBS GROWN AS ANNUALS

⚡ ALL ZONES

◐ PARTIAL SHADE

💧 REGULAR WATER

Fuchsia
Double Type

Popular, showy-flowered fuchsias are forms of *F. hybrida*, and are discussed under that heading. Other species are grown almost entirely by collectors, though the one described here, *F. magellanica*, is good for basic landscaping purposes. Fuchsias are evergreen or deciduous shrubs that are grown as annuals in most of the Northeast. Hybrids bloom well in pots or hanging baskets in regions with relatively cool summer nights. However, in areas with prolonged periods of hot, muggy weather, they often stop blooming by midsummer. The following types bloom from early summer to first frost. Flowers are unscented, frequented by hummingbirds.

F. hybrida. HYBRID FUCHSIA. Here belong nearly all garden fuchsias. Hundreds of varieties are available, with many color combinations. Sepals (top parts that flare back) are always white, red, or pink. Corolla (inside part of flower) may be almost any color possible within range of white, blue violet, purple, pink, red, and shades approaching orange. Flowers may be single- or double-petaled, varying in size from as small as a shelled peanut to as large as a child's fist. Plants vary from erect-growing shrubs 3–12 ft. high to trailing types grown in hanging containers.

Cultivars include 'Annabel', upright plant, white double flowers with pink flush and veining; 'Florabelle', semidouble, purple and red flowers; 'Gartenmeister Bonstedt', upright, small, slender, tubular red flowers; 'Jack Shahan', trailing, single flowers with rose pink corolla and lighter pink sepals; 'Lena', semidouble, magenta-purple corolla and pinkish white sepals.

Soil mix for containers or planting beds should be porous, water retentive, and rich in organic matter. In hot-summer climates, heavy mulching

Fuchsia Single Type

helps maintain soil moisture in beds. When foliage wilts in extreme heat, mist to cool it down. Apply light doses of complete fertilizer frequently. If plant becomes leggy, pinch branch tips to force side branching. Pick off old flowers as they start to fade.

F. magellanica. Zones 31, 32, 34, 39 (with winter protection), or all zones as annual. Many arching, 3-ft.-long stems loaded with drooping, 1½-in.-long, red-and-violet flowers. Leaves are oval, in groups of two or three, ½–1 in. long. Treat as herbaceous perennial in cold-climate areas. Roots are hardy with mulching; tops will die back with the first hard frost Grow only the hardiest cultivars, such as 'Riccartonii'. Be generous with mulch and do not expose plants to full sun. Full shade may be best in hottest areas.

Fumariaceae. This family consists of annuals and perennials, usually with irregularly shaped flowers. *Corydalis* and bleeding heart *(Dicentra)* are examples. This family is considered by many to be included in the poppy family (Papaveraceae).

FUNKIA. See HOSTA

GAILLARDIA

BLANKET FLOWER

Asteraceae (Compositae)

PERENNIALS AND ANNUALS

⚡ ZONES VARY BY SPECIES

☼ FULL SUN

💧 MODERATE WATER

Gaillardia

Native to central and western U.S. Low-growing summer bloomers with daisylike flowers in warm colors—yellow, bronze, scarlet. Thrive in heat, need good drainage. Easy to grow from seed and fine for cutting and borders; often reseed.

G. aristata. Perennial. Zones 31, 32, 34–45. This parent of the hybrid *G. grandiflora* has been replaced to a large degree by its offspring, but the wild form is still much used in prairie restoration and wildflower mixes. Grows 2–2½ ft. tall, with flower heads up to 4 in. wide. Colors range from yellow to red; most familiar form is red with a jagged yellow border on the ray flowers.

G. grandiflora. Perennial. Zones 31, 32, 34–45. Developed from native species *G. aristata* and *G. pulchella*. To 2–4 ft. high. Roughish gray-green foliage; flower heads 3–4 in. across, single or double petaled. Much variation in flower color: warm shades of red and yellow with orange or maroon bands. Exceptionally long bloom period for a perennial—from early summer until frost. Plants flower first year from seed. Can be short lived in hot, humid climates.

Many strains and varieties are available, including dwarf kinds and types with extralarge flowers. 'Goblin', 1 ft. tall, is an especially good compact variety with large, deep red flowers bordered in bright yellow. 'Goblin Yellow' is similar, but with yellow blooms. 'Baby Cole', another red-and-yellow type, grows 7–8 in. tall. The following varieties are all 2½ ft. tall: 'Burgundy', deep red; 'Tokajer', pure orange; 'Torchlight', yellow blooms bordered with red.

G. pulchella. Annual. To 1½–2 ft. high. Soft, hairy leaves. Bears 2-in.-wide flower heads in warm shades of red, yellow, gold; blossoms carried on long, whiplike stems. Easy to grow; sow seeds in warm soil after frost danger is past. 'Lorenziana' has no ray flowers (petals); instead, disc flowers are enlarged into little star-tipped bells, making blooms look like balls of bright fluff. Double Gaiety strain (1½ ft. tall) has flowers that range from near white to maroon; often bicolored. Lollipop strain is similar but only 10–12 in. tall.

GALANTHUS

SNOWDROP

Amaryllidaceae

BULBS

⚡ ZONES 31, 32, 34–45, EXCEPT AS NOTED

☼ ◐ FULL SUN OR PARTIAL SHADE

💧 REGULAR WATER DURING GROWTH AND BLOOM

☣ G. NIVALIS BULB IS POISONOUS IF INGESTED

Galanthus

Best adapted to cold climates. Closely related to *Leucojum* (snowflake) and often confused with it. White, nodding, bell-shaped blossoms are borne one per stalk. Inner flower segments have green tips;

G

G

larger outer segments are pure white. Plants have two or three basal leaves. Use in rock gardens or under flowering shrubs; naturalize in woodland; or grow in pots. Plant in autumn, in moist soil with ample humus; set 3–4 in. deep, 2–3 in. apart. Do not divide often; when necessary, divide right after bloom.

G. caucasicus. Zones 31, 32, 34, 39. To 6 in. high, with strap-shaped leaves to 5 in. long. Blooming time varies from late autumn to early spring. Flowers appear in winter in mild areas. They are 1¼-in.-long bells.

G. elwesii. GIANT SNOWDROP. Globular bells to 2 in. long on 1-ft. stems; two or three strap-shaped, 1¼-in.-wide leaves, 4 in. long (elongating to as much as 1 ft. after bloom). March–April bloom in cold climates. In southern part of range (where better adapted than *G. nivalis*), blooms January–February.

G. nivalis. COMMON SNOWDROP. More delicate version of *G. elwesii*, blooming about a week earlier. Dainty, 1-in.-long bells on 6–9-in. stems; leaves very narrow. 'Flore Pleno' and 'Lady Elphinstone' bear double flowers; 'Sandersii' has yellow markings instead of green; 'Pusey Green Tip' bears irregular double flowers, marked with green.

GALAX urceolata (G. aphylla)

Diapensiaceae

PERENNIAL

ZONES 31, 32, 34–43

PARTIAL OR FULL SHADE

REGULAR WATER

Galax urceolata

Native to mountain woodlands, Virginia to Georgia. Often used as ground cover, although it spreads slowly. Foliage, much used in indoor arrangements, gives this plant its real distinction. Growing in basal tufts, evergreen leaves are shiny, heart shaped, 5 in. across; in cold-winter regions, they turn bronzy in fall unless the plants are growing in deep shade. Foliage height ranges from 6 to 9 in.; in early summer, flower stems rise to 2½ ft., bearing slender foxtails of small white flowers at their tips.

Grow in acid soil with much organic material—preferably mulch of leaf mold. Locate under plants that appreciate the same conditions: dogwood, rhododendron, azalea, pieris. Space 1 ft. apart.

GALEOBDOLON luteum. See LAMIUM galeobdolon

GALIUM odoratum (Asperula odorata)

SWEET WOODRUFF

Rubiaceae

PERENNIAL

ZONES 31, 32, 34–43

PARTIAL OR FULL SHADE

REGULAR WATER

Galium odoratum

Attractive, low-spreading perennial that brings to mind deep-shaded woods. Slender, square stems 6–12 in. high, encircled every inch or so by whorls of six to eight aromatic, bristle-tipped leaves. Clusters of tiny white flowers show above foliage in late spring and summer. Leaves and stems give off fragrant, haylike odor when dried; they have been used traditionally to flavor May wine.

In the shade garden, sweet woodruff is best used as ground cover or edging along path. Will spread rapidly in rich soil with abundant moisture—can become a pest if allowed to grow entirely unchecked. Self-sows freely. Can be increased by division in fall or spring.

GALTONIA candicans

SUMMER HYACINTH

Liliaceae

BULB

ZONES 31, 32; OR DIG AND STORE

PARTIAL SHADE

REGULAR WATER DURING GROWTH AND BLOOM

Galtonia candicans

Native to South Africa. Straplike leaves, 2–3 ft. long; stout 2–4-ft. stems topped in summer with loose, spikelike clusters of fragrant white flowers—drooping, funnel-shaped, 1–1½ in. long, with three outer segments often tipped green. Plant behind low, bushy plants. Plant bulbs 6 in. deep in rich soil in fall; they will grow well for many years in mild-winter regions without lifting, dividing. In coldest zones, protect with a thick winter mulch; beyond hardiness range, dig and store.

GARDEN MYRRH. See MYRRHIS

GARLAND FLOWER. See HEDYCHIUM coronarium

GARLIC

Liliaceae

BULB

ALL ZONES

FULL SUN

REGULAR WATER

Garlic

For ornamental varieties, see *Allium*. Seed stores and some mail-order seed houses sell mother bulbs ("sets") for planting. In Zones 31, 32, plant October–December for early summer harvest. Where winters are cold, plant early in spring. Break bulbs up into cloves and plant base downward, 1–2 in. deep, 2–3 in. apart, in rows 1 ft. apart. Harvest when leafy tops fall over; air-dry bulbs, remove tops and roots, and store in cool place. Giant or elephant garlic has unusually large (fist-size) bulbs and mild garlic flavor. Same culture as regular garlic.

GARLIC CHIVES. See ALLIUM tuberosum

GAS PLANT. See DICTAMNUS albus

GAULTHERIA procumbens

WINTERGREEN, CHECKERBERRY, TEABERRY

Ericaceae

EVERGREEN GROUNDCOVER

ZONES 32, 34–45

PARTIAL SHADE

REGULAR WATER

Gaultheria procumbens

Native Newfoundland to Manitoba, south to Georgia and Alabama. Creeping stems; upright branches to 6 in. tall, with 2-in., oval, glossy dark leaves clustered toward tips. Leaves turn reddish with winter cold. When bruised, foliage emits strong wintergreen odor. Small, pinkish white urn-shaped summer flowers followed by scarlet berries. Both fruit and foliage have flavor of wintergreen (or teaberry). Use as small patches of ground cover in woodland garden; plant 1 ft. apart. 'Macrocarpa' is a compact, profusely fruiting variety.

GAURA lindheimeri

GAURA

Onagraceae

PERENNIAL

⚡ ZONES 31, 32, 34, 35, 37, 38 (coastal), 39

☼ FULL SUN

💧 REGULAR TO LITTLE WATER

Gaura lindheimeri

Native to Texas and Louisiana. Airy plant growing 2¼–4 ft. high. Stalkless leaves, 1½–3½ in. long, grow directly on stems. Branching flower spikes bear many 1-in.-long white blossoms that open from pink buds closely set on stems. Long bloom period (often from late spring into fall), with only a few blossoms opening at a time. Blossoms age to rosy color, then drop off cleanly, but seed-bearing spikes should be cut to improve appearance, prevent overly enthusiastic self-sowing, and prolong bloom. 'Corrie's Gold' has gold-edged leaves. 'Siskiyou Pink' has leaves mottled with burgundy and pink flowers opening from maroon buds. 'Whirling Butterflies' is a bit shorter and more compact than the species, with larger flowers.

Needs good drainage. Taproot makes it very drought tolerant. Clumps never need dividing; for additional plants, let some volunteer seedlings grow.

GAYFEATHER. See LIATRIS

GAYLUSSACIA brachycera

BOX HUCKLEBERRY

Ericaceae

EVERGREEN SHRUB

⚡ ZONES 32, 34, 36–39

☼ PARTIAL SHADE

💧 REGULAR WATER

Gaylussacia brachycera

Native to mountains of Pennsylvania to Virginia, Kentucky, and Tennessee. Uncommon in cultivation, box huckleberry can make an attractive 6–18-in.-high ground cover in well-drained, acid soil with ample organic content. Leathery, glossy dark green leaves to 1 in. long show reddish tints in full sun, turn bronze or purple in winter. Tiny, urn-shaped white or pinkish flowers are followed by edible bluish black berries that ripen in mid- to late summer. Spreads by underground stems, eventually covering large areas. In nature, some single plants have spread to form patches blanketing several hundred acres; it has been estimated that such patches may have started their growth up to 10,000 years ago.

GAZANIA

Asteraceae (Compositae)

PERENNIALS GROWN AS ANNUALS

⚡ ALL ZONES

☼ FULL SUN

💧 REGULAR TO MODERATE WATER

Gazania

Native to South Africa. Daisy flowers give dazzling color display during peak bloom in late spring, early summer. Gazanias grow well in almost any soil. Feed once in spring with slow-acting fertilizer. Carry gazanias through winter by taking cuttings in fall as you would for pelargoniums.

There are basically two types: clumping and trailing. Clumping gazanias (complex hybrids between a number of species) form a mound of evergreen leaves—dark green above, gray and woolly beneath, often lobed. Flowers 3–4 in. wide, on 6–10-in.-long stems; they open on sunny days,

close at night and in cloudy weather. You can buy clumping gazanias in single colors—yellow, orange, white, or rosy pink, with reddish purple petal undersides, often with dark blossom centers. Or you can get a mixture of hybrids (as plants or seeds) in different colors. Seed-grown kinds include Carnival (many colors, silver leaves); Chansonette (early blooming, compact; medium-size round flowers); Harlequin (many colors, eyed and banded); Mini-Star (compact, floriferous plants; named selections include 'Mini-Star Yellow', 'Mini-Star Tangerine'); Sundance (5-in. flowers, striped or banded); and Sunshine (big, multicolored flowers, gray foliage).

Named hybrids of special merit are 'Aztec Queen' (multicolored), 'Burgundy', 'Copper King', and 'Fiesta Red'; these are best used in small-scale plantings, although the last is sturdy enough for large expanses. 'Moonglow' is double-flowered bright yellow of unusual vigor; its blossoms, unlike most, stay open even on dull days.

Clumping gazanias serve as temporary fillers between young, growing shrubs and as a replaceable ground cover for relatively level areas not subject to severe erosion. Try in parking strips, as edgings along sunny paths, or in rock gardens.

Trailing gazanias (*G. rigens leucolaena*, formerly sold as *G. uniflora* or *G. leucolaena*) grow about as tall as clumping ones, but spread rapidly by long trailing stems. Foliage is clean silvery gray; flowers are yellow, white, orange, or bronze. New, larger-flowered hybrids are 'Sunburst' (orange, black eye) and 'Sunglow' (yellow). 'Sunrise Yellow' has large, black-eyed yellow flowers; leaves are green instead of gray. New hybrids are superior to older kinds in length of bloom, resistance to dieback. Trailing gazanias are useful on banks, level ground. Or grow them at top of wall and allow them to trail over. Attractive in hanging baskets.

GELSEMIUM
sempervirens

CAROLINA JESSAMINE

Loganiaceae

EVERGREEN TO SEMIEVERGREEN VINE

⚡ ZONES 31, 32

☼ ◑ ● BEST IN FULL SUN; TOLERATES SHADE

💧 REGULAR WATER

⚠ ALL PARTS ARE POISONOUS IF INGESTED

Gelsemium sempervirens

Native to southeastern U.S. Shrubby and twining vine; moderate growth rate to about 20 ft. Clean pairs of shiny, light green, 1–4-in.-long leaves on long, streamerlike branches. Evergreen to semievergreen. Fragrant, tubular yellow flowers, 1–1½ in. long, in late winter, early spring. Sometimes flowers sporadically in fall. 'Pride of Augusta' ('Plena') is a double-flowered form.

On trellis, vine will cascade and swing in wind; when trained on house, makes delicate green curtain of branches. Often trained on fences and mailboxes. Can get top-heavy; in this case, cut back severely. Also used as ground cover, especially on banks; keep trimmed to 3 ft. high. For best bloom and densest growth, plant in full sun, though plant will tolerate shade.

GENISTA

BROOM

Fabaceae (Leguminosae)

DECIDUOUS OR EVERGREEN SHRUBS

⚡ ZONES VARY BY SPECIES

☼ FULL SUN

💧 MODERATE TO LITTLE WATER

Genista

Leaves often small and short lived. Green branches give deciduous or sparsely leafed plants an evergreen look. Flowers yellow, sweet

G

pea shaped. Less aggressive than other brooms *(Cytisus);* will not run wild. Smaller kinds attractive in rock gardens, bank plantings. Need good drainage; tolerate rocky or infertile soil.

G. cinerea. Deciduous. Zones 31, 32. Upright shrub to 10 ft. high and 12 ft. across. Arching branches are lined with narrow grayish green leaves. In early to midsummer, bears slender clusters to 8 in. long of small, fragrant yellow flowers.

G. hispanica. SPANISH BROOM. Deciduous. Zones 31, 32. Forms a low, dense mound to 2½ ft. high and 5 ft. across. Spiny, with oblong medium green leaves. In late spring to early summer, bears clusters of golden yellow flowers near the tips of the stems.

G. lydia. Evergreen. Zones 32, 34. Nearly leafless shrublet, often sold erroneously as *Cytisus lydia.* Grows to 2 ft. high, with spreading habit. Makes a good ground cover. Profusion of flowers at ends of shoots in late spring. Sets little seed.

G. pilosa. Deciduous. Zones 31, 32, 34–41. Fairly fast growing, ultimately reaching 1–1½ ft. tall with 7-ft. spread. Intricately branched, gray-green twigs. Roundish, ¼–½-in.-long leaves. Blooms in spring. 'Vancouver Gold' is best selection.

G. sagittalis. Zones 32, 34, 37. Rather rapid grower to 1 ft. high, with wide spread. Leafless, upright, winged, bright green branchlets appear jointed. Makes sheet of golden flowers during bloom in late spring and early summer.

G. tinctoria. DYER'S GREENWEED, WOADWAXEN. Deciduous. Zones 31, 32, 34–45. Species grows to 6 ft., with undivided leaves to 2 in. long. 'Royal Gold', 2 ft. tall and as wide, is the only variety generally available; it bears yellow flowers on upright, 1–3-in.-long spikes in late spring or early summer. Cutting back after summer bloom will encourage some later flowering.

GENTIANA

GENTIAN

Gentianaceae

PERENNIALS

✿ ZONES 34, 36–43, EXCEPT AS NOTED

☼ ◐ FULL SUN OR PARTIAL SHADE

💧 REGULAR WATER

Gentiana

Low, spreading, or upright plants, generally with very blue tubular flowers. Though most are hard to grow, they are prized by rock garden enthusiasts. Need perfect drainage. Most require lime-free soil. If they thrive, they produce some of the richest blues in the garden.

G. acaulis. Leafy stems to 4 in. tall. Leaves 1 in. long. Rich blue flowers 2 in. long in summer. Grows well, but often fails to bloom.

G. andrewsii. CLOSED GENTIAN, BOTTLE GENTIAN. Native to eastern U.S. Fairly easy to grow in rich soil. Clump-forming plant to 2 ft. tall. Dark green leaves; dark blue flowers clustered at top of stem and in joints of upper leaves, in late summer or early fall. Flowers are usually fully closed, sometimes only partially closed.

G. asclepiadea. WILLOW GENTIAN. Native to Europe and western Asia. Similar to *G. andrewsii,* but the 1½-in. dark blue flowers open into stars. Flowers appear singly or in twos or threes in joints of upper leaves, in late summer or early fall. Appearance is that of arching, leafy spikes of blue flowers. Prefers partial shade. Not difficult. 'Alba' is a white form.

G. clusii (G. acaulis clusii). Similar to *G. acaulis,* but with larger flowers.

G. lutea. YELLOW GENTIAN. Zones 31, 32, 34–43. Upright and clump-forming, to 5 ft. high and 2 ft. across. Oblong, ribbed, blue-green leaves to 1 ft. long, clusters of star-shaped yellow flowers in leaf axils and at stem tips in midsummer.

G. makinoi. Zones 32, 34–41. Upright to 20 in. high and 6 in. across. Narrow oval leaves to 2 in. long; clusters of bell-shaped, tubular, light blue flowers with darker blue spots bloom in late summer.

G. saponaria. Zones 32, 34–43. Upright, to 3 ft., oval to lance-shaped leaves to 2½ in. long. In summer and autumn, clusters of blue flowers, closed at the mouth.

G. scabra. Zones 32, 34–43. Upright, to 1 ft. high and 8 in. across, with pointed, oval to lance-shaped, deep green leaves to 1½ in. long. In late summer bears clusters of bell-shaped, violet-blue flowers that often have white spots.

G. septemfida. Arching or sprawling stems 9–18 in. long. Oval leaves to 1½ in. long. Clusters of 2-in. dark blue flowers in late summer. Easy to grow. *G. s. lagodechiana* has sprawling stems that turn up at tips to display flowers at branch tips and among upper leaves.

G. sino-ornata. Trailing stems grow from 7-in. rosettes of bright green leaves; 2-in.-long flowers of brightest blue appear at stem ends in early fall. Fairly easy to grow in half shade.

G. verna. SPRING GENTIAN. Mat-forming plant 1½–4 in. tall. Dark blue, 1-in. flowers appear singly on short stems in spring. Difficult, fragile plant. Needs some lime.

Gentianaceae. The gentian family includes annuals and perennials from many parts of the world. Many have blue or purple flowers, including the gentians and *Eustoma.*

GEORGIA PLUME. See ELLIOTTIA

Geraniaceae. The cranesbill family of annuals and perennials (the latter sometimes shrubby) includes true geranium, *Erodium,* and *Pelargonium.*

GERANIUM

CRANESBILL

Geraniaceae

PERENNIALS

✿ ZONES VARY BY SPECIES

☼ ◐ AFTERNOON SHADE IN HOT-SUMMER AREAS

💧 REGULAR WATER, EXCEPT AS NOTED

Geranium

The common indoor/outdoor plant most people know as geranium is, botanically, *Pelargonium.* True geraniums, considered here, are hardy plants. Many types bloom over a long period, bearing flowers that are attractive though not as showy as those of pelargonium. Carried singly or in clusters of two or three, flowers have five overlapping petals that look alike. (Pelargonium blossoms also have five petals, but two point in one direction, the other three in the opposite direction.) Colors include rose, blue, and purple; a few are pure pink or white. Beaklike fruit that follows the flowers accounts for the common name "cranesbill." Leaves are roundish or kidney shaped, lobed or deeply cut; plants may be upright or trailing. Good in rock gardens, perennial borders; some are useful as small-scale ground covers.

The best climates for geraniums are cool- and mild-summer regions, where plants can grow in full sun or light shade. Give afternoon shade in hottest areas. All species appreciate moist, well-drained soil. Clumps of most types can be left in place for many years before they decline due to crowding; at that point, divide clumps in early spring. Increase plantings by transplanting rooted portions from a clump's edge.

G. 'Ann Folkard'. Zones 31, 32, 34–41. To 2 ft. high with a spread of 3 ft., chartreuse leaves, magenta flowers with black centers and black veining.

G. argenteum. Zones 32, 34, 39. To 3–5 in. high. Leaves basal, 1 in. across, with five to seven lobes; densely covered with silky, silvery hairs. Pink flowers with darker veins, 1½ in. across, with notched petals. Blooms late spring to early summer.

G. 'Brookside'. Zones 31, 32, 34–41. To 1½ ft. high, finely divided leaves, deep blue flowers with white centers.

G. cantabrigiense. Zones 31, 32, 34–43. Hybrid between *G. macrorrhizum* and *G. dalmaticum*. Similar to former, but with pink flowers. 'Biokovo' is white flowered. Blooms late spring to early summer.

G. cinereum. Zones 31, 32, 34–43. To 6 in. tall, much wider, with deeply cut dark green leaves. Inch-wide pink flowers with darker veining appear late spring–summer. 'Ballerina' has lilac pink flowers with purple veining; blooms over a long summer season. 'Lawrence Flatman' has slightly larger flowers of a deeper color. *G. c. subcaulescens* has deep purplish red flowers with black centers.

G. clarkei 'Kashmir White'. Zones 31, 32, 34–39. Grows 2 ft. tall. Finely cut leaves; 1½-in. white flowers veined with pink. Blooms late spring to early summer. 'Kashmir Purple', lavender-blue flowers veined in red, more vigorous than 'Kashmire White'. 'Kashmir Blue', pale blue flowers.

G. dalmaticum. Zones 31, 32, 34–43. Dwarf (6-in.) plant with glossy, 1½-in., finely cut leaves and bright pink, 1-in. flowers in spring. Useful in rock garden.

G. endressii. Zones 31, 32, 34–43. Bushy, 1–1½ ft. high. Leaves 2–3 in. across, deeply cut in five lobes. Flowers rose pink, about 1 in. across. Blooms late spring into fall in mild-summer areas; peters out in early summer in hot areas. 'Wargrave Pink' is a more compact form with salmon pink flowers.

G. himalayense (G. grandiflorum). Zones 31, 32, 34–43. Wiry, branching stems 1–2 ft. high. Leaves roundish, five lobed, long stalked, 1¾ in. across. Flowers in clusters, lilac with purple veins and red-purple eye, 1½–2 in. across. Blooms all summer. 'Birch Double' ('Plenum') has double flowers of somewhat lighter shade.

G. ibericum. Zones 31, 32, 34–37, 39–43. To 2 ft. tall, with 4-in., deeply cut leaves and 2-in. lavender blue flowers with purple veining. Late spring bloomer.

G. 'Johnson's Blue'. Zones 31, 32, 34–41. Hybrid resembling *G. himalayense* parent, but leaves are more finely divided. Blue-violet, 2-in.-wide flowers appear spring to fall.

G. macrorrhizum. Zones 31, 32, 34–43. To 8–10 in. high, spreading by underground roots. Inch-wide spring flowers are deep magenta; leaves with five to seven lobes are fragrant and have attractive autumn tints. Good ground cover for small areas, though it can overwhelm delicate smaller plants. 'Bevan's Variety' has deep reddish purple flowers, 'Cambridge' pure pink blooms. Other pinks include 'Ingwersen's Variety' and 'Marjorie's'. 'Spessart' ('Album') has white flowers with pink sepals and stamens.

G. maculatum. WILD CRANESBILL, SPOTTED CRANESBILL. Zones 31, 32, 34–45. Native to eastern North America; the only commonly cultivated native cranesbill. To 2 ft. tall and somewhat narrower, with deeply lobed leaves and an abundance of lilac pink, 1–1½-in. flowers in spring to early summer. 'Album' has white blooms.

G. magnificum. Zones 31, 32, 34–43. Hybrid between *G. ibericum* and *G. platypetalum*. Dark violet-blue summer flowers are similar to those of *G. platypetalum*, but larger. Grows to 2½ ft. high.

G. oxonianum. Zones 31, 32, 34–39. Hybrid between *G. endressii* and *G. sanguineum striatum*. 'Claridge Druce' is a vigorous spreader 2–3 ft. tall, 3 ft. wide, with finely cut grayish green leaves and large pink, dark-veined flowers blooming over a long period in summer.

G. phaeum. MOURNING WIDOW, BLACK WIDOW. Zones 32, 34–41. Grows to 2 ft. high, with open clusters of dark purple (nearly black) flowers in late spring to early summer. Tolerates deep shade. 'Lily Lovell' has large mauve purple flowers. 'Samobor' has purple-variegated leaves and deep burgundy blossoms.

G. platypetalum. Zones 31, 32, 34–43. Grows 16 in. tall. Dark violet-blue flowers to nearly 2 in. wide. Late spring bloomer.

G. pratense. Zones 32, 34–43. Common border perennial to 3 ft. Upright, branching stems; shiny green leaves, 3–6 in. across, deeply cut in seven lobes. Flowers about 1 in. wide, typically blue with reddish veins; often vary in color. Blooms late spring into summer. 'Mrs. Kendall Clark' has pale blue flowers with lighter veining.

G. psilostemon. Zones 31, 32, 34–41. Large (4-by-4-ft.) plant with big, deeply cut leaves and an early summer show of 1–1½-in. magenta flowers with darker centers. Leaves take on brilliant fall color. 'Ivan' is more compact, to 2 ft.; black-veined magenta flowers with a large black eye.

G. renardii. Zones 31, 32, 34–41. Compact plant 1 ft. tall and as wide, with handsome gray-green, lobed leaves with deeply etched veins. Early summer flowers are white with faint purple veining; overall effect is pearly gray. 'Phillippe Vapelle', blue-gray leaves, purple-blue flowers with dark veins.

G. sanguineum. BLOODY CRANESBILL. Zones 31, 32, 34–43. Grows 1½ ft. high; trailing stems spread to 2 ft. Leaves roundish, 1–2½ in. across, with five to seven lobes; turn bloodred in fall. Deep purple to almost crimson flowers, 1½ in. wide, bloom from late spring well into summer. 'Album' is somewhat taller than species and has white flowers. *G. s. striatum* (*G. s.* 'Prostratum', *G. lancastriense*), Lancaster geranium, is a dwarf form, lower and more compact, with light pink flowers heavily veined with red (its seedlings may vary somewhat); an excellent rock garden or foreground plant. Other 1–1½-ft. selections include 'John Elsley', pink with deeper pink veins; 'Max Frei', reddish purple; 'New Hampshire Purple', deep rosy purple; and 'Vision', reddish purple.

G. sylvaticum. Zones 31, 32, 34–41. Shade-loving plant to 3 ft. tall. Late spring to early summer flowers, 1 in. wide, from bluish to reddish purple. 'Album' has white flowers; 'Mayflower', large blue-violet flowers.

G. wallichianum. Zones 31, 32, 34, 39. Grows 1 ft. tall, 3 ft. wide. Lilac flowers with a white eye, throughout summer. 'Buxton's Variety' has pure blue flowers.

WHICH IS REALLY A GERANIUM?

Gardeners use the word "geranium" to speak of ivy geraniums, fancy-leafed geraniums, common geraniums, Lady Washington geraniums, and scented geraniums, all of which botanically are species of *Pelargonium*. Botanists define *Geranium* by the fact that all have five identical-looking overlapping petals in their flowers. For the botanical definition of *Pelargonium*, see that entry.

GERBERA jamesonii

TRANSVAAL DAISY
Asteraceae (Compositae)
PERENNIAL GROWN AS ANNUAL
✎ ALL ZONES
☼ ◖ PARTIAL SHADE IN HOTTEST AREAS
◐ REGULAR WATER

Gerbera jamesonii

Native to South Africa. Most elegant and sophisticated of daisies. Lobed leaves to 10 in. long spring from root crowns that spread slowly to form big clumps. Slender-rayed, 4-in. daisies (one to a stem) rise directly from crowns on 1½-ft., erect or slightly curving stems. Colors range from cream through yellow to coral, orange, flame, and red. Flowers are first rate for arrangements; cut them as soon as fully open and slit an inch at bottom of stem before placing in water. Blooms any time of year with peaks in early summer, late fall.

The wild Transvaal daisy was orange red. Plants sold as hybrids are merely seedlings or divisions in mixed colors. Specialists have bred duplex and double strains. Duplex flowers have two rows of rays and are often larger (to 5–6 in. across) on taller (2–2½-ft.) stems. In doubles, all flowers are rays and flowers vary widely in form—some flat, some deep, some swirled, some bicolored. Happipot strain has 4-in. flowers on 6-in.

stems. Double Parade strain has double flowers on 7–10-in. stems. Blackheart and Ebony Eyes strains have dark-centered flowers.

All types need excellent drainage; if drainage is poor, grow plants in raised beds. Plant 2 ft. apart with crowns at least ½ in. above surface. Feed frequently. Keep old leaves picked off. As house or greenhouse plant, grow in bright light with night temperature of 60°F/16°C.

Plant as seedlings from flats, as divisions or clumps, or from pots. To grow your own from seed, sow thinly in sandy, peaty soil at 70°F/21°C. Water carefully; allow 4 to 6 weeks to sprout. Takes 6 to 18 months to flower. Seed must be fresh to germinate well; seed specialists can supply fresh seed of single, double, or duplex strains. Doubles come about 60 percent true from seed.

GERMANDER. See TEUCRIUM

GERMAN IVY. See SENECIO mikanioides

GERMAN STATICE. See GONIOLIMON tataricum

GEUM

Rosaceae

PERENNIALS

☒ ZONES 32, 34–43

☼ ◐ PARTIAL SHADE IN HOT AREAS

◆ REGULAR WATER

Geum

Double, semidouble, or single flowers in bright orange, yellow, and red over long season (spring–late summer) if dead blooms are removed. Foliage handsome; leaves divided into many leaflets. Plants evergreen except in coldest winters. Good in borders and for cut flowers.

Ordinary garden soil; need good drainage. Grow from seed sown in early spring, or divide plants in autumn or early spring.

G. 'Borisii'. Plants sold under this name make 6-in.-high mounds of foliage and have foot-high leafy stems with bright orange-red flowers. Use in rock garden, front of border. True *G. borisii* has yellow flowers.

G. chiloense. Foliage mounds to 15 in. Leafy flowering stems reach about 2 ft.; flowers are about 1½ in. wide. Varieties include 'Dolly North', semidouble bright orange; 'Fire Opal', semidouble orange scarlet; 'Lady Stratheden', double yellow; 'Mrs. Bradshaw', double scarlet; and 'Princess Juliana', double copper. For the plant sold as 'Georgenberg', see *G. heldreichii*.

G. coccineum. Very similar to, and often confused with, *G. chiloense*. 'Red Wings', semidouble scarlet flowers with exceptionally long spring–autumn bloom season.

G. heldreichii (G. montanum heldreichii). Hybrid between *G. montanum* and another species. The 12–15-in.-high 'Georgenberg' has apricot-colored flowers.

G. montanum. Grows 4–8 in. tall, with one to three bright yellow, 1½-in.-wide flowers per stem. Useful in rock gardens.

G. reptans. Grows to 6 in. high and spreads by surface runners. Orange, 1½-in.-wide blossoms.

G. rivale. WATER AVENS. Lower growing than *G. chiloense* (to 1 ft. tall and as wide), with slightly nodding, ivory to pink flowers. 'Lionel Cox' has light yellow flowers.

G. triflorum. PRAIRIE SMOKE, OLD MAN'S WHISKERS. Native to North America. Stems to 20 in. tall bear clusters of nodding maroon flowers. Entire plant is often furry. Seeds have long, feathery gray "tails."

PRACTICAL GARDENING DICTIONARY

PLEASE SEE PAGES 449–523

GIANT GARLIC. See GARLIC

GIANT HOGWEED. See HERACLEUM

GIANT REED. See ARUNDO donax

GIANT SCABIOUS. See CEPHALARIA

GIANT SEQUOIA. See SEQUOIADENDRON giganteum

GILIA capitata

QUEEN ANNE'S THIMBLES, GLOBE GILIA

Polemoniaceae

ANNUAL

☒ ALL ZONES

☼ FULL SUN

◆ REGULAR WATER

Gilia capitata

This native of northwestern North America is grown in beds and borders for its lavender blue globe-shaped flowers with protruding stamens, borne in profusion in summer. Leaves are slender and feathery, and the overall plant is erect in habit, growing to 2 ft. high and about 9 in. wide. Prefers light, well-drained soil. Sow seeds where plants will grow in the garden, in spring or autumn.

GILLENIA trifoliata (Porteranthus trifoliatus)

BOWMAN'S ROOT

Rosaceae

PERENNIAL

☒ ZONES 31, 32, 34–43

◐ PARTIAL SHADE

◆ REGULAR WATER

Gillenia trifoliata

Woodland plant native from the north and northeast to the southeastern U.S.; little seen but deserving of wider use. Forms clumps of stiffish, upright, somewhat branching stems set with nearly stalkless leaves divided into three narrow, tooth-edged leaflets. Grows to 3 ft. or a little taller. In early summer, bears starlike white or pink flowers with red sepals. Open branching at flowering time gives an airy effect despite the erect stems. Foliage turns bronze red in autumn. Likes rich soil with ample organic material.

GINGER. See ZINGIBER officinale

GINGER LILY. See HEDYCHIUM

GINKGO biloba

MAIDENHAIR TREE

Ginkgoaceae

DECIDUOUS TREE

☒ ZONES 31, 32, 34–44

☼ FULL SUN

◌ ◆ REGULAR TO MODERATE WATER

Ginkgo biloba

Graceful tree, attractive in any season, especially in fall when leathery, light green leaves of spring and summer suddenly turn gold. Fall leaves linger (they practically glow when backlit by the sun), then drop quickly and cleanly to make golden carpet where they fall. Related to conifers but differs in having broad (1–4-in.-wide), fan-shaped leaves rather than needlelike foliage. In shape and veining, leaves resemble leaflets of maidenhair fern, hence tree's common name. Can grow to 70–80 ft., but most mature trees are 35–50 ft. May be gawky in youth, but becomes well proportioned with age—narrow to spreading or even umbrella shaped. Usually grows slowly, about 1 ft. a year, but under ideal conditions can grow up to 3 ft. a year.

Plant only male trees (grafted or grown from cuttings of male plants); female trees produce messy, fleshy, ill-smelling fruit in quantity. Named varieties listed below are male. Use as street tree, lawn tree. Plant in deep, loose, well-drained soil. Be sure plant is not root-bound in pot. Stake young tree to keep stem straight; young growth may be brittle, but wood becomes strong with age. In general, ginkgos are not bothered by insects or diseases, and they're very tolerant of air pollution, heat, and acid or alkaline conditions.

'Autumn Gold'. Upright, eventually rather broad and spreading.

'Fairmount'. Fast-growing, broadly pyramidal form. Straighter main stem than 'Autumn Gold', requires less staking.

'Pendula'. Horizontal or weeping branches.

'Princeton Sentry'. Fairly narrow, conical shape.

'Saratoga'. Erect, rounded, and somewhat smaller than other ginkgo varieties, with narrow leaves deeply split at the ends. Pendulous leaves give tree a graceful character.

GINSENG. See PANAX

GLADIOLUS

Iridaceae

Corms

🗡 Zones vary by type; or dig and store

☀ Full sun

💧 Regular water during growth and bloom

Gladiolus

All have sword-shaped leaves and tubular flowers, often flaring or ruffled, in simple or branching, usually one-sided spikes. Extremely wide color range. Bloom from spring to fall, depending on kind and time of planting. Superb cut flowers. Good in borders or beds behind mounding plants that cover lower parts of stems, or in large containers with low annuals at base. Thrips are a pest.

Plant in rich, sandy soil. Set corms about four times deeper than their height, somewhat more shallowly in heavy soils. Space big corms 6 in. apart, smaller ones 4 in. apart. Corms can be left in the ground from year to year in indicated zones; in colder areas, dig soon after first frost in autumn. Corms should be dried, then stored in single layer in flats or ventilated trays in a cool place (40 to 50°F/4 to 10°C).

Baby gladiolus. Zones 34–41 for winter-hardy types. Hybrid race resulting from breeding red-flowered *G. colvillei* with other species. Flaring, 2½–3¼-in. flowers in short, loose spikes on 1½-ft. stems. Flowers white, pink, red, or lilac; solid or blotched with contrasting color. When left in the ground, will form large clumps in border or among shrubs. Plant in fall or early spring for late spring bloom.

G. byzantinum (G. communis byzantinus). BYZANTINE GLADIOLUS. Zones 31, warmer parts of 32. Mainly maroon, sometimes reddish or coppery, 1–3-in. flowers in groups of 6–12 on 2–3-ft. stems. Narrower leaves than garden gladiolus. Plant in early spring for summer bloom.

G. callianthus (Acidanthera bicolor). ABYSSINIAN SWORD LILY. Perennial in Zones 31, protected areas of 32, but may not flower at all unless corms are dug and divided every year. Stems 2–3 ft. tall, bearing two to ten fragrant, creamy white flowers marked chocolate brown on lower segments. Each blossom 2–3 in. wide, 4–5 in. long. Excellent cut flowers. Plant in spring for bloom in late summer–fall. 'Murielae' is taller, with purple-crimson blotches.

Summer-flowering grandiflora hybrids. GARDEN GLADIOLUS. Perennial in Zones 31, 32, but usually lifted yearly even in those areas. Commonly grown garden gladiolus are a complex group of hybrids derived by variation and hybridization from several species. These are the best-known gladiolus, with widest color range—white, cream, buff, yellow, orange, apricot, salmon, red shades, rose, lavender, purple, smoky shades, even green shades. Individual blooms as large as 8 in. across. Stems are 4–5 ft. tall.

Newer varieties of garden gladiolus, to 5 ft. tall, have sturdier spikes bearing 12–14 open flowers at a time. They are better garden plants than older types and stand upright without staking. Another group, called miniature gladiolus, grows 3 ft. tall, with spikes of 15–20 flowers 2½–3 in. wide; useful in gardens and for cutting.

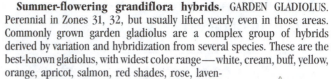

Gladiolus hybrid

High-crowned corms, 1½–2 in. wide, are more productive than older, larger corms (over 2 in. wide). After soil has warmed in spring, plant at 1- to 2-week intervals for 4 to 6 weeks for progression of bloom. Corms bloom 65 to 100 days after planting. If soil is poor, mix in complete fertilizer or superphosphate (4 lb. per 100 sq. ft.) before planting; do not place fertilizer in direct contact with corms. Treat with bulb dust (insecticide-fungicide) before planting. When plants have five leaves, apply complete fertilizer 6 in. from plants and water it in thoroughly. For cut flowers, cut spikes when lowest buds begin to open; keep at least four leaves on plants to build up corms.

GLAUCIDIUM palmatum

PAEONIACEAE

Perennial

🗡 Zones 32, 34–41

☀ ● Partial to deep shade

💧 Ample water

Glaucidium palmatum

This stately rhizomatous plant grows slowly to 2 ft. high. The elegant light green leaves are large and many-lobed, and the 2-in., pinkish lilac blooms, appearing in late spring and early summer, consist of petal-like sepals and bundles of gold stamens. Plant in a cool, sheltered spot in humusy, moist soil. Effective in mixed shady borders and woodland gardens.

GLAUCIUM flavum

YELLOW HORNED POPPY

Papaveraceae

Perennial

🗡 Zones 31, 32, 34, 39

☀ Full sun

💧 Regular water

Glaucium flavum

Often grown as a biennial, this short-lived perennial has handsome gray-green leaves growing in a basal rosette. Delicate, poppylike flowers of an intense yellow gold or orange are borne in summer atop long gray stems and are succeeded by attractive 4-in.-long seedpods. Flowers bloom only for a day or so, and not in profusion; group among other plants for foliage effect in a mixed border. Thrives in well-drained soil of average to low fertility.

FOR INFORMATION ON YOUR CLIMATE ZONE

PLEASE SEE PAGES 30–46

G

GLECHOMA hederacea (Nepeta hederacea)

GROUND IVY

Lamiaceae (Labiatae)

PERENNIAL

✂ ZONES 31, 32, 34–45

☼ ◐ ● SUN OR SHADE

💧 REGULAR WATER

Glechoma hederacea

Trailing plant with neat pairs of round, scalloped, bright green or white-edged leaves 1½ in. across, spaced along stems. Small, trumpet-shaped blue flowers in spring and summer not especially showy. Sometimes planted as small-scale ground cover or used to trail from hanging basket. To 3 in. tall with stems trailing to 1½ ft., rooting at joints. Can become a pest in lawns.

GLEDITSIA triacanthos

HONEY LOCUST

Fabaceae (Leguminosae)

DECIDUOUS TREE

✂ ZONES 32, 34–43

☼ FULL SUN

💧💧 REGULAR TO MODERATE WATER

Gleditsia triacanthos

Native to eastern U.S. Fast growing, with upright trunk and spreading, arching branches. To 35–70 ft. tall. Bright green, fernlike leaves to 10 in. long are divided into many oval, ¾–1½-in.-long leaflets. Late to leaf out; leaves turn yellow and drop early in fall. Inconspicuous flowers followed by broad, 1–1½-ft.-long pods filled with sweetish pulp and hard, roundish seeds.

Foliage casts filtered shade, allowing growth of lawn or other plants beneath. Small leaflets dry up and filter into grass, decreasing raking chores. Not good in narrow area between curb and sidewalk, since roots of old plants will heave paving. Stake tree until good basic branch pattern is established. Tolerant of acid or alkaline conditions, salt, drought, cold, heat, wind. Does best in areas with sharply defined winters, hot summers. Tree is susceptible to many pests, several of which are prevalent in humid-summer regions: mimosa webworm (chews leaves), pod gall midge (deforms foliage), honey locust borer (attacks limbs and trunks).

Trunks and branches of species are formidably thorny, and pods make a mess. Honey locusts for the garden are varieties of *G. t. inermis,* with no thorns and few or no pods. They include:

'Halka'. Fast growing, forms sturdy trunk early, has strong horizontal branching pattern. Can bear a heavy crop of seedpods.

'Imperial'. Spreading, symmetrical tree to about 35 ft. More densely foliaged than other forms; gives heavier shade.

'Moraine'. MORAINE LOCUST. Best known. Fast-growing, spreading tree with branches angled upward, then outward. Subject to wind breakage. Has greater resistance to webworms than do some of the newer selections.

'Rubylace'. Deep red new growth fading to bronzed green by midsummer, especially in warmest regions. Subject to wind breakage, webworm attack.

'Shademaster'. More upright and faster growing than 'Moraine'—to 24 ft. tall, 16 ft. wide in 6 years.

'Skyline'. Pyramidal and symmetrical.

'Sunburst'. Golden yellow new leaves; showy against deep green background. Summer color best in cooler climates. Defoliates early in response to temperature changes, drought. Prone to wind breakage. Very susceptible to foliage pests.

'Trueshade'. Rounded head of light green foliage.

GLOBE AMARANTH. See GOMPHRENA

GLOBEFLOWER. See TROLLIUS

GLOBE THISTLE. See ECHINOPS

GLOBULARIA cordifolia

GLOBE DAISY

Globulariaceae

EVERGREEN PERENNIAL

✂ ZONES 32, 34, 35, 37, 39

☼ FULL SUN

💧 MODERATE WATER

Globularia cordifolia

Globe daisy is a mat-forming plant to 5 in. tall and foot wide. Dark green, leathery leaves on creeping, rooting stems. In summer, bears small blue flowers gathered into tight, round heads on stalks standing above the foliage. They are not true daisies, although the flower heads resemble rayless daisies or small powder puffs. Provide good drainage. Use in rock gardens.

GLORIOSA DAISY. See RUDBECKIA hirta

GLORYBOWER. See CLERODENDRUM

GLORY-OF-THE-SNOW. See CHIONODOXA

GLOXINIA, HARDY. See INCARVILLEA

GLYCERIA maxima

MANNA GRASS

Poaceae (Gramineae)

PERENNIAL

✂ ZONES 31, 32, 34–41

☼ FULL SUN

💧 MORE THAN REGULAR WATER

Glyceria maxima

Found naturally in marshlands or in aquatic settings, this spiky grass grows vigorously to 32 in. high and spreads easily. Grows well in water, such as in a garden pond or any loamy and moist garden soil. Keep in container to prevent spreading. 'Variegata', the most common variety, features green-and-cream-striped leaves and is not quite as aggressive as the species. A very attractive plant for poorly drained soil.

GOAT'S BEARD. See ARUNCUS

GODETIA. See CLARKIA

GOLD DUST PLANT. See AUCUBA japonica 'Variegata'

GOLDEN ASTER. See CHRYSOPSIS

GOLDENCHAIN TREE. See LABURNUM

GOLDEN CLUB. See ORONTIUM aquaticum

GOLDEN CUP. See HUNNEMANNIA fumariifolia

GOLDEN FLEECE. See DYSSODIA tenuiloba

GOLDEN GARLIC. See ALLIUM moly

GOLDEN GLOW. See RUDBECKIA laciniata 'Hortensia'

GOLDEN LARCH. See PSEUDOLARIX kaempferi

GOLDEN MARGUERITE. See ANTHEMIS tinctoria

GOLDENRAIN TREE. See KOELREUTERIA paniculata

GOLDENROD. See SOLIDAGO

GOLDEN SEAL. See HYDRASTIS canadensis

GOLDEN STAR. See CHRYSOGONUM virginianum

GOLDEN TRUMPET. See ALLAMANDA cathartica

GOMPHRENA

GLOBE AMARANTH	
Amaranthaceae	
ANNUALS	
☀ ALL ZONES	
☀ ◑ FULL SUN OR PARTIAL SHADE	
● MODERATE WATER	

Gomphrena

Stiffly branching plants 9 in.–2 ft. tall, covered in summer and fall with rounded, papery, cloverlike heads ¾–1 in. wide. These may be dried quickly and easily, retaining color and shape for winter arrangements. Narrow oval leaves are 2–4 in. long.

G. globosa. White, pink, red, lavender, or purple flower heads top 1-ft. stems. Dwarf varieties for use as edging or bedding plants are 9-in. 'Buddy' (purple) and 'Cissy' (white). 'Strawberry Fields' grows 2 ft. tall, has 1½-in. heads. Planted closely in large pots—six to a shallow 10-in. pot—makes a long-lasting living bouquet.

G. haageana. To 2 ft. tall, with heads of tightly clustered, bright orange bracts that resemble inch-wide pine cones. Tiny yellow flowers peep from the bracts. Sold as 'Haageana Aurea' or simply 'Orange'.

GONIOLIMON tataricum
(Limonium tataricum)

GERMAN STATICE	
Plumbaginaceae	
PERENNIAL	
☀ ZONES 31, 32, 34–45	
☀ FULL SUN	
● MODERATE WATER	

Goniolimon tataricum

Dense clumps of dark green, narrowly oval leaves arise from a woody rootstock. Leafless flower stalks rise to 1½ ft., forking repeatedly into a broad, domed cluster to 1½ ft. wide. Tiny flowers are light purplish to white. The entire inflorescence can be dried for winter flower arrangements. Plant is heat tolerant.

Goodeniaceae. Members of this small family of perennials and shrubs—principally from the Southern Hemisphere, notably Australia—have irregularly lipped flowers. *Scaevola* is the most widely grown example.

GOOD KING HENRY. See CHENOPODIUM

FOR INFORMATION ON SELECTING PLANTS

PLEASE SEE PAGES 47–112

GOOSEBERRY

Grossulariaceae (Saxifragaceae)	
DECIDUOUS SHRUBS	
☀ ZONES 34–43 FOR BEST FRUIT PRODUCTION	
☀ ◑ FULL SUN OR PARTIAL SHADE	
● REGULAR WATER	

Gooseberry

For ornamental relatives, see *Ribes*. Same culture as currant; prune as for red and white currants. Like currant, prohibited in some areas where white pines grow. Grown for pies, canning. Lobed, somewhat maplelike leaves. Fruit often striped longitudinally, decorative. 'Fredonia' is a fairly open plant producing large, dark red fruit. 'Oregon Champion', 3–5-ft. thorny bush with green fruit, bears heavily. 'Pixwell', extremely hardy and with few thorns, has pink fruit. 'Poorman' has red fruit sweet enough to eat off bush. 'Welcome' has medium large, dull red fruit with tart flavor; plants are productive, nearly spineless.

GOOSE PLUM. See PRUNUS americana

GOPHER PLANT. See EUPHORBIA lathyris

GOURD

Cucurbitaceae	
ANNUAL VINES	
☀ ALL ZONES	
☀ FULL SUN	
● REGULAR DEEP WATERING	

Gourd

Many plants produce gourds. One of most commonly planted is *Cucurbita pepo ovifera*, yellow-flowered gourd that produces great majority of small ornamental gourds in many shapes and sizes. These small gourds, usually sold in seed mixtures, come in a host of shapes and patterns. They may be solid colors or striped, in varying combinations of yellow and green. Some are orange or white. Forms include round apple shapes, pear shapes, long-necked types, shorter-necked bottles, oval egg shapes, and squat, flattened shapes. Some have a ring of bumpy protuberances around the top or bottom and are referred to as "crown of thorns." The skins may be smooth or covered with warts and bumps.

Cucumis dipsaceus, hedgehog gourd or teasel gourd, bears small cylindrical, prickly gourds to 2 in. long, that look like burrs.

Cucurbita foetidissima, calabazilla, produces round green-and-yellow-striped gourds on long vines; perennial grown as annual but may not grow well in the North.

For two other garden-worthy gourds, see *Lagenaria siceraria* and *Luffa cylindrica* entries.

All grow fast and will reach 10–15 ft. Sow seeds when ground is warm. Start indoors if growing season is short. Gourds need all the summer heat they can get to develop fruit by frost. If planting for ornamental gourd harvest, give vines wire or trellis support to hold ripening individual fruits off ground. Plant seedlings 2 ft. apart or thin seedlings to same spacing. You can harvest gourds when tendrils next to their stems are dead, but it's best to leave them on the vine as long as possible—until the gourds turn yellow or brown and the rinds are hard. They can even stay on the vine through frosts, but a heavy frost can discolor them. Cut some stem with each gourd so you can hang it up to dry slowly in a cool, airy spot. When thoroughly dry, gourds can be carved or painted, then preserved with a coating of paste wax, lacquer, or shellac. They will usually last indefinitely if kept dry, but may form mold in damp areas.

GOUT WEED. See AEGOPODIUM podagraria

GRAMA GRASS, BLUE. See BOUTELOUA gracilis

Gramineae. See Poaceae

GRAPE

Vitaceae

DECIDUOUS VINES

☀ ZONES VARY BY VARIETY

☼ FULL SUN

💧 MODERATE WATER

▶ SEE CHART ON FOLLOWNG PAGES

Grape

For fruit, wine, shade, and fall color. A single grapevine can produce enough new growth every year to arch over a walk, roof an arbor, form a leafy wall, or provide an umbrella of shade over deck or terrace. Grape is one of the few ornamental vines with bold, textured foliage, colorful edible fruit, and dominant trunk and branch pattern for winter interest.

To get good-quality fruit, you must choose a variety that fits your climate, train it carefully, and prune it regularly.

There are several basic types of grapes. European grapes (*Vitis vinifera*) have tight skin, a generally high heat requirement, and cold tolerance to around 0°F/−18°C. These are the table grapes of the market, such as 'Thompson Seedless'. The classic wine grapes, such as 'Cabernet', 'Chardonnay', and 'Pinot Noir', are also European in origin. Although production of European wine grapes is increasing in the Northwest, Texas, tidewater Virginia, coastal Maryland, and eastern Long Island, these varieties are still grown primarily in California.

American grapes stem from *V. labrusca*, with some influence from other American native species and also often from *V. vinifera*. These are slipskin grapes of the 'Concord' type, which have a moderate summer heat requirement (as opposed to the European table grapes) and tolerate temperatures well below 0°F/−18°C. American grapes are used for jelly, in unfermented grape juice, and as flavoring for soft drinks; some wine, usually sweet, is also made from them. They grow throughout much of the U.S. but will not thrive in the Deep South; there, the grape of choice is the muscadine (*V. rotundifolia*), which bears large fruit in small clusters. Some muscadine varieties are self-fertile, while others require cross-pollination. (All other types of grapes are self-pollinating.)

Once established, grape vines grow rampantly. If all you want is a leafy cover for an arbor or patio, you need only train a strong vine up and over

---

DOUBLE WIRE

To grow a grapevine on a double wire rather than a single one, stretch 2 wires—the first at 2½–3 ft., the second at 5–6 ft.—between posts. When trunk tops lower wire during second summer, remove all side shoots; when it grows a foot above top wire, pinch off its tip. To develop parallel arms, choose strongest side shoot on each side of both wires and cut each to 2 buds. Remove all other side shoots.

---

its support and thin out tangled growth each year. But most people plant grapes for fruit, even if they want shade as well. For good fruit production, you'll need to follow more careful pruning procedures.

Grapes are produced on stems that develop from 1-year-old wood— stems that formed the previous season. These stems have smooth bark; older stems have rough, shaggy bark. The purpose of pruning is to limit the amount of potential fruiting wood, ensuring that the plant doesn't produce too much fruit and that the fruit it does bear is of good quality.

There are several pruning methods for grapes. The two most widely used are spur pruning and cane pruning; see chart for recommended method for each variety. Either technique can be used for training grapes on arbors. Whichever method you choose, the initial steps—planting and creating a framework—are the same. (See illustrations on p. 245 for details.) Pruning should be done in the dormant season—winter or earliest spring, before the buds swell.

ORNAMENTAL GRAPES

Grape vines are best known as the source of fruit for eating or processing into wine or juice. But some kinds are valuable landscape plants, grown for their colorful foliage. Two of the best are described here.

Ornamental grapes climb quickly, and feature handsome dark green, simple to lobed leaves that provide good color in fall. Small green flowers mature into attractive purplish fruit that forms in bunches. Train over an arbor, trellis, fence or pergola, or against a garden wall. Prefer well-drained soil rich in humus and of neutral to alkaline pH. Prune in midwinter and again in midsummer to contain growth, and more often if formal training is desired.

Vitis coignetiae. CRIMSON GLORY VINE. Zones 31, 32, 34–41. Grows to 50 ft. Large heart-shaped leaves to 1 ft. long are dark green in summer but turn brilliant red in autumn. The small, round, blue-black fruit is not edible. Fast growing and good for screening. Prefers loamy soil.

V. vinifera 'Purpurea'. PURPLELEAF GRAPE. Zones 31, 32, 34, 39. To 22 ft. Rounded, lobed leaves to 6 in. long, with irregularly toothed edges, turn plum-colored, then dark purple in autumn. The small, round, purple fruits are not good to eat.

GRAPE HYACINTH. See MUSCARI

GRASSES. The grasses in this book are either lawn or ornamental plants—except for corn, the only cereal commonly grown in home gardens. They are described under entries headed by their botanical names; to find these, check lists below. (All bamboos, which are grasses, are listed under Bamboo.)

Lawn grasses are *Agrostis*, bent grass, redtop; *Bouteloua*, blue grama grass; *Buchloe*, buffalo grass; *Cynodon*, Bermuda grass; *Festuca*, fescue; *Lolium*, ryegrass; *Poa*, bluegrass; *Zoysia*, zoysia.

Ornamental grasses are *Arrhenatherum*, bulbous oat grass; *Arundo*, giant reed; *Bouteloua*, blue grama grass; *Briza*, rattlesnake grass; *Calamagrostis*, feather reed grass; *Chasmanthium*, sea oats; *Coix*, Job's tears; *Cortaderia*, pampas grass; *Deschampsia*, hair grass; *Festuca*, fescue; *Hakonechloa*, Japanese forest grass; *Helictotrichon*, blue oat grass; *Imperata*, Japanese blood grass; *Milium effusum* 'Aureum', Bowles' golden grass; *Miscanthus*, eulalia grass, maiden grass, silver grass; *Molinia*, purple moor grass; *Muhlenbergia*, muhly grass; *Panicum*, switch grass; *Pennisetum*, fountain grass; *Phalaris*, ribbon grass; and *Stipa*, feather grass, needle grass.

GRASS NUT. See TRITELEIA laxa

GRECIAN LAUREL. See LAURUS nobilis

GREEN AND GOLD. See CHRYSOGONUM virginianum

GREEN CARPET. See HERNIARIA glabra

GREEN DRAGON. See PINELLIA

GROUND CHERRY. See PHYSALIS peruviana

GROUND IVY. See GLECHOMA hederacea

GROUNDSEL. See BACCHARIS halimifolia

FOR INFORMATION ON SELECTING PLANTS

PLEASE SEE PAGES 47–112

Grape Planting and Training

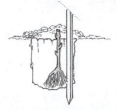

Planting: Plant bare-root grape deep in well-prepared soil, with only the top bud above soil level. Insert post or other support. Replace soil; cover exposed bud with lightweight mulch.

1st Summer: Let vine grow unchecked; don't try to train growth. The more leaves, the better the root development.

1st Winter: Select sturdiest shoot for trunk and remove all other shoots at their base. Shorten trunk to 3 or 4 lowest buds.

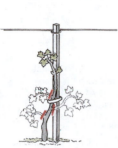

2nd Spring: Let buds grow into 6–8-in. shoots. Select a vigorous upright shoot to form the upper trunk, and tie loosely to post. Cut off all other shoots.

2nd Summer: When trunk reaches wire, cut its tip to force branching. Allow the 2 strongest developing shoots to grow, forming vine's arms; remove any others. Pinch any lateral shoots developing from arms to 10 in. long.

2nd Winter: Cut back all growth on trunk and arms; loosely tie arms to wire. Don't prune yet for fruit production; vines are too immature.

3rd Summer: Allow vine to grow. Remove any growth from trunk. Cane pruning and spur pruning differ from here on.

Cane Pruning from 3rd Winter: Cut back each arm to 12 buds; these will bear fruit the next summer. Select 2 strong lateral shoots near trunk and cut each to 2 buds; these are the renewal spurs. During next winter and every winter thereafter, remove fruiting canes at their base. Renewal spurs will have produced several new shoots from which new fruiting canes can be selected. Choose the 2 longest and strongest shoots and cut each to 12 buds; tie these shoots to wire. Select 2 next best shoots as renewal spurs and cut each to 2 buds.

Spur Pruning from 3rd Winter: Remove weak side shoots from arms. Leave strongest shoots (spurs) spaced 6–10 in. apart; cut each to 2 buds. Each spur will produce 2 fruit-bearing stems during next growing season. During next winter and every winter thereafter, remove upper stem on each spur and cut lower stem to 2 buds. Those buds will develop into stems that bear fruit the following summer.

Training on an Arbor

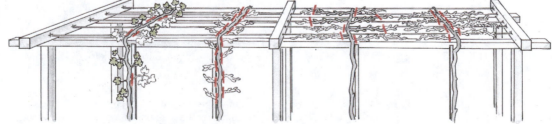

2nd Summer: When vine reaches top of arbor, bend it over and secure it as it grows across top. Remove side shoots to encourage tip to grow.

2nd Winter: Cut back main stem to point just beyond where you want the last set of branches. Cut off all side shoots. In spring, thin new shoots to 1 ft. apart.

3rd Winter, Cane Pruning: Cut back alternately to long canes (12 buds) and spurs (2 buds). Thereafter, follow cane pruning guidelines.

3rd Winter, Spur Pruning: Cut back each selected shoot (from previous summer's growth) to 2 buds. Thereafter, follow spur pruning guidelines.

GRAPE

G

VARIETY	ZONES	SEASON	PRUNING	COMMENTS
AMERICAN VARIETIES				
'Alden'	34–40	Early midseason	Spur	Large, firm, seeded reddish blue grape with light muscat flavor. For fresh eating, wine. Very productive. Good fall leaf color. Protect below –15°F/–26°C
'America'	31, 32, 34–36	Midseason	Cane	Seeded black grape for fresh eating, wine, juice. May succeed in warmer parts of areas farther north, but often tends to be too acid
'Bluebell'	34–43	Early	Cane	Seeded blue grape for fresh eating, juice, preserves. Good disease resistance. Hardy to at least –35°F/–37°C
'Buffalo'	34–42	Early	Cane	Seeded blue table and juice grape with spicy flavor. Performs well after a late frost
'Campbell Early'	32 (northern part), 34–42	Early midseason	Cane	Large seeded black grape of 'Concord' type for fresh eating, juice, wine. Colors before full sweetness develops; leave on vine a while. Tolerates heavy soil. In Zones 41 and 42, succeeds in areas with longest growing season
'Canadice'	34–42	Early	Spur	Seedless red grape will ripen even in cool areas. Very heavy bearing. Cane pruning often recommended, but should be spur-pruned, possibly thinned, to prevent overcropping. Hardy to about –20°F/–29°C if not overcropped
'Concord'	32 (northern part), 34–42	Midseason	Cane	Oldest cultivated American grape and the one most commonly used for juice, jelly. Seeded dark blue fruit. In Zones 41 and 42, succeeds in areas with longest growing seasons
'Delaware'	31, 32, 34–42	Midseason	Cane	Small pinkish grapes used for fresh fruit, juice, or wine. Vines are fairly productive and not very vigorous
'Diamond' ('Moore's Diamond', 'White Diamond')	32 (northern part), 34–42	Early midseason	Cane or spur	Seeded white grape with sweet, refined flavor. For fresh eating, juice, wine. In Zones 41 and 42, succeeds in areas with longest growing season
'Edelweiss'	34–43	Early	Cane	Seeded white grape for fresh eating, juice. Pick as soon as ripe. Excellent disease resistance. Hardy to –30°F/ –34°C
'Himrod'	34–42	Very early	Cane	Firm, seedless white grape with spicy flavor. For fresh eating, raisins. Very vigorous, suited to arbors. Protect below –15°F/–26°C
'Interlaken'	34-42	Very early	Cane or spur	Like 'Himrod', but sweeter and ripens a week earlier; vines are less vigorous but more productive. Protect below –15°F/–26°C
'Kay Gray'	31, 32–45	Early	Cane	Seeded white grape for table, juice, jelly. Hardy to –40°F/–40°C
'Lakemont'	34–42	Early midseason	Cane or spur	Seedless white table grape with higher acid content than 'Himrod' or 'Interlaken'; keeps well in cold storage. Protect below –15°F/–26°C
'Manito'	32 (northern part), 34–42	Early midseason	Cane	Seeded black table grape with fruity flavor. Widely adapted. In Zones 41 and 42, succeeds in areas with longest growing season

GRAPE

VARIETY	ZONES	SEASON	PRUNING	COMMENTS
'New York Muscat'	34–42	Early	Cane	Seeded blue-black grape with intense muscat flavor. For fresh eating, sweet wine. Moderately productive. Hardy to –20°F/–29°C
'Nitodal'	31, 32, 34, 35	Midseason	Cane	Seeded reddish blue table grape. Good in limy soils, hot climates
'Ontario'	32, 34–41	Early	Cane	Large yellow-green grapes. Developed in 1908 in New York State
'Price'	34–42	Very early	Spur	Heavy crop of very sweet, seeded blue grapes with refined 'Concord' flavor. For fresh eating, fresh juice. Ripens even in coolest areas. Protect below –15°F/–26°C
'Reliance'	34–42	Early midseason	Cane or spur	Seedless red grape for fresh eating, fresh juice. May be ready to eat before it colors up. Reliable, heavy bearer. Hardy to about -25°F/-32°C
'Steuben'	32 (northern part), 34–42	Midseason	Cane	Seeded blue grape with spicy flavor for fresh eating, juice. Very productive. Good disease resistance. In Zones 41 and 42, succeeds in areas with longest growing season
'Swenson Red'	34–43	Early	Spur	Red or reddish blue grape with excellent strawberrylike flavor, small seeds. Clusters may have distinctive dumbbell shape; vines may take a few years to develop full vigor, yield. Hardy to –30°F/–34°C
'Valiant'	31, 32, 34–45	Early	Cane or Spur	Small seeded blue grape makes good cooked juice. Colors before full sweetness develops; leave on vine a while. Has survived –50°F/–46°C. Not very disease resistant. Cane-prune in coldest areas
'Worden'	32, 34–42	Early	Cane	Large purple-black fruit on very productive vines. Clusters are larger than 'Concord'. Good table and wine grape
'Van Buren'	31, 32, 34–42	Early	Cane	Jet black skin, medium size grapes with sweet, juicy flesh. Fairly vigorous vine. Good table and wine grape
MUSCADINE VARIETIES				
'Carlos'	31, 32	Early to midseason	Spur	Seeded bronze grape with fine flavor. For juice, jelly, wine. Self-fertile
'Cowart'	31, 32	Early to midseason	Spur	Large seeded blue-black table and juice grape. Self-fertile
'Golden Isles'	31, 32	Midseason	Spur	Seeded bronze grape for table, wine, juice. Self-fertile
'Jumbo'	31, 32	Midseason to late	Spur	Huge black fruit. Needs pollinator
'Scuppernong'	31, 32	Midseason	Spur	The original muscadine variety. Bronze, speckled grape with distinctive aroma and flavor. Needs pollinator
'Triumph'	31, 32	Early midseason	Spur	Reliable, heavy crop of bronze to nearly yellow grapes with pineapple flavor. For juice, fresh eating, wine. Self-fertile

GUNNERA

Gunneraceae

PERENNIALS

ZONES 31, 32

PARTIAL SHADE

CONTINUOUSLY MOIST SOIL

Gunnera tinctoria

Big, bold, awe-inspiring plant to 8 ft. high, with giant leaves (4–8 ft. across) on stiff-haired stalks 4–6 ft. long. Leaves are lobed, conspicuously veined; new sets grow every spring. In the Northeast, foliage dies back completely in winter; provide a thick winter mulch over crowns. Corncoblike, 1½-ft. flower clusters form close to roots. Tiny fruits are red.

Best suited to regions with relatively cool summers, not-too-cold winters. A challenge to grow in eastern U.S., but a conversation piece if it succeeds. Grow in rich, moist, organic soil; feed regularly. Use beside a pond, in a bog garden, or dominating a bed of low, fine-textured ground cover.

G. manicata. Leaves carried fairly horizontally. Spinelike hairs on leafstalks and ribs are red. Leaf lobes are flatter, lack frills of *G. tinctoria*.

G. tinctoria (G. chilensis). Lobed leaf margins are toothed and somewhat frilled. The leaves are held in a bowl-like way, half upright and flaring.

DINOSAUR FOOD

Maybe not, but gunnera is such an exotic, jungly-looking plant that it's easy to imagine giant reptiles munching its huge leaves in a prehistoric forest. These statuesque plants are a good choice for anchors in mixed borders; they are striking at the edge of a pool, where their foliage will be mirrored in the water. Or try one in a large pot.

GYMNOCLADUS dioica

KENTUCKY COFFEE TREE

Fabaceae (Leguminosae)

DECIDUOUS TREE

ZONES 32, 34–43

FULL SUN

REGULAR TO MODERATE WATER

Native to eastern U.S. As a sapling, grows very fast, but slows down at 8–10 ft. Give it lots of space, since it ultimately reaches 60–100 ft. tall and 45–50 ft. wide. Unusual tree providing year-round interest.

Gymnocladus dioica

Handsome bark is dark gray to deep brown with rough, scaly ridges. The relatively few heavy, contorted branches and stout twigs make bare tree picturesque in winter. Attractive 1½–3-ft.-long leaves, divided into many 1–3-in.-long leaflets, emerge late in spring, usually in May. They are pinkish when expanding, deep bluish green in summer. Leaves sometimes turn an agreeable sunny yellow. In leaf, the tree casts light shade.

Male and female plants are separate. Narrow flower panicles at ends of branches in spring are up to 1 ft. long (and fragrant) on females, to 4 in. long on males. Blossoms on female trees are followed by flat, reddish brown, 6–10-in.-long pods containing hard black seeds. Pods persist through winter. Early settlers in Kentucky and Tennessee roasted the seeds to make a coffee substitute, giving the tree its common name.

Grows best in moist, rich, deep soil, but adapts to poor soil, drought, city conditions. Established tree can take much heat and cold. Prune in winter or early spring.

GYPSOPHILA

Caryophyllaceae

ANNUALS AND PERENNIALS

ZONES VARY BY SPECIES

FULL SUN

MODERATE WATER

Gypsophila

Much-branched slender-stemmed plants, upright or spreading, 6 in.–4 ft. tall, profusely covered in summer with small, single or double, white, pink, or rose flowers in clusters. Leaves blue green; few when plant is in bloom. Use for airy grace in borders, bouquets; fine contrast with coarse-textured plants. Dwarf kinds ideal in rock gardens.

Add lime to strongly acid soils. For repeat bloom on perennial species, cut back flowering stems before seed clusters form. Thick, deep roots of some perennial types difficult to transplant; do not disturb often.

G. cerastioides. Perennial. Zones 32, 34. Forms mat 3 in. tall, much broader, with gray leaves and clustered flowers varying from pink-veined white to pink. Use in rock garden, between paving stones.

G. elegans. Annual. All zones. Upright, 1–1½ ft. Lance-shaped, rather fleshy leaves to 3 in. long. Profuse single white flowers ½ in. across or more. Pink and rose forms available. Plants live only 5 to 6 weeks; for continuous bloom, sow seed in open ground every 3 to 4 weeks from late spring into summer. Excellent cut flower. Both 'Convent Garden' and 'Giant White' have larger flowers.

G. paniculata. BABY'S BREATH. Perennial. Zones 31, 32, 34–45. This is the classic filler in bouquets. Much branched to 3 ft. or more; leaves slender, sharp pointed, 2½–4 in. long. Single white flowers about 1/16 in. across, hundreds in a spray. 'Bristol Fairy' is an improved form, more billowy, to 4 ft. high, covered with double blossoms ¼ in. wide. Florists' favorite variety is 'Perfecta', which bears larger flowers. 'Compacta Plena' is a double white dwarf 1½ ft. tall; other dwarfs are double pink 'Pink Star' (1½ ft. tall) and 'Viette's Dwarf' (12–15 in. high). Grow all types from root grafts or stem cuttings.

G. repens. Perennial. Zones 31, 32, 34–43. Alpine native 6–9 in. high, with trailing stems 1½ ft. long. Leaves narrow, less than 1 in. long. Clusters of small white or pink flowers. Increase by cuttings in midsummer. Varieties include several 4-in.-high selections: white-flowered 'Alba' and pink-flowered 'Dubia' (with blooms borne on deep purplish stems) and 'Rosea'. Pink-blossomed 'Dorothy Teacher' is 2 in. high.

HACKBERRY. See CELTIS

HAKONECHLOA macra 'Aureola'

JAPANESE FOREST GRASS

Poaceae (Gramineae)

PERENNIAL

ZONES 31, 32, 34–41

PARTIAL OR FULL SHADE

REGULAR WATER

Hakonechloa macra 'Aureola'

Graceful, slender, leaning or arching stems to 1½ ft. carry long, slender leaves with gold stripes. Effect is that of a tiny bamboo. Spreads slowly by underground runners. Needs good, well-drained soil. Choice plant for woodland good, well-drained soil. Choice plant for woodland garden or for close viewing in a container. 'Albovariegata' has green leaves striped with white.

HALESIA

Styracaceae

DECIDUOUS TREES

ZONES 31, 32, 34–41

PART SHADE

REGULAR WATER

Halesia

Elegant trees native to southeastern U.S. Give best flower display in areas with winter cold; grow best in cool, deep, humus-rich soil. Attractive in woodland gardens, with rhododendrons and azaleas planted beneath.

H. carolina (H. tetraptera). SNOWDROP TREE, SILVER BELL. Moderate growth to 30–40 ft., with 20–35-ft. spread. Lovely in midspring, when clusters of snow-white, ½-in., bell-shaped flowers hang along length of graceful branches just as leaves begin to appear. Oval, finely toothed, 2–5-in.-long leaves turn yellow in fall. Interesting four-winged brown fruits hang on almost all winter. Train plant to a single trunk when young or it will grow as a large shrub. Flowers show off to best advantage when you can look up into tree.

H. diptera. TWO-WINGED SILVER BELL. Small (to 20–30 ft. tall), rounded, usually multitrunked. Flowers resemble those of *H. carolina*, but are more deeply lobed and bloom a week or two later. Fruits resemble those of *H. carolina* but have two rather than four wings. *H. d. magniflora* is a more profuse bloomer.

H. monticola. MOUNTAIN SILVER BELL. Similar to *H. carolina* but larger, eventually to 60–80 ft. tall. Leaves are also bigger (3–6 in. long), but tree casts only moderate shade. Flowers, fruit are also somewhat larger. 'Rosea' has light pink flowers.

Hamamelidaceae. The witch hazel family contains deciduous (rarely evergreen) trees and shrubs. Some have showy flowers; these include *Fothergilla*, witch hazel (*Hamamelis*), *Loropetalum*. Many of the deciduous kinds have brilliant fall color; examples are sweet gum (*Liquidambar*), *Parrotia*.

HAMAMELIS

WITCH HAZEL

Hamamelidaceae

DECIDUOUS SHRUBS OR SMALL TREES

ZONES VARY BY SPECIES

FULL SUN OR PARTIAL SHADE

MODERATE WATER

Hamamelis

Medium-size to large shrubs, sometimes treelike, usually with spreading habit and angular or zigzagging branches. Valued for bright fall foliage and interesting yellow to red blooms appearing in nodding clusters, usually in winter. Each flower consists of many narrow, crumpled petals; depending on whom you ask, blossoms resemble shredded coconut, mop heads, or spiders. Most types are fragrant and bloom over a long period. All appreciate rich, organic soil. Prune only to guide growth, remove poorly placed branches or suckers, or obtain flowering stems for winter bouquets.

H. intermedia. Zones 31, 32, 34, 39. Group of hybrids between *H. mollis* and *H. japonica*. Big shrubs (to 15 ft. high), blooming from late January in warmest part of range to mid-March in coldest areas. Often grafted; remove any growth originating from below graft. The following varieties are among the best:

'Allgold'. Upright shrub bearing deep yellow flowers, reddish at base; yellow fall foliage.

'Arnold Promise'. Late bloomer. Pure yellow, very fragrant flowers nearly conceal branches at peak of bloom. Exceptionally cold hardy.

'Carmine Red'. Spreading shrub with light red flowers; red-orange fall color. Vigorous.

'Diane'. Bright coppery red flowers with slight scent; fine ruddy gold fall color.

'Hiltingbury'. Spreading plant with pale copper blossoms; orange, red, and scarlet autumn leaves.

'Jelena' ('Copper Beauty', 'Orange Beauty'). Spreading plant with large leaves, large yellow flowers suffused with red, and orange-red fall foliage.

'Magic Fire' ('Fire Charm', 'Feuerzauber'). Upright plant with fragrant blossoms of coppery orange blended with red.

'Moonlight'. Upright shrub with strongly perfumed blossoms of light sulfur yellow, red at base; yellow fall foliage.

'Primavera'. Late bloomer producing large quantities of sweet-scented, primrose yellow flowers. Vigorous.

'Ruby Glow'. Erect; coppery red flowers; fine rusty gold fall color.

'Sunburst'. Heavy crop of radiant yellow, unscented blooms.

H. japonica. JAPANESE WITCH HAZEL. Zones 31, 32, 34–41. To 10–15 ft. tall, with loose, spreading habit. Fairly small, lightly scented yellow flowers, February–March. Chief distinction is brilliant fall foliage—shades of red, purple, and yellow. *H. j. flavopurpurascens* has yellow-orange flowers, purple at the base, and reddish yellow fall foliage. *H. j. arborea* is a larger form, to 20–25 ft. tall, with a profusion of yellow blossoms and yellow autumn leaves.

H. mollis. CHINESE WITCH HAZEL. Zones 31, 32, 34–41. Moderately slow-growing shrub to 8–10 ft. or small tree that may eventually reach 30 ft. Roundish leaves, 3½–6 in. long, are dark green and rough above, gray and felted beneath; turn good clear yellow in fall. Sweetly fragrant, 1½-in.-wide, rich golden yellow flowers with red-brown sepals bloom on bare stems, February–March. Effective against red brick or gray stone. Flowering branches excellent for arrangements. 'Early Bright' is an early-blooming variety. 'Pallida' has pale yellow flowers; 'Coombe Wood' bears slightly larger, more highly scented blooms than the species.

H. vernalis. OZARK WITCH HAZEL. Zones 31, 32, 34–41. Native to central and southern U.S. Slow-growing, rounded shrub to 10–15 ft., rarely taller. Leaves 2–5 in. long, medium to dark green, turning bright yellow in fall and holding for several weeks in favorable weather. Flowers are ½–¾ in. across, yellow (rarely orange or red), fragrant, and quite resistant to cold. Blooms January–March. 'Red Imp' has small red flowers.

H. virginiana. COMMON WITCH HAZEL. Zones 31, 32, 34–43. Native to eastern North America. Sometimes to 25 ft. tall but usually 10–15 ft. high; open, spreading, rather straggling habit. Moderately slow growing. The bark is the source of the liniment witch hazel. Roundish leaves similar to those of *H. mollis* but not gray and felted beneath; turn yellow to orange in fall. Fragrant, ¾-in.-wide, golden yellow blooms appear October–November and tend to be lost in colored foliage.

HARD FERN. See BLECHNUM

HARDY ORANGE. See PONCIRUS trifoliata

HARDY SUGAR CANE. See SACCHARUM arundinaceum

HARDY WATER CANNA. See THALIA

HAREBELL. See CAMPANULA rotundifolia

HARE'S TAIL GRASS. See LAGURUS

HARRY LAUDER'S WALKING STICK. See CORYLUS avellana 'Contorta'

HAWTHORN. See CRATAEGUS

HAY-SCENTED FERN. See DENNSTAEDTIA punctilobula

HAZELNUT. See CORYLUS, FILBERT

HEART LILY. See CARDIOCRINUM

HEATH. See DABOECIA cantabrica, ERICA

H

H

HEDERA

IVY

Araliaceae

EVERGREEN WOODY VINES

☘ ZONES VARY BY SPECIES

☼ ◐ ● SOME SHADE IN HOT AREAS

◗ ◗ REGULAR TO MODERATE WATER

Hedera

Spreads horizontally over the ground; also climbs on walls, fences, trellises. Sometimes a single planting does both—wall ivy spreads to become surrounding ground cover or vice versa. Dependable, uniform, neat. Holds soil, discouraging erosion and slippage on slopes. Roots grow deep and fill soil densely. Branches root as they grow, further knitting soil.

Ivy climbs almost any vertical surface by aerial rootlets—a factor to consider in planting against walls that must be painted. Chain link fence planted with ivy soon becomes wall of foliage.

Ivy must have shade in hot climates. Its only real shortcoming is monotony. All year long you get nothing from it but green or green and white (except in the case of *H. helix* 'Baltica').

Thick, leathery leaves are usually lobed. Mature plants will eventually develop stiff branches toward top of vine that bear round clusters of small greenish flowers followed by black berries. These branches have unlobed leaves; cuttings from such branches will have same kind of leaves and will be shrubby, not vining. The plain green *H. helix* 'Arborescens' is a variety of this shrubby type.

Most ivy ground covers need trimming around edges (use hedge shears or sharp spade) two or three times a year. Fence and wall plantings need shearing or trimming two or three times a year. When ground cover builds up higher than you want, mow it with rugged power rotary mower or cut it back with hedge shears. Do this in spring so ensuing growth will quickly cover bald look.

Many trees and shrubs can grow quite compatibly in ivy. But small, soft, or fragile plants will never exist for long with healthy ivy—it simply smothers them. Ivy can be a haven for slugs and snails; it also harbors rodents, especially when it is never cut back.

H. colchica. PERSIAN IVY. Zones 31, 32, 34. Oval to heart-shaped leaves, 3–7 in. wide, to 10 in. long (largest leaves of all ivies). 'Dentata' is faintly toothed; 'Dentata Variegata' is marbled with deep green, gray green, and creamy white. 'Sulphur Heart' ('Paddy's Pride') has central gold variegation.

H. helix. ENGLISH IVY. Zones 31, 32, 34, 39; hardiest varieties in 35, 37, and warmer parts of 38 and 41. Dull dark green leaves with paler veins are 2–4 in. wide at base and as long, with three to five lobes.

'Baltica', with whitish-veined leaves half as big as those of the species, is often considered hardiest variety of English ivy. Its leaves take on purplish tone in winter. Other exceptionally hardy varieties are 'Bulgarica', 'Hebron', 'Rochester', 'Thorndale', and '238th Street'.

Many small- and miniature-leafed forms of English ivy are useful for small-area ground covers, hanging baskets, and training to form intricate patterns on walls and in pots. These varieties are also used to create topiary shapes—globes, baskets, animals—on wire frames. Some small-leafed forms are 'Hahn's Self Branching', light green leaves, dense branching, best in part shade; 'Conglomerata', a slow-growing dwarf; and 'Minima', leaves ½–1 in. across with three to five angular lobes. Other varieties include 'Buttercup', 'California', 'Fluffy Ruffles', 'Gold Dust', 'Gold Heart', 'Heart', 'Needlepoint', 'Ripple', 'Shamrock', and 'Star'; select for leaf color and shape. These are most often grown as house plants, but if planted in protected sites, most are hardy in Zones 31, 32, 34, 39.

HEDYCHIUM

GINGER LILY

Zingiberaceae

PERENNIALS

☘ ALL ZONES INDOORS, SEE ALSO BELOW

☼ ◐ FULL SUN OR LIGHT SHADE

◗ AMPLE WATER

Hedychium

Foliage is handsome under good growing conditions. Leaves are on two sides of stems but grow in a single plane. In late summer or early fall, richly fragrant flowers in dense spikes open from cone of overlapping green bracts at ends of stalks. Southern specialist growers offer dozens of species and selections in heights from 2 to 9 ft., in colors that range from white and cream through pink to red, and a host of yellows, oranges, and salmons.

Remove old stems after flowers fade to bring on fresh new growth. Give soil high in organic matter. *H. coronarium* and the hybrid cultivars listed below are hardy outdoors in Zone 31 and warmer parts of Zone 32 if mulched well in winter. Elsewhere, and for other species in Zones 31, 32, grow in large containers outdoors in summer, back indoors in autumn. Let go dormant in winter by withholding water. Frosts in mild-winter areas can kill plants to ground, but new stalks appear in early spring. Useful near swimming pools, with palms, ferns, other tropical-looking plants.

H. coronarium. WHITE GINGER LILY, GARLAND FLOWER. Native to India, Indonesia. Grows 3–4 ft. high. Leaves 8–24 in. long, 2–5 in. across. Wonderfully fragrant white flowers in 6–12-in.-long clusters; good cut flowers.

H. gardnerianum. KAHILI GINGER. Native to India. Grows to 5 ft. high; 8–18-in.-long leaves 4–6 in. wide. Clear yellow flowers with red stamens, in 1½-ft.-long spikes. 'Compactum' is smaller.

H. greenei. Native to India. Grows to 4 ft., with orange-red flowers in 5-in. spikes.

H. 'Lemon Beauty'. To 5 ft., large, bright yellow flowers.

H. 'Peach Delight'. To 6 ft., very fragrant peachy orange flowers with deeper orange throat.

H. 'Pink Flame'. To 4–5 ft. high, large white flowers with pink flame-like marking on the lip.

HEDYOTIS caerulea. See HOUSTONIA caerulea

HEDYSARUM coronarium

FRENCH HONEYSUCKLE

Fabaceae

PERENNIALS

☘ ZONES 31, 32, 34–43

☼ FULL SUN

◗ REGULAR WATER

Hedysarum coronarium

Bushy plants with spikes of pealike flowers, handsome additions to beds and borders.

H. coronarium. Perennial, sometimes biennial. Native to Mediterranean area. Clusters of paired and rounded leaflets features clusters of deep red, pealike, fragrant flowers attractive to bees. Grows to 3 ft. high and 2 ft. across. Flowers, which crowd onto erect stems in spring and summer, are good for cutting. Locate at the back of the garden for best effect. Prefers well-drained, stony, or poor soil.

H. hedysaroides. Native to Europe. Forms clumps to 2 ft. high and 3 ft. wide. Compound leaves with pairs of oval leaflets. Loose spikes of red-violet or white flowers in mid- to late summer.

FOR INFORMATION ON YOUR CLIMATE ZONE

PLEASE SEE PAGES 30–46

HELENIUM

COMMON SNEEZEWEED

Asteraceae (Compositae)

PERENNIAL

⚡ ZONES VARY BY SPECIES

☼ FULL SUN

🔴 REGULAR WATER

Helenium

These long-blooming plants are related to sunflowers and asters. Durable and heat-loving, they are useful in beds and borders as cut flowers.

H. autumnale. COMMON SNEEZEWEED. Zones 31, 32, 34–43. Species is rarely grown; plants sold as such are usually hybrids between *H. autumnale* and other species. Leaves 2–4 in. long, toothed. Numerous branching, leafy stems to 1–6 ft. high, depending on variety. Blooms over a long period from midsummer to early fall; flowers are daisylike, with rays in yellow, orange, red, or copper shades surrounding a pompomlike, typically brown center.

Thrives in summer heat. Trim off faded blossoms to encourage more flowers. Better looking with scant fertilizer. Taller varieties need staking and are best suited to back of borders. Divide all types every few years. Plants can take some neglect. Drought tolerant, but look better with regular moisture.

The following named varieties are sometimes offered. Tall types grow to 4–5 ft., compact ones to about 3 ft. high.

'Baudirektor Linne'. Tall. Velvety red petals and a brown center.
'Butterpat'. Tall. Light yellow blossoms with a deeper yellow center.
'Crimson Beauty'. Compact. Dusky deep red flowers.
'Cymbal Star' ('Zimbelstern'). Tall. Gold blooms touched with bronze.
'Dunkel Pracht'. Tall. Dark red blossoms with a brown center.
'Gold Kugel' ('Gold Ball'). Compact. Dark-centered yellow blossoms.
'Moerheim Beauty'. Compact. Coppery red petals around a brown center.
'September Gold'. Compact. Bright yellow blossoms.
'Sunball' ('Kugelsonne'). Tall. Lemon yellow rays, chartreuse centers.
'Waldtraut'. Tall. Copper-tinged rays surrounding a dark center.
'Wyndley'. Compact. Butter yellow petals around a lime yellow center.

H. hoopesii. Zones 32, 34–45. Native to the western U.S. Upright to 3 ft. high, with basal clumps of grayish green, lance-shaped leaves. Clusters of bright yellow to orange daisylike flowers in early summer. Drought tolerant.

HELIANTHEMUM
nummularium

SUNROSE

Cistaceae

EVERGREEN SHRUBLETS

⚡ ZONES 32, 34

☼ FULL SUN

🔴 MODERATE WATER

Helianthemum nummularium

Commonly sold under this name are a number of forms as well as hybrids between this species and others. They grow about 6–8 in. high and spread to 3 ft. Leaves ½–1 in. long; may be glossy green above and fuzzy gray beneath, or gray on both sides. Delightful late spring to early summer display of clustered, 1-in.-wide, single or double flowers in bright or pastel colors—flame red, apricot, orange, yellow, pink, rose, peach, salmon, or white. Each blossom lasts only a day, but new buds continue to open. Shear plants back after flowering to encourage repeat bloom.

Specialists offer many named varieties. Especially noteworthy is one sold as *H. apenninum* 'Roseum' or merely as 'Wisley Pink', with comparatively large, pure pink flowers that contrast with the gray, furry foliage.

Let sunroses tumble over rocks, set in niche in dry rock wall, or grow in planters on sunny patio. Use them at seashore or in rock gardens; let them ramble over gentle slope. If used as ground cover, plant 2–3 ft. apart. In cold-winter areas, lightly cover plants with branches from evergreens in winter to keep foliage from dehydrating. Plants will be hardier if given soil that is neutral to alkaline, not too rich (good drainage is essential, though), and kept on dry side; object is to encourage hard, nonsucculent growth.

SUNFLOWERS THAT MAKE THE CUT

For cut-flower bouquets, try these ten sunflower varieties, all excellent for arranging: 'Autumn Beauty', 'Big Smile', 'Color Fashion Mixed', 'Double Sun Gold', 'Inca Jewels', 'Italian White', 'Music Box', 'Sunrich Lemon', 'Sunrich Orange', and 'Valentine'.

HELIANTHUS

SUNFLOWER

Asteraceae (Compositae)

ANNUALS AND PERENNIALS

⚡ ZONES VARY BY SPECIES

☼ FULL SUN

🔴 REGULAR WATER, EXCEPT AS NOTED

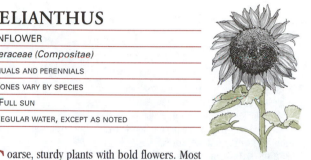
Helianthus

Coarse, sturdy plants with bold flowers. Most are tough and widely adapted. Perennial kinds spread rapidly, may become invasive. Tall kinds not for tidy gardens, may need staking. All bloom in late summer, fall.

H. angustifolius. SWAMP SUNFLOWER. Perennial. Zones 31, 32, 34. Native to eastern U.S. Grows 5–10 ft. tall, with narrow 6-in. leaves and sheaves of bright yellow, 2–3-in. daisies with dark brown centers. Likes ample moisture but adapts to ordinary garden conditions. Sometimes confused with *H. salicifolius*.

H. annuus. COMMON SUNFLOWER. Annual. All zones. From this rough, hairy plant with 2–3-in.-wide flower heads have come many ornamental and useful garden varieties. Best-known form is coarse, towering (to 10 ft.) plant with small rays outside and cushiony center of disk flowers, 8–10 in. across. Usually sold as 'Mammoth Russian'. 'Sunspot' carries flowers of like size on 2-ft. plants. People eat the roasted seeds; birds like them raw and visit flower heads in fall and winter. For children, annual sunflowers are big and easy to grow and bring sense of great accomplishment. Sow seeds in spring where plants are to grow. Large-flowered kinds need rich soil.

H. atrorubens. DARK-EYED SUNFLOWER. Perennial. Zones 31, 32, 34, 35, 37. Native to southeastern U.S. Grows 5–6 ft. tall, with coarse, bristly foliage and 2-in. yellow flower heads centered in dark purple. 'The Monarch' has semidouble flowers somewhat resembling the quilled flowers of a cactus-form dahlia.

H. decapetalus. THIN-LEAVED SUNFLOWER. Zones 31, 32, 34–41. Native to central and southeastern U.S. To 5 ft. high, spreads by rhizomes to form clumps. Tall stems are lined with lance-shaped to oval, medium green leaves. Yellow flowers to 3 in. across have brownish centers.

H. maximilianii. Perennial. Zones 31, 32, 34–43. Native to central and southwestern U.S. Clumps of 10-ft. stems clothed in narrow, 8–10-in. leaves and topped with narrow spires of 3-in. yellow flowers.

H. multiflorus (H. decapetalus). Perennial. Zones 31, 32, 34–43. Hybrid between *H. annuus* and a perennial species. To 5 ft. high, with thin, toothed, 3–8-in.-long leaves and numerous 3-in.-wide flower heads with yellow centers. Excellent for cutting. 'Capenoch Star' has single lemon yellow flowers with a large central brown disk. 'Loddon Gold' ('Flore Pleno') is a double-flowered form with deeper yellow blooms.

H

H

H. salicifolius (H. orgyalis). Perennial. Zones 31, 32, 34–43. Native to central U.S. Similar to *H. angustifolius,* but with narrower, more willowy, drooping leaves. The two species are sometimes confused in the nursery trade.

H. tuberosus. JERUSALEM ARTICHOKE. Perennial. Zones 31, 32, 34–41. Also grown as a commercial crop; tubers are edible and sold in markets as sunchokes. Plants 6–10 ft. tall, with bright yellow flower heads. Oval leaves 8 in. long. Spreads readily and can become pest. Best to harvest tubers every year and save out two or three for replanting. If controlled, makes a good, quick temporary screen or hedge.

Helianthus tuberosus

HELICHRYSUM

Helichrysum

	Asteraceae (Compositae)
	ANNUALS
✂	ALL ZONES
☼	FULL SUN
♦	MODERATE WATER

Best known are the strawflowers used in both fresh and dried arrangements. Others, though little known, are choice plants for landscape use. Some species are perennial in warm climates, but all are grown as annuals throughout the Northeast.

H. angustifolium. See *H. italicum*

H. bracteatum (Bracteantha bracteata). STRAWFLOWER. Annual. Grows 2–3 ft. high with many flower heads; dwarf forms also available. Known as "everlasting" because pompomlike, 2½-in. summer flowers are papery and last indefinitely when dried. Also good in fresh arrangements. Flowers may be yellow, orange, red, pink, or white (seeds come in mixed colors). Straplike leaves are medium green, 2–5 in. long. Plant seed in place in late spring or early summer (same time as zinnias). 'Dargan Hill Monarch' and 'Diamond Head' are shrubby perennial forms for mild-winter climates. Both have grayish green foliage and 3-in. golden yellow flower heads; the similar 'Cockatoo' has lemon yellow heads. Cut flowers for drying before they fully open.

H. italicum (H. angustifolium). CURRY PLANT. Spreading, branching to 2 ft. high, roughly as broad, with crowded, narrow, nearly white leaves to 1½ in. long. Leaves emit a strong fragrance of curry powder when bruised or pinched; though they are not used in curry, a few can add a pleasant aroma to a salad or meat dish. Bright yellow, ½-in. flower heads in clusters 2 in. across, midsummer to autumn.

H. petiolare. LICORICE PLANT. Woody-based plant with trailing stems to 4 ft. with white, woolly, inch-long leaves; insignificant flowers. Licorice aroma sometimes noticeable—in hot, still weather, for example, or when leaves are dry. Cultivars include:

'Limelight', also known as 'Aurea', has luminous light chartreuse leaves.

'Sky Net' bears creamy white flowerheads, ¾-in. across.

'Variegatum' has foliage with white markings.

'Roundabout', a miniature sport of 'Variegatum', sometimes reverts to its parent.

All varieties are useful for their trailing branches, which will thread through mixed plantings or mix with other plants in large pots or hanging baskets.

H. subulifolium. Mound-shaped plant to 20 in. tall, with glossy green, 5-in. leaves and bright, shining, orange-yellow summer flowers 1½ in. wide. Excellent for fresh or dried cut flowers.

FOR INFORMATION ON SELECTING PLANTS

PLEASE SEE PAGES 47–112

HELICTOTRICHON sempervirens (Avena sempervirens)

Helictotrichon sempervirens

	BLUE OAT GRASS
	Poaceae (Gramineae)
	PERENNIAL
✂	ZONES 31, 32, 34–41
☼	FULL SUN
♦	REGULAR WATER

Evergreen, 2–3-ft. fountains of bright blue-gray, narrow leaves resemble giant clumps of blue fescue (*Festuca glauca*), but are more graceful. Plants need full sun, good drainage. Combine with other grasses and broad-leafed plants, and with boulders in rock gardens. Pull out occasional withered leaves. Best appearance in cool end of range; becomes brown or gray in hot, humid summers.

HELIOPSIS helianthoides (H. scabra)

Heliopsis helianthoides

	OX-EYE
	Asteraceae (Compositae)
	PERENNIAL
✂	ZONES 31, 32, 34–45
☼ ◐	FULL SUN OR LIGHT SHADE
♦	REGULAR TO MODERATE WATER

As species name implies, resembles true sunflower, *Helianthus*. Clump-forming perennial to 5 ft. tall and half as wide, with 6-in., rough-textured, medium green leaves. Bright orange-yellow flower heads are 3 in. wide or wider. Blooms from July until frost. Plants are usually offered as *H. scabra,* a subspecies of *H. helianthoides.* Some of the best varieties are: 'Ballerina', an early bloomer to 3 ft., with semidouble deep yellow flowers; 'Karat', to 3½ ft., with single bright yellow flowers; and 'Summer Sun', to 3 ft., with single blossoms in rich golden yellow. Divide clumps of all types every few years.

HELIOTROPE, GARDEN. See VALERIANA officinalis

HELIOTROPIUM arborescens (H. peruvianum)

Heliotropium arborescens

	COMMON HELIOTROPE
	Boraginaceae
	TENDER PERENNIAL, TREATED AS ANNUAL
✂	ALL ZONES
☼ ◐	PARTIAL SHADE IN HOT-SUMMER CLIMATES
♦	REGULAR WATER
☣	ALL PARTS ARE POISONOUS IF INGESTED

Old-fashioned plant grown for delicate, sweet fragrance of its flowers. Treated as summer bedding annual 1½–2 ft. high. Flowers are dark violet to white, arranged in tightly grouped, curved, one-sided spikes that form rounded, massive clusters. Veined leaves have darkish purple cast. 'Black Beauty' and 'Iowa' are varieties with deep purple flowers; there are also dwarf forms under 1 ft. high. 'Marine' is compact, to 1½ ft. high, with deep violet-blue flowers. 'White Lady' has pink-tinged white flowers on foot-high plants.

Requires well-drained soil. Takes well to container growing; potted plants can be protected in winter and moved into patio or garden for spring and summer enjoyment.

HELIPTERUM roseum
(Acroclinium roseum)

PINK AND WHITE EVERLASTING, PINK PAPER DAISY

Asteraceae (Compositae)

ANNUAL

⧄ ALL ZONES

☼ ◑ FULL SUN TO PARTIAL SHADE

🌢 REGULAR WATER

Helipterum roseum

Top-notch flower for cutting, drying. Native to Australia. Grows 2 ft. tall, with scanty, narrow foliage and 1–2-in. pink or white daisies with papery "petals" that retain their color and form when dried. Grow in full sun in warm soil, sowing seeds after frost where plants are to grow. Thin to 6–12 in. apart. Useful for winter arrangements and garden color.

HELLEBORUS

HELLEBORE

Ranunculaceae

PERENNIALS

⧄ ZONES VARY BY SPECIES

◐ ● PARTIAL OR FULL SHADE

🌢 🌢 REGULAR TO MODERATE WATER

🌢 ALL PARTS ARE POISONOUS IF INGESTED

Helleborus

Distinctive, long-lived evergreen plants, blooming for several months in winter and spring. Basal clumps of substantial, long-stalked leaves, usually divided fanwise into leaflets. Flowers large, borne singly or in clusters, centered with many stamens. Good cut flowers; sear ends of stems or dip in boiling water, then place in deep, cold water.

Plant in good soil with lots of organic material added. Feed once or twice a year. Do not move often; plants reestablish slowly. Mass under high-branching trees on north or east side of walls, in beds bordered with ajuga, wild ginger, primroses, violets. Use in plantings with azaleas, pieris, rhododendrons, skimmia, and ferns.

H. argutifolius (H. lividus corsicus, H. corsicus). CORSICAN HELLEBORE. Zones 31, 32. Leafy stems to 3 ft. high. Pale blue-green leaves divided into three leaflets with sharply toothed edges. (Not to be confused with *H. lividus,* a rare plant with pale leaf veins and leaflets that have smooth edges or only a few fine teeth.) Clusters of large, firm-textured, light chartreuse flowers among upper leaves in early spring. After shedding stamens, flowers stay attractive until summer. Unlike most other hellebores, this species can take some sun and is drought tolerant.

H. atrorubens. Zones 31, 32, 34–41. To 1 ft. high and 1½ ft. across; lobed, dark green leaves divided into as many as 11 leaflets; leaves and stems sometimes tinged purple. In late winter to early spring, clusters of deep purple flowers with green shading inside. Needs neutral to alkaline soil.

H. cyclophyllus. Zones 31, 32, 34, 39. To 16 in. high and 1½ ft. across; pale green, lobed and toothed leaves, hairy on the underside. In late winter to early spring, clusters of as many as seven yellow-green flowers, outward-facing or drooping, and scented.

H. dumetorum. Zones 31, 32, 34, 39. To 1 ft. high; lobed and toothed leaves divided into up to 11 leaflets. In spring, clusters of drooping, cup-shaped green flowers to 1½ in. across.

H. foetidus. Zones 31, 32, 34, 39. Grows to 1½ ft. high. Attractive leaves—leathery, dark green, divided into 7–11 leaflets. Blooms February–April; flowers 1 in. wide, light green with purplish margin, in large clusters at branch ends. Good with naturalized daffodils. Self-sows freely where adapted. As species name implies, plant parts emit a somewhat unpleasant odor when bruised.

H. multifidus. Zones 31, 32, 34–41. To 1½ ft. high and 1½ ft. across; medium green, lobed and toothed leaves to 9 in. long, divided into many leaflets. In late winter to early spring, clusters of dark, almost metallic, green flowers, 1½–2 in. across. Several subspecies exist.

H. niger. CHRISTMAS ROSE. Zones 32, 34–45. Elegant plant to 1½ ft. tall, blooming at some time between December and early spring (timing depends on severity of winter). Lustrous dark green leaves divided into seven to nine leaflets with few, large teeth. White or greenish white, about 2-in.-wide flowers turn purplish with age. Named varieties are sometimes available. 'White Magic' has large white flowers that take on a hint of pink as they age.

H. nigercors. Zones 31, 32, 34, 39. To 1 ft. high and 3 ft. across; medium green, lobed and toothed leaves to 1 ft. long. In late winter to early spring, clusters of white flowers, sometimes tinged pink, to 4 in. across.

H. odorus. Zones 31, 32, 34, 39. To 1½ ft. high and as wide; deep green, lobed and toothed leaves to 16 in. long. In late winter to early spring, clusters of up to five fragrant, outward-facing green flowers to 3 in. across.

H. orientalis. LENTEN ROSE. Zones 31, 32, 34–41. Much like *H. niger* in growth habit, but easier to transplant. Basal leaves with 5–11 sharply toothed leaflets. Blooming starts in late winter and continues into spring. Flowering stems branched, with leaflike bracts at branching points and beneath flowers. Blossoms are white, greenish, purplish, or rose, often spotted or splashed with deep purple. Lenten rose is often mistakenly sold under the name "Christmas rose," but it differs from true Christmas rose in flower color and in having many small teeth on leaflets. Self-sows freely.

H. purpurascens. Zones 31, 32, 34–41. To 1 ft. high and as wide; leathery, medium green, lobed and toothed leaves to 11 in. long. In early to midspring, clusters of drooping, cup-shaped, purplish gray flowers tinged pink, flushed with light green inside. Can tolerate full sun in cool climates.

H. sternii. Zones 31, 32, 34, 39. To 14 in high and 1 ft. across; lobed, toothed or spiny leaves to 11 in. long have light veins and pinkish purple stalks. In early to late spring, clusters of many cup-shaped, pale green flowers tinged pink. Can tolerate full sun in cool climates.

HEMEROCALLIS

DAYLILY

Liliaceae

PERENNIALS

⧄ ZONES 31, 32, 34–45, EXCEPT AS NOTED

☼ ◑ FULL SUN OR LIGHT SHADE

🌢 REGULAR WATER

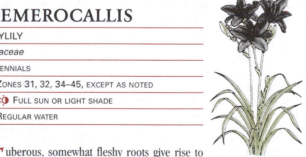

Hemerocallis

Tuberous, somewhat fleshy roots give rise to large clumps of arching, sword-shaped leaves—semievergreen or deciduous depending on type. Semievergreen types will grow in Zones 31, 32, 34, 39. There are also evergreen daylilies, but they need warmer climates than are present in the Northeast. Lilylike flowers in open or branched clusters at ends of generally leafless stems that stand well above foliage. Older yellow, orange, and rust red daylilies have mostly been replaced by newer kinds; both tall and dwarf varieties are available.

Although many species exist, only a few are offered by nurseries. Most of the daylilies available are hybrids; thanks to generations of crossing by scores of amateur and professional breeders, more than 20,000 named varieties have been registered by the American Hemerocallis Society, and hundreds more appear each year.

H

Use in borders with bearded iris, Michaelmas and Shasta daisies, red-hot poker, dusty miller, agapanthus. Mass on banks under high-branching, deciduous trees, along driveways and roadsides in country gardens. Group among evergreen shrubs, near pools, along streams. Plant dwarf daylilies in rock gardens, as edgings, low ground covers. Good cut flowers. Cut stems with well-developed buds; buds open on successive days, though each flower is slightly smaller than preceding one. Arrange individual blooms in low bowls. Snap off faded flowers daily.

Few plants are tougher or more trouble free than daylilies. They adapt to almost any kind of soil. Red-flowered daylilies need warmth to develop best color. Divide crowded plants in early spring or late fall.

H. altissima. Deciduous. Zones 31, 32, 34, 39. A lofty plant—leaves can grow to 5 ft. long, flower stems to 6 ft. high. Fragrant, 4-in. yellow flowers appear on branching stems in late summer and autumn. 'Statuesque' has 5-ft. stems, blooms in mid- to late summer.

H. citrina. Deciduous. To 4 ft. high, with arching leaves to 2½ ft. long. In midsummer, night-blooming, fragrant, pale yellow to greenish yellow star-shaped flowers are produced on stiff stems.

H. fulva. TAWNY DAYLILY, COMMON ORANGE DAYLILY. Deciduous. To 6 ft. high, with leaves to 2 ft. long or longer; tawny orange-red, 3–5-in.-wide, unscented flowers in summer. Rarely sold, but commonly seen in old gardens and along roadsides; a tough, persistent plant suitable for holding banks. The double-flowered 'Kwanso' is sometimes seen. Both species and variety have been largely replaced by hybrids.

H. hybrids. Deciduous, evergreen, and semievergreen. Deciduous types go completely dormant in winter and are hardier than evergreen types; they are the plants of choice in cold-winter regions. Semievergreen sorts may or may not retain leaves, depending on where they are grown. Modern hybrids grow 1–6 ft. tall and have flowers 3–8 in. across. Some have broad petals, others narrow, spidery ones; many have ruffled petal edges. Colors range far beyond the basic yellow, orange, and rusty red to pink, vermilion, buff, apricot, plum or lilac purple, creamy white, and near-white, often with contrasting eyes or midrib stripes that produce a bicolor effect. Many varieties are sprinkled with tiny iridescent dots known as diamond dust. Semidouble-flowered and double-flowered varieties exist.

To get what you want, buy plants in bloom (either in containers or in the field), or study specialists' catalogs, many of which have fine color photographs. To prolong the bloom season, look for reblooming (remontant) varieties; or select early, midseason, and late bloomers. Varieties listed as tetraploid (possessing twice the normal number of chromosomes) have flowers with unusually heavy-textured petals. Look for varieties that have received awards from the American Hemerocallis Society. The letters AM stand for Award of Merit, presented to ten varieties each year. HM means Honorable Mention, awarded to any plant receiving ten or more votes from the selection committee. SM stands for Stout Medal, the highest award a daylily can receive. SM winners include the long-blooming dwarf yellow 'Stella de Oro' and the free-blooming yellow tetraploid 'Mary Todd'. An old garden variety that retains its popularity amid the influx of new hybrid daylilies is 'Hyperion', a 4-ft.-tall plant with fragrant yellow flowers that bloom in midsummer.

H. lilio-asphodelus (H. flava). LEMON DAYLILY. Deciduous. Zones 31, 32, 34–43. To 3 ft. high, with 2-ft. leaves and fragrant, 4-in., pure yellow flowers in late May or June. Newer hybrids may be showier, but this species is still cherished for its delicious perfume and early blossom time.

HEMLOCK. See TSUGA

HEMP AGRIMONY. See EUPATORIUM cannabinum

HEN AND CHICKENS. See SEMPERVIVUM tectorum

HEN AND CHICKS. See ECHEVERIA

HEPATICA

LIVERLEAF

Ranunculaceae

PERENNIALS

ZONES 31, 32, 34–45, EXCEPT AS NOTED

PARTIAL OR FULL SHADE

REGULAR WATER

Hepatica

Low growers with leathery evergreen or semievergreen leaves and flowers consisting of petal-like sepals similar to those of some of the smaller anemones. (In fact, these plants were once classified as anemones.) Flowers appear early in spring, each rising on its own stalk above the clump of last year's leaves. A new crop of leaves follows bloom. Choice plants for woodland gardens or for the shaded rock garden. Little known in the U.S. except to wildflower fanciers, they are popular among plant collectors in Japan, where many varieties not yet grown here are cultivated. Provide neutral to mildly acid soil that is moist but well drained.

H. acutiloba. SHARP-LOBED HEPATICA. Native to eastern U.S. Leathery 4-in. rounded or kidney-shaped leaves divided into three sharp-pointed lobes. Flowers are lilac or white, ½–1 in. across, on stems 6–9 in. tall.

H. americana (H. triloba). Resembles the above, but leaves have rounded lobes and flowering stems are usually shorter, to 6 in. tall. Flowers typically light blue, but sometimes white or pink.

H. nobilis. Zones 32, 34–41. To 4 in. high. Medium green, round to kidney-shaped leaves to 2½ in. long are semievergreen, covered with soft hairs and purplish on the underside. Cup-shaped flowers may be white, blue, blue-violet, or pink, and usually appear before the leaves.

HEPTACODIUM miconioides

SEVEN SONS FLOWER

Caprifoliaceae

DECIDUOUS SHRUB OR SMALL TREE

ZONES 31, 32, 34–39, 41

FULL SUN OR LIGHT SHADE

REGULAR WATER

Heptacodium miconioides

This relative newcomer to the garden scene is a fountain-shaped shrub that eventually reaches 15–20 ft. tall, 8–10 ft. wide. It can be trained as a single- or multitrunked tree. Large, narrowly heart-shaped leaves are shiny green, deeply veined. No appreciable fall color. Creamy white, fragrant flowers in large clusters at branch ends open over a long season in late summer or fall. Blooms are succeeded by even showier masses of small fruits with bright purplish red calyxes. Common name derives from number of individual flowers in each of the clusters forming part of the larger inflorescence. Even winter bark is picturesque: thin, pale tan strips peel away to reveal dark brown bark beneath.

Seven sons flower is not fussy about soil and is usually free of pests and diseases. A shrub of much promise; it is sometimes referred to as the crape myrtle of the North.

DAYLILIES FOR DINNER

Daylily buds and blossoms are edible. Try unopened buds in salads or stir-fries, or chop them and use them to thicken soups. Flowers that are halfway or fully open make an interesting side dish when dipped in a light batter and fried in oil. Some cooks like to stuff the flowers with cheese or bread crumb mixtures or even meat before cooking.

HERACLEUM
mantegazzianum

GIANT HOGWEED

Apiaceae

PERENNIAL OR BIENNIAL

🌿 ZONES 31, 32, 34–43

☼ ● FULL TO PARTIAL SHADE

💧 REGULAR WATER

◊ MAY CAUSE RASH, INTESTINAL UPSET

*Heracleum
mantegazzianum*

This giant grows 8–10 ft. high, but may behave as a short-lived perennial if allowed to go to seed. Enormous clumps of large, showy green leaves, lobed like the fingers on a hand, and tiny white flowers gathered into huge flat clusters to 2 ft. across in summer are borne on hollow but ridged, purplish stems. Best in wild or spacious garden settings. Grows in moderately fertile to rich and well-drained soil. Has escaped into meadows and become a pest in some areas, so it is best to remove flower stalks before seeds have formed. Direct handling may result in skin rash, and ingestion will cause severe intestinal distress.

HERB-OF-GRACE. See RUTA graveolens

HERBS. This category includes all plants that at some time in history have been considered valuable for seasoning, medicine, fragrance, or general household use. As you look through lists of plants, you can recognize certain herbs because they bear the species name *officinalis*—meaning sold in shops, edible, medicinal, recognized in the pharmacopoeia. Today's herb harvest is used almost entirely for seasoning foods and for healing.

Herbs are versatile. Some creep along the ground, making fragrant carpets. Others are shrublike. Many make attractive pot plants. However, quite a few do have a weedy look, especially next to regular ornamental plants. Many are hardy and adaptable. Although hot, dry, sunny conditions with poor but well-drained soil are usually considered best, some herbs thrive in shady, moist locations with light soil rich in humus. And contrary to popular opinion, most herbs appreciate soil of average fertility.

Following are lists of herbs for specific landscape situations:

Kitchen garden. This can be a sunny raised bed near the kitchen door, planter box near the barbecue, or part of the vegetable garden. Plant basic cooking herbs: basil (*Ocimum basilicum*), chives, dill (*Anethum graveolens*), sweet marjoram (*Origanum majorana*), mint (*Mentha*), oregano (*Origanum vulgare*), parsley, rosemary (*Rosmarinus*), sage (*Salvia officinalis*), savory (*Satureja*), tarragon (*Artemisia dracunculus*), thyme (*Thymus*). The connoisseur may wish to plant angelica, anise (*Pimpinella anisum*), caraway (*Carum carvi*), chervil (*Anthriscus cerefolium*), coriander (*Coriandrum sativum*), common fennel (*Foeniculum vulgare*).

Ground cover for sun. Mother-of-thyme (*Thymus praecox arcticus*), lemon thyme (*T. citriodorus*), or woolly thyme (*T. pseudolanuginosus*).

Ground cover for sun or partial shade. Chamomile (*Chamaemelum nobile*).

Ground cover for shade. Sweet woodruff (*Galium odoratum*).

Perennial or shrub border. Common wormwood (*Artemisia absinthium*), salad burnet (*Sanguisorba minor*), lavender (*Lavandula*), monarda, rosemary, scented geraniums (*Pelargonium*).

Hedges. Formal clipped hedge—santolina, germander (*Teucrium*). Informal hedge—lavender, winter savory (*Satureja montana*).

Herbs for moist areas. Angelica, mint, parsley, sweet woodruff.

Herbs for partial shade. Chervil, costmary (*Chrysanthemum balsamita*), lemon balm (*Melissa officinalis*), parsley, sweet woodruff.

Herbs for containers. Crete dittany (*Origanum dictamnus*), chives, costmary, lemon verbena (*Aloysia triphylla*), sage, pineapple sage (*Salvia elegans*), summer savory (*Satureja hortensis*), sweet marjoram, mint, salad burnet.

Potpourris and sachets. Lavender, lemon balm, sweet woodruff, lemon verbena, monarda.

To dry leafy herbs for cooking, cut them early in day before sun gets too hot, but after dew has dried on foliage. (Oil content is highest then.) Leafy herbs are ready to cut from time flower buds begin to form until flowers are half open. (Exceptions: parsley can be cut any time; sage and tarragon may take on strong taste unless cut early in summer.) Don't cut perennial herbs back more than a third; annual herbs may be sheared back to about 4 in. from the ground. Generally you can cut two or three crops for drying during summer. Don't cut perennial herbs after September or new growth won't have chance to mature before cold weather.

Before drying, sort weeds and grass from herbs; remove dead or damaged leaves. Wash off loose dirt in cool water; shake or blot off excess moisture. Tie woody-stemmed herbs such as sweet marjoram or thyme in small bundles and hang upside down from line hung across room. Room should be dark (to preserve color), have good air circulation and warm temperature (about 70°F/21°C) for rapid drying to retain aromatic oils. If room is fairly bright, surround herb bundles with loose cylinders of paper.

For large-leafed herbs such as basil, or short tips that don't bundle easily, dry in tray with light wooden sides and window screen tacked to the bottom. On top of screen place double thickness of cheesecloth. Spread leaves out over surface. Stir leaves daily.

With good air circulation and low humidity, leafy herbs should be crumbly dry in a few days to a week. (If humidity is too high, try drying herbs in a paper bag in the refrigerator.) When herbs are dry, strip leaves from stems and store whole in airtight containers—dark glass is best—until ready to use. Label each container with name of herb and date dried. Check jars first few days after filling to make sure moisture has not formed inside. If it has, pour out contents and dry for a few more days.

To gather seeds, collect seed clusters such as dill, anise, fennel, caraway when they turn brown. Seeds should begin to fall out when clusters are gently tapped. Leave a little of stem attached when you cut each cluster. Collect in box. Flail seeds from clusters and spread them out in sun to dry for several days. Then separate chaff from seed and continue to dry in sun for another 1½–2 weeks. Store seed herbs same way as leafy ones.

EDIBLE HERB BOUQUETS

When cutting fresh herbs for the kitchen, don't worry about snipping more than you need. Put the extra cuttings in a vase of water and use them to decorate the table. They remain kitchen-useful as long as they stay perky (often a week or more). Basil, marjoram, mint, oregano, rosemary, sage, and thyme can be displayed and used this way.

HERCULES' CLUB. See ARALIA spinosa

HERNIARIA glabra

GREEN CARPET, RUPTURE WORT

Caryophyllaceae

PERENNIAL, SOMETIMES TREATED AS ANNUAL

🌿 ZONES 31, 32, 34–35

☼ ◐ ● SUN OR SHADE

💧 REGULAR WATER

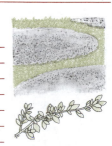

Herniaria glabra

Trailing plant under 2–3 in. tall with crowded, tiny, bright green leaves less than ¼ in. long. Bloom negligible. Where temperatures remain above −20°F/−29°C, grown as an evergreen perennial; foliage turns bronzy red in winter. In colder Zones 42–45, treated as an annual. Spreads

H

well by rooting stems, but won't grow out of control. Use it between stepping-stones, on mounds, around rocks, or in parking strips. Endures occasional footsteps, but not constant traffic. Provide well-drained soil.

HESPERALOE parviflora

Agavaceae

PERENNIAL

ZONES 31, 33, 35

FULL SUN

MODERATE TO LITTLE WATER

Hesperaloe parviflora

Native to Texas, northern Mexico. Makes dense, yuccalike clump of very narrow, swordlike, evergreen leaves 4 ft. long, about 1 in. wide. Pink to rose red, 1¼-in.-long, nodding flowers in slim, 3–4-ft.-high clusters bloom in early summer, with repeat bloom frequent in milder climates. On older plants, spikes can reach 8–9 ft. Good large container plant with loose, relaxed look. *H. p. engelmannii* is similar to species, but its 1-in.-long flowers are more bell shaped.

HESPERIS matronalis

DAME'S ROCKET

Brassicaceae (Cruciferae)

PERENNIAL OR BIENNIAL

ZONES 31, 32, 34–45

FULL SUN OR LIGHT SHADE

REGULAR WATER

Hesperis matronalis

An old-fashioned, cottage-garden plant, freely branched, to 3 ft. tall and as broad, with 4-in., toothed leaves and rounded clusters of ½-in., four-petaled, lavender to purple flowers. Flowers resemble those of stock and are fragrant at night. Grows readily from seed and often self-sows. Old, woody plants should be replaced by young seedlings. White and double-flowered forms exist but are rare.

HEUCHERA

CORAL BELLS, ALUM ROOT

Saxifragaceae

PERENNIALS

ZONES VARY BY SPECIES

LIGHT SHADE IN HOTTEST AREAS

REGULAR WATER

Heuchera

Compact, evergreen clumps of roundish leaves with scalloped edges. Slender, wiry stems 1–2½ ft. high bear open clusters of nodding, bell-shaped flowers ¼ in. or more across, in carmine, reddish pink, coral, crimson, red, rose, greenish, and white. Various types bloom between April and August. Flowers dainty, long lasting in cut arrangements, attractive to hummingbirds. Many recent introductions are grown more for leaf color than floral display.

Use in rock gardens or as ground cover; mass in borders or in front of shrubs; use as edging for beds of delphinium, iris, lilies, peonies, roses. Grow in well-drained, humus-rich soil. Divide clumps every 3 or 4 years in spring. Use young, vigorous, rooted divisions; discard older, woody rootstocks. Sow seed in spring.

H. americana. Zones 32, 34–43. Foliage mound 1–2 ft. high. Leaves 1½–4 ½ in. wide, green mottled white. Flower stalks to 3 ft. high bear tiny greenish white blossoms.

H. brizoides. Zones 32, 34–45. A group of hybrids between *H. sanguinea* and other species. As seed-grown plants, often called Bressingham Hybrids. Flowers come in white and shades of pink and red. 'June Bride' is a good white selection. 'Snowstorm' has deep reddish pink flowers above white-variegated leaves.

H. cultivars (selections and hybrids of *H. americanus* and other species). Zones 32, 34–43. 'Chocolate Ruffles', deep chocolate brown leaves with ruffled edges, purple undersides; 'Chocolate Veil', purple-brown leaves colored purple and silver between the veins, deep burgundy undersides; 'Garnet', deep red winter foliage, brighter red new foliage in spring; 'Lace Ruffles', ruffled and scalloped leaves mottled silvery white; 'Persian Carpet', pinkish burgundy leaves edged and veined in darker purple and with silvery highlights as well; 'Pewter Moon', purple leaves with strong central silvery zone; 'Pewter Veil', shining silvery leaves, small purple flowers; 'Plum Pudding', shiny maroon leaves patterned with silver between the veins; 'Ring of Fire', silvery, purple-veined leaves that develop a red rim in fall; 'Ruby Veil', 8-in. silvery leaves with veins that are red at leaf bases; and 'Velvet Night', deep bluish purple leaves.

H. cylindrica. Zones 31, 32, 34–43. Native to northwestern North America. Mound of foliage to 20 in. high; leaves are rounded to oval, lobed, with scalloped edges and deep green mottled with metallic lighter green. Grown for the foliage.

H. micrantha. Zones 31, 32, 34–43. Native to western U.S. Plant in protected spots in coldest part of range. Grows 1–2 ft. high. Long-stalked, roundish leaves are 1–3 in. long, hairy on both sides, toothed and lobed. Flowers are whitish or greenish, about ⅛ in. long, carried in loose clusters on leafy, 2–3-ft.-tall stems. Hybrid forms developed from *H. micrantha* are more widely adapted than the species itself. 'Palace Purple' has maplelike, rich brownish or purplish red leaves that retain their color all year; 'Ruffles' has leaves that are deeply lobed and ruffled around the edges.

H. sanguinea. CORAL BELLS. Zones 31, 32, 34–45. Native to Mexico and Arizona. Makes neat foliage tufts of round, 1–2-in. leaves with scalloped edges. Slender, wiry stems 1–2 ft. tall bear open clusters of nodding, bell-shaped bright red or coral pink flowers. Varieties with white, pink, or crimson flowers are available. 'Cherry Splash' and 'Frosty' display red flowers above variegated foliage.

H. villosa. Zones 31, 32, 34–41. Native to the Appalachian Mountains. Mound of foliage to 1½ ft. high. Leaves are triangular, lobed with scalloped edges, medium green. Summer flowers are white, occasionally pink, with green tips.

HEUCHERELLA tiarelloides

Saxifragaceae

PERENNIAL

ZONES 31, 32, 34–45

LIGHT SHADE

REGULAR WATER

Heucherella tiarelloides

Hybrid between *Heuchera brizoides* and foam flower (*Tiarella cordifolia*). Combines the flowering habit of the *Heuchera* parent with the heart-shaped leaves of foam flower in a low, clumping, evergreen perennial. Foot-high stems bear narrow sprays of many tiny pinkish bells in late spring or early summer, with a possible second bloom in autumn. Good varieties include 'Bridget Bloom', which produces its shell pink flowers over a long period. 'Pink Frost', another long bloomer, has pink flowers and roundish, mottled gray-green leaves. 'Quicksilver' has metallic silvery leaves with dark bronze veins; large pink flowers age to white. 'Silver Streak' has deeply lobed leaves that are pale silvery lavender and overlaid with deep maroon veins; small sprays of creamy lavender flowers. All forms make a good ground cover for woodland or shaded rock garden. Provide humus-rich soil and good drainage.

HIBISCUS

Malvaceae

SHRUBS, PERENNIALS, AND ANNUALS

⚡ ZONES VARY BY SPECIES

☼ FULL SUN

🔴 REGULAR WATER

Hibiscus

Several species are commonly grown. Most of these are cultivated for big showy flowers, though one is raised for colorful foliage and another for food.

H. acetosella. RED-LEAF HIBISCUS. In the Northeast grown from seed as an annual. Grows 3–5 ft. tall in a single growing season. The foliage, unlobed or lobed somewhat like a maple leaf, may be green or deep purplish red; only the red form is commonly grown, often as a coarse hedge. Cultivated for its foliage rather than the less conspicuous dark-centered red or yellow flowers. The plant may be better known as *H. eetveldeanus*.

H. coccineus. Perennial. Zones 31, 32, 34, 39. Shrubby perennial to 10 ft. high. Lance-shaped, lobed green leaves to 8 in. long. Dark red flowers to 6 in. across, with widespread petals in summer to early autumn.

H. eetveldeanus. See *H. acetosella*

H. grandiflorus. GREAT ROSE MALLOW. Perennial. Zones 31, 32. Bold in all aspects, the large, lobed, silvery gray leaves with a feltlike texture adorn vigorous plants that can reach 6 ft. or more with good growing conditions. Pale pink, 10-in. flowers appear in abundance from mid- to late summer.

H. moscheutos. PERENNIAL HIBISCUS, ROSE-MALLOW. Perennial. Zones 31, 32, 34–41. Largest flowers of all hibiscus, some reaching 1 ft. across, on a plant 6–8 ft. tall; bloom starts in late June and continues until frost. Oval, toothed leaves deep green above, whitish beneath. Plants die down in winter, even in mild climates. Feed at 6- to 8-week intervals during growing season. Protect from wind.

Seed-grown strains often flower the first year if sown indoors and planted out early. Southern Belle strain grows 4 ft. tall; Disco Belle, Frisbee, and Rio Carnival strains are 2–2½ ft. tall. Flowers, 8–12 in. wide, come in red, pink, rose, or white, often with a red eye. The many cutting-grown varieties include 'Blue River', 10-in. pure white flowers; and 'George Riegel', 10-in. ruffled pink blossoms with a red eye. Both of these varieties grow about 4 ft. high. Hybrid 'Lord Baltimore', to 6 ft. tall, produces 10-in. deep red flowers over an exceptionally long bloom period.

H. rosa-sinensis. CHINESE HIBISCUS, TROPICAL HIBISCUS. Tender evergreen shrub. Grow it in containers and shelter indoors over winter; or grow as annual, setting out fresh plants each spring. Also makes a good house plant that can be brought outdoors during the warm season.

One of showiest flowering shrubs. Grows to about 4 ft. tall in a pot, much taller outdoors where hardy. Glossy foliage varies somewhat in size and texture depending on variety. Growth habit may be dense and dwarfish or loose and open. Summer flowers single or double, 4–8 in. wide. Colors range from white through pink to red, from yellow and apricot to orange. Individual flowers last only a day, but the plant blooms continuously.

Requires excellent drainage; if necessary, improve soil or set plants in raised beds or containers. Fertilize monthly (potted plants twice monthly) April to early September, then let growth harden. To develop good branch structure, prune poorly shaped young plants when you set them out in spring. To keep a mature plant growing vigorously, prune out about a third of old wood in early spring. Pinching out tips of stems in spring and summer increases flower production.

H. sabdariffa. ROSELLE, JAMAICA SORREL, JAMAICA FLOWER. Annual. All zones. Tall (4–5 ft.), narrowish plant. Leaves oval, with three to five lobes. Grown for fleshy red base of yellow flowers. These are used in making sauce, jelly, cool drinks, and teas; dried, they are known as Jamaica flowers. Flavor is reminiscent of cranberry or red currant. Plants need long, hot summer to ripen flowers. Bloom begins as days shorten; early frosts prevent harvests. Grow like tomatoes; space plants 1½–2 ft. apart in rows. Can be used as narrow temporary hedge.

H. syriacus. ROSE OF SHARON, SHRUB ALTHAEA. Deciduous shrub. Zones 31, 32, 34–41. To 10–12 ft. tall, upright and compact when young, spreading and open with age. Easily trained to single trunk with treelike top or as an espalier. Leaves medium size, often with three coarsely toothed lobes. Foliage emerges later in spring than does that of most other deciduous shrubs; drops in fall without coloring. Resembles a bush covered with hollyhock flowers from mid- or late summer until frost. Blossoms are single, semidouble, or double, 2½–3 in. across; some have a conspicuously contrasting red to purple throat. Single flowers are slightly more effective, opening somewhat wider, but tend to produce many unattractive capsule-type fruits—which tend to produce many unwanted seedlings.

Easy to grow. Prefers heat, tolerates some drought. Prune to shape; for bigger flowers, cut back previous season's growth in winter, cutting down to two buds. Protect young plants with a winter mulch for first few years. The best varieties, some of them hard to find, include:

'Albus'. Single pure white 4-in. flowers.

'Anemoniflora' ('Paeoniflora'). Semidouble red blossoms with deeper crimson eye.

'Ardens'. Double purple flowers.

'Blue Bird'. Single blue blooms with deep red eye.

'Blushing Bride'. Double bright pink blossoms.

'Boule de Feu'. Double deep violet-pink flowers.

'Coelestis'. Single violet-blue flowers with reddish purple throat.

'Collie Mullens'. Double purplish lavender blossoms.

'Lucy'. Double deep rose flowers with red eye.

'Purpurea'. Semidouble purple blooms with red eye.

'Red Heart'. Single white blossoms with red eye.

'Woodbridge'. Single deep rose flowers with red eye.

Newer selections are sterile triploids, which have a long blooming season and set few or no seedpods. They include:

'Aphrodite'. Rose pink flowers with deep red eye.

'Diana'. Pure white blooms.

'Helene'. White flowers with deep red eye.

'Minerva'. Ruffled lavender pink blossoms with reddish purple eye.

H. trionum. FLOWER-OF-AN-HOUR. Tender annual to 30 in. high. Upright or spreading, to 2 ft. across. Lobed and toothed, hairy, dark green leaves. Trumpet-shaped, light yellow flowers with dark centers and deep purple stamens are borne from summer to early autumn.

HICKORY. See CARYA

HIPPOPHAE rhamnoides

SEA BUCKTHORN

Elaeagnaceae

DECIDUOUS SHRUB OR SMALL TREE

⚡ ZONES 34, 37–45

☼ FULL SUN

🔴🔴 REGULAR TO MODERATE WATER

Hippophae rhamnoides

Sea buckthorn is usually seen as an open, mounding shrub 8–10 ft. tall, although it can grow much taller. Spreads by suckering from roots. Branches are thorny. Leaves are narrow (¼ in. or less), to 3 in. long, silvery green to grayish green. Flowers are inconspicuous, but fruit on female plants is showy—bright orange, round or oval, to ⅓ in. long. Fruit lasts well through winter, apparently being too sour to appeal to birds. It can, however, be made into sauces or jam; it is high in vitamin C. To get fruit, you must have both male and female plants.

Sea buckthorn tolerates low temperatures, wind, poor soils (if they are reasonably well drained), and salt spray. A good screening plant for difficult situations.

FOR GROWING SYMBOL EXPLANATIONS

PLEASE SEE PAGE 113

H

HOGAN CEDAR. See THUJA plicata 'Fastigiata'

HOLCUS mollis
'Albovariegatus'

VARIEGATED CREEPING SOFT GRASS

Poaceae (Gramineae)

PERENNIALS

☘ ZONES 31, 32, 34, 39

☼ ◐ FULL SUN IN COOL CLIMATES, PARTIAL SHADE IN WARM CLIMATES

💧 REGULAR WATER

Holcus mollis

This handsome grass forms an effective, almost white carpet. Its flat leaves measure 6–8 in. long and are creamy white with a blue-green center stripe. Unlike the invasive all-green species, the variegated variety creeps controllably by underground roots, with one plant typically developing a 1½-ft. spread. Among the eight species of holcus, only this loosely tufted variety is cultivated as a garden plant. Use as a ground cover, at the front of a border, and in rock or informal wild gardens. Not grown for blooms. Benefits from cool spring and fall weather and from cutting back flower stalks before going to seed, since self-sown seedlings may revert to green. Cut back in midsummer where summers are hot and humid. Propagate by division in spring. Grow in sun to partial shade in moist, well-drained fertile soil.

HOLODISCUS discolor

ROCK SPIREA, OCEAN SPRAY

Rosaceae

PERENNIAL

☘ ZONES 31, 32, 34, 39

☼ ◐ FULL SUN TO PARTIAL SHADE

💧 REGULAR WATER

Holodiscus discolor

For an insight into growing this American shrub, it helps to know that in its native habitat out West ocean spray grows in the medium rich soil of mixed forests and the poor, thin soil of rocky outcrops. It grows well on dry, sandy sites, where its network of fine surface roots can help prevent erosion. Use as a garden specimen, massed in woodland gardens and informal shrub borders, or at the back of mixed borders. Cultivated for its white flower sprays, this spreading shrub has basal stems up to 10 ft. tall and 2–4-in. leaves with hairy undersides. Airy 10-in. clusters of tiny, white, cup-shaped flowers appear in June. In July, the flowers turn creamy white, and in fall the seed masses are reddish tan. Fragrant in warm weather. Prune deadwood and crowded or unproductive stems right after flowering.

HOLLY. See ILEX

HOLLY FERN. See CYRTOMIUM falcatum

HOLLYHOCK. See ALCEA rosea

HOLLYHOCK, miniature. See SIDALCEA

HOLY THISTLE. See SILYBUM marianum

HONEY LOCUST. See GLEDITSIA triacanthos

HONEYSUCKLE. See LONICERA

HOP. See HUMULUS

HOP HORNBEAM. See OSTRYA

HORDEUM jubatum

SQUIRREL TAIL GRASS

Poaceae (Gramineae)

PERENNIALS

☘ ZONES 31, 32, 34–43

☼ FULL SUN

💧 LESS THAN REGULAR WATER

Hordeum jubatum

Grown for its showy pinkish tan blooms, hordeum is a short-lived perennial grass with arching, light green leaves growing in thick clumps about 2 ft. high. The 5-in. nodding flower heads, which look like dense, silky, hanging tassels or tails, appear from early to midsummer. The blooms are excellent for cutting and also work well in dried arrangements. To dry, cut the flower stems near the base, gather into a little bunch, and hang upside down in a warm dry room until brittle. The plant, native to North America, Europe, and Asia, grows easily from seed, self-sows abundantly, and is sometimes considered a weed for its ability to take hold in dry, sunny fields, meadows, beaches, and roadsides. To cultivate, sow seed in early spring in any average soil and thin seedlings to 1 ft. apart.

HOREHOUND. See MARRUBIUM vulgare

HORNBEAM. See CARPINUS

HORSE BEAN. See BEAN, BROAD

HORSECHESTNUT. See AESCULUS

HORSERADISH

Brassicaceae (Cruciferae)

PERENNIAL

☘ ZONES 31, 32, 34–41

☼ FULL SUN

💧 REGULAR WATER

Horseradish

A large, coarse, weedy-looking plant grown for its large, white roots, which are peeled, grated, and mixed with vinegar or cream to make a condiment. Does best in rich, moist soils in cool regions. Grow it in some sunny out-of-the-way corner. Start with roots planted 1 ft. apart in late winter or early spring.

For an interesting foliage plant, consider growing a variegated from of horseradish, *Amoracia rusticana* 'Variegata'. This cultivar has green-and-white leaves, and offers the bonus of upright sprays of small white flowers in late spring to early summer. Variegated horseradish is not invasive like the regular green type—this variety spreads much more slowly.

HORSETAIL. See EQUISETUM hyemale

FRESH HORSERADISH

Through fall, winter, and spring, harvest pieces of horseradish roots from the outside of the root clump as you need them—that way you'll have your horseradish fresh and hot. Scrub and peel the roots, cutting away any dark parts; then grate them. Mix with vinegar, sweet cream, or sour cream—or simply sprinkle directly onto food.

HOSTA (Funkia)

PLANTAIN LILY

Liliaceae

PERENNIALS

⚘ ZONES 31, 32, 34–45

☼ ● PARTIAL OR FULL SHADE

🌢 REGULAR WATER

Hosta (Funkia)

Their real glory is in their foliage. The thin spikes of blue or white, trumpet-shaped flowers that appear for several weeks in summer are a dividend. There is tremendous variety in leaf size, shape, and color among the available species and named varieties; to appreciate the selection fully, you'll need to consult a specialist's catalog or visit a well-stocked nursery.

Leaves may be heart shaped, lance shaped, oval, or nearly round, carried at the ends of leafstalks that rise from the ground and radiate from the center of a clump. Leaves overlap to form symmetrical, almost shingled foliage mounds ranging in size from dwarf (as small as 3–4 in.) to giant (as big as 5 ft.). Leaf texture may be smooth, quilted, or puckery; surface may be glossy or dull; edges may be smooth or wavy. Colors range from light to dark green to chartreuse, gray, and blue. There are also combinations of colors, including variegations with white, cream, or yellow.

New varieties enter the scene in ever-increasing numbers. In few plants have the species undergone so many name changes; to be sure you are getting the one you want, buy the plant in full leaf or deal with an expert. The plants listed below are just a few of the many possibilities.

Generally, hostas are shade lovers, though some will tolerate sun. Most will grow in considerable sun in cool-summer regions. All forms go dormant (collapse almost to nothing) in winter, even in mild climates. All are splendid companions for ferns and plants with fernlike foliage, such as bleeding heart. Good in containers. In ground, plants last for years; clumps expand in size and shade out weed growth. Feeding once a year will bring on extra leafy splendor. Blanket of peat moss around plants will prevent mud from splattering leaves. Where slugs or snails are a problem, provide protection or try reportedly resistant selections (those with heavily textured or waxy leaves are the best bets).

H. crispula. CURLED-LEAF HOSTA. Ovate, 7-in.-long, dark green leaves with wavy, uneven margins and drooping, curly leaf tips. Foliage mound to 1½ ft. high. Many lavender flowers early in the season. Plant is sometimes confused with *H. fortunei* 'Albo-marginata', which blooms later.

H. decorata (H. 'Thomas Hogg'). Foot-high mound of oval leaves, 6 in. long, bluntly pointed at tips, dull green with silvery white margins. Dark violet flowers early.

H. fortunei. May be an ancient hybrid affiliated with *H. sieboldiana*. Variable plant known mainly for its many selections offering a wide range of foliage color. Typically, plants are 1–1½ ft. high, with oval leaves to 1 ft. long and lilac flowers. Young leaves of 'Albo-picta' are yellow with uneven green border; the yellow fades by summer. Leaves of 'Albo-marginata' have an irregular yellow border that fades to white; late bloom. 'Hyacinthina' has large gray-green leaves edged with a fine white line.

H. hybrids. The following list includes some of the best, most widely grown hostas.

'Antioch'. Broad green leaves with wide, creamy white margins. Lavender flowers well above 1½-ft. foliage mound.

'August Moon'. Spade-shaped, lightly crinkled, bright chartreuse leaves in 1½-ft. mound. White flowers.

'Big Mama'. Large, puckered, blue-green leaves in a 5-ft-wide clump. White flowers in early summer.

'Blue Angel'. Heavily veined blue-green leaves 16 in. long, nearly as wide, in an enormous 4-ft. mound. White flowers over long bloom period. Sun tolerant.

'Blue Ice', 4 in. high and 10 in. wide; blue-green, heart-shaped leaves; pale lavender flowers in early summer.

'Blue Mammoth'. Large, heavy, puckered, blue leaves in a clump almost 5 ft. wide. Pale lavender flowers in late spring.

'Blue Wedgwood'. Slightly wavy-edged, strongly veined, heart-shaped leaves in 1½-ft. mound. Pale lavender flowers early.

'Bright Lights'. Puckered yellow-green leaves have blue-green edging and splashes of blue-green in the center. White flowers in early summer. To 14 in. high and 2 ft. wide.

'Chartreuse Wiggles'. Dwarf (6-in. high), with lance-shaped, wavy-edged, chartreuse-gold leaves. Lavender flowers late.

'Dark Star'. Clump to 1½ ft. wide. Long, pointed, wavy leaves are blue-green with broad white edge. Lavender flowers on 2-ft. stems in mid-summer.

'Eternity', 1½ ft. high and 2½ ft. wide; golden, oval leaves; white flowers in midsummer.

'Eventide', 17 in. high and 3½ ft. wide; broad, pointed, blue-green leaves edged in white; white flowers in late spring.

'Francee'. Broadly heart-shaped leaves to 6 in. long with striking white edges form a 1½–2-ft. mound. Lavender flowers late. Sun tolerant.

'Frances Williams' ('Gold Edge', 'Gold Circle'). Mound to 2½–3 ft. high, made up of round, puckered, blue-green leaves boldly and irregularly edged in yellow. Pale lavender flowers early.

'Fringe Benefit'. Large, puckered, heart-shaped leaves with wide white edge. Lavender flowers in early summer.

'Ginko Craig'. Elongated, frosty green leaves with silver margins in a 1–1½-ft. mound. Abundant lavender flowers.

'Gold Edger'. Heart-shaped, 3-in., chartreuse-gold leaves. Foliage mound to 10 in. high. Masses of lavender flowers. Among the most sun tolerant; in fact, needs some sun for best color.

'Gold Standard'. Heart-shaped, bright golden leaves with a green margin form a 2-ft. mound. Pale lavender flowers. Sun tolerant.

'Grand Master'. Puckered blue-green leaves edged in creamy white form clumps to 20 in. high and 3 ft. wide. Pale lavender flowers in summer.

'Great Expectations'. To 20 in. high and 2½ ft. wide. Leaves have creamy center and blue-green edge. White flowers in early summer. Needs open shade or some morning sun.

'Guacamole'. Forms 2-ft.-wide clump. Yellow-green leaves with green edge, and large, white, fragrant flowers in late spring.

'Hadspen Blue'. Low (1 ft.), with slightly wavy, broadly oval blue leaves. Slug-resistant foliage. Many lavender flowers.

'Halcyon'. Heart-shaped, heavy-textured, blue-gray leaves in a 1½-ft. mound. Short spikes of rich lilac blue flowers.

'Honeybells'. Wavy-edged, yellow-green leaves in 2–2½-ft. mound. Lightly scented, pale lilac flowers.

'June'. Blue-edged leaves have a center that begins creamy white and gradually deepens to a dark yellow green. Clumps are 15 in. high and wide. Lavender blue flowers in early summer.

'Komodo Dragon'. Forms clumps 2½ ft. tall and up to 7 ft. across. Leaves are deep green, pointed, and rippled.

'Krossa Regal'. Big, leathery, frosty blue leaves arch upward and outward to make a 3-ft., vase-shaped plant. Slug-resistant foliage. Late bloom of lavender flower spikes can reach 5–6 ft.

'Lemon Lime'. Small plant just 6 in. tall and 8 in. wide. Leaves are golden chartreuse and fade slowly to light green. Flowers are pale lavender.

'Moonlight Sonata'. Large, rounded, thick blue-green leaves form 4-ft. clump to 20 in. tall. Fragrant white flowers on 2½-ft. stems in early summer.

'Night Before Christmas'. Vigorous plant to 1½ ft. Leaves are 8 in. long, with a dark green edge surrounding a white center that turns green late in the season. Lavender flowers bloom in early summer.

'Patriot'. Similar to 'Francee', but with a broader white edge. Lavender flowers in summer. Clumps grow 15 in. tall and 3 ft. across.

'Paul's Glory'. Gold leaves edged in blue; gold color lightens over the course of the season. Lavender flowers in late spring. Plants are 15 in. tall.

'Piedmont Gold'. Broadly heart-shaped, heavily veined, slightly wavy-edged, 7-in. leaves of glowing chartreuse gold in a 2–2½-ft. mound. White flowers. Sun tolerant.

'Pizzazz'. Forms clumps 1½ ft. high and 2 ft. wide. Rounded blue-green leaves have a pebbly texture and a wide border of creamy white. Light lavender flowers in early summer.

H

H

'Rhapsody', 3 ft. tall and 4 ft. wide; green leaves with broad white edge; lavender flowers in early summer.

'Royal Standard'. Glossy light green leaves, elongated and undulated, in a 2-ft. mound. Fragrant white flowers. Sun tolerant.

'Sagae'. Upright habit, forming clumps 2 ft. high and 3 ft. wide. Blue-gray leaves bordered with broad edge of creamy white. Pale lavender flowers on tall stems in summer.

'Shade Fanfare'. Leaves are pointed ovals to 7 in. long, green to gold with creamy white margin. Foliage mound to 1½ ft. high. Lavender flowers. Very sun tolerant.

'So Sweet'. Green leaves have a border that starts out gold and changes to creamy white. Fragrant white flowers in late summer. To 15 in. high.

'Sum and Substance'. Textured, shiny yellow leaves to 20 in. long form a mound to 3 ft. high, 5 ft. wide. Slug-resistant, very sun tolerant.

'Sun Power'. Pointed leaves of bright gold form vase-shaped clumps 22 in. high and 3 ft. wide. Light lavender flowers bloom in early summer.

'Wide Brim'. Blue-green leaves with broad creamy white edge form clumps 1½ ft. high. Light lavender flowers in late spring.

'Zounds'. Bright golden leaves with corrugated texture form clumps to 2 ft. tall and 3 ft. wide. White flowers in early summer.

H. lancifolia (H. japonica). NARROW-LEAFED PLANTAIN LILY. Leaves glossy deep green, 6 in. long, and lance shaped, the bases tapering into the long stalks. Foot-high foliage mound. Pale lavender flowers late.

H. montana. Oval- to heart-shaped leaves are prominently veined, vary in color from pale green to medium or dark green. White to grayish flowers in early summer to 2½ ft. high.

H. nakaiana 'Golden Tiara'. Foot-high mound of broadly heart-shaped leaves to 4 in. long, light green with gold edge. Purple flowers. Sun tolerant. 'Diamond Tiara', pale olive green leaves bordered in white and splashed with gray green. 'Grand Tiara', round golden leaves marked with green in the center. 'Platinum Tiara', golden leaves bordered in white.

H. plantaginea (H. grandiflora, H. subcordata). FRAGRANT PLANTAIN LILY. Leaves glossy bright green, to 10 in. long, broadly oval with parallel veins and quilted surface. Foliage mound 2 ft. high. Noticeably fragrant, large white flowers late. 'Aphrodite' is a double-flowered variety. 'Ming Treasure', light green leaves edged in yellow-green, fragrant white flowers in late summer; to 1½-ft. tall.

H. sieboldiana (H. glauca). Blue-green, broadly heart shaped leaves, 10–15 in. long, heavily veined and puckered. Many slender, pale lilac flower spikes nestle close to 2½-ft. foliage mound early in season. Foliage dies back early. 'Elegans' has the standard foliage, but leaves are covered in a blue-gray bloom; slug resistant.

H. sieboldii 'Kabitan'. Wavy, lance-shaped leaves to 5 in. long, chartreuse to yellow with thin green margins. White flowers rise above foot-high foliage mound.

H. tardiflora. Small plant (to 1 ft. high), with lance-shaped leaves to 6 in. long. Spikes of pale purple flowers, same height as foliage clump, come very late. More sun tolerant than most.

H. tokudama. Like *H. sieboldiana,* but smaller (to 1 ft.), with a more crepelike texture. Slug-resistant foliage. White flowers. 'Aureonebulosa' has gold leaves bordered in blue. 'Flavocircinalis', with irregular yellow margins, is more sun tolerant than the species.

H. undulata (H. media picta, H. variegata). WAVY-LEAFED PLANTAIN LILY. Wavy-edged, narrowly oval leaves, 6–8-in. long, in a 1½-ft. mound. Typical leaf has a creamy white center stripe, the balance of the leaf being green. Foliage is used in arrangements. Pale lavender flowers. 'Albo-marginata' has creamy white margins on leaves. 'Erromena' is an all-green variety.

H. ventricosa (H. caerulea). BLUE PLANTAIN LILY. So named for violet-blue blossoms, not for foliage color. Leaves are glossy deep green, broadly heart shaped, prominently veined, to 8 in. long, in a 2-ft. mound. Leaves of 'Aureo-maculata' are yellowish green with a green border. In 'Aureo-marginata' ('Variegata'), each leaf is green edged with creamy white; sun tolerant.

H. venusta. Small clumps of deep green, wavy-edged leaves to just 4 in. high and 10 in. across. Lavender flowers, midsummer into autumn.

HOUSELEEK. See SEMPERVIVUM

HOUSTONIA caerulea (Hedyotis caerulea)

BLUETS, QUAKER LADIES

Rubiaceae

PERENNIAL

ZONES 31, 32, 34–43

LIGHT SHADE

REGULAR WATER

Creeping perennial making small (2–3-in.) mounds of tiny oval leaves. Flowers appear singly on 2–2½-in. stalks in late spring. The ½-in.-wide, four-lobed flowers are pale blue (sometimes white) with a yellow eye. Individually small, they are profuse enough to create a charming effect in a moist, lightly shaded garden. Use in rock gardens, around stepping-stones, or as carpet for large potted shrubs like camellia or aucuba. In the wild, thrives among mosses in light shade under tall oak trees. Will also grow in poor lawns. In cool-summer areas, tolerates considerable sun.

Houstonia caerulea

HOUTTUYNIA cordata

Saururaceae

PERENNIAL

ZONES 31, 32, 34–41

SUN OR SHADE

AMPLE WATER

Underground rhizomes send up 2–3-in. leaves that look much like those of English ivy. When crushed, leaves give off a peculiar scent somewhat reminiscent of orange peel. Inconspicuous clusters of white-bracted flowers like tiny dogwood blossoms. Unusual ground cover that disappears completely in winter, even in mild climates. 'Variegata' ('Chameleon') has showy splashes of cream, pink, yellow, and red on foliage. 'Plena' has more prominent flowers consisting of several rows of white bracts; leaves are plain green. Plants can spread aggressively in wet ground. Attractive in container or, if curbed, in shady garden. Can grow in standing water; good for pond sites.

Houttuynia cordata

HOVENIA dulcis

JAPANESE RAISIN TREE

Rhamnaceae

DECIDUOUS TREE

ZONES 31, 32, 34–41

FULL SUN

REGULAR WATER

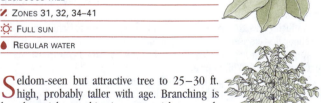

Seldom-seen but attractive tree to 25–30 ft. high, probably taller with age. Branching is largely upright, resulting in a narrowish to rounded head. Broadly oval, shiny dark green leaves are 4–6 in. long, prominently marked by three veins running lengthwise. No real fall color. Clustered greenish white flowers are inconspicuous but fragrant. Blooms are followed in early autumn by small reddish fruits partially enclosed by their stalks; stalks swell into edible

Hovenia dulcis

large, twisted, asymmetrical, fleshy red bodies a sweet, faintly raisinlike flavor. Attractive lawn, garden, or small street tree. No serious pest or disease problems.

HOWEA

Howea

Arecaceae (Palmae)

PALMS

ALL ZONES, TREATED AS HOUSE PLANTS

PARTIAL SHADE

REGULAR WATER

Native to Lord Howe Island in the South Pacific. These feathery palms are the kentia palms of florists, and are usually sold under the name "kentia." Reach about 8 ft. in a container. Give indirect light indoors. Move outdoors to shady deck or patio in summer.

Howeas are ideal pot plants—the classic parlor palms. Keep fronds clean and dust free to minimize spider mite problem.

H. belmoreana. SENTRY PALM. Less common than *H. forsterana*, smaller and more compact, with overarching leaves. Withstands some watering neglect, drafts, dust.

H. forsterana. PARADISE PALM. Larger than *H. belmoreana*, with longer leaves and long, drooping leaflets.

HUCKLEBERRY. See GAYLUSSACIA

HUMULUS

Humulus

HOP

Cannabaceae

PERENNIAL VINES

ZONES 31, 32, 34–45

FULL SUN

REGULAR WATER

Extremely fast-growing twining vines. Large, deeply lobed leaves attractive for summer screening on trellises or arbors. Hop vines will camouflage a run-down shed or an ugly fence. Train on a tripod of sturdy poles for vertical accent in the garden. Plants sold in nurseries are typically female (sexes are separate); no pollinator required.

Hops thrive in any average garden soil or in containers. Sow outdoors where plants are to grow when frost danger is past in spring, or indoors four to six weeks before the last expected frost, transplant outdoors after frost. Plants are likely to self-sow; pull up unwanted seedlings to keep plants from spreading.

H. japonicus. JAPANESE HOP. Perennial grown as annual. All zones. To 20–30 ft. Flowers do not make true hops. 'Variegatus' has foliage marked with white. Flowers in greenish clusters like pine cones. Sow seeds in spring where plants are to grow. Roots are perennial; tops die back in fall.

H. lupulus. COMMON HOP. This plant produces the hops used to flavor beer. Grow from roots (not easy to find in nurseries) planted in rich soil in early spring. Place thick end up, just below soil surface. Furnish supports for vertical climbing. Shoots appear in midspring and grow quickly to 15–25 ft. by midsummer. Leaves with three to five lobes, toothed. Squarish, hairy stems twine vertically; to get horizontal growth, twine stem tips by hand. Light green hops (soft, flaky, 1–2-in. cones of bracts and flowers) form in late summer. They're attractive and have fresh, piny fragrance. Cut back stems to ground after frost turns them brown. Regrowth comes the following spring. Tender hop shoots can be cooked as a vegetable. 'Aureus' has attractive chartreuse leaves in spring.

HUNNEMANNIA
fumariifolia

Hunnemannia fumariifolia

MEXICAN TULIP POPPY, GOLDEN CUP

Papaveraceae

PERENNIAL, USUALLY TREATED AS ANNUAL

ALL ZONES

FULL SUN

MODERATE TO LITTLE WATER

Related to California poppy (*Eschscholzia californica*). Bushy, open plant to 2–3 ft. high, with very finely divided blue-green leaves. Clear soft golden yellow, cup-shaped flowers with crinkled petals are about 3 in. across, bloom summer and early fall. Showy plant in masses. Blooms last for a week in water if cut in bud. Plant from nursery containers or sow seed in place in warm, sunny location; thin seedlings to 1 ft. apart. Reseeds. Needs excellent drainage. 'Sunlite' has clear yellow flowers.

HYACINTH BEAN. See DOLICHOS lablab

NATURALIZING A BLUEBELL PLANTING

Broadcast a handful of bulbs over an area and plant them where they fall. For a realistic effect, rearrange the bulbs before planting so they are closest together at one end of a group or toward the center—as though the colony originated at one spot and gradually increased outward. Mostly space bulbs about 6 in. apart.

HYACINTHOIDES
(Scilla, Endymion)

Hyacinthoides (Scilla, Endymion)

ENGLISH AND SPANISH BLUEBELLS, WOOD HYACINTH

Liliaceae

BULBS

ZONES VARY BY SPECIES

FULL SUN OR PARTIAL SHADE

REGULAR WATER DURING GROWTH AND BLOOM

These spring bloomers are still popularly known as *Scilla* (and sold by most dealers as such), but the current botanical name is *Hyacinthoides*. They resemble hyacinths but are taller, with looser flower clusters and fewer, narrower leaves.

Climate may determine which of the following two species is better for you. Spanish bluebell is the better choice in warmer regions; the English species prefers definite winter cold and moderate to cool summers. When grown near each other, they often hybridize, producing intermediate forms. Plant in fall—3 in. deep in mild climates, to 6 in. deep where winters are severe. Propensity for reseeding makes these plants good choices for naturalizing. Plant informal drifts among tall shrubs, under deciduous trees, among low-growing perennials. Clumps can be divided in autumn. The plants also thrive in pots and are good for cutting.

H. hispanica (Scilla campanulata, S. hispanica). SPANISH BLUEBELL. Zones 31, 32, 34–43. Prolific, vigorous, with sturdy, 20-in. stems bearing 12 or more nodding bells about ¾ in. long. Blue is the most popular color, 'Excelsior' (deep blue) the most popular variety. There are also white, pink, and rose forms. The inch-wide, straplike leaves can look a little ratty before they die back.

H

H. non-scripta (Scilla non-scripta). ENGLISH BLUEBELL, WOOD HYACINTH. Zones 31, 32, 34, 35, 37, 39. Fragrant flowers are narrower and smaller than those of Spanish bluebell, on 1-ft. stems that arch at the tip. Strap-shaped leaves are also narrower—only about ½ in. wide. 'Alba' is white flowered, 'Rosea' pink.

HYACINTHUS

HYACINTH

Liliaceae

BULBS

ZONES 31, 32, 34–45

FULL SUN OR HIGH SHADE

REGULAR WATER DURING GROWTH AND BLOOM

Hyacinthus

As garden plants, best adapted in cold-winter climates. Bell-shaped, fragrant flowers in loose or tight spikes rise from basal bundle of narrow bright green leaves. All are spring blooming. Where winters are cold, plant in September–October. In Zones 31–32, plant October–November.

H. amethystinus. See *Brimeura amethystina*

H. azureus. See *Muscari azureum*

H. orientalis. COMMON HYACINTH. Grows to 1 ft., with fragrant, bell-shaped flowers in white, pale blue, or purple blue.

Dutch hyacinth, derived from *H. orientalis* by breeding and selection, has large, dense spikes of waxy, bell-like, fragrant flowers in white, cream, buff, and shades of blue, purple, pink, red, and salmon. The size of the flower spike is directly related to the size of the bulb. Biggest bulbs are desirable for exhibition plants or for potting; next largest size is most satisfactory for bedding outside. Small bulbs give smaller, looser clusters with more widely spaced flowers. These are sometimes called miniature hyacinths.

Set the larger bulbs 6 in. deep, smaller bulbs 4 in. Hyacinth bulbs have invisible barbs on their surfaces that can cause some people's skin to itch; after handling, wash hands before touching face or eyes. Hyacinths look best when massed or grouped; rows look stiff, formal. Mass bulbs of a single color beneath flowering tree or in border. Leave bulbs in ground after bloom, continue to feed. Flowers tend to be smaller in succeeding years, but maintain same color and fragrance.

Choice container plants. Pot in porous mix with tip of bulb near surface. After potting, cover containers with thick mulch of sawdust, wood shavings, or peat moss to keep bulbs cool, moist, shaded until roots well formed; remove mulch, place in full light when tops show. Also grow hyacinths in water in special hyacinth glass, the bottom filled with pebbles and water. Keep in dark, cool place until rooted, give light when top growth appears; place in sunny window when leaves have turned uniformly green.

HYDRANGEA

Hydrangeaceae (Saxifragaceae)

DECIDUOUS SHRUBS OR VINES

ZONES VARY BY SPECIES

SOME SHADE IN HOT-SUMMER CLIMATES

REGULAR WATER

Hydrangea

Big, bold leaves and large clusters of long-lasting flowers in white, pink, red, or blue. Summer, fall bloom. Flower clusters may contain sterile flowers (conspicuous, with large, petal-like sepals) or fertile flowers (small, starry petaled); or they may feature a cluster of small fertile flowers surrounded by ring of big sterile ones (these are called lace cap hydrangeas). Sterile flowers last long, often holding up for months, gradually changing in color. Effective as single plants, massed, or in tubs on paved terrace.

Easy to grow in rich, porous soil. Fast growing, so prune to control size and form. Most hydrangeas bloom on the previous year's wood and should be pruned after flowering. (No flowering will occur if flower buds are killed in cold winters.) *H. arborescens* blooms on new growth and should be pruned in the late dormant season. On all types, to get biggest flower clusters, reduce number of stems; for numerous medium-size clusters, keep more stems.

H. anomala. CLIMBING HYDRANGEA. Deciduous vine. Zones 31, 32, 34–41. Climbs high by clinging aerial rootlets. Shrubby and sprawling without support. Roundish, 2–4-in.-long, green, heart-shaped leaves. Mature plants develop short, stiff, flowering branches with flat white flower clusters, 6–10 in. wide, in lace cap effect. Old plants have peeling, cinnamon-colored bark. *H. a. petiolaris (H. petiolaris)*, more common form in cultivation, differs hardly at all.

H. arborescens. SMOOTH HYDRANGEA. Deciduous shrub. Zones 31, 32, 34–43. Upright, dense to 10 ft. Oval, grayish green, 4–8-in. leaves. In basic species, most flowers in a cluster are fertile; the few sterile ones are not plentiful enough for full lace cap effect. Much showier is 'Annabelle', which produces enormous (to 1-ft.) globular clusters of sterile white flowers on a plant about 4 ft. tall. 'Grandiflora' has 6-in. clusters on a similarly sized plant.

H. aspera strigosa. Deciduous shrub. Zones 31, 32, 34, 39. Upright to 10 ft. high and wide. Lance-shaped, dark green leaves. Flat clusters of fertile blue to purple flowers surrounded by white sterile flowers, sometimes tinged with pink or mauve, in late summer to autumn.

H. macrophylla (H. hortensia, H. opuloides, H. otaksa). BIGLEAF HYDRANGEA, GARDEN HYDRANGEA. Deciduous shrub. Zones 31, 32, 34 (warmer parts), 39. Symmetrical, rounded habit; grows to 4–8 ft. or even 12 ft. high. Thick, shining, coarsely toothed leaves to 8 in. long; white, pink, red, or blue flowers in big clusters. In many varieties, blue or pink is determined by soil pH—bluest color produced in acid soil, reddest in alkaline soil. Plants can be made (or kept) blue by applying aluminum sulfate to soil; plants can be kept red or made redder by liming the soil or applying superphosphate in quantity. Treatment must be started well ahead of bloom to be effective.

Great performer in areas where winters are fairly mild, but disappointing where plants freeze to ground every year (may never bloom under these conditions, since flower buds are produced on old wood). Protect in colder part of range by mounding soil or leaves over base of plants.

There are hundreds of named varieties, and plants may be sold under many names. Florists' plants are usually French hybrids, shorter (1–3 ft. tall) and larger flowered than old garden varieties. Among the hardier garden varieties are 'All Summer Beauty', 3–4 ft. tall, with flower heads produced on current season's growth (unlike other bigleaf hydrangea varieties); 'Blue Wave', 6–7 ft. tall, with lace cap flowers; 'Domotoi', with double florets in large heads; 'Forever Pink', 3 ft. tall, with 4–5-in. flower heads; 'Goliath', with 15-in. flower heads; and 'Pia', a dwarf with tight clusters of heavy-textured small florets. Several lace cap varieties feature silver-variegated foliage: 'Silver Variegated Mariesii', 'Quadricolor', 'Tricolor', and 'Variegata'.

H. paniculata 'Grandiflora'. PEEGEE HYDRANGEA. Deciduous shrub. Zones 31, 32, 34–43. Upright, of coarse texture. Can be trained as a 25-ft. tree, but best as a 10–15-ft. shrub. Leaves 5 in. long, turn bronzy in fall. Mainly fertile flowers in upright 10–15-in. clusters, white slowly fading to pinky bronze. 'Kyushu' has glossy leaves. 'Praecox' blooms earlier. 'Tardiva' blooms later, has more pyramidal clusters with a mix of sterile and fertile flowers. 'Unique' has larger flower heads. 'White Moth' produces large round flowers in autumn.

H. quercifolia. OAKLEAF HYDRANGEA. Deciduous shrub. Zones 31, 32, 34–41. Broad, rounded shrub to 6 ft., with handsome, deeply lobed, oaklike, 8-in.-long leaves that turn bronze or crimson in fall. Elongated clusters of fertile and sterile white flowers in late spring and early summer turn pinkish purple as they age. Improvements on the species include 'Alice', deep green leaves turning burgundy in autumn, large flower clusters; 'Peewee', to 4 ft. high, chocolate to burgundy fall foliage, white flowers; 'Snow Queen', with larger flower clusters; and 'Snowflake', with extra petals for double-flowered effect. Stems and flower buds may be damaged where temperatures go much below −10°F/−23°C; in these areas, plant is best grown for its handsome foliage. Makes an attractive container plant that can be protected in cold weather.

H. sargentiana (H. aspera sargentiana). Deciduous shrub. Zones 31, 32. Upright to 10 ft. high and 8 ft. wide. Thick, bristly stems, wide, oval, dark green bristly leaves. In late summer to autumn, flat clusters of blue or purple fertile flowers surrounded by white sterile flowers.

H. serrata. Deciduous shrub. Zones 31, 32, 34, 39. Similar to *H. macrophylla*, but generally a smaller plant with smaller leaves, smaller flowers, and more slender stems. The lace cap variety 'Blue Billow', 3 ft. tall, maintains blue color in most soils. 'Preziosa', to 4 ft., has round pink flower clusters that age to red.

DRYING HYDRANGEA FLOWERS

The big blossoms of hydrangeas make good cut flowers and they dry well, too. Peegee hydrangea (*Hydrangea paniculata* 'Grandiflora') dries best, its creamy white flowers taking on pinkish tones before finally fading to light beige. Drying the flowers is a snap. Cut them when they begin to turn pinkish and feel somewhat papery. Stand the stems loosely in a tall container with a couple of inches of water in the bottom. Let the water evaporate naturally and the flowers will dry beautifully in their upright position.

Hydrangeaceae. The hydrangea family includes several woody-stemmed plants formerly listed under Saxifragaceae. *Hydrangea* and mock orange (*Philadelphus*) are examples.

HYDRASTIS canadensis

GOLDEN SEAL

Ranunculaceae

PERENNIAL

⚡ ZONES 32, 34, 35, 37, 39

☼ ● PARTIAL OR FULL SHADE

💧 REGULAR WATER

Hydrastis canadensis

Native to eastern U.S. Roots are used in herbal remedies. Makes an unusual ground cover in woodland or shade gardens. Plant grows from a thick yellow rootstock, sending up two deeply lobed 8-in. leaves and a 1-ft. stalk topped by two smaller leaves and an inconspicuous whitish to yellowish green flower. The blossom is followed by a large, showy red berry that resembles an outsize raspberry, though it isn't edible. Plant will grow in ordinary good garden soil, but it prefers plenty of leaf mold or compost. A modestly attractive choice for native plant enthusiasts.

Hydrophyllaceae. The waterleaf family, largely but not entirely native to North America, includes annuals, perennials, and a few shrubs. Many have flowers in clusters shaped like a shepherd's crook. *Nemophila* is among the few kinds sometimes grown in gardens.

HYLOMECON japonicum

WOOD POPPY

Papaveraceae

PERENNIAL

⚡ ZONES 32, 34–41

☼ ● PARTIAL TO DEEP SHADE

💧 REGULAR WATER

Hylomecon japonicum

This dainty rhizomatous woodland plant forms sizable clumps to 1 ft. high, and features pale green, featherlike leaves to 8 in. long. Deep yellow four-petaled flowers to 2 in. across bloom in late spring and early summer. Thrives in cool, shady woodland or wild garden settings. Does best in moist but well-drained, rich, and slightly acidic soil.

HYMENOCALLIS

Amaryllidaceae

BULBS

⚡ ALL ZONES; DIG AND STORE DECIDUOUS TYPES, OR GROW IN POTS

☼ ◑ FULL SUN OR PARTIAL SHADE

💧 REGULAR WATER DURING GROWTH AND BLOOM

🔻 BULBS ARE POISONOUS IF INGESTED

Hymenocallis

Clumps of strap-shaped leaves like those of amaryllis. The 2-ft. stems bear several very fragrant flowers in summer; blooms resemble daffodils in having a center cup, but cup is surrounded by six slender, spidery segments. Deciduous species maintain foliage throughout summer if watered, then die back in fall. Unusual plants for borders or containers. Plant in rich, well-drained soil after frost danger is past in spring. Set bulbs with tips 1 in. below surface. Deciduous sorts can be dug after foliage has yellowed (do not cut off fleshy roots), dried in an inverted position, and stored in open trays in a cool place.

H. festalis. Deciduous. Free flowering. Each stem bears four or more pure white flowers, the cup surrounded by very narrow curved segments. Leaves resemble those of *H. narcissiflora*.

H. latifolia (H. keyensis). SPIDER LILY. Evergreen. Native to Florida and the West Indies. Borne in clusters of 6–12, white flowers consist of 3-in. cup surrounded by 5-in.-long, spidery segments.

H. narcissiflora (Ismene calathina). BASKET FLOWER, PERUVIAN DAFFODIL. Deciduous. Leaves 1½–2 ft. long, 1–2 in. wide. White, green-striped flowers in clusters of two to five. Variety 'Advance' has pure white flowers, faintly lined with green in throat.

H. 'Sulfur Queen'. Deciduous. Primrose yellow flowers with light yellow, green-striped throat. Leaves like those of *H. narcissiflora*.

HYPERICUM

ST. JOHNSWORT

Hypericaceae

SHRUBS AND PERENNIALS, MOSTLY EVERGREEN

⚡ ZONES VARY BY SPECIES

☼ ◑ FULL SUN OR PARTIAL SHADE

💧 REGULAR TO MODERATE WATER

Hypericum

Large group of shrubs and perennials bearing yellow flowers resembling single roses with prominent sunburst of stamens in center. Open, cup-shaped, five-petaled blooms range in color from creamy yellow to gold; flowers may be solitary or in clusters. Neat leaves vary in form and color. Plants are useful for summer flower color and fresh green foliage. Various kinds used for mass plantings, ground covers, informal hedges, borders.

H. androsaemum. Semievergreen shrub. Zones 31, 32, 34, 39. Shade-tolerant European native. To 3 ft. tall, with stems arching toward the top. Leaves to 4 in. long, 2 in. wide. Clusters of ¾-in., golden yellow flowers at tops of stems and at ends of side branches in summer. Blossoms are followed by berrylike fruits that turn from red to purple to black as they age. Useful as tall ground cover at edge of woods, on shaded slopes, in a wild garden.

H. beanii (H. patulum henryi). Semievergreen, shrubby perennial; more perennial-like in colder part of range. Zones 31, 32. To 4 ft. tall, with light green, oblong leaves on graceful, willowy branches. Flowers brilliant golden yellow, 2 in. across, midsummer into fall. Good for low, untrimmed hedge, mass planting. Shabby winter appearance.

H. buckleii. Deciduous shrub. Zones 31, 32, 34–41. Forms low mat of oblong leaves; with clusters of bright yellow flowers in summer.

H. calycinum. AARON'S BEARD, CREEPING ST. JOHNSWORT. Evergreen to semievergreen shrublet; tops often killed in cold winters but come back in spring. Zones 31, 32, 34. Grows to 1 ft. high and spreads by vigorous underground stems. Short-stalked leaves to 4 in. long are medium green in sun, yellow green in shade. Flowers bright yellow, 3 in. across throughout summer. A tough, dense ground cover that competes successfully with tree roots, takes poor soil. Fast growing; will control erosion on hillsides. May invade other plantings unless confined. Plant from flats or as rooted stems; set 1½ ft. apart. Clip or mow tops every 2 or 3 years during dormant season.

H. coris. Evergreen shrublet. Zones 31, 32. Grows 6–12 in. or taller. Leaves narrow, ½–1 in. long, in whorls of four to six. Flowers yellow, ¾ in. across, in loose clusters, spring or early summer. Good ground cover or rock garden plant.

H. densiflorum. Deciduous shrub. Zones 31, 32, 34–41. Upright and bushy to 9 ft. Narrow, oblong leaves, golden yellow flowers mid- to late summer.

H. frondosum. Deciduous shrub. Zones 31, 32, 34, 39. Native to southeastern U.S. Grows 1–3 ft. tall, with mounding form. Blue-green leaves set off clusters of 1½-in. bright yellow flowers that bloom from midsummer to early autumn. 'Sunburst' forms a tight mound to 3 ft. tall and wide.

H. 'Hidcote' (H. patulum 'Hidcote'). Evergreen to semievergreen shrub; perennial that dies to the ground in coldest part of range. Zones 31, 32. To 4 ft. tall in mildest climates; in cold areas, freezes keep height closer to 2 ft. Leaves 2–3 in. long. Yellow, 3-in.-wide flowers all summer. Very prone to root rot and wilt in warm, humid areas.

H. kouytchense. Semievergreen shrub. Zones 31, 32. Twiggy, rounded growth 1½–2 ft. tall, 2–3 ft. wide. Pointed oval, 2-in. leaves; golden yellow, 2–3-in.-wide flowers, heavily produced in summer. Often sold as *H. 'Sungold'*.

H. moseranum. GOLD FLOWER. Evergreen shrub or perennial. Zones 31, 32, 34. Hybrid plant. Where hardy, may die back to roots during a severe winter. Mulch well for winter protection. Moundlike habit with arching, reddish stems. Leaves 2 in. long, blue green beneath. Golden yellow flowers, 2½ in. across, are borne singly or in clusters of up to five. Blooms in summer, possibly into fall. Cut back in early spring. 'Tricolor' has gray-green leaves tinged with pink and edged in white.

H. patulum henryi. See *H. beanii*.

H. prolificum. SHRUBBY ST. JOHNSWORT. Deciduous shrub. Zones 31, 32, 34–43. Upright and dense, to 3 ft. high. Narrow, glossy, blue-green leaves. Bright yellow flowers through much of the summer.

H. reptans. Evergreen shrublet. Zones 32, 34. Flat-growing plant that roots along ground. Leaves ¼–½ in. long, crowded along stems; flowers to 1¾ in. wide in summer. Rock garden plant. Protect from frosts in colder regions.

H. 'Rowallane'. Evergreen to semievergreen shrub; perennial that dies to the ground in coldest part of range. Zones 31, 32. Upright and rather straggly growth to 3–6 ft. Flowers bright yellow, 2½–3 in. across, profuse in late summer and fall. Leaves 2½–3½ in. long. Remove older branches annually.

H. 'Sungold'. See *H. kouytchense*.

HYPOESTES phyllostachya
(H. sanguinolenta)

FRECKLE FACE, PINK POLKA-DOT PLANT

Acanthaceae

PERENNIAL TREATED AS ANNUAL OR HOUSE PLANT

⚡ ALL ZONES AS ANNUAL

☼ ◑ FULL SUN OR LIGHT SHADE

● REGULAR WATER

Hypoestes phyllostachya

Though this tender plant is actually a perennial, it is almost always grown as bedding annual or house plant. Can reach 1–2 ft. tall. Slender stems bear oval, 2–3-in.-long leaves spotted irregularly with pink or white. A selected form known as 'Splash' has larger spots. Tiny,

inconspicuous lavender flowers are not always produced. For indoor use, plant in loose, peaty mixture in pots or planters. Feed with liquid fertilizer. Pinch tips to make bushy.

Hypoxidaceae. The star grass family consists of a small number of perennial plants growing from corms or rhizomes. Flowers have six equal segments and resemble those of the lily and amaryllis families. Yellow star grass (*Hypoxis*) and *Rhodohypoxis* are the only two commonly seen.

HYPOXIS hirsuta

YELLOW STAR GRASS

Hypoxidaceae

PERENNIAL

⚡ ZONES 31, 32, 34–41

☼ ◑ FULL SUN OR LIGHT SHADE

● ● REGULAR TO MODERATE WATER

Hypoxis hirsuta

Native from Maine to Florida and west to Texas. Usually found in dryish woodlands, growing in sandy or stony soil in full sun or light shade. Grassy, somewhat hairy, 1-ft.-long leaves rise from a short, cormlike rhizome. In spring and early summer, a 1-ft.-tall stem carries from one to seven bright yellow, starlike, inch-wide flowers. A second bloom may follow later. Interesting primarily to native plant enthusiasts or rock gardeners.

HYSSOP, ANISE. See AGASTACHE foeniculum

HYSSOPUS officinalis

HYSSOP

Lamiaceae (Labiatae)

PERENNIAL HERB

⚡ ZONES 31, 32, 34–45

☼ ◑ FULL SUN OR LIGHT SHADE

● ● REGULAR TO MODERATE WATER

Hyssopus officinalis

Compact growth to 1½–2 ft. Narrow, glossy dark green, pungent-smelling leaves on woody-based stems. Profusion of dark blue flower spikes throughout summer and into autumn; not a dramatic show, but pleasant looking. Selections with white, pink, or lavender blooms are available, though they may be difficult to find.

Start from seed sown in early spring, or from stem cuttings in late spring or early summer. Once established, may self-sow. Tolerates some drought but will thrive with routine watering if drainage is good. Tolerates trimming as a low hedge or knot garden border. Peppery leaves sometimes used in cooking.

IBERIS

CANDYTUFT

Brassicaceae (Cruciferae)

PERENNIALS AND ANNUALS

⚡ ZONES VARY BY SPECIES

☼ FULL SUN

● REGULAR WATER

Iberis

Free-blooming plants with clusters of white, lavender, lilac, pink, rose, purple, carmine, or crimson flowers. Perennial candytufts bloom from early spring to summer; can be used as winter annuals in mildest climates. Annual species bloom in spring and summer; they are most floriferous where summer nights are cool. Use all types for borders, cutting; perennials for edging, rock gardens, small-scale ground covers, containers.

All types need well-drained soil. In early spring or (in mild climates) fall, sow seed of annuals in place or in flats; set transplants 6–9 in. apart. Plant perennials in spring or fall. After bloom, shear lightly to stimulate new growth.

I. amara. HYACINTH-FLOWERED CANDYTUFT, ROCKET CANDYTUFT. Annual. All zones. Fragrant white flowers in tight, round clusters that elongate into hyacinthlike spikes on 15-in. stems. Narrow, slightly fuzzy leaves.

I. gilbraltarica. Perennial. Zones 31, 32. Resembles *I. sempervirens* but is less hardy to cold and bears flatter clusters of light pinkish or purplish flowers, sometimes white near center.

I. sempervirens. EVERGREEN CANDYTUFT. Perennial. Zones 31, 32, 34–45. Grows 8 in. to 1 ft. or even 1½ ft. high, spreading about as wide. Narrow, shiny dark green leaves are good looking all year. Pure white flower clusters carried on stems long enough to cut for bouquets. Lower, more compact varieties include 'Alexander's White', 6 in. tall, with fine-textured foliage; 'Kingwood Compact', also 6 in. high; 'Little Gem', 4–6 in. tall; and 'Purity', 6–12 in. tall, wide spreading. 'Snowflake', 4–12 in. tall and spreading to 1½–3 ft., has broader, more leathery leaves than the species; also has larger flowers in larger clusters on shorter stems. It is extremely showy in spring, with sporadic bloom through summer and fall. 'Snowmantle' is a similar vigorous variety. 'Autumn Snow' is a reliable spring and fall bloomer.

I. umbellata. GLOBE CANDYTUFT. Annual. All zones. Bushy plants 12–15 in. high. Lance-shaped leaves to 3½ in. long; flowers in pink, rose, carmine, crimson, salmon, lilac, and white. Dwarf strains Dwarf Fairy and Magic Carpet, available in the same colors, grow 6 in. tall.

IDESIA polycarpa

Flacourtiaceae	
DECIDUOUS TREE	
🌿 ZONES 31, 32, 34, 39	
☀ FULL SUN	
🔴 REGULAR WATER	

Idesia polycarpa

Native to central and western China and Japan. Grows to 50 ft. in loamy and well-drained soil, and is hardy as far north as Boston. Heart-shaped leaves measuring 5 by 5 in. Numerous clusters of yellow-green flowers in June, followed by pendulous bunches of small fruits that resemble grapes and turn brilliant orange red when ripe. Birds do not like these fruits, and they remain on the tree in excellent condition throughout the winter, providing great beauty in the bleakest months. Some trees produce all-male flowers and so do not fruit. Others are all-female and require a nearby male to fruit, and still others are both male and female. It would be prudent to plant several young trees. They begin to flower at a relatively young age; at that time, select a single male to be the pollinator and discard the rest, while retaining all female trees.

ILEX

HOLLY	
Aquifoliaceae	
EVERGREEN OR DECIDUOUS SHRUBS OR TREES	
🌿 ZONES VARY BY SPECIES	
☀ ◐ FULL SUN OR PARTIAL SHADE	
🔴 REGULAR WATER	

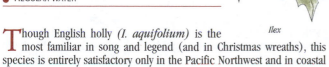
Ilex

Though English holly (*I. aquifolium*) is the most familiar in song and legend (and in Christmas wreaths), this species is entirely satisfactory only in the Pacific Northwest and in coastal northern California. In other areas, where temperatures cover a wider range, many other species are better choices. These include evergreen species grown for their attractive foliage and fruit as well as deciduous types grown principally for showy autumn and winter berries. In size, hollies range from foot-high dwarfs to trees 40–50 ft. tall. More than 400 species and countless hybrids exist. Smaller hollies are attractive as foundation plantings or low hedges; larger evergreen kinds make attractive, impenetrable tall hedges or screens.

All holly plants are either male or female, and as a rule both sexes must be present for the female to set fruit. Varieties described below are female unless otherwise noted. A few are self-fertile; these are also noted.

Most hollies prefer rich, moist, slightly acid garden soil with good drainage. (A few exceptions are noted.) All appreciate a mulch to deter weeds and keep soil cool and moist. Though hollies will grow in sun or part shade, choose a sunny spot for best berry production and most compact growth. Principal pests are scale, bud moth, and leaf miner.

I. altaclarensis. Evergreen tree. Zones 31, 32, 34. Hybrid between English holly and a species from the Canary Islands; resembles the former. 'Camelliafolia' has large, smooth-edged dark green leaves. 'J. C. Van Tol' bears regular crops of large dark red berries. 'Wilsonii' (also known as Wilson holly) can attain tree size, but is usually seen as a 6–8 ft. shrub; it has thick, leathery, rich green leaves up to 5 in. long.

I. aquifolium. ENGLISH HOLLY. Evergreen tree. Zones 31, 32, 34. The classic holly, but not the best choice for eastern gardens. Dislikes poor drainage, low temperatures, cold drying winds, and high humidity coupled with high temperatures. Has succeeded in ideal locations, but chancy; *I.* 'Nellie R. Stevens' (see page 266) is a better choice for achieving similar effect. Among the hardiest English holly selections are 'Balkans', which is the most cold tolerant and has both male and female forms; 'Boulder Creek'; and 'Zero' ('Teufel's Weeping').

I. aquipernyi. Evergreen shrub or small tree. Zones 31, 32, 34, 39. Hybrid between English holly and *I. pernyi*. May attain 20 ft. or more. The 2–4-in., spiny-edged leaves are closely set on branches. 'Aquipern' is a male selection; 'San Jose' and 'Brilliant' are female, with small red berries that set without pollination.

I. attenuata. Evergreen tree. Zones 31, 32. Hybrid between American holly (*I. opaca*) and a species native to the southeastern U.S. Dense, conical habit to 20–30 ft. tall; sparsely toothed foliage. 'East Palatka' and 'Foster's #2' (also known as Foster's holly) are widely planted female forms. 'Foster's #4' is a male plant. 'Nasa', a female holly, is known for its unusually narrow leaves.

I. ciliospinosa. Evergreen shrub. Zones 31, 32, 34–41. Upright with multiple stems, to 20 ft. high and 12 ft. wide. Oval leaves of dull dark green, to 2½ in. long with thin spines. Red berries.

I. cornuta. CHINESE HOLLY. Evergreen shrub or small tree. Zones 31, 32, but needs long warm season to set fruit. Very tolerant of heat and drought. Dense or open growth to 10 ft. or taller. Leaves typically glossy, leathery, nearly rectangular, with spines at the four corners and at tip. Berries exceptionally large, bright red, long lasting. Selections rather than species usually grown; fruit set, leaf form, and spininess vary. In the following list, those setting fruit do so without pollination.

'Berries Jubilee'. Dome-shaped plant to 6–10 ft., with large leaves and heavy crop of large, bright red berries. Leaves larger, spinier than those of 'Burfordii', on smaller plant.

'Burfordii'. BURFORD HOLLY. To 15 ft. tall and wide. Leaves nearly spineless, cupped downward. Heavy fruit set. Useful as espalier.

'Carissa'. Dwarf to 3–4 ft. high and 4–6 ft. wide at maturity. Dense growth, small leaves. Use for low hedge. No berries. Has been known to revert to 'Rotunda', the form from which it was developed.

'Dazzler'. Compact, upright growth. Glossy leaves have a few stout spines along wavy margins. Loaded with berries.

'D'Or'. Resembles 'Burfordii' but has bright yellow berries.

'Dwarf Burford' ('Burfordii Nana'). Resembles 'Burfordii' but somewhat smaller, to about 8 ft. tall and wide. Densely covered with small (1½-in.), light green, nearly spineless leaves. Dark red berries.

'Rotunda'. DWARF CHINESE HOLLY. Compact grower to 3–4 ft. tall, 6–8 ft. wide at maturity. Usually does not produce berries. A few stout spines and rolled leaf margins between spines make the medium light green leaves nearly rectangular.

I. crenata. JAPANESE HOLLY. Evergreen shrub. Zones 31, 32, 34, 37, except as noted below. Looks more like a boxwood than a holly. Dense, erect, usually 3–4 ft. high, sometimes to 20 ft. Narrow, fine-toothed leaves, ½–¾ in. long; berries are black. Extremely hardy and useful where winter cold limits choice of polished evergreens for hedges, edgings. Varieties include:

'Beehive'. Dense, compact mound with leaves ½ in. long, ¼ in. wide.

'Compacta'. Rounded shrub to 6 ft. tall. Dense habit, ¾-in. leaves. Many different plants sold under this name.

'Convexa'. Zones 31, 32, 34–41. Compact, rounded shrub to 4–6 ft. high, spreading wider. Leaves are ½ in. long, roundish, cupped downward at the edges. Use clipped or unclipped. Many different plants sold under this name.

'Dwarf Pagoda'. Exceptionally slow growing and dense—to 1 ft. in 8 years. Leaves less than ½ in. long.

'Glory'. Male plant (no fruit). Dense, rounded growth. Extremely hardy.

'Green Island'. Zones 31, 32, 34–41. Open, spreading growth to 3 ft. tall and twice as wide.

'Helleri'. Dwarf variety to 1 ft. high, 2 ft. wide; larger after many years, to 4 ft. tall and 5 ft. wide.

'Jersey Pinnacle'. Compact, dense, erect. To eventual 8 ft. tall, 2 ft. wide.

'Mariesii'. Often labeled as dwarf less than 1 ft. high, but old plants often grow much taller. Usually grows only 8 in. in first 10 years; erect habit.

'Soft Touch'. Grows 2 ft. tall, 3 ft. wide. Unlike other varieties, has soft, flexible branches.

I. decidua. POSSUMHAW. Deciduous shrub. Zones 31, 32, 34–41. Native to southeastern U.S. To 6–10 ft.; possibly small tree to 20 ft. Pale gray stems; shiny dark green leaves to 3 in. long. Orange to red berries last into winter or spring. 'Warren's Red', eventually 15–20 ft. tall, bears a heavy crop of large red berries. 'Council Fire' is lower growing. For fruit production, need a male pollinator such as 'Red Escort' or any male variety of American holly, such as 'Jersey Knight'.

I. 'Ebony Magic'. Evergreen shrub. Zones 32, 34, 35, 37. Hybrid with pyramidal form. Grows 8–10 ft. tall, possibly to 20 ft. Blackish purple bark; shiny dark green, spiny-edged leaves. Large orange-red berries last through spring. 'Ebony Male' often used for pollination.

I. 'Emily Brunner'. Zones 31, 32. Red-fruited, broadly pyramidal female to 20 ft., with large, spiny, glossy, 4½-in.-long, olive green leaves. Very popular landscape plant in warmer areas.

I. glabra. INKBERRY. Evergreen shrub. Zones 31, 32, 34–43. Native to eastern North America. To 10 ft. tall, with thick, dark green (olive green in winter), spineless leaves and black berries. More widely available is the dwarf form 'Compacta'; it grows to 4 ft. but can be sheared to make a 2-ft. hedge. 'Densa', 'Nordic', and 'Shamrock' are other dwarf varieties. 'Ivory Queen' has cream-colored berries.

I. 'Lydia Morris'. Zones 31, 32, 34, 39. Evergreen shrub to 22 ft. high. Dense and conical; glossy, diamond-shaped deep green leaves with spines. Red berries.

I. 'Mary Nell'. Zones 31, 32. Medium-size, red-fruited, upright, pyramidal female with bold, 3½-in-long, glossy, spiny leaves. Very popular landscape plant in warmer areas.

I. meserveae. Evergreen shrub. Zones 32, 34, 35, 37–39. Most plants in this category are hybrids between English holly and a cold-tolerant species from northern Japan. Apparently the hardiest of hollies that have true holly look. Dense, bushy plants 6–7 ft. tall, with purple stems and spiny, glossy blue-green leaves. Red-fruiting female varieties include 'Blue Angel', 'Blue Girl', and 'Blue Princess'; male pollinators include 'Blue Boy' and 'Blue Prince'. 'Golden Girl' has yellow berries. Red-fruited 'China Boy' and 'China Girl', both to 10 ft. tall, are crosses between Chinese holly and the northern Japanese species. They are slightly hardier and tolerate more summer heat than the Blue series.

I. 'Nellie R. Stevens'. Evergreen shrub or small tree. Zones 31, 32. Probably a hybrid between Chinese holly and English holly. Fast growing, densely conical to 15–25 ft. tall. Glossy, leathery, sparsely toothed leaves to 3 in. long. Sets fruit without a male holly, but forms a heavier crop if pollinated by male variety of Chinese holly.

I. opaca. AMERICAN HOLLY. Evergreen tree. Zones 31, 32, 34, 35, 39. Native to eastern U.S. Slow growing to 50 ft. tall; pyramidal or round-headed form. Leaves 2–4 in. long, spiny margined, dull or glossy green. Red berries. Hundreds of named varieties exist. Among the best are 'Canary', with yellow fruit'; 'Cardinal', many red berries on compact plant; 'Dan Fenton', with large leaves glossier than those typical of the species; 'Jersey Delight' and 'Jersey Princess'; 'Jersey Knight', a male pollen source; 'Merry Christmas'; ''Old Heavy Berry', large leaves and many red berries; Stewart's Silver Crown', with leaves edged in cream and marbled with gray green; and 'Yellow Berry', with bright yellow berries.

I. pedunculosa. Evergreen shrub or small tree. Zones 32, 34, 35, 37, 39. Exceptionally hardy for a broad-leafed evergreen. Native to China, Japan. Grows to 15 ft. or taller; awkward shape when young. Narrow, smooth-edged leaves 1–3 in. long and half as wide. The ¼-in. bright red berries dangle on 1–1½-in.-long stalks in autumn.

I. pernyi. Evergreen tree. Zones 31, 32, 34. Native to China. Slow growth to 20–30 ft. Glossy, 1–2-in.-long leaves, square at base, one to three spines on each side; closely packed against branchlets. Red berries set tightly against stems.

I. serrata. JAPANESE WINTERBERRY. Deciduous shrub. Zones 32, 34–41. To 15 ft. high and 10 ft. wide, bushy, with purple twigs. Dull green oval leaves to 3 in. long, with finely toothed edges. Fruit is usually red, sometimes yellow or white.

I. 'Sparkleberry'. Deciduous shrub. Zones 31, 32, 34–41. Vigorous to 15 ft. Toothed, oval, dark green leaves. Glossy red berries. 'Apollo' is the pollinator.

I. verticillata. WINTERBERRY, BLACK ALDER, MICHIGAN HOLLY. Deciduous shrub. Zones 31, 32, 34–43. Native to swamps of eastern North America. Unlike most hollies, thrives in boggy soils, but will succeed in any moist, acid, organic soil. To 6–10 ft. tall, rarely taller, eventually forming clumps by suckering. Leaves are oval, to 3 in. long and 1 in. wide. Female plants bear enormous crops of bright red berries that ripen in early fall and last all winter (or until they are eaten by birds). 'Afterglow' has orange to orange-red berries on a compact plant; 'Cacapon', 'Fairfax', and 'Winter Red' are standard-sized plants with dark red fruit; 'Red Sprite' is a large-berried dwarf selection. *I. v. chrysocarpa* has yellow berries. Pollinate with a male winterberry variety.

I. vomitoria. YAUPON. Evergreen shrub or small tree. Zones 31, 32. Native to southeastern U.S. Tolerates extremely alkaline soils better than other hollies. To 15–20 ft. tall, with narrow, inch-long, shallowly toothed dark green leaves. Can be grown as standard or sheared into columnar form; good topiary plant. Tiny scarlet berries borne in profusion without pollinator. Varieties include:

'Nana'. DWARF YAUPON. Low shrub. Compact to 1½ ft. high and twice as wide. Refined, attractive. Formal when sheared.

'Pendula'. Weeping branches show to best effect when plant is trained as standard.

'Pride of Houston'. Large shrub or small tree, upright, freely branching. Use as screen or hedge.

'Stokes' ('Stokes Dwarf', 'Shillings'). Dark green, closely set leaves. Compact. Smaller growing than 'Nana'.

'Yawkey'. Yellow-berried form.

ILLICIUM

ANISE TREE

Illiciaceae

EVERGREEN SHRUBS OR SMALL TREES

☀ ZONES 31, 32

◐ ● PARTIAL OR FULL SHADE

🌢 AMPLE WATER

Illicium

The anise trees are a little-used but attractive clan of shrubs or small trees noted for their anise-scented foliage and oddly shaped and colored flowers. Thick, leathery, glossy leaves; small flowers with many petal-like segments in early spring. Fruits that follow the blossoms are small, one-seeded pods arranged in a ring; the star anise of Chinese cookery is the fruit of *I. verum,* apparently not grown in the U.S. All like shade, ample moisture, and rich soil with abundant organic material. Big, bold foliage gives the impression of rhododendrons, so plants are useful for massing where rhododendrons will not thrive.

I. anisatum (I. religiosum). ANISE SHRUB. Native to Japan. Grows 6–10 ft. (possibly 15 ft.) tall, with glossy 4-in. leaves and inch-wide creamy to yellowish green flowers.

I. floridanum. FLORIDA ANISE TREE. Native Florida to Louisiana. Reaches 6–10 ft. or more, with leaves to 6 in. long; inch-wide maroon flowers have a scent most people find unpleasant. 'Halley's Comet' has somewhat larger, redder flowers than species; 'Album' is white flowered.

I. parviflorum. SMALL ANISE TREE. Grows 8–15 ft. tall, with 4-in. olive green leaves and inconspicuous, ½-in. yellow-green flowers. Can form small colonies by suckering. More tolerant of sun and dry soil than other anise trees, but equally at home in damp shade.

IMMORTELLE. See XERANTHEMUM annuum

IMPATIENS

BALSAM, TOUCH-ME-NOT, SNAPWEED

Balsaminaceae

PERENNIALS AND ANNUALS

🗲 ALL ZONES AS ANNUALS

☼ ◑ ● EXPOSURE NEEDS VARY BY SPECIES

💧 REGULAR WATER

Impatiens

Of the hundreds of species, only the following are widely grown. These are annuals or tender perennials treated as annuals; all are valuable for long summer bloom. Ripe seed capsules burst open when touched lightly and scatter seeds explosively.

I. balsamina. BALSAM. Summer annual. Erect, branching, 8–30 in. tall. Leaves 1½–6 in. long, sharply pointed, deeply toothed. Flowers large, spurred, borne among leaves along main stem and branches. Blossoms are solid colored or variegated, in shades of white, pink, rose, lilac, red. Compact, bushy, double camellia-flowered forms are most frequently used. Sow seeds in early spring; set out plants after frost in full sun (light shade in hot areas).

I. glandulifera. HIMALAYAN BALSAM. Summer annual. Sturdy, red-tinged stems to 6 ft. tall, lance-shaped leaves with toothed edges. Clusters of large, fragrant flowers, pink, lavender, rose purple, or white, with yellow spots on the inside. A bold and dramatic plant, but self-seeding may be a nuisance. Remove unwanted seedlings when young. Site in partial shade.

I. holstii. See *I. walleriana*

I. New Guinea hybrids. Perennials grown as summer annuals. A varied group of striking plants developed from number of species native to New Guinea, especially *I. hawkeri.* Plants can be upright or spreading; they usually have large leaves, often variegated with cream or red. Flowers are usually large (though not profuse); colors include lavender, purple, pink, red, orange. Many named kinds, ranging from spreading 8-in.-tall plants to erect 2-ft. types. 'Sweet Sue' and 'Tango', with bronzed foliage and bright orange, 2–3-in. flowers, can be grown from seed, as can Spectra hybrids. Grow in full sun or part shade. Good in pots, hanging baskets, borders.

I. niamniamensis 'Congo Cockatoo'. Perennial grown as indoor/outdoor container plant. Dark green, oval, scalloped leaves spiral up 3-ft. stems. Hooded, slender, red-and-yellow flowers in the leaf axils, most prolifically in summer. Site in partial shade.

I. oliveri (I. sodenii). POOR MAN'S RHODODENDRON. Perennial grown as indoor/outdoor container plant throughout the Northeast region. Shrubby to 4–8 ft. tall, 10 ft. wide. Bears many slender-spurred lilac, pale

lavender, or pinkish flowers 2¼ in. across. Glossy dark green leaves to 8 in. long in whorls along stems. Blooms in partial or deep shade; takes sun in cool-summer areas. Tolerates seacoast conditions.

I. sultanii. See *I. walleriana*

I. walleriana. BUSY LIZZIE. Perennial grown as summer annual. Includes plants formerly known as *I. holstii* and *I. sultanii.* Rapid, vigorous growth; tall varieties reach 2 ft. tall, dwarf kinds 4–12 in. high. Dark green, glossy, narrow, 1–3-in.-long leaves on juicy pale green stems. Flowers 1–2 in. wide, in all colors but yellow and true blue.

Strains exist in bewildering variety. Single-flowered kinds are best for massing or bedding; they nearly cover themselves with flowers. Doubles have attractive blooms like little rosebuds, but they don't match singles for mass show and are better grown in pots.

All types are useful for producing many months of bright color in partial or full shade. Grow from seed or cuttings; or buy plants in six-packs or pots. Space dwarf varieties 6 in. apart, big ones 1 ft. apart. If plants overgrow, cut them back as close as 6 in.—it's a tonic. New growth emerges in a few days; flowers cover it in 2 weeks. Plants often reseed in moist ground.

IMPERATA cylindrica 'Rubra' ('Red Baron')

JAPANESE BLOOD GRASS

Poaceae (Gramineae)

PERENNIAL

🗲 ZONES 31, 32, 34, 39

☼ ◑ FULL SUN OR PARTIAL SHADE

💧 REGULAR WATER

Imperata cylindrica '*Rubra' ('Red Baron')*

Clumping grass with erect stems 1–2 ft. tall, the top half rich blood-red. Striking in borders, especially where sun can shine through blades. Completely dormant in winter. Spreads slowly by underground runners. Rarely, if ever, flowers. The species form of this plant, cogongrass, is on the Federal Noxious Weed list; the cultivar is usually well-behaved, but remove any plants that revert to green—they are likely to become invasive.

INCARVILLEA

HARDY GLOXINIA

Bignoniaceae

PERENNIALS

🗲 ZONES VARY BY SPECIES

☼ ◑ LIGHT SHADE IN HOTTEST AREAS

💧 REGULAR WATER

Incarvillea

Not related to gloxinias but rather to the many trumpet vines (*Anisostichus, Campsis,* and the like). These are showy perennials from high elevations in India, Tibet, and China. Only one species is commonly seen, but others merit use. All have showy trumpet-shaped flowers carried in long, spikelike clusters above leaves divided featherwise into

I

many leaflets. Use in perennial borders or large rock gardens. Plants are deep rooted; they need reasonably deep soil and excellent drainage. In cold-winter regions, mulch plants after ground has frozen to prevent heaving.

I. arguta. Zones 31, 32; can be treated as annual elsewhere. A species only recently available in this country. To 5 ft. tall, sometimes becoming shrubby at base. Stems may flop, but flower clusters rise above foliage. Leaves to 8 in. long. Blooms in summer, bearing clusters of up to 20 rose pink (rarely white), 1½-in. flowers. Plants will bloom first year from seed if started early.

I. delavayi. Zones 31, 32, 34–41. Best known of the hardy gloxinias. Carrotlike roots are available from bulb growers in autumn; set them 8 in. deep in very well-drained soil. Leaves at base of plant are up to 1 ft. long. Bears 2½-in., yellow-throated, purplish pink flowers in early summer; blossoms are carried well above the foliage mass in an elongated spikelike cluster to 2 ft. tall. A white-flowered variety is available. 'Bee's Pink' has light pink flowers.

I. mairei. GARDEN GLOXINIA. Zones 31, 32, 34–43. To 20 in. high, plants have a long taproot. Basal clump of deep green, crinkled leaves to 10 in. long, comprised of pairs of oblong, toothed leaflets. Clusters of trumpet-shaped rose pink flowers with yellow throats and purple markings bloom in early summer.

I. olgae. Zones 31, 32, 34, 39. Woody, taprooted plant to 4 ft. high. Leaves are medium green, composed of pairs of oval leaflets. In early to midsummer, bears clusters of tubular flowers, rosy pink to light pink or white.

INCENSE CEDAR. See CALOCEDRUS decurrens

INDIAN CUCUMBER-ROOT. See MEDEOLA

INDIAN CUP. See SILPHIUM perfoliatum

INDIAN MOCK STRAWBERRY. See DUCHESNEA indica

INDIAN PINK. See SPIGELIA marilandica

INDIAN POKE. See VERATRUM

INDIAN RHUBARB. See DARMERA peltata

INDIAN TURNIP. See ARISAEMA triphyllum

INDIGO BUSH. See AMORPHA fruticosa, INDIGOFERA kirilowii

INDIGOFERA

INDIGO BUSH

Fabaceae (Leguminosae)

SHRUBBY PERENNIALS

 ZONES VARY BY SPECIES

☼ FULL SUN

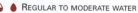 REGULAR TO MODERATE WATER

Indigofera

Plants in this genus are valued for their pealike flowers and attractive foliage. Grow them in rock gardens or mixed borders.

I. incarnata (I. decora). WHITE CHINESE INDIGO. Zones 31, 32, 34–41. Native to China and Japan. Low-growing ground cover to 1½ ft. high. Compound leaves composed of pairs of oval leaflets. Spikes of white pealike flowers with pink wings in summer.

I. kirilowii. Zones 31, 32, 34–43. Native to northern China, Korea, Japan. To 3–4 ft. high, with somewhat fernlike, bright green foliage. Small sweet pea–shaped rosy pink flowers carried in erect 4–5-in. spikes over a long bloom period in summer. Not fussy about soil or water but requires reasonably good drainage. Where winters are cold, it is killed to the ground, but comes back to bloom the next summer. Even in mild-winter areas, plants are more compact and attractive when cut back hard in earliest spring.

I. potaninii. Zones 31, 32, 34–41. Native to northwestern China. Long-blooming shrub to 5 ft. high and 6 ft. across. Compound gray-green leaves

---

composed of pairs of oval leaflets. Spikes of very small pink flowers appear from early summer to autumn.

INKBERRY. See ILEX glabra

INTERRUPTED FERN. See OSMUNDA claytoniana

INULA

ELECAMPANE

Asteraceae (Compositae)

PERENNIALS

ZONES 31, 32, 34–45, EXCEPT AS NOTED

☼ FULL SUN

WATER NEEDS VARY BY SPECIES

Inula

The elecampanes are medium-size to large perennials with big, daisy-like yellow flower heads characterized by many very narrow, sometimes drooping ray flowers around a central disk.

I. ensifolia. Grows to 2 ft. tall, making a dense, dark green clump of grassy leaves. Bright yellow daisies bloom at stem ends in late summer. 'Compacta' grows 8 in. high. Both species and variety need moderate water.

I. helenium. Native to Europe and Asia; naturalized in North America. Can reach 9 ft.; leaves at base of plant may be 2½ ft. long, upper leaves smaller. Clusters of 1-in. flowers in summer. Roots were once employed medicinally. Takes moist or wet soil.

I. hookeri. Zones 31, 32, 34–43. Native to the Himalayas. Forms clumps 2½ ft. tall and at least 2 ft. wide. Oblong, toothed, medium green leaves to 6 in. long. Flowers are pale yellow, with very slender rays surrounding a darker yellow central disk, and bloom in late summer to midautumn.

I. magnifica. Zones 31, 32, 34–41. To 6 ft. tall and 3 ft. wide. Vigorous plant with hairy, purple-streaked stems, dark green, oblong leaves to 10 in. long. Clusters of golden yellow flowers to 6 in. across in late summer. An excellent plant for bold back-of-the-border effects in midsummer. Regular to ample water; can grow in boggy conditions.

I. orientalis (I. glandulosa). Bushy growth to 1½–2 ft. tall. Orange-yellow, 3-in. flowers in summer. Regular water.

I. royleana. Exceptionally showy, with orange-yellow petals around a darker orange center to 5 in. across carried singly at tops of 2-ft. stems in late summer to early autumn. Rays tend to droop. Regular water. Best where summer nights are cool.

IPHEION uniflorum (Brodiaea uniflora, Triteleia uniflora)

SPRING STAR FLOWER

Amaryllidaceae

BULB

ZONES 31, 32, 34

☼ ◐ FULL SUN OR PARTIAL SHADE

REGULAR WATER DURING GROWTH AND BLOOM

Ipheion uniflorum

Native to Argentina. Flattish, bluish green leaves that smell like onions when bruised. Spring flowers 1½ in. across, broadly star shaped, pale to deep blue, on 6–8-in. stems. 'Wisley Blue' is a good bright blue selection. Use as edging, ground cover in semiwild areas, under trees, large shrubs.

Plant 2 in. deep in any good soil in fall. Easy to grow; will persist and multiply for years. Prefers dry conditions during summer dormancy, but will accept water if drainage is good. Will invade lawns, but only real turf fanatics will object.

IPOMOEA

MORNING GLORY

Convolvulaceae

PERENNIAL OR ANNUAL VINES

🗸 ALL ZONES AS ANNUALS

☼ FULL SUN

💧 REGULAR TO MODERATE WATER

Ipomoea

This genus includes many ornamental vines and the sweet potato; it does not include the weedy plant known as wild morning glory or bindweed *(Convolvulus arvensis)*. The plants described here may self-sow, but they do not spread by nearly ineradicable underground runners as does wild morning glory.

I. alba (Calonyction aculeatum). MOONFLOWER. Perennial climber, treated as summer annual. Fast growing (20–30 ft. in a season), providing quick summer shade for arbor, trellis, or fence. Luxuriant leaves 3–8 in. long, heart shaped, closely spaced on stems. Flowers fragrant, white (rarely lavender pink), often banded green, 6 in. across. Needs summer heat to bloom. Theoretically flowers open only after sundown, but they will stay open on dark, dull days. Seeds are hard; abrade them or soak them for 1 or 2 days for faster sprouting.

I. batatas. See Sweet Potato for edible varieties. Two ornamental cultivars grown as summer annuals are 'Blackie' with lobed, deep purple-black leaves, and 'Margarita', with heart-shaped chartreuse leaves. Both grow to 6 ft. in a container, 10 ft. or more on a trellis.

I. lobata (Mina lobata). SPANISH FLAG, EXOTIC LOVE. Perennial climber grown as an annual. To 15 ft. Lobed green leaves, slender clusters of small tubular flowers that open scarlet, then fade to orange, then yellow, then white; clusters may contain all colors at once.

I. multifida. CARDINAL CLIMBER. Annual climber to 6 ft. Triangular, medium green leaves to 5 in. long are divided into numerous narrow leaflets. Bright red, tubular flowers with flared mouth.

I. nil. MORNING GLORY. Summer annual. Includes rare large-flowered Imperial Japanese morning glories and a few varieties of common morning glory, including rosy red 'Scarlett O'Hara'. Early Call strain comes in a number of colors and is useful where summers are short. For culture, see *I. tricolor*.

I. quamoclit (Quamoclit pennata). CYPRESS VINE. Summer annual. Twines to 20 ft. Leaves 2½–4 in. long, finely divided into slender threads. Flowers are tubes 1½ in. long, flaring at mouth into five-pointed star; they are usually scarlet, rarely white.

I. tricolor. MORNING GLORY. Summer annual. Showy, single or double, funnel-shaped to bell-like flowers in solid colors of blue, lavender, pink, red, or white, usually with throats in contrasting colors; some bicolored or striped. Most types open only in morning, fade in afternoon. Bloom lasts until frost. Large, heart-shaped leaves.

Among most popular selections is 'Heavenly Blue', twining to 15 ft., with 4–5-in., pure sky blue flowers with yellow throat. Dwarf strain with white markings on leaves (known as Spice Islands or simply as Variegated) grows only 9 in. tall and spills to 1 ft. across; blooms in red, pink, blue, and bicolors.

Sow seed in place in full sun after frost. To speed sprouting, notch seed coat with knife or file (some growers sell scarified seed); or soak in warm water for 2 hours. For earlier start, start seed indoors, then set out plants 6–8 in. apart.

Use on fence or trellis or as ground cover. Or grow in containers; provide stakes or wire cylinder for support, or let plant cascade. For cut flowers, pick stems with buds in various stages of development, place in deep vase. Buds will open on consecutive days.

IPOMOPSIS

Polemoniaceae

BIENNIALS OR PERENNIALS GROWN AS ANNUALS

🗸 ALL ZONES

☼ FULL SUN

💧 REGULAR TO MODERATE WATER

Ipomopsis

Erect single stems, finely divided leaves, and tubular red (or yellow-and-red) flowers. They are startling in appearance, best massed; individual plants are narrow. Sow seed in spring or early summer for bloom the following summer.

I. aggregata (Gilia aggregata). Biennial. Native California to British Columbia, east to Rocky Mountains. To 2½ ft. tall. Flowers are red marked yellow (sometimes pure yellow), an inch or so long; borne in long, narrow clusters.

I. 'Hummingbird Mix'. Grow as annual. To 3 ft. tall; ferny leaves, flowers in shades of red, orange, yellow. Drought-tolerant. Attractive to hummingbirds; good cut flower.

I. rubra (Gilia rubra). Biennial or perennial. Native to southern U.S. To 6 ft. tall. Flowers red outside, yellow marked with red inside.

IRESINE

BLOODLEAF

Amaranthaceae

PERENNIALS

🗸 ALL ZONES AS INDOOR/OUTDOOR PLANTS

☼ FULL SUN

💧 REGULAR WATER

Iresine

Tender, upright-growing plants to 2–3 ft. tall, grown for attractive leaf color; flowers are inconspicuous. Tolerate seacoast conditions. Good in containers. Plants must be wintered indoors or treated as annuals. Pinch tips for bushiness. Easy to propagate by stem cuttings in fall or spring.

I. herbstii. Oval to round leaves, 1–2 in. long, usually notched at tip. Leaves purplish red with lighter midrib and veins; or green or bronzy, with yellowish veins. Stems are always red.

I. lindenii. Densely foliaged plant with bloodred, 2½-in.-long leaves, pointed instead of notched at tip.

Iridaceae. The large iris family includes many familiar (and unfamiliar) garden bulbs, corms, and fibrous-rooted perennials. Leaves are swordlike or grasslike, often in two opposing rows. Flowers may be simply arranged with six equal segments (as in *Crocus,* for example) or highly irregular in appearance (as in *Iris*).

IRIS

Iridaceae

BULBS AND RHIZOMES

🗸 ZONES VARY, ACCORDING TO SPECIES OR TYPE

☼ ◑ ● EXPOSURE NEEDS VARY BY SPECIES

💧 💧 💧 WATER NEEDS VARY BY SPECIES

Tall bearded iris

A large and remarkably diverse group of from 200 to 300 species, varying in flower color and form, cultural needs, and blooming periods (although the majority flower in spring or early summer). Leaves swordlike or grasslike; flowers showy, complex in structure. The three inner segments (the standards) are petals; they are usually erect or arching but, in some kinds, may flare to horizontal. The three outer segments (the falls) are petal-like sepals; they are held at various angles from nearly horizontal to drooping.

Irises grow from bulbs or rhizomes. In floral detail, there are three categories: bearded (each fall bears a caterpillarlike adornment), beardless (each fall is smooth), and crested (each fall bears a comblike ridge instead of a full beard).

Tall bearded irises (and other bearded classes) are the most widely sold iris types; many new hybrids are cataloged every year. Specialty growers abound. A small number offer various beardless classes and some species. Retail nurseries carry bulbous irises for fall planting.

Iris borer is potentially serious pest, found east of Rocky Mountains in Canada, south to Washington, D.C., west to Ohio and beyond. This borer is the larval stage of a dull brown moth that appears in late summer and early fall. Eggs laid in fall in dry debris close to the soil hatch the following spring. Larvae feed on leaf margins as they work toward the rhizomes, which they consume, leaving hollow shells. Telltale signs of infestation in summer are small "sawdust" piles around plant base. Thorough cleanup of garden debris before winter is first step in control. In early spring when new iris leaves reach 6 in. high, spray plants and soil with dimethoate. Repeat weekly until 2 weeks after last bloom.

BULBOUS IRISES

Irises that grow from bulbs have beardless flowers. Bulbs become dormant in summer and can be lifted and stored until planting time in fall.

Dutch and Spanish irises. Zones 31, 32, 34. The species that parented this group come from Spain, Portugal, Sicily, and northern Africa. (Dutch irises acquired their name because the hybrid group was developed by Dutch bulb growers.) Flowers come atop slender stems that rise up from rushlike foliage. Standards are narrow and upright; oval to circular falls project downward. Colors include white, mauve, blue, purple, brown, orange, yellow, and bicolor combinations—usually with a yellow blotch on falls. Dutch iris flowers reach 3–4 in. across, on stems 1½–2 ft. tall; these are the irises sold by florists. Bloom period is March–April in warm climates, May–June in colder climates. Spanish irises are similar but have smaller flowers that bloom about 2 weeks after Dutch irises.

Plant bulbs 4 in. deep, 3–4 in. apart, in October–November; give full sun. Apply a mulch in winter. Give regular water during growth. Bulbs can be left in the ground for several years where summers are dry; elsewhere, they should be lifted. After bloom, let foliage ripen before digging; store bulbs in cool, dry place for no more than 2 months before replanting. Dutch and Spanish irises are good in containers; plant five bulbs in a 5–6-in. pot.

The widely sold 'Wedgwood' is a Dutch hybrid hardy only in Zones 31, 32. Large flowers are lavender blue with yellow markings, blooming earlier than others (generally coinciding with 'King Alfred' daffodils). Bulbs are larger than those of average Dutch hybrid. Vigorous foliage is best masked by bushy annuals or perennials that will mature later in the season.

English irises. Zones 31, 32, 34, 39. The species *(I. latifolia)* from which named selections were made is native to the Pyrenees, where it grows in moist meadows. Early botanists first noticed the iris growing in southern England, where it had been taken by traders. Flowers are similar in structure to Dutch and Spanish irises, but falls are broader and decorated with a yellow hairline stripe. Colors include bluish purple, wine red, maroon, blue, mauve, white. Bloom time is early summer. Bulbs need cool, moist, acid soil; in fall, plant them 3–4 in. deep, 4 in. apart. Choose a partly shaded location in Zones 31, 32, full sun where summers are cool. Provide winter mulch, or lift and replant bulbs.

Reticulata irises. Zones 31, 32, 34, 39; in pots in colder zones. Bulbs covered by a netted outer covering give the group its name. These are classic rock garden and container plants, the flowers (like small Dutch irises) appearing on 6–8-in. stems in March–April (late January–early February in mild areas). Thin, four-sided blue-green leaves appear after bloom. Available species include *I. reticulata*, with 2–3-in. violet-scented flowers (purple, in the usual forms), and bright yellow–flowered *I. danfordiae*.

Pale blue–flowered *I. histrio* and large-flowered, blue-and-yellow *I. histrioides* may be carried by some specialists. Far more common are named hybrids such as 'Cantab' (pale blue with orange markings), 'Harmony' (sky blue marked yellow), 'J. S. Dijt' (reddish purple).

Bulbs are hardy to about −10°F/−23°C and need some subfreezing winter temperatures to thrive. Plant in autumn in well-drained soil in a sunny location; set bulbs 3–4 in. deep and as far apart. Bulbs need regular moisture from fall through spring. Soil should be kept dry during summer dormant period; in rainy climates, lift bulbs in summer or grow in pots so you can control moisture. Good for forcing. Divide only when vigor, flower quality deteriorate.

RHIZOMATOUS IRISES

Irises that grow from rhizomes (thickened, modified stems) may have bearded, beardless, or crested flowers; among this rhizomatous group are the most widely grown types. Leaves are swordlike, overlapping each other to form flat fans of foliage.

Bearded irises. Zones 31, 32, 34–45. The most widely grown irises fall into the bearded group. Many species, varieties, and years of hybridizing have produced a vast array of beautiful hybrids. All have upright standards, flaring to pendent falls that have characteristic epaulettelike beards. Tall bearded irises are the most familiar of these, but they represent just one subdivision of the entire group.

Bearded irises need good drainage. They'll grow in soils from sandy to claylike, but in clay soils plant in raised beds or on ridges to assure drainage, avoid rhizome rot. Plant in full sun in cool climates; in hottest regions, they'll accept light shade during the afternoon. July–October is best planting period; plant during July–August in cold-winter zones. In regions with mild winters and cool to moderate summers, plant throughout this period. Space rhizomes 1–2 ft. apart; set with tops just beneath soil surface, spreading roots well. Growth proceeds from the leafy end of rhizome, so point that end in direction you want growth initially to occur. For quick show, plant three rhizomes 1 ft. apart. Water to settle soil, start growth. Thereafter, water judiciously until new growth shows plants have rooted; then water regularly until fall rains or frosts arrive. If weather turns hot, shade newly planted rhizomes to prevent sunscald, possible rot. Where winters are severe, mulch new plantings temporarily with pine boughs to prevent heaving from alternate freezing, thawing. Remove mulch promptly in spring; rhizomes will rot under soggy mulch.

DIRECTING BEARDED IRIS

Rhizomes grow outward from the end with leaves; when planting, point that end in direction you want growth to take. For quick show, plant three rhizomes 1 ft. apart, two with growing ends pointed outward, the third aimed to grow into the space between them. On slopes, set rhizomes with growing end facing uphill.

From the time growth starts in late winter or early spring, water regularly until about 6 weeks after flowers fade; increases and buds for next year's flowers form during postbloom period. During summer, plants need less water. For best performance, feed plants with moderate-nitrogen fertilizer as growth begins in spring, then again after bloom has finished. If spring weather is cool and moist, leaf spot may disfigure foliage; use appropriate fungicide at first sign of infection. Remove old and dry leaves in fall.

Clumps become overcrowded after 3 or 4 years; quantity and quality of bloom decrease. Lift and divide crowded clumps at best planting time for your area. Save large rhizomes with healthy leaves, discard old and leafless rhizomes from clump's center. Break rhizomes apart or use a sharp knife to separate. Trim leaves, roots to about 6 in., let cut ends heal for several hours to a day before replanting. If replanting in the same soil, amend it with plenty of organic matter.

Dwarf and median irises. These irises generally have flowers shaped like the familiar tall beardeds, but they are smaller in flower size, plant size, and stature. Median iris is a collective term for the categories standard dwarf, intermediate and border bearded, and miniature tall bearded.

Miniature dwarf bearded irises. Grow to 8 in. tall; flowers large for size of plant. Earliest to bloom of bearded irises (about 6 weeks before main show of tall beardeds). Hardy, need winter chill. Plants multiply quickly. Shallow root systems need regular moisture and periodic feeding.

Standard dwarf bearded irises. Grow 8–15 in. tall. Flowers and plants are larger than miniature dwarfs. Profuse bloom. Best with some winter chill.

Intermediate bearded irises. Grow 15–28 in., bear flowers 3–5 in. across. Flower later than dwarfs but 1 to 3 weeks before tall bearded irises. Most are hybrids between standard dwarfs and tall bearded varieties, resemble larger standard dwarfs rather than border beardeds. Some give second bloom in fall.

Border bearded irises. Grow 15–28 in. tall—proportionately smaller versions of tall beardeds in the same great range of colors and patterns. Bloom period is same as for tall bearded.

Miniature tall bearded irises. Grow 15–28 in. high and flower with tall beardeds. But small flowers (2–3 in. wide), narrower foliage give them appearance of tall bearded irises reduced in every proportion. Good for cutting and arrangements—hence their original name, table irises.

Tall bearded irises. Among choicest perennials for borders, massing, cutting, although most are not very attractive in a mixed border after they finish flowering. Often best grown in beds of their own or hidden among plants that remain attractive all season, such as peonies. Adapted in all climates. Easy to grow, but subject to several insect and disease problems. Fancy, frilly modern hybrids need frequent division to maintain vigor, unlike the older cultivars, which could be left in place for years. Flower in midspring, on branching stems 2½–4 ft. high. All colors but pure red and green; patterns of two colors or more, blends produce infinite variety. Countless named selections available. Modern hybrids often have elaborately ruffled, fringed flowers. Two variegated-foliage varieties are sold. Leaves of 'Pallida Variegata' (often cataloged as 'Zebra') are striped with cream; leaves of 'Argentea' have white stripes. Both bear smallish blue lavender flowers on stems to 2 ft. high.

Remontant (or reblooming) tall bearded irises flower in mid- to late summer or fall, depending on variety and climate. Plants need fertilizer, regular moisture for best performance. Specialists' catalogs offer increasing numbers of remontant tall beardeds.

There are many tall bearded iris cultivars. Some good ones are: 'Babbling Brook', light blue flowers with pale yellow beard, ruffled; 'Bride's Halo', white with gold-edged standards and falls, frilled; 'Cup Race', large, white; 'Debby Rairdon', light yellow standards, falls white with yellow banding; 'Grand Waltz', orchid, laced and ruffled; 'Loop the Loop', white marked with medium blue-violet band around standards and falls; 'Mary Frances', light blue orchid; 'Navy Strut', deep indigo blue, ruffled and fluted; 'Pink Taffeta', pale rose pink, very ruffled; 'Stepping Out', white with violet markings on standards and falls, ruffled; 'Victoria Falls', powder blue with central white zone on falls; 'Winter Olympics', white, very wide, ruffled falls.

Aril and arilbred irises. The aril species and interspecies hybrids (characterized by an aril, or collar, on their seeds) offer strange and often remarkably beautiful flowers on unattractive plants. Exacting cultural requirements. Most species come from semidesert areas of the Near East and central Asia; plants need limy soil, perfect drainage, full sun, and no summer water (best suited to areas with scant or no summer rain). There are two main groups: *Oncocyclus* and *Regelias*. *Oncocyclus* include a number of species with huge, nearly globular flowers in lavender, gray, silver, maroon, and gold, often intricately veined and stippled with deeper hues. *Regelias* have smaller, narrower-petaled flowers, veined or unmarked. *Oncocyclus* are the most difficult to grow; somewhat easier are *Regelias* and hybrids between the two known as *Oncogelias*.

Arilbreds—hybrids between the arils and bearded irises—offer some of the arils' exotic beauty on plants nearly as easy to grow as tall beardeds, given well-drained, neutral to alkaline soil. Amount of aril ancestry can determine ease of culture: hybrids containing half aril ancestry or more usually are more demanding than those of one-quarter or three-eighths aril ancestry. Specialists' catalogs often state hybrid ancestries for this reason.

Beardless irises. Flowers in this group have smooth, "beardless" falls but otherwise differ considerably in appearance from one group or species to another. Rhizomes have fibrous roots (unlike fleshy roots of bearded types); most prefer or demand more moisture than bearded irises. Many can perform well from crowded clumps but will eventually need division. Timing varies; all should be dug and replanted quickly, keeping roots moist while plants are out of the ground.

The following five hybrid groups contain the most widely sold beardless irises. Also described are individual species (and their named selections) available from growers of specialty iris and perennials.

Iris ensata

Japanese irises. Zones 32, 34–45. Derived solely from *I. ensata* (formerly *I. kaempferi*), these irises feature sumptuous blossoms 4–12 in. across on slender stems to 4 ft. high. Flower shape is essentially flat. "Single" types have three broad falls and much-reduced standards, giving triangular flower outline; "double" blossoms have standards marked like the falls and about the same size and shape, resulting in circular flower outline. Colors are purple, violet, pink, rose, red, white—often veined or edged in contrasting shade. Plants have graceful, narrow, upright leaves with distinct raised midribs.

Plants need much moisture during growing, flowering period. Even though they are happy in boggy conditions, they easily tolerate ordinary garden soil, so long as it is moderately acid. Never give these plants lime. Plant rhizomes in fall or spring, 2 in. deep and 1½ ft. apart; or plant up to three per 12-in. container. Use in moist borders, at edge of pools or streams, or even in boxes or pots plunged halfway to rim in pond or pool during growing season.

'Eleanor Perry', red violet, double; 'Freckled Geisha', white edged in maroon, with wine-colored speckles, ruffled; 'Great White Heron', white with yellow markings, semidouble; 'Ise', pale blue with blue-purple veins; 'Light in Opal', pale orchid pink; opal iridescence; 'Over the Waves', white with light purple center, heavily ruffled; 'Pin Stripe', white, beautifully striped light blue; 'Reign of Glory', white with blue margins and stippling; 'Summer Storm', dark purple with orange markings, double; 'World's Delight', orchid pink.

Louisiana irises. Zones 31, 32, 34–43. Approximately four species from the lower Mississippi River basin and Gulf Coast compose this group of so-called swamp irises. Graceful, flattish blossoms on stems 2–5 ft. tall, carried above and among leaves that are long, narrow, and unribbed. The range of flower colors and patterns is extensive—nearly the equal of tall beardeds.

Specialists offer a vast array of named hybrids; some may carry the basic species as well. *I. brevicaulis (I. foliosa)* has blue flowers with flaring segments carried on zigzag stems among the foliage. *I. fulva* has coppery to rusty red (rarely yellow) blossoms with narrow, drooping segments. *I. giganticaerulea* is indeed a "giant blue" (sometimes white) with upright standards and flaring falls; stems may reach 4 ft. or more, with foliage in proportion. *I. hexagona* also comes in blue shades with upright standards, flaring falls. *I. nelsonii,* a natural hybrid population derived from *I. fulva* and *I. giganticaerulea,* resembles the *I. fulva* parent in flower shape and color (but also including purple and brown tones) and approaches the *I. giganticaerulea* parent in size.

'Ann Chowling', deep red with orange-yellow markings; 'Charjoy's David', red violet with greenish yellow markings; 'Chrome Dome', light yellow, nonfading; 'Clara Goula', creamy white with pale yellow markings; 'Full Eclipse', dark black violet; 'Shrimp Creole', rose-colored standards and falls; 'Shrimp Louis', shrimp pink standards, creamy red falls; 'This I Love', lavender pink, low growing.

Plants thrive in well-watered, rich garden soil as well as at pond margins; soil and water should be neutral to acid. Locate in full sun where summers are cool to mild; choose light afternoon shade where summers are hot. Plant in late summer; set rhizomes 1 in. deep, 1½–2 ft. apart. Mulch for winter where ground freezes.

Siberian irises. Zones 32, 34–45. The most widely sold members of this group are named hybrids derived from *I. sibirica* and *I. sanguinea* (formerly *I. orientalis*). Clumps of narrow, almost grasslike leaves (deciduous in winter) produce slender stems up to 4 ft. (depending on variety), each bearing two to five blossoms with upright standards and flaring to drooping falls. Colors include white and shades of blue, lavender, purple, wine, pink, and light yellow.

'Ausable River', sizable medium blue flowers; 'Blue Burgee', deep blue, flaring falls; 'Caesar's Brother', deep purple; 'Dewful', blue, productive; 'Dreaming Spires', lavender with flaring, royal blue falls; 'Ego', medium blue, ruffled; 'Ewen', wine red with yellow markings; 'Jewelled Crown', dark red flowers, gold and white markings on falls; 'Mabel Coday', mid-blue flowers, white signals; 'Navy Brass', navy blue with conspicuous brass markings; 'Orville Fay', large, medium blue with flaring falls; 'Superego', pale blue with darker blue falls; 'Tealwood', purple, flaring falls; 'White Swirl', white, flaring falls.

Give plants full sun (partial or dappled shade where summer is hot), neutral to acid soil. Set rhizomes 1–2 in. deep, 1–2 ft. apart. Plant in early spring or late summer. Water liberally from onset of growth until several weeks after bloom. Divide infrequently—when clumps show hollow centers—at best planting time for your region.

Spuria irises. Zones 31, 32, 34–43. In flower form, the spurias resemble Dutch irises. Older members of this group had primarily yellow or white-and-yellow blossoms; *I. orientalis* (universally known as *I. ochroleuca*) has naturalized in many parts of the West and South, its 3–5-ft. stems bearing white flowers with yellow blotches on the falls. Dwarf *I. graminea* bears narrow-petaled, scented, blue-and-maroon blossoms on foot-high stems. Modern hybrids show a great color range: blue, lavender, gray, orchid, tan, bronze, brown, purple, earthy red, and near black—often with a prominent yellow spot on the falls. Flowers are held closely against 3–6-ft. stems, rising above handsome clumps of narrow, dark green leaves. Flowering starts during latter part of tall bearded bloom and continues for several weeks beyond.

Plant rhizomes in late summer or early fall in rich, neutral to slightly alkaline soil; choose a spot in full sun to partial light shade. Set rhizomes 1 in. deep, 1½–2 ft. apart. Plants need plenty of moisture from onset of growth through bloom period but little moisture during summer. Divide clumps infrequently (not an easy task); mulch clumps for winter where temperatures drop to −20°F/−29°C or lower.

I. foetidissima. GLADWIN IRIS. Zones 31, 32. Native to Europe. Glossy evergreen leaves to 2 ft. make handsome foliage clumps. Stems 1½–2 ft. tall bear subtly attractive flowers in blue gray and dull tan; specialists may offer color variants in soft yellow and lavender blue, as well as 'Variegata', which has cream-striped evergreen leaves. Real attraction is large seed capsules that open in fall to show numerous round, orange-scarlet seeds; cut stems with seed capsules useful in arrangements. Grow in sun to shade in cool-summer regions, light or partial shade to full shade elsewhere. Extremely tolerant of aridity.

I. gracilipes. Zones 31, 32, 34–41. Crested iris to 6 in. high, with narrow grassy leaves to 1 ft. long. Lilac blue flowers, with a white patch veined in violet and a white crest tipped with yellow, bloom late spring–early summer. 'Alba', white flowers, much less vigorous than the species.

I. laevigata. Zones 32, 34–45. Smooth, glossy leaves reach 1½–2½ ft. high, to 1 in. wide. Flower stems grow to about the same height, bearing violet-blue blossoms with three upright standards and three drooping falls enlivened with yellow median stripes. Named color variants include white, magenta, and patterned purple-and-white. There also are varieties in which standards mimic falls in shape, pattern, and carriage, producing the effect of a double blossom. This is a true bog plant, growing best in constantly moist, acid soil—even in shallow water.

I. prismatica. Zones 31, 32, 34–43. Foliage and flowers suggest a small Siberian iris. Typical form grows about 1 ft. high, bearing dainty purple-and-white blossoms on branching, sinuous stems. A pure white form also exists. *I. p. austrina,* from the southern Appalachians, is a bit taller and coarser, with lilac blue blossoms. Give plants full sun and moist (but not boggy), acid soil. Rhizomes spread widely, forming loose colonies rather than tight clumps.

I. pseudacorus. YELLOW FLAG. Zones 31, 32, 34–45. Impressive foliage plant; under best conditions, upright leaves may reach 5 ft. tall. Flower stems grow 4–7 ft. (depending on culture), bear bright yellow flowers 3–4 in. across. Selected forms offer ivory and lighter yellow flowers, double flowers, variegated foliage, and plants with shorter and taller leaves. Plant in sun to light shade. Needs acid soil and more than average moisture; thrives in shallow water. Native to Europe but now found worldwide in temperate regions; seeds float, aiding plant's dispersal.

Several hybrids are excellent foliage plants with distinctive blossoms. All prefer ample water (but not pond conditions), sun to light shade. 'Gigantea' is large and vigorous, with particularly large flowers. 'Holden Clough' perhaps has *I. foetidissima* as the other parent. Flowers, 3–4 in. across, are soft tan heavily netted with maroon veins; stems grow to 4 ft.; leaves reach 4–5 ft. but tips arch over. Two of its seedlings are similar but larger. 'Phil Edinger' grows to 4½ ft. with arching foliage; 4–5-in. flowers are brass colored, heavily veined in brown. 'Roy Davidson' is similar, but flowers are dark yellow with fine brown veining and maroon thumbprint on falls. 'Variegata' leaves are striped creamy yellow in spring but turn all green by summer.

I. versicolor. BLUE FLAG. Zones 31, 32, 34–45. Widely distributed North American species, found in bogs and swamps in the Great Lakes region, Ohio Valley, and the Northeast. Grows 1½–4 ft. tall; narrow leaves are thicker in the center but not ribbed. Shorter-growing forms have upright leaves, but foliage of taller types may recurve gracefully. The typical wild flowers are light violet blue, but lighter and darker forms exist; a wine red variant has been sold as 'Kermesina'. Selections include pink 'Rosea' and 'Vernal' and others with violet red flowers. Like *I. pseudacorus,* thrives in sun to light shade, in moist, acid soil or shallow water.

Specialty growers offer hybrids between *I. versicolor* and other species such as *I. ensata, I. laevigata,* and *I. virginica.* Violet-flowered 'Gerald Darby', a hybrid with *I. virginica,* has striking wine red stems.

I. virginica. SOUTHERN BLUE FLAG. Zones 31, 32, 34–43. In plant and flower, this species is similar to *I. versicolor,* but it has a more southerly distribution in the wild. Distinguishing floral feature is longer standards. Flower colors include light to dark blue, wine red, pink, lavender, and white. A plant sold as 'Giant Blue' is distinctly larger in all parts, approaching *I. pseudacorus* in size. Plant in moist, acid garden soil or grow in shallow water. In deep ponds, plant in large pots barely submerged beneath the surface.

Crested irises. Botanically placed with beardless irises, they represent a transition between beardless and bearded: each fall bears a narrow, comb-like crest where a beard would be in bearded sorts. Slugs, snails are especially attracted to foliage, flowers. Several tender species and hybrids form bamboolike stems carrying foliage fans aloft; flower stems to 2 ft. are widely branched, bearing orchidlike sprays of fringed flowers in lavender to white with orange crests. These include *I. confusa, I. japonica, I. wattii,* and hybrids such as 'Nada' and 'Darjeeling'. Grow in sun where summer is cool, light shade elsewhere; plant in organically enriched soil. Regular water during growth. Grow in containers and move to shelter over winter.

I. cristata. Zones 32, 34, 39; hardy to −10°F/−23°C. Leaves 4–6 in. long, ½ in. wide. Slender, greenish rhizomes spread freely. Flowers white, lavender, or light blue with golden crests; specialty nurseries list named varieties. Give light shade, organically enriched soil, regular water. Divide just after bloom or in fall after leaves die down. 'Alba', white flowers; 'Shenandoah Sky', pale blue; 'Summer Storm', deep blue; 'Vein Mountain', pale blue with orange signals.

I. tectorum. ROOF IRIS. Zones 31, 32, 34–41. Foliage fans to 1 ft. tall look like those of bearded irises, but leaves are ribbed and glossy. Flowers suggest an informal bearded iris with fringed petals and crests in place of beards. Colors are violet blue with white crests, white with yellow crests;

standards are upright at first, open out to horizontal as flower matures. Give plants organically enriched soil, light shade, regular water. Short lived in regions of hot, dry summers. Native to Japan, where it is planted on cottage roofs. Its hybrid with a bearded iris, 'Paltec', will grow with bearded irises. Height is about 1 ft., the lavender flowers suggesting a bearded iris with beards superimposed on crests.

IRISH MOSS. See SAGINA subulata

ISATIS tinctoria

WOAD

Brassicaceae (Cruciferae)

PERENNIALS OR BIENNIALS

ZONES 31, 32, 34-43

FULL SUN

REGULAR WATER

Isatis tinctoria

When boiled in water, woad leaves release a substance that makes indigo, the blue dye. Today, taprooted woad grows in herb, medicinal, and medieval gardens for its historical associations and in meadow gardens for its clusters of bright yellow flowers. Home dyers also grow it to make traditional indigo dye. Introduced into the U.S., it has colonized western croplands and ranges, outcompeting native plants for food and water while it moves across the country. Woad usually grows 1-3 ft. tall but can grow to 5 ft. or more. It has blue-green leaves with cream midribs and a canopy of clustered, mustard yellow flowers, followed by hanging black seeds. Woad can grow on dry rocky sites or in moist, somewhat fertile, well-drained soil, always in full sun.

ISMENE calathina. See HYMENOCALLIS narcissiflora

ITEA virginica

VIRGINIA SWEETSPIRE

Grossulariaceae (Saxifragaceae)

DECIDUOUS SHRUB

ZONES 31, 32, 34, 39

FULL SUN OR PART SHADE

REGULAR WATER

Itea virginica

Native to eastern U.S. Erect shrub to 3–5 ft. tall or taller, spreading to form large patches where well adapted. Leaves are oval, dark green, to 4 in. long and 1½ in. wide. In fall, they turn purplish red or bright red; hang on the plant for a long time and may persist all winter in mild climates. Fragrant, ⅓–½-in., creamy white flowers are held in erect clusters; bloom in early summer. 'Henry's Garnet' is a superior selection with 6-in. flower clusters and garnet red fall color. On 'Saturnalia', fall foliage is a mix of orange, purple, and wine red.

A variety known as 'Beppu' or 'Nana' may be in fact a form of *I. japonica*. It is lower growing (to 2½ ft.) than *I. virginica,* with somewhat smaller flowers. Spreads rapidly by suckers. Somewhat less hardy than *I. virginica;* may be injured at 0° to −10°F/−18° to −23°C.

IWA-HIGE. See CASSIOPE

SPEAR. See TRITELEIA laxa

IVY. See HEDERA

IXIA

AFRICAN CORN LILY

Iridaceae

CORMS

ALL ZONES; DIG AND STORE, OR GROW IN POTS

FULL SUN

REGULAR WATER DURING GROWTH AND BLOOM

Ixia

Garden kinds are hybrids of several South African species, notably *I. maculata.* Swordlike leaves. Wiry, 18–20-in. stems topped with spikelike clusters of 1–2-in. blooms in cream, yellow, red, orange, pink, all with dark centers.

Grows best in slightly alkaline soil; incorporate lime into acid soil before planting. Plant corms 2–3 in. deep. Corms are not hardy in the Northeast, so treat as annual or dig and store bulbs over winter until time to replant. Potted corms can be stored in pots of dry soil.

IXIOLIRION tataricum (I. montanum)

Amaryllidaceae

BULB

ZONES 31, 32; OR DIG AND STORE, OR GROW IN POTS

FULL SUN

REGULAR WATER

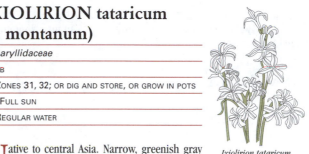

Ixiolirion tataricum

Native to central Asia. Narrow, greenish gray leaves. Wiry, 12–16-in.-high stems bear loose clusters of violet blue, trumpet-shaped, 1½-in. flowers in spring. Set bulbs 3 in. deep. Plant in fall. In Zones 31–32, needs a warm, sheltered site and mulch to protect leaves from spring frosts. In colder regions, plant in spring and treat as summer annual or dig after foliage dies back and store over winter. Where bulbs are left in ground, good drainage is essential to keep them from rotting over winter. Can also be grown in pots.

JACK-IN-THE-PULPIT. See ARISAEMA triphyllum

JACOB'S LADDER. See POLEMONIUM caeruleum

JAMAICA FLOWER, JAMAICA SORREL. See HIBISCUS sabdariffa

JAPANESE ANGELICA TREE. See ARALIA elata

JAPANESE ASTER. See KALIMERIS pinnatifida

JAPANESE BLOOD GRASS. See IMPERATA cylindrica 'Rubra'

JAPANESE FLOWERING APRICOT, JAPANESE FLOWERING PLUM. See PRUNUS mume

JAPANESE LACE FERN. See POLYSTICHUM polyblepharum

JAPANESE PAGODA TREE. See SOPHORA japonica

JAPANESE RAISIN TREE. See HOVENIA dulcis

JAPANESE SILVER GRASS. See MISCANTHUS sinensis

JAPANESE SNOWBALL. See VIBURNUM plicatum plicatum

JAPANESE SNOWBELL, JAPANESE SNOWDROP TREE. See STYRAX japonicus

JAPANESE SWEET SHRUB. See CLETHRA barbinervis

JAPANESE TORREYA. See TORREYA

I

JASIONE

SHEEP'S BIT

Campanulaceae (Lobeliaceae)

PERENNIAL, ANNUAL, OR BIENNIAL

⚡ ZONES VARY BY SPECIES

☼ ◐ FULL SUN OR LIGHT SHADE

💧 💧 MODERATE TO REGULAR WATER

Jasione
Sheep's bit

These summer bloomers with their pincushion flowers are good additions to beds and borders or rock gardens.

J. laevis (J. perennis). SHEPHERD'S SCABIOUS. Perennial. Zones 31, 32, 34. Clump of deep green basal leaves produces 1½-ft.-tall, essentially bare stalks with a few smaller leaves along their lower part. Blooms from midsummer until frost, bearing clusters of small blue flowers that form a tight 2-in. ball at top of each stalk. Common name comes from flowers' resemblance to those of *Scabiosa,* the pincushion flower. Requires good drainage and nonacid soil. Use in rock garden or at front of perennial border. 'Blue Light' produces 1–2-ft. flowering stems, blooms over a slightly longer period than the species.

J. montana. SHEEP'S BIT. Annual or biennial. All zones. To 20 in. high. Narrow, oblong leaves. Blue flowers in summer, sometimes tinged red or white.

JASMINUM

JASMINE

Oleaceae

EVERGREEN, SEMIEVERGREEN, OR DECIDUOUS VINES OR SHRUBS

⚡ ZONES VARY BY SPECIES

☼ ◐ FULL SUN OR PARTIAL SHADE

💧 REGULAR WATER

Jasminum

When one thinks of fragrance, jasmine is one of the first plants that comes to mind. Yet not all jasmines are fragrant; and despite its common name, the intensely sweet-scented Confederate or star jasmine is not a true jasmine at all, but a member of the genus *Trachelospermum.* All jasmines thrive in regular garden soil or an all-purpose potting mix, and need frequent pinching and shaping to control growth.

Jasmines are not hardy outdoors in most of the Northeast, but they make good container plants. Move pots outdoors to a partly shady location in summer, and bring them back indoors in autumn. Feed with all-purpose house plant fertilizer while in active growth, according to package directions.

J. fruticans. Evergreen or semievergreen shrub. Zone 31 or all zones in containers. Upright and dense to 5 ft. high outdoors. Leaves are dark green and divided into three leaflets. Clusters of small, mildly fragrant yellow flowers in summer.

J. nitidum. SHINING JASMINE, ANGELWING JASMINE. Evergreen to semievergreen vine. All zones in containers. Leathery, uncut, glossy medium green leaves to 2 in. long. Very fragrant flowers shaped like 1-in. pinwheels open from purplish buds in late spring and summer. Flowers are white above, purplish beneath, borne in clusters of three. Responds well to drastic pruning. Often sold as *J. magnificum.*

J. nudiflorum. WINTER JASMINE. Deciduous viny shrub. Zones 31, 32, 34, 39. Unsupported, to 4 ft. high and 7 ft. wide; can grow to 15 ft. tall if trained on a trellis or wall. Slender, willowy green stems stand out in winter landscape. Unscented, bright yellow, 1-in.-wide flowers appear in winter or early spring before leaves unfold. Handsome glossy green leaves have three leaflets. Best tied up at desired height and permitted to spill down in waterfall fashion. Good bank cover; spreads by rooting where stems touch soil. Attractive planted at top of retaining walls, with branches cascading over side. Cut back severely every few years to rejuvenate.

J. officinale. COMMON WHITE JASMINE, POET'S JASMINE. Semievergreen to deciduous twining vine. Zone 31, or all zones in containers.

Rapid growth to as much as 30 ft. outdoors. Glossy green leaves with five to seven leaflets, each 2 in. long. Very fragrant white flowers to 1 in. across; blooms all summer and into fall.

J. sambac. ARABIAN JASMINE. Evergreen shrub. All zones in containers. In Hawaii, it is also called pikake; it's a favorite flower for leis and is used in making perfume. In Asia, used in jasmine tea. To 5 ft. tall. Leaves undivided, glossy green, to 3 in. long. Blooms in summer, bearing clusters of powerfully fragrant, ¾–1-in. white flowers. Grow as small, compact shrub on trellis in container. 'Grand Duke' has double flowers.

> ## MORE JASMINE FLOWERS
> Jasmines growing as indooor/outdoor container plants can be encouraged to rebloom by cutting back the plants after they have flowered. Cut back long stems to right above a dormant bud, recognizable as a small bump on the stem, to stimulate new growth.

JEFFERSONIA

TWIN-LEAF

Berberidaceae

PERENNIALS

⚡ ZONES 31, 32, 34–41

◐ ● PARTIAL OR FULL SHADE

💧 AMPLE WATER

Jeffersonia

These early spring bloomers produce flowers before their leaves are fully developed, growing from a height of 4–8 in. in bloom to 10–12 in. thereafter. Young foliage is purplish red. Both species prefer soil high in organic matter.

J. diphylla. AMERICAN TWIN-LEAF. Native from New York State to the Deep South, this clump-forming perennial has deeply cleft, kidney-shaped leaves and 1-in.-diameter white flowers, each held atop a single erect stem. Prefers alkaline soil; add lime if necessary. Plant in woodland gardens or in collections of native plants.

J. dubia. Well-suited to rock and woodland gardens. Leaves are heart shaped, and the attractive bowl-shaped flowers are pale blue.

JERUSALEM ARTICHOKE. See HELIANTHUS tuberosus

JERUSALEM SAGE. See PHLOMIS

JETBEAD. See RHODOTYPOS

JEWEL MINT OF CORSICA. See MENTHA requienii

JOB'S TEARS. See COIX lacryma-jobi

JOE PYE WEED. See EUPATORIUM maculatum, E. purpureum

JOHNNY-JUMP-UP. See VIOLA tricolor

JOINT-FIR. See EPHEDRA

JONQUIL. See NARCISSUS, jonquilla hybrids

JOSEPH'S COAT. See AMARANTHUS tricolor

JUDAS TREE. See CERCIS siliquastrum

Juglandaceae. The walnut family consists of nut-bearing trees with leaves divided into many paired leaflets. Pecans and hickories (*Carya*), walnuts (*Juglans*), and wingnuts (*Pterocarya*) are examples.

JUGLANS. See WALNUT

JUJUBE. See ZIZIPHUS jujuba

JUNCUS effusus

SOFT RUSH	
Juncaceae	
PERENNIAL	
🌡 ZONES 31, 32, 34–45	
☀ ◑ FULL SUN OR LIGHT SHADE	
🌢 AMPLE WATER	

Juncus effusus

Somewhat resembles a grass. Round, leaflike stems are ⅛–¼ in. thick, to 2½ ft. tall, medium green turning brown with frost. Erect at first, they arch a little toward tips. Tiny, inconspicuous flowers are clustered at or near stem tips. 'Spiralis' has stems that coil in spirals. Use at edge of pond or stream, in the water, or among stones and pebbles.

JUNIPERUS

JUNIPER	
Cupressaceae	
EVERGREEN SHRUBS AND TREES	
🌡 ZONES VARY BY SPECIES	
☀ ◑ SUN; MOST TOLERATE LIGHT SHADE	
🌢 🌢 REGULAR TO MODERATE WATER	
▶ SEE CHART	

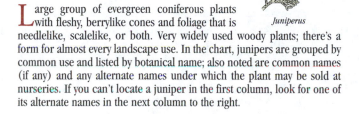

Juniperus

Large group of evergreen coniferous plants with fleshy, berrylike cones and foliage that is needlelike, scalelike, or both. Very widely used woody plants; there's a form for almost every landscape use. In the chart, junipers are grouped by common use and listed by botanical name; also noted are common names (if any) and any alternate names under which the plant may be sold at nurseries. If you can't locate a juniper in the first column, look for one of its alternate names in the next column to the right.

The ground cover group includes types ranging from a few inches to 2–3 ft. high. They are of two sorts: spreaders, which put down roots and spread out long, stiff branches; and creepers (mainly *J. horizontalis* varieties), which creep along the ground, rooting as they grow. If a spreader dies, the whole plant must be replaced; with a creeper, you may only lose the center. Low junipers are indispensable in rock gardens. As ground cover, space most varieties 5–6 ft. apart. In early years, mulch will help keep soil cool and weeds down.

Juniperus conferta

Shrub types range from low to quite tall, from spreading to stiffly upright and columnar. You can find a juniper in almost any height, width, shape, or foliage color. Fewer tree types are grown; they are valued for picturesque habit. Many of the larger junipers serve well as screens or windbreaks in cold-winter areas.

Junipers are subject to a number of pests and diseases. Among the most serious are bagworms (foliage is stripped from plant); blight (twig and branch dieback); twig borers (browning and dying branch tips); cedar-apple rust (disease alternating between junipers and apple trees causing twig dieback); juniper scale (no new growth, yellowed foliage); juniper webworm (webbing together and browning of foliage). To confirm a problem or decide on control measures, consult your Cooperative Extension Office or reputable local nursery.

Juniperus horizontalis

JUPITER'S BEARD. See CENTRANTHUS ruber

JUPITER'S DISTAFF. See SALVIA glutinosa

KAFFIR LILY. See SCHIZOSTYLIS coccinea

KAHILI GINGER. See HEDYCHIUM gardnerianum

JUNIPER

NAME	ALSO SOLD AS	ZONES	SIZE, HABIT	CHARACTERISTICS
GROUND COVERS				
Juniperus chinensis 'Parsonii' PROSTRATA JUNIPER	J. davurica 'Parsonii' J. prostrata J. squamata 'Parsonii'	31, 32, 34–43	To 1½ ft. by 8 ft. or more. Spreading	Slow growing. Dense short twigs on flat, rather heavy branches
J. c. procumbens JAPANESE GARDEN JUNIPER	J. procumbens	31, 32, 34–43	To 3 ft. by 12–20 ft. Spreading	Feathery yet substantial blue-green foliage on strong branches
J. c. p. 'Nana'	J. compacta 'Nana' J. procumbens 'Compacta Nana' J. procumbens 'Nana'	31, 32, 34–43	To 1 ft. by 4–5 ft. Curved branches spreading in all directions	Shorter needles and slower growth than *J. c. procumbens*. Can be staked into upright, picturesque shrub
J. c. 'San Jose'	J. c. procumbens 'San Jose' J. japonica 'San Jose' J. procumbens 'San Jose'	31, 32, 34–43	To 2 ft. by 6 ft. or more. Prostrate, dense, spreading	Dark sage green with both needle and scale foliage. Heavy trunked, slow growing

JUNIPER

NAME	ALSO SOLD AS	ZONES	SIZE, HABIT	CHARACTERISTICS
J. c. sargentii SARGENT JUNIPER	*J. sargentii J. sargentii viridis*	31, 32, 34–43	To 3 ft. by 10 ft. Ground hugging, spreading	Gray-green or green foliage. Feathery. Classic bonsai plant. 'Glauca' has blue-green foliage; 'Viridis' has bright green foliage
J. c. 'Saybrook Gold'		31, 32, 34–43	2–3 ft. by 6 ft. Arching, spreading, with drooping tips	Rich yellow foliage
J. communis 'Effusa'		31, 32, 34–45	To 1 ft. by 6 ft. Round, flat, spreading	Thin foliage shows off reddish brown stems
J. c. saxatilis	*J. c. montana J. c. sibirica*	31, 32, 34–45	To 1 ft. by 6–8 ft. Prostrate, creeping	Variable gray, gray-green foliage. Upturned branchlets like tiny candles. Native alpine
J. c. 'Windsor Gem'		31, 32, 34–45	To 8–10 in. by 5 ft., spreading	Similar to J. c. 'Effusa', but flatter, more open
J. conferta SHORE JUNIPER	*J. conferta littoralis.* Plants so named may be a grower's selected form	31, 32, 34, 39	To 3 ft. by 6–8 ft. Prostrate, creeping	Bright green, soft needles. Excellent for seashore and will stand heat if given moist, well-drained soil. 'Blue Pacific' is denser, bluer, more heat tolerant. 'Emerald Sea' is bright green
J. C. 'Silver Mist'		31, 32, 34, 39 To 1 ft.	Prostrate, creeping	Blue-green needles striped with silver-white. Salt tolerant
J. davurica expansa 'Aureovariegata'	*J. chinensis 'Alba'*	31, 32, 34–45	2–3 ft. by 4–5 ft. Mounding, spreading	Slow growing, with heavy, horizontal branches, patches of creamy yellow. Variegations can burn in hot sun
J. d. e. 'Parsonii'	*J. prostrata J. squamata 'Parsonii'*	31, 32, 34–45	To 1½ ft. by 8 ft. or more, spreading	Dense, short twigs on heavy, horizontal branches
J. horizontalis 'Bar Harbor' BAR HARBOR JUNIPER	*J. h. 'Blue Rug'*	31, 32, 34–45	To 1 ft. by 10 ft. Ground hugging, creeping	Fast growing. Feathery, blue-gray foliage turns plum color in winter. Foliage dies back in center to expose limbs as plant ages, especially in hot climates
J. h. 'Blue Chip'		34–45	To 1 ft. by 8–10 ft., creeping	Silvery blue foliage
J. h. 'Blue Mat'		31–45	9–12 in. by 6–7 ft., creeping	Dense mat of gray-green foliage
J. h. 'Douglasii' WAUKEEGAN JUNIPER		31, 32, 34—45	To 1 ft. by 10 ft., creeping	Steel blue foliage turns purplish in fall. New growth rich green
J. h. 'Emerald Spreader'		31, 32, 34—45	To 6 in. tall, creeping	Dense, feathery, bright green foliage
J. h. 'Glomerata'		31, 32, 34—45	To 6 in. tall, creeping	Deep green turning plum color in winter. Scale foliage gives soft look
J. h. 'Hughes'		31, 32, 34—45	To 6 in. tall, creeping	Showy silvery blue foliage
J. h. 'Marcellus'		31, 32, 34—45	To 5 in. tall, creeping	Blue-gray, soft-textured foliage
J. h. 'Mother Lode'		31, 32, 34—45	To 4 in. by 8–10 ft. Very flat juniper, creeping	Golden version of J. h. 'Wiltonii', the variety from which it was developed. Brilliant yellow foliage turns bronze yellow in winter

JUNIPER

NAME	ALSO SOLD AS	ZONES	SIZE, HABIT	CHARACTERISTICS
J. h. 'Plumosa' ANDORRA JUNIPER	*J. depressa plumosa*	31, 32, 34–45	To 1½ ft. by 10 ft., creeping	Gray green in summer, plum color in winter. Flat branches, upright branchlets. Plumy
H. j. 'Prince of Wales'		31, 32, 34–45	To 8 in. tall, creeping	Medium green foliage turns purplish in fall
J. h. 'Turquoise Spreader'		31, 32, 34–45	To 6 in. tall, creeping	Dense turquoise green foliage. Very flat
J. h. 'Wiltonii' BLUE CARPET JUNIPER	*J. h. 'Blue Rug'*	31, 32, 34–45	To 4 in. by 8-10 ft. Very flat, creeping	Intense silver blue. Dense, short branchlets on long, trailing branches. Similar to J. h. 'Bar Harbor' but tighter; it rarely exposes limbs
J. h. 'Youngstown'		31, 32, 34–45	To 1 ft. by 6 ft., creeping	Resembles J. h. 'Plumosa' but is flatter, more compact
J. h. 'Yukon Belle'		31, 32, 34–45	To 6 in. tall, creeping	Silvery blue foliage. Extremely cold hardy
J. sabina 'Arcadia'		31, 32, 34–45	To 1 ft. by 10 ft., spreading	Bright green, lacy foliage
J. s. 'Blue Danube'		31, 32, 34–45	To 14 in. by 10 ft. Dense, mounding, spreading	Soft, bright green foliage
J. s. 'Broadmoor'		31, 32, 34–45	To 14 in. by 10 ft. Dense, mounding, spreading	Soft, bright green foliage
J. s. 'Buffalo'		31, 32, 34–45	8–12 in. by 8 ft. Lower than tamarix juniper. Very wide spreading	Soft, feathery, bright green foliage
J. s. 'Calgary Carpet'		31, 32, 34–45	6–9 in. by 10 ft., spreading	Soft green foliage. Extremely cold hardy
J. s. 'Moor-Dense'		31, 32, 34–45	To 1½ ft. by 8 ft., spreading	Resembles J. s. 'Broadmoor' but is denser. Has layered look
J. s. 'Scandia'		31, 32, 34–45	To 1 ft. by 8 ft., spreading	Low, dense, bright green
J. s. 'tamariscifolia' TAMARIX JUNIPER TAM	*J. tamariscifolia*	31, 32, 34–45	To 1½ ft. by 10–20 ft. Symmetrically spreading	Dense blue-green foliage. Widely used
J. scopulorum 'Blue Creeper'		35, 41, 43	To 2 ft. by 6–8 ft., mounding, spreading	Bright blue-green color
J. virginiana 'Silver Spreader'	*J. v. prostrata*	31, 32, 34—43	To 1½ ft. by 6-8 ft., spreading	Silvery green, feathery, fine textured. Older branches become dark green
SHRUBS **J. chinensis 'Armstrongii'** ARMSTRONG JUNIPER		31, 32, 34—43	To 4 ft. by 4 ft. Upright	Medium green. More compact than Pfitzer juniper
J. c. 'Blaauw' BLAAUWS JUNIPER, BLUE SHIMPAKU		31, 32, 34—43	To 4 ft. by 3 ft. Vase shaped	Blue foliage. Dense. Compact

J

JUNIPER

NAME	ALSO SOLD AS	ZONES	SIZE, HABIT	CHARACTERISTICS
J. c. 'Fruitland'		31, 32, 34—43	To 3 ft. by 6 ft. Compact, dense	Like Pfitzer juniper but more compact
J. c. 'Gold Coast'	*J. 'Coasti Aurea'*	31, 32, 34—43		Similar or identical to J. c. 'Golden Armstrong'
J. C. 'Golden Armstrong'		31, 32, 34—43	To 4 ft. by 4 ft. Full, blocky	Between golden Pfitzer and Armstrong juniper in appearance
J. c. 'Hetzli' HETZ BLUE JUNIPER	*J. c. hetzi glauca J. glauca hetzi*	31, 32, 34—43	To 15 ft. Fountainlike	Blue-gray foliage. Branches spread outward and upward at 45° angle. Fast growing
J. c. 'Kaizuka' HOLLYWOOD JUNIPER	*J. c. 'Torulosa'*	31, 32, 34—43	To 15–30 ft. Irregular, upright	Rich green. Branches with irregular, twisted appearance. Give it plenty of room
J. c. 'Maney'		31, 32, 34—43	To 15 ft. Semierect, massive	Blue-gray foliage. Steeply inclined, spreading branches
J. c. 'Mint Julep'		31, 32, 34—43	4-6 ft. by 6 ft. Vase shaped	Mint green foliage, arching branches
J. c. 'Pfitzerana' PFITZER JUNIPER	*J. c. 'Pfitzeriana'*	31, 32, 34—43	5-6 ft. by 15-20 ft. Arching	Feathery, gray green. Sharp-needled foliage
J. c. 'Pfitzerana Aurea' GOLDEN PFITZER JUNIPER	*J. c. 'Pfitzeriana Aurea'*	31, 32, 34—43	3–4 ft. by 8–10 ft.	Blue-gray foliage with current season's growth golden yellow
J. c. 'Pfitzerana Compacta' NICK'S COMPACT PFITZER JUNIPER	*J. c. 'Pfitzereana Compacta'*	31, 32, 34—43	To 2 ft. by 4–6 ft. Densely branched	Compact. Gray-green foliage
J. c. 'Pfitzerana Glauca'	*J. c. 'Pfitzeriana Glauca'*	31, 32, 34—43	5–6 ft. by 10–15 ft.	Silvery blue foliage. Arching branches
J. c. 'Sea Green'		31, 32, 34—43	4–5 ft. by 4–5 ft. Arching, fountainlike	Compact, dark green
J. sabina SAVIN JUNIPER		31, 32, 34—45	Creeping or shrubby plant to 4–6 ft. by 5–10 ft.	Dark green foliage. Exceedingly tough plant
J. scopulorum 'Table Top Blue'		35, 41, 43	To 6 ft. by 8 ft.	Gray. Massive. Flat-topped
J. squamata 'Blue Carpet'		31, 32, 34—41	To 2 ft. by 4-6 ft.	Resembles J. s. 'Meyeri' in irregular branching habit, but is lower, more spreading and with bluer foliage
J. s. 'Blue Star'		31, 32, 34—41	To 2 ft. by 5 ft. Moundlike	Regular branching. Silver blue foliage turns a little darker in winter
J. s. 'Holger'		31, 32, 34—41	To 6 ft. by 6 ft.	Densely branched, broad, flat-topped. New growth yellow tipped
J. s. 'Meyeri' MEYER or FISHBACK JUNIPER		31, 32, 34—41	6-8 ft. by 2–3 ft. Upright	Oddly angled stiff branches. Broad needles. Blend of green, gray, and reddish foliage. Retains old dead foliage

J

JUNIPER

NAME	ALSO SOLD AS	ZONES	SIZE, HABIT	CHARACTERISTICS
COLUMNAR TYPES **J. chinensis 'Blue Point'**		31, 32, 34—43	To 7-8 ft. Broadly columnar	Dense, blue-green scale and needle foliage
J. c. 'Blue Vase'		31, 32, 34—43	4–5 ft. by 3–4 ft.	Dense, blue-green scale foliage
J. c. 'Columnaris' CHINESE BLUE COLUMN JUNIPER	*J. c 'Columnaris Glauca'* *j. excelsa 'Stricta'*	31, 32, 34—43	12-15 ft.	Blue-green, narrow pyramid. Prickly
J. c. 'Hetz's Columnaris'		31, 32, 34—43	12–15 ft.	Rich green. Dense column. Scale foliage predominant, branchlets threadlike
J. c. 'Robusta Green'		31, 32, 34—43	To 20 ft.	Brilliant green, dense-tufted column
J. c. 'Spartan'	*J. c. densaerecta 'Spartan'*	31, 32, 34—43	To 20 ft.	Rich green, dense column
J. communis 'Compressa'		31, 32, 34—45	To 2 ft.	Dwarf, for rock gardens
J. scopulorum 'Cologreen'		35, 41, 43	15–20 ft.	Narrow, bright green column
J. s. 'Green Ice'		35, 41, 43	To 15 ft. by 7–10 ft.	Dense branching, cold tolerance make it a good windbreak. Foliage is gray green.
J. s. 'Welchii'		35, 41, 43	To 8 ft.	Silvery green. Very narrow spire
J. s. 'Wichita Blue'		35, 41, 43	To 18 ft. or taller	Broad, silver blue pyramid
J. virginia 'Cupressifolia' HILLSPIRE JUNIPER	*J. v. 'Hilspire'*	31, 32, 34—43	15–20 ft.	Dark green, compact pyramid
J. v. 'Idyllwild'		31, 32, 34—43	To 15 ft. by 7 ft.	Broad pyramid with dark green foliage. Use for screening
J. v. 'Manhattan Blue'	*J. scopulorum 'Manhattan Blue'*	31, 32, 34—43	10–15 ft.	Blue-green compact pyramid
J. v. 'Skyrocket'	*J. scopulorum 'Skyrocket'*	31, 32, 34—43	10–15 ft.	Narrowest blue-gray spire
TREES **J. recurva 'Coxii'**		31, 32, 34	To 60 ft., usually much less	Erect, strongly weeping branches. Best in mild, moist climates
J. rigida 'Pendula' NEEDLE JUNIPER		31, 32, 34, 39	To 45 ft., usually much lower	Open growth, with drooping branchlets
J. scopulorum 'Tolleson's Blue Weeping'	*J. scopulorum 'Repandens'*	35, 41, 43	To 20 ft. or more, 10 ft. wide	Blue-green, drooping branchlets make a graceful weeping tree. 'Tolleson's Green Weeping' is similar, but dark green. Plants are not well adapted to hot, humid climates.
J. virginiana EASTERN RED CEDAR		31, 32, 34—43	40-50 ft. or more	Conical tree with dark green foliage that turns reddish in cold weather. Many varieties sold

J

KALE and COLLARDS

Kale

Brassicaceae (Cruciferae)

BIENNIAL GROWN AS ANNUAL

ALL ZONES

FULL SUN OR LIGHT SHADE

REGULAR WATER

Vegetable crops that live 1 or 2 years. The type of kale known as collards is a large, smooth-leafed plant resembling a cabbage that does not form a head. Planted in early spring or late summer, collards will yield edible leaves in fall, winter, and spring. 'Georgia' and 'Vates' are typical varieties. Curly-leafed kales (such as 'Dwarf Blue Curled' and 'Dwarf Siberian') form compact clusters of tightly curled leaves; they make decorative garden or container plants and supply edible leaves as well. So-called flowering kale (similar to flowering cabbage) has brightly colored foliage, especially toward centers of rosettes; it is edible.

For all types of kale and collards, harvest leaves for cooking by removing them from outside of clusters; or harvest entire plant. Exposure to frost sweetens the flavor, so try to postpone at least part of the harvest until plants have been touched by one or more light frosts. Mulch deeply or plant in cold frame to prolong harvest into winter. Far fewer pest and disease problems than most other cabbage-family crops.

KALIMERIS pinnatifida

Kalimeris pinnatifida

JAPANESE ASTER

Asteraceae (Compositae)

PERENNIAL

ZONES 31, 32, 34, 39

FULL SUN

REGULAR WATER

Perennial similar to *Boltonia asteroides*. Grows to 5 ft. tall, with finely cut leaves 3½ in. long and half as wide. Daisylike long-stemmed, inch-wide flowers in open clusters bloom over a long period in summer. Blossoms are white, tinged pink or blue. 'Hortensis' is a pure white form with semidouble flowers on a 3-ft. plant.

KALMIA latifolia

Kalmia latifolia

MOUNTAIN LAUREL, CALICO BUSH

Ericaceae

EVERGREEN SHRUBS

ZONES 31, 32, 34–41

FULL SUN OR PARTIAL SHADE

REGULAR WATER

LEAVES AND FLOWER NECTAR ARE POISONOUS IF INGESTED

Native to eastern North America from Canada to Florida, west across the Appalachians into states drained by the Ohio–Mississippi river systems. Elegant flowering shrub related to rhododendron, with somewhat similar showy flower clusters. Notable difference is that each long flower stalk bears a small bud resembling a fluted turban; buds open to chalice-shaped blooms with five starlike points. Plants share rhododendron's need for moist atmosphere and well-drained acid soil rich in humus, but take more sun. They tolerate full shade but bloom better with some light. Plants from southern forms grow better in warmer zones; those from northern seed sources grow better in cold-winter regions.

Slow growing to 6–8 ft. or taller, with equal spread. Glossy, leathery, oval leaves are 3–5 in. long, dark green on top, yellowish green beneath. Blooms in late spring; typically bears 1-in.-wide light pink flowers opening

from darker pink buds, but blossoms often have subtly different color in their throats and may have contrasting stamens. Flowers are carried in clusters to 5 in. across.

Many named varieties are available. They include:

'Bullseye', white flowers banded in red-purple.

'Carousel', white flowers banded in red and with bright purplish brown starburst patterning.

'Heart of Fire', red buds, deep pink flowers.

'Heart's Desire', deep red buds, burgundy flowers with white lip.

'Kaleidoscope', deep red buds, burgundy flowers with white lip; flowers brighter than 'Heart's Desire'.

'Nipmuck', deep red buds, flowers white to light pink, deep pink on back.

'Pink Charm', dark reddish pink buds, pink flowers.

'Pinwheel', maroon flowers edged in white, with white centers, scalloped edges.

'Raspberry Glow', dark burgundy buds, deep raspberry pink flowers.

'Richard Jaynes', red to raspberry pink buds, pink flowers with silvery sheen inside.

'Sarah', red buds, bright pinkish red flowers.

'Shooting Star', white flowers with backcurved "petals."

'Silver Dollar', light pink buds, large white flowers.

'Star Cluster', flowers are maroon in center, white around the edges.

'Sunset', red buds, near-red flowers.

'Yankee Doodle', red buds, yellow flowers with maroon bands and white throat.

Two dwarfs, both growing 2–2½ ft. tall and 4–5 ft. wide, are 'Elf', with nearly white blossoms, and 'Tiddlywinks', with medium pink blossoms opening from deep pink buds.

KALOPANAX septemlobus (K. pictus)

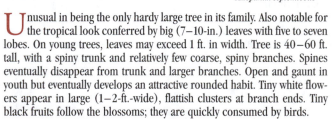

Kalopanax septemlobus

CASTOR ARALIA, TREE ARALIA

Araliaceae

DECIDUOUS TREE

ZONES 32, 34–41

FULL SUN

REGULAR WATER

Unusual in being the only hardy large tree in its family. Also notable for the tropical look conferred by big (7–10-in.) leaves with five to seven lobes. On young trees, leaves may exceed 1 ft. in width. Tree is 40–60 ft. tall, with a spiny trunk and relatively few coarse, spiny branches. Spines eventually disappear from trunk and larger branches. Open and gaunt in youth but eventually develops an attractive rounded habit. Tiny white flowers appear in large (1–2-ft.-wide), flattish clusters at branch ends. Tiny black fruits follow the blossoms; they are quickly consumed by birds.

KATSURA TREE. See CERCIDIPHYLLUM japonicum

KAYA. See TORREYA

KENILWORTH IVY. See CYMBALARIA muralis

KENTIA PALM. See HOWEA

KENTUCKY COFFEE TREE. See GYMNOCLADUS dioica

KENYA IVY. See SENECIO macroglossus

FOR INFORMATION ON YOUR CLIMATE ZONE

PLEASE SEE PAGES 30–46

KERRIA japonica

Rosaceae

DECIDUOUS SHRUB

⚡ ZONES 31, 32, 34–41

☀ ◐ ● TAKES FULL SUN IN COOL-SUMMER AREAS

💧 REGULAR WATER

Kerria japonica

Native to China. Open, graceful, rounded shrub to 6 ft. tall. Slender stems are yellowish green to bright green in winter, providing welcome color in cold climates. Toothed, heavily veined, somewhat triangular, 2–4-in.-long, bright green leaves unfold early in spring; turn yellow in fall. Flowers come in spring, sporadically into early summer; they look like small, single yellow roses. 'Pleniflora', more commonly planted than the species, has double golden, inch-wide blossoms and taller, suckering habit. 'Albiflora' has single pale yellow flowers. 'Golden Guinea' bears large, single flowers to 2½ in. across. 'Picta' ('Variegata') has white-edged leaves, single yellow flowers. 'Kinkan' has yellow-striped stems, single yellow blooms.

Give kerria room to display its arching form. It blooms on previous year's wood. Prune heavily after flowering, cutting out branches that have bloomed, all dead or weak wood, and suckers. The green branches are a favorite subject in Japanese wintertime flower arrangements.

KINGFISHER DAISY. See FELICIA bergeriana

KING'S SPEAR. See ASPHODELINE lutea

KINNIKINNICK. See ARCTOSTAPHYLOS uva-ursi

KIRENGESHOMA palmata

YELLOW WAX BELLS

Hydrangeaceae (Saxifragaceae)

PERENNIAL

⚡ ZONES 31, 32, 34, 35, 37, 39

◐ PARTIAL SHADE

💧 REGULAR WATER

Kirengeshoma palmata

Attractive plant to 4–4½ ft. tall. Dark purplish or reddish stalks carry deeply lobed and toothed leaves to 8 in. across; nodding flowers, in clusters of three, appear in joints of upper leaves and at top of stalks in late summer and early autumn. Blossoms drooping, narrowly bell shaped, 1½ in. long, pale yellow. A perennial of great elegance for partially shaded border or woodland garden.

The related and very similar *K. koreana* holds its flowers stiffly upright, and petals flare conspicuously at the tips.

KITAIBELA vitifolia

YUGOSLAVIAN MALLOW

Malvaceae

PERENNIALS

⚡ ZONES 31, 32, 34, 39

☀ FULL SUN

💧 REGULAR WATER

Kitaibela vitifolia

Native to damp meadows and copses in the former Yugoslavia, this vigorous, coarse-textured plant grows up to 9 ft. tall with long-stalked heart-shaped leaves up to 7 in. wide. Blooms in summer. Flowers are single or in clusters of two to four near the branch ends. Each blossom is 4 in. wide, with five white to pink petals around a central column of ragged

yellowish stamens. Use in wild gardens and meadow gardens. Grows best in deep, slightly fertile soil that is moist but well drained. To propagate, sow seed, take cuttings, or divide in spring. Sometimes short-lived.

KIWI, HARDY KIWI. See ACTINIDIA

KLEINIA. See SENECIO

KNAUTIA

Dipsacaceae

PERENNIALS

⚡ ZONES 31, 32, 34, 35, 37, 39

☀ FULL SUN

💧 REGULAR WATER

Knautia

Related to pincushion flower *(Scabiosa)*, with blossoms that are similar in structure—clustered in tight heads above ruffs of leafy bracts on bare stems. Leaves at base of plant are barely lobed, but upper leaves are deeply divided. The two species in cultivation are meadow plants that make few demands on the gardener; they are at home in cottage gardens, perennial borders, and meadow or roadside gardens. Flowers are good for cutting and can be dried for winter use.

K. arvensis. BLUE BUTTONS. Grows 1–4 ft. tall. Blue, 1½-in.-wide flower heads in summer.

K. macedonica. Grows 1½–2 ft. tall and as wide. Deep purplish red flower heads, early summer to fall.

KNIPHOFIA uvaria (Tritoma uvaria)

RED-HOT POKER, TORCH-LILY, POKER PLANT

Liliaceae

PERENNIAL

⚡ ZONES 31, 32, 34–41

☀ ◐ FULL SUN OR LIGHT SHADE

💧 💧 REGULAR TO MODERATE WATER

Kniphofia uvaria

Native to South Africa. Has been in cultivation long enough to give rise to garden varieties with some range in size, color. Typical plant is coarse, with large, rather dense clumps of long, grasslike leaves. Flower stalks (always taller than leaves) are about 2 ft. high in dwarf kinds, 3–6 ft. in larger kinds. The many drooping, orange-red or yellow, tubular flowers of the typical plant overlap, forming poker-like clusters 1 ft. long. Named varieties, in both dwarf and taller forms, come in soft or saffron yellow, creamy white, or coral.

Cultivars include 'Alcazar', salmon flowers; 'Border Ballet', cream to pink; 'Bressingham Comet', orange flowers with yellow base and red tips; 'Bressingham Flame', deep orange; 'Coral', pinkish melon; 'Earliest of All', blooms early, coral rose flowers; 'Little Maid', light green buds open to pale yellow flowers fading to ivory with age; 'Maid of Orleans', pale yellow buds open to yellow flowers fading to ivory with age; 'Peaches and Cream', lower flowers on spike are white, upper flowers are peach-colored; 'Pfitzeri' ('Wayside Flame'), orange red; 'Primrose Beauty', primrose yellow; 'Prince Igor', deep orange red; 'Rosea Superba', upper blossoms rosy red, lower ones white; 'Shining Sceptre', golden orange; 'Vanilla', creamy white.

Plants require excellent drainage. Bloom spring and summer; exact flowering time depends on variety. Cut out flower spikes after bloom. Where winter temperatures drop to 0°F/−18°C or below, tie foliage over clump to protect growing points. In warmer areas, cut foliage to ground in autumn. Clumps will grow undisturbed for many years. To increase plantings, carefully dig and remove young plants from clump's edge. Useful in large borders with other robust perennials such as daylilies, globe thistle.

K

K

KNOTWEED. See POLYGONUM

KOCHIA scoparia

SUMMER CYPRESS

Chenopodiaceae

ANNUAL

ALL ZONES

FULL SUN

REGULAR WATER

Kochia scoparia

To 3 ft. high, with branches densely clothed with narrow, soft, light green leaves, making plant too dense to see through. Grow individually for its gently rounded form, or group plants for low, temporary hedge or edging. Can be sheared into any shape. Plant from seed. Tolerates high heat and will perform well in short-summer areas.

K. s. trichophylla. MEXICAN FIRE BUSH, BURNING BUSH. Same as above, but foliage turns red at first frost. Can reseed profusely enough to become pest; hoe out unwanted seedlings when small.

KOELREUTERIA

Sapindaceae

DECIDUOUS TREES

ZONES VARY BY SPECIES

FULL SUN

REGULAR TO MODERATE WATER

Koelreuteria

Small trees native to Asia. Noted for large, loose clusters of yellow flowers followed by fat, papery fruit capsules resembling little Japanese lanterns; capsules are used in arrangements. Good patio, lawn, or street trees. Very adaptable to different soils as long as soil is fairly well drained. Control self-sown seedlings.

K. bipinnata (K. integrifoliola). CHINESE FLAME TREE. Zones 31, warmer parts of 32. To 20–40 ft. or taller; spreading and eventually flat topped. Leaves 1–2 ft. long, divided into many oval leaflets; turn yellow for short time before dropping. Flower clusters in late summer are similar to those of *K. paniculata*, but 2-in. fruit capsules are more colorful: orange, red, or salmon, appearing soon after flowers and persisting into fall. Stake and prune tree to develop high branching. Roots deep, not invasive; good tree to plant under.

K. paniculata. GOLDENRAIN TREE. Zones 31, 32, 34–41. To 20–35 ft., with 10–40-ft. spread. Open branching, giving slight shade. Leaves to 15 in. long with 7–15 oval, toothed or lobed leaflets, each 1–3 in. long. New leaves are purplish, turning bright green in summer; yellow to gold fall color unreliable. Very showy flower clusters, 8–14 in. long, in early to midsummer. Fruit capsules red when young, maturing to buff and brown shades; last well into autumn. Tree takes cold, heat, drought, wind. Prune to shape; can be gawky without pruning. 'September' blooms later than the species.

KOHLRABI

Brassicaceae (Cruciferae)

BIENNIAL GROWN AS ANNUAL

ALL ZONES

FULL SUN

REGULAR WATER

Kohlrabi

Cool-season vegetable related to cabbage. Edible part is an enlarged, bulblike portion of the stem, formed just above soil surface. Standard varieties are 'Early White Vienna' and 'Early Purple Vienna'; these are similar in size and flavor, differing only in skin color. Other white varieties include disease-resistant 'Triumph' and early 'Grand Duke'. Plants are very fast growing, ready to harvest in 50 to 60 days from seed. Sow seed ½ in. deep in rich soil, about 2 weeks after average date of last frost. Follow first planting with successive sowings 2 weeks apart. In areas with warm winters, plant again in late fall and early winter. Space rows 1½ ft. apart; thin seedlings to 4 in. apart. Harvest when round portions are 2–3 in. wide; slice and eat raw, or cook like turnips. Not usually bothered by pests or diseases.

KOLKWITZIA amabilis

BEAUTY BUSH

Caprifoliaceae

DECIDUOUS SHRUB

ZONES 31, 32, 34–41

FULL SUN OR PARTIAL SHADE

REGULAR WATER

Kolkwitzia amabilis

Native to China. Graceful, upright growth to 10–12 ft.; arching form in partial shade, denser and shorter in full sun. Gray-green leaves to 3 in. long sometimes turn reddish in fall. Blooms heavily in mid- to late spring, bearing clusters of small, yellow-throated pink flowers. Blossoms are followed by conspicuous pinkish brown, bristly fruits that prolong color display. Brown, flaky bark gradually peels from stems during winter.

'Pink Cloud' has darker pink flowers.

Adapts to many soils and climates. Flowers are borne on wood formed the previous year. Thin out oldest stems after blossoms have faded; or, to enjoy the fruit, prune lightly in early spring. Plant can be renewed by cutting to ground after bloom.

KOREAN FORSYTHIA. See FORSYTHIA ovata

KOREAN GRASS. See ZOYSIA tenuifolia

Labiatae. See Lamiaceae

LABURNUM

GOLDENCHAIN TREE

Fabaceae (Leguminosae)

DECIDUOUS LARGE SHRUBS OR SMALL TREES

ZONES VARY BY SPECIES

AFTERNOON SHADE IN HOT AREAS

REGULAR WATER

SEEDPODS ARE POISONOUS IF INGESTED

Laburnum

Upright growth; usually pruned into single-stemmed tree, but can be shrubby if permitted to keep basal suckers and low branches. Green bark; bright green leaves divided into three leaflets (like clover). Handsome in bloom: in mid- to late spring, bears yellow, sweet pea–shaped flowers in hanging clusters like wisteria. Use as a single tree in lawn or border; group in front of neutral background; or space regularly in long border of perennials, rhododendrons, or lilacs.

Provide well-drained soil. Prune and trim regularly to keep tidy. If possible, remove seedpods; not only are they toxic, but a heavy crop drains the plant's strength.

L. alpinum. SCOTCH LABURNUM. Zones 34–43. To 30–35 ft. tall. Flower clusters 10–15 in. long. 'Pendulum' has weeping branches.

L. anagyroides. COMMON GOLDENCHAIN. Zones 34–41. To 20–30 ft. tall; often bushy and wide spreading. Flower clusters 6–10 in. long. Like *L. alpinum*, it has a weeping variety, 'Pendulum'.

L. watereri. Zones 34–41. Hybrid between the two preceding species. To about 25 ft. tall. Flower clusters 10–20 in. long. 'Vossii' is the most widely grown and most graceful variety; it can be espaliered.

LADY BELLS. See ADENOPHORA

LADY FERN. See ATHYRIUM filix-femina

LADY PALM. See RHAPIS

LADY'S-MANTLE. See ALCHEMILLA

LADY'S SLIPPER. See CYPRIPEDIUM

LAGENARIA siceraria

WHITE-FLOWERED GOURD, HARD-SHELL GOURD, BOTTLE GOURD

Cucurbitaceae

ANNUAL

☀ ALL ZONES

☼ FULL SUN

🔴 REGULAR WATER

Lagenaria siceraria

This vigorous, fast-growing tender vine, native to the tropics in the Old World as well as South America, is grown for its hard-shelled fruits. Plants resemble pumpkin or cucumber vines, bear tendrils, and can climb as high as 30 ft. in a single season. Or they can be left to sprawl on the ground, where they will cover any obstacles in their path. The large, heart-shaped to rounded leaves can reach 9 in. across and are covered with soft, somewhat sticky, hairs. Male and female flowers are borne separately; both are solitary, white, and five-petaled. The female flowers have a slight swelling at the base, which becomes the fruit once the flower is pollinated. Males are carried on long, slender stalks and lack the swollen base. Blooms open at night and close the next day. The fruits that follow the flowers vary tremendously in shape, from small oval gourds to long, baseball-bat-shaped ones.

Gourds are named according to the shape of the fruit. Cannon Ball gourds bear small, round, pumpkin-shaped fruits. Bird House, sometimes called Martin House, gourds produce pear-shaped fruits usually ranging from 8 to 13 in. in diameter and about 15 in. long. Once dried, these are traditionally made into bird houses for purple martins or other bird species by drilling a hole on the side, adding small drainage holes in the bottom, and drilling the top and adding a hanger. Penguin or Powder Horn gourds bear somewhat funnel-shaped fruits with a narrow base that is as long as the bottom. Long-handled Dipper gourds have a small, rounded base with a straight or curved handle that can range from 3 to 4 or more ft. long. Short-handled Dipper gourds are similar, but have shorter handles. Snake gourds are long, thin, and twisted.

Gourds are warm-weather annuals requiring a long season to set and ripen fruit. In the Northeast, it is usually best to start seeds indoors in individual pots about 4 to 6 weeks before the last spring frost date. Transplant carefully after danger of frost has passed. They require full sun and rich, evenly moist, well-drained soil. Provide a sturdy trellis for climbing, let vines cover an arbor or large shrubs, or allow them to sprawl. If fruits are sitting on the soil, slip a piece of cardboard or leftover shingle under them to prevent rot. Handle fresh fruits carefully, as they are heavy and break easily; when dried, the gourds are quite strong. Harvest before the first fall frost and dry the fruits indoors in a warm (70°F), dry place for several months before using.

Hard-shell gourds delight many a craftsperson. They may be painted in various ways, sculpted, or etched with a burning tool. The American Gourd Society publishes an informative newsletter and has chapters throughout the country for devotees of this plant.

FOR INFORMATION ON SELECTING PLANTS

PLEASE SEE PAGES 47–112

LAGERSTROEMIA

CRAPE MYRTLE

Lythraceae

DECIDUOUS SHRUBS OR TREES

☀ ZONES 31, 32

☼ FULL SUN

🔴 MODERATE WATER

Lagerstroemia

The crape myrtles are among the most satisfactory of plants for hot-summer regions: showy summer flowers, attractive bark, and (in many cases) brilliant fall color make them year-round garden performers. Long, cool autumns yield the best leaf display; the first hard frost spoils the show. Mildew is a serious problem on susceptible varieties.

Most crape myrtles seen in gardens are varieties of *L. indica* or hybrids of that species with *L. fauriei*. The latter species has recently attracted notice for its hardiness and exceptionally showy bark.

All crape myrtles bloom on new wood and should be pruned in winter or early spring to increase next summer's flowers. On small, shrubby forms, remove spent flower clusters and thin out small twiggy growth; to maintain compactness and eliminate leggy look, cut branches nearly to the ground in spring. On large shrubs and trees, shorten branches by 1–1½ ft. in spring if you need to limit their size. Heavy watering and any fertilizing in summer can significantly decrease hardiness in marginal climates.

L. fauriei. JAPANESE CRAPE MYRTLE. Zone 32. Tree to 20–30 ft. with erect habit and outward-arching branches. Leaves light green, to 4 in. long and 2 in. wide, turning yellow in fall. Especially handsome bark: the smooth, gray outer bark flakes away to reveal glossy cinnamon brown bark beneath. Small white flowers are borne in 2–4-in.-long clusters; usually pauses after initial bloom, then flowers again in late summer. Resistant to mildew and best known as a parent of hardy, mildew-resistant hybrids with *L. indica*, though it is handsome in its own right. 'Fantasy', with even showier bark than the species, has a vase form—narrow below, spreading above; fast growing and very tall—to 50 ft. 'Townhouse' is shorter—to 30 ft.—multitrunked, and the best choice for those who wish to experiment with crape myrtle along the East Coast as far north as Cape Cod.

'Cherokee'. Compact growth to 12 ft. tall. Bright red flowers that repeat into September.

'Potomac'. Upright habit, to 20 ft. Clear pink flowers are easy to combine with other colors.

'Powhatan'. Compact growth, medium height. Flowers medium purple, productive, and long blooming.

'Tuscarora'. Wide-spreading habit, to 20 ft. tall. Dark coral-pink flowers. Orange-red autumn color; excellent, light-brown bark.

L. indica. CRAPE MYRTLE. Zones 31, 32. Shrub or tree where hardy, but capable of blooming from first-year regrowth if frozen to the ground. Behaves much like perennial in Zone 35. Variable in size (some forms are dwarf shrubs, others large shrubs or small trees) and habit (spreading to upright). Dark green leaves are 1–2½ in. long and somewhat narrower, usually tinted red on unfurling, often turning brilliant orange or red in fall. Crinkled, crepe-papery, 1–1½-in.-wide flowers in white or shades of pink, red, or purple are carried in dense clusters.

Trained as a tree, it develops an attractive trunk and branch pattern. Smooth gray or light brown bark peels off to reveal smooth, pinkish inner bark; winter trunk and branches seem polished.

The following list includes many of the best selections. Mildew can be a problem. Spray before plants bloom; or grow mildew-resistant hybrids of *L. indica* with *L. fauriei* (see list further down).

'Catawba'. Roundish, dense 6–10-ft. shrub (can be trained as a 15-ft. tree). Dark purple flowers. Orange-red fall color.

'Centennial'. Dwarf roundish shrub to 3 ft. high. Lavender flowers. Orange autumn foliage.

'Centennial Spirit'. Multistemmed large shrub or small tree to 20 ft. Dark red flowers. Orange-red fall color.

L

'Chica Pink' and 'Chica Red'. Compact, dense, 3–4 ft. tall and as wide. Bright pink or rosy red flowers. Yellow fall foliage.

'Glendora White'. Upright shrub to 9 ft. tall or, with training, a 25-ft. tree 20 ft. wide. White flowers. Red fall color.

'Peppermint Lace'. Somewhat erect shrub 6–7 ft. tall, or tree to 20 ft. high. Flowers are deep pink with a picotee edge of white. 'Prairie Lace' is similar in flower, but is a smaller (4–6-ft.) shrub. 'Queen's Lace', 12–14 ft. tall, is a hardier selection with similar flowers. All have red to red-orange fall foliage.

Petite series. These are semidwarf shrubs (5 ft. tall, 4 ft. wide) with names that describe their flower color: 'Petite Embers', 'Petite Orchid', 'Petite Pinkie', 'Petite Plum', 'Petite Red Imp', and 'Petite Snow'. Yellow fall foliage.

'Victor'. Compact shrub to 3 ft. tall. Dark red flowers. Red-tinged leaves turn reddish yellow in autumn.

The following are mildew-resistant hybrids between *L. indica* and *L. fauriei*. The products of a breeding program at the National Arboretum, they bear the names of Indian tribes.

'Acoma'. Spreading, arching shrub to 10 ft. tall and as wide. White flowers in 6–7 in. clusters. Reddish purple fall foliage.

'Comanche'. Large, spreading shrub to 12 ft. tall; can be trained as small tree. Bright red flowers. Reddish orange fall color.

'Hopi'. Shrubby plant 7 ft. tall, half again as wide. Pink flowers. Orange-red to dark red fall foliage.

'Muskogee'. Fast-growing large shrub or small tree to 20 ft. or more. Beige bark. Large clusters of lavender pink flowers. Red fall color.

'Natchez'. Fast-growing small tree to over 20 ft. tall and broad, with exceptionally handsome glossy brown bark. Large clusters of white flowers. Orange to red autumn foliage color.

'Seminole'. Shrub to 7–8 ft. tall and nearly as wide; can be trained into a 15–20 ft. tree. Large roundish clusters of pure medium pink flowers. Yellow fall color.

'Tonto'. Shrub to 8 ft. tall and 6 ft. wide, with beige bark. Bright magenta flowers.

'Tuskegee'. Small tree with multitrunked habit and horizontal branching; grows to 14 ft. high, 18 ft. wide. Deep pink to nearly red flowers. Orange-red fall foliage.

'Yuma'. Small multitrunked tree over 10 ft. tall and nearly as wide. Lavender flowers. Fall color yellowish to brownish red.

'Zuni'. Multistemmed shrub to 9 ft. tall and 8 ft. wide. Dark lavender (nearly purple) flowers. Orange-red to dark red fall foliage.

LAGURUS ovatus

HARE'S TAIL GRASS, RABBIT'S TAIL GRASS

Poaceae

ANNUAL GRASS

 ALL ZONES

☼ FULL SUN

🌢 REGULAR WATER

Lagurus ovatus

Grown largely for its showy flower heads—2-in.-long, creamy white, woolly tufts appearing throughout the summer—this upright grass has hairy light green foliage growing to 8 in. tall. Thrives in most well-drained soils of moderate fertility but does especially well in sandy soil. A good plant for the front of mixed and herbaceous borders, and for fresh and dried arrangements. If drying, pick just before flower heads are fully mature.

LAMB'S EARS. See STACHYS byzantina

FOR GROWING SYMBOL EXPLANATIONS

PLEASE SEE PAGE 113

Lamiaceae. Members of the mint family of herbaceous plants and shrubs are easily recognized by their square stems, leaves in opposite pairs, and whorled flowers in spikelike, sometimes branched, clusters. Many of the group are aromatic; the family contains most of the familiar kitchen herbs, including basil *(Ocimum)*, mint *(Mentha)*, oregano *(Origanum)*, and sage *(Salvia)*. Many have attractive foliage or flowers *(Coleus*, sage). This family was previously called Labiatae.

LAMIASTRUM galeobdolon. See LAMIUM galeobdolon

LAMIUM

DEAD NETTLE

Lamiaceae (Labiatae)

PERENNIALS

✎ ZONES 32, 34–43

◐ ● PARTIAL OR FULL SHADE

🌢 REGULAR WATER

Lamium

Leaves in opposite pairs are heart shaped, toothed, marked with white. Clustered flowers are pink, white, or yellow. All are vigorous growers that thrive in shade. One species is used as a ground cover.

L. galeobdolon (Galeobdolon luteum, Lamiastrum galeobdolon). YELLOW ARCHANGEL. Upright to 2 ft., slowly spreading to form tight clumps. Yellow flowers are unimportant. Best-known selection is 'Herman's Pride', with leaves evenly streaked and spotted with white. 'Compacta', compact habit, slower growth than 'Variegatum', leaves variegated silver. 'Silver Carpet' ('Silberteppich'), 6 in. high, yellow flowers. 'Silver Spangled', Zones 32, 34–41, big leaves heavily marked with silver, yellow flowers, less aggressive than 'Variegatum'. 'Variegatum', vigorous spreader with silver-marked leaves, yellow flowers.

L. maculatum. DEAD NETTLE, SPOTTED NETTLE. Running or trailing perennial used as a ground cover or in hanging baskets. To 6 in. tall, spreading 2–3 ft. Grayish green leaves have silvery markings. Pink flowers bloom spring into summer. Species is vigorous, even weedy, and is planted less frequently than its choicer varieties. These include 'Beacon Silver', with pink flowers and green-edged, silvery gray leaves; 'White Nancy', a 'Beacon Silver' with white blooms; 'Chequers', with pink blossoms and green leaves with a white center stripe; and 'Pink Pewter', with abundant pink flowers above silvery leaves edged gray green. All varieties nicely light up shady areas of the garden. They need some periodic grooming to remove old, shabby growth.

LANTANA

Verbenaceae

EVERGREEN SHRUBS GROWN AS ANNUALS

✎ ALL ZONES

☼ FULL SUN

🌢 MODERATE WATER

◆ FRUITS ARE POISONOUS IF INGESTED

Lantana

Fast growing, valued for profuse show of color all summer. Prone to mildew in shade or during prolonged overcast weather. Feed lightly. Too much water and fertilizer cuts down on bloom. Shrubby kinds used as annuals in beds or containers. Spreading kinds are effective spilling from raised beds, planter boxes, or hanging baskets. Crushed foliage has a pungent odor that some people find objectionable.

L. camara. One of two species used in hybridizing. Coarse, upright to 6 ft. Rough dark green leaves. Yellow, orange, or red flowers in 1–2-in. clusters.

L

L. montevidensis (L. sellowiana). WEEPING LANTANA. The other species used in breeding. This one is sold at nurseries. A little hardier than *L. camara,* it's a ground cover with branches trailing to 3 ft. or even 6 ft. Dark green, 1-in.-long leaves with coarsely toothed edges are sometimes tinged red or purplish, especially in cold weather. Rosy lilac flowers in 1–1½-in.-wide clusters. 'Lavender Swirl' is larger form that produces lavender, white, and mixed flower clusters. 'White Lightnin' is similar but has pure white flowers.

The following list gives some of the named kinds of lantana that are available. Some are merely forms of *L. camara,* or are hybrids between the forms. Others are hybrids between *L. camara* and *L. montevidensis.*

'Christine'. Cerise pink. Can be trained into small patio tree.

'Confetti'. Blossoms mix yellow, pink, and purple.

'Cream Carpet'. Cream with bright yellow throat.

'Dwarf Pink'. Light pink. Rather tender.

'Dwarf White'. White.

'Dwarf Yellow'. Yellow.

'Feston Rose'. Bicolored pink and yellow flowers.

'Gold Rush'. Rich golden yellow.

'Irene'. Compact. Magenta with lemon yellow.

'Lemon Swirl'. Yellow flowers, bright yellow band around each leaf.

'Radiation'. Rich orange red.

'Spreading Sunset'. Vivid orange red.

'Spreading Sunshine'. Bright yellow.

'Sunburst'. Bright golden yellow.

'Tangerine'. Burnt orange.

LARCH. See LARIX

LARIX

LARCH
Pinaceae
DECIDUOUS TREES
⚆ ZONES VARY BY SPECIES
☼ FULL SUN
⬤ REGULAR WATER

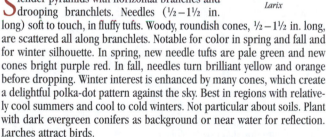

Larix

Slender pyramids with horizontal branches and drooping branchlets. Needles (½–1½ in. long) soft to touch, in fluffy tufts. Woody, roundish cones, ½–1½ in. long, are scattered all along branchlets. Notable for color in spring and fall and for winter silhouette. In spring, new needle tufts are pale green and new cones bright purple red. In fall, needles turn brilliant yellow and orange before dropping. Winter interest is enhanced by many cones, which create a delightful polka-dot pattern against the sky. Best in regions with relatively cool summers and cool to cold winters. Not particular about soils. Plant with dark evergreen conifers as background or near water for reflection. Larches attract birds.

L. decidua (L. europaea). EUROPEAN LARCH. Zones 36–45. Moderate to fast growth to 30–60 ft. Summer foliage color is grass green. Branches of 'Pendula' arch out and down; branchlets hang nearly straight down.

L. kaempferi. JAPANESE LARCH. Zones 32, 34, 36–45. Fast growing to 60 ft. or more but can be dwarfed in containers. Summer foliage is a soft bluish green. 'Pendula' has long, weeping branches.

L. laricina. AMERICAN LARCH. Zones 37–45. Native to northern U.S. and much of Canada. Slow to medium growth to 40–80 ft. tall. Bright blue-green summer foliage. Grows well in moist to boggy soils.

LARKSPUR. See CONSOLIDA ambigua

LATHYRUS

SWEET PEA
Fabaceae (Leguminosae)
ANNUAL OR PERENNIAL VINES
⚆ ZONES VARY BY SPECIES
☼ FULL SUN
⬤ ⬤ WATER NEEDS VARY BY SPECIES

Lathyrus

In this group is one of the best-known garden flowers—the delightfully fragrant and colorful sweet pea.

Throughout this book you will find flowers described as "sweet pea shaped." The flower of the sweet pea is typical of the many members of the pea family (Fabaceae). Each flower has one large, upright, roundish petal (banner or standard), two narrow side petals (wings), and two lower petals that are somewhat united, forming a boat-shaped structure (keel).

L. latifolius. PERENNIAL SWEET PEA. Zones 31, 32, 34–43. Strong-growing vine up to 9 ft., with blue-green foliage. Flowers usually reddish purple, often white or pink. Single colors are sometimes sold. Blooms all summer if not allowed to go to seed. Plants grow with little care, tolerate aridity. May escape and become naturalized. Use as bank cover, trailing over rocks, on trellis or fence.

L. odoratus. SWEET PEA. Spring or summer annual; some bloom in winter in greenhouse. All zones, but performance is curtailed by heat. Bears many spikelike clusters of crisp-looking flowers with a clean, sweet fragrance, in single colors and mixtures. Color mixtures include deep rose, blue, purple, scarlet, white, cream, amethyst on white ground, salmon, salmon pink on cream. Sweet peas make magnificent cut flowers in quantity. Bush types offer cut flowers the same as vine types and require no training.

To hasten germination, soak seeds for a few hours before planting. Treat seeds with fungicide. Sow seeds 1 in. deep and 1–2 in. apart. When seedlings are 4–5 in. high, thin to at least 6 in. apart. Pinch out tops to encourage strong side branches. Where climate prevents early planting or soil is too wet to work, start three or four seeds in each 2¼–3-in. peat pot, indoors or in protected place, and set out when weather has settled. Plant peat pots 1 ft. apart, thinning each to one strong plant. This method is ideal for bush types. Never let vines lack for water; soak heavily. To prolong bloom, cut flowers at least every other day and remove all seedpods. Regular monthly feeding with commercial fertilizer will keep vines vigorous and productive.

For vining sweet peas, provide trellis, strings, or wire before planting. Seedlings need support as soon as tendrils form. Freestanding trellis running north and south is best. When planting against fence or wall, keep supports away from wall to give air circulation.

The following describes vine-type sweet peas (grouped by time of bloom) and bush types.

Early flowering. (Early Flowering Multiflora, Early Multiflora, formerly Early Spencers.) The name "Spencer" describes a type of frilled flower (with wavy petals) that is now characteristic of almost all varieties. "Multiflora" indicates that the plants carry more flowers per stem than previous Spencer cultivars did. The value of early-flowering varieties is that they will bloom in winter when days are short. (Spring- and summer-flowering types will not bloom until days have lengthened to 15 hours or more.) Use these varieties for forcing in greenhouse. They are not heat resistant. Generally sold in mixed colors.

Spring flowering. (Spring-Flowering, Heat-Resistant Cuthbertson Type, Cuthbertson's Floribunda, Floribunda-Zvolanek strain.) Both mixtures and single-color named varieties are available in seed packets. Wide color range: pink, lavender, purple, white, cream, rose, salmon, cerise, carmine, red, blue. Royal or Royal Family is somewhat larger flowered and more heat resistant than the others. Plant just as soon as soil can be worked. In coldest areas, prepare soil for planting the preceding fall, and sow while ground is still soggy in spring.

Summer flowering. (Galaxy, Plenti-flora.) Available in named varieties and mixtures in wide color range. Heat resistant; bloom from early summer on. Large flowers are borne five to seven to each long stem. Plant in early spring.

Bush type. The so-called bush-type sweet peas are strong vines with predetermined growth, heights. Unlike vining types that reach 5 ft. and more, these stop their upward growth at 1–2½ ft.

Bijou. To 1 ft. Full color range in mixtures and single varieties. Four or five flowers on 5–7-in. stems. Useful and spectacular in borders, beds, window boxes, containers. Not as heat resistant or as long stemmed as Knee-Hi; performs better in containers.

Cupid. Grows 4–6 in. tall, 1½ ft. wide. Trails on ground or hangs from container.

Jet Set. Bushy, self-supporting plants 2–3 ft. tall. All colors.

Knee-Hi. To 2½ ft. Large, long-stemmed flowers, five or six to the stem. Has all the virtues and color range of the spring-flowering types, on self-supporting, bush-type vines. Provides cutting-type flowers in mass display in beds and borders. Growth will exceed 2½ ft. where planting bed joins fence or wall. Keep in open area for uniform height. Follow same planting dates as for spring-flowering sweet peas.

Little Sweethearts. Rounded bushes, 8 in. tall, bloom over a long season. Full range of colors. Patio strain grows 9 in. tall. Snoopea (12–15 in.) and Supersnoop (2 ft.) need no support, come in full range of sweet pea colors.

GETTING SWEET PEAS OFF TO A FINE START

In less-than-perfect soil, prepare ground for sweet peas like this. Dig trench 1–1½ ft. deep. Mix 1 part compost or other soil conditioner to 2 parts soil. As you mix, add complete commercial fertilizer according to label directions. Backfill trench with mix; plant seeds in it.

Lauraceae. The laurel family contains evergreen and deciduous trees and shrubs with inconspicuous flowers and (usually) aromatic foliage. Fruits are fleshy, containing a single seed. Examples are sweet bay *(Laurus)*, spicebush *(Lindera)*, and *Sassafras.*

LAUREL. See LAURUS nobilis, PRUNUS

LAURUS nobilis

SWEET BAY, GRECIAN LAUREL

Lauraceae

EVERGREEN SHRUB OR TREE

🗡 ALL ZONES; GROW IN POTS

☀ ◑ FULL SUN OR PARTIAL SHADE

💧 MODERATE WATER

Laurus

Slow growth to about 5 ft. when grown in a container. Natural habit is compact, broad-based—often that of a multi-stemmed, gradually tapering cone. Leaves are leathery, aromatic, oval, 2–4 in. long, dark green; traditional bay leaf of cookery. 'Saratoga' has broader leaves and a more treelike habit.

Not fussy about soil but needs good drainage. Takes well to clipping into standards or topiary shapes such as globes and cones. A classic formal container plant. Move to the protection of a greenhouse or cool, well-lighted room when temperatures reach about 20°F/−7°C.

LAVANDIN. See LAVANDULA intermedia

LAVANDULA

LAVENDER

Lamiaceae (Labiatae)

EVERGREEN SHRUBS OR SUBSHRUBS

🗡 ZONES VARY BY SPECIES

☀ FULL SUN

💧 MODERATE WATER

Lavandula

Native to Mediterranean region. Prized for its fragrant lavender or purple flowers; those of some species are used for perfume, sachets. Aromatic grayish or gray-green foliage. Plant as hedge or edging, in herb gardens, or in borders with plants needing similar conditions—nepeta, rosemary, santolina, verbena.

Lavenders require full sun, well-drained soil, little or no fertilizer. Their downfall is humidity accompanied by heat; they will succeed in cool coastal climates but not in steamy heat. Prune immediately after bloom to keep plants compact and neat. For sachets, cut flower clusters or strip flowers from stems just as color shows; dry in cool, shady place.

Since lavenders have been in cultivation for centuries and tend to interbreed, many varieties and hybrids have arisen, and names are difficult to sort out. Some of the names that follow may not agree with those you see on nursery labels.

L. angustifolia (L. officinalis, L. spica, L. vera). ENGLISH LAVENDER. Zones 31, 32, 34–41. Hardiest species and the one most widely planted. The classic lavender used for perfume and sachets. To 3–4 ft. high and wide. Narrow, smooth-edged gray leaves to 2 in. long; lavender, ½-in.-long flowers in 1½–2-ft.-high spikes in late spring or summer. Many varieties exist, among them the following:

'Alba'. To 3 ft. high, with pure white flower spikes above gray-green foliage.

'Compacta' ('Compacta Nana', 'Dwarf Blue'). Dark blue flowers on an 8–12-in. plant.

'Grey Lady'. To 1½ ft. tall. Silvery gray foliage, lavender blue flowers.

'Hidcote'. To 15–20 in. tall. Deep purplish blue flowers, gray foliage.

'Irene Doyle'. To 1½ ft. high. Lavender blue flowers in summer; re-blooms in early fall.

'Jean Davis'. Pale pink flowers above gray-green foliage on a 1½-ft. plant.

'Lavender Lady'. To 10 in. tall; gray foliage, lavender flowers. Fast grower, often blooming first year from seed.

'Mitcham's Gray'. Similar to 'Hidcote', but slightly taller and with lighter blue flowers.

'Munstead'. Compact plant to 1–1½ ft. Medium blue flowers. Long blooming; good for edging.

'Rosea'. Pink flowers on a 15-in. plant.

'Twickel Purple'. Dense, compact grower to 1½ ft. high, with heavy, thick spikes of light purple flowers.

L. intermedia. LAVANDIN. Zones 31, 32, 34–41. Group of hybrids between *L. angustifolia* and *L. latifolia.* All are vigorous, highly fragrant plants. About as hardy as English lavender parent, but more tolerant of warm, humid summers. Early to midsummer bloom. Includes 'Dutch', with 16-in. mounds of gray foliage and 3-ft. stems topped with dark purple flowers; 'Grappenhall', with dark violet spikes on 3½-ft. stems above 14-in. foliage mounds; 'Grosso', possibly the most fragrant of all, with compact, 8-in.-high mounds of silvery foliage and large, fat purple spikes on 2½-ft. stems; and 'Provence', a 2-ft. plant (to 3–4 ft. in bloom) with light purple flower spikes.

L. latifolia. SPIKE LAVENDER. Zones 32, 34, 39. Much like English lavender in appearance, but with broader leaves and much-branched flower stalks. Bloom period same as for English lavender.

PRACTICAL GARDENING DICTIONARY

PLEASE SEE PAGES 449–523

LAVATERA

TREE MALLOW

Malvaceae

ANNUALS OR EVERGREEN SHRUBS

🌡 ZONES VARY BY SPECIES

☀ FULL SUN

💧💧 REGULAR TO LITTLE WATER

Lavatera

Lavatera is named after the Lavater family of Zurich, but for many the word means "easy to grow." The flowers resemble single hollyhocks.

L. thuringiaca. Semievergreen shrub. Zones 31, 32. Flowers are purplish pink, 3 in. across, nearly everblooming. The variety 'Barnsley' has lighter pink flowers paling to white centers. 'Rosea' has pink flowers. Prune back to basal growth in early spring.

L. trimestris. ANNUAL MALLOW. All zones; best in cool-summer regions. Reaches a height of 3–6 ft. from spring-sown seed. Satiny flowers to 4 in. across; named varieties in white, pink, rosy carmine. Bloom extends from midsummer to frost if spent flowers are removed to halt seed production. Colorful, fast-growing summer hedge or background planting.

'Loveliness' grows 3–4 ft. high, bears deep rose blooms.

More compact (2–3-ft.) varieties include 'Mont Rose', rose pink; 'Mont Blanc', white; and 'Silver Cup', bright pink.

LAVENDER. See LAVANDULA

LAVENDER COTTON. See SANTOLINA chamaecyparissus

LAVENDER MIST. See THALICTRUM rochebrunianum

LEAD PLANT. See AMORPHA canescens

LEADWORT. See PLUMBAGO auriculata

LEATHERLEAF. See CHAMAEDAPHNE

LEATHERWOOD. See CYRILLA

LEDUM

Ericaceae

EVERGREEN SHRUBS

🌡 ZONES 34–45

☀ ◐ FULL SUN TO PARTIAL SHADE

💧 MORE THAN REGULAR WATER

Ledum

Relatives of heaths and heathers, rhododendrons and azaleas, ledums are slow-growing, mound-forming shrubs. They have narrow, leathery leaves that are aromatic when crushed. The white flowers are carried in clusters from late spring to early summer. Good site selection is essential to success: give these shrubs moist, cool, acid soil. They are ideal additions to bog gardens or other moist places, especially in peaty soil. Plants fail if their roots dry out. They also do not tolerate areas with hot summers.

L. groenlandicum. LABRADOR TEA. A small evergreen shrub reaching 2–4 ft. tall and spreading as far. Native from Greenland and Alaska to Canada and the northern U.S. Bears dark green, oval to slightly rounded leaves that have rust brown hairs underneath and 2-in.-wide clusters of ½–¾-in.-wide white flowers. 'Compactum' produces 1-ft.-tall, densely branched mounds of leaves and small clusters of flowers.

L. palustre. WILD ROSEMARY. A rounded, 1–4-ft.-tall shrub found from Europe and northern Asia to Canada and the U.S. Very narrow to linear leaves that are rust-colored underneath; bears 2-in.-wide clusters of ½-in. flowers.

FOR INFORMATION ON SELECTING PLANTS

PLEASE SEE PAGES 47–112

LEEK

Liliaceae

BIENNIAL GROWN AS ANNUAL

🌡 ALL ZONES

☀ FULL SUN

💧 NEVER LET DRY OUT

Leek

An onion relative that doesn't form distinct bulb. Plants grow 2–3 ft. tall; their edible, mild-flavored bottoms resemble long, fat green onions. Leeks need very rich soil. Best in cool weather. Sow in early spring; in coldest areas, sow indoors and set out plants in June or July. When plants have considerable top growth, draw soil up around fat, round stems to make bottoms white and mild. Keep soil out of bases of leaves. Begin to harvest in late autumn. Where winters are cold, dig up plants with roots and plant them closely in boxes of soil in cool but frost-free location, or mulch deeply before garden soil freezes. Where winters are mild, dig as needed from late fall until spring. Any offsets may be detached and replanted. If leeks bloom, small bulbils may appear in flower clusters; plant these for later harvest. Not bothered by many pests and diseases that attack onions.

Leguminosae. See Fabaceae

> ### WHITE-STEMMED LEEKS
> The easiest way to grow leeks with long white stems is to plant in trenches 6 in. deep. Set plants 3-4 in. apart in the trench. Gradually fill in soil as plants grow, adding only 1 in. of soil at a time. When plants are 8 in. tall, the trench can be filled completely.

LEIOPHYLLUM
buxifolium

SAND MYRTLE

Ericaceae

EVERGREEN SHRUB

🌡 ZONES 31, 32, 34–41

◐ ● PARTIAL TO FULL SHADE

💧 MORE THAN REGULAR WATER

Leiophyllum buxifolium

Native to the eastern U.S., the single species belonging to this genus is a densely branching shrub spreading by suckers. Compact and low-growing or prostrate habit; plants range from 1½ to 3 ft. tall and spread to 4–5 ft. The small, dark green, leathery leaves turn bronzy in winter. Close relatives of *Ledum* species, they bear rounded, 1-in.-wide clusters of pink buds in late spring and early summer that open into white, ¼-in.-wide, five-petaled flowers. Plants require moist, well-drained, acid soil that is somewhat sandy and rich in organic matter. They do not tolerate drought or heat. Use in a rock garden or with other broad-leafed evergreens with similar soil needs, such as smaller rhododendrons and azaleas. 'Nanum' is especially compact—from 2 to 4 in. and spreading to 1 ft.—and bears pink flowers.

LEMON BALM. See MELISSA officinalis

LEMON GRASS. See CYMBOPOGON citratus

LEMON THYME. See THYMUS citriodorus

L

L

LEMON VERBENA. See ALOYSIA triphylla

LENTEN ROSE. See HELLEBORUS orientalis

LEONOTIS ocymifolia

LION'S EAR, LION'S TAIL

Lamiaceae

TENDER PERENNIAL

✿ ALL ZONES, SEE BELOW

☼ FULL SUN

♦ REGULAR WATER

Leonotis

This native of South Africa, also known as *L. leonurus,* makes an excellent summer bedding accent plant, and is also grown in greenhouses in more northerly climates for its brilliantly colored whorls of tubular orange to reddish yellow flowers. Plant young plants outdoors in spring; they will bloom by midsummer. If growing under glass, plant in a soil-based potting mix; provide ample water in summer, but water sparingly throughout the winter. In summer months greenhouse plants can be taken outdoors and sunk, pots and all, in the garden. After flowering, cut back to encourage bushiness. Long-blooming and very effective, it loves heat and sun.

LEONTOPODIUM alpinum

EDELWEISS

Asteraceae (Compositae)

PERENNIAL

✿ ZONES 36–43

☼ FULL SUN

♦ REGULAR WATER

Leontopodium alpinum

Short-lived rock garden plant 4–12 in. high, with woolly white foliage and small flower heads closely crowded on tips of stems; a collar of slender leaves radiates out from below each flower head like the arms of a starfish. The tiny bracts of flower heads, also white and woolly, are tipped with black. Blooms early summer. Needs excellent drainage, cool temperatures.

LEOPARD PLANT. See LIGULARIA tussilaginea 'Aureo-maculata'

LEOPARD'S BANE. See DORONICUM

LESPEDEZA

BUSH CLOVER

Fabaceae (Leguminosae)

DECIDUOUS PERENNIAL OR SHRUB

✿ ZONES VARY BY SPECIES

☼ FULL SUN

♦ MODERATE TO LITTLE WATER

Lespedeza

Grow these bushy plants for their late-blooming pealike flowers that appear when most other shrub blossoms are long gone.

L. bicolor. Deciduous shrub. Zones 31, 32, 34–41. Erect to 6 ft. high and wide. Three-part lobed leaves, medium to dark green, composed of oval leaflets to 2 in. long. Slender clusters to 5 in. long of rose pink, sweet pea–shaped flowers in mid- to late summer.

L. thunbergii. Perennial. Zones 31, 32, 34, 39. Woody-based stems form a spreading, fountain-shaped plant 6 ft. tall and 10 ft. wide. Arching branches carry blue-green leaves with three 1½–2-in.-long leaflets. Blooms in late summer; drooping 6-in. clusters of rose pink, sweet pea–shaped flowers are carried in groups to form pendulous inflorescences 2–2½ ft. long. Cut plant to the ground in late fall or early spring; it will regrow rapidly and bear flowers on the new growth. Endures hot, dry sites and soil of low fertility. Needs good drainage. 'Gibraltar' is a more compact form (to 4½ ft.); 'Alba' and 'White Fountain' have white flowers. Use among other shrubs or in large perennial borders.

LETTUCE

Asteraceae (Compositae)

ANNUAL

✿ ALL ZONES

☼ ◑ PARTIAL SHADE IN HOTTEST CLIMATES

♦ REGULAR WATER

Lettuce

A short browse through a seed catalog, seed display rack, or selection of nursery seedlings will reveal enough variety to keep your salad bowl crisp and colorful throughout the growing season. There are four principal types of lettuce: crisphead, butterhead or Boston, loose-leaf, and romaine.

Widely sold in markets, crisphead is the most exasperating for home gardeners to produce. Heads form best when monthly average temperatures are around 55 to 60°F/13 to 16°C. In mild climates, this type of lettuce does well over a long season; in hot-summer areas, timing of planting is critical. Best varieties are various strains of 'Great Lakes', 'Imperial', and 'Iceberg'.

Butterhead or Boston types have loose heads with smooth green outer leaves and yellow inner leaves. Good varieties include 'Bibb' ('Limestone') and 'Buttercrunch'. 'Mignonette' ('Manoa') stands heat without bolting (going to seed).

Loose-leaf lettuce makes rosettes rather than heads. It withstands heat better than other types and is a summer mainstay in warm climates. Choice selections: 'Black-seeded Simpson', 'Oak Leaf', 'Slobolt', the red-tinged varieties 'Prizehead' and 'Ruby', and 'Salad Bowl', with deeply cut leaves.

Romaine lettuce has erect, cylindrical heads of smooth leaves, the outer ones green, the inner ones whitish. Tolerates heat moderately well. Try 'White Paris', 'Parris Island', 'Dark Green Cos', or 'Valmaine'.

Lettuces with bronzy to pinkish red leaves add color to a salad. 'Lollo Rosso', 'Red Sails', 'Red Oak Leaf', and 'Ruby' are loose-leaf varieties; 'Merveille des Quatre Saisons' and 'Perella Red' are butterheads; 'Rouge d'Hiver' is a romaine.

All types of lettuce need loose, well-drained soil. Sow in open ground at 10-day intervals for prolonged harvest. Barely cover seeds. Loose-leaf lettuce can be grown as close as 4 in. apart; thin all other types to 1 ft. apart. In cold-winter regions, begin sowing seed after frost, as soon as soil is workable; where summers are very short, sow indoors, then move seedlings outdoors after last frost. In mild-winter, cool-summer regions, sow in early spring for spring–summer harvest, then make further sowings in late summer or early fall for winter harvest.

PICKING LOOSE-LEAF LETTUCE

With this kind of lettuce you get three opportunities to harvest over a long period. Wait to thin until seedlings are big enough to eat, then use the thinnings for salads. Clip off just the outer leaves of larger plants as you need them. Finally, pull up whole plants. Finish harvesting when bloom stalks start to grow; before plants bolt to seed and turn bitter.

LEUCANTHEMUM. See CHRYSANTHEMUM

LEUCOJUM

SNOWFLAKE

Amaryllidaceae

BULBS

⚡ ZONES VARY BY SPECIES

☀ ◐ FULL SUN OR LIGHT SHADE

💧 REGULAR WATER DURING GROWTH AND BLOOM

Leucojum

Strap-shaped leaves and nodding, bell-shaped, white flowers with segments tipped green. Easy to grow and permanent. Naturalize under deciduous trees, in shrub borders or orchards, or on cool slopes. Plant 4 in. deep in fall. Do not disturb until really crowded; then dig, divide, and replant after foliage dies down.

L. aestivum. SUMMER SNOWFLAKE. Zones 31, 32, 34–43. Leaves 1–1½ ft. long. Stems 1½ ft. tall carry three to five 1-in. flowers. 'Gravetye Giant' is a bit taller and larger flowered than the species; it has as many as nine flowers per stem. In mild-winter areas, plants bloom in late winter; in colder regions, they bloom with daffodils.

L. autumnale. AUTUMN SNOWFLAKE. Zones 31, 32, 34–41. Narrow, grassy leaves to 6 in. long appear with, or right after, the flowers. Stems to 6 in. high bear two to four ½-in. white flowers in late summer to early autumn.

L. vernum. SPRING SNOWFLAKE. Zones 31, 32, 34–43. Flourishes in areas with definite winter cold. Leaves 9 in. long. In earliest spring, each foot-long stem bears a single large white flower (occasionally two per stem).

LEUCOTHOE

Ericaceae

EVERGREEN OR DECIDUOUS SHRUBS

⚡ ZONES VARY BY SPECIES

☀ ● PARTIAL OR FULL SHADE

💧 ● ● WATER NEEDS VARY BY SPECIES

◆ LEAVES AND NECTAR ARE POISONOUS IF INGESTED

Leucothoe

Related to *Pieris*. All have leathery leaves and clusters of urn-shaped white flowers. They need acid, woodsy, deep soil; do best in woodland gardens. Will tolerate full sun in cool climates if adequately watered. Best used in masses, since they are not especially attractive individually. Bronze-tinted winter foliage is a bonus.

L. axillaris. COAST LEUCOTHOE. Evergreen. Zones 31, 32, 34–41. Native to southeastern U.S. Spreading, arching growth to 2–4 ft. tall, 3–6 ft. wide. Leathery leaves to 4 in. long are bronzy when new. Flower clusters 1–3 in. long droop along stems in spring. Takes regular water.

L. fontanesiana (L. catesbaei). DROOPING LEUCOTHOE. Evergreen. Zones 32, 34–43. Native to southeastern U.S. Slow grower to 2–6 ft. high; branches arch gracefully. Leaves are leathery, 3–6 in. long; they turn bronzy purple in fall (bronzy green in deep shade). Spreads from underground stems. Blooms in spring, bearing drooping clusters of slightly fragrant, creamy white flowers resembling lily-of-the-valley. 'Rainbow', 3–4 ft. high, has leaves marked yellow, green, and pink. 'Lovita' is smaller than the species (2 ft. tall, 4 ft. wide), with smaller, darker green leaves that turn mahogany red in winter. 'Scarletta' is similar in size to 'Lovita'; its leaves are brilliant red on expanding, deep green in summer, and deep red in late fall and winter.

The species and its varieties take regular water. Can be controlled in height to make 1½-ft. ground cover in shade; just cut older, taller stems to ground. Blooming branches make decorative cut flowers. Where summers are hot and humid, various leaf spot diseases can cause serious disfiguration or defoliation.

L. populifolia. FLORIDA LEUCOTHOE. Evergreen. Zones 31, 32, 34, 39. Loose and arching, to 6 ft. high in gardens. Glossy green leaves to 4 in. long. Slender clusters of fragrant, creamy white flowers in late spring to early summer. Best species for humid areas. Regular to ample water.

L. racemosa. SWEETBELLS. Deciduous. Zones 31, 32, 34. Native to southeastern U.S. Grows 3–8 ft. tall, with 3-in. leaves that turn red before dropping from their red stems. White flowers in one-sided, 3-in. clusters form at ends of branches in late spring or early summer. A pink-flowering form is available. Endures dry shade.

LEVISTICUM officinale

LOVAGE

Apiaceae (Umbelliferae)

PERENNIAL HERB

⚡ ZONES 31, 32, 34–45

☀ FULL SUN

💧 REGULAR WATER

Levisticum officinale

This herb is sometimes grown for the celery flavor of its seeds, leaves, and stems. Reaches 2–3 ft. tall, sometimes even 6 ft. high. Leaves are cut and divided, glossy deep green; small greenish yellow flowers are borne in flattish clusters. Makes a dramatic specimen plant in the garden. Plants die back to ground in winter. Grow from seeds or divisions.

L

USING LOVAGE

Lovage got its name because it was once used in love potions. These days, it is valued as a celery substitute (it's easier to grow than celery). Use chopped leaves and stems in soups or salads, especially potato salad. Stems may be candied. Use seeds like celery seed.

LEWISIA

Portulacaceae

PERENNIALS

⚡ ZONES 34–41

☀ ◐ FULL SUN OR LIGHT SHADE

💧 LIGHT WATERING

Lewisia

Beautiful, often difficult plants for rock gardens, collections of alpine plants. All need excellent drainage; plant with fine gravel around crowns to prevent rot. Of the many offered by specialists, these are outstanding:

L. cotyledon. Native to northern California and southern Oregon. Rosettes of narrow, fleshy, evergreen leaves bear 10-in. stems topped by large, extremely showy clusters of 1-in. white or pink flowers striped with rose or red. Blooms spring to early summer. *L. c. howellii* is similar, but leaves are wavy edged and flowers somewhat larger. Can be grown in pots in fast-draining sterilized soil or growing mixes.

L. rediviva. BITTERROOT. Native to mountains of the West. State flower of Montana. Fleshy roots; short stems with short, succulent, strap-shaped leaves to 2 in. long that usually die back before flowers appear (seemingly from bare earth) in spring. Flowers, borne singly on short stems, look like 2-in.-wide rose or white water lilies. Not difficult if drainage is excellent.

L. tweedyi. Native to mountains, south-central Washington. Stunning big, satiny salmon pink flowers, one to three to a stem, bloom above fleshy, evergreen, 4-in. leaves. Prune out side growths to keep root crown open to air.

LIATRIS

GAYFEATHER

Asteraceae (Compositae)

PERENNIALS

ZONES 31, 32, 34–45

FULL SUN

REGULAR TO MODERATE WATER

Liatris

Showy plants native to eastern and central U.S. Basal tufts of narrow, grassy leaves grow from thick, often tuberous rootstocks. In summer or early fall, the tufts lengthen into tall stems densely set with slender leaves and topped by a narrow plume of small, fluffy purple (sometimes white) flower heads. Flowers of most species are unusual in opening from top of spike to bottom. Choice cut flowers.

These plants endure heat, cold, aridity, and poor soil. Fertilizing will give you larger flower spikes, but it also results in taller plants that need staking. Liatris is best used in mixed perennial borders, although the rosy purple color calls for careful placing to avoid color clashes.

L. callilepis. Plants grown and sold by Dutch bulb growers under this name are *L. spicata*.

L. ligulistylis. Grows 3–5 ft. tall, with reddish purple flowers that open from dark red buds.

L. microcephala. Only 12–14 in. tall, with grasslike leaves and rose purple flowers.

L. pycnostachya. KANSAS GAYFEATHER. To 4 ft. tall, with purple flowers. Likes moisture.

L. scariosa. To 2½ ft. high. The reddish purple flowers differ from those of most other gayfeathers in opening nearly all at once. Plant also prefers somewhat drier soil. 'September Glory' is taller, to 4–5 ft.; 'White Spire' is similar, but with white flowers.

L. spicata. Grows to 5 ft., with light purple flower heads tightly clustered in dense spikes. 'Alba' (3–4 ft.) is white flowered; 'Floristan White' (2–3 ft.) has a profusion of densely packed white blossom spikes good for cutting; 'Floristan Violet' has purple-pink flowers; 'Kobold' (2–2½ ft.) has deeper purple flowers and does not need staking; and 'Silvertips' (2½–3 ft.) has lavender flowers with a silvery finish.

LIBOCEDRUS. See CALOCEDRUS decurrens

LIGULARIA

Asteraceae (Compositae)

PERENNIALS

ZONES 32, 34, 36–43, EXCEPT AS NOTED

PARTIAL OR FULL SHADE

AMPLE WATER

Ligularia

Stately perennials with big leaves (1 ft. wide or wider in most species) and daisy flowers in yellow to orange. All need rich soil, ample moisture, and some shade; they do not tolerate heat or low humidity. Good around pools, along stream beds, in bog gardens.

L. dentata. Zones 32, 34, 36–41. Grown primarily for attractive roundish leaves, heart shaped at base. Sends up 3–5-ft. stems topped by big, branching heads of orange daisies in mid- to late summer. 'Desdemona' and 'Othello' have deep purple leafstalks, veins, and leaf undersurfaces; upper surfaces of leaves are green.

L. hessei 'Gregynog Gold'. Clump of heart-shaped, toothed leaves gives rise to stems as tall as 6 ft., bearing conical spikes of yellow-orange flowers in mid- to late summer.

L. macrophylla. Large, bold plant to 5½ ft. high. Oval basal leaves with toothed edges, to 2 ft. long and 1 ft. wide. Dense 1-ft. spikes of golden yellow flowers.

L. przewalskii. Similar to *L. stenocephala,* but leaves are deeply lobed and cut, flower stems are black, and bloom occurs a bit later.

L. stenocephala. Zones 32, 34, 36–41. Better known for flower spikes than foliage. Usually represented by variety 'The Rocket', with clumps of deeply cut leaves topped by tall (to 5-ft.), narrow spires of yellow daisies in early summer.

L. tussilaginea (L. kaempferi, Farfugium japonicum). Zones 31, warmer parts of 32; house plant or indoor/outdoor in all zones. Choice foliage plant for shady bed or entryways. Good container plant. Top hardy to 20°F/−7°C; plant dies back to roots at 0°F/−18°C, puts on new growth again in spring. Leaves, typically 6–10 in. across, rise directly from rootstock on 1–2-ft. stems; flower stalks 1–2 ft. tall bear a few 1½–2-in.-wide flower heads with yellow rays. Speckled variety 'Aureo-maculata', leopard plant, has thick, rather leathery leaves blotched with cream or yellow; leaves are nearly kidney shaped, but with shallowly angled and toothed edges. 'Argentea' has deep green leaves irregularly mottled (particularly on edges) with gray green and ivory. 'Crispata' ('Cristata') has curled and crested leaf edges.

L. wilsoniana. GIANT GROUNDSEL. Zones 32, 34, 36–41. Clump of broadly triangular leaves is topped in mid- to late summer by 5–6-ft. stems carrying dense, columnar spikes of golden yellow flowers.

LIGUSTRUM

PRIVET

Oleaceae

DECIDUOUS OR EVERGREEN SHRUBS OR SMALL TREES

ZONES VARY BY SPECIES

FULL SUN OR PARTIAL SHADE

REGULAR WATER

LEAVES, FRUITS CAUSE GASTRIC DISTRESS IF INGESTED

Ligustrum

Most widely used as hedges; can also be clipped into formal shapes and featured in tubs or large pots. All have abundant, showy clusters of white to creamy white flowers in late spring or early summer. Fragrance is described as pleasant to unpleasant (never wonderful or terrible). Flowers draw bees. Clipped hedges bear fewer flowers, since shearing removes most of the flower-bearing branches. Blossoms followed by small, berrylike blue-black fruits; birds eat them, thereby distributing seeds. Most privets are easily grown in any soil.

Nurseries sometimes misidentify certain privets. The smaller-leafed hardy privets used for hedging are often confused: *L. amurense, L. ovalifolium,* and *L. vulgare* look much alike, and any is likely to be sold as "common privet"—a name that belongs to *L. vulgare.*

L. amurense. AMUR PRIVET. Shrub. Zones 34–45. Deciduous in coldest areas, where it is much used for hedge and screen planting. Partially evergreen in milder climates but seldom planted there. Much like *L. ovalifolium* in appearance, but foliage is less glossy.

L. ibolium 'Variegata'. Semievergreen to deciduous shrub. Zones 31, 32, 34–41. Variegated form of a hybrid between *L. ovalifolium* and another Japanese privet. Resembles *L. ovalifolium* but has bright green leaves with creamy yellow edges.

L. japonicum. JAPANESE PRIVET, WAX-LEAF PRIVET. Evergreen shrub. Zones 31, 32. Dense, compact growth habit to 10–12 ft., but can be kept lower by trimming. Roundish oval leaves 2–4 in. long, dark to medium green and glossy above, distinctly paler to almost whitish beneath; have thick, slightly spongy feel. Excellent plant for hedges or screens, or for shaping into globes, pyramids, other shapes, or small standard trees.

'Howard' ('Howardii'). Two-toned shrub; leaves are yellow when new, aging to green. Both colors are usually present at once.

'Recurvifolium'. Leaves are somewhat smaller than in the species, wavy-edged, and twisted at the tip. Somewhat open grower.

'Rotundifolium' ('Coriaceum'). Grows 4–5 ft. high; has nearly round leaves to 2½ in. long. Partial shade in hot areas.

'Silver Star'. Grows 6–8 ft. high. Leaves are deep green, with gray-green mottling and startling creamy white edges. Provides a good contrast to deep green foliage.

'Texanum'. Very similar to the species but lower growing (to 6–9 ft.), with somewhat denser, lusher foliage. Useful as windbreak. Often sold as *L. texanum*.

'Variegatum'. Leaves have creamy white margins and blotches.

L. lucidum. GLOSSY PRIVET. Evergreen tree. Zones 31, 32. Makes a round-headed tree that eventually reaches 15–18 ft. Can be kept lower as a big shrub or may form multitrunked tree. Glossy, 4–6-in.-long leaves are tapered and pointed, dark to medium green on both sides. They feel leathery but lack the slightly spongy feel of *L. japonicum*'s leaves. Flowers in especially large, feathery clusters followed by profusion of fruit. Fine lawn tree. Can grow in narrow areas; good street tree if not planted near pavement or where fruit will drop on cars (see disadvantages noted below). Performs well in large containers. Or plant 10 ft. apart for tall privacy screen. Useful as windbreak.

Before planting this tree, carefully weigh the advantages listed above against the disadvantages. Eventual fruit crop is immense; never plant where fruits will fall on cars, walks, or other paved areas (they stain). Fallen seeds (and those dropped by birds) profusely sprout in ground cover and will need pulling. Many people dislike the flowers' odor, and fruiting clusters are bare and unattractive after fruit drop.

L. ovalifolium. CALIFORNIA PRIVET. Semievergreen shrub. Zones 31, 32, 34–39. Native to Japan. Grows rapidly to 15 ft. but can be kept sheared to any height. Dark green, oval, 2½-in.-long leaves. Set plants 9–12 in. apart for hedges. Clip early and frequently to encourage low, dense branching. Greedy roots. Well-fed, well-watered plants hold their leaves longest. Tolerates heat.

'Argenteum'. Leaves are edged in creamy white.

'Aureum'. GOLDEN PRIVET. Leaves have broad yellow edges. Sold as 'Variegatum'.

L. vicaryi. VICARY GOLDEN PRIVET. Deciduous shrub. Zones 32, 34–41. This one has yellow leaves; color is strongest on plants in full sun. To 4–6 ft. high, possibly to 12 ft. Best planted alone; color does not develop well under hedge shearing.

L. vulgare. COMMON PRIVET. Deciduous shrub. Zones 31, 32, 34–41. To 15 ft., unsheared. Dark green leaves less glossy than those of *L. ovalifolium,* root system less greedy. Clusters of black fruit conspicuous on unpruned or lightly pruned plants. 'Lodense' ('Nanum') is a dense dwarf form that reaches only 4 ft. with equal spread. 'Cheyenne' is hardier than the species, to Zone 43.

REJUVENATING A PRIVET HEDGE

After years of shearing, a deciduous privet hedge often develops a lot of dead shoots on the interior, covered with a sparse outer layer of foliage. Solve the problem by hand-pruning some of the branches to allow more light into the plants. For a very old, very bare hedge, cut back the branches to about 6 in. above the ground and start over. Shear the new hedge so the top is narrower than the bottom for denser, healthier foliage.

LILAC. See SYRINGA

Liliaceae. The lily family contains hundreds of species of ornamental plants, as well as such vegetables as asparagus and the whole onion tribe. Most grow from bulbs, corms, or rhizomes. Flowers are often showy, usually with six equal-size segments.

LILIUM

LILY

Liliaceae

BULBS

🌿 ZONES 31, 32, 34–45, EXCEPT AS NOTED

🔆 ROOTS IN SHADE; TOPS IN SUN OR FILTERED SHADE

🔴 NEVER LET ROOT ZONE DRY OUT

Lilium auratum

Most stately and varied of bulbous plants. For many years, only the species—the same plants growing wild in parts of Asia, Europe, and North America—were available, and many of these were difficult and unpredictable.

Around 1925, lily growers began a significant breeding program. They bred new hybrids from species with desirable qualities and also developed strains and varieties that were healthier, hardier, and easier to grow than the original species. They produced new forms and new colors; what is more important, they developed the methods for growing healthy lilies in large quantities. Today, the new forms and new colors are the best garden lilies, but it is still possible to get some desirable species.

Lilies have three basic cultural requirements: deep, loose, well-drained soil; ample moisture throughout the growing season; and coolness and shade at roots, with sun or filtered shade at tops where flowers form.

Plant bulbs as soon as possible after you get them. If you must wait, keep them in a cool place until you plant. If bulbs are dry, place them in moist sand or peat moss until scales get plump and new roots begin to sprout.

As noted above, lilies need deep, well-drained soil containing ample organic matter. If you want to plant in heavy clay or very sandy soil, add organic material such as peat moss, leaf mold, or composted ground bark. Spread a 3–4-in. layer of such material over the soil surface; broadcast complete fertilizer (follow directions for preplanting application) on top of it, then thoroughly blend both into the soil to a depth of at least 1 ft.

Before planting bulbs, remove any injured portions; then dust cuts with sulfur or an antifungal seed and bulb disinfectant. For each bulb, dig a generous planting hole (6–12 in. deeper than height of bulb). Place enough soil at bottom of hole to bring it up to proper level for bulb (see next paragraph). Set bulb with its roots spread; fill hole with soil, firming it around bulb to eliminate air pockets.

Planting depths vary according to size and rooting habit of bulb. General rule is to cover smaller bulbs with 2–3 in. of soil, medium bulbs with 3–4 in., and larger bulbs with 4–6 in. (but never cover Madonna lilies with more than 1 in. of soil). Planting depth can be quite flexible. It's better to err by planting shallowly than too deeply; lily bulbs have contractile roots that draw them down to proper depth. Ideal spacing for lily bulbs is 1 ft. apart, but you can plant as close as 6 in. for densely massed effect.

Lilies need constant moisture to about 6 in. deep. You can reduce watering somewhat after tops turn yellow in fall, but never allow roots to dry out completely. Flooding is preferable to overhead watering, which may help to spread disease spores. Pull weeds by hand if possible; hoeing may injure roots.

Viral or mosaic infection is a problem. No cure exists. To avoid it, buy healthy bulbs from reliable sources. Dig and destroy any lilies that show mottling in leaves or seriously stunted growth. Control aphids, which spread the infection. Control botrytis blight, a fungal disease, with appropriate fungicide. Moles and voles relish lilies.

Wait until stems and leaves turn yellow before you cut plants back. If clumps become too crowded, dig up, divide, and transplant them in spring or fall. If you're careful, you can lift lily clumps at any time, even in bloom.

Lilies are fine container plants. Place one bulb in a deep 5–7-in. pot or five in a 14–16-in. pot. First, fill pot one-third full of potting mix. Then place bulb with roots spread and pointing downward; cover with about an inch of soil. Water thoroughly and place in deep cold frame or greenhouse that is heated (in colder climates) just enough to keep out frost. During root-forming period, keep soil moderately moist. When top growth appears, add more soil mixture and gradually fill pot as stems elongate. Leave 1-in. space between surface of soil and rim of pot for watering. Move

L

pots onto partially shaded terrace or patio during blooming period. Later, if you wish to repot bulbs, do so in late fall or early spring.

Although the official classification of lilies lists eight divisions of hybrids and a ninth division of species, the following listings describe the lilies commonly available to gardeners. Advances in breeding are producing lilies with forms, colors, and parentage hitherto considered unlikely, if not impossible. Consult specialists' catalogs to learn about these new wonders, which are reaching the market faster than books can deal with them.

ASIATIC HYBRIDS

These are the easiest and most reliable for the average garden. Some have upward-facing flowers, while others have horizontally held or drooping flowers. Stems are strong, erect, and short (1½ ft.) to moderate (4½ ft.) in height. Colors range from white through yellow and orange to pink and red. Many have dark spots or contrasting "halos." They are the earliest to bloom (early summer). Examples are 'Citronella', yellow spotted with maroon; 'Connecticut King', deep yellow with wide open petals; 'Mont Blanc', large white flowers with brown spots in center. 'Enchantment', orange red spotted with black; 'Impala', bright yellow; 'Pink Floyd', creamy pink banded with rose pink; and 'Sancerre', pure white and unspotted.

AURELIAN HYBRIDS

Derived from Asiatic species, excluding *L. auratum* and *L. speciosum*. They have trumpet- or bowl-shaped flowers in midsummer. Flowers range from white and cream through yellow and pink, many with green, brown, or purple shading on their outer surfaces. Plants are 3–6 ft. tall, and each stem carries 12–20 flowers. Examples are 'African Queen', fragrant, yellow to apricot inside, brownish purple outside; 'Anaconda', coppery apricot; 'Black Dragon', white with maroon petal backs; 'Golden Splendour', yellow blooms from purple buds; 'Pink Perfection' varying shades of purple pink; and 'Thunderbolt', orange apricot blossoms.

ORIENTAL HYBRIDS

The most exotic of the hybrids. Bloom midsummer–early fall, with big (to 9-in.) fragrant flowers of white or pink, often spotted with gold and shaded or banded with red. Most are tall, with nodding flowers, but a few are dwarf and have upward-facing blooms. Examples are 'Casablanca', pure white; 'Journey's End', deep rosy pink with white edge, maroon band and spots; 'Pink Ribbons', light rose banded and spotted with deep rose; 'Sans Souci', light carmine wih white edge and darker carmine spots; 'Silver Elegance,' white with pale lavender spots; and 'Stargazer', rose red with white margins.

SPECIES AND VARIANTS

L. amabile. To 3–4 ft. tall, with one to eight blooms per stem; flowers are fragrant, orange red, with dark purplish dots. Midsummer bloom.

L. auratum. GOLD-BAND LILY. Mid- to late summer bloom on 4–6-ft. plants. Flowers fragrant, waxy white spotted crimson, with golden band on each segment.

L. candidum. MADONNA LILY. Zones 31, 32. Pure white, fragrant blooms on 3–4-ft. stems in late spring, early summer. Unlike most lilies, dies down soon after bloom, makes new growth in fall. Plant while dormant in August. Does not have stem roots; set top of bulb only 1–2 in. deep in sunny location. Bulb quickly makes foliage rosette that lives over winter, lengthens to blooming stem in spring. Subject to diseases that shorten its life. Cascade strain, grown from seed, is healthier than imported bulbs. The lily of medieval romance, a sentimental choice for many gardeners.

Lilium candidum

L. centifolium (L. leucanthemum centifolium). Grows 7–8 ft. high. Each stem bears 15–20 white flowers banded brownish purple on outside of petals. Late summer bloom.

L. cernuum. Only 12–20 in. tall, with lilac flowers often dotted dark purple. Midsummer bloom; perfectly hardy. Sun.

L. davidii. Zones 32, 34–45. A rhizomatous, 3–4-ft.-tall species native to western China bearing linear, finely toothed, dark green leaves. Clusters of 3-in.-wide, brilliant red flowers with recurved petals in midsummer.

L. formosanum. FORMOSA LILY. Zones 31, 32. A 2–6-ft.-tall species native to Taiwan with lance-shaped leaves and very fragrant, trumpet-shaped, 5–8-in.-long flowers in late summer to fall. Blooms are white and flushed with red purple on the outside. Compact *L. f. pricei* produces white flowers flushed dark purple red and stays under 2 ft. Bulbs may be short lived, but plants self-sow easily. Seed sown in pots early and set out after frost danger is past may bloom in the first season. Highly valued because it comes into bloom when other species have gone by and is very fragrant and showy.

L. henryi. Slender stems to 8–9 ft. topped by 10–20 bright orange flowers with sharply recurved segments. Midsummer bloom. Best in light shade.

L. lancifolium (L. tigrinum). TIGER LILY. To 4 ft. or taller with pendulous orange flowers spotted black. Late summer bloom. An old favorite; very easy to grow. Newer tiger lilies are available in white, cream, yellow, pink, and red, all with black spots.

L. lankongense. Zones 31, 32, 34–41. Grows 4–6 ft. tall; stems bear up to 36 nodding, powerfully fragrant, pale to deep pink flowers with purple spots. Mid- to late summer bloom.

L. martagon. TURK'S CAP LILY. Purplish pink, recurved, pendent flowers in early summer on 3–5-ft. stems. This lily is slow to establish but is long lived and eventually forms big clumps. *L. m. album*, pure white, is one of the most appealing lilies. It is a parent of the Paisley hybrids, a group with flowers in yellow, orange, and mahogany shades, most with maroon spots.

L. monadelphum. Zones 31, 32, 34–41. Clump-forming lily ranging 3–5 ft. tall. Lance-shaped leaves and showy clusters of 25–30 nodding, trumpet-shaped, yellow flowers in midsummer. Blooms are flushed purple outside and spotted with maroon or purple inside. Tolerates heavy, clayey soil and drier sites than most species.

L. philadelphicum. WOOD LILY, WILD ORANGE LILY. Zones 32, 34–43. Native East Coast wildflower 2–4½ ft. tall. Bears orange-red flowers spotted maroon in summer. Can be hard to establish and short lived. A site with sandy, acid soil is best.

L. pumilum. Each wiry, 1–1½-ft. stem carries 1–20 scented, coral red flowers. Blooms late spring–early summer. 'Yellow Bunting' is a brilliant yellow form.

L. regale. REGAL LILY. Superseded in quality by modern hybrid trumpet lilies but still popular and easy to grow. To 6 ft., with white, fragrant flowers in early to midsummer.

L. speciosum. Grows 2½–5 ft. tall. Large, wide, fragrant flowers with broad, deeply recurved segments, late summer; white, heavily suffused rose pink, sprinkled with raised crimson dots. 'Rubrum' is red, 'Album' pure white; there are also other named forms. Best in light shade (or at least afternoon shade); needs rich soil with plenty of leaf mold.

L. superbum. AMERICAN TURK'S CAP LILY. Zones 32, 34–43. A 5–10-ft.-tall species native to the East Coast, with rhizomatous bulbs. Bears clusters of 30–40 drooping 3-in.-wide orange flowers that have backcurved petals and are spotted or flushed with maroon. Best in moist, acid soil.

L. tigrinum. See *L. lancifolium*

LILY. See LILIUM

LILY-OF-THE-NILE. See AGAPANTHUS

LILY-OF-THE-VALLEY. See CONVALLARIA

LILY-OF-THE-VALLEY SHRUB. See PIERIS japonica

LILY TURF. See LIRIOPE and OPHIOPOGON

FOR INFORMATION ON YOUR CLIMATE ZONE

PLEASE SEE PAGES 30–46

L

LIMONIUM

STATICE, SEA LAVENDER

Plumbaginaceae

PERENNIALS, BIENNIALS, AND ANNUALS

☒ ZONES VARY BY SPECIES

☼ FULL SUN

🌢 MODERATE WATER

Limonium

Large, leathery basal leaves contrast with airy clusters of small, delicate flowers on nearly leafless, many-branched stems. Tiny flowers consist of two parts: an outer, papery envelope (the calyx) and an inner part (the corolla) that often has a different color. For spring–summer bloom of annual kinds, sow indoors and move to garden when weather warms up. Or sow outdoors in early spring for later bloom. All tolerate heat and many soils but need good drainage. They often self-sow.

L. bonduellii. Annual or biennial. All zones. Grows 2 ft. tall, with 6-in. basal leaves lobed nearly to midrib. Flower stems are distinctly winged; calyx is yellow, tiny corolla deeper yellow.

L. gmelinii. Perennial. Zones 32, 34–41. Basal rosette of spoon-shaped 5-in. leaves produces 2-ft., branching clusters of tiny blue flowers in mid- to late summer.

L. latifolium. Perennial. Zones 31, 32, 34–43. To 2½ ft. tall. Smooth-edged leaves to 10 in. long. Calyx is white and corolla bluish; pure white and pink kinds exist. Summer bloom. Vigorous plants may show a 3-ft.-wide haze of flowers.

L. sinuatum. Annual. All zones. Growth habit like *L. bonduellii,* with lobed leaves and winged stems, but calyx is blue, lavender, or rose and corolla is white. Widely grown as a fresh or dried cut flower.

L. suworowii. See *Psylliostachys suworowii*

L. tataricum. See *Goniolimon tataricum*

> ### STATICE LASTS LONG FRESH OR DRIED
> Cut for fresh bouquets after most flowers in each cluster have opened. For dried arrangements, cut after opening but before sun has faded them. With a rubber band, join several bunches together by stem bases; hang upside down in a dry spot out of bright sun until flowers dry.

LION'S EAR, LION'S TAIL. See LEONOTIS ocymifolia

Linaceae. The flax family of annuals, perennials, and shrubs displays cup- or disk-shaped flowers with four or five petals. Flowers are often showy. Individually short lived, they appear over a long season. The only family member covered in this book is flax *(Linum)*.

LINARIA

TOADFLAX

Scrophulariaceae

PERENNIALS AND ANNUALS

☒ ZONES VARY BY SPECIES

☼ ◐ FULL SUN OR LIGHT SHADE

🌢 MODERATE WATER

Linaria

Brightly colored flowers that resemble small, spurred snapdragons. Very narrow, medium green leaves. Easy to grow. Best in masses; individual plants are usually rather wispy.

L. cymbalaria. See *Cymbalaria muralis*

L. maroccana. BABY SNAPDRAGON, TOADFLAX. Annual. All zones. Grows to 1½–2 ft. high. Flowers in red-and-gold combination, rose, pink, mauve, chamois, blue, violet, or purple, blotched with different shade on the lip. Spur is longer than flower. Fairy Bouquet strain is only 9 in. tall and has larger flowers in pastel shades. Northern Lights strain blooms in reds, oranges, and yellows as well as bicolors. Seed in quantity for a show. Performs best during cool weather; sow in early spring after danger of frost is past, then again in late summer.

L. purpurea. Perennial. Zones 31, 32, 34–41. Narrow, bushy, erect growth to 2½–3 ft. Blue-green foliage; violet-blue flowers in summer. 'Canon Went' is a pink form. Short lived in hot, humid regions, but volunteer seedlings ensure resupply.

LINDEN. See TILIA

LINDERA

SPICEBUSH

Lauraceae

DECIDUOUS SHRUBS OR SMALL TREES

☒ ZONES VARY BY SPECIES

☼ ◐ FULL SUN OR PART SHADE

🌢 REGULAR WATER

Lindera

Large deciduous shrubs grown principally for the beauty of their bright yellow fall foliage. Flowers are attractive but not showy: small, greenish yellow, clustered at the joints of leafless shoots in earliest spring. Female plants have attractive fruits, but these are seldom seen unless plants of both sexes are present. Common name refers to the foliage, which is strongly aromatic when bruised or crushed. Although too large for most gardens, spicebushes are effective at the edge of woodland or as space fillers. Need good drainage; tolerate some drought.

L. benzoin. SPICEBUSH. Zones 31, 32, 34–43. Native to woodlands of eastern U.S. Grows 6–12 ft. tall and as wide. Light green leaves are 3–5 in. long, half as wide. Fall color and plant form are best in full sun; plants tolerate considerable shade but are loose and open if grown there. Fruit, noticeable after leaf fall, is bright red, ⅓–½ in. long. Species name describes the leaves' odor—a spicy scent reminiscent of benzoin, an aromatic gum once used in medicine and perfumery.

L. obtusiloba. JAPANESE SPICEBUSH. Zones 31, 32, 34–41. Native to Japan, Korea, and China. Larger than *L. benzoin* (10–20 ft. tall, somewhat narrower), with broader leaves (to 5 in. long, 4 in. wide). The shiny dark green leaves sometimes have a mitten shape, with one lobe or two as shallow divisions from the main leaf. Small (¼-in.) fruits turn from red to black. Fall color is an exceptionally brilliant yellow that holds for 2 weeks or more and develops even in considerable shade.

LINGONBERRY. See VACCINIUM vitis-idaea minus

LINNAEA borealis

TWINFLOWER

Caprifoliaceae

PERENNIAL

☒ ZONES 36–45

◐ ● PARTIAL OR FULL SHADE

🌢 REGULAR WATER

Linnaea borealis

Native to much of Northern Hemisphere. Flat, glossy evergreen mats with delicate 1-in.-long

L

leaves. Spreads by runners. Paired flowers appear on 3–4-in. stems. Flowers are pale pink, fragrant, trumpet shaped, ⅓ in. long. Collector's item or small-scale ground cover for woodland garden. Keep area around plants mulched with leaf mold to induce spreading. Tolerates some sun in cool-summer climates.

LINUM

FLAX

Linaceae

PERENNIALS AND ANNUALS

ZONES VARY BY SPECIES

☼ FULL SUN

◗ MODERATE WATER

Linum

These plants have erect, branching stems, narrow leaves, and abundant, shallow-cupped, five-petaled flowers that bloom from late spring into summer or fall. Each bloom lasts only a day, but others keep coming. The flax of commerce—*L. usitatissimum*—is grown for its fiber and seeds, which yield linseed oil.

Use in borders; some naturalize freely in uncultivated areas. Light, well-drained soil. Most perennial kinds live only 3 or 4 years and should be replaced regularly. Easy from seed; perennials also can be grown from cuttings. Difficult to divide.

L. flavum. GOLDEN FLAX. Perennial. Zones 31, 32, 34–41. Erect, compact, 12–15 in. tall, somewhat woody at base; grooved branches, green leaves. Flowers golden yellow, about 1 in. wide, in branched clusters. Often called yellow flax, a name correctly applied to closely related *Reinwardtia indica*. 'Compactum' is a smaller form.

L. grandiflorum 'Rubrum'. SCARLET FLAX. Annual. All zones. Bright scarlet flowers, 1–1½ in. wide, on slender, leafy, 1–1½ ft. stems. Narrow gray-green leaves. Also comes in a rose-colored form. Sow seed thickly in place in fall (in mild areas) or early spring. Quick color for borders or bulb cover. Good with gray foliage or white-flowered plants. Reseeds but doesn't become a pest. Often included in wildflower seed mixtures.

L. narbonense. Perennial. Zones 31, 32, 34–41. Wiry stems to 2 ft. high. Leaves blue green, narrow. Flowers large (1¾ in. across), azure blue with white eye, in open clusters. Best variety, 'Six Hills', has rich sky blue flowers.

L. perenne. PERENNIAL BLUE FLAX. Zones 31, 32, 34–41. Most vigorous blue-flowered flax. Stems to 2 ft., usually leafless below. Profuse bloomer, with branching clusters of light blue flowers that close in shade or late in the day. Self-sows freely.

LIP FERN. See CHEILANTHES

LIPPIA citriodora. See ALOYSIA triphylla

LIQUIDAMBAR

SWEET GUM

Hamamelidaceae

DECIDUOUS TREES

ZONES VARY BY SPECIES

☼ FULL SUN

◗◗ REGULAR TO MODERATE WATER

Liquidambar

Valuable for form, foliage, fall color, and easy culture. Moderate growth rate; young and middle-aged trees generally upright, somewhat cone shaped, spreading in age. Lobed, maplelike leaves. Flowers inconspicuous; fruits are spiny balls that ornament trees in winter, need raking in spring.

Give neutral or slightly acid, improved garden soil. Provide plenty of space for roots. Takes time to establish after planting. Stake well. Prune

only to shape. Trees branch from ground up and look most natural that way, but can be pruned high to expose a definite trunk.

Form surface roots that can be a nuisance in lawns or narrow parking strips. Good street trees in ample parking strip, however. Effective in tall screens or groves, planted 6–10 ft. apart. Brilliant fall foliage; fall color less effective in mildest climates or in mild, late autumns.

L. formosana. CHINESE SWEET GUM. Zones 31, 32. To 40–60 ft. tall, 25 ft. wide. Free-form outline; sometimes pyramidal, especially when young. Leaves with three to five lobes are 3–4½ in. across, violet red when expanding, then deep green. Yellow or red fall color.

L. orientalis. ORIENTAL SWEET GUM. Zones 31, 32. Native to Turkey. To 20–30 ft., spreading or round headed. Leaves 2–3 in. wide, deeply five lobed, lobes again lobed to produce a lacy effect. Leafs out early after short dormant period. Fall color varies from deep gold to bright red.

L. styraciflua. AMERICAN SWEET GUM. Zones 31, 32, 34–37, 39. Native to eastern U.S. Grows to 60–75 ft. in gardens; much taller in the wild. Narrow and erect in youth, with lower limbs eventually spreading to 20–25 ft. Good all-year tree. Branching pattern, furrowed bark, corky wings on twigs, and hanging fruit provide winter interest. Leaves five to seven lobed, 3–7 in. wide; deep green in spring and summer, turning purple, yellow, or red in fall. Even seedling trees give good fall color, though color may vary somewhat from year to year. To get desired and uniform color, choose trees while they are in fall leaf or buy budded trees of a named variety, such as the following:

'Burgundy'. Leaves turn deep purple red, hang late into winter or even early spring if storms are not heavy.

'Festival'. Narrow, columnar. Light green foliage turns to yellow, peach, pink, orange, and red.

'Gumball'. Dense, rounded shrub to 15 ft. high. Unremarkable fall color.

'Palo Alto'. Turns orange red to bright red in fall.

'Rotundiloba'. Lobes of leaves are rounded rather than sharp. Fall foliage is purple. Tree does not form fruit.

'Variegata'. Within a few weeks of unfurling, leaves develop streaks and blotches of yellow. They retain variegation throughout summer and early fall.

LIRIODENDRON
tulipifera

TULIP TREE

Magnoliaceae

DECIDUOUS TREE

ZONES 31, 32, 34–41

☼ FULL SUN

◗ REGULAR WATER

Liriodendron tulipifera

Native to eastern U.S. Fast growth to 60–90 ft., with eventual spread to 35–50 ft.; considerably larger in the wild. Straight, columnar trunk, with spreading, rising branches that form tall pyramidal crown. The 5–6 in. leaves are variously described as lyre shaped, saddle shaped, or truncated; they're like blunt-tipped maple leaves missing the end lobe. They turn from bright yellow green to bright yellow in fall.

Tulip-shaped flowers in late spring are 2 in. wide, greenish yellow, orange at base. Handsome at close range but not showy on the tree, since they are carried high up and well concealed by leaves. Trees don't usually bloom until they are 10 to 12 years old.

Nurseries may carry two slower-growing selections that are smaller than the species. 'Arnold' ('Fastigiata') has a rigidly columnar habit useful for narrow planting areas; it will bloom 2 to 3 years after planting. 'Majestic Beauty' has yellow-edged leaves.

Tulip trees thrive in deep, rich, well-drained neutral or slightly acid soil. Fairly weak wooded and subject to limb breakage from storms or ice; best used in wind-sheltered locations. Give them room; they make good large shade or lawn trees. Wide-spreading network of shallow, fleshy roots make them difficult to garden under. Control aphids as necessary.

LIRIOPE and OPHIOPOGON

LILY TURF

Liliaceae

EVERGREEN GRASSLIKE PERENNIALS

☘ ZONES VARY BY SPECIES

☼ ● SOME SHADE, EXCEPT AS NOTED

💧 💧 REGULAR TO MODERATE WATER

▶ SEE CHART NEXT PAGE

Liriope muscari

These two plants are similar in appearance: both form clumps or tufts of grasslike leaves and bear white or lavender summer flowers in spikelike or branched clusters (quite showy in some kinds). Last well in flower arrangements. Use as casual ground cover in small areas. Also attractive as borders along paths, between flower bed and lawn, among rock groupings, or in rock gardens. Grow well along streams and around garden pools. They compete well with roots of other plants; try under bamboo or to cover bare soil at bases of trees or shrubs in ground or in large containers. None satisfactory as mowed lawn. Tolerate indoor conditions in pots or planter. *Liriope* is hardier; *Ophiopogon* is suited only to the warmest Northeast zones, except for *O. planiscapus* 'Nigrescens', which is hardy to New York City.

Provide filtered sun to full shade; take full sun in cool-summer regions. Plant in well-drained soil. Become ragged and brown with neglect; cut back shaggy old foliage before new leaves appear. Plants don't need heavy feeding. To increase, divide in early spring before new growth starts.

Plants look best from spring until cold weather of winter. Extended frosts may cause plants to turn yellow; they take quite a while to recover. Can show tip burn on leaves if soil contains excess salts or if plants are kept too wet where drainage is poor.

LISIANTHUS. See EUSTOMA grandiflorum

LITHODORA diffusa

Boraginaceae

PERENNIAL

☘ ZONES 31, 32, 34, 39

☼ ☼ WILL TAKE FULL SUN IN ZONE 34

💧 MODERATE WATER

Lithodora diffusa

Prostrate, somewhat shrubby, slightly mounded, broad mass 6–12 in. tall. Narrow evergreen leaves, ¾–1 in. long; both foliage and stems are hairy. In late spring (and often later), plant is sprinkled with tubular, brilliant blue flowers ½ in. long. Loose, well-drained, lime-free soil. Use in rock gardens, spilling over walls. Best suited to mild-summer climates. 'Heavenly Blue' and 'Grace Ward' are selected varieties. Formerly *Lithospermum diffusum* or *L. prostratum*.

LITHOSPERMUM. See LITHODORA diffusa

LITTLE BLUESTEM. See SCHIZACHYRIUM

LIVERLEAF. See HEPATICA

LIVINGSTONE DAISY. See DOROTHEANTHUS bellidiformis

LIZARD'S TAIL. See SAURURUS cernuus

LOBELIA

Campanulaceae (Lobeliaceae)

PERENNIALS OR ANNUALS

☘ ZONES VARY BY SPECIES

☼ ☼ PARTIAL SHADE IN HOTTEST CLIMATES

💧 💧 AMPLE WATER

◈ MOST CONTAIN POISONOUS ALKALOIDS

Lobelia

Distinct differences separate the annual lobelia from the most familiar perennial kinds; the former is blue and spreading, the others red or blue and upright. On all types, the tubular, lipped flowers resemble those of honeysuckle or salvia.

L. cardinalis. CARDINAL FLOWER. Perennial. Zones 31, 32, 34–45. Native to eastern U.S. and to a few sites in mountains of Southwest. Erect, single-stemmed, 2–4-ft.-high plant with saw-edged leaves set directly on the stems. Spikes of flame red, inch-long flowers in summer. A bog plant in nature, it needs rich soil and constant moisture through the growing season.

Crossbreeding between this species and *L. splendens* (*L. fulgens*), which is closely related, has resulted in a number of hybrids. 'Queen Victoria' and 'Royal Robe' have deep purple-red foliage and scarlet flowers; 'Heather Pink' has soft pink flowers.

L. erinus. Annual. All zones. Popular and dependable edging plant. Compact or trailing growth habit with leafy, branching stems. Flowers, ¾ in. across, are light blue to violet (sometimes pink, reddish purple, or white) with white or yellowish throats. Blooms from early summer to frost in cool areas, but performs poorly in the heat and humidity of Zones 31 and 32. Takes about 2 months for seed sown in pots to grow to planting-out size. Moist, rich soil. Trailing kinds make a graceful ground cover in large planters or in smaller pots; the stems, loaded with flowers, spill over the edges.

'Cambridge Blue' has clear, soft blue flowers and light green leaves on compact 4–6-in. plant. 'Crystal Palace', also compact, has rich dark blue flowers, bronze green leaves. 'Rosamond' has carmine red flowers with white eyes. 'White Lady' is pure white. Three trailing varieties for hanging baskets or wall plantings are 'Hamburgia', 'Blue Cascade', and 'Sapphire'.

L. gerardii. Perennial. Zones 31, 32, 34–43. Hybrid between *L. cardinalis* and *L. siphilitica*; needs rich soil, constant moisture, part shade. 'Vedrariensis' grows to 4 ft., with coppery green foliage and bright royal purple flowers. 'Rosea', 2½ ft. high, has rose pink flowers. 'Ruby Slippers', 3 ft. tall, has dark red flowers.

L. siphilitica. Perennial. Zones 31, 32, 34–43. Native to eastern U.S. Leafy plants send up 3-ft. stalks set with blue flowers. Needs ample moisture, partial shade. 'Alba' has white flowers.

Lobeliaceae. See Campanulaceae

LOBULARIA maritima

SWEET ALYSSUM

Brassicaceae (Cruciferae)

ANNUAL

☘ ALL ZONES

☼ ☼ BEST IN FULL SUN, TOLERATES LIGHT SHADE

💧 REGULAR WATER

Lobularia maritima

Low, branching, trailing plant to 1 ft. tall, with narrow or lance-shaped leaves ½–2 in. long. Tiny, four-petaled white flowers crowded in clusters; honeylike fragrance. Blooms spring until frost in cold-winter regions;

L

LIRIOPE AND OPHIOPOGON

NAME	ZONES	GROWTH FORM	LEAVES	FLOWERS	COMMENTS
Liriope muscari BIG BLUE LILY TURF	31, 32, 34, 39	Forms large clumps but does not spread by underground stems. Rather loose growth habit, 1-1½ ft. high	Dark green. To 2 ft. long, ½ in. wide	Dark violet buds and flowers in rather dense, 6–8-in.-long spikelike clusters on 5–12-in.-long stems (resemble grape hyacinths). Followed by a few round, shiny black fruits.	Profuse flowers held above leaves in young plants, partly hidden in older plants. 'Lilac Beauty' has paler violet flowers. 'Variegata' has white-striped leaves. Many other varieties.
L. m. 'Border Gem'	31, 32, 34, 39	Dwarf clump to 8 in.	Leaves to 8 in. long	Lilac flowers	Use as edging. 'Little Beauty' is similar
L. m. 'Gold Banded'	31, 32, 34, 39	Large clump 1–1½ ft. high	Leaves broad, with narrow gold margins	Flowers as in *L. muscari*	Arching clumps
L. spicata CREEPING LILY TURF	31, 32, 34–43	Dense; spreads widely by underground stems. Grows 8–9 in. high	Narrow, deep green, soft, not as upright as *L. muscari.*	Pale lilac to white flowers in spikelike clusters barely taller than leaves	To get best effect, mow every year in spring prior to new growth. Good ground cover
L. s. 'Silver Dragon'	31, 32, 34–43	Similar in size to species	Leaves striped silvery white	Flowers pale purple on short spikes	Fine ground cover for shade; slower growing than species
Ophiopogon jaburan (often sold as *Liriope gigantea*)	31, 32	Eventually forms large clump growing from fibrous roots	Dark green, curved, firm leaves 1½–3 ft. long, about ½ in. wide	Small, chalk white flowers in nodding clusters, somewhat hidden by leaves. Metallic violent blue fruit.	Fruit is very attractive feature; good for cutting. 'Vittatus' has leaves striped lengthwise with white, aging to plain green. Similar to *L. muscari* 'Variegata'
O. japonicus MONDO GRASS	31, 32	Forms dense clumps that spread by underground stems, many of which are tuberlike. Slow to establish as ground cover	Dark green leaves ⅛ in. wide, 8–12 in. long. 'Nana' and 'Kyoto Dwarf' have half-sized leaves in tight clumps.	Flowers light lilac in short spikes usually hidden by the leaves. Blue fruit	Can be cut back. Easy to divide. Slow, sure spreader. Set divisions 6–8 in. apart. Roots will be killed at 10°F/-12°C. Looks best in partial shade
O. planiscapus *'Nigrescens'* ('Nigricans', 'Arabicus', 'Ebony Knight')	31, 32, 34, 39	Makes tuft 8 in. high and about 1 ft. wide	Leaves to 10 in. long. New leaves green but soon turn black	White (sometimes flushed pink) in loose spikelike clusters	Spreads slowly and does not make a solid cover. Interesting in containers. Valuable as novelty

often self-sows. In hot, humid regions, may go dormant during hottest period but resumes when weather cools. Seeds sometimes included in wildflower mixes or erosion-control mixes for bare or disturbed earth.

Easy, quick, dependable. Blooms from seed in 6 weeks; grows in almost any soil. Useful for carpeting, edging, bulb cover, temporary filler in rock garden or perennial border; between flagstones; in window boxes or containers. Attracts bees. If you shear plants halfway back 4 weeks after they come into bloom, new growth will make another crop of flowers, and plants won't become rangy.

Garden varieties better known than the species; these varieties self-sow, too, but seedlings tend to revert to taller, looser growth, less intense color, and smaller flowers. 'Carpet of Snow' (2–4 in. tall), 'Little Gem' (4–6 in.), and 'Tiny Tim' (3 in.) are good compact whites. 'Tetra Snowdrift' (1 ft.) has long stems, large white flowers. 'Rosie O'Day' (2–4 in.) and 'Pink Heather' (6 in.) are lavender pinks. 'Oriental Night' (4 in.) and 'Violet Queen' (5 in.) are rich violet purples.

LOCUST. See ROBINIA

LOLIUM

RYEGRASS

Poaceae (Gramineae)

ANNUAL OR PERENNIAL LAWN GRASSES

ZONES VARY BY SPECIES

FULL SUN

REGULAR WATER

Lolium

Not considered the choicest lawn grasses, but useful in special conditions and situations (lawns, pasture, soil reclamation). These are clumping, not running, grasses. To make tight turf, sow heavily. Ryegrass is often mixed with other lawn grass species for low-cost, large-area coverage in cool-summer climates.

L. multiflorum. ITALIAN RYEGRASS. All zones. Larger, coarser than perennial ryegrass. Basically an annual; some plants live for several seasons in mild climates. Fast growing, deep rooted. Hybrid between *L. multiflorum* and *L. perenne* is common or domestic ryegrass, often used as winter cover on soil.

L. perenne. PERENNIAL RYEGRASS. Zones 36, 38–45. Finer in texture than above, deep green with high gloss. Disadvantages are clumping tendency and tough flower and seed stems that lie down under mower blades. Advantages are fast sprouting and growth. Best in cool-summer climates. 'Manhattan' is finer, more uniform. Other varieties are 'Pennfine', 'Derby', 'Yorktown', 'Loretta'. Mow at 1½–2 in., higher in summer.

LONDON PRIDE. See SAXIFRAGA umbrosa

LONICERA

HONEYSUCKLE

Caprifoliaceae

EVERGREEN, SEMIEVERGREEN, OR DECIDUOUS SHRUBS OR VINES

 ZONES VARY BY SPECIES

☼ ◐ FULL SUN OR LIGHT SHADE

🌢 MODERATE WATER

Lonicera

These easy-to-grow plants exist in a great many species, most of them valued for tubular, often fragrant flowers. Vining kinds need support when they are starting out. When honeysuckles become overgrown, cut them to the ground; they regrow rapidly. Prune after flowering. Blossoms attract hummingbirds. Fruit provides food for many kinds of birds. Plants are generally not bothered by serious pests or diseases. Aphids are the chief problem, distorting buds and preventing flowering in parts of the East.

L. bella. BELLE HONEYSUCKLE. Deciduous shrub. Zones 32, 34–43. Large, vigorous hybrid shrub 8–10 ft. tall and spreading 8–12 ft. Bears blue-green leaves and in spring or early summer, white to pinkish blooms that fade to yellow. Red berries. 'Atrorosea' bears rose flowers with paler edges. 'Candida' produces pure white flowers.

L. brownii. Deciduous vine. Zones 31, 32, 34–45. Hybrid between *L. sempervirens* and *L. hirsuta*, a little-grown vine from the northeastern U.S. 'Dropmore Scarlet', the only selection extensively grown, climbs to 9–10 ft. It has blue-green leaves, those on the upper stem joining at the base; clusters of tubular scarlet flowers appear from early summer to frost.

L. fragrantissima. WINTER HONEYSUCKLE. Deciduous shrub, semievergreen in mild-winter areas. Zones 31, 32, 34–41. Arching, rather stiff growth to 8 ft. Leaves oval, dull dark green above, blue green beneath, 1–3 in. long. Creamy white flowers, ½ in. long, in late winter and early spring. Flowers richly fragrant (like *Daphne odora*) but not showy. Berrylike red fruit. Can be used as clipped hedge or background plant. Bring budded branches indoors for bloom.

L. heckrottii. GOLD FLAME HONEYSUCKLE, CORAL HONEYSUCKLE. Deciduous vine or small shrub, semievergreen in mild-winter climates. Zones 31, 32, 34–41. Vigorous to 12–15 ft., with oval, 2-in., blue-green leaves. Free blooming from spring to frost. Clustered 1½-in.-long flowers, bright coral pink outside and rich yellow within, open from coral pink buds. Train as espalier or on wire along eaves.

L. henryi. Evergreen vine. Zones 31, 32, 34–43. Twining woody vine climbing vigorously to 30 ft. Dark green, usually evergreen, leaves. Clusters of purple-red flowers with yellow throats from early to midsummer. Purple-black berries.

L. japonica. JAPANESE HONEYSUCKLE. Evergreen, semievergreen, or deciduous vine, depending on climate. Zones 31, 32, 34–41. Rampant—even invasive—and not recommended except for areas of poor, dry soil where little else will grow. Deep green, oval leaves; purple-tinged white flowers with sweet fragrance, late spring into fall.

Several varieties are grown, all better known than the species itself. 'Aureo-reticulata', goldnet honeysuckle, has leaves veined yellow, especially in full sun. 'Halliana', Hall's honeysuckle, most vigorous and widely grown, climbs to 15 ft., covers 150 sq. ft.; flowers pure white changing to yellow, attractive to bees. 'Purpurea', probably same as *L. j. chinensis,* has leaves tinged purple underneath and purplish red flowers that are white inside.

Of the above, 'Halliana' is the most commonly used as bank and ground cover and has escaped cultivation in the Mid-Atlantic and Southeast, moving into natural areas where its rampant growth quickly smothers native vegetation. Definitely not recommended for planting in the Northeast.

L. maackii. AMUR HONEYSUCKLE. Deciduous shrub. Zones 31, 32, 34–41. A large shrub or small tree 12–15 ft. high at maturity and spreading as far. Bears dark green leaves and pairs of fragrant white flowers along the stems. Blooms appear in early summer and fade to yellow. Red berries. Tolerates shade. This species can become invasive and is considered a noxious weed in some areas.

L. maximowiczii sachalinensis. Deciduous shrub. Zones 32, 34–41. These euphonious syllables denote an attractive dense, rounded shrub to 6–8 ft., with dark green leaves 1½–3 in. long and half as wide. The deep red, 1½-in.-long flowers are followed by red fruit. Fall color is bright yellow.

L. morrowii. MORROW HONEYSUCKLE. Deciduous shrub. Zones 31, 32, 34–43. A 6–8-ft. shrub that spreads 10–12 ft. Bears blue- to gray-green leaves and pairs of creamy white flowers in late spring or early summer that fade to yellow.

L. nitida. BOXLEAF HONEYSUCKLE. Semievergreen shrub, deciduous in coldest part of range. Zones 31, 32, 34, 39. To 4–6 ft. tall, with densely leafy branches. Tiny (½-in.), oval, shiny dark green leaves. Attractive bronze to plum-colored winter foliage. Late spring or early summer flowers are fragrant, creamy white, ½ in. long. Translucent blue-purple berries. Rapid growth, tending toward untidiness, but easily pruned as hedge or single plant. Takes salt spray. 'Baggesen's Gold' has golden foliage with better color in sun than in shade; 'Silver Beauty' has white-edged leaves.

L. periclymenum. WOODBINE HONEYSUCKLE. Deciduous vine. Zones 31, 32, 34–41. Resembles *L. japonica* but is less rampant, climbing to 20 ft. Whorls of 2-in.-long, fragrant flowers in summer, fall. Blooms of 'Serotina' are purple outside, yellow inside. 'Berries Jubilee' has yellow flowers followed by profusion of red berries. 'Belgica' is less vining, more bushy than most, with abundant white flowers flushed purple, fading to yellow; flowers and red fruit come in large clusters. 'Graham Thomas' has white flowers that turn copper-tinted yellow.

L. pileata. PRIVET HONEYSUCKLE. Evergreen or semievergreen shrub. Zones 31, 32, 34–41. Low, spreading plant to 3 ft. tall, with stiff horizontal branches. Dark green, 1½-in., privetlike leaves; small, fragrant white flowers in late spring; translucent violet purple berries. Good bank cover with low-growing euonymus or barberries. Does well at seashore. Give part or full shade in hot climates.

L. sempervirens. TRUMPET HONEYSUCKLE. Deciduous twining vine, shrubby if not given support. Zones 31, 32, 34–43. From late spring into summer, bears showy, unscented, orange-yellow to scarlet flowers—trumpet shaped, 1½–2 in. long, carried in whorls at ends of branches. Scarlet fruit. Oval, 1½–3-in.-long leaves are bluish green beneath. 'Cedar Lane' is a vigorous selection with deep red flowers. 'John Clayton' is compact and repeat-blooming, with yellow flowers and red fruit. 'Sulphurea' has yellow flowers in late spring. 'Superba', scarlet to orange-red flowers, repeat blooming. For 'Dropmore Scarlet', see *L. brownii*.

L. tatarica. Deciduous shrub. Zones 32, 34–43. Big, twiggy shrub to 10–12 ft. tall and wide, with bluish green foliage and white to pink flowers borne in pairs in late spring. Red berries follow. Most widely grown selection is 'Arnold Red', with dark red flowers. Too large for most gardens; use for shelter belt, screening, bird shelter.

L. tellmanniana. TELLMAN HONEYSUCKLE. Deciduous vine. Zones 31, 32, 34–41. Vigorous hybrid climbing to 15 ft. Handsome, bright green leaves, showy clusters of copper- to yellow-orange flowers from late spring to midsummer.

L. xylosteum. Deciduous shrub. Zones 32, 34–43. Mounding, arching growth to 10 ft. tall, 12 ft. wide. Grayish or bluish green leaves, white or pinkish flowers in late spring. Species is seldom seen. 'Claveyi' or 'Clavey's Dwarf' is most commonly grown; tends to stay 3–6 ft. tall, occasionally taller. Other dwarf selections are sometimes offered. All are useful for hedges or foundation plantings in harsh climates.

LOOFAH. See LUFFA

LOOSESTRIFE. See LYSIMACHIA punctata, LYTHRUM virgatum

LOROPETALUM chinense

Hamamelidaceae

EVERGREEN SHRUB

ZONES 31, 32

FULL SUN OR PARTIAL SHADE

REGULAR WATER

Loropetalum chinense

Generally 5–10 ft. tall. Neat, compact habit, with arching or drooping tiered branches. Leaves roundish, light green, soft, 1–2 in. long. Throughout the year, the occasional leaf turns yellow or red, providing a nice touch of color. White to greenish white flowers in clusters of four to eight at ends of branches. Each flower has four narrow, inch-long, twisted petals. Blooms most heavily in spring, but some bloom is likely at any time. 'Rubrum' ('Razzleberri') has purplish leaves and bright rosy pink flowers; 'Burgundy' is similar, if not identical.

Needs well-drained, nonalkaline soil. Subtly beautiful plant, good in foregrounds, raised beds, hanging baskets, woodland gardens, even maintained as a high ground cover.

LOTUS

Fabaceae (Leguminosae)

SHRUBBY PERENNIALS, OR GROWN AS ANNUAL

ZONES VARY BY SPECIES

FULL SUN OR PARTIAL SHADE

REGULAR WATER

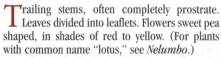

Lotus

Trailing stems, often completely prostrate. Leaves divided into leaflets. Flowers sweet pea shaped, in shades of red to yellow. (For plants with common name "lotus," see *Nelumbo*.)

L. berthelotii. PARROT'S BEAK. All zones. Trailing perennial with stems 2–3 ft. long, thickly covered with silvery gray foliage and very narrow, 1-in.-long scarlet blossoms. Blooms in summer and thrives in hot weather. Dies back in cold weather; suffers root rot in poor drainage. Set out young plants in spring and treat as an annual. Space 2 ft. apart as ground cover; cut back occasionally to induce bushiness. Also very effective in hanging baskets, as cascade over wall or rocks.

L. corniculatus. BIRD'S FOOT TREFOIL. Zones 31, 32, 34–41. Goes dormant throughout the Northeast. Use as ground cover or coarse lawn substitute in a small area. Makes mat of dark green, cloverlike leaves. Forms clusters of small yellow flowers in summer and fall. Seedpods at top of flower stems spread like bird's foot, hence common name. Sow seeds or set out plants. Should be mowed occasionally.

LOVAGE. See LEVISTICUM officinale

LOVE-IN-A-MIST. See NIGELLA damascena

LOVE-LIES-BLEEDING. See AMARANTHUS caudatus

PRACTICAL GARDENING DICTIONARY

PLEASE SEE PAGES 449–523

LUFFA cylindrica (L. aegyptiaca)

LOOFAH, VEGETABLE SPONGE, RAG OR DISHCLOTH GOURD

Cucurbitaceae

ANNUAL

ALL ZONES

FULL SUN

REGULAR WATER

Luffa cylindrica

This tropical vine in the gourd family produces the popular loofah scrubbers that sit by many American tubs and showers. These sponges are skeletons of mature fruit. The vigorous climbing vine grows 15-ft. stems and produces many attractive clusters of bright yellow, 2-in. male flowers and a few lone female flowers. Leaves are coarse and hairy. Smooth fruits are like giant cucumbers, measuring up to 2 ft. long and 5 in. wide. Native to India, where young fruits are eaten, luffa is a warm-season annual that grows best in deep, sandy loam. Start seeds indoors. After the last frost, set plants 2 ft. apart in rows spaced 5 ft. apart and grow on a 6-ft. trellis, since fruits touching the ground may rot. For bigger sponges, remove some of the setting fruit so the remaining ones can grow larger.

Grow luffa for fun or use it for a deciduous screen by growing it on a chain-link or other fence. To eat, harvest at 6 in. or less. For sponges, harvest mature fruit. Process sponges by soaking fresh or dry luffa gourds in warm water for a few days. Remove the flesh and seeds. Bleach the skeleton with hydrogen peroxide and then dry in sunlight.

LUNARIA annua (L. biennis)

MONEY PLANT

Brassicaceae (Cruciferae)

BIENNIAL

ZONES 31, 32, 34–43

AFTERNOON SHADE IN HOT CLIMATES

REGULAR TO MODERATE WATER

Lunaria annua

Old-fashioned garden plant, grown for silvery, translucent circles (about 1¼ in. across) that stay on flower stalks and are all that remain of ripened seedpods after outer coverings drop with seeds. Plants are 1½–3 ft. high, with coarse, heart-shaped, toothed leaves. Spring flowers resemble wild mustard blooms but are purple or white, not yellow. There is a form with variegated leaves.

Plant in an out-of-the-way spot in poor soil or in a mixed flower bed where shining pods can be admired before they are picked for dry bouquets. Tough, persistent; can reseed and become weedy.

LUNGWORT. See PULMONARIA

LUPINUS

LUPINE

Fabaceae (Leguminosae)

PERENNIALS, SHRUBS, AND ANNUALS

ZONES VARY BY SPECIES

FULL SUN

WATER NEEDS VARY BY SPECIES

Lupinus

Leaves are divided into many leaflets (like fingers of a hand). Flowers sweet pea shaped, in dense spikes at ends of stems. Hundreds of species, many of them native to western U.S.; occur in wide range of habitats, from beach sand to alpine rocks. The most commonly grown lupines are Russell Hybrids. Most lupines take poor conditions, but the hybrids prefer rich, slightly acidic, well-drained soil.

L. hartwegii. Annual. All zones. Native to Mexico. Grows 1½–3 ft. tall; comes in shades of blue, white, and pink. Easy to grow from seed sown in place in spring for summer bloom. Moderate water.

L. perennis. Perennial. Zones 31, 32, 34–43. Native to eastern U.S. To 2 ft. high, with purple flowers in late spring or early summer. Regular water.

L. polyphyllus. Perennial. Zones 34, 37–39. Native to moist places along the West Coast. Grows 1½–4 ft. tall, with dense clusters of blue, purple, or reddish flowers in summer. One important ancestor of the Russell Hybrids. Ample water.

L. Russell Hybrids. RUSSELL LUPINES. Perennials. Zones 34, 36–45. Best in cool areas of New England, northern tier of states, and adjacent southern Canada. Large, spreading plants to 4–5 ft. tall, with long, dense spikes of flowers in late spring or early summer. Blooms in white, cream, yellow, pink, blue, red, orange, purple, and bicolors. Little Lulu and Minarette strains are smaller growing—to 1½ ft.

Grow from seed or buy started plants in flats or pots. Keep soil moist; give plants good air circulation to prevent mildew. Often short lived, even in mild climates. Self-sown seedlings won't resemble parents.

'The Chatelaine', to 3 ft. high, pink-and-white bicolored flowers in early to midsummer; 'The Governor', to 3 ft. high, blue-and-white bicolored flowers in early to midsummer; 'My Castle', to 3 ft. high, deep rosy pink flowers in early to midsummer.

HELP LUPINE SEEDS ALONG

Lupine seeds are hard coated and often slow to sprout. They will germinate faster if you soak them in hot water or scratch or nick the seed coats with a file before planting.

LUZULA

WOODRUSH

Juncaceae

PERENNIALS

⚐ ZONES 31, 32, 34–43

☼ ● PARTIAL TO FULL SHADE

◆ MORE THAN REGULAR WATER

Luzula

These woodland residents, grown primarily for their foliage rather than their flowers, most closely resemble sedges or ornamental grasses. The leaves are grasslike and carried in handsome tufts or clumps; they are evergreen in warmer climates but semievergreen or deciduous in cold-climate regions. The species listed here are deciduous in the North, generally north of Zone 39. Tiny flowers, often brown in color, are produced in spring or summer, and are interesting but not ornamental. Use woodrushes in the shade or woodland garden. They thrive in moist, well-drained soil that is rich in organic matter.

L. nivea. SNOWY WOODRUSH. A 2-ft.-tall perennial native to Europe producing loose, 1½-ft.-wide clumps of linear leaves. Bears airy, 2-in.-long clusters of tiny off-white flowers in summer. Plants spread slowly by rhizomes. 'Snowbird' bears white flowers.

L. sylvatica. GREATER WOODRUSH. Vigorous, 2–2½-ft. species producing dense, 1½-ft.-wide clumps of dark green leaves. Native to Europe and southwestern Asia. Spreads strongly by suckers and makes a good ground cover for shade. Bears clusters of tiny brown flowers from spring to early summer. Tolerates drought as well as sunny sites. 'Marginata' bears dark green leaves edged in creamy white.

LYCHNIS

Caryophyllaceae

PERENNIALS AND ANNUALS

⚐ ZONES VARY BY SPECIES

☼ ◐ FULL SUN OR LIGHT SHADE

◆ ◆ WATER NEEDS VARY BY SPECIES

Lychnis

Hardy, old-fashioned garden flowers, all very tolerant of adverse soils. The different kinds vary in appearance but all offer eye-catching colors in summer. Plants are generally short lived and need to be replaced every few years.

L. arkwrightii. Perennial in Zones 31, 32, 34–41; sometimes grown as an annual. Complex hybrid involving several species. Remove faded flowers for repeat bloom. 'Dwarf Form' is a 10-in. plant with reddish green foliage and scarlet to orange-red flowers in few-flowered clusters. 'Vesuvius' is taller (to 2 ft.), with large orange-red flowers. Rich soil, regular water.

L. chalcedonica. MALTESE CROSS. Perennial. Zones 31, 32, 34–43. Loose, open, growing 2–3 ft. high, with hairy leaves and stems. Scarlet flowers in dense terminal clusters, the petals deeply cut. Plants effective in large borders with white flowers, gray foliage. There is a white variety, 'Alba'. Regular water.

L. coeli-rosa (Silene coeli-rosa, Agrostemma coeli-rosa, Viscaria coeli-rosa). Annual. All zones. Single, saucer-shaped, 1-in. flowers cover foot-tall plants over long summer bloom period. Blue and lavender are most common colors; white and pink are also available, most with contrasting lighter or darker eye spot. Leaves long, narrow, pointed. Good cut flowers. Sow seed in rich soil in early spring (in fall for winter and spring bloom in mild-winter climates). Regular water.

L. coronaria. CROWN-PINK, DUSTY MILLER, MULLEIN PINK, ROSE CAMPION. Perennial in Zones 31, 32, 34; treat as annual elsewhere. Grows 1½–2½ ft. tall, with attractive white, silky foliage and magenta to crimson flowers a little less than an inch across. Effective massed. 'Alba' has white flowers; 'Angel's Blush' bears white blossoms with a deep pink eye. All self-sow freely if fading flowers are not removed. Moderate water.

L. haageana. Perennial in Zones 31, 32, 34–41, but often treated as an annual. Red, orange, salmon, or white flowers in clusters of two or three blossoms throughout summer. Stems clothed in green leaves reach 1½ ft. high. Dies down shortly after bloom. Mulch to protect against extreme heat or cold. Though a hybrid, it comes fairly true from seed. Regular water.

L. viscaria. Perennial. Zones 31, 32, 34–43. Compact, low, evergreen clumps of grasslike leaves to 5 in. long. Pinkish purple, ½-in. flowers on 1½–2-ft. stalks. 'Alba' has white blooms. Foot-high 'Splendens' has magenta blossoms; 'Splendens Flore Pleno' is similar but double flowered. Two deep red bloomers are 8-in. 'Atropurpurea' and 1½-ft. 'Zulu'. 'Alpina' is a 4-in. dwarf with rosy pink blooms. Regular to moderate water.

LYCIUM chinense

MATRIMONY VINE, BOXTHORN

Solanaceae

DECIDUOUS SHRUB

⚐ ZONES 31, 32, 34

☼ FULL SUN

◆ ◆ REGULAR TO MODERATE WATER

Lycium chinense

Arching, often vinelike shrub to 12 ft.; branches sprawl or creep unless supported. Stems are usually thornless. Diamond-shaped bright green leaves to 3 in. long; small purplish blue flowers followed by bright red to orange-red fruit that is eaten by birds. Not especially attractive, but useful for bank cover, where branches will take root. Can thrive in poor soil and in ocean wind. Can be invasive; do not locate near choice garden plants.

L

LYCORIS

SPIDER LILY

Amaryllidaceae

BULBS

⚡ ZONES VARY BY SPECIES

☼ ◑ FULL SUN OR LIGHT SHADE

💧 REGULAR WATER DURING GROWTH AND BLOOM

Lycoris

Narrow, strap-shaped leaves appear in spring; foliage ripens and dies down before bloom starts. Clusters of red, pink, or yellow flowers appear on bare stems to 2 ft. tall in late summer, fall. Flowers are spidery looking, with long stamens and narrow, wavy-edged segments curved backward.

Grow in garden beds (where bulbs will survive winter) or as pot plants. Some kinds are tender, some half hardy. Bulbs available July–August. Set 3–4 in. deep (note exception for *L. squamigera*) in good soil. Don't disturb plantings for several years. When potting, set with tops exposed. Don't use pots that are too large, since plants with crowded roots bloom best.

L. aurea. GOLDEN SPIDER LILY. Zones 31, 32; or indoor/outdoor container plants. Bright yellow, 3-in. flowers.

L. radiata. RED SPIDER LILY. Zones 31, 32. Best known and easiest to grow. Coral red flowers with gold sheen; 1½-ft. stems. 'Alba' has white flowers. Will take light shade. Give winter protection.

L. sprengeri. Zones 31, 32. Similar to *L. squamigera*, but with slightly smaller purplish pink flowers.

L. squamigera (Amaryllis hallii). RESURRECTION LILY, MAGIC LILY, NAKED LADIES. Zones 31, 32, 34, 39. Clusters of fragrant, funnel-shaped, 3-in., pink or rosy lilac flowers on 2-ft. stems. Straplike leaves to 12 in. long. Hardiest species; overwinters in colder regions if bulbs are planted 6 in. deep in protected location, as against a south wall.

LYGODIUM

CLIMBING FERN

Schizaeaceae

PERENNIAL FERNS

⚡ ZONES VARY BY SPECIES

◑ ● PARTIAL TO FULL SHADE

💧 MORE THAN REGULAR WATER

Lygodium

Twining leaf stalks allow these unusual ferns to behave more like vines than their conventional land-bound cousins. The plants grow from short, branching, hairy rhizomes that remain in the soil: The vinelike, aboveground portions of the plants actually are individual fronds that range from 6 to 20 ft. or more in length. The stemlike leaf stalks or midribs of the fronds, called stipes, allow them to climb by twining around supports such as trellises or branches of other plants. Use climbing ferns to add a vertical accent to the shade garden. Provide a trellis or other support. They require moist, well-drained soil that is very rich in organic matter that remains damp from spring to fall; during winter, reduce watering but don't allow the soil to dry out completely.

L. japonicum. JAPANESE CLIMBING FERN. Zones 31, 32. A deciduous fern native to Japan, China, India, and Korea that bears very finely cut fronds and climbs from 6 to 10 ft. in height. Where not hardy, grow in pots which can be moved outdoors in summer and indoors in winter. When grown as a house plant, plants are evergreen and keep on growing all year. Cut back to new sprouts periodically, when the plants appear to lose vigor and look tired.

L. palmatum. HARTFORD FERN. Zones 31, 32, 34–45. A native species found from New England to Florida. Plants climb to 6 ft. and leaves are evergreen in warm climates. This species, native to bogs and swamps, is much more difficult to grow than *L. japonicum;* give it sandy or peaty, acid soil. Ideally, water with rainwater.

LYONIA mariana

STAGGERBUSH

Ericaceae

DECIDUOUS SHRUB

⚡ ZONES 31, 32, 34–41

☼ ◑ SHADE TO PARTIAL SHADE

💧 MORE THAN REGULAR WATER

Lyonia mariana

This attractive shrub grows to 6 ft. tall and features clusters of white or pink flowers ½ in. long that bloom on the leafless shoots of the previous year's growth. Dense, oblong foliage grows to 2½ in. long on abundant branches, making this specimen especially good for massing or as a garden screen. Thrives in moist, acid, boggy soil, especially along the coast.

LYSICHITON

SKUNK CABBAGE

Araceae

PERENNIALS

⚡ ZONES 31, 32, 34–41

☼ ◑ FULL SUN TO PARTIAL SHADE

💧 AMPLE WATER

Lysichiton

With its large, showy, glossy green leaves gathered in basal clusters and its arumlike blooms appearing in spring, this is a dramatic plant for the bog garden or pond's edge. Flowers are small and clustered on erect spadices, surrounded by attractive leaflike spathes. Grow in fertile soil, preferably enriched with organic matter, where roots can penetrate to a depth of at least 4 ft. Often takes a year or two to flower after planting.

L. americanus. YELLOW SKUNK CABBAGE. Appearing in April, the flowers on this West Coast native have yellow spathes and give off an unusual (some would say unpleasant) odor in warm weather or when bruised. Leaves are 3 ft. high.

L. camtschatcensis. WHITE SKUNK CABBAGE. Similar to the American species, but with white spathes and growing to a height of about 2 ft.

LYSIMACHIA

Primulaceae

PERENNIALS

⚡ ZONES VARY BY SPECIES

☼ ◑ FULL SUN OR PARTIAL SHADE

💧 MODERATE WATER

Lysimachia

Most are vigorous perennials capable of spreading by underground roots beyond allotted limits, especially if water supply is plentiful; of those listed, only *L. ephemerum* is well behaved. See that the more aggressive types do not invade choicer plantings. They are useful for naturalizing in woodland edges or barely maintained areas. Except as noted, bloom is in summer.

L. barystachys. Zones 31, 32, 34–41. Grows to 2 ft. tall, with narrow leaves and spikes of white flowers that start out horizontal and gradually turn upright.

L. ciliata. Zones 31, 32, 34–43. Erect plant to 3 ft., with opposite or whorled oval, 5-in. leaves. Small, nodding yellow flowers appear in upper leaf joints. 'Atropurpurea' is similar, but with red leaves. 'Firecracker' has purple, lance-shaped leaves.

L. clethroides. GOOSENECK LOOSESTRIFE. Zones 32, 34–45. Grows to 3 ft. high, with olive green foliage and gracefully curving spikes of white flowers.

L. ephemerum. Zones 32, 34–41. Grows to 3 ft., making a neat clump of leathery gray-green foliage. Long, slender clusters of long-lasting white flowers. Not invasive.

L. nummularia. MONEYWORT, CREEPING JENNY. Zones 31, 32, 34–43. Evergreen creeping plant with long runners (to 2 ft.) that root at joints. Forms pretty light green mat of roundish leaves. Yellow flowers about 1 in. across form singly in leaf joints. Summer blooming. Best use is in corners where it need not be restrained. Will spill from wall, hanging basket. Good ground cover (plant 1–1½ ft. apart) near streams. 'Aurea' has yellow leaves, needs shade.

L. punctata. LOOSESTRIFE. Zones 31, 32, 34–43. To 4 ft. tall. Erect stems have narrow leaves in whorls, with whorled yellow flowers on the top third. 'Alexander', ground cover 1½–2 ft. tall, has green leaves edged creamy white, yellow flowers; best in partial shade.

Lythraceae. The loosestrife family is represented in this book by *Cuphea,* crape myrtle *(Lagerstroemia),* and purple loosestrife *(Lythrum). Lysimachia punctata,* whose common name is loosestrife, is in the primrose family.

LYTHRUM virgatum

PURPLE LOOSESTRIFE

Lythraceae

PERENNIAL

⚊ ZONES 31, 32, 34–43

☼ FULL SUN

💧 REGULAR WATER; TOO MUCH MOISTURE ENCOURAGES INVASIVENESS

Lythrum virgatum

Showy plant for pond margins or moist areas but highly invasive and not recommended for planting. Included here because some nurseries still sell it. The 2-ft.-wide clumps put up 2½–5 ft.-high stems. Narrow leaves clothe lower portion of stems; the upper 8–18 in. are densely set with ¾-in. magenta flowers in late summer and fall.

L. virgatum has a bad reputation with lovers of native plants, since seedlings spring up so freely that native vegetation is crowded out. It has invaded wetlands in many areas, including parts of the Northeast. Hybrids (often sold as varieties of *L. salicaria,* a similar plant), including 'Roseum Superbum', 'Morden's Pink', 'Morden's Gleam', 'Pink Spires', and 'Rosy Spires', are said to be sterile, but they may interbreed and become a nuisance. In some regions, it is illegal to plant purple loosestrife and its variants—and doing so is unwise, even if not outlawed, wherever plants have ample moisture throughout the year.

MAACKIA

Fabaceae (Leguminosae)

DECIDUOUS TREE

⚊ ZONES VARY BY SPECIES

☼ FULL SUN

💧 REGULAR TO LITTLE WATER

Maackia

Related to locust *(Robinia)* and yellow wood *(Cladrastis lutea),* maackias are medium-size trees with a slow to moderate growth rate. Leaves are divided featherwise into many leaflets. Small, sweet pea-shaped summer flowers are creamy or yellowish white, crowded into upright, spikelike clusters to 4–6 in. long. These are followed by flat, 2–3-in.-long seedpods. Plants are not fussy about soil and have no significant pest or disease problems.

M. amurensis. AMUR MAACKIA. Zones 32, 34–43. Grows to a possible 60 ft., but may be only half that tall in gardens. Broad, rounded head; dark green foliage. Bark on trunk is an attractive bronze color, peels in curling flakes.

M. chinensis. CHINESE MAACKIA. Zones 32, 34–43. Smaller (to 20–30 ft.) and shrubbier than *M. amurensis,* with leaves divided into more and smaller leaflets. Foliage is silvery grayish green upon unfolding, then matures to dark green.

MACLEAYA (Bocconia)

PLUME POPPY

Papaveraceae

PERENNIALS

⚊ ZONES VARY BY SPECIES

☼ ☽ SUN OR LIGHT SHADE

💧 REGULAR WATER

Macleaya

These tall perennials are sometimes still listed as Bocconia, a name properly belonging to their shrubby tropical relatives. The two species described below resemble each other. Both have creeping rhizomes; tall, erect stems; large, deeply lobed leaves like those of edible fig tree; and small flowers in large, branching clusters. These plants look tropical, and their value lies in size and structure rather than flower color. Can be invasive if not controlled; plant among shrubs rather than amid delicate perennials.

M. cordata. Zones 32, 34–43. To 7–8 ft. tall, with 3-ft.-wide clumps of grayish green, 10-in. leaves and clouds of tiny white to beige flowers. Considered somewhat less invasive than *M. microcarpa.*

M. kewensis. Zones 31, 32, 34–43. Gray-green leaves and creamy flowers from early to late summer. 'Flamingo' has pinkish flowers.

M. microcarpa. Zones 31, 32, 34–43. Similar to *M. cordata,* but with pinkish beige flowers. Flowers of the cultivar 'Coral Plume' are more decidedly pink.

MACLURA pomifera

OSAGE ORANGE

Moraceae

DECIDUOUS TREE

⚊ ZONES 31, 32, 34–41

☼ FULL SUN

💧 💧 REGULAR TO LITTLE WATER

Maclura pomifera

Native Arkansas to Oklahoma and Texas. Fast growth to 60 ft. tall (though often less), with spreading, open habit. Young branches are thornier than mature ones. Wood is orange in color and very hard. Medium green leaves to 5 in. long. If there's a male plant present, female plants may bear inedible, 4-in. fruits (so-called hedge-apples) that somewhat resemble bumpy, yellow-green oranges. Withstands heat, cold, wind, poor soil, moderate alkalinity, wet or dry conditions. Easily propagated by seed, stem cuttings, root cuttings; easily transplanted. Named varieties exist; 'Wichita' is nearly thornless. Useful as big, tough, rough-looking hedge or background. Prune to any size from 6 ft. up. Pruned high, becomes a shade tree.

MADAGASCAR PERIWINKLE. See CATHARANTHUS roseus

MAGNOLIA

Magnoliaceae

DECIDUOUS OR EVERGREEN TREES AND SHRUBS

⚡ ZONES VARY BY SPECIES

☼ ◑ FULL SUN OR PARTIAL SHADE

🔴 REGULAR WATER

▶ SEE CHART NEXT PAGE

Magnolia soulangiana

Magnificent flowering plants with remarkable variety in color, leaf shape, and plant form. Magnolias are discussed here by general appearance; the chart on the following pages lists them alphabetically. New varieties and hybrids appear every year, but distribution is spotty in local nurseries. Mail-order specialists can supply many more kinds.

EVERGREEN MAGNOLIAS

To gardeners in mild-winter climates, the word "magnolia" usually means *M. grandiflora*, the classic southern magnolia with glossy leaves and huge, fragrant white flowers. Few trees can touch it for year-round beauty. And as cold-hardy selections have been developed in recent years, cultivation of this magnolia is spreading northward. North of Zone 32, site hardy selections carefully, as they all can suffer winter sunburn. Sweet bay *(M. virginiana)*, a hardier tree of smaller proportions, is semievergreen in the Northeast, and *M. v. australis* is completely evergreen at least as far north as Philadelphia. The two species are parents of the evergreen hybrids *M.* 'Freeman' and *M.* 'Maryland', which are similar to southern magnolia but slightly more cold tolerant.

DECIDUOUS MAGNOLIAS WITH SAUCER FLOWERS

This group includes the saucer magnolia *(M. soulangiana)* and its many varieties, often erroneously called tulip trees due to the shape and bright colors of their flowers. Also included here are the yulan magnolia *(M. denudata)* and lily magnolia *(M. liliiflora)*. All are hardy to cold, thriving in various climates—but all do poorly in hot, dry, windy areas, and early flowers of all forms are subject to frost damage. Related to these, but more tender to cold (and heat), are the big, spectacular Oriental magnolias from western China and the Himalayas—including *M. sprengeri* 'Diva'. Their early flowers are also subject to frost and storm damage.

DECIDUOUS MAGNOLIAS WITH STAR FLOWERS

This garden group includes *M. kobus, M. stellata* and its varieties (the star magnolias), and *M. salicifolia*. All are cold-hardy, slow-growing, early-blooming plants with wide climatic adaptability.

OTHER MAGNOLIAS

Less widely planted is a group of magnolias that bloom as leaves appear or after they unfurl; these are generally considered foliage plants or shade trees. Among them are *M. acuminata,* a big shade tree with inconspicuous flowers; *M. hypoleuca,* a big tree with large leaves and large but not noticeable flowers; and *M. fraseri* and *M. macrophylla,* medium-size trees with huge leaves and flowers.

MAGNOLIA CULTURE

For any magnolia, pick planting site carefully. Virtually all magnolias are hard to move once established, and many grow quite large. The best soil for magnolias is fairly rich, well drained, and neutral to slightly acid; if necessary, add generous amounts of organic matter when planting. Although you can grow most magnolias in somewhat alkaline soil, the plants may develop chlorosis.

Magnolias never look their best when crowded, and they may be severely damaged by digging around their roots. Larger deciduous magnolias are at their best standing alone against a background that will display their flowers and, in winter, their strongly patterned, usually gray limbs and big,

fuzzy flower buds. Small deciduous magnolias show up well in large flower or shrub borders and make choice ornaments in Oriental gardens. All magnolias are excellent lawn trees.

Balled-and-burlapped plants are available in late winter and early spring; container plants are sold any time. Do not set plants lower than their original soil level. Stake single-trunked or very heavy plants to prevent them from being rocked by wind, which will tear the thick, fleshy, sensitive roots. To avoid damaging the roots, set stakes in planting hole before placing tree. If you plant your magnolia in a lawn, try to provide a good-size area free of grass around the trunk. At least in the early years, keep a cooling mulch over the root area. Prevent soil compaction around root zone by keeping foot traffic to a minimum. Prune only when absolutely necessary; the best time is right after flowering, and the best technique is to remove the entire twig or limb right to the base. Magnolias seldom have serious pest or disease problems.

Magnolia grandiflora

Magnoliaceae. The magnolia family contains evergreen and deciduous trees and shrubs with large, showy flowers, usually with a large number of petals, sepals, and stamens. Tulip tree *(Liriodendron tulipifera)* and magnolia are examples.

MAGNOLIA ORDER OF BLOOM

Magnolias bloom in the following order, beginning in March or April in the Northeast: *M. denudata, M. salicifolia, M. stellata, M. kobus, M. loebneri, M. soulangiana, M. fraseri, M. acuminata, M. cordata, M. liliiflora, M. virginiana, M. sieboldii, M. wilsonii,* and finally, *M. macrophylla.*

MAHOBERBERIS

Berberidaceae

EVERGREEN OR SEMIEVERGREEN SHRUBS

⚡ ZONES 31, 32, 34–41

☼ ◑ FULL SUN TO PARTIAL SHADE

🔴 REGULAR WATER

Mahoberberis

Members of this hybrid genus are shrubs created by crossing barberries *(Berberis* spp.) with mahonias *(Mahonia* spp.). Plants bear somewhat leathery, dark green leaves that may be evergreen to semievergreen. The leaves remain on the plants in mild winters, but most leaves fall if temperatures dip below about −6°F/−21°C. These plants bear little, if any, flowers or fruit. Use them in shrub borders or other similar plantings. Prune out old, weak branches in late winter.

M. aquicandidula. Bears glossy, somewhat spiny, leathery, dark green leaves on stiff, open, 3–6-ft. plants. Foliage turns red to red purple in winter. *M. aquicandidula* is a cross between *Mahonia aquifolium* and *Berberis candidula.*

M. aquisargentii. A vigorous, 6-ft.-tall shrub with glossy leaves that turn bronze red to red purple in winter. Leaves on a single plant may be simple or compound and featherlike. A cross between *M. aquifolium* and *B. sargentiana.*

M. neubertii. A 4–6-ft.-shrub with a leggy habit and dull, semievergreen leaves. The result of a cross between *M. aquifolium* and *B. vulgaris.*

M

MAGNOLIA

VARIETY	ZONES	TYPE	HEIGHT	SPREAD	AGE AT BLOOM	FLOWERS	USES, CHARACTERISTICS, COMMENTS
Magnolia acuminata CUCUMBER TREE	31, 32, 34–43	Deciduous	60–80 ft.	25 ft.	12 yrs.	Small, greenish yellow, appear after leaves. Late spring, summer. Handsome reddish seed capsules, red seeds	Shade or lawn tree. Dense shade from glossy 5–9-in. leaves. Hardy to cold; dislikes hot, dry winds
M. a. cordata (*M. cordata*) YELLOW CUCUMBER TREE, YELLOW MAGNOLIA	31, 32, 34–41	Deciduous	To 35 ft.	To 35 ft.	12 yrs.	Larger (to 4 in.), chartreuse yellow outside, pure yellow within; appear as leaves start to expand. Mild lemon scent	Slow-growing lawn or border tree for large properties. Lower, shrubbier than *M. acuminata*. 'Miss Honeybee', with pale yellow flowers, is a good selection
M. 'Athene' (**Jury hybrid**)	31, 32, 34, 39 (possibly colder)	Deciduous	30 ft.	20 ft.	5–6 yrs.	Enormous, 10 in. wide. Pink, white inside	Bred to resemble the very tender *M. campbellii*. Hardy, but still experimental in the East. Opening flowers may be killed by late frosts.
M. 'Atlas' (**Jury hybrid**)	31, 32, 34, 39 (possibly colder)	Deciduous	30 ft.	20 ft.	5–6 yrs.	Incredible foot-wide blossoms held upright on branch. Soft pink	Bred to resemble the very tender *M. campbellii*. Hardy, but still experimental in the East. Blooms may avoid late frosts, but protect enormous flowers from wind.
M. biondii CHINESE WILLOW-LEAF MAGNOLIA	31, 32, 34–41	Deciduous	40 ft.	25 ft.	9–10 yrs.	White, tinted pink at base, 4 in. wide. Lightly fragrant with lemon scent.	Newly introduced from China and still rare. Blossoms very early and may be hit by late spring frosts.
M. brooklynensis 'Eva Maria'	31, 32, 34–41	Deciduous	Over 40 ft.	30 ft.	19 yrs.	Tulip shaped, about 4 in. wide, rose purple with shades of yellow-green in the petals	Cross between *M. acuminata* and *M. liliiflora*. Long blooming from about mid-May to mid-June
M. denudata (*M. conspicua*, *M. heptapeta*) YULAN MAGNOLIA	31, 32, 34–41	Deciduous	To 35 ft.	To 30 ft.	6–7 yrs.	White, fragrant, sometimes tinged purple at base. Held erect; somewhat tulip shaped, 3–4 in. long, spreading to 6–7 in. Early; often a few in summer	Tends toward irregular form—no handicap in informal garden or at woodland edge. Place it where it can be shown off against dark background or sky. Leaves 4–7 in. long. Cut flowers striking in arrangements.
M. 'Elizabeth'	31, 32, 34–41	Deciduous	To 40 ft.	To 20 ft.	2–6 yrs. from grafts	Fragrant medium yellow flowers, 6–7 in. wide. Color is lighter in milder-winter regions	A hybrid between *M. acuminata cordata* and *M. denudata*. Grow as single-trunk specimen or multitrunk shrub-tree
M. fraseri (*M. auriculata*)	31, 32, 34–41	Deciduous	To 50 ft.	20–30 ft.	10–12 yrs.	Creamy to yellowish white, 8–10 in. wide. Bloom late spring, when leaves are full grown. Rose red, 5-in. seed capsules showy in summer	Single lawn tree or woodland tree. Leaves 16–18 in. long, parchmentlike, in whorls at ends of branches. Effect is that of parasols. Handsome dark brown fall color
M. grandiflora SOUTHERN MAGNOLIA, BULL BAY	31, 32	Evergreen	To 80 ft.	To 40 ft.	15 yrs., sometimes much less. 2–3 years from grafts or cuttings	Pure white, aging buff; large (8–10 in. across), powerfully fragrant. Carried throughout summer, fall	Street or lawn tree, big container plant, wall or espalier plant. Unpredictable in form and age of bloom. Grafted plants more predictable but need pruning to become single-trunked tree. Can grow as multitrunked tree. Glossy, leathery leaves, 4–8 in. long. Messy fruit

M

MAGNOLIA

VARIETY	ZONES	TYPE	HEIGHT	SPREAD	AGE AT BLOOM	FLOWERS	USES, CHARACTERISTICS, COMMENTS
M. g. 'Edith Bogue'	31, 32, 34, 35, 37	Evergreen	To 35 ft.	To 20 ft.	2–3 yrs. from grafts	As in *M. grandiflora.* Young plants slower to come into heavy bloom than some other varieties	Shapely, vigorous tree, one of hardiest selections of *M. grandiflora.* Has withstood -24°F/-31°C. The one to try in coldest regions. Keep it out of strong winds
M. hypoleuca (*M. obovata*)	31, 32, 34–41	Deciduous	To 50 ft.	To 25 ft.	15 yrs.	To 8 in. across, creamy, fragrant. Appear in summer after leaves expand	Only for big lawn or garden. Coarse texture
M. kobus KOBUS MAGNOLIA	32, 34–41	Deciduous	To 30 ft.	To 20 ft.	15 yrs.	White, to 4 in. across; early	Cold-hardy, sturdy tree for planting single in lawn or in informal shrub and tree groupings. 'Wada's Memory' (*M. kewensis* 'Wada's Memory') blooms young, grows faster, has bigger flowers, coppery red new growth. *M. k. borealis* is much larger (to 75 ft.), with larger (6-in.) leaves
M. k. stellata (see *M. stellata*)							
M. Kosar-De Vos Hybrids (the 'Little Girl' series)	32, 34–43	Deciduous	To 12 ft.	To 15 ft.	4–5 yrs.	Flower color ranges from deep to pale purple (sometimes pink or white inside), depending on variety. Bloom in spring before leafout; sporadic rebloom in summer	Hybrids between *M. liliiflora* 'Nigra' and *M. stellata* 'Rosea'; bred to bloom later than *M. stellata* to avoid frost damage. Erect, shrubby growers bearing girls' names: 'Ann', 'Betty', 'Jane', 'Judy', 'Pinkie', 'Randy', 'Ricki', 'Susan'. Use in shrub border or singly in lawn
M. liliiflora (*M. quinquepeta*) LILY MAGNOLIA	31, 32, 34–41	Deciduous	To 12 ft.	To 15 ft.	4–5 yrs.	White inside, purplish outside; about 4 in. across. Selections sold as 'Gricilis', 'Nigra', and 'O'Neill' are dark purple red outside, pink inside. Blooms over long spring, summer season	Good for shrub border; strong vertical effect in big flower border. Spreads slowly by suckering. Leaves 4–6 in. long. 'Royal Crown', hybrid with *M. veitchii*, has pink, candle-shaped buds that open to 10-in. flowers. Good cut flower if buds taken before fully open.
M. loebneri	31, 32, 34–41	Deciduous	Slow to 12–15 ft.; can reach 50 ft.	12–15 ft.	3 yrs.	Narrow, strap-shaped petals like those of *M. stellata*, but fewer, larger. Blossoms of some selections are fragrant. Early	Hybrids between *M. kobus* and *M. stellata.* 'Ballerina' is white with faint pink blush; 'Leonard Messel' has pink flowers, deeper in bud; 'Merrill' ('Dr. Merrill') is a free-flowering white, hardy in Zone 43. Taller 'Spring Snow' has pure white flowers. Use in lawn or shrub border, at woodland edge
M. macrophylla BIGLEAF MAGNOLIA	31, 32, 34–45	Deciduous	Slow to 50 ft.	To 30 ft.	12–15 yrs.	White, fragrant, to 1 ft. across, appearing in late spring and early summer, after leaves are out	Show-off tree with leaves 1–2½ ft. long, 9–12 in. wide. Needs to stand alone. Needs some shade in warm climates
(**M. obovata x. M. virginiana**)	31, 32, 34 39	Semi-evergreen	30 ft.	15 ft.	8 yrs.	Creamy white, 6 in. wide, cup shaped, deliciously fragrant	Vigorous growth. Large leaves like *M. obovata* but dark green and glossy above like *M. virginiana*

M

MAGNOLIA

VARIETY	ZONES	TYPE	HEIGHT	SPREAD	AGE AT BLOOM	FLOWERS	USES, CHARACTERISTICS, COMMENTS
M. salicifolia ANISE MAGNOLIA	32, 34–41	Decid-uous	Slow to 18–30 ft.	To 12 ft.	2–10 yrs.	White, narrow petaled, to 4 in. across. Early	Usually upright with slender branches, graceful appearance. In front of trees, use as shrub border. Leaves (3–5 in. long) bronze red in fall. 'Kochanakee' and 'W. B. Clarke' are large flowered; bloom young and heavily. 'Miss Jack' has narrow, anise-scented leaves, blooms heavily
M. sieboldii (sometimes sold as *M. parviflora*) OYAMA MAGNOLIA	31, 32, 34, 39	Decid-uous	6–15 ft.	6–15 ft.	5 yrs.	White, cup shaped, centered with crimson stamens; fragrant. Begin blooming in late spring, extend over long period	Good for small gardens. Buds like white Japanese lanterns. Nice planted upslope or at top of wall so people can look into flowers. Leaves 3–6 in. long. Best in partial shade
M. soulangiana SAUCER MAGNOLIA (often erro-neously called TULIP TREE)	31, 32, 34–41	Decid-uous	To 25 ft.	To 25 ft. or more	3–5 yrs.	White to pink or purplish red, variable in size and form, blooming before leaves expand. Gener-ally about 6 in. across. Late winter into spring	Lawn ornament, anchor plant in big corner plantings. Hybrid of *M. denudata* and *M. liliiflora*. Seedlings highly variable; shop for named vari-eties. Foliage good green, rather coarse; leaves 4–6 in. (or more) long
M. s. 'Alba' ('Amabilis', 'Alba Superba')	31, 32, 34–41	Decid-uous	To 30 ft.	To 25 ft. or more	3–5 yrs.	Large, suffused pur-ple, opening nearly pure white. Early	Same uses as for *M. soulangiana*. Rather more upright in growth than most
M. s. 'Alexandrina'	31, 32, 34–41	Decid-uous	To 25 ft.	To 25 ft. or more	3–5 yrs.	Large. Color highly vari-able, from almost pure white to dark purple. Midseason	Same uses as for *M. soulangiana*. Large, rather heavy foliage. Variable habit, flower color; choose trees in bloom to get color you want. Delayed
M. s. 'Brozzonii'	31, 32, 34–41	Decid-uous	To 25 ft.	To 25 ft. or more	3–5 yrs.	Large (to 8 in. across). White, very slightly flushed purplish rose at base. Early	One of handsomest whites. Large, vigorous plant
M. s. 'Burgundy'	31, 32, 34–41	Decid-uous	To 25 ft.	To 25 ft. or more	3–5 yrs.	Large, well rounded; deep purple halfway up to petal tips, then light-ening to pink. Early	Earlier bloom than most makes it more susceptible to frost damage in cold areas
M. s. 'Coates'	31, 32, 34–41	Decid-uous	To 25 ft.	To 25 ft. or more	3–5 yrs.	Large, attractive; resemble those of *M. liliiflora* hybrid 'Royal Crown'. Midseason	Large, shrubby. Quick grower
M. s. 'Lennei' (*M. lennei*)	31, 32, 34–41	Decid-uous	To 25 ft.	To 25 ft. or more	3–5 yrs.	Very large, globe shaped, deep purple outside, white inside. Late	Spreading, vigorous plant with large leaves. Late bloom helps it escape frosts in cold areas

M

MAGNOLIA

VARIETY	ZONES	TYPE	HEIGHT	SPREAD	AGE AT BLOOM	FLOWERS	USES, CHARACTERISTICS, COMMENTS
M. s. 'Lennei Alba' (*M. lennei 'Alba'*)	31, 32, 34–41	Decid-uous	To 25 ft.	To 25 ft. or more	3–5 yrs.	Like those of *M. s.* 'Lennei', but white in color, slightly smaller, earlier (midseason)	Spreading, vigorous plant
M. s. 'Pink Superbia'	31, 32, 34–41	Decid-uous	To 25 ft.	To 25 ft. or more	3–5 yrs.	Large, deep pink, white inside. Early	Best where late frosts are not a prob-lem. Much like *M. s.* 'Alba' except for flower color
M. s. 'Rustica Rubra'	31, 32, 34–41	Decid-uous	To 25 ft.	To 25 ft. or more	3–5 yrs.	Large, cup shaped, deep reddish purple. Somewhat past mid-season. Big (6-in.) seed-pods of dark rose	Tall, vigorous grower for large areas. More treelike than many varieties
M. s. 'San Jose'	31, 32, 34–41	Decid-uous	To 25 ft.	To 25 ft. or more	3–5 yrs.	Large, white flushed pink. Blooms very early	Exceptionally early bloom puts it at risk for frost damage in cold areas
M. Spectrum	31, 32, 34–41	Decid-uous	25 ft.	15 ft.	10 yrs.	Deep reddish purple. Larger but similar to those of M. 'Galaxy'.	Sister seedling of M. 'Galaxy' with a somewhat wider growth habit, not quite as cold hardy, but does better in warm climates.
M. sprengeri 'Diva'	31, 32	Decid-uous	To 40 ft.	To 30 ft.	7 yrs. from grafts	To 8 in. wide, rose pink outside, white suffused pink with deeper lines inside. Scented. Early to midseason.	One of brightest colors; erect, spectac-ular flowers. Buds more frost resistant than those of *M. sargentiana robusta*. Hybrids between this and *M. liliiflora* are 'Galaxy' (large purple flowers open late in spring) and 'Spectrum' (larger but fewer flowers). Both are small trees
M. stellata STAR MAGNOLIA	31, 32, 34–41	Decid-uous	To 10 ft.	To 20 ft.	3 yrs.	Very early, white, about 3 in. wide, with 19–21 narrow, strap-shaped petals. Profuse bloom in late winter, early spring. Some varieties are fragrant	Slow growing, shrubby; fine for bor-ders, entryway gardens, edge of woods. Quite hardy, but flowers often nipped by frost in colder part of range. Fine texture in twig and leaf. Fair yellow-and-brown fall color
M. s. 'Centennial'	31, 32, 34–41	Decid-uous	To 10 ft.	To 20 ft.	3 yrs.	White, faintly marked pink, 5 in. across	Same uses as for *M. stellata*. Like an improved M. s. 'Waterlily'
M. s. 'Dawn'	31, 32, 34–41	Decid-uous	To 10 ft.	To 20 ft.	3 yrs.	To 40–50 pink petals	Same uses as for *M. stellata*
M. s. 'Rosea' PINK STAR MAGNOLIA	31, 32, 34–41	Decid-uous	To 10 ft.	To 20 ft.	3 yrs.	Pink buds; flowers flushed pink, fading to white. Very early	Same uses as for species. Various plants sold under this name. In cold regions, plant these early-flowering sorts in a northern exposure to delay bloom as long as possible, lessen frost damage
M. s. 'Royal Star'	31, 32, 34–41	Decid-uous	To 10 ft.	To 20 ft.	3 yrs.	White flowers with 25–30 petals. Fragrant. Blooms 2 weeks later than *M. stellata*	Same uses as for *M. stellata*. Faster growing

M

MAGNOLIA

VARIETY	ZONES	TYPE	HEIGHT	SPREAD	AGE AT BLOOM	FLOWERS	USES, CHARACTERISTICS, COMMENTS
M. s. 'Rubra'	31, 32, 34–41	Deciduous	To 10 ft.	To 20 ft.	3 yrs.	Rosy pink	More treelike in form than other *M. stellata* varieties
M. s. 'Waterlily'	31, 32, 34–41	Deciduous	To 10 ft.	To 20 ft.	3 yrs.	White. Larger flowers than *M. stellata*; broader, more numerous petals. Fragrant	Faster growing than most star magnolias. Leaves modest in size (2–4 in. long); finer foliage texture than other magnolias
M. veitchii VEITCH MAGNOLIA	31, 32, 34, 39	Deciduous	30–40 ft.	To 30 ft.	4–5 yrs.	Rose red at base, shading to white at tips, to 10 in. across. 'Rubra' has smaller, purple-red flowers. Early, before leaves emerge	Spectacular tree. Hybrid between *M. campbellii* and *M. denudata*. Fast growing and vigorous. Needs plenty of room and wind protection; branches are brittle. Blooms frequently frosted.
M. virginiana (*M. glauca*) SWEET BAY	31, 32, 34, 35, 37	Deciduous to evergreen	10–20 ft.	To 20 ft.	8–10 yrs.	Nearly globular, 2–3 in. wide, creamy white, fragrant. June–Sept.	Prefers moist, acid soil. Grows in swamps in eastern U.S. Deciduous shrub in colder areas; big semievergreen to evergreen tree in colder climates. Leaves grayish green, nearly white beneath, 2–5 in. long.
M. virginiana australis	31, 32, 34, 39	Evergreen	60 ft.	20–30 ft.	5–6 yrs.	Cream colored with a lemon fragrance. Cup shaped	Differs from *M. virginiana* in strong treelike habit, evergreen leaves, and later (3 weeks) commencement of flowering
M. virginiana australis 'Henry Hicks'	31, 32, 34 41	Evergreen to zone 41	60 ft.	20–30 ft.	5–6 yrs.	Cream colored with a lemon fragrance. Cup shaped	Differs from *M. virginiana* in strong treelike habit and pyramidal form, evergreen leaves, later bloom period, and hardier than var. australis.
M. wilsonii WILSON MAGNOLIA	32, 34, 35, 37	Deciduous	To 25 ft.	To 25 ft.	10 yrs.	White, with red stamens, pendulous, 3–4 in. across, fragrant. Late spring	Blooms at 4 ft. and tends to remain shrubby. Plant high on bank where people can look up at flowers. Best in light shade. Rich purplish brown twigs; narrow, tapered leaves, 3–6 in. long, with silvery undersides. Effect similar to that of *M. sieboldii*

M

MAHONIA

Berberidaceae

EVERGREEN SHRUBS

⬗ ZONES VARY BY SPECIES

☼ ◐ ● EXPOSURE NEEDS VARY BY SPECIES

🌢 ● WATER NEEDS VARY BY SPECIES

Mahonia

Related to *Berberis* and described under that name by some botanists. Easy to grow; good looking all year. Leaves divided into leaflets, usually with spiny-toothed edges. Bright yellow flowers in dense, rounded to spikelike clusters, followed by blue-black (sometimes red), berrylike fruit. Generally disease resistant, though in some regions foliage may be disfigured by small looper caterpillars. All species attract birds. The foliage of some species turns bronze or purple in winter.

M. aquifolium. OREGON GRAPE. Zones 31, 32, 34–41. Native British Columbia to northern California. Erect growth to 6 ft. tall or taller; spreads by underground stems. Leaves 4–10 in. long, with five to nine very spiny-toothed, oval, 1–2½-in. leaflets that are glossy green in some forms, dull green in others. Young growth ruddy or bronzy; scattered mature red leaves. Purplish or bronzy leaves in winter, especially in cold-winter areas or where plants are grown in full sun. Spring flowers in 2–3-in. clusters along stems; edible blue-black fruit with gray bloom (makes good jelly).

'Compacta' averages about 2 ft. tall and spreads freely to make broad colonies. New leaves glossy, light to coppery green; mature leaves matte medium green. 'Orange Flame', 5 ft. tall, has bronzy orange new growth and glossy green mature leaves that turn wine red in winter.

Oregon grape can take any exposure, though it does best with some wind protection in cold-winter areas. Plant in masses as foundation planting, in woodland, in tubs, as low screen or garden barrier. Control height and form by pruning; if any woody stems jut out too far, cut them down to ground (new growth fills in quickly). Needs little water.

M. bealei. LEATHERLEAF MAHONIA. Zones 31, 32, 34, 39. To 10–12 ft., with strong pattern of vertical stems, horizontal foliage. Leaves are over 1 ft. long, divided into 7–15 broad, thick, leathery leaflets up to 5 in. long; leaflets grayish or bluish green above, olive green below, with spiny-toothed edges. Very fragrant flowers in erect, 3–6-in.-long, spikelike clusters at branch ends in earliest spring. Powdery blue berries. Truly distinguished plant against stone, brick, wood, glass. Takes sun in cool-summer areas; best in part shade elsewhere. Plant in rich soil with ample organic material. Regular water.

M. nervosa. LONGLEAF MAHONIA. Zones 31, 32, 34, 39. Native British Columbia to northern California. Low shrub to 2 ft. tall (rarely to 6 ft. high). Spreads by underground stems to make good ground cover. Clustered at stem tips are 10–18-in.-long leaves with 7–21 glossy green, bristle-toothed, 1–3½-in.-long leaflets. Creates the impression of a stiff, leathery fern. Spring flowers in upright, 3–6-in.-long clusters. Blue berries. Best in shade; will take sun in cooler areas, becoming very compact. Use as woodland ground cover, facing for taller mahonias, low barrier planting. Moderate water.

M. repens. CREEPING MAHONIA. Zones 31, 32, 34–41. Native British Columbia to northern California, eastward to Rocky Mountains. Creeps by underground stems. To 3 ft. tall, with spreading habit. Dull bluish green leaves have three to seven spiny-toothed leaflets, turn bronzy in winter. Deep yellow spring flowers followed by blue berries in short clusters. Good ground cover in sun, partial shade. Needs little water.

MAIANTHEMUM
canadense

CANADIAN MAYFLOWER,
WILD LILY-OF-THE-VALLEY

Liliaceae

PERENNIAL

⚡ ZONES 32, 34–43

◐ ● PARTIAL SHADE TO FULL SHADE

Maianthemum canadense

Refined leaves and dainty white flowers that bloom in May make Canadian mayflower worth growing. This woodland wildflower has a 2-in.-long cluster of tiny fragrant blossoms topping a flowering stem and smooth leaves rounded at the base and pointed on top. Light red berries appear after the blooms. An effective shade-loving ground cover, mayflower stands 4–8 in. tall with an indefinite spread and is native to mature oak forests in eastern North America. It can form thick carpets in acid, humus-rich, leafy, moist, well-drained soil. Mayflower makes a wonderful addition to wildflower, woodland, and shrub gardens. It looks charming under blueberries, azaleas, and rhododendrons. Mulch lightly with leaves in fall or compost in spring, if desired. Propagate by dividing roots in early spring or fall or by sowing seed in spring or fall.

MAIDEN GRASS. See MISCANTHUS sinensis 'Gracillimus'

MAIDENHAIR FERN. See ADIANTUM

MAIDENHAIR TREE. See GINKGO biloba

MAIDEN PINK. See DIANTHUS deltoides

MAJORANA hortensis. See ORIGANUM majorana

MALABAR SPINACH. See BASELLA alba

FOR INFORMATION ON YOUR CLIMATE ZONE

PLEASE SEE PAGES 30–46

MALCOLMIA maritima

VIRGINIAN STOCK

Brassicaceae (Cruciferae)

ANNUAL

⚡ ALL ZONES

☼ FULL SUN

● REGULAR WATER

Malcolmia maritima

Grows to 8–15 in., single stemmed or branching from base, covered with nearly scentless, four-petaled flowers from spring to fall. Colors include white, yellow, pinks, lilacs, and magenta. Leaves are oblong. Sow in place at any time except in hot or very cold weather. Like sweet alyssum (*Lobularia maritima*), this plant blooms only 6 weeks after seeds are sown. Give it moderately rich soil. Good bulb cover.

MALE FERN. See DRYOPTERIS

MALOPE trifida

ANNUAL MALLOW

Malvaceae

ANNUAL

⚡ ALL ZONES

☼ FULL SUN

● REGULAR WATER

Malope trifida

This bushy shrub will grow to 3 ft. and features showy bowl-shaped and papery flowers 3 in. in diameter in white, pink, or purple. Toothed and rounded leaves are 3 in. across. 'Vulcan' has magenta pink blooms. Include in a mixed border where they will self-sow and provide plenty of blooms for cutting. Perfect in sandy coastal gardens, but only in cooler conditions away from excessive heat.

MALLOW. See MALVA

MALTESE CROSS. See LYCHNIS chalcedonica

MALUS

CRABAPPLE

Rosaceae

DECIDUOUS TREES, ONLY RARELY SHRUBS

⚡ ZONES 31, 32, 34–43

☼ FULL SUN

● ● REGULAR TO MODERATE WATER

▶ SEE CHART NEXT PAGE

Malus floribunda

Valued for brief bloom of handsome white, pink, or red flowers and for fruit that is edible, showy, or both; for crabapples used chiefly in cooking, see Crabapple. Over 600 kinds are cultivated, and new varieties appear every year; the selections listed here represent a far wider choice than any one nursery is likely to offer. Most types grow about 25 ft. high, although some are as low as 6 ft. or as tall as 40 ft. Leaves are pointed ovals, often fuzzy, from deep green to nearly purple; fall color is rarely noteworthy. Masses of single, semidouble, or double flowers with a musky sweet scent appear in spring, usually before the foliage unfurls. Tiny red, orange, or yellow apples ripen from midsummer into autumn; in some varieties, the fruit hangs on until late in the season, after

MALUS

NAME	SIZE, HABIT	FLOWERS	FRUIT	COMMENTS
'Adams'	Dense, round headed, to 20 ft.	Red buds open to single pink flowers	Red, over ½ in. wide, long lasting	Orange fall foliage. Good disease resistance
'Adirondack'	Columnar, to 10 ft. tall and 6 ft. wide	Red buds open to large waxy white flowers with red tinge	Red to orange red	Formal in appearance. High disease resistance
'Almey'	Upright, spreading, to 20 ft. (possibly taller)	Single scarlet flowers, white at base	Maroon, hangs on well	Purplish green foliage. Old-fashioned variety, very prone to disease except in areas of very low humidity. Newer, more resistant crabapples a better choice
'Ames White'	Dense, upright, to 20 ft.	Pink buds open to single white flowers	Yellow	High disease resistance
M. arnoldiana ARNOLD CRABAPPLE	Broad, to 20 ft. by 30 ft.	Red buds open to single pink flowers that fade to white; fragrant	Yellow and red	Susceptible to scab and fireblight
M. atrosanguinea CARMINE CRABAPPLE	Erect, dense, irregular, to 18 ft.	Single deep pink to red flowers; fragrant	Red turning brown; hangs on all winter	Summer foliage has purplish sheen. Moderate susceptibility to disease
'Brandywine'	Vigorous, shapely, to 15–20 ft. tall and wide	Double rose pink, fragrant	Yellowish green	Leaves have reddish cast. Moderate susceptibility to disease
'Callaway'	Attractive, round headed, to 25 ft.	Pink buds open to single white flowers	Deep red, large, long lasting	Low chilling requirement for bloom. High disease resistance
'Centurion'	Oval crowned to 25 ft. tall and 15–20 ft. wide	Red buds open to single red flowers	Shiny deep red, long lasting	Blooms young. High disease resistance
'Coralburst'	Small, dense, to 8–15 ft.	Coral pink buds open to small double rose pink flowers	Reddish orange, small; scant crop	Sometimes grown as a shrub. Fair disease resistance
M. coronaria WILD SWEET CRABAPPLE	Short trunk; broad, round-headed crown. To 30 ft.	Pink buds open to single flowers in pure white or pink-tinged white; fragrant	Yellowish green, large	Late blooming. Susceptible to rust
M. c. 'Charlotte'	Resembles *M. coronaria*	Large double pale pink flowers	Fruit similar to that of *M. coronaria*	Orange-red fall color. Like *M. coronaria*, late blooming and susceptible to rust
'Dolgo'	Willowy, spreading to 40 ft. tall and wide	Pink buds open to single white flowers	Purple, red, large. Good flavor, can be used for jelly	Moderate disease resistance
'Donald Wyman'	Broad, to 20 ft. by 25 ft.	Pink to red buds open to single white flowers	Shiny bright red, small, lasts through winter	Lustrous foliage. Good disease resistance
'Dorothea'	Dense, round headed, to 25 ft. tall and wide	Red buds open to large semi-double pink flowers	Bright yellow, small	Susceptible to scab, fireblight

M

MALUS

NAME	SIZE, HABIT	FLOWERS	FRUIT	COMMENTS
M. floribunda JAPANESE FLOWERING CRABAPPLE	Broad, dense, to 15–25 ft.	Deep pink buds open to single white flowers. Blooms fragrant, incredibly profuse	Yellow and red, small, do not last long	Moderate disease resistance
'Harvest Gold'	Vigorous, narrow, to 30 ft. tall and 15 ft. wide	Pink buds open to single white flowers. Late flowering	Yellow, showy, last until spring	High disease resistance
'Hopa'	Fast growth to 25 ft. by 20 ft.	Single rose red flowers, fragrant	Orange red, large, ripen and drop early. Good for jelly	Suckers freely. Old-fashioned variety, very prone to disease except in area of very low humidity. Newer, more resistant crabapples a better choice
M. hupehensis (*M. theifera*) TEA CRABAPPLE	Broad form; moderate growth to 15 ft. by 25 ft.	Single deep pink flowers fading to white; fragrant	Greenish yellow to red, small, not showy	Picturesque form and branching (branches are strongly angled from short trunk). Moderate disease resistance
'Indian Magic'	Round headed to 15–20 ft. tall and wide	Red buds open to single deep pink flowers	Shiny red to orange, small, long lasting	Moderate susceptibility to disease
'Indian Summer'	Round headed, to 18 ft. tall and wide	Single rose red	Bright red, long lasting	Good orange-red fall foliage color. High disease resistance
M. ioensis PRAIRIE CRABAPPLE	Round headed, to 20–30 ft. tall and wide	Pink buds open to large single white flowers; fragrant	Dull yellow-green, large	Susceptible to rust. Species rarely grown (see below)
M. i. 'Plena' BECHTEL CRABAPPLE	Round-headed, open, to 30 feet.	Double pink flowers; fragrant	Similar to species	Like species, highly susceptible to disease. M. i. 'Klehm's' is similar, but with higher disease resistance
M. i. 'Prince George'	Upright to 25 ft. tall and 15 ft. wide.	Double, light pink flowers with 50 petals	Bears little or no fruit Flowers well annually	Lack of fruit makes it an excellent patio tree. Disease resistant.
'Jewelberry'	Dwarfish, dense, to 8 ft. by 12 ft.	Pink buds open to single white flowers	Shiny red, ½ in. wide, long lasting	Bears young. Moderate disease resistance
'Katherine'	Slow growing to 20 ft. tall and wide	Deep pink buds open to large double pink flowers that quickly fade to white	Yellow with red cheek, very small	Fair disease resistance
'Liset'	Roundish, dense, to 15–20 ft. tall and wide	Crimson buds open to single flowers of deep red to crimson	Dark red to maroon, persistent	Deep purplish green leaves. Fair disease resistance
'Madonna'	Narrow, erect, to 20 ft. by 10 ft.	Pink buds open to double white flowers. Long bloom season	Yellow with red cheek, small	Bronze new growth. Good disease resistance
M. micromalus (*M. kaido*) MIDGET CRABAPPLE	Slow growth to 20 ft. by 15 ft.	Red buds open to single pink flowers. Profuse bloomer	Red or greenish, not showy	Susceptible to disease

MALUS

NAME	SIZE, HABIT	FLOWERS	FRUIT	COMMENTS
'Molten Lava'	Spreading, weeping, to 12 ft. tall and wide	Deep red buds open to single white flowers	Red orange, small, last well on tree	Attractive yellow winter bark. Good disease resistance
'Narragansett'	Broad, round headed, to 15 ft. tall and wide	Red buds open to single white flowers with faint touch of pink	Bright red, ½ in. wide, showy	High disease resistance
'Oekonomierat Echtermeyer' (*'Pink Weeper'*) WEEPING CRABAPPLE	Moderate growth rate to 15 ft., with weeping branches	Red buds open to single purplish red flowers	Purplish to reddish to greenish brown	Purplish foliage becomes purplish green in summer. Any branches growing erect should be pruned out. Disease prone
'Pink Perfection'	Round headed, to 20 ft. tall and wide	Red buds open to large double pink flowers	Yellow, insignificant	Susceptible to scab
'Pink Princess'	Low, broad, to 15 ft. by 12 ft.	Single rose pink	Deep, red, small, last well on tree	Reddish green foliage. Good disease resistance
'Pink Spires'	Narrowly upright to 25 ft.	Deep rose pink buds open to single rose pink flowers	Red-purple, persistent	New foliage red, maturing to bronzy green. Moderate disease resistance
'Prairifire'	Round headed, to 20 ft. tall and wide	Red buds open to single deep pinkish red flowers	Small, dark red, persistent	Leaves emerge reddish maroon, turn dark green. High disease resistance
'Profusion'	Upright, spreading, to 20 ft. tall and wide	Deep red buds open to single, deep purplish pink flowers	Dark red, long lasting	Purple foliage matures to bronzy green. Moderate disease resistance
'Purple Wave'	Broad, spreading, to 10–15 ft. tall and wide	Large single to semidouble rose red, fading to purplish pink	Dark purple red	Purplish foliage. Susceptible to scab, rust
M. purpurea 'Eleyi'	Irregular, open, to 20 ft. tall and wide	Single wine red flowers	Dark purple red. Profuse	Old-fashioned variety, very prone to disease except in areas of very low humidity. Newer, more resistant crabapples a better choice
M. p. 'Lemoine'	Dense, rounded habit, to 25 ft.	Deep purplish rose, the darkest color of any crabapple	Purplish red, annual	Good disease resistance makes this a better choice than 'Eleyi'
'Radiant'	Broad, round headed, to 20 ft. tall and wide	Deep red buds open to single deep pink flowers	Bright red, colors early; long lasting	Young leaves reddish, turning to green. Susceptible to scab
'Red Baron'	Narrow (to 20 ft. by 12 ft.), broadening in age	Very deep red buds open to single reddish pink flowers	Shiny dark red	Susceptible to scab
'Red Jade'	Irregular, weeping form; to 15 ft. tall and wide	Small single white flowers	Bright red, heavy crop, holds well into fall	Moderate disease resistance

M

M

leaves drop. Blooming and bearing may occur more heavily in alternate years. Birds are fond of small-fruited types.

Plant bare-root trees in winter or early spring; set out container plants any time. Crabapples prefer good, well-drained, deep soil, but they will grow in rocky or gravelly soils and in conditions ranging from acid to slightly alkaline. More tolerant of wet soil than flowering cherries or other flowering stone fruits; also hardier and longer lived than flowering stone fruits. Adapt to a variety of climates. All need some winter chill.

Malus sargentii

Crabapples may be bothered by aphids, Japanese beetles, spider mites, or tent caterpillars, but these pests are minor compared with potential disease problems: fireblight, apple scab, cedar-apple rust, and powdery mildew. In most parts of their range, where humidity is high and persistent, disease resistance of crabapple varieties is of great importance if you wish to avoid spraying. Where long, dry summers are the rule, diseases are less of a problem. Disease resistance (or lack of it) is noted in the chart.

Crabapples are fine lawn trees. Planted near fences, they will heighten screening effect, provide blossoms and fruit, and still give planting room for primroses, spring bulbs, or shade-loving bedding plants. Prune only to build good framework, correct shape, or remove suckers. Crabapples can be trained as espaliers.

MALVA

MALLOW

Malvaceae

PERENNIALS OR BIENNIALS

☼ ☽ ZONES VARY BY SPECIES

☼ ☽ LIGHT SHADE IN HOTTEST AREAS

🌢 REGULAR WATER

Malva

Related to and somewhat resembling hollyhock *(Alcea)*, but bushier, with smaller, roundish leaves. Easy to grow; need good drainage, average soil. Grow from seed; usually bloom first year. Use in perennial borders or for a quick tall edging. Plants not long lived.

M. alcea. Perennial. Zones 31, 32, 34–43. Grows to 4 ft. tall, 2 ft. wide. Saucer-shaped, 2-in.-wide pink flowers appear from late spring to fall. Common kind is 'Fastigiata', a narrower grower that looks much like a hollyhock.

M. moschata. MUSK MALLOW. Perennial. Zones 31, 32, 34–45. Erect, branching plant to 3 ft., with finely cut leaves and inch-wide (or somewhat larger) flowers, summer to fall. Entire plant emits a mild, musky fragrance if brushed or bruised. 'Rosea' has rose pink flowers; 2-ft.-tall 'Alba' is white flowered.

M. sylvestris. Perennial or biennial. Zones 31, 32, 34–45. Erect, bushy growth to 2–4 ft.; 2-in.-wide flowers appear all summer, often until frost. Common variety (often sold as *M. zebrina*) has pale lavender pink flowers with pronounced deep purple veining. 'Mauritiana' has deeper-colored flowers, often semidouble.

Malvaceae. The mallow family contains many hundreds of species of mainly herbaceous plants and some shrubs and trees, often with lobed leaves and showy flowers. Ornamental members include flowering maple *(Abutilon)*, *Hibiscus*, hollyhock *(Alcea)*, mallow *(Malva)*, and checkerbloom *(Sidalcea)*. Commercially, the family is important as the source of cotton.

FOR INFORMATION ON SELECTING PLANTS

PLEASE SEE PAGES 47–112

MANDEVILLA

Apocynaceae

EVERGREEN OR DECIDUOUS VINES

☼ ALL ZONES

☼ ☽ PARTIAL SHADE IN HOTTEST AREAS

🌢 REGULAR WATER

Mandevilla

Known for showy flowers, the genus *Mandevilla* includes plants that were formerly called *Dipladenia*. Flowers are saucer shaped, with tubular throats. Plants survive outdoors only in mildest regions; in the Northeast, they are treated as annuals or grown indoors in the winter and outdoors in summer, or in greenhouses.

M. 'Alice du Pont' (M. splendens, M. amabilis, Dipladenia splendens, D. amoena). Evergreen. To about 3 ft. in pots or tubs (where it is usually grown). Twining stems; dark green, glossy, oval, 3–8-in.-long leaves. Clusters of pure pink, 2–4-in.-wide flowers appear among leaves, spring–fall. Even very small plant in 4-in. pot will bloom. Plant in rich soil and provide frame, trellis, or stake for support. Pinch young plant to induce bushiness.

M. boliviensis. Evergreen. To about 3 ft. in a container. Glossy leaves. White flowers with yellow throats throughout the year.

M. laxa (M. suaveolens). CHILEAN JASMINE. Deciduous. Twines to 15 ft. or more. Leaves are long ovals, heart shaped at base, 2–6 in. long. Clustered summer flowers are white, 2 in. across, trumpet shaped, with powerful gardenialike fragrance. Provide rich soil.

M. splendens (M. amabilis, M. 'Profusa', M. sanderi). Evergreen. Similar to 'Alice du Pont', with same bloom period. 'Red Riding Hood', with deep red flowers, and white-blossomed 'Summer Snow' are lower growing and shrubbier than the species. Superb in hanging baskets.

MANNA GRASS. See GLYCERIA maxima

MAPLE. See ACER

MAPLE, FLOWERING. See ABUTILON

MARGUERITE. See CHRYSANTHEMUM frutescens

MARIGOLD. See TAGETES

MARJORAM. See ORIGANUM

MARRUBIUM

HOREHOUND

Lamiaceae (Labiatae)

PERENNIAL HERBS

☼ ☽ ZONES 31, 32, 34–45

☼ FULL SUN

🌢 🌢 REGULAR TO LITTLE WATER

Marrubium

Horehounds are a genus of woolly-leaved perennials native to the Mediterranean area. They tolerate dry conditions and thrive in well-drained soil of poor or average fertility. The two species described here are spreading and best used in informal gardens.

M. incanum. Grows to 20 in. tall and 2 ft. wide. Erect stems bear oblong to oval, gray-green leaves to 2 in. long with scalloped edges, covered with silky white hairs on underside. Whorls of small purplish white flowers backed by fuzzy gray calyces are borne in summer. One of the most reliable plants for silvery foliage in humid zones 31, 32.

M. vulgare. COMMON HOREHOUND. The horehound known to herb gardeners; grows 1–3 ft. high. Wrinkled, woolly, aromatic gray-green leaves; whorls of white flowers (similar to those of mint) on foot-long, branching stems. Needs little water but will take more if drainage is good;

otherwise, not fussy about soil. Sow seeds in spring in flats; transplant seedlings to 1 ft. apart. As garden plant, invasive and rather weedy looking, but can serve as edging in gray garden. Used for medicinal purposes and in candy. Foliage lasts well in bouquets.

MARSHALLIA grandiflora

BARBARA'S BUTTONS, LARGE-FLOWERED MARSHALLIA

Asteraceae

PERENNIAL

ZONES 31, 32, 34–41

FULL SUN OR PARTIAL SHADE

MORE THAN REGULAR WATER

Marshallia grandiflora

Lacy, buttonlike flower heads characterize this wildflower native to the East Coast. Unlike daisies and many other aster-family relatives, this species produces flower heads that consist solely of enlarged, delicately cut, petal-like disk florets, which make up the eyes of daisies and asters. They lack showy petals, more properly called ray florets, which characterize the blooms of daisies and asters. Plants produce a clump of glossy, lance-shaped leaves and range from 1–2 ft. tall in bloom. They grow naturally along streams and in other wet to boggy sites. Although they tolerate average soil with supplemental watering, they are best planted in rich soil that remains evenly moist.

MARSH MARIGOLD. See CALTHA palustris

MARSILEA quadrifolia

WATER CLOVER, PEPPERWORT

Marsiliaceae

AQUATIC FERN

ALL ZONES AS ANNUAL

FULL SUN

AMPLE WATER

Marsilea quadrifolia

Growing from slender rhizomes, this denizen of the water's edge resembles a bright green, floating four-leaf clover. In shallow water, the leaves, on slender 1-ft. stems, are held slightly above the surface. An attractive floating accent for small ponds or aquatic containers, marsilea should be treated as an annual or grown under glass throughout the Northeast region. Plant in pots in a heavy garden loam and sink 2 in. below the surface; can be invasive if not potted up. Also of interest are *M. drummondii,* with small, white-haired leaves, and *M. mutica,* with light green leaves streaked with brown.

> ### WATER CLOVER SOLVES A PROBLEM
> One of the best ways to prevent the growth of algae in a pond or garden pool is to cover the water surface with foliage, which blocks the light that algae need to grow. Water lilies and lotus, with their large leaves, are excellent providers of surface coverage. But in a very small pool, or a water garden in a shady location, water clover will do the job nicely.

MARY'S THISTLE. See SILYBUM marianum

MASK FLOWER. See ALONSOA

MASTERWORT. See ASTRANTIA

MATRICARIA recutita (M. chamomilla)

CHAMOMILE

Asteraceae (Compositae)

ANNUAL

ALL ZONES

FULL SUN

MODERATE WATER

Matricaria recutita

This is the chamomile whose dried flowers yield a fragrant tea with overtones of pineapple. Plant grows 2–2½ ft. tall, with finely cut, almost fernlike foliage and daisylike white-and-yellow flower heads an inch wide or less. Summer bloom. Grows easily in full sun and ordinary soil from seed sown in late winter or spring. Becomes naturalized.

Plants or seeds sold as *Matricaria* 'White Stars', 'Golden Ball', and 'Snowball' are varieties of *Chrysanthemum parthenium.* Chamomile sold as walk-on ground cover is *Chamaemelum nobile (Anthemis nobilis).* Its flowers yield medicinal-tasting, rather bitter tea.

MATRIMONY VINE. See LYCIUM chinense

MATTEUCCIA struthiopteris

OSTRICH FERN

Polypodiaceae

FERN

ZONES 32, 34–45

FULL SUN ONLY IN COOL, MOIST AREAS

AMPLE WATER

Matteuccia struthiopteris

Native to northern regions of North America. Hardy to extreme cold but an indifferent grower in mild-winter areas. Clumps are narrow at base, spread out at top like a shuttlecock. Unfolding young fronds (fiddleheads) are edible. Plant can reach 6 ft. in moist, moderate climates; grows only 1½–2 ft. tall in mountains where season is short, humidity low. Spreads by underground rhizomes and may become invasive. Dormant in winter. Attractive woodland or waterside plant. Needs rich, moist soil.

MATTHIOLA

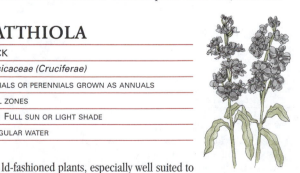

STOCK

Brassicaceae (Cruciferae)

BIENNIALS OR PERENNIALS GROWN AS ANNUALS

ALL ZONES

FULL SUN OR LIGHT SHADE

REGULAR WATER

Matthiola

Old-fashioned plants, especially well suited to the cottage garden. All have long, narrow gray-green leaves and luxuriant, scented flowers in erect, spikelike clusters. Best in cool weather.

M. incana. STOCK. Valued for fragrance, cut flowers. Oblong leaves to 4 in. long. Flowers single or double, 1 in. wide, with spicy-sweet scent. Colors include white, pink, red, purple, lavender, blue, yellow, cream. Blues and reds are purple toned; yellows tend toward cream.

Many strains available. Earliest bloomer is Trysomic Seven Weeks (blooms in 7 weeks), a branching plant to 12−15 in. tall. Ten Weeks, also branching, reaches 15−18 in. tall. Column stock and Double Giant Flowering are unbranched plants 2−3 ft. tall; they can be planted 6−8 in. apart in rows and are ideal for cutting. Giant Imperial strain is branched, 2−2½ ft. tall, comes in solid or mixed colors.

Stock needs light, fertile soil and good drainage. Plant in earliest spring to get flowers before hot weather; choose early bloomers. Plants take moderate frost but will not set flower buds if nights are too chilly. Where soil is not well drained in winter, plant in raised beds to avoid inevitable root rot.

M. longipetala bicornis. EVENING SCENTED STOCK. Foot-tall plant with lance-shaped leaves to 3½ in. long. Small purplish flowers are not showy, but emit a powerful fragrance at night.

MAY APPLE. See PODOPHYLLUM peltatum

MAYBUSH, MAYDAY TREE. See PRUNUS padus

MAYPOP. See PASSIFLORA incarnata

MAZUS reptans

Scrophulariaceae

PERENNIAL

🗓 ZONES 31, 32, 34, 39

☼ ◐ PARTIAL SHADE IN HOT CLIMATES

💧 REGULAR WATER

Mazus reptans

Slender stems creep and root along ground, send up leafy branches 1−2 in. tall. Narrowish bright green leaves are 1 in. long, with a few teeth along edges. Spring and early summer flowers are purplish blue with white and yellow markings, ¾ in. across; they appear in clusters of two to five. In shape, flowers resemble those of *Mimulus*. Use in rock garden or as small-scale ground cover; needs rich soil. Takes heavy foot traffic between pavers. Evergreen in mild-winter climates; in colder areas, freezes to ground but usually recovers quickly in spring if protected over winter by snow cover or light mulch. Self-sows to the point of becoming a nuisance in some gardens. Plant sold as *M. japonicus* 'Albiflora' is a white-flowering form of *M. reptans*.

MEADOW BEAUTY. See RHEXIA virginica

MEADOW RUE. See THALICTRUM

MEADOW SAFFRON. See COLCHICUM

MEADOWSWEET. See ASTILBE, FILIPENDULA ulmaria

MECONOPSIS cambrica

Papaveraceae

PERENNIALS

🗓 ZONES 34, 38 (COASTAL AREA), 39

◐ ● PARTIAL OR FULL SHADE

💧 REGULAR WATER

Meconopsis cambrica

Ardent collectors and shade garden enthusiasts sometimes attempt the many *Meconopsis* species offered by specialist seed firms. Most are difficult, but this one is not too hard to grow if given loose, acid soil and cool, humid, shady conditions. Does well on coast of Maine. Protect seaside plantings from wind. Plants self-sow without becoming invasive. In summer, produces orange or yellow, 3-in. poppies on 1−2-ft. stems. Gray-green, divided leaves. Tolerates full sun, some drought.

MEDEOLA virginiana

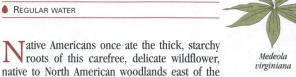

INDIAN CUCUMBER-ROOT

Liliaceae

PERENNIALS

🗓 ZONES 31, 32, 34–43

☼ ● PARTIAL SHADE, FULL SHADE

💧 REGULAR WATER

Medeola virginiana

Native Americans once ate the thick, starchy roots of this carefree, delicate wildflower, native to North American woodlands east of the Mississippi. The roots, white on the inside and measuring about an inch long, resemble cucumbers in looks and flavor. Plants produce 2-ft. stems without branches. Each stem has two leaf levels. Bottom leaves are up to 5 in. long and upper tier leaves are up to 2 in. long. From this level arise nodding greenish yellow flowers on 1-in. stalks in May and June. In late summer, plants develop attractive bright red to deep purple berries. *Medeola* suits shade gardens, informal native plant gardens, and woodland gardens. It prefers moist, somewhat acid soil. To increase, plant seed when fresh and ripe. Make sure before planting that seeds are free of pulp.

MEDLAR. See MESPILUS germanica

MEEHANIA

MEEHAN'S MINT

Lamiaceae

PERENNIALS

🗓 ZONES VARY BY SPECIES

◐ PARTIAL SHADE

💧 💧💧 REGULAR TO MORE THAN REGULAR WATER

Meehania

Like other mint-family plants, these low-growing, creeping perennials bear four-sided stems and tubular, two-lipped flowers. The blooms are carried in short, erect spikes and are arranged in whorls of three or more around the stems. Leaves are rounded to heart-shaped. Although plants tolerate sun and fairly dry soil, they are happiest in partial shade with rich, moist, well-drained soil. They spread, but are not as invasive as are true mints (*Mentha* spp.) or dead nettle (*Lamium galeobdolon*), both close relatives. Use them as ground covers in the shade or woodland garden.

M. cordata. CREEPING MINT, MEEHAN'S MINT. Zones 31, 32, 34–43. Native to rich woodlands in the eastern U.S., from Pennsylvania and Ohio south to North Carolinia and Tennessee. Plants form low, 1−1½-ft.-tall mounds and bear long, trailing stems. They produce upright, 2−3-in.-long spikes of pale violet, 1-in.-long flowers with white lips in spring.

M. urticifolia. Zones 31, 32, 34–41. An Asian native that forms 1−1½-ft. mounds; clumps spread to 6 ft. or more. Bears lance-shaped to somewhat triangular leaves and 1-ft.-tall spikes of 1½−2-in.-long violet flowers in late spring and early summer.

MEEHAN'S MINT. See MEEHANIA

FOR INFORMATION ON YOUR CLIMATE ZONE

PLEASE SEE PAGES 30–46

MELAMPODIUM

Asteraceae (Compositae)

ANNUALS AND PERENNIALS

☑ ZONES VARY BY SPECIES

☼ FULL SUN

◐ MODERATE WATER

Melampodium

These tough, drought-tolerant plants produce masses of small daisies over a long period. Provide well-drained soil.

M. leucanthum. BLACKFOOT DAISY. Short-lived perennial. Zones 35, 41, 43. To 1 ft. tall. Honey-scented white daisies with yellow centers bloom in spring and summer.

M. paludosum (Leucanthemum paludosum). BUTTER DAISY. Annual. All zones. To 1½ ft. tall. Deep yellow daisies appear throughout summer and into fall; no deadheading required. Tolerates heat and humidity. Start seeds indoors for earliest bloom; or sow in ground after soil has warmed.

Melastomataceae. The melastoma family consists almost entirely of tropical shrubs and trees with strongly veined leaves and symmetrical flowers, such as princess flower *(Tibouchina)*.

MELISSA officinalis

LEMON BALM, SWEET BALM

Lamiaceae (Labiatae)

PERENNIAL HERB

☑ ZONES 31, 32, 34–45

☼ ◐ SUN OR PARTIAL SHADE

◐ REGULAR WATER

Melissa officinalis

Grows to 2 ft. Light green, heavily veined leaves with lemon scent. White flowers unimportant. Shear occasionally to keep compact. Likes rich soil. Very hardy; self-sows, spreads rapidly. Propagate from seed or root divisions. Leaves used in drinks, fruit cups, salads, fish dishes. Dried leaves help give lemon tang to sachets, potpourris.

MELON, MUSKMELON, CANTALOUPE

Cucurbitaceae

ANNUALS

☑ ALL ZONES

☼ FULL SUN

◐ WATER MOST WHEN PLANTS ARE YOUNG

Melon

The true cantaloupe, a hard-shelled melon, is rarely grown in the U.S. Principal types cultivated here are muskmelons ("cantaloupes") and late melons. (See Watermelon for information on that fruit.)

Muskmelons are ribbed, with netted skin and usually salmon-colored flesh; they are more widely adapted than late melons. Varieties include 'Hale's Best', 'Honey Rock', and the hybrids 'Ambrosia', 'Mainerock', 'Samson', and 'Saticoy'. Hybrids are superior to others in disease resistance and uniformity of size and quality. (Choosing varieties resistant to mildew and other diseases is particularly important where summers are humid.) Other muskmelons include small, highly perfumed types from the Mediterranean, such as white-fleshed 'Ha-Ogen' and orange-fleshed 'Chaca' and 'Charentais'.

Late melons are a varied group including honeydew, casaba, 'Crenshaw', 'Honey Ball', 'Golden Beauty', and 'Persian'. Because they need a longer growing season than muskmelons, they are less widely cultivated. They dislike high humidity and grow best in areas with hot, relatively dry summers.

To ripen to full sweetness, melons need steady heat for 2½ – 4 months. Sow seed 2 weeks after average date of last frost; don't rush the season, since melons are truly tropical plants and will perish in even light frost. In regions where summers are cool or relatively short, start plants indoors in peat pots a few weeks before last frost date, then plant outdoors in light, well-drained soil in warmest southern exposure. Row covers permit earlier planting outdoors. Black plastic mulch under melons warms soil, speeds harvest, helps keep melons from rotting.

You can grow melons on sun-bathed trellises, but heavy fruit must be supported in individual cloth slings. They are best grown in hills or mounded rows a few inches high at center; you will need to provide considerable space. Make hills about 3 ft. in diameter and space them 3–4 ft. apart; encircle each with a furrow for irrigation. Make rows 3 ft. wide and as long as desired, spacing them 3–4 ft. apart; make furrows for irrigation along either side. Plant seeds 1 in. deep—four or five seeds per hill, two or three seeds every 1 ft. in rows. When plants are well established, thin each hill to the best two plants; thin rows to one strong plant per foot. Fill furrows with water from time to time (furrows let you water plants without wetting foliage), but do not keep soil soaked. Feed (again in furrow) every 6 weeks.

To make melons taste sweeter, hold off watering a week or so before you expect to harvest the ripe fruit. To determine if a melon is ready for harvest, lift fruit and twist; it will slip off the stem if ripe. A pleasant, perfumy fragrance also indicates ripeness.

MENISPERMUM
canadense

CANADA MOONSEED, YELLOW PARILLA

Menispermaceae

DECIDUOUS VINE

☑ ZONES 31, 32, 34–41

☼ ◐ SHADE TO PARTIAL SHADE

◐ REGULAR WATER

◊ FRUITS ARE POISONOUS WHEN INGESTED

Menispermum
canadense

This semiwoody climber can exceed 10 ft. in height and features vigorous clusters of heart- or shield-shaped leaves that cling to slender stems. Small, loose clusters of yellow-green flowers bloom in summer. Black fruit resembling grapes follows on flowering female plants and is likely to be poisonous if ingested. Perfect on trellis, fence, or garden walls, but because it suckers, avoid locating too near other plants. Prefers moderately fertile and well-drained soil. Prune in early spring and transplant suckers in fall or spring.

MENTHA

MINT

Lamiaceae (Labiatae)

PERENNIAL HERBS AND GROUND COVERS

☑ ZONES VARY BY SPECIES

☼ ◐ SUN OR PARTIAL SHADE

◐ REGULAR WATER

Mentha

Spread rapidly by underground stems. Can be quite invasive. They grow almost anywhere but perform best in light, medium-rich, moist soil.

Contain in pot or box to keep in bounds. Plants disappear in winter in colder part of range. Propagate from runners; replant every 3 years.

M. aquatica. WATER MINT. Zones 31, 32, 34, 39. Height ranges from ½ to 3 ft. Oval to oblong, scented, dark green leaves with toothed edges, 2½–3 in. long; reddish purple stems; rounded clusters of lilac pink flowers in summer. Grow in wet soil at edge of pond.

M. gracilis (M. gentilis). GOLDEN APPLE MINT. Zones 31, 32, 34, 35, 37, 39. To 2 ft. Smooth, deep green leaves, variegated yellow. Flowers inconspicuous. Use in flavoring foods. Foliage excellent in mixed bouquets.

M. piperita. PEPPERMINT. Zones 31, 32, 34–45. To 3 ft. Strongly scented, toothed, 3-in.-long leaves. Small purple flowers in 1–3-in. spikes. Leaves good for flavoring tea. *M. p. citrata*, called orange mint or bergamot mint, grows to 2 ft. and has broad, 2-in.-long leaves, small lavender flowers. It is used in potpourris or in flavoring foods. Crushed leaves have slight orange flavor.

M. pulegium. PENNYROYAL. Zones 31, 32. Creeping plant grows a few inches tall with nearly round 1-in. leaves. Small lavender flowers in tight, short whorls. Strong mint fragrance and flavor. Poisonous in large quantities but safe as a flavoring. Needs cool, moist site.

M. requienii. JEWEL MINT OF CORSICA. Zones 31, 32, 34, 39. Creeping, mat forming, to only ½ in. high. Tiny, round, bright green leaves give mossy effect. Tiny light purple flowers in summer. Delightful minty or sagelike fragrance when leaves are bruised or crushed underfoot.

M. spicata. SPEARMINT. Zones 31, 32, 34–45. To 1½–2 ft. Dark green leaves, slightly smaller than those of peppermint; leafy spikes of purplish flowers. Use leaves fresh from garden or dried, for lamb, in cold drinks, as garnish, in apple jelly.

M. suaveolens. APPLE MINT. Zones 31, 32, 34, 35, 37, 39. Stiff stems grow 1½–2½ ft. tall. Rounded leaves are slightly hairy, gray green, 1–4 in. long. Purplish white flowers in 2–3-in. spikes. Leaves have apple-mint fragrance. 'Variegata', pineapple mint, has leaves with white markings, faint fragrance of pineapple. Species is usually sold as *M. rotundifolia*.

MERRYBELLS. See UVULARIA

MERTENSIA virginica

VIRGINIA BLUEBELLS

Boraginaceae

PERENNIAL

✂ ZONES 31, 32, 34–45

◐ ● PARTIAL OR FULL SHADE

● REGULAR WATER

Mertensia virginica

A relative of forget-me-not *(Myosotis);* native to eastern U.S. Broadly oval, bluish green leaves form loose clumps that send up leafy, 1½–2-ft.-tall stems bearing loose clusters of nodding, 1-in. flowers. Buds are usually pink to lavender, but open to blue bells, sometimes with a pinkish cast. Appears and flowers early in spring; dies to ground soon after going to seed, usually by midsummer. Charming with naturalized daffodils or with ferns, trillium, bleeding heart in woodland garden.

Provide moist, rich soil. Use summer annuals to fill void after plants die back. Clumps can be left in place indefinitely; they will slowly spread. To get more plants, use volunteer seedlings or dig and divide clumps in early fall.

MESCAL. See AGAVE

PRACTICAL GARDENING DICTIONARY

PLEASE SEE PAGES 449–523

MESEMBRYANTHEMUM crystallinum

ICE PLANT

Aizoaceae

SUCCULENT ANNUAL

✂ ALL ZONES

☼ FULL SUN

● TAKES CONSIDERABLE DROUGHT

Mesembryanthemum crystallinum

The least ornamental of many plants commonly called *Mesembryanthemum* or ice plant, this is now considered the only true *Mesembryanthemum*. Use in hanging baskets, window boxes. *M. crystallinum* is a sprawling plant a few inches tall and several feet wide. Oval, flat, stalked, fleshy leaves grow to 4 in. long, turn red when water stressed. Leaves are covered with tiny transparent blisters that glisten like flecks of ice. Foliage is edible. Inch-wide, white to pinkish flowers in summer. Easy to grow from seed. In warm, humid climates, provide well-drained soil.

MESPILUS germanica

MEDLAR

Rosaceae

DECIDUOUS TREE

✂ ZONES 31, 32, 34, 39

☼ FULL SUN

● REGULAR WATER

Mespilus germanica

This native of Europe produces large, bowl-shaped, pink-tinged white flowers in late spring and early summer, followed by small, brown, flattened, apple-shaped fruits. Grown for its interesting gnarled habit and its fine russet color in autumn (as well as its edible fruit), it makes a good specimen for a small garden. Growing up to 20 ft., it can be kept closer to 6–8 ft. with modest pruning or can be espaliered against a wall. The fruits are highly acidic and must be eaten when just past ripe, after they have been exposed to the action of frost; they can also be made into preserves.

METASEQUOIA glyptostroboides

DAWN REDWOOD

Taxodiaceae

DECIDUOUS CONIFER

✂ ZONES 31, 32, 34–41

☼ FULL SUN

● BEST IN MOIST, NOT BOGGY SOIL

Metasequoia glyptostroboides

Thought to have been extinct for thousands of years, but found growing in a few isolated sites in China during the 1940s. Pyramidal tree bearing small cones. Soft, light green needles turn light bronze in autumn, then drop to reveal attractive winter silhouette. Branchlets tend to turn upward; bark is reddish in youth, becoming darker and fissured in age. Trees grow very fast in mild regions, moderately fast in cold-winter climates. They have reached about 90 ft., but they haven't been grown long enough in gardens to determine maximum height. Looks somewhat like bald cypress *(Taxodium distichum),* another deciduous conifer. While in leaf, also bears superficial resemblance to coast redwood.

Grows best in good, organic, well-drained soil with regular water. Good lawn tree, though in time surface roots may interrupt smooth flow of turf. Not suited to arid regions or seacoast, since dry heat and salty ocean winds will burn foliage.

MEXICAN FIRE BUSH. See KOCHIA scoparia trichophylla

MEXICAN FIRE PLANT. See EUPHORBIA heterophylla

MEXICAN FLAME VINE. See SENECIO confusus

MEXICAN SHELL FLOWER. See TIGRIDIA pavonia

MEXICAN SUNFLOWER. See TITHONIA rotundifolia

MEXICAN TULIP POPPY. See HUNNEMANNIA fumariifolia

MICHAELMAS DAISY. See ASTER novae-angliae, A. novi-belgii

MICROBIOTA decussata

SIBERIAN CARPET CYPRESS

Cupressaceae

EVERGREEN SHRUB

Zones 32, 34–45

Partial shade in hottest areas

Regular water

Microbiota decussata

Native to Siberian mountains and hardy to any amount of cold. Neat, sprawling shrub that resembles a trailing arborvitae. Grows to 1½ ft. tall, 7–8 ft. wide, with many horizontal or trailing plumelike branches closely set with scalelike leaves. Foliage green in summer, turning purplish, reddish brown in winter. More shade tolerant than junipers. Needs excellent drainage. Use as a bank cover.

MIGNONETTE. See RESEDA odorata

MILFOIL. See ACHILLEA millefolium

MILIUM effusum 'Aureum'

BOWLES' GOLDEN GRASS

Poaceae (Gramineae)

PERENNIAL GRASS

Zones 31, 32, 34, 39

Light shade

Ample water

Milium effusum 'Aureum'

Attractive clumping grass to 2 ft. tall, usually less. Bright greenish gold leaves erect, then arching and weeping. Effective for spot of color in woodland garden, shaded rock garden.

GOLDEN FOLIAGE

Rely on foliage as well as flowers for color in the garden. Plants with golden leaves add a warm glow, and light up shady spots. In addition to Bowles' golden grass, consider yellow sedge (*Carex stricta* 'Bowles's Golden') and golden hakone grass (*Hakonechloa macra* 'Aureola'). There are also golden-leaved hostas, coleus, and thymes, as well as many tree and shrub cultivars, both evergreen and deciduous. See the list, Plants with Colored Foliage, on page 63, for more possibilities.

MILK THISTLE. See SILYBUM marianum

MIMOSA. See ALBIZIA julibrissin

MIMULUS hybridus

MONKEY FLOWER

Scrophulariaceae

SHORT-LIVED PERENNIAL GROWN AS ANNUAL

ALL ZONES

PARTIAL OR FULL SHADE

REGULAR WATER

Mimulus hybridus

Smooth, succulent, medium green leaves form a mound to 1–1½ ft. high. Showy, velvety flowers are thought to resemble a grinning monkey face; they are funnel shaped, 2–2½ in. long, with two "lips." Colors range from cream through rose, orange, yellow, scarlet, and brown, usually with heavy brownish maroon spotting or mottling. Best suited to cool, moist climates, where it tolerates full sun. Use in shady borders; or plant in hanging baskets or window boxes. Sow seed in spring for summer bloom, or set out plants for spring show.

MINT. See MENTHA

MINT BUSH. See ELSHOLTZIA stauntonii

MIRABILIS jalapa

FOUR O'CLOCK

Nyctaginaceae

TUBEROUS-ROOTED PERENNIAL

ALL ZONES; SEE BELOW

FULL SUN

MODERATE WATER

ALL PLANT PARTS ARE POISONOUS

Mirabilis jalapa

Perennial in Zones 31, 32; frosts kill it to ground but roots survive. In colder climates, treat as summer annual; dig and store tuberous roots as you would dahlia roots. Strong, bushy habit gives this plant the substance and character of a shrub: erect, many-branched stems grow quickly to form a mounded clump 3–4 ft. high and wide. Deep green, oval, 2–6-in.-long leaves. Scented, trumpet-shaped flowers in red, yellow, or white, with variations of shades between. Blossoms open in midafternoon; bloom season runs midsummer through fall. Jingles strain is lower growing than old-fashioned kinds, has elaborately splashed and stained flowers in two or three colors. Four o'clock reseeds readily and has naturalized in many parts of the South.

MISCANTHUS

EULALIA GRASS, SILVER GRASS, MAIDEN GRASS

Poaceae (Gramineae)

PERENNIAL GRASSES

ZONES VARY BY SPECIES

SUN OR LIGHT SHADE

MUCH TO MODERATE WATER

Miscanthus

These are among the most popular ornamental grasses. All are large to very large clump-forming grasses; attractive flower clusters open as tassels and gradually expand into large plumes atop tall stalks in late summer or fall. Plumes are silvery to pinkish or bronze and last well into winter. Foliage is always graceful; may be broad or narrow, solid colored, striped lengthwise, or banded. In fall and winter, foliage clumps turn to shades of yellow, orange, or reddish brown, especially showy against snow

M

or an evergreen background. Need little care. Cut back old foliage to the ground before new foliage sprouts in spring; divide clumps when vigor declines.

M. floridulus (M. giganteus). GIANT CHINESE SILVER GRASS. Zones 31, 32, 34. Can reach 10–14 ft., with leaves to 2½ ft. long, 1½ in. wide. Silvery flower plumes rise another 1–2 ft. above foliage. Leaves turn purplish green in fall, then drop off, leaving tall bare stalks over winter.

M. sinensis. EULALIA GRASS, JAPANESE SILVER GRASS. Zones 31, 32, 34–41. Variable in size and foliage. Flowers are held well above foliage clumps and may be cut for fresh or dry arrangements. All are attractive in borders or as focal points in a garden. Many varieties are obtainable; new ones come to market every year. Here are a few of the choicest:

'Adagio'. To 2–4 ft., with gray foliage and pink flowers aging white.

'Autumn Light'. To 5–6 ft. Late bloom; red autumn foliage.

'Cabaret'. Clumps reach 6 ft. Leaves are striped with white. Reddish plumes turn creamy with age.

M. s. condensatus 'Silver Arrow'. To 5–7 ft. White-striped leaves; silvery plumes.

'Cosmopolitan'. Narrow, erect, to 6 ft. or taller. Broad leaves have broad white stripes.

'Gracillimus'. MAIDEN GRASS. To 5–6 ft. Best-known variety. Reddish flowers borne late. Slender, weeping foliage with narrow white midrib turns orange or tan in the fall.

'Graziella'. To 5–6 ft., with narrow leaves and silvery plumes high above foliage. Orange fall color.

'Kirk Alexander'. Low growing (to 3 ft.); leaves horizontally banded with yellow. Tan flowers.

'Malepartus'. To 6–7 ft., with broad leaves that turn orange in fall. Rose pink plumes fade to silvery white.

'Morning Light'. To 4–5 ft. Leaves have white midrib and narrow stripes along leaf edges for overall silvery appearance. Reddish bronze flowers. One of the most elegant varieties.

'Purpurascens'. Foliage clumps 3–4 ft. tall turn reddish orange in fall. Silvery plumes.

'Strictus'. PORCUPINE GRASS. Narrow, erect, to 5–6 ft., with creamy stripes that run across leaves. Copper flowers. A little more cold hardy than the species.

'Yaku Jima'. Smaller grower (to 3–4 ft.). Slender green leaves; tan flowers.

'Zebrinus'. Broadly arching clumps to 5–6 ft.; leaves banded crosswise with yellowish white. Flowers are coppery pink, aging to white.

MITCHELLA repens

PARTRIDGEBERRY, TWINBERRY

Rubiaceae

EVERGREEN PERENNIAL

ZONES 31, 32, 34–45

PARTIAL OR FULL SHADE

AMPLE WATER

Mitchella repens

Attractive small, creeping evergreen plant native to much of eastern North America. Roundish leaves less than 1 in. long, borne in pairs along trailing, rooting, somewhat woody stems. Paired small white flowers appear in late spring or early summer; these are followed by bright red berries less than ¼ in. wide. *M. r. leucocarpa* has white berries. Small-scale ground cover best seen near eye level—on a shady bank or above a wall. Provide steady moisture and soil with plenty of leaf mold or other organic matter.

MOCCASIN FLOWER. See CYPRIPEDIUM

MOCK ORANGE. See PHILADELPHUS

MOLE PLANT. See EUPHORBIA lathyris

MOLINIA caerulea

PURPLE MOOR GRASS

Poaceae (Gramineae)

PERENNIAL GRASS

ZONES 32, 34–41

FULL SUN OR LIGHT SHADE

AMPLE WATER

Molinia caerulea

Plant is long lived but slow growing, taking a few years to reach its full potential. Erect, narrow, light green leaves form a neat, dense clump 1–2 ft. tall and wide. In summer, yellowish to purplish flowers in narrow, spikelike clusters rise 1–2 ft. above clump; they turn to tan and last well into fall. Inflorescences are profuse, but have a narrow structure that gives clump a see-through quality; they make good cut flowers. In late fall, both leaves and flower clusters break off and blow away.

Notable cultivars developed from *M. c. arundinacea* include the following 'Karl Foerster' has leaves to 32 in. long, long purplish flower clusters on somewhat arching stems to 5 ft. 'Skyracer' has foliage clumps to 3 ft. tall; flowers bring it to 7–8 ft. 'Windspiel' is similar. Leaves of 'Variegata' are striped lengthwise with creamy white; foliage clump is 1–1½ ft. tall, with purple flowers adding 6–12 in.

MOLUCCELLA laevis

BELLS-OF-IRELAND, SHELL FLOWER

Lamiaceae (Labiatae)

ANNUAL

ALL ZONES

FULL SUN

REGULAR WATER

Moluccella laevis

About 2 ft. high. Flowers are carried almost from base in whorls of six. Showy part of flower is large shell-like or bell-like, apple green calyx, very veiny and crisp textured; small white tube of united petals in center is inconspicuous. As cut flowers, spikes of little bells are attractive and long lasting, either fresh or dried; be sure to remove unattractive leaves.

Needs loose, well-drained soil. Doesn't perform well in hot, humid climates. Sow seed in ground in early spring for summer bloom; in mildest climates, can be sown in fall for winter bloom. If weather is warm, refrigerate seed for a week before planting. For long spikes, fertilize regularly.

MOMORDICA charantia

BALSAM PEAR, BITTER MELON

Cucurbitaceae

ANNUAL VINE

ALL ZONES

FULL SUN

REGULAR WATER

Momordica charantia

Deeply lobed leaves; white, fringed flowers 1 in. across. Fruit to 8 in. long, cylindrical with tapered ends, ridged and warty, bright yellow when ripe, splitting to show scarlet seeds. Immature fruits cherished in Asian cooking despite bitter flavor. Showy ripe fruits are sometimes used in arrangements. Sprawls or climbs by tendrils. Sow seed when soil warms, feed generously, and provide a trellis or other support.

MONARCH-OF-THE-EAST. See SAUROMATUM venosum

MONARDA

BEE BALM, OSWEGO TEA, HORSEMINT

Lamiaceae (Labiatae)

PERENNIALS

ZONES VARY BY SPECIES

LIGHT AFTERNOON SHADE IN HOT AREAS

AMPLE WATER

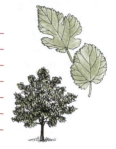
Monarda

Bushy, leafy clumps spread rapidly at edges and can be invasive. Dark green leaves grow 4–6 in. long, have strong, pleasant odor like blend of mint and basil. In summer, upright square stems are topped by tight clusters of long-tubed flowers much visited by hummingbirds. Plant 10 in. apart. Divide every 3 or 4 years. Not long lived where winters are warm, summers long and hot. Prone to mildew and other leaf diseases in dry soils and in very humid regions.

M. didyma. Zones 31, 32, 34–43. Native to eastern U.S. Basic species has scarlet flowers surrounded by reddish bracts. Garden selections and hybrids include scarlet 'Adam', pink 'Croftway Pink' and 'Granite Pink', 'Snow White', and dark red 'Mahogany'. A very old variety, 'Cambridge Scarlet', is still widely grown. Mildew-resistant varieties include red 'Jacob Kline'; pink 'Marshall's Delight'; lavender pink, 15-in. 'Petite Delight'; and wine red 'Raspberry Delight'. 'Violet Queen' is reddish violet. If spent flowers are removed, all varieties bloom over long period of 2 months or more. Don't let soil dry out.

M. fistulosa. Zones 31, 32, 34–45. Native from easternmost U.S. to Rocky Mountains. Lavender flowers to light pink encircled by whitish bracts are less showy than those of *M. didyma*. Best suited to wild garden.

MONDO GRASS. See OPHIOPOGON japonicus, under LIRIOPE and OPHIOPOGON

MONEY PLANT. See LUNARIA annua

MONEYWORT. See LYSIMACHIA nummularia

MONKEY FLOWER. See MIMULUS hybridus

MONKSHOOD. See ACONITUM

MONTBRETIA. See CROCOSMIA crocosmiiflora, TRITONIA

MOONFLOWER. See IPOMOEA alba

Moraceae. The mulberry family includes deciduous or evergreen trees, shrubs, and vines. Individual fruits are tiny and single-seeded but often aggregated into clusters. Fig (*Ficus*) and mulberry (*Morus*) are examples.

MORAINE LOCUST. See GLEDITSIA triacanthos 'Moraine'

MORINA longifolia

WHORLFLOWER

Morinaceae (Dipsaceae)

PERENNIALS

ZONES 31, 32, 34–41

FULL SUN TO PARTIAL SHADE

REGULAR MOISTURE

Morina longifolia

Grown for its spike of showy, waxy flowers that turn from white to pink to crimson, this evergreen perennial makes an unusual addition to beds and borders. Native to the Himalayas, whorlflower stands 2–4 ft. tall and 1 ft. wide, with skinny leaves up to 1 ft. long and 1 in. wide. Dark green foliage is scented and shiny, with spiny, serrated edges like a thistle. Leaves

---

and flowers occur in circles of three or more, giving the plant a tiered effect. Grow in poor to moderately fertile soil with excellent drainage. Cannot tolerate wet soil, severe winds, extreme cold, or intense heat and humidity. Use grouped in rock gardens and perennial borders. Seed heads good for dried arrangements.

MORNING GLORY. See CONVOLVULUS tricolor, IPOMOEA

MORUS

MULBERRY

Moraceae

DECIDUOUS TREES

ZONES VARY BY SPECIES

FULL SUN

WATER NEEDS VARY BY SPECIES

Morus

Leaves of variable form, size, and shape—often on same tree. Yellow fall color ranges from subdued to bright. Fruits look like miniature blackberries and are favored by birds. For creating shade in home gardens, the most important kinds are fruitless forms of *M. alba*.

M. alba. WHITE MULBERRY, SILKWORM MULBERRY. Zones 31, 32, 34–41. Native to China. Fast-growing tree can reach 30–50 ft. high and wide, though it is often smaller. Leaves to 6 in. long, nearly as wide, often lobed. Fruit-bearing (female) trees have inconspicuous flowers followed by sweet but rather insipid fruit that stains patios, clothing. 'Pendula' ('Teas' Weeping') is a low-growing, strongly weeping form—but a fruit producer. Fruitless (male) forms are better for home gardens, though they produce pollen in prodigious amounts. Good shade trees. Varieties include 'Chaparral' (weeping), 'Fan-San', 'Fruitless', 'Kingan', and 'Stribling' ('Mapleleaf').

Plants tolerate heat, alkaline soil, seacoast conditions. They take some aridity, but grow faster with regular water. Difficult to garden under because of heavy surface roots.

M. australis 'Unryu' (M. bombycis 'Unryu'). CONTORTED MULBERRY. Zones 31, 32, 34. Grows to 25 ft. tall, with twisted, contorted branches useful in dry floral arrangements or for winter silhouette. Fast growth means that branches may be cut freely with no harm to tree. Leaves to 6 in. long. Regular water.

M. nigra. BLACK MULBERRY, PERSIAN MULBERRY. Zones 31, 32, 34–41. To 30 ft. tall, with short trunk and dense, spreading head. Heart-shaped leaves to 8 in. long. Large, juicy, dark red to black fruit. Takes some aridity. 'Black Beauty' is smaller, to 15 ft. tall. 'Illinois Everbearing' produces an early summer crop of fruit followed by a smaller autumn crop. 'Wellington' is a heavy-fruiting variety.

M. papyrifera. See *Broussonetia papyrifera*

M. rubra. RED MULBERRY. Zones 31, 32, 34–41. Native to eastern and central U.S. Well-behaved tree with upright, spreading habit. Somewhat resembles *M. alba*, but fruit is red in color, a bit larger, and better tasting. Best in rich, moist soil.

MOSS, IRISH and SCOTCH. See SAGINA subulata

MOSS CAMPION. See SILENE acaulis, S. schafta

MOSS PINK. See PHLOX subulata

MOUNTAIN ASH. See SORBUS

MOUNTAIN GARLAND. See CLARKIA unguiculata

MOUNTAIN LAUREL. See KALMIA latifolia

MOUNTAIN MINT. See PYCNANTHEMUM virginianum

MOUNT ATLAS DAISY. See ANACYCLUS depressus

M

MOURNING BRIDE. See SCABIOSA atropurpurea

MOURNING WIDOW. See GERANIUM phaeum

MRS. ROBB'S BONNET. See EUPHORBIA robbiae

MUHLENBERGIA

Poaceae (Gramineae)

PERENNIAL GRASSES

🗡 ZONES VARY BY SPECIES

☼ ◑ FULL SUN OR LIGHT SHADE

💧 MODERATE TO LITTLE WATER

Muhlenbergia

These slender-leafed, fall-flowering native grasses are showy enough to stand out in the garden. All require good drainage and resist heat and drought.

M. capillaris. PINK MUHLY, PINK HAIR GRASS. Zones 31, 32, 34, 39. Native to sandy or rocky soils from New England, south to Florida and west to Texas and Mexico. Produces attractive clumps of glossy, linear leaves and airy, rich pink flower heads in fall. Clumps reach 3 ft. in bloom. 'Leuca' bears dark pink flowers.

M. lindheimeri. LINDHEIMER'S MUHLY. Zones 31, 32. Semievergreen species native to Texas and Mexico. Forms clumps of blue-gray leaves. Bears erect flower heads in fall, and plants reach 5 ft. in bloom.

MULBERRY. See MORUS

MULLEIN. See VERBASCUM

MULLEIN PINK. See LYCHNIS coronaria

MUSA

BANANA

Musaceae

TENDER PERENNIALS

🗡 ALL ZONES; SEE BELOW

☼ ◑ FULL SUN OR PARTIAL SHADE

💧💧 AMPLE WATER

Musa

While bananas are grown outdoors year-round in tropical climates, in the Northeast, they are either cultivated in greenhouses year-round or grown outdoors in the summer months—either in large tubs or in the ground—and overwintered indoors. The kinds described here include tall, medium, and dwarf plants, all fast-growing. They bear enormous, spectacular leaves—leaf blades can exceed 10 ft.—that add a striking tropical touch to summer beds and borders. Site them in a spot protected from wind because the leaves are easily tattered. Since all have soft, thickish stems and spread by suckers or underground roots to form clumps, they need to be grown in large tubs. Another option for plants grown outside during the summer is to cut the tops off the plants and dig the clumps before frost in fall. Contain the roots and attached soil in a sheet of plastic or large plastic bag. Cover them loosely and water sparingly over the winter months. Keep plants cool (60°F/16°C) over winter. Move to the garden after danger of frost has passed and the soil has warmed up. Bananas require rich, moist soil; feed and water regularly during the summer when they are growing actively.

M. acuminata 'Dwarf Cavendish' (M. cavendishii, M. nana). To 6–8 ft. tall, with leaves 5 ft. long, 2 ft. wide. Large, heavy flower clusters with reddish to dark purple bracts, yellow flowers. With ideal culture, plants overwintered in containers sometimes bear sweet, edible fruit. 'Enano Gigante' is similar, but its young leaves have red markings.

M. basjoo. JAPANESE BANANA. Hardy in Zones 31, 32. A 12–15-ft.-tall species with 10-ft.-long leaf blades. Bears drooping clusters of yellow or creamy colored flowers with brown bracts in summer. Yellow-green, 2½-in.-long fruits follow the flowers but are not good tasting. Provide winter mulch in Zones 31, 32; stems die back.

M. coccinea. SCARLET BANANA. Fairly compact, good for containers, grows to 5 ft. tall and as wide. Bears leaves with 3-ft.-long blades. Clusters of yellow flowers with red bracts in summer. Orange-yellow fruit 2 in. long.

M. ensete. See *Ensete ventricosum*

M. maurelii. See *Ensete ventricosum* 'Maurelii'

M. velutina. Compact species 4–5 ft. tall and 3 ft. wide. Suitable for containers. Bears leaves with red midribs and 3-ft.-long leaf blades. White flowers in summer; greenhouse-grown plants flower at other times of year. Pink fruit is 3½ in. long.

Musaceae. The banana family consists of giant herbaceous plants that resemble palm trees; the bases of the enormous leaves form a false trunk. *Ensete* and *Musa* are the only two members of the family.

MUSCARI

GRAPE HYACINTH

Liliaceae

BULBS

🗡 ZONES VARY BY SPECIES

☼ ◑ FULL SUN OR LIGHT SHADE

💧 REGULAR WATER DURING GROWTH AND BLOOM

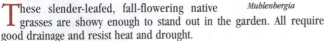

Muscari

Clumps of narrow, grassy, fleshy leaves appear in autumn and live through cold and snow. Small, urn-shaped, blue or white flowers in tight spikes appear in early spring. Plant 2 in. deep in fall, setting bulbs in masses or drifts under flowering fruit trees or shrubs, in edgings and rock gardens, or in containers. Very long lived. Lift and divide when bulbs become crowded. Plants self-sow under favorable conditions.

M. armeniacum. Zones 31, 32, 34–43. Bright blue flowers on 4–8-in. stems above heavy cluster of floppy foliage. 'Cantab' is lower growing, has neater foliage, and produces clear light blue flowers later than species. 'Blue Spike' has double blue flowers in a tight cluster at top of spike.

M. azureum (Hyacinthella azurea, Hyacinthus azureus). Zones 31, 32, 34–43. Between hyacinth and grape hyacinth in appearance. Stalks 4–8 in. high have tight clusters of fragrant, bell-shaped (not urn-shaped) sky blue flowers.

M. botryoides. Zones 31, 32, 34–45. Most cold hardy of the commonly grown grape hyacinths. Medium blue flowers on 6–12-in. stems. 'Album' has white flowers.

M. comosum. FRINGE HYACINTH, TASSEL HYACINTH. Zones 31, 32, 34–43. Unusual, rather loose clusters of shredded-looking flowers borne on 1–1½-ft. stems. In the species, blossoms are greenish brown on lower part of spike, bluish purple at top. 'Plumosum' ('Monstrosum'), feathered or plume hyacinth, bears violet blue to reddish purple flowers that look like shredded coconut.

M. latifolium. Zones 32, 34–43. Largest, possibly showiest of the grape hyacinths. Deep indigo blue flowers on 1-ft. stems. Plants have a single leaf.

M. tubergenianum. Zones 31, 32, 34–45. Stems to 8 in. tall. Flowers at top of spike are dark blue; those lower down are light blue.

FOR INFORMATION ON YOUR CLIMATE ZONE

PLEASE SEE PAGES 30–46

MUSTARD

Brassicaceae (Cruciferae)

ANNUAL

☑ ALL ZONES

☼ FULL SUN

🔴 REGULAR WATER

Mustard

Curly-leaf mustard somewhat resembles curly-leaf kale in appearance. It is usually cooked like spinach or cabbage; young leaves are sometimes eaten raw in salads or used as garnishes. Mustard spinach (tendergreen mustard) has smooth dark green leaves. It ripens earlier than curly mustard and is more tolerant of hot dry weather. 'Red Giant' ('Chinese Red'), with large, crinkled leaves with strong red shadings, is handsome enough for a border. Use mustard spinach when young as a salad green; older leaves are useful as boiled greens.

Mustard is fast and easy to grow; it will be ready for the table 35 to 60 days after planting. Sow in early spring and make successive sowings when young plants are established. Thrives in cool weather but quickly goes to seed in summer heat. Sow in late summer for fall use. Thin seedlings to stand 6 in. apart in rows. Harvest outer leaves as needed.

MYOSOTIS

FORGET-ME-NOT

Boraginaceae

PERENNIALS, BIENNIALS, AND ANNUALS

☑ ZONES 32, 34–45

☼ PARTIAL SHADE

🔴 REGULAR WATER

Myosotis

Both forget-me-not species feature exquisite, typically blue springtime flowers, tiny but profuse. Grow easily and thickly as ground covers. They perform best in cool, moist growing conditions—in woodland gardens, around pond edges, and along stream banks, for example.

M. scorpioides. Perennial. Similar in most respects to *M. sylvatica*, but grows lower and blooms over an even longer season, and roots live over from year to year. Flowers, about ¼ in. wide, are blue with yellow centers, pink, or white. Bright green, shiny, oblong leaves. Plant spreads by creeping roots.

M. sylvatica. Annual or biennial. To 6–12 in. Soft, hairy leaves, ½–2 in. long, set closely along stem. Tiny, clear blue, white-eyed flowers to ⅓ in. wide loosely cover upper stems. Flowers and seeds profusely for a long season, beginning in late winter or early spring. With habit of reseeding, will persist in garden for years unless weeded out. Often sold as *M. alpestris*. Improved varieties are available, best of which are 'Blue Ball' and 'Royal Blue Improved'.

MYRICA

WAX MYRTLE, BAYBERRY

Myricaceae

EVERGREEN OR DECIDUOUS SHRUBS OR TREES

☑ ZONES VARY BY SPECIES

☼ FULL SUN OR PARTIAL SHADE

🔴 WATER NEEDS VARY BY SPECIES

Myrica

Several species are useful as screen plants, informal hedges, or roadside plantings. Foliage is pleasantly aromatic. Although none is showy in flower, female plants bear attractive (though not conspicuous) small fruits.

M. cerifera. WAX MYRTLE. Evergreen shrub or tree. Zones 31, 32, 34, 39. Native to southeastern U.S. Grows to 15–20 ft., possibly taller. Leaves glossy dark green, to 3½ in. long. Grayish white fruits are heavily coated with a wax valued in candlemaking. Good specimen tree, hedge. Regular water.

M. gale. SWEET FERN, SWEET GALE. Deciduous shrub. Zones 36–45. Native to much of the Northern Hemisphere. Dense, erect growth to as tall as 6 ft., more typically 2–4 ft. Grown for fragrant leaves, to 2½ in. long. Takes regular moisture or boggy conditions.

M. pensylvanica (M. caroliniensis). BAYBERRY. Deciduous to semievergreen shrub. Zones 32, 34–44. Native to eastern U.S. Dense, compact growth to 9 ft. Leaves to 4 in. long, narrowish, glossy green, dotted with resin glands. Roundish fruit is covered with white wax—the bayberry wax used for candles. Tolerates seashore conditions—poor sandy or salty soil, wind. Fair tolerance for roadside salt. Regular water. *M. heterophylla* is similar to *M. pensylvanica*, but has somewhat larger leaves. Both species are semievergreen in the warmer parts of the Northeast, deciduous north of Zones 34 and 39.

MYROBALAN. See PRUNUS cerasifera

MYRRHIS odorata

GARDEN MYRRH, SWEET CICELY, SWEET CHERVIL

Apiaceae

PERENNIAL

☑ ZONES 32, 34–45

☼ PARTIAL SHADE

🔴 REGULAR WATER

Myrrhis odorata

This hardy herb grows 2–3 ft. tall with hollow stems, fernlike foliage, and umbrella-shaped clusters of starry white flowers that bloom in early summer. Sweet anise-flavored shoots, leaves, and seeds are used in cooking or are eaten raw in salads or with fruit. To enhance flavor, remove flowering stems as they appear. As an ornamental specimen it is a standout in an informal garden and will attract bees. Thrives in most soil conditions and will freely self-sow, but does not do well in excessive heat.

MYRTLE. See MYRTUS communis, VINCA

MYRTUS communis

MYRTLE

Myrtaceae

EVERGREEN SHRUB

☑ ALL ZONES

☼ ☼ FULL SUN OR PARTIAL SHADE

🔴 MODERATE WATER

Myrtus communis

Rounded form to 5–6 ft. high, 4–5 ft. wide. Glossy bright green leaves are pointed, 2 in. long, pleasantly aromatic when brushed or bruised. White, sweet-scented, ¾-in. flowers with many stamens bloom in summer; these are followed by bluish black, ½-in. berries. Any soil, but good drainage is essential. Not hardy in the Northeast, but an attractive container plant. Move outdoors to a deck or patio in summer, indoors over winter.

Named selections vary in foliage character and overall size. 'Variegata' fits basic description but has white-edged leaves. 'Boetica' is especially upright, with thick, twisted branches and larger, darker leaves. 'Buxifolia' has small leaves like a boxwood. Dwarf forms include 'Compacta', a small-leafed variety popular for edgings and low formal hedges; 'Compacta Variegata', similar but with white-margined foliage; and 'Microphylla', with tiny, closely set leaves.

M

NANDINA domestica

HEAVENLY BAMBOO, SACRED BAMBOO

Berberidaceae

EVERGREEN OR SEMIDECIDUOUS SHRUB

🌿 ZONES 31, 32

☼ ◑ ● SUN OR SHADE; COLORS BETTER IN SUN

💧 💧 REGULAR TO MODERATE WATER

Nandina domestica

Loses leaves at 10°F/−12°C; stems are damaged at 5°F/−15°C, but usually recovers fast. Belongs to the barberry family but is reminiscent of bamboo in its lightly branched, canelike stems and delicate, fine-textured foliage.

Slow to moderate growth to 6–8 ft. (you can keep plant to 3 ft. by pruning oldest canes to ground). Leaves intricately divided into many 1–2-in., pointed, oval leaflets, creating lacy pattern. Foliage expands pinkish and bronzy red, then turns to soft light green. Picks up purple and bronze tints in fall; often turns fiery crimson in winter, especially in sun and with some frost. Pinkish white or creamy white blossoms in loose, erect, 6–12-in. clusters at branch ends, late spring or early summer. If plants are grouped, shiny red berries follow the flowers; single plants seldom fruit heavily.

Best in rich soil with regular water, but its roots can even compete with tree roots in dry shade. Foliage may become chlorotic in alkaline soil. Most useful for light, airy vertical effects as well as for narrow, restricted areas. Good for hedge, screen, tub plant, bonsai. Dramatic with night lighting. Varieties include the following:

'Alba' (*N. d. leucocarpa*). Standard-size plant with creamy white berries and yellowish green foliage that turns yellow in fall. More subject to cold damage than the species.

'Compacta'. Lower growing than species (4–5 ft.), with narrower, more numerous leaflets; has very lacy look.

'Firepower'. Compact plant to 2 ft. tall and wide. Red-tinged summer foliage turns bright red in winter.

'Harbor Dwarf'. Low growing (1½–2 ft.), freely spreading. Underground rhizomes send up stems several inches from parent plant. Orange-red to bronzy red winter color. Good ground cover.

'Moyers Red'. Standard-size plant with broad leaflets. Brilliant red winter color in regions getting frost.

'Nana' ('Nana Purpurea', 'Atropurpurea Nana'). To 1–2 ft. tall. Coarse-foliaged plant with somewhat cupped or crinkled leaflets. Purplish green in summer, purplish red in winter. A slow spreader best used as an individual plant in a container or against a background of rock or gravel to emphasize its domed habit.

'Wood's Dwarf'. Rounded form to 3–4 ft. tall, densely foliaged, crimson orange to scarlet in winter.

NANKING CHERRY. See PRUNUS tomentosa

NARCISSUS

DAFFODIL

Amaryllidaceae

BULBS

🌿 ZONES 31, 32, 34–45, EXCEPT AS NOTED

☼ ◑ SUN; LATE KINDS LAST WELL IN LIGHT SHADE

💧 REGULAR WATER DURING GROWTH AND BLOOM

Narcissus

These spring-flowering bulbous plants are valuable in many ways. They are permanent, increasing from year to year; they stand up to cold and heat; they are useful in many garden situations; and they provide fascinating variety in flower form and color. Most offer early, midseason, and late varieties for extended bloom season. Most types are hardy to −30°F/−34°C (exceptions are noted). Finally, moles and deer won't eat them—good news for gardeners in areas where those creatures are common.

Narcissus Divisions (Groups)

Trumpet

Large-cupped

Small-cupped

Double

Cyclamineus Hybrid

Tazetta

Poeticus Narcissus

Split Corona

Triandrus Hybrid

N

Leaves are straight and flat (strap shaped) or narrow and rushlike. Flowers are composed of ring of segments (called the perianth) that are at right angles to the corona or crown (also called trumpet or cup, depending on its length) in center. Flowers may be single or clustered. Colors are basically yellow and white, but there are many variations—orange, red, apricot, pink, cream.

Flowers usually face sun; keep that in mind when selecting planting place. Use under trees and flowering shrubs, among ground cover plantings, near water, in rock gardens and patios, or in borders. Naturalize in sweeping drifts where space is available. Good in containers; fine cut flowers.

Plant bulbs as early in fall as you can get them. Look for solid, heavy bulbs. Number One double-nose bulbs are best; Number One round, single-nose bulbs are second choice. Plant with 5−6 in. of soil over tops of bulbs (4−5 in. for smaller bulbs). Set bulbs 8 in. apart and you won't have to divide for a number of years.

Let foliage mature and yellow naturally after bloom. Lift and divide clumps of daffodils when flowers get smaller and fewer in number; wait until foliage has died down. Don't forcibly break away any bulbs that are tightly joined to mother bulb; remove only those that come away easily. Replant at once, or store for only a short time—preferably not more than 3 weeks.

DAFFODILS IN CONTAINERS

For maximum show, set bulbs close together, the tips level with soil surface. Place pots in well-drained trench or cold frame and cover with 6−8 in. of moist peat moss, wood shavings, sawdust, or sand. Look for roots in 8 to 10 weeks (carefully tip soil mass from pot). Move pots with well-started bulbs to greenhouse, cool room, or sheltered garden spot to bloom. Keep well watered until foliage yellows; then plant in garden. You can sink pots or cans of bulbs in borders when flowers are almost ready to bloom, then lift containers when flowers fade.

Following are the 12 generally recognized divisions of daffodils and representative varieties in each division.

Trumpet daffodils. Trumpet is as long as or longer than surrounding flower segments. Yellows are the most popular; old variety 'King Alfred' best known, top seller, although newer 'Unsurpassable' and 'William the Silent' are superior. Other good yellows are 'Dutch Master', 'Lemon Glow' ('Lemon Yellow'), 'Primeur', 'Rijnveld's Early Sensation', and 'Spellbinder' (early blooming). White varieties include 'Cantatrice', 'Empress of Ireland', 'Mount Hood'. Bicolors with white segments, yellow cup, include 'Bravoure', 'Spring Glory', 'Trousseau'. Reverse bicolors like 'Spellbinder' have white cup and yellow segments.

Large-cupped daffodils. Cups are more than one-third the length of flower segments, but not as long as segments. Varieties include 'Camelot', 'Carlton', and 'Delibes' (orange-edged cup), yellow; 'Ice Follies', white; 'Ambergate', Binkie', 'Ceylon', 'Flower Record', 'Marion Lescault', and 'Mrs. R. O. Backhouse', bicolors.

Small-cupped daffodils. Cups less than or equal to one-third the length of segments. 'Barrett Browning', white petals, orange cup; 'Birma', yellow petals, red cup; 'Merlin', white petals, yellow cup edged orange-red; 'Mint Julep', pale greenish yellow petals, yellow cup with green eye.

Double daffodils. 'Cheerfulness', fragrant, creamy white; 'Sir Winston Churchill', creamy white with narrow orange petal segments interspersed; 'Tahiti', soft yellow with orange frills in center; 'Yellow Cheerfulness', fragrant, yellow.

Triandrus hybrids. Cups are short and flower segments usually recurved (flared back). Clusters of medium-size, slender-cupped, often nodding flowers. 'Thalia' is a favorite white with two or three beautifully proportioned flowers per stem. 'Silver Chimes' has six or more yellow-cupped white flowers per stem. Others include 'Petrel', white, fragrant; and 'Tresamble', white with recurved petals.

Cyclamineus hybrids. Early medium-size flowers with recurved segments. Gold, bright to creamy pale yellow, and white with yellow cup. Examples are 'Baby Doll', yellow; 'February Gold', yellow; 'Jenny', white; 'Jetfire', deep yellow with red-orange cup; 'Peeping Tom', yellow.

Jonquilla hybrids. Clusters of two to four rather small, very fragrant flowers with small, shallow cups. Yellow cultivars include 'Pipit' (fades to ivory), 'Quail' (bronzy yellow), 'Suzy', 'Sweetness', and 'Trevithian'. 'Bell Song' is pale ivory with pale pink cup.

Tazetta and Tazetta hybrids. Hardy to only about 10°F/−12°C, but excellent for forcing indoors in winter. These are polyanthus or bunch-flowered daffodils with small-cupped white and yellow flowers in clusters. Good forcing varieties include 'Geranium', paperwhite narcissus, and *N. tazetta* 'Orientalis' (Chinese sacred lilies). These, along with 'Cragford' (white, scarlet cup) and 'Grand Soleil d'Or' (golden yellow), can be grown indoors in bowls of pebbles and water. Keep dark and cool until growth is well along, then slowly bring into light. Hardier varieties to grow outdoors in warmest zones include 'Hoopoe' and 'St. Agnes'.

Poeticus narcissus. POET'S NARCISSUS. Late, white, fragrant flowers with shallow, broad, yellow cups edged red. 'Actaea' is largest; 'Cantabile' is fragrant, with white petals and green cup edged in yellow and red.

Species, varieties, and hybrids. Many species and their varieties and hybrids delight the collector. Most are small; some are true miniatures for rock gardens or very small containers.

N. asturiensis. Very early miniature trumpet flowers on 3-in. stems. Usually sold as *N.* 'Minimus'.

N. bulbocodium conspicuus. HOOP PETTICOAT DAFFODIL. Zones 31, 32, 34−41. To 6 in. tall, with little, upward-facing flowers that are mostly trumpet, with very narrow, pointed segments. Deep and pale yellow varieties.

N. cyclamineus. Zones 31, 32, 34−41. Backward-curved lemon yellow segments and narrow, tubular golden cup; 6 in. high.

N. jonquilla. JONQUIL. Cylindrical, rushlike leaves. Clusters of early, very fragrant, golden yellow flowers with short cups.

N. obvallaris (N. pseudonarcissus obvallaris). TENBY DAFFODIL. Miniature 8−10 in. high; upward-facing, golden yellow trumpet flowers in early spring.

N. poeticus recurvus. PHEASANT'S EYE DAFFODIL. Delicate-looking, 10−13 in. tall; large white petals, very small, red-rimmed yellow cup; spicy fragrance; very late blooming.

N. 'Rip Van Winkle' (N. pumulus plenus). Double-flowered, 4−6-in.-tall daffodil with yellow, dandelionlike blooms in early to midspring.

N. telemonous plenus (N. 'Van Sion'). Old-fashioned 12−14-in.-tall selection with pale yellow petals and a golden yellow trumpet filled with smaller petals. Blooms in early spring.

N. triandrus. ANGEL'S TEARS. Clusters of small white or pale yellow flowers on stems to 10 in. Rushlike foliage.

Split-corona daffodils. Cups are split into petal-like segments that spread back against the petals. Sometimes the cup segments are smooth, but cultivars with ruffled segments are also available. Cultivars include 'Bel Canto', with white petals and pale yellow cup; 'Cassata', white petals and lemon yellow cup that fades to white; 'Cum Laude', white petals, peachy yellow cup with green eye and salmon edge; 'Love Call', white petals, orange cup edged yellow; 'Palmares', with white petals and an apricot pink cup; and 'Printal', white petals, yellow-edged cup fading to white with yellow edge.

N

Miscellaneous. This group serves as a catch-all for a variety of new flower forms. Typical are 'Baccarat', light yellow with deeper yellow corona cut into six equal lobes; and 'Cassata', white with ivory split corona, the segments of which lie flat along the petals.

Miniature daffodils from various divisions. Not a narcissus division, these are miniature cultivars from various divisions: 'Baby Moon', fragrant, yellow; 'Chit Chat', yellow; 'Hawera', pale yellow with recurved petals; 'Minnow', fragrant, white petals, yellow cup; 'Segovia', white petals, small yellow cup; 'Sun Disc', rounded, overlapping petals, yellow with darker cup; 'Tete-a-Tete', yellow petals, yellow-orange cup, good for forcing.

NASTURTIUM. See TROPAEOLUM

NATAL IVY. See SENECIO macroglossus

NAVELWORT. See OMPHALODES

NEANTHE bella. See CHAMAEDOREA elegans

NECTARINE. See PEACH and NECTARINE

NEEDLE GRASS. See STIPA

NEEDLE PALM. See RAPHIDOPHYLLUM hystrix

NEILLIA

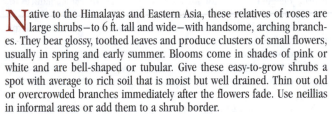

Rosaceae

DECIDUOUS SHRUBS

⚡ ZONES 31, 32, 34, 39

☼ ◐ FULL SUN TO PARTIAL SHADE

🔴 REGULAR WATER

Neillia

Native to the Himalayas and Eastern Asia, these relatives of roses are large shrubs—to 6 ft. tall and wide—with handsome, arching branches. They bear glossy, toothed leaves and produce clusters of small flowers, usually in spring and early summer. Blooms come in shades of pink or white and are bell-shaped or tubular. Give these easy-to-grow shrubs a spot with average to rich soil that is moist but well drained. Thin out old or overcrowded branches immediately after the flowers fade. Use neillias in informal areas or add them to a shrub border.

N. affinis. A species native to western China bearing dense, nodding, 3 ½-in.-long clusters of rose pink flowers in spring.

N. sinensis. CHINESE NEILLIA. Native to central China. Clump-forming shrub that spreads by suckers. Peeling brown bark. In late spring and early summer, bears 2½-in.-long clusters of densely packed, pinkish white, ½-in.-long flowers.

N. thibetica. Clump-forming shrub native to western China that spreads by suckers. In early summer, bears rose pink, ⅜-in.-long flowers in arching, 6-in.-long clusters.

NELUMBO (Nelumbium)

LOTUS

Nymphaeaceae

AQUATIC PLANTS

⚡ ALL ZONES

☼ ◐ FULL SUN OR PARTIAL SHADE

🔴 LOCATE IN PONDS, WATER GARDENS

Nelumbo

These are water plants. If you acquire started plants in containers, put them in pond with 8–12 in. of water over soil surface. If you get roots, plant in spring, horizontally, 4 in. deep, in 1–1½-ft.-deep container of fairly rich soil. Place soil surface 8–12 in. under water. Huge round leaves attached at center to leafstalks grow above water level. Large fragrant

flowers, growing above or below leaves, form in summer. Ornamental woody fruit, perforated with holes like a salt shaker, good for dried arrangements. Plants spread and will quickly fill a small pond. In a small pool or pond, plant in containers. Roots should not freeze; where the water may freeze to root level in winter, lift the tubers before the first hard frost and store them in a cool place over winter. Do not let the tubers dry out. Replant in spring when water is warm.

N. lutea (Nelumbium luteum). AMERICAN LOTUS. Similar to following but somewhat smaller in leaf and flower. Flowers are pale yellow. 'Yellow Bird' has wider, more rounded petals than those of the species.

N. nucifera (Nelumbium nelumbo). INDIAN or CHINESE LOTUS. Round leaves, 2 ft. or wider, carried 3–6 ft. above water surface. Pink, 4–10-in.-wide flowers carried singly on stems. Both tubers and seeds are esteemed in Chinese cookery, and the entire plant holds great religious significance for Buddhists. White, rose, and double varieties exist; dwarf forms suitable for pot culture are becoming available. Cultivars include 'Alba' with white flowers, 'Alba Striata', white flowers with red edges; 'Baby Doll', dwarf, excellent for tubs, small white flowers; 'Ben Gibson', long-lasting bicolored blossoms, yellow at the base, tipped pink; 'Chawan Basu', pink-and-cream flowers; 'Debbie Gibson', large, abundant, creamy white flowers; 'Pekinensis Rubra', flowers rosy red at first, aging to deep pink; 'Perry's Giant Sunburst', abundant, large, creamy white flowers on tall stems; 'Rosea Plena', double, deep rose pink.

NEMESIA

Scrophulariaceae

ANNUALS

⚡ ALL ZONES; BEST IN COOL WEATHER

☼ FULL SUN

🔴 REGULAR WATER

Nemesia

These South African natives are riotously colorful but somewhat touchy about weather—they don't like frost or heat. To enjoy a longer bloom season, remove fading flowers. Water during dry weather. Use as bedding plants, rock garden plants, in hanging baskets, as bulb covers.

N. caerulea (N. fruticans). Tender perennial grown as annual. Upright or spreading, to 2 ft. high; lance-shaped leaves. In summer, clusters of lavender blue, blue, or white flowers with yellow throats borne at tips of stems. 'White Innocence' has white flowers.

N. strumosa. The wild species reaches 1½ ft. high, but plants sold under this name are usually more compact hybrids between *N. strumosa* and *N. versicolor*. Hybrids include all colors except green, as well as bicolors such as 'Mello Red and White' and blue-and-white 'KLM'. Several strains are available in mixed colors. All types bear small flowers in clusters up to 4 in. wide; blossoms are cup shaped, with an enlarged lower lip.

N. versicolor. Resembles *N. strumosa*, but color range contains more blue, yellow, and white. Flowers of 'Blue Gem' are a rich pure blue with a white center.

NEMOPHILA

BABY BLUE EYES

Hydrophyllaceae

ANNUALS

⚡ ALL ZONES; BEST IN COOL WEATHER

☼ ◐ FULL SUN OR PARTIAL SHADE

🔴 REGULAR WATER

Nemophila

Native to western U.S. Trailing plants 6–12 in. high, with bell-shaped flowers to 1 in. across. Pale green, hairy, fernlike foliage gives plants a delicate appearance. Often used as low cover for bulb beds. Broadcast seed as soon as ground is workable in spring. Quickly killed by heat and humidity. Will reseed in favorable conditions (cool, moist weather).

N. maculata. FIVE-SPOT NEMOPHILA. Flowers are white with fine purple lines; one large purple spot appears near tip of each of the five lobes.

N. menziesii (*N. insignis*). BABY BLUE EYES. Blooms as freely in gardens as in the wild, bearing sky blue blossoms with a whitish center. Two unusual color forms are 'Snow Storm' (*N. m. atomaria*), with white flowers liberally dotted with black spots; and 'Pennie Black' (*N. m. discoidalis*), with blackish purple flowers rimmed in white.

NEPETA

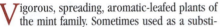

Lamiaceae (Labiatae)
PERENNIALS
▧ ZONES 32, 34–43, EXCEPT AS NOTED
☼ ◐ AFTERNOON SHADE IN HOT CLIMATES
◔ MODERATE WATER

Nepeta

Vigorous, spreading, aromatic-leafed plants of the mint family. Sometimes used as a substitute for lavender in cold-winter climates. Will tolerate regular moisture if soil is well drained.

N. cataria. CATNIP. To 2–3 ft. high, with downy gray-green leaves and clustered lavender or white flowers at branch tips in late spring, early summer. Easy grower in light soil; reseeds readily. Attractive to cats; some fall into a rapturous frenzy, rolling wildly on the plants. Sprinkle dried leaves over cats' food or sew some into toy cloth mouse. Some people use catnip to flavor tea.

N. faassenii. CATMINT. Makes soft, gray-green, undulating mounds to 1½ ft. high in bloom. The small aromatic leaves (like those of catnip) are attractive to cats, who enjoy nibbling foliage and rolling in plantings. Loose spikes of lavender blue flowers in late spring, early summer. If dead spikes prove unsightly, shear them back; this may bring on another bloom cycle. Set 1–1½ ft. apart for ground cover. Often sold as *N. mussinii.* 'Dropmore Hybrid' is taller than the species (to 2 ft.); 'Six Hills Giant' is taller still (2–3 ft.).

N. hederacea. See *Glechoma hederacea*

N. nervosa. Zones 31, 32, 34–41. Bushy and upright, less sprawling than *N. faassenii*. Medium green, lance-shaped leaves are slightly scented. Slender spikes of purple-blue flowers in midsummer to early autumn.

N. sibirica. Dark green clump to 2–3 ft. high, topped by 10-in. spikes of bright blue flowers in early summer. 'Souvenir d'Andre Chaudron' ('Blue Beauty'), larger flowered than the species, is a compact grower to 1½ ft. high.

NERIUM oleander

OLEANDER
Apocynaceae
EVERGREEN SHRUB
▧ ALL ZONES
☼ BEST IN HEAT AND STRONG LIGHT
◔ ◑ REGULAR TO LITTLE WATER
◆ ALL PARTS ARE POISONOUS IF INGESTED

Nerium oleander

Thrive where summers are warm and winters mild (plants are hardy to 15°F/−9°C). In the Northeast, grow in a large pot moved outdoors in summer and indoors over winter. Moderate to fast growth; most varieties grow about 6 ft. tall in a container. Ordinarily broad and bulky but easily trained into single- or multitrunked tree. Narrow, 4–12-in.-long leaves are dark green, leathery, and glossy, attractive in all seasons; a form with golden variegation is sometimes available.

Flowers 2–3 in. across, clustered at twig or branch ends, from mid- to late spring continuing into autumn. Many varieties are fragrant. Forms with double and single flowers are sold; colors range from white to shades of yellow, pink, salmon, and red. Varieties suitable for large containers

include the following: 'Sister Agnes', single white, is most vigorous grower; 'Mrs. Roeding', double salmon pink; 'Hawaii', single salmon pink flowers that drop cleanly.

Cultivars to grow in medium containers include: 'Algiers', deep red; 'Casa Blanca', white; 'Little Red, bright red; 'Marrakesh', red; 'Morocco', white; 'Peachblossom', fragrant, pink; 'Petite Pink', pink; 'Petite Salmon', salmon; 'Ruby Lace', bright red, with wavy-edged individual flowers; and 'Tangier', soft pink.

Oleanders need little water once established, but can take more. Provide a porous, all-purpose potting mix.

Prune in early spring to control size and form. Cut out old wood that has flowered. To restrict height, pinch remaining tips or prune them back lightly. To prevent bushiness at base, pull (don't cut) unwanted suckers.

Caution children against eating leaves or flowers; keep prunings, dead leaves away from hay or other animal feed; don't use wood for barbecue fires or skewers. Smoke from burning prunings can cause severe irritation.

NEVIUSIA alabamensis

SNOW WREATH
Rosaceae
DECIDUOUS SHRUB
▧ ZONES 31, 32, 34–41
☼ ◐ LIGHT SHADE OR FULL SUN
◔ MINIMAL TO SLIGHTLY LESS THAN REGULAR WATER

Neviusia alabamensis

This Alabama native is surprisingly hardy throughout much of New England, and grows 3–6 ft. high. Double-toothed, oval leaves. Attractive and unusual 1-in. white flowers comprised of many conspicuous stamens bloom in summer. Produces hard fruit that contains a single stone. Versatile in beds, borders, and on the margins of woodlands in well-drained and slightly dry soil that is moderately fertile. Prune only old and weak growth after flowers fade.

NEW JERSEY TEA. See CEANOTHUS americanus

NEW ZEALAND FLAX. See PHORMIUM

NEW ZEALAND SPINACH. See SPINACH, New Zealand

NICANDRA physaloides

SHOO-FLY PLANT, APPLE OF PERU
Solanaceae
ANNUAL
▧ ALL ZONES
☼ FULL SUN
◔ REGULAR WATER

Nicandra physaloides

This sturdy, many-branched, 4-ft.-tall plant produces 4-in.-long leaves with wavy edges and white-throated, pale violet-blue flowers in summer and early fall. Each bell-shaped bloom measures more than 1 in. across and lasts for just one day. 'Violacea' has white-centered violet-blue blooms, deep violet stems, and leaves covered with tiny violet hairs. Small, round, applelike fruits in lantern-shaped enclosures follow the flowers. Frequently found in old-fashioned southern gardens, this native of Peru is sometimes used to repel flies. Perfect in cottage gardens, wild gardens, beds and borders. Branches with ornamental fruit can be dried for flower arrangements.

Grows in ordinary garden soil with no special treatment. Start plants from seed 8 weeks before moving them into the garden, or sow outside for later flowering. Space plants 2 ft. apart. Plants may self-sow.

NICOTIANA

Solanaceae

TENDER PERENNIALS GROWN AS ANNUALS

☒ ALL ZONES

☀ ☽ FULL SUN OR PARTIAL SHADE

🌢 REGULAR WATER

⬧ ALL PARTS ARE POISONOUS IF INGESTED

Nicotiana

Upright-growing plants with slightly sticky leaves and stems. Usually grown for their fragrant flowers, which often open at night or on cloudy days; some kinds open during daytime. Flowers tubular, usually flaring at ends into five pointed lobes; grow near top of branched stems in summer. Large, soft, oval leaves. Some kinds reseed readily.

N. alata (N. affinis). Wild species is a 2–3-ft. plant with large, very fragrant white flowers that open toward evening. Seed is available. Selection and hybridization with other species have produced many garden strains that stay open day and night and come in colors ranging from white through pink to red (including lime green), but scent is barely noticeable in many.

Domino strain grows to 12–15 in. and has upward-facing flowers that can take heat and sun better than taller kinds. Nicki strain is taller (to 15–18 in.). The older Sensation strain is taller still (to 4 ft.) and looks more at home in informal mixed borders than as a bedding plant. Fragrance is erratic. If scent (especially during evening) is important, plant 'Grandiflora'.

N. langsdorffii. To 3–6 ft. tall. The branching stems are hung with drooping, inch-long, tubular light green flowers. No noticeable scent. Excellent for cutting.

N. sylvestris. To 5 ft. Intensely fragrant, long, tubular white flowers grow in tiers atop a statuesque plant. Striking in a night garden.

NIEREMBERGIA

CUP FLOWER

Solanaceae

PERENNIALS GROWN AS ANNUALS

☒ ALL ZONES

☀ FULL SUN

🌢 REGULAR WATER

Nierembergia

Flowers are tubular but flare into saucerlike or bell-like cups. Plant form varies by species, but all are covered with blooms during summer. Grow as annuals.

N. frutescens (N. scoparia). Shrubby plant to 1½ ft. high and 1 ft. wide. Narrow leaves to 2 in. long. Flowers are light blue fading to white at the edges, produced in midsummer to early autumn.

N. hippomanica violacea (N. h. caerulea). DWARF CUP FLOWER. Grows 6–12 in. high. Much-branched mounded plant, with very small, stiff leaves. Flowers are blue to violet. 'Purple Robe' is common variety. 'Mont Blanc' bears white flowers.

N. repens (N. rivularis). WHITE CUP. Prostrate 4–6-in. mat of bright green leaves. Blooms are white. For best performance, don't crowd it with more aggressive plants. Not as heat tolerant as dwarf cup flower.

FOR INFORMATION ON SELECTING PLANTS

PLEASE SEE PAGES 47–112

NIGELLA damascena

LOVE-IN-A-MIST

Ranunculaceae

ANNUAL

☒ ALL ZONES

☀ ☽ FULL SUN OR PARTIAL SHADE

🌢 REGULAR WATER

Nigella damascena

Branching to 1–1½ ft. high. All leaves, even those that form under collar beneath each flower, are finely cut into threadlike divisions. Blue, white, or rose flowers, 1–1½ in. across, are borne singly at ends of branches in spring. Curious papery-textured, horned seed capsules lend airiness to bouquets or mixed borders, are very decorative in dried bouquets. 'Miss Jekyll', with semidouble cornflower blue blossoms, is an outstanding variety; 'Miss Jekyll Alba' has white flowers; 'Persian Jewels' is a superior strain in mixed colors.

Plants come into bloom quickly in spring and dry up in summer heat. Sow seed on open ground where plants are to grow; long taproot makes transplanting unsatisfactory. Seed as soon as ground is workable after last frost. Self-sows freely.

NINEBARK. See PHYSOCARPUS

NODDING LADIES TRESSES ORCHID. See SPIRANTHES

NOLANA paradoxa

CHILEAN BELLFLOWER

Nolanaceae

TENDER PERENNIAL GROWN AS ANNUAL

☒ ALL ZONES

☀ FULL SUN

🌢 LESS THAN REGULAR WATER

Nolana paradoxa

This trailing plant, a South American native, bears prolific, 2-in.-wide blossoms similar to morning glories. The flowers open in sunlight and are deep blue with white throats and yellow interiors. Plants grow 4 in.–1 ft. high and thrive in poor, dry soil. Purple-streaked stems can be more than 1 ft. long. Leaves are about 1 in. long. *N. p. alba* and 'Snowbird' have white flowers; *N. p. violacea* has violet flowers; 'Blue Bird' is white-centered deep blue. A drought-tolerant choice for hanging baskets, window boxes, urns, edging, slopes, bedding, and rock and seaside gardens. Plant 6 in. apart after last frost in lean, sandy soil.

Nyctaginaceae. The four o'clock family includes annuals, perennials, shrubs, and vines with showy flowers or bracts. An example is four o'clock (*Mirabilis jalapa*).

NYMPHAEA

WATER LILY

Nymphaeaceae

AQUATIC PLANTS

☒ ALL ZONES

☀ PRODUCE FLOWERS IN SUN

🌢 LOCATE IN PONDS, WATER GARDENS

Nymphaea

Leaves float and are rounded, with deep notch at one side where leaf stalk is attached. Showy flowers either float on surface or stand above it on stiff stalks. Cultivated water lilies are largely hybrids that cannot be traced back to exact parentage. There are hardy and tropical types. Hardy kinds come in white, yellow, copper, pink, and red. Tropical types add blue and purple; recent introductions include an unusual greenish blue. Some tropicals in the white-pink-red color range are night bloomers; all others close at night. Many are fragrant.

When you buy water lilies, choose selections suitable for the depth of your pond; consult your supplier.

Hardy kinds are easiest for beginners. Plant them April–July. Set 6-in.-long pieces of rhizome on soil at pool bottom or in boxes, placing rhizome in nearly horizontal position with bud end up. In either case, top of soil should be 8–12 in. below surface of water. Enrich soil with 1 lb. of complete dry fertilizer (3–5 percent nitrogen) for each lily. Groom plants by removing spent leaves and blooms. They usually bloom throughout warm weather and go dormant in fall, then reappear in spring. In very cold areas, protect by covering pond or filling it deeper with water. Where water is likely to freeze to the bottom, lift and store indoors in cool location over winter.

Tropical kinds begin to grow and bloom later in summer but last longer, often up to first frost. Buy started tropical plants and set at same depth as hardy rhizomes. Tropical types go dormant but do not survive really low winter temperatures. Lift and store dormant tubers in damp sand over winter or buy new plants each year.

Nymphaeaceae. The water lily family consists of aquatic plants, usually with floating leaves and flowers. Two examples are lotus *(Nelumbo)* and water lily *(Nymphaea)*.

Nyssaceae. Deciduous trees from Asia and North America. Examples include sour gum *(Nyssa)* and dove tree *(Davidia)*.

NYSSA sylvatica

SOUR GUM, BLACK GUM, TUPELO, PEPPERIDGE

Nyssaceae

DECIDUOUS TREE

⚡ ZONES 31, 32, 34–43

☀ ◐ FULL SUN OR PARTIAL SHADE

💧 ◐ REGULAR TO MODERATE WATER

Nyssa sylvatica

Native to eastern U.S. Slow to moderate growth to 30–50 ft. or more, spreading to 20–30 ft. Pyramidal when young; spreading, irregular, and rugged in age. Crooked branches and dark bark make dramatic picture against winter sky. Dark green, glossy, 2–5-in.-long leaves emerge rather late in spring. Plants have separate sexes. Both male and female trees bear inconspicuous flowers; females will bear fruit if a male is growing nearby (though males sometimes set some fruit as well). Fruits are bluish black, shaped like small olives; birds like them. In autumn, leaves turn yellow and orange, then bright red before dropping. This is among the best native trees for consistent, blazing fall color.

Prefers moist, deep, well-drained, acid soil, but tolerates poor drainage, some drought. Does not thrive in polluted air. Excellent specimen or shade tree; very attractive in naturalized landscapes. Select a permanent location, since this tree's taproot makes it difficult to move later on.

N. aquatica, water tupelo, is similar, but has larger leaves and fruits. It grows in areas subject to flooding.

OAK. See QUERCUS

OAT GRASS, BLUE. See HELICTOTRICHON sempervirens

OAT GRASS, BULBOUS. See ARRHENATHERUM elatius bulbosum 'Variegatum'

OCIMUM basilicum

SWEET BASIL

Lamiaceae (Labiatae)

ANNUAL HERB

⚡ ALL ZONES

☀ FULL SUN

💧 REGULAR WATER

Ocimum basilicum

Somewhat bushy plant to 2 ft. tall, with green, shiny, 1–2-in.-long leaves and spikes of white flowers. Forms with purple or variegated leaves have purple flowers. Most popular basil for cooking. Used fresh or dry, it gives a pleasant, sweet, mild flavor to tomatoes, cheese, eggs, seafood, salads. There is a small-leafed dwarf kind that thrives in containers.

'Dark Opal', with large, dark purple bronze leaves and small lavender pink flowers, is attractive enough for borders and mass plantings; especially pleasing with dusty millers or 'Carpet of Snow' sweet alyssum. It grows 1–1½ ft. high, about 1 ft. wide. Other good purple-leafed varieties include 'Red Rubin', uniform dark color; and 'Purple Ruffles', deeply fringed and ruffled leaf edges.

Sow seeds of any basil in early spring; make successive sowings 2 weeks apart to have replacements for the short-lived older plants. Or set transplants out after last frost. Space plants 10–12 in. apart. Fertilize once during growing season with complete fertilizer. Keeping flower spikes pinched out will prevent seeding and subsequent death of plant.

OCONEE BELLS. See SHORTIA galacifolia

OENANTHE javanica

Apiaceae

PERENNIAL

⚡ ZONES 31, 32, 34–43

☀ FULL SUN

💧 MORE THAN REGULAR WATER

Oenanthe javanica

Spreads horizontally to 3 ft. and will grow to 16 in. high. Attractive dense foliage resembles the leaves of celery and grows to 6 in. long. Small, white, star-shaped flowers appear in clusters in summer. 'Flamingo' features leaves that are variegated pink, cream, and white. Suitable near the margins of pools or streams. Prefers moist and moderately fertile soil, but will also tolerate a dry location if shady. Site carefully; plant spreads rapidly.

OENOTHERA

EVENING PRIMROSE

Onagraceae

PERENNIALS

⚡ ZONES VARY BY SPECIES

☀ ◐ EXPOSURE NEEDS VARY BY SPECIES

💧 MODERATE WATER

Oenothera

Valued for showy, four-petaled, silky flowers in bright yellow, pink, or white. Some types display their blossoms during the day, but others open in late afternoon and close the following morning. Carefree plants that grow in tough, rough places. Can withstand light shade.

O. fruticosa (O. tetragona). SUNDROPS. Zones 31, 32, 34–45. Grows to 2 ft. high, spreading vigorously. Reddish stems and bright green foliage. Daytime display of 1½-in. bright yellow flowers all summer.

Thrives in full sun or light shade. Leaves of 'Summer Solstice' turn purplish red in autumn. 'Fireworks', 1½ ft. high, has brownish-tinted leaves, red stems, and red flower buds.

O. macrocarpa (O. missouriensis). Zones 34–37, 39, 41. Prostrate, sprawling stems to 10 in. long. Soft, velvety, 5-in. leaves. Blooms in late spring and summer, bearing bright yellow, 3–5-in.-wide flowers that open in the afternoon. Large winged seedpods follow the flowers. Best in full sun. Showy plant for rock garden or front of border.

O. speciosa. MEXICAN EVENING PRIMROSE. Zones 31, 32, 34–41. Often sold as *O. berlandieri* or *O. speciosa childsii*. Grows 10–12 in. high, with profuse showing of 1½-in. rose pink blooms in summer; flowers open in daytime, despite plant's common name. Stems die back after bloom. Spreads rapidly by underground stems and can invade other plantings. Full sun. 'Alba' is a white-flowered form; 'Woodside White' opens white but ages to pale pink; 'Siskiyou' is an especially vigorous, long-blooming variety with 2-in. light pink blossoms.

OKRA

Malvaceae

ANNUAL

☘ ALL ZONES

☼ FULL SUN

🔴 REGULAR WATER

Warm-season annual vegetable that grows well under same conditions as sweet corn. Plant when ground has warmed to 70°F/21°C. Soak seed 24 hours before planting to speed germination. Fertilize at least once in spring. Allow 50 to 60 days from planting to harvest. Pods grow on large, erect, bushy plants with tropical-looking leaves. Harvest pods every 2 or 3 days. Best size is 1–3 in. long; over-ripe pods are tough, and they shorten plant's bearing life. In containers, variety 'Red River' has tropical look. In large tub in warm spot, a single plant can yield enough to make it worth growing.

Okra

Oleaceae. The olive family includes about 900 species of trees and shrubs with opposite leaves and flower parts usually in fours. Typical members include privet *(Ligustrum)* and lilac *(Syringa)*.

OLEANDER. See NERIUM oleander

OMPHALODES

NAVELWORT

Boraginaceae

PERENNIALS

☘ ZONES VARY BY SPECIES

◑ LIGHT SHADE

🔴 REGULAR WATER

Omphalodes

A genus of perennials, biennials, and annuals from a variety of habitats in Asia, Europe, and northern Africa. They produce blue or white flowers and are related to forget-me-nots, which they resemble somewhat. Most species are shade plants, used in woodland gardens or shady rock gardens.

O. cappadocica. NAVELWORT. Zones 31, 32, 34, 39. Spreads by rhizomes to form clumps to 10 in. high, 16 in. across. Basal clump of oval to heart-shaped, medium green leaves covered with fine hairs. In early spring, clusters of small flowers, blue with white eye, bloom atop slender stems. 'Cherry Ingram' is a more compact plant with larger flowers of deeper blue. 'Starry Eyes', larger flowers with bluish white stripe at margin of every petal.

O. verna. BLUE-EYED MARY. Zones 31, 32, 34–41. Spreads slowly to become a small-scale ground cover to 8 in. high.. The 2-in. leaves are evergreen in milder parts of range. Spring flowers, ½ in. wide, are intense pure blue with a tiny white eye. Tolerates drought. 'Alba' has white flowers. 'Grandiflora' has blue flowers somewhat larger than those of the species.

Onagraceae. Most members of the evening primrose family have flower parts in fours, but otherwise are diverse in appearance and structure. They include *Clarkia, Fuchsia, Gaura,* and evening primrose *(Oenothera).*

ONION

Liliaceae

BIENNIAL GROWN AS ANNUAL

☘ ALL ZONES

☼ FULL SUN

🔴 REGULAR WATER

Onion

Grow onions from seed or sets (small bulbs). Sets are easiest for beginners, though seed gives larger crop for smaller investment and offers more choices in varieties. Planting can begin in early spring, as soon as soil is workable. Soil should be loose, rich, and well drained. Push sets just under soil surface so that point of bulb is visible; space a little wider than bulb size at maturity (closer if you want to harvest some as green onions). Sow seed ¼ in. deep, in rows 15–18 in. apart. Sow seed in early spring. When seedlings are pencil size, thin to same spacing as for sets, transplanting thinnings to extend planting. Trim back tops of transplants about halfway. In some areas, onion plants (field-grown, nearly pencil-size transplants or seedlings growing in pots) are available.

Onions are shallow rooted and need moisture fairly near the surface. Feed plants, especially early in season: the larger and stronger the plants grow, the larger the bulbs they form. Carefully eliminate weeds that compete for light, food, and water. When most of the tops have begun to yellow and fall over, dig bulbs and let them cure and dry on top of ground for several days. Then pull off tops, clean, and store in dark, cool, airy place.

Varieties differ in bulb size, shape, color, flavor, and storage life. Also keep in mind that onions form bulbs in response to day length. If you choose a type inappropriate for your area, it may make small premature bulbs or not bulb up at all. Long-day varieties need 14 to 16 hours of daylight and are grown in northern climates. They tend to be pungent and store well; examples are 'Early Yellow Globe', 'Ebenezer', 'Ruby', 'Southport White Globe', 'Sweet Spanish'. Short-day varieties, such as 'Vidalia', require 10 to 12 hours of daylight and are grown in southernmost climes. Intermediate-day types, requiring 12 to 14 hours of daylight, are suited to all growing areas; examples are 'Autumn Spice', 'Red Torpedo', 'Ringmaker'.

For ornamental relatives, see *Allium.*

ONOCLEA sensibilis

SENSITIVE FERN

Polypodiaceae

FERN

☘ ZONES 31, 32, 34–43

☼ FULL SUN

🔴🔴 MOIST TO WET SOIL

Onoclea sensibilis

Native to eastern U.S. Coarse-textured fern with 2–4-ft. sterile fronds divided nearly to midrib; fertile fronds smaller, with clusters of almost beadlike leaflets. Fronds come from underground creeping rhizome that can be invasive. Dies to the ground in winter. Fronds seem coarse to many gardeners, but fern is useful for planting along streams and ponds. Takes regular moisture, but won't be as big as in wetter conditions. Called sensitive fern because it is among the first plants to show frost damage in fall.

ONOPORDUM acanthium

COTTON THISTLE, SCOTCH THISTLE

Asteraceae

BIENNIAL

✹ ZONES 31, 32, 34–41

☀ FULL SUN

🌢 REGULAR WATER

Onopordum acanthium

Bees and butterflies are drawn to striking purple or white thistle flower heads 2 in. across, which bloom on stalks that branch like candelabra. Spiny gray-green leaves covered with soft hair can reach 14 in. long on massive, winged and woolly yellowish stems. Grows to 10 ft. tall in neutral or slightly alkaline soil and will self-sow. Best in large informal or stony gardens.

OPHIOPOGON. See LIRIOPE and OPHIOPOGON

OPUNTIA compressa (O. humifusa)

PRICKLY PEAR

Cactaceae

CACTUS

✹ ZONES 31, 32, 34–41

☀ FULL SUN

🌢 MODERATE TO LITTLE WATER

Opuntia compressa

Several species, including this one, are native to the northern U.S. and Canada. Though perfectly hardy in the coldest winters, they need excellent drainage to survive winter freezes and thaws; best grown in raised beds. These species are not easy to identify because of frequent name changes by botanists. Small, clump-forming plants to 1 ft. high and 3 ft. wide. Stems made up of jointed, flat, oval to rounded green pads, sometimes purple-tinged with brown spines. Showy, bright yellow flowers to 2½ in. across in late spring and summer, followed by edible red or purple fruit.

ORANGE CLOCK VINE. See THUNBERGIA gregorii

OREGANO. See ORIGANUM vulgare

OREGON GRAPE. See MAHONIA aquifolium

ORIENTAL ARBORVITAE. See PLATYCLADUS orientalis

ORIENTAL GARLIC. See ALLIUM tuberosum

ORIENTAL POPPY. See PAPAVER orientale

FOR INFORMATION ON SELECTING PLANTS

PLEASE SEE PAGES 47–112

ORIGANUM

Lamiaceae (Labiatae)

PERENNIALS

✹ ZONES VARY BY SPECIES

☀ FULL SUN

🌢 MODERATE TO LITTLE WATER, EXCEPT AS NOTED

Origanum

Mint relatives with tight clusters of small flowers and foliage with a strong, pleasant scent. Bracts in flower clusters overlap, giving effect of small pinecones. Not fussy about soil type.

O. dictamnus (Amaracus dictamnus). DITTANY OF CRETE. All zones; tender perennial grown as an annual. Native to Mediterranean area. Aromatic herb with slender, arching stems to 1 ft. long. Thick, roundish, somewhat mottled, woolly white leaves to ¾ in. long. Flowers pink to purplish, ½ in. long; rose purple fruit in conelike heads. Blooms summer to fall. Shows up best when planted individually in rock garden, container, or hanging basket.

O. 'Kent Beauty'. Zones 31, 32, 34–41. Ornamental hybrid, evergreen and shrubby, to just 4 in. high. Bright green leaves and showy pink to purple flowers and pink bracts. Needs good drainage.

O. laevigatum. Zones 32, 34. Sprawling, arching plant, with stems rooting at joints; bears branching clusters of purple flowers. 'Herrenhausen' has lilac pink flowers and purplish leaves in cool weather; 'Hopley's' has large heads of deep purplish pink flowers. Useful in dry gardens as bank or ground cover.

O. majorana (Majorana hortensis). SWEET MARJORAM. All zones; tender perennial grown as annual. To 1–2 ft. Small, oval gray-green leaves; spikes of white flowers in loose clusters at top of plant. Grow in fairly moist soil. Keep blossoms cut off and plant trimmed to prevent woody growth. Propagate from seeds, cuttings, or root divisions. It's a favorite herb for seasoning meats, salads, vinegars. Use leaves fresh or dried. Often grown in container indoors on window sill in cold-winter areas.

O. onites. POT MARJORAM. All zones, tender perennial grown as annual. To 2 ft. tall and as broad, with bright green aromatic leaves and flattish heads of tiny white or purplish flowers. Sometimes called Cretan oregano.

O. vulgare. OREGANO, WILD MARJORAM. Zones 31, 32, 34–45. Upright growth to 2½ ft. Spreads by underground stems. Medium-size oval leaves; purplish pink blooms. Grow in medium rich soil; needs good drainage. Keep trimmed to prevent flowering. Replant every 3 years. Fresh or dried leaves are used in many dishes, especially Italian and Spanish ones. 'Compactum' is a few inches tall, spreads widely, and seldom flowers. It can be used as a ground cover. 'Aureum' has gold leaves and pink flowers; 'Aureum Crispum', curly golden leaves, spreading habit. *O. v. hirtum*, Greek oregano, is stronger flavored than the species.

THE BEST OREGANO

Oreganos are confusing, and they're not always labeled correctly. If you want to grow oregano to use in cooking, you may want to avoid the common species, *Origanum vulgare*, in favor of the zestier Greek oregano. To be sure of getting the best flavor, buy plants locally and brush a leaf with your finger to sample the scent before making your purchase.

ORNAMENTAL GRAPE. See VITIS

ORNAMENTAL PEAR. See PYRUS

ORNAMENTAL PEPPER. See CAPSICUM annuum

O

ORNAMENTAL STRAWBERRY. See FRAGARIA

ORNITHOGALUM

Liliaceae

BULBS

🌡 ALL ZONES; DIG AND STORE; OR GROW IN POTS

☼ FULL SUN

💧 WATER NEEDS VARY BY SPECIES

🔹 ALL PARTS, ESPECIALLY BULB, ARE POISONOUS IF INGESTED

Ornithogalum

Leaves vary from narrow to broad and tend to be floppy. Flowers mostly star shaped, in tall or rounded clusters, appearing in late spring or early summer. Use in borders. Bulbs can be lifted and stored during winter; or they can be grown in pots and protected.

O. arabicum. STAR OF BETHLEHEM. Handsome clusters of 2-in., white, waxy flowers with beady black pistils in centers. Stems 2 ft. tall. Floppy bluish green leaves to 2 ft. long, 1 in. wide. In cool-summer climates, bulbs may not bloom second year after planting because they lacked sufficient heat. In-ground planting best in dry-summer areas. Excellent cut flower. Moderate water.

O. thyrsoides. CHINCHERINCHEE. Tapering, compact clusters of white, 2-in. flowers with brownish green centers. Flower stems 2 ft. high. Leaves bright green, upright, to 1 ft. long, 2 in. wide. May survive colder winters if given sheltered southern or southwestern location and protected with mulch. Like *O. arabicum,* best in dry-summer areas. Long-lasting cut flower. Moderate water.

O. umbellatum. STAR OF BETHLEHEM. Zones 31, 32; elsewhere, dig and store or grow in pots. Where hardy, may naturalize once established and become a pest. Clusters of 1-in.-wide flowers, striped green on outside, atop 1-ft. stems. Grasslike leaves about as long as flower stems. Cut flowers last well but close at night. Regular water.

ORONTIUM aquaticum

GOLDEN CLUB

Araceae

AQUATIC PERENNIAL

🌡 ZONES 31, 32, 34–41

☼ FULL SUN

💧 AMPLE WATER

Orontium aquaticum

This easy-to-grow native of the eastern U.S. reaches 1–1½ ft. tall. Oval to elliptical blue-green leaves are about 1 ft. long, with silvery undersides. Abundant, 4-in. white flower spikes topped with dozens of small golden flowers in spring are short-lived. Depending on planting depth, leaves may be submerged, floating, or held above the water surface. A highly attractive plant for bog gardens and the margins of ponds and pools, it should be given ample room for its thick rhizomes to spread. Plant in mud at the water's edge, or in large containers of heavy garden loam. For leaves to float, plant at least 1 ft. deep.

OSAGE ORANGE. See MACLURA pomifera

FOR GROWING SYMBOL EXPLANATIONS

PLEASE SEE PAGE 113

OSMANTHUS

Oleaceae

EVERGREEN SHRUBS

🌡 ZONES VARY BY SPECIES

☼ ☼ FULL SUN OR PARTIAL SHADE

💧 REGULAR TO MODERATE WATER

Osmanthus

All have clean, leathery, attractive foliage and inconspicuous but fragrant flowers. Plants aren't particular about soil; once established, they are fairly drought tolerant. Where plants are not hardy, grow them in pots moved outdoors in summer and indoors over winter.

O. fortunei. Zones 31, warmer parts of 32. Hybrid between *O. heterophyllus* and *O. fragrans*. Slow, dense growth to an eventual 20 ft. tall; often seen at height of about 6 ft. Leaves are oval, hollylike, up to 4 in. long. Small, fragrant white flowers bloom during fall. 'San Jose' is similar but has cream to orange flowers.

O. fragrans. SWEET OLIVE. Zone 31; elsewhere, grow in pots. Moderate growth to 10 ft. and more with age. Broad, dense, compact. Can be trained as small tree, espalier, container plant. Pinch out growing tips of young plants to induce bushiness.

Leaves glossy, medium green, oval, to 4 in. long, toothed or smooth edged. Tiny white flowers have powerful sweet, apricotlike fragrance. Bloom is heaviest in spring and early summer. *O. f. aurantiacus* has narrower, less glossy leaves than the species; its crop of wonderfully fragrant orange flowers is concentrated in early fall.

O. heterophyllus (O. aquifolium, O. ilicifolius). HOLLY-LEAF OSMANTHUS. Zones 31, 32. Grows 8–10 ft. tall (possibly to 20 ft.), with 2½-in., spiny-edged leaves. Resembles English holly, but leaves appear opposite one another on stems. Fragrant white flowers in late fall and winter.

'Goshiki'. Erect plant to 3½ ft. tall, 5 ft. wide. New leaves have pinkish orange markings that mature to yellow variegations on dark green. Flowers few to none.

'Gulftide'. Similar to 'Ilicifolius' but more compact.

'Ilicifolius'. Dense, symmetrical upright growth to 6–8 ft., eventually to 20 ft. Leaves dark green, strongly toothed, hollylike, to 2½ in. long. Fragrant white flowers in fall, winter, early spring.

'Purpureus' ('Purpurascens'). Same growth habit as species. Dark purple new growth, with purple tints through summer.

'Rotundifolius'. Slow growing to 5 ft. Roundish small leaves are lightly spined along edges.

'Variegatus'. Slow growing to 4–5 ft., with densely set leaves edged creamy white. Useful for lighting up shady areas. A bit less cold-tolerant than the species.

OSMUNDA

Osmundaceae

FERNS

🌡 ZONES VARY BY SPECIES

☼ ☼ 💧 EXPOSURE NEEDS VARY BY SPECIES

💧 DAMP TO WET SOIL

Osmunda

Three species of large, coarse, imposing deciduous ferns useful in naturalistic plantings. All like plenty of moisture but can survive with less, responding with smaller, less vigorous growth. Rhizomes have heavy growth of matted brown roots—the source of the osmunda fiber used for potting orchids.

O. cinnamomea. CINNAMON FERN. Zones 32, 34–45. Fern with erect sterile fronds to as tall as 5 ft., arching outward toward the top. Spores are borne on a different sort of frond—narrow, erect, much shorter, turning cinnamon brown as spores ripen. Unfolding young fronds (fiddleheads) are harvested for food. Fronds turn showy yellow to orange in fall. Full or light shade.

O. claytoniana. INTERRUPTED FERN. Zones 32, 34−45. If given ample water, grows as tall as 5 ft., more typically to 3 ft. Shorter in dryish soils. Each frond is "interrupted" in the middle by several short brown spore-bearing segments. Full or light shade.

O. regalis. ROYAL FERN, FLOWERING FERN. Zones 31, 32, 34−45. Large fern (to 6 ft.) with twice-cut fronds, each leaflet quite large. Coarser in texture than most ferns. Tips of fronds have modified segments that somewhat resemble flower buds; these produce the spores. Leaves turn yellow to brown in fall. 'Cristata' has crested fronds; 'Purpurascens' has purplish red new growth and stems that remain purple throughout the season. Light shade, but will thrive in sun in wet soil, even in mud. Especially attractive beside streams or ponds.

OSTEOSPERMUM

AFRICAN DAISY
Asteraceae (Compositae)
ANNUALS
◪ ALL ZONES
☼ FULL SUN
◓ ● REGULAR TO MODERATE WATER

Osteospermum

South African plants closely related to *Dimorphotheca* and often sold as such. Tender perennials treated as summer annuals in the Northeast. Profusion of daisylike flowers open only in sunlight. Medium green, narrowish oval leaves are smooth edged or with a few large teeth, 2−4 in. long. Plants look best with good garden soil and care, but will stand drought and neglect when established. Borders, mass plantings, slopes.

O. barberiae. Grows about 1½ ft. tall. Oblong to lance-shaped leaves to 6 in. long. Magenta flowers with dark purple or yellow centers. 'Lavender Mist', pale lavender.

O. 'Cream Symphony'. Creamy white flowers.

O. ecklonis. Grows 2−4 ft. tall, equally broad. Long stems bear 3-in. flower heads with white rays (tinged lavender blue on backs), dark blue center. Blooms early summer to frost.

O. fruticosum. TRAILING AFRICAN DAISY. Spreads rapidly by trailing, rooting branches. Will cover 2−4-ft. circle in a year; grows 6−12 in. high. Flowers to 2 in. wide, rays lilac above, fading nearly white by second day, deeper lilac beneath and in bud; dark purple center. 'African Queen' and 'Burgundy' have purple blooms. 'Whirlygig' has unusual white-and-blue flower heads with spoon-shaped, white-tipped petals; each petal is pinched in middle to reveal blue underside.

O. 'Lemon Symphony'. Lemon yellow flowers.

OSTRICH FERN. See MATTEUCCIA struthiopteris

OSTRYA

HOP HORNBEAM
Betulaceae
DECIDUOUS TREES
◪ ZONES VARY BY SPECIES
☼ ◑ FULL SUN OR LIGHT SHADE
◓ ● REGULAR TO MODERATE WATER

Ostrya

Hop hornbeams are so named because female flowers and fruit are enclosed in bractlike husks forming 1½−2½-in. clusters that resemble hops. Inch-long male catkins are attractive in winter. Trees are small to medium-size (seldom exceeding 40 ft.), slow growing. Foliage is dark green, turning yellow in fall. Attractive, but little used because of their slow growth—a fault to nurserymen, but a possible advantage to the gardener. Wood is hard, heavy, and dense.

O. carpinifolia. EUROPEAN HOP HORNBEAM. Zones 31, 32, 34, 35, 37, 39. Scarcely differs from the more common American species, *O. virginiana*.

O. japonica. Zones 31, 32, 34−41. Native to Japan and China. Oval to oblong, dark green leaves.

O. virginiana. AMERICAN HOP HORNBEAM, IRONWOOD. Zones 31, 32, 34−43. Native to eastern North America, where it is an understory tree.

OSWEGO TEA. See MONARDA

OXALIS

Oxalidaceae
PERENNIALS; SOME GROW FROM BULBS OR RHIZOMES
◪ ZONES VARY BY SPECIES
☼ ◑ FULL SUN OR LIGHT SHADE, EXCEPT AS NOTED
● REGULAR WATER

Oxalis

Leaves divided into leaflets; usually have three leaflets, like clover leaves. Flowers pink, white, rose, or yellow. Grow non-hardy species in containers in the Northeast; move outdoors in summer (or plant in the ground); grow indoors in winter.

O. acetosella. WOOD SORREL, SHAMROCK. Perennial. Zones 31, 32, 34−45. Low, mat-forming plant to 2 in. high, with three-part leaves and rose pink flowers with dark veins. Grow in rock or woodland garden; tolerates partial to light shade. One of several plants known as shamrock. See Shamrocks.

O. adenophylla. Zones 31, 32; container plant elsewhere. Dense, low (4-in.-high), compact tuft of leaves, each leaf with 12−22 crinkly, gray-green leaflets. Flowers are 1 in. wide, on 4−6-in. stalks, bell shaped, lilac pink with deeper veins, in late spring. Plant roots in fall. Needs good drainage. Good rock garden plant or companion to bulbs such as species tulips or the smaller kinds of narcissus, in pots or in the ground.

O. bowiei. BOWIE OXALIS. All zones. To 10 in. high. Long-stemmed leaves divided into three leaflets, often purple on the underside. Clusters of deep purple-pink flowers in summer.

O hirta. All zones. To 12 in., stems may be upright or drooping. Pale green leaves divided into three narrow to oblong leaflets. Large rose, lilac, or white flowers in autumn and winter.

O. purpurea. All zones. To 6 in. high. Green leaves with three leaflets are often purple on the underside. Pretty flowers of rose pink, violet, or white in autumn and winter.

O. tetraphylla 'Iron Cross' (O. deppei 'Iron Cross'). GOOD LUCK PLANT. All zones in pots. Four-part leaves resemble large four-leaf clover. Each leaflet has a v-shaped purple band at the base; together they form a cross shape in the center of the leaf. Funnel-shaped, purple-pink flowers about 1 in. across. When leaves die back after flowering, gradually withhold water to allow plant to have a dry dormant period.

O. versicolor. All zones in pots. Bulbs give rise to erect or spreading stems up to 6 in. tall. Leaves bear three deeply notched leaflets less than ½ in. wide. Flowers are white, over 1 in. wide, with yellow throat and purplish margins. The variety commonly seen is 'Candy Cane', with white flowers striped red. Striped buds especially colorful. Plant in fall for spring bloom.

OX-EYE. See HELIOPSIS helianthoides

O

OXYDENDRUM arboreum

SOURWOOD, SORREL TREE

Ericaceae

DECIDUOUS TREE

⚡ ZONES 31, 32, 34, 35, 37, 39

☀ FULL SUN

🔴 REGULAR WATER

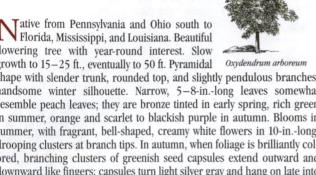

Oxydendrum arboreum

Native from Pennsylvania and Ohio south to Florida, Mississippi, and Louisiana. Beautiful flowering tree with year-round interest. Slow growth to 15–25 ft., eventually to 50 ft. Pyramidal shape with slender trunk, rounded top, and slightly pendulous branches; handsome winter silhouette. Narrow, 5–8-in.-long leaves somewhat resemble peach leaves; they are bronze tinted in early spring, rich green in summer, orange and scarlet to blackish purple in autumn. Blooms in summer, with fragrant, bell-shaped, creamy white flowers in 10-in.-long, drooping clusters at branch tips. In autumn, when foliage is brilliantly colored, branching clusters of greenish seed capsules extend outward and downward like fingers; capsules turn light silver gray and hang on late into winter. 'Chameleon' has especially showy fall foliage changing to red then yellow then lime green.

Grow in moist, acid, well-drained soil. Tolerates some drought, but not urban pollution. Will grow in partial shade, but best flowering and fall color in full sun. Among earliest and best trees for colorful autumn foliage in South. Not competitive; doesn't do well in lawns or under larger trees. Avoid underplanting with anything needing cultivation. Use as specimen in woodland garden, patio shade tree. Young plants make good container subjects.

OXYPETALUM caeruleum. See TWEEDIA caerulea

OYSTER PLANT. See SALSIFY

PACHISTIMA. See PAXISTIMA canbyi

PACHYSANDRA

SPURGE, PACHYSANDRA

Buxaceae

PERENNIAL GROUND COVERS

⚡ ZONES 31, 32, 34–43

◑🔴 LIGHT TO HEAVY SHADE

🔴 REGULAR WATER

Pachysandra

Two species of low-growing shrubby perennials used for ground cover in shady places. Slow but sure spreaders from underground runners, they are invaluable landscape plants. although overused. Hardy to cold; well able to compete with tree roots. Compact growth and clean, attractive foliage are their chief virtues. Flowers are not showy when viewed casually, but look attractive at close range. Provide moist, preferably somewhat acid soil, well amended with organic material. Too much sun causes yellowing foliage and poor growth.

P. procumbens. ALLEGHENY SPURGE, ALLEGHENY PACHYSANDRA. Semievergreen. Not as widely available as the Japanese species below. Grows 6–12 in. high; grayish green leaves are 2–4 in. long and 2–3 in. wide, clustered near top of stem. Leaves often mottled with gray or brownish markings. Small white or pinkish flowers are fragrant. Spreads more slowly than *P. terminalis*.

P. terminalis. JAPANESE SPURGE, JAPANESE PACHYSANDRA. Evergreen. Grows 8–12 in. high. Shiny dark green leaves are 2–4 in. long and ½–1½ in. wide; upper half of leaf has shallowly toothed edges. Small white flowers are borne in 1–2-in. spikes. 'Green Carpet' is shorter and denser in growth than the species, with shinier, deeper green leaves. 'Green Sheen' has especially glossy leaves; 'Silver Edge' ('Variegata') has creamy-edged foliage; fast-spreading 'Cut Leaf' has deeply dissected leaves.

Japanese spurge can stand very heavy shade and is very widely used as a ground cover under trees. Plant 6 in. apart for reasonably quick cover; apply a mulch and keep moist until established. Performs better in northern part of range. Seldom bothered by pests, but a leaf blight can cause serious damage if it gets out of hand; control with fungicides and, if possible, by limiting overhead watering.

PAEONIA

PEONY

Paeoniaceae

PERENNIALS AND DECIDUOUS SHRUBS

⚡ ZONES VARY BY TYPE

☀◐ AFTERNOON SHADE IN HOT CLIMATES

🔴 REGULAR WATER

Paeonia

Although a few species may be found in specialists' lists or in seed exchanges, most garden peonies are hybrids. The two basic types are herbaceous and tree peonies. Herbaceous types die to the ground in late fall; they are mostly descendants of *P. lactiflora*. Tree (actually shrub) peonies flower from permanent woody branches; they are chiefly descendants of *P. suffruticosa*. All peonies are extremely long-lived plants of significant size, demanding more than ordinary care in site preparation. In return, they can provide outstanding garden beauty for as long as you live.

Herbaceous peonies are planted in fall (preferably) or earliest spring as bare-root plants: compact rhizomes with several "eyes" (growth buds) and thick, tuberous roots. Tree peonies, practically all of them grafted onto herbaceous peony roots, may be planted in the same way. Many growers now offer tree peonies as container plants from spring to fall; they cost more than bare-root plants because of the time and labor involved in producing them.

Ideally, the planting site for peonies should be deeply dug several days before planting. Work in plenty of thoroughly decayed manure or compost and superphosphate; allow the soil to settle before planting. Set herbaceous peony roots with eyes 2 in. deep; deeper planting will prevent flowering. Set tree peonies so that the graft line is 3–4 in. below the soil surface (the object is to get the shrubby top to root on its own). Mulch the first year after the ground has frozen. Plants are unlikely to bloom the first year, but should bloom every year after that if fertilized after the flowering period and again in fall (the American Peony Society recommends 8-8-8).

During humid weather—particularly during cool, humid periods—the fungus disease botrytis is sometimes a problem: buds blacken and fail to develop, stems wilt and collapse. Prevent the problem by sanitation: in autumn, dispose of all leaves (also all stems on herbaceous peonies). As new growth emerges in spring, spray with copper fungicide.

WHY DIDN'T MY PEONY PUT ON A SHOW?

Poor flowering has many possible causes, including these: the plant is too young (wait a while); it was planted too deep or too shallow (lift during dormant season and replant at proper depth); flower buds were killed by a late freeze (wait until next year); extreme heat (plant early-flowering varieties); lack of nutrients (apply fertilizer); or the clump has been moved or divided too often (leave it alone).

PRACTICAL GARDENING DICTIONARY

PLEASE SEE PAGES 449–523

HERBACEOUS PEONIES

Perennials. 32, 34–45. Grow to 3–4 ft. tall. Large blossoms borne in late spring or early summer are 4–6 in. (even up to 10 in.) across; many varieties have a refreshing old rose scent. Flowers fall into three basic categories: single or semidouble, with one or two rows of petals; Japanese, with a single row of petals and a large central mass of narrow petal-like segments called staminodes; and double, with full flowers composed of many petals. In Zones 31, 32, singles and Japanese varieties tend to do better than full doubles, and early-season doubles are often more successful than mid- and late-season cultivars. All profit from light afternoon shade where summers are very hot.

Provide support for the heavy flowers. All types are choice cut flowers; cut just as buds begin to open. Leave at least three leaves on every cut stem, and do not remove more than half the blooms from any clump. The object is to preserve leaf growth to nourish the plant for next year. Remove faded flowers from plants to prevent seed formation.

There is no reason to divide a peony except to increase your stock. Dig in early fall, hose off soil, and divide into sections, making sure that each has at least three eyes; these appear at top of root cluster, at or near bases of past season's stems. Plant at once so that plants will get established before freezing weather.

There are many, many cultivars, some of the best of which are listed below.

Herbaceous Peony Cultivars. The Chinese peonies, derivatives of *P. lactiflora*, are the most numerous and popular kinds of herbaceous peonies. Also included here are the so-called hybrid peonies, resulting from crosses between Chinese peonies and species other than *P. lactiflora*. These flamboyant, easily grown and nearly permanent perennials are loosely classified into the following five general types based upon the structure of their blossoms.

Doubles. Five or more guard petals form the base for a dense, heaped, central mass of stamens and carpels that have been transformed to resemble petals. 'Baroness Schroeder' has large, round white flowers at first tinted light pink, midseason to late; 'Charlie's White' is white touched with yellow at the center, early; 'Cherry Hill', purplish red and very free flowering, very early; 'Diana Parks', large, fragrant, cardinal red blossoms, early; 'Dinner Plate', delicate pink, vigorous and somewhat fragrant, late; 'Emma Klehm', pink, deeply so inside, paler toward the edges, very late; 'Fairy's Petticoat', fades from pale pink to creamy white as it ages, very fragrant, early; 'Felix Supreme', red, vigorous and well known as a cut flower, midseason; 'Festiva Maxima', opens pale pink and fades rapidly to creamy white, often with red flecking, very fragrant, midseason; 'Henry Bockstoce', striking deep red flowers with falling guard petals, early; 'Kansas', red, marbled on the outer petals, excellent cut flower, midseason; 'Kelway's Glorious', one of the classic white lactifloras, large, saucer-shaped flowers with a warm, creamy center and excellent fragrance, midseason to late; 'Monsieur Jules Elie', large, unfading pink blossoms comprised of rounded outer petals around a raised mass of petals that are incurved in the manner of a chrysanthemum, early to midseason; 'Mrs. Franklin D. Roosevelt', one of the world's most beautiful peonies, with large, fragrant, waterlily-shaped blossoms opening pale pink and fading to near white, midseason; 'Myrtle Gentry', exceptionally fragrant, pale pink, late; 'Nick Shaylor' is loose in form, opens pale pink and fades to white with a blush center, not fragrant, very late; 'Pillow Talk', fluffy and full, pale rose pink, fragrant, midseason; 'Pink Lemonade', lovely blend of shell pink and pale yellow, fragrant, midseason; 'Raspberry Sundae', extraordinarily beautiful blend of large pink guard petals around a vanilla center topped by a tuft of deeper pink petals, fragrant, midseason; 'Red Charm', large, rich crimson, long lasting blossoms, midseason; 'Therese' opens semidouble pink becoming double and blush white, fragrant, midseason.

Semidoubles. Five or more guard petals surround a center of wide petals mixed with or encircling fertile pollen producing stamens. 'Coral Charm' has large, cupped flowers that are deep coral pink in bud, opening lighter coral, early; 'Cythera', low growing, spreads by runners to form a large clump, cup-shaped rose pink flowers on strong stems, early; 'Lovely Rose' opens deep pink, fading to pale pink with darker marbling and conspicuous white blotches at base of petals, early; 'Miss America',

blush pink buds, opens pure white with light yellow at the base of petals, fragrant, robust, early; 'Paula Fay', vivid pink flowers with petals that are crinkled at first, fragrant, early; 'Postilion', very large, glowing scarlet red flowers, very fragrant, early; 'Prairie Moon', usually semidouble but occasionally has single or nearly double blossoms, large, pale yellow, of exceptional beauty, early; 'Salmon Dream', pale salmon pink with a satiny sheen, midseason.

Japanese Varieties. Five or more enlarged outer guard petals surround a central mass of structures called staminodes (stamens with anthers that do not produce pollen). The staminodes are greatly enlarged and often are edged with yellow. 'Ama-No-Sode' has very large, 9-in. blossoms with mauve pink guard petals and a large central mass of pink-tipped yellow petaloids, midseason; 'Bowl of Beauty', bright pink guard petals surrounding the central mass of creamy yellow staminodes, fragrant, midseason to late.; 'Bu-Te', white with large, slightly ruffled petals and a small center of yellow staminodes, late midseason; 'Chocolate Soldier' has mostly Japanese type flowers but often produces single and sometimes double flowers on the same plant, dark reddish brown petals, very early; 'Comanche', magenta guard petals and yellow staminodes, exceptionally vigorous grower, midseason; 'Isani Gidui', vigorous grower with large blossoms comprised of a double ring of white guard petals around a mass of creamy yellow staminodes, fragrant, midseason; 'Westerner', vigorous grower with pale pink guard petals surrounding butter yellow staminodes, late.

Anemones. Five or more guard petals form the base for a central mass of transformed petal-like stamens that may be the same color or a different color from the petals. 'Barrington Belle' is very free flowering, with deep red guard petals and red or pink staminodes edged with gold, midseason; 'Gay Paree', brightest magenta guard petals surround creamy pink staminodes for a glowing combination, late midseason; 'Primevere', very fragrant and free flowering with essentially white flowers with a pale yellow center that ages white, midseason.

Singles. Five to ten petals surround a mass of fertile stamens and carpels. Although they are beautiful in all zones, the singles are especially valuable in regions where summer heat comes early (such as zones 31 and 32) and often fries the later blooming doubles and semidoubles just as they are coming into their glory. 'America' has an exceptional brilliant scarlet red blossom with a satiny sheen, yellow stamens, and light fragrance, early to midseason; 'Clair de Lune', cup-shaped blossoms comprised of palest yellow, somewhat crinkled, rounded petals around yellow stamens, somewhat fragrant, very early; 'Cream Delight', large blossoms with creamy white petals, side buds open to prolong the blooming season, early to midseason; 'Dawn Pink', large rose pink flowers with golden stamens, early to midseason; 'Firelight', cup-shaped with rose pink petals and long golden stamens, early; 'Illini Warrior', glossy, deep red flowers, somewhat fragrant, early; 'Krinkled White' is one of the first singles a gardener should acquire, large, crinkled white petals surround golden stamens, very free flowering, early; 'Red Velvet', satiny, ruby red petals and golden yellow stamens, late; 'Requiem' blooms profusely, waxy, creamy white petals surrounding a large center of golden stamens, exceptionally fragrant, midseason; 'Sea Shell', an all time favorite, vigorous and free flowering, with warm pink petals, good fragrance, late.

Herbaceous Peony Species. The blossoms of herbaceous peony species offer a certain simplicity and charm of bearing that can be completely lacking in the flamboyant modern hybrids. Excellent foliage characteristics and the possibility of beautiful seed pods are other attractions. Mail order nurseries that deal in rare plants are starting to list these wild 'unimproved' forms, often for quite expensive prices due to rarity and length of production time from seed. Any of the following plants could become a treasured heirloom in a northeastern garden.

P. anomala. Perennial. Zones 31, 32, 34–43. Native from the Ural Mts. to Siberia and Central Asia. The distinctive leaves are divided into up to a dozen or more lobes, depending upon the geographical form obtained. The blossoms are single, bright red with a mass of yellow stamens at the center, cup shaped, 3–4 in. wide, and borne individually on stems 1½–2 ft. tall. Late spring.

P. emodi. HIMALAYAN PEONY. Perennial. Zones 31, 32, 34, 39. Native to the western Himalayas. This exceptionally beautiful and graceful peony has cup-shaped, single, pure white blossoms with a central mass of yellow stamens. They are 5 in. wide, borne 2 to 4 per stem, and nod slightly among the handsomely lobed leaves. This treasure is 2–2½ft. high. Has a reputation of being difficult to grow and might best be placed in partial shade. Late spring.

P. mascula. Perennial. Zones 31, 32, 34–41. Native to Southern Europe. This peony has a number of geographical variants, one of the most garden worthy of which is subspecies *arietina,* native to E. Europe and Turkey. In its cultivated forms, this plant has single, pale pink to dark pinkish red blossoms, each 3–5 in. wide, on plants 2½–3 ft. tall. Late spring.

P. mlokosewitschii. CAUCASIAN PEONY, MOLLY THE WITCH. Perennial. Zones 31, 32, 34–41. Native to the Caucasus. Some gardeners consider this to be the world's most beautiful peony. It is without a doubt also one of the finest garden plants. Beautifully divided bluish green leaves set the stage in midspring for the gorgeous, single, bowl-shaped, lemon yellow blossoms, each 4–5 in. across, and comprised of eight rounded petals surrounding the central mass of golden stamens. To 3 ft. high, may be slow to establish. Midspring.

P. obovata. Perennial. Zones 31, 32, 34–41. Native to China. The single, cup-shaped blossoms are 3–4 in. wide and vary in color from white to purplish red depending upon the form obtained. Grows 2 ft. high. Considered somewhat difficult to grow and may be best in partial shade. Midspring.

P. officinalis. COMMON PEONY. Perennial. Zones 31, 32, 34–43. Native to Europe. This peony has been in European gardens for centuries and has many forms, both in the wild and in cultivation. The most usual wild type has single magenta flowers. 'China Rose' has single, cupped, salmon-pink blossoms with orange stamens. The large double flowers of 'Alba Plena' open with a blush of pink and quickly turn white. 'Rubra Plena' has a very rugged constitution and large, double, ruffled, satiny, bright crimson blossoms. In this country it is often called the "Memorial Day Peony."

P. tenuifolia. FERN-LEAF PEONY. Perennial. Zones 31, 32, 34–43. Native from S.E. Europe to S.E. Russia. Out of bloom it is hard to imagine that this plant could be a peony, with its deep green, glossy leaves dissected into numerous linear segments and nearly fernlike in appearance. Grows about 1½ ft. high. The single, globular, deep red blossoms are 2½–3 in. across and appear rather briefly in late spring. 'Plena' is also red, double, and considerably longer lasting. 'Rubra Plena' has double dark red flowers. 'Rosea' has single, pale pink flowers. 'Alba' is creamy white and very rare.

P. veitchii. Perennial. Zones 31, 32, 34, 39. Native to Western China. The beautiful leaves are deeply cut and form an excellent backdrop for the somewhat nodding, single, 2½–3½-in.-wide blossoms of magenta pink or white. Grows 2½ ft. high. Late spring.

P. wittmanniana. Perennial. Zones 31, 32, 34–41. Native to the N.W. Caucasus Mts. This outstanding peony has beautiful large leaves that are bronzy-green when young and dark green and glossy at maturity. The blossoms are 4–5 in. wide, bowl shaped, palest yellow to creamy white, and nestle among the foliage. Grows vigorously to 3–3⅔ ft. and makes a large clump. Late spring to early summer.

Paeonia Double Type

TREE PEONIES

Deciduous shrubs. Zones 31, 32, 34–43. Slow growth to an eventual 3–5 ft. tall, with handsome divided leaves and very large (to 10–12-in.) single to double flowers in early spring. They seldom reveal their true potential until they have spent several years in your garden, but the spectacular results are worth the wait. Relatively inexpensive imported small grafted plants are sometimes available, usually sold only by color (red, pink, white, yellow, purple); these are a good buy if you are very patient and can wait for them to attain good size. Catalogs offer named varieties of Japanese origin in white, pink, red, and purple. More recent and considerably more expensive (but worth it) are the yellow and orange hybrids resulting from crosses of *P. suffruticosa* with *P. delavayi* and *P. lutea.*

Tree peonies require less winter chill than herbaceous peonies. The flowers are fragile and should be sheltered from strong wind. Prune only to remove faded blooms and any dead wood. In coldest winter climates, shield from sun and wind with burlap curtain.

PAINTED DAISY. See CHRYSANTHEMUM coccineum

PAINTED TONGUE. See SALPIGLOSSIS sinuata

PAMPAS GRASS. See CORTADERIA selloana

PANAX

GINSENG

Araliaceae

PERENNIALS

✎ ZONES VARY BY SPECIES

● FULL SHADE

💧 MORE THAN REGULAR WATER

Panax

These woodland perennials are valued for their thick, fragrant root-stocks, used medicinally in many cultures. Each carrotlike root bears annual stems from which grow a circle of three hand-shaped leaves. In the center a cluster of minute, starry, greenish white flowers, followed later in the season by a bunch of berries, tops a flower stalk. Attractive in a wild, woodsy way, ginseng belongs in woodland gardens and herb gardens, but you have to wait 6 or 7 years before it's ready to harvest in the fall.

Ginseng needs moist, well-drained soil rich in organic matter and thrives in warm, humid weather during the growing season.

P. ginseng. KOREAN GINSENG. Zones 31, 32, 34–41. Grows 32 in. tall and 2 ft. wide, with erect stems and leaves to 5 in. long. Bears red berries after flowering in spring and early summer.

P. quinquefolius. AMERICAN GINSENG. Zones 32, 34–45. Native to eastern North America. Grows 1–3 ft. tall and 2 ft. wide, with leaves to 5 in. long. Produces decorative bright red berries after flowering. The rootstock is deep and branched.

PANICUM virgatum

SWITCH GRASS

Poaceae (Gramineae)

PERENNIAL GRASS

✎ ZONES 31, 32, 34–43

☼ ◑ FULL SUN OR LIGHT SHADE

💧 MUCH TO LITTLE WATER

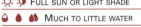

Panicum virgatum

Native to the tall grass prairie of the Midwest. Upright clump of narrow, deep green or gray-green leaves is topped by slender flower clusters; clump reaches 4–7 ft. high in bloom. Clusters open into loose, airy, delicate clouds of pinkish blossoms that fade to white, then brown. Foliage turns yellow in fall, gradually fades to beige. Both foliage and flowers persist all winter, providing interest in cold-weather gardens.

'Cloud Nine' is tall, to 6 ft., with bluish green leaves'; 'Dallas Blues' has powdery blue, pendulous leaves in upright, 5-ft. clumps. 'Haense Herms' is grown for red fall foliage, 'Heavy Metal' for stiffly upright silvery blue leaves that turn bright yellow in autumn; both reach 4–5 ft. high. 'Shenandoah' is most notable for its reddish purple autumn foliage; grows to 4 ft. tall. 'Strictum' is narrow, grows to 4 ft. high; leaves turn bright gold in autumn.

Plant tolerates many soils, moisture levels, and exposures, even salt winds. Attractive silhouette in winter. Use as accent in large informal flower border or as screening.

P

PANSY. See VIOLA

PAPAVER

POPPY

Papaveraceae

PERENNIALS AND ANNUALS

ZONES VARY BY SPECIES

FULL SUN

REGULAR TO MODERATE WATER

Papaver orientale

Poppies provide gay spring and summer color for borders and cutting. Give ordinary soil, good drainage; feed lightly until established. Perennials tend to be short lived. When using poppies as cut flowers, sear clipped stem ends in flame before placing in water.

P. alpinum (P. burseri). ALPINE POPPY. Perennial. Zones 32, 34–41; best adapted to colder climates. Rock garden plant with basal foliage rosette and 5–8-in.-high flower stalk. Blue-green, nearly hairless, divided leaves. Spring flowers are 1–1½ in. across, come in white, orange, yellow, salmon. Blooms first year from seed sown in fall or early spring.

P. atlanticum. Perennial. Zones 32, 34, 37. To 1½ ft. high, with jagged-edged, softly hairy leaves to 6 in. long. Bright orange, 3-in. flowers in summer.

P. nudicaule. ICELAND POPPY. Short-lived perennial in Zones 32, 34–45; grown as an annual in Zone 31. Divided leaves with coarse hairs. Slender, hairy stems 1–2 ft. high. Cup-shaped, slightly fragrant flowers to 3 in. across, in yellow, orange, salmon, rose, pink, cream, white. Sow seed in earliest spring for summer bloom; or set out summer-sown plants in autumn for bloom the following year. To prolong bloom, pick flowers frequently. Champagne Bubbles is most widely grown strain. Low-growing Wonderland strain (to 10 in.) comes in mixed or single colors. Misato Carnival strain has 6-in. flowers on 2–3-ft. stems.

P. orientale. ORIENTAL POPPY. Perennial. Zones 31, 32, 34–45. Needs winter chill for best performance. Height variable; some types are 16 in. tall, others reach 4 ft. Hairy, coarsely cut leaves. Single or double flowers are large to very large (to 11 in. across in some varieties); colors include white, pink, orange yellow, orange, scarlet, and dark red, usually with a dark blotch at base of each petal. A great many named varieties are sold; they bloom in late spring and early summer, then die back in midsummer.

Cultivars include 'Beauty of Livermore', with deep scarlet blooms that have black blotches at the base of each petal; 'Curlilocks', red-orange flowers with serrated petals and black blotches; 'Doubloon', stunning double orange flowers; 'Glowing Embers', scarlet blooms with ruffled petals; 'Harvest Moon', golden yellow blooms; 'Helen Elizabeth', salmon pink flowers that lack dark blotches; 'Mrs. Perry', pale salmon pink flowers with dark blotches; 'Snow Queen', white flowers with black blotches; 'Turkenlouis'('Turkish Delight'), scarlet flowers with dark blotches; and 'Wunderkind', bright pink flowers.

In all types, new leafy growth appears in fall, lasts over winter, and develops rapidly in spring. Set sprawling plants such as baby's breath nearby to cover the bare areas after the poppies die down. Plant dormant roots in fall with tops 3 in. deep. Set container-grown plants flush with soil line. Provide good drainage and room for air circulation. Divide crowded clumps in August, after foliage has died down.

P. rhoeas. FLANDERS FIELD POPPY, SHIRLEY POPPY. Annual. All zones, but best where summers are cool. Slender, branching, hairy-stemmed plant 2–5 ft. high. Short, irregularly divided leaves; single or double flowers 2 in. or wider, in red, pink, white, orange, scarlet, salmon, bicolors. Selections bearing single scarlet flowers with a black base are sold as 'American Legion' or 'Flanders Field'. Angels' Choir strain offers double flowers in a wide range of colors on 2–2½-ft. stems. Broadcast seed mixed with fine sand. Sow successively for bloom from spring through summer. Take cut flowers when buds first show color. Remove seed capsules (old flower bases) weekly to prolong bloom season. Notorious self-sower.

P. somniferum. OPIUM POPPY. Annual. All zones. To 4 ft. tall, with virtually hairless gray-green leaves and usually double, sometimes single, 4–5-in. flowers in white or rosy shades (pink and red to purple). Late spring bloom. Large, decorative seed capsules. Opium is derived from the sap of the green seed capsules; ripe ones yield large quantities of the poppy seed used in baking. Because of its narcotic properties, this species is not as widely offered as many other types.

Papaveraceae. The poppy family of annuals, perennials, and shrubs displays showy flowers usually borne singly. In addition to *Papaver*, members include California poppy *(Eschscholzia)*, *Glaucium*, and *Hunnemanniana*.

PAPER MULBERRY. See BROUSSONETIA papyrifera

PAPYRUS. See CYPERUS papyrus

PARADISE PALM. See HOWEA forsterana

PARROTIA persica

PERSIAN PARROTIA

Hamamelidaceae

DECIDUOUS SHRUB OR SMALL TREE

ZONES 31, 32, 34–41

FULL SUN

REGULAR TO MODERATE WATER

Parrotia persica

Native to Iran. Slow growing to 30 ft. or more, but most often seen as a shrub or multi-trunked tree to 15 ft. Young trees are fairly upright; older ones are wide-spreading, rounded. Choice and colorful; attractive all year. Most dramatic display comes in autumn: leaves usually turn golden yellow, then orange or rosy pink, and finally scarlet. Attractive smooth, gray bark; in mature trees, it flakes off to reveal white, tan, and green patches beneath. Blooms in late winter or early spring before leaves open. Flowers have dense heads of red stamens surrounded by woolly brown bracts; blooming plants have an overall reddish haze. New foliage unfurls reddish purple, matures to lustrous dark green. Leaves are ¾ in. long, oval, shallowly toothed along upper half.

Prefers slightly acid soil but tolerates alkaline and chalky soils. Will also withstand light shade. Pest resistant.

PARROTIOPSIS jacquemontiana

Hamamelidaceae

DECIDUOUS TREE OR SHRUB

ZONES 31, 32, 34–41

FULL SUN

REGULAR WATER

Parrotiopsis

Not often cultivated, this unusual specimen shrub or small tree is related to witch hazel, sweet gum, iron tree, and winter hazel. Grows to 20 ft. high. Alternate round leaves grow to 3 in. long and turn pale yellow in autumn. In spring, bears flowers resembling dogwoods—clusters of yellow stamens surrounded by 4–6 petal-like white bracts. Grows best in fertile, well-drained, acidic soil as a garden centerpiece separate from other trees or shrubs. Prune often during the early years to encourage development as a tree rather than a shrub.

P

PARROT'S BEAK. See LOTUS berthelotii

PARSLEY

Apiaceae (Umbelliferae)

BIENNIAL HERB TREATED AS ANNUAL

ALL ZONES

AFTERNOON SHADE IN HOT-SUMMER AREAS

REGULAR WATER

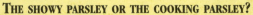
Parsley

Attractive edging for herb, vegetable, or flower garden; also looks good in boxes or pots. Plants are 6–12 in. high, with tufted, finely cut, dark green leaves. Use leaves fresh or dried as seasoning, fresh as garnish. Most satisfactorily grown anew every year. Buy plants at nursery or sow seed in place (in spring in cold-winter climates; in fall or early spring where winter is mild). Soak seed in warm water for 24 hours before planting. Even after soaking, it may not sprout for several weeks: according to folklore, parsley seeds must go to the devil and come back before sprouting. Thin seedlings to 6–8 in. apart.

> **THE SHOWY PARSLEY OR THE COOKING PARSLEY?**
> The Italian, flat-leafed parsley is the tastiest type for cooking. The curly varieties make the most attractive garnish and are appealing as a low border in a flower bed. A third type of parsley, called Hamburg parsley or parsley root, is grown for its white, carrot-shaped roots that taste like mild celery.

PARSNIP

Apiaceae (Umbelliferae)

BIENNIAL GROWN AS AN ANNUAL

ALL ZONES

FULL SUN

MAINTAIN EVEN SOIL MOISTURE

Parsnip

Needs deep, well-prepared, loose soil for long roots; roots of some varieties are 15 in. long. In cold-winter areas, plant seeds in late spring and harvest in fall; leave surplus in ground (under a thick layer of mulch) to be dug as needed in winter. Cold makes the roots sweeter. Soak seeds in water 24 hours before planting to improve germination. Sow ½ in. deep in rows spaced 2 ft. apart; thin seedlings to 3 in. apart.

PARTHENOCISSUS
(Ampelopsis)

Vitaceae

DECIDUOUS VINES

ZONES VARY BY SPECIES

SUN OR SHADE

REGULAR WATER

Parthenocissus

Cling to walls by sucker disks at ends of tendrils. Superb and dependable orange to scarlet fall leaf color. Flowers are insignificant. Attractive to birds. Think twice before planting them against wood or shingle siding; they can creep under it, and their clinging tendrils are hard to remove at repainting time.

P. henryana. SILVERVEIN CREEPER. Zones 31, warmer parts of 32. Native to China. To 20 ft.; less aggressive growth than the other species. Leaves have five 1–2½-in.-long leaflets; they open purplish, then turn dark bronzy green with pronounced silver veining and purple undersides. Color is best in shade, fades to plain green in strong light. Leaves turn rich red in autumn. Clings to walls, but needs some support to get started. Also good spilling over walls or as a small-scale ground cover.

P. quinquefolia. VIRGINIA CREEPER. Zones 31, 32, 34–43. Native to eastern U.S. Big, vigorous vine (to 30–50 ft. or more) that clings or runs over ground, fence, trellis, trees. Looser growth than *P. tricuspidata;* will drape its trailing branches over trellis, trees. Leaves divided into five separate 6-in. leaflets with saw-toothed edges; foliage turns bright to dull red in fall. Good ground cover on slopes; can control erosion. 'Engelmannii' has smaller leaves, denser growth.

P. tricuspidata. BOSTON IVY. Zones 31, 32, 34–41. Native to China, Japan. Semievergreen in mild-winter areas. Even more vigorous than *P. quinquefolia.* Glossy leaves to 8 in. wide are variable in shape, usually three lobed or divided into three leaflets; fall color varies from orange to burgundy. Clings tightly, grows fast to make dense, even wall cover. This is the ivy of the Ivy League; covers brick or stone in areas where English ivy freezes. Leaves of 'Beverly Brooks' and 'Green Showers' are larger than those of the species; leaves of 'Lowii' and 'Veitchii' are considerably smaller.

PARTRIDGEBERRY. See MITCHELLA repens

PASQUE FLOWER. See PULSATILLA vulgaris

PASSIFLORA

PASSION VINE

Passifloraceae

EVERGREEN, SEMIEVERGREEN, OR DECIDUOUS VINES

ZONES VARY BY SPECIES; OR GROW IN POTS

FULL SUN

REGULAR TO MODERATE WATER

Passiflora

Climb by tendrils to 20–30 ft.; bloom during warm weather. Flower parts can be seen to symbolize elements of the passion of Christ, hence plant's common name. The lacy crown represents a halo or crown of thorns; the five stamens, the five wounds; the ten petal-like parts, the ten faithful apostles.

Some of the passionflowers described below are hardy outdoors in Zones 31, 32, and one farther north, but all can be grown in containers in colder zones. Move the pots outdoors in summer and back indoors over winter. Provide a trellis to support the vines, or train them on wire hoops for a wreath effect. Plant in a porous, all-purpose potting mix.

Where hardy, the vigorous vines are likely to overgrow and tangle. To keep plant open and prevent buildup of dead inner tangle, prune annually after second year, cutting excess branches back to base or juncture with another branch. Tolerant of many soils outdoors. Use vines on trellises or walls for their vigor and bright, showy flowers; or use as soil-holding bank cover.

P. alatocaerulea (P. pfordtii). Evergreen or semievergreen. Dies to ground in colder part of range. Hybrid between *P. caerulea* and *P. alata,* a species not described here. Best known, probably least subject to damage from caterpillars. Three-lobed leaves 3 in. long. Fragrant, 3½–4-in. flowers, white shaded pink and lavender; deep blue or purple crown. Forms no fruit. In colder areas, give it a warm place out of wind, against wall or under overhang. Mulch roots in winter. Excellent windowsill bloomer.

P. 'Amethyst' ('Lavender Lady'). Evergreen. Profuse show of 4-in. lavender purple flowers with deep violet crown.

P. caerulea. BLUE CROWN PASSION FLOWER. Evergreen or semievergreen. Dies to ground in colder part of range. Five-lobed leaves, smaller than those of *P. alatocaerulea.* Flowers also smaller, in greenish white with white-and-purple crown. Edible small, oval fruit with orange rind and red seeds.

P. edulis. PASSION FRUIT. Semievergreen. Leaves three lobed, deeply toothed, light yellow green. Flowers white with white-and-purple crown, 2 in. across. Fruit produced in spring and fall: deep purple, fragrant, 3 in. long, delicious used in beverages, fruit salads, sherbets. 'Nancy Garrison' is a hardier version. There is also a yellow-fruited variety.

P. incarnata. WILD PASSION VINE, MAYPOP. Deciduous. Zones 31, 32, 34, 39; to Zone 41 with winter protection. Native to southeastern U.S. Hardiest of the passion flowers, surviving temperatures at least as low as −10°F/−23°C and possibly even lower. Dies to ground in colder part of range. Three-lobed leaves are 4–6 in. wide; freely produced flowers are 2–3 in. wide, white or pale lavender, with filaments banded in purple or pink. Yellow, 2-in. fruits are edible. Spreads vigorously from underground roots and can become an attractive pest. Although this plant is seldom sold in nurseries, it is easily grown from seed.

P. 'Incense'. Deciduous. Zones 31, 32. Hardy to 0°F/−18°C; holds its leaves through short cold spells, dies to ground when weather turns colder. Hybrid between *P. incarnata* and an Argentinian species. Flowers are 5 in. wide, violet with lighter crown, with sweet pea–like fragrance. Egg-shaped, 2-in. fruit has fragrant, tasty pulp; when ripe, it turns from olive to yellow green, then drops.

P. jamesonii. Evergreen. Glossy, three-lobed leaves. Profusion of long-tubed (to 4-in.) salmon to coral flowers. Fast bank or fence cover. This and similar plants are sold as 'Coral Seas'.

P. vitifolia. Evergreen. Grapelike, 6-in. deep green leaves set off bright red flowers 3½ in. long.

PASSION FRUIT. See PASSIFLORA edulis

PASSION VINE. See PASSIFLORA

PATRINIA

Valerianaceae

PERENNIALS

ZONES 31, 32, 34–41

EXPOSURE NEEDS VARY BY SPECIES

REGULAR WATER

Patrinia

Perennials with mounds of deeply cut or lobed leaves that produce stems bearing few or no leaves and flat-topped clusters of tiny yellow or white flowers. Summer bloom. They are useful for blending with other border perennials. Long-lasting cut flowers. All appreciate rich, well-drained soil.

P. scabiosifolia. Grows to 5–6 ft. and may require staking, but thinly foliaged flower stalks and open showers of yellow flower clusters give plant a see-through quality that makes it appropriate for either front or rear of border. Finely divided leaves to 6 in. 'Compact Selection' and 'Nagoya' grow only 1½–3 ft. tall. Cut flowers last several weeks and mix well with other kinds in arrangements. Full sun.

P. triloba. Grows 1 ft. tall and spreads slowly to make a small-scale ground cover. Glossy deep green, three- to five-lobed leaves are 2 in. long, finely divided. Yellow flowers. Grows best in light shade.

P. villosa. Leaves to 6 in. long, either divided or uncut. Sprawling flower stems to 1½ ft. hold showers of white blossoms. Full sun.

FOR INFORMATION ON YOUR CLIMATE ZONE

PLEASE SEE PAGES 30–46

PAULOWNIA tomentosa (P. imperialis)

EMPRESS TREE

Bignoniaceae

DECIDUOUS TREE

ZONES 31, 32, 34, 35, 37, 39

FULL SUN OR PARTIAL SHADE

REGULAR WATER

Paulownia tomentosa

Native to China. Somewhat similar to catalpa in growth habit, leaves. Fast growth to 40–50 ft., with nearly equal spread. Heavy trunk and heavy, nearly horizontal branches. Foliage gives tropical effect: light green, heart-shaped leaves are 5–12 in. long, 4–7 in. wide. No significant fall color. Brown flower buds the size of small olives form in autumn and persist over winter; they open before the leaves in early spring, forming 6–12-in.-long, upright clusters of trumpet-shaped, 2-in.-long, fragrant flowers of lilac blue with darker spotting and yellow stripes on the inside. Flowers are followed by 1½–2-in. seed capsules shaped like tops; these remain on tree with flower buds. Does not bloom well where winters are very cold (buds freeze) or very mild (buds may drop off).

Performs best in deep, moist, well-drained soil, though it will grow in many soils. Tolerates air pollution. Protect from strong winds. Plant where falling flowers and leaves are not objectionable. Not a tree to garden under because of dense shade, surface roots. If tree is cut back annually or every other year, it will grow as billowy foliage mass with giant-size leaves up to 2 ft. long; however, such pruning will reduce or eliminate flower production.

PAWPAW. See ASIMINA triloba

PAXISTIMA canbyi

Celastraceae

EVERGREEN SHRUB

ZONES 32, 34–43

PARTIAL SHADE IN HOT CLIMATES

REGULAR WATER

Paxistima canbyi

Native to mountains of Virginia and West Virginia. Slowly forms a mat 9–12 in. high, 3–5 ft. wide. Leathery leaves, ¼–1 in. long and ¼ in. wide, are shiny dark green, turning bronzy in fall and winter. Insignificant flowers. Useful as low edging, ground cover. Best in well-drained soil.

PEA

Fabaceae (Leguminosae)

ANNUAL

ALL ZONES

FULL SUN

REGULAR WATER

Pea

Sometimes called garden or English pea to distinguish it from Southern pea (a category including black-eyed pea, cowpea, and crowder pea).

Easy crop to grow when conditions are right, and delicious when freshly picked. Peas need coolness and humidity and must be planted at just the right time. If you have space and don't mind the bother, grow tall (vining) peas on trellises, strings, or screen; they reach 6 ft. or more and bear heavily. A good tall variety is 'Alderman'. Bush types are more commonly grown in home gardens; they require no support. Fine bush varieties are 'Green Arrow', 'Little Marvel', 'Morse's Progress No. 9', 'Freezonian', and 'Blue

Bantam'. An unusually good vegetable (and one popular in Asian cooking) is edible-pod snow or sugar pea; 'Mammoth Melting Sugar' is a tall vining variety, 'Dwarf Gray Sugar' a bushy one. 'Sugar Snap' is an edible-pod pea with full complement of full-size peas inside.

Peas need soil that is slightly acid to slightly alkaline, water retentive but fast draining. They are hardy and should be planted just as early in spring as ground can be worked. Where winters are mild and spring days quickly become too warm for peas, plant in February. Sow 2 in. deep in light soil, ½−1 in. deep in heavy soil or in winter. Moisten ground thoroughly before planting; do not supply supplemental irrigation until seedlings have broken through surface. Leave 2 ft. between rows and thin seedlings to stand 2 in. apart. Successive plantings several days apart will lengthen bearing season, but don't plant so late that summer heat will overtake ripening peas; most are ready to harvest in 60 to 70 days.

Plants need little fertilizer, but if soil is very light, give them one application of complete fertilizer. If weather turns warm and dry, supply water in furrows; overhead watering encourages mildew. Provide support for vining peas as soon as tendrils form. When peas begin to mature, pick all pods that are ready; if seeds ripen, plant will stop producing. Vines are brittle; steady them with one hand while picking with the other. Above all, shell and cook (or freeze) peas right after picking.

PEACH and NECTARINE

Peach and Nectarine

Rosaceae

DECIDUOUS FRUIT TREES

REGIONS VARY BY VARIETY

FULL SUN

REGULAR WATER

SEE CHART ON FOLLOWING PAGES

The peach and nectarine likely came originally from China and then spread through Asia to the Mediterranean basin countries and elsewhere in Europe. Spanish explorers brought the peach to the New World and it was found around 1600 in Mexico. Peaches and nectarines belong to the genus *Prunus* of the rose family Rosaceae and grow throughout the warmer temperate regions of both hemispheres. Trees will not tolerate severe cold and will not thrive where temperatures normally drop to −15 F.

In the New World, peaches and nectarines were primarily used for livestock food, brandymaking, and living fences. Thomas Jefferson even experimented with using peach wood for firewood because the tree grows rapidly. In the late 18th and early 19th centuries, many European peaches were also brought to America.

Most peaches grown in the United States have yellow flesh, but white flesh peaches that are favored in Asia and Europe are becoming popular. Yellow-fleshed peaches are high in vitamin A; white ones are lower.

Rootstocks. Major peach rootstocks are 'Lovell', 'Nemagard', and 'Citation'. 'Lovell' produces a tree about 15 ft. and is well-anchored, cold hardy with tolerance to wet soils. 'Nemagard' is a vigorous stock that needs well-drained soil; some nematode resistance. 'Citation', (a dwarfing rootstock of 50% of standard) anchors well, promotes early fruit production.

Site and location. In the colder regions of New England a slope where the temperature rises gradually in the spring is desirable. Often this is a southern slope promoting early bloom that gives a longer growing season for the fruit. Northern slopes expose the trees to damaging winds that destroy the buds. In more moderate climates where a southern slope would warm quickly and promote blossoming, a north slope is better. Peaches need a deep, well-drained loamy soil with a pH of 6−8.

Tree Characteristics. Trees are usually kept between 8 and 10 feet high, but will grow upright to 20 ft. To admit light and air circulation they are most often pruned in an open vase shape. The leaves are glossy green, with long points; they secrete a fluid attractive to ants and other insects. Five-petal flowers are both pink and white. Some varieties will produce very large flowers with a bright pink color.

Planting and Culture. Dormant trees are planted in the spring when the soil can be worked and are spaced about 20 ft. apart. Peaches and nectarine require little potassium or phosphorus but demand a great amount of nitrogen. Weed control by manual removal or mulching is important when the fruit is ripening to make large sweet fruit. After the "June drop"; thin the remaining fruit every 6−8 in. along the branches. Otherwise, all of the peaches will be small and the heavy tree load will increase the risk of broken limbs. During a drought, a mature tree during the ripening period needs at least 25 gallons of water a day.

Pollination. Most peach and nectarine varieties are self-fruit and do not require a pollinator to set a crop. One of the exceptions is J.H. Hale which must have another variety to set fruit.

Pests and Diseases. The most threatening insect pests are the peach tree and lesser peach tree borers. Insecticides and Integrated Pest Management practices will keep this pest under control. Keeping the tree healthy and free of bark damage, avoiding stubs or narrow crotches when pruning, and using a sticky agent around the trunk next to the soil line also helps. Other pests are the oriental fruit moth, Japanese beetles, and the plum curculio. The most challenging disease is the brown rot fungus that responds to fungicides and orchard sanitation. Removing all mummies and cultivation beneath the tree will help. Other diseases are bacterial leaf spot and canker.

PEACOCK MOSS. See SELAGINELLA uncinata

PEANUT

Peanut

Fabaceae (Leguminosae)

ANNUAL

ZONES 31, 32, 34−42

FULL SUN

REGULAR WATER

Best production where summers are long and warm. Tender to frost but worth growing even in the Northeast. Plants resemble small sweet pea bushes 10−20 in. high. After bright yellow flowers fade, a so-called peg (shootlike structure) develops at each flower's base, grows down into soil, and develops peanuts underground. For best performance, give fertile, well-drained soil; sandy or other light-textured soil is ideal for penetration by pegs.

The four basic classes of peanuts are Virginia and Runner types, with two large seeds per pod; Spanish, with two or three small seeds per pod; and Valencia, with three to six small seeds per pod. Buy seeds (unroasted peanuts) from mail-order seed firms. Plant as soon as soil warms up, setting nuts 1½−2 in. deep. Sow seeds of Virginia and Runner peanuts 6−8 in. apart; sow Spanish and Valencia peanuts 4−6 in. apart. Fertilize at planting time. In 110 to 120 days after planting, foliage yellows and plants are ready to dig; loosen soil, then pull up plants. Cure peanuts on vines in warm, airy place out of sunlight for 2 to 3 weeks, then strip from plants.

PICKING PEACHES

For the sweetest, juiciest peaches, pick the fruit when it is "tree ripe," that is, when the flesh at the stem end gives when pressed with your thumb. The earliest you should harvest is at the "firm ripe" stage, when the flesh at the bottom of the peach yields slightly to thumb pressure. Firm-ripe peaches will ripen fully indoors at room temperature.

To harvest peaches without bruising them, cup the fruit in your hand, then lift up and twist it slightly. The stem will detach cleanly and the tree will not be damaged, as can happen when the fruit is pulled downward.

PEACH AND NECTARINE

VARIETIES	RIPENING SEASON	FRUIT	COMMENTS
PEACH VARIETIES			
'Biscoe'	Midseason	Large size; red and yellow skin, rich, yellow to orange flesh	Moderately vigorous; very hardy flower buds with some resistance to bacterial spot. Good canner
'Canadian Harmony'	Midseason	Large freestone with golden yellow skin blushed red. Yellow flesh, reddish at the pit	Moderately vigorous and very hardy
'Golden Jubilee'	Midseason	Yellow with a bright red over color and the yellow flesh is red at the pit	High production with a heavy set, but somewhat self-thinning. From New Jersey
'Indian Blood Cling'	Midseason to late	Dark crimson skin, reddish flesh. Clingstone	Some resistance to brown rot and bacterial leaf spot. An old variety
'J. H. Hale'	Midseason to late.	Very large, golden yellow, rather smooth skin; ranks high in flavor	One of the few sterile peaches; needs another variety to pollinate it. Moderately vigorous, susceptible to bacterial spot
'Madison'	Midseason	Golden yellow skin with bright red blush and firm yellow flesh. Skin is particularly tender	Of medium vigor; tolerates spring frosts and bears heavily every year
'Raritan Rose'	Midseason	Medium to large with red skin and white flesh streaked red. High flavor	It is resistant to leaf curl but is susceptible to brown rot. Freezes well
'Redhaven'	Early	Nearly all red skinned; yellow flesh is slow to oxidize when exposed to ai.	One of the most planted varieties in the world. Very bud hardy; because of a heavy fruit, it must be thinned. It becomes freestone only after it is fully ripe
'Reliance'	Midseason	Yellow skin blushed a dull medium red and soft yellow flesh	From New Hampshire; very bud hardy with reports of survival at –25°F. Showy flowers; needs heavy thinning. Flavor only fair
'Veteran'	Midseason to late	Medium to large golden yellow fruit with a slight red blush	Bears early and blooms later than most peaches. Reliable in cold wet weather
'Wild Rose'	Early to midseason	Medium to large with smooth yellow-green skin mottled red. The white flesh is reddish around the pit	Large tree

P

PEACH AND NECTARINE

VARIETIES	RIPENING SEASON	FRUIT	COMMENTS
NECTARINE VARIETIES			
'Cherokee'	Early to midseason	Medium size; yellow semi-freestone of fair quality	Some resistance to spring frosts and large showy blooms
'Mericrest'	Midseason	Bright red skin with yellow flesh	Some disease resistance; considered as hardy as 'Reliance' peach
'Red Gold'	Late	Bright red skin with yellow flesh. Aromatic distinctive flavor	Winter-hardy with some disease tolerance. Heavy bearing

PEAR (Pyrus communis)

Rosaceae

DECIDUOUS FRUIT TREES

🌡 ZONES VARY BY VARIETY

☼ FULL SUN

💧 REGULAR WATER

▶ SEE CHART NEXT PAGE

Pear

The common pear is any of several species of the genus *Pyrus*, especially *Pyrus communis* of the rose family. Probably of European origin, hence the name, pears have been cultivated for thousands of years and there are thousands of named varieties. The British and European settlers introduced pears into America and the colonizing Spaniards took them into Mexico. They are cultivated in all the temperate zone countries of both hemispheres.

Commercially, pears rank second to apples of the world's deciduous fruits, except in the United States, where it ranks third to the second place peach. The most widely grown European pear is the 'Williams' Bon Chretien', known in America as the 'Bartlett'.

The European pears are generally distinguished by buttery smooth and sweet texture and flavor. Most are pyriform in shape (elongated at the stem and broad at the base). Skin colors vary from green to yellow with some bronze and red types. Unlike Asian pears, European pears must be harvested before full ripening on the tree.

Rootstocks. The major rootstocks are 'Old Home' with an interstem of 'Farmingdale' (OhxF), quince, and pear seedlings The 'Farmingdale' interstems will impart characteristics to the tree like dwarfing, cold hardiness, compatibility and disease resistance. Quince rootstock is dwarfing but is not compatible on all pears. Standard pear seedlings are usually grown from 'Bartlett' and 'Winter Nellis' seeds. 'Winter Nellis' is particularly cold hardy.

Soil Requirements. Pears will grow on most well-drained soils, but prefer, more than apples, a heavier loam soil.

Tree Characteristics. The pear tree is pyramidal in form with upright branching and on standard rootstock at maturity will be 30–40 ft. high. Quince and other dwarfing stock can reduce the height to 6–10 ft. Pear leaves are round to oval and leather-like. Most of the flowers of fruiting pears are white.

Planting and Culture. Plant near same depth as it grew in the nursery with care that the graft site on the stem is above ground. The site of the graft union is a slight bulge. Pear trees on standard rootstock should be spaced a minimum of 25 ft. and in 5–8 years will produce 3 bushels of fruit. On dwarf stock the plants should be spaced a minimum of 12 ft. The newly planted tree will benefit from annual mulch and a cup of bone

meal. It is important not to supply too much soluble nitrogen or to prune excessively. Both will stimulate succulent growth that is susceptible to fireblight.

Pollination. By planting two or more varieties the cross-pollination will insure good fruit set. 'Bartlett' and 'Seckel' will not cross-pollinate each other; so, a third variety would be needed with these two. Some good pollinators are 'Clapp's Favorite', 'Duchess', and 'Flemish Beauty'.

Pests and Diseases. Fireblight is a bacterial disease that will severely damage and even destroy young pear trees. Bees transmit it particularly at the time of bloom, aphids, psylla and other insects. It can also be spread by wind and rain. By the selection of less susceptible varieties, reduced nitrogen use, careful pruning and good orchard sanitation the disease can often be controlled. The pest that causes most damage is the pear psylla and it has become resistant to many insecticides. Dormant oil sprays and well-timed applications of insecticidal soap can reduce psylla populations.

PEAR, ASIAN or ORIENTAL

Rosaceae

DECIDUOUS FRUIT TREES

🌡 ZONES 32, 34–41

☼ FULL SUN

💧 REGULAR WATER

Pear, Asian or Oriental

Asian pears have been grown in the Orient for centuries and are becoming increasingly popular in the United States. They come from several species of the genus *Pyrus*, particularly *Pyrus pyrifolia* (*P. serotina*) and *Pyrus ussuriensis* of the rose family. All Asian pear varieties are selected seedlings or crosses from these species. Other names are apple pear and Nashi (the word pear in Japanese), as well as Oriental, Chinese and Japanese pears.

Asian pears will suffer tissue damage at temperatures below −15°F. A hardy rootstock is also required in the colder zones. Generally, Asian pears are less cold hardy than the European pears.

Asian pears are distinguished from the European pears by the more round shape, full ripening on the tree and the crispness of the flesh with sweet, sweet-tart and bland diverse flavors. Nashi skin colors are similar to those of the European ones but sometimes have white lenticels (grain-like dots).

Rootstocks. Asian pear cultivars are grafted to rootstocks *Pyrus betulaefolia*, *P. calleryana*, *P. serotina*, *P. ussuriensis* and *P. communis*. The most cold hardy are the *P. serotina* and *P. ussuriensis*, hardy to −40°F.

In warmer zones the *P. betulaefolia* is desirable for its vigor, production of large fruit, and its tolerance of wet soils. *P. calleryana* is not cold hardy and is only suitable as a rootstock for the Northeast.

Planting and Culture. Generally following the guidelines of the European pear. Most are pruned to a central leader shap, resembling, at maturity the Christmas tree profile. Most Asian pears bloom earlier than the European ones and in zones with a variable spring climate buds and blooms are subject to freezing. At the same time, many will set a very heavy fruit crop that requires hand thinning. If not properly thinned, the fruit size and quality will be diminished and the heavy fruit load will cause limb breakage. Fruiting will begin the third year after planting.

Pollination. Partially self-fruiting, most varieties will benefit from planting two or more cultivars. Asian pears also benefit from European pear pollen, like 'Bartlett', 'Harvest Queen', and 'Harrows Delight'. Varieties '20th Century' and 'Shinseiki' will usually set adequate crops even if planted singly. 'Kikusui' will not pollinate '20th Century' and 'Nitaka' is pollen sterile.

Pests and Diseases. The Asian pear can be severely damaged by codling moth. With the use of an insecticide and by thinning clusters to a single fruit, infestation can be reduced. In addition, the pear psylla will cause sticky fruit and can be reduced by the use of a delayed dormant spray. Asian pears are susceptible to fireblight and in the cooler areas will develop bacterial canker (*Pseudomonas*). For fireblight control select less susceptible varieties noted in the descriptions, carefully remove blighted material from the tree site and reduce nitrogen application that produces succulent susceptible growth.

Varieties (in order of ripening):

'Shinsui'. Early maturing, small to medium sized brown fruit with very sweet flesh. Varieties 'Nitaka and Kikusui will not pollinate it.

'Kosui'. Small to medium fruit with a light yellow skin slightly bronze russeted. The flesh is crisp, crunchy, and very sweet. The tree is vigorous growing but the leaves are subject to spray burn.

'Shinseiki'. Round, medium to large in size with a clear yellow skin and white, mild, sweet flesh. It is self-fruit, bears early and stores well. Pollinate with 'Bartlett' or 'Hosui'. It is moderately resistant to pseudomonas and fireblight.

'Yakumo'. Yellow-skinned smooth fruit with sweet, very juicy flesh sometimes said to have a melon flavor. The shape is oblong to oval. It will store well and is hardy to zone 43.

'Hosui'. is medium to large in size with brownish orange skin and off-white, sweet flesh. In cooler climates, the taste will have tartness. It is early blooming and can be pollinated with 'Bartlett', 'Chojuro', '20th Century' or 'Shinko'. In cold and wet springs it will develop pseudomonas. The fruit bruises easily.

'Kikusui'. Flat, with a yellowish green thin skin. Medium in size, the white flesh is sweet-tart and juicy. Pollinate with 'Bartlett', 'Chojuro' or '20th Century'. The tree is productive and early to bear.

'20th Century'. Also known as 'Nijisseki' and is the most popular variety in Japan and California. Medium in size and somewhat lopsided with a long stem, the skin is yellow with greenish mottling. Very juicy and crisp, it has a mild and bland flavor. Pollinate with 'Chojuro', 'Bartlett' or 'Hosui'. It will tolerate drought and heat but is subject to many diseases.

'Chojuro'. Flat, with russet-greenish skin and white, crisp flesh, that is reputed to have a butterscotch flavor. It is overbearing and should be heavily thinned. Crosses of 'Chojuro' and '20th Century' are often used to develop new varieties.

'Singo'. Tannish yellow skin with white, tender, juicy, very sweet flesh and excellent storage quality. A good pollinator for 'Korean Giant', it is hardy to zone 44, but will ripen properly only to Zone 42.

'Korean Giant'. Also called 'Olympic' and 'Hardy Giant'. Very large in size, the skin is a dark brown russet with sweet and juicy flesh. Pollinate with Singo. It store well.

'Shinko'. Medium in size and oval shaped with brownish green skin and a rich, distinctive flavor. Pollinate with 'Chojuro', '20th Century', 'Bartlett', or 'Hosui'. Both codling moth and fireblight are problems. It stores well.

'Ya Li'. From China, also known as 'Duckbill Pear'. It is one of the pear-shaped Asian varieties with greenish yellow skin and the white flesh is moderately sweet with some tartness. It may not ripen in cooler areas. The fall foliage is a wine-red. Pollinate with 'Bartlett'. It is one of the first to bloom and the last to ripen.

PEARL BUSH. See EXOCHORDA

PEARLY EVERLASTING. See ANAPHALIS

PEASHRUB. See CARAGANA

PECAN. See CARYA

PELARGONIUM

GERANIUM

Geraniaceae

ANNUALS

✎ ALL ZONES; OR INDOORS

☼ ☀ LIGHT SHADE IN HOT CLIMATES

💧 💧 REGULAR TO MODERATE WATER

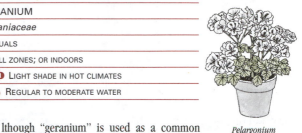

Pelargonium domesticum

Although "geranium" is used as a common name for *Pelargonium*, botanically speaking it's not really accurate. To the botanist, pelargoniums are perennials (grown as annuals in the Northeast) that endure light frosts but not hard freezes and have slightly asymmetrical flowers in clusters. Most come from South Africa. A true geranium, on the other hand, is one of many annual or perennial plants, most from the Northern Hemisphere, having symmetrical flowers borne singly or in clusters; some are weeds, some valued perennial border or rock garden plants.

To North American gardeners, a geranium is an ivy geranium, a common geranium, a regal or Lady Washington geranium, or a scented geranium, all of which are species or varieties of *Pelargonium*. Gardeners also use the word "geranium" for true geraniums.

Pelargonium tomentosum

Most garden geraniums can be divided among three species of *Pelargonium*: *P. domesticum*, Lady Washington geranium; *P. hortorum*, common geranium (this group also includes variegated forms usually referred to as fancy-leafed or color-leafed geraniums); and *P. peltatum*, ivy geranium. In addition, many other species have scented leaves. These plants are popular annual bedding plants or house plants. Move them indoors before the first frost or take cuttings for the following year.

All geraniums do well in pots. Common geraniums grow well in garden beds; Lady Washington geraniums are also planted in beds but tend to get rangy. Some varieties of Lady Washington are used in hanging baskets. Ivy geraniums are good in hanging containers or in raised beds. Use scented geraniums in close-up situations—in pots or in ground. For good bloom on potted geranium indoors, place it in a sunny window or in the brightest light possible.

Plant in any good, fast-draining soil. Remove faded flowers regularly to encourage new bloom. Pinch growing tips while plants are small to force side branches. Geraniums in pots bloom best when somewhat pot bound. Aphids, whiteflies, and spider mites are common pests.

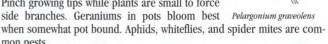

Pelargonium graveolens

P. domesticum. LADY WASHINGTON GERANIUM, MARTHA WASHINGTON GERANIUM, REGAL GERANIUM. Erect or somewhat spreading, to 3 ft. This species is more rangy than common geranium. Leaves are heart shaped to kidney shaped, dark green, 2–4 in. wide, with crinkled margins, unequal sharp teeth. Large, showy flowers 2 in. across (sometimes even larger) in loose, rounded clusters, in white and many shades of pink, red, lavender, purple, with brilliant blotches and markings of darker colors.

EUROPEAN PEAR VARIETIES

NAME	SEASONS	FRUIT	COMMENTS
'Anjou'	Midseason	Large pear with greenish yellow russet skin and a pink blush. Flesh is buttery, fine-grained, melting and aromatic. There is also a 'Red Anjou'	From Belgium, it was a favorite eating pear in Europe a hundred years ago. Needs a pollinator like 'Bosc' or 'Bartlett'
'Aurora'	Early	Large, yellow and russetted with a slight blush with smooth, melting flesh.	Ripens just before 'Bartlett'; will keep in storage longer than the 'Bartlett'
'Bartlett'	Early to midseason	Large, yellow skinned with a red blush. Flesh is smooth and juicy with a touch of tartness	Introduced from England in 1797; the standard and most widely grown of all pears. 'Seckel' and 'Magness' will not pollinate it. Subject to fireblight
'Bosc'	Midseason ripening	Medium size with golden skin and bronze russetting. Neck is gourd shaped. Tender juicy white flesh with a rich, slightly acid flavor	Will store for six months. Late blooming. When cooked, it will hold its shape.
'Clapp's Favorite'	Early	Very large, long necked lemon yellow pear with very sweet white flesh	Very susceptible to fireblight; will not store long
'Comice'	Late	French dessert fruit; large and roundish with green-yellow skin and a red blush. Flesh is buttery, juicy and firm with a rich sweet flavor	'Moonglow', 'Anjou', and 'Bartlett' are good pollinators. The tree is slow to begin bearing.
'Duchess'	Midseason	Large, greenish yellow russetted fruit with pink blush; crisp, firm flesh	Somewhat self-fertile; will bear two or three years after planting. A good pollinator for 'Bartlett'
'Flemish Beauty'	Midseason	Large roundish pear with clear yellow skin and a marbled and dotted red blush	Somewhat self-fertile and very hardy, it was at one time a leading commercial variety. Requires a good pollinator
'Kieffer'	Midseason	Large golden yellow cooking pear with crimson blush	Must be stored in a cool place until flavor develops. Self-fertile; resists fireblight. Extremely hardy
'Magness'	Midseason	Yellow skin with dark spot and light russet; flesh is sweet and almost free of grit cells. Medium sized, oval	Cross of 'Seckel' and 'Comice'; pollinator like 'Maxine' or 'Harrow Delight' is needed. Tree is slow to begin to bear. Some resistance to fireblight
'Maxine'	Early to midseason	Golden yellow with snow white flesh that has few grit cells. Flavor similar to many Asian pears	Some resistance to fireblight
'Moonglow'	Early to midseason	Medium to large with dull yellow skin with pink blush; white flesh is soft with mild flavor. Few grit cells	A seedling of 'Comice'. Somewhat resistant to fireblight
'Seckel' (Honey pear or sugar pear)	Midseason	Small yellowish brown fruit with pale russet and russet red blush. Fine-grained flesh extremely sweet and very juicy with spicy rich flavor	Introduced from Europe in 1790. A pollinator will increase yields; some fireblight resistance
'Tyson' (Early sugar pear)	Early	Medium size with yellow skin and spicy sweet flesh, but somewhat grainy at the core	Good pollinator; some resistance to fireblight
'Winter Nellis'	Very late	Dark brown and green, roughly russetted, juicy sweet flesh. Unattractive in appearance but unsurpassed for a late winter pear	Partially self-fruitful, sets heavier crops with a pollinator. Good pollinator for 'Bartlett'. Originated in Belgium in the early 19th century, used as a rootstock for pears

P

P. hortorum. COMMON GERANIUM, GARDEN GERANIUM. Most popular, widely grown. Shrubby, succulent stemmed, to 3 ft. or more; older plants grown in the open (in mild areas) become woody. Round or kidney-shaped leaves are velvety and hairy, soft to the touch, aromatic, with edges indistinctly lobed and scallop toothed; most varieties show zone of deeper color just inside leaf margin, though some are plain green. Fancy-leafed or color-leafed varieties have zones, borders, or splashes of brown, gold, red, white, or green in various combinations. Some also have highly attractive flowers. Single or double flowers are flatter and smaller than those of Lady Washington geranium, but clusters bear many more blossoms. Flowers are usually in solid colors. Many varieties in white and shades of pink, rose, red, orange, and violet.

*Pelargonium
hortorum*

There are also dwarf-growing, cactus-flowered, and other novelty kinds. Tough, attractive geraniums for outdoor bedding can be grown from seed, flowering the same summer. Widely available strains are Diamond and Elite (quick to reach bloom stage, compact, need no pinching); Orbit (distinct leaf zoning; broad, rounded flower clusters); and Sprinter (slow growing, very free flowering).

P. peltatum. IVY GERANIUM. Trailing plants to 2–3 ft. or longer. Leaves rather succulent, glossy bright green, 2–3 in. across, ivylike, with pointed lobes. Inch-wide single or double flowers in rounded clusters of five to ten; colors include white, pink, rose, red, and lavender. Upper petals may be blotched or striped. Many named varieties. 'L'Elegante' has white-edged foliage; other varieties have white or yellow veins in leaves. Summer Showers strain can be grown from seed; it comes as a mixture of white, pink, red, lavender, and magenta.

Scented geraniums. Many aromatic species are available; all fall into the 1–3-ft.-high range and bear clusters of small blossoms in white or rosy colors (flowers are secondary to the foliage in appeal). The common name of each refers to the plant's fragrance. Types include apple (*P. odoratissimum*), lemon (*P. crispum*), lime (*P. nervosum*), peppermint (*P. tomentosum*), and rose (*P. capitatum, P. graveolens*). All such scented kinds are more tolerant of hot, humid summers than other types. Good for herb garden, edgings, front of borders, window boxes, hanging baskets. Use fresh leaves of all types for flavoring jelly and iced drinks; use dried leaves in potpourri and sachets.

PELTANDRA

ARROW ARUM

Araceae

AQUATIC PERENNIALS

ZONES VARY BY SPECIES

FULL SUN TO SHADE

AMPLE WATER

Peltandra

With their handsome, arrow-shaped leaves and callalike flowers produced on tall spikes in early summer, these rhizomatous Northeast natives are good choices for a bog garden or the edges or ornamental ponds. Flowers are followed later in the season by berries, which often bend to the water's surface by late summer or early fall. Plant in containers or directly in the mud at water's edge in heavy soil high in organic matter; if planting in water, sink 3–5 in. below the surface. Easy to grow and not highly invasive.

P. sagittifolia (P. alba). WHITE ARROW ARUM. Zones 31, 32. The showier of the two species, it produces flowers with white leaflike spathes, followed by bronzy red berries.

P. virginica. GREEN ARROW ARUM. Zones 31, 32, 34–41. Foliage is clump-forming, deeply ribbed, glossy green. Spathes are pale green, sometimes edged with white, enclosing white to orange spikelike spadices; berries are green.

PELTIPHYLLUM peltatum. See DARMERA peltata

PELTOBOYKINIA
watanabei

Saxifragaceae

PERENNIAL

ZONES 32, 34–41

PARTIAL SHADE

MORE THAN REGULAR WATER

Peltoboykinia

Peltoboykinia contains two species of perennials grown for their handsome foliage—*P. watanabei* and the somewhat larger *P. tellimoides*. Both are native to moist woodlands in Japan and spread by creeping rhizomes to form mounds that are 2–3 ft. tall and wide. They bear lobed, toothed leaves that are peltate, meaning they are generally round in outline and the stem is attached in the center of the bottom side of the leaf blade. (Waterlilies and May apple, for example, also have peltate leaves.) In early summer, plants bear branched clusters of tiny, creamy yellow to greenish, 1/4–1/2-in.-long flowers. Select a site with rich, moist to boggy soil. Use these plants in moist woodland gardens or along ponds or streams.

PENNISETUM

FOUNTAIN GRASS

Poaceae (Gramineae)

PERENNIAL GRASSES

ZONES VARY BY SPECIES

EXPOSURE NEEDS VARY BY SPECIES

WATER NEEDS VARY BY SPECIES

Pennisetum

Fountain grasses are generally clump forming, with arching stems tipped with fat, furry flower plumes in summer. They are among the most graceful of ornamental grasses. Use them in containers, in perennial or shrub borders, as bank cover.

P. alopecuroides. Zones 31, 32, 34, 35, 37, 39. Bright green, 3–4-ft. foliage clumps are topped by pinkish plumes in early summer. Leaves turn yellow in fall, brown in winter. In 'Hameln', white plumes double the height of a 1–1½-ft. clump. In late summer, 'Moudry' has black plumes rising a foot or more above a 1½–2-ft. clump. 'Cassian' is a dwarf (2-ft.) selection with cream-colored flowers and yellow-tinted foliage that turns to orange and dark red in fall. 'Little Bunny' is like the species but dwarf, to 10 in. tall. 'Paul's Giant' reaches the uncommon height of 5 ft., has yellow-orange autumn foliage. Sun or light shade. Regular to moderate water. Can self-sow.

P. orientale. Zones 31, 32, 34, 35, 37, 39. The 1–1½-ft. clumps of leaves are topped by pinkish plumes that stand a foot or more above the foliage. Plumes mature to light brown and foliage turns straw color in winter. 'Tall Tales' makes an upright, arching clump to 4½ ft. tall, with tan blossoms rising another foot above the leaves. Growing conditions are the same as for *P. alopecuroides*.

P. setaceum. Perennial treated as annual. Dense, rounded clump to 4 ft. high. Coppery pink or purplish flowers, borne on 3–4-ft. stems, are held within the foliage clump or just above it. Full sun. Can take regular water, but is extremely drought tolerant when established. 'Rubrum' ('Cupreum', 'Purpureum'), reddish burgundy leaves and dark plumes. 'Eaton Canyon' (compact purple fountain grass) is a small version of 'Rubrum', 2½ ft. tall, with the same red-burgundy leaves.

P. villosum. FEATHERTOP. Perennial grown as an annual. To 2 ft. high and as wide. Narrow, arching green leaves, cylindrical, feathery white plumes in late summer–early autumn. Full sun to partial shade. Regular to moderate water, will tolerate drought.

P

PENNYROYAL. See MENTHA pulegium

PENSTEMON

BEARD TONGUE

Scrophulariaceae

PERENNIALS, EVERGREEN SHRUBS AND SHRUBLETS

✔ ZONES VARY BY SPECIES

☼ ◐ AFTERNOON SHADE IN HOT CLIMATES

◖ ◗ REGULAR TO MODERATE WATER

Penstemon

A few are widely grown; most are sold only by specialists. All have tubular flowers. Bright reds and blues are the most common colors, but there are penstemons in white and soft pinks through salmon and peach to deep rose, lilac, deep purple, and, rarely, yellow. Hummingbirds are attracted to the flowers. Of some 250 species, most are native to the western U.S. Need fast drainage. Usually short lived (3 to 4 years). Hybrids and selections tend to be easier than wild species to grow alongside regular garden plants.

P. ambiguus. PRAIRIE PENSTEMON, SAND PENSTEMON. Shrubby perennial. Zones 31, 32, 34–43. To 2 ft. high, with very narrow leaves and broad (rather than tall) clusters of white to pink flowers that resemble phlox. Early summer to early fall bloom.

P. barbatus. Perennial. Zones 31, 32, 34–43. Open, somewhat sprawling habit to 3 ft. tall. Bright green, 2–6-in.-long leaves. Long, loose spikes of 1-in. red flowers in midsummer to early fall. Selections include 'Elfin Pink', bright pink flowers on 1-ft. spikes; 'Pink Beauty', pink flowers on 2–2½-ft. spikes; 'Prairie Dusk', deep purple flowers on 2-ft. spikes; 'Prairie Fire', scarlet flowers on 2–2½-ft. spikes; 'Rose Elf', coral pink flowers on 2-ft. spikes, some rebloom; and 'Schooley's Yellow', lemon yellow flowers on 2-ft. spikes.

P. canescens. Perennial. Zones 31, 32, 34–41. Native to eastern U.S. To nearly 3 ft. high, oblong to lance-shaped leaves. Purple to violet flowers with darker markings bloom in summer.

P. digitalis. Perennial. Zones 31, 32, 34–43. Native to much of the eastern and midwestern U.S. Perennial to 5 ft. tall. Leaves to 7 in. long; flowers to 1½ in. long in white or pink shades, often with faint purple lines. Spring to early summer bloom. 'Husker Red', 2½–3 ft. tall, has maroon leaves and pale pink flowers.

P. gloxinioides. BORDER PENSTEMON, GARDEN PENSTEMON. Perennial treated as annual. Specific name has no botanical standing, but is widely used to refer to a hybrid group. Compact, bushy, upright growth to 2–4 ft. Tubular summer flowers in loose spikes at stem ends, in almost all colors but blue and yellow. Varieties include lavender 'Alice Hindley' ('Lady Hindley'), pink-tipped white 'Apple Blossom', rose pink 'Evelyn', bright red 'Firebird', rosy red 'Garnet', white (sometimes pink-flushed) 'Holly White', white-throated 'Huntington Pink', dark purple 'Midnight', and pale-throated purple 'Sour Grapes'. Cut back for second bloom on side branches.

P. hirsutus. Evergreen subshrub. Zones 31, 32, 34–45. Spreading or upright, to 32 in. high and 2 ft. across. Deep green, lance-shaped, toothed leaves; light violet flowers with white throat bloom in summer. 'Purpureus' has bright purple flowers.

P. laevigatus. Perennial. Zones 31, 32, 34–43. Native to eastern U.S. To nearly 4 ft. tall, lance-shaped, toothed leaves. Pale violet flowers, lighter on the inside, in summer.

P. pinifolius. Shrublet. Zones 31, 32, 34–43. Spreading, 4–6 in. high (rarely to 2 ft.), with crowded needlelike leaves ¾ in. long. Coral to scarlet, 1½-in.-long flowers in summer. Rock garden, low border plant, small-scale ground cover. 'Mersea Yellow' has bright yellow flowers.

FOR INFORMATION ON SELECTING PLANTS

PLEASE SEE PAGES 47–112

PENTAS lanceolata

STAR CLUSTERS

Rubiaceae

PERENNIAL GROWN AS ANNUAL

✔ ALL ZONES

☼ ◐ FULL SUN OR PARTIAL SHADE

◗ REGULAR WATER

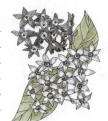

Pentas lanceolata

Grown as a perennial in Florida, but elsewhere it is a summer annual. Spreading, multistemmed plant to 2–3 ft. tall. Leaves are long, somewhat hairy ovals; stems are topped by tight, 4-in.-wide clusters of small, star-shaped flowers in white, pink, lilac, or red. Remove dead flowers for a long bloom season. Feed monthly in summer. If growing as a house plant, give it as much sunlight as possible by setting in a bright west or south window.

PEONY. See PAEONIA

PEPPER

Solanaceae

PERENNIALS GROWN AS ANNUALS

✔ ALL ZONES

☼ FULL SUN

◗ REGULAR WATER

Pepper

Peppers grow on attractive, bushy plants ranging from less than a foot high to 4 ft. tall, depending on variety. Use plants as temporary low informal hedge; or grow and display them in containers. The two basic kinds of peppers are sweet and hot.

Sweet peppers always remain mild, even when flesh ripens to red. This group includes big stuffing and salad peppers commonly known as bell peppers; best known of these are 'California Wonder' and 'Yolo Wonder'. Other good cultivars include 'Ace', extra early-bearing; 'Big Bertha', large fruit; 'King Arthur', large fruit on dwarf plants. Hybrid varieties have been bred for early bearing, high yield, or disease resistance. Big peppers are also available in bright yellow ('Golden Bell') and purple ('Purple Beauty'; purple types turn green when cooked). There are also orange cultivars (such as 'Orange Bell'), and peppers that ripen to chocolate brown ('Sweet Chocolate'). Other sweet types are thick-walled, very sweet pimientos used in salads or for cooking or canning; sweet cherry peppers for pickling; and long, slender Italian frying peppers and Hungarian sweet yellow peppers, both used for cooking.

Hot peppers range from tiny (pea-size) types to narrow, 6–7-in.-long forms, but all are pungent, their flavor ranging from the mild heat of Italian peperoncini to the near-incandescence of 'Habañero'. 'Anaheim' is a mildly spicy pepper used for making canned green chiles. 'Long Red Cayenne' is used for drying; other cayenne types include 'Super Cayenne II' and 'Ring-o-Fire'. 'Hungarian Yellow Wax (Hot)', 'Jalapeño', 'Fresno Chile Grande', and 'Serrano' are used for pickling. Mexican cooking utilizes an entire palette of peppers, among them 'Ancho', 'Mulato', and 'Pasilla'. Fiery peppers to use in Southeast Asian cuisine include 'Thai Dragon' and 'Thai Hot'.

Peppers need a long, warm growing season, and in most areas must be set outdoors as seedlings if they are to produce fruit. Buy nursery plants, or sow seed indoors 8 to 10 weeks before average date of last frost. When weather warms up and night temperatures remain consistently above 55°F/13°C, set transplants outdoors, spacing them 1½–2 ft. apart. Fertilize once or twice after plants become established, before blossoms set. Sweet peppers are ready to pick when they have reached good size, but they keep their flavor until red-ripe. Pimientos should be picked only when red-ripe. Pick hot peppers when they are fully ripe. Possible pests include aphids, whiteflies, cutworms, pepper maggots, and Colorado potato beetles.

PEPPERMINT. See MENTHA piperita

PERILLA frutescens

SHISO

Lamiaceae (Labiatae)

ANNUAL

✔ ALL ZONES

☼ ◑ FULL SUN OR LIGHT SHADE

◆ REGULAR WATER

Perilla frutescens

Sturdy, leafy warm-weather plant to 2–3 ft. tall. Deeply toothed, egg-shaped leaves to 5 in. long. Kind most commonly seen has bronzy or purple leaves that look much like those of coleus. *P. f. nankinensis* has darker purple-bronze leaves with curly edges. Leaves of Fancy Fringe strain are deeply cut and fringed, deep bronzy purple in color. Use leaves as vegetable or flavoring (they taste something like mint, something like cinnamon); fry long, thin clusters of flower buds as a vegetable in tempura batter. Extremely fast and easy to grow; self-sows freely. In Asia, seeds are pressed for edible oil.

PERIWINKLE. See CATHARANTHUS roseus, VINCA

PERNETTYA mucronata (Gaultheria mucronata)

Ericaceae

EVERGREEN SHRUB

✔ ZONES 32, 34

☼ ◑ PARTIAL SHADE IN HOT CLIMATES

◆ REGULAR WATER

Pernettya mucronata

Compact growth to 2–3 ft., spreading by underground runners to form clumps. Small, glossy dark green leaves; some turn red or bronzy in winter. Tiny, bell-shaped white to pink flowers in late spring are followed by colorful, long-lasting berries in purple, white, red, rose, pink, or near black, all with a metallic sheen. You'll get more fruit if several plants are grown for cross-pollination. Grow in acid, peaty soil. Can be invasive; control by cutting roots with spade. Top often needs regular pruning to stay attractive. Use as informal low hedge or border, in tubs or window boxes.

PEROVSKIA

RUSSIAN SAGE

Lamiaceae (Labiatae)

SHRUBBY PERENNIAL

✔ ZONES 31, 32, 34, 35, 37, 39

☼ FULL SUN

◆ MODERATE WATER

Perovskia

Woody-based clump with many upright, gray-white stems clothed in gray-green foliage. Leaves are 2–3 in. long and deeply cut on lower part of stem, become smaller and merely toothed toward top of stem. Each stem is topped with a widely branched spray of small lavender blue flowers; when plants are in full bloom in late spring and summer, flowers form a haze above the foliage. To extend flowering period, trim off spent blossoms. Mature clumps may reach 3–4 ft. high, with equal spread.

Often sold as *P. atriplicifolia*, but plants in circulation are probably hybrids between that species and *P. abrotanoides*. Widely grown 'Blue Spire', with deep violet blue blooms, is sometimes sold as *P. atriplicifolia* 'Superba' or *P.* 'Longin'. 'Blue Mist' (earliest-flowering variety) and 'Blue Haze' bear lighter blue blossoms. 'Filagran' has silvery, very finely cut leaves. Mass plants or use them individually in borders. Plants take any soil, as long as it is well drained. Extremely resistant to heat and drought. Best in warm summers, even where weather is humid. Cut nearly to ground each spring before new growth starts.

PERSIAN SHIELD. See Strobilanthes dyerianus

PERSICARIA. See POLYGONUM

PERSIMMON (Diospyros)

Ebenaceae

DECIDUOUS FRUIT TREES

✔ ZONES VARY BY SPECIES

☼ FULL SUN

◆ ◆ REGULAR TO MODERATE WATER

Persimmon

Of the two types of persimmons grown, the native species is a bigger, more cold-tolerant tree than the Asian species; however, the Asian type bears larger fruit that is sold in markets. Neither species is fussy about soil.

American persimmon *(Diospyros virginiana)* is native from Connecticut to Kansas and southward to Texas and Florida. It grows best in Zones 31, 32, 34–41. As a landscape tree, it is not as ornamental as the Asian species, and is probably best suited to wild gardens, where its tendency to form thickets from root suckers can be tolerated. Reaches 35–60 ft. tall, 20–35 ft. wide, with a broad, oval crown and attractive gray-brown bark fissured into a deep checkered pattern. Glossy, broad, oval leaves to 6 in. long turn yellow, pink, or reddish purple in fall. Fruit is round, yellow to orange (often blushed red), 1½–2 in. across; very astringent until soft-ripe, then very sweet. On wild species, fruit ripens in early fall after frost; some varieties do not require chill. Both male and female trees are usually needed to get fruit. 'Meader' is a self-fertile variety; its fruit is seedless if not pollinated.

TRY DRYING SOME PERSIMMONS

To dry persimmon fruit, pick it when hard-ripe with some stem remaining. Peel and hang by string in sun until it shrivels. Dried fruit has a flavor something like a date or very high quality prune.

Japanese or Oriental persimmon *(Diospyros kaki)* grows and fruits in Zones 31, 32. Reaches 30 ft. or more, with handsome, wide-spreading branch pattern. One of the best fruit trees for ornamental use; good small shade tree, espalier. Oval leaves, 6–7 in. long and 2–3½ in. wide, turn from glossy dark green to vivid yellow, orange, or red in autumn, even in mild climates. Brilliant orange, 3–4-in. fruits—the persimmons sold in markets—appear in fall and persist until winter unless harvested. This species sets fruit without pollination, though crops are often tastier and more abundant when pollinated. Varieties include:

'Chocolate'. Brown-flecked, very sweet flesh.

'Fuyu'. Nonastringent even when underripe; firm fleshed (like an apple), reddish yellow, about size of baseball but flattened like tomato. Similar but larger is 'Gosho', widely sold as 'Giant Fuyu'.

'Hachiya'. Shapeliest tree for ornamental use. This variety yields big (4-in.-long, 2½–3-in.-broad), slightly pointed persimmons. Pick before

P

fully ripe to save crop from birds, but allow to become soft-ripe before eating; astringent unless mushy.

'Tamopan'. Very large, turban shaped, astringent until fully ripe.

PERUVIAN DAFFODIL. See HYMENOCALLIS narcissiflora

PERUVIAN LILY. See ALSTROEMERIA

PETASITES japonicus

JAPANESE COLTSFOOT, FUKI

Asteraceae (Compositae)

PERENNIAL

 ZONES 31, 32, 34–41

☼ ◐ ● TAKES SUN IN COOL-SUMMER AREAS

💧 AMPLE WATER

Petasites japonicus

Giant perennial for growing in perpetually moist soil near the water. Creeping rhizomes give rise to huge (16-in.-wide), round leaves on long stalks; stalks are used as a vegetable (fuki) by the Japanese. Short spikes of fragrant white daisies appear in late winter before leaves emerge. Locate plant with care, since it is invasive and its thick rhizomes can be extremely difficult to eradicate. Varieties include 'Giganteus', with leaves up to 4 ft. wide on 5-ft. stalks, and 'Variegatus', with somewhat smaller leaves (to 2–3 ft.) boldly marked with creamy white.

PETRORHAGIA saxifraga

TUNIC FLOWER

Caryophyllaceae

PERENNIAL

 ZONES 32, 34–41

☼ FULL SUN

💧 REGULAR WATER

Petrorhagia saxifraga

Tunic flower, a European native, is grown for its loose clusters of white or pink, dark-veined, ½-in.-wide flowers that bloom for an extended period in summer. It has narrow, grassy, ½-in.-long green leaves forming a low mat. At 4 in. high, it creates an airy, delicate effect. It's available in a number of attractive varieties, including 'Alba', white blooms; and 'Alba Plena', double white flowers. 'Lady Mary', 'Pleniflora Rosea', and the compact 'Rosette' have double pink flowers. 'Splendens' has bigger pink blooms. 'Nana' is a dwarf. Handsome, long-lived, and good for edging. Grows well on slopes and banks, in rock gardens, or dry walls, and flourishes in poor, sandy, or fertile well-drained soil. It may self-sow abundantly but seedlings are easy to pull out by hand.

PETUNIA hybrida

PETUNIA

Solanaceae

TENDER PERENNIAL GROWN AS ANNUAL

 ALL ZONES

☼ FULL SUN

💧 REGULAR WATER

Petunia hybrida

Plants are low growing, bushy to spreading, with thick, broad leaves that are slightly sticky to the touch. Flower form varies from single and funnel shaped to very double and heavily ruffled (like carnations); the many colors include cream, yellow, pure white, and the whole range from soft pink to deepest red, light blue to deepest purple. Bicolors and picotees are available, as are types with contrasting veins on the petals and those with fluted or fringed edges. In most zones, plants bloom throughout summer until frost.

Plant in good garden soil. Single-flowered kinds tolerate alkalinity, will grow in poor soil if it's well drained. Plant 8–18 in. apart, depending on size of variety. After plants are established, pinch back halfway for compact growth. Feed monthly with complete fertilizer. Near end of summer, cut back rangy plants by about half to force new growth. In humid weather, botrytis disease can damage blossoms and foliage of most petunias; Multifloras are somewhat resistant. Smog damage (spotting on seedling leaves), tobacco budworm (flowers look tattered or fail to open) may be problems in some areas.

Described below are the three classes of petunias (the long-standing Grandiflora and Multiflora classes and the new Milliflora), the new ground cover variety, and a group of trailing hybrids. Petunias are generally labeled F_1 or F_2 hybrids. F_1 refers to first-generation hybrids, which are more vigorous and more uniform in color, height, and growth habit than their offspring, F_2 hybrids.

HYBRID GRANDIFLORA
Of the three classes, these bear the largest flowers but bloom the least profusely. Sturdy plants to 15–27 in. high, 2–3 ft. wide. Flowers usually single, ruffled or fringed, to 4½ in. across, in pink, rose, salmon, red, scarlet, blue, white, pale yellow, or striped combinations. Fluffy Ruffles strain has the largest blossoms, to 6 in. across. Cascade, Countdown, and Supercascade series have a cascading growth habit that makes them good for hanging baskets. Magic and Supermagic strains give heavy bloom on compact plants, bearing large (4–5-in.-wide) single flowers in white, pink, red, blue. Double Hybrid Grandifloras with heavily ruffled flowers come in all petunia colors except yellow.

HYBRID MULTIFLORA
Plants about same size as Grandifloras, but flowers are generally smooth edged and smaller (to 2 in. across), single or double. Neat, compact growth ideal for bedding, massed planting. Many named varieties in pink, rose, salmon, yellow, white, blue. Joy and Plum strains have single, satiny-textured flowers in white, cream, pink, coral, red, blue. 'Summer Sun' is a bright yellow petunia.

HYBRID MILLIFLORA
Newest class of petunias, with smaller flowers and more dwarf habit than Multiflora. Fantasy strain makes neat, compact mound to 10 in. high, with plentiful 1–1½-in. blooms in pink, red, blue, ivory. Good for pots, hanging baskets, window boxes.

'Purple Wave'. The first-ever ground cover petunia, growing 4–6 in. high, with 4-ft. spread. Abundance of vivid purple, 2–3-in. blossoms. Series now includes 'Misty Lilac Wave', pale lavender splashed with white; 'Pink Wave', bright pink; 'Rose Wave', rose pink. Good for banks, borders, containers, hanging baskets.

Supertunia. Another group of vigorously trailing hybrids, suited to pots, window boxes, hanging baskets, and use as annual ground cover in beds and borders. Cultivars include 'Cherry Cascade', cherry red with dark center; 'Priscilla', lavender with deeper purple flush down center of petals; 'Purple Sunspot', magenta purple with black center; 'Sun Lace', pink with yellow throat'; and 'Sun Snow', white.

STARTING PETUNIAS INDOORS

Get a jump on a short growing season by starting petunias indoors. Sow 10–12 weeks before last frost date. Mix the tiny seeds with sand to make sowing easier. Press lightly into soil but do not cover them. Move to garden when frost danger is past.

P

PHALARIS arundinacea

RIBBON GRASS, GARDENER'S GARTERS

Poaceae (Gramineae)

DECORATIVE PERENNIAL GRASS

🌿 ZONES 31, 32, 34–43

☀️ ◑ FULL SUN OR PARTIAL SHADE

💧 💧 💧 MUCH TO MODERATE WATER

*Phalaris
arundinacea*

Tough, tenacious, bamboolike grass that spreads aggressively by underground runners to form spreading, 2–3-ft.-high clumps. Deep green leaves turn buff in fall. Airy flower clusters are white, aging to pale brown. 'Picta' has green leaves with longitudinal white stripes. The following selections are less invasive: 'Dwarf Garters', a slow spreader half as tall as the species; and 1½–2-ft.-high 'Mervyn Feesey' ('Feesey's Form'), with white variegation strongly blushed with pink.

PHASEOLUS coccineus. See BEAN, SCARLET RUNNER

PHEASANT'S EYE. See ADONIS

PHELLODENDRON

CORK TREE

Rutaceae

DECIDUOUS TREE

🌿 ZONES VARY BY SPECIES

☀️ FULL SUN

💧 REGULAR WATER

Phellodendron

Despite their common name, these hardy trees are not the source of cork (that comes from an oak, *Quercus suber*), but rather derive their name from the conspicuous and ornamental corklike appearance of the bark. Leaves are strongly aromatic and provide good yellow color in fall. Small clusters of white or yellowish flowers are male and female on separate trees. Both are necessary to bear the dark, round fruits, which are ½-in. in diameter, taste of turpentine, and contain five small stones each. Attractive bark makes these trees fine specimen choices for larger gardens that can accommodate their spreading habits, which can exceed 40 ft.

P. amurense. AMUR CORK TREE. Zones 31, 32, 34–45. Spreads widely and grows to 45 ft. high. Stocky with pale gray bark. Lustrous leaves grow to 14 in. long and have 5 to 13 oval leaflets.

P. lavallei. LAVALLE'S CORK TREE. Zones 31, 32, 34–41. Reaches 30–45 ft. high and spreads widely. Thick with corklike gray-brown bark. Leaves are dull green with 5 to 13 leaflets and grow to 14 in. long.

P. sachalinense. SAKHALIN CORK TREE. Zones 31, 32, 34–45. Grows 30–45 ft. tall, finely channeled dark brown bark. Leaves are dull green on their top sides, blue green underneath, and grow to 1 ft. with 5 to 13 leaflets each.

PHILADELPHUS

MOCK ORANGE

Hydrangeaceae (Saxifragaceae)

DECIDUOUS SHRUBS

🌿 ZONES VARY BY SPECIES

☀️ ◑ PARTIAL SHADE IN HOTTEST AREAS

💧 💧 REGULAR TO MODERATE WATER

Philadelphus

Grown for typically white, usually fragrant flowers that bloom in late spring or early summer. Four-petaled, 1–2-in. blossoms range from

single through semidouble to double. Generally large, vigorous plants of fountainlike form with medium green foliage. Prune every year just after bloom, cutting out oldest wood and surplus shoots at base. To rejuvenate, cut to ground. Taller types are striking in lawns or as background and corner plantings; smaller kinds can be planted near foundations or used as low screens or informal hedges. Buy in bloom for best fragrance. Not fussy about soil, as long as drainage is good.

P. 'Buckley's Quill'. Zones 31, 32, 34, 39. Dense, compact growth to 4–5 ft., with clusters of fragrant double flowers. Petals are narrow and pointed.

P. coronarius. SWEET MOCK ORANGE. Zones 31, 32, 34–41. Old favorite. Strong growing, 10–12 ft. tall and wide. Oval, 1½–4-in.-long leaves. Clusters of very fragrant, 1½-in. flowers. 'Aureus' has bright golden leaves that turn yellow green in summer; it does not grow as tall as the species.

P. 'Galahad'. Zones 31, 32, 34–41. Compact, rounded growth to 4–5 ft. tall. Large, fragrant single flowers.

P. gordonianus. See *P. lewisii*

P. lemoinei. Zones 31, 32, 34, 39. This hybrid includes many garden varieties; most grow 5–6 ft. tall, and all have clusters of very fragrant flowers. Oval leaves to 2 in. long. 'Avalanche', more upright in habit, arching branches, many single, very fragrant flowers; 'Enchantment', double flowers; 'Fleur de Neige', very fragrant, single 1¼-in. flowers; 'Mont Blanc', profuse clusters of small, single, fragrant flowers on 3-ft. plants.

P. lewisii. WILD MOCK ORANGE. Zones 31, 32, 34–43. Native to western North America. Erect, arching habit (tall race from west of the Cascades is often called *P. gordonianus*). Oval leaves 2–4 in. long. Large, satiny, fragrant single flowers. 'Goose Creek' is a double-flowered selection. Plants tolerate some aridity.

P. purpureomaculatus. Zones 31, 32, 34–41. Group of hybrids including moderate-size shrubs with flowers showing purple centers. 'Belle Etoile' grows upright to 5 ft. tall; fragrant, fringed, single flowers to 2½ in. Oval leaves to 2 in. long.

P. virginalis. Zones 31, 32, 34–41. Another hybrid that has produced several garden varieties, usually with double flowers. Tall (6–8-ft.) varieties include 'Minnesota Snowflake' (reputedly hardy to −30°F/−34°C) and 'Virginal', both double, and 'Natchez', with 2-in. single flowers. Lower growing are double 'Glacier' (3–4 ft.) and 'Dwarf Minnesota Snowflake' (2–3 ft.).

P

PHLOMIS

JERUSALEM SAGE

Lamiaceae (Labiatae)

PERENNIALS OR SHRUBBY PERENNIALS

🌿 ZONES 31, 32, 34, 39

☀️ FULL SUN

💧 MODERATE WATER

Phlomis

Mediterranean natives related to sage (*Salvia*). Erect stems are set with whorls of tubular flowers in yellow, purple, or lavender; late spring and early summer bloom. Tolerate poor soil as long as drainage is good. Withstand considerable drought, but do better with moderate water.

P. russelliana. Spreads by runners, making clumps of large (to 8-in.), heart-shaped, furry leaves. Mats can be an effective weed-suppressing ground cover. Spikes with whorls of yellow flowers grow to 3 ft.

P. samia. Similar to *P. russelliana*, but with purplish pink flowers.

PHLOX

Polemoniaceae

PERENNIALS AND ANNUALS

ZONES VARY BY SPECIES

FULL SUN OR LIGHT SHADE, EXCEPT AS NOTED

REGULAR WATER, EXCEPT AS NOTED

Phlox

Most are natives of North America. Except for *P. drummondii* (annual phlox), the species described here are perennial. The many types of phlox show wide variation in growth form, but all have showy flower clusters. Tall kinds are excellent border plants; dwarf forms are mainstays in the rock garden. Unless otherwise noted, plants perform well in average garden soil with regular moisture. Two major problems affect phlox: red spider mites (which attack almost all species) and powdery mildew (*P. paniculata* is especially susceptible to this disease).

P. arendsii. Zones 31, 32, 34–43. Hybrid between *P. divaricata* and *P. paniculata*. To 1½ ft. high, with 1-in.-wide blossoms in clusters to 6 in. across, early summer. Cut off faded flowers for later rebloom. 'Anja' has reddish purple blooms, 'Hilda' lavender ones, 'Suzanne' white blossoms with red eye.

P. bifida. SAND PHLOX. Zones 31, 32, 34, 39. Clumps to 8–10 in. tall, with narrow light green leaves. Blooms spring–early summer, bearing profuse ½-in. lavender to white flowers with deeply notched petals. Likes full sun, excellent drainage. Drought tolerant.

P. buckleyi. SWORD-LEAF PHLOX. Zones 31, 32, 34, 39. Forms loose mat to 1½ ft. high. Sword-shaped leaves to 4 in. long; clusters of pink to bright purple flowers in early summer.

P. carolina. See *P. maculata*

P. 'Chattahoochee'. See *P. pilosa*

P. divaricata. SWEET WILLIAM PHLOX. Zones 31, 32, 34–43. To 1 ft. high, with slender, leafy stems and creeping underground shoots. Oval leaves 1–2 in. long. Blooms in spring, bearing open clusters of ¾–1½-in.-wide, somewhat fragrant blossoms in pale blue (sometimes with pinkish tones) varying to white. Use in rock gardens, as bulb cover. Give light shade and good, deep soil. Varieties include 'Arrowhead', with light lavender blue blossoms; 'Dirigo Ice', palest blue; 'Fuller's White'; *P. d. laphamii*, bright blue; and the compact 'London Grove', deep blue.

P. drummondii. ANNUAL PHLOX. All zones. Grows 6–18 in. tall, with erect, leafy stems more or less covered with rather sticky hairs. Flowers numerous, showy, in tight clusters at tops of stems. Bright and pastel colors (no blue or orange), some with contrasting eye. Tall strains in mixed colors include Finest and Fordhook Finest. Dwarf strains include Beauty and Globe, both with rounded flowers, and starry-petaled Petticoat and Twinkle. Bloom lasts from early summer until frost if faded flowers are removed. Plant in spring in cold regions, in fall in mild climates. Give full sun and light, rich loam.

P. glaberrima triflora. SMOOTH PHLOX. Zones 31, 32, 34–43. To 1½–2 ft. tall, with smooth, narrow, 3-in.-long leaves. Lavender pink flowers in late spring. This species is mildew free.

P. maculata (P. carolina, P. suffruticosa). THICK-LEAF PHLOX. Zones 31, 32, 34–45. To 3–4 ft. tall. Early summer flowers about ¾ in. wide, in 15-in.-long clusters, in colors ranging from white with pale pink eye to magenta. Shiny, mildew-resistant foliage. Varieties include 'Alpha', rose pink; 'Delta', white with pink eye; 'Miss Lingard' (white; best-known variety); 'Omega', white with purplish pink eye; and 'Rosalinde', deep rose pink.

P. nivalis. TRAILING PHLOX. Zones 31, 32, 34. Trailing plants form loose, 4–6-in.-high mats of narrow leaves. Purple, pink, or white, 1-in.-wide flowers in fairly large clusters, late spring–early summer. Excellent in rock gardens; needs good drainage. 'Camla' is a salmon pink variety.

P. ovata. MOUNTAIN PHLOX. Zones 31, 32, 34–41. To 15–20 in. tall, with smooth green, oval, mildew-free leaves to 6 in. long. Deep pink flowers in late spring.

P. paniculata. SUMMER PHLOX. Zones 31, 32, 34–43. To 3–5 ft. tall. Long, narrow, 2–5-in.-long leaves taper to a slender point. Fragrant, 1-in.-wide flowers in large, dome-shaped clusters throughout summer. Colors include white and shades of lavender, pink, rose, and red; blooms of some varieties have a contrasting eye. Plants do not come true from seed; most tend toward an uncertain purplish pink, though some are attractive. Thrives in full sun. Mulch to keep roots cool. Divide plants every few years, replanting young shoots from outside of clump.

Very susceptible to mildew at end of bloom season. To minimize problem, provide good air circulation: don't crowd plants and keep only six to eight stems on a mature plant. Spray with fungicide if necessary. Mildew-resistant cultivars include 'Bright Eyes', pale pink with red eye; 'Darwin's Joyce', light pink with darker eye, yellow-edged green leaves; 'David', white; 'Eva Cullum', pink with red eye; 'Franz Schubert', lilac pink; 'Katherine', lavender blue with white eye, very long blooming; 'The King', deep purple blue; 'Laura', purple with white eye; 'Miss Ellie', bright rose; 'Miss Holland', white with red eye; 'Miss Kelly', lilac with white eye; 'Miss Universe', white; 'Mt. Fuji', white; 'Sandra', scarlet; 'Shortwood', pink with darker pink eye; 'Sir John Falstaff', deep salmon pink with burgundy eye; and 'Starfire', bright red.

P. pilosa. PRAIRIE PHLOX. Zones 31, 32, 34–43. Forms a low (to 15-in.), mildew-free, semievergreen ground cover. Blue to pink or white blossoms in spring. 'Chattahoochee', now properly known as 'Moody Blue', has blue flowers with a red eye; 'Eco Happy Traveler' bears deep pink flowers; and 'Ozarkana' has light pink blooms with a white eye.

P. procumbens. Zones 31, 32, 34–43. Hybrid between *P. stolonifera* and *P. subulata*, but less widely creeping than either. Forms a mound of semievergreen foliage 6–12 in. tall, with purplish pink flowers in spring. 'Millstream Hybrid' has lavender pink flowers; 'O.G.K.' has rose pink blooms; 'Variegata' has pink blossoms and leaves edged in creamy white.

P. stolonifera. CREEPING PHLOX. Zones 31, 32, 34–45. Creeping, mounding plant to 6–8 in. high, with narrow evergreen leaves to 1½ in. long. Profusion of 1-in. lavender flowers in spring. Varieties include 'Blue Ridge', lavender blue; 'Bruce's White'; 'Sherwood Purple', deep lavender; and pink forms 'Home Fires', 'Melrose', and 'Pink Ridge'. Provide light shade.

P. subulata. MOSS PINK. Zones 31, 32, 34–45. Stiffish, ½-in., needle-like, evergreen to semievergreen leaves on creeping stems; forms mat to 6 in. high. Blooms late spring or early summer, with ¾-in.-wide flowers that range in color from white through pink to rose and lavender blue. Makes sheets of brilliant color in rock gardens. Provide loose, not-too-rich soil, moderate water. Specialists offer two dozen or more varieties; many of these are actually selections of other low-growing species or hybrids between such species and *P. subulata*. One variety, 'Tamanonagalei' ('Candy Stripe'), has rose pink blossoms edged in white, good fall rebloom; it is more drought tolerant than the average moss pink.

P. suffruticosa. See *P. maculata*

PHOENIX

DATE PALM

Arecaceae (Palmae)

PALMS

ALL ZONES

FULL SUN, EXCEPT AS NOTED

REGULAR WATER

Phoenix

Mostly large feather palms, but one is a dwarf. Trunks patterned with bases of old leafstalks. Not hardy in the Northeast; grow in pots moved outdoors in summer, indoors over winter.

P. canariensis. CANARY ISLAND DATE PALM. Grows to about 6–8 ft. tall in a container, with many gracefully arching fronds forming a crown. Young plants do well in pots for many years, often looking something like pineapples.

P. loureiri (P. humilis). Resembles smaller, more slender and refined *P. canariensis*. Slow grower to about 6 ft. tall in a pot. Leaves dark green, flexible. Does well in containers.

P

P. roebelenii. PYGMY DATE PALM. Native to Laos. Fine-leafed, small-scale, single-trunked palm; grows slowly to about 6 ft. Curved leaves form dense crown. Good pot plant. Does best in partial or full shade, but will not succeed in dark indoor corners.

P. rupicola. CLIFF DATE PALM. As stately as *P. canariensis*, but much smaller. Slender trunk; lower leaves droop gracefully.

PHORMIUM

NEW ZEALAND FLAX

Agavaceae

ANNUALS

ALL ZONES

FULL SUN OR LIGHT SHADE

MUCH OR LITTLE WATER

Phormium

Big, dramatic plants composed of many sword-like, stiffly vertical leaves in fan pattern. Flower stems reach high above leaves, bearing clusters of 1–2-in. blossoms in dull red or yellow. Perennials in warm climates; grow as summer annuals in the Northeast. Use as accent plants, near swimming pools. Sturdy, fast growing. Take poor drainage to a point; crown rot can be a problem in very poorly drained soil. Tolerate salt air and ocean spray, but not dune conditions. Good container plants. Increase by dividing large clumps.

P. tenax. NEW ZEALAND FLAX. Large, bold plant, reaching 1½–3 ft. as a summer container plant in the Northeast. Reddish brown flower stalks bear many dark red to yellowish flowers. Variants in leaf color are available. Among them are: 'Amazing Red', reddish brown with darker edges; 'Atropurpureum', purple red; 'Bronze', brownish red; 'Chocolate Baby', twisted, bronzy brown to bronze-green leaves; 'Dusky Chief', dusky reddish purple; 'Dwarf Burgundy', new foliage bronzy red, maturing to coppery green; 'Flamingo', leaves striped with zones of pink, red, yellow, and green; 'Pink Stripe', bronzy green leaves edged pink; 'Rubrum', deepest coloring, dark purplish red; 'Variegatum', green leaves striped with creamy white.

Numerous hybrids are grown for their brightly colored foliage. They are smaller than *P. tenax* and thus better adapted to containers and to gardens of modest size. Some are prevailingly yellow or apricot ('Apricot Queen', 'Golden Sword', 'Yellow Wave'), while others are dark purplish bronze ('Bronze Baby', 'Dark Delight'). Many are dazzling, with stripings and edgings of red, apricot, cream, green, or bronze ('Maori Chief', 'Maori Maiden', 'Maori Queen', 'Maori Sunrise', 'Sundowner'). A few are quite small ('Jack Spratt', 'Tom Thumb'). Some tend to revert to green or bronze; remove such growth at the base to preserve original color.

PHOTINIA

Rosaceae

EVERGREEN OR DECIDUOUS SHRUBS OR SMALL TREES

ZONES VARY BY SPECIES

FULL SUN

REGULAR TO MODERATE WATER

Photinia

Related to hawthorn, pyracantha. Densely foliaged plants, with large, elliptical to oval leaves and bright-colored new growth. In early spring, they bear flattish clusters of small white flowers. Good screens, background. Prune to shape; never allow new growth to get away and make long, bare switches. Attractive to birds. Susceptible to fireblight..

P. fraseri. REDTIP. Evergreen shrub or small tree. Zones 31, 32. Moderate to fast growth to 10–15 ft., spreading wider. Oval leaves to 5 in. long are bright, showy bronzy red when new, maturing to dark green. Flower clusters are not followed by berries. Good espalier or small single-stemmed tree. Cut branches excellent in arrangements. Resists mildew and

heat. Aphids may be a problem. Plant described here is properly known as 'Birmingham'; for many years, it was the only one sold, and the variety name was not attached. 'Indian Princess' (new growth is more orange than red) and 'Red Robin' are about half the size.

P. villosa. Deciduous shrub or small tree. Zones 31, 32, 34–41. Usually multistemmed, to 15 ft. tall and 10 ft. wide. The 1½–3-in.-long leaves are pale gold with rosy tints when expanding, dark green at maturity, bright red or yellow in fall. Flower clusters 1–2 in. across. Bright red fruit. Susceptible to powdery mildew.

PHYGELIUS

CAPE FUCHSIA

Scrophulariaceae

PERENNIALS

ZONES 31, WARMER PARTS OF 32

FULL SUN OR LIGHT SHADE

REGULAR WATER

Phygelius

Woody-based perennials that die to the ground in cold climates. Related to snapdragon and penstemon, but drooping flowers also suggest fuchsia. Plants grow 3–4 ft. tall and spread by underground stems or rooting prostrate branches. Tubular, curved flowers borne in loosely branched clusters at branch ends, summer–fall. Prune to keep plants neat; mulch roots in winter. Species can be started from seed, but named varieties should be grown from cuttings or by layering branches.

P. aequalis. Flowers dusty rose, in pyramidal clusters. 'Yellow Trumpet' has showy pale yellow flowers.

P. capensis. More open and sprawling than *P. aequalis*, with open clusters of orange to red flowers.

P. rectus. Hybrid between the previous two species. 'African Queen' has deep salmon orange flowers; 'Moonraker' bears pale yellow blooms; 'Pink Elf' has pale pink flowers with crimson lobes, on 30-in. plants; 'Winchester Fanfare' has deep rose flowers with yellow throats.

PHYLLOSTACHYS. See BAMBOO

PHYSALIS

Solanaceae

PERENNIALS AND ANNUALS

ALL ZONES

FULL SUN OR LIGHT SHADE

REGULAR WATER

Physalis

Fruit is surrounded by loose, papery husk (enlarged calyx of flower). First species below is ornamental; other two are edible.

P. alkekengi (P. franchetii). CHINESE LANTERN PLANT. Perennial often grown as annual. Plant is angularly branched, 1–2 ft. high. Long, creeping, whitish, underground stems; may become invasive without control. Long-stalked, light green leaves are 2–3 in. long. Flowers white, rather inconspicuous, appearing in leaf joints. Ornamental part of plant is calyx, which forms around ripened berry as loose, papery, bright orange-red, 2-in.-long, inflated envelope shaped like lantern. Fruit brightens garden in late summer and fall; dry, leafless stalks hung with gay lanterns make choice winter arrangements. Sow seed in spring in light soil. Increase by root division in fall or winter. 'Pygmy', 8-in. dwarf variety, makes a good pot plant.

P. ixocarpa. TOMATILLO. Annual of bushy, sprawling growth to 4 ft. Fruit about 2 in. wide, swelling to fill—or sometimes split—the baggy calyx. Fruit yellow to purple and very sweet when ripe, but usually picked green and tart and used (cooked) in Mexican cuisine.

P

P. peruviana. GROUND CHERRY, POHA. Tender perennial grown as annual. Bushy, 1½ ft. high. Leaves 2–4 in. long. Flowers bell shaped, ⅜ in. long, whitish yellow marked with five brown spots. Seedy yellow fruit is sweet, rather insipid; can be used for pies or preserves (remove papery husks before using in cooking). Grow in same way as tomatoes. Plants sprawl quite a bit and are slow to start bearing but are eventually productive where summers are long and warm. Several other species, including *P. pruinosa* and *P. pubescens,* are similar.

PHYSOCARPUS

NINEBARK

Rosaceae

DECIDUOUS SHRUBS

🌿 ZONES VARY BY SPECIES

☀️ ◐ ● SUN OR SHADE

💧 💧 REGULAR TO MODERATE WATER

Physocarpus

Ninebarks are so named because of their peeling bark, which strips off to reveal several layers. The plants resemble spireas and are closely related to them, bearing round clusters of tiny white or pinkish flowers in spring or early summer. All have lobed leaves. Of the two species described below, only *P. monogynus* has good fall color. Prune plants as needed after bloom; rejuvenate by cutting old stems to the ground.

P. monogynus. MOUNTAIN NINEBARK. Zones 35, 41, 43. Rocky Mountain and High Plains native. To 3–4 ft. tall, with 1½-in. leaves and few-flowered clusters of pinkish to white blossoms. Brilliant fall colors, typically orange and red.

P. opulifolius. COMMON NINEBARK, EASTERN NINEBARK. Zones 32, 34–45. Native to eastern and central North America. Upright and spreading to 5–10 ft. tall and wide. Leaves to 3 in. Many white or pinkish flowers in each cluster. Varieties are more attractive than species. Leaves of 'Lutea' are yellow when plant is grown in sunlight, yellow green in shade; 'Dart's Gold' is similar but brighter; 'Nugget', a compact plant to 6 ft., has leaves that unfold golden yellow, gradually age to lime green, then turn gold again in fall. *P. o. intermedius* grows 4–5 ft. tall and has smaller, darker green leaves than species.

PHYSOSTEGIA virginiana

FALSE DRAGONHEAD, OBEDIENT PLANT

Lamiaceae (Labiatae)

PERENNIAL

🌿 ZONES 31, 32, 34–45

☀️ ◐ FULL SUN OR PARTIAL SHADE

💧 REGULAR WATER

Physostegia virginiana

Slender, upright, leafy stems to 4 ft. Oblong leaves 3–5 in. long, with toothed edges and pointed tips. Funnel-shaped, 1-in.-long flowers in glistening white, rose pink, or lavender rose, carried in dense 10-in. spikes. Blooms from mid- to late summer into fall. Blossoms resemble snapdragons (hence the name "false dragonhead") and will remain in place if twisted or pushed out of position (hence the name "obedient plant"). The 3-ft. 'Bouquet Rose' has rose pink blossoms. The following varieties all grow 2 ft. high: rose pink 'Vivid'; white 'Summer Snow'; and 'Variegata', with bluish pink flowers and white-edged leaves.

Plant has a spiky form that makes it useful in borders, cut arrangements. Combine with taller asters or pincushion flower. Stake taller stems to keep upright. Cut to ground after bloom. Vigorous and notoriously invasive; divide every 2 years to keep in bounds.

FOR INFORMATION ON SELECTING PLANTS

PLEASE SEE PAGES 47–112

PICEA

SPRUCE

Pinaceae

EVERGREEN TREES OR SHRUBS

🌿 ZONES VARY BY SPECIES

☀️ ◐ FULL SUN OR LIGHT SHADE

💧 💧 REGULAR TO MODERATE WATER

Picea

Like firs, spruces are pyramidal and stiff needled, with branches arranged in neat tiers. But unlike firs, they have pendent cones, and their needles are attached to branches by small pegs that remain after needles drop. Most spruces are tall timber trees that lose their lower branches fairly early in life as they head upward; their canopies thin out noticeably as they age. Many species have dwarf varieties useful as foundation plantings, for rock gardens, in containers. Spruces grow best in regions where summers are cool or mild, not hot and humid.

Check spruces for aphids in late winter; if the pests are present, take control measures promptly to avoid defoliation in spring. Other common pests of spruce are bagworms (in eastern and central U.S.), spruce budworm (in northern regions), pine needle scale, and spider mites.

Prune only to shape. If a branch grows too long, cut it back to a well-placed side branch. To slow growth and make it more dense, remove part of each year's growth to force side branches. When planting larger spruces, don't place them too close to buildings, fences, or walks; they need space.

P. abies (P. excelsa). NORWAY SPRUCE. Zones 32, 34–45. Native to northern Europe. Fast growth to 100–150 ft. Stiff, deep green, attractive pyramid in youth; ragged in age, as branchlets droop strongly and oldest branchlets (those nearest trunk) die back. Extremely hardy and wind resistant; valued for windbreaks in cold areas. Tolerates heat and humidity better than most spruces. 'Columnaris' is narrow and columnar, to 60 ft. high. 'Inversa' has branches growing downward, prostrate habit. 'Nidiformis' (bird's nest spruce) is a slow-growing, spreading bushy shrub to 5 ft. high and 10 ft. wide, with an open "nest" in the center. 'Sherwoodii' is a rugged, picturesque shrub with compact but irregular growth habit; it was developed from a tree that at age 60 was only 5 ft. tall and 10 ft. across at base.

P. engelmannii. ENGELMANN SPRUCE. Zones 31, 32, 34–45. Native to western North America. Dense, slender pyramid, eventually exceeding 100 ft. tall and 30 ft. wide. Resembles blue-green forms of Colorado spruce, but has a narrower form and softer needles.

P. glauca. WHITE SPRUCE. Zones 35–45. Native to Canada and northern U.S. Cone-shaped tree to 60–70 ft., dense when young, with pendulous twigs and silver green foliage. Crushed needles have an unpleasant odor. Best where winters are very cold. The following two varieties are widely grown in gardens:

'Conica'. DWARF ALBERTA SPRUCE, DWARF WHITE SPRUCE. Also grows in Zones 32, 34. Compact, pyramidal tree, slowly reaching 7 ft. in 35 years. Short, soft needles are bright grass green when new, gray green when mature. Needs shelter from drying winds (whether hot or cold) and from strong reflected sunlight. Popular container subject. Often sold as *P. albertiana*.

P. g. densata. BLACK HILLS SPRUCE. Zones 35, 41, 43, 45. Slow-growing, dense pyramid; can reach 20 ft. in 35 years. 'Rainbow's End' is similar, but new growth is golden yellow.

P. omorika. SERBIAN SPRUCE. Zones 32, 34–41. Native to southeastern Europe. Narrow, conical, slow-growing tree to 50–60 ft. tall. Shiny dark green needles with silvery undersides. Retains branches to the ground for many years. Considered by some to be the most attractive spruce; one of the best for hot, humid climates. 'Nana' is a dwarf to 3–4 ft. tall (possibly to 10 ft. high), with short, closely packed needles. 'Pendula' has drooping, twisted branches.

P. orientalis. ORIENTAL SPRUCE. Zones 31, 32, 34–43. Native to Caucasus, Asia Minor. Dense, compact, cone-shaped tree with very short needles; grows slowly to 50–60 ft. high. Can tolerate poor soils if they are well drained, but may suffer leaf burn in very cold, dry winds. Highly rated by experts. 'Aurea' has a golden sheen over the foliage, new shoots are golden yellow, later changing to green. 'Skylands', to 20 ft. tall, has yellow new growth in sun. 'Weeping Dwarf' ('Pendula') is compact and slow growing with drooping branches.

P. pungens. COLORADO SPRUCE. Zones 32, 34–45. Slow to moderate growth rate. In gardens, reaches 30–60 ft. tall, 10–20 ft. wide; in the wild, grows to a possible 100 ft. tall, 25–35 ft. across. Very stiff, regular, horizontal branches form a broad pyramid. Foliage of seedlings varies in color from dark green through all shades of blue green to steely blue. The following varieties have consistent color:

'Fat Albert'. Compact, erect, broad, formal-looking blue cone. Slow growth (to 10 ft. in 10 years) makes it a good living Christmas tree.

'Glauca'. COLORADO BLUE SPRUCE. Distinctive gray-blue color.

'Hoopsii'. Beautiful, striking silvery blue color. Fast growing; needs early training to encourage erect, cone-shaped habit.

'Koster'. KOSTER BLUE SPRUCE. Bluer than 'Glauca'; growth habit sometimes irregular.

'Moerheimii'. Same blue as 'Koster', but shape is more compact and symmetrical.

'Montgomery'. Broad cone growing slowly to 2 ft. high, with strikingly blue foliage.

'Pendula'. WEEPING BLUE SPRUCE. Gray blue, with weeping branchlets. Stake main trunk while plant is young.

'Thomsen'. Similar in color to 'Hoopsii'. Vigorous, symmetrical habit.

PICKEREL WEED. See PONTEDERIA cordata

PIERIS

Ericaceae

EVERGREEN SHRUBS

ZONES VARY BY SPECIES

SOME SHADE, ESPECIALLY IN AFTERNOON

REGULAR WATER

LEAVES AND NECTAR ARE POISONOUS IF INGESTED

Pieris

Elegant in foliage and form all year, these plants make good companions for rhododendron and azalea, to which they are related. Whorls of leathery, narrowly oval leaves; clusters of small, typically white, urn-shaped flowers. Most plants form flower buds by autumn, so potential flower clusters are a subtle decorative feature over winter. Resembling strings of tiny greenish pink beads, the buds open late winter–midspring. New spring growth is often bright colored (pink to red or bronze), but matures to glossy dark green.

Same cultural needs as rhododendron and azalea. Need well-drained but moisture-retentive acid soil and summers that are cool to merely warm; do not thrive in hot, dry conditions. Choose a planting location sheltered from wind, where plants will get high shade or dappled sunlight at least during the warmest afternoon hours. Prune by removing spent flowers. Splendid in containers, in Oriental and woodland gardens, in entryways where year-round good looks are essential.

P. 'Brouwer's Beauty'. Zones 31, 32, 34–41. Upright, dense shrub to 10 ft. tall and 6 ft. wide. Glossy, deep green leaves to 3 in. long. Red buds open to clusters of white flowers.

P. floribunda (Andromeda floribunda). MOUNTAIN PIERIS. Zones 34–43. Compact, rounded shrub 3–6 ft. tall. Differs from the other species: new growth is pale green; mature leaves are dull dark green, 1½–3 in. long. Blossoms in upright clusters. Very hardy to cold. Tolerates sun, heat, and low humidity better than the others, but does not thrive in hot, humid regions.

P. 'Forest Flame' (P. 'Flame of the Forest'). Zones 31, 32, 34–41. Hybrid between *P. japonica* and a form of *P. forrestii*. Dense plant to 6–7

ft. high and ultimately as wide. Brilliant red new foliage fades to pink and cream, then matures to dark green. Blooms profusely, bearing broader, heavier flower clusters than those of *P. japonica*.

P. japonica (Andromeda japonica). LILY-OF-THE-VALLEY SHRUB. Zones 32, 34–41. Upright, dense, tiered growth to 9–10 ft. New growth is bronzy pink to red; mature leaves are glossy green, 3 in. long. Drooping clusters of white, pink, or nearly red flowers. Buds are often dark red. Many varieties, some rare. The following are grown for unusual habit or foliage:

'Bert Chandler'. New foliage turns from salmon pink through cream to white, then pale green.

'Compacta'. Grows to 6 ft. tall.

'Crispa'. Smaller than species (to 6–7 ft.), with handsome, wavy-edged leaves.

'Karenoma'. Compact growth to 3–6 ft., with upright flower clusters.

'Mountain Fire'. Fiery red new growth.

'Pygmaea'. Tiny dwarf less than 1 ft. tall, with very few flowers and narrow leaves to 1 in. long.

'Spring Snow'. Similar to 'Karenoma'.

'Variegata'. Slow grower with leaves marked with creamy white, tinged pink in spring. Prune out any green-leafed shoots.

The following varieties are grown principally for their flowers:

'Christmas Cheer'. Early-blooming bicolor with flowers in white and deep rose red; flower stalks are rose red.

'Coleman'. Pink flowers opening from red buds.

'Daisen'. Compact plant. Flowers are similar to those of 'Christmas Cheer', but leaves are broader.

'Dorothy Wyckoff'. Tall growing, with white flowers opening from deep red buds. Leaves turn purplish in winter.

'Pink'. Shell pink flowers fading to white.

'Purity'. To 3–4 ft. Late blooming; unusually large white flowers.

'Temple Bells'. Compact, tiered habit; a bit less cold tolerant than the species. Ivory flowers.

'Valley Rose'. Pink-and-white flowers; open habit.

'Valley Valentine'. Deep red buds and flowers.

'White Cascade'. Extremely heavy show of pure white blooms.

PIGGY-BACK PLANT. See TOLMIEA menziesii

PIMPERNEL. See ANAGALLIS

PIMPINELLA anisum

ANISE

Apiaceae (Umbelliferae)

ANNUAL HERB

ALL ZONES

FULL SUN

REGULAR WATER

Pimpinella anisum

Forms a clump of bright green, toothed leaves. Flowering stems with narrow, feathery leaves elongate to 2 ft.; stems are topped by umbrella-like clusters of tiny white flowers. Use fresh leaves in salads; use seeds for flavoring cookies, cakes, breads, confections.

Grows quickly in warm weather, but needs about 4 months to grow and mature a seed crop. Sow seeds indoors, then set out young plants when frost danger is past. Plants are taprooted and do not transplant easily once they begin to put on size. Grow in light, well-drained soil.

Pinaceae. Members of the pine family are evergreen trees with narrow, usually needlelike leaves and seeds borne on the scales of woody cones. Pine (*Pinus*), spruce (*Picea*), true cedar (*Cedrus*), larch (*Larix*), Douglas fir (*Pseudotsuga menziesii*), and hemlock (*Tsuga*) are examples.

P

P

PINCUSHION FLOWER. See SCABIOSA

PINE. See PINUS

PINEAPPLE

Bromeliaceae

BROMELIAD; CAN BEAR FRUIT

ALL ZONES; GREENHOUSE OR HOUSE PLANT

FULL SUN FOR FRUIT

REGULAR WATER

Pineapple

Plant is rosette of long, narrow leaves with saw-toothed edges. To grow it, cut leafy top from a market pineapple. Root base of top in water or fast-draining but moisture-retentive potting mix. When roots have formed, move pineapple to 7–8-in. pot of rich soil. Grow in greenhouse or sunny room where temperature stays above 68°F/20°C; move outdoors in summer. Water when soil is dry. Feed every 3 or 4 weeks with liquid fertilizer. Fruit forms (if you're lucky) in 2 years, on top of sturdy stalk in center of clump. Indoor-grown pineapple fruit is much smaller than commercial fruit. Sometimes available as a house plant is a variety with foliage variegated in pink, white, and olive green. *Ananas bracteatus tricolor* ('Striatus') has leaves striped cream, flushed and edged red-pink; pink fruit. Plants grown for foliage rather than fruit will take reduced light.

PINEAPPLE FLOWER. See EUCOMIS

PINELLIA

Araceae

TUBEROUS PERENNIAL

ZONES VARY BY SPECIES

PARTIAL TO FULL SHADE

REGULAR WATER

Pinellia

Members of the arum family, along with jack-in-the-pulpit, these shade lovers are hardy and easy to grow. Valued for their handsome leaves and interesting flowers. They do best in humus-rich, well-drained soil in woodland settings or shady rock gardens.

P. cordata. MINIATURE GREEN DRAGON. Zones 31, 32, 34, 39. To 6 in. or taller. Glossy, deep green arrowhead leaves with silver striping along the veins. Flower resembles a miniature jack-in-the-pulpit, blooming in late summer.

P. tripartita. GREEN DRAGON. Zones 31, 32, 34, 39. To 1 ft. tall, with three-lobed green leaves to 8 in. long. Green spathes are purple inside, with a strange-looking 10-in. tonguelike spadix in the center of the flower, bloom all summer.

PINK. See DIANTHUS

PINK POLKA-DOT PLANT. See HYPOESTES phyllostachya

PINKROOT. See SPIGELIA marilandica

SPRING PRUNING TO SHAPE A PINE TREE

To fatten up a rangy pine or to keep a young one teddy-bear chubby, cut back the candles of new growth by half (or even more) when the new growth begins to emerge in spring. Leave a few clusters untrimmed if you want growth to continue along a branch.

PINUS

PINE

Pinaceae

EVERGREEN TREES, RARELY SHRUBS

ZONES VARY BY SPECIES

FULL SUN

REGULAR TO LITTLE WATER

SEE CHART NEXT PAGE

Pinus

Pines are the great individualists of the garden, each species differing not only in its characteristics but also in the way it responds to wind, heat, and other growing conditions. Cone size and shape are an identifying feature of pines; another is the number of long, slender needles in a bundle. Most species have needles in groups of two, three, or five. Those with two needles tend to be more tolerant of unfavorable soil and climate than three-needle species, and three-needle pines more so than five-needle ones. As a group, pines are more adaptable than spruces or firs.

Pines tend to be pyramidal in youth, becoming more open or round topped with age. They grow best in full sun and will thrive in most soils that are reasonably well drained. Too much water results in yellow needles (with the yellowing appearing first in the older needles) and a generally unhealthy appearance—and can even cause sudden death. Most pines are fairly drought tolerant; exceptions are typically among the five-needle species. Pines rarely need fertilizer, and trees that receive it generally produce undesirable, rank growth.

A number of pests and diseases can afflict pines, but a healthy tree usually copes with such problems with little or no intervention. Trees most at risk are those weakened by drought or air pollution. Aphids, spider mites, scale, and bark beetles are possible wherever pines are grown. Most five-needle species are susceptible to white pine blister rust (a bark disease that can kill the tree), primarily in the Northeast and Northwest; currants and gooseberries are host plants to one part of the fungus's life cycle. Aphids usually show their presence by sticky secretions, sooty mildew, and yellowing needles. Birds are attracted to seeds contained in pinecones.

All pines can be shaped, and usually improved, by pruning. The best time to prune is in spring, when needles start to emerge from the spires of new growth (the so-called candles). Cutting back partway into these candles will promote bushiness and allow some overall increase in tree size; cutting out candles entirely will limit size. Don't cut the tree's leading shoot unless you want to limit its height. Careful pruning will allow you to maintain pines as hedges or screens.

PISTACIA chinensis

CHINESE PISTACHE

Anacardiaceae

DECIDUOUS TREE

ZONES 31, 32

FULL SUN

MODERATE WATER

Pistacia chinensis

Native to China. Slow to moderate growth to 30–60 ft. tall, with nearly equal spread. Young trees often gawky and lopsided, but older ones become dense and shapely if given reasonable care. Foot-long leaves consist of 10–16 paired dark green leaflets, each 2–4 in. long, ¾ in. wide. Good fall color; foliage turns luminous orange to red (sometimes shades of yellow). Trees are either male or female; if the two sexes are grown near each other, the female will bear small red fruits.

Tolerant of a wide range of soils, including alkaline types. Where verticillium wilt is present, minimize risk by providing good drainage and by watering as little as possible during dry periods. Very drought tolerant. Stake young tree and prune for the first few years to develop a head high enough to walk under. Reliable tree for street, lawn, patio, or garden.

PINE

NAME, NATIVE HABITAT	ZONES	GROWTH RATE, SIZE	GROWTH HABIT	NEEDLES AND CONES	COMMENTS
P. aristata BRISTLECONE PINE High mountains of West, very local and widely scattered	36–43	Very slow to 20 ft., possibly as tall as 45 ft.	Dense, bushy, heavy trunked, with ground-sweeping branches. In youth, symmetrical, narrow crowned; has mature look even then	Needles: in 5s, 1–1½ in., dark green, whitish beneath flecked with white dots of resin. Cones: 3½ in., dark purplish brown	So slow growing it is good for years in containers, rock gardens. Good bonsai plant. Needles persist for many years, many crowns extremely dense. Protect from winds in cold climates
P. banksiana JACK PINE From near the Arctic Circle southward to northern New York and Minnesota	37–45. Extremely cold hardy	Slow to moderate growth to 30–50 ft., often less	Symmetrical in youth; later irregular, picturesque. Sometimes shrubby	Needles: in 2s, olive green, curved or twisted, to 2 in. Cones: 1–2 in., pointed, yellowish brown	Tolerates poor soil, even sand. Useful for windbreaks, soil conservation
P. bungeana LACEBARK PINE Northern and central China	31, 32, 34–41. Hardy to –20°F/–29°C	Slow to 75 ft.	Often multitrunked, spreading. Sometimes shrubby. Picturesque	Needles: in 3s, 3 in., bright green. Cones: 2–2½ in., yellowish brown	Smooth, dull gray bark flakes off like sycamore bark to show smooth, creamy white branches and trunk. Brittle limbs can break under heavy snow loads
P. cembra SWISS STONE PINE Mountains of central Europe	34–45. Hardy to –35°F/–37°C	Extremely slow to 70 ft. or more	Spreading, short branches in narrow, dense pyramid; broad, open, and round topped in age	Needles: in 5s, 3-5 in., dark green. Cones: 3½ in., oval, light brown	Slow growth and dense, regular foliage make it good plant for small gardens. Handsome in youth. Resistant to white pine blister rust
P. densiflora JAPANESE RED PINE Japan	32, 34–41. Hardy to –20°F/–29°C	Rapid when young. May reach 100 ft., usually much less	Broad, irregular head. Often develops 2 or more trunks at ground level	Needles: in 2s, 2½–5 in., bright green or yellow-green. Cones: 2 in., oval or oblong, tawny brown	Intolerant of hot, dry, or cold winds. 'Oculus-draconis', dragon eye pine, has 2 yellow bands on each needle; viewed endwise, branch has concentric green and yellow bands. 'Pendula' is dwarf, sprawling; good in rock gardens
P. d. 'Umbraculifera' TANYOSHO PINE Japan	32, 34–41. Hardy to –20°F/–29°C	Slow to moderate, 12–20 ft.	Broad, flat topped, with numerous trunks from base. Spread greater than height	Same as for *P. densiflora*	Good for containers, rock gardens, Oriental gardens. Showy, flaking red-orange bark on young branches
P. flexilis LIMBER PINE Mountains of northern Arizona, Utah, Nevada, southeastern California; eastern slope of Rockies, from Alberta to Texas. Grows at 5,000–11,000 ft.	32, 34–43. Cold hardy.	Slow to moderate, to 20–30 ft. in gardens	Thick trunk, open round top, many limber branches that may droop at decided angle to trunk. Becomes dwarfed and more irregular at higher elevations	Needles: in 5s, to 3 in., slightly curved or twisted, dark green. Cones: to 5 in., oval or cone shaped, buff to buff-orange	Young plants rather straggly looking. Shapes well with shearing; can be used for bonsai. Good on rocky slopes. Tolerates wind, drought. 'Vandewolf's Pyramid' has regular form, blue-green color; 'Columnaris' is narrow; 'Pendulus' is weeping.

P

PINE

NAME, NATIVE HABITAT	ZONES	GROWTH RATE, SIZE	GROWTH HABIT	NEEDLES AND CONES	COMMENTS
P. h. brutia (*see P. brutia*)					
P. heldreichii leucodermis (*P. leucodermis*) BOSNIAN PINE Balkans, Greece, Italy	36–41. Very hardy to cold	Slow to 75 ft.	Erect, dense, oval to cone shaped	Needles: in 2s, short, stiff, dark green, persisting 5–6 years. Cones: 2–3 in., blue to bright brown, single or in clusters of 3	Pale gray bark. Slow growth, dense habit, and salt tolerance make it a good landscape tree, especially near ocean
P. koraiensis KOREAN PINE Korea and Japan	31, 32, 34–45. Very cold hardy	Slow growth to 30–50 ft., taller in old age	Loose cone shape, soft looking, branched to the ground	Needles: in 5s, 3–4½ in., bluish or grayish green. Cones: 3–6 in., cylindrical, bright brown	Attractive as single specimen or in groups. Very tolerant of soils and exposures. Relatively trouble free
P. mugo (*P. montana*) SWISS MOUNTAIN PINE Mountains of Spain, central Europe to Balkans	32, 34–45	Slow to variable heights	Extremely variable. Prostrate shrub, low shrub, or pyramidal tree of moderate size	Needles: in 2s, 2 in., dark green, stout, crowded. Cones: 1–2 in., oval, tawny to dark brown	Generally a bushy, twisted, somewhat open pine. *P. m. pumilio* is an eastern European form, shrubby and varying from prostrate to 5–10 ft. high. Very susceptible to scale
P. m. mugo MUGHO PINE Eastern Alps and Balkan states	32, 34–45	Slow to 4 ft.	From the start, a shrubby, symmetrical little pine. Many spread in age	Needles: Same as for *P. mugo*, but darker green. Cones: Same as for *P. mugo*, but a little shorter	Widely used in rock gardens, containers. Pick plants with dense, pleasing form
P. nigra (*formerly P. austriaca*) AUSTRIAN BLACK PINE Europe, western Asia	32 (color parts), 34–41. Hardy to –20°F/ –29°C	Slow to moderate, usually not more than 40 ft. in gardens	Dense, stout pyramid with uniform crown. Branches in regular whorls. In age, broad and flat topped	Needles: in 2s, 3–6½ in., very dark green, stiff. Cones: 2–3½ in., oval, brown	Tree of strong character that will serve either as landscape decoration or as windbreak in cold regions. Tolerant of urban and seacoast conditions. Problem of dieback has been especially severe in Midwest
P. parviflora JAPANESE WHITE PINE Japan and Taiwan	32, 34–41. Will survive –20°F/–29°C	Slow to moderate, to 20–50 ft. or more	In open ground, a broad pyramid, nearly as wide as high	Needles: in 5s, 1½–2½ in., bluish to green. Cones: 2–3 in., reddish brown	Widely used as bonsai or container plant. There are blue-gray ('Glauca') and dwarf forms

P

PINE

NAME, NATIVE HABITAT	ZONES	GROWTH RATE, SIZE	GROWTH HABIT	NEEDLES AND CONES	COMMENTS
P. peuce MACEDONIAN PINE Balkans and Greece	31, 32, 34–43	Slow, to 60 ft.	Narrow, pyramidal to conical	Needles: in 5s; to 4 in. long, dark bluish green. Cones: to 6 in. long, light brown, somewhat similar to *P. cembra*	Gray-brown bark, becomes scaly with age. Nice specimen plant. Tolerates poor soils
P. pumila JAPANESE STONE PINE Japan, Siberia, Northeastern China	32, 34–43	3–7 ft., variable according to the form grown	Low, spreading, dense shrub; appearance varies	Needles: in 5s, bluish green, to 2½ in. long. Cones: to 2½ in. long, purplish, turning yellowish or reddish brown	A natural dwarf, and the smallest of all pine species. The nearly prostrate growth makes it a choice plant for rock gardens and collections of dwarf conifers. 'Dwarf Blue' grows wider than tall; 'Jermyns' is more pyramidal
P. resinosa RED PINE Newfoundland to Manitoba, south to mountains of Pennsylvania, west to Michigan	36–45. Withstands extremes of heat and cold, but best in colder climates	Moderate to 50–80 ft.	Short trunked, densely branched, eventually a dense oval	Needles: in 2s, 5–6 in., dark green. Cones: 3–6 in., light brown	Orange-red bark in youth, reddish brown plates in maturity. Attractive tree for difficult situations, poor soils. Use for windbreak, shelter belt, erosion control
P. rigida PITCH PINE Northeast	32, 34–43 Medium, then	slow; to 60 ft. high Open,	pyramidal but irregular when young, becoming more gnarled and twisted with age, especially in exposed locations	Needles: in 3s, pointed, to 5 in. long, dark green. Cones: in clusters, to 4 in. long, oval, light brown	Adapts to poor, dry, sandy soils; salt tolerant. Sculptural, windswept appearance. 'Sherman Eddy' is compact, to 15 ft., with foliage in rounded tufts
P. strobus WHITE PINE, EASTERN WHITE PINE Newfoundland to Manitoba, south to Georgia, west to Illinois and Iowa	32, 34–41	Fast to 100 ft. or more	Symmetrical cone shape with horizontal branches in regular whorls. In age, broad, open, irregular. Fine textured, handsome	Needles: in 5s, 2–4 in., blue green, soft. Cones: 3–8 in., slender, often curved, light brown	Intolerant of strong winds, pollution, salts. Subject to white pine blister rust, white pine weevil (kills terminal shoots, causing tree to become bushy). Popular Christmas tree. Varieties include 'Fastigiata', among most beautiful of upright pines; 'Pendula', with weeping, trailing branches; 'Prostrata', a low, trailing form; 'Nana', suitable for pots, rock gardens for many years
P. sylvestris SCOTCH PINE Northern Europe, western Asia, northeastern Siberia	32, 34–45	Fast, then moderate to 70–100 ft.	In youth, a straight, well-branched pyramid. In age, irregular, open, and picturesque, with drooping branches	Needles in 2s, 1½–3 in., blue green, stiff. Cones: 2 in., gray to reddish brown	Popular as Christmas tree and in landscaping. Showy red bark in maturity; sparse foliage. Pick young trees for good green winter color; some turn yellowish. Wind resistant. Garden forms include dwarfs 'Nana' and 'Waterei', weeping 'Pendula', columnar 'Fastigiata'

P

PINE

NAME, NATIVE HABITAT	ZONES	GROWTH RATE, SIZE	GROWTH HABIT	NEEDLES AND CONES	COMMENTS
P. taeda LOBLOLLY PINE Southern New Jersey to Florida, East Texas and Oklahoma	32, 33	Fast to 50–90 ft.	Loose cone shape in youth; as it matures, loses lower branches to become a rather open-crowned tree	Needles: in 3s (rarely 2s), 6–10 in., dark yellow-green. Cones: 3–6 in., oval to narrowly conical, rust brown, in clusters of 2–5; scales are spine tipped	Tough tree, withstanding poor soils. Widely planted for pulp, lumber
P. thunbergiana *(P. thumbergii)* JAPANESE BLACK PINE Japan	32, 34–37, 39. Hardy to –20°F/–29°C	Fast in cool, moist climates; slow in arid regions. Height varies from 20 to 100 ft., depending on conditions.	Spreading branches from broad, conical tree, irregular and spreading in age, often with leaning trunk Needles: in 2s, 3–4½ in., bright green, stiff. Cones: 3 in., oval, brown	Handsome tree in youth. Takes well to pruning, even shearing. Excellent for bonsai or pots. Very salt tolerant.	'Majestic Beauty' stands up to smog. 'Thunderhead' is a dwarf (6 ft. at 10 years) with showy white winter buds and spring candles. Subject to nematodes
P. wallichiana *(P. griffithii, P. excelsa)* HIMALAYAN WHITE PINE Himalayas	32, 34, 37, 39. Needles turn brown at temperatures below –15°F/–26°C	Slow to moderate; reaches 40 ft. in gardens, 150 ft. in wild	Broad, conical, open. Often retains branches to the ground in age	Needles: in 5s, 6–8 in., blue green, drooping, soft. Cones: 6–10 in., light brown	Eventually large, but good form and color make it a good choice for featured pine in big lawn or garden. Resistant to white pine blister rust

P

PITCHER PLANT. See SARRACENIA

PLANE TREE. See PLATANUS

PLANTAIN LILY. See HOSTA

PLATANUS

PLANE TREE, SYCAMORE

Platanaceae

DECIDUOUS TREES

▰ ZONES VARY BY SPECIES

☼ ◑ FULL SUN OR LIGHT SHADE

🔴 REGULAR WATER

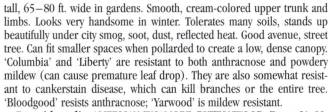

Platanus

All grow large, with heavy trunks and sculptural branch pattern. Older bark sheds in patches to reveal pale, smooth, new bark beneath. Big leaves (to 10 in. across) are rough surfaced and maplelike with three to five lobes; disappointing yellowish to brown autumn color. Ball-shaped brown seed clusters hang on threadlike stalks from bare branches through winter; these are prized for winter arrangements. Best in rich, deep, moist, well-drained soil. All are subject to anthracnose, which causes early leaf drop and twig dieback. Rake up and dispose of dead leaves, since fungus spores can overwinter on them.

P. acerifolia. LONDON PLANE TREE. Zones 31, 32, 34–41. Hybrid between *P. occidentalis* and *P. orientalis,* and often sold under the latter name. Grows 30–40 ft. tall in 20 years; may reach an eventual 70–100 ft.

tall, 65–80 ft. wide in gardens. Smooth, cream-colored upper trunk and limbs. Looks very handsome in winter. Tolerates many soils, stands up beautifully under city smog, soot, dust, reflected heat. Good avenue, street tree. Can fit smaller spaces when pollarded to create a low, dense canopy. 'Columbia' and 'Liberty' are resistant to both anthracnose and powdery mildew (can cause premature leaf drop). They are also somewhat resistant to cankerstain disease, which can kill branches or the entire tree. 'Bloodgood' resists anthracnose; 'Yarwood' is mildew resistant.

P. occidentalis. AMERICAN SYCAMORE, BUTTONWOOD. Zones 31, 32, 34–43. Very hardy. Native to eastern U.S. Similar to *P. acerifolia;* but has whiter new bark and a longer leafless period. Irregular habit, contorted branches. Occasionally grows with multiple or leaning trunks. Old trees near streams sometimes reach huge size. Best in a large wild garden.

P. orientalis. See *P. acerifolia*

PLATYCLADUS orientalis (Thuja orientalis)

ORIENTAL ARBORVITAE

Cupressaceae

EVERGREEN SHRUB

▰ ZONES 31, 32, 34–41

☼ ◑ FULL SUN OR LIGHT SHADE

🔴 REGULAR WATER

Platycladus orientalis

Foliage is carried in flattened sprays that are held vertically, forming a conical to pyramidal plant. Juvenile leaves are tiny and needlelike; mature leaves are minute, overlapping scales. Oval, ¾-in. cones are waxy blue green before ripening. Species (to 25 ft. high, 15 ft. wide) is rarely grown; nurseries offer more attractive, shrubbier selections 3–10 ft. high (see below). Widely used around foundations, by doorways or gates, in formal rows.

Less hardy to cold than American arborvitae *(Thuja occidentalis),* but tolerates heat and low humidity better. Tolerates many soils, but will not take boggy ones. Protect from strong winds. Bagworms and red spider mites are potential pests.

'Aureus' ('Aureus Nana', 'Berckmanii'). DWARF GOLDEN ARBORVITAE, BERCKMAN DWARF ARBORVITAE. Dwarf, compact, golden, globe shaped, usually 3 ft. tall, 2 ft. wide. Can reach 5 ft.

'Bakeri'. Compact, cone shaped, with bright green foliage. Grows 5–8 ft. high in 10 years.

'Beverlyensis'. BEVERLY HILLS ARBORVITAE, GOLDEN PYRAMID ARBOR-VITAE. Upright, globe shaped to conical; somewhat open habit. Branchlet tips golden yellow. In time, can reach 10 ft. tall and wide. Give it room.

'Blue Cone'. Dense, upright, conical; good blue-green color. To 8 ft. tall, 4 ft. wide.

'Bonita' ('Bonita Upright', 'Bonita Erecta'). Rounded, full, dense cone to 3 ft. tall. Dark green with slight golden tinting at branch tips.

'Fruitlandii'. FRUITLAND ARBORVITAE. Compact, upright, cone shaped, with deep green foliage.

'Minima Glauca'. DWARF BLUE ARBORVITAE. Grows 3–4 ft. tall and as wide. Blue-green foliage.

'Raffles'. Resembles 'Aureus' but is smaller, denser in growth, brighter in color.

'Westmont'. To 3 ft. tall, 2 ft. wide. Green foliage has yellow tips through the growing season.

PLATYCODON grandiflorus

BALLOON FLOWER

Campanulaceae (Lobeliaceae)

PERENNIAL

✿ ZONES 31, 32, 34–45

☀ ◐ AFTERNOON SHADE IN HOT-SUMMER AREAS

💧 REGULAR WATER

Platycodon grandiflorus

Inflated, balloonlike buds are carried on slender stalks at the ends of upright stems clad in broadly oval, 3-in. leaves. Buds open into 2-in., star-shaped blue-violet flowers with purple veins. Bloom begins in early summer and will continue for 2 months or more if spent blossoms (not entire stems) are removed. 'Albus' has blue-veined white flowers; 'Apoyama', dwarf to 9 in. high, deep violet-blue flowers; 'Hakone Double Blue', double flowers of deep violet blue; 'Komachi', blue flowers that remain balloon shaped; 'Plenum', semidouble pale blue flowers; 'Shell Pink', pale pink blossoms.

Plant is deep-rooted and takes 2 or 3 years to get well established. Dies back completely in fall, and new growth appears quite late in spring; mark position to avoid digging up fleshy roots. If you do unearth a root, replant it—or the pieces—right away.

BALLOON FLOWER IN BORDERS

With its decorative round buds, graceful star-shaped blossoms, and several-month-long bloom season, balloon flower is a nice choice for a summer border. Companion plants in shades of pink, deep to light blue, and white make for a lovely color combination; you might try astilbe, various kinds of bellflower *(Campanula),* coral bells *(Heuchera),* and mallow *(Malva).* Lush foliage plants such as hosta are good partners, too.

PLECTRANTHUS

SWEDISH IVY

Lamiaceae (Labiatae)

PERENNIALS

✿ ALL ZONES INDOORS

☀ ● SHADE OUTDOORS; BRIGHT LIGHT INDOORS

💧 REGULAR WATER

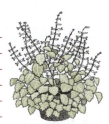

Plectranthus

Leaves somewhat thick, with scalloped edges and prominent veins. Small white or bluish flowers in spikes. Some species are excellent for summer bedding, or draping over the edges of planters. As greenhouse or house plants, grow in hanging pot or wall container that can be moved outdoors in summer. Among easiest plants to grow. Will root in water or soil. Many people remove flower buds before bloom to keep plants compact; others allow plants to bloom, then cut them back afterward. The following are the best known of many species and varieties:

P. argentatus. To 1 ft. high; spreading. Oval, grayish green leaves with scalloped edges. Terminal clusters of small, tubular, pale bluish white flowers. Good bedding plant.

P. australis. To 6 in. high; wide spreading. Shiny dark green leaves. Some forms have white-variegated foliage.

P. coleoides 'Marginatus'. To 2 ft. high; less trailing in habit than the others. Leaves green and gray green, edged in cream.

P. fosteri 'Marginatus' (P. coleoides 'Marginatus') to 10 in. high; stems grow upright, then trail. Oval, light green leaves with wide border of creamy white, scalloped edges. Can be used for summer bedding.

P. madagascariensis 'Variegated Mintleaf'. To 1 ft. high; creeping. Rounded, semisucculent leaves with scalloped edges, variegated white, smell minty when crushed. Can be used for summer bedding.

P. oertendahlii. To 6 in. high; wide spreading. Leaf veins are silvery above, purplish beneath. Leaf margins are purplish, scalloped.

PLEROMA. See TIBOUCHINA urvilleana

PLUM, FLOWERING. See PRUNUS

P

PLUM and PRUNE

Rosaceae

DECIDUOUS FRUIT TREES

✿ ZONES VARY BY VARIETY

☀ FULL SUN

💧 PERIODIC DEEP SOAKINGS

▸ SEE CHART NEXT PAGE

Plum and Prune

Like their cherry, peach, and apricot relatives, these are stone fruits belonging to the genus *Prunus*; for flowering plums, see Prunus. Three categories of edible plums and prunes are grown in the diverse climates of North America: European, Japanese, and hardy (see chart on pages 359–360). They tolerate many soil types, but do best in fertile, well-drained soil. Plants bloom in late winter or early spring. Harvest season is from June into September, depending on variety.

The two most widely grown groups are European *(P. domestica)* and Japanese *(P. salicina).* Damson plum *(P. insititia)* is often considered a type of European plum; it freely intercrosses with European plums. Prunes are European plum varieties with a high sugar content, a trait that allows them to be sun-dried without fermenting at the pit.

Compared to Japanese plums, European varieties as a group have a higher chill requirement, bloom later (and so are less subject to frost damage), ripen their fruit with less summer heat, and tend to be somewhat more cold hardy. European types are at their best in the Northeast.

A third category dominates in regions with severe winters, especially the Dakotas, Minnesota, and the Canadian prairies. This is a complex group of hardy hybrids involving Japanese plum, several species of native American wild plums, and the native sand cherry *(P. besseyi)*. Varieties with fruit approaching the size and quality of Japanese plums are sometimes called Japanese-American hybrids; those with considerably smaller fruit that is closer in flavor to wild plums are often referred to as cherry-plum hybrids.

The European plum likely originated about 2000 years ago in the Caucasus and Caspian region. Damson plums were mentioned in ancient writings as cultivated in the region of Damascus. Both may have been brought to America and grown from pits by the Pilgrims and other early colonists. Japanese plums have been traced to China and were introduced into the United States in the 1870s.

The fruits of the European plum range from red to green to yellow with purplish blue, the most common color. Japanese plums are yellow or red but never purplish blue. Damson plums are always purplish blue.

Tree characteristics. Plum trees will mature on most rootstocks from 20–30 ft. high, but dwarfing stock will reduce the size by fifty percent. Japanese plum will begin to bear in 3 to 4 years and European ones and Damsons in 4 to 5 years. In the colder parts of the Northeast, European plums and native species with a higher chill factors and later blooming times will be more successful than Japanese ones. Even in the warmer regions of the Northeast, the Japanese varieties are often frosted out. Train young trees to a vase shape opening up the center to admit sunshine, promote good air circulation, and prune out any tight vee-shaped crotches.

Soil requirements: Most plum trees grow well on a deep, well-drained soil and the European ones will tolerate a heavier soil. The pH should be above 6.0.

Rootstocks and propagation: The most popular of understocks for grafting European plums is the myrobalan. This give a vigorous, well anchored tree and is adaptable to many soil types. St. Julian, a rootstock with a number of strains, is used for all types of plums and peaches, as well. It is slightly dwarfing, tolerates many soil types, anchors well and will induce early bearing. The western sand cherry is used to produce a dwarf tree 6 to 8 feet tall.

Planting and culture: Use planting techniques as for other tree fruits and space European and Damson plums 18–24 ft. apart, Japanese 14–16 ft. and native species and those on dwarfing stock like the western sand cherry 10–14 ft. The planting site should be kept free of competing weeds by mechanical removal or mulching. A mulch of rotted manure a few inches deep applied annually will suppress weeds and provide the required nitrogen. Especially when the tree is young, it should be watered regularly when adequate rainfall is not available. Thinning the fruit to two inches apart after the "June drop" will improve both the size and quality of the plums. A few varieties like 'Santa Rosa' will self thin. Plum trees will begin to fruit three to five years after planting and, on maturity, in about 10 years will produce 3–5 bushels of fruit.

Pollination: When selecting varieties to plant, the pollination requirements must be carefully considered. It is often reported that European varieties are self-fertile, but will benefit from the pollen of another European variety. With Japanese plums, select two or more pollen compatible varieties for a good crop. The blooming period of the varieties for cross-pollination must overlap for all types of plums.

Pests and diseases: Plum curculio and leafhoppers, as well as the peach tree borer, are the major pest of the plum. Black knot caused by a fungus and brown rot are major diseases and are usually more prevalent in the more humid regions. Pests and diseases can be controlled with a regular spray program from your local agricultural extension service. Black knot can be greatly reduced by identifying the infected wood and pruning it out in the winter back to healthy tissue. Proper thinning of the fruit and removing mummies from the tree and debris from beneath the tree lessen brown rot.

Plumbaginaceae. The leadwort family consists of shrubs and perennials with clustered and funnel-shaped flowers: examples are thrift *(Armeria)* and two groups of plants commonly called plumbago *(Ceratostigma* and *Plumbago)*.

PLUMBAGO auriculata (P. capensis)

CAPE PLUMBAGO, LEADWORT

Plumbaginaceae

EVERGREEN TO SEMIEVERGREEN SHRUB OR VINE

ALL ZONES IN CONTAINER

FULL SUN

MODERATE TO LITTLE WATER

Plumbago auriculata

Grows to about 4 ft. high in a container. Fresh-looking, light to medium green leaves, 1–2 in. long. Inch-wide flowers in phloxlike clusters, varying (in seedling plants) from white to clear light blue. Select plants in bloom to get color you want. Typically blooms spring–fall. 'Alba' is white flowered; 'Imperial Blue' has sky blue blooms.

Grow in pots moved outdoors in summer, indoors over winter. Needs good drainage. For other plants called plumbago, see *Ceratostigma*.

PLUMBAGO larpentae. See CERATOSTIGMA plumbaginoides

PLUME CEDAR, PLUME CRYPTOMERIA. See CRYPTOMERIA japonica 'Elegans'

PLUME GRASS. See SACCHARUM

PLUME HYACINTH. See MUSCARI comosum 'Plumosum'

PLUME POPPY. See MACLEAYA

PLUM YEW. See CEPHALOTAXUS

POA

BLUEGRASS

Poaceae (Gramineae)

PERENNIAL AND ANNUAL GRASSES

ZONES VARY BY SPECIES

FULL SUN (EXCEPT FOR P. TRIVIALIS)

REGULAR WATER

Poa

One is the best-known cool-season lawn grass; the other two sometimes turn up in lawns, either intentionally or as an annual weed. Leaves of all have characteristic boat-prow tip.

P. annua. ANNUAL BLUEGRASS. All zones. Cool-season weed of lawns. Bright green, soft textured. Discourage it by maintaining thick turf of good grasses.

P. pratensis. KENTUCKY BLUEGRASS. Zones 32, 34–45. Rich bluegreen perennial lawn grass. Many selections are available as seed or sod. Mow at 2 in. high in spring and fall, at 3 in. high in summer. Use alone or in mixture with other grasses.

P. trivialis. ROUGH-STALKED BLUEGRASS. Zones 32, 34–45. Fine-textured, bright green perennial meadow and pasture grass. Occasionally used in shady lawn mixtures for its tolerance of shade and damp soil.

Poaceae. The grass family is undoubtedly the most important plant family in terms of usefulness to humans. All the world's important grain crops are grasses; the bamboos (giant grasses) are useful in building and crafts. Many grasses are used in lawns or as ornamental annual or perennial plants. Some botanists still use Gramineae as the family name for grasses.

P

PLUM

VARIETY	SEASONS	FRUIT	COMMENTS
EUROPEAN & DAMSON PLUM VARIETIES			
'Blue Damson'	Late	Small blue-black skin with green flesh; very tart	Suitable for jams, jellies and cooking. Cold hardy, heavy bearing and considered self-fruitful
'Burbank Grand Prize'	Midseason	Large oval; purplish skin with juicy sweet flesh. Hardy	Developed by Luther Burbank in California. Dessert quality. Of medium vigor and should be pollinated with Stanley
'Earliblue'	Early	Medium in size and blue in color with tender greenish yellow flesh	Resembling Stanley, it is shy bearing and the tree is slow to begin to produce
'Green Gage' (*Reine Claude*)	Midseason	Small to medium in size, greenish yellow skin with amber flesh. Very juicy	Brought from Italy to France in 1500, taken into England in the 18th century by Sir Thomas Gage
'Italian Prune' (*Fellenberg*) Italian or German prune.	Midseason	Large fruit is purple-skinned with a very sweet rich flavor when fully ripe	Fruit will hang on the tree two weeks after ripening. It is vigorous, late blooming and cold hardy. When cooked, the fruit turns a burgundy red
'Stanley'	Midseason	Large size with dark blue skin with a heavy bloom and juicy, sweet, greenish yellow flesh	The most widely plant European plum; was developed in New York in 1913. When cooked the flesh turns purplish red
'Sugar Plum'	Early midseason	Large in size with reddish purple skin and very sweet greenish yellow flesh. Medium in vigor. Lower chill requirement than most other European plums	Best eaten fresh. Not for processing
JAPANESE PLUM VARIETIES			
'Burbank'	Late midseason	Large, with purplish red skin and meaty sweet flesh	Best best picked before fully ripe on the tree. Thin properly. A good pollinator is 'Methley'
'Elephant Heart'	Midseason	Large, heart shaped plum with thick, bronze green skin that turns to a reddish purple when fully ripe. Distinctive flavor	It requires only 500 chilling hours. 'Santa Rosa' is a good pollinator

P

PLUM

VARIETY	SEASONS	FRUIT		COMMENTS
JAPANESE PLUM VARIETIES continued				
'Methley'	Early	Medium to large, with reddish purple fruit		Tree is vigorous and produces heavy annual crops. Good pollinator for early bearing varieties like 'Santa Rosa' and 'Shiro'
'Santa Rosa'	Midseason	Dark red skin with yellow flesh that is very fragrant. Large in size		Shy bearer and must have a pollinator, like 'Methley'. 'Santa Rosa' only produces well in the warmer areas of the northeast and is considered only moderately bud hardy
'Shiro I'	Early midseason	Small to medium in size with yellow skin with a pink blush and yellow flesh		Pollinate with 'Methley' or 'Santa Rosa'. The tree is productive, hardy and vigorous

PODOCARPUS

Podocarpaceae

EVERGREEN TREES OR SHRUBS

ZONES VARY BY SPECIES

FULL SUN OR PARTIAL SHADE

REGULAR TO MODERATE WATER

Podocarpus

Versatile plants grown for good-looking foliage, interesting form; adaptable to many garden uses. Good screen or background plants. Foliage generally resembles that of yews (*Taxus*), to which these plants are related, but leaves of the better-known species are longer, broader, and lighter in color than those of yews. If a male plant is growing nearby, females bear fruit after many years, producing small fleshy fruits rather than cones. Grow well (if slowly) in most soils, though they may develop chlorosis where soil is alkaline or heavy and damp. Some botanists now divide these plants into three genera (*Afrocarpus, Nageia, Podocarpus*).

P. macrophyllus. YEW PINE. Zones 31, 32, or father north in container moved indoors in winter. Shrub or tree. Native to China, Japan. To about 6 ft. tall in a container. Generally narrow and upright. Bright green leaves 4 in. long, ½ in. wide. Grow indoors or out, in tubs or open ground. Large shrub, screen, street or lawn tree (with staking and thinning). Limber enough to espalier. Easily pruned as clipped hedge, topiary. Very heat tolerant.

P. m. maki. SHRUBBY YEW PINE. Smaller, slower growing than species; reaches 6–8 ft. in 10 years. Dense, upright form. Leaves to 3 in. long, ¼ in. wide. One of the best container plants for outdoor or indoor use, and a choice shrub generally.

P. nagi (Nageia nagi). Tree. Not hardy in the Northeast; grow in container indoors over winter, outdoors in summer. Slow growth to about 8 ft. in a pot (80–90 ft. in its native Japan). Branchlets drooping, sometimes to a considerable length. Leaves 1–3 in. long, ½–1½ in. wide, leathery, smooth, sharp pointed. More treelike in youth than other species. Makes decorative foliage pattern against natural wood or masonry. Plant in groves for slender sapling effect.

P. alpinus. TASMANIAN PODOCARP. Zones 31, 32. Spreading shrub to 6 ft. tall, with yellow catkinlike flowers and bright red fruit.

P. nivalis. ALPINE TOTARA. Zones 31, 32. Evergreen shrub, to 25 ft. tall, with bronze-green leaves. Yellow catkinlike flowers; bright red fruit in autumn.

PODOPHYLLUM

Berberidaceae

PERENNIALS

ZONES VARY BY SPECIES

PARTIAL OR FULL SHADE

REGULAR WATER

RHIZOMES, LEAVES, STEMS, SEEDS POISONOUS IF INGESTED

Podophyllum

Odd herbaceous relatives of barberry, with thick, spreading underground rhizomes that send up stalks crowned with large, shield-shaped, deeply lobed leaves. Shoots with a single leaf are barren; those with two leaves bear a single 2-in.-wide flower (set between the leaves) followed by a juicy, 2-in.-long berry. Berries are edible but can have a powerful laxative effect. Attractive, slow-spreading deciduous ground cover plants for shady areas with rich, moist, woodsy soil.

P. hexandrum. Zones 32, 34, 37, 39. Native to Himalayas and China. Grows 1–1½ ft. high, with 10-in. umbrellalike leaves mottled brown. Leaves divided into three or five lobes, with each lobe further divided. White or pink flower; red berry.

P. peltatum. MAY APPLE, WILD MANDRAKE. Zones 31, 32, 34–43. Native to eastern U.S. To 1½ ft. high. Leaves to 1 ft. across, divided into five to nine lobes. White flower; yellow berry. Leaves pushing up through the forest duff are one of the earliest signs of spring in eastern woodlands. Dies down completely in summer.

P. pleianthum. CHINESE MAY APPLE. Zones 31, 32, 34, 39. Native to China and Taiwan. To 2½ ft. tall and 1½ ft. wide. Glossy leaves to 14 in. long, divided into six to ten lobes. Deep red to purple flowers; dark red fruit.

POISON IVY, POISON OAK. See RHUS

POKER PLANT. See KNIPHOFIA uvaria

Polemoniaceae. The phlox family consists mostly of annuals and perennials, including many wildflowers; examples are *Ipomopsis* and *Phlox*. Cup-and-saucer vine *(Cobaea)* is another member.

POLEMONIUM

Polemoniaceae

PERENNIALS

ZONES 31, 32, 34–43

PARTIAL OR FULL SHADE

REGULAR WATER

Polemonium

Lush rosettes of finely divided fernlike foliage; clusters of bell-shaped flowers, spring–summer. Combine nicely with bleeding heart, bellflower, ferns, hellebore, hosta, and lilies. Need good drainage. Grow from seed or from divisions made after bloom or in spring. Listed below are the types most commonly available in nurseries. All are good under trees.

P. caeruleum. JACOB'S LADDER. Clusters of lavender blue, pendulous, 1-in.-long flowers on leafy, 1½–2-ft.-high stems.

P. 'Firmament'. Hybrid between *P. caeruleum* and *P. reptans*. To 20 in. high, with bright blue flowers.

P. foliosissimum. To 2½ ft. high, with leafy stems and lavender blue flowers enhanced by bright orange stamens. Native to western U.S.; short lived where summer heat is accompanied by high humidity.

P. reptans. Wildflower in eastern woodlands and midwestern plains. Best known through its variety 'Blue Pearl', a profusely blooming blue-flowered dwarf with spreading growth to 9 in. high, 1½ ft. wide. Good in shaded, dampish rock garden.

POLIANTHES tuberosa

TUBEROSE

Agavaceae

TUBEROUS-ROOTED PERENNIAL

ALL ZONES (SEE BELOW)

FULL SUN OR PARTIAL SHADE

REGULAR WATER DURING GROWTH AND BLOOM

Polianthes

Native to Mexico. Noted for powerful, heady fragrance. Glistening white, tubular flowers are loosely arranged in spikelike clusters on stems to 3 ft. tall, late summer–fall. Long, narrow, grasslike basal leaves. Single forms are graceful, but double-flowered 'The Pearl' is most widely available; it's a good garden variety but not as long-lasting a cut flower as the single type.

To bloom year after year, tuberose needs a long (at least 4-month) warm season before flowering. Start indoors or plant outside after soil is warm. Set rhizomes 2 in. deep, 4–6 in. apart. If soil or water is alkaline, apply acid fertilizer when growth begins. Dig plants in fall after leaves have yellowed; cut off dead foliage. Let rhizomes dry for 2 weeks, then store them in a cool (40 to 50°F/4 to 10°C), dry place. Tuberose can also be grown in pots and moved to a protected area during cold weather. Divide clumps every 4 years.

Polygonaceae. The buckwheat family consists of annuals, perennials, shrubs, trees, and vines. Flowers lack petals, but sepals are often showy. Stems are jointed. Fruit is small, dry, single seeded. Representatives include rhubarb and knotweed *(Polygonum)*. True buckwheat—the pancake flour kind—is *Fagopyrum*, a crop plant of no ornamental value.

POLYGONATUM

SOLOMON'S SEAL

Liliaceae

PERENNIALS

ZONES 31, 32, 34–43, EXCEPT AS NOTED

WOODSY SHADE

REGULAR WATER

Polygonatum

Slowly spreading underground rhizomes send up stems that grow upright for a distance, then bend outward. On either side of the arching stems are broadly oval, bright green leaves arranged in nearly horizontal planes. Where leaves join stems, pairs or clusters of small, bell-shaped greenish white blossoms hang beneath the stems on threadlike stalks in spring. Small blue-black berries sometimes follow the flowers. Leaves and stems turn bright yellow in autumn before plant dies to the ground.

Attractive for form and flowers in woodland garden; good with astilbe, ferns, hellebore, hosta, wild ginger. Need loose, woodsy soil. Don't need dividing; to get more plants, remove rhizomes from a clump's edge in early spring. Attractive in containers. For false Solomon's seal, see *Smilacina*.

P. biflorum. Native to eastern North America. Bears 4-in. leaves on stems to 3 ft. tall. Flowers usually in pairs or threes.

P. commutatum. Carries 7-in. leaves on stems normally reaching 4–5 ft. high, possibly 7 ft. tall. Flowers in groups of two to ten. This species is considered to be a vigorous form of *P. biflorum*. It is sometimes sold as *P. canaliculatum*.

P. humile. Zones 31, 32, 34–41. Native to eastern Europe and western Asia. Grows to 8 in. tall and 20 in. wide. Bears 3-in. leaves with fine hairs. Flowers produced singly or in pairs.

P. odoratum (P. japonicum). Native to Europe, Asia. To 3½ ft. tall, with 4–6-in. leaves. Scented flowers usually borne in pairs, sometimes singly. 'Variegatum' has white-edged leaves carried on stems that are dark red until fully grown.

POLYGONUM

KNOTWEED

Polygonaceae

EVERGREEN OR DECIDUOUS PERENNIALS AND VINES

ZONES VARY BY SPECIES

FULL SUN, EXCEPT AS NOTED

REGULAR WATER, EXCEPT AS NOTED

Polygonum

Sturdy, sun-loving plants with jointed stems and small white or pink flowers in open sprays. Some kinds tend to get out of hand and need to be controlled. Botanists have reclassified these plants; the new names are given in parentheses below.

P. affine (Persicaria affinis). Evergreen perennial. Zones 31, 32. Tufted plant 1–1½ ft. tall. Leaves mostly basal, 2–4½ in. long, finely toothed, deep green turning to bronze in winter. Bright rose red flowers in dense, erect, 2–3-in. spikes, summer into fall. Informal border or ground cover. Tolerates some shade. 'Darjeeling Red' forms 3-in.-high mats with 10-in. spikes of flowers in deep pink aging to red; foliage turns red in fall. 'Dimity' has fatter, paler flower spikes. 'Superbum' is larger-leafed than the species, with somewhat taller spikes of pale pink flowers.

P. aubertii (Fallopia aubertii). SILVER LACE VINE. Deciduous. Zones 31, 32, 34–41. Fast growing: can cover 100 sq. ft. in a season. Heart-shaped, glossy, wavy-edged leaves 1½–2½ in. long. Small, creamy white flowers appear in a frothy mass from late spring until fall. Use as quick screen on fences or arbors, on hillsides, at seashore. You can prune severely (to ground) each year; bloom will be delayed until well into summer. Drought tolerant.

P

P. baldschuanicum (Fallopia baldschuanica). BOKHARA FLEECE-FLOWER. Deciduous vine. Zones 31, 32, 34–41. Much like *P. aubertii* in appearance, growth, vigor, and uses. Fragrant pink flowers, borne in large, drooping clusters, are somewhat larger than those of *P. aubertii*.

P. bistorta 'Superbum' (Persicaria bistorta 'Superbum'). Deciduous perennial. Zones 31, 32, 34–43. Forms a mound to 2½ ft. high, with leaves to 8 in. long. Flowers are pink aging to deep red, carried in dense, 4–6-in.-long, bottlebrushlike spikes held well above the foliage. Blooms in early summer, with sporadic repeat bloom until frost. Leaves turn bright red in autumn.

P. capitatum (Persicaria capitata). Evergreen perennial grown as summer annual. Rugged, trailing ground cover to 8 in. high, spreading to 20 in. Leaves 1½ in. long; new leaves are dark green, old ones tinged pink. Stems and small, round flower heads are pink. Has invasive roots and also reseeds freely. Takes sun or shade. Drought tolerant.

P. japonicum. JAPANESE KNOTWEED. Deciduous perennial. Zones 31, 32, 34–43. Tough, vigorous plant forming large clumps of red-brown, wiry, 4–8-ft. stems. Leaves nearly heart shaped, to 5 in. long. Greenish white flowers in late summer and fall. Extremely invasive, so do not plant it. Often called bamboo or Mexican bamboo because of jointed stalks.

P. j. compactum (P. reynoutria) is a lower, somewhat less rampant form, growing 10–24 in. high and spreading by creeping roots. In late summer, showy clusters of small, pale pink flowers open from red buds. Red-veined foliage turns red in fall before plant dies to the ground. Can be used with caution where an expansive soil-binding plant is needed, such as on a steep slope. Very long lived and difficult to eradicate once established.

P. vacciniifolium. (Persicaria vacciniifolia). Evergreen perennial. Zones 31, 32. Prostrate, with slender, leafy, branching red stems radiating 2–4 ft. Leaves ½ in. long, oval, turn red in fall. Rose pink late-summer flowers in dense, upright, 2–3-in. spikes on 6–9-in. stalks. Excellent bank cover or drapery for boulder in large rock garden.

P. virginianum (Persicaria virginiana). Deciduous perennial. Zones 31, 32, 34–41. Native to eastern U.S. Rhizome produces upright, leafy stems to 2–3 ft. high; spreads aggressively. Late to leaf out in spring. Species is green-leafed; it is less often grown than forms with variegated foliage. 'Variegata' has green leaves marbled with creamy white. 'Painter's Palette' is similar, but with a V-shaped reddish mark in center of each leaf; new leaves are creamy white splashed with light green and pink. Give part shade; protect from wind.

Polypodiaceae. The polypody family contains the vast majority of ferns. They differ from other ferns only in technical details concerning spore-bearing bodies (sporangia).

POLYPODIUM

Polypodiaceae

FERNS

🗡 ZONES VARY BY SPECIES

◐ ● PARTIAL OR FULL SHADE

💧 💧💧 AMPLE WATER

Widespread, variable group. Both types described here are hardy plants used in woodland gardens and shady rock gardens.

Polypodium

P. virginianum. AMERICAN WALL FERN, VIRGINIA POLYPODY. Zones 31, 32, 34–45. Native to eastern North America and eastern Asia. To 10 in. tall. Evergreen, with arching, narrow, dark green, leathery 10-in. fronds divided into pairs of lance-shaped to narrowly oblong lobes but not individual leaflets.

P. vulgare. COMMON POLYPODY. Zones 31, 32, 34–43. European native very similar to *P. virginianum*. Evergreen, to 10 in. tall, with fronds divided into deep lobes but not separate leaflets. 'Bifidum' has notched lobes; 'Cristatum' has ruffled lobes and tips; 'Jean Taylor' is dwarf, with finely cut, ruffled fronds.

POLYSTICHUM

Polypodiaceae

FERNS

🗡 ZONES VARY BY SPECIES

◐ ● PARTIAL OR FULL SHADE

💧 REGULAR WATER, EXCEPT AS NOTED

Polystichum

Hardy symmetrical plants with medium-size, evergreen (except on *P. braunii*) fronds. Among most useful and widely planted ferns, they combine well with other plants and are easy to grow. Do best in rich, organic, well-drained soil. Use in shady beds, along house walls, in mixed woodland plantings.

P. acrostichoides. CHRISTMAS FERN. Zones 31, 32, 34–45. Native to eastern North America. Grows to 1–1½ ft., with dark green leaves that make a fine contrast to snow or to the brown of dead leaves at Christmas time. Stiff fronds remain upright until pushed over by heavy snow or hard frost. In coldest climates, plant appreciates a leaf mulch.

P. aculeatum. PRICKLY SHIELD FERN, HARD SHIELD FERN. Zones 31, 32, 34–43. Native to Europe. Grows 2–4 ft. tall. Glossy, firm, fairly upright, once- or twice-cut fronds; final segments are tipped by soft prickles. Pale young fronds make an attractive show against the dark green mature ones.

P. braunii. BRAUN'S HOLLY FERN. Zones 31, 32, 34–41. Semi-evergreen to deciduous. Native to northern latitudes. Grows 1–3 ft. tall, with twice-divided fronds. Silvery green new growth.

P. polyblepharum. JAPANESE LACE FERN, TASSEL FERN. Zones 31, 32, 34–41. Native to Asia. Handsome, dense, lacy. Resembles *P. setiferum* but is taller, darker green, and somewhat coarser; fronds are a little more upright (to 2 ft. high). Usually sold as *P. setosum*.

P. setiferum. SOFT SHIELD FERN. Zones 31, 32, 34–41. Native to Europe. Finely cut fronds give effect of dark green lace, spread out in flattened vase shape. Many forms, 2–4½ ft. tall. 'Divisilobum' has frilly three- or four-leaflet fronds. 'Proliferum' makes plantlets on midribs of older fronds; these can be used for propagation. Other fancy varieties are sometimes sold under the name "English fern."

P. setosum. See *P. polyblepharum*

P. tsus-sinense. KOREAN ROCK FERN. Zones 31, 32, 34, 39. Native to eastern Asia. To 16 in. tall; dark green two-leaflet fronds further divided into narrow, toothed and pointed leaflets.

POMEGRANATE. See PUNICA granatum

PONCIRUS trifoliata

TRIFOLIATE ORANGE, HARDY ORANGE

Rutaceae

DECIDUOUS SHRUB OR TREE

🗡 ZONES 31, 32, 34–41

☀ FULL SUN

💧 REGULAR WATER

Poncius trifoliata

This unusual plant is a large, densely branched shrub or small tree that features stout, sharp spines on its branches. A relative of oranges and other citrus native to northern China. Ranges from 8 to 20 ft. in height and spreads 12–15 ft. Three-leaflet leaves turn yellow in fall. Plants bear fragrant, white, five-petaled flowers in late spring or early summer, followed by round, 1½–2-in.-wide, fuzzy-skinned fruits that resemble small oranges but are inedible. The fruit is ornamental well into winter and stands out against the green branches and spines. Use trifoliate orange as a thorny hedge, in shrub borders, or as a specimen. It can be trained against walls or fences. Plant it away from heavily trafficked areas, or it will impale unwary visitors. 'Flying Dragon' is a cultivar with twisted branches.

Pontederiaceae. The pickerel weed family contains aquatic or marsh plants with showy, usually blue flowers, among them pickerel weed *(Pontederia)* and water hyacinth *(Eichhornia)*.

PONTEDERIA cordata

PICKEREL WEED	
Pontederiaceae	
AQUATIC PLANT	
✂ ALL ZONES	
☼ ◑ FULL SUN OR LIGHT SHADE	
● LOCATE IN PONDS, WATER GARDENS	

Pontederia cordata

Grown as companion to water lilies; best planted in pots of rich soil placed in 1 ft. of water. Long-stalked leaves stand well above surface of water; these are heart shaped, to 10 in. long and 6 in. wide. Short spikes of bright blue flowers top 4-ft. (or shorter) stems. Gives wild-pond look to informal garden pool. Plant underwater at shorelines of natural ponds. Dormant in winter.

POOR MAN'S ORCHID. See SCHIZANTHUS pinnatus

POOR MAN'S RHODODENDRON. See IMPATIENS oliveri

POPCORN. See CORN

POPLAR. See POPULUS

POPPY. See PAPAVER

POPPY MALLOW. See CALLIRHOE involucrata

POPULUS

POPLAR, COTTONWOOD, ASPEN	
Salicaceae	
DECIDUOUS TREES	
✂ ZONES VARY BY SPECIES	
☼ FULL SUN	
● REGULAR DEEP WATERING	

Populus

Fast-growing, tough trees, best suited to rural areas and fringes of large properties. If they are planted in smaller gardens, their network of aggressive surface roots crowds out other plants, heaves pavement, and clogs sewer and drainage lines. Most poplars will sucker profusely if their roots are cut or disturbed. Plants are also subject to many pests and diseases. Nonetheless, some poplars are beautiful or distinctive enough to be widely sold despite their liabilities; many have good fall color. Leaves of most poplars are roughly triangular, sometimes toothed or lobed. Pendulous catkins appear before spring leafout; those on male trees are denser textured. Female trees later bear masses of cottony seeds that blow about and become a nuisance; for that reason, male (seedless) varieties are offered in nurseries.

P. alba. WHITE POPLAR. Zones 31, 32, 34–45. Native to Europe, Asia. Broad, wide-spreading tree to 40–60 ft. tall. Leaves are dark green above, white and woolly beneath, 2–5 in. long, usually with three to five lobes. A "lively" tree even in light breezes, with flickering white and green highlights. Poor fall color. Tolerates a wide range of soils. Suckers profusely.

Seedless variety 'Pyramidalis', the Bolleana poplar (often sold as *P. bolleana*), forms a narrow column and has a birchlike white trunk.

P. balsamifera (P. candicans). BALM-OF-GILEAD. Zones 35, 41–45. Native to northern climates. To 30–60 ft., broad topped. Leaves 4½–6 in. long. Two male selections are 'Idahoensis' ('Idaho Hybrid') and 'Mojave Hybrid'; both are large, fast-growing trees. The latter has nearly white bark.

STAY OUT OF ROOT TROUBLE

Do not plant any kind of *Populus* near pavement, sewer lines, septic tanks, or their leach lines. Also keep them out of lawns and small gardens. Their roots are invasive, and they form suckers. In the worst cases, they can heave up pavement and clog plumbing systems.

P. canadensis. CAROLINA POPLAR. Zones 31, 32, 34–43. Group of hybrids ranging in height from 40 to 150 ft. Toothed leaves to 4 in. long. Male varieties include fairly narrow 'Eugene' and disease-resistant 'Siouxland'.

P. maximowiczii. JAPANESE POPLAR. Zones 32, 34–43. Native to northeastern Asia. Handsome, broadly conical tree to 100 ft. tall. Smooth, gray-green bark; bright green leaves to 5 in. long. Males produce red catkins, females green, followed by the fluffy, cotton seeds.

P. nigra 'Italica'. LOMBARDY POPLAR. Zones 31, 32, 34–45. Male selection of European native. Beautiful columnar tree to 40–100 ft., with upward-reaching branches. Bright green, 4-in. leaves turn beautiful golden yellow in fall. Few problems in cold-winter, dry climates. In other regions, however, tree is subject to a canker disease that will soon kill it; in these areas, it is best used as a quick, temporary screen. 'Afghanica'—also sold as 'Theves' and as *P. n. thevestina*—has white bark.

P. simonii. Zones 31, 32, 34–45. Native to China. Columnar tree to 40 ft. tall, one of the balsam poplars. Leaves are yellow green and aromatic in spring, turn dark green, grow to 5 in. long. Catkins (red males, green females), appear in early spring and may be damaged by late frost.

P. tremula. EUROPEAN ASPEN. Zones 35–45. Native to Europe and Asia. Spreading tree to 70 ft. high and 30 ft. wide. Deep green leaves with coarsely toothed edges turn yellow in autumn; they quiver in the breeze like those of quaking aspen *(P. tremuloides)*. Catkins (grayish red male, green female) appear in early spring. Seedless variety 'Erecta', sometimes called Swedish columnar aspen, is narrow like Lombardy poplar, but it has red fall color and is less prone to canker.

PORCUPINE GRASS. See MISCANTHUS sinensis 'Strictus'

PORCUPINE PALM. See RHAPHIDOPHYLLUM hystrix

PORT ORFORD CEDAR. See CHAMAECYPARIS lawsoniana

PORTULACA

PORTULACA, ROSE MOSS	
Portulacaceae	
ANNUALS	
✂ ALL ZONES	
☼ ◑ FULL SUN OR VERY LIGHT SHADE	
● ● REGULAR TO LITTLE WATER	

Portulaca

Low-growing plants with fleshy leaves and stems. Generally, the brilliant flowers open fully only in bright light and close by midafternoon in hot weather. Plants bloom from late spring until frost, though quality may decline in late summer. Thrive in high temperatures, intense sunlight. Drought tolerant; ideal for dry, sunbaked places. Not fussy about soil.

Good for rock gardens, dry banks, edgings, hanging baskets. Plants don't require deadheading.

P. grandiflora. PORTULACA, ROSE MOSS. To 6 in. high, 1½ ft. across. Leaves cylindrical, pointed, 1 in. long. Trailing, branched reddish stems. Lustrous, roselike, 1-in.-wide flowers in red, cerise, rose pink, orange, yellow, white, pastel shades. Available as single colors or mixes, in either single-flowered or double strains. Prize Strain, Magic Carpet, Sunglo, Sunkiss are popular kinds. Afternoon Delight and Sundance strains stay open longer in the afternoon. Plants self-sow, though hybrid types don't come true from seed.

P. oleracea. PURSLANE. Unimproved form is a weed with tiny yellow flowers and edible stems and leaves. Warm weather and moisture encourage its growth. Control by hoeing or pulling before it goes to seed; don't let pulled plants lie about, since they can reroot or ripen seed.

PURSLANE A WEED?

The French call it *pourpier,* the Mexicans call it *verdolaga,* and both cultures use it in cooking. You can use purslane in salad, soup, pork stew, tomato sauce, and scrambled eggs.

Portulacaceae. The portulaca family contains annuals, perennials, and a few shrubs, usually with succulent foliage and frequently with showy flowers. Examples are *Lewisia* and *Portulaca.*

POSSUMHAW. See ILEX decidua

POTATO

Solanaceae

TUBEROUS-ROOTED PERENNIAL TREATED AS ANNUAL

☀ ALL ZONES

☼ FULL SUN

💧 EVENLY MOIST SOIL

⬥ GREEN SKIN AND RAW SHOOTS ARE TOXIC

Potato

Though not the most widely grown home garden vegetables, potatoes can be very satisfying: 2 lb. of seed potatoes can yield 50 lb. of potatoes for eating. The many pests and diseases that beleaguer commercial growers are not likely to plague home gardeners. One of the most damaging insect pests is Colorado potato beetle, found mainly in the eastern U.S. To avoid disease problems, the best tactic is to start with certified disease-free starter potatoes or disease-resistant varieties.

Can be grown from minitubers (these are planted whole) or from seed potatoes that you cut into 1½-in.-sq. pieces, each with at least two eyes. Since minitubers are uncut, they are less likely to rot in the ground. Home gardeners have access to an increasing number of potato varieties, including types with red, yellow, or bluish purple skins, sorts with yellow flesh, and even all-blue kinds. Shapes vary from round to fingerlike. Some varieties mature faster than others, but most take about 3 months.

Potatoes need sandy, fast-draining, fertile soil; tubers become deformed in heavy, poorly drained soil. Plant as soon as soil is workable in spring. Set minitubers or seed potato pieces 2 in. deep, 1–1½ ft. apart. Add loose soil as plant grows, taking care not to cover stems completely. The aboveground potato plant is sprawling and bushy, with much-divided dark green leaves somewhat like those of a tomato plant. Clustered inch-wide flowers are pale blue. Round yellow or greenish fruit is rarely seen.

Dig early potatoes (so-called new potatoes) when tops begin to flower; dig mature potatoes when tops die down. Dig carefully to avoid bruising or cutting tubers. Well-matured potatoes free of defects are the best keepers. Store in cool (40°F/4°C), dark place.

Another method of growing potatoes is to prepare soil so surface is loose, plant ½–2 in. deep, water well, and cover with a 1–1½-ft. layer of straw, hay, or dead leaves; surround with fence of chicken wire to keep loose material from blowing away. Potatoes will form on surface of soil or just beneath, requiring little digging. You can probe with your fingers and harvest potatoes as needed.

POTENTILLA

CINQUEFOIL

Rosaceae

EVERGREEN PERENNIALS AND DECIDUOUS SHRUBS

☀ ZONES VARY BY SPECIES

☼ ☼ SOME SHADE IN HOT CLIMATES

💧 MODERATE WATER

Potentilla

Hardy plants useful for ground covers and borders. Leaves are bright green or gray green, divided into small leaflets. Small, roselike, typically single flowers are cream to bright yellow; white; or pink to red. Cinquefoils generally are not at their best in hot, humid climates; they prefer cool nights and cool soils.

The genus includes perennial creeping plants used as ground covers and sturdy clumping plants for use in rock gardens or perennial borders. Leaves are divided fanwise into leaflets and are reminiscent of strawberry foliage. There are also shrubby potentillas most often sold as named forms of *P. fruticosa,* which is native to northern latitudes in North America, Asia, and Europe.

P. alba. Zones 32, 34–43. Perennial to 4 in. high and spreading, with 2½-in. bright green leaves with five leaflets. White, 1-in.-wide flowers in early spring; occasionally reblooms.

P. atrosanguinea. Zones 31, 32, 34–43. Sprawling, mounding perennial plant to 1½ ft. high, 2 ft. wide, with furry, three-leafleted leaves and 1-in. red blossoms in summer. A parent of several superior hybrids, including 1½-ft. 'Flamenco', with scarlet flowers and grayish foliage; 1½-ft. 'Gibson's Scarlet'; 1-ft. 'Vulcan', with deep red flowers; 15-in. 'William Rollisson', bearing semidouble bright orange blooms with a yellow center; and 1–1½-ft. 'Yellow Queen', which has semidouble bright yellow flowers.

P. fruticosa. SHRUBBY CINQUEFOIL. Zones 32 (cooler parts), 34–45. All have leaves divided into three to seven leaflets; some are distinctly green on top, gray beneath, while others look more gray green all over. All bloom cheerfully from late spring to early fall.

Fairly trouble-free. Best in well-drained soil with moderate water, but tolerate poor soils, drought, heat. Varieties with red or orange tinting should be lightly shaded, since they tend to fade quickly in hot sun. After the bloom period ends, cut out some of the oldest stems from time to time to make room for new growth. Here are some of the many varieties to be found in nurseries:

'Abbotswood'. To 3 ft., with dark blue-green leaves, 2-in. white flowers.

'Goldfinger'. Dense, dark green, to 3 ft. tall. Golden yellow, 1½-in. blooms.

'Goldstar'. Low mound to 2 ft., with 2-in. bright yellow flowers.

'Jackman's Variety'. To 4 ft. tall and somewhat wider, with 1½-in. bright yellow blossoms.

'Katherine Dykes'. Can reach 5 ft. but usually stays much lower; spreads at least as wide as high. Pale yellow, 1-in. flowers.

'Klondike'. Dense grower to 2 ft. high, with 1½–2-in. deep yellow flowers.

'Mount Everest'. Bushy, upright to 4½ ft.; 1½-in. pure white blossoms.
'Pixie Gold'. To 1–1½ ft. high, with ¾-in. yellow flowers.

'Primrose Beauty'. Silvery gray-green foliage on a 2–3-ft. plant. Pale yellow, 1½-in. flowers.

'Red Ace'. To 2 ft. high, 3–4 ft. wide. Flowers are 1½ in. wide, bright red with yellow center and yellow reverse. Flowers fade to yellow as they age (fading is very rapid in hot-summer climates or under poor growing conditions).

'Sunset'. To 2–2½ ft., with bright green foliage, 1½-in. yellow flowers shaded orange.

'Sutter's Gold'. To 1 ft. high, spreading to 3 ft. Clear yellow flowers about 1 in. across.

'Tangerine'. To 2½ ft. high, with 1½-in. bright yellow-orange blooms.

P. nepalensis. Zones 32, 34–43. Perennial to 1–2 ft. high. Leaves divided into five roundish leaflets; branching clusters of 1-in. purplish red blossoms in summer. Varieties are superior to the species for borders, cut flowers. 'Willmottiae' ('Miss Willmott'), 10–12 in. high, has salmon pink flowers. 'Melton Fire', 12–15 in. high, bears bright red flowers with yellow blending to a deep red center.

P. neumanniana 'Nana' (P. verna 'Nana'). Zones 31, 32, 34–43. Botanists keep running with the name of this plant and nurserymen never catch up. It has been known as *P. crantzii* and *P. tabernaemontanii.* The first of these may be *P. villosa;* the second is now called *P. neumanniana,* which is probably the correct name for this dainty-looking yet tough and persistent creeper. Grows 2–6 in. high. Bright green leaves divided into five leaflets; butter yellow, ¼-in. flowers in spring and summer. Stands more water than most cinquefoils. May turn brown in cold winters. Fast-growing ground cover, bulb cover. Good lawn substitute for no-traffic areas. Subject to a disfiguring rust in some regions.

P. recta 'Warrenii'. Zones 31, 32, 34–43. Perennial, to 15 in. tall, with leaves divided into five to seven leaflets. Profuse show of bright yellow, 1-in. flowers in late spring. Longer blooming and less weedy than the species. Tolerates a wide range of soils. Sometimes sold as *P. warrenii.* 'Macrantha' (which may be listed as *P. warrenii* 'Macrantha') is the same or a very similar plant.

P. tonguei. Zones 32, 34–41. Hybrid between *P. nepalensis* and another species. Creeping perennial plant with 1-ft.-long stems, leaves with three to five leaflets, and ½-in., red-centered apricot flowers.

P. tridentata 'Minima'. Zones 32, 34–43. Creeping ground cover with shiny, 1-in. leaves divided into three leaflets. Foliage turns red in fall. Small white flowers in spring and summer resemble those of strawberry.

P. warrenii. See *P. recta* 'Warrenii'

POTERIUM. See SANGUISORBA

POT MARIGOLD. See CALENDULA officinalis

PRAIRIE DOCK. See SILPHIUM

PRICKLY PEAR. See OPUNTIA compressa

PRICKLY POPPY. See ARGEMONE

PRIMROSE. See PRIMULA

PRIMULA

PRIMROSE

Primulaceae

PERENNIALS SOMETIMES TREATED AS ANNUALS

ZONES VARY BY SPECIES OR TYPE

TOLERATE FULL SUN IN COOL CLIMATES

WATER NEEDS VARY BY TYPE

▶ SEE CHART ON FOLLOWING PAGES

Primula

Primroses form a foliage rosette, above which rise circular, five-petaled flowers, each petal indented at the apex. Blossoms may be borne on individual stems, in clusters at stem ends, or in tiered, candelabralike clusters up the stem. Most are spring blooming, but a few bloom in early summer.

Specialists have organized the hundreds of species, selections, named hybrids, and hybrid strains into 34 sections, but primroses that are fairly easy to grow in home garden situations are fewer in number. A combination of moist, rich soil and cool, humid air is ideal for primroses. Some types thrive with regular water, while others need damp or even boggy soil. Most require some winter chill (polyanthus hybrids are a notable exception).

The greater the summer heat, the more protection from direct sun primroses need. Filtered or dappled sunlight and high shade are preferred exposures. Where the climate is less than favorable, primroses are sometimes treated as annuals.

Specialty nurseries, mainly in the Northwest, offer seeds and plants of many kinds of primroses. Fanciers exchange seeds and plants through primrose societies.

Primulaceae. The primrose family of annuals and perennials has single or variously clustered flowers with five-lobed calyxes and corollas. Examples are rock jasmine (*Androsace*), *Cyclamen*, and primrose (*Primula*).

PRINCE'S FEATHER. See AMARANTHUS hybridus erythrostachys

PRINCE'S PINE. See CHIMAPHILA

PRINCESS FLOWER. See TIBOUCHINA urvilleana

PRINSEPIA

Rosaceae

DECIDUOUS SHRUBS

ZONES VARY BY SPECIES

FULL SUN

REGULAR WATER

Prinsepia

These sturdy, medium-textured shrubs, members of the rose family native to China, have thorny arching stems and a rounded shape. They bear small, fragrant flowers in cream to white and round or oval purple-red fruits. Birds eat the ½-in. fruits, which are high in vitamin C, and use the shrubs for cover. Good additions to shrub borders and wildlife plantings. Because of their spiny stems and dense habit, they are also good for hedging and barriers. Prefer moist, well-drained, fertile soil without competition from other plants, but adapt to many weed-free soil types. When overgrown, they respond well to drastic pruning.

P. sinensis. CHERRY PRINSEPIA. Zones 32, 34–43. Grows 6–10 ft. high and wide. Healthy, disease resistant, and easily grown, it's good for low-maintenance hedges, screens, barriers, and difficult sites. Produces bright green leaves and fruits from July through September.

P. uniflora. HEDGE PRINSEPIA. Zones 35–38, 40, 41. Grows 4–5 ft. high and wide. It has handsome dark green leaves, but is hard to find in cultivation.

PRIVET. See LIGUSTRUM

PRIMULA

NAME	ZONES	LEAVES	FLOWERS	COMMENTS
Primula acaulis (*see P. vulgaris*)				
P. alpicola MOONLIGHT PRIMROSE	34–41	Long stalked, wrinkled, eventually forming wide clumps	Sulfur yellow (sometimes white or purple), spreading, bell shaped, in clusters on 20-in. stems. Powerfully fragrant. Summer	Somewhat tender in coldest areas. Regular water
P. auricula AURICULA	32, 34, 36–40	Evergreen rosettes of broad, leathery, toothed or plain-edged, gray-green leaves, sometimes with mealy, powdery coating that spots and runs in rain	White, cream, yellow, orange, pink, rose, red, purple, blue, or brownish, with white or yellow eye; carried in clusters on 6–8-in. stems. Fragrant. Early spring	Usually grown in pots for display. Some choice named varieties have green or near-black flowers with rings of mealy powder or rims of contrasting color. Regular water
B. beesianna	36–40	Long, tapering gradually into leafstalk; to 14 in. long (including stalk)	Somewhat variable, but usually reddish purple with yellow eye, in 5–7 dense whorls on 2-ft. stems. Mid- to late spring	Very deep rooted. Plentiful deep soakings
B. bulleyana	34–41	Like those of *P. beesiana*, but with reddish midribs	Bright yellow, from orange buds. Whorls on 2-ft. stems open over long season, mid- to late spring	Plants disappear in late fall; mark the spot. Older plants can be divided after bloom or in fall. Showy at woodland edge. Regular water
P. denticulata	34–45	About 6–12 in. long, only half grown at flowering time	Dense, ball-shaped clusters on foot-high, stout stems. Color ranges from blue violet to purple. Very early spring	Sometimes called drumstick primrose. Pinkish, lavender, and white varieties available. Not adapted to warm-winter areas. Regular water
P. elatior OXSLIP	31, 32, 34–43	Leaves: oval to oblong, to 8 in. long, with scalloped edges, medium green, with soft hairs on underside	Flowers: clusters of up to 12 yellow, tubular flowers to 1 in. long, on stiff, foot-long stems. Early-mid-spring	Provide moist but well-drained soil rich in organic matter
P. florindae	34–43	Broad, heart shaped, on long stems	Up to 60 yellow, bell-shaped, nodding flowers top 3-ft. stems in summer. Most fragrant and latest-blooming primrose	Will grow in a few inches of running water or in damp, low spot. Plants late to appear in spring. Hybrids have red, orange, or yellow flowers
P. japonica	32, 34–43	To 6–9 in. long, 3 in. wide	Stout stems to 2½ ft., each with up to 5 whorls of yellow-eyed purple flowers, late spring or early summer	'Miller's Crimson' is an excellent red variety. White and pink forms are also available. Needs lots of water; will grow at edge of pond, even in shallowest water
P. juliae hybrids (*Pruhonicensis hybrids*) JULIANA PRIMROSE	32, 34–43	Bright green, in tuftlike rosettes	White, blue, yellow, orange-red, pink, or purple, borne single or in clusters of 3–4-in. stems. Very early	Excellent for edging, woodland, rock garden. Regular water
P. polyantha POLYANTHUS PRIMROSES (*often called English primroses; this is a group of hybrids*)	32, 34–41	Clumps of fresh green, tongue-shaped leaves to 8 in. long, resembling leaves of romaine lettuce	1–2 in. across, in large, full clusters on stems to 1 ft. high. Almost any color. Blooms from winter to early or midspring. Adaptable and brilliant. Miniature Polyanthus have smaller flowers on shorter stalks	Fine large-flowered strains include Clarkeís, Concorde, Barnhaven, Pacific, Santa Barbara. Novelties include Gold Laced, with gold-edged mahogany petals. All excellent for massing, bulb companions, or containers. Treat as annuals in hot-summer areas. Regular water

P

PRIMULA

NAME	ZONES	LEAVES	FLOWERS	COMMENTS
P. pulverulenta	34, 37	A foot or more long, deep green, wrinkled	Red to red-purple, purple eyed, in whorls on 3-ft. stems thickly dusted with white meals. Late spring, summer	Bartley strain has flowers in pink and salmon range. A fine white with orange eye is available. Lots of water
P. sieboldii	34, 36–40	To 2–4 in. long, scalloped, toothed, on long, hairy stalks	Lilac with white eye, 1–1½ in. across, in clusters on 4–8 in. stems. Late spring	Hybrid strains available with white, pink or purple flowers. All types usually go dormant after flowering, enabling them to endure hotter summers better than other sorts of primroses. This is an excellent variety for the Northeast. Regular water
P. sinensis CHINESE PRIMROSE	Greenhouse or indoor plant	Evergreen, on long stalks; roundish, lobed, toothed, soft, hairy, 2–4 in. long. Hairs may irritate skin	White, pink, lavender, reddish, and coral; about 1½ in. across, many clustered on 4–8-in.-tall stems. Stellatas have star-shaped flowers in whorls. Winter	Tender. Favorite European pot plant; imported seed available from specialists. Regular water
P. veris COWSLIP	32, 34–41	Similar to those of polyanthus primroses	Bright yellow, fragrant, ½–1 in. wide, in early spring. Stems 4-8 in. high	Naturalize in wild garden or rock garden. Charming but not as sturdy as polyanthus primroses. Regular water
P. vialii (*P. littoniana*)	34, 36–40	To 8 in. long, 1½–2 in. wide, hairy, irregularly toothed; disappear in winter	Dense, narrow, 3–5 in.-long spikes of fragrant, ¼–½-in. wide flowers, violet blue opening from red buds. Stems erect, 1–2 ft. high. Late spring or early summer	Not long lived but quite easy from seed. Use in rock gardens. Rich, moist to damp soil
P. vulgaris (*P. acaulis*) PRIMROSE, ENGLISH PRIMROSE	32, 34–41	Tufted; much like those of polyanthus primroses	Flowers borne singly; vigorous garden strains often have 2 to 3 to a stalk. White, yellow red, blue, and bronze, grown, and wine. Early spring	Double varieties available. Blues and reds especially desirable. Use in woodland or rock garden, as edging. Nosegay and Biedermeier strains are exceptionally heavy blooming. Regular water

P

PROBOSCIDEA louisianica

UNICORN PLANT, DEVIL'S CLAW, RAM'S HORN

Pedaliaceae

ANNUAL

⚡ ALL ZONES

☀ ◐ FULL SUN TO PARTIAL SHADE

🔴 🔴🔴 REGULAR TO AMPLE WATER

Proboscidea

This native of the Midwest is occasionally grown for the tropical look of its wavy-margined, rounded, foliage, creamy white to purple funnel-shaped flowers held in open clusters, and unusual-looking seedpods. Pods are boat shaped and bear a pair of curved "horns." Grows to 1½ ft. high and 3 ft. wide. Does best in a moist, well-drained soil of moderate to high fertility. Plant in a mixed border or bed, or let it scramble at the base of a fence or trellis. Seed pods can be dried and used in everlasting arrangements.

PRUNE. See PLUM and PRUNE

FOR INFORMATION ON YOUR CLIMATE ZONE

PLEASE SEE PAGES 30–46

PRUNELLA

SELF-HEAL, HEAL-ALL

Lamiaceae (Labiatae)

PERENNIALS

⚡ ZONES 31, 32, 34–43

☀ ◐ FULL SUN OR LIGHT SHADE

🔴 REGULAR WATER

Prunella

Creeping perennials that form low, dense mats of foliage from surface and underground runners. Tight spikes of gaping, two-lipped mint-type flowers appear in summer, rising above foliage on bare stems a few inches to 1 ft. tall. Names are much confused, but all these plants are tough, tolerant, and deep rooted. Useful for small-scale ground cover and can endure the occasional footfall, but too invasive to risk planting near choice, delicate rock garden plants.

P. grandiflora. Largest species, with 4-in. leaves and purple flowers. Named varieties, sometimes sold as varieties of *P. webbiana*, include 'Pink Loveliness', 'Purple Loveliness' (lilac purple touched with white), and 'White Loveliness'.

P. vulgaris. Common species, with 2-in. leaves. Flowers are purple or pink. A form called *P. v. incisa* has deeply cut leaves.

P. webbiana. Similar to *P. grandiflora*, but with shorter leaves. There are purple and pink varieties.

PRUNUS

Rosaceae

🌿 EVERGREEN OR DECIDUOUS SHRUBS OR TREES

▨ ZONES VARY BY SPECIES

☼ FULL SUN, EXCEPT AS NOTED

💧 REGULAR TO MODERATE WATER

▶ SEE CHART ON FOLLOWING PAGES

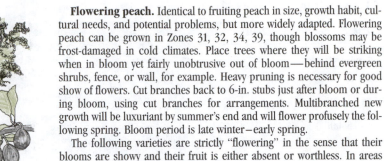

Prunus

Fruit trees that belong to *Prunus,* the "stone fruits," are described under their common names. See Cherry; Peach and Nectarine; Plum and Prune.

The ornamentals can be divided into two classes: evergreen and deciduous. Evergreens are grown in warm climates and are used chiefly as structure plants: hedges, screens, shade trees, street trees. Deciduous flowering trees and shrubs, closely related to the fruit trees mentioned above, are valued for their springtime display as well as for attractive shape and for form and texture of foliage. Many of these deciduous types offer a bonus of edible fruit.

EVERGREEN FORMS

P. laurocerasus. ENGLISH LAUREL. Zones 31, 32. Hardy to 5°F/−15°C; varieties listed below are hardier. Native from southeastern Europe to Iran. To 20 ft. tall, though generally seen as a lower clipped hedge. Leathery, glossy dark green leaves are 3−7 in. long, 1½−2 in. wide. Blooms in summer, bearing 3−5-in. spikes of creamy white flowers that are often hidden by leaves. Small black fruit appears in late summer and fall.

Where adapted, a fast-growing, greedy plant that's difficult to garden under or around. Regular water and nutrients will speed growth and keep top dense. Needs reasonably good drainage. Give partial shade in hot-summer areas. Tolerates salt spray. Stands heavy shearing but with considerable mutilation of leaves; best pruned by one cut at a time to remove overlong twigs just above a leaf. Best used as a tree or tall unclipped screen. The following are compact varieties:

'Otto Luyken'. Zones 31, 32, 34, 39. To 4 ft. tall, twice as broad. Leaves 2−4 in. long.

'Schipkaensis'. SCHIPKA LAUREL. Zones 31, 32, 34−41 (warmer parts). Usually 4−5 ft. high (possibly 10 ft. tall), wide spreading. Narrow leaves 2−4½ in. long.

'Zabeliana'. ZABEL LAUREL. Zones 31, 32, 34, 39. Narrow-leafed variety with branches angling upward and outward from base. Eventually reaches 6 ft., with equal or greater spread. More tolerant of full sun than species. Versatile plant; good for low screen, big foundation plant, bank cover (with branches pegged down), espalier.

DECIDUOUS FLOWERING FRUIT TREES

Flowering cherry. Zones vary by type; see chart. Cultural needs of all are identical. They require full sun and fast-draining, well-aerated soil; if your soil is substandard, plant in raised beds. Prune only to remove awkward or crossing branches; pinch back the occasional overly ambitious shoot to force branching. You can cut during bloom time and use branches in arrangements. Early to midspring bloom, depending on variety.

All are good trees to garden under. Use them as their growth habit indicates: large, spreading kinds make good shade trees, while smaller ones are indispensable in Oriental gardens. Foliage may sustain damage from insect pests. Plants growing in heavy soil are sometimes subject to root rot (for which there is no cure); an afflicted tree will usually bloom, then send out new leaves that suddenly collapse.

Flowering nectarine. Zones 31, 32, 34, 39. There is one important variety, 'Alma Stultz', a fast grower to 20 ft. high and wide. Blooms in early spring, covering itself with deliciously fragrant, 2−2½-in.-wide, waxy-petaled flowers in rosy white shaded pink, the color deepening with age. Flowers look something like azalea blossoms. Sparse crop of small, white-fleshed fruit is sometimes produced. Cultural needs and potential problems are the same as for peach.

Flowering peach. Identical to fruiting peach in size, growth habit, cultural needs, and potential problems, but more widely adapted. Flowering peach can be grown in Zones 31, 32, 34, 39, though blossoms may be frost-damaged in cold climates. Place trees where they will be striking when in bloom yet fairly unobtrusive out of bloom—behind evergreen shrubs, fence, or wall, for example. Heavy pruning is necessary for good show of flowers. Cut branches back to 6-in. stubs just after bloom or during bloom, using cut branches for arrangements. Multibranched new growth will be luxuriant by summer's end and will flower profusely the following spring. Bloom period is late winter−early spring.

The following varieties are strictly "flowering" in the sense that their blooms are showy and their fruit is either absent or worthless. In areas with late frosts, choose late bloomers; early bloomers are best in regions with hot, early springs.

'Early Double Pink'. Very early.

'Early Double Red'. Deep purplish red or rose red. Very early and brilliant, but color likely to clash with other pinks and reds.

'Early Double White'. Blooms with 'Early Double Pink'.

'Helen Borchers'. Semidouble clear pink, 2½-in.-wide flowers. Late.

'Icicle'. Double white flowers. Late.

'Late Double Red'. Later than 'Early Double Red' by 3 to 4 weeks.

'Peppermint Stick'. Double flowers striped red and white; may also bear all-white and all-red flowers on same branch. Midseason.

'Weeping Double Pink'. Smaller than other flowering peaches, with weeping branches. Requires careful staking and tying to develop main stem of suitable height. Midseason.

'Weeping Double Red'. Similar to above, but with deep rose red flowers. Midseason.

'Weeping Double White'. White version of weeping forms listed above.

Flowering plum. Zones vary by type; see chart. Flowers appear before leaves, from late winter to early spring. Less particular about soil than flowering cherries, nectarines, and peaches, but will fail if soil is waterlogged for prolonged periods. If soil is boggy, plant in raised beds, 6−12 in. above grade. Little pruning is needed. Potential pests include aphids, borers, scale, tent caterpillars. Possible diseases include canker and leaf spots. The most ornamental flowering plums, including purple-foliaged varieties, are described in the chart; for additional flowering plums, see listings for *P. americana, P. cistena,* and *P. maritima.*

> ### FLOWERING PLUM FOR INDOOR BLOOM
>
> Branches of flowering plum (or flowering cherry, peach, or nectarine) are beautiful for indoor decoration. For the longest-lasting bloom, cut branches when buds first begin to show color or when they have just opened. Follow proper pruning procedures when you cut branches: prune to thin or shape (don't just hack indiscriminately); always cut back to a side branch; and never leave stubs. Place branches in a deep container of water, not in florist's foam; strip off any buds or flowers that will be below water level.

ADDITIONAL DECIDUOUS SPECIES

P. americana. WILD PLUM, GOOSE PLUM. Shrub or small tree. Zones 31, 32, 34−45. To 15−20 ft. high, forming thickets. Profusion of clustered white, 1-in. flowers appears before the dark green leaves emerge. Fruit yellow to red, to 1 in. wide, sour but good for jelly. Extremely tough and hardy.

P. besseyi. WESTERN SAND CHERRY. Shrub. Zones 35, 41, 43, 45. Native from Manitoba to Wyoming, south to Kansas and Colorado. To 3−6 ft. tall. Good show of white flowers in spring, followed by sweet black cherries used for pies, jams, jellies. Withstands heat, cold, wind, drought. May not always fruit well in the Northeast.

P. cistena. PURPLE-LEAF SAND CHERRY, DWARF RED-LEAF PLUM. Shrub. Zones 32, 34−45. Dainty, multibranched hybrid to 6−10 ft. high. Can be trained as single-stemmed tree; good for small patios. Bears white to light pink flowers as leaves emerge, then covers itself in red-purple

P

PRUNUS—FLOWERING CHERRY AND PLUM

NAME	ZONES	GROWTH HABIT, FOLIAGE	HEIGHT, SPREAD	FLOWERS, SEASON, COMMENTS
FLOWERING CHERRY **Prunus 'Accolade'**	31, 32, 34, 39	Small tree with spreading branches, twiggy growth pattern. Very vigorous	To 20 ft. or more, equally wide	Semidouble pink, in large drooping clusters. Early. Hybrid between *P. sargentii* and *P. subhirtella*
P. 'Hally Jolivette'	31, 32, 34–41	Dense, broad, shrubby	To 6–8 ft., eventually to 15 ft. Slow grower	Semidouble light pink. Early; relatively long bloom. Can be used in shrub borders.
P. 'Okame'	31, 32, 34, 39	Upright, oval, fast growing. Dark green, finely textured foliage. Yellow-orange to orange-red fall color	To 25 ft. tall, 20 ft. wide	Single pink. Very early. Hybrid between *P. campanulata* and another species
P. sargentii SARGENT CHERRY	31, 32, 34–43	Upright, spreading branches from rounded crown. Orange-red fall foliage	To 40–50 ft. or more; not as wide as high	Single blush pink, in clusters of 2–4. Midseason. 'Columnaris' is narrower and more erect than typical *P. sargentii*
P. serrula BIRCH BARK CHERRY	31, 32, 34–41	Round headed; narrow, willow-like leaves. Valued for its beautiful glossy mahogany red bark	To 30 ft. and as wide	Bark more important than small white flowers almost hidden by new leaves. Midseason. Not at its best in hot, humid areas
P. serrulata JAPANESE FLOWERING CHERRY	31, 32, 34–41	The species is known through its many cultivated varieties, some of which are listed below		
P. s. 'Amanogawa'	31, 32, 34–41	Columnar tree. Use as you would small Lombardy poplar	To 20–25 ft. tall, 8 ft. wide	Semidouble light pink, with deep pink margins. Early midseason
P. s. 'Beni Hoshi' (*'Pink Star'*)	31, 32, 34–41	Fast grower with arching, spreading branches. Umbrella shaped in outline	To 20–25 ft. high and as wide	Single vivid pink; long, slightly twisted petals. Flowers hang below branches. Midseason
P. s. 'Kwanzan' (*'Kanzan'*, *'Sekiyama'*)	31, 32, 34–41	Branches stiffly upright, forming inverted cone. Orange fall foliage	To 30 ft. high, 20 ft. wide	Large, double, deep rosy pink, in pendent clusters displayed before or with red young leaves. Midseason. Tolerates heat and humidity well
P. s. 'Royal Burgundy'	31, 32, 34–41	Habit similar to that of 'Kwanzan'. Reddish purple foliage	Same as 'Kwanzan'	Like those of 'Kwanzan', but deeper pink
P. s. 'Shirofugen'	31, 32, 34–41	Wide horizontal branching	To 25 ft. and as wide	Double, long stalked, pink, fading to white. Latest to bloom; flowers appear with coppery red new leaves
P. s. 'Shirotae' (*'Mt. Fuji'*)	31, 32, 34–41	Strong horizontal branching	To 20 ft.; wider than high	Semidouble. Pink in bud; white when fully open, turning to purplish pink. Early
P. s. 'Shogetsu' (*'Shimidsu Sakura'*)	31, 32, 34–41	Spreading growth, arching branches	To 15 ft.; wider than high	Semidouble and very double pale pink, often with white centers. Late
P. s. 'Snow Fountains' (*'White Fountain'*)	31, 32, 34–41	Slightly curving trunk, branches weeping to ground. Yellow-and-orange fall foliage	To 6–12 ft. and as wide	Single white. Early
P. s. 'Snow Goose'	31, 32, 34–41	Erect, narrow at first, eventually becoming wider	To 20 ft. and as wide	Single white. Early. Reportedly disease resistant
P. s. 'Tai Haku'	31, 32, 34–41	Vigorous, with rounded crown. Good orange fall color	To 20–25 ft. and as wide	Largest blooms of any flowering cherry; single white, 2½ in. Late midseason

P

PRUNUS—FLOWERING CHERRY

NAME	ZONES	GROWTH HABIT, FOLIAGE	HEIGHT, SPREAD	FLOWERS, SEASON, COMMENTS
P. subhirtella 'Autumnalis'	31, 32, 34–41	Loose branching, bushy, with flattened crown, slender twigs	To 25–30 ft. and as wide	Double white or pinking white. Often blooms during warm autumn or winter weather as well as in early spring
P. s. 'Pendula' SINGLE WEEPING CHERRY, WEEPING HIGAN CHERRY	31, 32, 34–41	Usually sold grafted at 5–6 ft. high on upright-growing understock. Graceful branches hang down, often to ground	To 15–25 ft. and as wide	Single small pale pink, in profusion. Early
P. s. 'Rosea'	31, 32, 34–41	Wide-spreading, horizontal branching	To 20–25 ft. high, spreading to 30 ft.	Single pink, opening from nearly red buds. Profuse, very early bloom
P. s. 'Whitcombii'	31, 32, 34–41	Same at *P. s.* 'Rosea'	To 30 ft. high, spreading to 35 ft.	Single pink fading to white. Early
P. s. 'Yae-shidare-higan' DOUBLE WEEPING CHERRY	31, 32, 34–41	Same as *P. s.* 'Pendula'	Same as *P. s.* 'Pendula'	Double rose pink. Midseason
P. yedoensis YOSHINO FLOWERING CHERRY	31, 32, 34–41	Horizontal branches; graceful, open pattern	Fast to 40 ft., with 30-ft. spread	Single light pink to nearly white, fragrant. Early. Famous planting exists around the Tidal Basin in Washington, D.C.
P. y. 'Akebono' (sometimes called 'Daybreak')	31, 32, 34–41	Same as *P. yedoensis*	To 25 ft. and as wide	Flowers pinker than those of *P. yedoensis*. Early
FLOWERING PLUM				
P. blireiana (hybrid between *P. cerasifera* 'Atropurpurea' and *P. mume*)	32, 34, 39	Graceful, long, slender branches	To 25 ft. high, 20 ft. wide.	Leaves reddish purple, turning greenish bronze in summer. Flowers double, fragrant, pink to rose. Very little or no fruit
P. cerasifera CHERRY PLUM, MYROBALAN	32, 34, 39	Used at rootstock for various stone fruits. The species is not widely grown; its purple- and red-leafed varieties are more popular	Will grow to 30 ft. and as wide.	Leaves dark green. Flowers pure white. Small red plums, 1–1¼ in. across, are sweet but bland. Self-sows freely; some seedlings bear yellow fruit
P. c. 'Allred'	32, 34, 39	Upright, slightly spreading.	20 ft. tall, 12–15 ft. wide	Red leaves, white flowers. Red, 1¼-in.-wide, tart fruit is good for preserves, jelly
P. c. 'Atropurpurea' (*P.* 'Pissardii') PURPLE-LEAF PLUM	31, 32, 34, 39	Fast growing, rounded in form	25-30 ft. high	New leaves copper red, deepening to dark purple, gradually becoming greenish bronze in late summer. White flowers. Sets heavy crop of small red plums
P. c. 'Hollywood' (hybrid between *P. C.* 'Atropurpurea' and Japanese plum 'Duarte')	31, 32, 34, 39	Upright grower to 30–40 ft., 25 ft. wide	To 30–40 ft., 25 ft. wide	Leaves dark green above, red beneath. Flowers light pink to white. Good-quality red plums 2–2½ in. wide
P. c. 'Krauter Vesuvius'	31, 32, 34, 39	Upright, branching habit	To 18 ft. high, 12 ft. wide	Little or no fruit. Darkest foliage of all flowering plums. Light pink flowers, purple-black leaves
P. c. 'Mt. St. Helens'	31, 32, 34, 39	Upright, spreading, with rounded crown. Fast growth	To 20 ft. high and wide	A sport of 'Newport', it grows faster and leafs out earlier; it has richer leaf color and holds it later in the summer

P

foliage. May offer a summer crop of small blackish purple fruit. Pink-flowering 'Big Cis' forms a dense globe to 14 ft. high.

P. fruticosa. Like *P. besseyi*, but 2–3 ft. tall, with smaller red-purple fruit.

P. glandulosa. DWARF FLOWERING ALMOND. Shrub. Zones 31, 32, 34–43. Native to China, Japan. In early spring, before leaves appear, the many slender stems are transformed into wands of blossoms. Typically sold are the double-flowered selections 'Alboplena' (white) and 'Sinensis' (pink), both with 1–1¼-in. blooms like fluffy pompom chrysanthemums. Plants grow 4–6 ft. high, with clumps of upright, spreading branches and light green, 4-in., willowlike leaves. Prune heavily during or after flowering to promote strong new growth for next year's bloom. Can be used as flowering hedge. Suckers freely. Fireblight can be a problem.

P. maackii. AMUR CHOKECHERRY. Tree. Zones 35–45. Native to Manchuria and Siberia; extremely hardy to cold and wind. To 25–30 ft. tall. Main feature is handsome trunk bark, which is yellowish and peeling, like birch bark. Leaves strongly veined, rather narrow and pointed, to 4 in. long. Small white flowers in narrow clusters 2–3 in. long. Fruit is black.

P. maritima. BEACH PLUM. Zones 31, 32, 34–45. Native to Atlantic coast from Maine to Virginia. Suckering shrub to 6 ft. tall or taller, forming colonies. Dull green leaves are 1½–3 in. long, half as wide. White flowers are followed by ½–2-in., dark red to dark purple fruits that are cherished for preserves. Tolerates strong winds, salt spray.

P. mume. JAPANESE FLOWERING APRICOT, JAPANESE FLOWERING PLUM. Tree. Zones 31, 32, 34, 39. Blooms may be frosted in coldest areas. Neither true apricot nor true plum. Longer-lived, tougher, more trouble-free plant than other flowering fruit trees. Eventually develops into gnarled, picturesque 20-ft. tree. Leaves to 4½ in. long, broadly oval. Winter blossoms are small and profuse, with clean, spicy fragrance. Fruit is small, inedible. For profuse bloom on year-old wood, prune heavily; let tree grow for a year, then prune back all shoots to 6-in. stubs after bloom. The next year, cut back half the young growth to 6-in. stubs; cut back other half the next year. Continue this routine in succeeding years. Varieties include:

'Bonita'. Semidouble rose red.

'Dawn'. Large ruffled double pink.

'Peggy Clarke'. Double deep rose flowers with extremely long stamens and red calyxes.

'Rosemary Clarke'. Double white flowers with red calyxes. Very early.

'W. B. Clarke'. Double pink flowers on weeping plant. Effective large bonsai or container plant, focus of attention in winter garden.

P. padus. EUROPEAN BIRD CHERRY, MAYDAY TREE, MAYBUSH. Tree. Zones 34–45. Very cold hardy. Moderate growth to 15–20 ft., occasionally taller. Rather thin and open in habit while young. Dull dark green, oval leaves, 3–5 in. long, are among the first to unfold in spring. Big midspring show of small white flowers in slender, drooping, 3–6-in. clusters that nearly hide foliage. Small black fruit, much loved by birds, follows.

P. tenella. DWARF RUSSIAN ALMOND. Shrub. Zones 31, 32, 34–45. Native from Russia to central Europe. Bushy shrub to 5 ft. high and as wide. Glossy, dark green, oval to lance-shaped leaves to 3 in. long. In midspring, clusters of bright pink flowers to 1¼ in. across. Oval (almond-shaped) grayish yellow fruit. 'Alba' has white flowers; 'Fire Hill' has deep pink flowers.

P. tomentosa. NANKING CHERRY. Shrub. Zones 34–45. Like *P. besseyi*, extremely tough and cold hardy. To 6–8 ft. tall. Small, fragrant white flowers open from pinkish buds in spring; ½-in. scarlet fruit follows.

P. triloba. FLOWERING ALMOND. Small tree or treelike large shrub. Zones 34–41. Slow growth to 8–10 ft. (possibly 15 ft.) tall, with equal spread. Rather broad, 1–2½-in.-long leaves. Double pink flowers about 1 in. wide appear in early spring before leaf-out. A white form is sometimes available.

P. virginiana. CHOKECHERRY. Shrub or small tree. Zones 32, 34–45. Native Newfoundland to Saskatchewan, south to Kansas, east to North Carolina. To 20–30 ft. high, with suckering habit; 2–4-in. leaves. After leaf-out, tiny white flowers appear in slender, 3–6-in. clusters; these are followed by astringent, dark red to black fruit to ½ in. wide. 'Canada Red' ('Shubert') has leaves that open green, turn red as they mature. Rocky Mountain native *P. v. melanocarpa*, black chokecherry, has smoother leaves and blacker, sweeter fruit than the species.

PSEUDOCYDONIA sinensis

CHINESE QUINCE	
Rosaceae	
DECIDUOUS SHRUB OR SMALL TREE	
☀ ZONES 31, 32, 34, 39	
☼ FULL SUN	
● REGULAR WATER	

Pseudocydonia sinensis

Seldom seen, curious tree, usually 15–20 ft. high (rarely taller) and half as wide. Trunk is attractive, with bark that flakes off to reveal shades of brown, green, and gray. Trunks on old trees are often fluted. Roundish oval, dark green leaves to 4½ in. long turn yellow and red in fall. Spring bloom produces a scattering of flowers rather than a show—the pale pink, 1–1½-in. flowers are borne singly at ends of year-old twigs. Blossoms are followed by extraordinary fruits: fragrant yellow quinces to 7 in. long, weighing over a pound apiece. Fruits can be made into jam. Very susceptible to fireblight in warm, humid regions; control by pruning out damaged wood.

PSEUDOLARIX kaempferi (Chrysolarix kaempferi)

GOLDEN LARCH	
Pinaceae	
DECIDUOUS TREE	
☀ ZONES 32, 34–41	
☼ FULL SUN	
● REGULAR WATER	

Pseudolarix kaempferi

Slow growing to 40–70 ft. high, often nearly as broad at base. Wide-spreading branches, pendulous at tips, grow in whorls to form symmetrical, pyramidal tree. Foliage has a feathery look; 1½–2-in.-long, ⅛-in.-wide needles are clustered in tufts except near branch ends, where they are single. Needles are bluish green during growing season, then turn a magnificent golden yellow very briefly in autumn before dropping. Cones and bare branches make interesting winter patterns. Choose an open spot sheltered from winds. Best in deep, rich, well-drained, acid soil; performance is better in colder part of range. Fine for spacious lawns.

PSEUDOSASA. See BAMBOO

PSEUDOTSUGA menziesii glauca (P. taxifolia)

DOUGLAS FIR	
Pinaceae	
EVERGREEN TREE	
☀ ZONES 34–43	
☼ ☼ FULL SUN; TAKES PART SHADE IN YOUTH	
● ● REGULAR TO LITTLE WATER	

Pseudotsuga menziesii

Of the five (possibly eight) species of *Pseudotsuga*, only this one grows over a wide territory and is much cultivated. Also a popular Christmas tree. The Rocky Mountain form, *P. m. glauca*, grows more slowly than the species, to 50–70 ft. Trees are cone shaped and foliaged to the ground when young, then lose lower limbs as they age. Stiff, densely set, blue-green needles up to 1½ in. long radiate in all directions from the branches. Needles are sweetly fragrant when crushed. Ends of branches swing up. Pointed wine red buds form at branch tips in winter, open to apple green new growth in spring. Reddish brown, oval cones are about 3 in. long, have obvious three-pronged bracts. Unlike upright cones of true firs *(Abies),* these hang down.

Native range extends from Alaska through northern California, eastward into the Rocky Mountains, and southward into northern Mexico. The Rocky Mountain form, *P. m. glauca,* is the hardiest form and the best adapted to the Northeast. Compact, weeping, and other forms exist, but they are grown mostly in arboretums and botanical gardens. All tolerate wind and will grow in all soils except boggy ones.

PSYLLIOSTACHYS suworowii (Limonium suworowii)

STATICE

Plumbaginaceae

ANNUAL

☀ ALL ZONES

☼ FULL SUN

💧 REGULAR WATER

Psylliostachys suworowii

Rosettes of narrow, 8-in.-long leaves produce 1½-ft.-tall spikes of tiny lavender pink flowers in summer. Spikes are very slender, single or branched, and cylindrical, reminiscent of furry rats' tails. They are excellent in flower arrangements, fresh or dry.

Sow seed indoors, or sow in ground when danger of frost is over; then transplant seedlings or thin them to 1 ft. apart. The plant may be offered as *Statice suworowii.*

Cut statice to use in fresh or dried arrangements when most of the tiny flowers have opened. To dry the flowers, fasten several stems in a bunch with a rubber band, and hang bunches upside down in a dry, airy location out of direct light to air-dry.

> ### USING STATICE IN ARRANGEMENTS
>
> Statice—both the type described above and other species still classified in the genus *Limonium*—are colorful additions to fresh or dried arrangements. *Limonium* flowers are best used as fillers—small elements that fill space between larger blossoms that act as focal points in an arrangement. Use the slender spikes of *Psylliostachys* to add vertical line in arrangements with round or cup-shaped flowers.

PTELEA trifoliata

WAFER ASH, HOP TREE

Rutaceae

DECIDUOUS SHRUB OR SMALL TREE

☀ ZONES 31, 32, 34–43

☼ ◑ ● SUN OR SHADE

💧 💧 REGULAR TO MODERATE WATER

Ptelea trifoliata

Dense, rounded shrub or small, low-branching tree to 10–20 ft. tall (usually less) and equally broad. Leaves are divided into three 2–5-in. leaflets, turn from dark green to yellow in fall. They contain oil glands and are pungently aromatic when bruised; most people find the odor pleasant. Late spring flowers are small, greenish white, inconspicuous but fragrant. Winged seeds are disks to 1 in. wide, surrounded by a thin, flat, nearly circular rim. They look like wafers and have been used as a substitute for hops (hence the two common names).

PTERIDIUM aquilinum

BRACKEN

Polypodiaceae

FERN

☀ ZONES 31, 32, 34–43

☼ ◔ FULL SUN OR PARTIAL SHADE

💧 💧 ADAPTABLE

◆ FRONDS ARE POISONOUS IF INGESTED

Pteridium aquilinum

A worldwide native, bracken is represented by various subspecies that differ in minor details. Coarse, much-divided fronds rise directly from deep, running rootstocks. Grows from 2 ft. high to as tall as 7 ft. under good conditions. Occurs naturally in many places and can be tolerated in untamed gardens, but beware of planting it: deep rootstocks can make it a tough, invasive weed. Do not gather fronds to cook as fiddleheads, since they contain a slow poison.

PTEROCARYA fraxinifolia

CAUCASIAN WINGNUT

Juglandaceae

DECIDUOUS TREE

☀ ZONES 31, 32, 34–41

☼ FULL SUN

💧 💧 REGULAR TO MODERATE WATER

Pterocarya fraxinifolia

Moderate growth to 50 ft. or taller, and 50 ft. wide. Rounded in form, with spreading branches. Clearly shows its kinship to walnuts in its leaves, 8–18 in. long and divided into 7–27 finely toothed, oval leaflets. Bears 12–20-in.-long clusters of single-seeded, winged nuts that hang down from the branches.

Makes an attractive specimen or shade tree in a park or very large lawn; suckering habit and aggressive roots make it unsuitable for many home landscape uses.

Grows best in moist but well-drained soil, but tolerates drought and windy conditions when well established. Prune as needed in summer.

PTEROSTYRAX hispidas

EPAULETTE TREE

Styracaceae

DECIDUOUS TREE

☀ ZONES 31, 32, 34–41

☼ ◔ PARTIAL SHADE IN HOT CLIMATES

💧 REGULAR WATER

Pterostyrax hispidas

Native to Japan. Possibly reaches 40 ft., but more usually held to 15–20 ft. with 10-ft. spread. Trunk single or branched; branches open, spreading at top.

Light green leaves, gray green beneath, 3–8 in. long, rather coarse. Creamy white, fringed, lightly fragrant flowers in drooping clusters 4–9 in. long, 2–3 in. wide. Blooms in late spring or early summer. Small, furry gray fruit in clusters hangs on well into winter, are attractive on bare branches. *P. corymbosa,* little epaulette tree, is very similar, but more shrubby.

Prune to control shape, density. Best planted where you can look up into it—on bank beside path, above a bench, or in raised planting bed. It is a choice selection when planted at edge of woodland area or as focal point in large shrub border. Bark of trunk is prone to splitting after abrupt winter temperature shifts. To minimize this tendency, plant where trunk is shaded from morning sun.

P

PULMONARIA

LUNGWORT

Boraginaceae

PERENNIALS

⚡ ZONES 32, 34–43

☼ ● PARTIAL OR FULL SHADE

● REGULAR WATER

Pulmonaria

Low-growing shade lovers with quiet charm. Many kinds have foliage attractively dappled with gray or silver. The long-stalked leaves are mostly in basal clumps, though there are a few on the flower stalks. Bear drooping clusters of funnel-shaped blue or purplish flowers in spring, just before leaves emerge or at the same time. After flowering finishes, more leaves emerge from the base. If you keep plants well watered, foliage will remain ornamental throughout the growing season. All have creeping roots and can be used as small-scale ground covers in shaded areas. They work well with ferns, azaleas, rhododendrons, scillas, pink tulips under spring-flowering trees. Divide every 4 or 5 years, after flowering or in fall.

P. angustifolia. COWSLIP LUNGWORT. Tufts of narrowish, unspotted, dark green leaves. Clustered pink buds open to dark blue flowers on 6–12-in. stems. 'Azurea' has sky blue flowers; 'Blaues Meer' bears many bright blue flowers; 'Rubra' has soft red flowers.

P. longifolia. Slender, silver-spotted deep green leaves to 20 in. long. Blooms a bit later than the other species. 'Bertram Anderson' has deep blue flowers; leaves remain attractive throughout season.

P. montana (P. mollis, P. rubra). Hairy, unspotted light green leaves to 20 in. long, 5 in. wide. Blooms very early in spring. Flowering stems can reach 16 in. Blossoms may be white, blue, or red, the last most commonly seen. 'David Ward' has white-edged leaves and coral pink flowers. Blooms of 1-ft. 'Redstart' are an odd shade between salmon and brick red.

P. 'Roy Davidson'. Hybrid between *P. saccharata* and *P. longifolia*. Resembles *P. l.* 'Bertram Anderson' but has slightly wider leaves and flowers that open pink and deepen to blue.

P. saccharata. BETHLEHEM SAGE. To 1½ ft. high and spreading to 2 ft. wide, with blue flowers and silvery-spotted leaves. Specialists usually offer named selections; the following are compact, foot-high plants. 'Dora Bielefeld' has clear pink blooms; flowers of 'Mrs. Moon' open pink and turn blue; 'Pierre's Pure Pink' has pink flowers; 'Sissinghurst White' has white blooms. 'Janet Fisk', another variety with blooms that turn from pink to blue, has leaves that are silvery almost all over.

PULSATILLA
(Anemone pulsatilla)

PASQUE FLOWER

Ranunculaceae

PERENNIAL

⚡ ZONES VARY BY SPECIES

☼ ◑ FULL SUN OR LIGHT SHADE

● REGULAR WATER

Pulsatilla

Low-growing perennials from woody rootstock. Basal leaves are very finely cut, the segments covered with silky hairs. Each stem has several smaller, likewise silky leaves and is topped in spring by a cup-shaped, erect or nodding flower, 1½ to nearly 4 in. across, silky-hairy on the outer surfaces and centered with a yellow button of stamens. Blooms are followed by fluffy seed clusters almost as showy as the flowers; each seed is topped by a long, twisting, feathery appendage. Plants need very well-drained soil. Best adapted to cool, moist climates.

P. patens. EASTERN PASQUE FLOWER. Zones 32, 34–43. Native to North America, Russia, eastern Europe. To 6 in. tall and 4 in. wide. Medium green leaves grow to 5 in. long, with three to seven leaflets each

in turn divided into many narrow segments. [...] blue-violet or lilac, sometimes yellowish or cr[...]

P. vulgaris. PASQUE FLOWER. Zones 31, [...] and U.K. To 8 in. tall and as wide. Light green [...] very finely cut. Spring flowers range in colo[...] bluish purple, and red.

PUMPKIN

Cucurbitaceae

ANNUAL VINE

⚡ ALL ZONES

☼ FULL SUN

● WATER AT FIRST SIGNS OF WILTING

Pumpkin

Related to gourds, melons, squash. Wide range of fruit size, depending on variety. One of the best for a jumbo-size Halloween pumpkin is 'Atlantic Giant'. 'Small Sugar' is a smaller pumpkin with finer-grained, sweeter flesh. 'Sweetie Pie' and 'Jack Be Little' are 3-in.-wide miniatures useful as decorations. 'Lumina' is a novelty white pumpkin with orange flesh; it weighs 10–12 lbs. Seeds of all kinds are edible, but the easiest to eat are those of hull-less varieties like 'Trick or Treat'.

Pumpkin vines need lots of room: a single vine can cover 500 sq. ft., and even bush types can spread over 20 sq. ft. Where the growing season is short, start plants indoors. In most areas, sow seeds outdoors in late spring after soil has warmed. For vining pumpkins, sow five or six seeds 1 in. deep in hills 6–8 ft. apart; thin seedlings to two per hill. For bush pumpkins, sow a cluster of three or four seeds 1 in. deep, 2 ft. apart, in rows spaced 3 ft. apart; thin seedlings to one or two plants per cluster. Water regularly during dry periods, but keep foliage dry to prevent leaf diseases. In late summer, slide wooden shingles or other protection under fruit to protect it from wet soil (this is not necessary if soil is sandy). Depending on variety, pumpkins are ready to harvest 90 to 120 days after sowing, when shell has hardened. They're usually picked after first frost kills the plant. Pumpkins need rich soil, periodic fertilizer. They do not perform well in high heat and humidity. Same pests and diseases as squash.

> **GROW A GIANT PUMPKIN**
>
> As plant grows, cut off all but two branches. When flowering begins, take off all but one flower on each branch (your aim: two branches with one pumpkin on each). Every 2 feet along each branch, put a 4-in. mound of soil over branch so roots can form there.

PUNICA granatum

POMEGRANATE

Punicaceae

DECIDUOUS SHRUB OR SMALL TREE

⚡ ZONES 31, WARMER PARTS OF 32, OR INDOORS

☼ FULL SUN

● ● REGULAR WATER FOR FRUIT PRODUCTION

Punica granatum

Bear showy summer flowers with ruffled petals surrounding central clump of stamens. Some varieties yield fruit in fall. Narrow leaves open bronzy, then turn glossy bright green to golden green; brilliant yellow fall color except in climates with very mild winters. All varieties tolerate great heat and a wide range of soils, including alkaline soil that would kill most plants. Excellent pot plant; take outdoors in summer, indoors over winter. Prune late in dormant season, since plant blooms on new wood. Nonfruiting varieties need little water once established. Many cultivars,

P

‘Chico’, to 1½ ft. tall if pruned occasionally, double orange-red , ‘Nana’, to 3 ft., blooms when a foot tall, orange-red single flowers.

PURPLE BELLS, PURPLE BELL VINE. See RHODOCHITON atrosanguineum

PURPLE CONEFLOWER. See ECHINACEA purpurea

PURPLE HEART. See SETCREASEA pallida ‘Purple Heart’

PURPLE-LEAF PLUM. See PRUNUS cerasifera ‘Atropurpurea’

PURPLE MOOR GRASS. See MOLINIA caerulea

PURPLE OSIER. See SALIX purpurea

PURSLANE. See PORTULACA oleracea

PUSCHKINIA scilloides

Liliaceae

BULB

☘ ZONES 31, 32, 34–43

☼ ◑ FULL SUN OR LIGHT SHADE

◐ REGULAR WATER DURING GROWTH AND BLOOM

Puschkinia scilloides

Late winter or early spring bloomer closely related to squill (*Scilla*) and glory-of-the-snow (*Chionodoxa*). Performs best where ground freezes in winter. Bell-like flowers are pale blue or whitish with darker, greenish blue stripe on each segment, in spikelike clusters on 3–6-in. stems. Strap-shaped bright green leaves are broad, upright, a little shorter than flower stems. ‘Alba’ has white flowers. The most commonly sold variety is *P. s. libanotica,* a vigorous plant with pale blue, striped flowers like those of the species. Plant in autumn, placing 3–4 in. deep. Will grow for years without disturbance. Needs very little water during summer dormant period. Most effective in masses; good choice for naturalizing.

PUSSY TOES. See ANTENNARIA dioica

PYCNANTHEMUM virginianum

MOUNTAIN MINT, VIRGINIA MOUNTAIN MINT, PRAIRIE HYSSOP

Lamiaceae

PERENNIAL HERB

☘ ZONES 31, 32, 34–43

☼ ◑ FULL SUN TO PARTIAL SHADE

◐ REGULAR WATER

Pycnanthemum virginianum

Native to the eastern U.S., this fragrant member of the mint family has lance-shaped leaves and clusters of small white or pinkish flowers, produced from early summer to early fall. Highly aromatic when crushed, the leaves can be used in teas or as a flavoring, and are prescribed medicinally as an antispasmodic or mild stimulant. Flowers dry nicely and can be used in everlasting arrangements. Plant in an average to fertile, well-drained soil.

PRACTICAL GARDENING DICTIONARY

PLEASE SEE PAGES 449–523

PYRACANTHA

FIRETHORN

Rosaceae

EVERGREEN SHRUBS

☘ ZONES VARY BY SPECIES

☼ FULL SUN

◐ MODERATE WATER

Pyracantha

Grown for bright fruit, semievergreen to evergreen foliage, variety of landscape uses, and ease of culture. All grow fast and vigorously, with habit from upright to sprawling; nearly all have needlelike thorns. All have glossy green leaves, generally oval or rounded at ends, ½–1 in. wide, 1–4 in. long. All bear flowers and fruit on spurs along wood of last year’s growth. Spring flowers are small, fragrant, dull creamy white, carried in flattish clusters; they’re effective thanks to their profusion.

The real glory of firethorns is in the thick clusters of pea-size orange-red berries that light up the garden for months. Selections with red, orange, and yellow fruit are also available; if berry color is important, buy plants when in fruit. Depending on variety, berries color up from late summer to midautumn; some types hang on until late winter, when they’re cleared out by birds, storms, or decay. Dislodge old withered or rotted berries with a water jet or an old broom.

As shrubs and ground covers, firethorns look better and fruit more heavily if allowed to follow their natural growth habit. Prune only occasionally to check wayward branches. Plants can be espaliered; they can also be sheared as hedges, though at the expense of much fruit. Tolerate most soils but should not be overwatered. Potential pests include aphids and scale insects. In the humid Northeast, two serious problems are fireblight (which can kill the plant) and scab (which causes defoliation and turns fruit sooty); for best success, choose disease-resistant varieties.

P. coccinea. Zones 31, 32, 34, 39. Rounded growth to 8–10 ft. high (20 ft. trained against wall). Red-orange fruit. Best known for its varieties, which include the following:

‘Kasan’. Long-lasting orange-red berries. Spreading growth habit. Susceptible to scab.

‘Lalandei’ (very hardy, Zones 31, 32, 34–41) and ‘Lalandei Monrovia’ (Zones 31, 32, 34, 39). Similar varieties with orange berries. Susceptible to scab.

‘Wyattii’. Orange-red berries that color early. Very prone to fireblight and scab.

P. hybrids. This category includes some of the most desirable firethorns. Plants vary in size, habit, and cold hardiness.

‘Fiery Cascade’. Zones 31, 32, 34, 39. To 8 ft. tall, 9 ft. wide; berries orange turning to red. Good disease resistance.

‘Gnome’. Zones 31, 32, 34–41. Very cold hardy. Densely branched, 6 ft. high, 8 ft. wide. Orange berries. Very susceptible to scab.

‘Lowboy’. Zones 31, 32. Spreading plant to 2–3 ft. high. Orange fruit. Very prone to scab.

‘Mohave’. Zones 31, 32. To 12 ft. tall and wide. Heavy producer of big orange-red fruit that colors in late summer and lasts well into winter. Resistant to fireblight and scab.

‘Rutgers’. Zones 31, 32, 34–41. Spreading and bushy, to 3 ft. high and 9 ft. wide. Many orange red berries.

‘Teton’. Zones 31, 32, 34–41. Very cold hardy. Columnar growth to 12 ft. tall, 4 ft. wide. Golden yellow fruit. Resistant to fireblight and scab.

‘Watereri’. Zones 31, 32. To 8 ft. tall and wide. Very heavy producer of long-lasting bright red fruit.

‘Yukon Belle’. Zones 31, 32, 34, 35, 37, 39. Cold-hardiest orange-fruited firethorn. Dense growth, to 6–10 ft. high and wide.

PYRETHRUM marginatum. See CHRYSANTHEMUM pacificum

PYRETHRUM roseum. See CHRYSANTHEMUM coccineum

P

PYRUS

ORNAMENTAL PEAR

Rosaceae

EVERGREEN OR DECIDUOUS SHRUBS OR TREES

🌡 ZONES VARY BY SPECIES

☼ FULL SUN

🔴 REGULAR WATER

Pyrus

Fruiting pear is described under Pear. Following are ornamental species, grown for profuse flowers in late winter or early spring and for glossy, attractive leaves. Not fussy about soil, even growing well in heavy clay, but not at their best in shallow soil. Most are subject to fireblight (see Pear).

P. calleryana. Deciduous tree. Zones 31, 32, 34–41. Needs some winter chill. To 25–50 ft. tall, with strong horizontal branching pattern; young growth is thorny. Broadly oval, scalloped, glossy dark green, leathery leaves to 1½–3 in. long; turn rich purplish red in fall. Clustered pure white flowers are ¾–1 in. wide. Very early bloom; late freezes may destroy flower crop. Fruit very small, round, inedible. Less susceptible to fireblight than most pears. Available varieties include:

'Aristocrat'. Pyramidal, with branches that curve upward (a more stable structure than that of 'Bradford'). Fall color ranges from yellow to red. Very subject to fireblight in the South.

'Bradford'. Original introduction. Strongly vertical limbs (with no central leader), the branching pattern spreading with age; mature trees have a tendency to split. Has reached 50 ft. high, 30 ft. wide.

'Capital'. Narrowly columnar. Coppery fall color.

'Chanticleer' ('Cleveland Select', 'Stone Hill'). Narrow but not columnar; about 40 ft. tall, 15 ft. wide. Fall color varies from orange to reddish purple. Resistant to fireblight.

'Redspire'. Forms a shorter, narrower pyramid than 'Aristocrat'. Has especially large blossom clusters and yellow to red fall color. Quite prone to fireblight.

'Trinity'. Round-headed form to 30 ft. tall. Orange-red fall color.

'Whitehouse'. Narrowly columnar. Red to reddish purple fall color. Often gets a disfiguring leaf spot.

P. communis. See Pear

P. pyrifolia (P. serotina). SAND PEAR, JAPANESE SAND PEAR. Deciduous tree. Zones 32, 34–41. To 40 ft. tall. Like the common fruiting pear in appearance, but leaves are glossier and more leathery. Fall color ranges from brilliant orange red to reddish purple. Small, woody, gritty fruit. Improved forms of this tree, *P. p. culta* and its varieties, are grown for fruit by the Japanese and are becoming popular in the U.S.

P. salicifolia 'Pendula'. WEEPING WILLOW-LEAFED PEAR. Deciduous tree. Zones 32, 34–41. Elegant specimen plant to 15–25 ft. tall. Grown for silvery, willowlike foliage and beautiful weeping habit, showcased in winter when branches are bare. White flowers appear in early spring as silvery white new leaves emerge. Foliage slowly turns silvery green in summer. Fruit insignificant. Sometimes sold as 'Silver Frost'. Very susceptible to fireblight. Performance is better in cool climates.

P. ussuriensis. CHINESE PEAR. Deciduous tree. Zones 31, 32, 34–43. Conical to 40 ft. tall and 25 ft. wide. Glossy, deep green, broadly oval leaves to 4 in. long. Clusters of white flowers appear in mid-spring, followed by small, round green fruit.

QUAKER LADIES. See HOUSTONIA caerulea

QUAKING GRASS. See BRIZA maxima

QUAMOCLIT pennata. See IPOMOEA quamoclit

QUEEN OF THE MEADOW. See FILIPENDULA ulmaria

QUEEN OF THE PRAIRIE. See FILIPENDULA rubra

QUERCUS

OAK

Fagaceae

DECIDUOUS OR EVERGREEN TREES

🌡 ZONES VARY BY SPECIES

☼ FULL SUN

🔴🔴 SEE BELOW

Quercus

The oaks comprise 600 or so species of widely varying appearance and hardiness. Their common feature is the production of acorns—single nuts more or less enclosed in a cuplike organ made up of many closely set scales. Some oaks are widely planted over large parts of the country, while others have a limited range. Many wild-growing species may occur on rural or suburban properties but seldom, if ever, find their way into the nursery trade; these will not be discussed here.

Homeowners acquire oaks either by planting them or by inheriting trees that were present before the land was developed. Oaks that have been planted usually thrive without difficulty; inherited types probably require special attention. Protect trunks from earth-moving machinery with cribs of 2-by-4s or heavier timbers. Avoid piling excavated soil around trunks or above root systems (which extend somewhat beyond the branch spread); or provide drains for aeration and removal of excess water. Do not excavate or pave above the root zone without consulting a tree expert. Avoid compacting soil; when grading and other landscaping have been completed, be sure the tree has access to adequate water and air in the soil.

All oaks will take regular to moderate watering if they are planted out as young specimens. Mature trees will also take routine garden watering.

Caterpillars are the most serious potential pest of oaks. Gypsy moth caterpillars are most common in the East. Heavy infestation can cause defoliation; serious attacks for 2 or more years in a row can weaken or even kill a tree. However, gypsy moths tend to be cyclical problems, striking perhaps every 7 to 10 years. If control becomes necessary, consult a professional arborist or tree service; oak trees are too large for the limited spray equipment available to the home gardener.

Oak wilt, a fungus disease, has killed millions of oaks east of the Rockies. It is spread by oak bark beetles and by contact between healthy and infected roots; starting from the treetop down, leaves wilt, turn dull, curl, dry, and drop. Avoid pruning in spring, when bark beetles are most active. Don't plant a new oak within the root zone of a tree that has died.

Q. acutissima. SAWTOOTH OAK. Deciduous. Zones 31, 32, 34–41. Native to China, Korea, Japan. Moderate to fast growth to 35–45 ft. tall, usually with open, spreading habit. Deeply furrowed bark. Bristle-toothed, shiny dark green leaves are 3½–7½ in. long, a third as wide; they look like chestnut leaves. Foliage is yellowish on expanding, yellow to yellowish brown in fall; it may hang on late into winter. Fairly tolerant of various soils, though it prefers well-drained acid soil. Stands up well to heat and humidity. No serious problems. Good shade or lawn tree.

Q. alba. WHITE OAK. Deciduous. Zones 31, 32, 34–43. Native from Maine to Florida, west to Minnesota and Texas. Slow to moderate to 50–80 ft., taller in the wild. Pyramidal when young; in maturity, a majestic round-headed tree, often broader than tall. Leaves are 4–8 in. long, dark green above, lighter beneath, with deep, rounded lobes. Folklore has it that when the emerging leaves are as big as a mouse's ear, it is time to plant corn. Fall color varies from brown to wine red. Best in rich, deep, moist, preferably acid soil. One of the handsomest oaks, useful for timber, flooring, and barrel-making, but not widely planted because of its ultimate size and slow growth. Where it occurs naturally, however, it is among the most cherished of trees; it is the oak associated with treaty signings and other historic events.

Q. bicolor. SWAMP WHITE OAK. Deciduous. Zones 32, 34–43. Native Quebec to Georgia, west to Michigan and Arkansas. Slow to moderate growth to 50–60 ft., rarely taller, with equal or greater spread. Shallowly lobed or scalloped leaves are 3–7 in. long, a little more than half as wide, shiny dark green above, silvery white beneath. Fall color usually yellow,

Q

sometimes reddish purple. Bark of trunk and branches flakes off in scales. Tolerates wet soil; also thrives where soil is well drained. Drought resistant.

Q. cerris. TURKEY OAK. Deciduous. Zones 31, 32, 34, 39. Native to Europe. Round-headed, to 60 ft. high and wide. Blackish bark in squarish plates. Glossy, dark green leaves to 5 in. long, with pairs of triangular lobes. Acorns 1 in. long and half enclosed in a cup with backcurved scales.

Q. coccinea. SCARLET OAK. Deciduous. Zones 31, 32, 34–41. Native Maine to Florida, west to Minnesota and Missouri. Moderate to rapid growth in deep, rich soil. Can reach 60–80 ft. tall. High, light, open-branching habit. Bright green leaves are 3–6 in. long, a little more than half as wide, with deeply cut, pointed lobes. Foliage turns scarlet where autumn nights are cold. Deep roots. Good street or lawn tree. Fine to garden under.

Q. falcata. SOUTHERN RED OAK, SPANISH OAK. Deciduous. Zones 31, 32, 34–41. Native from Virginia to Florida, westward to southern Illinois and Arkansas. Moderate growth to 70–80 ft., eventually with rounded crown. Leaves 5–9 in. long, sometimes longer, with sharp-pointed lobes varying in number from three to nine. Fall color not significant. Tolerates relatively poor and dry soils as well as occasionally flooded soils.

Q. hemisphaerica. See *Q. laurifolia*

Q. imbricaria. SHINGLE OAK. Deciduous. Zones 32, 34–41. Native from Pennsylvania to Georgia, west to Nebraska and Arkansas. Slow growing and pyramidal in youth, eventually growing at a moderate rate into a rounded tree. Typical height is 50–60 ft., though tree sometimes reaches 100 ft. Shallowly ridged brown-gray bark. Oval, smooth-edged leaves are 2½–6 in. long, half as wide. Foliage is reddish on unfolding, dark glossy green in summer, yellowish brown to brownish red in autumn; often hangs on through winter. Thrives with pruning and can be trimmed into a hedge. Best in rich, deep, moist, well-drained soil; tolerates some drought.

The common name derives from one of the tree's uses: the wood was used for shingles. Sometimes called laurel oak because of its smooth, glossy leaves, but that name properly belongs to similar species *Q. hemisphaerica* and *Q. laurifolia*, less hardy evergreen or nearly evergreen oaks.

Q. laurifolia. LAUREL OAK. Zones 31, 32. Evergreen in southern part of range; loses leaves in winter in northern part. Native to coastal plain and piedmont from southern New Jersey to Florida, eastward to East Texas and southeast Arkansas. To 40 ft. or more in height, somewhat less in spread. Narrowly oval, smooth-edged, leathery leaves are shiny dark green, 1–4 in. long, ½–1¼ in. wide. *Q. hemisphaerica*, also called laurel oak, is similar.

Q. macrocarpa. BUR OAK, MOSSY CUP OAK. Deciduous. Zones 31, 32, 34–45. Native from Nova Scotia to Pennsylvania, westward to Manitoba and Texas. Rugged-looking tree growing slowly to 60–80 ft. high and at least as wide. Deeply furrowed dark gray bark. Leaves are glossy green above, whitish beneath, 4–10 in. long and half as wide, broad at tip, tapered at base. Yellowish fall color. Large acorns form in mossy cups. Similar to *Q. bicolor* but faster growing, more tolerant of adverse conditions. Needs lots of room.

Q. marilandica. BLACKJACK OAK. Deciduous. Zones 31, 32, 34, 39. Native to the eastern U.S. Small, scrubby tree to 40 ft. tall and 50 ft. wide. Rough-textured, dark brown bark. Broad-tipped leaves to 7 in. long, with three shallow lobes at the tip, glossy and dark green. Yellowish to brown fall color. Oval acorns. Needs acid soil.

Q. nigra. WATER OAK. Deciduous. Zones 31, 32, 34, 35. Native to lowland stream banks throughout southeastern U.S. Moderate to fast growth to 50–80 ft. tall, with conical or rounded canopy. Fairly narrow leaves, 1½–4 in. long, vary in shape from obovate to lobed; turn yellow to brown in fall, hang on late. Limbs subject to breakage by wind, snow, ice. Tolerates many soils, but not alkaline ones. Provide moist to wet conditions. Used as shade and street tree.

Q. palustris. PIN OAK. Deciduous. Zones 31, 32, 34, 43. Native from Massachusetts to Delaware, westward to Wisconsin and Arkansas. Moderate to fairly rapid growth to 50–80 ft. Slender and pyramidal when young, open and round headed at maturity. Smooth brownish gray bark becomes shallowly ridged with age. Lower

Quercus palustris

branches tend to droop almost to ground; if lowest whorl is cut away, branches above will adopt same habit. Only when fairly tall will it have good clearance beneath lowest branches. Glossy dark green leaves, 3–6 in. long and nearly as wide, are deeply cut into bristle-pointed lobes. In brisk fall weather, leaves turn yellow, red, and finally russet brown; may hang on in winter. Needs plenty of water; tolerates poorly drained soils. Widely used as lawn and street tree.

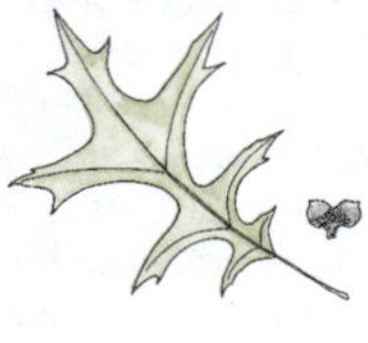

Q. phellos. WILLOW OAK. Deciduous. Zones 31, 32, 34–41. Native from New York to Florida, westward to Missouri and Texas. Fast to moderate growth to 50–90 ft. tall. Somewhat like *Q. palustris* in growth habit and spreading nature, this tree is grown and used in much the same way. Smooth gray bark becomes shallowly ridged in age. Leaves do not resemble those of other common oaks, but look more like willow leaves—2½–5 in. long, ⅓–1 in. wide, smooth edged. Foliage turns yellowish before falling; in warmer regions, dead leaves may hang on through winter. Most delicate foliage pattern of all oaks. Has no serious problems. Tolerates poorly drained soils.

Quercus phellos

Q. prinus. CHESTNUT OAK, BASKET OAK. Deciduous. Zones 31, 32, 34–41. Native from southern parts of Maine and Ontario southward to South Carolina and Alabama. Moderate growth to an eventual dense, rounded 60–70 ft. Bark often quite dark, even nearly black, becoming deeply furrowed with age. Unlobed leaves with coarse, rounded teeth are 4–6 in. long, 1½–3½ in. wide; in fall, their deep yellowish green color changes to yellow or yellowish brown. This tree tolerates poor, dry, rocky soil but looks better and grows faster with adequate water, good soil. Does not tolerate wet soils.

Q. robur. ENGLISH OAK. Deciduous. Zones 32, 34–41. Native to Europe, northern Africa, western Asia. Moderate growth to 40–60 ft. in gardens (to 90 ft. in wild), with rather short trunk and very wide, open head in maturity. Leaves 3–4½ in. long, half as wide, with three to seven pairs of rounded lobes. Leaves hold until late in fall and drop without much color change. 'Fastigiata', upright English oak, is narrow and upright (like Lombardy poplar) when young, branches out to broad, pyramidal shape when mature. Both this variety and the species are prone to mildew. Other varieties include 'Skymaster', a broad pyramid to 50 ft. tall and half as wide (narrower in youth); and 'Westminster Globe', a round-headed tree to 45 ft. tall and wide.

Q. rubra (Q. r. maxima, Q. borealis). RED OAK, NORTHERN RED OAK. Deciduous. Zones 31, 32, 34–45. Native from Nova Scotia to Pennsylvania, westward to Minnesota and Iowa. Fast growth to 60–75 ft. in gardens (over 100 ft. in wild). Broad, spreading branches and round-topped crown. With age, bark becomes quite dark and fissured. Leaves 5–8 in. long, 3–5 in. wide, with three to seven pairs of sharp-pointed lobes. New leaves and leafstalks are red in spring, turning dark red, ruddy brown, or orange in fall. Needs fertile soil and plenty of water. Stake young plants. High-branching habit and reasonably open shade make it a good tree for big lawns, parks, broad avenues. Deep roots make it good to garden under. Usually fairly trouble free.

Q. shumardii. SHUMARD RED OAK. Deciduous. Zones 31, 32, 34–41. Native from Kansas to southern Michigan, southward to North Carolina and Florida, westward to Texas. Similar to *Q. coccinea*, slightly less hardy. Yellow to red fall color. Tolerates drought, wide range of soils.

Q. variabilis. CHINESE CORK OAK. Deciduous. Zones 31, 32, 34–41. Native to China, Japan, Korea. Grows to 75–80 ft. tall. Thick, gray, corky bark. Glossy green leaves to 4 in. long, with pairs of pointed lobes, silvery gray on undersides. Acorns almost entirely enclosed in cup with long, curled scales.

Q. velutina. BLACK OAK. Deciduous. Zones 31, 32, 34–43. Native to eastern North America. Spreading, to 100 ft. tall, 80 ft. wide. Ridged, blackish brown bark. Oval, glossy green leaves with deep, pointed lobes. Reddish brown fall color. Rounded acorns. Needs acid soil.

FOR INFORMATION ON SELECTING PLANTS

PLEASE SEE PAGES 47–112

Q

QUINCE, FLOWERING. See CHAENOMELES

QUINCE, FRUITING
(Cydonia oblonga)

Rosaceae

DECIDUOUS SHRUB OR SMALL TREE

ZONES 31, 32, 34, 35, 37, 39

FULL SUN

MODERATE WATER

Quince

Slow to 10–25 ft. Unlike flowering quince (*Chaenomeles*), fruiting quince has thornless branches. Generally overlooked by planters of flowering fruit trees and home orchard trees, yet its virtues make common quince worth considering as an ornamental. Its winter form can be dramatic in pattern of gnarled and twisted branches. In spring, it bears white or pale pink, 2-in.-wide flowers at tips of leafed-out branches. Attractive, oval, 2–4-in. leaves, dark green above and whitish beneath; turn yellow in fall. Large, yellow, wonderfully fragrant fruit ripens in early fall.

Best in heavy, well-drained soil but tolerates wet soil. Avoid deep cultivation, which damages shallow roots and causes suckers. Prune only to form trunk and shape frame; thin out and cut back only enough to stimulate new growth. Do not use high-nitrogen fertilizer, as this results in succulent growth that is susceptible to fireblight. Remove suckers that sprout freely around the base of the tree; they rarely fruit and tend to weaken the tree.

Fruit is generally inedible when raw but useful in making jams and jellies. Fruit is also made into candy and blended with other fruits in pies. Some popular varieties are:

'Apple' ('Orange'). Old favorite. Round, golden-skinned fruit. Tender orange-yellow flesh.

'Champion'. Fruit golden yellow and sweet enough to be eaten raw. Very hardy and dependable.

'Cooke's Jumbo'. Large yellowish green fruit with white flesh. Can be nearly twice the size of other quinces.

'Pineapple'. Roundish, light golden fruit. Tender white flesh; pineapple-like flavor.

'Smyrna'. Round to oblong fruit with lemon yellow skin. Strong quince fragrance.

RADICCHIO. See CHICORY

RADISH

Brassicaceae (Cruciferae)

ANNUAL

ALL ZONES

FULL SUN OR LIGHT SHADE

MAINTAIN EVEN SOIL MOISTURE

Radish

You can pull radishes for the table as early as 3 weeks after you sow the seed (the slowest kinds take 2 months). To grow well, they need moist soil and some added nutrients. Supply nutrients by blending rotted manure into soil before planting, or—about 10 days after planting—feed beside row as for carrots, or apply liquid fertilizer. Sow seeds as soon as ground can be worked in spring and at weekly intervals until warm weather approaches (heat causes plants to go to seed, with roots becoming bitter in the process). In mild areas, radishes make a fall crop. Sow seeds ½ in. deep and thin to 1 in. apart when tops are up; space rows 1 ft. apart. Row covers will help protect against flea beetles, which attack foliage; will also deter root maggots by preventing adult flies from laying eggs.

Most familiar radishes are short, round, red or red-and-white types like 'Cherry Belle', 'Crimson Giant', and 'Scarlet White-tipped'. These should be used just as soon as they reach full size. Slightly slower to reach edible size are long white radishes, of which 'Icicle' is best known. Late radishes 'Long Black Spanish' and 'White Chinese' grow 6–10 in. long, can be stored in moist sand in a frost-free place for winter use. The last named, along with 'Alpine Cross' and similar very large, mild radishes, are sold as daikon (pronounced "dye-con").

Ranunculaceae. The immense buttercup family numbers nearly 2,000 species, among them numerous ornamental annuals and perennials. Members include *Anemone*, columbine (*Aquilegia*), *Clematis*, *Delphinium*, hellebore (*Helleborus*), and *Ranunculus*. Many are poisonous if eaten.

RANUNCULUS

Ranunculaceae

PERENNIALS WITH TUBEROUS OR FIBROUS ROOTS

ZONES VARY BY SPECIES

EXPOSURE NEEDS VARY BY SPECIES

REGULAR WATER

POISONOUS IF INGESTED

Ranunculus

A very large group (up to 250 species of widely different habit and appearance), but the ones listed are the only ones grown to any extent.

R. aconitifolius 'Flore Pleno'. WHITE BACHELOR'S BUTTONS. Zones 31, 32, 34–41. Fibrous-rooted perennial forms clumps to 2 ft. tall and 1½ ft. wide. Glossy dark green leaves have three to five toothed lobes arranged like fingers on a hand. Double, round white flowers on slender stems appear in late spring to early summer. Sun or shade.

R. acris. TALL BUTTERCUP. Zones 31, 32, 34–43. Fibrous-rooted perennial to 3 ft. tall and 9 in. wide. Medium green leaves to 3 in. long are lobed like fingers on a hand, the lobes toothed and sometimes further divided into segments. Round golden yellow flowers bloom on thin stems above the foliage in early to midsummer. 'Flore Pleno' has double flowers. Sun or shade.

R. asiaticus. PERSIAN RANUNCULUS, TURBAN RANUNCULUS. All zones (see below). Each large tuber produces many stalks to 1½ ft. or taller; in spring, each stalk bears one to four flowers, for a profuse show of blooms. Flowers are semidouble to fully double, 3–5 in. wide, in white and many shades of yellow, orange, red, pink, cream. Leaves are bright fresh green, almost fernlike. Popular strain is Tecolote Giants, available in single colors, mixed colors, and picotees. Bloomingdale is a dwarf (8–10-in.) strain.

Tubers are hardy to 10°F/−12°C; in Zone 31, plant in fall for bloom in winter, early spring. Everywhere else in the Northeast, plant as soon as ground is workable in spring. Needs full sun, perfect drainage (if necessary, plant in raised beds). Set tubers with prongs down, 2 in. deep (½–1 in. deep in heavy soil), 6–8 in. apart. Tubers rot if overwatered before roots form; you can start them in flats of moist sand, then plant after sprouts appear. Cover young sprouts with netting to protect from birds. Lift tubers when foliage yellows, cut off tops, and store in cool, dry place. Nursery-grown seedlings are sold in some areas. Good pot plant.

R. ficaria. LESSER CELANDINE. Zones 31, 32, 34–43. Tuberous-rooted perennial 2 in. high and 1 ft. wide. Glossy green heart-shaped leaves often toothed or scalloped. Yellow buttercup flowers to 1¼ in. across in early spring. 'Albus' has pale yellow flowers that fade to white; 'Bowles Double', double flowers with green centers fading to pale yellow; 'Brazen Hussy', shiny chocolate brown leaves, golden flowers. These plants can become invasive; site carefully. Partial to full shade.

R. repens 'Pleniflorus' (**R. r. 'Flore Pleno'**). CREEPING BUTTERCUP. Zones 31, 32, 34–43. Vigorous plant with thick, fibrous roots and runners growing several feet in a season, rooting at joints. Leaves glossy, roundish, deeply cut, toothed. Blooms in spring, bearing fully double, 1-in., button-shaped bright yellow flowers on 1–2-ft. stems. Ground cover in full sun to deep shade. Can be invasive. Basic species is single flowered and as aggressive as the variety (or more so).

RASPBERRY

Raspberry

Rosaceae

DECIDUOUS SHRUBS WITH BIENNIAL STEMS

ZONES 36–40, 42; also cooler parts of 41 and 43

☼ FULL SUN

● REGULAR WATER

Most popular and heavy bearing raspberries are red. There are two types: summer-bearing raspberries, which bear annually in summer on 2-year-old canes; and everbearing (also called fall-bearing) raspberries, which bear twice on each cane—in fall of first year, then in summer of second year. In both types, fruit follows loose clusters of white flowers. For ornamental relatives, see *Rubus*.

Raspberries need winter chill or cold and a slowly warming, lingering springtime to reach perfection. Good drainage is essential; if your soil is heavy clay, consider planting in raised beds. Slightly acid soil (pH 6 to 6.5) is ideal. Water need is greatest during flowering and fruiting. Feed at bloom time.

Plants are erect; they can be grown as free-standing shrubs and staked, but they are most easily handled if tied to wires fastened between two stout posts. The lower wire should be at 2½ ft., the upper one at 4–5 ft. The best time to plant is late winter or early spring. Set plants an inch deeper than they grew originally; space them 2½–3 ft. apart, in rows 7–9 ft. apart. Cut back the cane that rises from the roots, leaving only enough (about 6 in.) to serve as a marker.

Summer-bearing varieties should produce three to five canes the first year; these will bear the next year and should be cut out at ground level after fruiting. Second-year canes will appear all around parent plant and even between hills and rows. Remove all except 5–12 closely spaced, vigorous canes that come up near the crown. Tie these to top wire. In spring, before growth begins, cut them back to 4½–5½ ft. Fruit-bearing laterals will appear from these canes.

Everbearing raspberries differ slightly in pruning needs; they fruit in their first autumn on top third of cane and in their second summer on lower two-thirds of cane. Cut off upper portion that has borne fruit and leave lower portion to bear next spring. Cut out cane after it has fruited along its whole length.

You can follow the example of growers who cut everbearing canes to the ground yearly in fall after fruiting is finished; wait until late winter in cold regions. You'll sacrifice one of the crops in return for easy maintenance and a prolonged crop in summer. Use a powerful rotary mower in a large berry patch.

To control anthracnose and other fungus diseases, spray with lime sulfur during the dormant season and again when bloom time begins; this will also help control many insect pests. Cane borer may attack canes; prune out and destroy any damaged canes below entry points (pinhead-size holes in canes at or near ground level).

The following varieties are summer bearing unless otherwise indicated:

'Bababerry'. Everbearing. Needs little winter chill, stands heat well.

'Boyne'. Very hardy variety. Early ripening. Subject to anthracnose.

'Canby'. Large, bright red berries. Thornless.

'Cuthbert'. Medium-size berries of good quality.

'Durham'. Everbearing. Medium-size, firm berries of good quality. Starts to ripen 2 weeks before 'Indian Summer'. Good in North.

'Golden West'. Yellow berries. Excellent quality; tasty novelty.

'Heritage'. Everbearing. Small red berries are tasty, a bit dry.

'Indian Summer'. Everbearing. Small crops of large, tasty red berries. Fall crop often larger.

'Latham'. Older, very hardy variety for coldest regions. Mildews in humid-summer areas. Late ripening. Berries often crumbly.

'Meeker'. Large, firm bright red fruit on long, willowy branches.

'Newburgh'. Late-ripening variety. Large, light red berries. Takes heavy soil fairly well.

'New Washington'. Smallish fruit of high quality. Needs well-drained soil.

'Ranere' ('St. Regis'). Everbearing. Small, bright red berries.

'September'. Everbearing. Medium to small berries of good flavor. Fall crop the heavier one.

'Summit'. Everbearing. Can bear the first year. Heavy producer.

'Sumner'. Early variety with some resistance to root rot in heavy soils. Fine fruit.

'Willamette'. Large, firm, dark red berries that hold color and shape well.

RASPBERRY, BLACK or BLACKCAP

Raspberry, black or blackcap

Rosaceae

DECIDUOUS SHRUBS WITH BIENNIAL STEMS

ZONES 32, 34–43

☼ ◑ FULL SUN OR LIGHT SHADE

● REGULAR WATER

For ornamental relatives, see *Rubus*. Resemble regular red raspberry in many ways, but even less tolerant of mild climates. Blue-black fruit is firmer and seedier, with a more distinct flavor. Plants do not sucker from roots; new plants form when arching cane tips root in soil. No trellis needed. Head back new canes at 1½–2 ft. to force laterals. At end of growing season, cut out all weak canes and remove canes that fruited during current season. In late winter or early spring, cut back laterals to 10–15 in. on strong canes, 3–4 in. on weak ones. Fruit is produced on side shoots from these laterals. If you prefer trellising, head new canes at 2–3 ft. Subject to same pests and diseases as red raspberry.

Varieties usually sold are 'Brandywine'; 'Cumberland', an old variety; 'Morrison', large berry on productive vine; 'Munger', most popular commercial variety, and 'Royalty'. 'Jewel', a recent introduction, is disease resistant and vigorous; tip-pinch at 5 ft. 'Sodus', purple raspberry, is a vigorous hybrid of red and black raspberry; head new canes at 2½–3 ft.

RATIBIDA

Ratibida

Asteraceae (Compositae)

PERENNIALS

ZONES 31, 32, 34–43

☼ FULL SUN

● REGULAR WATER

Native to prairie and western states. Plants are stiffly erect, branched, roughly hairy, with deeply cut leaves. Flower heads resemble black-eyed Susan (*Rudbeckia*) but have fewer ray flowers and a round or cylindrical (rather than flat) central disk. Use in casual, natural-looking borders with grasses and other minimum-care perennials.

R. columnifera. MEXICAN HAT. To 2 ft. tall. Flowers have drooping ray flowers of yellow or brownish purple, and a tall, columnar brown disk. Effect is that of a sombrero with drooping brim.

R. pinnata. PRAIRIE or YELLOW CONEFLOWER. To 4 ft. tall, with yellow ray flowers and a nearly globular brown disk.

RATTAN PALM. See RHAPIS humilis

RATTLESNAKE GRASS. See BRIZA maxima

RATTLESNAKE MASTER. See ERYNGIUM yuccifolium

RAVENNA GRASS. See SACCHARUM ravennae

REDBUD. See CERCIS

RED-HOT POKER. See KNIPHOFIA uvaria

REDTOP. See AGROSTIS gigantea

RED VALERIAN. See CENTRANTHUS ruber

RED-VEINED DOCK. See RUMEX

RESEDA odorata

MIGNONETTE

Resedaceae

ANNUAL

⚡ ALL ZONES

☀ ◐ PARTIAL SHADE IN ZONES 31, 32

🔴 REGULAR WATER

Reseda odorata

To 1–1½ ft. tall; rather sprawling habit. Light green leaves. Not particularly beautiful plant, but well worth growing because of remarkable spicy-sweet flower fragrance. Small greenish flowers tinged with copper or yellow, in dense spikes that become loose and open as blossoms mature. Sow seed in early spring—or late fall or winter in mildest climates. Successive sowings give long bloom period. Best in rich soil. Plant in masses to get full effect of fragrance, or spot a few in flower bed to provide fragrance to scentless plantings. Suitable for pots. Strains have longer flower spikes and brighter colors, but they are less fragrant.

RESURRECTION FERN. See CHEILANTHES

RETINISPORA pisifera. See CHAMAECYPARIS pisifera

Rhamnaceae. The buckthorn family of shrubs and trees has small, usually clustered flowers and fruits that are either drupes (single seeded, juicy) or capsules. Family members include *Ceanothus, Rhamnus,* and Chinese jujube *(Ziziphus).*

RHAMNUS

Rhamnaceae

EVERGREEN OR DECIDUOUS SHRUBS OR TREES

⚡ ZONES 32, 34–45

☀ ◐ FULL SUN OR PARTIAL SHADE, EXCEPT AS NOTED

🔴 MODERATE WATER

Rhamnus

Small, clustered flowers are rather inconspicuous; plants are grown for form and foliage. Used chiefly as background plantings, hedges. Berrylike, typically pea-size fruits attract birds; volunteer seedlings may be a nuisance.

R. cathartica. COMMON BUCKTHORN. Deciduous shrub or small tree. To 15–25 ft. tall and wide. Glossy green, elliptical or oval leaves to 2½ in. long. Foliage drops late in season; fall color is poor. Short twigs often spine tipped. Black fruits. Tolerates drought, poor soil, wind. Useful hedge or small tree in coldest, driest regions. Full sun.

R. frangula. ALDER BUCKTHORN. Deciduous shrub or small tree. To 10–12 ft. (possibly 18 ft.) tall and as wide. Oval or obovate leaves to 3 in. long, glossy dark green turning yellow in autumn. Fruits turn from greenish yellow to red orange, dark red, and then black. 'Asplenifolia' has divided, fernlike leaves and grows slowly. 'Columnaris', tallhedge buckthorn, grows 12–15 ft. tall, 4 ft. wide. Set 2½ ft. apart for a tight, narrow hedge that can be kept as low as 4 ft.

RHAPIDOPHYLLUM hystrix

NEEDLE PALM

Palmaceae

PALM

⚡ ZONES 31, 32

☀ ◐ FULL SUN TO PARTIAL SHADE

🔴 REGULAR

Rhapidophyllum hystrix

Native to coastal areas from North Carolina to Florida but hardy farther north. This amazing palm has lived for years totally unprotected outdoors at the U.S. National Arboretum in Washington, D.C. Can withstand temperatures below 32°F/0°C, and is being successfully grown along the coast of southern New Jersey. Grown for its fan-shaped foliage, this nearly stemless palm grows slowly and forms large clumps. Leaf sheaths at the base of leafstalks are spiny to protect flowers and fruit. Each leafstalk bears a bright green leaf blade to 3 feet long with 5 to 12 lobes. Tiny purplish red flowers are cup shaped and hidden by the leaves. Plant grows overall to 6 ft. or more in height and spreads to 12 ft. Succeeds in moderately fertile, moist, but well-drained soil in the garden. North of Baltimore provide winter protection.

RHEUM palmatum

CHINESE RHUBARB

Polygonaceae

PERENNIAL

⚡ ZONES 31, 32, 34–41

☀ FULL SUN

🔴 🔴 REGULAR WATER, MORE THAN REGULAR WATER

Rheum palmatum

Standing up to 10 ft. tall and 6 ft. wide, this clump-forming ornamental rhubarb fills a lot of space and makes a dramatic accent in informal borders, damp gardens, and naturalistic sites. The huge leaves measure 2–3 ft. wide and are shaped like the rounded palm of a hand with five jagged lobes. The species has tall, upright, branched flower stems topped with pyramids of little cream, pink, or reddish blooms, followed by rusty brown fruits. In spring, impressive with its thick, reddish stems; in early summer, an imposing presence in bloom. Needs deep, fertile soil rich in organic matter and thrives with spring mulching and fertilization. Propagate by seed in the fall or by division in spring. Plant divisions 5 to 7 ft. apart.

'Bowles Crimson' has red blossoms. 'Atrosanguineum' has red flowers; new leaves are red but mature foliage is only red on the bottom. Var. *tanguticum* has bold, coarse leaves tinged purple and red, pink, or white flowers.

RHEXIA virginica

MEADOW BEAUTY

Melastomataceae

PERENNIAL

⚡ ZONES 31, 32, 34–41

☀ FULL SUN

🔴 🔴 CONSTANTLY MOIST SOIL

Rhexia virginica

A summer-blooming wildflower native from eastern Canada south to Florida where it grows in areas with moist to wet, acid, sandy soil. The 2-ft. plants, which usually have tuberous roots, bear oval leaves that are hairy on the upper surface and have hairy margins. From mid- to late summer, plants bear small clusters of 1½-in.-wide rose pink to purple-pink flowers. Use meadow beauty in bog gardens or moist, sunny wild gardens.

R

RHODIOLA

Crassulaceae

PERENNIALS

☀ ZONES VARY BY SPECIES

☼ FULL SUN

💧 REGULAR WATER

Rhodiola

These natives of the northern hemisphere, found in the wild on sea cliffs and in moist, rocky crevices on mountains, have fleshy, succulent-looking gray-green leaves along erect stems bearing rounded heads of small, star-shaped, sedumlike flowers. Growing from rhizomes, they're naturally suited to rock gardens but also work well at the front of mixed and perennial borders.

R. rosea. (Sedum rosea, Sedum rhodiola). ROSE ROOT. Zones 34–45. Stems are purple, and tips of leaves are tinted red; in late spring copper-colored buds appear, followed by copious yellow-green flowers. Does best in well-drained soil but tolerates damp conditions.

R. semenowii. Zones 31, 32, 34–43. To 2 ft. tall; narrow to oblong leaves to 2 in. long. Clusters of red buds open to greenish white to red-tinged flowers in summer.

RHODOCHITON
atrosanguineum

PURPLE BELLS, PURPLE BELL VINE

Scrophulariaceae

TENDER PERENNIAL VINE

☀ ALL ZONES AS ANNUALS, SEE BELOW

☼ FULL SUN

💧 REGULAR WATER

Rhodochiton

Often used as an annual, this rapidly growing climber may reach 10 ft. and blooms profusely the first year from seed. Stems are slender and twining, and heart-shaped leaves are an intense green. From summer often through first frost, produces an abundance of attractive bell-shaped maroon-purple calyxes from which extend tubular flowers of deep purple. The calyxes remain after the flowers drop, and the plant is full of bells. Use to screen porches and pergolas or cover an arbor or trellis; also attractive in hanging baskets. Performs best where summers remain cool

RHODODENDRON
(includes Azalea)

Ericaceae

EVERGREEN OR DECIDUOUS SHRUBS, RARELY TREES

☀ SEE BELOW

☼ GENERALLY BEST IN FILTERED SHADE

💧 CONSTANTLY MOIST SOIL AND HUMID AIR

❖ LEAVES ARE POISONOUS IF INGESTED

Rhododendron

Approximately 800 species belong to this huge group. The International Register lists more than 10,000 named varieties, of which perhaps 2,000 varieties are currently available. Botanists have arranged species into series and subseries; one of these series includes plants called azaleas. With careful selection, gardeners throughout the Northeast can find ways to grow members of this genus.

Rhododendrons and azaleas have much the same basic soil and water requirements. They require acid soil. They need more air in the root zone than many other garden plants but, at the same time, they need a constant moisture supply. In other words, they need soil that is both fast draining and moisture retentive. Yellowing, wilting, and collapse of plants indicate root rot caused by poor drainage. Soils rich in organic matter have the desired qualities; improve your soil with liberal quantities of organic matter. Plant azaleas and rhododendrons with top of root ball slightly above soil level. Never allow soil to wash in and bury stems. Rhododendrons are surface rooters and benefit from a mulch such as pine needles, oak leaves, and wood by-products such as fir bark or chips. Never cultivate around these plants.

Sun tolerance of azaleas and rhododendrons differs by species and variety. Too much sun causes bleaching or burning in leaf centers, though most can take full sun in cool-summer areas. Ideal location is in filtered shade beneath tall trees; east and north sides of house or fence are next best. Too-dense shade results in lanky plants that bloom sparsely. Any fertilizing should be done immediately after bloom. If leaves turn yellow while veins remain green, plants have iron deficiency called chlorosis; apply iron chelate to soil or spray with iron solution.

Though subject to many pests and diseases, plants are not usually beset by problems when well tended. Damage by root weevil adults, which notch leaves, is usually minor, but their larvae can girdle roots. Prevent new generations by controlling adults with contact insecticide. Lacebugs, which suck sap from leaf undersides, can be a severe problem in warm weather; spray with insecticidal soap or summer oil to control the wingless nymphs. Or use a systemic or contact insecticide to combat winged adults as well. Azalea petal blight fungus quickly ruins open blossoms of both azaleas and rhododendrons during warm, humid weather, turning the flowers brown and mushy. Because the spores form from resting bodies in petal debris from the previous year, thorough cleanup of infected blossoms will reduce infection both later in the season and in the following year. To control an infection, spray with a systemic fungicide; check with your Cooperative Extension Office for a specific recommendation.

Wind and soil salts burn leaf edges; windburn shows up most often on new foliage, salt burn on older leaves. Late frosts often cause deformed leaves. In extremely cold weather, sun and wind can severely damage plants; protect them by erecting a windbreak of burlap fastened to stakes. Protect roots against damage from alternate freezing and thawing by placing a mulch over the root system after the soil has frozen.

Prune evergreen azaleas by frequent pinching of tip growth from after flowering until July or August if you wish a compact plant with maximum flower production.

Prune large-flowered rhododendrons early in spring at bloom time if needed. Pruning in early spring will sacrifice some flower buds, but that is the best time for extensive pruning. Plant's energies will be diverted to dormant growth buds, which will then be ready to push out early in the growing season. Tip-pinch young plants to make them bushy; prune older, leggy plants to restore shape by cutting back to side branch, leaf whorl, or cluster of dormant buds. (Some varieties will not push new growth from dormant buds.) Clip or break off faded flower heads or spent clusters, taking care not to injure new buds and growth just beneath them.

RHODODENDRON RATINGS AND HARDINESS

Each plant in the list that follows includes a two-number rating (3/3, for example) assigned by the American Rhododendron Society. Flower quality is shown first and shrub quality second; 5 is superior, 4 above average, 3 average, 2 below average, 1 poor.

The list also gives each plant a hardiness rating, which indicates minimum temperatures a mature plant can tolerate without serious injury. Heights given are for plants 10 years old; older plants may be taller, and crowded or heavily shaded plants may reach up faster.

The bloom time given is approximate and varies with weather and location. The bloom season starts as early as January (in mildest climates) and extends through August; most types are spring bloomers. In the list below, "very early" corresponds to winter; "early" to early spring; "midseason" to midspring; "late" to late spring; and "very late" to summer.

KINDS OF RHODODENDRONS

Most people know rhododendrons as big, leathery-leafed shrubs with rounded clusters ("trusses") of stunning white, pink, red, or purple blossoms. But there are also dwarfs a few inches tall, giants that reach 40 or even 80 ft. in their native Southeast Asia, and a host of species and hybrids

R

in every intermediate size, in a color range including scarlet, yellow, near-blue, and a constellation of blends of orange, apricot, and salmon.

RHODODENDRONS IN CLAY OR ALKALINE SOIL?

They don't like it. Planting in raised beds that are 1–2 ft. above the original soil level is the simplest way to give these plants the conditions they need. Liberally mix organic material into top foot of native soil, then fill bed above it with a mixture that's 50 percent organic material, 30 percent soil, 20 percent sand. This mixture will hold air and moisture while allowing alkaline salts to leach through.

Ironclad hybrids for coldest winters. These can take temperatures to −25°F/−32°C: 'America', 'Boule de Neige', 'English Roseum', 'Ignatius Sargent', 'Nova Zembla', 'Parsons Gloriosum', 'PJM', 'President Lincoln', 'Roseum Elegans'.

Ironclad hybrids that tolerate hot summers. 'Anah Kruschke', 'Belle Heller', 'Cheer', 'Cynthia', 'English Roseum', 'Fastuosum Flore Pleno', 'Holden', 'Nova Zembla', 'PJM', 'Roseum Elegans', 'Scintillation'.

The following list of named varieties give some idea of their adaptability to different northeastern climates and garden roles. These are the generally available kinds, representing only a portion of the best rhododendrons grown in our region.

'America'. 3/3. −25°/−32°C. To 5 ft. tall and wide. Dark red. Late.

'Anah Kruschke'. 2/3. −10°F/−23°C. To 5 ft. Lavender purple. Color not the best, but plant has good foliage, tolerates heat, is not fussy about soil. Midseason.

'Anna Rose Whitney'. 4/3. 5°F/−15°C. Compact grower to 5 ft., with excellent foliage. Big trusses in rich, deep pink. Midseason.

'Azurro'. 3/4. −15°F/−26°C. Compact plant to 4 ft. Rich purple with red blotch. Late.

'Belle Heller'. 4/3. −10°F/−23°C. To 5 ft. Pure white with gold blotch. Midseason. Sun and heat tolerant.

'Blue Diamond'. 5/4. 0°F/−18°C. Compact, erect growth to 3 ft. Small leaves. Lavender blue flowers cover plant early to midseason. Takes considerable sun in cool climates.

'Blue Ensign'. 4/3. −15°F/−26°C. Compact, well-branched, rounded plant to 4 ft. Leaves tend to spot. Lilac blue flowers have a striking dark spot in the upper petal. Midseason.

'Blue Peter'. 4/3. −10°F/−23°C. Broad, sprawling growth to 4 ft.; needs pruning. Large trusses of lavender blue flowers blotched with purple. Midseason.

'Boule de Neige'. 3/3. −25°F/−32°C. To 5 ft. Rounded plant with bright green leaves and snowball-like clusters of white flowers. Midseason.

'Bow Bells'. 3/4. 0°F/−18°C. Compact, rounded growth to 4 ft. Rounded leaves; bronzy new growth. Bright pink, bell-shaped flowers in loose clusters. Midseason.

R. carolinianum. 3/3. −25°F/−32°C. Native to mountains of the Carolinas and Tennessee. To 3–6 ft. tall and as broad or broader. Leaves turn purplish in cold winters. Tight clusters of pink flowers in midseason. 'Album' is similar but bears white flowers.

R. catawbiense. 3/3. −25°F/−32°C. Native to mountains from West Virginia to Alabama. To 5 ft., eventually much larger. Lavender purple flowers in midseason. Ancestor of many heat-tolerant varieties. 'Album' has pink buds opening to white flowers with greenish yellow blotch.

'Cheer'. 3/3. −10°F/−23°C. Mound-shaped, glossy-leafed plant to 4 ft. Pink flowers. Early. Heat tolerant.

'Christmas Cheer'. 2/4. −5°F/−21°C. To 3 ft. Pink to white flowers in tight trusses. Very early bloom compensates for any lack in flower quality. Can take full sun.

'Cinnamon Bear'. 5/5. −10°F/−23°C. Low, dense, to 4 ft. Rosy pink buds open to pink flowers. Midseason. Furry brown leaves an additional attraction.

'Cynthia'. 4/3. −15°F/−26°C. To 6 ft. Rosy crimson with blackish markings. Midseason. Old favorite for background. Heat tolerant.

Dexter Hybrids. -10°F/-23°C. Evergreen, with open growth. Height, flower color vary; fragrant flowers. 'Dexter's Spice', white flowers, midseason.

'Dora Amateis'. 4/4. −15°F/−26°C. To 3 ft. tall. Compact, rather small-foliaged plant; spreading, good for foreground. Profuse bloomer with green-spotted white flowers. Early midseason.

'Elizabeth'. 4/4. 0°F/−18°C. Broad grower to 3 ft. tall, with medium-size leaves. Blooms very young. Bright red, waxy, trumpet-shaped flowers in clusters of three to six at branch ends and in upper leaf joints. Main show early; often reblooms in autumn. Very susceptible to fertilizer burn, salts in water. There is a red-leafed form.

'English Roseum'. 3/4. −25°F/−32°C. Erect shrub to 6 ft. Lavender blooms with yellowish green petal blotches. Midseason. Hardy to both cold and heat.

'Furnival's Daughter'. 5/4. −5°F/−21°C. To 5 ft. Bright pink flowers with deep red blotch. Midseason.

'Ginny Gee'. 5/5. −5°F/−21°C. Striking 2-ft. plant with small leaves, dense growth. Covered with small flowers in early midseason. Blooms range from pink to white, with striped and dappled patterns.

'Golfer'. 4/5. −15°F/−26°C. Low, broad, dense, to 1 ft., with silvery, furry coat on leaves. Bright pink. Midseason.

'Gomer Waterer'. 3/4. −15°F/−26°C. To 5 ft. White flushed lilac. Late midseason. Old-timer.

'Halfdan Lem'. 5/4. −5°F/−21°C. Well shaped, vigorous, to 5 ft. Luminous red trusses stand out against deep green foliage. Midseason.

'Hallelujah'. 5/5. −15°F/−26°C. To 4 ft. Rose red flowers in midseason stand above thick, beautiful forest green foliage. Takes full sun. Very strong grower. Fine-looking plant with or without flowers.

'Holden'. 3/3. −15°F/−26°C. Compact grower to 4 ft. Rose red flowers marked with deeper red. Midseason. Heat tolerant.

'Ice Cube'. 4/3. −20°F/−29°C. To 5 ft. Cone-shaped clusters of creamy white flowers with a small yellow flare. Midseason to late.

'Ignatius Sargent'. 2/2. −25°F/−32°C. To 5 ft., with open growth habit, large leaves. Deep rose pink flowers. Midseason to late.

'Janet Blair'. 4/3. −15°F/−26°C. Vigorous plant to 6 ft. tall and spreading. Large, ruffled pastel flowers blend pink, cream, white, and gold; rounded trusses. Midseason to late.

'Lodestar'. 4/4. −20°F/−29°C. To 5 ft. Large white or palest lilac flowers marked deep greenish yellow. Midseason to late.

'Lord Roberts'. 3/3. −10°F/−23°C. To 5 ft. Handsome dark green foliage and rounded trusses of black-spotted red flowers. Midseason to late. Plants grown in sun have more compact growth, bloom more profusely.

'Mars'. 4/3. −10°F/−23°C. To 4 ft. Dark red. Late midseason. Handsome form, foliage, flowers.

'Mrs. Furnival'. 5/5. −10°F/−23°C. Compact growth to 4 ft. Tight, round trusses of clear pink flowers with light brown blotch in upper petals. Late midseason.

R. maximum. ROSEBAY RHODODENDRON. -20°F/-29°C. Evergreen, with open growth to 15 ft.; deep green, oblong leaves. Rose, pink, or white flowers spotted green or orange. Late. Needs shade.

R. mucronulatum. 4/3. −25°F/−32°C. Deciduous azalealike rhododendron with open growth to 5 ft. Makes up for bare branches by very early bloom. Flowers are generally bright purple. There is a pink form, 'Cornell Pink'.

'Nova Zembla'. 3/3. −25°F/−32°C. To 5 ft. Profuse red flowers come late in the season. Hardy to both cold and heat.

'Parsons Gloriosum'. 2/2. −25°F/−32°C. To 5 ft., upright but fairly compact. Pinkish lavender flowers. Midseason to late.

'Patty Bee'. 5/5. −10°F/−23°C. Dense, moundlike growth to 1½ ft. Leaves are small, giving plant a finely textured look. Trumpet-shaped yellow flowers cover plant in midseason.

'Pink Pearl'. 3/3. −5°F/−21°C. To 6 ft. or more; open, rangy growth without pruning. Rose pink, tall trusses in midseason. Dependable grower and bloomer in all except coldest climates.

R

'PJM'. 4/4. −25°F/−32°C. To 4 ft. Lavender pink blooms come early. Foliage turns mahogany in winter. Takes heat as well as cold.

'President Lincoln'. 2/3. −25°F/−32°C. To 6 ft. Lilac-toned lavender pink with bronze blotch. Midseason to late.

'Purple Splendour'. 4/3. −10°F/−23°C. Informal growth to 4 ft. Ruffled, deep purple blooms blotched black purple. Midseason. Easy to grow.

R. racemosum. 3/3. −10°F/−23°C. Several forms include 6-in. dwarf, 2½-ft. compact upright shrub, and tall 7-footer. Small pink flowers in clusters of three to six all along stems. Early. Easy to grow; sun tolerant in cooler areas.

'Ramapo'. 3/4. −20°F/−29°C. Dense, spreading growth to 2 ft. in sun, taller in shade. New growth is dusty blue green. Violet blue flowers cover plant in midseason. Fine for rockeries.

'Roseum Elegans'. 2/3. −25°F/−32°C. Vigorous plant to 6 ft., with small trusses of pinkish lilac flowers. Midseason to late. Hardy to both cold and heat.

'Sappho'. 3/2. −5°F/−21°C. To 6 ft. White with dark purple spot in throat. Midseason. Easy to grow; gangly without pruning. Use at back of border.

'Scarlet Wonder'. 5/5. −10°F/−23°C. Outstanding dwarf (to 2 ft. tall) of compact growth. Shiny, quilted foliage forms backdrop for many bright red blossoms. Midseason.

'Scintillation'. 4/5. −15°F/−26°C. Compact 5-ft. plant covered in lustrous, dark green leaves. Rounded trusses carry gold-throated pink flowers. Midseason. Heat tolerant.

'Sham's Candy'. 3/3. −20°F/−29°C. To 5 ft. with narrow deep green leaves. Cone-shaped trusses of deep pink flowers with yellow-green blotch. Midseason to late.

'Sumatra'. 4/4. −15°F/−26°C. Dwarf to 2 ft. tall. Deep pure red flowers. Midseason.

'Taurus'. 5/4. 0°F/−18°C. Vigorous, upright to 6 ft.; well covered with forest green leaves. Brilliant red flowers with black spotting on upper lobes come in large, round trusses. Midseason bloom comes only after plants reach 4 to 6 years old.

'Trinidad'. 4/4. −20°F/−29°C. To 4 ft. Cream flowers edged in red. Midseason to late.

'Trude Webster'. 5/4. −10°F/−23°C. Strong 5-ft. plant, with large leaves. Huge trusses of clear pink flowers come in midseason. One of the best pinks.

'Vulcan'. 3/4. −5°F/−21°C. To 4 ft. Bright brick red flowers. Midseason to late. New leaves often grow past flower buds, partially hiding flowers.

R. yakushimanum. 4/4. −20°F/−29°C. Dense, spreading growth to 3 ft. Gray-felted new foliage; older leaves have heavy tan or white felt beneath. Clear pink bells changing to white. Late midseason. Selections range from 'Ken Janeck', a large (and large-leafed) form with very pink flowers, to 'Yaku Angel', with pink-tinged buds opening to pure white. There are also a number of hybrids that are as good in cold climates as they are in milder ones, among them 'Mardi Gras', 'Mist Maiden', 'Yaku Sunrise', and 'Yaku Princess' (this last selection is part of a good series of hybrids, all with monarchic names).

KINDS OF EVERGREEN AZALEAS

The evergreen azaleas fall into more than a dozen groups and species, though an increasing number of hybrids have such mixed parentage that they don't conveniently fit into any group. The following includes some of the most popular groups. Except as noted, bloom season is early (see "Rhododendron ratings and hardiness," page 380, for explanation of bloom season terms). In greenhouses, plants can be forced for winter bloom. Plant sizes vary within the groups.

Gable Hybrids. Zones 31, 32, some to 39. Bred to produce azaleas of Kurume type that take 0°F/−18°C temperatures. In colder part of range, they may lose some leaves. Bloom heavily in midseason. Frequently sold are 'Caroline Gable', bright pink; 'Herbert', purple; 'Louise Gable', pink; 'Pioneer', pink; 'Purple Splendor'; 'Purple Splendor Compacta' (less rangy growth than 'Purple Splendor'); 'Rosebud', pink; and 'Rose Greeley', white.

Girard Hybrids. Zones 31, 32. Hardy to −5°F/−21°C or somewhat colder. These originated from Gable crosses. Examples are 'Girard's Fuchsia', reddish purple; 'Girard's Hot Shot', orange red with orange-red fall and winter foliage; and 'Girard's Roberta', with 3-in. double pink flowers.

Glenn Dale Hybrids. Zones 31, 32, some to 39. Hardy to 0°F/−18°C. Developed primarily for hardiness, but they do drop some leaves in cold winters. Some are tall and rangy, others low and compact. Growth rate varies from slow to rapid. Some have small leaves like Kurume Hybrids; others have large leaves. Familiar varieties are 'Anchorite', orange; 'Aphrodite', pale pink; 'Buccaneer', orange red; 'Everest', white; 'Geisha', white with red stripes; 'Glacier', white; and 'Martha Hitchcock', white-edged magenta.

Kaempferi Hybrids. Zones 31, 32, 34, 39. Based on *R. kaempferi*, the torch azalea, a cold-hardy plant with orange-red flowers. These are somewhat hardier than Kurume Hybrids, to −15°F/−26°C, taller and more open in growth, nearly leafless in coldest winters. Profuse bloom. Among those sold are 'Fedora', salmon rose; 'Holland', late, large red; 'John Cairns', orange red; and 'Palestrina', white.

Kurume Hybrids. Zones 31, 32. Hardy to 5 to 10°F/−15 to −12°C. Compact, twiggy plants, densely foliaged with small, glossy leaves. Small flowers are borne in incredible profusion. Plants mounded or tiered, handsome even out of bloom. Widely used as house plants. Grow well outdoors in half sun. Many varieties available; the most widespread are 'Coral Bells', pink; 'Hexe', crimson; 'Hino-crimson', bright red; 'Hinodegiri', cerise red; 'Sherwood Orchid', red violet; 'Sherwood Red', orange red; 'Snow'; and 'Ward's Ruby', dark red.

North Tisbury Hybrids. Zones 31, 32, 34, 39. Hardy to about 0°F/−18°C. You can see a common, notable ancestry in most of these plants (*R. nakaharai*). Their low, spreading habit and very late bloom (into midsummer) make them naturals for hanging baskets and ground covers. Some of the best are 'Alexander', very hardy, with bronze fall foliage and red-orange blooms; 'Pink Cascade', pink; and 'Red Fountain', with dark red-orange blooms around the Fourth of July.

Satsuki Hybrids. Zones 31, 32. Includes azaleas referred to as Gumpo and Macrantha hybrids. Hardy to 5°F/−15°C. Plants low growing, some true dwarfs; many are pendent enough for hanging baskets. Large flowers come late. Popular varieties: 'Bunkwa', blush pink; 'Flame Creeper', orange red; 'Gumpo', white; 'Gumpo Pink', rose pink; 'Hi Gasa', bright pink; 'Rosaeflora', rose pink; 'Shinnyo-No-Tsuki', violet red with white center.

R. mucronatum ('Indica Alba', 'Ledifolia Alba'). Zones 31, 32, 34, 39. Spreading growth to 6 ft. (but usually 3 ft.); large, hairy leaves. White or greenish flowers 2½–3 in. across; early. 'Indica Rosea' ('Ledifolia Rosea') has white flowers flushed and blotched with rose; it blooms very early (about a month before the species). 'Sekidera' is white flushed with reddish purple. 'Delaware Valley White' is slightly more cold tolerant than other varieties.

KINDS OF DECIDUOUS AZALEAS

Very few deciduous shrubs can equal deciduous azaleas in show and range of color. Flowers of their evergreen relatives can't match these in the yellow, orange, and flame red range or in bicolor contrasts. Fall foliage is often brilliant orange red to maroon. Deciduous azaleas tend to be less particular about soil and watering than most evergreen types. Many deciduous species are native to the eastern and southern U.S. Selections of these species and hybrids are increasingly popular. See "Rhododendron ratings and hardiness" (page 380) for bloom season terminology. In warm, humid regions, powdery mildew can be a serious problem for many Ghent, Knap Hill, and Mollis hybrids.

Ghent Hybrids. Zones 32, 34–41. Many are hardy to −25°F/−32°C. Upright growth variable in height. Flowers generally smaller than those of Mollis Hybrids. Colors include shades of yellow, orange, umber, pink, and red. Midseason.

Knap Hill–Exbury Hybrids. Zones 32, 34–41. Hardy to −25°F/−32°C. Plants vary from spreading to upright, from 4 to 6 ft. tall. Flowers are large (3–5 in. across), in clusters of 7–18, sometimes ruffled or fragrant, white through pink and yellow to orange and red, often with contrasting blotches.

R

Both Knap Hill and Exbury azaleas come from same original crosses; first crosses were made at Knap Hill (in England), and subsequent improvements were made at both Exbury (also in England) and Knap Hill. The "Rothschild" azaleas are Exbury plants. Ilam Hybrids are from same original stock, further improved in New Zealand.

Midseason to late bloom. If you want to be sure of color and flower size, choose from named varieties. Some of the best are 'Cannon's Double', pink; 'Gibraltar', orange; 'Homebush', double deep pink; 'Klondyke', golden tangerine; and 'Oxydol', white with yellow markings. Don't automatically consider all seedlings inferior plants, however—but do select them in bloom.

Mollis Hybrids. Zones 32, 34−41. Hardy to −25°F/−32°C. Hybrids of *R. molle* and *R. japonicum*. Upright growth to 4−5 ft. high; 2½−4-in.-wide flowers are carried in clusters of 7−13. Blossom color ranges from chrome yellow through poppy red. New growth has a light skunky fragrance, but foliage turns a lovely yellow to orange in autumn. Very heavy bloom in midseason.

Northern Lights Hybrids. Zones 34−45. Developed by the University of Minnesota; hardy to −40°F/−40°C. Grow 2−4 ft. tall, produce ball-shaped trusses of fragrant sterile flowers (they won't set seed) late in the season. Most widely available are 'Apricot Surprise', 'Orchid Lights', 'Rosy Lights', and 'White Lights'. Foliage can have the skunky odor of the group's Mollis ancestors.

Viscosum Hybrids. Zones 32, 34−41. Hardy to −15°F/−26°C. Hybrids between Mollis azaleas and *R. viscosum*. Deciduous shrubs with colors of Mollis but fragrance of *R. viscosum*. Late.

R. alabamense. ALABAMA AZALEA. Zones 31, 32. Hardy to −5°F/−21°C. Native to Alabama, Georgia. Grows 5−6 ft. tall and spreads by suckering to form colonies. Highly fragrant white flowers usually blotched with yellow. Early.

R. arborescens. SWEET AZALEA. Zones 32, 34−41. Hardy to −10°F/−23°C. Native to mountains from Pennsylvania to Alabama. Erect, open shrub to 8 ft. (possibly 20 ft.) tall. Fragrant white to pale pink flowers appear late, after leaves have expanded.

R. atlanticum. COAST AZALEA. Zones 31, 32, 34−41. Hardy to −15°F/−26°C. Native from Delaware to South Carolina. Suckering shrub to 3−6 ft. tall, with white to pink fragrant (and somewhat sticky) flowers early, before leaves expand (or as they expand).

R. austrinum. FLORIDA AZALEA. Zones 31, 32. Hardy to 5°F/−15°C. Native to northern and western Florida and southern parts of Georgia, Alabama, Mississippi. To 8−10 ft. tall, with fragrant flowers that may be pale yellow, cream, pink, orange, or red in color. Early.

R. bakeri. CUMBERLAND AZALEA. Zones 31, 32, 34−41. Hardy to −15°F/−26°C. Native to mountains of Kentucky, Virginia, Tennessee, Georgia, Alabama. Grows 3−8 ft. tall. Flowers range from yellow and orange to (usually) red. Late midseason. Does not tolerate heat.

R. calendulaceum. FLAME AZALEA. Zones 31, 32, 34−41. Hardy to −25°F/−32°C. Native to mountain regions from southern Pennsylvania to Georgia. To 4−8 ft. or taller. Clusters of 2-in.-wide yellow, red, orange, or scarlet flowers. Late. A very important parent of many hybrid deciduous azalea races.

R. canadense. RHODORA. Zones 36−43. Hardy to −25°F/−32°C. Native from eastern Canada to Pennsylvania. Open, lanky shrub to 3−4 ft. Clusters of 1½-in. reddish purple flowers in early midseason as leaves expand. Needs cool climate.

R. canescens. PIEDMONT AZALEA. Zones 31, 32, 34−41. Hardy to −5°F/−21°C. Native from North Carolina to Texas. Large (to 10-ft.), suckering shrub with fragrant white to pink or rose flowers. Early. Sun or shade.

R. flammeum. OCONEE AZALEA. Zones 31, 32, 34, 37. Hardy to −15°F/−26°C. Native to South Carolina, Georgia. Fairly compact shrub to 6 ft., with clusters of 1¾-in. flowers in midseason. Color is typically bright red but may vary to yellow or orange.

R. japonicum. JAPANESE AZALEA. Zones 31, 32, 34−41. Hardy to −10°F/−23°C. Upright, fast growth to 6 ft. tall. Salmon red flowers, 2−3 in. wide, are carried in clusters of 6−12. Midseason. *R. j. aureum* has rich yellow flowers.

R. luteum (R. flavum). PONTIC AZALEA. Zones 31, 32, 34−41. Hardy to −15°F/−26°C. Native to Eastern Europe, Asia Minor. To 8 ft. Fragrant, single yellow flowers with darker blotch. Midseason.

R. oblongifolium. TEXAS AZALEA. Zones 31, 32. Hardy to −5°F/−21°C. Native to East Texas, Oklahoma, and Arkansas. To 6 ft. tall. Slightly fragrant white flowers to 1 in. long appear in midseason, after leaves emerge.

R. periclymenoides (R. nudiflorum). PINXTERBLOOM AZALEA. Zones 31, 32, 34−43. Hardy to −15°F/−26°C. Native from Massachusetts to Ohio and North Carolina. Often called "honeysuckle" in its native range. Suckering shrub growing 2−3 ft. high (occasionally much taller). Pale pink (usually) to deep pink, fragrant, 1½-in. flowers appear in midseason, as leaves expand.

R. prinophyllum (P. roseum). ROSESHELL AZALEA. Zones 32, 34−43. Hardy to −25°F/−32°C. Native from southern Quebec to Virginia, west to Missouri and Oklahoma. To 4−8 ft. tall, occasionally much taller; bright pink (sometimes white), 1½-in. flowers with strong clove fragrance. Blooms in midseason, before or with leaves. One of the parents of the extremely hardy Northern Lights Hybrids.

R. prunifolium. PLUMLEAF AZALEA. Zones 31, 32, 34−41. Hardy to −15°F/−26°C. Native to Georgia and Alabama. To 10 ft., with orange-red to bright red flowers. This is the latest blooming of all azaleas.

R. schlippenbachii. ROYAL AZALEA. Zones 31, 32, 34−43. Hardy to −20°F/−29°C. Native to Korea. Densely branched shrub to 6−8 ft. Leaves in whorls of five at tips of branches. Large (2−4-in.), pure light pink, highly fragrant flowers in clusters of three to six. Early midseason. A white form is also available. Good fall color: yellow, orange, scarlet, crimson. Foliage resists mildew. Protect from full sun.

R. vaseyi. PINKSHELL AZALEA. Zones 32, 34−41. Hardy to −20°F/−29°C. Native to mountains of North Carolina. Upright, irregular habit; plant spreads to about 15 ft. wide. Light pink flowers are borne in clusters of five to eight in midseason.

R. viscosum. SWAMP AZALEA. Zones 31, 32, 34−45. Hardy to −25°F/−32°C. Native to damp or wet ground, Maine to Alabama. To 5−8 ft. tall. Flowers are white (occasionally pink), 2 in. long, sticky on the outside, with a powerful clove scent. Very late.

RHODOHYPOXIS baurii

Hypoxidaceae

BULBLIKE TUBER

🗡 ZONES 31, 32; OR GROW IN POTS

☀ FULL SUN

🔴 REGULAR WATER DURING GROWTH AND BLOOM

Rhodohypoxis baurii

Tufts of narrow, 2−3-in. leaves are nearly obscured by masses of 1-in. white, pink, or rose red flowers over a long spring−summer season. Dormant in winter. Tubers multiply quickly with good drainage, adequate water. Protect from winter rains or snow with pane of glass or shingle. If grown in pots, turn pots on side in winter or store over winter in cold frame. Excellent plant for rock garden, stone sink garden, or pots.

RHODOTYPOS scandens

JETBEAD, WHITE KERRIA

Rosaceae

DECIDUOUS SHRUB

🗡 ZONES 31, 32, 34−41

☀ ◐ FULL SUN, BUT PARTIAL SHADE TOLERATED

🔴 REGULAR

Rhodotypos scandens

Spreading shrub features bright green foliage and showy four-petaled white flowers to 1½ in. across borne singly in late spring. Glossy black berries form in groups of four to five after flowers, persist until spring, go dormant for a year, then develop into seedlings around the original plant. Prune out older wood once flowers have faded. Does best in moderately fertile and well-drained soil with an occasional dressing of compost. Suitable for informal shrub borders or woodland settings.

RHUBARB

Polygonaceae

PERENNIAL GROWN FROM RHIZOME

🌿 ZONES 31, 32, 34–45; BEST IN ZONES 34–45

☼ ◐ SOME SHADE IN HOTTEST CLIMATES

🌢 WATER FREELY DURING ACTIVE GROWTH

◆ LEAVES ARE POISONOUS IF INGESTED; USE STEMS ONLY

Rhubarb

Big, elongated, heart-shaped, crinkled leaves and red-tinted leafstalks are showy enough to qualify for display spot in garden. Delicious, tangy leafstalks are used like fruit in sauces and pies. Flowers are insignificant, in spikelike clusters. Preferred varieties are 'Victoria', with greenish stalks; and 'Cherry' ('Crimson Cherry'), 'MacDonald', and 'Strawberry', all of which have red stalks.

Plant divisions (containing at least one bud) in late winter or early spring. Set tops of divisions at soil line; space 3–4 ft. apart. Permit plants to grow for two full seasons before harvesting. During next spring, you can pull off leafstalks for 4 or 5 weeks; older, huskier plants will take up to 8 weeks of pulling. Harvest leafstalks by grasping near base and pulling sideways and outward; do not cut with a knife, since cutting leaves a stub that will decay. Never remove all leaves from a single plant. Stop harvesting when slender leafstalks appear. After harvest, feed and water freely; cut out any blossom stalks that appear. Plants won't die back completely in mildest winters.

A related species, *Rheum palmatum* (Chinese rhubarb), offers several ornamental cultivars that make a bold, sculptural statement in beds and borders. 'Astrosanguineum' ('Atropurpureum') has red-pink flowers and leaves that are red-purple when young and turn slowly to dark green; 'Bowles' Crimson' has dark red flowers and deep red undersides to leaves.

RHUS

SUMAC

Anacardiaceae

EVERGREEN OR DECIDUOUS SHRUBS OR TREES

🌿 ZONES VARY BY SPECIES

☼ FULL SUN

🌢 🌢 REGULAR TO LITTLE WATER

Rhus

Of the ornamental sumacs, deciduous kinds are extremely hardy; they are noted for brilliant fall leaf color and, on female plants, showy clusters of (usually) red fruits. They tend to produce suckers, especially if their roots are disturbed by cultivation. Evergreen species are less hardy. All species of sumac thrive in almost any soil, as long as it is well drained; soggy soils can kill them.

R. aromatica. FRAGRANT SUMAC. Deciduous shrub. Zones 31, 32, 34–43. Native to eastern North America. Fast growing to 3–5 ft. tall, sprawling much wider. Leaves to 3 in. long, with three leaflets; fragrant when brushed against or crushed. Foliage turns red in fall. Tiny yellowish flowers in spring, small red fruit in late summer. Coarse bank cover, ground cover for poor or dry soils. Two available varieties are 'Gro-low' (to about 2 ft.) and 'Green Mound' (to 4 ft.).

R. chinensis. CHINESE SUMAC. Zones 31, 32, 34–41. Native to China and Japan. Upright, spreading, deciduous shrub or small tree to 24 ft. tall. Leaves grow to 16 in. long, with pairs of toothed, oval leaflets, a single terminal leaflet, and prominent central midrib. Foliage is bright green in summer, yellow to orange or reddish in autumn. Large, showy clusters of yellowish white flowers adorn the sizable plants in late summer. In the

Northeast frost intervenes before the fruits have a chance to mature.

R. copallina. SHINING SUMAC. Zones 31, 32, 34–43. Native from Maine to Ontario, south to Florida and Texas. Deciduous shrub or tree to 30 ft. high and wide, dense and compact when young and becoming more open with age. Dark green leaves to 14 in. long are divided into pairs of oval to oblong leaflets, with a single terminal leaflet and a prominent central midrib. Leaves turn rich shades of red in autumn. Erect clusters of yellow-green flowers in summer, followed by red fruit. Good choice for naturalistic landscaping in poor soil.

R. cotinus. See *Cotinus coggygria*

R. glabra. SMOOTH SUMAC. Deciduous shrub or small tree. Zones 31, 32, 34–45. Native to much of North America. Upright to 10 ft., sometimes treelike to 20 ft. In the wild, spreads by underground roots to form large patches. Looks much like *R. typhina*, but usually grows lower and does not have velvety branches. Leaves divided into 11–23 rather narrow, 2–5-in.-long, toothed leaflets, deep green above and whitish beneath; turn scarlet in fall. Inconspicuous flowers are followed by showy, erect clusters of scarlet fruit that remain on bare branches from fall well into winter. Garden use same as for *R. typhina*. 'Laciniata' has deeply cut, slashed leaflets, giving it a fernlike appearance.

R. typhina. STAGHORN SUMAC. Deciduous shrub or small tree. Zones 31, 32, 34–45. Upright to 15 ft. (sometimes 30 ft.) tall, spreading wider. Very similar to *R. glabra*, but branches are covered with short, velvety brown hairs and resemble a deer's antler "in velvet." Leaves divided into 11–31 toothed, 5-in.-long leaflets; foliage is deep green above, grayish beneath, turns rich red in fall. Tiny greenish blossoms in 4–8-in.-long clusters appear in early summer; these are followed by clusters of fuzzy crimson fruit that lasts all winter, gradually turning brown. 'Laciniata', with deeply cut leaflets, does not grow quite as large as the species and is said to have richer fall color.

Both *R. typhina* and *R. glabra* take extreme heat and cold. Big divided leaves give tropical effect; fall show is brilliant (for best effect, plant among evergreens). Bare branches make fine winter silhouette; fruit is decorative. Both species will grow in large containers. Their aggressive colonization by root suckers can be a problem, especially in small gardens.

ABOUT THE ITCHY RHUS RELATIVES

Poison ivy and poison oak were once members of *Rhus*, but they have now been reclassified as *Toxicodendron radicans* and *T. diversilobum*, respectively. Both can cause severe dermatitis on contact; even breathing smoke from burning plants can be harmful. If either plant is on your property (the three-leaflet leaves turn bright red in fall), destroy it with chemical brush killer.

RIBBON GRASS. See PHALARIS arundinacea

RIBES

CURRANT, GOOSEBERRY

Grossulariaceae (Saxifragaceae)

EVERGREEN OR DECIDUOUS SHRUBS

🌿 ZONES VARY BY SPECIES

☼ ◐ FULL SUN OR PARTIAL SHADE

🌢 MODERATE WATER

Ribes

Those without spines are called currants; those with spines are known as gooseberries. The following species are grown ornamentally (though some bear edible fruit); see Currant and Gooseberry for strictly fruiting types. Members of this tribe are still banned in a few areas where white pines grow, because they are alternate hosts to white pine blister rust.

R

R. alpinum. ALPINE CURRANT. Deciduous. Zones 34–45. Native to Europe. Dense, twiggy growth to 4–5 ft. (rarely taller). Roundish, toothed, lobed, ½–1½-in.-wide leaves appear very early in spring. Yellow flowers and fruit not showy. Good hedge. Dwarf forms are 'Green Mound' and gold-leafed 'Aureum'.

R. nigrum. BLACK CURRANT. Deciduous. Zones 34, 36, 38–43. To 6 ft. tall, with three-lobed, deep green, oddly scented leaves. Drooping clusters of whitish flowers turn to juicy, shiny black fruits with blackberry-currant (sweet-tart) flavor. Fruit used in jams, jellies, sauces. Rust-immune varieties include 'Consort', 'Coronet', and 'Crusader'.

R. odoratum. CLOVE CURRANT. Deciduous. Zones 34–45. To 6 ft. high and as wide. Bright green leaves have 3–5 toothed lobes, turn purple and red in autumn. Native to the Midwest and High Plains. Flowers have carnation fragrance. Old variety 'Crandall' has large, shiny black fruit with the rich, sweet-tart flavor of *R. nigrum.*

R. sanguineum. PINK WINTER CURRANT, RED FLOWERING CURRANT. Deciduous. Zones 32, 34, 37, 39. Native from British Columbia to northern California. To 4–12 ft. tall, with 2½-in.-wide, maplelike leaves. Blooms in spring, producing small, deep pink to red flowers, 10–30 in each 2–4-in.-long, drooping cluster. Blue-black berries have a whitish bloom. Most commonly sold is *R. s. glutinosum* (more southerly in origin), with clusters of 15–40 flowers; pink, red, and white varieties are available. 'King Edward VII' has dark red flowers. Needs excellent drainage where summers are warm and moist or humid.

RICINUS communis

	CASTOR BEAN
	Euphorbiaceae
	SHRUB USUALLY TREATED AS ANNUAL
⚡	ALL ZONES
☼	FULL SUN
🌢	REGULAR WATER
⬥	SEEDS (OR BEANS) ARE HIGHLY POISONOUS

Ricinus communis

Bold and striking plant. Can provide tall screen or leafy background in a hurry; grows to 6–15 ft. in a season. Should not be planted in areas where small children play—the poisonous seeds are attractive. Foliage or seeds occasionally cause severe contact allergies as well. To prevent seed formation, pinch off the burrlike seed capsules while they are small.

Large-lobed leaves are 1–3 ft. across on vigorous young plants, smaller on older plants. Unimpressive small, white flowers are borne in clusters on foot-high stalks in summer, followed by attractive prickly husks that contain seeds. Grown commercially for castor oil extracted from seeds. Many horticultural varieties: 'Carmencita' has dark red-bronze leaves and red flowers; 'Dwarf Red Spire' is lower-growing plant (to 6 ft.) with red leaves and seedpods; Gibsonii' is a dwarf (to 4 ft.) with dark stems and dark reddish purple leaves with a metallic sheen; 'Zanzibarensis' has very large green leaves.

ROBINIA

	LOCUST
	Fabaceae (Leguminosae)
	DECIDUOUS SHRUBS OR TREES
⚡	ZONES VARY BY SPECIES
☼	FULL SUN
🌢	MODERATE TO LITTLE WATER
⬥	BARK, LEAVES, AND SEEDS ARE POISONOUS IF INGESTED

Robinia

Leaves divided like feathers into many roundish leaflets; clusters of sweet pea–shaped, white or pink flowers midspring to early summer.

Locusts are fairly fast growing and well adapted to dry, hot conditions. Will take poor soil. Drawbacks: wood is brittle, roots aggressive, plants often spread by suckers.

R. ambigua. Zones 31, 32, 34–43. Tree. Name given to hybrids between *R. pseudoacacia* and *R. viscosa,* a seldom-grown pink-flowering locust. The following are best-known varieties:

'Decaisneana'. To 40–50 ft. tall, 20 ft. wide. Flowers like those of *R. pseudoacacia* but pale pink.

'Idahoensis'. IDAHO LOCUST. Tree of moderately fast growth to shapely 40 ft. Bright magenta rose flowers in 8-in. clusters; one of showiest of locusts in bloom.

'Purple Robe'. Resembles 'Idahoensis' but has darker, purple-pink flowers, reddish bronze new growth; blooms 2 weeks earlier and over a longer period.

R. hispida. BRISTLY LOCUST. Zones 31, 32, 34–41. Shrub. Native to the southeastern U.S. Erect, to 8 ft. high, spreading by suckers to 10 ft. wide. Bristly stems, deep green leaves to 1 ft. long, divided into 9–13 oval leaflets. Drooping clusters of rosy pink flowers in late spring to early summer, followed by brownish seedpods.

R. pseudoacacia. BLACK LOCUST. Zones 31, 32, 34–43. Tree. Native to eastern and midwestern U.S. Fast growth to 75 ft., with rather open and sparse-branching habit. Deeply furrowed brown bark. Thorny branchlets. Leaves divided into 7–19 leaflets 1–2 in. long. Flowers white, fragrant, ½–¾ in. long, in dense, hanging clusters 4–8 in. long. Beanlike, 4-in.-long pods turn brown and hang on tree all winter.

Little valued in its native territory except as a source of honey and fence posts, it has been widely planted (and has subsequently escaped) in much of the western U.S. and in Europe. It manufactures its own fertilizer through nitrogen-fixing root nodule bacteria and can colonize the poorest soil. Given some pruning and training in its early years, it can be a truly handsome flowering tree, but locust borer limits its usefulness in many regions. Locust leaf miner is also a damaging pest in some areas.

Often used as street tree, but not good in narrow parking strips or under power lines. Wood is extremely hard; suckers are difficult to prune out where not wanted. Varieties include the following:

'Frisia'. New growth nearly orange; mature leaves yellow, turning greener in summer heat. Thorns and new wood are red.

'Pyramidalis' ('Fastigiata'). Very narrow, columnar tree.

'Tortuosa'. Slow growing, with twisted branches. Few flowers in blossom clusters.

'Umbraculifera'. Dense, round headed. Usually grafted 6–8 ft. high on another locust to create a living green lollipop. Very few flowers.

ROCKCRESS. See ARABIS

RODGERSIA

	Saxifragaceae
	PERENNIALS
⚡	ZONES 32, 34–41
☼	PARTIAL SHADE
🌢	AMPLE WATER

Rodgersia

Native to China, Japan. Large plants with imposing leaves and clustered tiny flowers in plumes somewhat like those of astilbe. Primary feature is handsome foliage, which often takes on bronze tones in late summer. Plants spread by thick rhizomes, need rich soil. Can tolerate full sun in cool-summer climates. The different species hybridize freely. Dormant in winter; provide winter mulch in cold climates. Showy in moist woodland or bog gardens.

R. aesculifolia. To 6 ft. Leaves are divided like fingers of hand into five to seven toothed, 10-in. leaflets; they resemble those of horsechestnut (*Aesculus*). Shaggy brown hairs on flower stalks, leaf stems, major leaf veins. White flowers.

R. henricii. Resembles *R. aesculifolia,* but leaves taper to a long point and flowers are purplish red.

R. pinnata. To 4 ft. Leaves have five to nine 8-in. leaflets. Red flowers.

R. podophylla. To 5 ft. Coppery green leaves divided into five 10-in. leaflets. Creamy flowers.

R. sambucifolia. To 3 ft. Leaves have up to 11 leaflets. Flat-topped flower clusters are white or pink.

R. tabularis. See *Astilboides tabularis.*

ROHDEA japonica

CHINA LILY, SACRED LILY

Liliaceae

PERENNIAL

ZONES 31, 32, 34, 39

PARTIAL TO FULL SHADE

REGULAR WATER

Rohdea japonica

This species is grown for its rosettes of leathery, dark green leaves that are produced in handsome, hostalike clumps. The leaves, which are evergreen, are lance shaped to somewhat rounded and reach 1–1½ ft. long. Plants bear dense spikes of greenish white, bell-shaped flowers in spring that usually are hidden among the leaves. The flowers are followed by red berries. Use China lily in shade and woodland gardens. It can also be grown in containers.

ROSA

ROSE

Rosaceae

DECIDUOUS OR EVERGREEN SHRUBS

ALL ZONES, EXCEPT AS NOTED

FULL SUN OR LIGHT SHADE

REGULAR WATER, EXCEPT AS NOTED

Rosa

The rose is undoubtedly the best-loved flower and most widely planted shrub in temperate parts of the world. Although mostly deciduous, can be evergreen in mild climates. Centuries of hybridizing have brought us the widest possible range of form and color. There are foot-high miniatures, tree-smothering climbers, flowers the size of a thumbnail or a salad plate, and all possible variations in between. Red, pink, and white are traditional rose colors, but you also find cream, yellow, orange, and blended and bicolor flowers, as well as magenta, purple, lavender, and even tan and brown.

Growing roses is not difficult, provided you choose types and varieties suited to your climate, buy healthy plants, locate and plant them properly, and attend to their basic needs—water, nutrients, any necessary pest and disease control, and pruning. Despite the delicate appearance of their blooms, roses are often quite resilient plants.

CLIMATE

Every year, the American Rose Society rates modern roses (and an increasing number of old roses) on a scale of 1 to 10. The higher the rating, based on a national average of scores, the better the rose. The highest rated roses are likely to perform well in most climates and so are good choices for novice growers. But a rating does not tell the entire story: a rose with a low rating may do especially well in certain regions but fail in others. The following general tips will help guide your selection.

In cool-summer areas, you should, if possible, avoid varieties having an unusually great number of petals. Many of these tend to "ball," opening poorly or not at all. Also, in the absence of heat, dark-colored flowers may appear "muddy" rather than clear and vibrant, while pastel colors are usually clear and attractive. The overcast and fog prevalent in many cool-summer areas also encourage foliar diseases—primarily mildew, rust, and black spot. Choose varieties noted for disease resistance; then be sure to plant them in open areas where air circulation is good.

In cold-winter areas (Zones 34–45), the widely marketed modern roses—hybrid teas, grandifloras, and floribundas—are not completely hardy; some form of winter protection is needed to guarantee their survival from year to year (see "Winter protection," page 388). Many of the old roses (usually those that flower in spring only) and a number of the species and their hybrids survive winters in the coldest zones with scant or no protection from the cold.

In any region, the best place to see roses suitable for your climate is a local municipal or private rose garden. The varieties that are performing well are obviously good choices for your garden.

BUYING PLANTS

All roses are available as bare-root plants from late fall through early spring. Either plant in fall before ground freezes (then protect plants over winter), or plant in early spring after soil has thawed.

The majority of modern roses sold are budded plants: growth eyes of the desired varieties are budded onto understock plants that furnish the root systems. The understocks are carefully selected to promote rapid top growth of the desired roses and make root systems capable of thriving in a wide range of soils and climates. However, many old roses, species and their hybrids, and virtually all miniatures are "own-root" plants raised from cuttings. Ultimately, it makes no difference whether the plant is budded or own-root: either can grow well and produce fine flowers. Budded plants do offer more uniform root quality than you find among own-root plants, and budded plants often are larger at time of purchase than are own-root ones. But both kinds will be equally husky within a year or two. Own-root roses have one advantage, however: if an own-root plant is killed to the ground by cold (or mowed down by accident), it will regrow from the roots as the rose you want, not as understock. Under similar conditions, regrowth from roots of the budded plant will be the understock rose rather than the desired variety.

Bare-root plants are the best buy, and they are graded 1, 1½, or 2 according to strict standards. Plants graded 1 and 1½ are the most satisfactory, number 1 being the best. Number 2 plants may take longer to develop into decent bushes than the huskier numbers 1 and 1½. Retail nurseries and mail-order suppliers of modern roses usually offer only number 1 plants, and they will often replace plants that fail to grow. Old roses, shrub roses, and species roses (most commonly available by mail order) may be offered as budded plants that conform to the numbered grading standards, but some growers offer own-root (not budded) plants that may or may not be up to number 1 size. Catalogs usually state what size plant to expect.

During bare-root planting time, retail nurseries also may offer a selection of "boxed" roses with root systems encased in cardboard cartons. Supermarkets, discount stores, and some retail nurseries sell dormant roses that have roots encased in moist material and enclosed in long, narrow bags. These packaged roses may be good value, but you should buy them as soon as they appear for sale. Those that are displayed indoors on store shelves may be dried out or encouraged into premature growth by the indoor heating. Be prepared, too, for a number of these bargain roses to be mislabeled.

Grandiflora Rose 'Camelot'

If you wish to plant roses during their growing season, you can buy roses growing in containers. This way, you can see and evaluate unfamiliar varieties before purchase and quickly fill in gaps in your garden. But container roses are more expensive than bare-root plants. Best time to buy container-grown roses is in mid- to late spring—when plants are fairly well rooted in the containers and can be set out before stressful summer heat arrives. For standard bush and climbing roses, look for robust plants growing in large (preferably 5-gal.) containers; this guarantees that root systems will have received little or no pruning to fit the container. Also, try

R

to buy only roses planted in containers toward the end of the most recent dormant season; they generally will be in better condition than plants that have been in containers for a year or more. Avoid plants showing considerable dead or twiggy growth. Miniature roses usually are sold in containers that range from 4-in. pots to 2-gal. cans. Healthy new growth and foliage are signs of a good miniature plant, regardless of container size.

The presence of a plant patent number on a variety's name tag is no assurance of quality. It simply means that for a variety's first 17 years in commerce, the patent holder receives a royalty on each plant sold. Many fine roses that bear no patent number on name tags once were patented but have been in commerce for longer than the 17-year patent lifespan.

LOCATION AND PLANTING

For best results, plant roses where they will receive full sun all day. Avoid planting where roots of trees or shrubs will steal water and nutrients intended for roses. To lessen any problem with foliar diseases, plant roses where air circulates freely (but not in path of regular, strong winds). Generous spacing between plants will also aid air circulation. How far apart to plant varies according to the growth habit of the roses and according to climate. The colder the winter and shorter the growing season, the smaller the bushes will be; where growing season is long and winters are mild, bushes can attain greater size. But some varieties are naturally small, others tall and massive—and those relative size differences will hold in any climate. In Zones 34–45, you might plant most vigorous sorts 3 ft. apart, whereas the same roses could require 6-ft. spacing in milder zones.

Soil for roses should drain reasonably well; if it does not, the best alternative is to plant in raised beds. Dig soil deeply, incorporating organic matter such as ground bark, peat moss, or compost; this preparation will help aerate dense clay soils and will improve moisture retention of sandy soils. Add complete fertilizer to soil at the same time, and dig supplemental phosphorus and potash into planting holes; this gets nutrients down at the level where roots can use them.

Healthy, ready-to-plant bare-root roses should have plump, fresh-looking canes (branches) and roots. Plants that have dried out slightly in shipping or in nursery can be revived by burying them, tops and all, for a few days in moist soil, sand, or sawdust. Just before planting any bare-root rose, it is a good idea to immerse entire plant in water for several hours to be certain all canes and roots are plumped up. Plant according to directions for bare-root planting (see page 484), making sure that holes are large enough that you can spread out roots without bending or cutting them back. Just before planting, cut back broken canes and broken roots to below breaks. Set plant in hole so that bud union ("knob" from which canes grow) is just above soil level. Even growers in cold-winter climates find this successful, and plants produce more canes when planted this way, as long as plants are well protected during winter. After you have planted a rose and watered it well, mound a mixture of ½ soil and ½ peat moss or sawdust over bud union and around canes to conserve moisture. Gradually (and carefully) remove soil or other material when leaves begin to expand.

If you plan to plant new roses in ground where existing bushes have been growing for 5 or more years, dig generous (at least 1½-ft.-wide, 1½-ft.-deep) planting holes and replace old soil with fresh soil from another part of the garden. A condition known as "specific replant disease" inhibits growth of new roses planted directly in soil of established rose gardens.

ROUTINE CARE

All roses require water, nutrients, some pruning, and, at some point in their lifetimes, pest and disease control. (Exceptions are some antique and species roses that thrive on little water once established.)

Water. For best performance, the most popular garden roses need watering at all times during the growing season. Inadequate water slows or halts growth and bloom. Water deeply so that entire root system is moistened. How often to water depends on soil type and weather. Big, well-established plants need more water than newly set plants, but you will need to water new plants more frequently to get them established.

Basin flooding is a simple way to water individual rose plants, and if you have a drip irrigation system, many plants can be watered this way at one time. If you sprinkle, do it early in the day to be sure foliage dries off by nightfall. Even if you irrigate in basins, give plants an occasional sprinkling to clean dust off foliage (if rain doesn't do it for you).

Mulch, spread 2–3 in. deep, will help save water, prevent soil surface from baking hard, keep soil cool in summer, deter weed growth, and contribute to healthy soil structure (well aerated, permeable by water and roots).

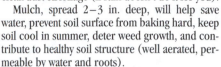

Floribunda Rose 'Cathedral'

Nutrients. Regular applications of fertilizer will produce the most gratifying results. Give first feeding just as growth begins. Time fertilizer application in relation to bloom period. Ideal time to make subsequent feedings is when a blooming period has ended and new growth is just beginning for next cycle of bloom. Depending on expected arrival of freezing temperatures, stop feeding in late summer or fall, generally about 6 weeks before earliest normal hard frost.

Dry commercial fertilizer, applied to soil, is most frequently used. A variation on that type is slow-release fertilizer that provides nutrients over prolonged period; follow directions on package for amount and frequency of applications. Liquid fertilizers are useful in smaller gardens utilizing basin watering. Most liquid fertilizers can also be sprayed on rose leaves, which absorb some nutrients immediately.

Pest and disease control. Certain controls usually are needed during the growing season.

Principal rose pests are aphids, spider mites, and (in some areas) Japanese beetle, rose midge, and thrips. If you don't want to rely on natural predators, start controlling aphids when they first appear in spring and repeat as needed until they are gone or their numbers severely reduced. Spider mites are hot-weather pests capable of defoliating and weakening plants—especially those that are underwatered and weak. Best control for voracious Japanese beetle is at the grub stage. Likewise, rose midge larvae in the soil are the more vulnerable life-cycle stage, susceptible to applications of diazinon in granular or liquid drench form. Thrips do their damage inside flower buds, discoloring petals or disfiguring them so that buds may not open. Contact insecticide sprays can't reach most thrips hidden in petals; systemic insecticides are more successful.

Powdery mildew, rust, and black spot are the Big Three of foliar diseases. First line of defense for all three is thorough cleanup of all dead leaves and other debris during the dormant season; this is simplest right after you have pruned plants. Then, before new growth begins, spray plants and soil with dormant-season spray of horticultural oil or lime sulfur (calcium polysulfide). This will destroy many disease organisms (as well as insect eggs) that might live over winter to reinfect plants in spring. During the growing season, apply controls for diseases prevalent in your area. Preventive measures usually are recommended for disease control; unchecked infections can weaken plants, especially if defoliation occurs from rust or black spot.

Two other foliar diseases, anthracnose and downy mildew, can occur to a lesser extent on roses. Anthracnose is similar to black spot and responds to the same treatment. Downy mildew begins in the upper reaches of a plant after leaves have fully formed, appearing in moist weather when temperatures are below 80°F/27°C. Foliage of infected plants shows irregular, purplish blotches, then turns yellow (sometimes with patches of green remaining) and falls off. On stems, the fungus shows as purplish mottling; infected stems are likely to die by the end of the year without treatment. To combat downy mildew during the growing season, spray infected plants with a fungicide containing zinc and manganese. Where the disease has appeared, use a dormant spray containing zinc or copper after winter pruning and rose garden cleanup.

Chlorosis—evidenced by leaves turning light green to yellow while veins remain dark green—is not a disease but a symptom, usually of iron deficiency. Iron chelate corrects chlorosis most quickly; iron sulfate also is effective but slower to act.

Leaves that show irregular patterning in yellow or cream indicate that the plant is infected with a mosaic virus. Some plants show the virus consistently; others display symptoms just occasionally. Although plants may appear to grow with vigor, virus infection does impair overall strength and productivity—and it can make foliage unsightly. Fortunately, it is not transferable from plant to plant by insects or pruning; it is transmitted in propagation—from infected rootstock or budwood. Commercial rose producers now are diligently working to eliminate virused stock. If you have a virused plant that is growing poorly or is unattractive, remove it from the garden.

DISEASE-PREVENTIVE SPRAY

To prevent black spot and prevent or control powdery mildew, spray roses every 4–7 days with a solution of 1 tablespoon baking soda to 1 gallon of water, with a few drops of insecticidal soap or horticultural oil to help it stick.

Pruning. Done properly each year, pruning will contribute to the health and longevity of your rose plants. Sensible pruning is based on several facts about the growth of roses. First, blooms are produced on new growth. Unless pruning promotes strong new growth, flowers will come on spindly outer twigs and be of poor quality. Second, the more healthy wood you retain, the bigger the plant will be; and the bigger the plant, the more flowers it can produce. Nutrients are stored in woody canes, so a larger plant is a stronger plant. Therefore, prune conservatively; never chop down a vigorous 6-ft. bush to 1½-ft. stubs unless you want only a few huge blooms for exhibition. (Exception: in cooler parts of the Northeast, where plant may freeze back to its winter protection, you will remove dead wood in spring and may be left with equivalent of severely pruned plant.) Third, the best pruning time for most roses (certain climbers and shrub types excepted) is at the end of dormant season (late February and early March) when growth buds begin to swell. Exact time will vary according to locality.

General pruning guidelines. The following pruning practices apply to all roses except certain shrub and species roses. Special instructions for pruning those roses are included later in this section.

Use sharp pruning shears; make all cuts as shown in the Practical Gardening Dictionary under Pruning Cuts. Remove wood that is obviously dead and wood that has no healthy growth coming from it; branches that cross through the plant's center and any that rub against larger canes; branches that make bush appear lopsided; and any old and unproductive canes that strong new ones have replaced during past season. Cut back growth produced during previous year, making cuts above outward-facing buds (except for very spreading varieties: some cuts to inside buds will promote more height without producing many crossing branches). As a general rule, remove one-third to no more than one-half the length of previous season's growth (except when removing winter-damaged canes, as noted above). The ideal result is a V-shaped bush that has a relatively open center.

If any suckers (growth produced from understock, not the rose variety growing on it) are present, completely remove them. Dig down to where suckers grow from understock and pull them off with downward motion; that removes basal growth buds that would have produced additional suckers in subsequent years. Let the wound air-dry before you replace the soil around it.

Be certain you are removing a sucker rather than a new cane growing from the bud union of the budded variety. Usually you can note a distinct difference in foliage size and shape, as well as in size of thorns, on sucker growth. If in doubt, let the presumed sucker grow until you can establish its difference from cane. A sucker's flowers will be different; a flowerless, climbing cane from a bush rose is almost certainly a sucker.

Consider cutting flowers as a form of pruning. Cut off enough stem to support flower in vase, but don't deprive plant of too much foliage. Leave on plant a stem with at least two sets of five-leaflet leaves. Prune to outward-growing bud or to five-leaflet leaf.

The most widely planted modern roses—hybrid teas and grandifloras—can be pruned successfully according to these guidelines. A few additional tips apply to other popular types:

Floribunda, polyantha, and many shrub roses are grown for quantities of flowers, so amount of bloom rather than quality of individual flower is the objective. Cut back previous season's growth only by one-fourth, and leave as many strong new canes and stems as plant produced. Most produce more canes per bush than do hybrid teas and grandifloras. If you have a hedge of one variety, cut back all plants to uniform height.

Climbing roses may be divided into two general types: those that bloom in spring only (including a large category known as natural climbers, discussed in "Climbing roses," page 390), and those that bloom off and on in other seasons as well as in spring (including the very popular climbing sports of hybrid tea roses). All climbers should be left unpruned for the first 2 or 3 years after planting; remove only dead, weak, and twiggy wood, allowing plants to get established and produce their long, flexible canes. Most bloom comes from lateral branches that grow from long canes, and most of those flowering branches develop when long canes are spread out horizontally (as along a fence). Types that bloom only in spring produce strong new growth after they flower, and that new growth bears flowers the following spring. Prune these climbers just after they bloom, removing oldest canes that show no signs of strong new growth. Repeat-flowering climbers (many are climbing sports of bush varieties) are pruned at the same time you'd prune bush roses in your locality. Remove oldest, unproductive canes and any weak, twiggy growth; cut back lateral branches on remaining canes to within two or three buds from canes.

Pillar roses are not quite bush or climber. They produce tall, somewhat flexible canes that bloom profusely without having to be trained horizontally. Prune pillar roses according to general guidelines for bush roses.

Tree roses, more properly called "standards," are an artificial creation: a bush rose budded onto a 2–3-ft.-high understock stem. Be sure to stake trunk securely to prevent its breaking from weight of bush it supports. A ½-in. metal pipe makes good permanent stake; use cross tie between stake and trunk to hold them secure. General pruning guidelines apply, with particular attention to maintaining symmetrical plant.

Miniature roses should be pruned back to at least half the height they attained during the previous year, removing all weak and twiggy stems. Some growers prune miniatures severely—back to the lowest outward-facing growth buds on the previous year's new stems.

Winter protection. Where winter low temperatures regularly reach 10°F/−12°C and lower, some winter protection is needed for nearly all modern roses. Low temperatures can kill exposed canes; repeated freezing and thawing will kill canes by rupturing cells; and winter winds can fatally desiccate exposed canes because plants are unable to replace moisture from frozen soil.

A healthy, well-ripened plant withstands harsh winters better than a weak and actively growing one. Prepare plants for winter by timing your last fertilizer application so that bushes will have ceased putting on new growth by expected date of first sharp frost. Leave the last crop of blooms on plants to form hips (fruits), which will aid the ripening process by stopping growth. Keep plants well watered until soil freezes.

Polyantha Rose 'Margo Koster'

After a couple of hard freezes have occurred and night temperatures seem to remain consistently below freezing, mound soil over base of each bush to height of 1 ft. Get soil from another part of garden; do not scoop soil from around roses, exposing surface roots. Cut excessively long canes back to 2–4 ft. (the lower figure applies in the colder northern regions); then, with soft twine, tie canes together to keep them from whipping around in wind. When mound has frozen, cover it with evergreen boughs, straw, or other fairly lightweight material that will act as insulation to keep mounds frozen. Your objective is to prevent alternate freezing and thawing of mound (and canes it covers), maintaining plant at constant temperature of 15 to 20°F/−9 to −7°C. A 3−4-ft.-high wire-mesh cylinder filled with noncompacting insulating material (such as straw, hay, oak leaves, or pine needles) may preserve much of the cane growth it encloses.

Remove protection in early spring when you are reasonably certain hard frosts will not recur. Gradually remove soil mounds as they thaw; do it carefully to avoid breaking new growth that may have begun sprouting under the soil. Use of manufactured Styrofoam rose cones eliminates the labor of mounding and unmounding; just a bit of soil around the cone's base plus a rock or brick on top will hold it in place over the bush. Disadvantages are cost and limited availability of cones; the need to cut rose down to fit cone over it, perhaps requiring more severe pruning than is usually necessary; moisture condensation inside cone as days begin warming. To avoid condensation problem, get cones with removable tops that can be opened on warm late-winter days.

You should mound climbing roses in same manner, but in addition you need to protect all of their canes. Where winter lows range from −10 to 5°F/−23 to −15°C, wrap canes in burlap stuffed with straw or similar material for insulation. Where temperatures normally go below −10°F/ −23°C, remove canes from their support, gently bend them to ground, secure them in that position, and cover with soil. A wiser plan in such climates is to plant only climbers known to be successful in your area or reputed to be hardy in similar climates.

Standards (tree roses) may be insulated in the same manner as for climbers, but they still may not survive, since the head of the tree is the most exposed. Some rosarians wrap with straw and burlap, then construct a plywood box to cover the insulated plant. Others dig their standards each year and pack the roots loosely in soil or other medium in a cool garage, basement, or shed, then replant in spring. A simpler technique is to grow standards in large containers and move them in fall to cool shed or garage where temperatures won't drop below 10°F/−12°C.

TYPES OF ROSES

A renewed interest in old roses, continued developments of new hybrids, and breeding programs directed toward producing landscape shrubs have led to a greatly expanded offering of roses to the gardening public. For convenience, the following sections describe three broad categories: modern roses, old roses, and species and species hybrids.

Modern roses. Types described below constitute the majority of roses offered for sale and planted by hundreds of thousands each year. Those that have been All-America Rose Selections, recognized on the basis of their performance in nationwide test gardens, are indicated by "AARS"; those with an asterisk (*) before their names have been rated 8.0 or higher by the American Rose Society.

Hybrid teas. This, the most popular class of rose, outsells all other types combined. Flowers are large and shapely, generally produced one to a stem on plants that range from 2 ft. to 6 ft. or more, depending on the variety and climate. Many thousands of varieties have been produced since the first rose in the class, 'La France', appeared in 1867; hundreds are cataloged, and new ones appear each year. The most popular ones are listed in the following color groups:

Red: 'Chrysler Imperial' (AARS), *'Mr. Lincoln' (AARS), *'Olympiad' (AARS).

Pink: 'Bewitched' (AARS), 'Brigadoon' (AARS), *'Century Two', *'Color Magic' (AARS), *'Dainty Bess' (single), 'Duet' (AARS), *'First Prize' (AARS), *'Miss All-American Beauty' (AARS), 'Perfume Delight' (AARS), *'Royal Highness' (AARS), 'Secret' (AARS), 'Sheer Bliss' (AARS), *'Tiffany' (AARS), *'Touch of Class' (AARS).

Multicolors, blends: 'Broadway' (AARS), 'Chicago Peace', *'Double Delight' (AARS), *'Granada' (AARS), 'Just Joey', 'Medallion' (AARS), 'Rio Samba' (AARS), 'Seashell' (AARS), 'Voodoo' (AARS).

Orange, orange tones: 'Brandy' (AARS), *'Folklore', *'Fragrant Cloud', 'Tropicana' (AARS).

Yellow: *'Elina', 'Graceland', 'King's Ransom' (AARS), 'Oregold' (AARS), 'Midas Touch' (AARS), *'Peace' (AARS), 'Summer Sunshine', 'Sunbright'.

White: *'Garden Party' (AARS), 'Honor' (AARS), 'John F. Kennedy', *'Pascali' (AARS), *'Pristine'.

Lavender: 'Blue Girl', 'Blue Ribbon', 'Heirloom', *'Lady X', *'Paradise' (AARS).

Grandifloras. Vigorous plants, sometimes 8−10 ft. tall, with hybrid tea−type flowers borne singly or in long-stemmed clusters. Some are derived from crosses between hybrid teas and floribundas; others are just extra-vigorous, cluster-flowering segregates from ordinary hybrid tea ancestry. They're good for mass color effect, for number of cuttable flowers produced per plant, and as background or barrier plants.

Red: 'Love' (AARS), 'Olé'.

Pink, pink blends: *'Aquarius' (AARS), 'Camelot' (AARS), *'Earth Song', *'Pink Parfait' (AARS), *'Queen Elizabeth' (AARS), *'Sonia', *'Tournament of Roses' (AARS).

Orange, blends: 'Arizona' (AARS), 'Montezuma', 'Solitude' (AARS).

Yellow: *'Gold Medal'.

White: 'White Lightnin' (AARS).

Lavender: 'Lagerfeld'.

Floribundas. Originally developed from hybrid teas and polyanthas (see below), these are noted for producing quantities of flowers in clusters on vigorous and bushy plants. Plant and flower sizes are smaller than those of most hybrid teas. Some have flowers of elegant hybrid tea shape; others are more informal. These are plants for providing mass color. Use for informal hedges, low borders and barriers, as container plants.

Red: *'Europeana' (AARS), 'Impatient', *'Sarabande' (AARS), *'Showbiz' (AARS), *'Trumpeter'.

Pink: *'Betty Prior', *'Bridal Pink', 'Cherish' (AARS), 'Gene Boerner' (AARS), 'Pleasure' (AARS), *'Sexy Rexy', 'Sweet Inspiration' (AARS), *'Sweet Vivien'.

Orange, blends: *'Apricot Nectar' (AARS), *'Cathedral', *'First Edition' (AARS), 'Gingersnap', 'Marina', *'Orangeade', 'Redgold' (AARS), *'Summer Fashion'.

Yellow: *'Sun Flare' (AARS), *'Sunsprite'.

White: *'Evening Star', *'French Lace' (AARS), *'Iceberg', *'Ivory Fashion' (AARS).

Lavender: *'Angel Face' (AARS), 'Intrigue' (AARS).

Polyanthas. Original members of this class appeared in the late 19th century, the result of crosses with *R. multiflora*. Small flowers (under 2 in. across) come in large sprays; plants are vigorous and usually low growing, nearly everblooming, and quite disease resistant. 'Margo Koster' has coral orange, very double flowers that resemble ranunculus; it has sported to produce color variants in white, pink, orange scarlet, and red. 'The Fairy' produces huge clusters of small, light pink flowers on a plant that can reach 4 ft. high. 'China Doll' is a knee-high plant with larger, deeper pink flowers in smaller clusters. With light pruning two 19th-century classics make sizable bushes that resemble bushy Noisettes (see under "Old roses," page 390). 'Cécile Brunner' (often called the Sweetheart Rose) has light pink flowers of perfect hybrid tea form; 'Perle d'Or' (sometimes called Yellow Cécile Brunner) is similar except for its apricot orange flower color.

Miniature roses. These are perfect replicas of modern hybrid teas and floribundas but plant size is reduced to 1−1½ ft. (grown in the ground) with flowers and foliage in proportion. Derived in part from *R. chinensis minima* (presumably through its forms 'Rouletii' and 'Pompon de Paris'), they come in all colors of modern hybrid teas. Plants are everblooming. Grow them outdoors in containers, window boxes, and rock gardens or as border and bedding plants. You can grow them indoors: pot in rich soil in 6-in. (or larger) containers, and locate in a cool, bright window. Miniatures are hardier than hybrid teas but still need winter protection in Zones 34−45. Shallow roots demand regular water and fertilizer, mulch. Nearly all are own-root, cutting-grown plants.

Many new miniatures appear on the market each year. Among the best are these, all rated 8.5 or higher:

Red, orange: 'Orange Sunblaze', 'Peggy', 'Starina'.

Pink: 'Coral Sprite', 'Cupcake', 'Millie Walters', 'Pierrine', 'Pink Meillandina'.

Blends: 'Dreamglo', 'Earthquake', 'Jean Kenneally', 'Little Artist', 'Little Jackie', 'Loving Touch', 'Magic Carrousel', 'Minnie Pearl', 'Party Girl', 'Rainbow's End', 'Shortcake', 'Wow'.

Yellow: 'Morain', 'My Sunshine', 'Rise 'n' Shine'.

White: 'Pacesetter', 'Snowbride'.

Lavender, purple: 'Ruby Pendant', 'Winsome'.

Climbing roses. Modern climbing roses may be divided into two general categories: natural climbers (large flowered, except for miniatures) and climbing sports of bush roses (hybrid teas, grandifloras, floribundas, polyanthas, miniatures). Here are popular varieties of natural climbers:

Red: *'Altissimo' (single), 'Blaze', *'Don Juan', *'Dortmund', *'Dublin Bay', 'Solo', 'Tempo'.

Pink: 'Blossomtime', *'Clair Matin', *'Galway Bay', *'Hi Ho' (miniature), *'Jeanne Lajoie' (miniature), 'New Dawn', *'Pink Perpétué', *'Rhonda'.

Orange, blends: *'America' (AARS), *'Compassion', *'Handel', 'Joseph's Coat', *'Royal Sunset', 'Spectra'.

Yellow: 'Golden Showers' (AARS), 'Royal Gold'.

White: *'City of York', 'Lace Cascade', 'White Dawn'.

Here are popular varieties of climbing sports:

Red: 'Cl. Chrysler Imperial', 'Cl. Crimson Glory'.

Pink: 'Cl. Cécile Brunner' (polyantha), 'Cl. China Doll' (polyantha), 'Cl. Dainty Bess', 'Cl. First Prize', 'Cl. Queen Elizabeth'.

Orange, blends: 'Cl. Double Delight', 'Cl. Granada', 'Cl. Mrs. Sam McGredy', 'Cl. Peace'.

White: *'Cl. Iceberg'.

Shrub roses. Significant breeding is under way to develop roses for general landscape use. These are collectively known as shrub roses. Emphasis is on plants that will provide attractive floral displays (even good-looking individual blossoms), disease-resistant foliage, and individuals that will survive cold winters with no special protection. Mail-order rose specialists lead the way in offering these plants, but retail nurseries are offering them more and more. Here is an overview of types available.

Hybrid musk roses. These were developed in the first three decades of the 20th century from the multiflora rambler 'Trier', which was distantly descended from the musk rose through the Noisettes. The hybrid musks are large (6–8-ft.) shrubs or small climbers that will perform well in dappled or partial shade as well as in sun. Most are nearly everblooming, with fragrant, clustered flowers in white, yellow, buff, pink shades, red. Popular varieties include 'Buff Beauty', buff apricot; 'Cornelia', coral; 'Felicia', pink; 'Kathleen', single pink, like apple blossoms; 'Penelope', salmon; 'Will Scarlet', red.

English roses. This is a rapidly expanding group of hybrids. England's David Austin has bred various old roses (albas, centifolias, gallicas) with modern roses in order to capture the forms and fragrances of old roses in repeat-flowering plants that offer the color range of modern hybrids. The group is extremely varied and includes low shrubs as well as plants that are determined to be climbers regardless of pruning. Many have Shakespearean or Chaucerian names; over 80 are in commerce. Popular varieties include 'Abraham Darby', pink-yellow-apricot blend, upright to climbing plant; 'Charles Austin', apricot, bushy plant; 'Fair Bianca', creamy white, spreading bush; 'Gertrude Jekyll', deep pink, tall and upright; 'Graham Thomas', rich yellow, tall plant; 'Mary Rose', rose pink, tall and upright; 'Othello', dusky dark red, tall bush or climber.

Ground cover roses. A number of European and American breeders are producing roses that spread their canes widely but build up to no more than 2 ft.—perfect for covering slopes, forming traffic-proof covers on level ground, or for container culture. Vigor, disease resistance, profusion of bloom are the hallmarks of these roses. Examples are 'Essex', 'Flower Carpet', 'Nozomi', 'Pink Bells', 'Rosy Carpet'.

Hardy roses. Two breeding programs have produced numerous varieties that will survive northern winters with virtually no special protection. Some of them resemble floribundas and grandifloras; ancestries include various hardy species plus modern hybrid teas and floribundas. Many of these feature country names: 'Country Dancer', 'Hawkeye Belle', 'Maytime', 'Prairie Princess'. Others are mostly larger shrubs to small climbers, derived in part from *R. rugosa;* most are cluster flowered, like large floribundas. Many are named for explorers: 'Alexander Mackenzie', 'Henry Kelsey', 'John Cabot', 'William Baffin'.

Patio roses. Larger than miniatures, smaller than floribundas, these plants (mostly of European origin) are bushy, profuse flowering, usually no more than 2 ft. tall. They're good providers of mass color as border and container plants. Examples are 'Amorette' and 'Hakuun', white; 'Minilights', soft yellow; 'Pink Pollyanna', pink; 'Yellow Jacket', yellow.

Miniature Rose

Other shrub roses. Many modern shrub roses of complex ancestry can't be pigeonholed into categories according to species affiliation or specific characteristic. The plants may be spreading or upright; they are usually 3 ft. or greater in height, and their flowers come in small to large clusters. These include such gems as 'Alchymist'; 'Ballerina' (classed as hybrid musk but more like a giant polyantha); 'Erfurt'; the various Meidiland roses ('Bonica', 'Pink Meidiland', 'Red Meidiland', 'White Meidiland'); 'Pearl Drift'; 'Sally Holmes'; and 'Sea Foam'. Check individual descriptions of catalog offerings to find appealing candidates that meet your specific landscape needs.

Old roses. Among rosarians, the dividing line between old and modern roses is 1867—the year that the first hybrid tea was introduced. Old roses are varieties that belong to the various rose classes that existed prior to 1867 (even though some varieties in these classes were introduced as late as the early 20th century). Old roses may be divided into two categories. The old European roses comprise the albas, centifolias, damasks, gallicas, and moss roses—the oldest hybrid groups derived from species native to Europe and western Asia. Most flower only in spring; many are hardy in the coldest climates with little or no winter protection. The second group contains classes derived entirely or in part from East Asian roses: Chinas, Bourbons, damask perpetuals, hybrid perpetuals, Noisettes, and teas. Original China and tea roses were brought to Europe from eastern Asia; 19th-century hybridizers greatly increased their numbers and also developed the other classes from crosses with European roses. Repeat flowering is a characteristic of these classes; hardiness varies, but nearly all need winter protection in coldest zones.

Alba roses. Developed from *R. alba,* the White Rose of York, and associated with England's War of the Roses. Spring flowers range from single to very double, white to delicate pink. Upright plants are vigorous and long lived, with green wood and handsome, disease-resistant gray-green foliage. Garden varieties include white 'Alba Semiplena', 'Alba Maxima', and 'Mme. Legas de St. Germain' and these in shades of pink: 'Celestial', 'Félicité Parmentier', and 'Königin von Dänemark'. 'Great Maiden's Blush' bears pinkishwhite, richly scented flowers.

Centifolia roses. The roses often portrayed by Dutch painters; developed from *R. centifolia,* the cabbage rose. Centifolia roses are open growing with prickly stems; stems reach 6 ft. tall but arch with weight of blossoms. Intensely fragrant spring flowers typically are packed with petals, often with large outer petals that cradle a multitude of smaller petals within. Colors include white, pink shades. 'Rose des Peintres' is a typical rich pink cabbage rose; 'Paul Ricault' produces silken, deep pink flowers on an upright plant; 'Tour de Malakoff' is a tall, rangy plant with peonylike blossoms of pink fading to grayish mauve. Dwarf varieties (3 ft. or less) are 'Petite de Hollande', 'Pompon de Bourgogne', and 'Rose de Meaux'.

Climbing Rose 'Climbing Mrs. Sam McGredy'

Damask roses. Originating with *R. damascena.* Plants reach 6 ft. or more, typically with long, arching, thorny canes and light or grayish green, downy leaves. The summer damasks flower only in spring; forms of these are cultivated to make attar of roses (used in the perfume industry). Available varieties include 'Celsiana', blush pink; 'Leda', white with crimson markings; 'Mme. Hardy', white; and 'Versicolor'('York and Lancaster'), with petals that may be pink, white, or blend of pink and white. The autumn damask rose, *R. d.* 'Semperflorens' *(R. d. bifera),* flowers more than once in a year; slender buds open to loosely double, clear pink blossoms. This is the "Rose of Castile" of the Spanish missions.

Gallica roses. Cultivated forms of *R. gallica,* the French rose. Fragrant spring flowers run from pink through red to maroon and purple shades. Plants reach 3 – 4 ft. tall with upright to arching canes bearing prickles but few thorns and dark green, often rough-textured leaves. Grown on their own roots, these plants will spread into clumps from creeping rootstocks. Historic 'Officinalis', known as the Apothecary Rose, is presumed to be the "Red Rose of Lancaster" from the War of the Roses; flowers are semidouble, cherry red, on a dense, medium-height plant. Its sport, 'Versicolor'—generally known as 'Rosa Mundi'—has pink petals boldly striped and stippled red. Other gallicas include 'Belle de Crécy', pink aging to violet; 'Cardinal de Richelieu', slate purple; 'Charles de Mills', crimson to purple; and 'Tuscany', dark crimson with gold stamens.

Moss roses. Two old rose classes—centifolia and damask—include variant types that feature mosslike, balsam-scented glands that cover unopened buds, flower stems, and sometimes even leaflets. The moss of centifolias is soft to the touch; that of damask mosses is more stiff and prickly. Flowers are white, pink, red, often intensely fragrant. 'Communis' and 'Centifolia Muscosa' ('Muscosa') are typical pink centifolias with moss added; 'White Bath' is 'Centifolia Muscosa' done in white. Other available varieties are 'Comtesse de Murinais', pale pink to white; 'Gloire des Mousseux', deep pink; 'Mme. Louis Lévêque', salmon pink; 'Nuits de Young', dark red; 'William Lobb', dark red to purple. Repeat-flowering mosses include 'Alfred de Dalmas', creamy pink; 'Gabriel Noyelle', apricot; 'Henri Martin', red; and 'Salet', bright pink.

China roses. The first two China roses to reach Europe (around 1800) were really cultivated forms of *R. chinensis* that had been selected and maintained by Chinese horticulturists. Flowers were pink or red, under 3 in. across, in small clusters, on 2–4-ft.-high plants. 'Old Blush' ('Parson's Pink China'), one of the original two, is still sold; other available China roses include red 'Cramoisi Supérieur' ('Agrippina'), white 'Ducher', and crimson 'Louis Philippe'. China rose ancestry was the primary source of repeat-flowering habit in later 19th- and early 20th-century roses. Modern miniature roses owe their reduced stature to *R. chinensis minima,* presumably through its forms 'Rouletii' and 'Pompon de Paris'.

Bourbon roses. The original Bourbon rose was a hybrid between *R. chinensis* and the autumn damask (*R. damascena* 'Semperflorens'). Later developments were shrubs, semiclimbers, and climbers with flowers in white, pink shades, and red, mostly quite fragrant. Best known today are 'La Reine Victoria', 'Madame Ernst Calvat', 'Madame Pierre Oger', and 'Souvenir de la Malmaison' (all pink), and the supremely fragrant 'Madame Isaac Pereire' (magenta red). A famous Bourbon-China hybrid, 'Gloire des Rosomanes', gained widespread distribution as an understock (called "Ragged Robin") in commercial rose production. Occasionally it is offered as a hedge plant; growth is upright to fountainlike, with coarse foliage and semidouble, cherry red flowers throughout the growing season.

Damask perpetuals. This was the first distinct hybrid group to emerge, beginning around 1800, combining the China roses with old European rose types. Ancestries vary, but all appear to include China roses and the autumn damask (*R. damascena* 'Semperflorens'); generally they were known as Portland roses after the first representative, 'Duchess of Portland'. All are short, bushy, repeat-flowering plants with centifolia- and gallica-like flowers. Among those sold are 'Comte de Chambord', cool

pink; 'Duchess of Portland', crimson; 'Jacques Cartier', bright pink; and 'Rose du Roi', crimson purple.

Hybrid perpetuals. In the 19th and early 20th centuries, before hybrid teas dominated the catalogs, these were *the* garden roses. They are big, vigorous, and hardy to about −30°F/−34°C with minimal winter protection. Plants need more water and fertilizer than hybrid teas in order to produce repeated bursts of bloom. Prune high, thin out oldest canes, arch over remaining canes to encourage bloom in quantity. Watch for rust. Flowers often are large (to 6 or 7 in.), full, and strongly fragrant; buds usually are shorter, plumper than standard hybrid tea buds. Colors range from white through pink shades to red and maroon. Varieties still sold include 'Frau Karl Druschki', white; 'Général Jacqueminot', cherry red; 'Mrs. John Laing', rose pink; 'Paul Neyron', deep pink, peonylike flower; 'Ulrich Brünner Fils', carmine red.

Noisette roses. The union of a China rose (*R. chinensis*) and the musk rose (*R. moschata*) produced the first Noisette rose, 'Champneys' Pink Cluster', a repeat-flowering shrubby climber with small pink flowers in medium-size clusters. Crossed with itself and China roses, it led to a race of similar roses in white, pink shades, and red; crossed with tea roses, it yielded large-flowered, climbing tea-Noisettes. All are best in milder climates (Zones 31 and warmer parts of 32). Small-flowered Noisettes include 'Aimée Vibert Scandens', white; 'Blush Noisette', light pink; and 'Fellenberg', cherry red. Larger-flowered tea-Noisettes are 'Alister Stella Gray', yellow; 'Crepuscule', orange; 'Lamarque', white; 'Madame Alfred Carrière', white; 'Maréchal Niel', yellow; and 'Rêve d'Or', buff apricot.

Tea roses. A race of elegant, virtually everblooming, relatively tender roses best in Zones 31 and warmer parts of 32. Plants are long lived, building on old wood and disliking heavy pruning. Flowers are in pastel shades—white, soft cream, light yellow, apricot, buff, pink, and rosy red; flower character varies, but many resemble hybrid teas in flower quality. In crosses with hybrid perpetuals, tea roses were parents of the first hybrid teas. Available varieties include 'Duchesse de Brabant', warm pink, tuliplike; 'Lady Hillingdon', saffron; 'Maman Cochet', creamy rose pink; 'Marie van Houtte', soft yellow and pink; 'Mlle. Franziska Krüger', pink and cream to orange; 'Monsieur Tillier', dark pink and brick red; and 'White Maman Cochet', creamy white shaded pink. The cross of a tea and the tea ancestor *R. gigantea* produced 'Belle Portugaise' ('Belle of Portugal'), a rampant, spring-flowering climber bearing large pale pink blossoms.

Species and species hybrids. Among this diverse assemblage of wild species and their hybrids are excellent shrub and climbing roses, useful for mass floral effect and for the attractiveness of both plant and foliage.

R. carolina. CAROLINA ROSE. Deciduous shrub. Zones 31, 32, 34–43. Native to the eastern U.S. Grows to 3 ft. tall and spreads by underground stems. Single red flowers. Red fruits.

R. eglanteria (R. rubiginosa). SWEET BRIAR, EGLANTINE. Deciduous shrub or climber. Zones 31, 32, 34–45. Vigorous growth to 8–12 ft. Prickly stems. Dark green leaves have the fragrance of green apples, especially after rain. Flowers single, pink, 1½ in. across, appearing singly or in clusters in late spring. Red-orange fruit. Can be used as hedge, barrier, screen; plant 3–4 ft. apart and prune once a year in early spring. Can be held to 3–4 ft. Good hybrid forms are 'Lady Penzance', 'Lord Penzance'.

R. foetida (R. lutea). AUSTRIAN BRIER. Deciduous shrub. Zones 32, 34–41. Slender, prickly stems 5–10 ft. long, are erect or arching in habit. Leaves dark green, smooth or slightly hairy, they are especially susceptible to black spot; may drop early in fall. Flowers (appearing in mid- to late spring) are single, bright yellow, 2–3 in. across, with odd scent. This species and its well-known variety 'Bicolor', Austrian Copper rose, are the source of orange and yellow in modern roses. 'Bicolor' is a 4–5-ft.-tall shrub with brilliant coppery red flowers, their petals backed with yellow. Its form 'Persiana', Persian Yellow rose, has fully double, yellow blossoms.

All forms perform best in warm, fairly dry, well-drained soil and in full sun. Need reflected heat in cool-summer areas. Prune only to remove dead wood.

R. glauca (R. rubrifolia). Deciduous shrub. Zones 31, 32, 34–45. Foliage, not flower, is the main feature of this species: the 6-ft. plant is covered in leaves that combine gray green and coppery purple. Small, single spring flowers are pink, forming small, oval hips that color red in fall.

R. harisonii. HARISON'S YELLOW ROSE. Deciduous shrub. Zones 31, 32, 34–45. Thickets of thorny stems to 6–8 ft.; finely textured foliage; flowers (in late spring) profuse, semidouble, bright yellow, fragrant. Occasionally reblooms in fall in warmer climates. Showy fruit. Hybrid between *R. foetida* and *R. spinosissima*. Very old rose that was taken westward by pioneers from New York. Vigorous growing, disease free, hardy to cold, and (once established) resistant to aridity. Useful deciduous landscaping shrub.

R. moyesii. Deciduous shrub. Zones 32, 34, 39. Large, loose shrub is best as background plant or featured shrub-tree specimen. Spring bloom is a glorious display of bright red single flowers to 2½ in. across, carried singly or in groups of two. A second display comes in fall, when the large, bottle-shaped hips ripen to brilliant scarlet. 'Geranium' is a selection with somewhat shorter, more compact growth and red flowers in clusters of up to five. The hybrid 'Sealing Wax' offers pink flowers, also on a smaller and more compact bush.

From a hybrid tea crossed with a form of *R. moyesii,* 'Nevada' makes a large, arching shrub with light green leaves and dark stems. In spring, stems are covered with 4-in., pink-tinted, single white flowers, with lesser displays following later in the year. 'Marguerite Hilling' is a pink sport.

R. multiflora. Deciduous shrub. Zones 31, 32, 34–45. Arching growth on dense, vigorous plant 8–10 ft. tall and as wide. Susceptible to mildew, spider mites. Many clustered, small white flowers (like blackberry blossoms) in mid- to late spring; sweet fragrance akin to that of honeysuckle. Profusion of ¼-in. red fruit, much loved by birds, in fall. (The fruit display has a down side: profuse volunteer seedlings, which put this rose in the "weed" category.) Has escaped cultivation and invaded pasturelands, fields, and other open places in the Northeast. Promoted as hedge but truly useful for this purpose only on largest acreage—far too large and vigorous for most gardens. One of the most widely used understocks in commerical rose production, but species form not recommended for home gardens.

A number of distinctive climbing roses, known as multiflora ramblers, are hybrids of this species. Best known are several "blue ramblers": 'Bleu Magenta', crimson purple fading to gray violet; 'Rose-Marie Viaud', crimson purple to violet and lilac; 'Veilchenblau', maroon purple to gray lilac; and 'Violette', maroon purple to grayish plum.

R. pimpinellifolia (R. spinosissima). SCOTCH ROSE, BURNET ROSE. Deciduous shrub. Zones 32, 34–45. Suckering, spreading shrub 3–4 ft. tall. Stems upright, spiny, bristly, closely set with small, ferny leaves. Handsome bank cover on good soil; helps prevent erosion. Spring flowers white to pink, 1½–2 in. across; fruit dark brown to blackish. Its form 'Altaica' can reach 6 ft. tall, with larger leaves and 3-in. white flowers garlanding branches. Several hybrids are noteworthy. 'Stanwell Perpetual' produces blush pink, double blossoms from spring to fall on a mounding, twiggy plant with small gray-green leaves. 'Frühlingsmorgen' is best known of several German hybrids; tall, arching bush bears large, single yellow flowers edged cherry pink and centered with maroon stamens. 'Golden Wings' makes a 6-ft. bush that flowers throughout the growing season; 4-in. blossoms are single, light yellow with red stamens.

R. roxburghii. CHESTNUT ROSE. Deciduous shrub. Zones 31, 32, 34–41. Spreading plant with prickly stems 8–10 ft. long. Gray, peeling bark. Light green, very finely textured, ferny foliage; new growth bronze and gold tipped. Immune to mildew. Buds and fruit are spiny, like chestnut burrs. Flowers—generally double, soft rose pink, very fragrant—appear in mid- to late spring. Normally a big shrub for screen or border, but if stems are pegged down it makes good bank cover, useful in preventing erosion.

R. rugosa. SALTSPRAY ROSE, RAMANAS ROSE. Deciduous shrub. Zones 32, 34–45. Vigorous, very hardy shrub with prickly stems. To 3–8 ft. tall.

Leaves bright glossy green, with distinctive heavy veining that gives them crinkled appearance. Flowers are 3–4 in. across and, in the many varieties, range from single to double and from pure white and creamy yellow through pink to deep purplish red, all wonderfully fragrant. Blooms spring, summer, early fall. Bright red, tomato-shaped fruit, an inch or more across, is seedy but edible and sometimes used in preserves.

All rugosas are extremely tough and hardy, withstanding hard freezes, wind, aridity, salt spray at ocean. They make fine hedges; plants grown on their own roots will make sizable colonies and help prevent erosion. Foliage remains quite free of diseases and insects, except possibly aphids. Among most widely sold rugosas and rugosa hybrids are 'Blanc Double de Coubert', double white; 'Frau Dagmar Hartopp', single pink; 'Hansa', double purplish red; 'Will Alderman', double pink. Two unusual rugosa hybrids are 'F. J. Grootendorst' and 'Grootendorst Supreme'; their double flowers with deeply fringed petals resemble carnations more than roses.

R. virginiana. VIRGINIA ROSE. Deciduous shrub. Zones 31, 32, 34–45. Native to the eastern U.S. Grows to 6 ft. (can be kept to 3 ft. with pruning) and spreads by underground stems. Single pink flowers, bright red fruit, red and orange autumn foliage. Twigs are red in winter. Good landscape plant.

R. wichuraiana. MEMORIAL ROSE. Vine. Deciduous in Zones 31, 34, 39; evergreen or partially evergreen in Zone 32. Trailing stems grow 10–12 ft. long in one season, root in contact with moist soil. Leaves 2–4 in. long, with five to nine smooth, shiny, ¼–1-in. leaflets. Midsummer flowers are white, to 2 in. across, in clusters of six to ten. Good ground cover, even in relatively poor soil. Wichuraiana ramblers, produced in the first 20 years of this century, are group of hybrids between the species and various garden roses. Pink 'Dorothy Perkins' and red 'Excelsa' produce smothering spring displays of small, formless flowers that obscure the often-mildewed leaves. Larger, better-shaped flowers and glossy, healthier leaves are found in 'Albéric Barbier', creamy white; 'François Juranville', coral pink; 'Gardenia', light yellow; 'Paul Transon', coppery salmon; and 'Sander's White Rambler', white.

R. xanthina hugonis (R. hugonis). FATHER HUGO'S ROSE, GOLDEN ROSE OF CHINA. Deciduous shrub. Zones 32, 34–41. Dense growth to 8 ft. Stems arching or straight, with bristles near base. Handsome foliage; leaves deep green, 1–4 in. long, with 5–11 tiny leaflets. Blooms profusely in mid- to late spring. Branches become garlands of 2-in.-wide, yellow, faintly scented flowers. Useful in borders, for screen or barrier plantings, against fence, trained as fan on trellis. Will take high filtered afternoon shade. Prune out oldest wood to ground each year to shape plant, get maximum bloom.

Rosaceae. The rose family contains an immense number of plants of horticultural importance. In addition to roses, family members include strawberry, bramble fruits (blackberry, raspberry), many flowering and fruiting trees (apple, crabapple, pear, plum), firethorn (*Pyracantha),* and *Spiraea*, as well as other ornamental trees, shrubs, and perennials.

ROSCOEA

Zingiberaceae

PERENNIALS

ZONES VARY BY SPECIES

FULL SUN TO PARTIAL SHADE

REGULAR WATER

Roscoea

These relatives of ginger are grown for their delicate, orchidlike blooms that appear in summer or early fall. Smooth, glossy, lance-shaped leaves and 1-ft. flower stalks emerge from a cluster of fleshy roots. Flowers have long tubes, a hooded upper petal, and two spreading lower petals. Plant in beds, border, woodland, wildflower, and rock gardens. They appreciate mild winters and cool, humid summers. Grow best when planted in spring 5 in. deep in moist, cool soil rich in organic matter. Mulch heavily with compost

R

in winter, when the plant dies back to the ground. Increase the plant by division in spring or by seed in winter or fall. May self-sow.

R. alpina. Zones 31, 32, 34, 39. Himalayan native. Rock garden plant growing up to 6 in. high. Flower stems usually bear a single purple flower with a white tube. Blooms in summer.

R. purpurea. Zones 31, 32, 34–41. To 1 ft. tall and 6–8 in. wide. Its bluish purple, thin-textured flowers sometimes have white veins and throats. They appear on flower stalks in groups of two to four. Blooms in late summer. Strong and hardy.

ROSE. See ROSA

ROSELLE. See HIBISCUS sabdariffa

ROSE-MALLOW. See HIBISCUS moscheutos

ROSEMARY. See ROSMARINUS officinalis

ROSE MOSS. See PORTULACA

ROSE OF SHARON. See HIBISCUS syriacus

ROSINWEED. See SILPHIUM

ROSMARINUS officinalis

ROSEMARY

Lamiaceae (Labiatae)

EVERGREEN SHRUB OR HERB

✄ ZONES 31, 32; OR IN POTS

☼ FULL SUN

💧 MODERATE TO LITTLE WATER

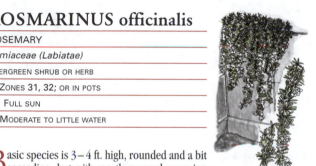
Rosmarinus officinalis

Basic species is 3–4 ft. high, rounded and a bit spreading, but with mostly upward-sweeping branches. Narrow, almost needlelike, inch-long leaves usually glossy green above, grayish white beneath, aromatic when brushed or bruised. Bear small clusters of small, typically lavender blue flowers over long winter–spring bloom period. Plants must have well-drained soil in regions with summer rainfall and warm to hot temperatures. Prune as needed, making all cuts to side branches or into leafy stems. Where not hardy, grow in containers moved outdoors in summer, indoors over winter.

Selections include the following. Foliage of all types has culinary use.

'Arp'. The hardiest rosemary; takes temperatures to −10°F/−23°C. Open grower to 4 ft. Bright blue flowers.

'Collingwood Ingram' (*R. ingramii*). To 2–2½ ft. high, spreading to 4 ft. or more. Branches curve gracefully. Flowers in rich, bright shade of blue violet. Tallish bank or ground cover with high color value.

'Huntington Carpet' ('Huntington Blue'). To 1½ ft. high; spreads quickly yet maintains dense center. Pale blue flowers.

'Ken Taylor'. Resembles 'Collingwood Ingram' but is lower growing and has a greater tendency to trail.

'Lockwood de Forest' (*R. lockwoodii, R. forestii*). Resembles 'Prostratus', but with lighter, brighter foliage and bluer flowers.

'Majorca Pink'. Erect shrub to 2–5 ft. Lavender pink flowers.

'Miss Jessup's Upright'. Very upright to 4 ft.; pale blue flowers. Suitable for formal herb gardens.

'Old Salem'. Dense, erect growth to 3 ft.; pale blue flowers. Fairly cold hardy under snow cover.

'Prostratus'. DWARF ROSEMARY. To 2 ft. high with 4–8-ft. spread. Will trail over wall or edge of raised bed to make curtain of bright to dark green. Pale lavender blue flowers. Slightly less cold hardy than most other types of rosemary.

'Tuscan Blue'. Rigid, upright branches to 6 ft. or taller grow directly from base of plant. Rich green leaves, blue-violet flowers.

ROWAN. See SORBUS aucuparia

ROYAL FERN. See OSMUNDA regalis

RUBBER TREE, HARDY. See EUCOMMIA ulmoides

Rubiaceae. The widespread and varied madder family contains herbs, shrubs, and trees with opposite or whorled leaves and (usually) clustered flowers. Among its members are partridgeberry (*Mitchella*), *Pentas,* and sweet woodruff (*Galium*).

RUBUS

BRAMBLE

Rosaceae

DECIDUOUS OR EVERGREEN SHRUBS OR GROUND COVERS

✄ ZONES VARY BY SPECIES

☼ ◐ FULL SUN OR LIGHT SHADE

💧 REGULAR TO MODERATE WATER

Rubus

Best known for edible members blackberry and raspberry (see separate entries), the brambles include many ornamental plants, most of them without prickles or thorns. Provide good drainage.

R. cockburianus. GHOST BRAMBLE. Deciduous shrub. Zones 31, 32, 34–41. Forms a thicket to 8 ft. high and wide, with prickly, arching stems that appear white in winter. Oval, deep green leaves to 8 in. long are covered with white hairs on the underside and divided into up to 9 oblong leaflets. Clusters of purple flowers at the stem tips in summer.

R. deliciosus. ROCKY MOUNTAIN THIMBLEBERRY, BOULDER RASPBERRY. Deciduous shrub. Zones 35–41. To 3–5 ft., with arching, thornless branches. Bright green, lobed leaves are nearly round. White spring flowers to 2–3 in. wide look like single roses. Fruit attracts birds. Hybrid between this species and *R. trilobus* is *R. tridel* 'Benenden', which grows 8–10 ft. tall.

R. pentalobus (R. calycinoides, R. fockeanus). Evergreen shrub, ground cover. Zones 31, 32. Creeping stems make a mat that spreads 1 ft. a year. Densely packed green leaves are ruffled, nearly round; look crinkled above, felty beneath. Some leaves turn red or bronze in winter or in full sun. Small white flowers like those of strawberry; edible salmon-colored berries. 'Emerald Carpet' is the selection most commonly seen.

R. spectabilis 'Olympic Double'. Deciduous shrub. Zones 35–41. Showy, bright pink double flowers, 2 in. wide, appear in spring.

RUDBECKIA

Asteraceae (Compositae)

PERENNIALS AND BIENNIALS

✄ ZONES VARY BY SPECIES

☼ ◐ FULL SUN OR LIGHT SHADE

💧 REGULAR TO MODERATE WATER

Rudbeckia

Garden rudbeckias are descendants of wild plants native to North America. All are tough and easy to grow, thriving in any except soggy soils. Showy yellow or orange flowers brighten summer and fall borders. Good cut flowers. Cutting also encourages rebloom late in season. Divide perennials when they become crowded, usually every few years.

R. fulgida. Perennial. Zones 31, 32, 34–43. Native to the eastern U.S. To 3 ft. tall, with branching stems and 5-in.-long leaves. Yellow, 2–2½-in.-wide summer flowers with black to brown center. Spreads by rhizomes, forming large clumps. Varieties more often grown than species. Among

R

most popular is *R. f. sullivantii* 'Goldsturm', bearing 3-in. black-eyed Susan flowers on 2–2½-ft. stems. Some nurseries offer the taller, more variable seed-grown Goldsturm strain. 'Little Suzy' grows only 12–14 in. tall and is very floriferous.

R. hirta. GLORIOSA DAISY, BLACK-EYED SUSAN. Zones 31, 32, 34–43. Native to the Midwest. Biennial or short-lived perennial; often grown as annual because it blooms first summer from seed sown in early spring. To 3–4 ft. tall, with upright branching habit and rough, hairy stems and leaves. Daisylike single flowers 2–4 in. wide, with orange-yellow rays and purplish black center.

Gloriosa Daisy strain has 5–7-in.-wide single daisies in yellow, orange, russet, or mahogany, often zoned or banded. 'Irish Eyes' has golden yellow flowers with a light green center that turns brown as it ages. 'Pinwheel' has mahogany-and-gold flowers. 'Marmalade' (2 ft.) and 'Goldilocks' (8–10 in.) are lower growing, can be used at front of border or as ground cover. Gloriosa Double Daisy strain has somewhat smaller (to 4½-in.) double flower heads, nearly all in lighter yellow and orange shades.

R. laciniata. Perennial. Zones 31, 32, 34–43. Native to central and eastern North America. To 3 ft. tall, with deeply lobed, light green leaves. Blooms summer–fall, bearing 2–3½-in.-wide flowers with drooping yellow rays around a green central disk. Very heat tolerant. The following two varieties are more widely grown in gardens. 'Hortensia' ('Golden Glow'), to 6–7 ft. tall with double bright yellow flowers, makes a good summer screen or tall border plant. Aphids seem to like it. Does not seed, but spreads rapidly (sometimes aggressively) by underground stems and is easily divided. Less aggressive is 'Goldquelle', a 2½-ft.-tall plant with double yellow blooms.

R. maxima. Perennial. Zones 31, 32, 34, 35, 37, 39. Native to North America. Large (to 5-in.) bluish gray leaves form a mound to 2–3 ft. tall and wide. In midsummer, 5–6-ft. stems bear flower heads with a 2-in. brown center cone and drooping yellow rays.

R. nitida. Perennial. Zones 31, 32, 34, 35, 37, 39. Native to the southern U.S. Similar to *R. laciniata* but shorter. More widely grown than the species is 'Herbstsonne' ('Autumn Sun'), a 4–6-ft. plant bearing single yellow flower heads with a bright green central disk.

R. purpurea. See *Echinacea purpurea*

R. subtomentosa. SWEET CONEFLOWER. Perennial. Zones 32, 34–43. Native to the Midwest. To 28 in. tall and 1 ft. wide, with upright, branching habit. Oval leaves to 5 in. long, covered with soft gray hairs. Flowers to 3 in. across, with yellow rays surrounding a dark purple-brown central disk, bloom in autumn.

R. triloba. BROWN-EYED SUSAN. Biennial. Zones 32, 34–43. Native to the eastern U.S. and Canada. Forms clumps to 5 ft. tall and 3 ft. wide, with a branching habit. Oval, lobed leaves to 5 in. long. Flowers to 1½ in. across, with orangy yellow rays surrounding a purple-black central disk, bloom in late summer and autumn.

RUE. See RUTA graveolens

RUE ANENOME. See ANEMONELLA thalictroides

RUMEX sanguineus

BLOODY DOCK, BLOODY SORREL, RED-VEINED DOCK

Polygonaceae

PERENNIAL

☀ ZONES 31, 32, 34, 39

☼ ◐ ● FULL SUN TO SHADE

💧 REGULAR WATER

Rumex sanguineus

Grown for its attractive foliage, this clump-forming plant, which grows to 1–2 ft. tall, has long, narrow light green leaves with intensely colored maroon to red veining. The small, star-shaped midsummer flowers,

opening green then going to a pinkish brown, are insignificant; cutting them back may encourage foliage growth. A good plant for the rock, shade, or wild garden, it flourishes in well-drained, neutral soil but does well in a wide variety of conditions. In cooler climates, the plant is likely to self-seed. Aphids can be a problem.

RUPTURE WORT. See HERNIARIA glabra

RUSSIAN OLIVE. See ELAEAGNUS angustifolia

RUSSIAN SAGE. See PEROVSKIA

RUTABAGA. See TURNIP and RUTABAGA

Rutaceae. Besides rue *(Ruta)*, the rue family includes many perennials, shrubs, and trees, most important of which are the citrus clan. Most members have oil glands in leaves or other parts and are aromatic. Cork tree *(Phellodendron)*, trifoliate orange *(Poncirus)*, and *Skimmia* are other notable members.

RUTA graveolens

RUE, HERB-OF-GRACE

Rutaceae

PERENNIAL HERB

☀ ZONES 31, 32, 34–41

☼ FULL SUN

💧💧 REGULAR TO MODERATE WATER

💧 MAY CAUSE DERMATITIS

Ruta graveolens

To 2–3 ft., with aromatic, fernlike blue-green leaves. Small, greenish yellow flowers are followed by decorative brown seed capsules. Sow seeds in flats; transplant to 1 ft. apart. Needs good garden soil; add lime to strongly acid soil. Cut back in early spring to encourage bushiness. Seed clusters can be dried for use in wreaths or swags. 'Blue Beauty' and 'Jackman's Blue' are dense, compact varieties with fine blue-gray color. 'Blue Mound' and 'Curly Girl' are even more compact.

Rue owes its status as an herb to history and legend rather than to any medicinal or culinary use. It was once thought to ward off disease, guard against poisons, and aid eyesight. It was also used to make brushes for sprinkling holy water. Sap causes dermatitis in some people.

RYEGRASS. See LOLIUM

SACCHARUM

PLUME GRASS, SUGAR CANE

Poaceae

PERENNIAL GRASSES

☀ ZONES VARY BY SPECIES

☼ FULL SUN

💧 REGULAR WATER

Saccharum

Though most species in this genus of clump-forming grasses grow only in tropical and subtropical climates, several are winter hardy. Grown in borders and as specimens for their showy foliage (attractive as a cut and dried flower) and dramatic plumed inflorescences, they thrive in sheltered sites in well-drained soil.

S. arundinaceum. HARDY SUGAR CANE. Zones 31, 32, 34, 39. Grows to 10 ft. tall and wide, with white-margined grayish green leaves topped in midfall with purplish pink pampaslike plumes.

S. ravennae. RAVENNA GRASS. Zones 31, 32, 34, 39. Huge clumps more than a yard wide and 14 ft. tall are comprised of arching gray-green leaves with burgundy-colored stems that take on a purple tint in fall. Produced in late summer and early fall, flower plumes are silver gray to purple. A bold, yet elegant grass sure to stand out in any landscape.

SACRED LILY. See ROHDEA japonica

SAFFLOWER. See CARTHAMUS tinctorius

SAFFRON, MEADOW. See COLCHICUM

SAGE. See SALVIA

SAGE, RUSSIAN. See PEROVSKIA

SAGINA subulata

IRISH MOSS, SCOTCH MOSS

Caryophyllaceae

PERENNIAL

☘ ZONES 32, 34–43

☼ ◑ FULL SUN OR PARTIAL SHADE

🔴 REGULAR WATER

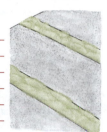
Sagina subulata

Of two different plants of similar appearance, *Sagina subulata* is the more common. The other is *Arenaria verna*, usually called *A. v. caespitosa*. Both make dense, compact, mosslike masses of slender leaves on slender stems. But *A. verna* has tiny white flowers in few-flowered clusters, while *S. subulata* bears flowers singly and differs in other technical details. In common usage, however, green forms of the two are called Irish moss, while golden green forms (*A. v.* 'Aurea' and *S. s.* 'Aurea') are called Scotch moss.

Both *Sagina* and *Arenaria* are grown primarily as ground covers for limited areas. They're useful for filling gaps between paving blocks. In cool-summer gardens, they can self-sow and become pests.

Although they look like moss, these plants won't grow well under conditions that suit true mosses. They need good soil, good drainage, and occasional feeding with slow-acting, nonburning fertilizer. They take some foot traffic and tend to hump up in time; control humping by occasionally cutting out narrow strips, then pressing or rolling lightly. Control slugs, snails, cutworms. Cut squares from flats and set 6 in. apart for fast cover. To avoid lumpiness, plant so that soil line of squares is at or slightly below the surface.

SAGITTARIA

ARROWHEAD

Alismataceae

PERENNIALS

☘ ZONES VARY BY SPECIES

☼ ◑ FULL SUN TO PARTIAL SHADE

🔴 AMPLE WATER

Sagittaria

These aquatic plants, some fully submerged but most extending above the water's surface, derive their name from the elegant arrow-shaped leaves borne by many of the species. Preferring still water, they grow from rhizomes, some of which are edible. Blooms, appearing in July and August, are generally white and three petaled, held on a tall stalk. Useful at the edges of ponds and in aquatic containers, to add height and foliage interest.

S. engelmanniana. Zones 31, 32, 34, 39. Linear to lance-shaped arrowhead leaves to 10 in. long, rising above the surface of the water; flowers on 2-ft. stems.

S. latifolia 'Flore Pleno'. DOUBLE GIANT ARROWHEAD. Zones 31, 32, 34–41. Grows to 2 ft. tall, with double blooms.

S. sagittifolia 'Flore Pleno'. DOUBLE COMMON ARROWHEAD. Zones 31, 32, 34–41. Double white blooms produced throughout the summer.

SAGO PALM. See CYCAS revoluta

ST. JOHNSWORT. See HYPERICUM

Salicaceae. The willow family consists of deciduous trees or shrubs with flowers in catkins and (generally) with silk-tufted seeds that blow about. Besides willow *(Salix)*, examples are cottonwood and poplar *(Populus)*.

SALIX

WILLOW

Salicaceae

DECIDUOUS SHRUBS OR TREES

☘ ZONES VARY BY SPECIES

☼ FULL SUN

🔴 LOTS OF WATER

Salix

Fast-growing, somewhat weak-wooded trees. Take any soil; most even tolerate poor drainage. All have shallow, invasive roots and are hard to garden under. Most are subject to borers, blights, cankers, and other problems. Weeping willows are best used as single trees near stream or lake, although they can, with training, become satisfactory shade trees for patio or terrace. They leaf out very early in spring and hold leaves late. Shrubby willows are grown mainly for catkins ("pussy willows") or colored twigs, as screen plants, or for erosion control on banks of streams and rivers. For this last purpose, types native to the region are best. The many willow species hybridize readily; as a result, names are much confused in the nursery trade.

S. alba. WHITE WILLOW. Tree. Zones 31, 32, 34–45. Upright growth to 75–100 ft. Yellowish brown bark. Narrow, 1½–4-in.-long leaves are bright green on top, silvery beneath; may turn golden yellow in fall. The following forms are valued for colorful twigs:

'Britzensis' ('Chermesina'). Young twigs turn radiant orange red in winter. For best display, cut back clump to about a foot high just before spring growth begins. Stems will grow as much as 8 ft. in a single season.

S. a. tristis (S. babylonica aurea, S. 'Niobe'). GOLDEN WEEPING WILLOW. Pendulous habit. To 80 ft. high; wider than tall. Young stems are bright yellow. Among the most attractive weeping willows.

S. a. vitellina. Brilliant yellow winter twigs. Cut back heavily, as for 'Britzensis'.

S. babylonica. WEEPING WILLOW. Tree. Zones 31, 32, 34, 39. To 30–50 ft., with equal or greater spread. Smaller than *S. alba tristis,* with longer (3–6-in.) leaves and even more pronounced weeping habit. Greenish or brown branchlets. 'Crispa' ('Annularis'), ringleaf or corkscrew willow, has leaves twisted and curled into rings or circles; it is a somewhat narrower tree than the species.

S. blanda. WISCONSIN WEEPING WILLOW. Tree. Zones 31, 32, 34–41. To 40–50 ft. or more, spreading wider. Hybrid of *S. babylonica* but less strongly weeping, with broader leaves of a more bluish green color. 'Fan', fan giant blue weeping willow, is resistant to borers and blight.

S. caprea. FRENCH PUSSY WILLOW, PINK PUSSY WILLOW. Shrub or small tree. Zones 31, 32, 34–41. To 25 ft. tall. Broad leaves 3–6 in. long, dark green above, gray and hairy beneath. Male plants produce fat, woolly pinkish gray catkins about 1 in. long in early spring before leaf-out. Can be kept to shrub size by cutting to ground every few years. 'Pendula', Kilmarnock willow, forms a trailing mound suitable for ground cover; it can also be grafted onto an upright trunk and used as a small weeping tree. 'Weeping Sally' is the female form.

S

S. discolor. PUSSY WILLOW. Shrub or small tree. Zones 31, 32, 34–45. To 20 ft. tall. Slender stems are red brown; 2–4-in. leaves are bright green above, bluish beneath. Catkins of male plants (usually only kind sold) are the feature attraction—soft, silky, pearl gray, grow to 1½ in. long.

S. elaeagnos. ROSEMARY WILLOW. Shrub. Zones 32, 34–43. Dense and upright, to 10 ft. tall and 15 ft. wide. Narrow, deep green leaves resemble those of rosemary, turn yellow in fall. Slender green catkins in spring. Stems are reddish brown.

S. 'Flame'. Shrub or small tree. Zones 31, 32, 34–41. Hybrid to 15–20 ft. high, with compact, dense habit. Branch tips curl upward and inward. Foliage turns a good golden yellow rather late in autumn. Spectacular orange-red bark in winter.

S. 'Golden Curls'. Shrub or small tree. Zones 31, 32, 34, 39. Hybrid between *S. matsudana* 'Tortuosa' and *S. alba tristis*. To 30 ft. tall, with somewhat weeping and twisting branches, somewhat curled leaves, and bright yellow bark on new growth. After establishing a framework, cut back hard in winter to keep colorful new growth coming on.

S. gracilistyla. ROSE-GOLD PUSSY WILLOW. Upright, spreading shrub. Zones 31, 32, 34, 39. To 6–10 ft. tall. Narrowly ovate, 2–4-in.-long leaves are gray green above, bluish green beneath. Male plants produce plump, 1½-in.-long, furry gray catkins with numerous stamens with rose-and-gold anthers. Cutting branches for arrangements will curb plant's size. Every 3 or 4 years, cut back whole plant to short stubs; you'll be rewarded by especially vigorous shoots with large catkins. *S. g. melanostachys* has black catkins with red anthers.

S. lanata. WOOLLY WILLOW. Shrub. Zones 41–45. Upright and bushy, 6–10 ft. high, but can be kept to 2–4 ft. with pruning. Rounded, dark green leaves to 2½ in. long, covered with gray woolly hairs that make leaves appear gray. Yellow catkins in spring—males are golden, females grayish. Can be grown as a hedge. Needs a cool climate.

S. matsudana. HANKOW WILLOW. Tree. Zones 31, 32, 34, 39. Upright, pyramidal growth to 40–50 ft. Narrow, bright green, 2–4-in.-long leaves. Can thrive on less water than most willows. 'Navajo', globe Navajo willow, is a large, spreading, round-topped tree to 70 ft. tall. 'Tortuosa', dragon-claw willow, grows 30 ft. tall and 20 ft. wide, has branches fantastically twisted into upright, spiraling patterns; it is valued for winter silhouette and for cut branches for arrangements. 'Umbraculifera', globe willow, reaches 35 ft. high and has an umbrella-shaped top with upright branches, drooping branchlets.

S. purpurea. PURPLE OSIER, ALASKA BLUE WILLOW. Shrub. Zones 34–43. To 10–18 ft. high, with purple branches and narrow, 1–3-in. leaves that are dark green above, markedly bluish beneath. 'Gracilis' ('Nana'), dwarf purple osier, has slimmer branches and narrower leaves; it is usually grown as clipped hedge and kept 1–3 ft. high and wide.

S. 'Scarlet Curls'. Shrub or small tree. Zones 31, 32, 34, 39. Resembles 'Golden Curls', but bark on new growth is red.

S. udensis 'Sekka' (S. sachalinensis 'Sekka'). JAPANESE FANTAIL WILLOW. Shrub or small tree. Zones 31, 32, 34–41. Wide-spreading male plant to 10–15 ft. high. Narrow leaves are 2–4 in. long, green above, silvery beneath. Silvery catkins to 2 in. long. Main feature is the branch structure: branches are flattened, often 1–2 in. wide, twisted and curled, picturesque in arrangements.

SALPIGLOSSIS sinuata

PAINTED TONGUE

Solanaceae

ANNUAL

◪ ALL ZONES

☼ FULL SUN

◆ REGULAR WATER

Salpiglossis sinuata

Upright, open habit, to 2–3 ft. tall. Sticky leaves and stems. Leaves to 4 in. long, narrowly oblong. Flowers much like petunias in shape and

---

size (2–2½ in. wide), but more unusual in color—shades of mahogany red, reddish orange, yellow, purple and pink tones, marbled and penciled with contrasting color. Bolero (2 ft.), Friendship (15 in.), and Splash (2 ft.) are compact strains.

Provide rich, well-drained soil. Stake tall types. Pinch out tips of growing plants to induce branching. Best bloom in late spring and early summer, but regular deadheading will keep flowers coming until frost in cool-summer climates. Good background plant for border; also a handsome cut flower.

SALSIFY

OYSTER PLANT

Asteraceae (Compositae)

BIENNIAL OFTEN GROWN AS AN ANNUAL

◪ ALL ZONES

☼ FULL SUN

◆ REGULAR WATER

Salsify

Grown for its edible root, which looks something like parsnip and has creamy white flesh that tastes a little like oysters. Plant grows to 4 ft. tall; leaves are narrow, grasslike. Plant in rich, deep, sandy soil, spaded deep. Culture is same as for parsnips. It takes about 150 days to grow to maturity. Cooked, mashed salsify, mixed with butter and beaten egg, can be made into patties and sautéed until brown to make mock oysters. If plant is allowed to overwinter in mild climates, it will produce flower stalk topped by large head of lavender purple, dandelionlike flowers followed by white, cottony seeds.

SALT BUSH. See BACCHARIS halimifolia

SALVIA

SAGE

Lamiaceae (Labiatae)

ANNUALS, BIENNIALS, PERENNIALS, SHRUBS

◪ ZONES VARY BY SPECIES

☼ FULL SUN, EXCEPT AS NOTED

◆ REGULAR WATER, EXCEPT AS NOTED

▸ SEE CHART ON FOLLOWING PAGES

Salvia

The sages, along with the ornamental grasses, became horticultural stars in the 1980s and 1990s. Botanical gardens and collectors have introduced scores of new species and selections from Mexico, South America, Eurasia, and Africa, along with superior forms of our native species. Some are annual bedding plants, others are border perennials, and still others serve as shrubs or ground covers. Where available as nursery plants, many of the tender perennials and shrubs are sometimes grown as annuals in cold-winter climates.

Flower colors range from white and yellow through pink to scarlet, and from pale lavender to true blue and dark purple. What they have in common is a floral arrangement in which whorls of two-lipped flowers are either distinctly spaced along the flower stalks or so tightly crowded they look like one dense spike. Inflorescences in some species are branched. Many salvias are aromatic, some strongly so; some are sweet scented, while others, such as common sage *(S. officinalis)*, have a more savory fragrance.

At least 60 species and an additional 40 to 50 selections are grown. The chart on the following pages lists many of the best *Salvia* species and cultivars for gardens in the Northeast.

S

SALVIA

NAME, TYPE	ZONES	GROWTH HABIT	FLOWERS	COMMENTS
Salvia argentea SILVER SAGE Biennial	31, 32, 34–45	Flat 1-ft. rosette of white, furry, 6–9-in.-long leaves	Branched flowering stems to 4 ft.; white summer flowers, tinged pink or yellow.	Use at front of border for striking foliage. Grow as an annual in colder climates
S. azurea grandiflora *(S. pitcheri)* Perennial	31, 32, 34–43	To 5 ft., with smooth or hairy 2–4-in. leaves	Gentian blue, ½-in.-long blooms provide mass of color, summer-frost	Tolerant of heat, humidity. Not always permanent in wet winters
S. coccinea Perennial, but usually a self-seeding annual	All zones	Bushy, to 2–3 ft., with dark green furry leaves	Flowers red, in 4-in. spikes, spring-fall	'Brenthurst' is a pink furry form. 'Lady in Red' is a shorter selection good for foreground planting
S. elegans PINEAPPLE SAGE Perennial grown as an annual	All zones	To 2–3 ft.; light green leaves have fruity scent and taste	Red flowers in short spikes, autumn	Use leaves in cool drinks, fruit salads. Plant is large and open; give it plenty of space
S. farinacea MEALY-CUP SAGE Perennial grown as an annual	All zones	Fast growth to 2–3 ft., grayish green leaves	Spikes of small blue flowers rise above foliage mound in summer	Plants are perennial where winter temperatures remain above 10 F/-12 C, but blooms best when treated as annual. 'Mina' (1 ft.) and 'Victoria' (1½ ft.) are dwarfs
S. leucantha MEXICAN BUSH SAGE Shrub	31, 32, annual farther north	To 3–4 ft., with graceful arching stems, grayish green foliage	Long velvety purple spikes set with small white flowers arch outward in summer, fall	Takes some aridity, sun or light shade. Cut old stems to the ground. All-purple and pink forms exist. Annual in colder climates
S. nemerosa Perennial	31, 32, 34–41	Narrow, erect plant to 3 ft. with narrow, 4-in. roughish leaves	Velvet blue flowers in narrow spikes above foliage, summer-fall	Species rarely seen. 'East Friesland', 2½ ft. is widely sold. Pink 'Rose Queen' is lower, now so vigorous. See also 'S. superba'
S. officinalis COMMON SAGE Perennial	31, 32, 34–41	To 2½ ft., with aromatic, wrinkled gray-green leaves	Lavender blue flowers in short spikes above the foliage, summer	All varieties good for seasoning. 'Berggarten', nonflowering, has biggest leaves, is longest lived (but least pungent). Colored varieties are 'Icterina', yellow and green leaves; 'Purpurascens', purplish tints; and 'Tricolor', gray, white, and purplish pink. 'Nana' is a dwarf
S. patens GENTIAN SAGE Perennial	All zones as annual	To 2–3 ft., compact, with large, long-stalked leaves	Flowers 2 in. long, pure blue, in clusters to 16 in. long; summer, fall	Fertilize for repeat bloom

S

SALVIA

NAME, TYPE	ZONES	GROWTH HABIT	FLOWERS	COMMENTS
S. pratensis MEADOW SAGE Perennial	31, 32, 34–41	To 3 ft., with large (6-in.), rough basal leaves	Spikes of lavender blue flowers on branching stems, spring	'Haematodes' is most commonly grown form. Makes a great show but bloom period is short. Reseeds. Needs warm, well-drained site. Grow as an annual in colder climates
S. sclarea CLARY Perennial or biennial	31, 32, 34–41	Rough, gray-green, highly aromatic leaves to 8 in. long	Flowers white to lilac in big branching clusters to 3 ft., spring-summer	'Turkestanica' has pink flower stalks, white-and-pink flowers. Species and variety can be grown as annuals in all zones
S. splendens SCARLET SAGE Perennial usually grown as annual	All zones	Branched plant 1–3 ft. tall, depending on strain or variety, with bright green foliage	Flowers scarlet, in tall, dense clusters; also available in pink, purple, white, in tall or dwarf strains. Summer	Grow from seed or buy young plants from nurseries. Effective with gray-foliaged plants Cultivars include 'Blaze of Fire', 'Bonfire', 'Carabiniere Scarlet', 'Flare', 'Rambo', 'Scarlet Queen', and 'St. John's Fire'
S. superba Perennial	31, 32, 34–41	Erect, branched, 2–3 ft. plants with narrow leaves; narrow, erect flower spikes top each stalk	Flowers violet blue or purple, summer-fall	Closely related to *S. nemorosa*. Plants often sold under either name are 'Blue Hill', dark blue, tall, nearly everblooming; 'Lubeca', tall, early flowering, deep violet; 'May Night', low growing, with deep blue flowers; 'East Friesland' and 'Rose Queen' (see under *S. nemorosa*)
S. sylvestris Perennial	31, 32, 34–41	Erect, branched, to 1½ ft. high and wide; scalloped, oblong to lance-shaped leaves	Dense clusters of small summer flowers, pinkish purple to violet or blue	Hybrid between *S. nemerosa* and *S. pratensis*
S. uliginosa Perennial	31, 32, 34, 39	Clumping plant with erect stems 6–7 ft. tall, with narrow, bright green, highly aromatic leaves	Flowers pale blue and white in erect, branched clusters to 5 in. long, summer-fall	Plant spreads by rhizomes to make big clumps. Divide from time to time. Much or little water. Provide winter protection
S. verticillata LILAC SAGE Perennial	31, 32, 34–41	Clumps 1½–2 ft. tall, composed of broad, hairy, heart-shaped leaves	Branched flower stalks to 2½ ft. carrying purple-blue flowers appear in summer (spring-fall in mild-winter areas)	Sun or light shade. 'Purple Rain' is a superior form with long, arching spikes of purple flowers
S. viridis (*S. horminum*) Annual	All zones	Single stemmed or branched plants to 1½ ft. tall	Flowers insignificant, but leaflike bracts in pink, white, or blue are showy in summer. Long-lasting cut flowers, fresh or dried	'Claryssa' is a superior selection with pink, blue, purple, or white bracts. 'Oxford Blue' has blue bracts; 'Pink Sundae', bright pink; 'White Swan', white with green veins. All are excellent cut flowers and can be dried

SAMBUCUS

ELDERBERRY

Caprifoliaceae

DECIDUOUS SHRUBS OR TREES

☑ ZONES VARY BY SPECIES

☼ ◑ FULL SUN OR LIGHT SHADE

🔴 REGULAR WATER

⬥ UNCOOKED FRUITS OF RED-BERRIED SPECIES CAN CAUSE NAUSEA, VOMITING, DIARRHEA IF INGESTED

Sambucus

In their natural state, these are rampant, fast-growing, wild-looking plants—but they can be tamed to a degree. Use them as you would spiraea or other large deciduous shrubs. In large gardens, they can be effective as a screen or windbreak. To keep them dense and shrubby, prune hard: in late dormant season, cut back all previous year's growth to a few inches. New growth sprouts readily from stumps.

Elders are a confusing lot, and botanists in different regions tend to assign different names to the same plant. There are black-, blue-, and red-fruited elders; birds eat the fruit of all types, but the fruit of redberried species can cause nausea in humans if consumed raw in large quantities.

S. canadensis. AMERICAN ELDERBERRY. Zones 31, 32, 34–45. Native to central and eastern North America. Spreading, suckering shrub to 6–8 ft. high. Foliage is almost tropical looking; each leaf has seven 2–6-in.-long leaflets. Flat, creamy white flower clusters to 10 in. wide in early summer, followed by tasty purple-black fruit. Fruit used for pies; both flowers and fruit used for wine. Strictly fruiting varieties include 'Adams', 'Johns', and many more; plant any two for pollination. Ornamental varieties include 'Aurea', with golden green foliage (golden in full sun) and red berries; and 'Laciniata', cutleaf or fernleaf elder, with finely cut foliage and dark berries.

S. nigra. BLACK ELDER, EUROPEAN ELDER. Zones 32, 34, 39. Native to Europe, Africa, Asia. Resembles *S. canadensis* but grows larger (tree to 20–30 ft.) and bears less flavorful berries (which are usually mixed with other fruits in jellies). Species is rarely seen, but smaller-growing (6–8-ft.) ornamental forms are available. 'Alba Variegata' has white berries, leaves edged in creamy white. Types bearing the standard purple-black berries include 'Aurea', with yellow new growth; 'Laciniata', with finely divided, fernlike leaves; and 'Purpurea' (*S. n. porphyrifolia*), with deep purple leaves and pinkish flowers.

S. pubens. SCARLET ELDER. Zones 34–43. Native to northern latitudes in North America. Shrubby plant, usually 2–4 ft. high, possibly reaching 15 ft. Leaves divided into five or seven 2–4-in.-long leaflets. Blooms in late spring, with tall (to 5-in.), loose flower clusters; inedible bright red fruit follows the flowers.

S. racemosa. RED ELDERBERRY, EUROPEAN RED ELDERBERRY. Zones 34–43. Native to northern latitudes in North America, Europe, Asia. Bushy shrub 8–10 ft. tall. Leaves divided into five or seven smooth, sharply toothed leaflets. Small, creamy white flowers in dome-shaped clusters to 2½ in. wide, late spring into summer; inedible bright red berries. 'Plumosa Aurea' has finely divided golden leaves.

SAND CHERRY. See PRUNUS, Additional Deciduous Species

SAND PEAR. See PYRUS pyrifolia

FOR INFORMATION ON SELECTING PLANTS

PLEASE SEE PAGES 47–112

SANGUINARIA canadensis

BLOODROOT

Papaveraceae

PERENNIAL

☑ ZONES 32, 34–43

◑ ☼ PARTIAL OR FULL SHADE

🔴🔴 AMPLE WATER

Sanguinaria canadensis

A North American native, this member of the poppy family gets its common name from the orange-red juice that seeps from cut roots and stems. Big, deeply lobed grayish leaves. Blooms in spring, bearing lovely (but ephemeral) white or pink-tinged, 1½-in. flowers carried singly on 8-in. stalks. Plant dies back in mid- to late summer. For damp, shaded rock or woodland garden where it can spread. 'Multiplex' has double flowers.

SANGUISORBA

BURNET

Rosaceae

PERENNIALS

☑ ZONES VARY BY SPECIES

☼ ◑ LIGHT SHADE IN HOT CLIMATES

🔴 REGULAR WATER

Sanguisorba

Perennials that grow from creeping rhizomes. Leaves are divided featherwise into toothed roundish or oval leaflets. Flowers are small, carried in dense, feathery spikes resembling small bottlebrushes. Often sold as *Poterium*.

S. canadensis. GREAT BURNET, CANADIAN BURNET. Zones 31, 32, 34–45. Bright green, 3–6-ft.-tall clumps put up 8-in. spikes of white flowers in late autumn. Dies to ground even in mild climates.

S. minor. GARDEN BURNET, SALAD BURNET. Zones 31, 32, 34–43. Can grow to 1½ ft. tall, with roundish red flower heads 1 in. long, but is usually kept clipped to a few inches to maintain a supply of fresh new leaves for culinary use. Leaves have a light cucumberlike flavor and are used in salads, soups, cool drinks. Can be used as an edging for border planting or herb garden. Evergreen in all but the coldest-winter regions.

S. obtusa. Zones 31, 32, 34–41. To 4 ft. tall, with grayish green leaves and 4-in. pink flower spikes in summer. Evergreen in all but the coldest winters.

S

SANTOLINA

Asteraceae (Compositae)

EVERGREEN SUBSHRUBS

☑ ZONES 32, 34–35, 39, EXCEPT AS NOTED

☼ FULL SUN

🔴 ⬥ REGULAR TO LITTLE WATER

Santolina

These have attractive foliage, a profusion of small, round, buttonlike flower heads in summer, and stout constitutions. Good as ground covers, bank covers, or low clipped hedges. Grow in any soil. All plants are aromatic if bruised and look best if kept low by pruning. Clip off spent flowers. Cut back to a few inches tall in early spring. May die to ground in coldest areas, but will come back from roots.

S. chamaecyparissus (C. incana). LAVENDER COTTON. Can reach 2 ft., but looks best clipped to 1 ft. or less. Brittle, woody stems are densely clothed with rough, finely divided, whitish gray leaves. Unclipped plants produce bright yellow flower heads. Set 3 ft. apart as ground cover, closer as edging for walks, borders, foreground plantings. Replace if woodiness takes over. 'Nana' is smaller than the species, to 1 ft. tall and 2–3 ft. wide. 'Lemon Queen', 2 ft. tall and wide, has lemon yellow flowers.

S. pinnata (S. ericoides). To 2–2½ ft. tall, with narrow, saw-edged dark green leaves and cream-colored flowers. *S. p. neapolitana,* 12–15 in. tall, has silvery foliage and bright yellow buttons.

S. rosmarinifolia (S. virens). Zones 31, 32. To 2 ft., with narrow, green-and-silvery leaves like those of rosemary. Leaves may have tiny teeth or none at all. Bright yellow flowers.

SANVITALIA procumbens

CREEPING ZINNIA

Asteraceae (Compositae)

ANNUAL

⚡ ALL ZONES

☼ FULL SUN

◉ REGULAR TO MODERATE WATER

Sanvitalia procumbens

Not really a zinnia, and in fact looks like a tiny sunflower. Grows only 4–6 in. high but spreads or trails to 1 ft. or more. Leaves are like miniature (to 2-in.-long) zinnia leaves. Flower heads nearly 1 in. wide, with dark purple-brown center and bright yellow or orange rays. Bloom lasts from midsummer until frost. Varieties are 'Mandarin Orange' and double-flowered 'Gold Braid'.

Needs good drainage. Resents transplanting, so sow seeds where plants will grow—as early as early April in mildest-winter climates, as late as May or even June where soil is slow to warm up. Heat resistant. Plant in hanging baskets or pots, or use as temporary filler in border, edging, or cover for slope or bank.

SAPONARIA

Caryophyllaceae

PERENNIALS

⚡ ZONES VARY BY SPECIES

☼ FULL SUN

◉ REGULAR TO MODERATE WATER

Saponaria

Generally low growing; closely related to *Lychnis* and *Silene.* Easy to grow in well-drained soil. Useful as border or rock garden plants.

S. lembergii 'Max Frei'. Zones 32, 34, 37. Hybrid between two Mediterranean species. Compact, trailing plant 6–15 in. tall, with blue-green foliage and a midsummer show of inch-wide, bright reddish pink flowers.

S. ocymoides. Zones 34–45. Trailing habit to 1 ft. high and 3 ft. across. Oval dark green leaves. In spring, plants are covered with small pink flowers in loose bunches shaped much like those of phlox. Useful for covering walls and as ground cover. Intolerant of hot, humid summers. 'Alba' is a white form; 'Rubra Compacta' has deeper pink flowers.

S. officinalis. SOAPWORT, BOUNCING BET. Zones 31, 32, 34–45. To 2 ft. tall, spreading by underground runners. Dark green leaves. Loose clusters of 1-in. red, pink, or white flowers in midsummer. If vigorously rubbed with water, plant produces suds. This is a tough plant; before the days of herbicides, it could be seen growing in the cinders along railroad rights-of-way. 'Rosea Plena', with double light pink flowers, is the common garden form. 'Rubra Plena' has crimson blooms that turn paler as they age.

S. pumilio (S. pumila). Zones 32, 34, 37, 39. Forms a small, tight, bright green cushion to 1 ft. high, 2 ft. wide. Relatively large purplish pink flowers are borne singly on branch ends in spring, making a ring of blossoms around base of plant.

SAPPHIREBERRY. See SYMPLOCOS paniculata

SARCOCOCCA hookeriana humilis (S. humilis)

SWEET BOX

Buxaceae

EVERGREEN SHRUB

⚡ ZONES 31, 32

☼◉ PARTIAL OR FULL SHADE

◉ REGULAR TO MODERATE WATER

Sarcococca hookeriana

Native to Himalayas, China. Low growing, seldom more than 1½ ft. high; spreads by underground runners to 8 ft. or more. Grown for handsome, dark green, waxy foliage and for tiny, powerfully fragrant white flowers hidden in foliage in late winter or early spring. Oval, pointed leaves (1–3 in. long, ½–¾ in. wide) are closely set on branches. Small, berry-like, glossy blue-black fruit. Useful ground cover in shaded areas—under overhangs, in entryways, beneath low-branching evergreen trees. Maintains slow, orderly growth and polished appearance in deepest shade. Tolerates sun in cool-summer climates. Grows best in soil rich in organic matter; add peat moss, ground bark, or the like to planting bed. Scale insects are the only pests.

SARGENT CHERRY. See PRUNUS sargentii under PRUNUS, Flowering Cherry (chart)

SARRACENIA

PITCHER PLANT

Sarraceniaceae

PERENNIALS

⚡ ZONES VARY BY SPECIES

☼ FULL SUN

◉ CONSTANTLY MOIST SOIL

Sarracenia

These fascinating, carnivorous plants are native to acidic bogs from the Canadian Arctic south to Florida. Plants grow from short, thick rhizomes that produce clumps of hollow, trumpet- or urn-shaped leaves that form the exotic-looking pitchers designed to trap unwary insects. Pitchers range from 2 in.–3 ft. tall and often have a hood that partially covers the top of the pitcher. In spring, nodding, solitary flowers appear on erect stalks that hold them above the pitchers.

In the garden, plant pitcher plants in a bog or other wet place in full sun. They require acid soil that is rich in organic matter and that remains constantly wet. Pitcher plants also can be grown in containers set in water. Where not hardy, container-grown plants can be overwintered in a cool sunny sunroom or greenhouse. Plants do not have to catch insects for survival—they manufacture food by photosynthesis like all other green plants. Do not try to supplement their diets by feeding them bits of meat or other scraps. When adding these natives to your garden, be sure to purchase nursery-propagated plants. Unscrupulous dealers still collect pitcher plants from the wild and sell them, thus depleting natural populations. Nursery-propagated plants are far superior and easier to establish.

S. flava. YELLOW PITCHER PLANT. Zones 31, 32, 34, 39. Native wildflower from Virginia southward producing slender, 1–3-ft.-tall, yellow-green pitchers with raised hoods sheltering the tops. Bears yellow, 4-in.-wide flowers in spring. Plants form 3-ft.-wide clumps with time.

S. leucophylla (S. drummondii). WHITE TRUMPET. Zones 31, 32, 34, 39. Species native from Missouri east and south to Florida producing 3-ft.-wide clumps of 1–3½-ft.-tall, slender, trumpet-shaped pitchers that are white netted with purple near the top and on the hoods. Bears purple, 3–4-in.-wide flowers in spring.

S

S. minor. HOODED PITCHER PLANT. Zones 31, 32, 34, 39. Native from North Carolina to Florida. Bears trumpet-shaped, 1–2-ft.-tall green pitchers marked with purple veins and patches of yellow or white near the tops. Pitchers are nearly closed at the tops by hoods marked with white. Bears yellow flowers in spring.

S. purpurea. PURPLE PITCHER PLANT, COMMON PITCHER PLANT. Zones 31, 32, 34–45. Hardy native from Canada to New Jersey that bears rounded, green pitchers marked with red veins. The pitchers are 2–20-in. long and borne horizontally along the ground, with the openings pointing up. They turn red in fall. Plants produce new pitchers all season and clumps reach 3 ft. with time. Bears dark red, 2-in.-wide flowers in spring.

S. 'Dixie Lace'. Zones 31, 32, 34, 39. Handsome hybrid with yellow to yellow-brown pitchers netted with red veins. Pitchers are semierect (carried at a 45-degree angle), and plants form 1½-ft.-wide clumps. Bears maroon red flowers in spring. Produces new pitchers all season long.

S. 'Ladies in Waiting'. Zones 31, 32, 34, 39. Hybrid selection bearing erect, 2-ft. tall pitchers that are green at the base and red speckled with white at the top. Bears maroon red flowers in spring. Produces new pitchers all season long.

SARUMA henryi

UPRIGHT WILD GINGER

Aristolochiaceae

PERENNIAL

ZONES 31, 32, 34–41

PARTIAL TO FULL SHADE

REGULAR WATER

Saruma henryi

A native of China that is relatively new in the garden trade, *Saruma* is related to wild gingers *(Asarum),* but does not resemble them in growth habit. Plants reach 2 ft. high and bear fuzzy, heart-shaped, 5-in.-wide light green leaves. They produce ¾-in.-wide butter yellow flowers atop the stems from early spring through late summer. With time, clumps spread to about 3 ft. Use this species as an exotic addition to the woodland or shade garden. Plants will self-sow.

SASA. See BAMBOO

SASSAFRAS albidum

SASSAFRAS

Lauraceae

DECIDUOUS TREE

ZONES 31, 32, 34–41

FULL SUN

REGULAR WATER

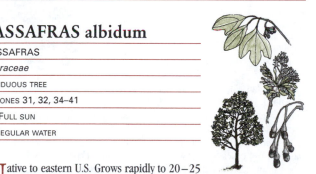
Sassafras albidum

Native to eastern U.S. Grows rapidly to 20–25 ft. high, then more slowly to an eventual 50–60 ft. Often shrubby in youth; with age, becomes dense and pyramidal, with heavy trunk and rather short branches. Dark reddish brown, furrowed bark. Interesting winter silhouette. Leaves 3–7 in. long, 2–4 in. wide; they may be oval, mitten shaped, or lobed on both sides. Excellent fall color—shades of yellow, orange, scarlet, and purple. Yellow flowers aren't showy, but clusters outline the bare branches in early spring. Male and female flowers on separate trees; when the two sexes are grown near each other, the female tree bears dark blue, ½-in. berries on bright red stalks.

Pleasantly aromatic tree; bark of roots was sometimes used for making tea, which had a flavor reminiscent of root beer. The tree's volatile oil, which contains safrole, is carcinogenic in animals; the bark is safrole-free.

Performs best in well-drained, nonalkaline soil; won't take prolonged drought. Hard to transplant; small trees transplant best.. Tends to produce suckers, especially if roots are cut during cultivation. Gypsy moths eat the foliage; Japanese beetles also favor sassafras.

HERBAL USES FOR SASSAFRAS

Although sassafras tea is no longer generally recommended, sassafras has some traditional external applications that are still considered safe and effective. Sassafras poultices have been used to treat wounds and sores of the skin, and also to relieve the itching caused by poison ivy and poison oak.

SATUREJA

Lamiaceae (Labiatae)

ANNUALS AND PERENNIALS

ZONES VARY BY SPECIES

FULL SUN

REGULAR TO MODERATE WATER

Satureja

These aromatic plants serve many culinary purposes.

S. hortensis. SUMMER SAVORY. Annual. All zones. Upright to 1½ ft.; loose, open habit. Rather narrow, aromatic leaves to 1½ in. long; use fresh or dried as mild seasoning for meats, fish, eggs, soups, beans, vegetables. Whorls of delicate pinkish white to rose flowers in summer. Light, rich soil. Good pot plant.

S. montana. WINTER SAVORY. Shrubby perennial. Zones 31, 32, 34, 39. Low, spreading, 6–15 in. high. Stiff, narrow to roundish leaves to 1 in. long; not as delicate in flavor as summer savory. Use leaves fresh or dried; clip at start of bloom season for drying. Profuse summer bloom; whorls of small white to lilac flowers, attractive to bees. Light, well-drained soil. Use in rock garden, as dwarf clipped hedge in herb garden.

SAUROMATUM venosum (S. guttatum)

VOODOO LILY, MONARCH OF THE EAST

Araceae

TUBEROUS PERENNIALS

ZONES 31, 32; ELSEWHERE, GROW IN POTS

PARTIAL SHADE

REGULAR WATER

Sauromatum venosum

Resembling a very elongated jack-in-the-pulpit, voodoo lily blooms in early spring from tubers up to 6 in. thick. The blooms, pollinated by flies, stink like rotten meat for a few hours a day for a few days when mature. They have a 2–4-in. stalk, a 2–4-in. cylindrical lower part, and 1–2-ft. long, inch-wide, twisted purplish green blade with interior spots of blackish purple. Large, compound leaves rise on spotted yard-high stalks a few weeks after the flowers have gone by. This foliage lends a decidedly tropical appearance to the garden until frost.

Treated as an oddity, voodoo lily can bloom without soil or water, although that will finish off the plant. North of Zone 32, specimens may also survive cold winters outdoors in a sheltered site with a 1-ft. covering of loose mulch. Plant tubers 6 in. deep. Also good in pots, which can be brought indoors in winter and set outdoors and sunk into the ground in summer. Voodoo lily needs rich, moist, humusy soil during its growth period. When grown in pots, it requires dryness during winter dormancy.

S

SAURURUS cernuus

LIZARD'S TAIL, SWAMP DRAGON, WATER DRAGON

Saururaceae

PERENNIAL

ZONES 31, 32, 34–43

FULL SUN TO PARTIAL SHADE

MORE THAN REGULAR WATER

Saururus cernuus

Native to eastern North America, lizard's tail is a vigorous, bog-dwelling species that bears somewhat heart-shaped leaves topped by narrow, arching, tail-like spikes of fragrant white flowers in summer. Plants range from 1 to 2 ft. high. They spread vigorously and become invasive in water gardens, especially shallow, earth-bottomed ones. Grow this plant in soil that remains constantly moist: It also grows in standing water to a depth of 6 in. To restrict its spread, keep it in containers set with the rims 1–2 in. above the soil surface.

SAVORY. See SATUREJA

SAXIFRAGA

SAXIFRAGE

Saxifragaceae

PERENNIALS

ZONES VARY BY SPECIES

EXPOSURE NEEDS VARY BY SPECIES

REGULAR WATER

Saxifraga

Some saxifrages are native to mountainous areas of North America; most are from Europe. They do best in rock gardens where summer heat and humidity are not intense. Require good drainage and light soil; rot easily in soggy soil. Most grow in full sun or light shade, but those listed here—all evergreen species—are shade plants.

S. rosacea (S. decipiens, S. sternbergii). Zones 32, 34–41. Cushion-forming, spreading plant—typical "mossy" type of saxifrage. Spreads fairly rapidly. Narrow, fleshy leaves are divided into three to five narrow lobes. Foliage turns crimson in late fall. In spring, flower stalks to 8–9 in. high display wide-open white flowers. Needs a cool, semishaded location; dies out in hot, muggy weather. Many named varieties and hybrids exist, with flowers in pink, rose, and red. 'Carnival' has red flowers that fade to pink, then white.

S. stolonifera (S. sarmentosa). STRAWBERRY GERANIUM. Zones 31, 32; house plant anywhere. Creeping plant that makes runners like strawberry. Nearly round, white-veined leaves to 4 in. across, pink underneath; blend well with pink azaleas. White flowers to 1 in. across, in loose, open clusters to 2 ft. tall, late summer–fall. Can be used as house plant in hanging baskets or pots; good ground cover where hard freezes are infrequent. Give bright indirect light indoors, partial or full shade outdoors.

S. umbrosa. Zones 32, 34. Rosettes of green, shiny, tongue-shaped leaves 1½ in. long. Blooms in spring, with open clusters of pink flowers on wine red stalks. Does best in full shade. Good ground cover for small areas; effective near rocks, stream beds. This species generally goes by the common name "London pride," but that name actually belongs to *S. urbium*, a hybrid between *S. umbrosa* and the similar *S. hirsuta*.

Saxifragaceae. The saxifrage family once included a number of shrubs, but these now occupy their own families—Hydrangeaceae and Grossulariaceae (currants and gooseberries). Remaining in Saxifragaceae are a number of herbaceous plants, including *Astilbe, Bergenia*, coral bells *(Heuchera)*, and of course saxifrage *(Saxifraga)*.

SCABIOSA

PINCUSHION FLOWER

Dipsacaceae

ANNUALS AND PERENNIALS

ZONES VARY BY SPECIES

FULL SUN

REGULAR TO MODERATE WATER

Scabiosa

Stamens protrude beyond curved surface of flower head, giving illusion of pins stuck into a cushion. Bloom begins in midsummer, continues until frost if flowers are cut. Plants do not thrive in hot, humid climates, but they are easy to grow in cooler regions. Good in mixed or mass plantings. Excellent for arrangements.

S. atropurpurea. PINCUSHION FLOWER, MOURNING BRIDE. Annual. All zones. Usually sold as *S. grandiflora*. To 2½–3 ft. tall. Oblong, coarsely toothed leaves. Many long, wiry stems carry flowers to 2 in. wide or more, in colors ranging from blackish purple to salmon pink, rose, and white.

S. caucasica. PINCUSHION FLOWER. Perennial. Zones 32, 34–43. To 1½–2½ ft. high. Leaves vary from finely cut to uncut. Flowers 2½–3 in. across; depending on variety, color may be blue to bluish lavender or white. Excellent for cut flowers. Give part shade in hot-summer areas. Fama strain has branching stalks of light blue, 3-in. flowers with unusually large ray flowers around the edge. House Hybrids strain contains a mixture of white and blue shades. 'Alba' is white flowered; 'Blue Perfection' bears lavender blue blooms with fringed petals.

S. columbaria. Perennial. Zones 32, 34. To 2 ft. tall. Finely cut gray-green leaves. Flowers to 3 in. across come in lavender blue, pink, or white, depending on the variety. 'Butterfly Blue' grows to 1 ft. high, bears 2-in. blooms.

S. ochroleuca. Biennial or short-lived perennial. Zones 32, 34. To 2 ft. tall, with light yellow flowers to 2½ in. across.

S. stellata. Annual. All zones. To 1½ ft. tall. Many heads of pale blue, 1½-in. flowers; these quickly turn to papery bronze drumsticks, useful in dry arrangements.

SCAEVOLA

Goodeniaceae

PERENNIALS GROWN AS ANNUALS

ALL ZONES

FULL SUN

REGULAR TO MODERATE WATER

Scaevola

Australian natives with fan-shaped flowers (all petals on one side) in blue shades. As annuals in the Northeast, bloom late spring–frost. Good for hanging baskets, as ground covers, spilling over walls.

S. aemula. Fleshy-stemmed, sprawling plants used mainly in hanging baskets or to cascade over walls. Lavender blue, 1½-in. flowers produced along branches. Available mainly through varieties: 'Blue Wonder', blue flowers; 'Purple Fanfare' ('Diamond Head'), purple blue; 'Purple Shamrock', purple blue flowers larger than those of most other scaevolas, on bushy, 14-in. plants; 'White Charm', white flowers; and 'Sun Fan', small, light blue flowers, heat tolerant.

S. 'Mauve Clusters'. More wide spreading, smaller flowered than *S. aemula;* stems not as fleshy. Forms mats to 4–6 in. high, eventually 3–5 ft. across. Lilac mauve, ½-in.-wide flowers. Set plants 3 ft. apart for ground cover.

PRACTICAL GARDENING DICTIONARY

PLEASE SEE PAGES 449–523

S

SCHISANDRA chinensis

CHINESE MAGNOLIA VINE

Schisandraceae

DECIDUOUS VINE

⚡ ZONES 31, 32, 34–43

☀ ◑ FULL SUN OR PARTIAL SHADE

🌢 REGULAR WATER

Schisandra chinensis

Glossy, oblong, dark green leaves contrast with clusters of fragrant, creamy pink, cup-shaped flowers on this twining climber that can be trained over a garden wall, gazebo, or arbor. Small bright red berries follow flowering on female vines, but both sexes must be present to ensure fruit. Thrives in moist, sandy soil and will grow 20–30 ft. high.

SCHIZACHYRIUM scoparium

LITTLE BLUESTEM, PRAIRIE BEARD GRASS

Gramineae

PERENNIAL GRASS

⚡ ZONES 31, 32, 34–41

☀ FULL SUN

🌢 REGULAR WATER

Schizachyrium scoparium

This finely textured native American prairie grass features slender leaves 1–1½ ft. long and will grow in clumps to 4 ft. high. Summer foliage colors range from bright green to subtle blue to purple. In fall, color varies from tan to copper and even orange. One outstanding cultivar, 'The Blues', features distinctive blue stems covered with a delicate whitish film. Summer flowers of this species develop into fluffy seed heads that sparkle when backlit. Erect stems withstand snow and make it a good choice for the winter garden. Does not require fertile soil, but prefers good drainage and will not survive conditions that are excessively moist. Ideal for meadows and for transition areas between tended and natural gardens, or as a specimen plant in a more formal setting.

SCHIZANTHUS pinnatus

POOR MAN'S ORCHID, BUTTERFLY FLOWER

Solanaceae

ANNUAL

⚡ ALL ZONES

◑ FILTERED SHADE

🌢 REGULAR WATER

Schizanthus pinnatus

Grows to 1½ ft. high. Great quantities of small orchidlike flowers, with varicolored markings on pink, rose, lilac, purple, or white background. Blossoms look quite showy against the plant's ferny foliage, make long-lasting cut flowers. Buy potted plants, or start seeds indoors about 4 weeks ahead of outdoor planting time (germination is slow). Plants are sensitive to both frost and heat. Plan for summer bloom where summer temperatures are moderate. Provide a location sheltered from wind. Good container plant. Often grown in greenhouses and conservatories.

FOR GROWING SYMBOL EXPLANATIONS

PLEASE SEE PAGE 113

SCHIZOPHRAGMA hydrangeoides

JAPANESE HYDRANGEA VINE

Hydrangeaceae

DECIDUOUS VINE

⚡ ZONES 31, 32, 34, 39

◑ PARTIAL SHADE

🌢 REGULAR WATER

Schizophragma hydrangeoides

Resembles *Hydrangea anomala*, the climbing hydrangea. Climbs by holdfasts to 30 ft. Leaves are dark green, 3–5 in. long, oval, pointed, toothed. Broad clusters of flowers appear summer–fall; they resemble lace cap hydrangeas, but the showy white parts are the enlarged (to 1½-in.) sepals of the outermost flowers. In contrast to hydrangea, in which sterile flowers contain several showy sepals, sterile flowers of this plant have one sepal each. 'Moonlight' has blue-green foliage with a silvery cast. Use species or variety in shaded areas to climb masonry walls or trees.

SCHIZOSTYLIS coccinea

CRIMSON FLAG, KAFFIR LILY

Iridaceae

RHIZOMATOUS PERENNIAL

⚡ ZONES 31, 32; OR GROW IN POTS

☀ ◑ LIGHT SHADE IN HOT CLIMATES

🌢🌢 AMPLE WATER DURING ACTIVE GROWTH

Schizostylis coccinea

South African native hardy to 10°F/−12°C; except in Zones 31 and 32, grow in pots and protect in winter. Narrow, evergreen, 1½-ft.-long leaves resemble those of gladiolus. In autumn, slender 1½–2-ft. stems bear spikes of showy flowers—crimson, starlike, 2½ in. wide. Each blossom lasts 4 days, others follow; excellent cut flowers. Divide clumps when overgrown. Varieties include 'Alba', with white flowers; 'Mrs. Hegarty', pale pink; 'Oregon Sunset', watermelon red; 'Sunrise', bright pink; 'Viscountess Byng', soft pink. Water generously from spring through bloom; cut back on water at other times.

SCIADOPITYS verticillata

UMBRELLA PINE

Taxodiaceae

EVERGREEN TREE

⚡ ZONES 31, 32, 34, 35, 37, 39

☀ ◑ AFTERNOON SHADE IN ZONES 31, 32

🌢 REGULAR WATER

Sciadopitys verticillata

Grows to 100–120 ft. in its native Japan, but not likely to exceed 25–40 ft. in gardens here. Very slow grower. Young plant is symmetrical, dense, rather narrow; older plant opens up and branches tend to droop. Small, scalelike leaves grow scattered along branches, bunched at branch ends. At branch and twig ends grow whorls of 20–30 long (3–6-in.), narrow, flattened, firm, fleshy needles of glossy dark green (they radiate out like spokes of umbrella). In time, 3–5-in.-long woody cones may appear.

Choice decorative tree for open ground or container use. Plant in rich, well-drained, neutral or slightly acid soil. Leave unpruned, or thin to create Oriental effect. Good bonsai subject. Boughs are beautiful and long lasting in arrangements. These are trees for connoisseurs, scarce because of their extremely slow growth.

S

SCILLA

SQUILL, BLUEBELL

Liliaceae

BULBS

⚘ ZONES VARY BY SPECIES

☼ ◑ FULL SUN OR LIGHT SHADE

💧 REGULAR WATER DURING GROWTH AND BLOOM

☣ ALL PARTS ARE POISONOUS IF INGESTED

Scilla

All have basal, strap-shaped leaves and clusters of bell-shaped or star-like flowers in winter or spring. Best planted in informal drifts among shrubs, under deciduous trees, among low-growing spring perennials. Good in pots, for cutting. All need some winter chill. Plant cold-hardy species 2–3 in. deep, about 4 in. apart. All types are dormant in summer.

S. bifolia. Zones 31, 32, 34–41. First to bloom in early spring. Carries up to eight turquoise blue, inch-wide, starlike flowers on each 8-in. stem. There are white, pale purplish pink, and violet blue varieties. Each bulb produces only two leaves.

S. hispanica. See *Hyacinthoides hispanica*

S. nonscripta. See *Hyacinthoides non-scripta*

S. siberica. SIBERIAN SQUILL. Zones 34–45. Blooms very early, with loose spikes of intense blue flowers on 3–6-in. stems. 'Spring Beauty', with darker blue stripes, is choice. Also comes in white, purplish pink, and violet blue varieties.

S. tubergeniana (S. mischtschenkoana). Zones 31, 32, 34–43. Blooms in winter to very early spring, at about same time as snowdrops and winter aconite. Flowers are pale blue with a darker blue stripe down center of each flower segment. Four or more flowers to each 4-in. stalk; three or more stalks to each bulb.

SCOTCH BROOM. See CYTISUS scoparius

SCOTCH HEATHER. See CALLUNA vulgaris

SCOTCH MOSS. See SAGINA subulata

Scrophulariaceae. The figwort family consists principally of annuals and perennials. Most have irregular flowers, with four or five lobes often arranged as two lips. Some examples are snapdragon (*Antirrhinum*), foxglove (*Digitalis*), *Nemesia*, beard tongue (*Penstemon*), and wishbone flower (*Torenia*).

SCUTELLARIA

SKULLCAP

Lamiaceae

PERENNIALS AND SUBSHRUBS

⚘ ZONES VARY BY SPECIES

☼ ◑ FULL SUN TO PARTIAL SHADE

💧 REGULAR WATER

Scutellaria

Cultivated for their attractive tubular flowers in shades of purple, pink, yellow, and white, this group of summer-blooming plants includes both short and tall varieties that usually have square stems.

S. alpina. Subshrub. Zones 31, 32, 34–43. Grows 6–12 in. tall, with prostrate, hairy stems full of oval, 1-in. leaves. Groups of 1-in. violet flowers with white to yellow lower lips top 2–3-in. stalks. Needs well-drained, gravelly soil in a fairly dry location. Well suited to rock gardens.

S. altissima. Zones 31, 32, 34, 39. Grows 1–3 ft. high. Spikelike flower stems are studded with blooms that have long, soft yellow to blue coloring on top and white lower lips. Use in woodland and wild gardens. Plants

flourish in average soil in sun to partial shade. May self-sow. Increase by seed or division.

S. indica. Zones 31, 32. Erect plant to 1 ft. high, with hairy leaves and flower stalks covered with two-lipped, long-tubed blue or white flowers. Prefers well-drained, gravelly soil. Good for rock gardens.

S. orientalis. Zones 31, 32, 34–41. This mat-forming rock garden plant has horizontal stems and hairy grayish leaves. Flowers are yellow above and have a reddish lower lip and purple or chartreuse hairy bracts. Likes well-drained alkaline sites.

S. incana. Zones 31, 32, 34–41. Native to the central and eastern U.S. Growing wild in moist woodland areas, this hairy plant, 2–3 ft. tall, has erect stems with 2–4-in. grayish green leaves. It produces light blue flowers in showy groups, blooming later than some other skullcaps. Grow it in borders with other late bloomers such as aster, coneflower, and helenium. Gray seed heads look attractive after blooming has finished.

SEA BUCKTHORN. See HIPPOPHAE rhamnoides

SEA HOLLY. See ERYNGIUM

SEA KALE. See CRAMBE maritima

SEA LAVENDER. See LIMONIUM

SEA PINK. See ARMERIA

SEDGE. See CAREX

SEDUM

STONECROP

Crassulaceae

SUCCULENT PERENNIALS

⚘ ZONES VARY BY SPECIES

☼ ◑ FULL SUN OR LIGHT SHADE, EXCEPT AS NOTED

💧 MODERATE TO LITTLE WATER, EXCEPT AS NOTED

Sedum

They come from many parts of the world and vary in hardiness, cultural needs; some are among hardiest succulent plants. Some are tiny and trailing, others upright. Leaves fleshy, highly variable in size, shape, and color; evergreen unless otherwise noted. In cold climates, leaves of evergreen types may turn red. Flowers usually small, starlike, in fairly large clusters, sometimes brightly colored. Some flower in spring, others in summer and fall.

Smaller sedums are useful in rock gardens, as ground or bank cover, in small areas where unusual texture, color are needed. Some of the smaller types are prized by collectors of succulents, who grow them as potted or dish garden plants. Larger types good in borders or containers. Most propagate easily by stem cuttings—even detached leaves will root and form new plants. Soft and easily crushed, they will not take foot traffic; otherwise they are tough, low-maintenance plants. Set ground cover kinds 10–12 in. apart.

The botanically precise will note that several plants sold as *Sedum* have been reassigned to the genus *Hylotelephium;* changes are indicated below.

S. acre. GOLDMOSS SEDUM. Zones 31, 32, 34–43. To 2–5 in. tall, with upright branchlets from trailing, rooting stems. Tiny light green leaves; clustered yellow flowers in spring. Extremely hardy but can get out of bounds, become a weed. Use as ground cover, between stepping-stones, or on dry walls.

S. album. Zones 31, 32, 34–43. Often sold as *S. brevifolium*. Creeping plant 2–6 in. high. Leaves to ½ in. long, light to medium green, sometimes red tinted. White or pinkish summer flowers. Ground cover. Roots from smallest fragment, so beware of placing it near choice, delicate rock garden plants. 'Coral Carpet' has orange new growth, turns reddish bronze in winter.

S. anglicum. Zones 31, 32, 34–43. Low, spreading plant 2–4 in. tall. Dark green leaves to ⅛ in. long. Pinkish white spring flowers. Ground cover.

S. cauticolum (Hylotelephium cauticolum). Zones 31, 32, 34–43. Arching stems to 8 in. long are set with blue-gray, slightly toothed leaves. Clusters of small rose red flowers top stems in late summer or early fall. Dies to ground in winter.

S. dasyphyllum. Zones 31, 32, 34–41. Low, spreading mat with tiny, closely packed gray-green leaves and small white flowers with pink streaks. 'Riffense' has especially plump, succulent, blue-gray leaves. Partial shade.

S. ellacombianum. Zones 31, 32, 34–45. Sometimes offered as a variety of *S. kamtschaticum*. Differs in being a shorter plant (to 6 in. high) with more compact growth, unbranched stems, and scalloped rather than toothed leaves.

S. kamtschaticum. Zones 31, 32, 34–45. Trailing stems to 1 ft. long are set with thick, somewhat triangular, 1–1½-in., slightly toothed leaves. Summer flowers age from yellow to red. Useful in colder climates as small-scale ground cover, rock garden plant. 'Golden Carpet' has abundant bright golden flowers and leaves resembling those of *S. ellacombianum*. 'Variegatum' has cream-edged leaves. *S. k. floriferum* is a more profuse bloomer than the species, with smaller, lighter yellow flowers. Its variety 'Weihenstephaner Gold' bears abundant bright yellow blossoms opening from red buds in late spring.

S. lineare. Zones 31, 32, 34–43. Often sold as *S. sarmentosum*. Spreading, trailing, rooting stems to 1 ft. long, closely set with narrow light green leaves 1 in. long. Flowers yellow, star shaped, profuse in late spring, early summer. Ground cover. Vigorous spreader. 'Variegatum', with white-edged leaves, is a good container plant.

S. sarmentosum. See *S. lineare.*

S. sieboldii (Hylotelephium sieboldii). Zones 31, warmer parts of 32. Spreading, trailing, unbranched stems to 8–9 in. long. Leaves in threes, nearly round, stalkless, toothed in upper half, blue gray edged red. Plant turns coppery red in fall, dies to ground in winter. Each stem shows a broad, dense, flat cluster of dusty pink flowers in autumn. Beautiful rock garden or hanging basket plant. Light shade. 'Variegatum' has leaves marked yellowish white.

S. spathulifolium. Zones 31, 32, 34–41. Spoon-shaped blue-green leaves tinged reddish purple, packed into rosettes on short, trailing stems. Light yellow flowers, spring–summer. Ground cover, rock garden plant. Very drought tolerant. 'Cape Blanco' is a selected form with good leaf color. 'Purpureum' has deep purple leaves.

S. spectabile (Hylotelephium spectabile). Zones 31, 32, 34–43. Upright or slightly spreading stems to 1½ ft. tall, well set with blue-green, roundish, 3-in. leaves. Pink flowers in dense, 6-in.-wide, dome-shaped clusters atop stems in late summer, autumn. If stems are not cut after bloom, flower clusters mature into brownish maroon seed clusters atop bare stems. Dies to ground in winter. 'Brilliant' has deep rose red flowers, 'Carmen' is soft rose, 'Meteor' is carmine red, and 'Ruby Jewel' is deep maroon. Full sun. Regular to moderate water. Species resembles *S. telephium* in foliage and flowers, and in the developing seed heads that put on a long-lasting show.

S. spurium. Zones 31, 32, 34–43. Low grower with trailing stems. Leaves thick, an inch or so long, nearly as wide, dark green or bronze. Pink summer flowers in dense clusters at ends of 4–5-in. stems. For rock garden, pattern planting, ground cover. 'Coccineum', often known by the name "dragon's blood," has bronzy leaves, rosy red flowers.

S. telephium (Hylotelephium telephium). Zones 31, 32, 34–43. To 2 ft. high. Resembles *S. spectabile*, but leaves are somewhat narrower. Like *S. spectabile*, it is showy over a long season, dies down in winter. 'Indian Chief' has deep pink flowers. Hybrid 'Autumn Joy' has blossoms of bright salmon pink turning to russet; hybrid 'Mohrchen' has pink flowers and purple new growth. 'Atropurpureum' (often listed as a variety of *S. maximum*, a species no longer considered distinct from *S. telephium*) has burgundy leaves all season and dusty pink flowers. Full sun. Regular to moderate water.

S. 'Vera Jameson'. Zones 31, 32, 34–43. Hybrid with the habit and flowers of *S. sieboldii*, but with purple leaves.

SELAGINELLA

SPIKE MOSS

Selaginellaceae

PERENNIALS

ZONES VARY BY SPECIES

FULL SUN TO PARTIAL SHADE

REGULAR

Selaginella

Elegant rhizomatous evergreens have creeping spiked stems and are grown mostly for their scalelike ornamental foliage. Grow as trailing ground cover in a moist woodland garden, or to add interest and texture to hanging baskets. Can be cultivated as specimen plants for terrariums and indoor decoration. Prefers moderately fertile soil that is well-drained and rich in humus.

S. braunii. TREELET SPIKE MOSS. Zones 31, 32, 34–41. Erect frond-like stems to 1½ ft. high arise all at once in late spring. Gives a lacy, ferny effect not unlike the foliage of arborvitae. Turns straw colored in winter. Spreads.

S. kraussiana. TRAILING SPIKE MOSS. Zones 31, 32, 34, 39. To 1 in. high and wide spreading. Bright green and mossy with trailing stems. As a ground cover gives a carpetlike effect.

S. uncinata. PEACOCK MOSS. Zones 31, 32, 34, 39. To 2 in. high; metallic blue-green leaves form on short trailing stems that take root. Spreads widely. Prefers bright filtered sunlight rather than shade.

SELF-HEAL. See PRUNELLA

SEMPERVIVUM

HOUSELEEK

Crassulaceae

SUCCULENT PERENNIALS

ZONES 31, 32, 34–41

FULL SUN

REGULAR TO LITTLE WATER

Sempervivum

Evergreen perennial plants with tightly packed rosettes of leaves. Little offsets cluster around parent rosette. Flowers star shaped, in tight or loose clusters, white, yellowish, pink, red, or greenish, pretty in detail but not showy. Summer bloom. Blooming rosettes die after setting seed, but easily planted offsets carry on. Many species, all good in rock gardens, containers, even in pockets on boulders or pieces of porous rock. Need good drainage.

S. arachnoideum. COBWEB HOUSELEEK. Tiny gray-green rosettes, ¾ in. across, of many leaves joined by fine hairs that give a cobweb-covered look to plant. Spreads slowly to make dense mats. Bright red flowers on 4-in. stems; seldom blooms.

S. tectorum. HEN AND CHICKENS. Rosettes gray green, 4–6 in. across, spreading quickly by offsets. Leaves tipped red brown, bristle pointed. Flowers red or reddish in clusters on stems to 2 ft. tall. Easy to grow in rock gardens, borders, pattern planting.

S

FOR INFORMATION ON SELECTING PLANTS

PLEASE SEE PAGES 47–112

SENECIO

Asteraceae (Compositae)

PERENNIALS, SHRUBS, VINES

▨ ZONES VARY BY SPECIES

☼ ◐ ● EXPOSURE NEEDS VARY BY SPECIES

◖ ◗ ◕ WATER NEEDS VARY BY SPECIES

Senecio

Daisy relatives that range from garden cineraria and dusty miller to vines, shrubs, perennials, succulents, even a few weeds. Succulents are often sold as *Kleinia,* an earlier name.

S. aureus. GOLDEN GROUNDSEL. Perennial. Zones 31, 32, 34–43. Native to eastern North America. To 2 ft. high. Clump of bright green, toothed leaves is topped in spring by flat clusters of deep yellow, ½–1-in.-wide daisies. Full sun or part shade. Good bog garden plant.

S. cineraria. DUSTY MILLER. Shrubby perennial in Zones 31, 32; grown as annual in colder climates. To 2–2½ ft. tall and spreading. Woolly white leaves cut into many blunt-tipped lobes. Clustered heads of yellow or creamy yellow flowers, during summer. Gets leggy unless sheared occasionally. Full sun. Provide good drainage, moderate water. Striking in night garden.

> **WILL THE REAL DUSTY MILLER PLEASE STAND UP?**
>
> Many plants answer to the name; all have whitish, silvery, or grayish foliage, grow in full sun, and tolerate some drought. A number of plants are sold by this common name; the best known is *Centaurea cineraria.* Two are species of *Senecio: S. cineraria* and *S. vira-vira.* Others include *Artemisia stellerana* and *Lychnis coronaria.*

S. confusus. MEXICAN FLAME VINE. Not hardy in the Northeast, but can be grown as a summer annual. Twines to 8–10 ft. Light green, rather fleshy leaves are 1–4 in. long, ½–1 in. wide, coarsely toothed. Large clusters of ¾–1-in., startling orange-red blooms with golden centers appear at branch ends; 'São Paulo' is deeper orange, almost brick red. Plants bloom all year where winters are mild. Provide light soil, regular water. Full sun or light shade. Use on trellis or column, let cascade over bank or wall, or plant in hanging basket.

S. leucostachys. See *S. vira-vira*

S. macroglossus. KENYA IVY, NATAL IVY, WAX VINE. Evergreen vine in warm climates; grown as house plant in the Northeast. Twining or trailing vine to 6½ ft., with thin, succulent stems and thick, 2–3-in.-wide, waxy or rubbery leaves. Leaves are shaped like ivy leaves, with three, five, or seven shallow lobes. Tiny yellow daisies in summer. Leaves of 'Variegatus' are boldly splashed with creamy white. Outdoors, give part shade and moderate water. As house plant, grow in sunny window and water only when soil is dry.

S. mikanioides. GERMAN IVY. Vine. Grown as house plant in the Northeast. Twines to 18–20 ft. outdoors, much smaller indoors. Ivylike, roundish leaves with five to seven sharply pointed lobes, each ½–3 in. long. Winter flowers are small yellow daisies without rays. Good screening vine or trailing plant for window boxes. Full sun or part shade. Moderate water.

S. vira-vira (S. leucostachys, S. cineraria 'Candissimus'). DUSTY MILLER. Subshrub. Zones 31, 32, or grow as annual. To 4 ft. tall, with broad, sprawling habit. Leaves like those of *S. cineraria* but more strikingly white and more finely cut into much narrower, pointed segments. Creamy white summer flowers are not showy. In full sun, it is brilliantly white and densely leafy; in part shade, it is looser and more sparsely foliaged, with larger, greener leaves. Tip-pinch young plants to keep them compact. Moderate water.

SENSITIVE FERN. See ONOCLEA sensibilis

SENTRY PALM. See HOWEA belmoreana

SEQUOIADENDRON giganteum (Sequoia gigantea)

BIG TREE, GIANT SEQUOIA

Taxodiaceae

EVERGREEN TREE

▨ ZONES 32, 34, 36–39

☼ FULL SUN

◖ MODERATE, DEEP WATERING

Sequoiadendron giganteum

Old specimens exceed 300 ft. tall and have the most massive trunk in the world (to 30 ft. in diameter), yet young trees ("young" in terms of a 3,000-year life span) are neat, handsome trees for larger gardens, reaching height of 60–100 ft. Foliage is gray green, each leaf a pointed scale overlapping the next like a prickly cypress. Dark reddish brown cones to 3½ in. long. Lower branches hang on for many years, forming a dense pyramid. Lowest branches sometimes root where they touch ground, forming secondary "trees" that blend into the original. Removing lower branches reveals a fissured, craggy trunk covered with dark red-brown bark. 'Pendulum' has drooping branches and must be staked to coax it into vertical habit.

Primary use is as featured tree in large lawn (roots may surface there) or other open space. Though native to semiarid mountains of central California, will tolerate the humid-summer region from southern New England through mid-Atlantic states. However, outside its natural habitat, it is subject to fungus diseases that can disfigure or kill it. Prefers deep soils. Requires excellent drainage in hot, humid regions.

SERVICEBERRY. See AMELANCHIER

SETCREASEA pallida 'Purple Heart' (Tradescantia pallida 'Purpurea')

PURPLE HEART, PURPLE QUEEN

Commelinaceae

PERENNIAL

▨ ALL ZONES; SEE BELOW

☼ FULL SUN

◖ MODERATE WATER

Setcreasea pallida 'Purple Heart'

Creeping plant related to wandering Jew. Stems a foot or more high, inclined to flop over. Leaves rather narrowly oval and pointed, strongly shaded with purple, particularly on undersides. Pale or deep purple flowers not showy. Use discretion in planting, since the vivid foliage can create a harsh effect. Pinch back after bloom. Not hardy in the Northeast, but can be grown as summer annual or house plant. Outdoors, use as ground cover, bedding plant, or pot plant. Give house plants strong indirect light.

SEVEN SONS FLOWER. See HEPTACODIUM miconioides

SHADBLOW. See AMELANCHIER

FOR INFORMATION ON SELECTING PLANTS

PLEASE SEE PAGES 47–112

S

SHALLOT

Liliaceae

SMALL ONIONLIKE BULB

ALL ZONES

FULL SUN

REGULAR WATER

Shallot

Prized in cooking for its distinctive flavor. Plant either sets (small dry bulbs) or nursery plants in fall in Zones 31 and 32, early spring in cold-winter areas. Leaves 1–1½ ft. high develop from each bulb. Tiny lavender or white flowers sometimes appear. Ultimately two to eight bulbs will grow from each original bulb. At maturity (early summer if fall planted, late summer if spring planted), bulbs are formed and tops yellow and die. Harvest by pulling clumps and dividing bulbs. Let outer skin dry for about a month so that shallots can be stored for 4 to 6 months.

Some seed firms sell sets; nurseries with stocks of herbs may sell growing plants. If you use sets, plant so that tips are just covered. Golden brown skins of Dutch shallots enclose white cloves. Coppery skins of red shallots conceal purple cloves.

SHAMROCKS. Around St. Patrick's Day, nurseries and florists sell "shamrocks." These are small potted plants of *Medicago lupulina* (hop clover, yellow trefoil, black medick), an annual plant; *Oxalis acetosella* (wood sorrel), a perennial; or *Trifolium repens* (white clover), also a perennial. The last is most common. All have leaves divided into three leaflets, symbolic of the Trinity. They can be kept on a sunny windowsill or planted out, but they have little ornamental value and are likely to become weeds.

SHASTA DAISY. See CHRYSANTHEMUM maximum

SHELL FLOWER. See ALPINIA zerumbet, MOLUCCELLA laevis

SHELL GINGER. See ALPINIA zerumbet

SHEPHERDIA

Elaeagnaceae

DECIDUOUS SHRUBS

ZONES 34–45

FULL SUN

REGULAR TO LITTLE WATER

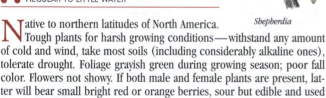

Shepherdia

Native to northern latitudes of North America. Tough plants for harsh growing conditions—withstand any amount of cold and wind, take most soils (including considerably alkaline ones), tolerate drought. Foliage grayish green during growing season; poor fall color. Flowers not showy. If both male and female plants are present, latter will bear small bright red or orange berries, sour but edible and used for jams and jellies. Birds like the fruit.

S. argentea. SILVER BUFFALOBERRY. Spreading, suckering plant grows 6–10 ft. (possibly 18 ft.) tall, with spine-tipped branchlets. Longish oval leaves to 1 in., silvery on both surfaces. Grayer appearance than *S. canadensis*.

S. canadensis. RUSSET BUFFALOBERRY. Rounded habit; grows 6–8 ft. tall. Leaves to 2 in. long, half as wide; they are green above and silvery with brown scales beneath, giving overall grayish green effect.

SHEPHERD'S SCABIOUS. See JASIONE laevis

SHIELD FERN. See DRYOPTERIS, POLYSTICHUM

SHISO. See PERILLA frutescens

SHOOTING STAR. See DODECATHEON

SHORTIA

Diapensiaceae

PERENNIALS

ZONES 34–41

WOODSY SHADE

AMPLE WATER

Shortia

Beautiful, small, spring-blooming evergreen plants that spread slowly by underground stems. *S. galacifolia* is native to the U.S.; the other two species are native to Japan. Intolerant of heat. Need acid, leafy, or peaty soil. Grow with azaleas or rhododendrons.

S. galacifolia. OCONEE BELLS. Native to mountains of North and South Carolina. Forms clump of glossy green, round or oval leaves 1–3 in. long, with scallop-toothed edges. Each of the many 4–6-in.-high stems is topped with a single, nodding, 1-in.-wide white bell with toothed edges.

S. soldanelloides. FRINGE BELLS. Round, coarsely toothed leaves form clumps similar to those of *S. galacifolia,* but flowers are pink to rose in color, with deeply fringed edges.

S. uniflora 'Grandiflora'. Like *S. galacifolia* but with indented and wavy-edged leaves and flowers that are large fringed bells of clear soft pink.

SHRUB BUSH CLOVER. See LESPEDEZA thunbergii

SHUNGIKU. See CHRYSANTHEMUM coronarium

SIBERIAN CARPET CYPRESS. See MICROBIOTA decussata

SIBERIAN WALLFLOWER. See ERYSIMUM hieraciifolium

SIDALCEA

CHECKERBLOOM, MINIATURE HOLLYHOCK

Malvaceae

PERENNIAL

ZONES 31, 32, 34–41

FULL SUN

REGULAR WATER

Sidalcea

Most commonly grown forms are hybrids, typically 2–3 ft. high, with rounded, lobed leaves and silky-petaled 1–2-in. flowers like little hollyhocks. They include 'Brilliant', with carmine red flowers; 'Elsie Heugh', bright pink blossoms with fringed petals; 'Loveliness', shell pink flowers; and 'Oberon', rose pink flowers. 'Puck' is compact, to 16 in. high, with dark pink flowers. 'Party Girl', with deep pink blooms, is taller (to 3½ ft.). Plants bloom all summer if faded flowers are removed. These and other improved garden plants were developed mainly from *S. malviflora,* a species with bright pink or lavender pink flowers, and *S. candida,* a white-flowered native of the High Plains. Performance is best in cool, fairly dry climates. Provide good drainage. Divide clumps every few years.

S

SILENE

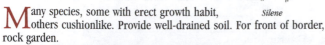

Caryophyllaceae

PERENNIALS

ZONES VARY BY SPECIES

FULL SUN OR PARTIAL SHADE

WATER NEEDS VARY BY SPECIES

Silene

Many species, some with erect growth habit, others cushionlike. Provide well-drained soil. For front of border, rock garden.

S. acaulis. CUSHION PINK, MOSS CAMPION. Zones 32, 34–45. Mosslike mat of small, narrow, bright green leaves. Reddish purple, ½-in. flowers, borne singly in spring. Regular water.

S. alpestris (S. quadrifolia). Zones 32, 34–41. Low creeper to 8 in. high. Produces a fine show of small double white flowers in spring, with scattered bloom later. Moderate water.

S. coeli-rosa. See *Lychnis coeli-rosa*

S. schafta. MOSS CAMPION. Zones 32, 34–41. Forms tufts of upright, rather wiry stems to 6–12 in. high. Small, tongue-shaped leaves. Rose purple flowers, one or two to a stalk, late summer into fall. 'Splendens' is deep rose pink. Moderate water.

S. uniflora (S. vulgaris maritima). Zones 32, 34–43. Forms a low cushion of gray-green foliage. Abundant white summer flowers; each flower is nearly enclosed by a balloonlike calyx. Moderate water.

S. virginica (Melandrium virginicum). FIRE PINK. Zones 32, 34–43. Native to eastern and central U.S. Narrow, lance-shaped leaves in a clump to 2–3 ft. high. Clusters of crimson flowers with notched petals in late spring or early summer. Hybrid 'Longwood', with fringed, deep pink flowers, forms an evergreen mound to 8 in. high. Regular water.

SILK TREE. See ALBIZIA julibrissin

SILPHIUM

PRAIRIE DOCK, ROSINWEED

Asteraceae

PERENNIALS

ZONES VARY BY SPECIES

FULL SUN TO PARTIAL SHADE

REGULAR WATER

Silphium

Found naturally in open fields and prairie lands, these tall and erect plants have coarse ovate leaves and few branches, and emit a strong turpentine-like odor. Yellow flowers resembling sunflowers bloom in clusters. Spreads in clumps and is best suited to wild or woodland gardens, or at the back of a border garden. Does best in fertile, moist soil that is neutral to slightly alkaline, but can tolerate ordinary soil, and even clay.

S. lacinatum. COMPASS PLANT, PILOT PLANT, POLAR PLANT. Zones 31, 32, 34–41. Stout, hairy stems grow to 8 ft., with paired fernlike leaves 1 ft. long that point in exactly opposite directions, hence the common names. Bright yellow flowers to 5 in. across bloom late summer into autumn.

S. perfoliatum. CUP PLANT, INDIAN CUP. Zones 31, 32, 34–41. Another bold 8-footer, but with coarse, upright, square stems clasped by the bases of the opposite leaves to form the cups referred to in the common name. The upper portions of the stately plants are covered in midsummer by loose clusters of bright yellow flowers.

S. terebinthinaceum. PRAIRIE DOCK. Zones 32, 34–45. Tall, erect stems arise from mostly basal clumps of 2-ft.-long leaves. In mid- to late summer these 8–10-ft. stalks are crowned with 3-in. sunflowerlike blooms.

SILVER BELL. See HALESIA carolina

SILVERBERRY. See ELAEAGNUS commutata, E. pungens

SILVER GRASS. See MISCANTHUS

SILVER LACE VINE. See POLYGONUM aubertii

SILVER SAGE. See SALVIA argentea

SILVER SPREADER. See ARTEMISIA caucasica

SILYBUM marianum

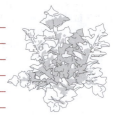

MILK-, BLESSED-, HOLY-, MARY'S-THISTLE

Asteraceae

ANNUAL OR BIENNIAL

ZONES 31, 32, 34–43

FULL SUN

REGULAR WATER

Silybum marianum

Hardy and erect, this thistlelike plant is grown for its spiny stems and ornamental shiny white or green foliage. Lance-shaped leaves with their thorny teeth and distinctive milky veins and splotches have inspired the myth that the markings were caused as the Blessed Mary nursed the infant Jesus. Rose purple flowers to 2½ in. across are enclosed by spiny bracts and bloom summer to autumn in the second year. Grows 3–5 ft. high in poor to moderately fertile soil that is well drained and neutral to slightly alkaline. Suitable in wild gardens or informal borders or in rock gardens. Self-seeds easily.

SINARUNDINARIA. See BAMBOO, Fargesia

SINOCALYCANTHUS chinensis (Calycanthus chinensis)

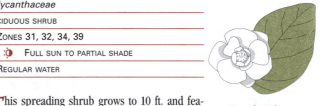

Calycanthaceae

DECIDUOUS SHRUB

ZONES 31, 32, 34, 39

FULL SUN TO PARTIAL SHADE

REGULAR WATER

Sinocalycanthus chinensis

This spreading shrub grows to 10 ft. and features shiny green, oval leaves to 6 in. long. Striking white cup-shaped flowers tinged with pink bloom singly in early summer. Grows best in moderately fertile but humus-rich and well-drained soil. Best in shrub borders or natural garden settings where it can be protected from drying winds.

SISYRINCHIUM

BLUE-EYED GRASS

Iridaceae

PERENNIALS

ZONES VARY BY SPECIES

FULL SUN OR LIGHT SHADE

REGULAR TO MODERATE WATER

Sisyrinchium

Related to iris. Narrow, rather grasslike leaves. Small flowers, made up of six segments, open in sunshine. Pretty but not showy, best suited for informal gardens or for naturalizing.

S. angustifolium. Zones 32, 34–43. Native to eastern U.S. Grows 6–18 in. tall, with narrow dark green leaves and clusters of ½-in. blue flowers in summer.

S. bermudianum (S. graminoides). BERMUDA BLUE-EYED GRASS. Zones 31, 32, 34–41. Native to the West Indies. Grows 5–6 in. tall with narrow leaves and clusters of blue flowers with yellow centers in summer.

S. 'Devon Skies'. Zones 31, 32, 34, 39. Large blue flowers.

S. 'Quaint and Queer'. BROWN-EYED GRASS. Zones 31, 32, 34, 39. Grows to 10 in. tall, with flat, narrow leaves and clusters of chocolate brown flowers in late spring.

S. 'Mrs. Spivey'. Zones 31, 32, 34, 39. White flowers.

SKIMMIA

Rutaceae

EVERGREEN SHRUBS

ZONES 31, 32

PARTIAL OR FULL SHADE

REGULAR WATER

Skimmia

Slow growing and compact, with glossy, rich green leaves neatly arranged along the branches. In spring, tiny white flowers open from clusters of pinkish buds held well above foliage. Hollylike red fruit appears in fall and winter if pollination requirements are met. Individual plants are dense mounds; when massed, they form a solid foliage cover. Good under windows, beside shaded walks, flanking entryways, in containers. Blend well with all shade plants.

Prefer moist, highly organic, acid soils. Mites are the main pests; they give foliage a sunburned look. Thrips may also attack.

S. foremanii. Hybrid between *S. japonica* and *S. reevesiana.* Resembles *S. japonica* but is more compact, with broader, heavier, darker green leaves. Plants may be male, female, or self-fertile.

S. japonica. Variable in size. Slow growth to 2–5 ft. or taller, 3–6 ft. wide. Oval, blunt-ended leaves to 3–4 in. long and 1 in. wide, mostly clustered near twig ends. Flowers are borne in 2–3-in. clusters; they are larger and more fragrant on male plants. If a male plant is present, female plants produce bright red berries—attractive enough to make planting both sexes worth the effort. A form with ivory white berries is available. Male variety 'Macrophylla' is a rounded, spreading shrub to 5–6 ft. tall, with large leaves and flowers.

S. reevesiana (S. fortunei). Dwarf, dense-growing shrub 2 ft. tall. Self-fertile, with dull crimson fruit. Fragrant flowers.

SKULLCAP. See SCUTTELARIA

SMILACINA racemosa

FALSE SOLOMON'S SEAL, FALSE SPIKENARD

Liliaceae

PERENNIAL

ZONES 31, 32, 34–43

WOODSY SHADE

REGULAR WATER

Smilacina racemosa

Commonly seen in shaded woods throughout much of North America. Grows 1–3 ft. tall; spreads by creeping rhizomes to form dense colonies. Each single, arching stalk has several 3–10-in.-long leaves with hairy undersides; foliage turns golden yellow in autumn. Stalks are topped by fluffy, conical clusters of small, fragrant, creamy white flowers in spring. Red autumn berries with purple spots follow the blooms; fruit is favored by wildlife. Good for naturalizing in wild garden. Needs rich, loose, moist, slightly acid soil. Resembles true solomon's seal (*Polygonatum*).

SMOKE TREE. See COTINUS coggygria

SNAKESHEAD. See FRITILLARIA meleagris

SNAPDRAGON. See ANTIRRHINUM majus

SNAPWEED. See IMPATIENS

SNEEZEWEED. See HELENIUM autumnale

SNOWBALL, FRAGRANT. See VIBURNUM carlcephalum

SNOWBELL. See STYRAX

SNOWBERRY. See SYMPHORICARPOS

SNOW BUSH. See BREYNIA distiacha

SNOWDROP. See GALANTHUS

SNOWDROP TREE. See HALESIA carolina

SNOWFLAKE. See LEUCOJUM

SNOW-IN-SUMMER. See CERASTIUM tomentosum

SNOW-ON-THE-MOUNTAIN. See EUPHORBIA marginata

SOAPWORT. See SAPONARIA officinalis

SOCIETY GARLIC. See TULBAGHIA violacea

Solanaceae. Members of the potato family bear flowers that are nearly always star or saucer shaped and five petaled; fruits are berries or capsules. Plants are frequently rank smelling or even poisonous, but many are important food crops—eggplant, pepper, potato, tomato. Others are garden annuals, perennials, shrubs, or vines—amethyst flower (*Browallia*), *Nicotiana*, and *Petunia*, to name a few.

SOLENOSTEMON scutellarioides. See COLEUS hybridus

SOLIDAGO and SOLIDASTER

GOLDENROD

Asteraceae (Compositae)

PERENNIALS

ZONES 31, 32, 34–45, EXCEPT AS NOTED

FULL SUN OR LIGHT SHADE

MODERATE WATER

Solidago

Goldenrods are not as widely grown as they deserve, largely due to the mistaken belief that their pollen causes hay fever (in fact, other plants are responsible). Although a few of the hundred-plus species are weeds in many regions, many are choice garden plants. All have leafy stems rising from tough, woody, spreading rootstocks; all bear small yellow flowers in large, branching clusters from mid- or late summer into fall. All are tough plants that thrive in not-too-rich soil. Use in borders with black-eyed Susan or Michaelmas daisy, or naturalize in meadows or edge-of-woodland gardens. For a similar plant, try the goldenrod relative *Solidaster luteus,* also described in this entry.

Solidago 'Golden Baby'. Hybrid, dwarf plant to 2 ft. tall, with airy plumes of bright golden yellow flower heads, 6–8 inches long, in midsummer.

S. rugosa. Hairy-stemmed plant to 5 ft. tall, with flowers on widely branching, arching stems. 'Fireworks' makes a more compact, 4-ft. clump, with bright yellow flower clusters that spray out from the plant like fireworks.

S. sempervirens. Zones 31, 32. Grows 2–6 ft. tall, with very large clusters of deep golden flowers.

S. sphacelata 'Golden Fleece'. Zones 31, 32, 34–41. Stands just 1½–2 ft. high when in bloom. Low foliage mound makes it a good ground cover. Set 15 in. apart, plants will form a solid mat in a year.

S. virgaurea. To 3 ft. tall, with flower clusters in a tight spikelike inflorescence or a looser cluster with upright branches. Not as well known as its varieties or hybrids. 'Cloth of Gold', to 18–20 in. tall, has a long bloom season beginning in midsummer. 'Strahlenkrone' ('Crown of Rays') is a stiff, erect 2-footer with wide, flat, branched flower clusters. 'Goldenmosa', probably the best known, grows 2½–3 ft. tall, has very large flower clusters reminiscent of florists' mimosa.

Solidaster luteus. Hybrid of goldenrod and a perennial aster. To 2 ft. tall. Plant resembles goldenrod but has larger, softer yellow flowers like small asters. Unlike most goldenrods, needs staking to remain upright. 'Lemore' has light yellow rays.

SOLOMON'S SEAL. See POLYGONATUM

SOPHORA

Fabaceae (Leguminosae)

DECIDUOUS TREES OR SHRUBS

☀️ ZONES 31, 32, 34–41

☼ ◐ FULL SUN OR PARTIAL SHADE

🌢 MODERATE WATER

Sophora

Handsome flowering plants with showy, drooping clusters of sweet pea–shaped blossoms followed by seedpods. Leaves are divided into numerous leaflets.

S. davidii. Deciduous shrub. To 8 ft. high and 10 ft. wide, bushy or spreading. Grayish green leaves, to 3½ in. long, are divided into up to 17 leaflets. Clusters to 6 in. long of blue-violet–and–white flowers in late spring and early summer.

S. japonica. JAPANESE PAGODA TREE, CHINESE SCHOLAR TREE. Deciduous tree. To 50–75 ft. high and wide. Young wood smooth, dark gray green. Old branches and trunk gradually take on rugged look of oak. Dark green, 6–10-in. leaves are divided into 7–17 oval leaflets; no fall color. Small, yellowish white flowers are carried in branched, foot-long sprays at branch ends in summer. Pods are 2–3½ in. long, narrowed between big seeds for a bead necklace effect. Appreciates well-drained soil. Tolerates heat, drought, city conditions.

'Regent' is an exceptionally vigorous, uniform grower. Other varieties include 'Pendula', to 25 ft., with weeping branches; and 'Princeton Upright', similar to 'Regent' but more erect in habit. The spreading forms are good shade trees for lawn or patio, though stains from flowers and pods may be a problem on paved surfaces and parked cars.

SORBARIA

FALSE SPIRAEA

Rosaceae

DECIDUOUS SHRUBS

☀️ ZONES VARY BY SPECIES

☼ ◐ FULL SUN OR LIGHT SHADE

🌢 REGULAR WATER

Sorbaria

These shrubs spread by suckering and will cover large areas if not curbed. Fernlike leaves are finely divided into many toothed leaflets; poor fall color. Foliage effect is lush, almost tropical, especially in rich, moist soil; in drier conditions, plant size is reduced. Stems are topped in summer by branching pyramidal clusters bearing clouds of tiny white blossoms that attract bees.

These eventually fade to brown and are best cut off at that time. Thin clumps drastically or cut back almost to ground in early spring; blooms appear on new wood.

S. aitchisonii. Zones 32, 34, 39. Larger overall than *S. sorbifolia*—grows 6–12 ft. tall, with leaves to 14 in. long and flower clusters to 1½ ft. long. Blooms mid- to late summer.

S. sorbifolia. Zones 32, 34–45. Grows 3–8 ft. tall (possibly to 10 ft.), with foot-long leaves and foot-long flower clusters in early summer.

SORBUS

MOUNTAIN ASH

Rosaceae

DECIDUOUS TREES OR SHRUBS

☀️ ZONES VARY BY SPECIES

☼ ◐ FULL SUN OR LIGHT SHADE

🌢 ● REGULAR TO MODERATE WATER

Sorbus

Valued for showy flowers and showier fruit. Blossoms are grouped in broad, flat clusters scattered over foliage canopy in spring; they develop into hanging clusters of small, berrylike fruit that colors up in late summer or early fall. Fruit is typically red or orange red, but white, pink, and golden forms are occasionally available. Birds eat the fruit, but usually not until after leaves have fallen. Foliage is typically finely cut and somewhat fernlike, although some less widely planted species have undivided leaves. Some have good fall color; these are noted below.

Provide good, well-drained soil. Like many other members of the rose family, they are subject to fireblight, which can be a problem in the Northeast. Borers and cankers are problems for trees under stress. Where adapted, they are good small garden or street trees, though fruit can be messy over paving.

S. alnifolia. KOREAN MOUNTAIN ASH. Tree. Zones 32, 34–43. Broad, dense, to 40–50 ft. tall. The name *alnifolia* refers to the leaves, which are undivided (like those of alder); they are 2–4 in. long, toothed, dark green, turning yellow to orange in fall. Red-and-yellow fruit. Tolerates heat and humidity better than other mountain ashes.

S. americana. AMERICAN MOUNTAIN ASH. Tree, sometimes large shrub. Zones 32, 34–45. Native to mountains of eastern North America. To 30 ft. tall. Leaves to 10 in. long, divided into 11–17 leaflets; dark green above, paler beneath, turning yellow in fall. Orange-red fruit. Attractive in native range, but not considered a choice or long-lived tree elsewhere.

S. aria. WHITEBEAM. Tree. Zones 32, 34, 39. To 30–45 ft. tall, with a dense crown of simple, undivided, 2–4-in.-long leaves—dark green above, whitish beneath. Variable fall color; best forms are yellow in autumn. Red or orange-red fruit.

S. aucuparia. EUROPEAN MOUNTAIN ASH, ROWAN. Tree. Zones 34–43. Naturalized in North America. To 20–40 ft. or taller. Sharply rising branches form a dense, oval to round crown. Leaves are 5–9 in. long, with 9–15 leaflets; they are dull green above, gray green below, turning tawny yellow to reddish in autumn. Orange-red fruit. 'Cardinal Royal' has especially large, bright red berries. 'Fastigiata' is a narrow, erect form; 'Blackhawk', another columnar form, is resistant to fireblight.

S. decora. SHOWY MOUNTAIN ASH. Tree or shrub. Zones 31, 32, 34–45. Upright, to 25 ft. high and 15 ft. wide. Deep blue-green leaves to 6 in. long, with up to 15 leaflets, turn orange to red in autumn. Red fruit.

S. hupehensis. Tree. Zones 34–41. Eventually to a possible 50 ft. tall, usually much less. Leaves to 7 in. long, with 13–17 leaflets, turn orange red in fall. White fruit. The form in cultivation is fireblight-resistant 'Coral Cascade', with red fruit and red fall foliage.

S. hybrida. Tree. Zones 34–41. Hybrid of *S. aria* and *S. aucuparia*. Erect habit to 20–30 ft. Leaves are 2½–4 in. long; they have one or two pairs of leaflets at the base, but tips are merely lobed (like oak leaves). Red fruit.

S. reducta. Shrub. Zones 32, 34, 39. To 2 ft. high, 3 ft. wide, spreading by underground runners. Leaves to 4 in. long, with 9–15 small leaflets; turn bronze red in autumn. Pink fruit. For rock garden or bonsai.

S. thuringiaca. Tree. Zones 34, 39. Hybrid between *S. aucuparia* and a species with undivided leaves. To 40 ft. tall, with leaves either deeply lobed and toothed or having one pair of leaflets beneath a large terminal leaflet. Bright red fruit.

S. tianshanica. TURKESTAN MOUNTAIN ASH. Shrub or small tree. Zones 34, 39. To 16 ft. tall. Leaves 5–6 in. long, with 9–15 leaflets. Bright red fruit. Neat form, slow growth; excellent plant for small garden. 'Red Cascade' is compact, oval crowned.

SORGHASTRUM nutans 'Sioux Blue'

BLUE INDIAN GRASS

Gramineae (Poaceae)

PERENNIAL GRASS

ZONES 31, 32, 34–43

FULL SUN

REGULAR MOISTURE

Sorghastrum nutans

Grown for its metallic blue leaves and very upright habit, blue Indian grass is an ornamental variety of tall prairie grass. Native to much of the U.S., including the Northeast, it has narrow leaves to 2 ft. long and flowering stems up to 6 ft. high. Because it tolerates heat and humidity and is free of fungal rusts, it is especially valued in the mid-Atlantic states, but it is excellent in borders throughout the Northeast region. Has yellow fall color and stays erect through winter, especially when grown in sun. Use flowers, which appear in midsummer, fresh or dried in arrangements. Gives three seasons of interest in the garden. Winter color is papery tan. Cut back early each spring to about 6 in. and fresh grass will grow. Adaptable to many soils and drought tolerant once established. The species, *Sorghastrum nutans*, grows up to 7 ft. tall and self-sows with abandon.

SORREL, WOOD. See OXALIS

SOUR GUM. See NYSSA sylvatica

SOURWOOD. See OXYDENDRUM arboreum

SOYBEAN

Fabaceae

ANNUAL

ALL ZONES

FULL SUN

REGULAR WATER

Soybean

Traditionally a farm crop, today soybeans are finding their way into home vegetable gardens. Not only are they easy to grow, soybeans are the most protein-rich members of the pea family. The bushy, 1–2-ft.-tall plants produce small clusters of hairy pods filled with two to four flattened, round seeds. While cultivars of soybeans grown agriculturally also are edible, seed companies are now offering selections developed especially for eating at the fresh, shell stage, when they have a tender-firm texture and somewhat buttery flavor that resembles lima beans. Soybeans eaten at this stage are called *edamame* in Japan; they are sometimes called green vegetable soybeans in this country. Cultivars developed for fresh use—'Envy', 'Butterbeans', and 'Sayamusume' are three—have larger seeds, tend to be easier to shell, and tend to mature more quickly than agricultural cultivars, but their flavor is similar. Grow soybeans as you would snap beans—give them full sun with rich, moist,

well-drained soil. Plant them outdoors a week after the last frost date. Harvest when the shells have plumped up but are still green and soft. To prepare them for eating, boil them for 5 minutes. (They contain a chemical that inhibits the digestion of proteins, which is destroyed by boiling, and they should not be eaten raw.) Like other pea-family plants, soybeans have the ability to fix nitrogen in the soil: Dig spent plants into the soil after harvest or pull and compost them.

SOUTHERNWOOD. See ARTEMISIA abrotanum

SPANISH BLUEBELL. See HYACINTHOIDES hispanica

SPANISH DAGGER. See YUCCA gloriosa

SPARAXIS tricolor

HARLEQUIN FLOWER

Iridaceae

CORM

ALL ZONES; DIG AND STORE; OR GROW IN POTS

FULL SUN

REGULAR WATER DURING GROWTH AND BLOOM

Sparaxis tricolor

Native to South Africa. Makes a clump of sword-shaped leaves. Small, funnel-shaped flowers in spikelike clusters on 1-ft. stems over long period in late spring. Flowers come in yellow, pink, purple, red, and white, usually blotched and splashed with contrasting colors. Closely related to ixia and similar to it in uses and culture.

SPEARMINT. See MENTHA spicata

SPEEDWELL. See VERONICA

SPICEBUSH. See LINDERA

SPIDER FLOWER. See CLEOME hasslerana

SPIDER LILY. See LYCORIS

SPIDERWORT. See TRADESCANTIA virginiana

SPIGELIA marilandica

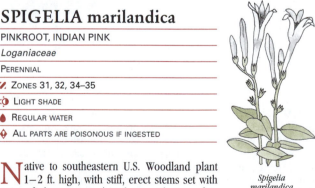

PINKROOT, INDIAN PINK

Loganiaceae

PERENNIAL

ZONES 31, 32, 34–35

LIGHT SHADE

REGULAR WATER

ALL PARTS ARE POISONOUS IF INGESTED

Spigelia marilandica

Native to southeastern U.S. Woodland plant 1–2 ft. high, with stiff, erect stems set with pairs of glossy green, 4-in. leaves. Clusters of 2-in., trumpet-shaped flowers; blossoms are red on the outside and yellow inside, facing upward to show a yellow five-pointed star at the mouth. Early summer bloom. Easy to grow if given light shade and moist, acid soil. With enough moisture, will tolerate full sun. Although once used medicinally, the plant is poisonous.

SPIKE MOSS. See SELAGINELLA

SPIKENARD. See ARALIA racemosa

S

SPINACH

Chenopodiaceae

ANNUAL

ALL ZONES

FULL SUN

KEEP SOIL EVENLY MOIST

Spinach

Leafy cool-season vegetable. Matures slowly during fall, winter, and spring; long daylight of late spring and heat of summer make it go to seed quickly. Requires rich, fast-draining soil. Make small sowings at weekly intervals to get successive harvests. Space rows 1½ ft. apart. After seedlings start growing, thin plants to 6 in. apart. One feeding will encourage lush foliage. When plants have reached full size, harvest by cutting off entire clump at ground level. Leaf miner is often a pest.

SPINACH, NEW ZEALAND

Tetragoniaceae

PERENNIAL USUALLY GROWN AS ANNUAL

ALL ZONES

FULL SUN

REGULAR WATER

New Zealand Spinach

Warm-season vegetable used as substitute for true spinach, which needs cool weather to succeed. Harvest greens from plants by plucking off top 3 in. of tender stems and attached leaves. A month later, new shoots grow up for another harvest. Plant is spreading, 6–8 in. high. Sow seed in early spring after frost danger is past. Feed once or twice yearly with complete fertilizer. Though heat and drought tolerant, also thrives in cool, damp conditions.

SPINDLE TREE. See EUONYMUS europaeus

SPIRAEA

Rosaceae

DECIDUOUS SHRUBS

ZONES VARY BY SPECIES

FULL SUN OR LIGHT SHADE

REGULAR TO MODERATE WATER, EXCEPT AS NOTED

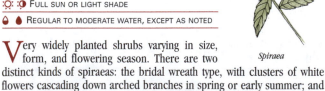

Spiraea

Very widely planted shrubs varying in size, form, and flowering season. There are two distinct kinds of spiraeas: the bridal wreath type, with clusters of white flowers cascading down arched branches in spring or early summer; and the shrubby type, typically growing knee-high and bearing pink, red, or white flowers clustered at ends of upright branches in summer to fall.

Like other members of the rose family, these are subject to various pests and diseases, but tend not to be seriously bothered. Tough, easy to grow. With few exceptions, not fussy about soil. Prune the mostly spring-blooming, bridal-wreath spiraeas after flowers have finished; cut to the ground wood that has bloomed. Prune the summer-blooming, shrubby spiraeas in winter or earliest spring; they generally need less severe pruning than bridal wreaths. If you remove spent flower clusters, plants will produce a second (but less lavish) bloom.

S. alba. MEADOWSWEET. Zones 31, 32, 34–43. Native to eastern North America. Erect and spreading, to 5 ft. high. Oblong, toothed leaves to 4 in. long. Cone-shaped clusters of white flowers in summer.

S. albiflora. See *S. japonica* 'Albiflora'

S. arguta. GARLAND SPIRAEA. Zones 31, 32, 34–43. Hybrid growing to 7–8 ft. high, bushy and rounded. Light green, oblong leaves to 1½ in. long. Clusters of white flowers in spring. 'Compacta' grows 3 ft. tall, with smaller flowers. 'Graciosa' is early blooming.

S. billardii. Zones 31, 32, 34–43. Hybrid between *S. douglasii* and a European species. Resembles *S. douglasii* in form, flowers, and requirement for acid soil and ample water. 'Triumphans' bears a profusion of purplish rose blossoms.

S. brachybotrys. Zones 31, 32, 34–43. Hybrid to about 8 ft. tall, with arching branches. Narrowly oval to oblong, dark green leaves to 2 in. long. Clusters of rose pink flowers in summer.

S. bumalda. Zones 31, 32, 34–43. Name given to a group of hybrids between varieties of *S. japonica*. All are low, shrubby spiraeas that bloom summer to fall. Selections include:

'Anthony Waterer'. Several forms; the best grows 3–4 ft. tall and slightly wider. All have flat-topped, carmine pink flower clusters and maroon-tinged young foliage; some have cream-edged leaves.

'Coccinea'. Like 'Anthony Waterer', but grows 2–3 ft. tall and bears brighter flowers.

'Dolchica'. To 1½–2½ ft. tall, with deeply cut leaves and bright pink flowers. Purplish new growth.

'Froebelii'. Resembles 'Anthony Waterer' but grows slightly taller.

'Goldflame'. Resembles 'Froebelii', but leaves are bronzy on unfolding, then yellow to chartreuse in summer and reddish orange before falling. Pink flowers. Prune out any green-leafed stems.

'Goldmound'. Compact 1–3-ft. shrub with yellow to chartreuse foliage, pink flowers. Sometimes considered a variety of *S. japonica*.

'Limemound'. Resembles 'Goldmound' but is somewhat hardier. Pink flowers; lime green foliage that turns orange red in fall.

S. cantoniensis (S. reevesiana). DOUBLE BRIDAL WREATH. Zones 31, 32. Upright grower to 5–6 ft., with arching branches. White flowers wreathe leafy branches, late spring to early summer. In colder part of range, the small dark green leaves turn red in fall; in mild-winter areas, they remain on the plant without changing color.

S. japonica. Zones 32, 34–41. Upright shrubby spiraea to 4–6 ft. tall, with flat clusters of pink flowers carried above sharply toothed, oval green leaves. Best known through its selections, which are typically lower than the species and bloom between summer and fall. These include:

'Albiflora' (*S. albiflora*). Rounded, compact shrub 1–1½ ft. tall, with white flowers.

'Alpina'. DAPHNE SPIRAEA. Low (1-ft.) mound with pink flowers. Foliage turns red and orange in fall.

'Fortunei'. Unusually tall (to 5 ft.), with pink flowers.

'Little Princess'. Resembles 'Alpina' but is larger (to 2½ ft. tall).

'Magic Carpet'. To 1½–2 ft. tall. Reddish bronze new growth contrasts with chartreuse to yellow older foliage. Pink flowers.

'Neon Flash'. To 3–4 ft. tall, 4–5 ft. wide. Purplish-tinted foliage, bright rosy pink flowers.

'Norman'. To 1½–2 ft. tall, with deep pink flowers and dark purple autumn foliage.

'Shirobana' ('Shibori'). To 2–3 ft. tall, with flowers of white, light pink, and deep rose pink on the same plant.

S. nipponica tosaensis 'Snowmound'. Zones 32, 34–43. Compact, spreading plant to 2–3 ft. tall. Profusion of white flowers in late spring or early summer. Narrow dark green leaves have little autumn color.

S. prunifolia 'Plena'. BRIDAL WREATH SPIRAEA, SHOE BUTTON SPIRAEA. Zones 32, 34–41. Graceful, arching branches on a suckering, clump-forming plant to 6 ft. tall and wide. In early to midspring, bare branches are lined with small double white flowers resembling tiny roses. Small dark green leaves turn bright shades of red, orange, and yellow in autumn.

S. thunbergii. Zones 31, 32, 34–43. Showy, billowy, graceful shrub 3–5 ft. tall, with many slender, arching branches. Round clusters of small single white flowers appear all along bare branches in early spring. Blue-green, extremely narrow leaves turn soft reddish brown in fall.

S. tomentosa. HARDHACK, STEEPLEBUSH. Zones 32, 34–45. Native to eastern U.S. and northern Europe. Spreads by suckering to form thickets

S

to 5 ft. tall. Rose pink flowers in 6-in. clusters, summer to fall. Best in acid soil with ample water. Useful in wild gardens.

S. trilobata 'Swan Lake'. Zones 32, 34–43. Like a small version of *S. prunifolia* 'Plena'. To 3–4 ft. tall, with a massive show of tiny white flowers in mid- to late spring. Small leaves often have three lobes. 'Fairy Queen' is more compact, seldom exceeding 3 ft.

S. vanhouttei. Zones 31, 32, 34–43. Widely planted hybrid between *S. cantoniensis* and *S. trilobata*. The classic bridal-wreath spiraea. Arching branches form a fountain to about 6 ft. high by 8 ft. or wider. Leafy branches are covered with circular, flattened clusters of single white blossoms in mid- to late spring, continuing into early summer in colder regions. Dark green foliage may turn purplish in fall.

S. veitchii. VEITCH SPIRAEA Zones 32, 34–43. Native to China. Tallest species, reaching 12 ft. high, with arching stems. Oblong leaves, clusters of white flowers in early summer.

SPIRANTHES
cernua odorata

NODDING LADIES' TRESSES ORCHID

Orchidaceae

PERENNIAL

❄ ZONES 31, 32, 34–45

☼ PARTIAL SHADE

💧 MORE THAN REGULAR WATER

Spiranthes cernua odorata

A native, terrestrial orchid found growing in woodlands from Pennsylvania to Tennessee and south to Texas and Florida. Produces low rosettes of narrow, 2–10-in. leaves topped by erect, 2-ft.-tall racemes of white, ¼-in.-long, fragrant flowers in fall. Where happy, plants spread slowly by underground rhizomes to from handsome clumps. Select a site with moist soil rich in organic matter. When adding this native orchid to your garden, be sure to purchase only nursery-propagated plants, not ones collected from the wild. 'Chadd's Ford' is an award-winning selection, vigorous and relatively easy to grow. The spikes of bloom start to appear in September and continue until frost.

SPLEENWORT. See ASPLENIUM

SPOROBOLUS

DROPSEED

Gramineae (Poaceae)

PERENNIAL GRASSES

❄ HARDINESS VARIES BY SPECIES

☼ ◑ FULL SUN TO PARTIAL SHADE

💧 💧 REGULAR TO LESS THAN REGULAR WATER

Sporobolus

Two dropseeds are cultivated in American gardens. Both are easy-to-grow, clump-forming, drought-tolerant, North American perennials that bloom in summer.

S. airoides. ALKALI DROPSEED. ZONES 31, 32, 34–41. Makes a 3-ft. mound of narrow grayish green leaves that turn yellow in fall and tan in winter. Elegant spikes of open flowers appear on curving stems up to 5 ft. high, typically in early summer. Native to alkaline meadows and vales of the western and midwestern U.S., it's well suited to use in both meadow and prairie gardens.

S. heterolepis. PRAIRIE DROPSEED. Zones 31, 32, 34–43. Native to prairies from the Northeast to the South and West. The leaves are so fine that they resemble a fountainlike mass of shiny green hairs in a small, thick mound up to 15 in. high. Fall color is rich orange, while winter color is pale and coppery. Pungent-scented flowers appear in late summer on 2-ft.

stems. Elegant in form, slow growing, clump forming, and adaptable to many soil and light conditions, prairie dropseed makes a good specimen or ground cover, ideal in both formal and informal settings.

SPRING STAR FLOWER. See IPHEION uniflorum

SPRUCE. See PICEA

SPURGE. See PACHYSANDRA

SQUASH

Cucurbitaceae

ANNUAL

❄ ALL ZONES

☼ FULL SUN

💧 REGULAR WATER

Squash

There are two forms of squash. Summer squash are planted for a warm-weather harvest and eaten in the immature state; this group includes scalloped white squash (pattypan squash), yellow crookneck and straight-neck varieties, and cylindrical, green or gray zucchini or Italian squash. Winter squash is grown for harvest in late summer or fall; it stores well and is used for baking and pies. Varieties come in many sizes, colors, and shapes (turban, acorn, and banana are a few); all have hard rinds and firm, close-grained, good-tasting flesh. In both forms of squash, blossoms and tiny, developing fruit at base of female flowers can be picked as delicacies.

Summer squash yields prodigious crops from just a few plants (within 50 to 65 days after sowing) and continues to bear for weeks. Vines are large (2½–4 ft. across at maturity) and need plenty of room; if space is limited, look for bush varieties. 'Early Summer Crookneck' and 'Early Prolific Straightneck' are good yellow summer squash. 'Early White Bush' (white) and 'Scallopini Hybrid' (green) are choice scalloped varieties. 'Ambassador Hybrid', 'Aristocrat Hybrid', and 'Burpee Hybrid' are productive zucchini varieties. Zucchini and scalloped squash also come in golden yellow variants. Novelties include 'Gourmet Globe', a round, striped zucchini, and 'Kuta', a whitish squash that can be eaten like summer squash at 6 in. or allowed to ripen into a 1-ft. winter squash.

Winter squash is planted and grown on vines like pumpkins, and typically needs more space than summer squash. Most are ready to harvest 60 to 110 days after sowing. Types for storing include the small 'Table Queen', 'Acorn', 'Butternut', and 'Buttercup', and the large 'Hubbard', 'Blue Hubbard', and 'Jumbo Pink Banana'. Spaghetti squash looks like any other winter squash, but when you open it after cooking, you find that the nutty-tasting flesh is made up of long, spaghettilike strands. 'Turk's Turban' resembles its namesake. Winter squash doesn't grow well in high heat and humidity.

Bush varieties of summer squash can be planted 2 ft. apart in rows. If planted in circles (hills), they need more room; allow a 4-ft. diameter for each plant. Runner-type winter squash needs 5-ft. spacing in rows, 8-ft.-diameter hills. The few bush varieties of winter squash can be spaced as for bush varieties of summer squash. Provide rich soil, periodic fertilizer. Roots need regular moisture, but leaves and stems should be kept as dry as possible to prevent leaf diseases such as powdery mildew. Late squash should stay on vines until thoroughly hardened; harvest these with an inch of stem and store in cool place (about 55°F/13°C).

DEFEATING THE SQUASH VINE BORER

If borers bother your squash vines, try these tactics in addition to timing plantings. To prevent borers, watch for the adult moth—it's orange and black and resembles a wasp. Moths lay eggs at base of stems in late June or early July, a bit earlier in mild parts of the Northeast. If you spot moths, check around base of stems or just under the soil for very tiny red and orange eggs. Crush any you find.

S

Pests include squash bug (set out boards or burlap as traps and destroy your catch each morning) and squash vine borer (plant early or late to avoid peak midsummer damage). Control cucumber beetles, which can spread incurable bacterial wilt disease as they chew holes in leaves and flowers.

SQUILL. See SCILLA

STACHYS

LAMB'S EARS, BETONY

Lamiaceae (Labiatae)

PERENNIALS

ZONES VARY BY SPECIES

FULL SUN OR LIGHT SHADE

MODERATE WATER

Stachys

All have paired, typically rough or hairy leaves and spikelike clusters of small, usually two-lipped flowers. All are tough, tolerant plants. Of the 300-odd species, only a few are commonly grown. Provide well-drained soil. Plants often die out in center; divide and replant outer sections.

S. byzantina (S. lanata, S. olympica). LAMB'S EARS. Zones 31, 32, 34–43. Dense, ground-hugging rosettes of soft, thick, rather tongue-shaped, woolly white leaves to 4 in. long, 1 in. wide; clumps spread by surface runners. Some (not all) rosettes send up 1–1½-ft. flowering stems with small leaves and whorls of small purple flowers in late spring to early summer; these are attractive but become dowdy when they fade. Plant is more useful for foliage effect, so many people cut off or simply pull out flowering stems. Continued rain can smash the plants down and make them mushy, and frost can damage leaves, but recovery is strong.

'Silver Carpet' does not produce flower spikes and is somewhat less vigorous than the species. 'Countess Helene von Stein', commonly called 'Big Ears' (the plant, not the countess), has longer, broader leaves than the species and produces fewer flowering stems. There are also harder-to-find lime green and variegated forms.

Use all forms for contrast with dark green foliage and with leaves of different shapes, such as those of strawberry or some sedums. Good edging plants for paths, flower beds; highly effective edgings for bearded iris. Excellent ground covers in high, open shade.

S. macrantha (S. grandiflora). BIG BETONY. Zones 31, 32, 34–45. Dense, foot-high clump of long-stalked, heart-shaped, wrinkled, roughly hairy, scallop-edged green leaves to 3 in. across. Showy purplish pink flowers, carried two or three whorls to a spike, held 8 in. above leaves. Spreads rapidly in rich, moist soil. Most common form is 'Robusta', to 2 ft. high; its blossom spikes bear four or five whorls of flowers. 'Superba' has deep violet blossoms. 'Alba' is a white-flowered form.

S. officinalis. BETONY. Zones 31, 32, 34–45. Similar to *S. macrantha*, but leaves are elongated (to 5 in. long) and may be hairy or nearly smooth. The purplish or dark red flowers are densely packed into short spikes atop leafy stems. Little grown except by herb fanciers, but white-blooming 'Grandiflora Alba' and pink-blooming 'Grandiflora Rosea' are attractive 2-ft. plants for perennial border or woodland edge.

STACHYURUS praecox

Stachyuraceae

DECIDUOUS SHRUB

ZONES 31, 32, 34, 39

FULL SUN OR LIGHT SHADE

REGULAR WATER

Slow to 10 ft., with spreading, slender, polished chestnut brown branches. Pendulous flower

Stachyurus praecox

stalks 3–4 in. long, each with 12–20 unopened buds, hang from the branches in fall–winter. In late winter, buds open into pale yellow or greenish yellow, bell-shaped flowers ⅓ in. wide. Greenish yellow, berrylike fruit in summer. Bright green, toothed leaves, 3–7 in. long, taper to sharp tip. Leaves often somewhat sparse. Fall color pleasant (but not bright) rosy red and yellowish. Grow under deciduous trees to shelter winter buds from heavy freezes.

STAPHYLEA

BLADDERNUT

Staphyleaceae

DECIDUOUS SHRUBS

ZONES VARY BY SPECIES

SUN OR SHADE

REGULAR WATER

Staphylea

Deciduous suckering shrubs with paired leaves divided into leaflets. Tightly clustered, greenish to yellowish white flowers bloom in spring or summer. Common name comes from the fruit, which is an inflated bladderlike capsule containing a few seeds; bladders are green, turning light brown. Plants tolerate a wide variety of soils. Most are too big for small gardens, but have their place at the woodland edge or in large shrub borders.

S. bumalda. JAPANESE BLADDERNUT. Zones 31, 32, 34–41. To 4–6 ft. tall, with leaves divided into three 2½-in. leaflets. The off-white spring flowers, borne in 1–3-in. clusters, are followed by inch-long fruit.

S. colchica. COLCHIS BLADDERNUT. Zones 31, 32, 34, 35, 37, 39. To 12 ft. tall; leaves have three or five 3-in. leaflets. Yellowish white spring flowers in 2–4-in. clusters have a coconut fragrance. Fruit to 3 in. long.

S. pinnata. EUROPEAN BLADDERNUT. Zones 31, 32, 34, 35, 37, 39. To 10–15 ft. tall. Leaves have three to seven 4-in. leaflets. Drooping, 4–5-in. clusters of white flowers appear in early summer are followed by 1½-in. fruit.

S. trifolia. AMERICAN BLADDERNUT. Zones 31, 32, 34–43. To 10–15 ft. tall, usually somewhat broader. Leaves have three 4-in. leaflets. Greenish white spring flowers in 1½–2-in. clusters, followed by 1–1½-in. fruit.

STAR CLUSTERS. See PENTAS lanceolata

STAR OF BETHLEHEM. See ORNITHOGALUM

STATICE. See LIMONIUM

STEEPLEBUSH. See SPIRAEA tomentosa

STEPHANANDRA incisa

Rosaceae

DECIDUOUS SHRUB

ZONES 32, 34–43

FULL SUN OR LIGHT SHADE

REGULAR WATER

Stephanandra incisa

Mounding shrub 4–7 ft. tall, with arching branches that may root when they contact damp soil. Leaves are 1–2 in. long, deeply lobed, the lobes toothed; turn from bright green to dull reddish or purplish orange in autumn. Tiny white spring flowers, carried in loose, 1–2½-in. clusters, are not showy. Use for massing or informal hedge or screen, tall bank cover for weed and erosion control. More commonly used is 'Crispa', 2–3 ft. tall and 4–5 ft. wide, with good reddish purple fall color; useful bank or ground cover. Both species and variety dislike alkaline soil.

STERNBERGIA lutea

Amaryllidaceae

BULB

ZONES 31, 32; OR GROW IN POTS

FULL SUN

REGULAR WATER DURING GROWTH AND BLOOM

Sternbergia lutea

Narrow, 6–12-in. leaves appear in fall simultaneously with flowers and remain green for several months after blooms have gone. Golden yellow, 1½-in. flowers resemble large crocuses on 6–9-in. stems and provide a pleasant autumn surprise in borders or rock gardens, near pools. Good cut flower. Dies to the ground in spring. Plant bulbs as soon as they become available (in August or September). Set 4 in. deep, 6 in. apart. Clumps bloom well only after 2 or 3 years; wait at least 6 to 8 years before dividing.

In colder climates, grow in pots. Place four or five bulbs in a pot, setting them 2 in. deep. Don't be in a hurry to repot, since plants bloom better when pot-bound.

STEWARTIA

Theaceae

DECIDUOUS SHRUBS OR TREES

ZONES VARY BY SPECIES

LIGHT SHADE IN HOT CLIMATES

REGULAR WATER

Stewartia

These are all-season performers. They show off fresh green leaves in spring, white flowers like single camellias in summer, and colorful foliage in fall; winter reveals a distinctive pattern of bare branches and smooth bark that flakes off in varying degrees, depending on species. *S. koreana* and *S. pseudocamellia* have the showiest bark; it flakes off to show a patchwork of green, gray, brown, rust, terra-cotta, and cream.

Best in well-drained, acid soil with high content of organic matter. Good in woodland garden and as foreground specimens against backdrop of larger, darker-leafed trees.

S. koreana. KOREAN STEWARTIA. Tree. Zones 32, 34, 39. Pyramidal growth to 20–25 ft.; may eventually reach 50 ft. Leaves are 1–4 in. long, turn orange to red orange in fall. Flowers, carried on short stalks among leaves, reach 3 in. wide and have yellow-orange stamens. Probably a variety of *S. pseudocamellia.*

S. malacodendron. SILKY STEWARTIA. Shrub or small tree. Zones 31, 32. Virginia native. To 10–15 ft. tall and wide. Shoots and undersides of 2–4-in. leaves are downy. Blossoms are 3½ in. wide, have purple stamens with blue anthers. Bark not as effective as on other species.

S. monadelpha. TALL STEWARTIA. Tree. Zones 31, 32. To 25 ft. tall, with slender, upward-angled branches. Leaves are 1½–3 in. long, turn brilliant red in fall. Flowers to 1½ in. wide. Older limbs and trunk have smooth, cinnamon brown bark.

S. ovata. MOUNTAIN STEWARTIA. Shrub or small tree. Zones 31, 32, 34, 39. Native to southeastern U.S. To 10–15 ft. tall and wide. Leaves grow 2–5 in. long, turn orange to scarlet in fall. Flowers, 3 in. wide, have frilled petals. Bark is not as handsome as on some other species. *S. o. grandiflora* has 4-in. flowers with lavender anthers; it will bloom even as a young plant.

S. pseudocamellia. JAPANESE STEWARTIA. Tree. Zones 32, 34, 39. Forms a pyramid that may reach 30–40 ft. after many years. Leaves to 2½–3 in. long; fall color bronze to purple. Flowers are more cup shaped than those of *S. koreana;* they reach 2½ in. wide, have orange anthers.

S. sinensis. Tree. Zones 31, 32, 34, 39. Native to China. Cone-shaped, to 70 ft. tall. Leaves are dark green, oval to elliptical, with toothed edges; they turn bright red in fall. Fragrant white flowers 2 in. across in midsummer. Peeling, reddish brown bark.

STIPA

FEATHER GRASS, NEEDLE GRASS

Poaceae (Gramineae)

PERENNIAL GRASSES

ZONES 31, 32, 34, 39

FULL SUN

WATER NEEDS VARY BY SPECIES

Stipa

Feather or needle grasses have large, open, airy inflorescences that can impart lightness and motion to the garden. Of the 150 or so species, a few have special merit.

S. gigantea. GIANT FEATHER GRASS. Clumps of narrow, arching leaves grow 2–3 ft. tall. Open, airy sheaves of yellowish flowers shimmer in a broad cloud reaching to 6 ft. in height and breadth. Regular water; established plants endure some drought.

S. tenuissima (Nasella tenuissima). MEXICAN FEATHER GRASS, TEXAS NEEDLE GRASS. Very thin bright green leaves form erect clumps that arch outward toward the top. Numerous thin flowering stems divide and redivide into almost hairlike fineness, green at first, then golden. Single or scattered clumps are effective among ground cover or boulders, on slopes. Larger plantings can create effective erosion control. Water regularly, but let soil dry out between irrigations. Can self-sow.

STOCK. See MATTHIOLA

STOKESIA laevis

STOKES' ASTER

Asteraceae (Compositae)

PERENNIAL

ZONES 31, 32, 34–43

FULL SUN

REGULAR WATER

Stokesia laevis

Native to southeastern U.S. A rugged and most adaptable plant. Much branched, with stiff, erect stems 1½–2 ft. high. Smooth, firm-textured, medium green leaves, 2–8 in. long, sometimes toothed at base, evergreen (to semievergreen in cold climates). Leafy, curved, finely toothed bracts surround tight flower buds; in summer or early autumn, these open to 3–4-in.-wide, asterlike flower heads in blue, purplish blue, or white. Each blossom has a central button of small flowers surrounded by a ring of larger ones. Long-lasting cut flower. Grows best in well-drained soil. Provide winter cover of evergreen boughs or straw in coldest regions. Good in pots.

Choices include 10-in.-high 'Bluestone', medium blue; and the 1½-ft.-tall varieties 'Blue Danube', with lavender blue blossoms and a long bloom season extending into winter in mildest climates; 'Klaus Jelitto', light blue; 'Mary Gregory', creamy yellow; 'Silver Moon', white; and 'Wyoming', deep purple. 'Omega Skyrocket' grows to 3 ft., with blue flowers. 'Purple Parasols' bears frilly, dark purple flowers on foot-high stems.

STONECRESS. See AETHIONEMA

STONECROP. See SEDUM

FOR GROWING SYMBOL EXPLANATIONS

PLEASE SEE PAGE 113

S

STRAWBERRY

Rosaceae

PERENNIALS

✿ 31, 32, 34–45

☼ FULL SUN

💧 REGULAR WATER

▶ SEE CHART NEXT PAGE

Strawberry

Plants have toothed, roundish, medium green leaves and white flowers. They grow 6–8 in. tall, spreading by long runners to about 1 ft. across.

June-bearing types produce one crop per year in late spring or early summer; generally, they are the highest-quality strawberries you can grow. Day-neutral or everbearing kinds flower and set fruit over a longer season. Their harvest tends to peak in early summer, then continue (often unevenly) through fall; the exact fruiting pattern depends on the variety. Everbearers put out fewer runners than June bearers.

Strawberries of one variety or another can be grown in every part of the U.S. and most of populous Canada, though success is difficult where soil and water salinity are very high. Varieties tend to be regionally adapted; check the accompanying chart for some of the best selections, and look for other good choices in local nurseries.

To bring in a big crop of berries, plant in rows—on flat ground if soil drains well, or on a raised mound (5–6 in. high) if soil is heavy or poorly drained. Set plants 14–18 in. apart in rows spaced 2–2½ ft. apart. For a small harvest, you can grow a dozen or so plants in a sunny patch in a flower or vegetable garden, or put them in boxes or tubs on the patio.

Planting season is usually determined by when local nurseries offer plants. In the Northeast, plant in early spring for harvest the following year. Set out everbearing plants in spring for summer–fall berries; pinch off the earliest blossoms to increase plant vigor.

Plant carefully. The crown should be above soil level (a buried crown will rot); topmost roots should be ¼ in. beneath soil level (exposed roots will dry out). Mulch to deter weeds, conserve moisture, and keep berries clean.

Strawberry plants need about 1 in. of water per week throughout the growing season, even more moisture when bearing fruit. Drip irrigation is ideal to help reduce disease problems, but overhead irrigation is satisfactory. Feed June bearers twice a year—very lightly when growth begins and again, more heavily, after fruiting. Everbearing types prefer consistent light fertilization. Heavy feeding of either type in spring leads to excessive plant growth, soft fruit, and fruit rot.

Most varieties reproduce by runner plants; some make few or no offsets. Pinch off all runners to get large plants with smaller yields of big berries; let runner plants grow 7–10 in. apart for heavy yields of smaller berries. When your plants have made enough offsets, pinch off additional runners. Do not let the planting become too dense, since that leads to much lower yields, diseases, and poor-quality fruit.

Most perennially grown June bearers benefit greatly from renovation. After the harvest is over, cut off the foliage; you can use a lawn mower set high so it won't injure the crowns. If diseases were a problem, dispose of the leaves. Water and fertilize to encourage new growth. This is also a good time to reduce a dense planting by removing the old "mother" plants and leaving the younger, more productive "daughter" plants.

Some home gardeners are following the example of commercial growers who treat strawberries as annuals. Plants are installed in summer or early fall, usually with a plastic mulch; they are not allowed to make offsets. After harvest, the plants are removed and a new planting made. Benefits are healthier plants, fewer weeds, and bigger fruit. 'Chandler' is especially well adapted to this system, but almost any variety can be grown this way if planted at just the right time (you may have to experiment).

Strawberries need a winter mulch in cold climates. Cover the planting with a 4–6-in. layer of straw or other light, weed-free organic material. When temperatures warm in spring, rake the mulch between the plants.

Plants are subject to many diseases: fruit rots (botrytis, anthracnose, leather rot), leaf diseases (leaf spot, leaf scorch, leaf blight), crown diseases (anthracnose), root diseases (verticillium wilt, red stele, black root rot), and viruses. Root weevils, aphids, mites, and slugs and snails are among potential pests. To help reduce problems, install only certified disease-free plants; also remove diseased foliage and ripe or rotten fruit. Replace plants with new ones as they begin to decline, usually after three years.

Ornamental types are discussed under *Fragaria*.

STRAWBERRY BUSH. See EUONYMUS americana

STRAWBERRY GERANIUM. See SAXIFRAGA stolonifera

STRAWBERRY SHRUB. See CALYCANTHUS floridus

STRAWFLOWER. See HELICHRYSUM bracteatum

STREPTOPUS

TWISTED STALK

Liliaceae

PERENNIALS

✿ ZONES VARY BY SPECIES

☽ PARTIAL SHADE

💧 REGULAR WATER

Streptopus

Woodland natives that resemble Solomon's seal (*Polygonatum*). They bear arching stems with alternate leaves that are rounded with pointed tips and bases that either are stalkless or clasp the stalk. Small, nodding, bell- or wheel-shaped flowers appear in the leaf axils in early summer. Blooms are borne singly or in pairs and are followed by round berries. Plants grow from a branching rootstock and form clumps with time. Suited to woodland wildflower or shade gardens.

S. amplexifolius. Zones 31, 32, 34–41. Native from North America to Greenland, Europe, Asia, and Japan. Grows 1½–3½-ft. tall. Bears stem-clasping leaves and nodding, greenish white, ½-in.-long flowers, either singly or in pairs. Berries are ½ in. wide and red.

S. roseus. Zones 31, 32, 34–45. Native to northeastern North America. Grows 1–2½ ft. tall. Bears stalkless leaves that do not clasp the stem and solitary, nodding, ½-in.-long flowers that are rose pink or purple. Flowers are followed by red, ½-in.-wide berries.

STROBILANTHES

Acanthaceae

PERENNIAL SUBSHRUBS, ANNUALS

✿ ZONES VARY BY SPECIES

☼ ☽ FULL SUN TO PARTIAL SHADE

💧💧 REGULAR TO AMPLE WATER

Strobilanthes

Varying widely by species, these generally tropical plants bear five-lobed funnel-shaped or tubular flowers of blue, purple, white, or, rarely, yellow, usually borne in clusters or spikes.

S. atropurpureus. Perennial subshrub. Zones 31, 32, 34–41. The hardiest species, this clump-forming subshrub dies to the ground each winter throughout the Northeast. Erect, branching stems can grow up to 6 ft., with a 6–10-ft. spread. Purple salvialike flowers, borne in large clusters, are produced abundantly throughout the summer.

S. dyerianus. PERSIAN SHIELD. Tender perennial grown as annual. All zones. A striking plant, bearing large leaves variegated maroon purple and silver with deep maroon undersides. Pale blue funnel-shaped flowers appear on top of short spikes in autumn. Grow as a summer annual or under glass; entire plants or rooted cuttings can overwinter in a warm greenhouse. Very sun and heat resistant in containers or bedded out, so long as soil is moisture retentive. One of those rare plants that projects its presence across the garden and brightens anything it is combined with.

STRAWBERRY

NAME	DESCRIPTION	ADAPTABILITY	RESISTANCE
JUNE-BEARING VARIETIES			
'Allstar'	Large, firm, light red fruit with good flavor. Consistent production	Widely adapted, but best in Mid-Atlantic, Northeast, eastern Canada	Resistant to red stele, verticillium wilt, leaf diseases
'Annapolis'	Early, consistent production of medium-large fruit	Mid-Atlantic, Northeast, eastern Canada	Resistant to red stele
'Camarosa'	Large, attractive, firm fruit over a long period	All zones in annual production	Susceptible to mites
'Chandler'	Large juicy berries produced over long period. Very good flavor, good texture	All zones in annual production	Some resistance to leaf spot
'Delmarvel'	Early berry with excellent flavor. Moderate yields	Southeast, Mid-Atlantic	Some resistance to anthracnose. Resistant to red stele
'Earliglow'	Early crop of medium-size berries of excellent flavor and quality. Moderate yields	Widely adapted, but best in Southeast, Mid-Atlantic, Northeast, eastern Canada	Resistant to red stele. Tolerates fruit rot better than many other varieties
'Honeoye'	Large, firm fruit. Excellent, consistent production	Widely adapted, but best in Mid-Atlantic, Northeast, eastern Canada	Resistant to leaf diseases. Susceptible to red stele, verticillium wilt and, in the Pacific Northwest, viruses
'Jewel'	Large, firm fruit with good flavor. Reliable producer	Widely adapted, but best in Mid-Atlantic, Northeast, eastern Canada	Resistant to leaf diseases. Reportedly tolerant of bacterial leaf spot. Susceptible to red stele
'Kent'	Large, firm, dark red fruit. Excellent production. Cold-hardy variety from Canada	Widely adapted, but best in Mid-Atlantic, Northeast, eastern Canada	Resistant to leaf diseases. Susceptible to red stele
'Northeaster'	Early crop of large berries with very good flavor	Northeast, eastern Canada	Resistant to red stele
'Scott'	Large, firm, midseason berries, mild flavor. Freeze well	Eastern U.S.	Resistant to red stele, partially resistant to verticillium wilt. Resistant to leaf diseases
'Sparkle'	Deep, bright red, flavorful fruit ripens late June. Not harmed by late frosts	Northern climates	Resistant to red stele, partially resistant to leaf spot
'Sunrise'	Medium-size, light red, firm fruit	Eastern U.S.	Resistant to red stele and verticillium wilt. Withstands mildew
'Winona'	Reliable production of very good quality fruit in northern climates. Especially cold-hardy	All zones	Resistant to red stele

S

STRAWBERRY

NAME	DESCRIPTION	ADAPTABILITY	RESISTANCE
DAY-NEUTRAL/ EVERBEARING VARITIES **'Ozark Beauty'**	Deep red, firm, large, flavorful fruit. Bears in June and continues through summer; productive	Adapted to the Northeast	Resistant to verticillium wilt.
'Tribute'	Medium to large with excellent flavor	All zones	Resistant to red stele and verticillium wilt
'Tristar'	Medium-size berries with excellent flavor	All zones	Resistant to red stele and mildew. Moderately susceptible to viruses

STYLOPHORUM
diphyllum

CELANDINE POPPY

Papaveraceae

PERENNIAL

ZONES 31, 32, 34–43

PARTIAL TO FULL SHADE

REGULAR WATER

Stylophorum diphyllum

This wildflower native to eastern North America produces mounds of handsome, 8–12-in.-long leaves that are lobed in a pinnate, or featherlike, fashion. From spring to summer they bear clusters of showy, saucer-shaped, four-petaled flowers that are rich yellow and 1–2 in. across. Plants thrive in rich, moist soil and are ideal additions to shade and woodland gardens. They self-sow with enthusiasm, but excess seedlings are easy to pull up where they are not wanted.

Styracaceae. The storax family includes trees and shrubs with bell-shaped, usually white flowers. Members are Halesia, epaulette tree (Pterostyrax), and Styrax.

STYRAX

Styracaceae

DECIDUOUS TREES OR SHRUBS

ZONES VARY BY SPECIES

FULL SUN OR PARTIAL SHADE

REGULAR WATER

Styrax

Neat, well-behaved flowering trees of modest size for patios or lawns; make a nice contrast in front of larger, darker-leafed trees. The species described below put on a show of white, bell-shaped flowers in hanging clusters. Easy to garden under, since roots are deep and nonaggressive. Provide good, well-drained, nonalkaline soil.

S. americanum. AMERICAN SNOWBELL. Shrub. Zones 31, 32, 34, 39. To 10 ft. high and 8 ft. wide, rounded form. Dark green, oblong leaves to 3 in. long, sometimes toothed. Bell-shaped white flowers with backcurved petals appear in early to midsummer.

S. japonicus. JAPANESE SNOWDROP TREE, JAPANESE SNOWBELL. Tree. Zones 32, 34, 39. To 30 ft. tall, with slender, graceful trunk; branches often strongly horizontal, giving tree a broad, flat top. Oval, scallop-edged leaves to 3 in. long; turn from dark green to red or yellow in fall. Faintly fragrant, ¾-in. white flowers hang in small clusters on short side branches. Leaves angle upward from branches while flowers hang down, giving the effect of parallel green and white tiers. Prune to control shape; tends to be shrubby unless lower side branches are suppressed. Splendid tree to look up into; plant it in raised beds near outdoor entertaining areas, or on a high bank above a path. 'Pendula' ('Carillon') is a shrubby variety with weeping branches; 'Pink Chimes', also shrubby, is a more upright form with pink flowers. 'Rosea' is upright and has pink flowers. 'Sohuksan' has darker green leaves.

S. obassia. FRAGRANT SNOWBELL. Tree. Zones 32, 34, 35, 37, 39. To 20–30 ft. tall, rather narrow. Oval to round, deep green, 3–8-in.-long leaves. Where frosts come very late, leaves may color yellow in autumn. Fragrant flowers to 1 in. long are carried in drooping, 6–8-in. clusters at branch ends and may be partly obscured by foliage. Blooms a little earlier than *S. japonicus*. Good against background of evergreens, or for height and contrast above border of rhododendrons and azaleas.

S. wilsonii. FRAGRANT SNOWBELL. Tree. Zones 31, 32. To 8 ft. tall. Clusters or single bell-shaped white flowers appear in early summer. Leaves are oval to diamond-shaped.

SUGARBERRY. See CELTIS laevigata

SUGAR CANE. See SACCHARUM

SUMAC. See RHUS

SUMMER CYPRESS. See KOCHIA scoparia

SUMMER FORGET-ME-NOT. See ANCHUSA capensis

SUMMER HYACINTH. See GALTONIA candicans

SUMMER LILAC. See BUDDLEIA davidii

SUMMERSWEET. See CLETHRA alnifolia

SUNDROPS. See OENOTHERA fruticosa

SUNFLOWER. See HELIANTHUS

SUNROSE. See HELIANTHEMUM nummularium

SWAMP DRAGON. See SAURURUS cernuus

SWAMP MILKWEED. See ASCLEPIAS incarnata

SWAN RIVER DAISY. See BRACHYCOME iberidifolia

FOR INFORMATION ON SELECTING PLANTS

PLEASE SEE PAGES 47–112

SWEDISH IVY. See PLECTRANTHUS

SWEET ALYSSUM. See LOBULARIA maritima

SWEET BALM. See MELISSA officinalis

SWEET BAY. See LAURUS nobilis, MAGNOLIA virginiana

SWEETBELLS. See LEUCOTHOE racemosa

SWEET BOX. See SARCOCOCCA hookeriana humilis

SWEET CONEFLOWER. See RUDBECKIA subtomentosa

SWEET FERN, SWEET GALE. See MYRICA gale

SWEETLEAF. See SYMPLOCOS paniculata

SWEET OLIVE. See OSMANTHUS fragrans

SWEET PEA. See LATHYRUS odoratus

SWEET POTATO

Convolvulaceae

PERENNIAL GROWN AS ANNUAL

☑ ZONES 31, 32

☼ BEST IN FULL SUN

🔴 REGULAR WATER

Sweet Potato

Not a potato, but the thickened root of a trailing tropical vine closely related to morning glory *(Ipomoea)*. Bush and short vine varieties also available. Needs long, hot, frost-free growing season—easiest to grow in the South. Also requires well-drained soil (preferably sandy loam) and plenty of room. Start with certified disease-free slips (rooted cuttings) from a garden center or mail-order nursery. Look for resistant varieties. To avoid buildup of disease organisms in the soil, don't grow sweet potatoes in the same location two years in a row.

There are two classes of sweet potatoes. One has soft, sugary yellow-orange flesh (examples are 'Centennial', 'Gold Rush', 'Vineless Puerto Rico'); the other has firm, dry whitish flesh (members of this group include 'Yellow Jersey', 'Nemagold'). The sweet yellow-orange type is incorrectly labeled "yam" when sold in grocery stores. Most varieties are ready to harvest 110 to 120 days after planting.

Plant in late spring when soil temperature has warmed to 70°F/21°C. Work in a low-nitrogen fertilizer before planting; too much nitrogen produces leafy growth at the expense of roots. Set slips so that only stem tips and leaves are exposed; space 1 ft. apart, in rows 3 ft. apart. To ensure good drainage, mark off rows and create a ditch between them to form planting ridges. Row covers provide added heat and keep out many pests. Harvest before first frost; if tops are killed by sudden frost, harvest immediately. Dig carefully to avoid cutting or bruising roots. Flavor improves in storage (starch is converted to sugar). Dry roots in sun, then cure by storing for 10 to 14 days in warm (about 85°F/29°C), humid place. Store in cooler environment (but not below 55°F/13°C) until ready to use.

Sweet potatoes are sometimes grown for decorative foliage—leaves are heart shaped in some varieties, cut or lobed in others. Ornamental varieties are discussed under *Ipomoea*.

SWEETSHRUB. See CALYCANTHUS floridus

SWEETSPIRE. See ITEA virginica

SWEET SULTAN. See CENTAUREA moschata

SWEET WILLIAM. See DIANTHUS barbatus

SWEET WOODRUFF. See GALIUM odoratum

SWISS CHARD

Chenopodiaceae

BIENNIAL GROWN AS ANNUAL

☑ ALL ZONES

☼ FULL SUN

🔴 REGULAR WATER

Swiss Chard

A form of beet grown for leaves and stalks instead of roots. One of the easiest and most practical of vegetables for home gardens. Sow big, crinkly, tan seeds ½–¾ in. deep in spaded soil, anytime from early spring to early summer. Thin seedlings to 1 ft. apart. About 2 months after sowing (plants are generally 1–1½ ft. tall) you can begin to cut outside leaves from plants as needed for meals. New leaves grow up in center of plants. Yield all summer and seldom bolt to seed (if one does, pull it up and throw it away).

Regular green-and-white chard looks presentable in flower garden. 'Bright Lights', a recent introduction, has pink, orange, yellow, and white stalks; it is a showstopper in the garden and in the vegetable basket. 'Rhubarb' chard has red stems and reddish green leaves; it looks attractive in garden beds or containers. Its leaves are valuable in floral arrangements and tasty when cooked, too—sweeter and stronger flavored than green chard. Cook leaves and leafstalks separately, since stalks take longer.

SWITCH GRASS. See PANICUM virgatum

SYCAMORE. See PLATANUS

SYMPHORICARPOS

SNOWBERRY, CORALBERRY

Caprifoliaceae

DECIDUOUS SHRUBS

☑ ZONES VARY BY SPECIES

☼ ◑ 🔴 EXPOSURE NEEDS VARY BY SPECIES

💧 MODERATE WATER

Symphoricarpos

North American natives. Low growing, often spreading by root suckers. Small, pink-tinged or white flowers in clusters or spikes. Attractive round, berrylike fruit remains on stems after leaves drop in autumn; nice in winter arrangements, attracts birds. Use as informal hedge or to control erosion on slopes.

S. albus (S. racemosus). COMMON SNOWBERRY. Zones 32, 34–45. Upright or spreading shrub 2–6 ft. tall. Leaves roundish, dull green, ¾–2 in. long (to 4 in. and often lobed on sucker shoots). Pink flowers in spring, followed by white fruit from late summer to winter. *S. a. laevigatus* bears more and bigger fruit than the species. Best fruit production in sun. Not a first-rate shrub, but useful in its tolerance of poor soil, urban air, and shade. Withstands neglect.

S. chenaultii. Zones 32, 34–43. Hybrid. Resembles parent *S. orbiculatus,* but red fruit is lightly spotted white and leaves are larger. 'Hancock' is 1-ft. dwarf valued as woodland ground or bank cover. High shade.

S. orbiculatus (S. vulgaris). CORALBERRY, INDIAN CURRANT. Zones 32, 34–45. Resembles *S. albus,* but bears a profusion of small purplish red fruit in clusters. These are bright enough and plentiful enough to provide a good fall to winter show. Full sun.

FOR GROWING SYMBOL EXPLANATIONS

PLEASE SEE PAGE 113

SYMPHYTUM officinale

COMFREY

Boraginaceae

PERENNIAL HERB

ZONES 31, 32, 34–43

PARTIAL SHADE IN HOT-SUMMER AREAS

REGULAR WATER

LEAVES ARE POISONOUS IF INGESTED

Symphytum officinale

Deep-rooted, clumping plant to 3 ft. high. Furry leaves with stiff hairs; basal leaves to 8 in. long or more, upper leaves smaller. Flowers not showy, ½ in. long, usually dull rose in color but sometimes white, cream, or purple. Leaves can be dried and brewed to make a medicinal tea, but this use is no longer recommended. Plants die back to the ground in fall. To keep leaf production high, cut out flowering stalks and mulch each spring with compost. Grow from root cuttings.

Although comfrey has a long history as a folk remedy, think hard before establishing it in your garden. Plant spreads freely from roots and is difficult to eradicate. Herb enthusiasts claim that comfrey accumulates minerals, enriches compost. 'Uplandicum' is a nicely variegated cultivar.

SYMPLOCOS paniculata

SAPPHIREBERRY, SWEETLEAF

Symplocaceae

DECIDUOUS SHRUB

ZONES 32, 34–41

FULL SUN

REGULAR WATER

Symplocos paniculata

To 10–20 ft. tall; wider than tall in maturity. Can be trained as a low-branching or multitrunked small tree. Dark green leaves to 3½ in. long and half as wide. In late spring or early summer, 2–3-in. clusters of small, fragrant white flowers bloom on previous year's wood. Main draw is the autumn show of sapphire blue, ⅓-in. fruits that garland the branches. Berries are much appreciated by birds. Single plants set little or no fruit, so plant groups of seedlings; cutting-grown plants from a single parent are not self-fertile. Some growers sell groups of three seedlings as a single plant to ensure fruiting. Use for screening or in a large shrub border.

S

SYRINGA

LILAC

Oleaceae

DECIDUOUS SHRUBS, RARELY SMALL TREES

ZONES VARY BY SPECIES

FULL SUN; TOLERATES PARTIAL SHADE IN WARMEST CLIMATES

REGULAR WATER

Syringa

A garden staple in cold-winter regions, cherished for big, flamboyant, usually fragrant flower clusters at branch tips. Best known are common lilac *(S. vulgaris)* and its many varieties, but there are other species of great usefulness. All are medium-size to large shrubs with no special appeal when out of bloom. Individual flowers are tubular, flaring into four petal-like lobes (in single types) or into a clutch of "petals" (in double kinds). Floral show comes from number of small flowers packed into dense pyramidal to conical clusters. Depending on climate, bloom occurs from early spring (in the earliest kinds) to early summer, always after leaves have formed.

Provide well-drained, neutral to slightly alkaline soil; if soil is strongly acid, dig lime into it before planting. Most lilacs bloom on wood formed

the previous year, so prune just after flowering ends. Remove spent flower clusters, cutting back to a pair of leaves; growth buds at that point will make flowering stems for next year. Renovate old, overgrown plants by cutting a few of oldest stems to the ground each year. For the few types that bloom on new growth, prune in late dormant season. Stem borer, scale, and leaf miner are the major pests; powdery mildew, leaf spot, and bacterial blight may be problems.

S. chinensis (S. rothomagensis). CHINESE LILAC. Zones 32, 34–43. Hybrid between common lilac and *S. persica*. To 15 ft. high, usually much less. More graceful than common lilac, with finer-textured foliage and twigs. Profusion of airy, open clusters of fragrant rose purple flowers. 'Alba' has white flowers.

S. henryi 'Lutece'. Zones 31, 32, 34–45. Grows to 10 ft. tall and blooms later than most other lilacs, in early June. A hybrid between *S. josikaea* and *S. villosa*, it has flowers of light purple pink.

S. hyacinthiflora. Zones 32, 34–43. Group of fragrant hybrids between common lilac and *S. oblata*, a Chinese species. Resemble common lilac, but generally bloom 7 to 10 days earlier. 'Assessippi' (single lavender), 'Excel' (single lilac blue), 'Grace McKenzie' (single lilac blue), and 'Mt. Baker' (single white) are very early blooming. Other varieties include 'Alice Eastwood' (double magenta), 'Blue Hyacinth' (single lavender), 'Clarke's Giant' (single lavender, larger flowers), 'Esther Staley' (single magenta), 'Gertrude Leslie' (double white), 'Pocahontas' (single purple), 'Purple Heart' (single purple), and 'White Hyacinth' (single white).

S. josikaea. HUNGARIAN LILAC. Zones 32, 34–43. Dense, upright growth to 12 ft. Dark green foliage. Lilac purple, slightly fragrant flowers in narrow clusters 4–7 in. long.

S. laciniata (S. persica laciniata). Zones 31, 32, 34, 35, 37, 39. To 8 ft. tall, with open habit and good rich green foliage color. Leaves to 2½ in. long, divided nearly to midrib into three to nine segments. Many small clusters of fragrant lilac-colored blooms.

S. meyeri 'Paliban'. Zones 32, 34–43. Dense, neat habit to 4–5 ft. high, somewhat wider. Fine-textured, mildew-resistant foliage. Starts flowering when only a foot high. Profusion of reddish purple buds open to softly fragrant light pink flowers. Sometimes sold as *S. palibiniana* or *S. velutina*.

S. microphylla 'Superba'. Zones 32, 34–41. Compact grower to 7 ft. tall. Mildew-resistant leaves. Deep red buds open to fragrant, single bright pink flowers. Sometimes reblooms in September.

S. oblata dilatata. KOREAN EARLY LILAC. Zones 34–43. Vigorous and upright when young, more spreading with age, to 15 ft. tall and wide. Fragrant pinkish lilac flowers bloom earlier than other lilacs, in early May. Leaves turn purple in autumn.

S. patula 'Miss Kim'. Zones 32, 34–43. Dense, twiggy, rounded habit to eventual 8–9 ft., but stays at 3 ft. for many years. Sometimes grafted high to make standard tree. Purple buds open to very fragrant icy blue flowers. Leaves may turn burgundy in fall.

S. pekinensis. PEKING LILAC. Zones 32, 34–43. Spreading shrub to 15 ft. high and wide, with arching branches. Creamy white, scented flowers; dark green leaves.

S. persica. PERSIAN LILAC. Zones 31, 32, 34–41. Graceful, loose form to 6 ft. high, with arching branches and 2½-in.-long leaves. Many clusters of fragrant pale violet flowers appear all along branches.

S. prestoniae. Zones 34–45. Group of extra hardy hybrids developed in Canada. Flowers come on new growth at the end of the lilac season, after common lilac has bloomed. Bulky, dense plants resemble common lilac, but they are shorter (to 6–10 ft.) and individual flowers are smaller and not particularly fragrant. Good selections include 'Donald Wyman' (dark rosy purple), 'Isabella' (lilac), 'Jessica' (violet), 'Minuet' (pale lilac), 'Miss Canada' (true bright pink), 'Nocturne' (bluish lilac), and 'Royalty' (purple to violet). For 'James MacFarlane' (sometimes sold as a member of this group), see *S. swegiflexa*.

S. reticulata (S. japonica, S. amurensis japonica). JAPANESE TREE LILAC. Zones 32, 34–43. Can be grown as large shrub to 30 ft. tall, or easily trained as single-trunked tree. Smooth bark, something like cherry bark in glossiness. Leaves to 5 in. long. White flower clusters, to 1 ft. long, produced on new growth late in lilac season. Flowers showy, but scent is like that of privet flowers. 'Ivory Silk' is compact, to 12 ft. high, and starts blooming while young.

S. swegiflexa. Zones 32, 34, 39. Hybrid between two Chinese species, *S. reflexa* and *S. sweginzowii*; sometimes known by the name "pink pearl lilac." To 12 ft. tall. Deep reddish buds open to fragrant single pink flowers in clusters to 8 in. long. Blooms on new growth, 3 weeks after common lilac. 'James MacFarlane' is best-known variety.

S. vulgaris. COMMON LILAC. Zones 32, 34–45. Can eventually reach 20 ft. tall, with nearly equal spread. Suckers strongly. Prune out suckers on grafted plants (no need to do so on own-root plants). Leaves roundish oval, pointed, dark green, to 5 in. long. Blooms in midspring, bearing pinkish or bluish lavender flowers in clusters to 10 in. long or more ('Alba' has pure white flowers). Fragrance is legendary; lilac fanciers swear that the species and its older varieties are more fragrant than newer types. Excellent cut flowers.

Varieties, often called French hybrids, number in the hundreds. They generally flower a little later than the species and have larger clusters of single or double flowers in a wide range of colors. Singles are often as showy as doubles, sometimes more so. All lilacs require 2 to 5 years to settle down and produce flowers of full size and true color. Here are just a few of the many choice varieties:

'Capitaine Baltet' (magenta), 'Charles Joly' (double dark purplish red), 'Congo' (red-violet buds open to deep lilac purple flowers), 'Katherine Havemeyer' (purple buds open to blue-violet flowers), 'Lucie Baltet' (single light pink), 'Miss Ellen Willmott' (double pure white), 'Ludwig Spaeth' (single reddish purple to dark purple), 'Monge' (large, single dark reddish purple flowers), 'President Lincoln' (single Wedgwood blue), 'President Poincaré' (double two-tone purple), 'Sensation' (single wine red with white picotee edge), 'William Robinson' (double pink).

Newer hybrids include 'Krasavitsa Moskvy' ('Beauty of Moscow'), with large clusters of pink buds opening into double white flowers; 'Nadezhda' ('Hope'), with deep purple buds opening into lilac blue double flowers; and 'Primrose', with pale yellow blooms (paler in warm climates).

TAGETES

MARIGOLD

Asteraceae (Compositae)

Annuals and perennials

Zones vary by species

Full sun

Regular water, except as noted

Tagetes

Robust, free-branching, nearly trouble-free plants ranging from 6 in. to 4 ft. tall, with flowers from pale yellow through gold to orange and brown maroon. Leaves finely divided, ferny, usually strongly scented. Annuals will bloom early summer to frost if old flowers are picked off. Handsome, long-lasting cut flowers; strong aroma from leaves, stems, and flowers permeates a room, but some odorless varieties are available. Easy to grow from seed, which sprouts in a few days in warm soil; to get earlier bloom, start seeds in flats or buy flat-grown plants.

T. erecta. AFRICAN MARIGOLD, TALL MARIGOLD. Annual. All zones. Original strains were 3–4-ft.-tall plants with single flowers. Modern strains more varied; most have fully double flowers. They range from dwarf Guys and Dolls and Inca series (12–14 in.) through Galore, Lady, and Perfection (16–20 in.) to Climax (2½–3 ft.). Novelty tall strains are Odorless and First Whites (28–30 in.). 'Snowbird' (1½ ft.) is a white marigold with uniform habit and color. Triploid hybrids, crosses between African and French marigolds, have exceptional vigor, bear profusion of 2-in. flowers over a long bloom season. Generally shorter than other *T. erecta* strains, they range from 10-in. Nugget to 12–14-in. Fireworks, H-G, Solar, and Sundance.

T. filifolia. IRISH LACE. Annual. All zones. Mounds of bright green, finely divided foliage, 6 in. tall and as wide, resemble unusually fluffy, round ferns. Used primarily as edging plant for foliage effect, but tiny white flowers are attractive.

T. lucida. MEXICAN TARRAGON. Perennial grown as an annual. All zones. Single, usually unbranched stems grow to 2–2½ ft. Narrow, uncut, smooth dark green leaves have strong scent and flavor of tarragon. Unimpressive yellow flowers are less than ½ in. wide.

T. patula. FRENCH MARIGOLD. Annual. All zones. Varieties from 6–18 in. tall, in flower colors from yellow to rich maroon brown; flowers may be fully double or single, and many are strongly bicolored. Best for edging are the dwarf, very double Janie (8-in.), Bonanza (10-in.), and Hero (10–12-in.) series in a range of colors from yellow through orange to red and brownish red. The Aurora and Sophia series have flowers that are larger (2½ in. wide) but not as double.

Make a tall marigold plant stand straight

To make tall marigold plants stand as firmly as possible (perhaps stoutly enough not to need staking), dig planting holes extra deep, strip any leaves off lower 1–3 in. of stem, and plant with stripped portion below soil line.

T. tenuifolia (T. signata). SIGNET MARIGOLD. Annual. All zones. Infrequently planted. Smaller flower heads than French marigold, but incredibly profuse in bloom. Finely cut foliage. Golden orange 'Golden Gem' ('Ursula') and bright yellow 'Lemon Gem' both form 8-in. mounds.

TALL BUTTERCUP. See RANUNCULUS acris

TALLHEDGE BUCKTHORN. See RHAMNUS frangula 'Columnaris'

TAMARIX

TAMARISK

Tamaricaceae

Deciduous shrubs or trees

Zones vary by species

Full sun

Moderate to very little water

Tamarix

These large shrubs or small trees are useful in areas where wind, salt, and poor soil are challenges, as in seacoast gardens. Only demands are sun and good drainage. Tend to be invasive in mild-winter climates and in rich soil; better behaved in more northerly regions. Tiny, scalelike, light green or bluish foliage on airy, arching, reddish branches; in spring or summer, narrow plumes of small pink or rose blossoms appear at branch ends. Prune regularly to maintain graceful effect. Locate where plant won't be prominent while out of leaf. There is much confusion in labeling of tamarisks in nurseries and among botanists.

T. hispida. KASHGAR TAMARISK. Zones 31, 32, 34–41. Smaller than other species, to 4 ft. high; good choice for smaller gardens. Fluffy, bright pink flower clusters in late summer. Blooms on new wood; prune in late winter or very early spring.

T. parviflora. Zones 31, 32, 34–43. To 12–15 ft. tall, usually not as wide. Light pink blossoms in late spring. Blooms on old wood; prune right after bloom.

T. ramosissima (T. pentandra). Zones 31, 32, 34–45. To 10–15 ft. tall, usually not as wide. Rosy pink flowers in spring or early summer. Blooms on new wood; prune late winter or very early spring. 'Cheyenne Red' has deeper pink blooms than the species; 'Summer Glow' has bright pink flowers and blue-tinged foliage; 'Rosea' bears rich pink flowers later in summer.

TAMPALA. See AMARANTHUS tricolor

TANACETUM

Asteraceae (Compositae)

PERENNIAL HERBS

ZONES VARY BY SPECIES

FULL SUN

REGULAR TO MODERATE WATER

Tanacetum

Most kinds of *Tanacetum* have finely divided leaves (often highly aromatic) and clusters of daisylike flower heads. Some have gray to nearly white foliage.

T. balsamita. See *Chrysanthemum balsamita*

T. coccineum. See *Chrysanthemum coccineum*

T. parthenium. See *Chrysanthemum parthenium*

T. ptarmiciflorum. See *Chrysanthemum ptarmiciflorum*

T. vulgare. TANSY, COMMON TANSY. Zones 31, 32, 34–43. Coarse garden plant to 3 ft. with finely divided bright green aromatic (some say smelly) leaves, and small yellow button flowers. Thin clumps yearly to keep in bounds; tansy can be very aggressive and self-seeds prolifically. No longer used medicinally, though still grown in herb gardens. *T. v. crispum*, fern-leaf tansy, to 2½ ft., has finely cut foliage and yellow buttonhead flowers, is more decorative than the species.

THE MANY USES OF TANSY

Tansy has been used by herbalists and householders for centuries. The crushed leaves have a strong medicinal-piney scent, and have been used as a substitute for pepper. The aroma comes from a bitter substance called thujone, which is toxic in large amounts and is also present in wormwood. Tansy was planted near doorways or sprigs hung in homes to repel ants, flies, and fleas. In 16th and 17th century England it was strewn on floors to freshen the air in buildings.

The yellow button flowers can be used as fresh cut flowers or dried for use in everlasting arrangements, wreaths, and swags. The flowers and young leaves are also useful in dyeing, yielding green and yellow shades.

TANSY. See TANACETUM vulgare

TARO. See COLOCASIA esculenta

TARRAGON, FRENCH. See ARTEMISIA dracunculus

TARRAGON, MEXICAN. See TAGETES lucida

TASSEL FERN. See POLYSTICHUM polyblepharum

Taxaceae. The yew family contains needle-leafed evergreens with single-seeded fruit surrounded by a fleshy coat. Yew (*Taxus*) is the most notable example.

Taxodiaceae. The taxodium family includes evergreen (and some deciduous) coniferous trees, usually with small cones containing two to six seeds on each scale. Members include *Cryptomeria*, dawn redwood (*Metasequoia*), umbrella pine (*Sciadopitys*), giant sequoia (*Sequoiadendron*), and *Taxodium*.

TAXODIUM

Taxodiaceae

DECIDUOUS OR EVERGREEN TREES

ZONES VARY BY SPECIES

FULL SUN

MUCH OR LITTLE WATER

Taxodium

Conifers of great size with shaggy, cinnamon-colored bark and graceful sprays of short, narrow, flat, needlelike leaves. Female flowers produce round, fragrant, 1-in. cones. The following species are native to the southeastern U.S. but adapt widely to much colder and drier climates. Both are very tough, tolerant trees.

T. ascendens. POND CYPRESS. Deciduous. Zones 31, 32, 34–41. Resembles bald cypress (*T. distichum*) in most details and is believed by some experts to be a variety of that species. Somewhat narrower and more erect than bald cypress; trunk not as strongly buttressed. Leafs out late in spring. In the wild, found on higher ground around ponds; doesn't actually grow in the water, as bald cypress does. 'Nutans' is the main form grown. 'Prairie Sentinel' is very narrow.

T. distichum. BALD CYPRESS. Deciduous. Zones 31, 32, 34–43. Can grow into 100-ft.-tall, broad-topped tree in the wild, but young and middle-aged garden trees are pyramidal to 50–70 ft. high. Foliage sprays delicate and feathery, with narrow, about ½-in.-long leaves of a pale, delicate, yellow-toned green. Foliage turns orange brown before dropping. Interesting winter silhouette.

Any soil except strongly alkaline. Takes extremely wet conditions (even grows in swamps), but also tolerates rather dry soil. Trunk is buttressed near base. Develops knobby growths called "knees" when growing in waterlogged soil. Bagworms may be troublesome in some years. Requires only corrective pruning, to remove dead wood and unwanted branches. Outstanding tree for stream bank or edge of lake or pond.

TAXUS

YEW

Taxaceae

EVERGREEN SHRUBS OR TREES

ZONES VARY BY SPECIES

FULL SUN OR PARTIAL SHADE

REGULAR TO MODERATE WATER

FRUIT (SEEDS) AND FOLIAGE ARE POISONOUS IF INGESTED

Taxus

Yews are conifers—but they do not bear cones. Instead, they produce fleshy, scarlet (rarely yellow), cup-shaped, single-seeded fruit. In general, yews are more formal, darker green, and more tolerant of shade and moisture than most cultivated conifers. Long lived; tolerant of much shearing and pruning, since they sprout from bare wood. Excellent for hedges, screens.

Easily moved even when large, but since plants grow at a slow to medium rate, big ones are luxury items. They take many soils, but do not thrive in strongly alkaline or strongly acid ones. Do not take extreme heat. Reflected heat from hot south or west wall will burn foliage. Even cold-hardy kinds show needle damage when exposed to dry winds, very low temperatures. Only female plants produce berries, but many do so without male plants nearby; varieties described below are female, except as noted. Subject to vine weevils, mealybugs, scale insects, various fungus diseases. During prolonged hot, dry weather, hose off plants every 2 weeks.

T. baccata. ENGLISH YEW. Zones 32, warmest parts of 34. To 25–40 ft., sometimes taller, with wide-spreading branches forming broad, low crown. Needles ½–1½ in. long, dark green and glossy above, pale beneath; spirally arranged. Garden varieties are far more common than the species. These include:

'Adpressa'. Usually sold as *T. brevifolia*, name correctly belonging to the native western yew. Wide-spreading, dense shrub to 4–5 ft. high.

'Aurea'. Broad pyramid to 25 ft. tall after many years. New foliage is golden yellow from spring to fall, then turns green.

'Repandens'. SPREADING ENGLISH YEW. Long, horizontal, spreading branches make 2–4-ft.-high ground cover, spreading to 8–10 ft. after many years. Useful low foundation plant. Will arch over wall.

'Stricta' ('Fastigiata'). IRISH YEW. Dark green column to 20 ft. or taller. Has larger needles and more crowded, upright branches than does English yew. Branches tend to spread near top, especially in snowy regions or where water is ample. Branches can be tied together with wire. Plants that outgrow their space can be reduced by heading back and thinning; old wood sprouts freely. There is a form with yellowish white variegation on leaves.

T. canadensis. CANADIAN YEW. Zones 34–45. To 6 ft. high and 8 ft. wide–often wider than it is tall when mature. Needles ½–¾ in. long, glossy deep green above, lighter green beneath, reddish in winter; arranged in two rows along twigs. Cannot tolerate hot, dry conditions; needs shade in winter.

T. cuspidata. JAPANESE YEW. Zones 32, 34–41. To 50 ft. in Japan; usually grown as compact, spreading shrub in U.S. Needles ½–1 in. long, dark green above, tinged yellowish beneath; usually arranged in two rows along twigs, making flat or V-shaped spray. The most commonly grown varieties are:

'Capitata'. Plants sold under this name are probably ordinary *T. cuspidata* in its upright, pyramidal form. Dense growth to 10–25 ft., possibly taller. Can be held lower by pinching new growth. Fruits heavily.

'Densa'. Low and wide, to 4 ft. high and 20 ft. across; very dark green needles.

'Expansa'. Open centered and vase shaped, wider than it is high; to about 10 ft. tall.

'Nana'. Often sold as *T. brevifolia*. Slow-growing male variety to 3 ft. tall, 6 ft. wide in 20 years, eventually to a possible 20 ft. tall. Makes a good low barrier or foundation plant for many years.

'Thayerae'. Wide-spreading shrub, to 8 ft. tall and 15 ft. across, with flattened top.

T. media. Zones 32, 34–41. Group of hybrids between Japanese yew and English yew. Intermediate between the two in color and texture. Of dozens of selections, these are among the most widely offered:

'Beanpole'. Narrow, upright to 18 ft. tall and just 1½ ft. wide.

'Brownii'. Compact, rounded plant to 4–8 ft. tall, possibly larger. Male variety. Good low, dense hedge.

'Densiformis'. Zones 32, 34–43. Dense and bushy, to 4 ft. high and 6 ft. wide; bright green color.

'Everlow'. Low and spreading, to 1½ ft. high and 5 ft. wide; dark green foliage; tolerates drying winds.

'Green Wave'. 3–4 ft. tall, forms a mound. Arching branches.

'Hatfieldii'. Broad column or pyramid to 10 ft. or taller; good dark green color. Male variety.

'Hicksii'. Narrow, upright grower to 10–12 ft. or taller; slightly broader at center than at top or bottom, widening with age.

'Kelseyi'. Dense and upright, to 12 ft. tall; very dark green needles.

'Tauntonii'. Low and spreading, to 4 ft. high and 6 ft. wide. Tolerates heat better than most and also resists winter burn.

'Vermeulen'. Rounded, compact, and slow-growing, to 8 ft. high and 9 ft. across.

'Wardii'. To 6 ft. tall, 20 ft. across; flat-topped. Dark green leaves.

TEABERRY. See GAULTHERIA procumbens

FOR GROWING SYMBOL EXPLANATIONS

PLEASE SEE PAGE 113

TELEKIA speciosa

Asteraceae

PERENNIAL

ZONES 31, 32, 34–41

PARTIAL SHADE

AMPLE WATER

Telekia speciosa

Native to wetlands and watersides in eastern Europe, this daisylike plant produces abundant sprays of large, yellow, fragrant flowers, 2–3 in. across, throughout the summer and into the fall. The toothed leaves are quite large; the plants themselves can grow to 6 ft. tall with a 3-ft. spread. Thriving in moist, slightly alkaline soil of moderate fertility, they are easy to grow and are well suited to naturalistic and woodland gardens and the edges of ponds, or wherever a big, bold background plant is wanted.

TETRADIUM daniellii. See EVODIA daniellii

TEUCRIUM

GERMANDER

Lamiaceae (Labiatae)

EVERGREEN SHRUBS OR PERENNIALS

ZONES VARY BY SPECIES

FULL SUN

MODERATE WATER

Teucrium

Tough plants, enduring poor, rocky soils. They can't stand wet or poorly drained soils but will tolerate regular watering where drainage is good.

T. canadense. Perennial. Zones 31, 32, 34–41. Wild plant grows to 3 ft. tall, bearing white to rose flowers. The form offered in nurseries is a dwarf evergreen creeper to 8 in. high, with pale pink summer flowers.

T. chamaedrys. Shrubby perennial. Zones 31, 32, 34, 39. To 1 ft. high, spreading to 2 ft.; many upright, woody-based stems densely set with toothed, ¾-in.-long, dark green leaves. Red-purple or white flowers in loose spikes (white-flowered form is looser). Use as edging, foreground, low clipped hedge, or small-scale ground cover. Shear back once or twice a year to force side branching. 'Prostratum' is 4–6 in. high, spreading to 3 ft. or more.

T. montanum. Shrub. Zones 31, 32, 34, 39. Low, creeping to semi-upright dwarf shrub. Narrow oblong leaves to ¾ in. long, covered with white hairs underneath. Clusters of creamy white flowers at ends of stems in summer. Suitable for rock gardens or front of borders.

T. pyrenaicum. Perennial. Zones 31, 32, 34, 39. To 8 in. high. Green leaves to 1 in. long, nearly round, with notched edges. Clusters of white or white-and-purple flowers at stem tips in summer. Suitable for rock gardens or front of borders.

THALIA dealbata

HARDY WATER CANNA

Marantaceae

PERENNIAL

ZONES 31, 32, 34, 39

FULL SUN

AMPLE WATER

Thalia dealbata

This native of the Gulf Coast to Missouri thrives in the water or at water's edge. The tall, slender leaves, growing from the base of the plant, are cannalike; small purple blooms atop tall, slender stalks are borne in

T

panicles. Reaching a height of from 2 to 6 ft., plants thrive in rich soil well amended with organic matter; crown can be submerged in up to 2 in. of water. Will grow in part-sun but blooms will be diminished. Lends a tropical accent to ponds, water margins, and large aquatic containers. Roots need to be overwintered indoors, in a pool in a greenhouse, north of Zone 32.

THALICTRUM

MEADOW RUE

Ranunculaceae

PERENNIALS

⚊ ZONES VARY BY SPECIES

◐ ☀ LIGHT SHADE TO FULL SUN

💧 REGULAR WATER

Thalictrum

Foliage clumps, often blue green in color, resemble those of columbine. In late spring or summer, plants send up sparsely leafed stems topped by puffs of small flowers, each consisting of four sepals and a prominent cluster of stamens. Superb for airy effect; delicate tracery of leaves and flowers is particularly effective against dark green background. Pleasing contrast to sturdier perennials. Foliage is a good addition to flower arrangements.

All meadow rues thrive in dappled sunlight at woodland edges and tolerate full sun in coolest regions. Grow in moist, humus-rich soil. Protect from wind. Divide clumps every 4 or 5 years.

T. alpinum. Zones 32, 34–41. To 6–12 in. high, with green leaves, greenish purple sepals, yellow stamens. Good for rock garden.

T. aquilegiifolium. Zones 32 (cooler parts), 34–41. To 2–3 ft. tall, with bluish green foliage. Earliest of the meadow rues to bloom. Clouds of fluffy stamens (the white or greenish sepals drop off) appear for a couple of weeks in mid- to late spring. Rosy lilac is the usual color; white and purple selections are available. 'Atropurpureum' has dark purple flowers; 'Thundercloud', rosy purple with dark purple stamens. If left in place, spent flowers are followed by attractive, long-lasting seed heads. Heat tolerant.

T. delavayi (T. dipterocarpum). CHINESE MEADOW RUE. Zones 31, 32, 34–41. To 3–4 ft. (even 6 ft.) tall, with thin, dark purple stems that need support. Green foliage. Lavender to violet sepals, yellow stamens. 'Hewitt's Double' has double lilac-colored flowers; bloom lasts 2 months or longer.

T. flavum glaucum (T. speciosissimum). Zones 31, 32, 34–41. To 3–5 ft. tall; stems need staking. Blue-green foliage; summer flowers similar to those of *T. aquilegiifolium*, but color is lemon yellow. Heat tolerant.

T. kiusianum. Zones 31, 32, 34–41. Forms a low mat 4 in. high and 1 ft. across. Leaves are deep bluish green. Light mauve pink flowers in early summer.

T. minus. Zones 32, 34–43. A somewhat variable species. The form most often sold ('Adiantifolium') reaches 3 ft. when in flower. Bluish green foliage; flowers consist of yellow stamens (greenish sepals drop off).

T. rochebrunianum. Zones 32, 34–41. Forms green-foliaged clumps to 4–6 ft. tall, with sturdy stems that don't need staking. White or lavender sepals with pale yellow stamens. 'Lavender Mist', with violet sepals, is a superior selection.

Theaceae. The tea family consists of evergreen or deciduous trees and shrubs with leathery leaves and five-petaled flowers that have a large number of stamens. *Camellia*, *Franklinia*, and *Stewartia* are important representatives.

FOR GROWING SYMBOL EXPLANATIONS

PLEASE SEE PAGE 113

THELESPERMA

GREENTHREAD

Asteraceae

ANNUALS, BIENNIALS, OR PERENNIALS

⚊ ALL ZONES

☀ FULL SUN

💧💧 MODERATE TO LITTLE WATER

Thelesperma

A group of annuals, biennials, and perennials native to the American West, the greenthreads have daisylike flowers similar to those of coreopsis. Plants often self-sow. The species listed here are annuals or often behave as annuals, and tolerate dry conditions.

Seedlings do not transplant well; direct-sow in spring where plants are to grow. Plant in informal or naturalistic gardens. Deer usually avoid these plants. Seed is available from midwestern or western wildflower seed specialists. Grow in alkaline soil with very good drainage and some organic matter.

T. burridgeanum. BURRIDGE GREENTHREAD. Annual. Native to Texas. To 3 ft. tall, branched stems with 4-in. leaves divided into pairs of narrow, threadlike leaflets of medium green. Summer flowers are 1½ in. across, reddish brown tipped with yellow, with purplish brown central disk. Easy to grow.

T. filifolium. GREENTHREAD, FALSE GOLDEN WAVE. Annual or biennial. Native to central Texas. Aromatic leaves to 5 in. are divided into pairs of oblong leaflets. Summer flowers are 2 in. across, yellow tinged reddish brown, with brown central disk. Self-sows freely and often behaves as an annual.

THELYPTERIS

Thelypteridaceae (Polypodiaceae)

FERNS

⚊ ZONES VARY BY SPECIES

◐ ● PARTIAL OR FULL SHADE

💧💧 AMPLE WATER

Thelypteris

The plants commonly sold under this name have undergone more name changes than is usual even for ferns. Botanically current names are noted in parentheses below; nurseries may not have caught up. Species grown in North America are deciduous and commonly thrive in shade, although some tolerate sun if moisture is plentiful. All have their place in fern collections or wild gardens, in areas with moist conditions. They are found growing wild in bogs and swamps throughout the temperate regions of the world.

T. decursive-pinnata (Phegopteris decursive-pinnata). Zones 31, 32. Deciduous, to 32 in. high. Pale green fronds are once- or twice-divided into narrow, linear leaflets.

T. hexagonoptera (Phegopteris hexagonoptera). BROAD BEECH FERN. Zones 31, 32, 34–43. Medium green, triangular fronds to 1½–2 ft. long and wide. Fronds are once-divided, with each division deeply cut and toothed.

T. noveboracensis (Parathelypteris noveboracensis). NEW YORK FERN. Zones 32, 34–45. Pale green, 1–2-ft.-long fronds are once divided, with the segments deeply lobed. A vigorous colonizer, it can be used as a ground cover in shade—or even in full sun if kept moist.

T. palustris. MARSH FERN. Zones 31, 32, 34–45. Spreads rapidly by rhizomes. Fronds occur singly or in tufts and are of two kinds: sterile and fertile. Sterile fronds are 6–24 in. long and half as wide, tapered at both ends, once-divided, with segments deeply lobed. Fertile fronds are 1–3 ft. long, sturdier and stiffer than the sterile ones.

T. phegopteris (Phegopteris connectilis). NARROW BEECH FERN. Zones 32, 34–43. Resembles *T. hexagonoptera*, but fronds are somewhat shorter and narrower.

T

THERMOPSIS

FALSE LUPINE, BUSH PEA

Fabaceae (Leguminosae)

PERENNIALS

⚡ ZONES VARY BY SPECIES

☀ ◐ FULL SUN OR LIGHT SHADE

🌢 REGULAR WATER

Thermopsis

These easy-to-grow perennials resemble lupines. Silvery leaves are divided into leaflets that spread like fingers on a hand; erect, spikelike clusters of sweet pea–shaped yellow flowers appear in spring. Because of their tendency to spread by underground rhizomes, they are best in informal or wild gardens. Need little care. Somewhat drought resistant.

T. caroliniana. Zones 31, 32, 34–45. Native to the Carolinas and Georgia. To 3–4 ft. tall, with 10-in. flower clusters. More heat tolerant than the other species.

T. lupinoides. Zones 34–45. Native to Eurasia, Alaska. To 2 ft. tall, with densely packed, 10-in. flower clusters.

T. montana. Zones 34–41. Native to western North America. To 2–4 ft. tall, with 8-in. flower clusters.

THRIFT. See ARMERIA

THUJA

ARBORVITAE

Cupressaceae

EVERGREEN SHRUBS OR TREES

⚡ ZONES VARY BY SPECIES

☀ ◐ PARTIAL SHADE IN HOT-SUMMER AREAS

🌢🌢 REGULAR TO MODERATE WATER

Thuja

Neat, symmetrical, geometrical plants that run to globes, cones, cylinders. Juvenile foliage is feathery, with small, needlelike leaves; mature foliage is scalelike, carried in flat sprays. Foliage in better-known varieties is often yellow green or bright golden yellow. Urn-shaped cones with overlapping scales are ½ in. long, green turning brownish.

Although arborvitaes will take both damp and fairly dry soils, they grow best in well-drained soil. Need humidity and suffer where summers are hot and dry. They are subject to some problems, including bagworms and heart rot. Generic name is sometimes spelled *Thuya.*

T. occidentalis. AMERICAN ARBORVITAE, EASTERN ARBORVITAE. Zones 32, 34–45. Native to eastern U.S. Upright, open growth to 40–60 ft., with branches that tend to turn up at ends. Leaf sprays bright green to yellowish green. Foliage turns bronze in severe cold. The species itself is seldom seen, but smaller garden varieties are common. Among these, the taller ones make good informal or clipped screens, while lower kinds are often used around foundations, along walks or walls, as hedges. Some good varieties are:

'Brandon'. Fast growth to 12–15 ft. tall, 3–4 ft. wide. Useful as screen.

'Douglasii Pyramidalis'. Vigorous-growing pyramid to 15 ft. or taller.

'Elegantissima'. Narrow and pyramidal, to 15 ft. high and 5 ft. wide. Dark green foliage has yellow tips that turn brown in winter.

'Emerald' ('Emerald Green', 'Smaragd'). Neat, dense-growing, narrow cone to 10–15 ft. tall, 3–4 ft. wide. Holds its color throughout winter.

'Fastigiata' ('Pyramidalis', 'Columnaris'). Tall, narrow, dense, columnar plant to 25 ft. high, 5 ft. wide; can be kept lower by pruning. Good plant for tall hedges and screens (6 ft. or more), especially in cold regions and damp soils. Set 4 ft. apart for neat, low-maintenance screen.

'Globosa' ('Little Gem', 'Little Giant', and 'Nana' are similar varieties). GLOBE ARBORVITAE, TOM THUMB ARBORVITAE. Dense, rounded, with bright green foliage. Usually 2–3 ft. tall with equal spread; eventually larger.

'Hetz Midget'. Low, dense globe to 4 ft. high; good green color.

'Holmstrup'. Slow growing and pyramidal, to 10 ft. tall. Bright green foliage. Good hedge or screen.

'Nigra'. Tall, dense, dark green cone to 20–30 ft. tall, 4–5 ft. wide.

'Pendula'. Pyramidal, to 15 ft. high, with weeping branchlets.

'Rheingold' ('Improved Ellwangeriana Aurea'). Cone-shaped, slow-growing, bright golden plant with a mixture of scalelike and needlelike leaves. Even very old plants seldom exceed 6 ft.

'Rosenthalii'. Slow growing and pyramidal, to 15 ft. tall. Dark green foliage. Good hedge or screen.

'Spiralis'. Narrow pyramid to 45 ft. tall, branchlets in a spiral around stem. Dark green foliage.

'Techny'. Slow-growing pyramid with broad base, to 15 ft. tall. Dark green foliage. Good hedge or screen; does well in the North.

'Umbraculifera'. Globe shaped in youth, gradually becoming flat topped. At 10 years it should be 4 ft. tall and wide.

'Wareana'. Dense, pyramidal, to 8 ft. tall. Bright green foliage. Does well in North.

'Woodwardii'. Widely grown dense, globular shrub of rich green color. May attain considerable size with age, but it's a small plant over reasonably long period. If you can wait 72 years, it may be 8 ft. high by 18 ft. wide.

'Yellow Ribbon'. To 8–10 ft. tall, 2–3 ft. wide, with bright yellow foliage throughout the year.

T. orientalis. See *Platycladus orientalis*

T. plicata. WESTERN RED CEDAR. Zones 32, 34–37, 39. In gardens, typically grows to 50–70 ft. tall, 15–25 ft. wide. Slender, drooping branchlets, set closely with dark green leaf sprays. Unlike many forms of *T. occidentalis,* this species has foliage that does not discolor in cold weather. Single trees are magnificent in large lawns, but lower branches spread quite broadly and trees lose their characteristic beauty when these are cut off. An alternative to the more pest-ridden *Cupressocyparis leylandii.* A few varieties are:

'Aurea'. Younger branch tips golden green.

'Fastigiata'. HOGAN CEDAR. Very dense, narrow, erect; fine for tall screen.

'Hillieri'. Irregularly shaped dense, broad shrub with thick, short, heavy branches.

'Stoneham Gold'. Dense, slow-growing dwarf (6 ft. tall, 2 ft. wide) with orange new growth.

'Striblingii'. Dense, thick column 10–12 ft. tall, 2–3 ft. wide. For moderate-height screen planting or use as an upright sentinel.

'Virescens'. Narrow, fast growth.

'Watnong Green'. Fast growth; broad, conical form.

'Zebrina'. Broadly cone shaped, to 50 ft. tall. Yellow-striped foliage.

THUJOPSIS dolabrata

FALSE ARBORVITAE, DEERHORN CEDAR, HIBA CEDAR

Cupressaceae

EVERGREEN TREE

⚡ ZONES 32, 34–37, 39

☀ ◐ FULL SUN OR PARTIAL SHADE

🌢🌢 REGULAR TO MODERATE WATER

Thujopsis dolabrata

Pyramidal, coniferous, often shrubby, of very slow growth to 30–50 ft. tall, 10–20 ft. wide. Foliage resembles that of *Thuja,* but twigs are coarser, glossy, branching in staghorn effect. Best where summers are cool, humid. Plant as single tree where foliage details can be appreciated. Slow growth makes it good container plant. 'Nana' is a dwarf variety to 3 ft. high; 'Variegata' has white branch tips.

THUNBERGIA

Acanthaceae

VINES OR SHRUBS

ALL ZONES; SEE BELOW

PARTIAL SHADE IN HOTTEST AREAS

REGULAR WATER

Thunbergia

Tropical plants noted for showy flowers. Those described here grow fast enough to bloom the first season and can thus be treated as annuals. Provide rich, well-drained soil. Good greenhouse plants.

T. alata. BLACK-EYED SUSAN VINE. Perennial vine grown as summer annual. Small, trailing or twining plant with triangular, 3-in. leaves. Flowers are flaring tubes to 1 in. wide in orange, yellow, or white, all with purple-black center. Start seed indoors; set plants out in good soil in sunny spot as soon as weather warms. Use in hanging baskets or window boxes or as ground cover; or train on strings or low trellis.

T. gregorii (T. gibsonii). ORANGE CLOCK VINE. Perennial grown as summer annual. Twines to 6 ft. tall or sprawls over ground to cover 6-ft. circle. Leaves 3 in. long, toothed. Flowers tubular, flaring, bright orange, borne singly on 4-in. stems. Plant 3–4 ft. apart to cover a wire fence, 6 ft. apart as a ground cover. Plant above a wall, over which vine will cascade, or grow in a hanging basket. Showy and easy to grow.

THYME. See THYMUS

THYMOPHYLLA tenuiloba. See DYSSODIA tenuiloba

THYMUS

THYME

Lamiaceae (Labiatae)

EVERGREEN SHRUBBY PERENNIALS

ZONES 31, 32, 34–43

PARTIAL SHADE IN HOTTEST AREAS

MODERATE WATER

Thymus

Members of the mint family with tiny, usually heavily scented leaves and masses of colorful little flowers in late spring or summer. Diminutive plants well suited to herb garden, rock garden; prostrate, mat-forming types make good ground covers for small spaces. Attractive to bees. Provide warm, light, well-drained soil; restrain plants as needed by clipping back growing tips.

T. citriodorus. LEMON THYME. Hybrid to 4–12 in. high; erect or spreading. Lemon-scented foliage; summer flowers of palest purple. Leaves of 'Argenteus' are splashed with silver, those of 'Aureus' with gold.

T. herba-barona. CARAWAY-SCENTED THYME. Grows quickly to form a thick, flat mat of tiny dark green leaves with caraway fragrance. Clusters of rose pink flowers in midsummer.

T. lanuginosus. See *T. pseudolanuginosus*

T. praecox arcticus (T. serpyllum, T. drucei). MOTHER-OF-THYME, CREEPING THYME. Main stems form a flat mat, with branches rising 2–6 in. high. Roundish dark green leaves; clusters of small, purplish white flowers in summer. Good for small areas or filler between stepping-stones where foot traffic is light. Soft and fragrant underfoot. Leaves can be used for seasoning and in potpourri. Among the many garden forms are the following:

'Album'. Pure white flowers.

'Coccineum'. Deep pink flowers.

'Linear Leaf Lilac'. Needlelike leaves, red stems, lilac flowers.

'Longwood'. Strong grower with furry gray leaves and 4-in. spikes of lilac flowers.

'Minus'. Tiny, dense, compact, slow-growing plant with pink flowers. 'Elfin' is even tinier.

'Pink Ripple'. Larger than the species. Lemon-scented foliage, salmon pink blooms.

'Reiter's'. Profuse rose red blooms.

T. pseudolanuginosus (T. lanuginosus). WOOLLY THYME. Forms flat to undulating mat 2–3 in. high. Stems densely clothed with small, woolly gray leaves. Sparse, seldom-seen midsummer bloom of pinkish flowers in leaf joints. Becomes slightly rangy in winter. Use in rock crevices, between stepping-stones, to spill over bank or raised bed, to cover small patches of ground. 'Hall's Woolly' is not as furry but blooms more heavily.

T. vulgaris. COMMON THYME. To 6–12 in. high. Narrow to oval, gray-green leaves. Tiny lilac flowers in dense whorls in late spring or summer. Low edging for flower, vegetable, or herb garden. Good container plant. Use leaves fresh or dried for seasoning fish, shellfish, poultry stuffing, soups, vegetables. Many of the varieties, such as silver-variegated 'Argenteus', are not as hardy to cold as the species. 'Aureus' has golden leaves.

TIARELLA

FOAMFLOWER, SUGAR-SCOOP

Saxifragaceae

PERENNIALS

ZONES VARY BY SPECIES

PARTIAL OR FULL SHADE

REGULAR WATER

Tiarella

Clump-forming perennials spread by rhizomes (and by stolons, in the case of *T. cordifolia*). Leaves arise directly from rhizomes; foliage is evergreen, though it may change color in autumn. Selections with year-round colorful foliage are becoming popular; look for new introductions in addition to ones described below. Narrow, erect flower stems carry many small white (sometimes pinkish) flowers. Useful in shady rock gardens; make pretty ground covers but will not bear foot traffic.

T. cordifolia. FOAMFLOWER. Zones 32, 34–43. Rapid spreader. Forms foot-wide clumps of light green, lobed, 4-in. leaves that show red-and-yellow fall color. Flower stalks 1 ft. tall. 'Brandywine' has light green leaves with broad red centers; runs vigorously, has pale pink flowers. Leaves of 'Dunvegan' are deeply cut and heavily veined with maroon; 'Eco Running Tapestry' has fuzzy green leaves patterned in black; 'Filigree Lace' forms a dense mound of ruffled leaves and bears white flowers. 'Iron Butterfly' has large, deeply cut leaves. 'Slickrock' is a compact grower with 8-in. flower stalks.

T. wherryi (T. cordifolia collina). Zones 32, 34–41. Resembles *T. cordifolia*, but has no stolons and spreads more slowly. Flower clusters are somewhat more slender; flowers are sometimes pink tinted. Leaves of 'Eco Red Heart' have dark red centers and veins. 'Oakleaf' has deeply lobed leaves, pink flowers.

TIBOUCHINA urvilleana (T. semidecandra)

PRINCESS FLOWER, GLORYBUSH

Melastomataceae

EVERGREEN SHRUBS OR TREES

ALL ZONES; SEE BELOW

PARTIAL SHADE IN HOT AREAS

REGULAR WATER

Tibouchina urvilleana

Tropical shrubs of Brazilian origin, with open growth to 5 ft. high. Branch tips, buds, and new growth shaded with velvety hairs in orange and bronze red. Velvety, 3–6-in.-long leaves are often edged red; older leaves add spots of red, orange, or yellow, especially in winter. Clusters of brilliant royal purple, 3–5-in.-wide flowers. Prefers rich, well-drained, slightly acid soil. Has a tendency to legginess and should be pruned lightly

T

after every bloom cycle. Resprouts quickly after pruning. Pinch tips of young plants to encourage bushiness. Not hardy in the Northeast, but can be grown in container moved outdoors in summer, indoors over winter. Protect from strong winds when outdoors.

TIGER FLOWER. See TIGRIDIA pavonia

TIGRIDIA pavonia

TIGER FLOWER, MEXICAN SHELL FLOWER

Iridaceae

BULB

☀ ZONE 31; OR DIG AND STORE; OR GROW IN POTS

☼ ◑ PARTIAL SHADE IN HOTTEST AREAS

🔴 REGULAR WATER DURING GROWTH AND BLOOM

Trigridia pavonia

Leaves narrow, ribbed, swordlike, 1–1½ ft. long; flower stalks (1½–2½ ft. tall) have shorter leaves. Showy, 3–6-in.-wide flowers have three large segments forming triangle, joined with three smaller segments to form center cup. Larger segments usually white or vivid solid color—orange, pink, red, yellow. Smaller segments usually spotted or blotched with darker colors. (Immaculata strain features solid colors, unspotted.) Plants bloom in summer; each flower lasts one day, but others follow for several weeks.

Plant in spring, after weather warms up. Plant in rich, porous soil, setting bulbs 2–4 in. deep, 4–8 in. apart. During active growth, feed every 2 weeks with mild solution of liquid fertilizer; or apply slow-release fertilizer once, when bulbs break ground. Can be left in ground only in Zone 31; divide every 3 or 4 years. In the rest of the Northeast, dig and store bulbs after foliage turns yellow; break bulbs apart just before replanting in spring. Can also be grown in pots and protected in winter. Easily grown from seed and may bloom first year. Spider mites may require control; they cause yellowish or whitish streaks on foliage.

TILIA

LINDEN

Tiliaceae

DECIDUOUS TREES

☀ ZONES VARY BY SPECIES

☼ FULL SUN

🔴 REGULAR WATER

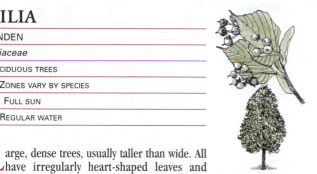

Tilia

Large, dense trees, usually taller than wide. All have irregularly heart-shaped leaves and small, fragrant, yellowish white flowers in drooping clusters, late spring–early summer. Flowers develop into nutlets, each with an attached papery bract. Stately good looks, moderate growth rate have made lindens favorite park and street trees in Europe.

Best growth in deep, rich, moist soil. Autumn color varies from negligible to good yellow. Young trees need staking and shaping; older trees require only corrective pruning. Aphids can cause disagreeable drip of honeydew and sooty mold.

T. americana. AMERICAN LINDEN, BASSWOOD. Zones 31, 32, 34–45. Native to eastern and central North America. To 60–80 ft. tall, 30–50 ft. wide. Straight-trunked tree with a narrow crown. Dull dark green leaves to 4–6 in. long, nearly as wide. 'Redmond' is a pyramidal form with glossy foliage.

The southern native *T. heterophylla,* white basswood, was once considered a separate species but has now been merged with *T. americana.* It is less cold-hardy (Zones 31, 32) than the species and has silvery leaf undersides.

T. cordata. LITTLE-LEAF LINDEN. Zones 32, 34–43. The most cold-hardy linden. Native to Europe. Dense pyramid to 60–70 ft. or taller. Leaves 1½–3 in. long and as wide (or wider), dark green above, silvery beneath. Excellent medium-size lawn or street tree. Given space to develop its symmetrical crown, it can be a fine patio shade tree (but expect bees in flowering season). Can be sheared into hedges. Very tolerant of city conditions. Japanese beetle may be a problem in some regions. Selected forms include 'Chancellor', 'Glenleven', 'Greenspire', 'June Bride' (especially heavy bloomer), and 'Olympic'.

T. euchlora. CRIMEAN LINDEN. Zones 32, 34–43. Hybrid between *T. cordata* and another species. To 40–60 ft. tall, a little more than half as wide. Slightly pendulous branches. Leaves 2–4 in. long, rich glossy green above, paler beneath. Casts more open shade than *T. cordata.*

T. heterophylla. See *T. americana*

T. platyphyllos. LARGE-LEAVED LINDEN. Zones 31, 32, 34–41. Native to Europe. Broadly columnar, to 100 ft. tall. Deep green, broadly oval to rounded leaves to 6 in. long, lighter green beneath, turn yellow in autumn.

T. tomentosa. SILVER LINDEN. Zones 32, 34–41. Native to Europe, western Asia. To 50–70 ft. tall, a little more than half as wide. Leaves are 3–5 in. long, light green above, silvery beneath; they turn and ripple in the slightest breeze. More tolerant of heat and drought than other species. 'Sterling' has silvery young leaves and an especially handsome winter silhouette.

TI PLANT. See CORDYLINE terminalis

TITHONIA rotundifolia (T. speciosa)

MEXICAN SUNFLOWER

Asteraceae (Compositae)

PERENNIAL GROWN AS ANNUAL

☀ ALL ZONES

☼ FULL SUN

🔴 REGULAR WATER

Tithonia rotundifolia

Husky, gaudy, rather coarse plant with spectacular flowers, velvety green leaves. Grows rapidly to 6 ft. tall. Blooms from summer to frost, bearing 3–4-in.-wide flower heads with orange-scarlet rays and tufted yellow centers. Use as a temporary screen. 'Torch', to 4 ft., makes a bushy summer hedge; 'Yellow Torch' has golden yellow flowers. 'Goldfinger' and 'Sundance' are 3-footers for smaller gardens. All have inflated hollow stems; cut with care for bouquets to avoid bending stalks. Sow seed in place in spring, in well-drained, not-too-rich soil. Tolerant of drought, humidity, intense heat. Attractive to butterflies, hummingbirds.

TOADFLAX. See LINARIA

TOAD LILY. See TRICYRTIS

TOLMIEA menziesii

PIGGY-BACK PLANT

Saxifragaceae

PERENNIAL

☀ ZONES 31, 32, 34, 39; OR INDOORS

☼ ◑ PARTIAL OR FULL SHADE

🔴 🔴 TOLERATES WET SOIL

Tolmiea menziesii

Native to Coast Ranges from northern California northward to Alaska. Chief asset is abundant production of attractive 5-in.-wide basal leaves—shallowly lobed and toothed, rather hairy. Leaves can produce

T

new plantlets at junction of leafstalk and blade. Tiny, rather inconspicuous reddish brown flowers top 1–2-ft.-high stems. Hardy outdoors in Zones 31, 32, 34, 39; in all zones can be grown as annual or moved outdoors in summer, indoors over winter. Good annual ground cover for shade. As house plant, needs filtered light, cool temperatures, frequent watering. Makes handsome hanging basket plant. Mealybugs, spider mites are occasional pests. Start new plants any time of year: take leaf with plantlet and insert in moist potting mix so base of plantlet contacts soil.

TOMATILLO. See PHYSALIS ixocarpa

TOMATO

Solanaceae

PERENNIAL GROWN AS ANNUAL

ALL ZONES

FULL SUN

REGULAR WATER

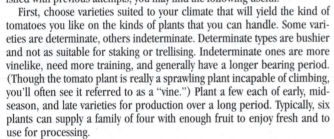

Tomato

Easy to grow and prolific, tomatoes are just about the most widely grown of all garden plants, edible or otherwise. Amateur and commercial growers have varying ideas about how best to grow tomatoes; if your own particular scheme works, continue to follow it. But if you're a novice or you're dissatisfied with previous attempts, you may find the following useful.

First, choose varieties suited to your climate that will yield the kind of tomatoes you like on the kinds of plants that you can handle. Some varieties are determinate, others indeterminate. Determinate types are bushier and not as suitable for staking or trellising. Indeterminate ones are more vinelike, need more training, and generally have a longer bearing period. (Though the tomato plant is really a sprawling plant incapable of climbing, you'll often see it referred to as a "vine.") Plant a few each of early, midseason, and late varieties for production over a long period. Typically, six plants can supply a family of four with enough fruit to enjoy fresh and to use for processing.

Set out tomato plants in spring after frost danger is past and the soil has warmed. To grow your own plants from seed, sow seeds 5 to 7 weeks before you intend to set out plants. Sow in pots of light soil mix or in a ready-made seed starter (sold at garden supply stores). Cover seeds with ½ in. of fine soil. Firm soil over seeds. Keep soil surface damp. Place seed container in cold frame or sunny window—a temperature of 65 to 70°F/18 to 21°C is ideal, although a range of 50°F/10°C at night to 85°F/29°C in the day will give acceptable results. When seedlings are 2 in. tall, transplant them into 3- or 4-in. pots. Keep in sunny area until seedlings reach transplant size. When buying tomato plants, look for compact ones with sturdy stems; avoid plants that are tall for their pots or that already have flowers or fruit.

Plant in a sunny site in well-drained soil. Tomato plants prefer neutral to slightly acid soil; plan to add lime to very acid soil or sulfur to alkaline soil the autumn before setting out plants. Space plants 1½–3 ft. apart (staked or trained) to 3–4 ft. apart (untrained). Make planting hole extra deep. Set seedlings in hole so lowest leaves are just above soil level. Additional roots will form on buried stem and provide a stronger root system.

Tomato management and harvest will be most satisfying if you train plants to keep them mostly off the ground (left alone, they will sprawl and some fruit will lie on soil, often causing rot, pest damage, and discoloration). Most common training method for indeterminate varieties is to drive a 6-ft.-long stake (at least 1 by 1 in.) into ground a foot from each plant. Use a soft tie to hold the plants to these stakes as they grow.

Slightly easier in the long run, but more work at planting time, is to grow each plant in wire cylinder made of concrete reinforcing screen (6-in. mesh). Screen is manufactured 7 ft. wide, which is just right for cylinder height; most indeterminate vines can grow to top of such a cylinder. Put stakes at opposite sides of cylinder and tie cylinder firmly to them. As vine grows, poke protruding branches back inside cylinder every week. Reach through screen to pick fruit.

Tomato plants need regular moisture at the root level. Since they are deep rooted, water heavily when you do water. If soil is fairly rich, you won't need to fertilize at all. But in ordinary soils, give light application of fertilizer every 2 weeks from the time first blossoms set until end of harvest; or give a single application of slow-release fertilizer.

Pests of tomato plants include Colorado potato beetles and whiteflies. If you see large green caterpillars with diagonal white stripes feeding upside down on leaf undersides, you have hornworms; handpick them or spray young caterpillars with *Bt* or *Btk*. Tomatoes are prone to a long list of diseases. Early blight (also called alternaria blight) shows up on leaves as dark spots with concentric rings inside, and on fruit as sunken lesions with same ring pattern. Sprays of liquid copper fungicide will control early blight and several other diseases; consult a local nursery or your Cooperative Extension Office for spray schedule. If plants are growing strongly, then suddenly wilt and die, the cause is probably verticillium wilt, fusarium wilt, or both. Pull and dispose of such plants. Diseases live over in soil, so plant in a different location every year and try varieties resistant to wilt or certain other diseases (see introduction to "Tomato varieties," below).

Some tomato problems—leaf roll, blossom-end rot, cracked fruit—are physiological; these can usually be corrected (or prevented) by maintaining uniform soil moisture. A mulch will help conserve moisture in very hot or dry summers.

If you have done everything right and your tomatoes have failed to set fruit in the spring, use hormone spray on blossoms. Tomatoes often fail to set fruit when night temperatures drop below 55°F/13°C. In chilly-night areas, select cold-tolerant varieties (especially small-fruited strains). Fruit-setting hormone often speeds up bearing in the earlier part of the season. Tomatoes can also fail to set fruit when temperatures rise above 100°F/38°C, but hormones are not effective under those conditions.

Harvest fruit when it is fully red and juicy; keep ripe fruit picked to extend season. When frost is predicted, harvest all fruit, both green and partly ripe. Store in a dry place out of direct sunlight at 60 to 70°F/16 to 21°C; check often for ripening.

TOMATO VARIETIES

Following are types of tomatoes you can buy as seeds or started plants. The number of varieties is enormous and increases every year. There are tomatoes for every taste and every region of the country. It's a good idea to consult a knowledgeable nursery, your Cooperative Extension Office, and other gardeners to find out which varieties will flourish in your local climate and soil.

If certain diseases or nematodes cause trouble locally, you may be able to grow varieties that resist one or more problems. Keys to resistance you may see on plant labels or in catalog descriptions include V (verticillium wilt), F (fusarium wilt), FF (Race 1 and Race 2 fusarium), T (tobacco mosaic virus), N (nematodes), A (alternaria leaf spot), and L (septoria leaf spot). For example, a variety labeled VFFNT resists verticillium wilt, two races of fusarium wilt, nematodes, and tobacco mosaic virus.

Main crop or standard tomatoes. 'Celebrity', 'Big Boy', and 'Better Boy' are widely grown. Old varieties 'Marglobe' and 'Rutgers' are still popular in many regions.

Early tomatoes. These varieties set fruit at lower night temperatures than other tomatoes do. 'Early Girl', 'Burpee's Early Pick', 'Pilgrim', 'First Lady', and 'Dona' are representative. Such tomatoes are often successful in cool-summer climates such as New England.

Cool-summer tomatoes. These will ripen fruit where accumulated summer heat is too low for most tomatoes. 'Oregon Spring', 'Swift', 'Manitoba', and 'Stokesalaska' will grow in far northern and mountain areas. Nurseries in cool-summer areas may offer locally adapted varieties.

Hybrid tomatoes. Some suppliers tout certain tomatoes as hybrids. They are usually referring to first-generation offspring of controlled parent lines, sometimes indicated by F_1 after the name. These varieties are more predictable and uniform in growth and fruit quality. Some are giants like 'Beefmaster' and 'Big Beef', but hybrid paste tomatoes are also available.

Novelty tomatoes. Among these are yellow and orange varieties such as 'Orange Queen', 'Mountain Gold', 'Husky Gold', and 'Lemon Boy'. 'Caro Rich' is very high in vitamin A and beta carotene. Those who have a special taste for novelties can grow tomatoes with deep reddish brown flesh ('Black Prince'), white tomatoes ('New Snowball', 'White Beauty'), tomatoes with

T

striped fruit ('Green Zebra', 'Tigerella'), and even one with fruit that is green when fully ripe ('Evergreen'). 'Long Keeper' will stay fresh in storage for 3 months, and 'Stuffer' and 'Yellow Stuffer' yield large, nearly hollow fruits that resemble bell peppers.

Large-fruited tomatoes. These grow to full size in areas where both days and nights are warm. Fruits can weigh a pound or even more. 'Beefsteak', 'Beefmaster', and 'Big Beef' are typical. 'Burpee's Supersteak Hybrid' can produce 2-lb. fruits, and 'Delicious' has produced a tomato weighing 7 lb. 12 oz.

Paste tomatoes. These bear prodigious quantities of small oval fruits with thick meat and small seed cavities. Sometimes called plum tomatoes, they are favorites for canning, sauces, and tomato paste. They are also good for drying. 'Roma', 'San Marzano', 'Viva Italia', and the yellow 'Italian Gold' are examples.

Small-fruited tomatoes. Fruits range in size from currants to large marbles. Shapes and colors are indicated by names: 'Red Cherry', 'Red Pear', 'Yellow Cherry', 'Yellow Pear'. Those with very small fruits include 'Sweet 100', 'Supersweet 100', 'Sweet Million', and 'Gardener's Delight'. Small-fruiting types that grow on small plants suitable for pots or hanging baskets include 'Tiny Tim', 'Small Fry', and 'Patio'.

Heirloom tomatoes. Varying in size, appearance, and plant habit, these represent old varieties that have been maintained by enthusiasts in different parts of the country. Most are grown for excellent flavor. 'Brandywine' is a currently popular heirloom variety.

TORCH-LILY. See KNIPHOFIA uvaria

TORENIA fournieri

WISHBONE FLOWER	
Scrophulariaceae	
ANNUAL	
PARTIAL SHADE	
REGULAR WATER	

Torenia fournieri

Compact, bushy, to 1 ft. high. Blooms summer to fall; light blue flowers with deeper blue markings and bright yellow throats look like miniature gloxinias. Stamens arranged in wishbone shape. White-flowered and pink-flowered forms are also available. Sow seed in pots; transplant to garden after frosts. Prefers cool, moist soil and some shade (will tolerate full sun in coolest climates). Use in borders, pots, window boxes. Plants in the ground can be lifted for winter bloom indoors in a sunroom.

TORREYA nucifera

JAPANESE TORREYA, KAYA	
Taxaceae	
CONIFEROUS EVERGREEN TREE	
ZONES 31, 32, 34–41	
FULL SUN OR DAPPLED SHADE	
REGULAR WATER	

Torreya nucifera

This handsome conical evergreen is the hardiest of the seven species in the genus and will survive in sheltered northeastern gardens. Can grow to 75 ft. in Japan where it is native, and in the Northeast can develop into a large bush or into a tree up to 50 ft. high. It has deep green, yewlike, lance-shaped leaves 1 in. long with sharply pointed tips. Female cones are olive green and oblong and grow to 1 in. long. Grow in fertile, moist, but well-drained soil where the atmosphere is humid and the tree will be sheltered from the wind.

TOUCH-ME-NOT. See IMPATIENS

TOVARA virginiana. See POLYGONUM virginianum

TRACHELIUM caeruleum

Campanulaceae (Lobeliaceae)	
PERENNIAL GROWN AS ANNUAL	
ALL ZONES	
FULL SUN OR PARTIAL SHADE	
REGULAR WATER	

Trachelium caeruleum

Grows to 2½ ft. tall and wide. Clumps of stems are clothed with narrow, sharply toothed dark green leaves and topped by broad, dome-shaped clusters of tiny bluish violet flowers (good for cutting) over a long summer bloom season. If sown early, it will bloom first year (and so can be treated as an annual). Tough, undemanding plant.

TRACHYCARPUS fortunei

WINDMILL PALM	
Arecaceae (Palmae)	
PALM	
ZONE 31; OR INDOORS	
FULL SUN OR PART SHADE	
REGULAR WATER	

Trachycarpus fortunei

Native to China. Moderate to fast growth to 30 ft. in warm-winter areas; may reach 10 ft. or more in pots indoors. Trunk is dark, usually thicker at top than at bottom. Fan-leafed palm with leaves 3 ft. across, carried on toothed, 1½-ft. stalks. May become untidy and ruffled in high winds. Except in Zone 31, grow in a pot moved outdoors in summer, indoors over winter. Sometimes sold as *Chamaerops excelsa*.

TRACHYMENE coerulea
(Didiscus coeruleus)

BLUE LACE FLOWER	
Apiaceae (Umbelliferae)	
ANNUAL	
ALL ZONES	
FULL SUN	
REGULAR WATER	

Trachymene coerulea

Upright stems to 2 ft. tall, clad with finely divided leaves. Numerous small, lavender blue flowers in 2–3-in.-wide, flat-topped clusters that are quite lacy in appearance. Good cut flower; its lacy appearance is a nice complement to bulbs and perennials. Grow in light, rich, well-drained soil. Sow seeds in place or in peat pots (taproot makes transplanting difficult) in early spring for summer bloom. Cover the seeds completely, as darkness enhances germination. Does not perform well in heat. Where summers are hot and winters mild, sow in fall for winter to spring bloom. Close spacing and deadheading encourages more bloom. Stake if necessary, in sites where it is not supported by neighboring plants with stronger stems.

PRACTICAL GARDENING DICTIONARY

PLEASE SEE PAGES 449–523

TRADESCANTIA

SPIDERWORT

Commelinaceae

PERENNIALS

ZONES VARY BY SPECIES

PARTIAL OR FULL SHADE, EXCEPT AS NOTED

REGULAR TO AMPLE WATER

Tradescantia

Most are long-trailing, indestructible plants, typically grown indoors in strong light (but not direct sun) or outdoors in shady sites. Indoor types are grown in hanging baskets and often called inch plant or wandering Jew. The two species described here are outdoor plants.

T. andersoniana. See *T. virginiana*

T. ohiensis. Zones 31, 32, 34–41. Similar to *T. virginiana*, but leaves are glaucous (covered with a grayish bloom). To 3 ft. tall, narrow leaves; flowers blue, rose purple, or white.

T. pallida 'Purpurea'. See *Setcreasea pallida* 'Purple Heart'

T. virginiana. Zones 31, 32, 34–43. Border perennial for sun or shade. Grows in 1½–3-ft.-tall clumps, with long, deep green, erect or arching grasslike foliage. Three-petaled flowers open for only a day, but buds come in large clusters and plants are seldom out of bloom during late spring, summer. Named garden varieties available in white, shades of blue, lavender, purple, gradations of pink from pale pink to near red. Ample water preferred but will tolerate drier soils. If plants look unsightly by midseason, shear to the ground. Plants will recover rapidly and probably bloom again. Divide clumps when crowded. Often sold as *T. andersoniana*.

TRAILING AFRICAN DAISY. See OSTEOSPERMUM fruticosum

TRANSVAAL DAISY. See GERBERA jamesonii

TREE ARALIA. See KALOPANAX septemlobus

TREE MALLOW. See LAVATERA

TREE-OF-HEAVEN. See AILANTHUS altissima

TRICYRTIS

TOAD LILY

Liliaceae

PERENNIALS

ZONES VARY BY SPECIES

PARTIAL SHADE

AMPLE WATER

Tricyrtis

Woodland plants that resemble false Solomon's seal (*Smilacina*) in foliage. Though not especially showy, the late summer to fall flowers are interesting—complex, heavily spotted, somewhat orchidlike. Each 1-in. flower has three petals and three sepals with a column of decorative stamens and styles rising from the center. Flowers appear at leaf bases and in terminal clusters. Need woodsy soil.

T. formosana. Zones 31, 32, 34, 39. May be the same as a species offered as *T. stolonifera*. To 2½ ft. tall; spreads by stoloniferous roots but is not invasive. Stems are more upright than those of *T. hirta*, and flowers are mostly in terminal clusters. Green leaves mottled with deeper green. Clusters of brown or maroon buds open to flowers in white to pale lilac densely specked with purple. Begins blooming a little earlier than *T. hirta*. Blossoms of 'Amethystina' are typically lavender blue spotted in dark red, with a white throat. 'Gates of Heaven' has golden leaves and purple flowers; 'Moonlight' has gold-variegated leaves and white flowers; 'Samurai' has white-edged leaves and purple-speckled white flowers.

T. hirta. Zones 32, 34–41. To 3 ft. tall, with arching stems. Flowers, appearing in leaf joints all along the stems, are white to pale lilac, densely peppered with purple. 'Alba' has white flowers flushed with green; 'Albomarginata' has white-edged leaves and purple flowers; 'White Towers' has arching stems and upward-facing white flowers in the leaf axils. 'Miyazaki' and 'Miyazaki Gold' are improved forms that bloom more profusely; the latter has yellow-edged leaves; 'Sinonome' has sizable flat, fragrant white flowers splashed with reddish purple.

T. latifolia (T. bakeri). Zones 31, 32, 34–41. To 2½ ft. tall and 3 ft. wide. Upright to arching stems; broadly oval to oblong leaves to 6 in. long, glossy medium green with darker green spots when young. Branched clusters of greenish yellow flowers, yellow inside, with brown spots, in early to midsummer.

T. macropoda. Zones 31, 32, 34–41. To 27 in. tall. Upright stems, oblong to oval leaves to 3 in. long. Branched clusters of purple-white flowers with purple spots.

T. 'Tojen'. Zones 31, 32, 34–41. To 2 ft. tall. Very large, thick leaves. Clusters of lavender pink flowers with pale pink throats in mid- to late summer.

TRIFOLIUM repens

WHITE CLOVER, WHITE DUTCH CLOVER

Fabaceae (Leguminosae)

PERENNIAL

ZONES 31, 32, 34–45

FULL SUN OR PARTIAL SHADE

REGULAR WATER

Trifolium repens

There are scores of clover species, most of them field crops. All have ability to take nitrogen from air and put it into the soil through action of root bacteria. White clover is sometimes used to mix with lawn grass seed. Can stain clothing of children who play on it; white flower heads attract bees. Prostrate stems root freely and send up lush cover of leaves with three (rarely a lucky four) ¾-in. leaflets. *T. r. minus* is one of the shamrocks.

TRILLIUM

WAKE ROBIN

Liliaceae

PERENNIALS

ZONES 31, 32, 34–43

PARTIAL OR FULL SHADE

REGULAR WATER

Trillium

Bloom in early spring; need some winter chill. Each stem is topped with a whorl of three leaves; from center of these rises a single flower with three maroon or white petals. Plant the thick, deep-growing, fleshy rhizomes in shady, woodsy site. Left undisturbed, they will gradually increase. Plants die to the ground in mid- to late summer. In addition to species listed below, many others are offered by native plant specialists.

T. catesbaei (T. stylosum). Resembles *T. grandiflorum* but has pink flowers.

T. cernuum. NODDING TRILLIUM. To 2 ft. high. Pointed, diamond-shaped, medium green leaves. Nodding flowers are usually light pink, but are sometimes reddish brown or white, with backcurved petals and purple stamens.

T. erectum. PURPLE TRILLIUM. To 2 ft. high, with 7-in. midgreen leaves and 2-in., erect, brownish purple flowers. Sometimes known by the name "stinking Benjamin" due to the odd odor of its flowers. A white form also exists.

T

T. grandiflorum. Stout stems 8–18 in. high. Leaves 2½–6 in. long. Flowers are nodding, to 3 in. across, white aging to rose. 'Flore Pleno' has double flowers.

T. luteum. YELLOW TRILLIUM. To 16 in. tall. Medium green leaves are oval and pointed, to 6 in. long, mottled with lighter green. Flowers are stemless, yellow to greenish, and faintly lemon-scented, with narrow upright petals.

T. recurvatum. BLOODY BUTCHER. To 15 in. high. Leaves spotted in reddish purple; purple-brown flowers.

T. sessile. To 1 ft. high, with purple-spotted leaves and dark purplish red flowers.

T. undulatum. PAINTED TRILLIUM, PAINTED WOOD LILY . To 20 in. high, with upright or somewhat nodding, 1½-in. white flowers marked reddish purple within. This plant is considered difficult; needs cool conditions and acid soil.

T. vaseyi. SWEET TRILLIUM. To 2 ft. high. Broad leaves to 8 in. long. Fragrant, dark magenta flowers to 6 in. wide, on 1½-ft. stems appear in early summer.

TRITELEIA

Amaryllidaceae

CORMS

ZONES 31, 32

FULL SUN

REGULAR WATER DURING GROWTH AND BLOOM

Triteleia

Plants under this name were formerly known as *Brodiaea*. All have narrow, grassy leaves that usually die back before flowers bloom. Flowers are funnel-shaped with pointed petals, carried in clusters at tips of bare stems. Blooms from spring to early summer.

T. laxa (B. laxa). GRASS NUT, ITHURIEL'S SPEAR. Flower stalk to 2½ ft.; purple-blue, 1½-in. trumpets.

T. 'Queen Fabiola'. Flower stalk to 2½ ft. tall; deep violet flowers. Good cut flower.

T. tubergenii. Flower stalk to 2½ ft. tall; light blue flowers.

TRITOMA uvaria. See KNIPHOFIA uvaria

TRITONIA (Montbretia)

Iridaceae

CORMS

ALL ZONES; DIG AND STORE; OR GROW IN POTS

FULL SUN

REGULAR WATER DURING GROWTH AND BLOOM

Tritonia

Native to South Africa. Related to freesia, ixia, and sparaxis. Clumps of narrow, sword-shaped leaves give rise to branched stems carrying short, spikelike clusters of brilliant flowers in late spring. Long-lasting cut flowers.

Set corms 2–3 in. deep, 3 in. apart, in well-drained soil. Plant in early spring. After bloom, foliage dies back. Dig corms in fall and store over winter, or grow in pots. Good in rock gardens, borders.

T. crocata. Often called flame freesia. Stems to 1–1½ ft., bearing orange-red, funnel-shaped, 2-in. flowers. *T. c. miniata* has bright red blooms; 'Princess Beatrix' has deep orange flowers. Others come in white and shades of pink, salmon, yellow, and apricot.

T. hyalina. Bright orange flowers with narrower segments than those of *T. crocata*, with transparent area near base. A little smaller than *T. crocata*.

TROCHODENDRON
aralioides

WHEEL TREE

Trochodendraceae

EVERGREEN TREE

ZONES 32, 34, 39

FULL SUN TO PARTIAL SHADE

MORE THAN REGULAR WATER

Trochodendron aralioides

The wheel tree may grow 60 ft. tall in its native Japan, Korea, and Taiwan, but in the Northeast it's a broadleaf evergreen shrub growing 10–20 ft. high and 5–10 ft. wide. With its rich, glossy, midgreen foliage and bright green flowers, wheel tree makes an effective contrast with darker, more common broadleaf evergreens such as rhododendron and leucothoe. The wheel tree's leaves are up to 6 in. long and 3 in. wide, and its stems are scented when crushed or bruised. Flowers lack petals, the conspicuous parts being slender-stalked stamens arranged around the edges of small green disks. These blossoms appear in 3-in.-long, terminal groups. Little brown fruits follow the flowers. An unusual specimen plant that looks good with other broadleaf evergreens and deciduous trees. It thrives in a sheltered spot away from wind and harsh winter sun and grows best in rich, moist, well-drained loam.

TROLLIUS

GLOBEFLOWER

Ranunculaceae

PERENNIALS

ZONES 32, 34–43

FULL SUN OR PARTIAL SHADE

AMPLE WATER

Trollius

Clumps of finely cut, shiny dark green leaves put up 2–3-ft.-tall stems terminating in yellow to orange, roundly cupped to globe-shaped flowers. Some types begin blooming in spring, others in summer; remove faded flowers to prolong bloom. Excellent cut flowers.

Intolerant of drought, heat. Continually damp ground near a pond or stream is ideal planting site. If growing in regular garden bed, liberally amend soil with organic matter and keep well watered. Divide clumps when they thin out in the middle.

T. cultorum. Name given to a group of hybrids between T. *europaeus* and two Asiatic species. Grow 2–3 ft. tall and resemble T. *europaeus* in most details. Bloom comes at some time from spring into summer, depending on hybrid. Choices include 'Alabaster' with pale yellow flowers' 2-ft. 'Earliest of All', with pale orange-yellow blooms; 2-ft. 'Golden Queen', deep orange; and 2½-ft. 'Lemon Queen', soft yellow.

T. europaeus. To 1½–2 ft. tall. Globular, lemon yellow flowers, 1–2 in. across, in spring. Some varieties have orange blooms. Somewhat more tolerant of dry soil than other species. 'Superbus' has very large yellow flowers, up to 4 in. wide.

T. ledebouri. Plant sold by nurseries under this name grows 3 ft. tall, bears 2-in., golden orange, cup-shaped flowers in summer. 'Golden Queen' reaches 4 ft., has 4-in. blossoms.

T. yunnanensis. Grows 2-2½-ft. tall. Cup-shaped bright yellow flowers in late spring and early summer, to 2½ in. across, but often much smaller. From Southwest China.

FOR INFORMATION ON YOUR CLIMATE ZONE

PLEASE SEE PAGES 30–46

T

TROPAEOLUM

NASTURTIUM

Tropaeolaceae

ANNUALS

✓ ALL ZONES

☼ ◐ EXPOSURE NEEDS VARY BY SPECIES

🔴 REGULAR WATER

Tropaeolum

Distinctive appearance, rapid growth, and easy culture are three of nasturtiums' many strong points. Less conspicuous, but odd and pretty, is *T. peregrinum,* the canary bird flower.

T. majus. GARDEN NASTURTIUM. Two main kinds. Climbing types trail over the ground or climb to 6 ft. by coiling leaf stalks; dwarf kinds are compact, to 15 in. tall. Both have round, shield-shaped, bright green leaves on long stalks. Broad, long-spurred flowers, to 2½ in. across, have a refreshing fragrance, come in colors ranging through maroon, red brown, orange, yellow, and red to creamy white. Good cut flowers. Young leaves, flowers, and unripe seedpods have peppery flavor like watercress and may be used in salads.

Dwarf forms are most widely sold. You can get seeds of mixed colors in several strains, or a few separate colors, including cherry rose, mahogany, and gold. Both single- and double-flowered forms are available. All types are easy to grow in most well-drained soils; they do best in sandy soil. Sow in early spring; plants grow and bloom quickly, and will often reseed unless stopped by heat or humidity. Full sun or light shade. Somewhat drought tolerant. Aphids can be a problem.

T. peregrinum. CANARY CREEPER, CANARY BIRD FLOWER. Climbs to 10–15 ft. Leaves are deeply five lobed. Flowers ¾–1 in. across, canary yellow, frilled and fringed, with green, curved spur. Sow in spring for bloom from summer until frost. Provide support, such as stakes or netting; or allow plant to climb into a shrub. Needs light shade.

TRUMPET CREEPER, TRUMPET VINE. See CAMPSIS

NASTURTIUMS FOR DINNER

Adventurous gardeners can enjoy nasturtiums in the kitchen as well as in the garden. The flowers, leaves, and seed pods are all edible, with a tangy, peppery flavor similar to that of watercress. You may taste an additional light note of perfume in the flowers, which are mildly fragrant.

Chop young leaves and flowers into salads, or blend them into savory herb butters. Immature seed pods can be pickled in brine and used as a substitute for capers.

TSUGA

HEMLOCK

Pinaceae

EVERGREEN TREES AND SHRUBS

✓ ZONES VARY BY SPECIES

☼ ◐ FULL SUN OR PARTIAL SHADE

🔴 REGULAR WATER

Tsuga

These are mostly big trees with unusually graceful appearance. Branches horizontal to drooping. Needlelike leaves are banded with white beneath, flattened and narrowed at the base to form distinct, short stalks.

Small, oval, medium brown cones hang down from branches. Bark is deeply furrowed, cinnamon colored to brown.

All hemlocks need some winter chill; all are shallow rooted. Best in acid soil and high summer humidity, with protection from hot sun and wind. Take well to heavy pruning; make excellent clipped hedges, screens. Easily damaged by salt and drought. Subject to various pests and diseases, but damage is not always serious if plants are well grown. Recently, a woolly adelgid (an aphid) has caused the decline and even death of many hemlocks in the Northeast.

T. canadensis. CANADA HEMLOCK. Zones 32, 34–43. Native from Nova Scotia to Minnesota, southward along mountain ranges to Alabama and Georgia. Dense, pyramidal tree to 40–70 ft. or taller, half as wide. Tends to grow two or more trunks. Outer branchlets droop gracefully. Dark green needles, about ½ in. long, are mostly arranged in opposite rows on branchlets. Fine lawn tree or background planting; outstanding clipped hedge. 'Pendula', Sargent weeping hemlock, grows slowly to 10–20 ft. tall and twice as wide, with pendulous branches; with careful pruning, can easily be kept to handsome, 2–3-ft., cascading mound suitable for a large rock garden. Numerous other dwarf, weeping, and variegated selections are sold.

T. caroliniana. CAROLINA HEMLOCK. Zones 32, 34–41. Native to mountains in the southeast U.S. Resembles *T. canadensis* but is somewhat slower growing, a little stiffer in habit, and darker green in color. Longer needles are arranged all around the twigs instead of in opposite rows. More tolerant of polluted air and city conditions than *T. canadensis,* but not as well adapted to lowlands of eastern seaboard.

T. chinensis. CHINESE HEMLOCK. Zones 31, 32, 34–41. Native to China. Broadly cone-shaped to domed tree to 140 ft. tall. Glossy dark green leaves. Peeling, fissured, pinkish beige bark. New shoots are yellow green, turning yellowish gray.

T. diversifolia. NORTHERN JAPANESE HEMLOCK. Zones 32, 34, 39. Native to Japan. Dense, broadly conical tree with a rounded top, to 90 ft. tall, with notched needles. Does well in the eastern U.S., and has a neat, graceful appearance.

T. sieboldii. SOUTHERN JAPANESE HEMLOCK. Zones 32, 34, 39. Native to Japan. Dense and pyramidal, to 90 ft. tall. Glossy dark green foliage. Handsome ornamental tree.

TUBEROSE. See POLIANTHES tuberosa

TULBAGHIA

Amaryllidaceae

PERENNIALS

✓ ZONES 31, 32

☼ FULL SUN

🔴 REGULAR WATER

Tulbaghia

Many narrow leaves grow from central point to make broad clumps, from which rise long stems bearing clusters of star-shaped flowers. Suffer frost damage at 20 to 25°F/−7 to −4°C, but recover quickly.

T. fragrans (T. simmleri). Gray-green, 1-in.-wide leaves to 12–14 in. long or longer. Fragrant, lavender pink flowers, 20–30 on 1½–2-ft. stalk. Blooms midwinter–spring. Good cut flower.

T. violacea. SOCIETY GARLIC. Bluish green, narrow leaves to 1 ft. long. Rosy lavender flowers, 8–20 in cluster on 1–2-ft. stem. Some bloom most of year, with peak in spring and summer. Leaves, flower stems have onion or garlic odor if cut or crushed. Unsatisfactory cut flower for this reason (but can be used as seasoning). 'Variegata' has creamy stripe down the center of each leaf. 'Silver Lace' has white-margined leaves. 'Tricolor' is another variety with white-edged leaves; its foliage is suffused with pink in spring.

T

TULIPA

TULIP

Liliaceae

BULBS

ZONES 31, 32, 34–45

FULL SUN

REGULAR WATER DURING GROWTH AND BLOOM

Tulipa

Tulips vary considerably in color, form, height, and general character. Some look stately and formal, others dainty and whimsical; a few are bizarre. Bloom comes at some time from March to May, depending on type.

Use larger tulips in colonies or masses with low, spring-blooming perennials such as aubrieta, basket-of-gold, candytuft, rockcress, or sweet William phlox, or with annuals such as forget-me-not, sweet alyssum, pansy, or viola. Plant smaller, lower-growing species in rock gardens, near paths, in raised beds, or in patio or terrace insets for close-up viewing. Tulips are superb container plants; the more unusual kinds, such as Double Early, Rembrandt, and Parrot strains, seem more appropriate for containers than for garden beds.

Nearly all hybrid tulips and most species (wild) tulips need an extended period of winter chill for best performance. Best results are obtained the first spring after the bulbs are purchased. In successive years, the size, number, and height of the blooms decline. Tulip bulbs form offsets that need several years to get to blooming size, but as the offsets mature, they draw energy from the mother bulb. The resulting decline in flowering causes many gardeners to replace their bulbs every year, or surely by the third year. A few species and some cultivars labeled as "perennializers" may persist for five or more years, but this cannot be guaranteed. You can encourage repeat bloom by planting the bulbs deeply (three times deeper than the height) in a place where they will bake during summer dormancy, by fertilizing with a complete fertilizer high in nitrogen before bloom, by preventing seed formation, and by allowing foliage to yellow and wither before removing it after bloom. In areas with warm, wet summer soil, bulbs are prone to rot and shouldn't be expected to bloom for more than a year or two.

Bulbs can be planted under deciduous trees that leaf out after tulip flowers fade. Light shade helps prolong bloom of late-flowering kinds. Good light should come from overhead; otherwise, stems will lean toward light source. Rich, sandy soil is ideal, although tulips will grow in any good soil with fast drainage. They do not like soil where tulips were recently growing—choose an entirely different site, or put in fresh soil to the requisite planting depth. Set bulbs three times as deep as they are wide (a little shallower in heavy soils), from 4 to 8 in. apart depending on ultimate size of plant. Plant bulbs as early as mid-September in coldest areas, around mid-October to early November in Zones 31, 32.

To protect tulips from burrowing animals, plant in baskets of ¼-in. wire mesh. Thwart ground squirrels and other animals that like to dig up bulbs by securing chicken wire over new plantings.

Tulips have been classified into many divisions and reclassified over time. The following divisions are accepted internationally and are based upon the characteristics of the flowers.

Single Early tulips. Large single flowers of red, yellow, or white grow on 10–16-in. stems. Much used for growing or forcing indoors in pots. Also grown outdoors. Varieties include 'Apricot Beauty', soft salmon pink; 'Diana', white; 'Flair', buttercup yellow flamed vermilion; 'Keizerskroon', scarlet edged yellow; 'Purple Prince', lilac purple with red-purple interior.

Double Early tulips. Double peonylike flowers to 4 in. across bloom on 6–12-in. stems. Same colors, same bloom season as Single Early tulips. In rainy areas, mulch around plants or surround with ground cover to keep mud from splashing short-stemmed flowers. Effective massed in borders for early bloom. 'Abba', tomato red; 'Monte Carlo', yellow; 'Peach Blossom', rosy pink; 'Schoonord', white.

Triumph tulips. Single flowers on medium-tall (20-in.), sturdy stems, valuable in providing continuity of bloom. 'Arabian Mystery', deep purple with white edge; 'Attila', light purple violet; 'Bellona', golden yellow; 'Coleur Cardinal', scarlet with purple flush; 'Don Quichotte', deep rose with purple sheen; 'Dreaming Maid', lavender pink shading to near white at edges; 'New Design', pink flushed pale yellow, with fuchsia pink edges.

Darwin hybrids. Spectacular group bred from old Darwin tulips and huge, brilliant species *T. fosteriana*. Have enormous, brightly colored flowers on 24–28-in. stems. Most are in scarlet-orange to red range; some have contrasting eyes or penciling; some measure 7 in. across. Pink, yellow, and white varieties exist. 'Apeldoorn', cherry red; 'Elizabeth Arden', deep salmon pink flushed purple; 'Golden Apeldoorn', golden yellow; 'Ivory Floradale', ivory white; 'Pink Impression', rosy pink.

Single Late tulips. Single flowers on tall (18–30-in.) stems, often have contrasting edges. Late blooming. This group includes the old Darwin and Cottage tulips. Make good cut flowers. 'Kingsblood', deep cherry red with scarlet tips; 'Queen of Bartigons', salmon pink; 'Queen of Night', dark maroon black; 'Temple of Beauty', salmon rose, lily-shaped flowers; 'Union Jack', white flamed red.

Lily-flowered tulips. Once included in Cottage division; now separate group. Flowers are long and narrow, with long, pointed segments. Graceful, slender stemmed, fine in garden (where they blend well with other flowers) or for cutting. Stems 20–26 in. tall. Late blooming. Full range of tulip colors. 'Ballade', reddish magenta edged cream; 'China Pink', soft pink with white base; 'Red Shine', deep red; 'West Point', bright primrose yellow; 'White Triumphator', white.

Fringed tulips. Single flowers, red, pink, yellow, violet, or white, with fringed edges, often in a different color. Late blooming. Use in garden or for cut flowers. 'Burgundy Lace', wine red with lighter fringe; 'Fancy Frills', ivory blending to rose pink, with light pink fringe; 'Fringed Elegance', yellow with thin red edge and pale yellow fringe.

Viridiflora tulips. Flowers edged or blended green with other colors—white, yellow, rose, red, or purple—on 10–20-in. stems. Late blooming. 'Esperanto', pinkish red with green stripes that fade to reddish brown; 'Groenland', soft rose with soft green stripes; 'Spring Green' ivory with feathery, soft green stripes.

Rembrandt tulips. Because the streaks and variegations on these tulip flowers are caused by a transmittable virus, they can no longer be imported and should not be planted. Tulips now sold as Rembrandts are multicolor tulips of genetic, not viral, origin and come from other tulip classes. Often sold in mixtures. Varieties include 'Beauty of Volendam' (Triumph), white with deep burgundy rose feathering; 'Sorbet' (Single Late), white with raspberry pink flames.

Parrot tulips. Late-flowering tulips with large, long, deeply fringed and ruffled blooms striped and feathered in various colors. Many have descriptive names, e.g., 'Blue Parrot', 'Red Parrot'. Good in containers, unusual cut flowers. 'Apricot Parrot', soft apricot with tinges of peach, cream, yellow, and green; 'Estella Rijnveld', red flamed white; 'Flaming Parrot', bright yellow flamed red.

Double Late tulips (often called peony-flowered). Large, heavy blooms like peonies. They range from 18 to 22 in. tall; flowers may be damaged by rain or wind in exposed locations. 'Angelique', pale rose pink with light and dark pink accents, shading to cream on the edges; 'Maywonder', deep rose; 'Miranda', red with yellow base; 'Mount Tacoma', white.

Kaufmanniana tulips. Varieties and hybrids of *T. kaufmanniana*, 5–10 in. tall, very early blooming, in white, pink, orange, and red, often with markings, some with leaves patterned brown. Flowers open wide like water lilies.

T. kaufmanniana. WATERLILY TULIP. Medium-large creamy yellow flowers marked red on outside and yellow at center. Stems 6 in. tall. Very early bloom. Permanent in gardens.

Many choice named varieties, including 'Ancilla', white (soft pink outside) with yellow base outlined in red; 'Johann Strauss', ivory (currant red edged yellow outside) with yellow base; 'Stresa', golden yellow (currant red edged yellow outside) with deep red markings at base.

Tulipa kaufmanniana

T

Fosteriana tulips. Hybrids and varieties of *T. fosteriana.* Single, bowl-shaped flowers. Midseason blooming.

T. fosteriana. To 10 in. high. Large single flowers to 8 in. across, bright red with yellow-edged purple-black base. Light gray-green leaves to 1 ft. long. 'Juan', deep orange with yellow base; 'Princeps', bright scarlet; 'Red Emperor' ('Mme. Lefeber'), fiery red, 16 in. high; 'White Emperor', white.

Greigii tulips. Varieties and hybrids of *T. greigii* resemble those of *T. kaufmanniana,* with leaves usually heavily spotted and streaked with brown, to 1 ft. high. Flower early or midseason. Grow in rock garden or bed or border.

T. greigii. Scarlet flowers 6 in. across, on 10-in. stems. Foliage mottled or striped with brown. Early blooming.

'Czar Peter', white with wine rose feathering, reddish inside; 'Oratorio', rose pink with apricot pink interior and black base; 'Plaisir', carmine red with yellow edges and black-and-yellow base, vermilion inside.

Miscellaneous tulips. This group includes species and hybrids not included in other divisions. Most species tulips—wild tulips—are low growing and early blooming, with shorter, narrower leaves than garden hybrids, but there are exceptions. Generally best in rock gardens or wild gardens where plantings can remain undisturbed for many years.

Outstanding species, all from the Miscellaneous group, include:

T. acuminata. Flowers have long, twisted, spidery segments of red and yellow on 1½-ft. stems. Late blooming.

T. bakeri. See *T. saxatilis.*

T. batalinii. Single, soft yellow flowers on 6–10-in. stems. Very narrow leaves. Midseason.

T. clusiana. LADY or CANDY TULIP. Slender, medium-size flowers on 9-in. stems. Rosy red on outside, white inside. Grows well in mild-winter areas. Give sheltered position in colder areas. Midseason.

T. c. chrysantha (*T. stellata chrysantha*). To 6 in. tall. Outer segments rose carmine, shading to buff at base; inner segments are bright yellow. Midseason.

T. eichleri. Big scarlet flowers with black bases margined buff on 1-ft. stems. Early.

T. linifolia. Scarlet, black-based, yellow-centered flowers on 6-in. stems in midseason. Handsome with *T. batalinii.*

T. praestans. Cup-shaped, orange-scarlet flowers, two to four to 10–12-in. stem, in midseason. Variety 'Fusilier' is shorter, has four to six flowers to a stem.

T. saxatilis (*T. bakeri*). Fragrant, yellow-based pale lilac flowers open nearly flat, one to three to each 1-ft. stem. Early bloom. 'Lilac Wonder', rosy purple with yellow base.

T. stellata chrysantha. See *T. clusiana chrysantha*

T. sylvestris. Yellow, 2-in. flowers, one or two on 1-ft. stem. Late. Good in warm-winter areas.

T. tarda (*T. dasystemon*). Each 3-in. stem has three to six upward-facing, star-shaped flowers with golden centers and white-tipped segments. Early.

T. turkestanica. Vigorous tulip with up to eight flowers on each slender, 1-ft. stem. Flowers slender in bud, star shaped when open, gray green on outside, off-white with yellow base inside. Very early bloom.

T. whittallii. Orange inner petals with dark basal blotch; outside flushed green and buff.

> ### USING TULIPS AS CUT FLOWERS
>
> Tulips make lovely additions to cut flower bouquets and arrangements, if given a bit of special handling. Long-stemmed varieties are best for cutting. Cut when the buds are beginning to show color. Cut off the white base of the stem, and wrap the stems and flowers in florists's tissue or newspaper before conditioning, to help keep the stems straight. Stand in cool water nearly up to the base of the flowers for several hours or overnight before arranging the flowers.

TULIP TREE. See LIRIODENDRON tulipifera, MAGNOLIA soulangiana

TUPELO. See NYSSA sylvatica

Turnip

TURNIP and RUTABAGA

Brassicaceae (Cruciferae)

BIENNIALS GROWN AS ANNUALS

ALL ZONES

FULL SUN

REGULAR WATER

Both are cool-season crops. Although turnips are best known for roots, foliage is also a useful green vegetable. Turnip roots come in various colors (white, white topped with purple, creamy yellow) and shapes (globe, flattened globe); some varieties are grown for leaves only. Rutabaga is a tasty turnip relative with large yellowish roots; its leaves are palatable only when very young, since they turn coarse as they mature. Turnip roots are quick growing and should be harvested and used as soon as big enough to eat; rutabaga is a late-maturing crop that stores well in the ground. Flavor of rutabaga improves with light frost.

Grow both in rich, loose, well-drained soil. Plant in early spring for early summer harvest, or in summer for fall harvest. Sow seeds ½ in. deep, 1 in. apart. Thin turnips to 2–6 in. apart for roots, 1–4 in. apart for greens. Thin rutabaga to 5–8 in. apart; it needs ample space for roots to reach full weight of 3–5 lb.

Roots of both turnip and rutabaga are milder flavored if soil is kept moist, become more pungent under drier conditions. Turnip roots are ready to harvest about 75 days after sowing, rutabaga in 90 to 120 days. Cabbage root maggot is a pest of turnip (it is less likely to infest rutabaga); see Cabbage for controls.

TURTLEHEAD. See CHELONE

TWEEDIA caerulea (Oxypetalum caeruleum)

Asclepiadaceae

TWINING PERENNIAL

ALL ZONES AS ANNUAL

FULL SUN

REGULAR WATER

Tweedia caerulea

Twining perennial to 3 ft., grown as warm-season annual in the Northeast, blooming from late summer to fall from seed sown in early spring. Leaves are 4 in. long. Star-shaped, 1-in. flowers, pale blue aging to lilac, grow along the stems and at branch ends. Upward-pointing milkweed pods follow the blossoms and provide an extended period of interest. Tip-pinch young plants to force branching. Good cut flower. Takes any well-drained soil.

TWINBERRY. See MITCHELLA repens

TWINFLOWER. See LINNAEA borealis

TWINSPUR. See DIASCIA barberae

TWISTED STALK. See STREPTOPUS

TYPHA

CATTAIL

Typhaceae

PERENNIALS

ZONES 31, 32, 34–45

FULL SUN TO SHADE

AMPLE WATER

Typha

Native to North America, Europe, Africa, and Asia, these rhizomatous plants grow robustly, and often invasively, at the edges of ponds, streams, and pools. Long, slender leaves emerge from the base of the plant; tiny flowers are held in sausage-shaped spikes at the top of tall stalks. Thrives in almost any moist soil. Cut flowers are prized for fresh and dried arrangements. Plants attract wildlife, especially water birds.

T. angustifolia. NARROW-LEAVED CATTAIL. To 5 ft. tall. Highly invasive, with long, narrow leaves and brown flower spikes produced in midsummer. Will quickly form a dense screen or backdrop. To avoid undue spread, plant in large containers, replanting every several years.

T. minima. DWARF CATTAIL. Growing only to 1–2½ ft. high and 1–1½ ft. across, this elegant dwarf has narrow blue-green leaves and dark brown, plump flower spikes produced in mid- to late summer. Perfect for small aquatic containers.

Ulmaceae. The elm family contains trees and shrubs, usually deciduous, with inconspicuous flowers and fruit that may be nutlike, single-seeded and fleshy, or winged. Elm *(Ulmus)*, hackberry *(Celtis)*, and *Zelkova* are representative.

ULMUS

ELM

Ulmaceae

DECIDUOUS OR SEMIEVERGREEN TREES

ZONES VARY BY SPECIES

FULL SUN

REGULAR WATER

Ulmus

Once much-prized shade trees, elms have fallen on hard times. Dutch elm disease (spread by a bark beetle) has killed millions of American elms throughout North America and can attack most other elm species. Many of the larger elms are attractive fare for various beetles, leafhoppers, aphids, and scale, making them either time consuming to care for or messy (or both). Beyond their pest problems, elms have other drawbacks. Their root systems are aggressive and near the surface, making it difficult to grow any other plants beneath. Many types produce suckers. Branch crotches are often narrow, splitting easily in storms. Despite their flaws, elms are widely planted, valued for their fast growth, moderate shade, and environmental toughness. Researchers continue to devote much effort to finding disease-resistant varieties. All elms are fairly soil tolerant, and all have handsome oval leaves. Poor yellow fall color, except as noted.

U. alata. WINGED ELM. Deciduous. Zones 31, 32, 34, 39. Native to southeastern U.S. To 20–40 ft. tall, not quite as wide. Open, airy canopy. Leaves 1–2½ in. long, finely toothed, dark green turning pale yellow in fall. Common name derives from corky outgrowths ("wings") on twigs and young branches. Degree of winging varies among seedlings—the wings really stand out on some, while on others they're almost nonexistent. Your best bet is to get a cutting-grown tree from a parent with good bark characteristics. Clusters of small reddish seeds in spring. 'Lace Parasol' is a weeping form (to 8 ft. tall, 12 ft. wide after 45 years) now being introduced in the nursery trade.

U. americana. AMERICAN ELM. Deciduous. Zones 31, 32, 34–45. Native to eastern North America. This majestic, arching tree once graced lawns and streets throughout its range, but it has been decimated by Dutch elm disease. Fast growth to 100 ft. or taller with nearly equal—sometimes greater—spread. Main branches upright, outer ones pendulous. Rough-surfaced, 3–6-in.-long, toothed dark green leaves; great variation in shade of yellow fall color. Leafs out very late where winters are mild. Papery, pale green seeds in spring are messy.

Long search for disease-resistant varieties with classic vase shape seems to have been fruitful. 'Valley Forge' and 'New Harmony' are being tested and made available to the public.

U. carpinifolia. SMOOTH-LEAFED ELM. Deciduous. Zones 31, 32, 34–41. Native to Europe. To 70–90 ft. tall, with upright branches, weeping branchlets. Shiny deep green leaves to 2–3½ in. long. Prone to many pests and diseases, though moderate in susceptibility to Dutch elm disease.

U. glabra. SCOTCH ELM. Deciduous. Zones 32, 34–41. Native to Europe. Fairly upright habit to 70–100 ft. tall. Leaves 3–6 in. long, sharply toothed, rough surfaced, on very short stalks. Rarely planted today, but old trees are sometimes seen. 'Camperdownii', Camperdown elm, generally 10–20 ft. tall, has weeping branches that reach to ground and make a tent of shade. 'Pendula' is similar, but has a flatter top.

U. hollandica. DUTCH ELM. Deciduous. Zones 32, 34–41. Group of hybrids between Scotch elm and smooth-leafed elm. Most grow to 100 ft. or taller and sucker freely. All are prone to Dutch elm disease.

U. parvifolia. CHINESE ELM, LACEBARK ELM. Semievergreen or deciduous, depending on winter temperatures and individual tree's heredity. Zones 31, 32, 34, 35, 37–39. Fast growth to 40–60 ft. tall. Extremely variable in form, but generally spreading, with long, arching, eventually weeping branchlets. On trunks of older trees, bark sheds in patches (somewhat as bark of sycamore does), creating beautiful mottling in many specimens. Leathery dark green leaves are ¾–2½ in. long, evenly toothed; mediocre display of yellow to reddish orange in fall. Good resistance to Dutch elm disease, elm leaf beetle, and Japanese beetle.

Consult local authorities about hardy selections; some survive subzero temperatures. Two unusual dwarf varieties may interest bonsai specialists: 'Frosty', a shrub only 3 ft. high, has leaves edged with tiny white teeth; 'Hokkaido' is a very slow-growing miniature tree (to 1 ft. tall in 20 years) with tiny leaves.

A word of caution: A less desirable species, *U. pumila*, Siberian elm, is sometimes sold as Chinese elm.

U. procera. ENGLISH ELM. Deciduous. Zones 32, 34–41. To 120 ft. tall. Tall trunk with wide-spreading or upright, dense crown of branches. Leaves 2–3½ in. long, sandpapery, medium green; hang on longer in autumn than those of American elm. Similar to American elm in susceptibility to Dutch elm disease. Suckers profusely.

U. pumila. SIBERIAN ELM. Deciduous. Zones 31, 32, 34–45; used chiefly in Zones 43–45 where climate limits tree choices. To 50–70 ft. tall, not quite as wide. Leaves ¾–2 in. long, smooth, dark green. Endures cold, heat, aridity, and poor soil. Has brittle wood and weak crotches, and—though resistant to Dutch elm disease—is not a desirable tree. Possibly useful in holding soil against erosion; fast growth also makes it suitable for windbreak or shelterbelt. Papery, winged seeds disperse seedlings over wide area. Very susceptible to elm leaf beetles.

UMBRELLA PINE. See SCIADOPITYS verticillata

UMBRELLA PLANT. See CYPERUS alternifolius

UPRIGHT WILD GINGER. See SARUMA henryi

FOR GROWING SYMBOL EXPLANATIONS

PLEASE SEE PAGE 113

T

URSINIA anthemoides

DILL-LEAF URSINIA

Asteraceae (Compositae)

TENDER PERENNIAL GROWN AS ANNUAL

✔ ALL ZONES

☼ FULL SUN

● REGULAR WATER

Ursinia anthemoides

Native to South Africa, this daisylike perennial grows quickly from seed and is therefore treated as an annual in more northerly gardens. Growing to 16 in., with a 1-ft. spread, the plant has delicate, ferny, lightly fragrant foliage and a bushy habit. Appearing in summer, the flowers have slender, golden yellow rays with purple undersides; centers are ringed with purple, with an interior purple dot. Hot, humid summers tend to cut back on flower production. Thrives in sandy, well-drained soil. Grow at the front of a mixed or flower border, or include in cottage gardens or informal foundation plantings. Cut flowers are attractive, but close up at night and in weak light.

UVULARIA

BELLWORT, MERRYBELLS

Liliaceae

PERENNIALS

✔ ZONES 32, 34–43

◐ ● LIGHT OR DEEP SHADE

● REGULAR WATER

Uvularia

Attractive woodland plants native to eastern and central North America. Underground rhizomes send up erect stems, nodding toward the tip. Leaves are smooth and bright green, held close to stems in two ranks. Drooping, bell-shaped, pale yellow flowers hang from joints of upper leaves in spring. Foliage remains attractive all summer, dies back in winter. For woodland or shaded rock garden with moist, acid soil. Doesn't make a bold show, but looks attractive close up.

U. grandiflora. LARGE MERRYBELLS. To 2½ ft. tall, with gray-green foliage and 2-in. bells.

U. perfoliata. To 2 ft. tall, with blue-green leaves that seem to surround the stem. Bells are 1½ in. long.

U. sessilifolia. STRAWBELL. To 1½ ft. tall, with yellow-green foliage and 1¼-in. bells.

VACCINIUM

Ericaceae

EVERGREEN OR DECIDUOUS SHRUBS

✔ ZONES VARY BY SPECIES

☼ ◐ ● EXPOSURE NEEDS VARY BY SPECIES

● ● ● WATER NEEDS VARY BY SPECIES

Vaccinium

Excellent ornamental shrubs with clusters of bell-shaped flowers and colorful, edible fruit that attracts birds. Species described here are evergreen shrubs; those described under Blueberry are deciduous. All require rich, organic, acid soil. Good for woodland gardens.

V. angustifolium. See Blueberry

V. corymbosum. See Blueberry

V. macrocarpon. CRANBERRY. Zones 32, 34, 36–45. Native from Newfoundland to Minnesota, south to North Carolina. Creeping plant 2–6 in. high, spreading and rooting from stems. Narrow, ¾-in.-long leaves are dark green in summer, turning coppery or purplish red in winter. Tiny pinkish spring flowers are followed by tart red fruits in autumn. Commercial producers grow cranberries in bogs—beds that can be

flooded to control weeds and pests, provide winter protection, and make harvesting easier. Gardeners can use cranberry as an attractive small-scale ground cover in damp soil and full sun.

V. vitis-idaea. COWBERRY, FOXBERRY. Zones 32, 34–41. Native to Europe. Slow growth to 1 ft. high, spreading to 3 ft. wide by underground stems. Glossy dark green leaves to 1 in. long; new growth often tinged bright red or orange. Clustered white or pinkish spring flowers followed by sour red berries something like tiny cranberries; these are valued for preserves, syrups. Handsome little plant for small-scale ground cover, informal edging around larger plantings. Needs moist or damp soil. Prefers part or full shade, but with ample water will take full sun in cool-summer areas. North American native *V. v. minus*, lingonberry, is hardier to cold, also growing in Zones 42–45. Has smaller leaves (to ½ in.), is attractive in pots.

Valerianaceae. The valerian family of perennial herbs (rarely shrubs), has clustered small flowers. In addition to *Valeriana*, members include red valerian (*Centranthus*) and *Patrinia*.

VALERIANA officinalis

VALERIAN, GARDEN HELIOTROPE

Valerianaceae

PERENNIAL HERB

✔ ZONES 31, 32, 34–43

☼ ◐ FULL SUN OR PARTIAL SHADE

● ● REGULAR TO MODERATE WATER

Valeriana officinalis

Both true heliotrope (*Heliotropium*) and red valerian (*Centranthus ruber*) are more common than *Valeriana officinalis*. Tall, straight stems grow to about 4 ft. high; most leaves remain fairly close to ground. Leaves are light green, borne in pairs that are further divided into eight to ten pairs of narrow leaflets. Tiny, fragrant flowers are white, pink, red, or lavender blue, in rounded clusters at ends of stems. Plant spreads and can become invasive. Roots are strong smelling and are widely used in herbal preparations said to have sedative qualities. Start new plants from seeds or divisions. Grow in mixed herb or flower borders but don't allow it to crowd other plants.

VALLOTA speciosa

SCARBOROUGH LILY

Amaryllidaceae

BULB

✔ ALL ZONES, INDOORS

◐ BRIGHT INDIRECT LIGHT

● REGULAR WATER DURING ACTIVE GROWTH

Vallota speciosa

Native to South Africa. Strap-shaped evergreen leaves are 1–2 ft. long. Clusters of bright orange-vermilion, funnel-shaped, 2½–3-in.-wide flowers grow on 2-ft. stalks. Blooms summer and early fall. A white-flowered form is rarely available. Survives outdoors year-round where frosts are very light and infrequent, but is not hardy in the Northeast. It is, however, an excellent pot plant for patio or indoors. Set bulbs with tips just below surface. Plant blooms best when roots are crowded. Fertilize monthly during active growth. Water regularly except during semidormant period in winter and spring, but never let plant dry out completely.

FOR INFORMATION ON SELECTING PLANTS

PLEASE SEE PAGES 47–112

U

VANCOUVERIA

Berberidaceae

PERENNIALS

⚡ ZONES VARY BY SPECIES

☽ PARTIAL SHADE

🌢 REGULAR WATER

Vancouveria

Native to woodlands of northwestern U.S. These are close relatives of *Epimedium*, and like it, they are used as ground covers in shady spots. Bloom in late spring, early summer. Leaves are divided into numerous leaflets; cut foliage is attractive in bouquets. All species need cool, moist, acid conditions. Difficult to establish in hot-summer climates.

V. chrysantha. Evergreen. Zones 31, 32, 34, 39. To 8–16 in. tall. Bronze-tinged gray-green leaves, 1½ in. long and wide. Small yellow flowers, 4–15 to the stalk, each flower ½ in. wide.

V. hexandra. Deciduous. Zones 31, 32, 34–41. To 4–16 in. tall. Leaflets are 1–2½ in. long, light green; fresh appearance all summer. Flower stalks usually topped with three drooping white flowers to ½ in. across, petals and sepals sharply bent backward.

V. planipetala (V. parviflora). INSIDE-OUT FLOWER. Deciduous. Zones 31, 32, 34, 39. To 2 ft. tall. Light to medium green, 1½-in., shallowly lobed leaflets. White flowers are tiny—only about ⅛ in. wide—but are carried in large clusters (25–50 blossoms per cluster).

VARIEGATED GINGER. See ALPINIA sanderae

VENIDIUM fastuosum

CAPE DAISY, NAMAQUALAND DAISY

Asteraceae (Compositae)

TENDER PERENNIAL GROWN AS ANNUAL

⚡ ALL ZONES

☼ FULL SUN

🌢 REGULAR WATER

Venidium fastuosum

This South African plant is grown for its showy daisy flowers. Plants are upright, shrubby, and 2–3 ft. high, with gray hairs covering the hollow stems and fiddle-shaped leaves. The 4-in.-wide flower heads like to face the sun. Flowers have dark purple to almost black centers and golden rays with a shiny blackish purple spot at the base. They look lovely in beds, borders, containers, or fresh arrangements, but the rays close in cloudy weather and at night. Grow in well-drained soil away from extremes of cold, heat, and humidity. Sow seed outdoors in spring or, preferably, start indoors 6 weeks before the last frost date. Set seedlings outdoors about 1 ft. apart after all danger of frost has passed. Pinch early shoots to encourage branching, and stake before plants get too large. Apply fertilizer regularly once established.

VERATRUM viride

INDIAN POKE

Liliaceae

PERENNIAL

⚡ ZONES 31, 32, 34–45

☽ PARTIAL SHADE

🌢🌢 MORE THAN REGULAR WATER

🌢 ALL PARTS HIGHLY TOXIC IF INGESTED

Veratrum viride

This bold and vigorous rhizomatous perennial, native to much of southern North America, can grow to 6 ft. high and features impressive, dark green ribbed leaves. Clusters of star-shaped green to yellow-green flowers bloom in summer on terminal panicles to 2 ft. long. Perfect for damp, shady sites near ponds or streams, or in woodland or wild gardens. It

prefers fertile, humusy, moist but well-drained soil. Be sure soil does not dry out. Avoid ingestion or direct contact with skin since plant is highly toxic.

VERBASCUM

MULLEIN

Scrophulariaceae

BIENNIALS AND PERENNIALS

⚡ ZONES VARY BY SPECIES

☼ FULL SUN

🌢 MODERATE WATER

Verbascum

Large group of rosette-forming, summer-blooming plants that send up 1–6-ft. stems closely set with nearly flat, five-petaled, circular flowers about an inch across. Both foliage and stems are often covered in woolly hairs. Taller mulleins make striking vertical accents. Grow all in well-drained soil. Cut off spent flowers of perennial kinds to encourage a second round of blooming. Leave spikes of biennial species in place for reseeding. Mulleins self-sow freely—and some are downright weedy, such as the attractive roadside weed *V. thapsus*.

V. blattaria. MOTH MULLEIN. Zones 31, 32, 34–43. Biennial. Low clumps of smooth, dark green, cut or toothed leaves. Purple-centered, pale yellow or white flowers on stems 1½–2½ ft. high.

V. bombyciferum 'Arctic Summer'. Biennial. Zones 32, 34–41. Foot-high rosettes of furry, gray-green, oval leaves. Powdery white stems to 6 ft. or more bear yellow flowers.

V. chaixii. Perennial. Zones 31, 32, 34–41. Leaves to 6 in. long, less conspicuously furry than those of *V. bombyciferum* 'Arctic Summer'. Red-eyed, pale yellow flowers in narrow, often branched spikes to 3 ft. high. 'Album' has white flowers with purple centers.

V. hybrids. Perennials. Zones 32, 34, 39. These include the Cotswold and Benary hybrids. Flower spikes in white, cream, and shades of pink or purple are carried on 3–4-ft. stems. Named selections in separate colors exist, such as the popular 'Pink Domino'.

V. olympicum. Perennial. Zones 32, 34, 39. Large white leaves with soft, downy hairs form a rosette to 3 ft. across. Many stems to 5 ft. high carry bright yellow flower spikes.

V. phoeniceum. PURPLE MULLEIN. Perennial. Zones 32, 34–43. Leaves are smooth on top, hairy underneath. Slender spikes of purple flowers on 2–4-ft. stems.

VERBENA

Verbenaceae

PERENNIALS, SOME GROWN AS ANNUALS

⚡ ZONES VARY BY SPECIES

☼ FULL SUN

🌢 MODERATE WATER

Verbena

Most produce their clusters of small, five-petaled, tubular blossoms in summer. Perennial species usually have purple flowers and are often treated as annuals. Low verbenas make good ground covers, hanging basket plants; taller sorts are good in borders. Most thrive in heat, tolerate drought. They dislike continually wet conditions, so provide good air circulation and well-drained soil. Most are susceptible to mildew and spider mites.

V. bipinnatifida. Perennial. Zones 31, 32, 34–43. Native from Great Plains to Mexico. Grows 8–15 in. high, with finely divided leaves and blue flowers. Spreads by self-sowing in most climates.

V. bonariensis. Perennial in Zones 31, warmer parts of 32; annual in colder climates. Native to South America, but naturalized in southeastern U.S. and California. Airy, branching stems to 3–6 ft. carry purple flowers. Leaves mostly in 1½-ft.-high basal clump. Plant's see-through quality makes it suited for foreground or back of border. Self-sows freely.

V

V. canadensis. Perennial in Zones 31, 32, 34–41, but usually treated as annual in all zones. Native from Virginia to Florida west to Colorado and Mexico. To 1½ ft. high, with rosy purple flowers. There is a compact (6-in.-high) form suitable for rock gardens; white- and pink-flowering forms are also sold. 'Homestead Purple', to 6–10 in. high and spreading to 2 ft., has dark green leaves and deep purple flowers; it thrives in hot, humid climates. When growing the species or its varieties as perennials, provide good winter drainage; in colder part of range, cover with light winter mulch.

V. hybrida (V. hortensis). GARDEN VERBENA. Tender perennial treated as annual. All zones. Many-branched upright and bushy or low and spreading plant 6–14 in. high and 1½–3 ft. across. Oblong, 2–4-in., bright green or gray-green leaves with toothed margins, divided and lacy in some cultivars. Flowers in flat, compact clusters to 3 in. wide. Colors include white, pink, bright red, purple, blue, and combinations. Many cultivars exist, including:

Babylon Series. Bushy and early blooming, mildew resistant; flowers in pink, bright rose, lilac, lavender.

'Camp Joy'. Spreading habit; flowers combine shades of pink from soft to bright.

'Homestead Purple'. Bushy and tall, to 1½ ft.; heat tolerant; rich, bright purple flowers.

'Imagination'. Low and spreading, finely divided leaves; dark violet blue flowers; good basket plant.

Novalis Series. Upright and branched; flowers are scarlet, rose pink, or deep blue with white eye, white, scarlet, or bright rose without eye.

Patio Temari Hybrids. Upright and bushy; flowers in purple blue, rose pink, hot pink, and pale pink.

'Peaches and Cream'. Spreading and bushy; soft orangey pink flowers fade to peachy yellow, then ivory.

'Showtime Trinidad'. Upright and bushy; deep rose pink flowers.

Tapien Hybrids. Low and spreading, disease and heat tolerant; flowers in pink with dark eye, salmon, soft pink, blue violet, lavender.

Temari Hybrids. Spreading and disease resistant; flowers in red, burgundy, purple, coral pink, pale blue.

V. peruviana (V. chamaedryfolia). Perennial in warm climates, but treated as annual in all zones. Spreads rapidly, forming a very flat mat. Leaves are neat, small, closely set. Flat-topped clusters of scarlet-and-white flowers on slender stems cover foliage. Hybrids—with flowers in white, pinks, or reds—spread more slowly, have slightly larger leaves and stouter stems.

V. rigida (V. venosa). Perennial in Zones 31, 32; can be grown as annual. Native to South America, but naturalized in southeastern U.S. To 10–20 in. high, spreading. Rough, strongly toothed, dark green leaves to 2–4 in. long. Lilac to purple-blue flowers in cylindrical clusters on tall, stiff stems. Blooms in 4 months from seed. 'Flame', to 4 in. high, is a selection with bright scarlet flowers; grow from cuttings.

V. 'Sissinghurst'. Perennial. Zones 31, 32. Evergreen plant a few inches high and spreading to 4 ft. wide. Rose pink flowers.

V. 'Taylortown Red'. Perennial. Zones 31, 32. Evergreen spreader to 1 ft. tall, 6 ft. wide. Bright red flowers.

V. tenuisecta (V. erinoides). MOSS VERBENA. Perennial. Zone 31; annual elsewhere. Native to South America, but naturalized in Deep South. To 8–12 in. high, with finely cut leaves. Rose violet to pink flowers. 'Alba' is a white-flowered form. The species is sometimes offered as *V. pulchella gracilior.*

VERBENA, LEMON. See ALOYSIA triphylla

Verbenaceae. The immense verbena family contains annuals, perennials, shrubs, and a few trees and vines. Leaves are usually opposite or in whorls, flowers in spikes or spikelike clusters. Fruit may be berries or nutlets. Glorybower (*Clerodendrum*), *Lantana*, *Verbena*, and chaste tree (*Vitex*) are examples.

VERNONIA
noveboracensis

IRONWEED	
Asteraceae (Compositae)	
PERENNIAL	
▨ ZONES 31, 32, 34–41	
☼ ◑ FULL SUN OR LIGHT SHADE	
◑ ◑ ◐ ◑ MUCH TO LITTLE WATER	

Vernonia noveboracensis

Seldom considered for gardens, this meadow plant is a handsome choice for the back of the border or for a contrasting color scheme with goldenrod and black-eyed Susan. Clumps of leafy stems to 6–8 ft. tall are topped in late summer by broad, flat clusters of fluffy, brilliant purple flower heads. These should be clipped off before they develop into the rust-colored seed clusters that give the plant its name (unless you want plant to naturalize from volunteer seedlings). Grows in wet or dry soils and needs no coddling.

VERONICA

SPEEDWELL	
Scrophulariaceae	
PERENNIALS	
▨ ZONES VARY BY SPECIES	
☼ FULL SUN, EXCEPT AS NOTED	
◑ ◑ WATER NEEDS VARY BY SPECIES	

Veronica

Handsome plants ranging from 4 in. to 2½ ft. in height. Small flowers (¼–½ in. across) in white, rose, pink, or pale to deep blue are massed for an effective color display. Use in sunny borders and rock gardens. Prostrate, mat-forming kinds are generally less tolerant of damp conditions than bushy kinds and should be watered less often. Named varieties are not easily assigned to a species; authorities differ.

V. alpina. Zones 32, 34–45. Creeping rootstock forms low rosette of foliage that sends up spikelike flower clusters in spring or early summer; in warmer part of range, often reblooms in fall. Varieties include 10-in. 'Alba', with white flowers; 10-in. 'Barcarolle', rose pink; and 1-ft. 'Corymbosa', deep blue. The hybrid 'Goodness Grows', 1–2 ft. tall, has an extra-long bloom period, producing violet blue blossoms from late spring to frost if old flowers are removed. Regular water.

V. austriaca teucrium 'Crater Lake Blue'. Zones 31, 32, 34–41. 1½ ft. tall, forming a mat 2 ft. across. Oblong gray-green leaves to 3 in. long with toothed or scalloped edges. In summer, spikes of deep but bright blue flowers on straight stems. Moderate to regular water.

V. gentianoides. GENTIAN SPEEDWELL. Zones 32, 34–43. Creeping rootstock forms a dense mat of glossy dark green leaves, topped in spring by leafy stems carrying 10-in. spikes of ice blue flowers with darker veining. 'Variegata' has leaves marked with white. More tolerant of moist soils than other mat-forming species; do not let soil dry out.

V. grandis holophylla. Zones 32, 34–43. Many stems to 2 ft. tall are densely clothed with waxy, glossy dark green leaves ending in spikelike clusters of blue flowers. These appear all summer if old clusters are deadheaded. 'Lavender Charm' ('Blue Charm') grows 1½–2 ft. tall. 'Icicle', to 1½ ft., has white flowers. Regular water.

V. incana. SILVER SPEEDWELL. Zones 32, 34–43. Furry, silvery white, mat-forming foliage clumps. Deep blue flowers on 10-in. stems in summer. Varieties include 15-in. 'Minuet', with pink flowers; 10-in. 'Pavane', rose pink; 15-in. 'Red Fox', deep rose pink; 1½-ft. 'Saraband', deep blue; and green-leafed, 15-in. 'Romilley Purple', deep violet purple. Moderate to little water.

V. longifolia subsessilis (V. subsessilis). Zones 32, 34–43. Clumps of upright stems to 2 ft. tall are topped in midsummer by spikes of deep blue flowers about ½ in. wide; deadhead to prolong bloom. Stems are leafy and rather closely set with narrow, pointed leaves. Regular water.

V. pectinata. Zones 34–43. Prostrate mat spreads by creeping stems that root at joints. Roundish, ½-in.-long leaves with scallop-toothed or deeply cut edges. Profuse spring or early summer bloom; flowers are deep blue with white centers, in 5–6-in. spikes among the leaves. 'Rosea' has rose pink flowers. Good in rock gardens or wall crevices. Full sun or part shade. Moderate to little water.

V. peduncularis. Zones 31, 32, 34, 39. Low and mat forming, to 4 in. tall and 2 ft. across. Glossy green, purple-tinged oval to lance-shaped leaves with toothed edges. Small spikes of deep blue flowers with white eye in spring and summer; long blooming. 'Georgia Blue' is vigorous and free blooming. Moderate water.

V. prostrata (V. rupestris). Zones 32, 34–43. Small leaves to ¾ in. long. Tufted, hairy stems; some are prostrate and form mats of hairy foliage, while others grow upward to 8 in. tall and are topped by short clusters of pale blue flowers in late spring or early summer. 'Alba' bears white blooms, 'Mrs. Holt' pale pink ones. 'Trehane' has golden yellow leaves, bright blue flowers. Moderate to little water.

V. repens. Zones 31, 32, 34, 39. Shiny green, ½-in. leaves clothe prostrate stems, give mosslike effect. Clusters of tiny lavender to white flowers in spring. Good as a small-scale ground cover, filler between stepping-stones, or cover for small bulbs. Moderate to little water. Tolerates some shade.

V. saturejoides. Zones 32, 34–43. Roundish, ½-in. leaves closely overlap on stems. Dark blue flowers in short, compact spikes appear in spring. Fine rock garden plant; stems spread by creeping roots. Moderate to little water.

V. spicata. Zones 31, 32, 34–43. Rounded green clumps send up spikelike flower clusters to 2 ft. tall. Long summer bloom period if plants are deadheaded. Varieties include 'Blue Fox', to 20 in. high; 'Blue Peter', 2 ft., with dark blue flowers; 'Icicle', 2 ft., with pure white flowers; and rosy pink 'Heidekind', to 10 in. high. All take regular water. Need good drainage.

V. 'Sunny Border Blue'. Zones 32, 34–43. Compact plant with crinkled foliage. Dark violet blue flowers in spires to 2 ft. tall over an exceptionally long bloom season, starting in late spring or early summer. Deadheading prolongs the show until frost. Regular water.

V. 'Waterperry' ('Waterperry Blue'). Zones 32, 34–41. Low, trailing plant roots as it spreads. Leaves are roundish, bronze-tinted ovals ½ in. long. Round flowers in loose clusters are pale blue, veined deeper blue. Spring bloom is followed by sporadic flowering throughout summer and fall. Use for bulb cover, in rock garden, poolside. Mat-forming plant but prefers regular water.

VERONICASTRUM virginicum (Veronica virginica)

CULVER'S ROOT

Scrophulariaceae

PERENNIAL

ZONES 32, 34–43

FULL SUN OR LIGHT SHADE

REGULAR WATER

Veronicastrum virginicum

Native to eastern U.S. Resembles a very tall *Veronica*. Stems to 5–7 ft. high, clothed with whorls of toothed, 6-in., lance-shaped leaves. Stems branch in the upper portions and are topped by slender spikelike clusters (to 9 in. long) of tiny pale blue or white flowers. Pink varieties exist. Useful plant for background in large borders. Makes a striking pattern against dark background, such as tall hedge or woodland edge, but too much shade makes it floppy. Likes fertile, well-drained, slightly acid soil.

VIBURNUM

Caprifoliaceae

DECIDUOUS OR EVERGREEN SHRUBS, SMALL TREES

ZONES VARY BY SPECIES

FULL SUN OR PART SHADE, EXCEPT AS NOTED

REGULAR WATER, EXCEPT AS NOTED

Viburnum

Large and diverse group of plants with clustered, sometimes fragrant flowers followed by single-seeded, often brilliantly colored fruit much appreciated by birds. In general, heaviest fruit set occurs when several different named varieties or seedlings that bloom at the same time are planted together. Some viburnums are valuable for winter flowers. Many deciduous kinds have poor or inconsistent fall color. Some evergreen types are used principally as foliage plants. A few species, as noted, can be grown as small trees.

Viburnums prefer slightly acid soil but are very tolerant, even accepting heavy soils. Many have a wide range of climate adaptability. Where summers are long and hot, most evergreen kinds look better with some sun protection. Prune to prevent legginess; some evergreen kinds can be sheared. Aphids, thrips, spider mites, scale, and root weevils are potential pests in many regions. However, plants are not usually seriously troubled. Keep any sulfur sprays off foliage.

V. bodnantense. Deciduous. Zones 31, 32, 34–41. To 10 ft. or more. Oval leaves 1½–4 in. long are deeply veined, turn dark scarlet in fall. Loose clusters of very fragrant flowers, deep pink fading paler, bloom fall–spring. Red fruit is not showy. This plant is a hybrid; there are several varieties. Best known is 'Dawn' ('Pink Dawn'). Flower buds freeze in coldest winters.

V. burkwoodii. Deciduous. Zones 31, 32, 34–41. Hybrid to 6–12 ft. tall, 4–8 ft. wide. Leaves to 3½ in. long, glossy dark green with white, hairy undersides; turn purplish red in cold weather. Very fragrant white flowers open in late winter or early spring from dense, 4-in. clusters of pink buds. Blue-black fruit is not showy. Early growth is straggly; mature plants are dense. Can be trained as espalier.

'Chenault' (*V. chenaultii*). Denser, more compact, slightly later blooming, more deciduous in mild climates than the species.

'Mohawk'. Zones 31, 32, 34–43. To 7 ft. tall. Red buds are showy long before they expand into white flowers. Bright orange-red fall color. Resistant to bacterial leaf spot.

V. carlcephalum. FRAGRANT SNOWBALL. Deciduous. Zones 31, 32, 34–41. Hybrid plant to 6–10 ft. tall and wide. Leaves 2–3½ in. long, dull grayish green, downy beneath; turn reddish purple in autumn. Long-lasting, waxy white, perfumed flowers in showy, dense, 4–5-in. clusters in spring.

V. carlesii. KOREAN SPICE VIBURNUM. Deciduous. Zones 31, 32, 34–43. To 4–8 ft. tall and wide. Leaves are like those of *V. carlcephalum*; inconsistent reddish fall color. Sweetly fragrant, 2–3-in. clusters of white flowers open from pink buds in spring. Blue-black summer fruit is not showy. Best in part shade during summer, in sun during spring, winter. The hybrid 'Cayuga', hardy into Zones 43, grows 5 ft. tall and has white flowers opening from pink buds.

V. cassinoides. WITHE-ROD. Deciduous. Zones 31, 32, 34–43. Native to eastern and central North America. Attractive dense, rounded plant 5–6 ft. (possibly to 10 ft.) tall, with dull dark green leaves; red-orange to red-purple fall color. Flat clusters of white flowers bloom in late spring or early summer; these are followed by showy, mixed-color clusters of green, pink, red, and blue fruits that eventually turn black. Tolerates damp soil, wind, seacoast conditions.

V. dentatum. ARROWWOOD VIBURNUM. Deciduous. Zones 31, 32, 34–45. Native from New Brunswick to Minnesota, south to Georgia. To 6–10 ft. tall (or taller) and as wide. Cream-colored flowers in late spring are followed by blue-black, ¼-in. fruit. Dark green, 4-in. leaves turn yellow, orange, or deep red in autumn. 'Morton' has deep burgundy fall color; 'Ralph Senior' and 'Synnestvedt' have red, yellow, and orange fall color. Plants tolerate heat, cold, and wet soil. Use as screen or tall hedge.

V

V. dilatatum. LINDEN VIBURNUM. Deciduous. Zones 32, 34−41. To 8−10 ft. tall and not quite as wide. Nearly round, 2−5-in. gray-green leaves; inconsistent rusty red fall color. Tiny, creamy white, somewhat unpleasant-smelling flowers in 5-in. clusters, late spring or early summer. Showy bright red fruits are produced most heavily where summers are warm; they ripen in early fall, hang on into winter. Outstanding named varieties include the following:

'Catskill'. Compact growth to 5−8 ft. tall, 8−10 ft. wide, with smaller leaves than species. Dark red fruit. Fall color is a combination of yellow, orange, and red.

'Erie'. Rounded habit to 6 ft. tall, 10 ft. wide. Coral fruit. Leaves turn yellow, orange, and red in autumn. Highly disease resistant.

'Iroquois'. To 9 ft. tall, 12 ft. wide. Selected for heavy production of larger, darker red fruit. Orange-red to maroon fall foliage.

V. farreri (V. fragrans). Deciduous. Zones 31, 32, 34, 35, 37, 39. Loose habit, to 8−12 ft. tall and as wide. Smooth green leaves are oval, heavily veined, 1½−3 in. long; turn soft russet red to reddish purple in fall. Fragrant white to pink flowers in 2-in. clusters appear before leaves open, in winter or early spring. Blossoms survive to 20 to 22°F/−7 to −6°C; they freeze in colder temperatures. Bright red fruit. Prune to prevent leggy growth. 'Album' has pure white flowers. Pink-flowered 'Nanum' is lower growing (to 2 ft.).

V. hybrids. This group includes plants of complex ancestry. The following, all spring bloomers, are widely offered:

'Chesapeake'. Semievergreen. Zones 31, 32, 34, 39. To 6 ft. tall, 10 ft. wide, with wavy-edged, glossy dark green leaves. Small, fragrant white flowers open from pink buds; dull red to black fruit follows.

'Conoy'. Evergreen. Zones 31, 32, 34, 39. Dense, rounded plant to 5 ft. tall, 8 ft. wide. Lustrous dark green leaves, whitish beneath, take on maroon tinge in winter in colder part of range. Creamy white, slightly fragrant flowers; long-lasting red berries. Tolerates shearing.

'Eskimo'. Semievergreen. Zones 31, 32, 34, 35, 37, 39. Dense, compact habit to 5 ft. tall and wide. Shiny dark green foliage; unscented white flowers in 3−4-in., snowball-like clusters.

V. juddii. Deciduous. Zones 31, 32, 34−41. Hybrid plant to 4−8 ft. tall. Bushier and more spreading than *V. carlesii* but similar to it in other respects, including fragrance.

V. lantana. WAYFARING TREE. Deciduous. Zones 34−41. Large (10−20-ft.), rounded, multistemmed shrub with 2−5-in. dark green leaves that turn an inconsistent purplish red in fall. Flat, 3−5-in. clusters of creamy flowers in midspring develop into yellow fruits that gradually age to red, then black; all colors are sometimes present at once. Berries of 'Mohican' hold their red color longest. This species tolerates drought and lime soils better than most other viburnums.

V. lentago. NANNYBERRY. Deciduous. Zones 32, 34−45. Native to eastern and central North America. Will grow as single-trunked tree to 30 ft. tall or as massive shrub to lesser height. Creamy white flowers in flat, 4−6-in. clusters in spring. Edible fruit is red at first, turning to blue black. Glossy dark green, 2−4-in.-long leaves turn an inconsistent purplish red in fall. Good in dappled shade of taller trees, at woodland edge. Takes moist or dry soils.

V. macrocephalum (V. m. 'Sterile'). CHINESE SNOWBALL. Deciduous. Zones 31, 32, 34, 39. To 12−20 ft. tall, with broad, rounded habit. Leaves oval to oblong, 2−4 in. long, dull green. Spectacular big, rounded, 6−8-in. flower clusters in spring (or anytime during warm weather) are composed of sterile blossoms that are lime green at first, changing to white. No fruit. Can be trained as espalier.

V. opulus. EUROPEAN CRANBERRY BUSH. Deciduous. Zones 31, 32, 34−45. To 8−15 ft. tall and wide, with arching branches. Lobed, maplelike dark green leaves to 2−4 in. long and wider than long; fall color may be yellow, bright red, or reddish purple. Creamy white spring flowers consist of 2−4-in. clusters of small fertile blossoms ringed with larger sterile blossoms for a lace cap effect. Large, showy red fruit, fall−winter. Takes moist to boggy soils. Control aphids. Varieties include:

'Aureum'. To 10 ft. tall. Golden yellow foliage needs some shade to prevent sunburn.

'Compactum'. Same as *V. opulus* but smaller: 4−5 ft. high and wide.

'Nanum'. To 2 ft. tall, 2 ft. wide. Needs no trimming as low hedge. Cannot take poorly drained, wet soils. No flowers, fruit.

'Roseum' ('Sterile'). COMMON SNOWBALL. To 10−15 ft. Resembles *V. opulus,* but flower clusters are like snowballs: 2−2½ in. across, composed entirely of sterile flowers (so no fruit). Aphids are especially troublesome on this form.

V. plicatum plicatum. JAPANESE SNOWBALL. Deciduous. Zones 31, 32, 34−43. To 8−15 ft. tall and wide. Oval, 3−6-in. long, strongly veined, dull dark green leaves turn purplish red in fall. Showy, 3-in. snowball-like clusters of white sterile flowers in midspring look like those of *V. opulus* 'Roseum', but this plant is less bothered by aphids. Horizontal branching pattern gives plant a tiered look, especially when in bloom: flower clusters are held above the branches, while leaves hang down. No fruit. Tolerates occasionally wet soils.

V. plicatum tomentosum. DOUBLEFILE VIBURNUM. Deciduous. Zones 31, 32, 34−43. A truly beautiful viburnum. Resembles Japanese snowball, but midspring flower display consists of small fertile flowers in flat, 2−4-in. clusters edged with 1−1½-in. sterile flowers in lace cap effect. Fruit is red aging to black, showy, not always profuse. Takes moist to wet soils. Selections include the following:

'Cascade'. To 10 ft. tall, with wide-spreading branches, large sterile flowers.

'Mariesii'. To 10 ft. tall, 12 ft. wide. Has larger flower clusters, larger sterile flowers than the species.

'Newport'. To 5−6 ft. tall and wide.

'Pink Beauty'. To 8−10 ft. tall, with light pink flowers that fade to white in warm temperatures.

'Shasta'. More horizontal habit than the species (to 10 ft. tall, 15 ft. wide), with large sterile flowers.

'Shoshoni'. To 5 ft. tall, 8 ft. wide.

'Summer Snowflake'. To 5−8 ft. tall. Blooms from spring to fall.

'Watanabe', 'Nana Semperflorens', and 'Fujisanensis' ('Mt. Fuji') are similar, if not identical, to 'Summer Snowflake'.

V. prunifolium. BLACK HAW. Deciduous. Zones 31, 32, 34−43. Native to eastern U.S. Upright to 15 ft. and spreading as wide. Can be trained as small tree. Common name comes from dark fruit and plant's resemblance to hawthorn (*Crataegus*). Oval, finely toothed leaves to 3 in. long turn purplish to reddish purple in autumn. Abundant clusters of creamy white flowers in spring are followed by edible blue-black fruit in fall, winter. Use as dense screen or barrier, attractive specimen shrub. Best in full sun. Tolerates drought.

V. rhytidophyllum. LEATHERLEAF VIBURNUM. Evergreen. Zones 31, 32, 34−41. Narrow, upright growth to 6−15 ft. tall. Leaves narrowish, to 4−10 in. long, deep green and wrinkled above, densely fuzzy underneath. Yellowish white spring flowers in 4−8-in. clusters. Fruit is scarlet, aging to black. Tattered-looking plant where cold winds blow. Leaves droop in cold weather. Tolerates deep shade. Some find this plant striking; others consider it coarse. 'Alleghany' and 'Willowwood' are hybrids similar to the parent. Hybrid 'Pragense' has a finer texture than the parent.

Viburnum rhytidophyllum

V. sargentii. Deciduous. Zones 34−43. Upright, rounded growth to 12−15 ft. tall and wide. Lobed, somewhat maplelike, 2−5-in.-long leaves. Foliage is bronze purple when new, dark green in summer; may turn yellow to red in fall. White to cream blossoms in late spring; 2−4-in. clusters of small fertile flowers, edged with 1-in. sterile flowers in lace cap effect. Bright red fruit colors up in late summer and fall, hangs on into winter. 'Onondaga', to 6 ft. or taller, has foliage that emerges deep maroon and holds a maroon tinge when mature; its white lace cap flowers are tinged purple.

V. setigerum. TEA VIBURNUM. Deciduous. Zones 31, 32, 34−41. To 8−12 ft. tall, rather erect, multistemmed, often bare at the base. (Plant lower shrubs around it for concealment.) Leaves, once used for making tea, are 3−6 in. long, dark green or blue green, turning purplish in fall. White spring flowers in 1−2-in. clusters are not striking, but heavy production of scarlet fruit makes this the showiest of fruiting viburnums.

V. trilobum. CRANBERRY BUSH. Deciduous. Zones 34–45. Native to Canada, northern U.S. To 10–15 ft. tall. Leaves look much like those of *V. opulus;* they emerge reddish tinged, mature to dark green, turn yellow to red purple in fall. White lace cap flowers appear in midspring, followed by fruit (edible in this species) similar to that of *V. opulus.* 'Compactum' grows 6 ft. tall; 'Wentworth' has berries larger than those of the species.

V. wrightii. Deciduous. Zones 31, 32, 34–41. Similar to *V. dilatatum* except for its larger leaves, which may turn a good red in fall. Useful tall hedge.

VINCA

PERIWINKLE, MYRTLE

Apocynaceae

PERENNIALS

⚊ ZONES VARY BY SPECIES

☽ ● PARTIAL OR FULL SHADE

⬤ MODERATE WATER

Vinca

Trailing, arching stems that root where they touch the soil make these evergreen plants useful as ground and bank covers. Shiny dark green leaves are oval to oblong. Lavender blue, five-petaled, pinwheel-shaped flowers appear in leaf joints in spring. Tolerate sun if well watered.

V. major. Zones 31, 32; variegated form grown as an annual. The larger, more aggressive species. Leaves to 3 in. long, flowers to 2 in. across. Spreads rapidly; where hardy, can be extremely invasive in areas that are sheltered and forested. Will mound up 1–2 ft. high. Shear close to ground occasionally to bring on new growth. 'Variegata' has leaves irregularly edged creamy white, and is widely grown as an annual in window boxes and hanging baskets.

V. minor. DWARF PERIWINKLE. Zones 31, 32, 34–43. Miniature version of *V. major,* with smaller leaves and flowers and a height of just 6 in. More restrained, less likely to invade adjacent plantings, although it, too, has become a pest. Among the many varieties are 'Alba', with white flowers; 'Atropurpurea', deep purple flowers and small leaves; 'Aureola', light blue flowers, yellow veins in leaf centers; 'Bowles' Variety', larger leaves, deeper blue flowers; 'Miss Jekyll', small grower with white flowers; 'Ralph Shugert', white-edged leaves, blue flowers, autumn rebloom. 'Sterling Silver' is a blue-flowered form with green leaves specked with pale green and edged in cream. 'La Grave' is similar to (if not the same plant as) 'Bowles' Variety'.

V. rosea. See *Catharanthus roseus*

VIOLA

VIOLA, VIOLET, PANSY

Violaceae

PERENNIALS, SOME TREATED AS ANNUALS

⚊ ZONES VARY BY SPECIES

☀ ☽ ● EXPOSURE NEEDS VARY BY SPECIES

⬤ REGULAR WATER

Viola

Botanically speaking, violas, pansies, and violets are all perennials belonging to the genus *Viola.* However, pansies and violas are usually treated as annuals; they are invaluable for spring-through-summer color in the Northeast. Many garden centers also sell pansies for fall color as well. In Zones 31, 32 they flower in mild periods through most of winter. Pansies and violas provide mass color in borders and edgings, as ground covers for spring-flowering bulbs, and in containers. Violets are more often used as woodland or rock garden plants. Pansies and violas take sun or shade; except as noted, violets thrive in part or full shade.

V. blanda. SWEET WHITE VIOLET. Zones 31, 32, 34–43. Native to eastern North America. To 2–3 in. tall, spreading by runners. Fragrant early

spring flowers are white veined purple, with sharply reflexed petals. Likes humus-rich soil.

V. cornuta. VIOLA, TUFTED PANSY. Zones 31, 32, 34–43 for kinds grown as perennials, and all zones as annuals. To 6–8 in. high, with smooth, wavy-toothed, somewhat oval leaves. Purple, pansylike flowers, about 1½ in. across, have slender spur. Modern strains and varieties have larger flowers with shorter spurs, in solid colors of purple, blue, yellow, apricot, ruby red, and white. Crystal strain has especially large flowers in clear colors. Set out nursery plants or sow seed as for pansy.

Some nurseries offer English violas—named varieties propagated by cuttings or division. These form clumps to 2 ft. wide and are reliably perennial. Varieties include 'Better Times', 2-in. yellow flowers; 'Columbine', creamy white flowers liberally splashed with purple; 'Etain', pale yellow flowers with purple borders; 'Mt. Spokane', white flowers with a shading of palest blue; and 'Whiskers', cream-colored flowers marked with thin purple lines.

V. cucullata (V. obliqua). MARSH BLUE VIOLET. Zones 32, 34–43. Native to eastern and central North America. Leaves to 4 in. wide. Blue, ¾-in.-wide flowers in early spring. Good ground cover, but self-sows and can become a nuisance. 'Freckles' has white flowers liberally dotted with purple; comes true from seed.

V. dissecta. Zones 31, 32, 34–41. Native to Japan. To 4 in. high. Three-part leaves divided into lance-shaped leaflets. Fragrant, pale rose pink flowers in spring.

V. koreana. KOREAN VIOLET. Attractive miniature species, under 2 in. tall in bloom, with leaves marbled silver, in the manner of hardy cyclamen. Most flowers do not open, but go directly to seed. May self-seed abundantly in a sheltered, shady location. 'Stylettas' is even more handsomely mottled, and more likely to produce mauve pink flowers in spring.

V. labradorica. Zones 31, 32, 34–45. Native to northeastern U.S., Canada, Greenland. Tiny violet 3 in. high or less, with roundish, 1-in. leaves tinged purple and tiny lavender blue flowers in spring. Spreads aggressively by runners and can invade choice small perennials; volunteer seedlings can earn it weed status. Useful small-scale ground cover in shade or filler between stepping-stones or paving blocks.

V. odorata. SWEET VIOLET. Zones 31, 32, 34–43. The violet of song and story. Spreads by long runners at moderate rate. Dark green, heart-shaped leaves, toothed on margins. Fragrant, short-spurred flowers in deep violet, bluish rose, or white. Deep purple 'Royal Robe', a large plant with long stems (to 6 in.), is widely grown. 'Royal Elk' has single, fragrant, long-stemmed violet-colored flowers. 'Charm' grows in clumps, has small white flowers. 'Rosina' is pink flowered. Plant size varies from 2 in. for smallest varieties to 8–10 in. for largest.

Plants tolerate full sun in cool-summer areas. Remove runners and shear rank growth in late fall for better spring flower display. For heavy bloom, apply a complete fertilizer in very early spring, before flowering. These violets can become genuine pests if allowed to spread into other perennial plantings or lawns.

Parma violets are hybrids of imprecise ancestry but derived in part from *V. odorata,* which they resemble. Hardy to about 10°F/−12°C—possible outdoors only in Zone 31, but can be grown in cold frames into New England. Flowers are very double and intensely fragrant. 'Duchesse de Parme' (lavender), 'Marie Louise' (deep violet), and 'Swanley White' represent the range of colors available. Plants prefer cool winters and mild summers. Beyond their hardiness range, grow these violets in containers and keep in a cool greenhouse (or in a cool indoor room) over winter.

V. palmata. EARLY BLUE VIOLET. Zones 32, 34–43. Native to eastern U.S. Plants bear violet blue, white-centered violets on 8-in. stems in spring. Leaves are divided into several toothed lobes. Slow to spread.

V. pedata. BIRD'S-FOOT VIOLET. Zones 32, 34–43. Native to eastern North America. So named because its finely divided leaves resemble a bird's foot. Blooms early spring to early summer; inch-wide flowers on 4-in. stems are usually two-toned violet blue with darker veins. Forms clumps; does not spread by runners. Not as easy to grow as other violets; likes excellent drainage, filtered sun or high shade, acid conditions.

V. priceana. See *V. sororia*

V

V. sororia (V. priceana). CONFEDERATE VIOLET. Zones 31, 32, 34–43. Leaves are somewhat heart shaped, to 5 in. wide. Blooms spring to early summer; flowers are ½–¾ in. across, white, heavily veined with violet blue, flat-faced like pansies. No runners. Self-sows readily; best in woodland garden. Good ground cover among rhododendrons.

V. tricolor. JOHNNY-JUMP-UP. All zones as annual. To 6–12 in. tall, with oval, deeply lobed leaves. Purple-and-yellow spring flowers resemble miniature pansies. Flowers of 'Molly Sanderson' are so deep a purple that they appear black. Self-sows profusely. Like pansy, takes sun or shade.

V. t. hortensis. See *V. wittrockiana*

V. wittrockiana (V. tricolor hortensis). PANSY. All zones as annual. Many strains with flowers 2–4 in. across, in white, blue, mahogany red, rose, yellow, apricot, purple; also bicolors. Petals often striped or blotched; Crown and Crystal Bowl strains have unblotched flowers. Plants grow to about 8 in. high. F_1 and F_2 hybrids more free flowering, heat tolerant. To prolong bloom of pansies, pick flowers (with some foliage) regularly, remove faded blooms before they seed. In hot-summer areas, plants get ragged by midsummer and should be removed.

Set out nursery plants in spring for summer bloom or in early fall for autumn color. Or start plants from seed. Sow seed in mid- to late summer and overwinter seedlings in a cold frame until spring planting time; or sow seed indoors in January or February, plant out in spring.

VIOLET. See VIOLA

VIPER'S BUGLOSS. See ECHIUM vulgare

VIRGINIA BLUEBELLS. See MERTENSIA virginica

VIRGINIA CREEPER. See PARTHENOCISSUS quinquefolia

VIRGINIAN STOCK. See MALCOLMIA maritima

VISCARIA coeli-rosa. See SILENE coeli-rosa

Vitaceae. The grape family contains vines that climb by tendrils and produce berries. In addition to grape, best-known representatives are Boston ivy and Virginia creeper (both species of *Parthenocissus*).

VITEX

CHASTE TREE

Verbenaceae

DECIDUOUS OR EVERGREEN SHRUBS OR TREES

🌡 ZONES 31, 32, 34, 39

☀ FULL SUN

💧 REGULAR WATER

Vitex

Large group of mostly tropical and subtropical trees, only a few are grown in the U.S. They have handsome, divided leaves and clustered flowers. Deciduous species are root hardy and can be treated as perennials in colder parts of their range. All tolerate seacoast conditions.

V. agnus-castus. CHASTE TREE. Deciduous shrub or small tree. Native to southern Europe, western Asia. In the New York/Philadelphia region, grows to about 8–10 ft. high. In cooler regions where it typically freezes to the ground in winter, this plant is a shrubby perennial, generally reaching just 3–5 ft. tall. In Washington, D.C., and farther south, it grows as a small tree.

Aromatic leaves are divided fanwise into five to seven narrow, 2–6-in.-long leaflets that are grayish green above, gray beneath. No real fall color. Small, fragrant, lavender blue flowers in 6–12-in. spikes at branch ends and in leaf joints, summer–fall. Varieties include 'Alba' and 'Silver Spire', with white flowers; 'Latifolia' (sometimes sold as *V. macrophylla*), a sturdy plant with large leaflets; and 'Rosea', with pinkish flowers.

Thrives in heat. Tolerant of various soils, but prefers well-drained soil. Good in shrub border. If trained high, makes a good small shade tree.

Plants treated as perennials should be cut to within 1 ft. of ground in spring; they will bloom on new growth.

V. negundo. Deciduous shrub or small tree. Native to southeast Africa, eastern Asia. Similar to *V. agnus-castus*, but a little larger and slightly more cold hardy; 5–8-in. flower spikes aren't as showy. 'Heterophylla' has delicate-looking, finely lobed leaflets. In coldest areas, treat as perennial, as for *V. agnus-castus*.

VITIS. See GRAPE

VOODOO LILY. See SAUROMATUM venosum

WAFER ASH. See PTELEA trifoliata

WAKE ROBIN. See TRILLIUM

WALDSTEINIA

BARREN STRAWBERRY

Rosaceae

PERENNIALS

🌡 ZONES 32, 34–41

☀◐ FULL SUN OR LIGHT SHADE

💧 REGULAR WATER

Waldsteinia

These creeping, strawberrylike, evergreen ground covers spread by runners to make 3–4-in.-high mats. Glossy bright green leaves are divided into three leaflets; in cold climates, they may take on bronze tones in winter. Yellow, ¾-in. flowers in spring and early summer are followed by tiny, inedible fruit. For fast cover, plant 1 ft. apart in well-drained soil. Better in cool-summer areas than where summers are hot and humid.

W. fragarioides. Native to eastern North America. Leaves larger than those of *W. ternata*, with leaflets to 3 in. long.

W. ternata. Native to Siberia, China, Japan. Similar to *W. fragarioides*, but has more compact growth and shorter leaflets (to 1½ in. long).

WALLFLOWER. See ERYSIMUM

WALNUT (Juglans)

Juglandaceae

DECIDUOUS TREES

🌡 ZONES VARY BY SPECIES

☀ FULL SUN

💧 REGULAR WATER

Walnut

Large, spreading trees suitable for big properties. All produce oval or round, edible nuts in fleshy husks; those of native species have a wild flavor, those of English walnut are the ones sold commercially. Among the drawbacks of these trees are their large size; shallow, competitive roots (roots of black walnut even inhibit growth of some other plants); and wind-borne pollen, which causes an allergic reaction in many people. Moreover, trees tend to be out of leaf for a long time—and they are often messy when in leaf (drip and sooty mildew from aphid exudations) and in fruit (husks from nuts can stain).

J. cinerea. BUTTERNUT. Zones 32, 34–45. Native from New Brunswick to Georgia, west to Arkansas and North Dakota. To 50–60 ft. (possibly to 100 ft.) tall, with broad, spreading canopy. Resembles black walnut—but tree is smaller, leaves have fewer leaflets (11–19), and nuts are oval or elongated rather than round. Flavor is good, but shells are thick and hard to crack.

J. nigra. BLACK WALNUT. Zones 31, 32–43. Native from Massachusetts to Florida, west to Texas and Minnesota. Can reach 150 ft. tall (though often attains only half that height in gardens), with high-branched, oval- to round-headed habit. Furrowed blackish brown bark. Leaves have 15–23 leaflets, each 2½–5 in. long. Richly flavored nuts, 1–1½ in. across, are thick shelled and very hard. Some varieties, however, are easier to crack. Black walnut inhibits the growth of many other plants; consult your Cooperative Extension Office for a list of plants that will grow near it.

J. regia. ENGLISH WALNUT. Zones 32, 34–41, if cold-hardy strains are grown. Native to southwest Asia, southeast Europe. To 60 ft. high, with equal spread. Fast growing, especially when young. Trunk and heavy, horizontal or upward-angled branches are covered with smooth gray bark. Leaves have five to seven (rarely more) 3–6-in.-long leaflets. This species bears the familiar walnuts sold commercially; most are produced in California, Oregon, and Washington.

Many varieties are available; choosing the right one is critical. In most of the Northeast, choose a walnut described as Carpathian or Hardy Persian; most offered are seedlings, but grafted, named varieties exist. In areas with late frosts, get a variety that leafs out late and releases its pollen late, such as 'Hansen'. Check with your Cooperative Extension Office or a local nursery for best choices in your area.

WARMINSTER BROOM. See CYTISUS praecox

WASHINGTON THORN. See CRATAEGUS phaenopyrum

WATER AVENS. See GEUM rivale

WATERCRESS

Brassicaceae (Cruciferae)

PERENNIAL

Zones 31, 32, 34–35

Full sun or partial shade

Grows naturally in running streams

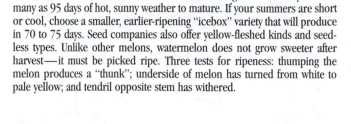
Watercress

To 10–15 in. high. Small, roundish leaflets are edible, with a sharp, spicy flavor. Flowers are insignificant. Can be started from seed or cuttings. Plant seed in flats or pots; transplant seedlings to wet place in garden or to a wet stream bank, where they will grow rapidly. Or insert cuttings of watercress from the market into wet soil or near a stream; these root readily. (If you intend to plant watercress near a stream, make sure the water is free from pollution before you set out plants.) You can also grow watercress in pots of soil placed in a tub of water; change water at least weekly by running a hose slowly into tub. Plants are more cold hardy in water.

WATER DRAGON. See SAURURUS cernuus

WATER HAWTHORN. See APONOGETON distachyus

WATER HYACINTH. See EICHHORNIA crassipes

WATER LILY. See NYMPHAEA

WATERMELON

Cucurbitaceae

ANNUAL

All zones

Full sun

Water most heavily when plants are young

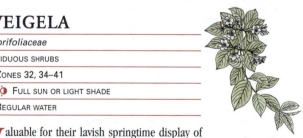
Watermelon

Needs a long growing season, more heat than most other melons, and more space than other vine crops—about 8 ft. by 8 ft. for each hill (circle of seed). Other

than that, culture is as described under Melon. Large varieties may need as many as 95 days of hot, sunny weather to mature. If your summers are short or cool, choose a smaller, earlier-ripening "icebox" variety that will produce in 70 to 75 days. Seed companies also offer yellow-fleshed kinds and seedless types. Unlike other melons, watermelon does not grow sweeter after harvest—it must be picked ripe. Three tests for ripeness: thumping the melon produces a "thunk"; underside of melon has turned from white to pale yellow; and tendril opposite stem has withered.

WATSONIA

Iridaceae

PERENNIALS

31, 32, OR ALL ZONES, DIG AND STORE

Full sun

Regular water

Watsonia

Native to South Africa. Somewhat similar to gladiolus, but flowers are smaller and more tubular, appearing on taller, branched stems. Narrow leaves to 2½ ft. long. Good cut flowers. Where hardy, leave undisturbed for many years, allowing large clumps to form. Divide only when quality declines. Elsewhere, dig in fall and store indoors over winter.

W. beatricis. Zone 31, warmer parts of 32. Bright apricot red, 3-in. flowers on somewhat branched, 3½-ft. stems in summer. Selected hybrids come in colors from peach to nearly scarlet.

W. pyramidata. Rose pink to rose red, 2½-in. flowers in spikelike clusters on branched, 4–6-ft. stems, late spring–early summer. Many excellent large-flowered hybrids in pink, white, lavender, and red. Needs regular water during growth and bloom; can tolerate it during dormant season if soil is well drained. In cold climates, dig corms after foliage dies down; replant in early spring.

WAX MYRTLE. See MYRICA

WAX VINE. See SENECIO macroglossus

WAYFARING TREE. See VIBURNUM lantana

WEIGELA

Caprifoliaceae

DECIDUOUS SHRUBS

Zones 32, 34–41

Full sun or light shade

Regular water

Weigela

Valuable for their lavish springtime display of funnel-shaped, 1-in.-long flowers. When weigelas finish blooming, their charm fades; they aren't attractive out of bloom. Most are rather stiff, coarse-leafed plants, becoming rangy unless pruned. No real fall color.

After flowering, cut back branches that have bloomed to unflowered side branches. Leave only one or two of these to each stem. Cut some of the oldest stems to ground. Thin new suckers to a few of the most vigorous. A simpler method you can employ every other year is to cut back entire plant about halfway just after blooms fade. Resulting dense new growth will provide plenty of flowers the next spring. Use as backgrounds for flower border, as summer screen, in mixed shrub border.

W. florida (W. rosea). Fast growth to 6–10 ft. tall, 9–12 ft. wide, with branches often arching to the ground. Leaves 2–4½ in. long, half as wide. Pink to rose red flowers are borne singly or in short clusters all along previous season's shoots. The many varieties and hybrids include:

'Bristol Ruby'. To 6–7 ft. tall and nearly as wide, with ruby red flowers. Some repeat bloom in midsummer and fall.

'Candida' ('Alba'). To 5 ft. tall, with white flowers tinged green.

'Java Red'. Compact growth to 2½–4 ft. Deep red flowers and red-tinted deep green foliage.

'Minuet'. Dwarf (to 2–3 ft. high), with purplish leaves and flowers that blend red, purple, and yellow.

'Newport Red' ('Vanicekii', 'Cardinal', 'Rhode Island Red'). To 6 ft. tall, with brilliant red flowers. Young stems are bright green in winter.

'Pink Delight'. Compact growth to 3–4 ft. tall. Deep pink flowers.

'Pink Princess'. Loose, open habit to 6 ft. tall. Lilac pink blossoms.

'Red Prince'. To 6 ft. tall, with nonfading red flowers; some rebloom in late summer.

'Variegata'. Compact growth to 4–6 ft. tall. Deep rosy red flowers; bright green leaves edged pale yellow to creamy white. Popular and showy.

W. middendorffiana. Dense, broad plant to 3–4 ft. tall. Dark green, wrinkled leaves 2–3 in. long, half as wide. Sulfur yellow flowers with orange markings are clustered at ends of branches. Best in cool, moist place; less rugged than other weigelas.

W. praecox. Similar to *W. florida*, but blooms several weeks earlier and grows to about 6 ft. tall. Pink to rose flowers with yellow throats.

WELSH POPPY. See MECONOPSIS cambrica

WESTERN RED CEDAR. See THUJA plicata

WESTERN SAND CHERRY. See PRUNUS besseyi

WHEEL TREE. See TROCHODENDRON aralioides

WHITE BACHELOR'S BUTTON. See RANUNCULUS aconitifolius 'Flore Pleno'

WHITEBEAM. See SORBUS aria

WHITE CEDAR. See CHAMAECYPARIS thyoides

WHITE CLOVER, WHITE DUTCH CLOVER. See TRIFOLIUM repens

WHITE KERRIA. See RHODOTYPOS scandens

WHITE MUGWORT. See ARTEMISIA lactiflora

WILD GINGER. See ASARUM

WILD INDIGO. See BAPTISIA

WILD MANDRAKE. See PODOPHYLLUM peltatum

WILD MARJORAM. See ORIGANUM vulgare

WILD PLUM. See PRUNUS americana

WILLOW. See SALIX

WINDFLOWER. See ANEMONE

WINDMILL PALM. See TRACHYCARPUS fortunei

WINTER ACONITE. See ERANTHIS hyemalis

WINTERBERRY. See ILEX verticillata

WINTER CREEPER. See EUONYMUS fortunei

WINTERGREEN. See GAULTHERIA procumbens

WINTER HAZEL. See CORYLOPSIS

WINTERSWEET. See CHIMONANTHUS praecox

WISHBONE FLOWER. See TORENIA fournieri

FOR GROWING SYMBOL EXPLANATIONS

PLEASE SEE PAGE 113

WISTERIA

Fabaceae (Leguminosae)

DECIDUOUS VINES

ZONES VARY BY SPECIES

FULL SUN, EXCEPT AS NOTED

WATER YOUNG ONES WELL, OLDER ONES LESS

Wisteria

Twining, woody vines of great size, long life, and exceptional beauty in flower. So adaptable they can be grown as trees, shrubs, or vines. All have large bright green leaves divided into many leaflets, spectacular clusters of blue, white, or pinkish blossoms, and velvety, pealike pods to about 6 in. long. Fall color subdued, in yellow shades. Plants are not fussy about soil, but need good drainage; in alkaline soil, watch for chlorosis and treat with iron chelates or iron sulfate.

Pruning and training are important for control of size and shape and for bloom production. Let newly planted wisteria grow to establish framework you desire, either single-trunked or multitrunked. Remove stems that interfere with desired framework and pinch back side stems and long streamers. For single-trunked form, rub off buds that develop on trunk. For multiple trunks, select as many vigorous stems as you wish and let them develop; if plant has only one stem, pinch it back to encourage others to develop. Remember that main stem will become good-size trunk, and that weight of mature vine is considerable. Any support structure should be sturdy and durable; do not use a tree as a support.

Tree wisterias can be bought already trained; or you can train your own. Remove all but one main stem and stake this one securely. Tie stem to stake at frequent intervals, using plastic tape to prevent girdling. When plant has reached height at which you wish head to form, pinch or prune out tip to force branching. Shorten branches to beef them up. Pinch back long streamers and rub off all buds that form below head. Replace stakes and ties as needed. Wisterias can be trained as big shrubs or multistemmed, small, semiweeping trees; permit well-spaced branches to form the framework, shorten side branches, and nip long streamers. Unsupported plants make vigorous bank cover.

In general, wisterias do not need fertilizer. Prune blooming plants every winter: cut back or thin out side shoots from main or structural stems, and shorten back to two or three buds the flower-producing spurs that grow from these shoots. You'll have no trouble recognizing fat flower buds on these spurs.

In summer, cut back long streamers before they tangle up in main body of vine; save those you want to use to extend height or length of vine and tie them to support—eaves, wall, trellis, arbor. If old plants grow rampantly but fail to bloom, withhold all nitrogen fertilizers for an entire growing season (buds for the next season's bloom are started in early summer). If that fails to produce bloom the next year, you can try pruning roots in spring—after you're sure no flowers will be produced—by cutting vertically with spade into plant's root zone.

W. brachybotrys (W. venusta). SILKY WISTERIA. Zones 32, 34, 35, 37, 39. Often sold as *W. b.* 'Alba'. Silky-haired leaves 8–14 in. long, divided into 9–13 leaflets. Flowers are white, very large, long-stalked, slightly fragrant, in short (4–6-in.) clusters that open all at once during leaf-out. 'Violacea' has purple-blue flowers. Older plants (especially in tree form) bloom remarkably profusely.

W. floribunda. JAPANESE WISTERIA. Zones 31, 32, 34–41. Leaves are 12–16 in. long, divided into 15–19 leaflets. Fragrant, 1½-ft. clusters of violet or violet-blue flowers appear during leaf-out. Clusters open gradually, starting from the base; this prolongs bloom season but makes for a less spectacular burst of color than that provided by Chinese wisteria. Many varieties are sold in white, pink, and shades of blue, purple, and lavender, usually marked with yellow and white. 'Longissima' ('Macrobotrys') has long (1½–3-ft.) clusters of violet flowers. 'Longissima Alba' bears white flowers in 2-ft. clusters; 'Ivory Tower' is similar. 'Rosea' is a good lavender pink variety. 'Plena' has very full clusters of double flowers in deep blue violet. 'Texas Purple' blooms at an early age.

W

W. frutescens. AMERICAN WISTERIA. Zones 31, 32, 34. Native from Virginia to Florida and Texas. Leaves 7–12 in. long, divided into 9–15 leaflets. Less vigorous, thinner stems, later bloom, smaller pods than the other species. Fragrant, pale lilac flowers marked with yellow blotch appear in dense, 4–6-in.-long clusters in late spring–summer after leaf-out; blossoms are followed by 2–4-in. pods. White-flowered 'Nivea' blooms a little earlier than the species.

W. sinensis. CHINESE WISTERIA. Zones 31, 32, 34–35, 37, 39. Leaves are 10–12 in. long, divided into 7–13 leaflets. Plants bloom before leaves expand in spring. Clusters of violet-blue, slightly fragrant flowers are shorter (to 1 ft.) than those of Japanese wisteria, but make quite a show by opening all at once nearly all along the cluster. 'Alba' is a white-flowered form. 'Caroline' and 'Cooke's Special' are grafted forms. Plants will bloom in sun or considerable shade.

WITCH HAZEL. See HAMAMELIS

WOADWAXEN. See GENISTA tinctoria

WOODBINE. See LONICERA periclymenum

WOOD FERN. See DRYOPTERIS

WOOD HYACINTH. See HYACINTHOIDES non-scripta

WOODRUFF, SWEET. See GALIUM odoratum

WOODSIA obtusa

BLUNT-LOBED WOODSIA, COMMON WOODSIA

Thelypteridaceae (Polypodiaceae)

FERN

⚡ ZONES 31, 32, 34 –43

☼ ◑ FULL SUN OR LIGHT SHADE

🌢 REGULAR WATER

Woodsia obtusa

Small deciduous fern. Fronds 12–15 in. long, 4 in. wide, bright green in shade, gray green in sun. May be once-cut (into deeply lobed segments) or twice-cut. Fronds are produced throughout the growing season. Likes well-drained soil that is neutral or even slightly alkaline. Use in woodland or rock garden.

WOOD SORREL. See OXALIS acetosella

WOODWARDIA

CHAIN FERN

Blechnaceae (Polypodiaceae)

DECIDUOUS ferns

⚡ ZONES 31, 32, 34–41

◑ PART SHADE, EXCEPT AS NOTED

🌢 AMPLE WATER

Woodwardia

Medium to large, usually coarse-textured ferns with rich green fronds. Name comes from chainlike pattern of spore cases beneath frond segments. Most like shade beneath canopy of tall trees, but some will withstand full sun if roots are kept wet.

W. areolata. Native to eastern and southeastern U.S. To 2½ ft. high, with deeply lobed fronds, the lobes finely toothed. Spore-bearing fronds are narrower. Can take considerable sun.

W. virginica. Native to eastern and southern U.S. To 1–2 ft. tall, with twice-cut fronds that are bronzy green when they emerge. Likes wet soil and can even grow with roots submerged.

WORMWOOD. See ARTEMISIA

XANTHOCERAS
sorbifolium

YELLOWHORN

Sapindaceae

DECIDUOUS SHRUB OR SMALL TREE

⚡ ZONES 31, 32, 34–41

☼ FULL SUN

🌢 REGULAR WATER

Xanthoceras sorbifolium

Little-known plant worthy of greater garden use. Usually seen as a multistemmed shrub 8–10 ft. tall, but can attain stature of a small tree (20–25 ft.). Leaves are 1 ft. long, with many narrow, toothed dark green leaflets; they hang on late in fall. White, 1-in.-wide flowers appear in spring, clustered at branch ends or in joints of uppermost leaves; throat of each blossom has a yellow blotch that darkens to red. Flowers are followed by leathery, 2-in. pods filled with dark seeds; seeds are reminiscent of buckeyes. Tolerates windy conditions, some drought. Yellowhorn needs summer heat for good growth and bloom. Propagate by seed or root cuttings.

XANTHORHIZA
simplicissima

YELLOWROOT

Ranunculaceae

DECIDUOUS SHRUB

⚡ ZONES 31, 32, 34–43

☼ ◑ ● SUN OR SHADE

🌢 🌢 🌢 AMPLE TO MODERATE WATER

Xanthorhiza simplicissima

Native to eastern U.S. Thicket-forming ground cover to 2–3 ft. high. Lacy, celerylike leaves usually divided into five toothed leaflets to 2½ in. long. Foliage is shiny bright green in summer, golden yellow and orange in autumn; drops fairly late. Roots and inner bark are yellow. Nodding clusters of tiny, star-shaped purplish flowers before spring leaf-out are attractive though not showy.

Extremely cold hardy. Prefers moist, well-drained, slightly acid soil, but tolerates heavy soils and dry sandy soils. Spreads fastest in damp, shady places; thrives along stream banks. Rejuvenate an overgrown planting by cutting it to the ground in spring. Plant root divisions in spring or fall. No serious pests or diseases.

XERANTHEMUM annuum

COMMON IMMORTELLE

Asteraceae (Compositae)

ANNUAL

⚡ ALL ZONES

☼ FULL SUN

🌢 REGULAR WATER

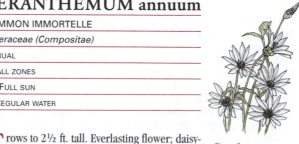
Xeranthemum annuum

Grows to 2½ ft. tall. Everlasting flower; daisy-like heads of papery bracts to 1½ in. across in pink, lavender, white, shades of purple. Scant foliage is silvery green. Sow seed directly in the ground in spring for summer to fall bloom. Accepts almost any soil. Cut flowers can be dried for use in winter bouquets.

X

YUCCA

Agavaceae

EVERGREEN PERENNIALS, SHRUBS, TREES

⚡ ZONES VARY BY SPECIES; OR INDOORS

☼ FULL SUN

💧 WATER NEEDS VARY BY SPECIES

Yucca

Yuccas grow over much of North America, and hardiness depends on species. All have tough, sword-shaped leaves and large clusters of white or whitish, rounded to bell-shaped flowers. Some are stemless, while others reach tree size. Best in well-drained soil.

Group with agaves, cacti, or succulents, or grow with various softer-leaved tropical foliage plants. Taller kinds make striking silhouettes, and even stemless species provide important vertical effects when in bloom. Some have stiff, sharp-pointed leaves; keep these away from walks, terraces, and other well-traveled areas. (Some people clip off the sharp tips with nail clippers.)

Young plants of some species can be used as indoor plants. They withstand dry indoor atmosphere and will grow well in hot, sunny windows. Buy gallon-can size or smaller; set out in garden ground when plants become too large for the house. Successful indoors are *Y. filamentosa, Y. gloriosa, Y. recurvifolia.*

Y. filamentosa. ADAM'S NEEDLE. Zones 31, 32, 34–43. Native to southeastern U.S. Stemless. Stiff leaves grow to 2½ ft. long, 1 in. wide, with long, loose fibers at edges. Blooms late spring to summer; yellowish white, 2–3-in.-wide flowers, lightly fragrant in the evening, are carried in tall, narrow clusters to 4–7 ft. or taller. Similar in appearance to *Y. flaccida* and *Y. smalliana.* One of the hardiest, most widely planted yuccas in colder regions. Varieties include 'Concava Variegata', with cream-edged leaves tinted pink in cold weather; 'Ivory Tower', with outfacing rather than drooping flowers; 'Bright Edge', with leaves edged in yellow; and 'Garland Gold', with leaves having a broad gold center stripe. Regular water.

Y. flaccida. Zones 31, 32, 34–43. Native to southeastern U.S. Stemless. Differs from *Y. filamentosa* in having less rigid leaves, straight fibers on leaf edges, and somewhat shorter flower clusters. Regular water.

Y. glauca. SOAPWEED. Zones 35, 41, 43. Native to central and southwestern U.S. Stiff, narrow, 1–2½-ft.-long leaves form a clump 3–4 ft. wide. Stem is low or prostrate. Leaves are grayish green, edged with a hairline of white and a few thin threads. White summer flowers bloom on a spike 4–5 ft. tall. Regular water.

Y. gloriosa. SPANISH DAGGER, SOFT-TIP YUCCA. Zones 31, 32. Native to southeastern U.S. Generally multitrunked to 10 ft. tall. In colder part of range, plant is usually stemless. Leaf points are soft and will not penetrate skin. Summer bloom. Good green color blends well with tropical-looking, lush plants. Needs regular water, but too much moisture may produce black areas on leaf margins.

Y. recurvifolia (Y. pendula). Zones 31, 32. Native to southeastern U.S. Single, unbranched trunk to 6–10 ft. tall; may be lightly branched in age. Can be cut back to keep single trunked. Spreads by offsets to make large groups. Beautiful blue-gray-green leaves are 2–3 ft. long, 2 in. wide, sharply bent downward. Leaf tips are spined but bend to the touch; they are not dangerous. Less stiff and metallic looking than most yuccas. Large white flowers in late spring or early summer are borne in loose, open clusters 3–5 ft. tall. Easy to grow under all garden conditions where hardy.

Y. smalliana. ADAM'S NEEDLE, BEAR'S GRASS. Zones 31, 32, 34–43. Native to southeastern and south-central U.S. Similar to *Y. filamentosa*, but has narrower, thinner, flatter leaves and smaller individual flowers. Regular water.

ZAMIA

Zamiaceae (Cycadaceae)

CYCADS

⚡ ALL ZONES, INDOORS

☼ FILTERED SHADE

💧 REGULAR WATER

Zamia

Of 100 or so species, only the following two are often seen. They have short trunks usually marked with scars from old leaf bases; trunks may be completely or partially buried. Circular crowns of leaves resemble stiff fern fronds or small palm fronds. In the Northeast, zamias are grown as houseplants and need strong interior light. Slow growing and costly, but will last many years with good care.

Z. furfuracea. CARDBOARD PALM. Native to Mexico. Short, sometimes subterranean trunk. Fronds up to 3 ft. long (usually much less) with as many as 12 pairs (usually fewer) of extremely stiff, leathery, dark green leaflets to 4½ in. long, 1½ in. wide. Leaflets may have a few teeth toward the tip.

Z. pumila (Z. floridana). COONTIE. Native to Florida, Cuba, West Indies. Short trunk is largely below soil level. Fronds to 3 ft. long, with as many as 30 pairs of dark green leaflets. Leaflets grow to 5 in long, are narrower than those of *Z. furfuracea.*

ZANTEDESCHIA

CALLA

Araceae

RHIZOMES

⚡ ALL ZONES; GROW IN POTS

☼◐ PARTIAL SHADE IN HOT AREAS

💧 WATER NEEDS VARY BY TYPE

Zantedeschia

Native to South Africa. Basal clumps of long-stalked, shiny, rich green, narrow- or lance-shaped leaves, sometimes spotted white. Flower bract (spathe) surrounds central spike (spadix) that is tightly covered with tiny true flowers.

Common calla (*Z. aethiopica*) is basically evergreen, going only partly dormant even in colder parts of range. It is soil tolerant and will thrive in moist, even boggy, soil all year. Grown as a container plant throughout the Northeast. Alternatively, you can dig garden-planted rhizomes in fall and pot them up for winter storage indoors. It does not like being stored; keep soil slightly moist and do not let it dry out completely. Gardeners in Zones 31, 32 often succeed with this species in the ground.

The other species described here die to the ground yearly. They need slightly acid soil and regular water during growth and bloom, followed by a resting period in which, ideally, water is withheld. Store potted rhizomes dry in their containers. Start rhizomes indoors and plant outdoors when frost danger is past in spring. Set rhizomes of common calla 4–6 in. deep, those of other species 2 in. deep.

Z. aethiopica. COMMON CALLA. Forms large clump of unspotted deep green leaves 1½ ft. long, 10 in. wide. Pure white or creamy white, 8-in.-

long spathes on 3-ft. stems appear mostly in spring and early summer. 'Green Goddess' is a robust variety with large spathes that are white at the base, green toward the tip. 'Hercules', larger than species, has big spathes that open flat, curve backward. 'Childsiana' is 1 ft. tall. 'Minor' grows 1½ ft. tall, with 4-in. spathes.

Z. elliottiana. GOLDEN CALLA. To 1½–2 ft., with bright green, white-spotted leaves 10 in. long, 6 in. wide. Spathes 4–5 in. long, changing from greenish yellow to rich golden yellow, late spring or early summer. Tolerates full sun, even in hot-summer areas.

Z. rehmannii. RED or PINK CALLA. To 1–1½ ft., with narrow, lance-shaped, unspotted green leaves 1 ft. long. Pink or rosy pink spathes to 4 in. long in spring. 'Superba', a deeper pink, improved variety, is generally sold rather than species. Hybrids of this and other calla lily species are available; flower colors range through pinks and yellows to orange and buff tones, with some purplish and lavender tones on yellow grounds.

ZANTHOXYLUM

Rutaceae

DECIDUOUS SHRUBS OR SMALL TREES

ZONES VARY BY SPECIES

FULL SUN

REGULAR WATER

Zanthoxylum

Z. americanum. Tree or shrub. Zones 32, 34–45. Native to eastern North America. Spreading, to 25 ft. tall. Medium green leaves to 1 ft. long, divided into pairs of oval to oblong leaflets. Aromatic bark. Small yellow-green flowers in spring, followed by bumpy, rounded red fruit.

Z. piperitum. JAPAN PEPPER. Shrub. Zones 31, 32, 34, 39. Native to China, Japan, Korea. Compact, dense growth to 8–20 ft. tall. Handsome dark green leaves 3–6 in. long, divided into 11–23 oval, 2-in.-long leaflets; may turn yellow in autumn. Flat, ½-in.-long spines grow in pairs along stems. Green flowers are inconspicuous. Small, aromatic red fruits have black seeds that are pulverized and used as a seasoning in Japan. Leaves have a peppery flavor, slightly numbing to the tongue; they too are used in Japanese cuisine, typically as a garnish floating on soups. Used this way, they are called sansho.

Z. simulans. PRICKLY ASH. Shrub or tree. Zones 31, 32, 34–41. Native to China, Taiwan, and Japan. Spreading, to 20 ft., with spines. Dark green leaves to 8 in. long, divided into oval, toothed leaflets, turn yellow to reddish in autumn. Tiny green flowers in summer are followed by bumpy, round red fruit.

ZELKOVA

Ulmaceae

DECIDUOUS TREES

ZONES 31, 32, 34–41

FULL SUN

REGULAR TO MODERATE WATER

Zelkova

Closely related to elms and sometimes used as a substitute for the ill-fated American elm, which has fallen victim to Dutch elm disease. (Zelkova, too, can get the disease, but the infection is rarely fatal.) Good shade trees, with colorful autumn foliage.

Z. serrata. SAWLEAF ZELKOVA. Native to Japan, Taiwan, and South Korea. Grows at a moderate to fast rate, eventually reaching a height and spread of 60 ft. or more. Silhouette ranges from urn shaped to quite spreading. Like beech, zelkova has smooth gray bark; on old trees, bark often flakes off to reveal orange patches. Leaves are 2–3½ in. long, 1½ in. wide, similar to those of elm but rougher in texture, with sawtooth margins. Fall foliage color varies from yellow to dark red to dull reddish

brown. Nurseries offer several selections that approach the vase shape of American elm; of these, 'Halka' is the fastest growing and the best elm mimic. 'Green Vase' has a narrower vase shape than the vigorous 'Village Green'.

Z. sinica. Native to China. Broad and upright, 40–50 ft. tall, may be multitrunked. Peeling bark is mottled gray, orange, and brown. Dark green, oval, toothed leaves to 4½ in. long turn yellow or orange in fall. Zelkovas take wide range of soils. Water deeply to encourage deep rooting; established trees are fairly tolerant of drought, wind. You will need to train and prune young trees to establish a good framework; thin out crowded ascending branches. Foliage may be visited by Japanese beetles and by elm leaf beetles if local elms have died.

ZENOBIA pulverulenta (Andromeda speciosa)

Ericaceae

SEMIEVERGREEN TO DECIDUOUS SHRUB

ZONES 31, 32, 34–41

PARTIAL SHADE

AMPLE WATER

Zenobia pulverulenta

Native from North Carolina to Florida. Slow growth to 2–4 ft. or possibly 6 ft. tall, with open, loose, arching habit. Pale green leaves are 1–2 in. long, half as wide; new growth heavily dusted with bluish white powder for a pearly gray effect. Fall foliage is yellowish with a red tinge. White, bell-shaped, ½-in.-wide, anise-scented flowers bloom in loose clusters at ends of branches, late spring to early summer. Sometimes spreads by underground stems. Related to heaths and heathers; needs well-drained, acid soil.

ZEPHYRANTHES

ZEPHYR FLOWER, FAIRY LILY

Amaryllidaceae

BULBS

ALL ZONES; GROW IN POTS

FULL SUN

REGULAR WATER DURING GROWTH AND BLOOM

Zephyranthes

Clumps of grassy leaves give rise to slender, hollow stems, each bearing a single funnel-shaped flower with six segments. Flowers of some kinds resemble lilies; those of other types look like crocuses. In the wild, flowers bloom after a rain (hence another common name, "rain lily"), and they may appear in the garden after a good soaking.

Need little care. Pretty in rock garden or foreground of border. Excellent pot plant for patio or greenhouse. Plant in late summer or early fall; set bulbs 1–2 in. deep. Container plants bloom better when somewhat pot-bound.

Z. atamasco. Hardy outdoors in Zone 31, warmer parts of 32; mulch over winter. Elsewhere, bring container plants indoors for winter and keep soil just slightly moist. Native to southeastern U.S. Semievergreen leaves to 1½ ft. long, ¼ in. wide. Pink-striped buds open to fragrant, crocuslike, pure white blossoms in midspring.

Z. candida. Zones 31, 32. Large clumps of glossy evergreen leaves to 1 ft. long. Glossy-textured, crocuslike flowers are 2 in. long, pure white outside, tinged rose inside, borne singly on stems as long as leaves. Blooms in late summer, early fall.

Z. hybrids. Zones 31, warmer parts of 32. Most widely offered is *Z. ajax* (a cross between *Z. candida* and *Z. citrina*), a free-flowering plant with light yellow blossoms. Other hybrids available from mail-order specialists include 'Alamo', with deep rose pink flowers flushed yellow;

Z

'Apricot Queen', yellow flowers stained pink; 'Prairie Sunset', large light yellow flowers suffused with pink; and 'Ruth Page', rich pink blooms.

ZEPHYR FLOWER. See ZEPHYRANTHES

Zingiberaceae. The ginger family contains tropical or subtropical perennials with fleshy rhizomes and canelike stems clothed with sheathing leaf stalks; usually bear large leaves. Flowers are irregular in form, in spikes or heads, often showy or with showy bracts. Many are aromatic or have fragrant flowers. Includes *Alpinia*, ginger lily (*Costus, Hedychium*), and true ginger (*Zingiber*).

ZINGIBER officinale

TRUE GINGER

Zingiberaceae

PERENNIAL WITH THICK RHIZOMES

🗲 ALL ZONES; GROW IN POTS

◑ PARTIAL SHADE

🌢 WATER HEAVILY AFTER GROWTH STARTS

Zingiber officinale

Rhizomes are the source of ginger used in cooking. Stems 2–4 ft. tall. Narrow, glossy bright green leaves to 1 ft. long. Summer flowers (rarely seen) are yellowish green, with purple lip marked yellow; not especially showy. Ginger needs heat and humidity. Buy roots (fresh, not dried) at grocery store in early spring; cut into 1–2-in.-long sections with well-developed growth buds. Let cut ends dry, then plant just below surface of rich, moist soil; pot culture is common. Water cautiously until top and root growth are active. Feed once a month. Plants are dormant in winter; keep indoors and reduce watering so soil is just slightly moist. Harvest roots at any time—but allow several months for them to reach some size.

ZINNIA

Asteraceae (Compositae)

ANNUALS

🗲 ALL ZONES

☼ FULL SUN

🌢 REGULAR WATER, EXCEPT AS NOTED

Zinnia

Long-time garden favorites for colorful, round flower heads in summer and early fall. Hotweather plants, they do not gain from being planted early, but merely stand still until weather warms up. Subject to mildew in foggy places, if leaves are habitually wet at night, and when autumn brings longer nights, more dew and shade. Sow seeds where plants are to grow (or set out nursery plants) May to July. Give good garden soil and feed generously. Most garden zinnias belong to *Z. elegans*.

Z. angustifolia (Z. linearis). Annual. Compact plants to 16 in. tall. Leaves very narrow. Inch-wide flower heads are orange; each ray has a paler stripe. Blooms in 6 weeks from seed, continues late into fall. 'Classic' grows 8–12 in. tall, to 2 ft. wide. There are also white and yellow forms. Good in hanging baskets.

Z. elegans. Annual. Plant height ranges from 1–3 ft., leaves to 5 in., flower head size from less than 1 in. to as much as 5–7 in. across. Forms include full doubles, cactus flowered (with quilled rays), and crested (cushion center surrounded by rows of broad rays); colors include white, pink, salmon, rose, red, yellow, orange, lavender, purple, and green.

Many strains are available, from dwarf plants with small flowers to 3-ft. sorts with large blooms. The Mini series and Thumbelina strain are extra-

dwarf types (to 6 in. tall). Other small-flowered kinds on larger (1-ft.) but still compact plants are Cupid and Buttons; still taller (to 2 ft.) but small flowered are the Lilliputs. Dreamland and Peter Pan strains have 3-in. blooms on bushy dwarf plants to 1 ft.; Whirligig has large bicolored flowers on 1½-ft. plants. Large-flowered strains with 2–3-ft. plants include Border Beauty, Burpeeana California Giants, Dahlia-flowered, Giant Cactus–flowered, Ruffles, State Fair, and Zenith. 'Rose Pinwheel', with single daisy-type rose pink flowers, is a 1½–2-ft.-tall hybrid.

Z. grandiflora. Perennial grown as annual in the Northeast. Native to high plains, the Southwest, Mexico. To 10 in. tall, spreading by seeds or runners. Leaves to 1 in. long, ⅛ in. wide. Flower heads are 1½ in. wide, bright yellow with orange eye. In its native range, it will bloom spring to fall if watered during dry season. Very drought tolerant once established.

Z. haageana. Annual. Plants compact, 1–1½ ft. tall; narrow, 3-in. leaves. Double strains Persian Carpet (1 ft. tall) and Old Mexico (16 in. tall) have flowers in mahogany red, yellow, and orange, usually mixed in the same flower head. Colorful, long blooming.

ZIZIPHUS jujuba

CHINESE JUJUBE

Rhamnaceae

DECIDUOUS SHRUB OR SMALL TREE

🗲 ZONES 31, 32, 34, 39

☼ FULL SUN

🌢 MODERATE WATER

Ziziphus jujuba

Slow to moderate growth to eventual 20–30 ft. tall, with rounded habit. Usually grown as tree, but sometimes seen as large shrub. Spiny, gnarled, somewhat pendulous branches. Glossy bright green, 1–2-in.-long leaves with three prominent veins. Foliage may turn a good yellow in autumn. Clusters of small yellowish flowers bloom in late spring; these are followed in fall by shiny, reddish brown, ½–2-in.-long fruits with a sweet, applelike flavor. Candied and dried, fruits resemble dates. Two thornless, grafted varieties: 'Lang' (1½–2-in. fruits, bears young); 'Li' (2-in. fruits).

Very decorative, but also tough—withstands drought, heat, saline and alkaline soils. Grows better in good garden soil. Thrives in lawns. Prune in winter to shape, encourage weeping habit, or reduce size.

ZOYSIA

Poaceae (Gramineae)

PERENNIAL GRASSES

🗲 ZONES 31, 32, 34, 39

☼◑ THRIVE IN SUN, TOLERATE SOME SHADE

🌢 REGULAR WATER

Zoysia

They tend to spread slowly, are fairly deep rooted. Dormant and straw colored during the winter; turn green in spring. Use for lawns, ground covers. Plant using sod, sprigs, stolons, or plugs. (Stolons give much faster cover than plugs.) Mow lawns ¾ in. high.

Z. 'Emerald'. EMERALD ZOYSIA. Hybrid between *Z. japonica* and *Z. tenuifolia*. Wiry, dark green, prickly-looking turf; hard to cut.

Z. japonica 'Meyer'. MEYER ZOYSIA. Resembles bluegrass. Turns brown earliest in winter, turns green latest in spring.

Z. matrella. MANILA GRASS. Also similar to bluegrass in appearance. Holds color a little better than Meyer zoysia.

Z. tenuifolia. KOREAN GRASS. Creeping, fine textured, bumpy. Makes a beautiful grassy meadow or gives mossy Oriental effect in areas impossible to mow or water often.

ZUCCHINI. See SQUASH

Z

PRACTICAL GARDENING DICTIONARY

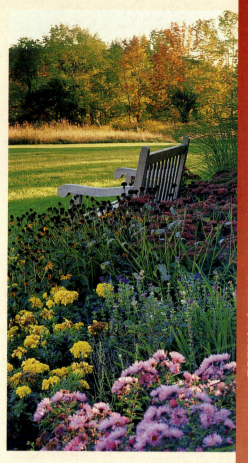

Success in gardening, as in any other endeavor, involves an understanding of certain basic principles and procedures. In the pages that follow, you'll find the fundamental information and step-by-step instructions you need to plant and care for your garden. The Practical Gardening Dictionary begins with a glossary that defines words that you will encounter throughout these pages and throughout the gardening world. Following the glossary, arranged in an easy-to-use alphabetical format, an illustrated guide offers advice on topics such as making compost, choosing and using fertilizers, plant propagation and planting techniques, pruning, soil management, watering and water conservation, and buying and caring for tools. You'll also find help in dealing with garden problems—diseases, insects, animal pests, and weeds—based on the principles of Integrated Pest Management, with emphasis on the least toxic means of control. Look to these pages, too, for information on selecting and growing all the major categories of plants, from annuals and biennials through ornamental grasses and perennials to shrubs, trees, vegetables, and vines.

Use the following guide to help you locate topics of interest:

Glossary

Acid soil. A soil with a pH below 7.

Alkaline soil. A soil with a pH above 7.

Alternate leaves. See Opposite leaves.

Annual. A plant that completes its life cycle in one year or less.

Anther. See *Flower*.

Axil. The inner angle between a leaf (or other organ of a plant) and the stem from which it springs. Organs in the axil, such as flowers and buds, are called axillary.

Balled-and-burlapped (B-and-B). Refers to specimen shrubs and trees sold for planting with a large ball of soil around the roots, wrapped in burlap or a synthetic material to hold the soil together. Usually available from late fall to early spring.

Bare-root. Refers to deciduous shrubs and trees and some perennials sold for planting with the soil removed from their roots. Usually sold in winter and early spring.

Bedding plant. Any plant suitable for massing in beds for its colorful flowers or foliage. Most bedding plants are annuals or perennials that are grown as annuals.

Biennial. A plant that germinates and produces foliage and roots during its first growing season, then blooms, produces seed, and dies during its second growing season.

Bolt. To produce seeds or flowers prematurely; the term usually refers to annual flowers and vegetables. Bolting most frequently occurs when plants that prefer cool weather (lettuce, for example) are set out too late in the year or when unseasonably hot weather rushes growth.

Bracts. Modified leaves growing just below a flower or flower cluster; not all plants have them.

Broad-leafed. Used to describe evergreen shrubs or trees, this term refers to plants that have foliage year-round—boxwood and camellia, for example—but are not conifers (such as juniper), which have needlelike or scalelike leaves.

Bud. An undeveloped or rudimentary organ or shoot of a plant. A flower bud develops into a blossom, while a growth bud produces shoots or leafy growth. Terminal buds (also called apical buds) are produced at the end of a shoot. Lateral buds (also called axillary buds) are produced in the axil of a plant. Latent buds lie dormant beneath the bark; if a branch breaks or is cut off near a latent bud, that bud may develop into a new shoot.

Budding. A method of propagation in which a bud (the scion) from one plant is inserted beneath the bark of another related plant.

Bud union. The point at which a shoot or bud (scion) unites with the rootstock.

Bulb. In layman's terms, any plant that grows from a thickened underground structure may be referred to as a bulb. Botanically speaking, however, not all such underground structures are really bulbs. A true bulb consists of an underground stem base that contains an embryonic plant surrounded by scales—modified leaves that overlap each other. Bulblike structures include corms, rhizomes, tubers, and tuberous roots.

Calyx. See *Flower*.

Cane. An elongated flowering or fruiting stem, usually arising directly from the roots. Examples of cane-producing plants include barberry, forsythia, rose, raspberry, and grape.

Cane pruning. A method of pruning grapevines. See *Grape* in the A to Z Plant Encyclopedia.

Catkin. A slender, spikelike, often drooping flower cluster. Alder and birch are two familiar trees that bear catkins.

Chill requirement. Many bulbs, perennials, and deciduous shrubs and trees (fruit trees in particular) need a certain amount of cold weather to grow and bloom well in the following year. In mild-winter areas where these plants do not receive the necessary winter chill, their performance is often disappointing: they leaf out late, fail to flower or fruit well, and often decline in health and vigor. For certain such plants—apples and lilacs, for example—varieties have been developed that require less winter chill. In milder-winter areas, bulbs that require winter chilling can be stored in the vegetable bin of the refrigerator before planting; chill them for the length of time the supplier recommends.

Compound leaf. See *Leaf*.

Conifer. A more precise term for some of the plants many people simply call evergreens, such as cedar, juniper, and pine. Leaves of most are narrow and needlelike or tiny and scalelike. A few conifers, including larch and dawn redwood, are deciduous. All conifers bear seeds in cones or in modified conelike structures (juniper berries, for example). Yew and podocarpus bear single seeds on fleshy bases, but thanks to their needlelike foliage, they are sometimes grouped with conifers.

Corm. A swollen underground stem base composed of solid tissue (unlike the scales of a true bulb).

Corolla. See *Flower*.

Crown. This word has two meanings. A tree's crown is its entire branch structure, including foliage. "Crown" also refers to the point at which a plant's roots and top structure join, usually at or near the soil line.

Cultivar. This coined word is shorthand for "cultivated variety." Cultivars are genetically distinct plants, maintained in cultivation by human effort; they may be of hybrid origin or simply selected varieties of plants that occur in the wild. Cultivar names are enclosed in single quo-

tation marks and are not italicized, as in *Lobelia erinus* 'Crystal Palace'.

Deadhead. To remove spent flowers. By preventing a plant from setting seed, deadheading both prolongs the bloom season and eliminates unwanted seedlings. It also keeps the garden looking tidy.

Deciduous. This term describes any plant that naturally sheds all of its leaves at any one time (usually in fall).

Defoliation. Refers to the unnatural loss of foliage, usually to the detriment of the plant's health.

Dieback. This occurs when a plant's stems die for part of their length, beginning at the tips. Causes of dieback include inadequate moisture, nutrient deficiency, poor climate adaptation, and severe injury from pests or diseases.

Dormancy. The annual period when a plant's growth processes greatly slow down. For many plants, dormancy occurs with the onset of winter, as days grow shorter and temperatures colder.

Double flower. See *Flower forms*.

Drainage. The downward movement of water through the soil. When this process occurs quickly, the soil is well drained; when it occurs slowly, the soil is poorly drained.

Espalier. A tree or shrub trained so that its branches grow in a flat pattern—against a wall or fence, on a trellis, along horizontal wires.

Established plant. A plant that is firmly rooted and producing good foliage growth.

Evergreen. Unlike deciduous plants, evergreens never lose all their leaves at one time. See also Broad-leafed; Conifer.

Fertilization. The fusion of male and female gametes (fertile reproductive cells) following pollination.

Fertilize. To apply nutrients (fertilizer) to a plant.

Flower. The part of a seed-bearing plant that contains the reproductive organs.

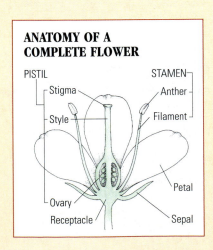

ANATOMY OF A COMPLETE FLOWER

PISTIL — STAMEN
— Stigma — Anther
— Style — Filament
— Ovary — Petal
— Receptacle — Sepal

Flower forms: single, semidouble, double.
The basic flower forms are single, with one row of petals containing the minimum number of petals for the blossoms of that particular species (usually four, five, or six); semidouble, with two or three times the minimum number of petals, usually in two or three rows; and double, with multitudinous densely packed petals that typically produce a rounded blossom shape.

Fruit. A general term used to describe the mature ovary of a plant, containing one to many seeds. Fruits may be soft and fleshy, as in the case of peaches or apples, or dry, like an acorn or dried pea pod.

Genus (plural: Genera). Plant families are subdivided into groups of more closely related plants called genera.

Harden off. To adapt a plant that has been grown indoors or in a greenhouse or other shelter to outdoor conditions. Over a week or more, the plant is exposed to increasing periods of time outside, so that when it is planted in the garden it can make the transition with a minimum of shock.

Hardy. In horticultural terms, a plant's hardiness is its resistance to, or tolerance of, frosts or freezing temperatures. The word does not mean tough, pest resistant, or disease resistant.

Herbaceous. The opposite of "woody," describes a plant with soft or fleshy (nonwoody) tissue. In the strictest sense, the term refers to plants that die to the ground each year and regrow stems the following growing season. Commonly, it refers to any nonwoody plant—annual, perennial, or bulb.

Humus. The soft brown or black substance formed in the last stages of decomposition of animal or vegetable matter.

Hybrid. A distinct plant resulting from a cross between two species, subspecies, varieties, cultivars, strains, or any combination of the above; or, less commonly, between two plants from different genera.

Inflorescence. A group of individual flowers borne on a single stem.

Leader. The central upward-growing stem of a single-trunked tree or shrub.

Leaf. The main photosynthetic organ of most plants. A simple leaf is a single unit, while a compound leaf is divided into separate segments called leaflets. In a palmately compound leaf, the leaflets grow from one point at the end of a stem. In a pinnately compound (once-divided) leaf, the leaflets are arranged along a central axis; a bipinnately compound leaf is twice pinnate or twice-divided.

Leaflet. A division or segment of a compound leaf. See *Leaf.*

Microclimate. The climate of a small area or locality (such as a backyard or even just a portion of it) as opposed to that of a larger region. Microclimates are determined by such factors as hills, hollows, and the location of houses and other structures.

Naturalize. To set out plants or bulbs randomly, without a precise pattern, and leave them in place to spread at will, as they would in the wild.

Node. The joint in a stem where a bud, branch, or leaf starts to grow. The area of stem between nodes is the internode.

Offset. A young plant that develops by natural vegetative reproduction, usually at or near the base of the parent plant.

Open-pollinated plants. Varieties or cultivars of plants produced from natural, random pollination.

Opposite leaves; alternate leaves. Leaves are opposite when they spring from opposite sides of the same node on a stem. Alternate leaves arise from opposite sides of different nodes.

Organic matter. Any material originating from a living organism—peat moss, ground bark, compost, or manure, for example—that can be dug into soil to improve its condition.

Ovary. See *Flower; Fruit.*

Peat moss. A highly water-retentive, spongy organic soil amendment, peat moss is the partially decomposed remains of any of several mosses. It increases soil acidity. Sphagnum peat moss is generally considered the highest in quality.

Perennial. A perennial is a nonwoody plant that lives for more than 2 years and sometimes for many years.

Petal. See *Flower.*

Pistil. See *Flower.*

Pollination. The transfer of pollen from the male reproductive organs to the female ones, which leads to fertilization and seed production.

Rhizome. A modified stem growing horizontally under or at the soil surface. It may be long and slender, as in some perennials (and in perennial weeds like blackberry), or thick and fleshy, as in many irises.

Root-bound. Plants suffer from this condition when they grow in the same container for too long. The roots become tangled and matted and grow in circles.

Rootstock. The part of a budded or grafted plant that furnishes the root system and sometimes part of the branch structure. Understock has the same meaning.

Runner. See *Stolon.*

Self-seed, self-sow. Refers to a plant shedding fertile seeds that produce seedlings, usually near the parent plant.

Species. Each genus is subdivided into groups of individuals called species. Each species is generally a distinct entity (though it may closely resemble other species in the genus), reproducing from seed with only a small amount of variation.

Spore. A simple type of reproductive cell capable of producing a new plant. Certain kinds of plants—including algae, fungi, mosses, and ferns—reproduce by spores.

Sport. A mutation: a spontaneous variation from the normal pattern. In horticulture, a sport is usually seen as a branch that differs notably from the rest of the plant.

Stamen. See *Flower.*

Standard. A plant trained to resemble a small tree, with a single, upright trunk topped by a rounded crown of foliage. In some standards, the trunk and top are joined by grafting. The "tree rose" is a familiar example of a standard.

Stolon. A stem that creeps along the soil surface, taking root at intervals and forming new plants where it roots. Bermuda grass spreads by stolons.

Sucker. In a grafted or budded plant, sucker growth originates from the rootstock rather than from the desired grafted or budded part of the plant.

Taproot. A thick central root that may penetrate deeply into the ground. In some plants, such as carrots and parsnips, taproots are storage organs.

Tender. The opposite of hardy plants, tender plants have a low tolerance for frost or freezing temperatures.

Tendrils. Specialized growths along the stems or at the ends of leaves on some vines. Tendrils wrap around supports, enabling the vine to climb.

Thin. With regard to pruning, to thin is to remove entire branches, large or small, back to the main trunk, a side branch, or the ground. Seedlings or developing fruits may also be thinned; in this case, the term refers to removing excess plants or fruits so that the remaining ones are spaced far enough apart to grow well.

Tuber. A swollen underground stem with multiple growth points scattered over its surface. The potato is a familiar example.

Underplanting. Planting one plant beneath another, such as setting out a ground cover under a tree.

Understock. See *Rootstock.*

Variegation. Striping, edging, or other markings in a color different from the primary color of a leaf or petal.

Water sprout. In trees, any strong vertical shoot growing from the main framework of trunk and branches is properly called a water sprout, though the word "sucker" may also be used.

Whorl. Three or more leaves, branches, or flowers growing in a circle from a node on a stem or trunk.

Woody. This word describes a plant with hardened (woody) stems or trunks. An herbaceous plant, in contrast, has soft stems.

A

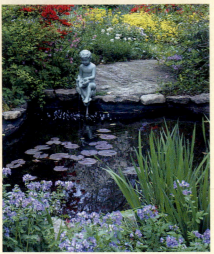

Successful gardens of every kind result from understanding basic gardening principles and procedures.

Practical Guide to
GARDENING

This section offers an introduction to the basic techniques of growing all sorts of plants. You will find information on annuals, bulbs, perennials, trees and shrubs, vegetables, and other plant categories. Look in the following pages for guidance on when to plant hardy and tender annuals, how to double-dig soil, how to take cuttings to propagate new plants, what to use to get rid of cucumber beetles, how to keep raccoons out of the garden, and lots more useful, hands-on information.

It is important to remember that gardening is an art, not a science, and that the best ways of doing things vary from one gardener to another. Each garden is a unique combination of soil, moisture, light, and temperatures, and growing conditions vary from year to year and place to place. Plants do not perform in exactly the same way in every garden, and the same horticultural techniques do not produce exactly the same results for every gardener.

Do not be afraid to experiment in your garden. Use the information in this section as a basic guide to good gardening practices, but feel free to modify the techniques according to what proves most effective for you. As you gain experience, you will learn what works best for you by a process of trial and error. There are no hard and fast rules in gardening. Part of the joy of gardening is the opportunity to observe and participate in the web of life that is a garden, and to try out different plants and gardening techniques. Use the information that follows as a solid foundation on which to build as you discover which techniques are most effective for you.

Annuals

Annuals are plants that germinate, grow shoots and leaves, flower, set seed, and die within a period of less than a year. Biennials (page 453), in contrast, take two growing seasons to complete their life cycle, while perennials (page 470) live for more than 2 (and sometimes for many) years. Though the annual-biennial-perennial distinction seems clear on paper, in the garden it is somewhat blurred. For example, some tender perennials (those that cannot survive freezing temperatures), such as geranium *(Pelargonium)* and some kinds of salvia and verbena, flower year after year in mild-winter climates but are grown as annuals where winters are cold. A few hardier perennials, such as snapdragon *(Antirrhinum majus),* are grown as annuals even where they are hardy because older plants don't perform as well as young ones.

Favorite annuals are listed in Annuals for Seasonal Color in A Guide to Plant Selection, beginning on page 47.

Annuals such as these zinnias, salvias, and dusty millers are colorful all season long.

PLANTING ANNUALS. The best planting time for annuals depends on your climate and the specific plant. *Cool-season annuals,* such as calendula, sweet pea *(Lathyrus odoratus),* and some primroses *(Primula),* grow best in the cool soil and mild temperatures of fall and early spring. Also called hardy annuals, these plants can withstand fairly heavy frosts. Indeed, if they are to bloom vigorously, they must develop roots and foliage during cool weather. Gardeners in cold-winter areas should plant them in very early spring, as soon as the soil can be worked. In the milder parts of the Northeast, they can be sown in fall for bloom in winter and early spring. To achieve the earliest flowers, timing is important: plant while the days are still warm enough to encourage growth but when day length is decreasing. Plant too soon, and the plants will start blooming before winter sets in and then go dormant; plant too late, and you probably won't get flowers until later in spring. In mild-winter regions, cool-season annuals can also be planted in late winter or very early spring for spring bloom.

Some hardy annuals will bloom all summer if deadheaded regularly or sheared back when flowering slows. Others, such as pansies, stop blooming when the weather becomes too hot.

Warm-season annuals, also known as tender annuals, comprise a large group of plants, including cosmos, sunflower *(Helianthus annuus),* and zinnia. These plants grow and flower best in the warm months of late spring, summer, and early fall. They are cold tender and may perish in a late frost if planted too early in spring. Set them out after all danger of frost has passed in spring. Many warm-season annuals will bloom all summer.

You can start annuals from seed sown in containers or, in many cases, directly in the garden (see page 486 for more on starting seeds). Many annuals are also sold as started plants in nurseries; for best results, choose those that are relatively small, with healthy foliage and few or no flowers. Plants with yellowing leaves and those that are leggy, root-bound, too big for their pots, or already in full bloom will establish only slowly in the garden, and they'll usually flower poorly. (See page 483 for directions on planting from containers.)

To get your annuals off to a good start, prepare the garden soil carefully before setting out transplants or sowing seed. You'll find information on preparing planting beds on page 482.

CARING FOR ANNUALS. The key to success with annuals is to keep them growing steadily, through attention to watering, fertilizing, and deadheading.

Water the bed thoroughly after you plant; thereafter, water enough to keep soil moist, but not soggy. Young seedlings or transplants may need water once a day in warm weather, but as they become established they'll be able to get by with less. Apply a 1- to 2-inch layer of mulch (such as compost, ground bark, or pine needles) to conserve water and discourage weeds from establishing. When spreading mulch, keep it 1 to 2 inches away from plant stems to encourage good air circulation and prevent stems from rotting at the base. When starting from seeds, wait until seedlings are several inches tall before mulching them.

Mixing a complete fertilizer into the soil before planting will generally supply annuals with nutrients sufficient for at least half the growing season. In cold-winter areas, an additional feeding after bloom begins will carry the plants through their season. Where winters are warmer and the growing season correspondingly longer, give supplemental feedings both after flowering starts and again in late summer.

As their flowers fade, annuals put their energy into ripening seeds. If you regularly deadhead — that is, remove dead flowers and any seedpods — the plant will usually

bear more flowers in a continued effort to produce seeds. Deadheading also keeps the garden tidy. To do the job, just pinch or cut off individual flowers or shear the flower heads with pruning or hedge shears, taking care not to remove more than a third of the plant.

Biennials

Biennials typically complete their life cycle in 2 years—in contrast to annuals (page 452), which live for less than a year, and perennials (page 470), which live for more than 2 years. During their first year, biennials grow from seed into leafy but nonblooming plants. They live through the winter (experiencing the period of cold temperatures that most require for bloom); then, in the following year, they flower, set seed, and die. This is the life cycle you'll observe if you start seeds yourself. Biennials sold in nurseries, though, usually bloom the year you buy them, since the grower has taken care of the first phase of growth for you.

Familiar biennials include Canterbury bell *(Campanula medium),* hollyhock *(Alcea rosea),* and common foxglove *(Digitalis purpurea),* as well as vegetables such as carrot and onion. Breeders have developed strains of some biennials (including hollyhock and foxglove) that grow as annuals; these bloom the first year from seed, assuming the seed is sown early in spring. You'll also find hollyhock and foxglove strains that grow as short-lived perennials.

To grow biennials, sow seeds in containers or directly in the garden at the time indicated on the seed packet, typically mid- to late spring or summer. (For more on starting seeds, see page 486.) Transplant young plants into the garden in early fall, setting them in well-prepared soil; water as needed. Where the ground freezes, place a protective mulch of straw or chopped leaves around the plants, taking care not to smother the foliage rosettes. In spring, feed with a complete fertilizer as soon as new growth begins to show.

Bulbs

Commonly lumped together as "bulbs" are a multitude of plants with underground structures that serve as storage organs, accumulating nutrient reserves that will ensure the plant's survival through dormancy and supply

energy for its growth and bloom in the year to come. The five bulb types recognized by botanists—true bulbs, corms, tubers, rhizomes, and tuberous roots—are described on page 454.

SELECTING AND PLANTING BULBS. Choose plump, firm bulbs that feel heavy for their size; avoid any that are soft, squashy, or shriveled. Many kinds of bulbs are graded by size. Larger-circumference bulbs generally yield more flowers, but they're also the priciest. If you're planting a large quantity it's more economical to buy midsize specimens (they'll build up after a year or two to bloom as lavishly as larger bulbs).

AVOID WILD BULBS

Certain bulbs have been dug so extensively in the wild that they are fast vanishing from their native habitats; many of these are considered endangered species. Wild-dug sorts that have been offered for sale in the United States include species anemones and narcissus (rather than named varieties or hybrids) as well as various species of cyclamen, winter aconite *(Eranthis),* fritillary *(Fritillaria),* snowdrop *(Galanthus),* snowflake *(Leucojum),* and sternbergia. To avoid contributing to the disappearance of such plants from the wild, buy only bulbs labeled "commercially propagated" or "from cultivated stock." If the bulbs are not labeled, ask about their origin before purchasing.

THE FIVE BULB TYPES AND WAYS TO DIVIDE THEM

The characteristics of each bulb type are summarized below, along with advice on how to divide each type. For information on the best time to divide and replant specific bulbs, consult the A to Z Plant Encyclopedia. The photos show bulbs oriented the way they should be planted.

True bulb. A true bulb is an underground stem base containing an embryonic plant surrounded by scales—modified leaves that overlap each other. A basal plate at the bottom of the bulb holds the scales together and produces roots. Most true bulbs have a protective papery outer skin called a tunic. Lilies, however, lack a tunic, making them more susceptible to drying and damage than other true bulbs; be sure to handle them with care. Most true bulbs produce offsets (also called increases). To divide, simply separate these from the mother bulb.

Narcissus

   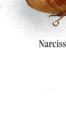

Muscari   Iris (bulbous)   Leucojum

Lilium, Oriental Hybrid

Corm. A corm is a swollen underground stem base, but unlike a true bulb, it's composed of solid tissue rather than scales. Roots grow from a basal plate at the corm's bottom; the growth point is at the top. Many corms have a tunic formed from the dried bases of the previous season's leaves. Each corm lasts for a single year; as it shrinks away, a new corm and, in many species, small increases *(cormels)* form on top of it. To divide, separate healthy new corms and any cormels from the old corms (cormels may take 2 to 3 years to reach flowering size).

Crocus

Watsonia   Freesia

Like most plants, bulbs need good drainage. If your soil drains very poorly, plant on a slope or in raised beds.

You can plant bulbs in a separate bed or set them among other plants, digging an individual hole for each bulb. (See page 482 for information on preparing a planting bed.) Work a complete fertilizer into the soil in the bed; or, if you're planting bulbs in individual holes, dig up to a tablespoon of fertilizer into the bottom of each hole, then cover with about 2 inches of compost or soil and plant the bulb.

In most soils, true bulbs and most corms should be planted about three times as deep as the bulb is wide. In hot climates or sandy soils, plant slightly deeper; in heavy soils, plant slightly shallower. The chart on page 453 demonstrates how deep and how far apart to plant some widely grown winter- and spring-blooming bulbs; for depth and spacing for other bulbs, check the entries in the A to Z Plant Encyclopedia.

CARING FOR BULBS. Bulbs need water while they're growing actively. For most sorts, this period begins after planting and continues until the foliage dies back, until flowering is finished, or—for some types—until autumn. If you must supplement rainfall, water deeply enough to penetrate the root zone; the roots grow beneath the bulb.

When growth begins, apply a complete fertilizer to enhance the quality of the current season's flowers. After bloom ends, much or all of a bulb's stored nutrients are depleted; to ensure a good show next year, those nutrients must be replenished. As long as the leaves are green and growing, they'll continue to manufacture food

NATURALIZING BULBS

A number of bulbous plants can be planted in meadows, fields, or light woodlands, where they'll form a wildflowerlike carpet of bloom year after year. Consult the A to Z Plant Encyclopedia to see if the bulbs you want to naturalize are good candidates for this treatment and to check their climate, exposure, and moisture needs.

The traditional naturalizing method is to broadcast a handful of bulbs over the desired planting area, then plant them where they fall. To achieve the most realistic effect, you may need to adjust the pattern slightly: the drift should be denser at one end or toward the center, as if the bulbs began to grow in one spot, then gradually spread to colonize outlying territory. Once you have the pattern you want, use a trowel or bulb planter to set the bulbs at their preferred depths.

Following bloom, fertilize the bulbs and allow the foliage to remain until it withers. After a number of years, overcrowding may cause a decrease in the number of flowers; when this happens, it's time to dig, divide, and replant.

Some bulbs like these narcissus naturalize beautifully and provide a carpet of color every spring.

Rhizome. A rhizome is a thickened stem growing partially or entirely below ground. Its roots grow directly from the underside. The primary growing point is at one end of the rhizome; additional growing points form along the sides. To divide, cut into sections that have visible growing points.

Iris (rhizomatous)

Zantedeschia

Tuber. Tubers, like corms, are swollen underground stem bases, but they lack the corm's distinct organization. There is no basal plate, so roots can grow from all sides. Instead of just one (or a few) growing points, a tuber has multiple growth points scattered over its surface; each is a scalelike leaf with a growth bud *(eye)* in its axil. Some tubers, such as cyclamen and begonia, are perennial; they increase in size each year. Others (the potato is the best-known example) are annual; as new tubers grow, the old ones disintegrate. To divide either kind of tuber, cut it into sections, making sure each has one or more growing points.

Begonia

Cyclamen

Tuberous roots. While the other four bulb types are specialized stems, a tuberous root is a true root, thickened to store nutrients. Fibrous roots for the uptake of water and nutrients grow from its sides and tip. Tuberous roots grow in a cluster, with the swollen portions radiating out from a central point. The growth buds are at the bases of old stems rather than on the roots themselves. To divide, cut the root cluster apart so each division contains both roots and part of a stem base with one or more growth buds.

Dahlia

for the coming year, so it's vital to leave them on the plant—bedraggled and weary though they may appear!—until they yellow and pull away easily. (If you want to hide the dying foliage, try overplanting with annuals or a ground cover.) After flowering is finished, it's also important to apply a complete fertilizer such as a 10-10-10 formula or a "bulb food" high in phosphorus and potassium. For these last two nutrients to be effective, they must reach the root zone (see "Fertilizers," page 462); scratch the fertilizer into the soil or apply it in narrow trenches dug near the bulbs, then water thoroughly.

Composting

Composting is a natural process that converts raw organic materials into a valuable soil conditioner you can use to improve a soil's

---

COMPOSTING WITH WORMS

Worm composting, or vermicomposting, is an efficient way to compost kitchen scraps in a small amount of space. Red wiggler worms and ready-made bins for housing them are sold by mail-order and in some nurseries. (Red wigglers also are commonly sold for fish bait and can be purchased at fish and tackle shops.) Or house worms in a covered homemade wooden bin (about 2 feet square and 8 to 15 inches deep). If you are planning to keep your worms indoors, you will need a tray under the bin to catch any spills. Place the bin in a shaded rain-protected location where it won't freeze or be exposed to direct sun, which will cause it to overheat and kill the worms. Next, fill the bin with bedding by making a 50–50 mix of topsoil and manure, then mixing that with equal parts of shredded newspaper. Soak the mix overnight, then squeeze out excess moisture and fluff it up. Wait for 24 hours to see if it heats up before adding worms. If it does heat up, wait a few more days before adding worms because the heat will be detrimental to the worms.

Add the worms by spreading them on top of the bedding; 2 pounds of worms is usually sufficient and will process about 7 pounds of fruit and vegetable scraps weekly. Begin feeding them kitchen scraps—lightly at first until you gauge how much they can consume—by spreading the scraps on top of the bedding. (Cover the scraps with a layer of straw, if you like, and pull it back whenever you add new scraps.) Give the worms fruit and vegetable scraps, coffee grounds, and grains, but avoid meats and greasy foods. After 3 to 6 months, you can begin harvesting the compost, which looks like dark, rich soil. When you harvest, add additional bedding and gently turn and fluff up the remaining material.

COMPOSTING SYSTEMS

You can make compost in a freestanding pile or a homemade structure, or use a purchased manufactured composter.

■ **Freestanding compost piles.** These piles should be at least 3 feet high and wide; at this size, their mass is great enough to generate the microbial activity needed for heating the materials. The upper size limit is about 5 feet high and wide; a pile larger than that may not receive enough air at its center. When siting the pile, allow space alongside for turning.

■ **Wire cylinders or hoops.** For these, use welded wire, chicken wire, or snow fencing, supporting it with stakes if necessary. The cylinder or hoop should be about 4 feet in diameter and 3 to 4 feet tall. To turn the pile, lift the cylinder and move it to one side; then fork the materials back into it.

■ **Three-bin systems.** Bin systems are more complex than freestanding piles or those corralled with wire, but they also offer a more flexible way to make compost. The left bin holds new green and brown material; the center one contains partly decomposed material, while the right bin holds finished or nearly finished compost. Turn the material in each bin weekly, moving decomposed material to the right. (The last bin will be empty for a few weeks at the start.)

■ **Manufactured composters.** These include various sorts of *tumblers*, systems that make it easier to turn materials and produce finished compost quickly. Most are turned with a crank, but some roll on the ground or are turned with foot treads. Such devices provide a tidy way to make compost, and are especially practical in small gardens.

Another manufactured composter is the *static compost bin*, in which the contents sit without turning (though occasional aerating with a spading fork is helpful). You add new materials at the top; the finished compost is removed through a door at the base. Though tidy, these units produce only fairly small amounts of compost—and they do so rather slowly.

Freestanding pile

Wire cylinder

Static bin

Tumbler

4 by 4   1 by 1   2 by 6

Three-bin system

2 by 2 spacer
between 2 by 6s

structure, boost its nutrient content, and make it more water retentive. Besides being good for your garden, composting lightens the load at the landfill: you recycle garden debris at home rather than consigning it to the dump.

A pile of leaves, branches, and other garden trimmings will eventually decompose with no intervention on your part. This type of composting is called *slow* or *cold composting*. With a little effort, however, you can speed up the process. If you create optimum conditions for the organisms responsible for decay (by giving them the mixture of air, water, and carbon- and nitrogen-rich nutrients they need), the compost pile will heat up quickly and decompose in only a few months. Such *hot composting* also destroys many (though not all) pathogens and weeds.

You can make compost in a freestanding pile or use some sort of enclosure (see page 456). Regardless of the method, though, the fundamentals of composting are the same.

GATHER MATERIALS. You'll need approximately equal amounts by volume of brown matter and green matter. *Brown matter* is high in carbon and includes dry leaves, hay, sawdust, straw, wood chips, and woody prunings. *Green matter* (which is not necessarily green in color) is high in nitrogen; it includes grass clippings, fruit and vegetable scraps, coffee grounds, tea bags, crushed eggshells, and manure from cows, horses, goats, poultry, and rabbits. The compost will heat up faster if you collect the ingredients in advance and assemble the pile all at once. Don't use bones, cat or dog waste, dairy products, meat scraps, badly diseased or insect-infested plants, or pernicious weeds that might survive composting (such as bindweed and quackgrass).

CHOP MATERIALS. Shredding or chopping large, rough materials into smaller pieces (ideally no larger than $3/4$ inch to 2 inches) allows decay-producing organisms to reach more surfaces and thus speeds up the composting process. Use a shredder-chipper or lawn mower; or chop the materials with a machete on a large wooden block. Shredding dry leaves is a good idea, too; just run a lawn mower over them.

BUILD THE PILE. Building the pile like a layer cake makes it easier to judge the ratio of brown to green materials. Start by spreading a 4- to 8-inch layer of brown material over an area at least 3 feet square; then add a layer of green material 2 to 8 inches deep. (Layers of grass clippings should be only 2 inches deep; less-dense green materials can be layered more thickly.) Add another layer of brown material and sprinkle the pile with water. Mix these first three layers with a spading fork. Continue adding layers, watering, and mixing. To heat up efficiently, the pile should be about 3 feet tall, giving it a volume of one cubic yard.

COMPOST TROUBLESHOOTING

PROBLEM	POSSIBLE CAUSES	SOLUTIONS
Rotten odor	Too wet Lacks oxygen	Turn pile to aerate; layer in dry material such as sawdust, dry leaves.
Ammonia odor	Excess nitrogen (green material)	Turn pile; layer in dry material such as sawdust, dry leaves.
Pile not heating up	Too dry Too much dry or woody material	Turn pile, adding water. Add fresh green material such as grass clippings, fruit or vegetable scraps; bury scraps in pile.
Pile is attracting rodents and flies	Fruit or vegetable scraps are on the surface Meat or dairy scraps have been added	Always bury kitchen scraps inside the pile. If meat or dairy scraps are present, remove them. Turn pile to increase temperature. If a rodent problem continues, use a covered bin made of fine-mesh wire.

TURN THE PILE. In just a few days, the pile should have heated up dramatically. In time, it will decompose on its own, but you can hurry things along by turning the contents to introduce more oxygen—which is needed by the organisms responsible for decomposition. Using a spading fork or pitchfork, restack the pile, redistributing it so that the materials originally on the outside are moved to the pile's center, where they'll be exposed to higher heat. If necessary, add water; the pile should be as moist as a wrung-out sponge. Turn the pile weekly, if possible, until it is no longer generating internal heat and most of the materials have decomposed.

USE THE COMPOST. Finished compost is dark and crumbly, with an earthy aroma. Mix it into your planting beds or use it as a mulch. If some of the material from the pile's exterior is still coarser than you prefer for a soil amendment, use it as a rough mulch or simply incorporate it into your next compost pile. To obtain fine-textured compost to use as potting soil or for starting seeds, sift the finished compost through a screen with $1/2$-inch mesh.

Container Gardening

Growing plants in containers lets you have a garden even when the space for one is limited or nonexistent: you can install a planter box below a window or use containers to turn a tiny balcony or patio into a leafy haven. Gardeners with plenty of room appreciate containers, too, valuing the versatility they offer. Blooming pot plants bring seasonal color to garden beds, a porch, or the front steps and are easily replaced with new ones when their flowers fade. In addition, containers give you the chance to experiment with new plant combinations and with kinds not suited to the native conditions. For instance, if your soil is alkaline or claylike but you're longing to raise acid-loving plants or those that demand fast drainage, just fill their pots with the sort of soil they need. Plants too tender for your winters can be moved to shelter when cold weather hits.

PREPARING CONTAINERS. Choose containers with at least one drainage hole, so water won't accumulate around plant roots. Scrub used containers with a solution of 1 part household bleach to 9 parts hot water. Cover the drainage hole(s) with a small piece of fine wire screen to keep soil from washing out.

CHOOSING A POTTING MIX. A good potting soil allows roots to grow easily; it should be fast draining yet moisture retentive. Quick drainage means roots won't run the risk of suffocating in soggy soil, while good water retention saves you from having to water too often. Regular garden soil, even good loam, is too dense for container use. For best success, most gardeners turn to packaged potting mixes, which don't contain

A SUBSTITUTE FOR PEAT

For potting mixes, many gardeners prefer sphagnum peat moss over ground bark: peat breaks down more slowly, and unlike bark, it won't compact in the container and limit aeration. There are, however, concerns over the ecological damage that may result from the overmining of some peat bogs. One good alternative to peat is coir dust, which is available by mail-order and in some nurseries. A by-product of the coconut fiber industry, it's sold in bales and in compressed "bricks" that expand when soaked in water to make about 9 quarts of fluffy material. Used in potting mixes, it breaks down slowly and retains moisture and air well; it's also useful as a soil additive or mulch in the garden. Keep in mind, though, that coir dust won't help acidify the soil the way peat does, since its pH is closer to neutral (5.7 to 6.2).

C

soil; they're mixtures of organic materials (such as ground bark, sphagnum peat moss, and/or compost) plus mineral matter such as perlite, vermiculite, pumice, or sand. Limestone may be added to balance the acidity of peat moss; fertilizers and wetting agents (see Soil Polymers, page 500) also may be included. Since potting mixes consisting of ingredients such as bark and peat can be very difficult to wet (water seems to run right through them), before planting, prewet the mix thoroughly. An easy way to accomplish this is to fill a five gallon bucket with mix, add water, and let it soak overnight. Before planting, flush the mix with water once or twice to eliminate excess salts. (For precautions on using packaged potting mixes, see page 489.)

A 2-cubic-foot bag of potting mix holds enough to transplant 8 to 10 plants from 1-gallon nursery cans into individual 10- to 12-inch pots or to fill a 36- by 8- by 10-inch planter box. For large planting projects, though, you may want to make your own mix. For a basic no-soil mix, combine ⅔ cubic yard nitrogen-stabilized ground bark, coir dust, or sphagnum peat moss; ⅓ cubic yard washed 20-grit sand; 6 pounds 0-10-10 granular fertilizer; and 10 pounds dolomite or dolomite limestone.

WATERING. Because they have only a limited area from which to draw moisture, container plants must be watered more often than those grown in the ground. In hot or windy weather, some (especially those in hanging baskets) may need watering several times a day; in cool weather, it may be sufficient to water weekly or even less often. Test with your finger: if the soil is dry beneath the surface, it's time to water.

Apply water over the entire soil surface until it flows from the pot's drainage holes. This moistens the entire soil mass and prevents any potentially harmful salts from accumulating in the mix. If the water drains too fast—virtually the instant you pour it in—there's probably air space between the soil and the container walls. In this case, completely submerge the container in a tub of water for about half an hour; or, for large pots, set a hose on the soil surface near the plant's base and let water trickle slowly into the mix.

A drip irrigation system (see page 513) can make watering container plants almost effortless. Kits designed for this purpose are widely available.

FERTILIZING. Container plants need regular feeding, since the necessary frequent watering leaches nutrients from the potting mix. Apply a liquid fertilizer every 2 weeks during the growing season, following the directions on the label. Or mix a controlled-release type (see page 462) into the potting mix before planting.

REPOTTING. If roots are crowded and protruding from the drainage holes, the plant has outgrown its container and needs a roomier home. Because you want to keep the soil mass fairly well filled with roots, it's best to shift to a

TOP: Buckwheat is a fast-growing cover crop that needs warm weather to grow well; its flowers attract beneficial insects. BOTTOM: Nitrogen-containing nodules on fava bean roots

slightly larger container rather than a much bigger one. If the pot is too large, the ratio of soil to roots will be too great for the roots to absorb all the moisture after watering—a situation that often leads to root rot. Select a new container that allows just an inch or two of fresh mix on all sides of the root mass. If the root ball is compacted (with tightly twined roots), make four shallow vertical cuts down its sides with a sharp knife to encourage the roots to move out into the new soil.

If you want to keep an older plant in the same large pot indefinitely, you can root-prune it periodically. Gently turn the plant out of its container and use a sharp knife to shave off an inch or two from all four sides and the bottom of the root ball; then return the plant to the container, adding fresh soil mix around and beneath the roots.

Cover Crops

Also known as green manure, cover crops are legumes or grasses planted expressly to improve garden soil. They also help prevent erosion and effectively loosen soil compacted by heavy equipment during the construction of new homes. Most cover crops are planted in fall (6 to 8 weeks before the first hard frost) and dug into the soil in spring. As they decay, they break down into humus, which improves the soil's structure and increases its ability to hold moisture. Legumes such as fava beans, Austrian peas, clovers, and vetch also add extra nitrogen, thanks to their association with so-called nitrogen-fixing bacteria (genus *Rhizobium*). These bacteria draw nitrogen from air in the soil and "fix" it in nodules on a legume's roots; when the plants eventually decompose, the nitrogen is released back into the soil.

Grass or cereal cover crops such as rye, barley, buckwheat, and mustard don't contribute extra nitrogen to the soil, but they do produce plenty of organic matter. Gardeners often combine legumes and grasses as cover crops to enjoy the benefits of both.

Before planting, till or dig the area and rake it smooth. Treat legume seeds with an inoculant powder (available from seed companies that sell cover-crop seeds) to be certain that *Rhizobium* bacteria are present. Broadcast seeds at the rate recommended by the supplier and rake again to cover them. In spring, dig in the cover crop by hand (for small areas) or with a tiller, then wait until most of the stems and leaves have decayed before planting the garden. You can also cut the stems and leaves and add them to your compost pile, then dig just the lower stems and roots into the soil.

Diseases

Although few gardens escape diseases entirely, the advice and photos in this section will help you prevent most common diseases and, if problems do occur, assist you in identifying them and taking action.

The Integrated Pest Management (IPM) approach discussed on page 471 applies to dealing with diseases as well as with other kinds of pests. IPM aims to maintain an attractive, productive garden with minimal use of synthetic (chemical) controls; its goal is to reduce diseases and pest populations to tolerable levels, not to eradicate them entirely (which is rarely possible in any case).

PLANT PATHOGENS. Covered here are plant diseases caused by several kinds of organisms. Bacteria, fungi, and viruses are responsible for most leaf, stem, and flower diseases; the most widespread soilborne diseases are due to fungi. (Plant problems brought on by other factors are sometimes mistaken for diseases; this is true of iron-deficiency chlorosis, page 481, and sunburn, page 481.)

Fungi are microscopic, typically multicellular organisms. Some obtain their food parasitically from green plants, causing diseases in the process. Many produce multitudinous tiny reproductive bodies called spores, which can be disseminated in numerous ways—by wind, insects, splashing water from rain or irrigation, garden equipment, and handling. Given the right conditions, each spore will germinate and grow, producing a new infection.

A number of diseases resulting from fungal infection are described on the following pages.

Bacteria are single-celled organisms. Like fungi, they cannot create their own food supply, so they feed on organic matter, including plants. Unlike fungi, however, the bacteria that afflict plants must remain inside their host or in plant debris to survive. They do not produce spores but multiply rapidly by cell division. Since they require both moisture and warmth for reproduction, the diseases they cause are generally less prevalent in dry summers than in rainy or humid regions. Nonetheless, garden watering can provide the moisture they need to flourish. Bacteria are spread by insects, splashing water, garden equipment, and handling.

The bacterial disease fireblight is described on page 460.

Viruses are ultramicroscopic particles capable of invading plant tissue and reproducing in it, usually at the expense of the host plant. They produce a variety of symptoms, including stunting and other abnormalities in growth; spots or discoloration on leaves; and damaged fruit. (Some attractive plants, such as variegated-leaf abutilon and certain tulips with bizarrely striped flowers, owe their variegation to a virus.) Most garden plants are susceptible to at least one viral disease; especially prone to attack are a number of vegetables, including beans, cucumbers, squash, tomatoes, and peppers.

Viral diseases are commonly spread by plant-eating insects such as aphids, leafhoppers, and whiteflies. Depending on the virus, spread can occur via infected seeds and pollen; through pruning, grafting, budding, and other forms of vegetative propagation; and, in some cases, by contaminated hands, clothing, and tools.

To prevent these diseases, plant resistant varieties (if available) and buy certified virus-free stock. Control virus-spreading insects; remove weeds, which are hosts for some viruses. If you find a virus-infected plant, the best course of action is to destroy it. There are no chemical controls at this time.

PREVENTING DISEASES. Because many diseases cannot effectively be controlled once their symptoms become apparent, prevention is of prime importance. Whenever possible, plant resistant varieties; many are noted in the entries in the A to Z Plant Encyclopedia, and your Cooperative Extension Service can also give you information on this score. Choose certified and disease-free plants and seeds to avoid introducing pathogens into your garden.

Give your plants the climate, exposure, and amount of moisture they prefer: a sun-loving plant sited in the shade may be more susceptible to fungal diseases, and one that does best in dry conditions may succumb to certain root and foliage diseases if overwatered. Allow plenty of space between plants to ensure sufficient air

circulation. Also fertilize according to each plant's needs; too much or too little fertilizer can increase susceptibility to some diseases.

Use soil solarization (see page 518) to destroy soil-dwelling pathogens. Control weeds, since they may harbor pathogens; control insects that may spread diseases. Clean up the garden each fall so disease organisms can't overwinter in plant debris.

MANAGEMENT OPTIONS. If diseases do appear in your garden, immediately remove diseased annuals and vegetables to keep the problem from spreading. On larger plants (including perennials), remove diseased flowers, leaves, and, if possible, branches. Discard all infected material in the trash, not the compost heap. Disinfecting tools used on afflicted plants by dipping them between cuts in a solution of 1 part household bleach to 9 parts water may help prevent the spread of some diseases.

TOP TO BOTTOM: Anthracnose, Damping off, Fireblight

PLANT DISEASES. Discussed on the following pages are some of the plant diseases you're most likely to encounter in your garden. Many diseases that affect only one kind of plant—such as peach, rose, or elm *(Ulmus),* for example—are treated in the appropriate entry in the A to Z Plant Encyclopedia. For lawn diseases, see page 467.

Anthracnose. Caused by a number of fungi, anthracnose appears early in the growing season. It affects many different plants but seldom kills them. Symptoms depend on the particular plant, but you'll typically see sunken, gray or tan to dark brown spots on leaves, stems, fruit, or twigs. Leaves may wither and drop.

The spores that cause anthracnose are spread by rain and garden sprinkling. To discourage the disease, avoid overhead watering and use a mulch to decrease splashing of rain or sprinkler water. Give plants sufficient space for good air circulation; grow vining plants on trellises to keep them dry. Whenever possible, plant resistant varieties. Remove infected leaves, fruit, twigs, and branches, then destroy them to prevent reinfection.

To prevent anthracnose, you may use fungicides containing lime sulfur (during the dormant season), copper compounds, or chlorothalonil. Consult your Cooperative Extension Office or a commercial sprayer for information on the best chemical spray for your area and the appropriate time to apply it.

Blackspot. A fungal disease that attacks many roses. It appears at first as rounded black spots on the leaves, which eventually turn yellow between the spots and finally drop off. This fungus also can cause dark cankers on rose stems. Pick off and destroy (do not compost) any afflicted leaves, and prune out any stems that show cankers. Spray plants every 7 to 10 days with fungicidal soap or sulfur; add a few drops of liquid dish soap to the spray as a spreader sticker. The best approach to blackspot is to plant resistant roses: Hybrid teas are among the most susceptible, but plant breeders are releasing disease-resistant selections every year. Many shrub roses are resistant and rugosa roses are immune to this disease. Also, prune plants to improve air circulation near the center of the plants. Rake up and destroy leaves and replace mulch around the bases of the plants to reduce the number of blackspot spores that overwinter.

Damping off. A variety of fungi may be responsible for this disease, which affects young seedlings, causing them to collapse at or near the soil surface. In some cases, seeds rot before they can sprout.

To prevent damping off, use pasteurized potting soil for containers; thoroughly clean and disinfect used containers before planting in them (scrub them with a solution of 1 part household bleach to 9 parts hot water). Provide good air circulation around seedlings, thinning them if necessary to eliminate crowding, and do

D

not overwater. You can buy some seeds pre-treated with fungicides. A biological fungicide containing live strains of the soil bacterium *Streptomyces griseoviridis* (Mycostop), which protects against damping-off fungi, can be used to treat seeds, potting soil, or seedlings. (Mycostop may not be registered in all states.)

Fireblight. Resulting from infection by a bacterium, this disease attacks only members of the rose family that produce pomes (applelike fruits), including apple, cotoneaster, crabapple, hawthorn, pear, pyracantha, and quince. Fireblight causes shoots (and sometimes the entire plant) to blacken and die suddenly; affected parts look as though they have been scorched by fire.

During moist weather, especially in early spring when temperatures are above 60°F/16°C, the bacteria are carried to blossoms by splashing water and by flies and other insects. Once in the blossoms, they're transported to other flowers by honeybees; the infection then spreads to the shoots and limbs. The bacteria survive in infected twigs and cankers, ready to infect blossoms again the following spring.

Whenever possible, plant resistant cultivars. To protect blossoms from infection, spray at 3- or 5-day intervals during the bloom season with copper compounds. A product containing fosetyl-al (Aliette) can be used on ornamentals.

To control the pathogen once it has appeared, prune out and discard diseased branches, making cuts at least 6 to 8 inches below blighted tissue. Disinfecting tools between cuts with a solution of 1 part household bleach to 9 parts water may help to keep the disease from spreading.

Leaf spot. Caused by a wide range of fungi and bacteria, leaf spots are variable in appearance. A plant that has small, round, light green spots that turn brown may have bacterial leaf spot. Cherry leaf spot causes round, red or purplish spots; as the disease progresses the centers drop out of the spots. Round yellow spots that turn brown with gray centers indicate early blight. Anthracnose also causes leaf spots, see page 459 for details on this disease. All leaf spot diseases may cause lesions on stems. They also cause stunted growth and spotted or deformed fruit. The first line of defense is to pick off and destroy (do not compost) any afflicted leaves. Rake up and destroy any leaves that fall off the plant as well, to reduce the number of overwintering spores. Space and prune plants (by thinning out stems) to increase air circulation. Spray plants with a sulfur or copper-based fungicide every 7 to 10 days if the problem is severe. Many gardeners simply replace plants severely affected with leaf spot diseases, and planting resistant cultivars is a good way to eliminate the problem entirely.

Powdery mildews. These diseases are caused by fungi which can infect leaves, buds, flowers, and/or stems, depending on the host plant and

TOP TO BOTTOM: Powdery mildew, Pythium root rot, Rust

the particular fungus. The disease first appears as small white or gray circular patches on plant tissue, then spreads rapidly to form powdery areas of fungal filaments and spores. New growth may be stunted; blossoms may fail to set fruit or may produce fruit covered with powdery fungus. Most powdery mildews thrive in humid air, but the spores—unlike those of other fungi—need dry surfaces, such as leaves, stems, and flowers, to become established.

To prevent powdery mildews, plant resistant varieties; many are noted in the entries in the A to Z Plant Encyclopedia. Be sure to give plants sufficient light and air circulation.

To control the fungi, pick off and destroy infected leaves and flowers and thin stems to improve air circulation. If necessary, spray with sulfur, potassium bicarbonate, triadimefon,

copper soap fungicide, neem oil, or triforine. Rose growers have had some success controlling powdery mildews with baking soda mixtures, potassium bicarbonate, or antitranspirants such as Cloud Cover or Wilt-Pruf.

Root rots, water molds. Certain fungi (notably *Pythium* and *Phytophthora*) produce mobile spores that can swim short distances through water in the soil and attack plant roots. The fungi kill roots and also invade the crowns of plants, sometimes girdling them. Diseased plants wilt, and their leaves discolor, become stunted, and drop prematurely. Branches or even the entire plant may die. Root rot and water mold fungi are most active in warm soils (55 to 80°F/13 to 27°C), but they can survive in dry, cold ones, becoming active when favorable conditions arise. Many plants are susceptible, especially if they are overwatered or planted in heavy, poorly drained soils.

To prevent the problem, improve drainage (see page 499) or plant in raised beds. Do not overwater. Use resistant plants.

Rust. Most strains of the 4,000 or so types of rust fungi are specific to particular plants; rose rust will not infect hollyhocks, for example, and hollyhock rust will not infect roses. The first sign of infection is the appearance of powdery pustules on leaf undersides; these are usually yellow to rusty brown but may be purple or another color. As the disease progresses, leaf undersides become covered with powdery masses of spores, and the upper surfaces may be spotted with yellow; eventually, the whole leaf may turn yellow, then drop.

Prevent rust by planting resistant varieties. Give plants the best possible air circulation. Remove infected leaves immediately; in winter, clean up all fallen leaves and debris. If watering from overhead, be sure plants will have time to dry before dusk.

Sprays that are sometimes effective (depending on the kind of rust and the infected plant) include copper soap fungicide, sulfur, triadimefon, and triforine.

Sooty mold. Commonly seen on the leaves and twigs of many trees and shrubs, sooty mold is caused by a fungus that grows on honeydew produced by sap-sucking insects such as scale, aphids, mealybugs, and whiteflies. Sooty mold is considered fairly harmless (since it does not feed on plants), but extremely heavy infestations can block sun from reaching leaves, which may then turn yellow and drop prematurely. To prevent the problem, control honeydew-excreting insects. Wash or wipe the fungus from leaves as soon as possible.

Verticillium wilt. A widespread and destructive disease, verticillium wilt results from infection by a fungus that invades and plugs the water-conducting tissues in the roots and stems of plants. It can affect crops such as tomatoes and strawberries, as well as roses and some trees. A common symptom is wilting or death of one side of the plant. Leaves turn yellow or brown, then die; as the disease progresses, entire branches die. Small plants may be destroyed in one season, but mature trees may live on (though in compromised health) for long periods. The fungus can survive in the soil for years, even in the absence of host plants.

Plant resistant selections when these are available. In areas where verticillium wilt is present, grow susceptible crops in containers filled with pasteurized potting mix. Soil solarization can be effective in destroying the fungus.

Mildly affected trees or shrubs may recover from an attack. You can aid recovery by deep but infrequent irrigation. If a plant has been

TOP TO BOTTOM: Sooty mold, Tobacco mosaic, Verticillium wilt

PRODUCTS FOR DISEASE PREVENTION AND CONTROL

You'll find a number of products aimed at disease prevention or control. These include *preventatives*, products that prevent diseases from occurring but cannot control them once they become established; *eradicants*, which help control diseases once they have appeared (many simply protect new growth); and *systemics*, materials that are taken up by plant roots and act as preventatives, eradicants, or both. The controls described here are the most useful and commonly available ones; other, generally less widely sold products are mentioned in the descriptions of specific diseases beginning on page 458.

Synthetic fungicides are manufactured compounds that do not normally occur in nature. *Natural fungicides and bactericides*, in contrast, are products whose active ingredients originate in a plant, animal, or mineral, or whose action results from a biological process. Be aware that "natural" does not mean "harmless"; some of these products can still harm people or plants if they are used incorrectly.

When using any product, *read the label directions carefully and follow them exactly.* The package will state the plants and diseases for which the control is registered for use; it is illegal to use it on a plant or to control a disease not so listed.

The following products are listed by the accepted common name of the *active ingredient*—the actual chemical that prevents or controls the disease or diseases listed on the package label. Some widely used trade names, if they differ from the common name, are noted in parentheses. Before you buy, read the label to make sure you're getting the active ingredient you want. (For more on reading and understanding pesticide labels, see page 478.)

NATURAL FUNGICIDES AND BACTERICIDES

- **Baking soda, sodium bicarbonate.** You can buy baking soda sprays, but it's easy to make your own by mixing 2 teaspoons each of baking soda and fine-grade horticultural oil with 1 gallon of water. This mixture helps control black spot and powdery mildew on roses. Commercial versions contain a "sticker" ingredient to help keep the spray on the plant. If you mix your own, add a dash of common dish soap to the mix to serve as a spreader sticker.

- **Copper compounds (Bordeaux mixture).** General-purpose fungicides and bactericides used to prevent fireblight, peach leaf curl, shot hole, brown rot, and other foliar diseases. Toxic to fish.

- **Copper soap fungicide.** Broad-spectrum fungicide used to control many plant diseases, including rust, black spot, and powdery mildew.

- **Lime sulfur, calcium polysulfide.** Used as a spray in winter (when plants are dormant) to prevent various leaf spots and peach leaf curl. Very caustic; wear goggles and plastic gloves when applying.

- **Neem oil (Rose Defense, others).** Used to prevent and control black spot, powdery mildew, and some other foliar diseases. (Also used as an insecticide and miticide.) Toxic to fish.

- **Potassium bicarbonate (Remedy, others).** Used to control powdery mildew. May not be registered in all states.

- **Sulfur (Sulfur dust, others).** Controls powdery mildew, rust, and other diseases. Do not use in conjunction with horticultural oil sprays or when the outdoor temperature is above 85°F/29°C.

SYNTHETIC FUNGICIDES

- **Chlorothalonil (Daconil, others).** Broad-spectrum liquid fungicide used to prevent powdery mildew, leaf spots, gray mold, scab, and a variety of lawn and other diseases. Toxic to fish.

- **Triadimefon (Fungi-Fighter; formerly Bayleton).** Wettable powder; systemic used for prevention or eradication of powdery mildew, rust, and some lawn diseases. Toxic to fish.

- **Triforine (Funginex).** Liquid systemic for prevention and eradication of powdery mildew, rust, black spot, and a variety of other diseases. You must wear goggles and a face mask during application. Keep animals out of treated areas.

neglected, apply fertilizer; do not, however, fertilize infected trees and shrubs that show lush growth, since excess nitrogen may favor the disease's development. Prune out dead branches. Clean tools of any soil, which can carry the fungus to other parts of the garden.

Fertilizers

When they're actively growing, plants need a steady supply of nutrients. Though many of these are present in soil, water, and air, the gardener may need to supply others. Most likely to require supplemental feeding are fast-growing annuals (such as vegetables and flowering plants), lawns, perennials, fruit trees, and immature plants of numerous kinds. Mature trees and shrubs, on the other hand, may need little or no fertilizing. The entries in the A to Z Plant Encyclopedia cover fertilizing needs and schedules for many plants. General guidelines are also given in the listings for annuals (page 452), bulbs (page 453), ground covers (page 465), lawns (page 465), perennials (page 470), shrubs (page 497), trees (page 504), and vegetables (page 506). A soil test (see page 499) is a good way to determine any nutrient deficiencies in your soil; your Cooperative Extension Office is another excellent source of information on nutrient needs specific to your area.

FERTILIZER TYPES AND FORMS. Visit almost any nursery and you'll encounter a bewildering array of fertilizers in different forms and formulas. To decide which ones to buy, start by reading the labels. Every fertilizer label states the percentage by weight the product contains of the three macronutrients used in mineral form: nitrogen (N), phosphorus (P), and potassium (K). These nutrients are always listed in the order N-P-K. For example, a fertilizer labeled

10-8-6 contains 10 percent nitrogen, 8 percent phosphorus, and 6 percent potassium. The label also tells you the source of each nutrient.

Nitrogen is often listed on fertilizer labels as nitrate or some form of ammonium (many products contain it in both forms). Fertilizers containing nitrogen in the nitrate form are water soluble and fast acting, especially in cool soils, but they are easily leached away by rain or irrigation (thus requiring fairly frequent replenishment) and can pollute surface and ground water if used to excess. Fertilizers in the form of ammonium, those from organic sources (such as blood meal), and IBDU (isobutylidene diurea, a synthetic organic fertilizer) are released more slowly and last longer in the soil, because they must be converted into nitrate form by soil microbes before plant roots can absorb them.

Phosphorus is expressed on product labels as phosphate, P_2O_5, and listed as "available phosphoric acid." Potassium is expressed as potash, K_2O, and may be described in various ways, including "available phosphate" and "water-soluble potash." It is important to note that, unlike nitrogen, phosphorus and potassium do not move readily through the soil in solution. They must therefore be applied near plant roots to do the most good. Dig these nutrients into the soil when planting or scratch them into the soil around existing plants.

Complete fertilizers contain the three macronutrients N, P, and K; some may also include secondary and/or micronutrients (which will be listed on the label). *Simple fertilizers* supply just one macronutrient. Most familiar are the nitrogen-only types, such as ammonium sulfate (21-0-0), and phosphorus-only superphosphate (0-20-0). Falling between complete and simple types are *incomplete fertilizers,* which contain two of the three major

elements; an example is 0-10-10, providing phosphorus and potassium but no nitrogen.

Natural and chemical fertilizers. You can buy fertilizers in either natural (organic) or synthetic (chemical) form.

Natural fertilizers, derived from dead organisms, include fish emulsion and fish meal, all kinds of animal manures, and meals made from blood, bone, alfalfa, cottonseed, soybeans, and kelp and other seaweed. There are also powdered mineral products such as granite dust and rock phosphate. Most contain lower levels of nutrients than chemical products. They release their nutrients more slowly, as well: rather than dissolving in water, they are broken down by microorganisms in the soil, providing nutrients as they decay (decomposition proceeds more quickly in warm, moist soils than in cold or dry ones). Thanks to this slow nutrient release, natural fertilizers are much less likely to burn roots than are chemical types.

Many natural fertilizers are high in just one major nutrient. Blood meal, for example, supplies only nitrogen (N-P-K ratio 12-0-0), while rock phosphate (0-3-0) provides only phosphorus. Some manufacturers combine several natural fertilizers in a single package to produce a complete fertilizer.

Chemical fertilizers are derived from the chemical sources listed on the product label. Compared to natural fertilizers, they usually provide higher levels of nutrients and are faster acting, especially in cold soils; they typically cost less, too. They're a good choice for greening up lawns in spring and giving plants suffering from nutrient deficiencies a quick tonic. Keep in mind that chemical products can burn roots if applied too heavily.

Liquids or solids? Both natural and chemical fertilizers are sold in liquid or solid forms.

Liquid fertilizers, including fish emulsion and water-soluble crystals, deliver nutrients to the roots immediately. They're easy to use, especially on container plants, and if you follow label directions for dilution you'll run no risk of burning roots. Liquid fertilizers must be reapplied frequently, since their nutrients leach through the root zone rapidly.

Solid fertilizers are usually sold as granules or pellets. They can be broadcast or spread over lawns and ground covers, scratched or dug into the soil around other plants, and dug into the soil when preparing new planting beds.

Other solids include *controlled-release fertilizers,* sold as spikes, tablets, or beadlike granules that release nutrients gradually over a fairly long period—typically 3 to 9 months—if the soil receives regular moisture. Dig granules into soil at planting time or scratch them into the soil surface (they're useful for fertilizing container plants). Use a mallet to pound spikes into the ground; dig holes for tablets.

General- and special-purpose fertilizers. The various fertilizers labeled "general-purpose"

Fertilizer forms, clockwise from left, include soluble crystals (mounded and dissolved in water), dry granules, organic fish meal, and controlled-release pellets.

or "all-purpose" usually contain equal or nearly equal amounts of the macronutrients N, P, and K (a 10-10-10 formula, for example). They are intended to meet most plants' requirements throughout the growing season.

Other fertilizers are formulated for specific needs. High-nitrogen blends (such as 29-3-4) help keep lawns green and growing quickly, while higher-phosphorus mixes (6-10-4, for example) are intended to promote flowering and fruiting. Some packaged fertilizers are formulated for particular types of plants, such as bulbs and roses. Those designed for acid lovers such as camellias, rhododendrons, and azaleas are especially useful.

Another special kind of fertilizer is *foliar fertilizer*. Such products are liquids applied to leaves, which can absorb nutrients through openings in the leaves called stomata; some solutions are high in the macronutrients, while others offer an effective way to apply micronutrients. To avoid burning leaves, water plants thoroughly before spraying them, follow dilution directions, and don't apply the fertilizer at all if outdoor temperatures will rise above 85°F/29°C.

You can also buy formulas that combine fertilizers with insecticides (chiefly for roses) or with weed killers, fungicides, or moss killers (all for lawns). An organic weed-and-feed for lawns is made with corn gluten. These products are appropriate if you need the extra ingredient every time you fertilize; if not, it's more economical to buy it separately. Before using any such products, read the label carefully—as you would for any fertilizer—to check for instructions and precautions. The herbicides included in some combination products, for example, can damage plants with roots growing into the application area.

PLANT NUTRIENTS

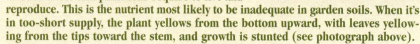

The nutrients plants need are divided into three groups: macronutrients, secondary nutrients, and micronutrients.

Macronutrients. These are nutrients that plants need in fairly large quantities. Three—carbon, oxygen, and hydrogen—are found in air and water; plants use the others in mineral form.

Nitrogen (chemical symbol N) is used in the synthesis of proteins, chlorophyll, and enzymes—all substances that plant cells require to live and reproduce. This is the nutrient most likely to be inadequate in garden soils. When it's in too-short supply, the plant yellows from the bottom upward, with leaves yellowing from the tips toward the stem, and growth is stunted (see photograph above).

Phosphorus (P) promotes flowering and fruiting, strong root growth, and the transfer of energy from one point in the plant to another. Plants deficient in phosphorus show stunted growth and reduced yield of fruit; in some, you may see purplish areas on the leaf undersides.

Potassium (K) is important for regulating the synthesis of proteins and starches that make sturdy plants. It also helps increase resistance to diseases, heat, and cold. Symptoms of deficiency include reduced flowering and fruiting, spotted or curled older leaves, and weak stems and roots.

Secondary nutrients. Plants need these in about the same amounts as they do the macronutrients. However, since they're less likely to be deficient in most soils than are the macronutrients, they're commonly called secondary nutrients.

Calcium (Ca) plays a fundamental role in cell formation and growth, and most roots require some calcium right at the growing tips.

Magnesium (Mg) forms the core of the chlorophyll molecules in the cells of green leaves.

Sulfur (S) acts with nitrogen in the manufacture of protoplasm for plant cells.

Micronutrients. Also known as trace elements, micronutrients are required in very small quantities; in fact, excess amounts can be toxic. Among them are *zinc* (Zn) and *manganese* (Mn), both thought to function as catalysts in the utilization of other nutrients; and *iron* (Fe), essential for chlorophyll formation (see page 481 for information on iron-deficiency chlorosis).

APPLYING FERTILIZERS

Before planting a new bed, work in a fertilizer containing phosphorus and potassium. This puts these essential nutrients at the level in the soil where they are readily available to plant roots.

Using a cultivator, gently scratch the soil beneath plants with roots growing close to the surface. Apply a granular fertilizer and water thoroughly. Roots of larger plants may extend several feet beyond the reach of the foliage, so be sure to spread fertilizer widely enough to reach all the roots.

Liquid fertilizers can be applied with a watering can. You can also use an injector device to run the fertilizer through a drip watering system. A simple siphon attachment (above) draws a measured amount of fertilizer from concentrate in a pail and dilutes it as it is mixed with water from a hose.

Frost and Cold Protection

Wherever you garden, the best defense against cold damage is to choose trees, shrubs, and screen and hedge plants hardy in your climate zone. Use tender plants for summer display in borders, or plant them in containers that can be moved to shelter when the weather turns frigid.

EXTENDING THE SEASON. Inevitably in the Northeast cold weather marks the beginning and end of each growing season. Fortunately for gardeners, there are some simple ways to lengthen the gardening season at both ends—by getting an earlier start in spring and warding off fall frosts. See Winter Protection for information on steps you can take to get plants ready for the dormant season. Here are some techniques to consider for stretching your growing season.

KNOW YOUR GARDEN'S MICROCLIMATES. That is, learn which areas tend to be warmer and which are colder. Microclimates can help extend the season whether you are growing vegetables or planting spring bulbs. For the earliest displays of spring bulbs like daffodils and crocuses, for example, look for protected sites that tend to stay warmer in winter. Bulbs planted at the base of a south-facing wall will bloom earlier than ones on exposed or north-facing sites. When selecting a site to grow vegetables or annuals, consider that sites exposed on all sides (particularly the north) tend to warm up later in spring and cool off more quickly in fall. When compared to a protected site (sheltered on one or more sides by hedges, walls, fences, or other windbreaks) such sites will probably have later spring frosts and earlier fall frosts, meaning a shorter growing season. Other locations prone to late frosts include hollows and low, enclosed areas—commonly called frost pockets—that catch cold air as it sinks, then hold it motionless.

Mulch and chopped-up Christmas tree branches provide some protection for young or tender plants.

USE SEASON EXTENDERS. Hot caps, temporary cold frames, and other season-extension devices are commonly used to get an early start in the spring vegetable garden. They also are useful for getting annuals off to a quick start in beds and borders. See page 507 for more information on season extenders. Keep in mind that season extenders and temporary shelters such as sheets laid on plants overnight also can be used to protect plants from early fall frost. Sometimes an early spell of cold weather is followed by several weeks of warm temperatures, and protecting plants for one or two nights can buy an extra month of growing season.

Although season extenders are great for a wide variety of plants, it's best not to depend on them to keep tender annuals alive that were planted outdoors too early. Heat-loving annuals such as coleus and ornamental peppers—as well as tender perennials such as cannas and dahlias—won't really begin growing until the soil warms up to about 60°F/15°C. They may survive colder temperatures, but plants kept warm and indoors until the weather settles usually perform best during the rest of the season.

WATCH THE WEATHER. Frost that hits in early fall (before the growing season ends) or in spring (after growth is underway) is much more damaging than one striking when plants already are semidormant or dormant. In spring and fall, be alert for signs of an impending freeze: still air, clear skies, low humidity, and, of course, low temperatures. It's wise to check TV and radio weather bulletins as well. If you notice danger signals late in the afternoon, protect at-risk plants out in the garden with temporary shelters such as sheets, floating row covers, even cardboard boxes overnight. Move container-grown plants into the garage or onto a protected porch. Remove coverings during the day unless the threat of frost continues. (For ways to protect vegetables from frost and extend their productivity, see page 507.)

WINTER PROTECTION. Whether you live in mild Zone 32, or northern climates such as Zones 44 and 45, where winters are frigid and the frost-free growing season is short, it is best to grow plants that are hardy in your zone. Plants that are undamaged by normal cold winter temperatures in your area will inevitably be healthier than ones that are routinely damaged each year. Still, it can be tempting to experiment with plants that are not reliably hardy where you live. Careful siting and winter protection can help such plants survive.

Since lush, rank growth is more likely to be damaged by freezing temperatures, it is a good idea to take steps to condition or prepare even hardy plants for cold weather. Water and fertilize the garden as needed in late spring and early summer, while plants are growing the fastest. In late summer, taper off feeding plants to slow their growth, which will also slow naturally as cooler temperatures and shorter days arrive. This helps discourage new growth that won't have time to

mature before cold weather arrives. Reducing water also helps harden growth—but apply enough to keep the soil moist through the onset of the frost season, since moist soil holds and releases more heat than dry soil does.

Once the ground has frozen completely, protect marginally hardy perennials and other low-growing plants with a thick layer of coarse mulch such as evergreen boughs or saltmarsh hay. Leave this mulch in place until new growth emerges in spring—but remove it gradually then to prevent frost damage to new shoots. Most hardy trees and shrubs need no further protection. Some roses are marginally hardy and need to be protected. With roses, the aim is to keep the roots and bud union alive and to preserve as many live canes as possible; see page 388 for information.

Broad-leafed evergreens often suffer in winter because the leaves continue to transpire and thus lose moisture (particularly on relatively warm, windy days). If the soil is frozen, however, the roots cannot take up water to replace what has been lost, and the plant becomes desiccated. To minimize damage to these plants, water thoroughly before the ground freezes, then apply a thick mulch of oak leaves, pine needles, wood chips, or ground bark. The mulch limits the penetration of frost into the ground, allowing the deepest roots to continue absorbing moisture; it also protects surface roots from alternate freezing and thawing. Careful siting is important as well: when you plant broad-leafed evergreens, avoid locations where bright sun—especially in early morning—will strike frozen plants. To avoid rupturing plant tissues, thawing should be gradual.

Don't hurry to prune frost-damaged plants. Cutting them back too soon may stimulate tender new growth that will be nipped by later frosts, and you may mistake leafless but living stems for dead ones. When new growth begins in spring, you can remove wood that is clearly dead.

Grasses. See Lawns (at right); Ornamental Grasses (page 469).

Ground Covers

Gardeners rely on ground covers to blanket the soil with dense foliage, adding beauty and variety to the garden and suppressing weeds at the same time. Though lawn grasses (see entry at right) are doubtless the best-known cover for bare ground, the term "ground cover" is typically used to refer to other, nongrassy plants, among them shrubs, vines, and many perennials. If chosen carefully, they require considerably less maintenance and water than lawns do. Ground cover plants usually produce a relatively even surface, though heights range from a few inches to knee-high or even taller.

Japanese spurge *(Pachysandra terminalis)* is an invaluable ground cover for shady places.

PLANTING GROUND COVERS ON A SLOPE

When setting plants on a steep slope where erosion may occur, arrange them in staggered rows. Make an individual terrace for each plant and create a basin or low spot behind each one to catch water. Set the crowns of the plants high, so they won't become saturated and rot after watering.

CHOOSING GROUND COVERS. When selecting ground covers, start by considering your site. Is it level or sloping, sunny or shady? How much water will be available for the plants? Also decide if you want a ground cover you can walk across or one that will serve as a traffic barrier. Settle on a deciduous cover or an evergreen one; decide if you want flowers or prefer just plain foliage. Ask yourself how the ground cover will fit in with the garden's other plants and hardscape. As you consider all these questions, you'll zero in on the right plants for your situation. For ideas, consult Ground Covers and Lawn Substitutes in A Guide to Plant Selection, beginning on page 47.

PLANTING AND CARING FOR GROUND COVERS. In warmer parts of the Northeast, groundcovers can be planted in spring or fall. In the coldest areas, wait until spring to plant. Most ground covers grow best in well-prepared soil; for these, ready the planting area as directed on page 482, adding plenty of organic matter. Some kinds of ground covers, however, can be planted directly in native soil with little or no amendment. This group includes various tough, shrubby types, many of them natives.

Before planting, install landscape fabric (see page 468) to help control weeds, if desired.

When planting ground covers purchased in small pots or flats, set them in holes the same depth as and slightly wider than the root ball. For directions on setting out plants from gallon-size containers, see page 485. The required spacing varies with the plant; check entries in the A to Z Plant Encyclopedia for details.

Water thoroughly after planting, then keep the soil moist (but not soggy) as the plants settle in. Apply a mulch to help conserve moisture and to prevent weed seeds from growing.

Once ground covers are established, their water needs vary depending on the particular plant and the soil in which it is growing. Fertilizer requirements differ, too. As a rule of thumb, though, most woody, shrubby ground covers (especially drought-tolerant sorts) have fairly low nutrient needs; many get along with little or no fertilizing. Perennial ground covers with softer, lusher growth generally have higher nutrient requirements and should receive an annual feeding in spring.

Herbs

The word "herb" applies to any plant that, at some time in history, has been valued for seasoning, medicine, fragrance, or general household use. Within this broad category, you'll find tall, willowy plants like dill as well as low, fine-textured creepers (some kinds of thyme, for example) that spread along the ground to form a fragrant carpet. Many herbs are annuals and biennials grown for their leaves and seeds; others, such as French tarragon and oregano, are perennials; still others are tough shrubs like rosemary, as useful in the landscape as in the kitchen.

Herbs have numerous garden uses. They can, of course, be grouped together in an all-herb garden, be it a sunny corner of the vegetable plot, a special raised bed, or a traditional circular planting centered with a birdbath or sundial. They also make excellent container plants—and pot culture is a good way to grow them near the kitchen door, handy for snipping. And many herbs add texture and interest to the perennial or shrub border.

Basil

PLANTING AND CARING FOR HERBS. Choose a planting spot that receives 6 to 8 hours of full sun each day. Well-drained soil is essential; if drainage is poor, dig in plenty of organic matter or plant in raised beds. Work in a complete fertilizer before planting. Herbs aren't heavy feeders, so this should suffice for the entire season.

Most perennial and shrubby herbs are easier to start from transplants than from seed. Nurseries offer many kinds in spring, typically in 2- or 4-inch pots; some are also sold in gallon containers. Annual and biennial herbs (such as basil, cilantro, dill, and parsley), on the other hand, can successfully be started from seed.

Lawns

The classic lawn—lush, green, and crisply mowed—has long been a basic landscaping element. Today, however, water conservation is an important issue everywhere, and attention has naturally focused on the huge amount of water needed to keep lawns alive and green. Research has shown that the grasses traditionally favored for turf (Kentucky bluegrass, bent grasses, fine fescues, perennial ryegrass) require more water per square foot than almost any other kind of garden plant. Moreover, up to half the water used by a typical single-family household is applied outdoors, primarily to lawns—and most homeowners give the lawn more water than it really needs.

Responding to these findings, some communities now restrict the amount of lawn that can be planted around new homes. Many gardeners, too, have reconsidered the value of a lawn. Some have eliminated it entirely, replacing it with one of the alternatives discussed under Water Conservation (page 512); others have sharply reduced its size. Besides demanding less water than a large expanse does, a small lawn requires less labor, time, and money to maintain.

If you do include a lawn in your landscape, you can do more to save on time and water than just keep it small. Opt for a simple geometric shape; it will allow you to irrigate without overspray, and it's easier to mow. Keeping the lawn fairly level makes good sense, too, since it minimizes runoff and makes mowing safer. Finally, be sure you choose the right grass for your climate, prepare and plant the site carefully, and maintain the lawn properly.

L

PLANTING A NEW LAWN. When you plant a new lawn—whether from seed or sod—proper site preparation is essential. Remove any existing sod with a sod cutter (available from rental yards); for easier removal, you can kill the sod with an herbicide such as glyphosate before using the cutter. It's wise to have the soil's pH tested (see page 499) before you plant. Sow cool-season grasses approximately six weeks before the first fall frost date. In warmer regions, sow warm-season grasses in late spring or early summer.

Till the site to a depth of about 8 inches and spread it with a 3- to 4-inch layer of an organic amendment, such as commercial compost. Also apply a complete fertilizer and any materials recommended by the soil test lab to adjust the pH. Till again; rake the area smooth and water it thoroughly. Let the soil settle for a few days; then sow the seed or lay the sod as shown in the photographs on facing page.

CARING FOR LAWNS. To look their best, lawns require consistent watering and fertilizing as well as regular mowing.

Watering. To encourage deep rooting and conserve water, irrigate lawns as deeply and infrequently as possible. In most areas, once or twice a week should be adequate during warm weather; in hotter regions, you'll probably have to water more often. During cooler times of year, you can cut back on watering. Check with local water agencies or your Cooperative Extension Office for guidelines, which are often based on evapotranspiration (ET)—a weather-based, localized measurement of how much water a plant uses and how much evaporates from the soil.

To decide how thirsty the lawn really is, you can also perform a few informal tests. First, just step on the grass: if the blades don't spring back from your footprint, it's time to water. Or push a screwdriver into the soil; if it doesn't penetrate easily, the lawn probably needs water. A soil sampling tube (see page 513) will give a more accurate indication of the soil's moisture content.

Many sprinklers apply water faster than the soil can absorb it. To prevent runoff, water in cycles; sprinkle until just before runoff or puddling occurs (typically 10 to 15 minutes), then repeat the cycle in an hour. Adjust sprinklers so they don't overshoot onto paving.

To improve water penetration and reduce runoff, aerate and dethatch your lawn every few years. Local nurseries offer information and equipment to help you with these tasks.

Fertilizing. Most lawns are heavy feeders, requiring regular applications of high-nitrogen fertilizer. Give cool-season lawns two applications of fertilizer in spring and two in fall. Fertilize warm-season lawns monthly in late spring and summer (feed Bermuda grass only lightly in summer, to restrain its growth). Numerous bagged lawn fertilizers, both synthetic and natural, are sold; check the packages for recommended application rates.

CHOOSING THE RIGHT LAWN GRASS FOR YOUR AREA

Lawn grasses fall into two categories: *cool-season* and *warm-season* (subtropical). Each group comprises a variety of plants with varying water needs. For more information on specific grasses, consult the individual listings in the A to Z Plant Encyclopedia. Whatever grass you choose, it pays to buy top-quality grasses, because hybridizers are releasing new grasses every year that feature better insect and disease resistance as well as improved vigor and drought tolerance. When buying grass seed, don't settle for the cheapest brand available. Cheap grass seed can contain a large portion of weed seeds (the percentages are listed on the label) as well as inert matter such as soil and stones.

Though they require care, lawns set off your home like no other ground cover.

Cool season grasses easily withstand winter cold but their growth slows down when warm weather arrives and they do not grow well in areas with hot, dry summers—or in years when the weather is unusually hot and dry. All grow well throughout the Northeast, although most require regular watering in the summer months to remain green. Cool-season grasses are often sold as mixes of several kinds; even if one of them is not adapted to the soil or sun/shade conditions in your garden, chances are that others in the package will do as well. While many homeowners prefer a pure bluegrass lawn, for example, combining bluegrass with fine fescue creates a blend that is fairly drought tolerant and tolerates more shade than pure bluegrass would. Blends of grasses are especially valuable for problem areas—such as high traffic areas or shady spots—because they are especially selected to thrive in these tough conditions. Warm season grasses, such as Bermuda grass, are not appropriate north of Zone 32.

GRASSES FOR THE NORTHEAST

Bent grasses (*Agrostis*). Fine-textured grasses requiring ample water and more care than other lawn grasses. Grow in acid soil, in sun or light shade. Mow at ½ to ¾ inch. Sold as seed, sod.

Crested wheatgrass (*Agropyron cristatum*). Light bluish green grass makes tough, very drought-tolerant lawn for sunny areas; grown primarily in the Midwest. Goes dormant and turns brown in hot weather. Mow at 2 inches. Sold as seed.

Fine fescue (*Festuca rubra* and others). Fine-bladed grasses that succeed in well-drained soil in shaded sites. Fairly drought tolerant. Sometimes blended with Kentucky bluegrass or perennial ryegrass or used to overseed warm-season grasses in the South. Mow at 1½ to 2 inches. Sold as seed.

Tall fescue (*Festuca elatior;* also called coarse fescue). Tough grass that tolerates heat and some drought and flourishes in sun or shade. It freezes out in the coldest climates. Newer selections (dwarf tall fescue) are finer bladed, deeper green. Mow at 2 to 3 inches. Sold as seed, sod.

Kentucky bluegrass (*Poa pratensis*). Classic grass for cooler regions. Needs regular water. Takes sun, light shade. Mow at 1 to 2½ inches. Sold as seed, sod.

Perennial ryegrass (*Lolium perenne*). Deep green grass that does best in sun. Needs frequent watering. Used as year-round lawn in cooler areas or to overseed winter-dormant grasses. Mow at 2 inches. Sold as seed, sod.

Bermuda grass (*Cynodon dactylon*). Zones 31–32 only. Good, drought-tolerant lawn for large, sunny areas. Invades shrub plantings and flower beds by seed and spreading roots if not contained. Mow at 1 inch. Sold as seed. Hybrid Bermuda grass is finer-textured and does not self-sow; mow at ½ to ¾ inch. Sold as sod, sprigs, plugs.

Zoysia (*Zoysia*). Tolerates drought and heat; takes sun or shade. Mow at 1 to 2 inches. Sold as sod, sprigs, plugs. It goes dormant and turns brown in winter, but greens up again in spring.

L

If you cut back on watering because of drought, hold back on fertilizer as well.

Mowing. To keep a lawn healthy, mow it regularly; grass is weakened if allowed to grow too long between mowings. When the blades are about one-third taller than the recommended height (see the descriptions of individual lawn grasses on page 466), it's time to mow. Leave clippings on the lawn to decompose and add nutrients to the soil unless they are quite long (long clippings might smother the grass).

LAWN PROBLEMS. To avoid lawn problems, plant grass that's well adapted to your area and care for it properly. If you do encounter problems, the following information will help you identify and correct them. (For a discussion of weeds that bother lawns, see page 518.)

Chinch bugs. These small (1/6-inch-long), grayish black insects suck sap from grass blades (especially in hot weather), attacking bluegrass, Bermuda grass, and zoysia grass. Symptoms are brown or yellow patches, especially in dry locations; patches eventually die. To confirm presence of these pests, push a can with both ends removed into the soil just where grass is beginning to brown and fill it with water; if present, chinch bugs will float to the surface.

To control, eliminate thatch. Keep lawn moist to promote beneficial fungi that attack chinch bugs. For chemical control, use diazinon.

Fairy ring. This fungal disease is common in lawns growing in soil high in organic matter or containing wood debris (such as boards or old roots). Symptoms include small circular patches of dark green grass surrounding areas of dead or light-colored grass. Mushrooms may or may not be present.

To control, apply a nitrogen fertilizer and keep the lawn wet for 3 to 5 days. Also aerate the lawn. There are no chemical controls.

Chinch bug

Fairy ring

SEED OR SOD

Lawn grass is sold in several forms; seed and sod are used in the Northeast. If you seed, weed diligently after planting.

Seed is the least expensive way to start a lawn, and it's offered for a wide variety of grasses. Read the package label carefully. It should list the named varieties of the grass or grasses included and indicate a high rate of germination for those grasses; it should also show a low percentage of crop or weed seeds in relation to the percentage of lawn grass seeds.

Fall seeding is recommended for most grasses, since cool-season grasses germinate well then and fall and winter rains help establish the lawn. In the coldest climates, seed in early fall, so the lawn can grow before winter.

SOWING GRASS SEED

1 After preparing the site, scatter seed. A mechanical spreader helps sow seed evenly.

2 Lightly rake seed into the soil to distribute it as evenly as possible.

3 Spread a very thin layer of mulch, such as aged or nitrogen-fortified sawdust, over the area; roll with an empty roller to press seed into soil. Water thoroughly, then keep the seedbed moist with frequent watering until the seed sprouts.

LAYING SOD

1 After preparing the site, moisten the soil. Unroll the strips and lay them out with their ends staggered, pressing the edges together firmly.

2 Use a knife to trim sod so it fits snugly around paving and other obstacles.

3 To press roots firmly into the soil, roll the lawn with a roller half-filled with water. Water the new lawn once daily (more often in hot weather) for 6 weeks.

Rust. Rust fungi can afflict Kentucky bluegrass, perennial ryegrass, tall fescue, and zoysia lawns. Infected lawns have an overall yellowish to reddish color; small, reddish pustules form in circular or elongated patches on older leaf blades and stems. Blades eventually shrivel and die.

To control, apply adequate (but not excessive) nitrogen fertilizer. For rust spores to germinate, leaf surfaces must be wet for 4 hours; water in the morning so that grass will dry out during the day. The fungicides triadimefon and chlorothalonil may be effective.

Sod webworms. The larvae of several kinds of moths, these pests attack all turf grasses. Small dead patches appear in spring and gradually enlarge during summer. Pale moths fly close to the lawn in a zigzag pattern at dusk. To confirm presence of sod webworms, drench an affected patch of lawn with a solution of 1 tablespoon dishwashing soap and 1 gallon water. Larvae will float to the surface; if you find 15 or more per square yard, treat the lawn.

To control, try parasitic nematodes (see page 472). For chemical control, use a product containing permethrin (a pyrethroid).

White grubs. These 1- to 1½-inch grubs are the larvae of several species of beetles; they have three pairs of legs and curl into a C shape when exposed. They feed on roots of all turf grasses. Distinct, irregularly shaped brown patches appear in afflicted lawns; symptoms are most severe in late summer. Sections of dead turf pull up easily.

To control, apply parastic nematodes (see page 472), first checking to be sure the species you buy is recommended for use against white grubs. Chemical controls include carbaryl and imidacloprid; these work best if you first dethatch the lawn.

TOP TO BOTTOM: Rust, Sod webworms, White grubs

Mulching

Mulching is the process of applying organic or inorganic materials to the surface of the soil around plants. Mulches are valuable for several reasons. They help hold moisture in the soil; insulate soil from extreme or rapid changes of temperature; prevent most weed seedlings from becoming established (and make it easier to remove any that do grow); keep mud from splashing up onto foliage, flowers, fruit, and surfaces such as house walls; help prevent erosion; and make your garden beds look tidy. Before applying either organic or inorganic mulches, clear away existing weeds.

ORGANIC MULCHES. Organic mulches, derived from once-living matter, break down slowly, improving the soil and adding nutrients as they decompose. Choices include chopped leaves, compost, grass clippings (apply in thin layers, letting each layer dry before applying another), pine needles, shredded bark, ground bark, wood chips, sawdust, straw, and coir dust (see page 457). Other good organic mulches are agricultural by-products such as cocoa beans, crushed nut hulls or shells and pomace, the pulpy remains of grapes or apples that have been pressed to make wine or juice. (Let pomace dry before using it.)

Apply organic mulches in a 2- to 4-inch-thick layer on paths and around plants, but take care not to let mulch touch plant stems or cover the plants' crowns: too much moisture near the crown can cause rot.

INORGANIC MULCHES. Examples of inorganic mulches include gravel, river rock, and other kinds of stones; black plastic; and landscape fabrics. Stones make permanent mulches that can discourage weeds effectively; check with the supplier for the amount you need. Black plastic both warms the soil and suppresses weeds, making it especially useful in vegetable gardens.

Landscape fabrics—unlike plastic—are porous, allowing air, water, and dissolved nutrients to reach the soil. Sold in nurseries and garden supply centers, these fabrics are best used in permanent plantings around trees and shrubs; they aren't really suited for beds of vegetables or annuals, where you change plants often. Install them as shown at right (you can lay

LAYING LANDSCAPE FABRIC. Unroll fabric, then use scissors or a knife to cut X-shaped slits for plants. Tuck the flaps back in around the plants' bases.

them around existing plants or cut slits in them to accommodate new ones). After installation, cover the fabric with a 2- to 3-inch layer of a weed-free organic mulch.

Native Plants, Gardening with

Native plants give your garden a sense of place, making it part of the overall landscape of the region where you live. They attract wildlife, drawing birds, butterflies, lizards, and insects to the garden. And because they're naturally suited to the climate, they're generally self-sufficient, needing little care once established.

The Northeast is home to a number of native plant communities, including oak/hickory and beech/maple forests, oak woodland, coniferous forest, and various kinds of meadows and wetlands. Local native plant societies, demonstration gardens at botanical gardens and parks, and field guides can all teach you more about groups of plants indigenous to your area.

Your garden may offer enough diversity in growing conditions to accommodate natives from different communities. A hot, dry, sunny slope with well-drained soil is an excellent site for a mix of meadow wildflowers. A damp, low-light spot will suit shade-loving natives adapted to moist locales; a little-watered area beneath trees is right for those that prefer dry shade. A permanently wet, even boggy area is ideal for moisture-loving species.

HOW MUCH MULCH SHOULD YOU BUY?

Bulk quantities of organic mulch are sold by the cubic yard. Determine how many square feet you want to cover (multiply the area's length by its width), then consult the chart below to determine the approximate amount of mulch you need.

HOW MUCH MULCH TO USE

To cover this area	2 inches deep	3 inches deep	4 inches deep
100 square feet	⅔ cubic yard	1 cubic yard	1⅓ cubic yards
250	1⅔	2½	3⅓
500	3⅓	5	6⅓
1,000	6⅔	10	13⅓

L

PLANTING AND CARING FOR NATIVE PLANTS.
If natives are to thrive in your garden over the long term, you'll need to pay special attention to getting them established. Be sure to select species that are adapted to the soil conditions and sun exposure in your yard. When setting out container-grown plants, start with young ones that are not root-bound—they may not be much to look at when first planted, but they'll adapt more successfully than larger plants. Water immediately after planting, being sure to saturate the soil. Then water carefully and steadily for the first summer or two: don't inundate the plants, but don't let them dry out, either. Once you've nursed your natives through their first 2 years (and assuming you have planted them where the natural conditions suit them), they should do well with little or no supplemental watering. In general, Eastern natives don't require fertilizing (and some are actually weakened by it). A light mulch is beneficial, but to avoid rot, keep it away from the plants' crowns.

Joe Pyeweed, native to much of the East Coast, thrives with little care throughout the Northeast.

Organic Gardening

Also known as chemical-free or natural gardening, organic gardening is often associated with raising crops that are safer to eat, but its principles apply to any sort of garden, not just the vegetable plot and the fruit orchard. Organic gardeners (and farmers) strive to produce the healthiest plants possible with minimal impact on the environment and minimal risk to all creatures—human and otherwise—who enjoy the garden. They avoid using chemical fertilizers and pesticides, focusing instead on creating healthy soil, which in turn promotes healthy plants less susceptible to insects and disease. They aim for biological diversity in their gardens, choosing plants that will attract a wide variety of organisms, including the beneficial insects that help keep damaging pests under control.

ELEMENTS OF AN ORGANIC GARDEN. As noted below, many aspects of organic gardening are covered elsewhere in these pages.

Building healthy soil. Healthy garden soil is home to earthworms and numerous other beneficial creatures. Its structure is hospitable to plant roots—neither too dense nor too loose, fast draining yet moisture retentive. To achieve this kind of soil, amend your planting beds with organic amendments such as compost and manure (see pages 455–457 and 500–501 for more on composting and soil amendments). Cover crops (page 458) also help. Fertilizers, too, can boost a soil's nutrient content; organic gardeners prefer natural products (page 462), which, though slower acting than chemical ones, provide a more sustained release of nutrients and encourage beneficial soil-dwelling organisms.

Controlling pests and diseases. Be diligent about monitoring the garden, so you know which problems are present and what natural controls (beneficial insects, for example) may already be at work. Physical controls such as barriers, handpicking, and water jets (page 471) can curtail insect damage. Choosing plant varieties resistant to specific diseases and pests is important; you'll find many such varieties listed in the A to Z Plant Encyclopedia. Crop rotation prevents diseases and insects that are specific to certain plants from building up in any one part of the garden. For more on disease and pest control, including a discussion of Integrated Pest Management (IPM) using beneficial insects and biological controls, see pages 471-473.

Controlling weeds. To keep weeds down, use mulches (see page 468; organic mulches also help improve the soil). Physical management techniques such as pulling and hoeing (page 517) are also effective.

Ornamental Grasses

Grown for their graceful form and varying textures, ornamental grasses provide a handsome foil to shrubs and perennials. Many are excellent container plants, too. Like lawn grasses, ornamental sorts can be divided into warm- and cool-season types. *Warm-season grasses* include most species of *Miscanthus, Molinia, Panicum,* and *Pennisetum;* they grow from spring through summer, bloom in fall, and then go dormant. Their foliage and flowering plumes remain attractive—albeit dry and brown—through the winter.

Cool-season grasses are typically evergreen or semievergreen, though some die back in cold climates. They begin new growth in early spring (fall in warmer regions), then flower in spring and summer. The group includes *Deschampsia, Festuca, Helictotrichon sempervirens,* and *Sesleria,* as well as the sedges *(Carex).*

For help in choosing these plants, see Ornamental Grasses on page 67. Be aware that a few ornamental grasses can be invasive, spreading too extensively in the garden or wild lands; these are noted in the entries in the A to Z Plant Encyclopedia.

Ornamental grasses planted in drifts bring texture, movement, and subtle colors to gardens and landscapes.

PLANTING AND CARING FOR ORNAMENTAL GRASSES. Garden care for ornamental grasses is more or less the same as that you'd give perennials. Most should be planted in spring, though cool-season sorts can also be set out in late summer or early fall. Before planting, work organic matter (such as compost) and a complete fertilizer into the soil. Don't bury the plants' crowns when you set them in, as this can lead to rot. A mulch will help keep down weeds and conserve soil moisture, but again, be careful not to let it pile up around the grasses' crowns.

Ornamental grasses vary greatly in their moisture needs—some require water regularly, others only rarely. Check the listings in the A to Z Plant Encyclopedia for details. If planted in well-prepared beds and mulched, most ornamental grasses can do without feeding, but if they're growing poorly it's wise to give them an application of general-purpose fertilizer in early spring.

These plants all benefit from an annual cleanup in late winter. Cut back warm-season grasses just as you see new growth emerging at the plants' bases, using pruning shears to trim dead foliage and flowering stems to within a few inches of the ground. (If you have a number of large clumps, electric hedge shears or a mechanical weed trimmer will make quick work of this project.) Evergreen cool-season grasses needn't be cut back every year. Instead, clean them up by removing dead foliage; you can often simply "comb" out old growth by running your fingers through the clumps. After a few years, however, the grasses may develop a great deal of unattractive or dead leaves; at this point, cut them back by two-thirds in late winter or early spring to encourage fresh new growth.

Divide ornamental grasses in early spring every few years or so, when the clump's center dies out. To divide, dig up the clump; if it's very large, you may first need to cut it into sections with a sharp spade or an ax. Then cut off and replant vigorous sections from the outside of the clump.

O

Perennials

The general category of perennials encompasses plants with widely varying habits of growth, but all have at least one thing in common: they live for more than 2 years, in contrast to annuals and biennials (pages 452 and 453), which complete their life cycles within 1 and 2 years, respectively. Some perennials die down to the ground at the end of each growing season, then reappear at the start of the next. These include hosta and peony *(Paeonia)* and are often called "herbaceous" plants. Others, such as Shasta daisy *(Chrysanthemum maximum)* and coral bells *(Heuchera),* go through winter as low tufts of leaves, ready to grow when spring arrives. A third type of perennial is truly evergreen, its foliage persisting almost unchanged throughout the winter months. Thrift *(Armeria maritima)* and yucca are two examples.

PLANTING PERENNIALS. Perennials are sold both containerized and bare-root. Nurseries and garden centers offer them in containers ranging from cell-packs to 1-gallon pots; for information on planting these, see page 483.

Nurseries and mail-order catalogs also sell some perennials bare-root during their dormant period. As the name implies, bare-root plants have had most or all of the soil removed from around their roots, which are then surrounded with organic packing material and enclosed in plastic bags. If you'll be planting bare-root perennials within a day or two after purchase or receipt, open the bags slightly, add a little water, and hold them in a cool place. If planting must be delayed by more than a few days, however, pot up the plants in small containers or heel them in—plant them temporarily in a shallow trench in the garden. Before setting out bare-root perennials in their permanent location, prepare the soil as described on page 482. Then plant as shown below.

STAKING PERENNIALS
Some perennials are naturally inclined to sprawl or flop over. To display their blooms most effectively and to keep them from smothering neighboring plants, you'll need to prop them up. These illustrations show three useful staking techniques.

Metal hoop support

Bamboo stake and tie; cork at tip of stake protects eyes from injury

Stakes and string

CARING FOR PERENNIALS. Routine watering during growth and bloom will satisfy most perennials. There are, of course, exceptions— some plants prefer drier soil, while others demand lots of moisture. These are noted in the A to Z Plant Encyclopedia. Keep in mind that young plants require more frequent watering than older ones with deeper, more extensive root systems. A layer of mulch helps conserve water as well as suppressing weeds and improving the soil as it decomposes. Once perennials are established in the garden, feed them once annually in late winter or early spring, using a complete fertilizer.

Throughout the bloom season, deadhead your perennials (that is, remove the spent flowers), both to keep the plants tidy and to prevent them from diverting energy to seed production. Of course, you may not want to deadhead in all cases. Certain perennials, for example, have attractive seedheads many gardeners prefer to leave in place until winter or early spring, both for decoration and to provide food for seed-eating birds.

Later in the year (in fall or winter), it's a good idea to clean up most perennials by removing old, dead, and fallen foliage, flowers, and stems. Besides neatening up the garden, such a cleanup deprives pests (especially snails and slugs) of hiding places and helps eliminate any disease organisms that may be living on garden debris.

Many gardeners in cold-winter climates mulch perennials over the winter to protect them from alternate freezing and thawing. As soon as the ground freezes, apply a lightweight mulch that won't pack down into an airtight mass; evergreen boughs, saltmarsh hay, and pine needles are all good choices.

Over time, many perennials form such thick clumps that the plants are too crowded to turn in a good performance. When this happens, dig and divide as described on page 492.

PLANTING BARE-ROOT PERENNIALS

 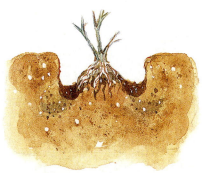 

1 Remove organic packing material and soak the roots in water for about 30 minutes.

2 Dig a hole about twice as wide as the root system. Then make a cone of soil in the center to support the roots.

3 Set the plant on the cone of soil and spread the roots evenly. Fill with soil so that the crown of the plant is level with or slightly above the soil, then water well.

Pests and Pest Management

Chemical-based pesticides were introduced in the 1940s, ushering in a long era of pest control through attempted eradication. Beyond being generally unsuccessful, this approach has often been actively harmful to a wide range of nontarget organisms, including humans and other animals, birds, and beneficial insects. In recent years, recognizing that gardens are complex and interdependent systems, more and more gardeners have rejected the "elimination" method: far from solving a problem, wiping out a particular pest simply upsets the garden's natural balance. The focus today has shifted to maintaining a diversified garden, where pests are largely kept in check by natural forces. If one or more pests do cause excessive damage, gardeners first attempt to manage the situation by using physical or biological controls. Chemicals are employed only as a last resort.

The balanced, safety-conscious attitude described above reflects the goals and methods of *Integrated Pest Management (IPM)*, an approach first developed for commercial agriculture but just as appropriate for the home garden. Its primary aim is to prevent problems. When diseases or pest infestations do arise, a number of integrated techniques are brought into play to reduce them to tolerable levels—not to eliminate them completely.

PREVENTING AND IDENTIFYING PROBLEMS. To thwart problems before they start, IPM begins with good cultural practices. Choose healthy plants adapted to your climate and garden conditions; whenever possible, select varieties resistant to diseases and pests prevalent in your area. Plant carefully and follow up with proper watering, fertilizing, garden cleanup, and other care as needed. Use soil solarization (page 518), a technique that reduces or eliminates some soil-dwelling pests and weed seeds. In the vegetable garden, rotate crops to prevent the buildup of specific pests (page 473).

Another basic aspect of IPM is regular garden monitoring. If you check your plants frequently, you're more likely to spot problems before they get out of hand. Note the general condition of each plant; then look for fungal growth, holes in leaves or fruit, sap oozing from bark, and wilted branches. Check for insects hiding on leaf undersides, in bark fissures, or beneath fallen leaves. A hand lens is useful for spotting tiny pests like spider mites.

Because beneficial or harmless creatures sometimes resemble damaging pests, it's important to identify the organisms you find accurately. For help with identification, check the photos and descriptions, pages 472–475 or consult your Cooperative Extension Office.

MANAGEMENT OPTIONS. Even if your garden inspection reveals a few pest problems, you may not need or want to employ controls. Keep in mind that the truly pest-free garden does not exist, and learn to accept some marred fruit,

flowers, or foliage. More extensive damage doesn't automatically require control, either: it may sometimes be better simply to remove and replace an afflicted plant than to attempt a cure.

If you decide that a problem is serious enough to warrant action on your part, it's time to formulate a pest management strategy. Within the guidelines of IPM, you'll begin with physical and biological controls, turning to chemicals only when all else fails.

Physical controls. These nontoxic controls include a number of techniques.

Handpicking. Remove and destroy slugs, snails, caterpillars, and other pests. To get rid of some pests, you may need to pluck and destroy entire leaves (a tactic that can also help control some foliage diseases).

Pruning. Remove and destroy entire branches infested with a pest or disease.

Spraying with water. A strong jet can knock many pests from plants and often kill them.

Erecting barriers. Certain physical structures can prevent pests from reaching susceptible plants. These include row covers (page 507); more permanent plant cages made by fastening screening to frames of wood or PVC pipe; and plant collars (paper cups, plastic cartons, or empty cans with both ends cut out) that protect seedlings from cutworms and other insects. Other barriers are discussed in the descriptions of individual pests.

Using traps. You can trap pests in various ways. Colored sticky traps are designed to catch specific insects; some are attracted to the color red, others to white or yellow, for example. Pheromone traps are also used. Pheromones

TOP: Plastic cartons prevent cutworms from reaching vegetable seedlings. BOTTOM: Yellow sticky cards attract and trap whiteflies.

are chemicals involved in communication between insects of the same species; they're placed in traps with sticky materials and used in commercial farming to monitor the presence of particular pests, thus helping to time sprays precisely. Some pheromone traps are used to control pest caterpillars (notably codling moth) by mass trapping of males.

Biological controls. When you use biological controls, you're relying on living organisms—beneficial insects, for example—to destroy garden pests. This sort of control occurs naturally in the garden all the time. To draw beneficials to your garden and encourage them to remain, provide food in the form of nectar-producing flowering plants, and be sure to avoid chemical sprays that will indiscriminately destroy both helpful and harmful creatures. You can purchase and release some beneficial insects. See page 472 for more information on beneficials and plants that attract them.

Certain microorganisms are also classed as biological controls. The best-known of these is *Bacillus thuringiensis (Bt)*, a bacterium that, once ingested by susceptible pest larvae, causes them to stop feeding and eventually die. Many different strains have been identified, each effective against specific types of larvae. *Bt* does not affect other, nontarget creatures. For more on biological controls, see page 472.

Chemical controls. As a last resort, IPM turns to various sorts of pesticides, first selecting the least toxic controls (products such as insecticidal soap, for example). If these are not successful, the use of stronger chemicals (synthetics) may be warranted. For lists of both natural and synthetic pesticides, see page 477.

LOCATING BIOLOGICAL PEST AND DISEASE CONTROLS

Many biological pest and disease control products are sold by mail-order companies specializing in gardening products. These include Harmony Farm Supply, Graton, CA; M & R Durango Inc., Bayfield, CO; Peaceful Valley Farm Supply, Grass Valley, CA; and Rincon-Vitova Insectaries Inc., Ventura, CA. In addition, the California Environmental Protection Agency publishes a free guide, *Suppliers of Beneficial Organisms in North America*. To obtain the guide, write to the California Department of Pesticide Regulation, Environmental Monitoring and Pest Management Branch, 830 K Street, Sacramento, CA 95814-3510; or call (916) 324-4100. The Bio-Integral Resource Center publishes a *Directory of Least-toxic Pest-control Products*, updated yearly; write to P.O. Box 7414, Berkeley, CA 94707 or call (510) 524-2567.

P

BENEFICIALS

Some of the beneficial creatures that are described here are naturally present in Northeastern gardens; others, as noted, can be introduced to reduce various pest populations. Beneficials that attack specific pests are noted in the descriptions below. Spiders and centipedes are also important predators, as are toads, frogs, and birds.

Assassin bugs. These slim, ½- to ¾-inch-long insects have long legs and even longer angled antennae. Some species are brilliant red or black; others are brown or gray. They prey on many insects, stabbing their victims with a long, curved beak.

Damsel bugs are dull gray or brown, about ½ inch long, and very slender, with a long, narrow head. Nymphs resemble the adults, but they're smaller and have no wings. Both adults and nymphs feed on aphids, leafhoppers, and small caterpillars.

Ground beetles range from ½ to 1 inch long; most are shiny black, though some are also marked with bright colors. The smaller species eat other insects, caterpillars, cutworms, and soil-dwelling maggots and grubs. Some larger species eat slugs and snails and their eggs.

Lacewings. An adult lacewing is an inch-long, flying insect with lacy, netted wings and long antennae. The immature or larval form looks something like a ½-inch-long alligator; it has visible legs and is equipped with pincers at the mouth end. Lacewing larvae devour aphids, leafhoppers, mealybugs, mites, psyllids, thrips, whiteflies, and other insects; adults of most species feed only on nectar, pollen, and honeydew from garden plants. Larvae are commercially available.

Lady beetles. Also known as ladybugs, these familiar garden helpers and their larvae (which look like ¼-inch-long, six-legged alligators with orange and black spots or stripes) feed on aphids, mealybugs, and the eggs of many insects. Mail-order suppliers and garden centers sell lady beetles, but once released they often fly away rather than staying in your garden. Freeing them at night or keeping them in cages for the first few days may encourage them to remain.

Minute pirate bugs. Both the adults (⅛-inch-long, black-and-white bugs) and pale orange nymphs feed on thrips, spider mites, and insect eggs. Also called flower bugs, they occur naturally in gardens; they can also be purchased for release.

Parasitic nematodes. Parasitic nematodes, widely available from garden-supply catalogs, include several species of microscopic worms. Also known as beneficial or predatory nematodes, they're effective against several hundred kinds of insects, including cucumber beetles, cutworms, flea beetles, grubs, root weevils, and sod webworms. They attack the larvae, releasing a toxic bacterium that kills the host. Read directions carefully, since effectiveness depends on proper soil conditions and release techniques.

Parasitic wasps. Many species of naturally occurring parasitic wasps lay their eggs in the larvae, pupae, or eggs of other insects, thus destroying them. These tiny wasps are not harmful to humans. One type offered in many garden catalogs is the trichogramma wasp, which lays its eggs within the eggs of many moths and butterflies. Several species are sold; check with the seller to get the one best adapted to your situation.

Soldier beetles are narrow, ¾-inch-long, typically red or orange beetles with leathery-looking black, gray, or brown wing covers. The adults eat aphids and other soft-bodied insects; the tiny soil-dwelling larvae attack smaller insects. Adults also feed on pollen and nectar.

Syrphid flies. Also known as flower or hover flies, these insects are important naturally occurring beneficials. Adults have golden bodies banded with yellow; they look a bit like bees but have only one set of wings. While adults feed only on nectar and pollen, the larvae (tapered green or gray maggots with small fangs) consume dozens of aphids each day.

Tachinid flies. The gray, bristled adults look something like houseflies. They feed only on nectar, but their tiny, spined green larvae parasitize pests such as armyworms, cutworms, stinkbugs, and smaller beetle larvae. There are many species, each attacking specific insects.

Assassin bug

Damsel bug

Ground beetle

Lacewing

Parasitic wasp

Soldier beetle

Syrphid fly

Tachinid fly

P

PLANTS THAT ATTRACT BENEFICIAL INSECTS

Certain flowering plants provide sources of food that many beneficials need at various times during their life cycle. Integrate them into a border or plant them in swaths around the garden. Mix many kinds: the wider the range of food and shelter you provide, the more varieties of insects you'll attract (and the more likely they are to stay). Plan your plantings so some are in flower throughout the growing season.

Coreopsis *(Coreopsis)*
Corn cockle *(Agrostemma githago)*
Cosmos *(Cosmos bipinnatus)*
Dill *(Anethum graveolens)*
Fennel *(Foeniculum vulgare)*
Feverfew *(Chrysanthemum parthenium)*
Mints *(Mentha)*
Orange coneflowers *(Rudbeckia)*
Oregano *(Origanum)*
Purple coneflowers *(Echinacea)*
Shasta daisies *(Chrysanthemum maximum)*
Sweet alyssum *(Lobularia maritima)*
Thymes *(Thymus)*
Yarrow *(Achillea)*

Plant a wide variety of flowers to attract beneficials.

PLANT PESTS. Some of the pests most commonly encountered in Northeastern gardens are discussed here. A number of pests that afflict only one kind of plant—ash trees *(Fraxinus)*, apples, or tomatoes, for example—are treated in the appropriate entry in the A to Z Plant Encyclopedia.

The controls mentioned for each pest are discussed in order of toxicity, from least to most toxic. Bear in mind that whenever you use chemical controls, whether natural or synthetic, *you risk killing beneficials* along with the target pests.

Ants. On their own, most ants aren't serious pests; some are even important natural enemies of harmful insects. Certain species, however, nurture and protect sap-sucking insects such as aphids, mealybugs, soft scales, and whiteflies. These pests in turn produce honeydew, which encourages the growth of sooty mold (page 460).

To prevent ants from tending sap-sucking insects on trees, place sticky barriers (commercial brands include Tree Tanglefoot Pest Barrier and Stickum) around the trunks; also prune off any branches that touch the ground to eliminate alternate paths up into the plant. Diatomaceous earth can be effective in deterring ants. Bait or ant stakes can be used on the ground near trails or nests.

Aphids. These soft, oval insects range from pinhead to matchhead size and may be black, pink, white, or pale green. They cluster together on young shoots, buds, and leaves. Both adult and immature aphids (nymphs) damage a wide range of plants by piercing the leaves and stems and sucking out plant juices. Some aphids transmit viral diseases.

Prevent aphids from damaging vegetables by planting under row covers (page 507). Reflective aluminum mulches (available from nurseries and mail-order sources) deter flying adult aphids from laying eggs.

Because numerous creatures keep aphid populations in check, the best control tactic is often to do nothing and leave the pests to the mercy of natural controls: lady beetles, lacewing larvae, soldier beetles, syrphid flies, predatory midges, parasitic wasps, and even lizards and some small birds. To encourage beneficials, grow plants that attract them (see box at left).

You can blast aphids from plants with strong jets of water; they can also be killed by spraying with insecticidal soap.

Horticultural oil, used as a dormant spray in winter, will kill the overwintering eggs of aphids on deciduous trees. Natural pesticides containing pyrethrins can be used. Other pesticides are also effective in controlling aphids but should be called upon only when infestations are severe. These include diazinon, malathion, and (on nonedible plants) acephate.

Bagworms. These tricky pests are most often mistaken for pine cones on evergreens, but actually, they are small moths. They spend most of their lifecycle on evergreens and other trees and shrubs, where they disguise themselves in hanging silken bags covered with needles or bits of leaves from their host trees. (A close look at the bags during warm summer weather will reveal that they move—a sure sign that they are not pine cones!) Infested trees develop defoliated patches. To control them, cut the bags off by hand, collect them in a plastic bag, and discard in the trash. Spraying plants with BTK (a special formulation of *Bacillus thuringensis*) in early spring also is effective. Pheromone traps set out in August will also attract males and discourage future generations.

Borers. Several symptoms signal the presence of borers in a tree, including a pile of sawdust-

TOP TO BOTTOM: Ants, Aphids (with ants), Spotted cucumber beetle

P

like material near the base of a trunk with a gummy trail up the trunk to a small hole. Dogwoods infested with borers develop lumpy swellings near the base of the trunk, or may have limbs or bark that falls off. The best way to prevent these pests is to avoid damaging the bark. Keep lawnmowers and string trimmers away from the trunk—the injuries they cause make it easier for borers to attack. If you do see evidence of borers, try to cut out the site with a sharp knife, or stick a long, thin wire up through the hole to stab and kill the pest. Keep plants healthy with regular water, mulch, and fertilizer. Remove badly infested trees.

Cucumber beetles. Two kinds of cucumber beetles—both about ¼ inch long—cause trouble in Eastern gardens. The spotted cucumber beetle looks a bit like a greenish yellow lady beetle with 12 black spots on its back; the striped cucumber beetle is yellowish orange and marked with three black stripes. Adult beetles chew holes in leaves and flowers and damage stems of cucumbers, melons, squash, and other vegetables; the spotted kind also feeds on roses and other garden plants. Both can spread diseases. The larvae, which live underground, may damage roots.

Cutworm

Earwig

Flea beetle

Galls

Leaf miners

P

Flea beetles. These tiny ($\frac{1}{10}$-inch-long) oval, shiny beetles may be blue black, brown, or bronze; they jump like fleas when disturbed. Adult flea beetles riddle leaves with small holes. They feed on many vegetable crops and are especially damaging to seedlings; they also spread diseases.

Adult flea beetles overwinter in weeds and garden debris; a fall cleanup will remove these havens. Protect seedlings with row covers. To control flea beetles, use azadirachtin (neem extract) or diazinon.

Gall-forming insects and mites. Galls—distorted swellings on plant leaves, stems, or flowers—are caused by the larvae of several hundred different species of wasps, midges, mites, aphids, and other invertebrates. Despite their unsightliness, most leaf galls are harmless. Prune off those on smaller branches or simply remove the whole branch. Large galls (and large branches) are usually better left in place, since pruning them out may harm the plant.

Leaf miners are the larvae of certain moths, beetles, and flies. They tunnel within foliage, leaving twisting trails on the surface. Adult leaf miners are rarely seen. Various species attack vegetables, ornamental and fruit trees, annuals, and perennials. The damage is mostly cosmetic, although yield of some crops may be reduced.

Protect vegetables by planting under row covers (page 507), thus preventing the adult insects from reaching the plants to lay eggs. Handpicking infested leaves is helpful. Parasitic wasps are natural enemies of leaf miners and lay their eggs on larvae or near leaf miner egg sites. Azadirachtin (neem extract) may discourage adults from laying eggs on leaf surfaces. Once the insect is inside the leaf, chemical control is difficult; the systemic insecticide acephate can be used on nonedibles.

Mealybugs have an oval body with overlapping soft plates and a white, cottony covering. They are closely related to scale insects—but unlike scales, most mealybugs can move around (slowly). They suck plant juices, causing stunting and, in some cases, death. Sooty mold (page 460) may grow on the honeydew they excrete. Mealybugs are houseplant pests everywhere; outdoors, they're only troublesome in warm-winter areas. For any infestation inside and for minor infestations outside, daub the pests with a cotton swab dipped in rubbing alcohol. Outdoors, hose plants with water jets (or insecticidal soap sprays) every 2 to 4 weeks to remove adult and immature mealybugs and their eggs as well as sooty mold. Control ants (page 473), which nurture mealybugs for their honeydew.

Beneficial insects, including lacewings, lady beetles, and syrphid flies, help control these pests. You can introduce the mealybug destroyer (*Cryptolaemus montrouzieri*), a lady beetle relative whose adults and larvae both consume

Protect young plants by using row covers (page 507). Natural controls include birds and tachinid flies. You can handpick these beetles, dropping them into a bucket of soapy water. For major infestations, spray with a natural insecticide containing pyrethrins. Parasitic nematodes will reduce larval populations. Chemical controls include malathion and carbaryl.

Cutworms. A large variety of hairless larvae of night-flying moths make up the diverse group called cutworms. They feed at night and on overcast days; during the daylight hours, they hide underground, curled up in a C shape. Most cut off young plants at ground level—hence their name.

To help prevent cutworm damage, clear and till garden beds to destroy eggs, larvae, and pupae before you sow seeds. To protect transplants, encircle each with a can (with both ends removed) or a paper cup or plastic carton with the bottom cut out; it should extend 1 to 2 inches both into the soil and above ground.

Encourage or introduce natural predators such as parasitic nematodes and ground beetles. Spreading diatomaceous earth around young seedlings may deter cutworms.

Earwigs. These familiar pests aren't all bad—they prey on aphids and other insects. On the negative side, they destroy young seedlings and damage flower petals, some soft fruits, and corn silk. To prevent earwig damage, keep the garden clean, removing hiding places such as weedy areas and dead foliage.

Several kinds of traps are effective. At night, when earwigs are active, place moistened rolled-up newspapers, rolls of corrugated cardboard, or short sections of garden hose in the garden; in the morning, dispose of the insects that have crept inside. You can also trap earwigs in a short cat food or tuna can containing ½ inch of vegetable oil. Place several such cans around the garden and dispose of them as they fill with the corpses of earwigs unable to resist the lure of the drink.

mealybugs; it needs warm temperatures, so it's most effective in greenhouses and during the warmer months outdoors. For severe infestations, spray with horticultural oil, azadirachtin (neem extract), pyrethrins, acephate (on nonedibles), diazinon, or malathion.

Mites. To the naked eye, these tiny spider relatives look like flecks of red, yellow, or green. Signs of mite infestation include yellow-stippled leaves (where the pests have sucked plant juices) and a tan or bronze cast to the foliage. Heavily infested plants are weakened and may eventually die. To check for the presence of mites, hold a piece of white paper under the affected foliage and tap the plant: the pests will drop onto the paper, looking like specks of pepper, then try to crawl away. Also, look for spiderlike webs around stem tips and other leaves. Of the many kinds of mites, several are host-specific (such as citrus bud mites), but others—notably spider mites—attack a variety of outdoor and indoor plants.

Dust that settles on leaves encourages mites, so hose off plants frequently to keep the pest population down. Increased humidity also helps. Drought-stressed plants are more susceptible to mites.

Many natural predators help keep mites in check. You can purchase lacewing larvae and several species of predatory mites that prey on spider mites.

Mites can often be washed from foliage with water jets; insecticidal soap is also effective. Spraying with horticultural oil in late winter smothers mites and eggs (it can be applied in summer as well). On some plants (check the product label for listings), you can control mites with sulfur dusted on leaf undersides (do not use sulfur in combination with oil sprays). Neem oil is a miticide. Chemical miticides are available in some areas.

Pillbugs and sowbugs. These familiar creatures are soil-dwelling crustaceans, not insects. Pillbugs roll up when disturbed into black balls about the size of a large pea; sowbugs are usually gray and don't roll up. Their principal food is decaying vegetation (which they help break down into humus), but they also eat very young seedlings, the skins of melons and cucumbers, and berries.

To limit these pests' populations, remove hiding places, such as boards lying on the ground and weedy areas with decaying foliage. Lift ripening fruit off the ground with pebbles or strawberry baskets. Plastic mulch is helpful, because the soil under it gets too hot for the pests' comfort. Chemical control is generally not required.

Root weevils. A number of root weevils and their larvae can harm plants. In some species, such as the black vine weevil, both adults and larvae are harmful; the adults feed on leaves, flowers, and bark of rhododendron, yew, grape and other plants, while the larvae consume

roots, especially those of young plants. Billbugs are root weevil larvae that damage lawns.

Parasitic nematodes help control root weevil larvae. Azadirachtin (neem extract) and some pyrethroids are effective against adults. Acephate can be used to control adults on nonedible plants.

Scales. Though related to mealybugs and aphids, scales differ in having a waxy, shell-like covering that camouflages them and protects them from some natural enemies (and insecticides). Scales are classified as "armored" (hard) or soft; soft scales are more mobile and excrete a sticky honeydew.

An adult scale lives under its waxy shell, which sticks to the host plant. Running from the underside of the insect into the plant tissue is a tiny filamentous mouth part, through which the scale sucks plant juices. Scale eggs hatch beneath the shell; in spring or summer, the young scales ("crawlers") leave the protective cover to seek their own feeding sites.

Mealybugs

Pillbug

Black vine weevil (a type of root weevil)

Many naturally occurring parasites and predators, including several species of lady beetles, control or limit scale populations; a few of these are sold for release in the garden or greenhouse. In dry weather, you can help treat scale-infested plants by hosing them off frequently, since dust inhibits the various scale parasites and predators. Get rid of ants (page 473), which tend to protect soft scales.

You can control light infestations by picking scales off the plant or scraping them off with a plastic scouring pad. On deciduous plants, you can kill some adult scales in winter with horticultural oil. In summer, horticultural oil, used at a growing-season dilution, is an effective control for both adults and crawlers. Scales are vulnerable to insecticides when in the crawler stage. To check for crawlers, wrap double-sided sticky tape around branches; if you find trapped crawlers, apply controls. Horticultural oil, insecticidal soap, and synthetic insecticides such as diazinon or malathion may be effective against crawlers.

Mites

Sowbug

Scales

Slugs and snails. Often considered the worst garden pests, slugs and snails are similar creatures: a slug is simply a snail without a shell. These mollusks have toothlike jaws that rasp large, ragged holes in leaves and flowers. Seedlings and new transplants may be eaten entirely. For the most part, they hide by day and feed at night, although they may be active on gray or rainy days.

Try to eliminate these pests' favorite daytime hiding places—weedy areas, boards, stones, unused flower pots. You can protect newly planted seedlings by encircling them with a 3- to 4-inch-high "fence" made from copper strips; such strips can also be stapled to raised beds and wrapped around tree trunks and containers. Wood ashes and diatomaceous earth also make good barriers.

If done regularly, handpicking is effective. Go hunting after dark (with a flashlight) or early in the morning. You can also trap these creatures. A wide plank elevated about an inch off the ground offers a daytime hiding place from which you can collect and dispatch the pests. Shallow containers filled with beer or a solution of 1 teaspoon each active baking yeast and sugar to 1 cup water may lure slugs and snails to their deaths.

Commercial baits containing iron phosphate (Sluggo, Escar-Go) are fairly effective, causing the mollusks to stop feeding and die within a few days. These baits are considered nonhazardous to humans, pets, and wildlife. Commercial baits containing metaldehyde are sold as pellets, meal, or emulsion. Set them out in late evening and clear them away (along with dead pests) in the morning, since they can be toxic to birds and pets.

P

Thrips are almost microscopic—the light or dark brown adults less than $1/20$ inch long, with narrow, feathery wings, the wingless, light green or pale yellow nymphs even smaller. Both adults and nymphs feed by rasping soft flower and leaf tissue, then sucking plant juices. In heavy infestations, both flowers and leaves are discolored and fail to open normally, looking twisted or stuck together. If you look closely, you'll see stippled, puckered areas on flowers and foliage. Leaves may take on a silvery or tan cast similar to that caused by mites—but if thrips are present, you'll see numerous small, black, varnishlike fecal pellets on leaf undersides.

Natural enemies include lacewing larvae, minute pirate bugs, predaceous thrips and mites, and spiders. Insecticidal soaps and horticultural oil can be used to help control thrips. Acephate (on nonedibles) and malathion can also be effective.

Snail

Damage from thrips

Whiteflies

Whiteflies are small (about $1/8$-inch-long) winged insects that fly up in clouds when you brush or touch an infested plant. The immature form is a nearly transparent wingless nymph; it excretes honeydew as it feeds, attracting ants and promoting the growth of sooty mold (page 460). Both adults and nymphs suck plant juices. Affected foliage may first show yellow stippling, then curl and turn brown. Whiteflies thrive in the warm, still air of greenhouses. In warm climates, they're also found outdoors all year, but in colder regions they cause outdoor problems only during summer. In such chilly-winter zones, they do not overwinter outside; garden infestations originate from indoor plants or purchased transplants. To protect your garden, inspect greenhouse and indoor plants and eliminate any whiteflies you find. And no matter what your climate, when you buy new garden plants—particularly bedding plants, which may have started their lives in a greenhouse—carefully examine leaf undersides for adults and nymphs.

Natural enemies, which can be attracted to or introduced into the garden, include lacewing larvae and *Delphastus pusillus,* a species of lady beetle known as whitefly predator. Two species of tiny parasitic wasps, *Encarsia formosa* and *Eretmocerus californicus,* can be released to help control whiteflies in greenhouses.

Handpicking heavily infested leaves helps reduce whitefly populations. Yellow sticky traps (available commercially) can trap significant numbers of the pests. Water jets work well; hose off infested plants every few days, hitting both sides of all leaves. Insecticidal soap can be more effective than water and is less hazardous to natural enemies than other insecticides. Other controls include azadirachtin (neem extract), horticultural oil, and pyrethrins.

Woolly adelgid. A serious pest of hemlocks (*Tsuga* spp.) in the East, woolly adelgids form cottony, white egg masses along the twigs from late winter into early spring. Nymphs suck sap from needles all summer, causing needles to drop and eventually weakening and killing plants. Adults overwinter on the plants. The best control is to spray plants in late winter or very early spring with horticultural oil at a dormant-season dilution (be sure to do this before plants resume growth in spring). Then spray in early summer and fall with horticultural oil at the growing-season dilution. Read the label carefully for recommended dilutions.

DISPOSING OF PESTICIDES

You may need to dispose of pesticides (including fungicides and herbicides) if you have mixed up more solution than you need or if you have a product that is no longer considered safe due to changes in its registration status. (Until you can dispose of such pesticides properly, keep them—and all others—secured in a locked cabinet.)

Never pour any pesticide down any type of drain, including a storm drain; it could pollute the water supply and harm the environment. Instead, contact your city or county public works department, garbage company, or Cooperative Extension Office to find out where you can discard such products. Many communities sponsor hazardous waste disposal sites, which typically accept used motor oil and leftover paint as well as undiluted pesticides in their original containers and diluted solutions that you have mixed. Since federal law requires that products containing hazardous ingredients be labeled, carefully pour leftover solutions into a glass or plastic container with a tight-fitting lid; write the product name (name of active ingredient and trade name) and its dilution ratio on the container. Empty any powdered or granular pesticide (such as a lawn-care product applied with a spreader) into a heavy-duty garbage bag; then seal and label the bag.

PRODUCTS FOR PEST CONTROL

Sold in liquid, powder, or granular form, pesticides carry one or more active ingredients. Their availability is constantly shifting: new products continue to arrive on the market, while older ones may be withdrawn if research reveals them to be health or environmental hazards.

The lists below cover the most useful and widely available natural and synthetic pesticides for the gardener. Others, generally targeting only one kind of pest, are mentioned in the individual pest descriptions beginning on page 473 for information. *Synthetic pesticides* are manufactured compounds that do not normally occur in nature. *Natural pesticides*, in contrast, are products whose active ingredients originate in a plant, animal, or mineral, or whose action results from a biological process (as in the case of *Bacillus thuringiensis*; see page 471). Be aware that "natural" does not mean "harmless"; some natural products can still harm people or plants if they are used incorrectly.

Sources for some less-common natural pesticides are given on page 471.

When using any pesticide, *read the label directions carefully and follow them exactly.* The package will clearly state the plants and pests on which the control is registered for use, and it is illegal to apply it to a plant or pest not so listed.

The products described below are listed by the accepted common name of the *active ingredient*—the actual chemical that controls the pest or pests listed on the package label. Some widely used trade names, if they differ from the common name, are noted in parentheses. Before you buy, read the label to make sure you're getting the active ingredient you want. (For more on reading and understanding pesticide labels, see page 471.)

NATURAL PESTICIDES

- **Azadirachtin, neem oil** (Bioneem; Fruit, Nut, and Vegetable Spray; Rose Defense; others). Azadirachtin (neem extract) is derived from a tropical tree *(Azadirachta indica).* It repels pests and, once ingested, interrupts their growth cycle, killing larvae as well as adults. Effective against aphids, beetles, caterpillars, grasshoppers, leaf miners, mealybugs, root weevils, whiteflies, others. Neem oil (primarily the oil of the neem seed) controls insects in egg, larval, and adult stages; it also controls mites and some plant diseases. Mix with warm water before spraying. Both azadirachtin and neem oil can kill nontarget insects such as honeybees and lady beetles. Toxic to fish.

- ***Bacillus thuringiensis, Bt.*** A bacterium that controls many pest larvae. *Bt kurstaki* (Btk) is lethal to certain caterpillars, including cabbage worm, geranium budworm, and tomato hornworm; other Bt strains are effective against the larvae of mosquitoes, fungus gnats, Colorado potato beetles, and elm leaf beetles.

- **Diatomaceous earth.** A powdery substance made from the skeletons of microscopic marine organisms. Effective against pests such as ants, aphids, cutworms, slugs, snails. Works by matting on the insect and damaging its protective coat (not by lacerating its exoskeleton or membrane and causing death by desiccation, as is widely thought). Be sure to use the insecticidal product, not the one intended for swimming pool filters. Wear a breathing mask during application to avoid inhaling the dust. Diatomaceous earth can kill nontarget insects.

- **Horticultural oils.** Highly refined petroleum oils that smother pests, pest eggs, and disease spores. In winter, during the dormant season, they are applied to control insect eggs, some overwintering insects, and certain diseases. In summer, these oils are used at a lower rate, sprayed on foliage of many plants to combat insects such as aphids, mealybugs, mites, scales, thrips, and whiteflies. Before using horticultural oils on plants in leaf, test-spray a small portion of the plant to be sure foliage will not be damaged.

- **Insecticidal soap.** Made not from detergent, but from potassium salts of fatty acids found in plants and animals. Effective against pests such as aphids, mealybugs, mites, scales, thrips, and whiteflies. Hard water inactivates it, so mix the concentrate with soft water, distilled water, or rainwater. Toxic to earthworms.

- **Pyrethrins** (Bug Buster-O, others). Derived from compounds found in the dried flowers of *Tanacetum cinerariifolium.* Both a contact and a stomach poison; lethal to many pests. Breaks down quickly in sunlight; to give it more time to act, apply after sundown. Some products combine pyrethrins with other pesticides. Toxic to fish. The dried flowers, known as pyrethrum, are also sold as an insecticide.

- **Sulfur.** Dusted or sprayed over plants to control mites and psyllids as well as some plant diseases. Do not use sulfur in conjunction with horticultural oil spray or when air temperature is above 85°F/29°C. Can irritate the eyes.

SYNTHETIC PESTICIDES

- **Acephate** (Orthene). A systemic poison (one absorbed by the plant and incorporated into its tissues), this broad-spectrum product is used against aphids, beetles, caterpillars, grasshoppers, leaf miners, mealybugs, thrips, root weevils, whiteflies, other pests. Do not use on edible crops. Toxic to honeybees and birds.

- **Carbaryl** (Sevin). Broad-spectrum contact insecticide. Controls most chewing insects but is not effective against many sucking types—in fact, it often increases problems with the latter by destroying their natural predators. Registered for use on edible crops. It ia highly toxic to honeybees, fish, and earthworms.

- **Diazinon.** Broad-spectrum contact insecticide that controls ants, aphids, beetles, caterpillars, mealybugs, scales, white grubs, other pests. Often used on lawn pests. Highly toxic to birds, moderately toxic to honeybees and fish. Future registration limitations are possible.

- **Imidacloprid** (Merit). Controls a variety of pests of lawns and ornamentals. Toxic to fish.

- **Malathion.** Broad-spectrum contact insecticide that controls aphids, beetles, caterpillars, mealybugs, scales, thrips, whiteflies, other pests. Registered for use on edible crops. Toxic to honeybees, birds, and fish. Future registration limitations are possible.

- **Pyrethroids.** Synthetic versions of plant-based pyrethrins, pyrethroids are increasingly being used in pesticides and are effective against many garden and household pests. Active ingredients include **permethrin, cyfluthrin,** and others. Less hazardous to humans, birds, and mammals than many other pesticides; toxic to honeybees and fish.

P

READING A PESTICIDE LABEL

Precautionary statements: This section may start with the headline "Precautionary statements" or with a repeat of the signal word found on the front of the label. Information is customized for product type and its associated toxicity-level category. It tells you of known hazards to humans, domestic animals, and the environment.

First aid instructions: Indicates the immediate action required if the product is ingested or inhaled or comes into contact with the skin or eyes.

Directions for use: Indicates how much of the product to use and how to mix and apply it.

Plants: Lists the plants that can safely be treated by the pesticide. If it can be used on edible crops, also tells you how many days before harvest the product can be applied.

Note to physicians: Specifies the action a physician should take in the event the product is ingested or inhaled or comes into contact with the skin or eyes.

Controls: Lists the pests that the product is formulated to control.

Product name: Provides the pesticide's trade name, often includes marketing information that positions the product against its competitors and attracts the eye of potential buyers. Sometimes the accepted common name of the active ingredient is included as part of the brand name, especially if that name has become familiar to the public.

Active ingredients: Lists the accepted common name of the pesticide's active ingredient. Learn to identify pesticides by their common names and look here first to find out exactly what is in the pesticide before purchasing it. The chemical name of the pesticide may also be included in this section.

Signal word: Look for words such as *Caution, Warning, Danger,* or *Poison.* These words signal the toxicity-level category associated with the pesticide. Additional information will be found on the back of the container, under the section "Precautionary statements."

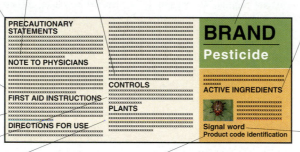

PRECAUTIONARY STATEMENTS

NOTE TO PHYSICIANS

FIRST AID INSTRUCTIONS

DIRECTIONS FOR USE

CONTROLS

PLANTS

BRAND
Pesticide

ACTIVE INGREDIENTS

Signal word
Product code identification

Storage & disposal: Specifies how to safely store and dispose of the product.

Product code identification: Provides the number assigned to the product by the manufacturer and the Environmental Protection Agency (EPA) to identify it. Use this number when contacting the manufacturer or EPA about the pesticide.

BIRDS AND MAMMALS. Most gardeners welcome some—though not all—wildlife into their gardens. (See page 473 for ways to draw wildlife to your yard.) Certain birds and animals, however, can cause significant damage to plants. Some of the Northeast's worst troublemakers are discussed below, along with suggestions for controlling them.

Birds. For the most part, gardeners see birds as friends who can play a significant role in controlling pests such as caterpillars (including cutworms and sod webworms), grasshoppers, and scales. Some kinds of birds, however, can be a nuisance at certain times, eating newly planted seeds (including lawn seed), tender seedlings, transplants, fruits, nuts, or berries.

Providing alternate foods can sometimes reduce damage to the fruits and berries you want to harvest; try planting elderberries *(Sambucus),* fruiting mulberries *(Morus),* or hawthorns *(Crataegus).* Reflectors, fluttering objects, and scarecrows may reduce damage briefly, but birds soon become accustomed to them. The best solution is to use screen or netting. Broad-mesh (¾-inch) nylon or plastic netting is popular for trees, since it readily admits air, water, and sunlight. Enclose fruit trees with netting 2 to 3 weeks before fruit ripens, tying it around the trunk beneath the lowest branches or securing it to the ground so birds can't find an opening.

Row covers (page 507) are the easiest way to protect sprouting seedlings and maturing vegetables, because they require no support. You can also make wooden or plastic pipe frames

TOP: Starling BOTTOM: Netting over strawberries

with screen, aviary wire, or netting attached to cover the top and all sides. Such frames are mobile and reusable, and they can be designed to make harvesting easy.

Chipmunks. These tunneling rodents eat seeds, roots, bulbs, nuts, and other plant material. They especially delight in uprooting newly planted bulbs and seedlings--even if they don't eat them. Chipmunks can be caught in Hav-a-Heart traps (bait them with peanut butter) and relocated, but populations usually are high and new individuals will replace the relocated ones. Another option is to cover newly planted areas temporarily with hardware cloth or screen to discourage chipmunks from digging up new bulbs, seedlings, or plants. They are more likely to leave established plantings alone. Spraying plants with repellents such as those used for deer also can be effective. Domestic cats also make effective predators.

Deer. As wild vegetation becomes less available during summer droughts or winter snows, deer move into gardens to forage. They develop feeding patterns, visiting tasty gardens regularly (most often in the evening). Fond of a wide array of flowering plants, especially roses, they'll also eat the foliage or fruit of nearly anything you grow for the table. For a list of plants that deer usually ignore, see Plants that Resist Deer in A Guide to Plant Selection, beginning on page 47.

Fencing is the most certain protection. On level ground, a 7- to 8-foot woven wire fence will usually keep deer out; on slopes, you may need

P

Deer

Rabbit

to erect a 10- to 11-foot barrier to guard against animals jumping from higher ground. A horizontal "outrigger" extension on a fence makes it harder for deer to clear. Because deer cannot high-jump and broad-jump at the same time, double fencing has worked for many gardeners: construct a pair of parallel 4- to 5-foot fences spaced 4 to 5 feet apart. Low-growing plants can be set out in the area between the fences.

If fencing your entire garden is impractical, put chicken-wire cages around young plants and cylinders of wire fencing around larger specimens. Cover raised beds with mesh or row covers (page 507).

Commercial deer repellents can work if sprayed often enough to keep new growth covered with repellent and to replace what rain and irrigation wash away. Changing the type of repellent may be helpful, since deer get used to smells. Do not apply repellents to edible plants unless the label indicates you can do so; some are not safe to eat.

Groundhogs. Also called woodchucks, these large rodents can eat their way through a vegetable garden in short order. Although trapping and relocating or killing groundhogs are options, new individuals usually arrive to replace them. The best control is a fence about 3 feet high installed next to a 6-inch trench. For best results, install the fence before the groundhogs discover the delights of your vegetable garden: once they get in the habit of dining there, it is much more difficult to discourage them.

Rabbits. These common pests eat a wide variety of plants—from vegetables to annuals, perennials, bulbs (especially tulips), and other ornamentals. They also eat the bark of trees and shrubs. A fence is the best option for eliminating rabbits. While it doesn't have to be tall (as low as 2 feet is fine), it does need to extend 2 to 3 inches below the soil surface to prevent these pests from burrowing under it. For individual plants—such as tulips or other ornamentals planted in a bed or border—individual barriers are quite effective. Construct cylinders of chicken-wire and set them around plants to be protected. (Again, make sure they are set into the soil.) Repellents such as those used for deer also are effective.

Raccoons. Raccoons can be a real pest in vegetable gardens. They eat almost anything, but they are especially fond of ripe sweet corn. You will know they've been in your corn patch when you find chewed ends of cobs, scattered kernels, shredded husks, and broken cornstalks littering the garden. Raccoons can be hard to keep away—they can climb and they are wily. Here are some tactics to try in outwitting them. Sprinkle ammonia around the garden periodically, and reapply after rain. Sprinkle red or black pepper onto the silks on each ear of corn; reapply after rain.

Plant squash with the corn—the prickly stems and leaves may keep raccoons away. Plant vines all around the outside of the corn patch and let them sprawl. Raccoons like to have a clear view in all directions around them as they eat, and the tangled vines will interfere with visibility.

If you have only a small corn patch, cover each ripening ear with a paper bag fastened with a rubber band. Enclose the plants in a wire mesh cage tall enough to accommodate their full height.

Finally, try lighting the garden at night. If all else fails, install an electric fence.

Squirrels. Most troublesome in areas that border fields or wild lands, ground squirrels live in underground burrows, where they store food, raise their young, and hide from predators such as foxes, hawks, and owls. They are most active in midmorning or late afternoon (except in very hot weather); most hibernate in winter. When they're up and about, they scurry here and there causing trouble—nibbling through tomato patches, gnawing roots and bark, climbing trees after fruits and nuts.

Keep ground squirrels out of trees with metal rodent guards around the trunks. Poison baits and traps can be effective; check with your local Cooperative Extension Office for methods legal in your area, or hire a pest-control professional.

Voles. These small rodents (just 5 to 8 inches long when mature) have short ears and tails. They feed on a wide variety of vegetables, grasses, bulbs, and tubers and gnaw on the bark of trees, sometimes girdling them; damage to bark may occur just above or below ground. Voles travel in aboveground runways, usually hidden beneath tall grasses or ground covers, that connect the openings to their short, shallow burrows.

You can control voles by managing the vegetation they use for cover: mow weeds, remove heavy mulches (especially those close to trees), and cut back ground covers. Protect the lower trunks of shrubs and young trees with hardware cloth cylinders, being sure to bury the bottom edges so voles can't dig beneath them.

Trapping can be an effective control. Use simple wooden mouse traps, baited with peanut butter or apple slices. Place these along the runways and check them daily. Keep small children and pets away from areas where you have set traps. Baits are sometimes used; check with your Cooperative Extension Office for types available in your area.

Raccoon

Vole

P

Plant Anatomy and Growth

Knowledge of the basic parts of a plant and the role each plays in the plant's growth and reproduction is one of the fundamentals of successful gardening. The box below describes the functions of flowers, leaves, roots, and stems. Though we often think of these elements as separate entities, in fact, their functions are interrelated, and plant growth and reproduction could not proceed without the contributions of each part.

In addition, plants must interact with aspects of the environment—air, water, sunlight, and soil—if they are to grow and reproduce. Understanding these interactions helps gardeners manipulate environmental factors to maximize plant growth.

For more on flowers see Parts of a Complete Flower, page 450. Seed germination is illustrated on page 486.

Plant Conservation

Plants, both wild and cultivated, supply food for humans and other animals; habitats for insects and wildlife; and medicines, timber, and other essential products. However, it is estimated that more than 34,000 species—some 12.5 percent of all known higher plants (ferns, conifers, and flowering plants)—are either extinct in the wild or threatened with extinction.

P

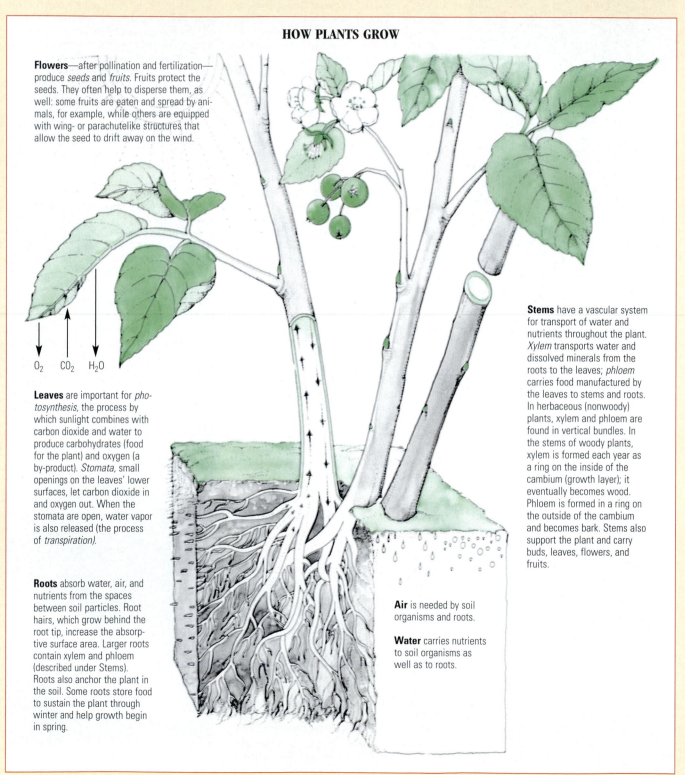

HOW PLANTS GROW

Flowers—after pollination and fertilization—produce *seeds* and *fruits*. Fruits protect the seeds. They often help to disperse them, as well: some fruits are eaten and spread by animals, for example, while others are equipped with wing- or parachutelike structures that allow the seed to drift away on the wind.

O_2 CO_2 H_2O

Leaves are important for *photosynthesis,* the process by which sunlight combines with carbon dioxide and water to produce carbohydrates (food for the plant) and oxygen (a by-product). *Stomata,* small openings on the leaves' lower surfaces, let carbon dioxide in and oxygen out. When the stomata are open, water vapor is also released (the process of *transpiration).*

Roots absorb water, air, and nutrients from the spaces between soil particles. Root hairs, which grow behind the root tip, increase the absorptive surface area. Larger roots contain xylem and phloem (described under Stems). Roots also anchor the plant in the soil. Some roots store food to sustain the plant through winter and help growth begin in spring.

Stems have a vascular system for transport of water and nutrients throughout the plant. *Xylem* transports water and dissolved minerals from the roots to the leaves; *phloem* carries food manufactured by the leaves to stems and roots. In herbaceous (nonwoody) plants, xylem and phloem are found in vertical bundles. In the stems of woody plants, xylem is formed each year as a ring on the inside of the cambium (growth layer); it eventually becomes wood. Phloem is formed in a ring on the outside of the cambium and becomes bark. Stems also support the plant and carry buds, leaves, flowers, and fruits.

Air is needed by soil organisms and roots.

Water carries nutrients to soil organisms as well as to roots.

Camassias in the wild

Concerned gardeners can take some steps to help preserve such plants.

Avoid buying plants dug from their native habitat. Though most plants available to gardeners are commercially propagated, some rare species are still routinely dug in the wild, especially those that are slow growing or difficult to propagate. Bulbs falling into this group are listed on page 453. Other plants threatened by wild collection include trilliums and other spring-blooming wildflowers; native orchids; Jack-in-the-pulpit (*Arisaema* species); several kinds of carnivorous plants; and various palms and ferns.

Don't include invasive plants in your garden if you live near wild lands. Such plants may escape and take over the habitat of natives, crowding them out. For more on invasive plants, see page 517.

Support the conservation of plants in their natural habitats, botanical gardens, and seed banks. Various preserves and other protected areas in the U.S. and abroad practice *in situ* (on-site) conservation: they maintain plants along with the insects, birds, animals, and soil and disease organisms normally associated with them in the wild, preserving the natural diversity of the ecosystem. Such sanctuaries include nature preserves, wildlife refuges, and state and national parks.

Botanical gardens feature *ex situ* (off-site) conservation. They are important repositories of samples of rare and endangered plants and also maintain some that have already become extinct in the wild.

Seeds, especially those of crop plants and their wild relatives, are conserved in special seed banks. They are first dried, then stored at low temperatures, remaining viable for many years.

Plant Disorders, Environmental and Cultural

Some plant problems are caused not by disease organisms or pests but by environmental or cultural factors. Drying winds and extremes of temperature may hinder plant growth, for example. Other plant problems are related to soil conditions such as excess road salt; under- or overfertilizing (see page 463 for information on nitrogen deficiency); and too much or too little water (see pages 512–513). Besides damaging plants directly, cultural and environmental problems can stress plants and make them more vulnerable to insects and diseases.

If you aren't certain why a plant is languishing, get help before you act. Simply assuming that a pest or disease is the culprit can result in the needless—and useless—application of pesticides. Regular garden monitoring and, when necessary, consultation with nursery personnel or your Cooperative Extension Office can assist you in identifying the precise causes of problems in your garden.

CHLOROSIS. This disorder affects pin oaks (*Quercus palustris*), rhododendron, and azalea, especially when these plants are growing in soils that do not have an acid pH. Chlorosis also affects some vegetables and annuals. Leaves lose their green color from the edges inward; leaf veins usually remain green. The newest leaves are the most noticeably affected; they may be unusually small and either completely white or bright yellow in color. Chlorosis is usually caused by a deficiency of iron (though it occasionally results from lack of another mineral, such as zinc or manganese). When plants are chlorotic, the soil itself is not necessarily iron poor; it may simply be alkaline (with a high pH), a condition under which iron becomes unavailable to roots. Soggy, poorly aerated soils also delay or hinder the release of iron to plant roots.

Adjusting soil pH by adding organic matter or, if necessary, sulfur, is the best long-term solution to chlorosis. Improving drainage is also helpful. Chelated iron, applied according to the directions on the label, can temporarily correct the problem.

SALT DAMAGE. Stunted plants that wilt and have dried out leaves—despite adequate rainfall—often signal salt damage. Salts damage plant roots and also can build up on foliage. In the Northeast, de-icing salts commonly used on roads and walkways often are the culprit. Near the coastline, wind-blown sea salt may be the problem. Excess fertilizer and urine from pets also can cause symptoms of salt damage. To remove excess salts in the soil, water heavily. Avoid using de-icing salts on walkways. Substitute sand, sawdust, or wood ashes wherever possible. Cheap fertilizer also works as a de-icer and is less damaging to plants than sodium chloride. For sites along roadways, use salt-tolerant plants. See Soil for suggestions of salt-tolerant plants.

SOIL COMPACTION. Soil that is compacted causes a variety of diseaselike symptoms, because it has such a profound effect on plant roots. Plants growing in compacted soil are stunted, tend to wilt easily, have yellowed leaves, and bloom poorly. Because compacted soil doesn't have sufficient pore space for water and air and tends to drain poorly, plants growing in it wilt more quickly during dry weather and succumb to wet soil more quickly during wet weather. Soil compaction is a notorious problem on construction sites, and few trees and other plants survive having the soil compacted around their roots (not to mention the root damage caused by construction vehicles). On construction sites, erect fences around trees you want to save well before construction begins: fences should go around the drip line of trees to keep vehicles off their roots.

If compacted soil is a problem in your garden, the best solution is double digging the soil and adding plenty of organic matter. See page 482 for information on double digging. As an alternative, construct a raised bed over a site where soil compaction is a problem. If foot traffic is causing the problem, a fence may be the answer—or adding stepping stones to keep feet on a pathway and off garden beds. Finally, keeping the soil mulched—and avoiding walking on prepared soil—helps prevent soil compaction.

SUNBURN, SUNSCALD. Overexposure to sunlight can damage leaves, fruits, and bark. Symptoms include bleached-out, yellowish, or brown foliage; pale-colored, sunken, often wrinkled areas on fruits; and bark that turns dark brown, splits, and dies. Damaged tissue may be invaded by disease-causing organisms. Most likely to experience sunburn or sunscald are plants moved into the sun from shaded locations (as from a nursery to a home garden) and those that have been heavily pruned, reducing the leafy cover that shades bark and fruits.

To prevent sunburn and sunscald, transplant in cool, even rainy, weather, if possible. If conditions are warm, shade new transplants with shadecloth, burlap stapled to wooden frames, or broad, flat pieces of wood placed in the ground on the sunny side of the plants. Use burlap or tree-wrapping paper (available at nurseries) to wrap trunks of newly planted or

P

TRAVELERS' ALERT: BRINGING PLANTS HOME

Think twice before packing those plants. The U.S. government regulates the importation of plants, seeds, fruits, and vegetables from foreign countries to America, and from Hawaii, Puerto Rico, and the U. S. Virgin Islands to the mainland. The regulations are intended to prevent the introduction of insects, diseases, and potentially invasive plants. Thus, plants must be free of leaf mold and of sand or other soil, and seeds must be cleaned. For more information on bringing home plants or seeds, contact the Animal and Plant Health Inspection Service of the U. S. Department of Agriculture: USDA APHIS, Plant Protection and Quarantine, 4700 River Road, Unit 136, Riverdale, MD 20737-1236, Attn: Permit Unit. You can also call (301) 734-8645 or visit the service's web site (www.aphis.usda.gov).

heavily pruned trees. Or protect exposed tree trunks by painting them with water-based interior white latex paint, diluted by half with water. Finally, note that plants adapted to shaded conditions will exhibit sunburn symptoms if planted in a too-bright location. Always be sure to select plants suited to the site.

Planting Beds, Raised Beds

Before sowing seeds or setting out annuals, perennials, or vegetables, you'll want to prepare a planting bed. In most gardens, the simple sort of bed described below will suffice. In some cases, however—notably when soil or drainage is poor—constructing raised beds may be a better choice.

MAKING A PLANTING BED. Good soil preparation is the first step toward success with seeds sown directly in the garden and with small plants set out from pots or flats. Begin by eliminating weeds (see pages 517–518). Then loosen the soil with a spading fork or tiller; it should be slightly damp when you work it, not wet or bone-dry. Dig down 10 to 12 inches if you can, breaking up clods and removing stones as you go. Spread a 3- to 4-inch-thick layer of organic matter (such as compost or nitrogen-fortified ground bark or sawdust) over the area. As noted in Fertilizers (page 462), both phosphorus and potassium benefit plants most when placed near the roots, so it's best to work a fertilizer high in these nutrients (such as a 5-10-10 or similar formula) into the soil before planting, rather than applying it to the surface afterwards.

Raised beds can be simple mounds of earth or they can be enclosed as shown above

Also add any amendments needed to alter soil pH at this time. Incorporate all amendments evenly with a spading fork or tiller, then level the bed with a rake.

MAKING RAISED BEDS. Besides solving problems involving poor soil and poor drainage, raised beds have other advantages. Their soil warms earlier in spring, and because it is typically not walked upon, it remains loose and easier for roots to penetrate. You can also fill these beds with particular types of soil to suit specific plants—acid soil for blueberries, for example. The simplest raised beds are made by piling amended soil, either purchased or dug from pathways or other parts of your garden, on the area you want to plant. It's a good idea to loosen the area's existing soil as much as possible first, to ease penetration by water and roots.

Many gardeners go a step farther and provide some sort of enclosure for their raised beds. Two-inch-thick wood is most common, but rocks or cinder blocks can also be used. Plan to make enclosed beds at least 8 inches high; a height of 12 inches gives roots even more growing space. The bed can be any length that fits the space and available building materials, but it's usually best to limit its width to about 4 feet, so that you can reach the center of the bed from either side. If rodents are a problem, line the bottom of the bed with hardware cloth, fastening it to the sides. Fill raised beds with good topsoil amended with plenty of organic matter, such as compost or nitrogen-fortified ground bark or sawdust.

Planting Techniques

Proper planting techniques depend on the plant and how it is sold. Many plants—annuals, vegetables, and some perennials and ground covers—are sold as seedlings in small containers or flats during the growing season. Larger plants, such as shrubs, trees, and certain vines and more mature perennials, may be offered in several ways: in containers of various sizes during the growing season; as bare-root plants during the dormant season; or with the

---

P

DOUBLE DIGGING

This soil preparation technique helps amend soil in the upper level of a planting bed and breaks up soil on the lower level to allow roots to grow deeper. It's hard work, but the results last for years. Before double digging, remove weeds from the plot.

1 Dig a trench one spade-blade deep along one side of the plot. Mound the soil from this trench nearby.

2 Loosen soil in the bottom of the trench with a spading fork; mix organic matter into the loosened soil.

3 Dig a second trench one spade-blade deep alongside the first. Shovel the excavated soil into the first trench, along with organic matter and a fertilizer high in phosphorus and potassium (such as a 5-10-10 product).

4 Loosen the soil in the bottom of the second trench and mix in organic matter.

Continue to dig trenches across the plot in the same way. Fill the last trench with soil saved from the first.

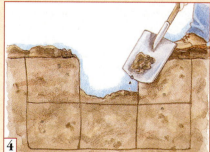

root ball enclosed in burlap, typically from late fall to early spring. The following pages discuss planting all of the above types. For information on starting seeds, see pages 486–489; for tips on planting bulbs, see pages 453–454.

PLANTING ANNUALS AND PERENNIALS. Nurseries offer seedlings of both annuals and perennials, giving you a head start over raising the plants from seed yourself. Many of these, as well as vegetables and some ground covers, are sold in plastic cell-packs, individual plastic pots, peat pots, and flats. (Some perennials, perennial vegetables, and strawberries may also be sold bare-root during their dormant season; for planting instructions, see page 484.) Before planting annuals and perennials, make a planting bed as described on page 482.

At the nursery, choose stocky young plants with good leaf color and a root ball that holds together but is not tangled or matted. Root-bound plants won't grow as well as younger ones, even if you cut or loosen coiled roots.

PLANTING BARE-ROOT SHRUBS AND TREES. Bare-root plants are sold in late winter and early spring by retail nurseries and mail-order companies. Many deciduous plants are available this way, including fruit and shade trees, flowering shrubs, roses, grapes, and cane fruits.

Though venturing out in the cold and wet of winter to set out bare-root plants takes a certain amount of determination, the effort is worthwhile. Such plants typically cost only 40 to 70 percent as much as the same varieties purchased in containers later in the year; beyond that, they

PLANTING ANNUALS AND PERENNIALS

1 Dig a hole for each plant, making it the same depth as the container and an inch or two wider.

2 With your fingers, lightly separate matted roots. If there's a pad of coiled roots at the bottom of the pot, cut or pull it off so that new roots will form and grow into the soil.

3 Place each plant in its hole so that the top of the root ball is even with the soil surface. Firm soil around the roots; then water each plant with a gentle flow that won't disturb soil or roots.

REMOVING PLANTS FROM CONTAINERS

SMALL POTS. To remove plants from small pots, turn the pot upside-down while holding the plant in place between your fingers. The plant should slip out easily.

FLATS. Separate the plants in a flat by cutting straight down around each one with a putty knife or spatula. Or gently separate the plants from each other with your fingers.

CELL-PACKS. Plants in plastic cell-packs are easy to remove from the container, since each plant is in an individual cube of soil. Turn the cell-pack over and push down on the bottom of each cell with your thumbs.

PEAT POTS. These plants are not removed from their pots, but go into the ground pot and all; the roots then grow through the pot into the soil, while the pot eventually decomposes. Make sure the pots are moist before planting by letting them stand in a shallow container of water for several minutes. If they're dry, they'll absorb moisture too slowly from the soil and the roots may have trouble breaking through them, resulting in a stunted plant. It's also important to cover the tops of the pots with soil, since exposed peat acts as a wick, drawing moisture from the soil. If covering the peat would bury the plant too deeply, break off the pot's rim to slightly below the soil level inside the pot.

Small pot

Planting flat

Cell pack

P

usually establish more quickly and grow better initially than containerized plants. This faster growth is in part due to the fact that when you set out a bare-root plant, you refill the planting hole with soil dug from that hole—and the plant's roots thus grow in just one kind of soil. When you plant a containerized or balled-and-burlapped plant, on the other hand, you put two soils, usually with different textures, in contact with each other. The juxtaposition of two different soils can make it difficult for water to penetrate uniformly into the rooting area.

When buying from a local nursery, select bare-root plants with strong stems and fresh-looking, well-formed root systems. Avoid any with slimy roots or dry, withered ones; also reject any that have already leafed out.

It's best to plant bare-root plants as soon as possible after purchase. If bad weather prevents immediate planting, heel in the plants by laying them temporarily in a trench dug in a shady spot in the garden and covering the roots with moist soil or potting mix; it's important not to let the roots dry out. Before planting, soak the roots for at least 4 hours (or preferably overnight) in a bucket of water. Just before planting, cut any damaged or broken roots back to healthy tissue.

Dig a planting hole as shown at right. In areas with heavy clay or hardpan (see page 499), a wider hole will give the roots more growing space. Once you've dug the hole, set in the plant as illustrated below.

SETTING OUT PLANTS FROM CONTAINERS.
Many deciduous broadleaf trees and shrubs, as well as most perennials, are offered in containers. But that's not the only reason containerized plants are popular. You can buy them throughout the growing season, in a variety of sizes (from 1-gallon pots to hefty wooden boxes for large specimen shrubs and trees) and a range of prices; they're relatively easy to transport; and

DIGGING THE PLANTING HOLE

To plant trees and shrubs, dig a planting hole with sides that taper outward into the soil. Make the hole at least twice as wide as the roots of the plant. Roughen the sides with a spading fork; if the sides are smooth, it can be difficult for roots to penetrate the soil. To keep the plant from settling too much after planting and watering, make the hole a bit shallower than the root ball or root system, then dig deeper around the edges of the hole's bottom. This leaves a firm plateau of undug soil to support the plant at the proper depth.

they needn't be planted immediately. Furthermore, because you can buy these plants with flowers, fruit, or autumn leaf color on display, you're able to see exactly what you are getting.

When selecting container-grown plants, look for healthy foliage and strong shoots. Check the leaves and stems to be sure no insects are present. Do your best to avoid root-bound plants. Two common signs of this condition are roots protruding above the soil level and husky

roots growing through the container's drainage holes; additional indicators are plants that are large for the size of the container, leggy plants, and dead twigs or branches. If you do end up with a root-bound plant, be sure to loosen the roots before planting as shown on page 485.

To remove plants from gallon or larger size plastic containers, tap sharply on the bottom and sides to loosen the root ball. The plant should slide out easily. With fiber or pulp pots, tear the pot away from the root ball, taking care not to damage the roots. Plant as shown in the illustrations on page 485.

PLANTING BALLED-AND-BURLAPPED SHRUBS AND TREES.
Some kinds of woody plants have root systems that won't survive bare-root transplanting; others are evergreen and cannot be bare-rooted. Instead, such plants are dug from the field with a ball of soil around their roots, and the soil ball is then wrapped in burlap or a synthetic material and tied with twine or wire. These are called balled-and-burlapped (B-and-B) plants. Some deciduous trees and shrubs (large specimens, in particular), evergreen shrubs such as rhododendrons and azaleas, and various conifers are sold this way.

When buying B-and-B plants, look for healthy foliage and an even branching structure. The covering should be intact so the roots are not exposed, and the root ball should feel firm and moist.

B-and-B plants can be damaged if handled roughly. Always support the bottom of the root ball when moving the plant; don't pick the plant up by the trunk or drop it, which might shatter the root ball. Because a B-and-B plant is usually quite heavy, it's a good idea to have the nursery deliver it or have a friend help you move it to and from your vehicle in a sling of stout canvas. Once home, you can move the plant by sliding it onto a piece of plywood and pulling it

PLANTING BARE-ROOT SHRUBS AND TREES

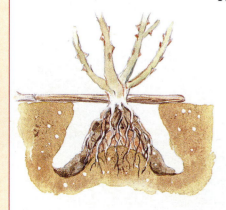

1 Make a firm cone of soil in the planting hole. Spread the roots over the cone, positioning the plant at the same depth as (or slightly higher than) it was in the growing field. Use a shovel handle or yardstick to check the depth.

2 Hold the plant upright as you firm soil around its roots. When backfilling is almost complete, add water. This settles the soil around the roots, eliminating any air pockets. If the plant settles below the level of the surrounding soil, pump it up and down while the soil is saturated to raise it to the proper level.

3 Finish filling the hole with soil; then water again. Take care not to overwater while the plant is still dormant, since soggy soil may inhibit the formation of new roots. When the growing season begins, make a ridge of soil around the hole to form a watering basin; water when the top 2 inches of soil are dry.

P

to the planting spot. For planting directions, see page 486.

Note: Most shrubs and trees grow best if planted in the soil native to your garden, rather than in amended soil, but B-and-B plants are sometimes an exception. They are generally grown in clay or heavy soil that holds together well when the plants are dug up and wrapped. If you have medium- to heavy-textured garden soil (such as fairly heavy loam or clay), there's no need to amend the soil you return to the planting hole. If the B-and-B soil is denser than that in your garden, however, the plant may have a hard time getting established. The heavy soil around its roots will absorb water more slowly than the surrounding garden soil—so the B-and-B's soil can be dry even if the garden soil is kept moist. To avoid this problem, mix an organic amendment such as compost or nitrogen-fortified ground bark or sawdust into the soil removed from the planting hole, using about one shovelful of amendment for every three shovelfuls of soil. Use this blend to fill in around the roots.

Plant Propagation

In gardening usage, "propagation" is a general term for the various ways of starting new plants. Plants can be propagated either sexually or asexually. *Sexual propagation* involves the union of male and female parts of a flower to produce seed. Plants grown from seed reflect the characteristics of both their parents. In *asexual (vegetative) propagation,* the new plant has a single parent; it is produced from a vegetative part (root, stem, bud, or leaf) of just one plant. This new plant is a *clone,* genetically identical to its parent and maintains uniformity—assuring, for example, that each plant of the rose 'Queen Elizabeth' is like every other. Methods of asexual propagation include taking cuttings, dividing plants, layering, budding, and grafting.

DEALING WITH ROOT-BOUND PLANTS

1 It is important to loosen coiled roots before planting so they will grow into the soil. With your hands, tease the roots apart. Then cut off any extralong roots with clippers.

2 Another method is to spray the soil away from the root ball with a strong jet of water, then loosen and uncoil the roots.

3 A third—and more drastic—method is to make several vertical slits in the root ball with a knife to stimulate new root growth.

PLANTING FROM A CONTAINER

1 Dig a hole as shown on page 484. Spread roots out over the central plateau of firm soil. The top of the root ball should be 1 to 2 inches above surrounding soil.

2 Backfill with the unamended soil you dug from the hole, adding the soil in stages and firming it around the roots with your hands as you work.

3 Make a berm of soil to form a watering basin. Irrigate gently. Spread a layer of mulch around the plant, keeping it several inches away from the stem or trunk.

P

PLANTING BALLED-AND-BURLAPPED PLANTS

1 Measure the root ball from top to bottom. The hole should be a bit shallower than this distance, so that the top of the root ball is about 2 inches above the surrounding soil. Adjust the hole to the proper depth; then set in the plant.

2 Untie the covering. If it's burlap, it will eventually rot and need not be completely removed; just spread it out to uncover about half the root ball. If the covering is a synthetic material, remove it entirely. If you are planting in a windy site, drive a stake in alongside the root ball. Fill the hole with soil to within 4 inches of the top and water gently.

3 Continue to fill the hole, firming the soil as you go. Make a berm of soil to form a watering basin; then water the plant. If you staked the plant, loosely tie it to the stake. As the plant becomes established, keep the soil moist but not soggy.

SOWING SEEDS. Starting plants from seed is an economical way to get lots of plants. It also gives you plenty of choices—whether you're growing flowering plants or vegetables, you'll find many more varieties offered in seed catalogs than at the local nursery.

Many annuals, wildflowers, and vegetables can be seeded directly in the garden, either broadcast over a bed to give a planted-by-nature look or sown in the traditional rows of a vegetable or cutting garden. Many other plants, however, are best raised from seed sown in containers. These include slow-growing kinds as well as warm-season vegetables and annuals that may need to be started when the soil is still too cold and wet for in-ground planting.

Seeds of some kinds of plants have specialized requirements for germination. For example, seeds of plants native to areas with cold winters normally need a period of low temperatures before they will sprout. In the wild, this happens naturally: the seeds mature in late summer or autumn, are moistened by rain in fall and chilled throughout the winter, then sprout in spring. Gardeners can mimic this cold period by stratifying the seeds—either sowing them in containers that are set outdoors for the winter, or placing them between layers of moist paper towels enclosed in a plastic bag, then refrigerating them for a month or two.

Some seeds—including those of false indigo (*Baptisia*), lupine (*Lupinus*), and locust (*Robinia*)—have a hard seed coat that does not allow water to penetrate. Before they can germinate, they must be scarified. In nature, scarification may be accomplished by soil fungi and bacteria that partially decompose the seed

SEED GERMINATION

Seeds cannot germinate until certain favorable environmental conditions are met. These include adequate moisture, a preferred temperature, and a loose-textured soil that provides oxygen to the sprouting seed. (Seeds of some species also require light, meaning that no newspaper or other covering should be placed over the planted seeds; seed packets note this requirement.) Once these conditions occur, the *radicle*—the embryonic root—emerges from the seed and begins growing downward; root hairs and lateral roots develop from it. The lower part of the stem (the *hypocotyl*) pulls the *cotyledons* or seed leaves upward and into the light. Food stored in the cotyledons nourishes the seedling until the first true leaves begin photosynthesis. (In some species, such as peas, the cotyledons remain underground during germination.)

Some familiar plants—grasses, corn, orchids, lilies—have only one cotyledon and are called *monocots*. Plants with two cotyledons are called *dicots*.

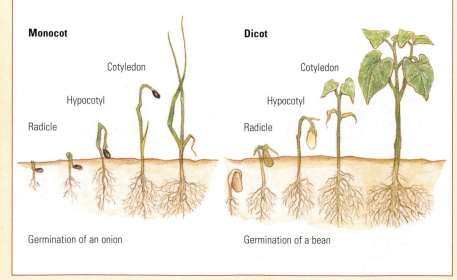

Germination of an onion

Germination of a bean

coat; it also occurs when birds or animals consume and then excrete the seeds, having digested the seed coat. Gardeners can scarify seeds by artificial means, nicking the seed coat with a file or scratching it with sandpaper.

Sowing seeds outdoors. Whether you're broadcasting a wildflower mixture, sowing several kinds of annuals for a showy border, or planting rows of vegetables, start by preparing a planting bed (see page 482).

Planting seeds in rows. Make furrows in the planting bed, following the seed packet instructions for depth of furrows and spacing between them. If possible, lay out the rows in a north-south direction, so that both sides will receive an equal amount of sunlight during the day. Form the furrows with a hoe, rake, or stick; for perfectly straight rows, use a board or taut string as a guide, as shown below.

Sow seeds evenly, spacing them as the packet directs. You can tear off a small corner of the packet and tap the seeds out as you move along, or pour a small quantity into your palm and scatter pinches of seed as evenly as possible. Larger seeds, such as beans, can be placed individually by hand.

Water the furrows with a fine spray; then keep the soil surface moist but not dripping wet until the seeds sprout. After the seedlings are up and growing, gradually cut back on watering, but be sure you keep the root zone moist. Thin seedlings once they've developed two sets of true leaves but while they're still small. Thinned plants can be transplanted into any empty spaces in the rows.

Broadcasting seeds. In addition to beds of wildflowers, this method (shown above) gives a natural-looking planting of other easy-to-grow annuals, such as sweet alyssum *(Lobularia maritima)*, Chinese forget-me-not *(Cynoglossum amabile)*, and nasturtium *(Tropaeolum majus)*.

Sowing seeds in containers. Many plants get off to a better start when sown in containers and transplanted to garden beds later in the season. It's easier to provide plants in containers with the warm temperatures and bright light they need for quick growth, and easier to protect them from insects and birds as well. The information on the seed packet will help you decide when to plant. Most annual flowers and vegetables should be sown 4 to 8 weeks before it's time to transplant them outdoors.

Container choices. Convenience, cost, and reusability all determine which containers you select. If you're reusing old pots, scrub them out and soak them for 30 minutes in a solution of 1 part household bleach to 9 parts hot water to prevent infection by damping-off fungi (page 459), which destroy seedlings.

Plastic flats with no dividers are an old favorite. They're readily available from garden supply stores and mail-order catalogs, and free when you buy seedlings at nurseries.

Plastic cell-packs and 2- to 4-inch plastic pots (recycled from nursery purchases) are easy to obtain and use.

BROADCASTING SEEDS IN A PREPARED BED

1 For a patterned planting, outline the areas for each kind of seed with gypsum, flour, or stakes and string. You may want to put a label in each area.

2 To achieve a more even distribution, shake each kind of seed (or an entire wildflower seed mixture) in a covered can with several times its bulk of white sand.

3 Scatter the seed-sand mixture as evenly as possible over the bed or individual planting areas; then rake lightly, barely covering the seeds with soil. Take care not to bury them too deeply.

4 Spread a very thin layer of mulch (such as sifted compost) over the bed to help retain moisture, keep the surface from crusting, and hide the seeds from birds.

5 Water with a fine spray. Keep the soil surface barely damp until the seeds sprout; once seedlings are up, gradually decrease watering frequency.

6 When seedlings have two sets of true leaves, thin those that are too closely spaced. Transplant the thinned seedlings to fill empty spaces in the bed.

Stretch string between two stakes and plant beneath it. Lay a board on the soil surface, then plant along its edge.

BUYING AND STORING SEEDS

Be sure the seeds you buy are fresh; they should be dated for the current year. For many plants, seed may be sold in three different forms: loose, pelletized, and in tapes. Loose seeds, traditionally sold in packets, are familiar to all gardeners. Pelletized seeds, also sold in packets, are individually coated (like small pills) to make handling and proper spacing easier. Seed tapes are strips of biodegradable paper with seeds embedded in them, properly spaced for growing to maturity. You just unroll the tape in a prepared furrow and cover it with soil.

Store extra seeds in an airtight jar or other container in a cool, dry place. With proper storage, many kinds of seeds remain viable for a year, and some stay good for several years.

P

Peat pots are inexpensive but not reusable. However, because you plant seedlings pot and all, such pots minimize disturbance to roots. Keep them moist after seeding (so roots can penetrate them easily).

Plastic foam flats with tapered individual cells are sold by nurseries and through mail-order catalogs. They come in several cell sizes; some have capillary matting that draws water from a reservoir, making seedling care easier.

In addition to the containers listed above, you can use recycled household items—plastic cups, cut-down milk cartons, foil baking pans. Be sure to punch several drainage holes in any container that lacks them, since seedlings will die if water collects around their roots.

ABOVE, TOP: Various seed-starting trays and pots are available at nurseries and through mail-order catalogs.
ABOVE, BOTTOM: Plant two seeds in each cell of plastic foam flat; later thin to one seedling per cell.

Peat pots go into the garden with seedlings.

SOWING SEEDS IN CONTAINERS

1 Fill each container to within ½ inch of the rim with damp mix, firming it gently with your fingers or a block of wood. Scatter seeds thinly over the surface of the planting mix. Check the seed packet for recommended planting depth and cover with the proper amount of mix. (A general rule of thumb is to cover seeds to a depth equal to twice their diameter.) Label each container with the plant name and sowing date. Moisten lightly. Many gardeners cover the containers loosely with damp newspaper; this helps keep soil moist but still allows air to get in, preventing the growth of fungi. (Don't cover if the seeds need light to germinate, however; see page 486.)

Place the containers in a warm spot. When the seeds germinate, uncover the containers, if necessary; then move them to a spot where they'll be in bright light, such as a greenhouse or a sunny window. (Or give them 12 to 14 hours of fluorescent light each day, setting the light 6 to 8 inches above the tops of the plants.) Water when the surface of the soil feels dry, spraying with a fine mist.

2 When the seedlings develop their second set of true leaves, it's time to transplant them. (If you don't need many plants, just thin the seedlings to one plant per pot—or thin flat-grown ones to a distance of 2 inches apart—and skip transplanting them to larger containers.) To transplant, fill new containers such as 4-inch plastic pots with dampened potting mix. Remove the seedlings from their original pot by squeezing its sides and turning it upside down, keeping one hand around the soil ball. Once the soil ball is out of the pot, carefully pull it apart with both hands and set it down on a flat surface.

3 Separate the fragile rootballs with a toothpick or skewer, or tease them apart with your fingers.

4 Poke a hole in the new container's planting mix. Handle each seedling by the leaves to avoid damaging the tender stem; support the root ball with your finger. Place each seedling in its new container and firm the mix around it. Water immediately, then set pots in bright light; keep them out of direct sunlight for a few days to let the seedlings recover from transplanting. Fertilize weekly with a fertilizer sold for starting seeds or a liquid type diluted to half-strength.

About 10 days before the seedlings are ready to plant outdoors, harden them off so they can withstand bright outdoor sun and cooler temperatures. Stop fertilizing them and set them outside for several hours each day in a wind-sheltered spot receiving filtered light. Over the next week or so, gradually increase exposure until the plants are in full sun all day (shade lovers are an exception; they shouldn't be exposed to day-long sun). Then set them out in the garden as illustrated on page 483.

1

2

3

4

P

Growing medium. Buy a seed-starting mix or potting soil sold at the nursery, or make your own medium by combining 1 part each of peat moss or finely shredded bark and perlite. Before using purchased mixes, flush them with water once or twice to eliminate excess salts. The mix should be moist but not soggy when you plant seeds.

Note: Vermiculite is sometimes recommended as an ingredient in homemade growing mixes. However, the Environmental Protection Agency has warned that some brands of vermiculite may be contaminated with small amounts of potentially cancer-causing asbestos. If you do use vermiculite, to be on the safe side mix it with other ingredients outdoors or in a well-ventilated area, keep it damp, and avoid bringing dust from the product into the house on clothing.

CUTTINGS. Plants can be propagated from cuttings in several ways, depending on the plant part used as propagation material. Any plant that produces sprouts from its roots will grow from root cuttings. Some kinds of plants will root successfully from a leaf or a portion of a leaf. Stem cuttings—in which roots are induced to grow from sections of stem—are described as softwood, semihardwood, or hardwood, depending on the maturity of the stems; see pages 490 and 491 for directions.

Root cuttings. Numerous perennials and other plants can be propagated by root cuttings. Among many others, these include bear's breech *(Acanthus),* Japanese anemone, globe thistle *(Echinops),* Oriental poppy *(Papaver orientale),* trumpet vine *(Campsis),* blackberry, and raspberry.

Make root cuttings when the plant is dormant—in late fall or early winter, for most species. You can dig up an entire plant or just a section of its roots. With a sharp knife, remove vigorous, healthy pieces of root 2 to 4 inches long; those growing close to the crown will form new plants most quickly. (Note that rooting hormone is not needed, and in fact may actually

Strobilanthes, an annual foliage plant, can be propagated through leaf cuttings.

ROOT CUTTINGS

To start a few root cuttings, insert them upright in a pot. For a larger number, lay the cuttings in a flat.

THREE TYPES OF LEAF CUTTINGS

Rex begonias are propagated by making cuts in the large veins on the underside of mature leaves. Lay the leaf flat, cut side down, on the rooting medium; then enclose the container in a plastic bag. In time, new plants will grow at the point where each vein was cut.

To root leaf cuttings of sedum or African violet *(Saintpaulia ionantha),* insert a young leaf with an inch or two of stem into the rooting medium. Enclose the container in a plastic bag to retain humidity. New plants form at the base of the stem. Prickly pear *(Opuntia)* can also be propagated from leaf cuttings. Use an entire pad as each cutting, inserting the base into moist rooting medium. A new plant will form at the base of the leaf.

To root leaf cuttings of mother-in-law's tongue *(Sansevieria),* cut a leaf into 3- to 4-inch-long sections. Insert these pieces into the rooting medium.

delay rooting.) If you have only a few cuttings, you can place them upright in a container filled with damp potting mix, with the top cut ends (those that were closest to the crown on the parent plant) just at soil level. For larger numbers of cuttings, fill a flat to within an inch of the top with potting mix; lay the cuttings flat on top of the mix, then cover them with about ½ inch more mix.

Water the planted containers well. Then place them in a growing area such as a greenhouse or cold frame and provide protection from direct sun. Once stems and green leaves have formed, move the containers into full light and water them as needed. When the young shoots are several inches tall and new roots have formed (check by gently digging up a cutting), transplant them to individual pots and feed with liquid fertilizer.

Leaf cuttings. Some plants can form roots from a leaf or a portion of one. Three examples are shown above. For rooting medium, use a mix of 1 part peat moss and 1 part vermiculite, perlite, or coarse builder's sand.

P

SOFTWOOD AND SEMIHARDWOOD STEM CUTTINGS

Taken during the active growing season from spring until late summer, softwood cuttings are the easiest stem cuttings to take and the fastest to root. They are made from relatively soft, flexible new growth. Semihardwood cuttings are taken somewhat later in the growing season, usually in summer or early autumn. A suitable semihardwood stem is firm enough to snap if bent sharply; if it just bends, it's too mature for satisfactory rooting.

In addition to deciduous and evergreen shrubs and trees, many perennials may be propagated by softwood and semihardwood cuttings.

ROOTING THE CUTTINGS

1 Prepare containers first. Use clean pots or flats with drainage holes. Fill them with a half-and-half mixture of perlite and peat moss, or with perlite alone. Dampen the mixture.

2 Gather cuttings early in the day, when plants are fresh and full of moisture. The parent plant should be healthy and growing vigorously. With a sharp knife or bypass pruners, cut off an 8- to 12-inch length of stem.

Prepare the cuttings by removing and discarding any flower buds, flowers, and side shoots. Then slice the stem into 3- to 4-inch pieces, each with at least two nodes (growing points). Make each cut just below a node, since new roots will form at this point. Strip the lower leaves from each cutting.

3 Dip the lower cut ends of the cuttings in liquid or powdered rooting hormone; shake off any excess. (Many plants will root without the use of hormones.)

Using the end of a sharp pencil, make holes in the rooting medium an inch or two apart; then insert the cuttings. Firm the medium around the cuttings and water with a fine spray. Label each container with the name of the plant and the date. Set containers in a warm spot that's shaded but not dark.

Enclose each container in a plastic bag, fastening the bag closed to maintain humidity. Open the bag for a few minutes every day to provide ventilation.

4 Once the cuttings have taken hold and are growing roots, they will begin to send out new leaves. To test for rooting, gently pull on a cutting; if you feel resistance, roots are forming. At this point, expose the cuttings to drier air by opening the bags; if the cuttings wilt, close the bags again for a few days.

When the plants seem acclimated to open air, transplant each to its own pot of lightweight potting soil. By the next planting season, the new plants should be ready to go out in the garden.

P

HARDWOOD CUTTINGS

Take hardwood cuttings at the onset of the dormant season, in late fall or early winter. For deciduous plants, wait to take the cuttings until just after the leaves fall. Most deciduous shrubs and trees, and some evergreens, can be propagated by this method. It is best to plant the cuttings in a protected nursery area where the soil is moist but well drained and reasonably fertile. You might wish to add some slow-release fertilizer to poor soil. The nursery area can be a shaded cold frame with the lid off, or a spot in the garden out of direct sun and wind. Root the cuttings as explained below.

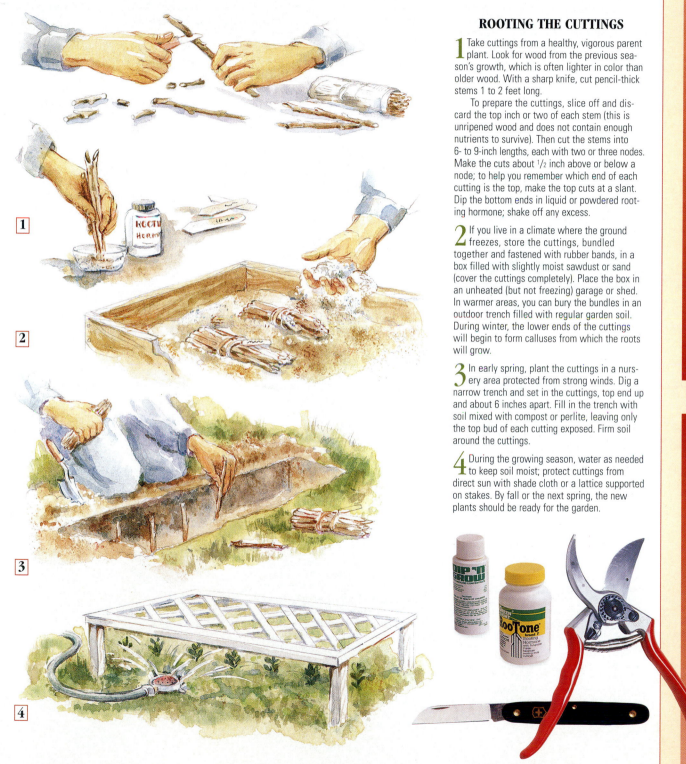

ROOTING THE CUTTINGS

1 Take cuttings from a healthy, vigorous parent plant. Look for wood from the previous season's growth, which is often lighter in color than older wood. With a sharp knife, cut pencil-thick stems 1 to 2 feet long.

To prepare the cuttings, slice off and discard the top inch or two of each stem (this is unripened wood and does not contain enough nutrients to survive). Then cut the stems into 6- to 9-inch lengths, each with two or three nodes. Make the cuts about 1/2 inch above or below a node; to help you remember which end of each cutting is the top, make the top cuts at a slant. Dip the bottom ends in liquid or powdered rooting hormone; shake off any excess.

2 If you live in a climate where the ground freezes, store the cuttings, bundled together and fastened with rubber bands, in a box filled with slightly moist sawdust or sand (cover the cuttings completely). Place the box in an unheated (but not freezing) garage or shed. In warmer areas, you can bury the bundles in an outdoor trench filled with regular garden soil. During winter, the lower ends of the cuttings will begin to form calluses from which the roots will grow.

3 In early spring, plant the cuttings in a nursery area protected from strong winds. Dig a narrow trench and set in the cuttings, top end up and about 6 inches apart. Fill in the trench with soil mixed with compost or perlite, leaving only the top bud of each cutting exposed. Firm soil around the cuttings.

4 During the growing season, water as needed to keep soil moist; protect cuttings from direct sun with shade cloth or a lattice supported on stakes. By fall or the next spring, the new plants should be ready for the garden.

P

491

DIVISION. Division is the easiest way to propagate many perennials, bulbs, and shrubs that form suckers or clumps of stems with rooted bases. In essence, the process involves separating one plant into several rooted, self-supporting plants. Besides giving you new plants, division rejuvenates overgrown plants, increasing quantity of bloom and improving overall appearance.

Most plants can be divided either in fall or early spring. If you plan to divide in fall and you live in a cold-winter climate, do the job early enough in the season to let roots get established before freezing weather arrives (generally 6 to 8 weeks before the first hard frost). Avoid dividing plants in the heat of summer, since it is difficult for divisions to become established then.

A day or two before dividing, thoroughly moisten the soil around the clump to be divided. To make the plants easier to handle, cut back the stems of larger perennials, leaving about 6 inches of foliage. (When dividing shrubs, cut stems back to 6 to 12 inches long.) If you'll be planting in a new bed, prepare the soil (see page 482) before you divide, so the divisions won't have to spend too long out of the ground. If you're replanting in the same location as the parent clump, keep the divisions in a shady spot covered with damp newspapers while you replenish the soil.

For division of bulbous plants, see pages 454–455; turn to page 469 for information on dividing ornamental grasses.

LAYERING. Layering is a technique that encourages new roots to form on branches still attached to the parent plant. The parent supplies the layer—the new plant—with water and nutrients during the rooting process. When roots have formed, the new plant is detached and transplanted.

Ground layering. Also called simple layering, ground layering is an easy way to produce a few

DIVIDING PERENNIALS

1 Loosen the soil in a circle around the clump, cutting 6 to 12 inches beyond the plant's perimeter with a shovel or spading fork. Then dig under the roots to free them from the soil. Lift the whole clump out of the ground; or, if it's too heavy to lift, cut it into sections. Set the clump (or pieces) in a convenient working spot such as a path.

2 Gently tease some soil from the root ball so you can see what you are doing. For larger, fibrous-rooted perennials such as daylilies (*Hemerocallis*), hose off as much of the soil as possible.

3 Now make the divisions. Look at the plant, noting natural dividing points between stems or sections. You can easily divide some perennials by pulling the clumps apart by hand. Those with mats of small, fibrous roots can be cut with a knife, small pruning saw, or trowel; types with thick, tough roots may require a sharp-bladed shovel or an axe. Try to divide the clumps into good-sized sections, which will grow and bloom more quickly than small divisions. Trim any damaged roots, stems, or leaves from the divisions.

4 Replant the divisions as soon as possible, then keep them well watered while they get established. You can also plant divisions in containers (a good idea if they're very small) to set out later or share with other gardeners.

GROUND LAYERING

1 In spring, select a young, healthy, pliable shoot growing low on the plant to be layered. Loosen the soil where the shoot will be buried and work in a shovelful of compost. Dig a shallow hole in the prepared area.

With a sharp knife, make a cut where the shoot will touch the soil; cut about halfway through the shoot, starting from the underside. Dust the cut with rooting hormone powder and insert a pebble or wooden matchstick to hold it open.

Lay the shoot (the layer) in the hole and fasten it down with a piece of wire or a forked stick. Some gardeners tie the layer's tip to a stake to help it grow upwards.

2 Fill in the hole, firming the soil around the layer. A rock or brick can be placed on top to help hold the layer in place.

During the growing season, keep the soil around the layer moist. Adding a few inches of mulch will help retain moisture.

When you are sure roots have formed (this may take anywhere from a few months to more than a year; gently dig into the soil to check), cut the new plant free from the parent. Dig it up, keeping plenty of soil around the roots, and move it to its intended location.

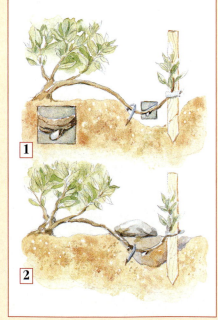

AIR LAYERING

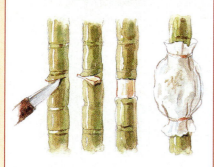

Air layering is most successful if done while a plant is growing actively. To encourage such growth in houseplants, fertilize the plant to be layered, then place it in a sunny window. When new leaves appear, proceed with layering.

Begin below a node. Make a slanting cut (insert a wooden matchstick to keep it open) or remove a ring of bark. Dust cut with rooting hormone, encase in damp sphagnum moss, and cover with plastic wrap to keep moss moist.

If layering is successful, roots will appear in the moss after several months; you can then sever the newly rooted stem from its parent and pot it. At this point, it's usually a good idea to remove about half the new plant's leaves to prevent excessive moisture loss through transpiration while it gets established.

If no roots form, the cut you made will form a callus, and new bark will eventually grow over it.

T-BUDDING

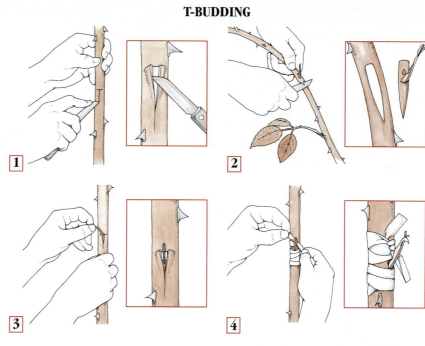

1 Choose a stock stem $1/4$ to $1/2$ inch in diameter. Make a T-shaped cut in the bark; the top of the T should extend about a third of the way around the stem. Gently pry up the corners of the T. If the bark does not pull away easily, it may be too early in the season; try again in a week or two.

2 Select a bud (located at the base of a leaf) from the budwood plant; remove the leaf but retain its stalk to use as handle. Be sure to take a vegetative bud, which is usually small and pointed, rather than a larger, plumper flower bud. Cut a shield-shaped patch containing the bud, beginning about $1/2$ inch below the bud and finishing about 1 inch above it; leave a bit of wood attached to the back of the bud shield.

3 Push the bud shield down between the flaps of the T-cut, being careful not to damage the bud. Cut off the top of the shield to make it even with the horizontal cut of the T. All of the shield should fit between the bark flaps.

4 Bind the budding site snugly with plastic grafting tape or rubber budding strips, starting beneath the bud and finishing above it. Cover the top of the T, but leave the bud exposed.

---

new plants, though it may take as long as a year. This technique can be used to propagate many shrubs and perennials that have low-growing or trailing branches. See the steps below.

Air layering. Air layering involves the same principle as ground layering, but it's used for branches higher on a plant. It is often employed to propagate large house plants—overgrown rubber plants *(Ficus elastica),* for example, but it's also successful in some outdoor trees and shrubs, including citrus, witch hazel *(Hamamelis),* magnolia, and rhododendron.

BUDDING AND GRAFTING. These methods involve joining parts of two different—but closely related—plants so that they will grow as one. With a steady hand and a little practice, you can learn to use budding and grafting to propagate roses, grapes, and fruit and ornamental trees or to add one or more new varieties to an existing fruit or nut tree. The part that becomes the upper or aboveground portion of

the plant is known as the *scion;* it may be a piece of a branch or a single bud. The scion gives the new plant the desired qualities of flowering, fruiting, or form. The part that provides the roots is called the *stock, rootstock,* or *understock.* In some cases, the stock is a young plant chosen because it causes the new plant to be hardier, more disease resistant, or smaller in size (as in dwarf fruit trees, for instance). In other cases, the stock may be a mature tree that you want to graft over to a new variety.

Successful budding and grafting depend upon uniting the *cambium* layers of scion and stock—the thin layer of growing cells just inside the bark. When these layers join with each other, new growth can occur. Use a very sharp knife to make all cuts: the cleaner the cut, the better the chance for a successful union. T-budding and cleft grafting are illustrated here. Other methods include chip budding, patch budding, whip grafting, and side grafting; consult a plant propagation manual for details on these.

Budding. Also called bud-grafting, this operation is carried out in summer or early fall when plants are actively growing. Roses and some other flowering shrubs, as well as grapes and fruit trees, are propagated by this method. Budding involves inserting a growth bud (the scion) from one plant beneath the bark of a related plant (the stock). The stock is either a pencil-thick rooted cutting of a sort known to produce a strong root system or a seedling plant of such a species. Usually, buds are inserted just a few inches above the soil. (They are occasionally placed in small branches in the upper portion of a tree.) If the plants are compatible and the budding operation is successful, the bud will unite with the stem into which it was inserted. It will remain plump but dormant throughout fall and winter, then begin to grow in spring, when all the plant's buds burst into growth. At this point, the stem is cut back to just above the new, growing bud. The flowers, fruit, and leaves arising from the implanted bud will have the characteristics of the plant from which it was taken.

P

Grafting. This technique unites a short length of stem—the scion—with a stock. The stock plant may be either a slim seedling to be grafted near ground level or an old fruit tree to be grafted on its major limbs. Cleft grafting (illustrated at right) is popular for converting fruit and nut trees to new varieties. Cleft grafts are made in early spring, when the growth buds of the stock are just beginning to swell. However, the scion wood should still be dormant when the graft is made—so gather it in late fall or winter. Cut ¼- to ½-inch-thick tip growth, making sure each piece has 3 or 4 buds. Bundle the cut stems together, label them, and place in a sealed plastic bag in the refrigerator. Some mail-order companies offer scion wood in winter.

Pruning

Pruning tasks vary in scope—from removing large tree limbs to pinching out new growth on perennials—and your goals in pruning will differ, too. Here are a few reasons why you may need or want to prune.

To maintain the health of your plants. Trees and shrubs will be healthier and more attractive if you remove branches that are badly diseased, dead, or rubbing together. Plants that have become too densely branched should be thinned to allow air and sunlight to reach their inner leaves and stems, helping to discourage some diseases.

To direct growth. Each time you make a pruning cut, you stop growth in one direction and encourage it in another, since growth continues in the buds and branches left behind.

To remove undesirable growth. Prune out wayward branches and remove suckers (stems growing up from the roots) and water sprouts (upright shoots growing from the trunk and branches). It should not, however, be necessary to cut back a plant continually to keep it in bounds. If it requires such treatment, it was probably a poor choice for its location and should be replaced with a plant that will naturally remain smaller.

To increase quality or yield of flowers or fruit. Most fruit trees and many flowering trees and shrubs need regular pruning to produce a good annual crop of fruit or blossoms. Specifics of pruning these plants are given in the A-to-Z Plant Encyclopedia.

To maintain safety. Remove split or broken branches that threaten to fall, injuring people or damaging buildings or cars. Also prune away any branches that obscure oncoming traffic from view.

To create hedges or topiary. Suitable plants can be shaped in various ways through regular shearing.

P

CLEFT GRAFTING

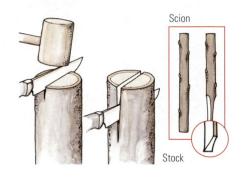

1 Prepare the stock by splitting it several inches down into a smooth, straight-grained section (so the split will be even). Shape the bottom end of the scion into a long, gradually tapering wedge; the outside edge of the wedge should be slightly thicker than the inside (as shown in the cross-section diagram).

Scion

Stock

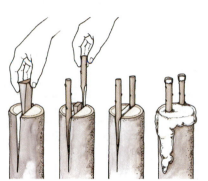

2 Use a wedge or large screwdriver to hold open the split stock while you work. Insert the scion (or two, as illustrated) into the stock, carefully placed so that the cambium layers of stock and scion(s) match. After the scion(s) are properly placed, remove the wedge and cover the entire union with grafting wax. Also coat the top of the scion(s) so they won't dry out. If the graft is successful, buds on the scion wood will show growth during spring.

PRUNING AND PLANT GROWTH

Some kinds of pruning cuts are made near a growth bud. Because subsequent growth varies depending on the bud's location, learning about growth buds will help you decide where to make cuts.

The terminal bud grows at the tip of a shoot, causing that shoot to grow longer. Actively growing terminal buds produce hormones that move down the stem and inhibit the growth of other buds on that stem.

Lateral buds grow along the sides of the shoot at leaf attachment points (nodes); they produce the sideways growth that makes a plant bushy. These buds stay dormant until the shoot has grown long enough to diminish the influence of the hormones produced by the terminal bud, or until the terminal bud is pruned off; then they begin to grow.

Latent buds lie dormant beneath the bark. If a branch breaks or is cut off near a latent bud, that bud may develop into a new shoot.

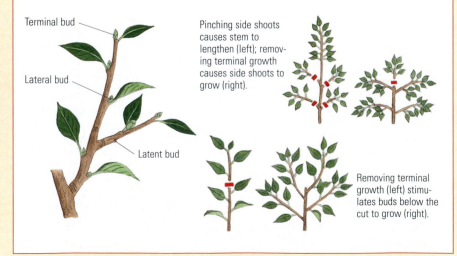

Terminal bud

Lateral bud

Latent bud

Pinching side shoots causes stem to lengthen (left); removing terminal growth causes side shoots to grow (right).

Removing terminal growth (left) stimulates buds below the cut to grow (right).

FOUR TYPES OF PRUNING CUTS. Most pruning involves four basic techniques: thinning, heading, shearing, and pinching. What sets these methods apart is where you cut in relation to growth buds and side branches.

Thinning. Most of the cuts you make when pruning should be thinning cuts. Such cuts can direct growth, eliminate competing or old stems, reduce overall size, and open up a plant's structure.

To thin, you remove an entire stem or branch, taking it back to its point of origin or to its junction with another branch. You might cut a branch back to the trunk, to the parent branch from which it arose, or (in the case of plants that send up stems directly from the roots) all the way to the ground. When removing one branch at a branch junction, be sure the remaining branch is at least one-third the diameter of the one being removed. If it's any smaller than that, it will be unable to assume the terminal role, and the effect will be more like that resulting from a heading cut (see below).

When you remove a branch, you of course also remove the buds on that branch. Thinning cuts can cause bud growth elsewhere on the plant, but they're much less likely than heading cuts to stimulate clusters of shoots. Thus, thinning lets you reduce the bulk of a plant with minimal regrowth.

Heading. Heading cuts remove just part of a stem or branch—not the whole thing, as thinning cuts do. Such cuts can be made back to a bud or to a twig or branch too small to take over the terminal role (less than one-third the diameter of the branch you're removing). Heading stimulates the growth of lateral buds just below the cut. (Shearing and pinching, discussed below, are also forms of heading.)

For maintenance pruning of most woody plants, heading is a less desirable technique than thinning. Though it may initially make a plant smaller and more compact, this situation won't last for long: once headed, the plant will produce vigorous new growth from lateral buds. If you head a wayward shoot instead of thinning it out, you can expect a candelabrum of shoots to grow in its place. Continual heading thus ruins the natural shape of most woody plants. It is, however, useful when your goal is precisely to induce vigorous growth beneath a cut—when you want to force branching at particular locations to fill a hole in the tree's crown; train young fruit trees; increase bloom production in roses or other flowering shrubs; or rejuvenate old or neglected shrubs.

Shearing. An indiscriminate form of heading, shearing does not involve careful, precise cutting just above a growing point. Instead, you simply clip a plant's outer foliage to create an even surface, as in hedges or topiary. However, because the plants best suited to shearing have lateral buds and branches close together on their stems, almost every cut ends up near a growing point.

Pinching. This is the simplest, most basic pruning cut. Using your thumb and forefinger or a pair of hand shears, you nip off the tips of new growth, removing the terminal bud. This stops the shoot from growing longer and stimulates branching. Pinching is used primarily on annuals and perennials to make them bushy and encourage the production of more flowers.

MAKING PRUNING CUTS. When pruning, always cut back to a part that will continue to grow—to the trunk, another branch, a bud, or even to the plant's base, if it sends up stems from the roots. At these points of active growth, callus tissue will start to grow inward from cells at the end of the cut; in time, the wound will seal off. Clean cuts callus over faster than ragged

TYPES OF PRUNING CUTS

Pinching

Shown here are three types of pruning cuts: pinching removes the terminal growth; heading removes part of the shoot; and thinning eliminates the entire shoot.

Heading
Heading cuts produce clusters of shoots from buds below the cuts.

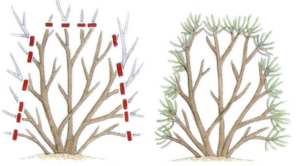

Shearing
Shearing, which is really random heading, produces an outer layer of dense, twiggy growth from buds below the cuts.

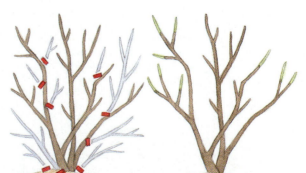

Thinning
Thinning cuts open up a plant and cause the least amount of regrowth.

P

CUTTING ABOVE A BUD

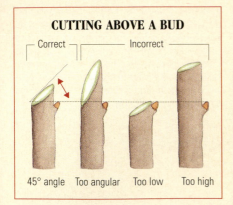

Correct   Incorrect

45° angle   Too angular   Too low   Too high

POSITIONING PRUNING SHEARS

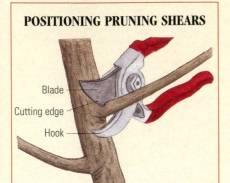

Blade

Cutting edge

Hook

To make a proper close pruning cut, hold the pruning shears with the blade closer to the growth that will remain on the plant. A stub results when you reverse the position and place the hook closer to the plant.

REMOVING A BRANCH

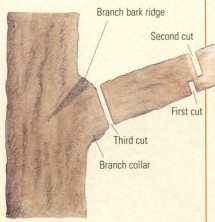

Branch bark ridge

Second cut

First cut

Third cut

Branch collar

1 About a foot from the branch base, make a cut from the underside approximately a third of the way through.

2 About an inch farther out on the branch, cut through the top until the branch rips off. The branch should split cleanly between the two cuts.

3 Make the final cut by placing your saw just outside the branch bark ridge and cutting downward and just outside of the branch collar. (If the crotch is very narrow, cut upward from the bottom to avoid cutting into the branch collar.)

ones, so it's important to use an appropriate, well-sharpened pruning tool (for more on tools, see page 501). Forcing a tool to cut a branch bigger than it's designed to handle can result in ragged, uneven cuts (and can damage the tool).

The precise placement of a cut is usually also important. If you cut too close to a bud, it's likely to die. If you cut too far away from it, on the other hand, you'll leave a stub which, though still attached to the plant, is no longer involved in its active metabolism. In time, the stub will wither and die, then decay and drop off to leave an open patch of dead tissue—an invitation to disease or insect infestation.

When cutting back to a bud, look for a healthy specimen pointing in the direction you want the new shoot to grow. A proper cut will be about ¼ inch away from the bud, sloping away at approximately a 45° angle. Its lowest point should be opposite the bud and even with it, and it should slant upward in the direction the bud is pointing (see illustration at left).

When removing a branch, don't make a flush cut. Position your shears or saw just outside the *branch collar,* the wrinkled area or bulge at the branch's base where it meets another branch or the trunk. Also refrain from cutting into the *branch bark ridge* (the raised bark in the branch crotch). Leaving these areas intact keeps decay to a minimum.

If you need to remove larger branches (any that are too big to support in one hand while sawing with the other), make the cut in three steps to avoid ripping the bark and tearing the tissue around the collar, as shown at left. If the limb in question is very heavy or high in a tree, however, it's wisest to hire a professional arborist. This is also the best course for repairing storm-damaged trees and for pruning around power lines.

WHEN TO PRUNE. In general, pruning is best done in late winter (when plants are dormant) or during mid- to late summer; specific pruning times are given for many plants described in the A-to-Z Plant Encyclopedia. Dead or badly diseased wood is an exception: it should be removed as soon as you spot it. (Be sure, however, that dead-looking wood truly is dead. Freeze-damaged tissue that looks beyond help is sometimes in fact still alive; see page 465.) The best time to prune also depends in part on whether the plant is deciduous or evergreen.

Deciduous trees and shrubs—those that drop their leaves in fall—are typically pruned in late winter or early spring, just before or just as they resume growth. When the plants are leafless, it's easier to see their overall shape and to spot broken and awkwardly placed branches. To avoid cold damage to exposed tissues, prune after the danger of heavy frost is past. Flowering trees and shrubs demand a little extra attention to timing—you'll need to know whether they bloom on old or new wood before you decide just when to prune. Plants that bear flowers in spring on wood that grew the preceding year should be pruned only after flowering is finished; if you prune in late winter, you'll cut off the

flower buds. Woody plants that produce flowers later in the growing season on the current season's growth, however, can be pruned in late winter without sacrificing blossoms, since the new (flowering) wood will grow after pruning. Check to see which category your plants belong to—older branches are usually darker, less pliable, and woodier looking than new growth.

Many deciduous plants can also be pruned in midsummer, after the growth flush of spring and early summer has slowed. This is a good time to thin out excess growth; moreover, vigorous shoots such as suckers and water sprouts are less likely to regrow if removed in summer. In cold-winter areas, be sure to complete such summer pruning no later than a month before the usual first-frost date, since pruning may stimulate tender new growth susceptible to cold damage.

Broad-leafed evergreen trees and shrubs don't drop their foliage, but growth of most slows down to a level approaching dormancy during the coldest time of year. Most can be pruned late in this dormant period (late winter or early spring) or in summer. For flowering broad-leafed evergreens, however, timing is more precise; as for deciduous flowering plants, you'll need to prune with an eye toward preserving flower buds. For evergreens flowering on last season's growth, prune after bloom; for those that bloom on new wood, prune before spring growth begins.

Conifers, in many cases, don't require any pruning. For those that do, timing depends on the growth habit of the conifer in question. These typically evergreen plants (which bear needles or scalelike leaves) fall into two broad classes: those with branches radiating out from the trunk in whorls and those that sprout branches in a random fashion.

Fir *(Abies),* spruce *(Picea),* and most pines *(Pinus)* are examples of whorl-type conifers. They produce all their new growth in spring, with buds appearing at the tips of new shoots as well as along their length and at their bases. (On pines, the new shoots are called candles, since that's what they look like until the needles grow.) Prune these conifers in early spring. You can cut new shoots back about halfway to induce more branching; or you can cut them out entirely to force branching from buds at their bases. Be sure to make cuts above potential growth buds or back to existing branches. Cutting back into an old stem—even one that bears foliage—won't force branching unless you're cutting back to latent buds.

Random-branching conifers, including cedar *(Cedrus),* cypress *(Cupressus),* juniper *(Juniperus),* arborvitae *(Platycladus and Thuja),* yew *(Taxus),* and hemlock *(Tsuga),* grow in spurts throughout the growing season rather than just in spring. They can be pruned much as deciduous and broad-leafed evergreens are. New growth will sprout from the branches below your cuts as long as the remaining part of the branch bears some foliage; most won't develop new growth from bare branches (hemlock and yew are exceptions). You usually have more leeway in timing for pruning random-branching conifers than you do for whorl-branching types, though the best time for the job is usually right before spring growth begins.

Shrubs

Shrubs are woody plants that live for many years. They are typically planted to provide long-lasting features in a landscape, forming a framework to help unite the garden's various elements. Many establish a permanent woody structure in their youth, then increase in size by growing new branches from older ones. Others produce shorter-lived woody stems (canes) each year from the base, with a few to many new stems emerging as the older ones decline.

In form, shrubs may be rounded, vase shaped, conical, or columnar; in size, they range from ankle-high dwarfs to plants as tall as small trees. In contrast to trees, though, most have foliage all the way to the ground, rather than only at the top of a bare trunk.

SELECTING SHRUBS. So many different shrubs are available that you may have some difficulty choosing the best ones for your garden. Start by considering adaptability: select plants that will thrive in your climate and soil conditions. (Check the A to Z Plant Encyclopedia for specific information on the shrubs you're considering.) It's also important to think about mature size. That cute tuft of greenery from a gallon can may look fine in a 4- by 4-foot space for a while, but if it ultimately will reach 12 feet in all directions, it's the wrong plant for the spot. In the same vein, bear in mind that the most attractive shrubs are those allowed to grow according to their natural inclinations, without excessive pruning. (Shrubs intended for hedges are an exception; in this case you can control size by pruning. For a list of good shrubs for hedges as well as those that can serve as privacy screens, see Plants for Hedges and Screens in A Guide to Plant Selection, beginning on page 47.) You'll also want to decide whether a deciduous or an

Viburnum trilobum, a graceful, stately shrub, provides abundant white flowers in spring and showy berries that birds adore in fall.

ESPALIER

This is a method of training a tree or shrub so that its branches grow in a flat pattern against a wall or fence. The branches are tied to a support—usually a trellis made of wire. The illustration below shows several espalier forms.

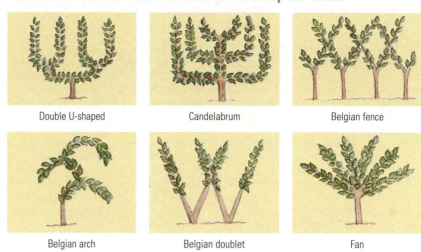

Double U-shaped   Candelabrum   Belgian fence

Belgian arch   Belgian doublet   Fan

REJUVENATING SHRUBS THAT GROW FROM THE BASE

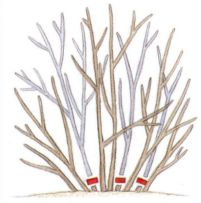 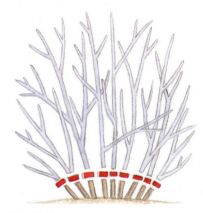

Gradually
Remove about a third of the oldest growth annually for 3 years.

Drastically
If the shrub withstands severe pruning, cut back the whole plant before new spring growth begins.

---

evergreen shrub best suits your purposes. Finally, consider ornamental features such as foliage texture, variegated or unusually colored leaves, attractive flowers, and colorful fruits.

PLANTING AND CARING FOR SHRUBS. Shrubs may be sold bare-root, in containers, or balled-and-burlapped (B-and-B). See pages 482–486 for planting directions for each type. How the plant is sold also affects the best time of year for planting. Bare-root plants must be set out soon after you purchase them in late winter or very early spring; this is also an ideal time to plant B-and-B shrubs. You can plant container-grown shrubs at any time during the growing season, but to avoid stressing them, it's best to plant in spring or fall rather than in the heat of summer.

Water newly planted shrubs immediately, then keep the soil moist but not soggy as the plants settle in. Mulching will help conserve water and prevent weed growth around shrubs. Future watering needs depend on the particular shrub. Once established (after a year or two in the garden), many native shrubs and other popular ornamentals survive on rainfall alone, while those native to moist sites will need supplemental water in dry summers.

Fertilizer needs vary, too. Some shrubs (notably roses) do best with regular fertilizing, and other flowering sorts may also benefit from at least an annual application of fertilizer. But many shrubs grow well with no supplemental nutrients. If the shrub puts out strong new growth with good color each year, it's doing well

S

without feeding—but if new growth is scant, pale, or weak, it should be fertilized.

To prune shrubs, follow the principles outlined on pages 494–496. Shrubs that have become overgrown—with long, straggling, tangled branches—may require rejuvenation, a rather severe form of pruning. This method works best on shrubs that send up stems (canes) from the roots. Some can even take drastic rejuvenation, which involves cutting back all stems almost to the ground before new spring growth begins. Shrubs so pruned may need several seasons to recover fully, but in the long run they'll be more compact and attractive. Plants amenable to this treatment include glossy abelia (*Abelia × grandiflora*), barberry (*Berberis*), forsythia, mock orange (*Philadelphus*), shrubby willows (*Salix*), and spiraea.

On other cane-producing shrubs, it's safest to proceed much more gradually with rejuvenation, spreading the pruning over a period of 3 years. In either case, once you've gotten rid of the old stems, keep the shrub under control by continuing to remove a few of the oldest stems each spring.

Soils and Soil Management

Understanding your soil and learning how to improve it will help make the garden more productive. Soil texture affects watering and fertilizing schedules, and, in some cases, it determines the kinds of plants you'll be able to grow.

Soil supports roots and provides them access to nutrients, water, and air. Most roots grow in the uppermost soil layer, called *topsoil,* which is relatively active biologically and is most directly affected by weather. Below the topsoil is the *subsoil.* It is less affected by microorganisms and weather, and while it may contain plant nutrients, it is not as hospitable to roots as topsoil. Discussions of soil quality and improvement generally focus on topsoil.

Soil is composed of mineral particles, living and dead organic matter, and pore spaces containing water and air. Good garden soil is approximately 45 percent minerals, 5 percent (or more) organic matter, and 50 percent pore spaces. The *mineral* portion is composed of rock broken down into tiny particles, while *organic matter* includes leaves, stems, roots, materials added by gardeners, and myriad soil-dwelling micro- and macroorganisms.

The network of *pore spaces* determines a soil's permeability to water and air and its water-holding capacity. This network includes large pores *(macropores)* and small ones *(micropores).* Macropores permit water and air to enter the soil easily and allow excess water to drain away. Micropores are responsible for a soil's water-holding capacity: they hold water against the force of gravity, making it available when needed by plants. The proportion of macro- to micropores affects soil quality. Soils that contain a preponderance of large pores are loose in texture; they are well aerated but cannot retain water for long and need more frequent

irrigation. Soils with many small pores, on the other hand, are dense types that can hold a lot of water but not much air.

SOIL TEXTURE. Texture describes the size of a soil's mineral particles. These include large, coarse sand particles, smaller silt particles, and tiny particles of clay.

Clay soils. Also called adobe, gumbo, or simply "heavy" soils, clay soils are composed of flattened, platelike, microscopic particles that pack closely together, leaving little pore space for either water or air. But because these particles offer the largest surface area per volume of all soil particles, clay soils can hold the greatest volume of nutrients in soluble form. They also hold water for a longer time after getting wet. Drainage (the downward movement of water) is slow in clay soils, so the loss of soluble nutrients through leaching is slow as well. Due to their high density, clay soils are the slowest to warm in spring.

Sandy soils. Sand particles are comparatively large, and they're irregularly rounded rather than flattened. Their size and shape allow for much larger pore spaces between particles than in clay soils; consequently, sandy soils contain lots of air and drain well. In a given volume of sandy soil, the surface area of the particles is less than in the same volume of clay—so the volume of soluble nutrients in sandy soil is correspondingly lower. And because sandy soil drains quickly and thus loses nutrients faster than clay, plants in sand need watering and feeding more often than those growing in clay. Sandy soils warm more quickly in spring than clay soils.

Loam. Loam is considered the ideal garden soil. It contains a mix of all three particle types—clay, silt, and sand—but none predominates. With a combination of large and small pore spaces, it drains well (but doesn't dry out too fast), loses nutrients at only a moderate rate, and contains enough air for healthy root growth.

Determining soil texture. To identify the texture of your garden soil, thoroughly wet a patch of soil, then let it dry out for a day. Now pick up a handful of soil and squeeze it firmly in your fist. If it forms a tight ball and has a slippery feel, it's predominantly clay. If it feels gritty and doesn't hold its shape at all but simply crumbles apart when you open your hand, it's sandy. If it is slightly crumbly but still holds a loose ball, it's closer to loam.

SOIL STRUCTURE. While a soil's *texture* is defined by the size of its primary particles, its *structure* is determined by the way those particles bind together to form small clumps, called *aggregates.* In soil with a good structure, the pores between and within the aggregates are large enough to let air and water pass through

easily, yet small enough to retain some water for plant roots to use.

Though you can't change a soil's basic texture, you *can* improve its structure by adding organic matter. Such improvement is especially important in fine-textured (clay) soils, since it increases porosity: organic matter helps bind the small particles together into larger aggregates. Gypsum and lime, both inorganic amendments, are sometimes used to improve structure in clay soils; for advice on using them, consult soil professionals or your Cooperative Extension Office.

In sandy soils, organic matter lodges in the pore spaces and acts like a sponge, holding water and nutrients.

Be aware that soil structure can be damaged, especially in soils high in clay. Running heavy machinery over the soil or even walking on planting areas compresses the pore spaces, as does tilling soil when it's too wet. Always let soil dry out until it's barely moist before working it.

SOIL PROBLEMS. Some of the soil problems that result in poor plant growth may be due to factors other than basic soil texture or structure. Here are a few of the most common such problems—and practical ways to deal with them.

SOIL TEXTURE AND TYPE

The size of a soil's mineral particles determines its texture and designates its type: clay, sand, or loam. Clay has the smallest particles, sand the largest; silt particles are intermediate in size. Loam, the ideal garden soil, contains a mix of all three particle sizes.

SOIL PARTICLES

Clay
Less than 1/12,500 in.

Silt
Up to 1/500 in.

Fine sand
Up to 1/250 in.

Medium sand
Up to 1/50 in.

Coarsest sand
1/12 in.

TESTING YOUR SOIL'S DRAINAGE. To check drainage, dig a 2-foot-deep hole and fill it with water. After it drains, fill it again. If this second amount of water drains away quickly (usually in an hour or less), the drainage is good. If it remains for several hours or longer, the soil drains poorly.)

THE pH SCALE

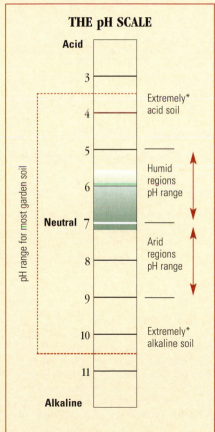

pH range for most garden soil

Acid

3

4 — Extremely* acid soil

5

6 — Humid regions pH range

Neutral — 7

8 — Arid regions pH range

9

10 — Extremely* alkaline soil

11

Alkaline

▢ pH range preferred by acid-loving plants

▢ pH range preferred by most garden plants

*Soils nearing extremes require professional intervention to modify pH.

POOR DRAINAGE. For most plants, good drainage is essential for healthy growth. If the soil drains poorly, water remains in the pore spaces rather than draining away, and air, necessary both to roots and beneficial soil-dwelling organisms, is thus unable to enter the soil. Soil texture, a low-lying location, or hardpan (see below) can all contribute to poor drainage.

As noted above, clay soils often drain poorly. To improve the situation, work in plenty of organic matter. Planting in raised beds filled with good, well-drained soil is another option.

Poor drainage may also occur naturally in the garden's low spots. Solving the problem may require installing drainage tiles to carry away excess water. If this is impractical, consider adapting your garden to the site and growing plants suited to moist areas.

Hardpan is an impervious layer of soil that can cause trouble when it lies near the surface. Hardpan is found naturally in some regions— in the Southwest, for example, where the most common natural hardpan layer is called caliche. It can also be created, as when builders spread excavated subsoil over the soil surface and then repeatedly drive heavy equipment over it. In either case, though a thin layer of topsoil may conceal the hardpan, roots cannot penetrate it nor water drain through it.

If the hardpan layer is thin, it may be possible to break it up by having the soil plowed to a depth of 1 foot or more. If plowing is impractical, you may be able to drill through the hardpan with a soil auger when planting, creating a drainage chimney. Thick hardpan, however, may require the installation of a subsurface drainage system, a project that usually requires hiring a contractor. Growing plants in raised beds filled with good soil is another alternative.

Soil pH. Soil ranges from acid through neutral to alkaline. This characteristic is stated as a pH number. Soil with a pH of 7 is neutral—neither acid nor alkaline. A pH below 7 indicates acidity, while one above 7 indicates alkalinity. The soil's degree of acidity or alkalinity primarily affects the availability of certain nutrients. If the pH is extreme in either direction, key nutrients are chemically "tied up" in the soil and not available to plant roots. The best way to determine your soil's pH is to have the soil tested (see Testing Your Soil, below).

Acid soil is most common in regions where rainfall is heavy and is often associated with sandy soils and those high in organic matter. Though most plants grow well in mildly acid soil, highly acid conditions are inhospitable. Adding calcium carbonate (lime) is often suggested to raise pH. Follow the recommendations of your soil test lab for amounts to apply.

Alkaline soil, found in many regions of the West where rainfall is typically light, is uncommon in the Northeast. Alkaline soil is high in calcium carbonate (lime). Many plants grow well in moderately alkaline soil; others, notably blueberries, rhododendrons, and azaleas, will not thrive in such soils because the alkalinity reduces the availability of certain elements (including iron and zinc) necessary for their growth.

Sulfur can be used to lower soil pH; follow the testing lab's advice for amounts to apply. You can also lower the pH of alkaline soil over time with regular (at least annual) applications of organic amendments such as compost or well-composted (aged) manure. Another option for growing plants that need acid soil is to plant them in containers or raised beds filled with an appropriate soil mix. (However, if your water is alkaline, these remedies are unlikely to be effective.)

TESTING YOUR SOIL

A soil analysis will disclose your soil's pH (acidity or alkalinity) and can also reveal nutrient deficiencies. The simple test kits sold at nurseries can give you a general indication of your soil's condition; for a more precise reading, have the test done at a laboratory. In some states, the Cooperative Extension Service will test your soil, but even if it does not, it should be able to direct you to commercial soil laboratories. Or look in the yellow pages under "Laboratories—Analytical." The lab will tell you where and how to collect soil to be tested.

Or, write to one of the following labs for information on submitting a soil test: A&L Analytical Laboratories, Inc., 411 N. Third Street, Memphis, TN 38105; Peaceful Valley Farm Supply, P.O. Box 2209, 125 Spring Hill Drive, Grass Valley, CA 95945, website: www.groworganic.com.

To use this pH soil test kit, mix the provided solution with a bit of soil; the resulting color is compared with the color chart to that indicates pH.

S

Salty soils. Salty soils are found near the seashore and in arid regions. They can also result from the overuse of fertilizers, de-icing salts and fresh manures. Excess salts in the soil affect plants by "pulling" water from the roots, making it difficult for plants to take up enough moisture or nutrients; symptoms include scorched and yellowed leaves or browned and withered leaf margins. Seed germination is also inhibited. *If deicing salts are the problem, reduce their use if possible. Along roadways and in seaside gardens, use salt-tolerant plants.* To correct the condition, you can improve drainage by adding organic matter and leach the soil periodically with water to wash the salts below the plants' root zones.

ORGANIC SOIL AMENDMENTS. The decaying remains of plants and animals, organic matter is vital to maintaining the fertility of all soils and is especially necessary in soils high in clay and sand. Gardeners incorporate organic soil amendments to improve or maintain a soil's structure and to encourage healthy populations of beneficial soil-dwelling microorganisms.

As organic matter decomposes, it releases nutrients that increase fertility. However, the nitrogen released by decaying organic matter isn't immediately available to plants. It must first be converted by various microorganisms (bacteria, fungi, actinomycetes, and others) into ammonia, then into nitrites, and finally into nitrates, which can be absorbed by plant roots. The final product of the breakdown of organic matter is humus, a soft, sticky material that decomposes slowly and improves soil structure.

The microorganisms that ultimately produce humus require a certain amount of soil moisture, air, and warmth. Soils high in organic matter tend to contain relatively high populations of these organisms. Earthworms are also plentiful in soils rich in organic matter; as they tunnel along, they improve drainage and aeration, while their castings add nutrients.

Many types of organic amendments are available in the Northeast, either commercially packaged or sold in bulk. One choice is manure, which contains more nutrients than most other amendments (manures should be aged well to avoid adding excess salts to the soil). Compost is an excellent amendment; see page 455 for more on homemade compost. Municipal compost is made from grass clippings, leaves, and tree prunings gathered and composted by municipal agencies, then sold or given to local residents. Mushroom compost, a by-product of mushroom farming, is available in some areas; it tends to be high in salts, so use it in smaller quantities than other composts.

Peat moss increases acidity and is thus often used to amend soils around acid-loving plants. There is, however, concern over the ecological damage that may result from the depletion of this natural resource. Some gardeners prefer to use coir dust—a by-product of the coconut fiber industry—instead. For more on this renewable resource, see page 457.

SALT-TOLERANT PLANTS

For plantings along roads and walkways where de-icing salts inevitably find their way onto the soil, or in gardens at the seashore, the best approach is to choose plants that tolerate salt. In such sites, it is a good idea to water heavily several times during the summer to leach some of the salts from the soil. Use the list below to get started; your local Cooperative Extension Service also may have lists of suggested plants suitable for your area.

TREES

Acer platanoides (Norway maple)

Acer ginnala (amur maple)

Amelanchier (serviceberries)

Chamaecyparis (false cypresses)

Gleditsia triacanthos (common honey locust)

Hippophae rhamnoides (sea buckthorn)

Ilex opaca (American holly)

Liquidambar (sweet gums)

Nyssa sylvatica (black tupelo)

Syringa (lilacs)

Pinus nigra (Austrian pine)

Pinus sylvestris (Scotch pine)

Pinus thumbergii (Japanese black pine)

Taxodium distichum (bald cypress)

SHRUBS

Calluna vulgaris (heather)

Cotoneaster (cotoneasters)

Forsythia (forsythia)

Hibiscus syriacus (rose-of-sharon)

Hydrangea (hydrangeas)

Juniperus (junipers)

Myrica (bayberries)

Pinus mugo (Swiss mountain pine)

Rosa rugosa (rugosa rose)

Vaccinium (blueberries)

Viburnum dentatum (arrow-wood viburnum)

Taxus (yews)

PERENNIALS AND GROUNDCOVERS

Ajuga (bugleweeds)

Armeria maritima (thrift)

Eryngium maritimum (sea holly)

Gaillardia grandiflora (blanket flowers)

Hedera (ivies)

Hemerocallis (daylilies)

Hibiscus moscheutos (rose mallow)

Hosta (hostas)

Sedum (sedums)

Sempervivum (hen-and-chicks)

Solidago (goldenrods)

SOIL POLYMERS

When added to soil, tiny gel-like soil polymers absorb hundreds of times their weight in rain or irrigation water that would otherwise drain away—holding it (and the dissolved nutrients it contains) for plants to use. The gel's ability to retain water means that plants still have a steady source of moisture when the soil itself is dry, helping them to grow better (since they don't suffer from wide fluctuations in moisture)—and letting you stretch the time between waterings. Soil polymers are most often used in potting mixes; in fact, some kinds come with a polymer already incorporated. However, they're also useful in outdoor planting beds in areas with limited rainfall.

Various brands of polymers are available. Sorts containing polyacrylamide are the longest lasting, staying effective for up to 10 years. To do their job, polymers must be mixed into the soil, since root hairs have to grow into the particles to extract water. Mix the dry gel with water to expand the particles, then blend them evenly into the soil at the rate recommended by the manufacturer. Note that if you add too great an amount of gel, the particles will ooze to the surface when the soil is moistened by rain or irrigation.

If you add raw (green or uncomposted) organic matter to your soil as an amendment, it may be proprotionally higher in carbon than in nitrogen. During the time soil organisms are breaking down high-carbon materials, they require nitrogen and may temporarily compete with plants for nitrogen available in the soil. (Of course, once the organic material has decomposed, it will release extra nitrogen into the soil.) For this reason, high-carbon soil amendments such as sawdust, wood shavings, and ground bark should be bolstered with nitrogen before use. If you use unfortified amendments, mix a nitrogen fertilizer into them.

Using organic amendments. Be generous when adding organic amendments. When preparing a new planting bed, spread a 3- to 4-inch layer of amendment over the soil and dig or till it into the top 9 to 12 inches. Around established plantings, you can add organic material to the soil by spreading it over the soil surface as a mulch; earthworms, microorganisms, and water will help mix it into the top layer of soil. (Note that peat moss is not very effective as a mulch; once it dries out, it's hard to moisten again, and it may blow away. To use peat as an amendment, always mix it into the top few inches of soil.) If the established plants are deep rooted—as are most mature trees and shrubs, for example—you can gently work the amendment into the top inch or so of soil, using a three-pronged cultivator.

Tools

Stores, nurseries, and specialized mail-order catalogs offer gardening tools in bewildering array. This section describes a number of useful tools—many of them quite versatile—and offers tips for selecting them and using them comfortably and efficiently.

SHOVELS. With their wide, dished heads, *round-point shovels* are efficient soil movers. Use them to loosen soil, pick it up, and transfer it to a pile or wheelbarrow; they're also a good choice for digging planting holes. Select a larger round-point shovel (such as one with a 9-inch-long, 12-inch-wide head) for general digging. If you're working in a confined space, you may find it more convenient to use a *floral shovel,* which has a smaller (6- by 8-inch) head and a shorter handle.

Round-point shovels vary in lift—the angle formed between the ground and the shovel handle when the shovel head is laid flat on the ground. To make digging easier by minimizing the amount of bending you'll have to do, choose a tool with generous lift.

Square-nose shovels and *scoops* are not meant for digging. They're used to scoop up loose material such as compost or gravel from a flat surface and move it to a different spot. They come in various sizes; choose one that will pick up the greatest amount of material you can lift repeatedly without tiring.

SPADES. In contrast to shovels, spades have longer, narrower, relatively flat heads. They're used to prepare soil for planting, to dig narrow, straight-sided trenches, and, sometimes, to prune roots. Most familiar and most generally useful is the *English garden spade,* which has an almost flat blade (about 7 inches wide by 11 inches long) and forward-turned steps (the ledge at the top of the blade where you place your foot when you dig). The handle—often a short D type—extends almost straight up from the blade with little or no lift.

Border spades are smaller, with blades about 6 inches wide and 8 inches long. As the name indicates, they're handy in confined spaces such as flower beds or borders. At the opposite extreme in size are various spades with long, narrow blades, such as *transplanting spades,* which have slightly dished blades about 5 inches wide and 14 or 16 inches long.

SPADING FORKS. Substitutes for spades in clay or rocky soils, spading forks (also called digging forks) help fracture large clods of soil, breaking them into smaller clumps. They should have four tines that are square or rectangular in cross section and about ½ inch wide. Tines this thick help concentrate your pulling strength, and they don't bend easily. Like spades, they come with shorter D handles or longer straight handles.

MANURE FORKS. These tools (as well as pitch forks and compost forks) aren't for spading. Instead, they're used to move manure or piles of prunings or to turn compost. Various styles in various sizes and overall weights are available, with four or more tines. For a long-lasting fork, look for one with forged rather than welded tines. A T-shaped handle makes turning compost easier.

HOES. You'll find hoes designed for a variety of jobs, including cultivating, moving soil, digging furrows, and removing weeds. *Conventional* or *American-style garden hoes* have flat front edges to cut weeds off at ground level and sharp corners that work like small picks. The most common kind has a 6-inch-wide blade. Narrower (2½-inch-wide) blades are useful for light jobs in tight spots; a wider (8-inch) blade is ideal for paths and driveways.

So-called V hoes come in blade sizes varying from 1 by 3 inches to 4 by 6 inches. The most common is the *Warren hoe,* which is especially useful in vegetable gardens. Use the point to make small furrows, and the sides—well sharpened—to slice weeds.

Eye hoes and *grape hoes* are heavy-duty hoes with wide, deep blades set perpendicular to the handle. They are used for breaking ground, chopping tough weeds, scraping away dense growth, and moving soil.

A number of hoes are intended specifically for weeding. These hoes have little or no blade surface and are used with the blade parallel to the ground (or nearly so). They come in a wide variety of sizes and shapes, including circle, diamond, stirrup, rectangle, arrowhead, and scuffle. However, there are only three variables in the way they function: they may be push hoes, draw hoes, or scuffle hoes (which cut on both the push and draw strokes). When using any of these hoes, the idea is to run the blade just under the soil surface to cut off weeds at ground level. Disturb the soil as little as possible to avoid bringing more weed seeds to the surface, where they will be able to germinate.

RAKES. *Garden* or *soil rakes* have thick steel tines, either straight or curved. The tines may be attached to the handle directly by a tang or socket, or indirectly by a curving bow. The bow type has more spring or resilience. These rakes are used to break up clods of dirt, level the soil, tamp seedbeds to make them firm, and work amendments into the top few inches of a planting bed.

DIGGING AND HOEING

Learning to dig and hoe properly can literally save your back. When digging with a shovel, don't drive the tool into the ground at a low angle, bend over to lever the soil loose, and then lift with your back bent. Instead, drive the shovel blade straight down, as close to your body as you can manage comfortably. The shovel handle will angle away from you. When you've driven the blade in as far as possible, step back with the foot that is not on the shovel's step or tread and pull the handle toward the center of your chest. Then, grasping the handle at the top with one hand and sliding the other hand toward the bottom, bend your knees and lower your body, keeping your back straight. Lift the shovelful of soil, using the strength of your legs, not your back.

Using a spade involves the same techniques, except that you'll usually be turning the soil over in a bed instead of lifting and moving it.

When using a hoe, rake, or cultivator, stand sideways to the work—as if you were using a kitchen broom. Grasp the handle with your thumbs wrapped around it near the top. As you work, flex your knees slightly and pull the tool across the front of your body. This position keeps your back straight and, if you hit a buried rock or large root, you'll naturally pull with the strong muscles in your upper legs instead of straining your lower back.

SELECTING TOOLS: HANDLES AND HEADS

When choosing tools for your garden, look for high-quality tools that fit your body type. For example, shovels, spades, and spading forks are available with either shorter "D"-type handles or long handles. "D" handles are best for shorter, smaller gardeners (though they're also useful in confined spaces), but tall people are usually more comfortable using long-handled tools. Look for hoes, cultivators, and rakes that are at least as tall (preferably an inch taller) than you are; this allows you to use them in a standing rather than a stooping position.

Handles made of straight-grained, knot-free wood are generally the best choice for most garden tools (make sure handle and head are attached with a rivet that passes all the way through the handle). Tubular aluminum handles are easily bent, while tubular fiberglass ones can be shattered, especially on heavily used digging tools. What's more, these handles are usually narrower in diameter than wooden ones and thus more tiring to grasp for long periods.

Forging—heating metal until it is almost molten, then pounding it into shape—produces a denser tool head that is less likely to bend or break and takes an edge better than less-expensive stamped steel. Highly polished, forged stainless steel tools are preferred by some gardeners because they don't rust and they slide easily into the soil. However, they're somewhat more brittle than tools made of conventional carbon steel, making them more difficult to sharpen and more likely to fracture if used improperly.

GARDEN TOOLS

Hedge shears

Hand pruners

Weeder

Trowel

Bulb planter

Shovel Digging spade Spading fork

Scuffle hoe

Edger

Leaf rake

Wheelbarrow

Gloves

Hat

Soil rakes are available with six, eight, 14, or 16 tines. Select a rake with some weight in its head; if it's too light, you'll have to work harder to provide the downward force needed to break clods or move soil.

Leaf rakes have wide, thin, flat, springy tines. In the best ones, the tines are closely spaced and curve downward and slightly inward at the tip; they're arranged in a curving fan with a stabilizing brace about 8 inches up from the tip of the tines. Metal tines will last longer than those made of bamboo or polypropylene. In addition to raking leaves, these rakes are useful for gathering grass clippings and other lightweight materials into piles.

A leaf rake should be light but sturdy, allowing you apply firm pressure to the ground with a minimum of effort. Widths may be as great as 4 feet—ideal for large properties with lots of deciduous trees. Smaller versions (only 8 or 10 inches wide) are useful for raking between shrubs and perennials.

A *thatching rake* is used to clear thatch out of lawn grasses. It has semicircular metal tines that are attached with the rounded edge facing forward. When you use this rake, you keep the head on the ground. Pulled through dense grass, the tines rip out thatch; the push or forward stroke clears material from the tines.

CULTIVATORS. These tools may have only one tine or two to five tines, spaced 1½ to 2 inches apart. The tines may be long or short, curved or straight; the tine ends are pointed in some models, flattened to form a lozenge-shaped tooth in others. Use cultivators to break up compacted soil around plants, keeping it loose and friable, and to work amendments into the upper few inches of soil; they are also effective for weeding.

Select a narrow cultivator if you plan to cultivate between closely spaced plants or if your soil is heavy; the fewer the tines, the more concentrated your pulling force will be. A cultivator with tines arranged in a V shape rather than lined up in a row is also easier to pull through heavy soils. If plants are widely spaced, a four- or five-tine cultivator is more practical; it also works best in sandy or well-amended soils.

A single-tine cultivator is known as a *finger hoe*. If you sharpen the sides of its tooth or tine, you can use it both for nicking weeds out of small spaces and for cultivating.

HALF-MOON EDGER. This tool is used to maintain a neat edge between lawn and adjacent beds of flowers or ground covers. You can also use it to edge between lawn and paving.

HAND TOOLS. In addition to scaled-down versions of hoes and cultivators, hand tools include knives, dibbles, specialized weeders—and, of course, the indispensable trowel.

Trowels. Though principally planting tools, trowels are also useful for cultivating, weeding, and scooping fertilizers and other soil amendments from bags.

A trowel should be both strong and sharp; the best are made of forged steel and have a wooden handle driven and pinned into a socket at the top of the blade. For general use, select one with a shallowly dished blade about 4 inches wide and 6 inches long. *Transplanting trowels* are narrower (about 3 inches wide), tapered, and deeply dished; they may have marks on the blade to help you gauge planting depth. *Potting trowels* are even narrower—about 2½ inches wide—and only shallowly dished. *Crevice* or rockery trowels are just 1 inch wide; they are invaluable for weeding as well as for planting a rock garden.

Knives. A sturdy knife comes in handy for diverse tasks: dividing roots of plants, opening bags of soil or soil amendments, carving points on the ends of wooden stakes. The *Japanese farmer's knife* (Hori Hori) features a slightly dished blade that can be used as a trowel; one side of the blade is saw-toothed, while the other has a sharp edge that can cut roots and burlap.

Dibbles. These are used to poke holes in prepared soil to plant bulbs, bedding plants, and vegetable starts. They are usually carrot-shaped, with an iron point and a rounded or T-shaped handle.

Weeders. Look for a hand weeder with a bent shaft or with a ball attached to the shaft to serve as a fulcrum, giving you leverage to pop weeds out of the ground. The weeder's head should be small and forked.

PRUNING TOOLS. Shears and saws for pruning come in many different forms and sizes—not surprising, when you consider that pruning cuts and techniques (not to mention the plants being pruned) vary, too (see "Pruning," page 494).

Hand pruners. Many gardeners take this tool with them whenever they go into the garden, carrying it in a leather case that clips to a belt or pants pocket. There are two basic types. *Bypass pruners* have a curved hook and a curved blade. The branch to be cut rests against the hook; the blade cuts it, passing the hook as it slices through the branch. In some models, the cutting blade bends away from the handle at an angle up to 45°; this gives you more cutting power and minimizes strain on your wrists. *Anvil pruners* have a flat anvil (instead of a hook) and a straight blade; the blade cuts through the branch until it hits the anvil.

Hand pruners should not be used on any branch thicker than your little finger; doing so risks damaging the plant, the tool, or both. Use a lopper or a saw instead.

Loppers. These powerful branch cutters have long handles that give you much more leverage than the short handles of hand pruners. They range from 1 to 3 feet in length and may have either bypass or anvil construction. Smaller

loppers can substitute for hand pruners if you lack the hand strength needed to operate the latter; they're also good for cutting among thorny branches without scratching your hands and arms. The cutting capacity of loppers (that is, the diameter of branch they can cut) is the distance between the center of the blade and the center of the hook or anvil when the blades are opened at right angles to each other. The largest loppers will cut 3-inch-thick branches. A good in-between size for most garden jobs, capable of cutting branches up to 2 inches thick, is a 26-inch model. Be sure to select loppers with strong handles, preferably bolted on. A shock absorber, located below the pivot point, saves wear on your arms.

Pruning saws. If a branch is too large to cut with hand pruners or loppers, use a pruning saw. In contrast to carpenter's saws, most medium pruning types cut on the pull rather than the push stroke. They may have straight or curved blades; a curved one fits more easily into tight spots between branches. They may also have fixed or folding blades. Some models come with gullets—deep slots every fourth tooth or so that accumulate and release sticky sawdust, so that the cutting teeth don't get gummed up.

Older-style saws have teeth bent slightly to right and left. When used, such a saw makes a wide kerf (slot), preventing binding. Newer types omit this feature; instead, each tooth is ground on three edges. These models (sometimes referred to as *Japanese-style saws*) cut much more rapidly and deliver a smoother cut. They can snap if you apply too much force or try to cut on the push stroke, and they cannot be resharpened, but most gardeners feel that their ease of use and cutting speed more than make up for any drawbacks. A 13-inch Japanese-style saw with a fixed blade is a good choice for most gardens; it easily cuts branches 1 to 5 inches in diameter. Call an arborist if you need to cut larger branches.

T

Using the right tool for every job makes the work easier and the results more successful.

CARING FOR GARDEN TOOLS

Given proper care, well-made tools not only make gardening easier but will last for generations. All tools need cleaning after use, and any tool with an edge—be it a shovel, spade, hoe, or pruning tool—should be kept sharp. When blades eventually become dull, it's easiest to have a professional restore them; many garden supply and hardware stores can recommend a reliable sharpening service.

Cleaning tools. To remove accumulated sap and rust from pruning shears, use a little oil and steel wool; you can also buy special oil/solvent mixtures (such as CLP Shear Oil) to clean sap and dirt from pruning tools and to lubricate them. To maintain the smoothest operation, occasionally disassemble the tool and work a dab of synthetic white lithium grease onto the pivot bolt and into the area around the bolt hole.

Clean the sawdust from pruning saws after each use and remove any sap and rust with steel wool and oil. Apply a thin coat of paraffin to the blade before using.

A barbecue brush (with scraper) is handy for cleaning digging tools. Use the scraper to remove layers of dirt and mud as you work in the garden. The bristles give a final cleanup before you store the tool. Many gardeners keep a bucket of coarse sand mixed with a couple of quarts of used automotive oil in the tool shed. Before putting tools away, they drive the heads into the sand; this both removes soil and oils the tool, preventing rust.

Once a year, give tool heads a thorough cleaning. Remove rust with medium steel wool and a little oil; then use paint thinner to clean off the oily residue. Finally, apply a rust-proofing paint.

Maintaining wooden handles. Wooden handles on all types of garden tools last for many years if kept clean and oiled. Wipe them off after every use and, once a year or so, sand the handles lightly and apply a coat of boiled linseed oil with a cloth. If the oil soaks in completely, apply another coat, then buff the handle.

Pole pruning tools. Look to these when you need extra reach for cutting high branches. They typically come with both shears and a saw, which you attach to a pole. To make the shears work, you pull a cord or press a lever to draw the blade through the branch; most will cut through branches ¾ to 1 inch thick. The saw is usually a standard pull-cut curved saw. The poles come in various lengths; some are telescoping, while others fit together in sections. In either case, they're easiest to use if they're fairly stiff.

Hedge shears. In addition to trimming hedges, these are useful for shearing flowering shrubs and cutting back perennials. For heavy-duty pruning of hedges with dense, woody growth, select shears with a short (7-inch) blade. One blade will often be serrated and notched; the notch helps hold bigger twigs in place while you cut. Hedge shears with longer blades (up to 11 inches) are meant for light-duty shearing of leafy tip growth; the longer blades will shear a larger area with each stroke. Be sure any hedge shears you buy are equipped with shock absorbers.

SPRAYERS. Garden sprayers are used to apply fungicides, pesticides, herbicides, and foliar fertilizers. Many styles and sizes are available. If you don't do much spraying, a 1-quart, hand-pumped compression sprayer is a good choice; it allows you to mix small amounts of chemicals, avoiding waste. Select one with a brass spray nozzle and sturdy innards. For more extensive spraying, choose a 2-gallon capacity hand pump model. It should have a polyethylene tank and a brass valve wand, adjustable brass nozzle, and pump. An extra-long hose allows you to leave the sprayer on the ground and move around as you spray.

Trees

Trees are the backbone of the garden, providing shade and shelter and bringing year-round beauty through their foliage, flowers, fruits, bark, and branch structure. The distinction between a tree and a large shrub is sometimes blurred, but trees typically are tall plants with one dominant trunk (though some kinds may have several trunks) topped by a crown of foliage. In contrast, most shrubs are smaller and have foliage all the way to the ground.

SELECTING TREES. Because trees are so important to the landscape and are generally slow growing, it's worth taking the time to choose them carefully. Start by considering the points below; also consult local nursery personnel and look at the trees in your neighborhood to see which ones perform particularly well. Trees (pages 103–105) in A Guide to Plant Selection lists trees suitable for many purposes and situations.

Landscape function. What role should the tree play in your garden? If you need a source of shade, choose a tree with a wide canopy. Deciduous trees give you summer shade (and can significantly reduce air-conditioning expenses), then admit sun to warm the house after their leaves drop in fall. If you want to block views into your home or garden, choose relatively tall, dense trees. If you're looking for a specimen tree to serve as a garden focal point, search for interesting foliage or a striking display of blossoms or berries—or outstanding fall color. Fruit trees have special appeal, providing delicious fruit as well as lovely form and flowers.

Climate adaptability. Be sure that any tree you consider planting is well adapted to your climate zone.

Cultural preferences. Match the needs of each tree to the conditions in your garden. Select those that will grow well in the soil you have, with the amount of water they'll receive naturally or that you can provide.

Deciduous versus evergreen. Deciduous trees start their growth with a burst of new leaves (and often flowers) in early spring, then remain in leaf through summer. In autumn, the foliage drops to reveal bare limbs, often changing color before it falls.

Evergreen trees include both broad-leafed evergreens and conifers (though there are a few deciduous conifers); both kinds serve well as screens and windbreaks. Broad-leafed evergreens have the same sort of foliage as deciduous plants, but they keep their leaves year-round. Older leaves may fall intermittently throughout the year or in one season, but there's always enough foliage to give the tree a well-clothed look. Most conifers have leaves that are narrow and needlelike or tiny and scalelike; they may drop some leaves year-round.

Growth rate and size. Different trees grow at different rates. If you need a tree to shade a south-facing window or provide privacy, select a fast-growing sort for quick results—but take care not to choose one that will outgrow its site. In fact, it's important to visualize the ultimate height and spread of a tree you consider for any role: not only is an overly large one out of scale in most gardens, but it will eventually crowd structures and other plants and may ultimately have to be removed.

Root system. A tree with a network of greedy surface roots is a poor candidate for planting in a lawn or garden, since it will hog most of the water and nutrients. The same tree may be just right, however, at the garden's fringes or along a country drive. Some trees have surface roots that can lift and crack nearby pavement, making them less-than-ideal choices for a patio, entryway, or parking strip.

Maintenance. Trees that produce a fair amount of litter from falling leaves, flowers, or

T

fruits shouldn't be planted beside a patio, in a lawn, or near a swimming pool—you'd be spending far too much time cleaning up. Such trees are better candidates for background areas, where the litter can remain where it falls. In regions with regular high winds or heavy annual snowfall, avoid trees with weak or brittle wood: they can be hazardous to people and property, and removing broken limbs can both ruin the tree's beauty and cost you a tidy sum.

Pest and disease problems. Make sure the trees you're considering aren't overly susceptible to pests or diseases. Keep in mind that a particular tree may be trouble free in one climate but plagued with problems in another.

Longevity. Some trees can be planted for future generations to enjoy; others grow quickly but decline quickly as well. Trees planted for screening or shade should be long lived, but for specimen planting, shorter-lived kinds may be an excellent choice. Plant these, however, only where removal will be relatively easy and won't compromise your overall landscape. Many attractive flowering trees, for example, run their course in about 20 years, but when they die you can fill the resulting gap with another tree of the same sort.

PLANTING AND CARING FOR TREES. Many deciduous trees are sold bare-root during the dormant season from late fall through early spring. Deciduous trees as well as conifers and broad-leafed evergreens may also be sold balled-and-burlapped from early fall into the following spring, or in containers throughout the year. For instructions on planting all types, see pages 483–486.

The exposed trunk of a newly planted tree needs protection from drying winds, hot sun, freezing temperatures, gnawing animals (such as rabbits, deer, and rodents), and damage from carelessly wielded lawn mowers or string trimmers. To keep it free from harm, wrap it in loosely tied burlap or a manufactured trunk wrapping material. Remove the wrapping after a year, when the bark has become thicker and tougher (don't leave wrapping in place longer than this, since it can eventually girdle the tree).

All trees, even drought-tolerant kinds, need regular water during the first several years after planting, until their roots have grown deep enough to carry them through dry periods. Once established, however, many kinds require only infrequent irrigation.

Regular fertilizing, too, is needed for a few years after planting. By ensuring a good supply of nitrogen for the springtime growth surge, you'll encourage young trees to get established quickly. Once a tree is well settled in, though, it may grow satisfactorily with no further feeding—and in fact, fertilizing a tree that continues to put out healthy, vigorous new growth is a waste of both time and fertilizer. Feeding may be in order, however, if a tree's new growth is weak, sparse, or unusually pale, or if it has a fair amount of dieback that cannot be ascribed to over- or underwatering.

TRAINING AND PRUNING. Most young trees benefit from some early training or pruning. The idea is to encourage the development of a sturdy trunk from which radiate strong, well-placed main limbs (scaffold branches). Conifers are an exception: they seldom need training unless they develop more than one leader (central upward-growing stem). If that occurs, remove the weaker of the two stems. Deciduous and broad-leafed evergreen trees, on the other hand, are more likely to require training, but don't rush the job. Prune newly planted trees as little as possible: just remove dead, broken, or rubbing branches and the weaker limb of a double leader (if present). Wait a full year—until the tree's roots are growing well—before doing more than this. Prune the tree gradually over the next 3 to 5 years, but don't remove too much wood in any one year.

Though you may be tempted to begin training a tree by removing lower limbs, it's best to leave these in place for the first few years, as shown at left. (Don't remove the lower limbs of conifers such as spruces, firs, and others with a strongly pyramidal shape at all. They look most natural when allowed to branch all the way to the ground.)

STAKING YOUNG TREES

A young tree will develop a sturdier trunk if it grows unsupported and can sway in the breeze. Stake it only if it is planted in an extremely windy location or if the main trunk is too weak to stay upright on its own. Use ties that won't bind or cut into the bark, such as wide strips of canvas or rubber; fasten each tie around the tree and both stakes in a figure-8 pattern, as shown below. The tree should be able to move an inch in either direction.

To figure out where to attach the ties to a weak trunk, run your hand up the trunk until you find the point where the top no longer flops over. Cut off the stakes an inch or so above the ties. In a windswept site, a young tree's roots may need anchoring to keep them in firm contact with the soil; use stakes and ties only a foot above ground level for this kind of staking. In both cases, sink stakes at right angles to the prevailing wind. Remove them after about a year or as soon as the tree appears to be self-supporting.

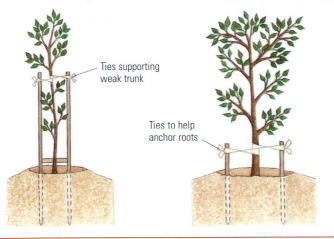

Ties supporting weak trunk

Ties to help anchor roots

FORMING A STRONG TREE TRUNK

Young trees develop a strong trunk more quickly if their lower branches are left in place for the first few years after planting; these branches also help shade the trunk. During this time, shorten the side branches only if they become too long or vigorous, pruning during the dormant season or just before spring growth begins. Once the trunk is at least 2 inches thick, begin removing the lower branches gradually, over a period of several years.

WHAT'S WRONG WITH TOPPING?

Topping—reducing the height of a mature tree by sawing off its top limbs—is the fastest way to ruin a tree's appearance. It doesn't reduce height for long, either. Unlike a bushy hedge that soon sprouts new growth even after severe shearing, an older tree does not grow back in a natural-looking way when its upper limbs are pruned to stubs. Instead, it sends out scores of weak shoots from buds near the cutoff points, and these shoots are often taller, coarser, denser, and more weakly attached than the natural top was. Topping may also shorten a tree's life, both because the resultant large wounds are exposed to decay and insect attack and because the process removes much of the leafy growth needed to manufacture food for the plant.

Though some topped trees can eventually recover their form, it may take decades. A good professional arborist will not top a tree that has grown too large for its space, but instead will gradually scale it back by making thinning cuts to groups of branches in the upper part of the canopy.

As the tree grows, encourage well-placed scaffold branches by selecting shoots at fairly evenly spaced intervals, both up the trunk and spiraling around it. Whenever possible, favor wide-angled branches forming more-or-less U-shaped crotches over narrow-angled ones that have V-shaped crotches. If the angle is very narrow, branches tend to be weakly attached to the trunk and split off easily. Remove badly placed and superfluous branches before they become too large, keeping the ultimate shape of the tree in mind. Also remove suckers, water sprouts, and lateral branches growing toward the center of tree.

For more on pruning methods, including instructions for removing large limbs, see page 496.

Vegetable Gardening

Growing your own vegetables is rewarding and enjoyable. In return for your efforts, you'll harvest food that's fresh and bursting with flavor. To make your vegetable patch a success, plan before you plant. If you're new to vegetable gardening, start small: an area of just 100 to 130 square feet can provide a substantial harvest. As you gain experience, you may elect to expand the plot.

To decide which vegetables to plant, first list the kinds your family really enjoys. Then consider how much room each type requires. If space is limited, raise those that give a good yield for the area they occupy. Beans, tomatoes, and some summer squash, for example, can overwhelm you with produce from a postage stamp-size plot. At the other extreme are melon and squash varieties that grow on long vines; these, as well as corn, require a great deal of space relative to their yield.

Because vegetables grow best with at least 6 hours of full sun each day, be sure to choose a sunny planting area. To avoid both shade and root competition, locate the garden away from trees and large shrubs. It's also important to choose a spot protected from cold winds in spring and hot, dry winds in summer. Steer clear of "frost pockets"—low-lying areas that may experience frosts later in spring and earlier in fall than other parts of the garden. To make watering and other routine tasks easier, aim for a level site; if only sloping land is available, try to find a south- or southeast-facing slope to take full advantage of the sun. Lay out rows along the slope's contours to minimize water runoff and erosion. On very steep sites, constructing terraces will make gardening much easier.

PLANTING VEGETABLES. The first step toward a satisfying vegetable garden is careful soil preparation: you'll be rewarded with faster growth and a substantially larger harvest. Follow the steps on page 482 for preparing your planting bed. The size and shape of the bed (or beds) will depend on several factors. You may choose to plant vegetables in *rows,* separated by paths that give you access to the plants and let you easily till or hoe the soil. This layout works well for tall-growing plants like corn and for those that need support, such as tomatoes and pole beans. Other plants, however, grow best in *hills*—that is, grouped in a cluster (though not necessarily on a mound). This method is useful for sprawling plants such as most varieties of melons and winter squash. Smaller-growing vegetables, such as beets, carrots, spinach, and lettuce, can be grown efficiently in *wide beds.* In this arrangement, you prepare a bed about 3 feet wide, then broadcast the seeds over it rather than sowing them in rows. Paths on either side allow access to the plants.

If your soil is very poor or does not drain well, you may elect to grow your vegetables in raised beds (see page 482) filled with a mixture of compost and good topsoil.

You can start vegetables by planting seeds outdoors in the garden or by setting out transplants you have either started yourself or purchased from a nursery. Sorts requiring a long growing season—peppers and tomatoes, for example—need many weeks of warm temperatures before they produce fruit and are best set out as transplants. But other types, including beans, carrots, corn, and peas, do not transplant well and grow best if started from seed sown directly in the garden. For more on sowing seeds and on starting and setting out transplants, see pages 483–488.

CARING FOR VEGETABLES. For the best harvest, keep your vegetables growing steadily throughout the season, trying to avoid any checks in their development. Those started from seed sown in the ground usually require thinning, so that each plant will have enough space to develop properly. Thin plants when they're a few inches tall, spacing them as indicated in the descriptions in the A to Z Plant Encyclopedia or on the seed packet.

Provide a steady supply of moisture from planting until harvest. Until they're well established, transplants will need frequent watering—enough to keep the soil moist but not soggy. Rows or beds of seeds and young seedlings likewise need steady moisture, sometimes requiring sprinkling as often as two or three times a day in hot weather. As transplants and seedlings grow and their roots reach deeper, you can water less often—but when you do, be sure to moisten the entire root zone. To water the garden, use sprinklers, furrows, or a drip system (see pages 514–516).

Mulching the garden is important: it conserves moisture and suppresses weed growth. An organic mulch such as straw or compost also improves soil structure as it decomposes, making the top few inches looser and more crumbly. However, because organic mulches also keep the soil cool, it's best not to apply them until warm weather arrives; don't put them down too early in spring. A mulch of black plastic sheeting, on the other hand, helps warm the soil quickly—making it especially useful for growing heat-loving crops such as melons and eggplant in regions with cool or short summers. After preparing the soil, cover it with black plastic; then cut small holes where you want to sow seeds or set out plants.

For many vegetables, the fertilizer applied when you prepare the bed at planting time will be sufficient for the entire season. However, heavy feeders (such as corn) and those requiring a long growing season, including tomatoes and some varieties of cabbage and broccoli, may need one or two follow-up feedings. Lightly scratch dry granular fertilizer into the soil (keep it off plant foliage), then water it in thoroughly; or use a water-soluble fertilizer.

As is true for the garden as a whole, caring for a vegetable plot involves preventing pest and disease damage. You'll find information on many

V

diseases and pests and advice for controlling them on pages 458–461, 471–478, and in the entries for specific vegetables in the A to Z Plant Encyclopedia. The following measures will also help keep your garden productive and healthy.

Keep the garden clean. Composting or discarding spent plants and tilling the soil (especially in fall) can help you avoid trouble, since some insects and diseases overwinter or spend certain developmental stages on plant debris.

Plant resistant varieties when available. Seed packets and plant tags may bear code letters noting inbred resistance to certain serious problems. Tomatoes, for example, may be designated V, F, N, and/or T, indicating resistance to verticillium wilt, fusarium wilt, harmful nematodes (which cause root knots), and tobacco mosaic virus, respectively.

Mix different kinds of plants. Large expanses of just one sort can result in large populations of pests fond of that plant. Mixed plantings encourage more kinds of insects, including beneficial species that prey on the troublemakers.

Encourage natural controls such as toads, lizards, many birds, and beneficial insects (see page 472). Avoid chemical sprays, if possible—and be aware that even sprays made from natural ingredients can harm helpful creatures as well as pests, leaving the garden vulnerable to new attack.

Change the location of crops from season to season to prevent the buildup of diseases and insects specific to certain kinds of vegetables in any one part of the garden.

Vines

Versatile additions to almost any landscape, vines can be used to frame entryways, decorate bare walls and fences, mask unsightly sheds, and cover arbors with foliage and flowers. Defined in the most basic terms, a vine is simply a flexible shrub that doesn't stop extending its growth—it just keeps getting taller or longer, depending on whether you train it vertically or horizontally. And if unsupported, it won't climb at all; it will simply sprawl across the ground (some vines are grown in this manner for use as ground covers).

SELECTING VINES. Like trees and shrubs, vines vary widely in their characteristics. They may be deciduous, semievergreen, or evergreen. Some provide greenery alone; others bear decorative fruits or blossoms.

Think about ultimate size and weight, too: some vines are lightweight enough to adorn a flimsy trellis without damaging it, but others eventually become weighty enough to pull down and destroy all but the sturdiest supports. As noted below, the vine's particular method of attachment will also determine the kind of support you'll need to provide. *(continued on page 510)*

SEASON EXTENDERS

Warm-season vegetables may need protection from frost when they are first planted in spring, then again as temperatures begin to dip in fall. In spring, individual plants can be protected with various plastic or paper caps known as hotcaps. Also available is a special plastic hotcap for tomatoes; it consists of water-filled cylinders that trap heat effectively.

Floating row covers (shown at right) made of polyethylene, polyester, or polypropylene are one of the most useful tools for protecting plants from cold temperatures (and from certain insect pests, as well). Sold in rolls, these fabriclike covers can be laid directly over seeded beds or plants or propped on stakes; they serve as miniature greenhouses. They are extremely lightweight, transmit 80 to 95 percent of the sunlight that strikes them, and allow both water and air to pass through. Burying the cover's edges in the soil will seal out insect pests, though any pests already on the plants may proliferate (remove covers when plants begin to bloom to admit pollinating insects).

WARM-SEASON AND COOL-SEASON VEGETABLES

Depending on the weather they need for best growth, vegetables are classed as warm-season or cool-season. *Warm-season vegetables* require both warm soil and high temperatures (without significant cooling at night) to grow steadily and produce a harvest. They include traditional summer crops such as snap beans, corn, cucumbers, melons, peppers, tomatoes, and squash. (So-called winter squashes such as acorn, hubbard, and banana are also warm-season crops; the name refers not to the planting season, but to the fact that the fruits can be stored for winter consumption.) For almost all of these vegetables, the fruit (rather than the leaves or roots) is the edible part. Warm-season vegetables are killed by frost, so don't plant them until after the last frost in spring unless you give them cold protection; see "Season Extenders," above.

Cool-season crops grow best at temperatures an average of 10 to 15°F/6 to 8°C below those needed by warm-season types. Most will endure short spells of frost. Many familiar cool-season vegetables are grown for their leaves or roots (lettuce, spinach, carrots, and radishes, for example), while in others (such as broccoli, cauliflower, and artichokes) the immature flowers are harvested. A few—peas and broad beans—produce edible seeds. Success with cool-season crops depends on bringing plants to maturity in cool weather; in hot conditions, many of them become bitter tasting and may bolt to seed rather than producing edible parts. They should thus be planted in very early spring—so that the crop will mature before summer heat settles in—or in late summer, for a crop that matures during fall. In warmer regions, cool-season vegetables can be planted in a cold frame from late summer to early fall to provide harvests in late fall, winter, and early spring. Some crops, such as kale, taste better after they have been exposed to light frost.

V

The charts below indicate approximate planting dates for warm-season and cool-season vegetables. In most zones a second sowing of cool weather crops may be made in late summer or early fall for harvest in fall. These dates are noted on the line below the dates given for spring sowing. To learn the planting dates for your area, find your climate zone (see pages 30–46), then look up the crops on the charts. If you garden in a colder part of your zone, use the later in the range of dates for spring planting, and earlier ones for late-summer and fall planting. Also, keep in mind that localized microclimates may influence planting times; keeping year-to-year records will help you customize this information for your garden.

PLANTING DATES FOR COOL-SEASON VEGETABLES

VEGETABLE NAME	ZONE 32	ZONE 34	ZONE 35	ZONE 36	ZONE 37	ZONE 38
BEETS (S)	late March–early May	early April–mid May	early April–mid May	early April–early May	mid April–late May	mid April–late May
BROCCOLI (T) (S)	early March–late April / early–mid August	mid March–mid May / mid–late July	late March–early April / late July	late March–mid May / late May–early June	early April–late May / early July	early April–late May / late June–mid July
BRUSSELS (T) SPROUTS (S)	early–mid March / early–mid August	mid–late March / late July–early August	late March–early April / early August	late March / early–mid June	early April / mid July	early April–late May / mid–late July
CABBAGE (T) EARLY CVS: MIDSEASON CVS: LATE CVS:	early March–early May / early–mid April / early–mid May	mid March–mid May / mid–late April / mid–late May	late March–early May / late April / late May	mid March–mid May / late April / late May–early June	late March–late May / early May / early June	late March–early June / early–mid May / early–mid June
CARROTS (S)	early March–mid May / early–mid August	mid March–late May / late July–mid August	mid–late March / early August	late March–late May / mid–late July	early April–early June / early–mid July	early–mid April / early–mid July
CAULIFLOWER (T) (S)	mid March–mid May / early–mid August	early April–mid May / late July–mid August	late March–late April / early August	early April–early May / mid–late July	mid April–late May / early–mid July	mid April–late May / early–mid July
CELERY (T)	mid March–mid May	early April–late May	early April–early May	early April–late May	mid April–early June	mid April–mid June
CHARD (S,T)	early April–mid May / late July–early August	mid April–mid May	early–mid April	late April–late May	early–late May	early May–early June
KOHLRABI (T, S)	early–mid March / early–mid August	mid–late March	(S) late March	(S) late March–early May / early August	(S) early April / mid–late July	(S) early–mid April / mid–late July
LETTUCE (T,S) LEAF LETTUCE (S)	mid March–early May also early–mid September	early April–mid May / mid–late August	late March–early May / late August	early April–early May / mid–August	mid April–late May / early August	mid April–late May / late July–early August
ONIONS (S) (T)	early–mid March / mid March–early April	early–late March / early–mid April	mid–late March / late March–late April	late March–early April / early–mid April	early April / mid April	early–mid April / mid April–early May
PEAS (S)	mid–late March / mid–late August	late March–early April / late July–mid August	late March–early April	early–mid April / late July–early August	mid April / mid July	mid–late April / mid–late July
POTATOES (SEED POTATOES)	mid March–early April	early–mid April	early–mid April	early–mid April	mid April	mid–late April
RADISHES (S)	early–late March / early–mid October	mid March–early April / mid–late September	late March–early April / late September	late March–early April / mid September	early–mid April / late August	early–late April / late August–mid Septemb
SPINACH (T) (S)	mid March–early April / early–mid March / mid–late September	early–mid April / mid–late March / early–mid September	late March–early April / mid March / mid September	early–mid April / late March–early April / early September	mid April / early April / mid August	mid April–early May / early–late April / mid–late August
TURNIPS (S)	mid March–early April / early–mid September	early–mid April / mid–late August	late March–early April / late August	late March–early April / mid August	mid April / early August	mid April–early May / late July–early August

S = plant from seed; T = set out transplants

'Golden' beets

'Sultan' cabbage

'Danvers' carrots

Kohlrabi

'Oakleaf' lettuce

'Green Arrow' peas

ZONE 39	ZONE 40	ZONE 41	ZONE 42	ZONE 43	ZONE 44	ZONE 45
mid April–late May	early–late May	early–late May	early–late May	mid May–mid June	mid May–mid June	mid May–mid June
early April–late May / mid–late July	mid April–late May / late June	mid April–late May / early July	mid April–late May	late April–mid June	early May–mid June	early May–mid June
early April / late July	mid April / early–mid July	mid April / mid July	mid April	late April	early May	early May
late March–late May / early May / late May–early June	early April–late May / mid May / mid June	mid April–early June / mid May / mid June	early April–early June / mid May / mid June	late April–mid June / late May	late April–late June / early June	late April–late June / early June
early April–late May / late July	mid April–mid June / late June	mid April–mid June / early July	mid April–mid June	late April–late June	early May–early July	early May–early June
mid April–late May / late July	late April–mid May / late June	early–late May / early July	early–late May	mid May–mid June	mid May–mid June	mid May–mid June
mid April–late May	early May–mid June	early May–mid June	early May– mid June	mid May–late June	mid May–late June	mid May–mid June
early–late May	mid May–early June	mid May–early June	mid May–early June	late May–mid June	early–mid June	early–late June
(S) early–mid April / early–mid August	(S) mid April / mid July	(S) mid April / mid July	(S) mid April / mid June	(S) late April	(S) early May	(S) early May
mid April–late May / late August	late April–mid May / late July	early–late May / early August	early–late May / early August	mid May–mid June / mid–late July	mid May–mid June / mid July	mid May–mid June / early July
early–mid April / mid–late April	mid April / late April	mid April / late April–early May	mid April / late April	late April / mid May	early May / mid May	early May / mid May
mid–late April / late July	late April–early May / early–mid July	late April / mid July	mid–late April / mid July	late April–early May / late June–early July	mid May	mid May
mid–late April	early May	early May	early May	mid May	mid May	mid May
mid–late April / mid September	late April / late August	late April / early September	late April / early September	late April–early May / mid–late August	early–mid May / mid August	early–mid May / early August
mid–late April / early–mid April / early September	early May / mid April / early August	early May / mid April / mid August	early May / mid April / mid August	mid May / early May / mid July–mid August	mid May / early May / early August	late May / mid May / mid July
mid–late April / late August	early May / late July	mid April / early August	early May / early August	mid May	mid May	mid May

V

Warm season tips: To keep the garden in good shape during hot summer weather, be sure it receives adequate moisture. A mulch of loose organic material helps conserve moisture and moderate soil temperatures. To extend the harvest of spring crops as long as possible, keep them well watered and mulched, and keep the plants picked. Providing some shade in the hottest part of the day can help, too. Plan now for a second harvest of cool-season crops in fall. Start seeds or set out transplants in summer for a second crop.

PLANTING DATES FOR WARM-SEASON VEGETABLES

VEGETABLE NAME	ZONE 32	ZONE 34	ZONE 35	ZONE 36	ZONE 37	ZONE 38
BEANS (S)	mid–late April	late April–mid May	early May	early–mid May	mid–late May	mid May–early June
CORN (S)	mid–late April	late April–mid May	early May	early–mid May	mid–late May	mid May–early June
CUCUMBERS (S,T)	mid–late April	late April–early May	late April	late April–early May	mid May	mid–late May
EGGPLANT (T)	mid–late April	late April–mid May	early–mid May	early–mid May	mid–late May	mid May–early June
MUSKMELONS (S,T)	mid–late April	late April–mid May	early May	early–mid May	mid–late May	mid May–early June
PEPPERS (T)	late April–early May	early–late May	mid–late May	mid–late May	late May	late May–mid June
SUMMER SQUASH (S,T)	mid–late April	late April–mid May	early May	early–mid May	mid–late May	mid May–early June
WINTER SQUASH (S,T)	mid–late April	late April–mid May	early May	early–mid May	mid–late May	mid May–early June
TOMATOES (T)	mid–late April	late April–mid May	early May	early–mid May	mid–late May	mid May–early June
WATERMELON (S,T)	mid–late April	late April–mid May	early May	early–mid May	mid–late May	mid May–early June

S = plant from seed; T = set out transplants

Once you have a good idea of what you're looking for—an evergreen flowering vine for a delicate wooden trellis, say—narrow the list down to just those plants suited to your climate zone. For ideas, see Vines and Vinelike Plants in A Guide to Plant Selection, beginning on page 47.

METHODS OF ATTACHMENT. Some vines twine around their supports with stems, others with tendrils; some cling with special growths such as suction disks, while others need to be tied to their support to climb along it.

Twining vines. The new growth of these vines twists or spirals as it elongates, coiling around a support or even around growth on the same or nearby plants. Nearly all twining vines make too tight a spiral to encircle a post, so it's best to support them with cord or wire.

Vines with tendrils. Specialized growths along the stems or at the ends of leaves reach out and wrap around anything within reach—a wire or cord, another stem of the same vine, an adjoining plant. The tendrils grow out straight until they make contact, then contract into a spiral. Give such vines narrow supports that the tendrils can easily grasp.

Clinging vines. Special growths along the stems of these vines attach to flat surfaces. Some clingers have tendrils equipped at their tips with suction disks that grip the support; others have "claws" that hook into small irregularities or crevices of a flat surface. Another type of clinger has aerial rootlets along its stems that tenaciously hang on to all but absolutely smooth, slick surfaces. Bear in mind that all of these clinging devices—known collectively as holdfasts—can damage brick, wood, concrete, and other building materials.

Vines that require tying. Some vines have no means of attachment. They simply thread their way through and over other plants, depending on this living support to hold their stems in place. A few (climbing roses, for example) have thorns on their stems; these help secure the stems in place as they scramble but offer no permanent support. In the garden, these sorts of plants must be tied to their supports.

PLANTING AND CARING FOR VINES. Most vines are sold in containers; a few deciduous kinds (roses and grapes, for example) are available bare-root. See pages 483–485 for container and bare-root planting guidelines.

Many vines grow well in ordinary soil with an annual application of fertilizer in spring. To look their best, almost all require yearly pruning. Check the A-to-Z Plant Encyclopedia for comments on the specific needs of each vine.

'Santa Cruz' melon

'Fiesta' hot pepper

'Spookster'
pumpkin

'Park's Crookneck'
squash

'Ruby Red' Swiss chard

'Better Boy' tomato

ZONE 39	ZONE 40	ZONE 41	ZONE 42	ZONE 43	ZONE 44	ZONE 45
mid–late May	late May	late May	late May–early June	mid June	mid June	mid June
mid–late May	late May	late May	late May–early June	mid June	mid June	mid June
mid May	late May	late May	late May	early June	mid June	early–mid June
mid–late May	late May	late May	late May–early June	mid June	mid June	mid June
mid–late May	late May	late May	ate May–early June	early–mid June	mid–late June	mid June
late May–early June	early June	early June	early June	mid–late June	late June	mid–late June
mid–late May	late May	late May	late May–early June	mid June	mid–late June	mid June
mid–late May	late May	late May	late May–early June	mid June	mid–late June	mid June
mid–late May	late May	late May	late May–early June	mid June	mid June	mid June
mid–late May	late May	late May	late May–early June	early–mid June	mid–late June	mid June

VINE ATTACHMENTS

Twining stems

Tendrils

Suction (holdfast) discs

Aerial rootlets

Scrambles;
no means of attachment

V

Water Conservation

In most years, Northeastern gardens are blessed with enough rain to support a wide variety of plants without much supplemental watering. That's especially true for established trees and shrubs and many perennials and herbs. In dry summers, however, most homeowners depend on regular watering—especially of lawns and vegetable gardens—to keep their gardens going. There are some simple, practical steps you can take to reduce the amount of supplemental water your yard requires. This doesn't just save money on your water bill: having a water-conserving landscape can make all the difference during dry years, when watering restrictions may limit how much you can water, if you can at all.

LOCATE PLANTS WISELY. If you mix plants that need little or no irrigation with those that require regular moisture, you'll be wasting water on the undemanding plants (and may even harm them). To avoid this situation, try to organize your garden into *hydrozones*—groups of plants with similar water needs. Doing so will simplify irrigation while giving each plant the right amount of moisture. The concept of hydrozoning was developed for arid and semi-arid climates, but it can be applied anywhere that gardeners need to supplement rainfall. High-water-use plants are typically located nearest the house, while those needing less water are planted progressively farther away. (For a list of drought-tolerant plants, see Plants for Dry Gardens in A Guide to Plant Selection, beginning on page 47.) This scheme frees you from dragging hoses to the far reaches of the garden or extending an irrigation system farther than necessary.

RECONSIDER YOUR LAWN. Most conventional lawn grasses use water at a rate disproportionate to other plants, largely because they have a shallow root system that dries out quickly (especially in sandy soil). Consider reducing the size of your lawn or choosing a lawn alternative such as an unthirsty ground cover, gravel, or hard surface such as brick, other paving, or a wooden deck. If you feel that a lawn is a necessary component of your garden, select a grass requiring less water than the more familiar types; see page 466 for less-thirsty turf grasses adapted to your climate.

MULCH YOUR PLANTINGS. An organic mulch spread several inches thick over planting beds acts as an insulating blanket, slowing evaporation from the soil and keeping it cooler than it would be if left unprotected. Rocks and gravel also do the job. Black plastic sheeting, sold in rolls, conserves moisture and suppresses weeds. You can also buy rolls of various plastic materials, known collectively as landscape fabrics. For more on all these mulches, see page 468.

CONSERVING WATER ON SLOPES

Plants on slopes are often challenging to irrigate, since water can run downhill faster than it can seep into the root zone. To prevent wasteful runoff, make basins or terracing to channel water directly to plant roots, as shown below.

Individual basin. Make a wide basin. Build up on the low side to increase water-holding capacity.

Terracing. Headers help control runoff. Because surface reservoir is small, water must be applied slowly.

ELIMINATE RUNOFF. Don't waste water by irrigating paved surfaces. If your sprinkler system showers water over a sidewalk, patio, or driveway, replace the heads with models that deliver water only where it is needed; or, if necessary, redesign the system.

Sloping land and heavy clay soils invite runoff—due to gravity in the first case, slow water penetration in the second. To avoid runoff in such sites, adjust the rate at which water is applied. If you use sprinklers, you can improve penetration by watering in successive short intervals, giving the water time to soak in between each spell of sprinkling. On slopes, terraces and basins can also help prevent runoff (see above).

USE LOW-VOLUME WATERING DEVICES. Soaker hoses are effective and easy to install. Drip irrigation (see page 515) offers an excellent way to reduce water use. You can also upgrade an existing underground sprinkler system: install low-volume sprinkler heads or, if you're more ambitious, convert it entirely to a drip system, using the parts and kits available at hardware stores.

USE TIMERS. With the simplest timers, you set the dial for the length of time you want the water to run or the number of gallons of water you want to apply; then you turn on the water. The timer turns the faucet off for you.

More sophisticated timers operate on batteries or household current. You set them to a schedule; they turn the water on and off as programmed. Such timers assure that your garden will be watered whether you're at home or away. What's more, you can select a schedule that will give your plants the precise amount of water they need to thrive.

The flaw of automatic controllers is that they follow your schedule regardless of weather:

they'll turn on the water during a deluge or apply amounts of water appropriate for hot summer temperatures on a cool fall day. To solve this problem, reset the controller to take seasonal rainfall and weather conditions into account. Or use electronic attachments that function as weather sensors. By linking a soil moisture sensor to the controller, for example, you can trigger the sprinklers to switch on only when the sensor indicates that soil moisture has dropped to the point where water is needed. Another useful attachment is a rain shutoff device; it accumulates rainwater in a special collector pan, turning off the controller when the pan is filled to a prescribed depth and triggering it to resume watering when the collected water has evaporated. Before installing either of these sensors, be sure they are compatible with the automatic controller.

Watering

Plants, like animals, need water to live. A seed must absorb water before it can germinate. Roots can take up nutrients only when water is present in the soil, and water transports nutrients throughout plants. Water is also essential for photosynthesis.

WATERING GUIDELINES. A number of interrelated factors—including soil texture, the particular plants and their ages and root depths, and the weather—determine how much water your plants need and how often they need it.

A soil's ability to absorb and retain water is closely related to its composition. Clay soils absorb water slowly and drain slowly too, retaining water longer than other soils. Sandy soils, in contrast, absorb water quickly and drain just as rapidly. Loam soils absorb water fairly quickly and drain well, but not too fast.

Absorption patterns vary, too: though water moves primarily downward, it also moves laterally to some extent. Lateral movement is greatest in clay soils; in sandy ones, most water seeps straight down and there is little horizontal movement.

To improve absorption and drainage in clay and to make sandy soils more moisture retentive, work in organic amendments. (For more on soil texture and organic amendments, see pages 497–501.)

Once their roots are established, different plants have widely differing water needs. Those native to semiarid and arid climates, called *xerophytes,* have evolved features that allow them to survive with little water and low relative humidity. They may have deep root systems, for example, or water-retaining leaves that are small, hairy, or waxy. Many familiar garden plants, however, are adapted to moist soil and high relative humidity. Called *mesophytes,* they usually have broad, thin leaves that lose moisture readily.

Keep in mind that *all* young plants, including xerophytes, require more frequent watering than mature ones until their root systems become well established. And many annuals and vegetables require regular moisture throughout the growing season if they are to bloom well or produce a good crop.

The depth of a plant's root zone also influences watering practices; typical root depths of trees, shrubs, and other plants are shown above right. Applying enough water to moisten the entire root zone encourages roots to grow throughout that zone, while shallow watering keeps them near the soil surface. Deeper roots have access to more moisture and can go longer between waterings; they're also less subject to stress from heat and drying winds than shallow roots are.

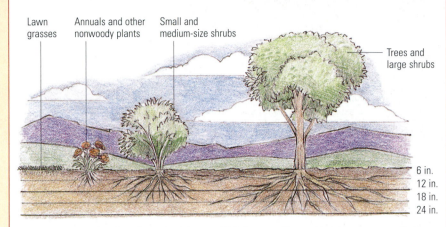

COMPARATIVE ROOT DEPTHS

Lawn grasses

Annuals and other nonwoody plants

Small and medium-size shrubs

Trees and large shrubs

6 in.
12 in.
18 in.
24 in.

The rooting depths illustrated here will help you determine the amount of water needed to supply moisture to your plants' root zones. Even in the case of large trees, most of the feeder roots are within the top 2 feet of soil, though taproots (which serve to anchor the tree) may penetrate farther. It's also important to note that the feeder roots of trees and shrubs extend well beyond the plant's leafy top or canopy; be sure to apply water to all of the root area.

Root hairs of underwatered plants will dry out and die, causing the plant to slow its growth, wilt, and eventually die. But you don't want to overdo it, either. It's important to learn how often you must water to keep the root zone moist. Watering below the root zone is wasteful, since the water is not used—and beyond that, keeping the soil too moist can cause as many problems as letting it get too dry. Roots need air as well as water, and they absorb both from the pore spaces between soil particles. When water penetrates the soil, it displaces the air in the pores; then, as it drains away, evaporates, and is taken up by roots, the pore spaces fill with air again. If water is applied too often, the pore spaces never have a chance to drain. They remain filled with water, cutting off the roots' air supply. This lack of oxygen makes roots susceptible to various water-mold fungi, which in turn can lead to rot.

To check how far water penetrates your soil, water for a set amount of time (say, 30 minutes). Wait for 24 hours, then use a soil sampling tube (shown at right) or dig a hole to check for moisture. Sampling tubes are especially useful in lawns or around established trees and shrubs; they let you test moisture at deeper levels without digging a hole that might disturb roots. A metal rod or a long screwdriver pushed into the ground can also serve as a soil probe. It will move easily through moist soil but slow down or stop when it reaches dry soil, allowing you to estimate how deeply the moist area extends. You'll soon learn to judge how long to water each plant or group of plants to soak the root zone thoroughly.

Weather affects water needs as well. When it's hot, dry, and windy, plants use water quickly, and young or shallow-rooted ones sometimes

cannot absorb it fast enough to keep foliage from wilting. Such plants need frequent watering to keep moisture around their roots. During cool, damp weather, on the other hand, plants require much less water.

Because the factors just discussed—soil texture, plant characteristics and age, and weather—are variable, following a fixed watering schedule year-round (or even all summer) isn't the most efficient way to meet your plant's needs. Before you water, always test the soil for moisture (see above) and look at plants for signs of wilting.

SOIL TEXTURE AND WATER PENETRATION

Applied to sand (left), 1 inch of water penetrates about 12 inches. Applied to loam (center), 1 inch of water reaches about 7 inches. Applied to clay (right), 1 inch of water soaks only 4 to 5 inches.

USING A SOIL SAMPLING TUBE

This device allows you to check soil moisture at deeper levels than you can reach with a trowel, without disturbing plant roots too much. Push the tube into the ground, pull it out, and examine the soil in the sample. If it is dry or only slightly moist, it's time to water. If the top layer is damp and the rest is dry, you need to water longer to ensure deeper penetration. A soil sampling tube is also useful for detecting compacted layers of soil, checking how deeply roots penetrate, and taking samples for soil tests.

W

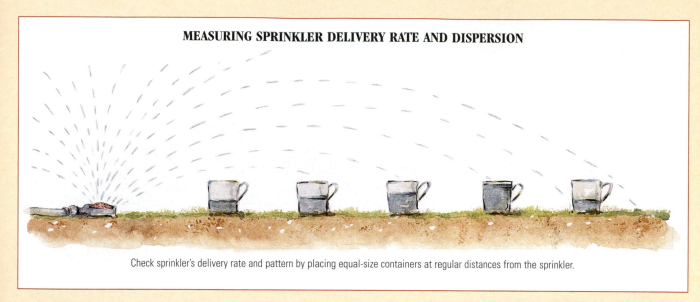

MEASURING SPRINKLER DELIVERY RATE AND DISPERSION

Check sprinkler's delivery rate and pattern by placing equal-size containers at regular distances from the sprinkler.

WATERING METHODS. Methods for applying water range from simple hand-held sprayers to hose-end sprinklers to more complex underground rigid-pipe systems and drip systems. The method or methods appropriate for your garden depend on how often you need to water, the size of your garden, and how much equipment you want to buy.

Hand watering. Watering with a hand-held nozzle may be relaxing pastime, but it's usually inadequate for plants; it takes too long to truly soak the soil. Hand watering is, however, useful for new transplants, seedlings, and container plants, since you can apply the water gently and put it exactly where it's needed.

Sprinkling. Water can be applied through sprinklers attached to the end of a hose or via an in-ground sprinkler system. In either case, the sprinklers apply a high volume of water over a large surface. Many plants, particularly those that like a cool, humid atmosphere, thrive with overhead sprinkling. This method also rinses dust from foliage and discourages certain pests (especially spider mites). But sprinkling has some negative aspects as well. It can be wasteful: wind may carry off some water before it even reaches the ground, and water that falls on or runs off onto pavement is lost too. In humid climates, sprinkling encourages some foliage diseases such as black spot and rust—though you can minimize this risk by sprinkling early in the morning, so that leaves dry quickly as the day warms. Another potential drawback is that plants with weak stems and/or heavy flowers bend and sometimes break under a heavy load of water.

The wide assortment of portable, hose-end sprinklers includes stationary models that resemble salt shakers or rings; oscillating, rotating, and impulse sprinklers; and "walking" types that slowly roll through the area to be watered. When selecting a sprinkler, look for one with a coverage pattern that most closely matches the area to be irrigated; the shape and size of the space the sprinkler covers should be listed on the package.

Permanent underground sprinkler systems offer some advantages over hose-end watering. They free you from moving hoses and sprinklers and can be automated to operate even if you're away from home for an extended period. And recent refinements in the design of the sprinklers have improved such systems' efficiency: the newer sprinklers produce less runoff and overspray onto buildings, walkways, and fences and distribute water more evenly. For such a system to work properly, though, it must be well designed; consult with a licensed landscape contractor or a company specializing in irrigation systems.

Sprinkler application rates. To sprinkle effectively with a portable or an underground system, you need to know how fast water penetrates your soil and the delivery rate of your sprinklers. As the illustration on page 513 shows, 1 inch of water (from sprinkling or rainfall) moistens about 12 inches in sandy soil, 7 inches in loam, and 4 to 5 inches in clay. Thus, if you want to water to a depth of 12 inches, you'll need to apply about an inch of water to sandy soil, 2½ to 3 inches to clay soil.

To determine delivery rate, place a number of equal-size containers (straight-sided coffee cups, for example) at regular intervals outward from the sprinkler, as shown above. (If you are testing an underground system, place the containers among the sprinkler heads.) Then turn on the water and note how long it takes to fill a container with an inch of water. This test will also show you the delivery pattern. If the containers fill unevenly, move portable sprinklers to achieve more even coverage, or check the sprinkler heads of underground systems to see if they need adjusting or replacing.

Root irrigators. This device—which resembles a giant hypodermic needle—is useful for getting water to root zones of trees growing near sidewalks, patios, or other areas with a minimum of open soil. It also helps get water deep into the soil on sloping land, where deep penetration without runoff can be a problem. Attach the tool to the end of a garden hose; then insert it into the ground as you turn the water on. Water travels down a hollow probe and shoots out of holes at the tip. Some models also supply fertilizer as they water.

Flooding. Flooding or soaking is an effective way to supply sufficient water to the deep, extensive root systems of large shrubs and trees. Form two concentric rings of soil and flood the outer ring as shown below. For freshly planted trees and shrubs, make the outer ring just outside the outer edge of the rootball; move it farther out as the plant grows.

If you grow vegetables or flowers in rows, you can build adjoining basins for large plants like squash or make furrows between rows (see page 515). To minimize damage to roots, it's best to construct the furrows when the plants are young, before their root systems have spread. Broad, shallow furrows are generally better than deep, narrow ones: the wider the

Flood the basin around this newly planted conifer to deliver water to the roots. As the tree grows, enlarge the basin. To avoid overwatering, remove the basin during rainy seasons.

furrow, the wider the root area you can soak, since water moves primarily downward rather than laterally. And a shallow furrow is safer for plants—nearby roots are less likely to be disturbed when you scoop out the furrow, and they're likewise less apt to be exposed by a strong flow of water through it.

Soil soaker hoses. Soaker hoses, the forerunners of drip irrigation systems, are still useful for slow, steady delivery of water. They're long tubes made of perforated or porous plastic or rubber, with hose fittings at one or both ends. When you attach a soaker to a regular hose and turn on the water supply, water seeps or sprinkles from the soaker along its entire length. You can also water wide beds by snaking soakers back and forth around the plants; trees and shrubs can be watered with a soaker coiled over the outermost edges of the root zone. You'll probably need to leave soakers on longer than you would sprinklers; to determine timing, check water penetration with a trowel or soil sampling tube.

Drip irrigation. The term "drip irrigation" describes the application of water not only by drip emitters but also by microsprays. These have two traits in common: they operate at low pressure, and they deliver a low volume of water compared to standard sprinklers. Because the water is applied slowly on or near the ground, there should be no waste from runoff and little or no loss to evaporation. You position the emitters to deliver water just where the plants need it; you control penetration by varying the time

WATERING IN FURROWS AND BASINS

Furrows 3 to 6 inches deep help irrigate straight rows on level ground. Bubbler on hose end softens flow of water. Note that furrows don't work well in very sandy soils, since the water moves primarily downward and has little horizontal movement.

Basins with sides 3 inches high hold water around large plants such as tomatoes and peppers. On level ground, link basins to make watering easier.

the system runs and/or the emitters' delivery capacity (rated in gallons per hour—gph). You can also regulate the volume of water delivered to each plant by varying the type and number of emitters you set up for each.

In addition to water conservation, drip systems offer the advantage of flexibility. You can tailor them to water individual plants by providing each with its own emitter(s), or distribute water over larger areas with microsprays. A standard layout might include hookups to two or more valves and several kinds of parts.

Because the lines are aboveground (they're easily concealed with mulch) and are made of limber plastic, changing the system is simple: just add or subtract lines or emitters as needed.

Your drip system can be simply attached to a hose end or provided with fittings to allow it to be screwed into a hose bibb. Or, if you prefer, you can connect it permanently to your main water source. Like underground irrigation systems, drip systems should be outfitted with a backflow preventer. In addition, a filter is necessary (even when you're using municipal supplies

DRIP IRRIGATION COMPONENTS

Timer

Backflow preventer

Pressure regulator

Compression fitting

Emitter line

Emitter line (cutaway view)

Filter

Stakes (to hold lines in place)

Microspray

Drip emitters

Tubing

Punch (to make holes for emitters in tubing)

Goof plugs (to close off emitter holes)

Compression fittings (to connect lines and other components)

A SAMPLE DRIP SYSTEM

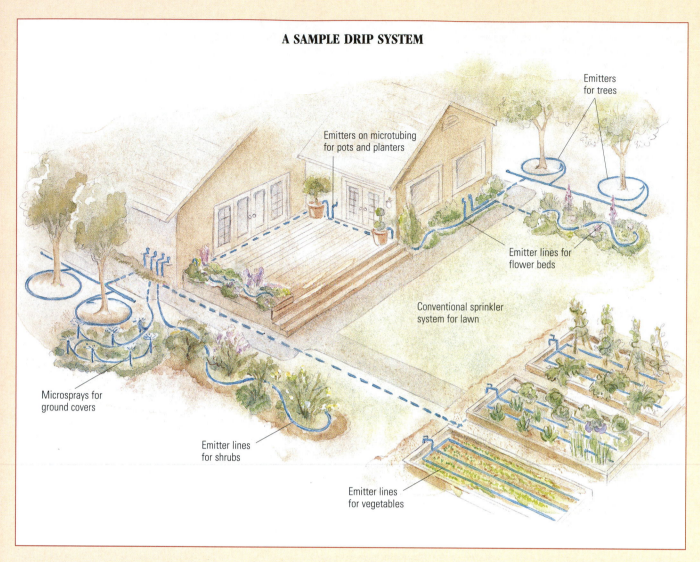

Emitters for trees

Emitters on microtubing for pots and planters

Emitter lines for flower beds

Conventional sprinkler system for lawn

Microsprays for ground covers

Emitter lines for shrubs

Emitter lines for vegetables

of clean water) to keep the small openings on drip emitters and microsprays from becoming clogged. A pressure regulator is also needed—drip systems are designed to run best at a much lower pressure than is found in most household water supplies. The regulator protects the fittings from blowing apart under excess force and allows the watering devices to work properly.

Emitters for drip systems. Emitters vary in shape, size, and internal mechanism, but all operate on the principle of dispensing water slowly; flow rates of most types range from ½ to 2 gph. You insert the emitters directly into ½- or ⅜-inch drip irrigation tubing or into thinner microtubing positioned to run from the larger tubing to each plant. Non-pressure compensating emitters work well on flat or relatively level ground and with lines less than 200 feet long. But when water pressure will be lowered by gravity or friction (on hillsides or with long lines), opt for pressure-compensating emitters. These deliver the same amount of water throughout the system.

You can also purchase emitters factory-installed in polyethylene tubing. These may be referred to as "in-line" emitters or emitter lines. Spaced 1, 1½, 2, or 3 feet apart, they deliver ½, 1, or 2 gph and are available in non-pressure compensating and pressure-compensating versions. Some emitter lines are infused with a small amount of herbicide to prevent root intrusion; these can be buried to water lawns.

While the standard emitters simply drip, types that deliver water in other ways are available as well. *Misters* produce a fine spray—a good way to increase humidity for plants like fuchsia, tuberous begonia, and ferns. *Microsprays* are low-volume equivalents of standard sprinklers, useful for irrigating closely spaced or dense plantings, such as ground covers and flower beds.

Weeds

Weeds are plants growing where gardeners don't want them to grow. They rob desirable plants of water, nutrients, and sunlight, they may harbor insects and diseases—and they're frequently unattractive.

Whether a plant is labeled a weed depends on several factors. Some plants, such as bindweed and quack grass, are regarded as weeds wherever they grow. Others may be considered weeds in some situations, garden plants in others: yarrow (*Achillea*) is an annoying weed when it invades a lawn, for example, but some yarrows are handsome perennials for beds and borders. Certain plants spread so aggressively that they're often thought of as weeds; examples include some kinds of asters, bamboos, mint (*Mentha*), Mexican evening primrose (*Oenothera speciosa*, often sold as *O. berlandieri*), sweet woodruff (*Galium odoratum*), and Jerusalem artichoke (*Helianthus tuberosus*). And some ornamentals have gone beyond invading the garden alone, jumping the fence to overwhelm natives in wild lands (see box, page 517).

Despite their frankly undesirable qualities (from the gardener's point of view), weedy plants do have their positive side. An assemblage of weeds can hold the soil on a steep bank, preventing erosion. Other weeds provide nectar and shelter for beneficial insects and butterflies. When they die and decompose, weeds add humus to the soil. And even the dreaded poison ivy is important to the deer, birds, and rabbits who eat its berries.

W

CLASSIFYING WEEDS. Identifying weeds is an important step in choosing the best way to manage these pests. They are often classified by the length of their life cycle. *Annual weeds* (like annual garden plants) grow shoots and leaves, flower, set seed, and die within a period of less than a year. Most members of this group are summer annuals, which germinate in spring or summer and die by fall. Winter annual weeds begin growth in fall or early winter, then set seed in early spring while the weather is still cool. *Biennial weeds* produce a cluster or rosette of leaves in their first year of growth; in the following year, they flower, set seed and die. Both annuals and biennials reproduce by seed. Almost all *perennial weeds,* which live for several years, also reproduce by seed—but once mature, most of them produce spreading roots, stolons, rhizomes, bulbs, or tubers as well.

You'll find descriptions of some of the most common Eastern weeds in each of these groups on pages 518–522, along with suggestions for controlling them. You can also consult your Cooperative Extension Office for advice on identifying and controlling locally troublesome weeds.

MANAGEMENT OPTIONS. As is true for other kinds of pests, it is rarely possible to eradicate weeds entirely. You can, however, substantially reduce infestations and prevent further problems through physical controls—employing methods that range from hand pulling through mowing, flaming, and mulching—as well as soil solarization (see page 518). If these measures are unsuccessful, chemical management may be needed.

Physical controls. When you're confronted with a weed problem, turn to these methods first.

Hand pulling or *hoeing* is your first line of defense against most weeds. If you're diligent for several consecutive years about pulling or hoeing out annual and biennial weeds before they set seed, their numbers will decline significantly. These methods will also help control perennial weeds, as long as you catch the plants while they're young. Once perennials have passed the seedling stage, though, it's usually necessary to dig out their roots; if you just pull up or cut off the tops, the pests can resprout from fragments left behind. Even with assiduous digging, you'll probably need to repeat the process several times to manage tough perennial weeds. Some useful tools for weeding are illustrated on page 502.

Don't leave pulled or hoed-out weeds on bare ground, since they may take root again. Leafy annual or biennial types that do not yet have flowers or seeds can safely be relegated to the compost pile, as can the top growth of perennial weeds (before seeding). But roots of perennials (dandelions and quack grass, for example) should be tossed in the trash rather than composted—as should any weeds that have set seed.

Rototilling or *discing* will do the job on annual and biennial weeds in larger areas, such as orchards, vacant lots, roadsides, or plots intended for future gardens. These methods not only knock down weeds but also incorporate them into the soil, where they decay to form humus. However, perennial weeds usually sprout again from the roots or crowns—and some kinds even grow more abundantly after tilling.

Using rotary mowers or *weed eaters* is another good choice for seasonal weed control in larger areas. Both tools cut the weeds: weed eaters leave the severed tops behind, while mowers grind them up as they cut them.

Smothering effectively kills weeds in areas earmarked for future planting. After mowing or cutting off the top growth, put down a layer of heavy cardboard, newspapers (in a layer at least two dozen sheets thick; thicker for woody weeds), or black plastic. Overlap these materials so weeds can't grow through the cracks. Anchor the covering with a layer of bark chips or other organic mulch. Leave these smothering materials in place for at least a full growing season; allow a year or more for tough or perennial weeds.

Flaming offers another way to knock down weeds. Powered by propane or a mixture of propane and butane, flamers are not meant to burn weeds; instead, they heat them to the point at which their cell walls burst. Though this damage is drastic enough to kill many young weeds, types with deep perennial roots usually regrow; destroying these requires several treatments. Take care when using flamers around mulches, and never use them in dry, fire-prone areas.

Presprouting is a useful technique for preparing planting areas for vegetables, perennial beds, or new lawns in parts of the garden plagued by weeds. Add needed amendments, till the soil, water, and then wait a week or two for weed seeds to germinate. When they're only a few inches high, scrape them away. Then sow or transplant your vegetables, flowers, or lawn, disturbing the soil as little as possible to avoid bringing more weed seeds to the surface.

WEEDS OF WILD LANDS

While most of the plants brought from other parts of the world to ornament gardens (or provide timber or food) are welcome and well behaved, some have escaped from cultivation and invaded wild lands throughout the East. Unchecked by the natural forces that helped control them in their homelands, they thrive, displacing local native plants; they change the structure of the ecosystems they enter, threatening diversity and destroying wildlife habitats. Native plant societies maintain lists of problem plants in each state; a few of the worst offenders are noted here.

Giant reed *(Arundo donax)* has become a serious invader of riparian areas in warmer climates, while ailanthus *(Ailanthus altissima),* also called tree of heaven, is a common weed tree throughout our region. Purple loosestrife *(Lythrum salicaria)* has overrun thousands of acres of wetlands. Garlic mustard *(Alliaria officinalis)* is another vigorous weed, common to the Northeast, as well as other regions.

Gardeners can help stem the spread of invasive plants by not using them near natural areas, as in gardens of rural or vacation homes. Native plant societies as well as other organizations, such as garden clubs and volunteer groups at state and national parks, often sponsor programs for eradication of these native plants in wild lands (and for restoration of native species).

Purple loosestrife has overrun natural wetlands throughout the United States. Though it is still sold by some nurseries, home gardeners should not plant it.

W

Soil solarization controls many kinds of weed seeds as well as harmful fungi, bacteria, and some nematodes.

Once you've destroyed weeds in a garden area, take steps to prevent their reappearance. **Mulching** bare soil is an effective deterrent to weed growth; see page 468 for information on choosing and using mulches, including landscape fabrics. **Ground covers,** sometimes called living mulches, are effective in preventing weed growth: like organic and inorganic mulches, they keep sunlight from reaching weeds and their seeds. You'll usually have to do some hand weeding or apply a mulch for the first few seasons after you plant a ground cover, but as it grows and spreads to form a tight carpet, weed growth is much reduced. For more on ground covers, see page 465.

Chemical controls. Synthetic herbicides are not recommended for food gardens. In home ornamental gardens, they should be your last resort, called into play only when other methods have failed. Beyond the risks they may pose to health and the environment, many of these chemicals can damage desirable plants if they drift through the air or run off in irrigation or rainwater. Some persist in the soil for long periods, injuring later plantings. And often the entire process of herbicide use—selecting an appropriate product, reading the label, mixing and applying the spray, cleaning up—takes more effort than simply pulling or digging out the weeds.

If you use herbicides, always make sure the product is safe for the desirable plants growing in and near the areas to be treated. Also keep in mind that you can be held responsible for any damage to neighboring properties resulting from herbicides you use (do not apply them on windy days). See page 521 for lists of natural and synthetic herbicides as well as explanations of terms used in describing herbicides, such as pre-emergence and postemergence.

ANNUAL WEEDS. Most of these weeds can be controlled by diligent hand weeding and hoeing. This should be carried out before the weeds go to seed, since most annual weeds produce prodigious amounts of seed. To discourage the growth of these weeds in lawns, maintain a thick turf (for more on lawns, see pages 565–568). Mulches are effective in reducing the germination of annual weeds in garden areas; most such weeds can also be destroyed by soil solarization (see 518). If chemical control is needed, use a pre-emergence herbicide labeled for the weed in question. Apply it in fall for winter annual weeds, in early spring for summer annuals. For postemergence treatment, spot-treat annual weeds with herbicidal soaps or products containing glufosinate-ammonium or glyphosate, taking care not to get these chemicals on desirable plants. Selective postemergence herbicides that are effective on particularly troublesome annual weeds are mentioned below.

SOIL SOLARIZATION

Soil solarization takes advantage of the sun's heat, trapped under clear plastic sheeting, to control many kinds of weed seeds as well as harmful fungi, bacteria, and some nematodes. The process is carried out in summer and works best in regions that have hot, sunny weather for 4 to 8 weeks straight; daytime temperatures above 80°F/27°C are ideal. Solarization isn't very effective in coastal climates with summer fog, nor does it work well in very windy areas.

Plan to solarize areas you intend to use for fall vegetables, ornamental beds, or lawn. Follow these steps.

1 Cultivate soil, clearing it of weeds, debris, and large clods of earth. It is important to get rid of growing weeds, because clear plastic—unlike black plastic—doesn't halt growth of plants in the soil beneath it.

2 Make a bed at least 2 feet wide (narrower beds make it difficult to build up enough heat to have much effect). Carve a small ditch around perimeter and rake to level surface.

Soak soil to a depth of 1 foot: moist soil conducts heat better than dry soil and initiates germination of weed seeds. Both seeds and any seedlings will then be killed by heat.

3 Cover soil with 1- to 4-mil clear plastic; use UV-resistant plastic if it's available, since it won't break down during solarization. Stretch plastic tightly so that it is in contact with the soil. Bury the edges in the perimeter ditch. An optional second layer of plastic increases heat and makes solarization more effective; use soda cans as spacers between the two sheets.

Leave plastic in place for 4 to 6 weeks (8 weeks for really persistent weeds); then remove it. Don't leave it down longer than 8 weeks, or soil structure may suffer.

You can now plant. After planting, avoid cultivating more than the upper 2 inches of soil, since weed seeds at deeper levels may still be viable.

Top to bottom: Annual bluegrass; Crabgrass; Henbit; Knotweed

Biennial weeds such as mallows are controlled in the same way as annual ones.

Annual bluegrass (*Poa annua*). Winter annual, though there are perennial forms. Forms a bright light green tuft of softly textured grass. A weed in lawns; also troublesome in flower borders and winter vegetable crops.

Crabgrass (*Digitaria species*). Summer annual. This shallow-rooted weed thrives in hot, moist areas. Seeds germinate in early spring in warmer climates, later in colder areas. As the plant grows, it branches out at the base; stems can root where they touch the soil. It is typically found in lawns and flower beds that receive frequent surface watering; infrequent deep watering can dry out crabgrass roots, killing the weeds or diminishing their vigor. Corn gluten meal is used as a pre-emergence herbicide for crabgrass; it also acts as a fertilizer, thickening lawns and thus suppressing weed growth. For postemergence treatment around ornamentals, use herbicides that kill grasses, such as fluazifop-butyl or sethoxydim.

Henbit (*Lamium amplexicaule*). Biennial or winter annual that is especially problematic in spring and fall. Bears creeping stems with rounded leaves and clusters of small, two-lipped, pink or purple flowers. Plants bloom in spring to early summer and again in fall, and the seeds germinate from fall to spring. Plants also spread by rooting at the leaf nodes. Pull up plants beginning in late winter and continue through early summer. Watch for new seedlings in fall. Remove all sections of stem and roots; otherwise plants will re-root and reappear.

Knotweed (*Polygonum aviculare*). Annual. A weed often found on poor, compacted soil; bears long, slender, sprawling stems with narrow, bluish green leaves. Tiny flowers are carried in clusters in the leaf axils from summer to fall. Pull plants when they are young or hoe them up. Get the blade of the hoe slightly under the soil surface to pull up the crown of the plant.

Lambs' Quarters (*Chenopodium album*). Summer annual. Coarse, leafy weed grows 2 to 6 feet high; its green to reddish green, fleshy leaves are simple or toothed, and bear irregular spikes of tiny flowers at shoot tips. It is common in gardens and orchards and on roadsides.

Mallow (*Malva neglecta*). Winter or summer annual or biennial, depending on climate. Also known as cheeseweed (the fruits resemble a round of cheese), these broad-leafed weeds have rounded, lobed leaves and pinkish white flowers. They grow quickly, ranging in height from a few inches to 4 feet tall, and are found in lawns, in gardens, and on roadsides. Pull when young; older plants develop a deep taproot.

Prickly lettuce (*Lactuca serriola*). Annual, winter annual, or biennial. This common weed bears a rosette of wavy-edged or toothed leaves and stems that exude milky sap when broken. The small, pale yellow flowers are borne on tall, branched stems from midsummer to fall and are followed by dandelion-like seedheads. Like dandelions, the seeds are carried on the wind. Pull plants or hoe them up as soon as you see them. Remove the crown of the plant before they flower and set seed. This species can transmit diseases to cultivated lettuces.

Purslane (*Portulaca oleracea*). Summer annual. A prostrate broad-leafed weed with fleshy stems and leaves (which are edible, with a tart, lemony flavor) and small yellow flowers, purslane thrives in moist conditions but can withstand considerable drought. Though it's easy to pull or hoe, pieces of stem reroot readily, so be sure to remove them from the garden. Related to the garden flower known as ornamental purslane, portulaca, or rose moss.

Sowthistles (*Sonchus species*). Summer annual. These upright, 1- to 4-foot tall weeds have stout taproots, hollow stems, and milky sap that oozes out when a leaf or stem is broken. The yellow flowers look like those of dandelions. Common in gardens, they may grow in lawns as well.

Spotted spurge (*Chamaesyce maculata;* also listed as *Euphorbia maculata*). Summer annual, though seeds can germinate as early as February

Top to bottom: Lambs' quarters; Mallow; Prickly lettuce

W

Purslane

Sowthistle

in warm regions. This weed is particularly aggressive: not only does it produce large quantities of seed, it also sets seed just a few weeks after germination—and the seeds may germinate immediately. It grows from a shallow taproot and forms a low mat of branching stems that exude a milky juice when cut or broken.

PERENNIAL WEEDS. Described below are some of the Northeast's most troublesome perennial weeds. Management options are described from least to most toxic—physical controls first, then chemical ones. In general, growth of perennial weeds can be controlled with landscape fabrics installed so that no light reaches the soil (note that these must be applied *after* clearing the area of weeds; see page 517). Organic mulches are not as effective,

since seeds or plants sprouting from roots left in the ground often grow through them.

Bermuda grass *(Cynodon dactylon).* A fine-textured and fast-growing perennial, Bermuda grass is frequently planted as a lawn in warm climates. It spreads by underground stems (rhizomes), aboveground runners (stolons), and, in common Bermuda grass, by seed—and easily becomes a difficult-to-control weed in shrub borders, flower beds, and lawns planted to other kinds of grasses; especially south of Pennsylvania. If you have a Bermuda lawn, use 8-inch-deep barriers or edging to prevent it from advancing into other parts of the garden.

Dig up stray clumps before they form sod, being sure to remove all the underground stems; any left behind can start new shoots. Repeated pulling and digging are usually necessary to stop this weed. Seeds and shallow rhizomes of Bermuda grass are destroyed by soil solarization, but deeply buried rhizomes will survive.

For chemical control, you can use a pre-emergence herbicide containing pendimethalin or oryzalin to prevent seeds from growing. Postemergence products include herbicides that kill grasses, such as fluazifop-butyl or sethoxydim; these are effective against most grasses and can be sprayed over some broad-leafed ornamentals without harming them (check the product label). Bermuda grass growing in cool-season lawn grasses can be treated with some products containing triclopyr, as indicated on the label. Spot-treat actively growing Bermuda grass with glyphosate, taking care not to get it on desirable plants.

Bindweed *(Convolvulus arvensis).* Also called wild morning glory or field bindweed, this weed grows in open areas throughout the East, usually in loam to heavy clay soil. Its 1- to 4-foot-long stems crawl over the ground and twine over and around other plants. The trumpet-shaped flowers are white to pink.

Once established, bindweed forms a deep, extensive root system, so hand-pulling seldom controls it—the stems break off, but the weed returns from the root. To kill it, cultivate or hoe every 6 weeks throughout the growing season; this eventually weakens the root system. Don't let bindweed set seed: the hard-coated seeds can sprout even after lying dormant in the soil for 50 years! Seeds (but not roots) can be killed by soil solarization.

An herbicide containing trifluralin may provide pre-emergence control around many ornamentals. In midsummer, when bindweed is growing vigorously but has not yet set seed, spot-treat isolated patches with glyphosate, taking care to avoid contact with desirable plants.

Dandelion *(Taraxacum officinale).* Familiar as a lawn weed throughout the Northeast, dandelions form a deep, fleshy taproot as they

mature. They spread by windborne seeds that follow the familiar yellow blossoms.

If dandelions are growing in your lawn, the turf is probably thin and undernourished. A healthy lawn can outcompete this weed, so thicken the turf by overseeding and proper fertilizing, watering, and mowing. Pull dandelions from lawns and gardens while they're small, before they produce a deep taproot and set seed. Once the taproot has formed, it's necessary to remove all of it to get rid of the plant, since new plants can sprout from even a small piece. A dandelion weeder with a forked blade

Bermuda grass

Bindweed

Dandelion

PRODUCTS FOR WEED CONTROL

Herbicides are classified according to what stage of weed growth they affect, as well as by how they damage their target weeds.

Pre-emergence herbicides work by inhibiting the growth of germinating weed seeds and very young seedlings; they do not affect established plants. To be effective, they must thus be applied before the seeds sprout. Before applying these chemicals in ornamental gardens, remove any existing weeds. Some pre-emergence products are formulated to kill germinating weeds in lawns; these may be sold in combination with fertilizers, which increase the vigor of the lawn and improve its ability to compete against weeds. (Such dual-purpose products should not, however, be treated solely as fertilizers and reapplied whenever the lawn needs feeding—for that purpose, use a regular lawn fertilizer.)

Follow label directions carefully; some pre-emergence products must be watered into the soil, while others are incorporated into it. Note that some may also harm seeds you sow later in the season; check the label to learn how long the product you use remains active in the soil.

Postemergence herbicides act on growing weeds rather than on seeds. They damage plants in different ways. Those that are translocated must be absorbed by the plant through its leaves or stems; they then kill it by interfering with its metabolism. *Contact* herbicides kill only the plant parts on which they are sprayed; regrowth can still occur from roots or unsprayed buds.

The natural and synthetic herbicides listed here are widely available. *Synthetic herbicides* are manufactured compounds that do not normally occur in nature. *Natural herbicides*, in contrast, are products whose active ingredients originate in a plant or mineral.

When using any herbicide, *read the label directions carefully and follow them exactly*. The package will clearly state the weeds the product controls and the other plants, if any, around which it can be safely used; it is illegal to apply it to any plant not designated as a target.

The following products are listed alphabetically by the accepted common name of the *active ingredient*—the actual chemical that controls the weed or weeds listed on the package label. Some widely used trade names, if they differ from the common name, are noted in parentheses. Before you buy, read the label to make sure you're getting the active ingredient you want. (For more on reading and understanding herbicide labels, see page 478.)

NATURAL HERBICIDES

- **Corn gluten meal (Suppressa, others).** Pre-emergence. Used to control some germinating weed seeds in lawns. This product is also a fertilizer, serving to thicken lawns and thus suppress weed growth (some research indicates that this may be its primary contribution to weed control).

- **Herbicidal soap (Superfast, others).** Post-emergence. Contact herbicides that degrade quickly. Kill top growth of young, actively growing weeds; most effective on annual weeds. Made from selected fatty acids (as are insecticidal soaps).

SYNTHETIC HERBICIDES

- **Fluazifop-butyl.** Postemergence. A translocated herbicide that controls actively growing grasses. Can be sprayed over many broad-leafed ornamentals without damaging them; check the label.

- **Glufosinate-ammonium (Finale).** Postemergence. Contact herbicide that damages or kills many kinds of weeds. Take care not to apply to desirable plants.

- **Glyphosate (Roundup).** Postemergence. Translocated herbicide that kills or damages any plant it contacts. Effective on a broad range of troublesome weeds, but must be used with care to avoid contacting desirable plants.

- **Oryzalin (Surflan).** Pre-emergence. Used to control annual grasses and many broad-leafed weeds in warm-season turf grasses and in gardens.

- **Pendimethalin (Prowl).** Pre-emergence. Used to control many grasses and broad-leafed weeds in turf and in ornamental plantingss. Toxic to fish.

- **Sethoxydim (Grass-Getter).** Postemergence. Translocated herbicide that controls many grasses growing in ornamental plantings; check the label.

- **Triclopyr (Brush-B-Gon, Turflon Ester).** Postemergence. Translocated herbicide. Depending on formulation, used on cool-season turf to control broad-leafed weeds and Bermuda grass; also used to control hard-to-kill woody plants. Use with care to avoid damaging desirable plants.

- **Trifluralin.** Pre-emergence. Controls many grasses and broad-leafed weeds in turf and ornamental plantings. Toxic to fish.

Nutsedge

is helpful. A hand weeder with a bent shaft (or a ball attached to the shaft) to serve as a fulcrum increases leverage, helping to pop dandelions out of the ground.

For chemical control in lawns, use a postemergence product labeled for dandelions in turf; these typically combine several herbicides. Spot-treating with glyphosate will partially control dandelions in gardens, but take care not to get the chemical on desirable plants.

Nutsedge, yellow *(Cyperus esculentus).* Yellow nutsedge resembles a grass, but its stems are solid and triangular in cross-section. True grasses, in contrast, have hollow stems that are oval or flat in cross-section. Nutsedge leaves grow from the base in groups of three; grass leaves grow in sets of two. Small, roughly round tubers (nutlets) form at the tips of the roots; the weed spreads by these tubers as well as by seed.

Remove yellow nutsedge when it's young—when plants have fewer than five leaves or are less than 6 inches tall. Older, taller plants are mature enough to produce tubers; when you dig or pull the plant, the tubers remain in the soil to sprout. Repeatedly removing the top growth eventually weakens the tubers. Soil solarization provides only partial control.

For postemergence chemical control, try glyphosate, being careful not to get the chemical on desirable plants. It is most effective on young plants; it will not kill mature tubers or those that have become detached from the treated plant.

W

Poison ivy *(Toxicodendron radicans)*. Poison ivy, usually found in shady areas and at the edges of woodlands, it sprawls along the ground until it finds something to climb; then it becomes a vine. Its leaves are divided into three leaflets with scalloped, toothed, or lobed edges. A resin on the leaves, stems, fruits, and roots of both plants causes severe contact dermatitis in most people. Plants are spread by birds, who eat the fruits and disperse the seeds.

Poison ivy is most effectively controlled with an appropriately labeled herbicide, such as triclopyr or glyphosate; take care to avoid getting these chemicals on desirable plants. Repeated applications are needed as new leaves grow.

Quack grass *(Elytrigia repens)*. Also known as couch grass or devil's grass, this aggressive weed invades both lawns and gardens. It can reach 3 feet tall but stays much lower in mowed areas. It produces an extensive network of long, slender, branching, yellowish white rhizomes that can spread laterally 3 to 5 feet.

Because it reproduces readily from even small pieces of rhizome left in the soil, quack grass is difficult to manage. Before planting, thoroughly dig the area and remove all visible pieces of rhizome; this will slow the weed's growth for a few years.

Poison ivy

Quackgrass

WOODY WEEDS

Rosa multiflora

Woody weeds can be extremely troublesome once they take hold. Here are some control strategies:

Dig up the roots. The entire root system must be removed, for often new plants will grow if just a small piece of root remains in the ground. Special tools are available; a three-pronged claw weeder is effective on vines and other shallow-rooted plants.

Mow repeatedly. Regular mowing keeps seedlings from growing. It can eliminate bittersweet, multiflora rose, poison ivy, and other pests.

Use an herbicide. For well-established, deep-rooted, aggressive spreaders such as Japanese honeysuckle and multiflora rose, it's almost impossible to dig out the entire root system. Careful application of an environmentally friendly but effective herbicide, such as a glyphosate product, may be best.

For chemical control, use herbicides that control grassy weeds, such as fluazifop-butyl or sethoxydim. Or spot-treat with an herbicide containing glyphosate, taking care to avoid contact with desirable plants.

Wildlife, Gardening to Attract

Making your garden attractive to wildlife—songbirds, hummingbirds, butterflies, toads, lizards, frogs, and other creatures—is primarily a matter of providing shelter, water, and food. It's also important to avoid using pesticides. Try to emphasize native plants, since they're familiar to the local wildlife and adapted to your climate. Also remember that a garden teeming with wildlife is not overly tidy; parts of it are left to grow naturally, providing safe havens for creatures of all sorts. See A Guide to Plant Selection (beginning on page 47) for lists of plants attractive to butterflies and hummingbirds, including kinds that provide food for butterfly larvae (caterpillars).

Tall trees. These provide shelter, food (seeds or fruits, depending on species), and nesting places for birds; they also protect the garden from strong winds.

Hummingbird feeder. Prepare a solution of 1 part granulated white sugar to 4 parts water; bring it to a boil, let it cool, and fill the feeder with it. Keep the feeder clean; hummers can develop a deadly infection from dirty feeders.

Birdbath. To provide some protection from cats and other predators, place it in an open area; a location 10 to 20 feet from protective shrub cover offers a good safety zone. In freezing weather, thaw the bath's water with boiling water or use a birdbath heater.

A WILDLIFE GARDEN

Hedgerow. Provides food, shelter, and nesting sites for birds. Plant a variety of low to medium-tall shrubs and small trees. Include as many fruit-bearing types as possible, as well as kinds that feed butterfly larvae.

Low ground covers. These provide a safe cover for birds and other creatures.

Brush pile. Instead of hauling away or shredding tree prunings and other brush, make piles to shelter birds and other wildlife.

Flower borders. Include a wide selection of flowering plants that provide nectar for butterflies, beneficial insects, and hummingbirds, as well as species whose foliage feeds butterfly larvae. Let plants go to seed to furnish food for songbirds.

Nesting boxes. Install nesting boxes away from the activity around feeders and face them away from prevailing weather. Mount on metal poles to keep cats and raccoons at bay.

Meadow. Plant native grasses, wildflowers, and low shrubs for food, shelter, and nest-building materials.

Pond. Provides water for birds and a habitat for frogs and turtles. Birds are especially attracted to the splashing water of a small fountain. Make a "beach" at one side to provide shallow water and an easy entrance to the deeper part of the pond. An "island" (a large rock) in the center provides refuge for turtles and frogs. Add water plants for more shelter.

Vines. Flowering vines provide shelter, nesting sites, and nectar; many species also bear berries and foliage that are sources of food for birds and butterfly larvae.

Rocky area. Gives shelter to lizards and toads.

Bird feeders. Locate feeders near trees or shrubs so birds can fly to cover; keep them off the ground to protect the clientele from cats. Set up feeders in fall and maintain them through winter when natural foods are scarce. Keep feeders clean. Besides seeds (sunflower, millet, safflower, thistle, and so on), birds enjoy suet, offered in mesh bags or special feeders.

Tulips

RESOURCE DIRECTORY

Gardeners in the northeastern United States and Canada can look to many sources for help and inspiration. Arboretums, botanical gardens, display gardens, and extensive plant collections throughout the East Coast offer countless ideas for choosing plants and garden designs. Public gardens feature native and exotic plants in landscape settings, giving you an idea of how they will thrive in your own garden. Nurseries and mail-order suppliers throughout the region offer a wide range of plants—from perennials to trees and shrubs, vegetables and herbs to bulbs, heirloom roses to ornamental grasses. The array of plants is always expanding, with different varieties and colors of perennials, annuals, bulbs, trees, shrubs, herbs, and vegetables being introduced every year.

Botanical Gardens, Arboretums, Display and Estate Gardens

The many outstanding public gardens described in these pages range in size from the small and intimate to enormous estates covering hundreds of acres. Some were designed by well-respected landscape architects such as Frederick Law Olmstead, who helped design the Arnold Arboretum at Harvard University. Others were created by gardening enthusiasts, such as Pierre S. du Pont who developed what is now the acclaimed Longwood Gardens.

If you're starting a new garden, or adding to an existing one, a visit to a public garden can give you some fresh ideas to use on your own property: lively flower combinations, innovative bed shapes, and the interesting use of containers and garden accessories. Best of all, you can see which plants thrive in your area and how they look when fully grown.

Mail-Order Suppliers

Local nurseries and garden centers, too numerous to list in this resource directory, offer a good supply of popular plants and seeds. But if you're looking to become a more adventurous gardener, you may want to grow something new and different such as red corn, a rose pink sunflower, or chocolate-scented flowers. These unusual plants may not be easy to find at your nearby garden supplier. That's when it's time to turn to the many mail-order sources. Many catalogs offer a wide range of different plants, while others specialize in a particular type of plant, or in hard-to-find or exotic species. Turn to pages 534–539 to learn which catalogs can provide the selections you're looking for.

Many mail-order suppliers also have web sites on the Internet where they advertise or sell their products. Gardeners can search for typical or obscure plants, browse electronic catalogs, and pose planting and growing questions by e-mail to company representatives. These web sites, where you can often also purchase plants (make sure you're using a safe server before disclosing credit card information), are often great sources of gardening information.

Keep in mind that catalogs can be tantalizing—and it's easy to make impulse buys. Before you spend a lot of money, form a clear idea of your needs by assessing your budget, the space you want to fill, your soil conditions, and the amount of sun and shade the different parts of your garden receive. Sketch a garden plan on paper before purchasing plants, keeping in mind harmonious plant combinations, compatible bloom times, and plants' colors and heights, as well as their water, light, and maintenance needs. Try to estimate as closely as possible how many plants you'll need before you start buying.

Once you've assessed your needs, review the catalog's plant descriptions carefully. A good catalog will give a physical description of the plant, as well as soil and light requirements, hardiness to cold, planting instructions, bloom time, and mature growth measurements. In deciphering plant descriptions, learn to tell the difference between truly helpful information and marketing tactics. The wise shopper will learn to decode of the typical words and phrases catalogs use.

"Start seeds indoors" describes seeds that require some extra care. These may germinate slowly or need more warmth, or the seedlings may demand extra time or attention before being planted outside. "Sow in place" usually means that the plant may not survive being transplanted; it's wise to follow this advice.

Beware of a plant that is described as "vigorous." This term sometimes implies that the plant could grow so quickly and invasively that it could outcompete other plants in its path. This may not be a problem for you, but if your garden has limited space, look instead for compact, bush, or dwarf varieties.

Plants that "self-sow readily" are usually annuals and biennials (but can also be trees or shrubs) that you plant once and continue to enjoy year after year: a new crop of seeds germinates and grows each year with no work on your part. Whether you want this plant duplicated throughout your garden is up to you and how much you like the plant.

Most catalogs allow you to specify the best shipping dates for your plants—this should correspond to the best time in your area to actually plant your purchases. Most companies will help you determine the proper ship date for your zone. Remember to order early to get the best selection of plants and to ensure optimal planting times.

In addition to checking shipping dates, also check on the catalog company's guarantee policy. Most reputable companies guarantee that their plants will be in excellent condition when received, and if you follow the planting and care advice and your plant does not thrive, the company will replace the plant or refund your money within a reasonable amount of time. And don't order blindly on price alone. If something sounds too good to be true, beware—it probably is! In general, catalogs offer a discount for buying larger quantities.

Scientific Plant Names

Everywhere you look, whether in public gardens, nurseries, catalogs, or books, you'll come across Latin plant names. To learn more about what they mean and why they are important, turn to pages 540–541. For information on the most accepted pronunciations of plant names, turn to pages 542–543.

Botanical Gardens and Arboretums

Botanical gardens and arboretums display plants from around the world as well as local native species, often in landscape settings. Some have demonstration gardens filled with flowers, fruits, and vegetables; some include displays featuring irrigation devices, mulches, fencing, or paving. Many offer classes in gardening techniques, host special events, operate horticultural libraries, and sell hard-to-find plants. Some are living laboratories, overseeing the propagation and preservation of endangered plants. The botanical gardens and arboretums described below, listed alphabetically by state, are the major establishments (and a few lesser-known ones) you can visit throughout the eastern United States and Canada. Many of the gardens have web sites where you can check on what's in bloom and daily special attractions. Call before visiting the gardens as hours are subject to change.

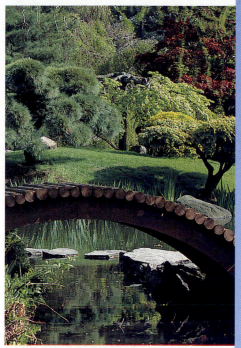

Brooklyn Botanic Garden, New York

CONNECTICUT

Bartlett Arboretum
University of Connecticut

151 Brookdale Road
Stamford, CT 06903
(203) 322-6971
Open daily 8:30 to sunset

This 63-acre arboretum has a large collection of plants and shrubs, including a variety of nut trees, a mixed-hardwood forest, and a unique collection of native, Japanese, Korean, and European azaleas and rhododendrons. Also a woodland trail leading to a reflecting pond. There are 5 acres of display gardens, including low-maintenance perennials and annuals, a garden of All America Selections, and a wildflower garden.

The Connecticut College Arboretum

270 Mohegan Avenue
Box 5201
Connecticut College
New London, CT 06320
(860) 439-5020
www.conncoll.edu/ccrec/greennet/arbo
Open daily sunrise to sunset

Spread out over 750 acres, this arboretum serves as a refuge for native plants and animals and some exotic ornamentals, as well as providing a research facility for students and faculty of Connecticut College. There is an impressive selection of trees, shrubs, and woody vines that are indigenous to eastern North America. Visit in June to see the lovely display of blooming mountain laurel. Other highlights are the wildflower garden and the tropical greenhouse, featuring a large display of cacti and orchids.

MAINE

Coastal Maine Botanical Gardens

P.O. Box 234
Boothbay, ME 04537
(207) 633-4333
Open daily, weather permitting

Encompassing 128 acres of unspoiled land, this botanical garden is dedicated to preserving and displaying coastal Maine's habitats and flora. A network of trails takes you along the shoreline under a canopy of evergreen and deciduous trees. Lovely stone outcroppings, knolls, and ledges are decorated with ferns, mosses, lichen, and wild blueberries.

MASSACHUSETTS

The Arnold Arboretum of Harvard University

125 Arborway
Jamaica Plain, MA 02130
(617) 524-1718
www.arboretum.harvard.edu
Open daily from dawn to dusk

Founded in 1872, the 265-acre Arnold Arboretum has one of the country's finest collections of 14,000 hardy trees, shrubs, and vines, grouped together by family. Most notable are the crabapple, rose, conifer, rhododendron, and bonsai collections. A stunning display of one of the largest collections of lilacs is a popular attraction in mid-May. Along the Chinese Path are flowering trees and shrubs brought to the Arboretum from China and Japan in the early 1900s.

Berkshire Botanical Garden

Routes 102 & 183
P. O. Box 826
Stockbridge, MA 01262
(413) 298-3926
www.berkshirebotanical.org
Open May to October, daily 10 to 5

Located in the heart of the Berkshires are 15 acres of woodlands, perennial and annual gardens, a terraced organic herb and vegetable garden, a pond garden, a rock garden, and water garden. The garden's many lectures, demonstrations, and workshops, as well as much of the garden's maintenance, are led by local volunteers.

Garden in the Woods

New England Wild Flower Society
180 Hemenway Road
Framingham, MA 01701-2699
(508) 877-7630
www.newfs.org
Open April 15 to June 15, daily 9 to 5; in May until 7; June 16 to October 31, Tuesday to Sunday 9 to 5

Originally a private garden, these 32 acres of natural woodlands and 13 acres of gardens display the largest landscaped collection of native plants.in the Northeast, including many rare and endangered species. Three miles of trails lead to individual gardens, including a woodland garden, rock and pond plantings, New England bog plantings, and a Western habitat-inspired area with prickly pear cactus and other plants that survive in sun and drought. The meadow and wildlife gardens provide food and shelter for many animals and insects.

NEW JERSEY

New Jersey Botanical Garden/Skylands

Ringwood State Park
Morris Road
Ringwood, NJ 07456
(732) 962-7527
www.njbg.org
Open daily 8 to 8

In 1984, 96 acres surrounding Skylands, a Tudor-style manor house, was designated as New Jersey's official botanical garden. The nine formal perennial and annual gardens are separated from the wilder, more naturalistic heather and wildflower gardens by a half-mile stretch of crab apple trees. This Crab Apple Vista is particularly impressive when in full bloom in mid-May, along with the flowering azalea and lilac gardens. Lovely stone statuary are sprinkled throughout the gardens.

The Rutgers Gardens

Cook College
Rutgers University
112 Ryders Lane
New Brunswick, NJ 08901
(732) 932-8451
Open daily dawn to dusk

A series of teaching, research, and botanical gardens spread over 50 acres on the Rutgers University campus. In addition to a shade tree collection, a rhododendron and azalea garden, and an evergreen garden, this is also home to one of the largest collections of American hollies in the world. There are a variety of flower and vegetable gardens and greenhouses, and trails through a large untouched forest. One of the most intriguing sights is its bamboo forest with towering thin bamboo trees that have multiplied rapidly over the years.

NEW YORK

Brooklyn Botanic Garden

1000 Washington Avenue
Brooklyn, NY 11225
(718) 623-7200
www.bbg.org
Open April to September, Tuesday to Friday 8 to 6, weekends and holidays 10 to 6; October to March, Tuesday to Friday 8 to 4:30, weekends 10 to 4:30

A 52-acre oasis of many specialty gardens within the garden allows visitors to forget about the surrounding urban setting. Some of the most popular sights include the flowering cherry and magnolia trees and the spring bulb display. The Cranford Rose Garden has 5,000 plants representing 1,200 varieties. The newly renovated Japanese Hill and Pond Garden contains both common and unusual plants, wisteria-covered pergola, and a symbolic Torii—a fixture of Japanese gardens. The 1-acre Children's Garden teaches young enthusiasts how to plant and care for vegetables and flowers.

Cornell Plantations

One Plantations Road
Ithaca, NY 14850
(607) 255-3020
www.plantations.cornell.edu
Open daily sunrise to sunset

This botanical garden and arboretum is adjacent to Cornell University's campus. The gardens include herbs, flowers, vegetables, peonies, rock gardens, native wildflowers, rhododendrons, and ground covers. The arboretum specializes in trees and shrubs that are hardy in New York State. The Herb Garden contains 17 theme beds, including herbs used for natural dyes, herbs associated with sacred rituals or religion, culinary herbs, and herbs with significance in literature and folklore. Plantations also manages 3,000 acres of natural areas of bogs, meadows, woodlands, and gorges around central New York.

New York Botanical Garden, New York

Mary Flagler Cary Arboretum, New York

Institute of Ecosystem Studies
Mary Flagler Cary Arboretum

N.Y. 44A, Box R
Millbrook, NY 12545

(914) 677-5359

www.ecostudies.org

Open April to September, Monday to Saturday 9 to 6, Sunday 1 to 6; October to March, Monday to Saturday 9 to 4, Sunday 1 to 4

This arboretum surrounding an ecological research and education center, offers both nature trails and informal gardens highlighting low-maintenance plants that thrive in this part of the Hudson River Valley. Individual beds within the perennial garden focus on a particular theme—flowers that attract butterflies or hummingbirds, shade-loving perennials, an ornamental grass bed. The two newest beds are the Water Garden and Xeriscape Bed.

New York Botanical Garden

200th Street and Kazimiroff Blvd.
Bronx, NY 10458

(718) 817-8700

www.nybg.org

Open April to October, Tuesday to Sunday and Monday holidays 10-6; November to March, Tuesday to Sunday and Monday holidays 10-4

Encompassing 250 acres, this is one of the oldest and largest public gardens in the world. The grounds include dramatic rock outcroppings, ponds, meadows, wetlands, natural forest, waterfalls, as well as gardens. Among the 47 different gardens and plant collections are the Peggy Rockefeller Rose Garden, which contains 2,700 rose bushes. The demonstration gardens include a fragrance garden, an autumn garden, and a wildlife garden. The recently renovated Enid A. Haupt Conservatory showcases tropical, subtropical, and desert plants from around the world within its Victorian glass walls.

Planting Fields Arboretum State Historic Park

P.O. Box 58
Oyster Bay, New York 11771

(516) 922-9200

www.plantingfields.com

Open daily 9 to 5

Situated on a 400-acre estate on the North Fork of Long Island, this lovely arboretum was designed by the prestigious Olmstead Brothers landscape firm. An impressive collection of beeches, cedar, magnolias, rhododendrons, azaleas, linden, and oak trees surround the Elizabethan-style manor house. The holly collection has more than 100 different types of American, Asian, English, and hybrid forms. The unique 5-acre Synoptic Garden has trees and shrubs, all suitable for Long Island gardens, arranged alphabetically by botanical name. Other specialized gardens include roses, perennials, camellias, and an Italian pool garden.

Holden Arboretum, Ohio

OHIO

Cleveland Botanical Garden

11030 East Boulevard
Cleveland, OH 44106

(216) 721-1600

www.cbgarden.org
Open daily dawn to dusk

Not far from downtown Cleveland, this botanical garden and research facility has 7 acres of landscaped grounds including 5 gardens, open grassy areas, and woodland paths. The Western Reserve Herb Society Garden has a formal English knot garden and more than 300 herb species. The formal Mary Ann Sears Swetland Rose Garden showcases the best hybrid roses for northeast Ohio. The Wildflower Garden contains many of Ohio's native trees, shrubs, and wildflowers.

Holden Arboretum

9500 Sperry Road
Kirtland, OH 44094

(440) 946-4400
www.holdenarb.org

Open Tuesday to Sunday 10 to 5

One of the largest in the country, this 3,400-acre arboretum is dedicated to collecting and displaying woody plants for ornamental and scientific purposes. Among the collections of specific trees and shrubs are lilacs, viburnums, crab apples, and rhododendrons. The colorful new Butterfly Garden has ornamental grasses and summer-blooming perennials that are favorites of butterflies and hummingbirds. The Hedge Garden of 27 different evergreen and deciduous trees are meticulously maintained to illustrate proper pruning.

PENNSYLVANIA

Hershey Gardens

P.O. Box 416
170 Hotel Road
Hershey, PA 17033

717-534-3493

www.hersheygardens.org

Open daily April to September 9 to 6; in October open daily 9 to 5; Evening hours until 8 on Friday to Sunday from Memorial Day to Labor Day

Originally built in 1937 as a 3-acre rose garden, Hershey Gardens has now grown to a 23-acre botanical display garden containing 275 different variety of roses and more than 7,000 other plants. Special collections include dwarf and weeping conifers, hollies, rhododendron, and Japanese maples. Specimen trees include the giant sequoia, blue atlas cedar, bald cypress, and European beech. The Butterfly House and Garden contains 300 butterflies and an assortment of annuals, perennials, and flowering shrubs that attract butterflies as well as hummingbirds.

BOTANICAL GARDENS AND ARBORETUMS

Lewis Ginter Botanical Garden, Virginia

Historic Bartram's Garden

54th Street and Lindbergh Boulevard
Philadelphia, PA 19143
(215) 729-5281
www.libertynet.org/bartram
Open daily March to December 10 to 5; closed
January and February except by appointment

Situated on the banks of the Schuylkill River is
this country's oldest botanical garden, designed
by botanist and plant scholar John Bartram. A
self-taught Quaker who lived from 1699 to 1777,
Bartram traveled around the country and
brought plants back to this site, many of which
are still thriving today. On a 27-acre hillside
leading from the 1730 stone house down to the
river are hundreds of trees and shrubs originally cataloged by Bartram. Other highlights
include a wildflower meadow and a kitchen
garden comprised of raised beds of herbs used
for culinary and medicinal purposes. A fragrant
Common Flower Garden has herbaceous plants
and bulbs that were propagated for exchanging
with other collectors.

Morris Arboretum and Gardens of the University of Pennsylvania

100 Northwestern Avenue
Philadelphia, PA 19118
(215) 247-5777
www.upenn.edu/morris
Open all year except Thanksgiving and the
week between Christmas and New Years. Daily
10 to 4; April to November until 5 on Saturday
and Sunday

This lush 92-acre Victorian-style park is filled
with flower beds, old and rare trees, winding
paths, streams, arches, and sculpture. There is
also a Japanese rock garden and a slope of hollies that ends in an azalea meadow. The formal
All-America Rose Selection Garden is surrounded by a row of wisteria.

RHODE ISLAND

Blithewold Mansion, Gardens & Arboretum

101 Ferry Road
Bristol, RI 02809
(401) 253-2707
www.blithewold.org
Open daily 10 to 5

This 33-acre estate overlooks Narragansett Bay
and Bristol Harbor. Its sweeping lawn is
adorned with 1,500 trees and shrubs and 250
types of woody plants, both native and exotic
species. Most notable is the 90-foot Giant
Sequoia, the largest of its kind on the East Coast.
The surrounding gardens are connected by
gravel paths and include a rose garden, water
and rock gardens, a nut grove, and the bosquet.
Children and adults alike will enjoy strolling
through the Bamboo Grove, where fast-growing
stalks reach up to 30 feet high.

VIRGINIA

Lewis Ginter Botanical Garden

1800 Lakeside Avenue
Richmond, VA 23228
(804) 262-9887
www.lewisginter.org
Open daily 9 to 5 except Thanksgiving,
Christmas Day, and New Year's Day

This large botanical garden surrounding a lake
has 17 distinct gardens on 24 acres of landscaped
grounds. The most notable is the diverse perennial garden, one of the largest on the East Coast.
The formal Victorian garden is accented with colorful annuals, topiaries, and boxwoods. The Bog
Garden has a unique collection of pitcher plants,
rushes, and sedges. The fragrant Herb Garden is
also laced with euphorbia and shrub roses. An
exotic and serene Asian Valley has a large collection of camellias, Japanese maples, and azaleas.

WASHINGTON, D.C.

United States National Arboretum

3501 New York Avenue N.E.
Washington, DC 20002
(202) 245-2726
www.ars-grin.gov/na
Open daily 8 to 5 except Christmas Day

This 446-acre federally-funded arboretum has
many impressive plant collections and gardens.
The Gotelli Dwarf and Slow-Growing Conifer
Collection includes 1,500 specimens of fir,
cedar, false cypress, juniper, spruce, hemlock
and more displayed along a hillside allowing
visitors to fully appreciate their interesting
shapes, colors, and forms. The half-mile trail
through the Fern Valley winds through ferns,
wildflowers, and native trees and shrubs. Other
highlights include the bonsai collection, medita-
tive gardens, and dogwood collections.

CANADA

Montréal Botanical Garden

4101 Sherbrooke Street East
Montreal, Quebec H1X 2B2
Canada
(514) 872-1400
www.ville.montreal.qc.ca/jardin
Open daily 9 to 5, until 7 in summer

Set in the heart of Montreal, this botanical garden exhibits plants from around the world,
including 21,000 plant species displayed in 10
greenhouses and 30 themed gardens. The Chinese Garden is the largest outside Asia. The
Japanese Garden features typical Japanese
plants and landscape styles. The greenhouses
are filled with orchids, tropical ferns, begonias
and gesneriads, and tropical rainforest plants.

Royal Botanical Gardens

680 Plains Road West
Burlington, Ontario L7T 4H4
Canada
(905) 527-1158
www.rbg.ca
Open daily 9:30 to dusk

Stretched out for 11 miles along the northwest
shore of Lake Ontario, the 2,700-acre complex
includes five major garden areas and 30 miles
of trails through meadows, marshes, undeveloped forests, and a wildlife sanctuary. The Lak-
ing Garden, filled with peonies, perennials,
daylilies, and ornamental grasses, is particularly spectacular in June when the thousands of
irises are in bloom. The Rock Garden showcases flowering cherries, annuals, azaleas, and
100,000 spring-blooming bulbs. The Lilac Dell
boasts 800 different types of lilacs.

Estate Gardens and Other Public Historic Gardens

Elizabeth Park Rose Garden, Connecticut

L eft to posterity by pioneering gardeners and enthusiastic plant collectors, grand old estates and living museums throughout the eastern United States and Canada celebrate flora and fauna of their own regions and abroad. A number of these gardens are open to the public and are described below (listed alphabetically by state). Visit them for gardening inspiration, a peek into gardening styles from long ago, and the chance to view plants tested by time. Check out the web sites before you go to see what's in bloom and to learn about special events--and always call before visiting as hours are subject to change.

CONNECTICUT

Caprilands Herb Farm

534 Silver Street
Coventry, CT 06238
(860) 742-7244
www.caprilands.com
Open daily 9 to 5

A 50-acre herb farm lovingly started and attended to by enthusiast Adelma Simmons. Low stone walls and brick paths divide the herb beds arranged around a particular plant or theme. More than 360 varieties of herbs are grown here, and each bed is given a descriptive and sometimes whimsical name. For example, The Bride's Garden has plants with heart-shaped foliage alongside plants traditionally related to love (forget-me-nots, lemon verbena).

Cricket Hill Garden

Peony Heaven
670 Walnut Hill Road
Thomaston, CT 06787
(860) 283-1042
www.treepeony.com
Open Thursday to Sunday 10 to 4 from May to mid-June. Other times, call for appointment

This magnificent display of colorful and fragrant Chinese tree peonies is best viewed during the height of the bloom season at the end of May. Revered in ancient China as a symbol of wealth and prosperity, the more than 150 varieties of tree peonies that bloom here have such descriptive names as Lotus that Shines in the Sun and Fairy's Glow. Some of the more common herbaceous types of peonies also grows on this 3-acre hillside, overlooking a pond and woodlands.

Elizabeth Park Rose Garden

c/o Friends of Elizabeth Park
P.O. Box 370361
West Hartford, CT 06137
(860) 242-0017
www.elizabethpark.org
Open daily dawn to dusk

Located on Prospect and Asylum Avenues on the Hartford/West Hartford border, this 102-acre free public park is bursting with 15,000 colorful rose bushes. Among the highlights at this garden are the many elaborate arches covered with ramblers. The oldest municipal rose garden in the country, this former estate also has an All-America Rose Selection Test Garden, a heritage rose garden, various perennial and annual beds, a rock garden, an herb garden, dahlia beds, and over 100 varieties of specimen trees.

Gertrude Jekyll Garden at the Glebe House Museum

Hollow Road
Woodbury, CT 06798
(203) 263-2855
Open daily dawn to dusk

The distinguished English garden designer and writer Gertrude Jekyll had a profound influence on many American gardens. However this is the only extant garden in the country she actually designed. This classic English cottage-style garden includes a mixed perennial border with bee balm, black-eyed Susans, peonies, and cosmos; and a shade garden with turtlehead, hosta, and cardinal flower. There is also a rose allee, foundation plantings, and a kitchen herb garden.

DELAWARE

Nemours Mansion and Gardens

P.O. Box 109
1600 Rockland Road
Wilmington, DE 19899
(302) 651-6912
www.kidshealth.org/nf/mansion
Open May 1 to November 30 Tuesday to Sunday by guided tour only. Reservations are recommended for individuals and required by groups. Tours are given Tuesday to Saturday at 9, 11, 1, and 3; on Sunday no tour at 9

Located in the scenic Brandywine region, this 300-acre estate was home to Alfred I. du Pont. The lush one-third mile long Main Vista leading from the 102-room mansion has landscaped French-style gardens, fountains, urns, a maze, pools, and statuary surrounded by natural woodlands. The elaborate Sunken Garden contains masses of flowers, marble and bronze statues, grand fountains, and ornate staircases. The highlight of the Southern Gardens is the 8,500 square foot annual and perennial border.

Winterthur Museum, Garden and Library

Route 52
Winterthur, DE 19735
(302) 888-4600; (800) 448-3883
www.winterthur.org
Open year-round Monday to Saturday 9 to dusk, Sunday 12 to dusk. Closed Thanksgiving, Christmas, and New Year's Days

This 60-acre garden on the grounds of the former country estate of Henry Francis du Pont is naturalistic and free-flowing. The 8-acre Azalea

Woods is bursting with color in Spring when the white oaks and American beech trees contrast with flowering dogwood and white, pink, lavender, salmon, and red azalea and rhododendrons. The Sundial Garden has fragrant flowering shrubs surrounding an antique sundial and is a striking contrast to the evergreen Pinetum, a collection of pines, firs, spruces, cedars, and flowering quince.

MAINE

Celia Thaxter's Garden

Appledore Island
Isles of Shoals, ME 03908
(607) 255-3717
www.sml.cornell.edu/p-vctg.htm
Open Sundays from July to Labor Day.
Reservation are required for ferry from Portsmouth, New Hampshire

This colorful cottage garden located on a rocky island off the coast of Maine was the home of the 19th-century poet Celia Thaxter. Using her book, *An Island Garden*, illustrated by the impressionist Childe Hassam, volunteers were able to recreate the garden after it had been destroyed by fire after her death.

Wild Gardens of Acadia

Sieur De Monts Spring
P.O. Box 896
Bar Harbor, ME 04609
(207) 288-3338
Open daily dawn to dusk

Located within Acadia National Park, this 1-acre garden amongst meadows, woodlands, bogs, heath, and ponds features 400 species of plants, flowers, and fruits native to Mount Desert Island. Visitors follow a winding path, lined with ferns, to view the impressive wildflower collection. Twelve sections of gardens show the different habitats on the island and the typical plants that thrive in each condition. The center of the garden has a variety of plants that attract birds, including maple-leafed viburnum, roses, fall-blooming witch hazel, and sweet pepperbush.

MARYLAND

Brookside Gardens

1800 Glenallan Avenue
Wheaton, MD 20902
(301) 949-8231
Open daily 9 to sunset except Christmas Day

This 50-acre public garden has a glass conservatory filled with seasonal and lush tropical plants, as well as formal and informal gardens. The Gude Garden is a serene Japanese-style garden of ponds, trees, shrubs, and a teahouse. There is also a perennial garden, a yew garden, a water garden filled with pink lotus blossoms, a rose garden, and a fragrance garden. There is also a large collection of viburnum, and more than 400 varieties

Mohonk Mountain House Gardens, New York

of rhododendrons and azaleas. Set within the Wheaton Regional Park with plenty of indoor displays, this is a good place to visit in the winter.

Ladew Topiary Gardens

3535 Jarrettsville Pike
Monkton, MD 21111
(410) 557-9466
Open April 15 to October 31, Monday to Friday 10 to 4, Saturday and Sunday 10:30 to 5

The 15 gardens set on this 22-acre site are filled with whimsical and intricate displays of scenes created entirely of topiaries-carefully pruned and trained trees and shrubs. A fox-hunting scene, complete with horses, hounds, and a fox, as well as a giraffe and an elaborate flock of swans are just some of the topiaries found on the grounds. Other garden displays include a romantic Victorian Garden of lantana, smoke bush, and heliotrope, and single-color gardens featuring plants with either pink, yellow, or white blooms.

William Paca Garden

186 Prince George Street
Annapolis, MD 21401
(410) 263-5553; (800) 603-4020
www.annapolis.org/paca.htm
Open March 1 to December 31, Monday to Saturday 10 to 4, Sunday 12 to 4; January to February, Friday and Saturday 10 to 4, Sunday 12 to 4

This restored 18th-century garden was the former home of William Paca, one of the signers of the Declaration of Independence. The 2-acre garden includes a fish-shaped pond, vegetable garden, and a wilderness garden, European garden favorites, and American native plants popular from 1765 to 1780. The rose parterre contains 9 antique varieties of roses.

MASSACHUSETTS

Mount Auburn Cemetery

580 Mt. Auburn Street
Cambridge, MA 02138
(617) 547-7105
Open daily 8 to 5, until 7 during daylight savings time

This 174-acre active cemetery has more than 5,000 native and foreign trees (700 varieties). Its meticulously maintained grounds are enhanced with lakes, rolling hills, and sweeping vistas. More than 50,000 annuals are planted each year throughout the grounds along with bulbs, ground covers, and shrubs. Also of interest are the headstones and the collection of artwork. Founded in 1831 as the nation's first rural cemetery, there is no picnicking, jogging, or bicycling allowed on the grounds in consideration of those interred there and their visitors.

Naumkeag

5 Prospect Hill Road
Stockbridge, MA 01262
(413) 298-3239
www.thetrustees.org
Open daily from Memorial Day to Columbus Day 10 to 5

The gardens surrounding the 46-acre Victorian mansion designed by Stanford White live up to its Native American name: Haven of Peace. Designed as a series of "outdoor rooms" the gardens include the Afternoon Garden, the Evergreen Garden, and Rose Garden. The striking Blue Steps are surrounded by white birches, concrete arches, and a fountain pool. Under the shade of maple, pine, and spruce trees is a mossy Linden Walk, inspired by the linden allees seen in Germany.

NEW HAMPSHIRE

Fuller Gardens

10 Willow Avenue
North Hampton, NH 03862

(603) 964-5414
www.fullergardens.org

Open mid-May to mid-October, daily 9 to 6

This Colonial Revival-style garden was designed by landscape architect Arthur Shurtleff with later enhancements by the Olmstead Brothers. The former summer estate of the late Massachusetts governor Alvan T. Fuller, this seaside gardens includes more than 2,000 rose bushes, including hybrid teas, grandifloras, and floribundas. There's also a Japanese garden with a Koi pond, a hosta display, several perennial borders, and colorful annual gardens.

Moffatt-Ladd House Garden

154 Market Street
Portsmouth, NH 03801

(603) 436-8221

Open daily June 15 to October 15, Monday to Saturday 10 to 5, Sunday 1 to 5

This colonial house was built in 1763 by wealthy sea captain John Moffat as a wedding present to his son. The 1-acre gardens were originally planned by Alexander Hamilton Ladd. Descendants of the house lived here until 1913 when it opened to the public. The formal gardens are formed by a series of four terraces; there are

Wave Hill, New York

also pear trees, old brick walks, grass steps, beehives, and an herb garden.

NEW JERSEY

Leonard J. Buck Garden

11 Layton Road
Far Hills, NJ 07391

(908) 234-2677
www.park.co.somerset.nj.us/

Open Monday to Friday 10 to 4, Saturday 10 to 5, Sunday 12 to 5; Closed weekends and major holidays December to March. Call first to check on weather conditions during winter months

Begun in the late 1930s, this is a series of alpine and woodland naturalistic gardens located in a 33-acre wooded stream valley. Tucked among the outcroppings are many rare and exotic rock garden plants, making this one of the best rock gardens in the Northeast. Woodland trails lined with wildflowers, ferns, and various flowering trees and shrubs wind through the rock gardens. There are also large dawn redwood trees from China, royal azaleas, and rhododendrons.

NEW YORK

The Conservatory Garden

Fifth Avenue and 105th Street
New York, NY 10021

(212) 360-2766
www.centralparknyc.org

Open daily 8 to dusk

Located in the northeast corner of Central Park, this garden has three main sections, each complemented with statues, fountains, and flowers beds styled after classic European gardens. The focus of these gardens is on the composition of the plants' different shapes and textures. The large lawn of the Central Garden is flanked by a double row pink and white flowering crabapple trees.

Innisfree Gardens

Tyrrel Road
Millbrook, NY 12545

(914) 677-8000

Open May 1 to October 20, Wednesday to Friday 10 to 4, Saturday, Sunday and legal holidays 11 to 5

Modeled after a Chinese "cup garden" originating in Chinese paintings from a thousand years ago, visitors to this garden stroll around a lovely glacial lake from one three-dimensional picture to another. There are streams, waterfalls, retaining walls, and rock formations as well as pleasant sitting areas. This subtle landscape also includes islands of willow trees, a lotus pool, rocks covered with sedums and lichens, and wildflowers. Originally owned by Walter

and Marion Beck from 1930 to 1960, the garden got its name from the poem by William Butler Yeats.

Mohonk Mountain House Gardens

100 Mountain Rest Road
New Paltz, NY 12561

(914) 255-1000
www.mohonk.com

Open daily dawn to dusk

The 15 acres of cultivated gardens on the grounds of this National Historic Landmark resort include a rose garden, herb gardens, water gardens, rock gardens, perennial gardens, and cutting gardens. The formal Victorian-style Show Garden contains 78 concentric beds of annuals, rustic vine-covered arbors, and specimen trees and shrubs. Miles of scenic trails lead through the surrounding grounds and Shawangunk Mountain.

Old Westbury Gardens

71 Old Westbury Road
Westbury, NY 11568

(516) 333-0048
www.oldwestburygardens.org

Open late April to October, Wednesday to Monday, 10 to 5; Open Sundays in November; in December open Wednesday to Monday, 11 to 4

Listed on the National Register of Historic Places, this 150-acre Long Island estate has a variety of gardens, sweeping lawns, rolling fields, meadows, woodlands, lakes, and ponds. The English-style formal gardens and perennial borders are a combination of geometric allees and softer, more romantic gardens. The Primrose Path has forget-me-nots, azaleas, rhododendrons, astilbes, foxgloves, and Japanese anemones planted among the different species of primroses that bloom throughout the season.

Wave Hill

675 West 252nd Street
Bronx, NY 10471-2899

(718) 549-3200
www.wavehill.org

Open daily Tuesday to Sunday; October 15 to April 14, 9 to 4:30; April 15 to October 14, 9 to 5:30; open until dusk on Wednesdays from May 31 to August 30. Closed Mondays except Memorial Day, Labor Day, and Columbus Day

This 28-acre public garden in the Bronx overlooks the Hudson River and the New Jersey Palisades. Built in 1843, the property was originally a private country estate. Highlights here are the Flower Garden and the Wild Garden. The Flower Garden, enclosed by a rustic cedar fence, is reminiscent of 1920s private gardens, and features combinations of vintage and modern perennials, annuals, shrubs, and bulbs. The flowers change with the seasons, but the conifers provide a permanent backdrop.

OHIO

Kingwood Center

900 Park Avenue West
Mansfield, OH 44906

(419) 522-0211

Open daily April 1 to October 31, 8 to dusk;
November 1 to March 31, 8 to 5

The former estate of Charles Kelley King, president of the Ohio Brass Company, these 47 acres of lawn, woods, and gardens surround a 27-room French Normandy mansion built in 1926. 50,000 tulips bloom in spring followed by a richly-colored sweep of annuals. Highlights include the perennial garden, an herb garden, free-form beds of bearded irises, a rose garden, and a peony garden.

Stan Hywet Hall and Gardens

714 North Portage Path
Akron, OH 44303

(330) 836-5533
www.stanhywet.org

April 1 to December 31 open daily 9 to 6; end of January to March open Tuesday to Saturday 10 to 4, Sunday 1 to 4

Stan Hywet, Old English for "stone quarry", is the 65-room Tudor Revival estate of Franklin A. Seiberling, co-founder of Goodyear Tire, and his family. The 70 acres of landscaped grounds, vistas, and apple orchards include a naturalistic lagoon, a Japanese garden, a rose garden, a formal West Terrace, a cutting garden, and the Elliptical Garden.

Stan Hywet Hall and Gardens, Ohio

PENNSYLVANIA

Chanticleer Gardens

786 Church Road
Wayne, PA 19087

(610) 687-4163
www.chanticleergarden.org

Open April to October, Wednesday to Saturday 10 to 5; June to August open Friday until 8

Located just west of Philadelphia, near Valley Forge, this 31-acre garden contains tropicals, perennials, container plantings, woodlands, and wildflowers. A new Ruin Garden is currently being constructed around the foundation of a house that once stood on the property. The Tropical Teacup garden showcases plants native to the tropics and sub-tropics that also thrive in the heat of the Pennsylvania summer including passion flowers, taro, pineapple lilies, tropical gingers, and banana plants.

RHODE ISLAND

Green Animals

380 Cory's Lane
Portsmouth, RI 02871

(401) 683-1267

Owned and operated by
The Preservation Society of Newport County
424 Bellevue Avenue
Newport, RI 02840

(401) 847-1000

Open daily May 1 to October 31, 10 to 5

An historic topiary garden with 80 meticulously maintained topiaries in the shapes of birds, animals, arches, spirals, and various geometric forms. The topiaries, made mostly from boxwoods and yews, are set in flower gardens. In addition to the formal topiaries, there are also perennial and annual beds, vegetable and herb gardens, and fruit tree orchids on the 7-acre grounds overlooking Narragansett Bay.

Shakespeare's Head

21 Meeting Street
Providence, RI 02903

(401) 831-7440

Call for hours of operation

This small but elaborate colonial garden is jointly owned by the Providence Preservation Society and the Junior League. The renovated historic house on the grounds was originally built in 1772 and in 1939 its gardens were restored using terraces to conform to the hilly site. The garden is now a replica of a typical Colonial Garden, and a plant list is available documenting the dates each plant would have been used. The garden contains boxwood hedges, quince and crab apple trees, lilacs, geometrically shaped flower beds, and an herb garden. The best time to visit the garden is in the spring.

The Elms

Newport, RI

Owned and operated by the Preservation Society of Newport County (see above)

www.newportmansions.org

One of the many historic mansions that line Newport's Bellevue Avenue, this French-style chateau was the summer home of millionaire miner Edward Berwind. The 11-acre grounds include many specimen trees, large fountains, and two 18th-century marble teahouses with copper roofs that flank the entrance to the elaborate sunken garden. At the center of the sunken garden, currently undergoing a major renovation, is an elaborate cistern decorated with dancing cherubs surrounded by large rectangular beds of begonias and ageretum edged by boxwood.

VERMONT

Shelburne Museum

U.S. Route 7
Shelburne, VT 05482

(802) 985-3334
www.shelburnemuseum.org

Open daily late May to late October 10 to 5; late October to late May 1 to 5 except major holidays

The gardens of this 37-building American folk art museum, housing a collections of early American arts and crafts, are interspersed throughout its 45-acre grounds. More than 400 lilac bushes bloom in the spring. The Bostwick Garden has a display of annuals and perennials framed by a stone wall. Old-fashioned rose bushes are scattered around the grounds, often surrounding wooden benches where visitors can relax and enjoy the setting.

VIRGINIA

Colonial Williamsburg Gardens

Colonial Parkway
P.O. Box 1776
Williamsburg, VA 23187

(757) 229-1000; (800) HISTORY
www.colonialwilliamsburg.org

Nestled amongst the homes, shops, and buildings of this 18th-century restoration are more than 100 gardens spread over more than 90 acres. The Colonial Revival-style gardens include a kitchen garden filled with fruits and vegetable (including varieties that existed in the eighteenth century) a parterre garden featuring blue and white larkspurs and edging boxwoods, and a Ballroom Garden with boxwood parterres and holly topiaries. Geometrically shaped beds in the Elkanah Deane garden hold anemones, bulbs, annuals, and perennials surrounded by lindens.

Monticello

Route 53, P.O. Box 316
Charlottesville, VA 22902
(804)984-9822
www.monticello.org

Open daily March to October 8 to 5; November to February 9 to 4:30. Closed Christmas Day

The grounds surrounding the home where Thomas Jefferson lived from 1769 to 1834 include 27 beds of different vegetables, oval-shaped flower beds filled with a variety of plants, a winding walk alongside a colorful flower border, two orchards, and two vineyards. An 18-acre ornamental grove includes magnolia, aspen, chinaberry, and wild crab apple. Trees were among Jefferson's favorite plants and many native and exotic species grow throughout the property, including a red cedar, European larch, cooper beech, and a giant tulip poplar believed to be from his original garden.

George Washington's Mount Vernon Estate and Garden

George Washington Memorial Parkway
P.O. Box 110
Mount Vernon, VA 22121
(703) 780-2000
www.mountvernon.org

Open daily April to August 8 to 5; March, September, October 9 to 5; November to February 9 to 4

The grounds and gardens of this historic, 18th-century plantation home of America's first president are much the same as when Washington first planted them. The formal composition of the Upper Garden includes larkspur, foxglove, cardinal flower, heliotrope, and other flowers neatly laid out in brick-edged beds. Fruit trees and vegetables are also grown here. On the grounds are a kitchen garden, a botanical garden, a fruit garden and nursery, and a large variety of trees, including a dozen from Washington's original planting.

Woodlawn Plantations

9000 Richmond Highway
Alexandria, VA 22309
(703) 780-4000
www.nthp.org/main/sites/woodlawn.htm

Open March to December daily 10 to 5; also open President's Day

This 1805 house and grounds were a gift from George Washington to his foster daughter Eleanor "Nelly" Custis and his nephew, Lawrence Lewis. In the 1950s the property was acquired by the National Trust for Historic Preservation and opened to the public. The grounds include two formal rose bed parterres containing more than 36 beds of roses bordered in dwarf English boxwood separated by gravel paths. Surrounding are circular beds of pink crape myrtle. Many of the roses are varieties known before 1850 including gallica, moss, cabbage, tea, China, damask, hybrid, and perpetuals.

George Washington's Mount Vernon Estate and Garden, Virginia

WASHINGTON, DC

Dumbarton Oaks

1703 32nd Street NW
Washington, DC 20007
(202) 339-6400
www.doaks.org

Open daily (except national holidays and during inclement weather), April to October 2 to 6; November to March 2 to 5

Once the country estate of diplomat Robert Bliss and his wife Mildred, these grounds were designed by landscape designer Beatrix Farrand with elements from traditional French, English, and Italian gardens. The steep, sloping terrain to the north and east of the mansion on the property has an array of terraces and theme gardens, including Forsythia Hill, Crabapple Hill, and Cherry Hill. The tiny Star Garden, accented with astrological motifs, is enclosed by a white azalea hedge. The formal Rose Garden, has nearly 1,000 rose bushes.

CANADA

Edwards Garden

775 Lawrence Avenue East
Toronto, Ontario M3C 1P2
Canada
(416) 392-8186
Open daily 8 to 8

This former estate garden situated on the Wilket Creek ravine combines formal gardens and roses on the uplands, rhododendrons in the valley, and surrounding natural woodlands. Virginia bluebells, euphorbia, golden corydalis, and ferns grow in the rock garden. The 35-acre garden is filled with bulbs in the spring, annuals, lilacs, and perennials in the summer, and colorful chrysanthemums in the fall. On the sheltered ravine are mature hemlock and birch trees with underplantings of wildflowers.

Jardins de Métis

200 Route 132
Grand-Métis, Quebec G0J 1Z0
Canada
(418) 775-2221
www.jardinsmetis.com

Open daily 8:30 to 5; mid-June to September open until 6:30

Situated on the confluence of the Métis and St. Lawrence rivers, this 45-acre garden was created by Lady Elsie Reford, who inherited the property from her uncle in 1919. During the 1920s she planted thousands of species of plants, including many exotic and native perennials, in a naturalistic setting. In 1961 the garden was acquired by the city of Quebec and opened to the public. The blue poppy, the garden's symbol, blooms throughout the grounds in July. Because spring comes late in this region, the tulips bloom in June. In the Allée Royale (or Long Walk) an English-style border blooms all summer with phlox, large pink peonies, delphinium, lilies, dianthus, and roses.

Mail-Order Suppliers

Do you have a perfect spot in your garden for a 'Blue Bird' hibiscus, a deep yellow dahlia the size of a dinner plate, or a prized heirloom tomato? Though you may not readily find these particular plants in your local nursery, you can order them through the mail. There are hundreds of mail-order catalogs that offer favorite mainstream plants in addition to unusual, obscure, and heirloom varieties. Some sell a variety of plants and accessories. Others specialize in roses, perennials, trees and shrubs, ornamental grasses, fruit and berries, herbs, vegetables, seeds, bulbs, or garden supplies. Many of these catalogs also have informative web sites where you can order catalogs, purchase plants, browse and search an on-line catalog, communicate through e-mail with a professional gardener, and gain a wealth of related information. Below are some reputable companies that ship quality plants. Call, write, or make an on-line request for a catalog. Some firms charge a modest price for a catalog, but the price is well worth the rewards that will follow in your garden. Always order early for the best selection. Addresses and phone numbers are subject to change.

Viola wittrockiana, 'Jolly Joker Poker Face', pansy

FLOWERS AND VEGETABLES: SEEDS

W. Atlee Burpee & Company

300 Park Avenue
Warmister, PA 18974

(800) 888-1447; fax (800) 487-5530
www.burpee.garden.com
www.burpee.com

Flower and vegetable seeds and plants, including heirloom varieties; also herbs, bulbs, and lilies.

D.V. Burrell Seed Growers Co.

P.O. Box 150
Rocky Ford, CO 81067-0150

(719) 254-3318; fax (719) 254-3319

Vegetable, flower, and herb seeds and supplies. Catalog gives growing suggestions for best germination of seeds. Also sells books.

Comstock, Ferre, & Co.

263 Main Street
Wethersfield, CT 06109

(860) 571-6695; fax (860) 571-6595
www.tiac.net/users/comstock

Seeds of annuals, perennials, and everlastings. Older varieties of vegetables and disease-resistant newer varieties.

Gurney's Seed & Nursery Company

110 Capital Street
Yankton, SD 57079

(605) 665-1671; fax (605) 665-9718
www.vgmarketplace.com
www.gurneys.com

Catalog offers a wide selection of all types of seeds and plants, including fruit trees, roses, nuts, berries, and vegetables. Also offers canning supplies.

Johnny's Selected Seeds

1 Foss Hill Road
Albion, ME 04910-9731

(207) 437-4301; fax in U.S. (800) 437-4290; fax outside U.S. (207) 437-2165
www.johnnyseeds.com

Specializes in flowers and vegetables that grow well in cold, Northern climates. Catalog describes germination and growing conditions in detail.

Park Seed Company

1 Parkton Avenue
Greenwood, SC 29647-0001

(800) 845-3369; (864) 223-8555; fax (800) 275-9941
www.parkseed.com

Wide selection of new and unusual flower and vegetable seeds and plants, as well as bulbs. Also offers propogating supplies.

Select Seeds Antique Flowers

180 Stickney Hill Road
Union, CT 06076-4617

(860) 684-9310; fax (800) 653-3304
www.selectseeds.com

Seeds and plants of rare, old-fashioned flowers, originally found in gardens 50 or more years ago, many of them hard to find elsewhere. Specializes in antique sweet peas, fragrant flowers, and flowering vines.

Stokes Seed, Inc.

P.O. Box 548
Buffalo, NY 14240-0548

(716) 695-6980; fax (888) 834-3334
www.stokeseeds.com

Color seed catalog includes 2,500 vegetable and flower seeds plus helpful gardening accessories. Complete cultural information given on all varieties.

Thompson & Morgan

P.O. Box 1308
Jackson, NJ 08527-0308

(800) 274-7333; fax (888) 466-4769
www.thompson-morgan.com

Very large selection of rare and unusual flower, and vegetable seeds, plus a comprehensive list of standard cultivars. Fully illustrated catalog gives helpful descriptions of plants.

Vesey's Seeds, Ltd.

York
Prince Edward Island
Canada C0A 1P0

(800) 363-7333; (902) 368-7333; fax (800) 686-0329
www.veseys.com

To request a catalog in the U.S., write:
P.O. Box 9000
Calais, ME 04619-6102

Wide selection of vegetables and flowers. Speciality is short-season varieties for Canada and New England.

Lilium martagon, Turk's cap lily

Kalimeris pinnatifida, Japanese aster

ROSES

Antique Rose Emporium

9300 Lueckemeyer Road
Brenham, TX 77833

(800) 441-0002; fax (979) 836-0928
www.weareroses.com

Old garden roses grown on their own root selected for long bloom and fragrance. Catalog gives detailed historical and growing information. Also sells rose books.

Corn Hill Nursery

2700 Route 890
Corn Hill, New Brunswick E4Z 1M2
Canada

(506) 756-3635; fax 506-756-1087

Wide selection of roses of all kinds. Catalog gives winter hardiness of each rose and suggests which roses are best suited to different climate. Also fruit trees.

Heirloom Old Garden Roses

24062 Riverside Drive NE
St. Paul, OR 97137

(503) 538-1576; fax (503) 537-5902
www.heirloomroses.com

Catalog offers more than 500 old garden and shrub roses along with detailed descriptions and photos of roses. Also gives suggestions for successful rose growing, and useful books.

Jackson & Perkins

1 Rose Lane
Medford, OR 97501

(800) 292-4769; (800) 872-7673
www.jacksonandperkins.com

Wide selection of different types and color of roses, including, hybrid tea, floribunda, English, miniature, and climbing roses. Separate catalog sells perennials, bulbs, lillies, and garden accessories.

Lowe's Roses

6 Sheffield Road
Nashua, NH 03062-3028

(603) 888-2214; fax (603) 888-6112
www.loweroses.com

Most of the old, species, and modern shrub roses are propagated to order, so will take some time to deliver. Also some grafted roses.

Nor'East Miniature Roses, Inc.

P.O. Box 307
Rowley, MA 01969

(978) 948-7964; fax (978) 948-5487
www.shore.net/~nemr/
www.noreast-miniroses.com

Wide variety of miniature roses including climbing, fragrant, tree, and microminis. Newest varieties include 'Scentsation', 'Jilly Jewel', and 'Y2K'. Catalog also lists roses by color.

Paeonia 'Cinnabar Ramparts', peony

The Roseraie at Bayfields

P.O. Box R
Waldoboro, ME 04572-0919

(207) 832-6330; fax (800) 933-4508
www.roseraie.com

More than 300 varieties of old garden roses grown for Northern climates, including gallicas, damasks, portlands, and hybrid perpetual. Also sells rose fertilizers, and rose supports and trellises. Printed brochure lists roses, but the most helpful information, description of plants, and useful growing tips can be found on the web site.

BULBS, CORMS, AND TUBERS

Charles H. Mueller Co.

7091 North River Road
New Hope, PA 18938

(215) 862-2033; fax (215) 862-3696
www.chmuellerco.com

Specialty is spring-blooming bulbs, such as daffodils, tulips, and hyacinth. Catalog also offers autumn crocus, alliums, tuberous begonias, caladiums, and summer-blooming bulbs.

Dutch Gardens

P.O. Box 200
Adelphia, NJ 07710-0200

(800) 818-3861; (908) 780-7220
www.dutchgardens.com

Large selection of spring-blooming Dutch bulbs. Separate catalog for summer-flowering bulbs, including lilies, amaryllis, dahlias, gladiolus.

Euscaphis japonica

McClure & Zimmerman

P. O. Box 368
108 West Winnebago
Friesland, WI 53935
(920) 326-4220; fax (800) 374-6120
www.mzbulb.com
Usual and hard-to-find spring- and fall-planted bulbs, corms, tubers, and rootstock. Catalog has pen and ink drawings of flowers.

Iris pallida 'Variegata'

John Scheepers, Inc.

23 Tulip Drive
Bantam, CT 06750
(860) 567-0838; fax (860) 567-5323
www.johnscheepers.com
Very large variety of all kinds of bulbs. Company is owned by same family as Van Engelen (see below), but sells bulbs in smaller quantities. Large selection of amaryllis for indoor bloom. Illustrated catalog.

Van Bourgondien Bros.

P.O. Box 1000
245 Farmingdale Road
Babylon, NY 11702-0598
(800) 622-9997; fax (800) 327-4268
www.dutchbulbs.com
Many varieties of new and unusual spring- and summer-blooming bulbs, including dutch tulips, callas, gladiolus, dahlias, and Oriental and heirloom lillies. Also Japanese tree peonies.

Van Dyck's

P.O. Box 430
Brightwaters, NY 11718-0430
(800) 248-2852; fax (800) 639-2452
www.vandycks.com
Tulips, hyacinth, daffodils, iris, crocus and other spring- and fall-flowering bulbs. Also ferns and perennials.

Van Engelen, Inc.

23 Tulip Drive
Bantam, CT 06750
(860) 567-8734; fax (860) 567-5323
www.vanengelen.com
Bulk quantities (usually 50-100, depending upon variety) of a wide selection of Dutch bulbs. For smaller quantities, see sister company, John Scheepers. Large collection of alliums.

PERENNIALS, ANNUALS, TREES, AND SHRUBS

Bluestone Perennials

7211 Middle Ridge Road
Madison, OH 44057
(800) 852-5243; fax (440) 428-7198
www.bluestoneperennials.com
Catalog offers more than 800 varieties of perennials, including shrubs, herbs, ground covers and grasses.

Carroll Gardens

444 East Main Street
Westminster, MD 21157
(800) 638-6334; fax (410) 857-4112
www.carrollgardens.com
Large selection of roses, perennials, herbs, vines, trees, and shrubs. Catalog gives detailed description and growing requirements of plants.

Mellinger's Inc.

2310 West South Range Road
North Lima, OH 44452-7444
(800) 321-7444; (330) 549-9861; fax (330) 549-3716
www.mellingers.com
All kinds of plants, seeds, bulbs, perennials, grasses, trees, and shrubs. Selection of lawn and garden supplies.

Roslyn Nursery

211 Burrs Lane
Dix Hills, NY 11746
(631) 643-9347; fax (516) 484-1555
www.roslynnursery.com
Specializes in rare and exotic varieties of rhododendrons. Also offers azaleas, camellias, trees, perennials, ground covers and grasses.

Zantedeschia 'Schwartzwald', calla lily

André Viette Farm & Nursery

P.O. Box 1109
Fishersville, VA 22939
(800) 575-5538; (540) 943-2315; fax (540) 943-0782
www.viette.com
More than 3,000 varieties of plants, including poppies, iris, peonies, and daylilies. In catalog, plants are grouped by use or growing conditions, sun or shade, or by type.

Wayside Gardens

1 Garden Lane
Hodges, SC 29695-0001
(800) 845-1124; fax (800) 817-1124
www.waysidegardens.com
Hard-to-find and unusual perennials as well as classic favorites. Also wide variety of trees,

Ilex aquifolium 'Aureomarginata', holly

shrubs, roses, and edible ornamentals. Detailed descriptions of plants and growing conditions.

White Flower Farm

P.O. Box 50
Route 63
Litchfield, CT 06759-0050

(800) 503-9624; fax (800) 496-1418
www.whiteflowerfarm.com

Extensive collection of shrubs, ornamental grasses, and perennials, including many unusual varieties. Detailed plant and growing descriptions. Catalog and web site is a handy plant reference guide, with helpful cultural instructions sent with each order. Fall catalog also sells bulbs.

NATIVES, WILDFLOWERS, AND GRASSES

Kurt Bluemel, Inc.

2740 Greene Lane
Baldwin, MD 21013-9523

(800) 248-7584; fax (410) 557-9785
www.bluemel.com

Catalog lists many ornamental grasses, unique bamboo, perennials, ferns, sedges, and rushes. Plants are also listed by categories, such as "fragrant and aromatic" or "grasses for cut flowers."

Garden Place

6780 Heisley Road
P.O. Box 388
Mentor, OH 44061-0388

(888) 255-3059; (440) 255-3705; fax (888) 255-9535
www.springbrookgardens.com

Retail division of Springbrook Gardens. All kinds of perennials, including ornamental grasses and ground covers. Grasses grown from

division. Catalog lists plants by color, height, use, and gives growing tips.

Limerock Ornamental Grasses

70 Sawmill Road
Port Matilda, PA 16870

(814) 692-2272; fax (814) 692-9848

Extensive collection of ornamental grasses including miscanthus, pennisetum, rushes and sedges. Catalog gives full descriptions of grasses, growing conditions and uses in garden, planting and spacing instructions, as well as garden plan designs

Niche Gardens

1111 Dawson Rd.
Chapel Hill, NC 27516

(919) 967-0078; fax (919) 967-4026
www.nichegdn.com

Specializes in nursery-propagated wildflowers, perennials, ornamental grasses, trees, and shrubs. Helpful plant descriptions, including planting suggestions, explanation of growth habits, and instructions for caring for plants.

Tripple Brook Farm

37 Middle Road
Southampton, MA 01073

(413) 527-4626; fax (413) 527-9853
www.tripplebrookfarm.com

Northeastern native plants, including grasses, hardy bamboos, flowering shrubs, and fruit trees.

Underwood Shade Nursery

P.O. Box 1386
North Attleboro, MA 02763-0386

(508) 222-2164; fax (508) 222-5152
www.underwoodshadenursery.com

Native, hybrid, and exotic woodland shade-tolerant plants, including wildflowers, ferns, perennials, ground covers, and ornamental grasses.

Phormiun tenax, New Zealand flax

Claytonia virginica, spring beauty

FRUITS, NUTS, AND BERRIES

Adams County Nursery, Inc.

P.O. Box 108
26 Nursery Road
Aspers, PA 17304

(717) 677-8105; fax (717) 677-4124
www.acnursery.com

Wide selection of bare-root fruit trees, including apple, pear, sweet and sour cherry, plum, and apricot. Also support systems for trees. Catalog gives helpful growing tips and ideas for getting the best crop.

Edible Landscaping

P.O. Box 77
361 Spirit Ridge Lane
Afton, VA 22920

(800) 524-4156; (804) 361-9134; fax (804) 361-1916
www.eat-it.com

Fruit for Mid-Atlantic gardeners, including hardy kiwi, figs, Oriental persimmons, citrus, and pear. Also nuts, coffee, and bamboo.

Henry Leuthardt Nurseries, Inc.

P. O. Box 666
East Moriches, NY 11940-0666

(631) 878-1387; fax (631) 874-0707

Specializes in espaliered apple and pear trees. Many old varieties of plum, peaches, apple, and pear trees. All kinds of berries and grapes.

Indiana Berry & Plant Co.

5218 West 500 South
Huntingburg, IN 47542

(800) 295-2226; (812) 683-3055; fax (802) 683-2004
www.indberry.com

Strawberries, blackberries, raspberries, rhubarb, grapes, elderberries, paw-paws, kiwi, currants, cranberries, and asparagus.

'Bright Lights' Swiss chard

J.E. Miller Nurseries, Inc.

5060 West Lake Road
Canadaigua, NY 14424

**(800) 836-9630; (716) 396-2647; fax
(716) 396-2154**
www.millernurseries.com

Large selection of fruit and nut trees, berries, grapes (including wine grapes), male asparagus, and plums. Asian pear varieties and 30 types of antique apples.

Nourse Farms, Inc.

41 River Road
South Deerfield, MA 01373

(413) 665-2658; fax (413) 665-7888
www.noursefarms.com

Virus-indexed varieties of strawberries as well as blackberries, raspberries, blueberries, currants, gooseberries, and rhubarb. Also horseradish and asparagus.

St. Lawrence Nurseries

325 State Highway 345
Potsdam, NY 13676

(315) 265-6739
www.sln.potsdam.ny.us

Informative catalog of organically-grown, cold-hardy fruit and nut trees. Catalog lists plants according to hardiness, fruit color, and harvest season and includes a great deal of cultural information.

HERBS AND VEGETABLES

Companion Plants

7247 N. Coolville Ridge Road
Athens, OH 45701

(740) 592-4643; fax (740) 593-3092
www.companionplants.com

More than 600 varieties of common and hard-to-find herb plants and seeds from around the world. Large selection of plants native to the Northeast, and seven mushroom kits. Informative chart with companion planting suggestions

The Cook's Garden

P.O. Box 5010
Hodges, SC 29653

(800) 457-9703; fax (800) 457-9705
www.cooksgarden.com

Herb and vegetable seeds for the serious kitchen gardener, including some organic seed and heirloom varieties. Good plant descriptions along with planting and growing tips. Also seeds of flowers and ornamentals, and a few books. Color illustrations throughout catalog.

Heirloom Seeds

P.O. Box 245
West Elizabeth, PA 15088-0245

(412) 384-0852; fax (412) 384-0852
www.heirloomseeds.com

Large variety of seeds of open-pollinated heirloom vegetables, including beans, cucumbers, lettuce, squash, and spinach. Also gardening books, supplies, and non-toxic pest-control products.

Jersey Asparagus Farms, Inc.

105 Porchtown Road
Pittsgrove, NJ 08318

**(800) 499-0013; (856) 358-2548; fax
(856) 358-6127**
www.jerseyasparagus.com

Specializes in Jersey male hybrid asparagus, which is fairly disease resistant and high yielding.

Shepherd's Garden Seeds

30 Irene Street
Torrington, CT 06790-6658

(860) 482-3638; fax (860) 482-0532;
www.shepherdseeds.com

European vegetable and herb seeds and plants for the cook and gardener. Many heirloom varieties. Also flowers, fruit plants, and potato starts, as well as tools and gifts.

Tomato Growers Supply Company

P.O. Box 2237
Fort Myers, FL 33902

**(888) 478-7333; (941) 768-1119; fax
(941) 768-3476**
www.tomatogrowers.com

More than 400 varieties of tomato seeds, and 150 varieties of sweet and hot pepper seeds. Also sells related books, equipment, and growing supplies.

Vermont Bean Seed Company

Garden Lane
Fair Haven, VT 05743-0250

**(803) 663-0217; (802) 273-3400; fax
(888) 500-7333**
www.vermontbean.com

Large selection of beans and vegetables seeds. Also flower, small fruit, and herb seeds and growing supplies.

Heirloom tomatoes

Well-Sweep Herb Farm

205 Mount Bethel Road
Port Murray, NJ 07865

(908) 852-5390; fax (908) 852-1640
www.wellsweep.com
Wide variety of herbs, scented geraniums, and common and unusual perennials. Also offers herb gifts, supplies, and books.

kneeling bench

TOOLS, SUPPLIES, AND ACCESSORIES

BioLogic Company

P.O. Box 177
Willow Hill, PA 17271

(717) 349-2789; fax (717) 349-2789
www.biologicco.com
Supplies three different strains of beneficial nematodes to help control harmful insects in the garden, such as white grubs, cut worms, and black vine weevils. All are safe and organic pest controls.

Charley's Greenhouse Supply

17979 State Route 536
Mt. Vernon, WA 98273

(800) 322-4707; fax (800) 233-3078
www.charleysgreenhouse.com
Greenhouses, lighting for indoor gardens, irrigation and propagation supplies, potting sheds, orchids, tools, and benches.

Gardener's Supply Company

128 Intervale Road
Burlington, VT 05401

(888) 833-1412; fax (800) 551-6712
www.gardeners.com
Wide array of gardening products and furniture, including greenhouses, decorative items, flower supports, clothing, tools, gifts, and plants.

Gardens Alive!

5100 Schenley Place
Lawrenceburg, IN 47025

(812) 537-8650; fax (812) 537-5108
www.gardens-alive.com
Natural and organic lawn and gardening supplies, such as fertilizers designed for specific plants, weed controls, beneficial insects, botanicals, and mineral pesticides.

A.M. Leonard, Inc.

P.O. Box 816
Piqua, OH 45356-0816

(800) 543-8955; (937) 773-2694; fax (800) 433-0633
www.amleo.com
Large selection of horticultural and landscaping tools, equipment, clean-up supplies, and accessories.

Peaceful Valley Farm Supply

P.O. Box 2209
Grass Valley, CA 95945

(888) 784-1722; fax (530) 272-4794
www.groworganic.com
Broad selection of tools and supplies for organic gardeners. Sells beneficial insects, weed and pest control, organic soil supplements, vegetable and cover crop seed, row covers, and composting supplies.

seeder

Smith & Hawken

P.O. Box 6900
2 Arbor Lane
Florence, KY 41022-6900

(800) 776-3336; fax (606) 727-1166
www.smithandhawken.com
Teak outdoor furniture, gardening tools and supplies, clothing and accessories, composting equipment, and gifts for gardeners.

Womanswork

P.O. Box 543
York, ME 03909-0543

(800) 639-2709; fax (207) 363-0805
www.womansworkgloves.com
Specializes in top-quality work and gardening gloves made to fit women's hands. Also sells gloves for men and children.

Well-Sweep Herb Farm, New Jersey

Dianthus barbatus, sweet william

Demystifying Scientific Plant Names

Scientific plant names can be intimidating to gardeners. So why have they been used around the world for hundreds of years? Why do we use them in this book? And why do the plants sold at nurseries most often have scientific names printed somewhere on their labels? There's good reason: common names for plants are often confusing and misleading. A single common name can apply to different plants in different parts of the country or the world. It can be used for two or more plants that not only look different but vary tremendously in growth habit, needs, and bloom season.

Scientific Names Are Precise

Scientific names are more precise than common names. If you ask simply for "dusty miller," you may well get the response: "Which one?" All of the plants with that common name are perennials known for their silvery foliage, but they differ in other ways. Among the dusty millers, *Centaurea cineraria* has typically purple thistlelike flowers; *Senecio cineraria* has small yellow blooms; *Senecio vira-vira* bears white flowers; and *Lychnis coronaria* has magenta blossoms.

Other plants with the same common name often are not at all similar. "Black-eyed Susan," for example, applies to a golden-flowered perennial (*Rudbeckia hirta*) and to a vine most often planted as a summer annual (*Thunbergia alata*). "Angel's tears" is a bulb grown for its clusters of white flowers (*Narcissus triandrus*) and is also a ground cover with inconspicuous flowers (*Soleirolia soleirolii*).

Multiple common names for a plant can also cause confusion. If you call a certain plant "sour gum," while another person knows it as "tupelo" and yet another says "pepperidge," you may not know you're all talking about the same tree—*Nyssa sylvatica.*

So the real reason for learning scientific names is a practical one: they provide the most accurate means we have for putting a verbal handle on a plant. You can't be sure what you are getting unless you order a plant by its scientific name.

Scientific Names Offer Clues

Scientific names, if you break them down, can tell you something about the plants. The first part of a scientific name is the genus name, which is usually a classical name. The second part is the species name, which is usually a descriptive word and often simple to decipher.

Descriptive words used again and again in species names are listed opposite. When you know the meanings of these words, many names become easy to understand and helpful in identifying plants. *Collinsia heterophylla,* for example, combines *hetero* (heterogeneous or various) with *phylla* (leaves) to mean "various-size leaves." Some of the leaves are lanceolate and others oblong.

The common names that are direct translations are among the easiest to remember. Bigleaf hydrangea (*Hydrangea macrophylla*) does have large leaves. *Macro* means large, *phylla* means leaves.

Some of the scientific names are so much like English words that there is no question as to their meaning. *Prostratum, compacta, deliciosa, fragrans,* and *pendula* all say something immediately recognizable.

Chamaecyparis pisifera 'Filifera Aurea', false cypress

A GUIDE TO BOTANICAL NAMES

Color of Flowers or Foliage

albus—white
argenteus—silvery
aureus—golden
azureus—azure, sky blue
caesius—blue-gray
coeruleus—dark blue
candidus—pure white, shiny
canus—ashy gray, hoary
carneus—flesh colored
cereus—waxy
citrinus—yellow
coccineus—scarlet
concolor—one color
croceus—yellow
cruentus—bloody
discolor—two colors, separate colors
glaucus—covered with gray bloom
incanus—gray, hoary
luteus—reddish yellow
purpureus—purple
rubens, ruber—red, ruddy
rufus—ruddy

Portulaca grandiflora, rose moss

Form of Leaf (folius—leaves or foliage)

acerifolius—maplelike
angustifolius—narrow
aquifolius—spiny
buxifolius—boxwood-like

Chrysogonum virginianum, golden star

ilicifolius—hollylike
laurifolius—laurel-like
parvifolius—small
populifolius—poplarlike
salicifolius—willowlike

Shape of Plant

adpressus—pressing against, hugging
altus—tall
arboreus—treelike
capitatus—headlike
compactus—compact, dense
confertus—crowded, pressed together
contortus—twisted
decumbens—lying down
depressus—pressed down
elegans—elegant, slender, willowy
fastigiatus—branches erect and close together
humifusus—sprawling on the ground
humilis—low, small, humble
impressus—impressed upon
nanus—dwarf
procumbens—trailing
prostratus—prostrate
pumilus—dwarfish, small
pusillus—puny, insignificant
repens—creeping
reptans—creeping
scandens—climbing

Where It Came From

The suffix *-ensis* (of a place) is added to place-names to specify the habitat where the plant was first discovered.

africanus—of Africa
alpinus—of the alps
australis—southern
borealis—northern
campestris—of the field or plains
canadensis—of Canada
canariensis—of the Canary Islands
capensis—of the Cape of Good Hope area
chilensis—of Chile
chinensis—of China
hortensis—of gardens
insularis—of the island
littoralis—of the seashore
montanus—of the mountains
rivalis, rivularis—of brooks
sylvestris—of the woods or country
virginianum—of Virginia

Plant Parts

dendron—tree
flora, florum, flori, florus—flowers
phyllus—leaf or leaves

Plant Peculiarities

armatus—armed
baccatus—berried, berrylike
barbatus—barbed or bearded
campanulatus—bell or cup shaped
ciliaris—fringed
cordatus—heart shaped
cornutus—horned
crassus—thick, fleshy
decurrens—running down the stem
densi—dense
diversi—varying
edulis—edible
floridus—free flowering

fruticosus—shrubby
fulgens—shiny
gracilis—slender, thin, small
grandi—large, showy
-ifer, -iferus—bearing or having; e.g., *stoloniferus,* having stolons
laciniatus—fringed or with torn edges
laevigatus—smooth
lobatus—lobed
longus—long
macro—large
maculatus—spotted
micro—small
mollis—soft, soft-hairy
mucronatus—pointed
nutans—nodding, swaying
officinalis—medicinal
obtusus—blunt or flattened
-oides—like or resembling; e.g., *jasminoides,* like a jasmine
patens—open, spreading growth
pinnatus—constructed like a feather
platy—broad
plenus—double, full
plumosus—feathery
praecox—precocious
pungens—piercing
radicans—rooting, especially along the stem
reticulatus—net-veined
retusus—notched at blunt apex
rugosus—wrinkled, rough
saccharatus—sweet, sugary
sagittalis—arrowlike
scabrus—rough feeling
scoparius—broomlike

Malva sylvestris 'Zebrina', mallow

Oxalis purpureus

Schizanthus pinnatus, poor man''s orchid

Our Spelling	As In
a	hat, hand
ay	baby
ah	hall
ai	air
e	met, bed
ee	we
i	tin
ye	wine
o	hot
oe	romance
u	must, burr
oo	rumor
ew	human
uh	comma, consider, sinister, vapor, minus

Pronunciation Guide

Scientific names are the universal language for plants, but they are pronounced differently in various parts of the world, even among English-speaking countries. Because these names come from Latin and Greek, there is no absolute, approved, obligatory pronunciation for them —we say them as we choose. What follows is a list of the most-often-used ways to say many scientific plant names.

Salpiglossis

A

Abelia—uh-BEE-lee-uh
Abeliophyllum—a-bee-li-o-FIL-uhm
Abies—AY-bi-eez
Abutilon—uh-BEW-tuh-lon
Acer—AY-sir
Achillea—ak-i-LEE-uh
Aconitum—ak-oe-NYE-tuhm
Actaea—ak-TEE-uh
Actinidia—AK-ti-NID-ee-uh
Adiantum—ad-ee-AN-tuhm
Aesculus—ES-kew-luhs
Aethionema—ee-thi-oe-NEE-muh
Agapanthus—ag-uh-PAN-thuhs
Agave—uh-GAH-vay
Ageratum—ah-JER-uh-tuhm
Ailanthus—uh-LAN-thuhs
Ajuga—uh-JEW-guh
Alonsoa—al-on-ZOE-uh
Amelanchier—am-uh-LANG-kee-uhr
Anemone—uh-NEM-uh-nee
Anisodontea—uh-NIS-oh-DON-tee-uh
Aquilegia—ak-wuh-LEE-jee-uh
Arabis—AIR-uh-bis
Aralia—uh-RAY-lee-uh
Arctostaphylos—ahrk-toe-STAF-i-luhs
Arctotheca—ahrk-toe-THEE-kuh
Arisaema—a-riss-EE-muh
Arrhenatherum—a-ree-na-THEE-rum
Artemisia—ahr-tuh-MEE-zee-uh
Asarina—AS-a-rin-uh
Aspidistra—as-puh-DIS-truh
Astilbe—uh-STIL-bee
Avena—av-EE-na

Anisodontea

B

Baccharis—BAK-uh-ris
Berberis—BUR-buh-ris
Bergenia—bur-GEN-ee-uh
Betula—BET-ew-luh
Bidens—BYE-denz

Brachycome—brak-ik-OE-mee
Broussonetia—broo-so-NESH-ee-uh
Buddleia—BUD-lee-uh

C

Caladium—kuh-LAY-dee-uhm
Calendula—kuh-LEN-dew-luh
Callirhoe—kal-LI-ro-ee
Callistephus—ka-LIS-tuh-fuhs
Campanula—kam-PAN-ew-luh
Caryopteris—ka-ri-OP-ter-is
Castanea—cas-TAY-nee-uh
Celosia—see-LOE-shee-uh
Centaurea—sen-tah-REE-uh
Cephalanthus—sef-a-LAN-thus
Cephalaria—sef-a-LAY-ri-uh
Ceratostigma—sair-ah-toe-STIG-muh
Cercidiphyllum—ser-sid-I-FIL-um
Cercis—SIR-suhs
Chamaecyparis—kam-uh-SIP-uh-ris
Cheilanthes—ki-LAN-theez
Chelone—ke-LOE-nay
Chimaphila—ki-MAF-I-la
Chionanthus—kye-oe-NAN-thuhs
Chrysogonum—kris-OG-uh-nuhm
Cimicifuga—sim-I-SIF-ew-guh
Clematis—KLEM-uh-tis
Cleome—KLEE-oe-mee
Clivia—KLYE-vee-uh
Cobaea—ko-BEE-uh
Colchicum—KAHL-chi-kuhm
Convallaria—kon-vuh-LAIR-ee-uh
Convolvulus—kon-VOL-vew-luhs
Coreopsis—koer-ee-OP-suhs
Cotinus—koe-TYE-nuhs
Cotoneaster—kuh-toe-nee-AS-tuhr
Crataegus—kruh-TEE-guhs
Crocosmia—kroe-KOZ-mee-uh
Cuphea—KEW-fee-uh
Cynoglossum—sin-OE-GLOS-uhm
Cytisus—SIT-I-sus

Clematis

D

Daboecia—duh-BEE-shee-uh
Daphne—DAFF-nee
Decaisnea—de-KAYN-I-uh
Dennstaedtia—den-STET-I-uh
Deutzia—DOOT-zee-uh or DOYT-zee-uh
Dracaena—druh-SEE-nuh
Dryopteris—drye-OP-ter-uhs
Duchesnea—dew-KEZ-nee-uh

E

Echeveria—ek-uh-VAIR-ee-uh
Echinacea—ek-uh-NAY-see-uh
Echinops—EK-uh-nops
Echium—EK-ee-uhm
Elaeagnus—el-ee-AG-nuhs
Epigaea—ep-I-JEE-uh
Equisetum—ek-wuh-SEE-tuhm
Eremurus—air-uh-MEWR-uhs
Erica—ee-RYE-kuh (correct, but universally pronounced AIR-ik-uh)
Eryngium—e-RIN-ji-um
Eschscholzia—e-SHOELT-see-uh
Euonymus—ew-ON-uh-muhs
Exochorda—ek-so-KOER-duh

F

Fatshedera—fats-HED-uh-ruh
Foeniculum—fee-NIK-ew-lum
Forsythia—for-SITH-ee-uh
Fragaria—fruh-GAIR-ee-uh
Fraxinus—FRAK-suh-nuhs
Fuchsia—FEW-shee-uh

G

Gaillardia—gay-LAHR-dee-uh
Gazania—guh-ZAY-nee-uh
Genista—je-NIS-tuh
Gentiana—jen-shee-AY-nuh
Gerbera—GUR-bur-uh
Geum—JEE-uhm

Gleditsia—gluh-DIT-see-uh
Gomphrena—gom-FREE-nuh
Gypsophila—jip-SOF-uh-luh

H

Halesia—HAYLZ-ee-uh
Hamamelis—ham-uh-MEE-luhs
Hedera—HED-uh-ruh
Helianthemum—hee-lee-AN-thuh-muhm
Helianthus—hee-lee-AN-thuhs
Heliopsis—hee-lee-OP-suhs
Heliotropium—hee-lee-oe-TROE-pee-uhm
Hemerocallis—hem-uh-roe-KAL-uhs
Heuchera—HEW-kuh-ruh
Hibiscus—hye-BIS-kuhs
Hippophae—hi-POF-ay-ee
Hosta—HOS-tuh
Hydrangea—hye-DRAIN-jee-uh
Hymenocallis—hye-muh-noe-KAL-uhs
Hypericum—hye-PEER-i-kuhm

Heliopsis

I

Iberis—eye-BEE-ruhs
Idesia—eye-DEE-zee-uh
Ilex—EYE-lex
Impatiens—im-PAY-shuhnz
Incarvillea—in-kar-VIL-ee-uh
Ipomoea—ip-oe-MEE-uh
Iresine—ir-uh-SYE-nee

J

Jasminum—JAZ-muh-nuhm
Jassione—jas-I-OE-nee
Juniperus—joo-NIP-uh-ruhs

K

Kniphofia—nip-HOE-fee-uh
Kochia—KOE-kee-uh
Koelreuteria—ke-roo-TEE-ree-uh
Kolkwitzia—koel-KWIT-zee-uh

L

Lagerstroemia—lay-guhr-STREE-mee-uh
Lathyrus—LATH-uh-ruhs
Leiophyllum—leye-oe-FIL-um
Liatris—lye-AT-ruhs
Liriodendron—leer-ee-oe-DEN-druhn
Liriope—luh-RYE-oe-pee
Lobelia—loe-BEE-lee-uh
Lonicera—loe-NIS-uh-ruh
Lychnis—LIK-nis
Lysimachia—lye-suh-MAY-kee-uh

M

Maackia—ma-AY-ki-uh
Macleaya—ma-KLAY-uh
Malus—MAY-lus
Mandevilla—man-duh-VIL-uh

Matthiola—ma-thee-OE-luh
Melaleuca—mel-uh-LOO-kuh
Mespilus—MES-pi-lus
Mimulus—MIM-ew-luhs
Musa—MEW-zuh
Myosotis—mye-oh-SO-tuhs
Myrica—mi-RYE-kuh

N

Nandina—nan-DEE-nuh
Narcissus—nahr-SIS-uhs
Nerium—NEE-ree-uhm
Neviusia—nev-I-EW-si-uh
Nicotiana—ni-koe-shee-AY-nuh
Nierembergia—nee-rem-BURG-ee-uh
Nyssa—NIS-uh

O

Oenothera—ee-no-THEE-ruh
Omphalodes—om-fa-LOE-deez
Osmanthus—oz-MAN-thuhs
Osteospermum—os-tee-oe-SPUR-muhm
Oxalis—ok-sal-is
Oxydendrum—OK-see-DEN-druhm

P

Pachysandra—pak-ee-SAN-druh
Papaver—puh-PAY-vuhr
Parthenocissus—PAHR-thuh-noe-SIS-uhs
Pelargonium—pel-ahr-GOE-nee-uhm
Pennisetum—pen-uh-SEE-tuhm
Penstemon—PEN-stuh-muhn
Phalaris—FAL-a-ris
Philadelphus—fil-uh-DEL-fuhs
Photinia—foe-TIN-ee-uh
Phyllitis—fi-LYE-tis
Physalis—FYE-suh-luhs
Picea—pye-SEE-uh
Pieris—pee-AIR-uhs
Pinus—PYE-nuhs
Pittosporum—pi-TOS-puh-ruhm,
Platanus—PLAT-uh-nuhs
Platycladus—plat-i-KLAD-uhs
Podocarpus—poe-doe-KAR-puhs
Polianthes—pol-ee-AN-theez
Polygonatum—pol-ee-GON-uh-tuhm
Portulaca—por-tew-LAK-uh
Potentilla—poe-ten-TIL-uh
Primula—PRIM-ew-luh
Proboscidea—proe-bo-SID-ee-uh
Pseudotsuga—soo-doe-TSOO-guh
Pyrus—PYE-ruhs

Q

Quercus—KWER-kuhs

R

Ranunculus—ra-NUN-kew-luhs
Rheum—REE-um
Rohdea—ROE-dee-uh

Rosmarinus—roez-muh-RYE-nuhs
Rudbeckia—rud-BEK-ee-uh

S

Saccharum—sak-KAR-um
Salpiglossis—sal-pi-GLOS-uhs
Sanvitalia—san-vi-TAY-lee-uh
Sarracenia—sar-a-SEE-ni-uh
Scabiosa—skay-bee-OH-suh
Schisandra—skye-ZAN-dra
Schizanthus—ski-ZAN-thuhs
Sciadopitys—sye-a-DOP-I-tis
Scilla—SIL-uh
Sempervivum—sem-per-VYE-vuhm
Senecio—suh-NEE-shee-oe
Sequoia—suh-KWOY-uh
Spiraea—spye-REE-uh
Symplocos—SIM-pluh-koes

T

Tagetes—tuh-JEE-teez
Taxodium—taks-OE-dee-uhm
Thuja—THOO-yuh
Thymus—TYE-muhs
Tibouchina—tib-oo-KYE-nuh
Tigridia—tye-GRID-ee-uh
Tolmiea—tol-MEE-uh
Trachymene—truh-KIM-uh-nee
Tradescantia—trad-es-KAN-shee-uh
Tropaeolum—troe-PEE-uh-luhm
Tsuga—TSOO-guh

Senecio

Tibouchina

V

Vaccinium—vak-SIN-ee-uhm
Venidium—ve-NID-I-um
Verbascum—vur-BAS-kuhm
Verbena—vur-BEE-nuh
Viburnum—vye-BUR-nuhm
Vinca—VING-kuh
Viola—Vi-OH-luh
Vitex—VEE-teks

W–Z

Weigela—wye-JEE-luh
Wisteria—WIS-teer-ee-uh
Xanthorriza—san-thoe-RYE-zuh
Xeranthemum—sir-an-thuh-MUM
Yucca—YUK-kuh
Zantedeschia—zan-tuh-DES-kee-uh
Xeranthemum—sir-an-thuh-MUM
Zelkova—zel-KO-vuh
Zephyranthes—ZEF-urh-an-THEES
Zizyphus—ZIZ-uh-fuhs
Zoysia—ZOY-see-uh

INDEX

Gardening Terms and Topics

INDEX
Scientific and Common Names

Italic page numbers refer to pages on which there are relevant photographs. The **boldface** page number after each scientific name refers to the plant's encyclopedia entry. The page number after a common name also refers to the encyclopedia entry; to find more page references to a common name, look under the scientific name in parentheses.

Acknowledgments

SPECIAL CONTRIBUTORS

Robert S. Hebb
*Former Director
of Horticulture,
Cary Arboretum of the New
York Botanical Garden,
New York, New York;
Former Director,
Lewis Ginter Botanic Garden,
Richmond, Virginia*

Thomas Burford
*Fruit Tree Consultant;
Author:* Apples: A Catalog of
International Varieties
Monroe, Virginia

John Emmanuel
*Assistant Director
of Horticulture,
Wave Hill,
Bronx, New York*

Gary Koller
*President, Koller and
Associates Garden Design,
Boston, Massachusetts;
Former Assistant Director
for Horticulture,
Arnold Arboretum of Harvard
University, Jamaica Plains,
Massachusetts*

Nan Sinton
*Director of Programs,
Horticulture Magazine*

Kathy Tracy
*Proprietor,
Avant Gardens,
Dartmouth, Massachusetts*

CONTRIBUTORS

Nancy Adams
John K. Arbogas
Dr. David Bar-Zvi
David Barkely
Susan Beebe
Robert Beyfuss
Dr. Toni Bilik
Linda Blue
William Brown
Deborah Brown
Christy Bubolz
Thomas Buob
Scott Byars
Wayne Cahilly
Brian Caldwell
Scott Chadwell
Gerald Clingman
Patricia P. Cobb
Steven M. Cohan
Paul Cooper
Robert Crasweller
Joe Dektor
Terry Del Valle
Gerald Draheim
Randall Drinkard
R. Edmonds
Brian Eshenauer
Miklos Faust
John Fech
Chad Finn
Rick Foster
Steve Fouch
Barry Fugatt
Frank Funderbunk
Floyd Giles
Robert Goerger
Duane Greene
Austin Hagen
Thurston Handley
John Harris
Edward Hedborn
Greg Heilig
Michael D. Henshaw
Peter Heus
David Himelrick
Jeff Iles
Randal Jackson
Jules Janick
Ricky Kemery
Mark Kepler
Jack Kerrigan
Mohamad W. Khan
Tom Kirby
Dean Krauskopf
Karen Krueger
Ralph Kulm
Donna Lamb
John Lankenau
Stephanie Larimer
Barbara Larson
Verna Litton
Thomas MacCubbin
Jim McCausland
Bray McDonald
Stephanie Mallozzi
Sue Mearing
Chip Miller
Craig Minor
Ann Munson
Sally Muspratt
Don Neal
Phil Normandy
Krista Oakley
Thomas Obourn
Dom Parise
Wilma R. Penland
Len Perry
Ed Poenicke
Marvin R. Pritts
Earl Puls, Jr.
Freddie Rasberry
Sherry Rindels
David Robson
Dan Rogalla
Lon J. Rombough
Jeff Schulz
David Seavey
Mandy Self
Roseann Sherry
Brenda Simons
Dr. Lois Berg Stack
Chris Strand
George H. Taylor
Roy L. Taylor
Paul Thompson
Tom Tiddens
Ann Upton
Steven VanderMark
Celeste Vander Mey
Richard Verville
Carl Wagner
Jim Ward
Norman Warminski
William C. Welch
Dr. Joe White
Tom Whitlow
Dave Williams
J. Craig Williams
Dee Wookey
Keith Zanziger
Thomas Zundel

EDITORS

Susan Lang
John R. Dunmire
Philip Edinger
Joseph F. Williamson
Lance Walheim

Photography Credits

The sources for the photographs in the book are listed below. Except as noted for pages 48–112, credits from left to right are separated by semicolons; credits from top to bottom are separated by dashes.

Back cover: Jerry Pavia (5); Nancy Rotenberg (right, bottom).

1: Karen Bussolini; 2: Ken Druse–Nancy Rotenberg; 3: Ian Adams; 4: Jerry Pavia–Clifton Carr–Jerry Pavia; 5: Jerry Pavia–Albert Squillace–Dency Kane; 6: Nancy Rotenberg; 7: Karen Bussolini; 8: Jerry Pavia–Susan Roth; 9: Karen Bussolini; Karen Bussolini courtesy Sydney Eddison–Karen Bussolini; 10: Nancy Rotenberg–Roger Foley; 11: Ken Druse–Roger Foley; 12,13: Leonard Phillips; 14: Karen Bussolini; 15: Ken Druse; 16: Jerry Pavia (2)–Roger Foley; 17, 18: Alan and Linda Detrick; 19: Lynn Karlin–Ian Adams; 20: Karen Bussolini, courtesy Carolyn Roehm–Karen Bussolini; 21: Karen Bussolini courtesy Carolyn Roehm; 22, 23: Karen Bussolini; 24: Betsy Pinover Schiff courtesy Pamela Scurry, owner and designer, from *Gardens in the City*, Harry N. Abrams, 1999; 25: Ken Druse; 26: Jerry Pavia–Alan and Linda Detrick (2); 27: Nancy Rotenberg–Carole Ottesen; 28: Karen Bussolini courtesy Sydney Eddison–Karen Bussolini courtesy Bunny Williams; 29: Celia Pearson–Karen Bussolini; 30: Steve Mulligan–Paul Rezendes; 31: Steve Mulligan–Ian Adams; 32: Dency Kane; 33: Albert Squillace; Jerry Pavia; Albert Squillace; 34: John Bildahl–Karen Bussolini; 35: Ian Adams–Mark Turner; 36: Carr Clifton; 37: Alison Shaw–Janet Davis; 38: Ian Adams; 39: Carr Clifton; Jerry Pavia–Janet Davis; 40: Paul Rezendes–Rob and Ann Simpson; 47: Ken Druse

48-112: all by Jerry Pavia except as follows: 48: Bob Hebb (top right); 49: Bob Hebb (left, 3rd from top); 50: Albert Squillace (3rd from top) 51: Alan and Linda Detrick (2nd from top); 52: Ian Adams (left, 3rd from top and bottom; right, top and bottom); 53: Dency Kane (left, 2nd from top), Bob Hebb (right, 2nd from top), Ian Adams (3rd from top); 54: Dency Kane (left, top), Karen Bussolini (right, top), Albert Squillace (right, 2nd from top), Janet Davis (right, 3rd from top); 60: Karen Bussolini (left, 3rd from top); 61: Alan and Linda Detrick (right, bottom); 63: Albert Squillace (left, 2nd from top and bottom); 64: Albert Squillace (top); 68: Albert Squillace (left, 3rd from top, and right, 3rd from top); 69: Albert Squillace (right, 3rd from top, and bottom); 70: Albert Squillace (left, 3rd from top); 73: Alan and Linda Detrick (right, bottom); 74: Albert Squillace (right, top); 76: Albert Squillace (left, bottom); 77: Bob Hebb (left, 3rd from top), Chani Yammer (right, 2nd from top); 78: Albert Squillace (left, bottom and right, 2nd from top); 79: Albert Squillace (left, 3rd from top and right, 2nd from top); 80: Albert Squillace (left, 2nd from top and right, 3rd from top), Bob Hebb (left, bottom), Alan and Linda Detrick (right, bottom); 81: Albert Squillace (left, 2nd from top), Ian Adams (left, 3rd from top); 82: Albert Squillace (right, bottom); 83: Lori Stein (left, bottom); 84: Albert Squillace (left, 2nd from top); 86: Albert Squillace (right, 2nd from top); 91: Chani Yammer (right, 3rd from top); 94: Albert Squillace (left, all except bottom); 96: Albert Squillace (right, 2nd from top and bottom); 97: Albert Squillace (left, top, and right, 2nd from top); 98: Albert Squillace (right, 2nd from top); 99: Albert Squillace (left, 3rd from top, and bottom; right 3rd from top); 101: Bob Hebb (left, bottom), Chani Yammer (right, 3rd from top), Albert Squillace (right, bottom); 102: Albert Squillace, all; 103: Albert Squillace (left, 3rd from top, and bottom, and right, top), Lori Stein (right, 3rd from top); 104: Albert Squillace (2nd from top, 4th from top); 105: Albert Squillace (top, 2nd, 3rd from top, and bottom); 106: Chani Yammer (left, bottom), Albert Squillace (right, all); 107: Albert Squillace (left, 2nd from top), Chani Yammer (left, bottom); 108: Albert Squillace (right, bottom); 110: Albert Squillace (right, bottom); 111: Ian Adams (left, top), Bob Hebb (left, 2nd from top), Albert Squillace (left, bottom; right, top and bottom).

449: Ken Druse; 452: Ken Druse (2)–Albert Squillace; 454–455: Celia Pearson; 456, 458: Norman Plate; 459: Derek Fell (2)–Phil Degginger/Color-Pic; 460: Alan and Linda Detrick (2)–Peter Gregg/Color-Pic; 461: William J. Weber, Visuals Unlimited–Phil Degginger/Color-Pic–Steven Sibbett; 462: Glenn Christiansen; 463: Ray Maleike–Saxon Holt; Norman Plate (2); 464: Walter Chandoha; 465: Michael Thompson; 466: Roger Foley; 467: Scott and Company–Bill Knoop–Norman Plate (6); 468: Norman Plate–Max Badgley (2)–Dr. Richard S. Cowles; 469: Paul Rezendes; Chani Yammer; 471: Crandall and Crandall; 472: Ron West (3); Max Badgley–Ron West (4); 473: Albert Squillace; Bill Johnson–Dwight Kuhn–Ed Degginger/Color-Pic; 474: Ed Degginger/Color-Pic; Bill Beatty–Ed Degginger/Color-Pic; Scott Camazine–Dwight Kuhn; 475: Alan and Linda Detrick; Ann and Rob Simpson–Phillip Roullard (2)–Max Badgley; Dwight Kuhn; 476: Ed Degginger/Color-Pic–Phillip Roulard–Ann and Rob Simpson; 478: Crandall and Crandall–Charles Mann; 479: Alan and Linda Detrick–Ian Adams; Ian Adams–Dwight Kuhn; 481: Ian Adams; 482: Albert Squillace; 487, 488: Norman Plate; 489: Albert Squillace; 491: Norman Plate; 497: Albert Squillace; 499: Norman Plate–Scott Atkinson; 502, 503: Ian Reeves; 506: Chani Yammer; 507, 508: Albert Squillace; 509: Chani Yammer; Jerry Pavia; Albert Squillace; Jerry Pavia (3); 510: Albert Squillace; 511: Albert Squillace; Jerry Pavia (4); Chani Yammer; 513, 514: Norman Plate; 515: Ian Reeves; 517: Albert Squillace; 519: Em Ahart–Ed Degginger–Alan and Linda Detrick (2); Phillip Roullard; Jessie M. Harris; Gerald D. Tang; 520: Alan and Linda Detrick–Jessie M. Harris; R. Cowles–Alan and Linda Detrick–Bill Johnson; 521: Gerald D. Tang; 522: Rob and Ann Simpson–R. Cowles; Ed Degginger; 524: van Bourgondien, www.dutchbulbs.com; 525: Dency Kane; 526: Derek Fell–Dency Kane; 527: Ian Adams; 528: Leonard Phillips; 529: Dency Kane; 530: Ken Druse; 531: Albert Squillace; 532: Ian Adams; 533: Lori Stein; 534: Alan and Linda Detrick; 535: Jerry Pavia (2); Cricket Hill Garden; 536: Bob Hebb–Albert Squillace; van Bourgondien, www.dutchbulb.com; 537: Jerry Pavia (2); Bob Hebb; 538: Dwight Kuhn (2); 539: Ian Reeves–Albert Squillace; Ian Reeves; 540: Jerry Pavia; Chani Yammer; Jerry Pavia; 541: Jerry Pavia–Jerry Pavia; Chani Yammer; Albert Squillace; 542: Jerry Pavia; Albert Squillace; Jerry Pavia–Jerry Pavia; 543: Jerry Pavia; Jerry Pavia; Albert Squillace; 559: Ken Druse.